MW00774606

DATE DUE

ENCYCLOPEDIA OF
Interpersonal
VIOLENCE

Editorial Board

ENCYCLOPEDIA OF
Interpersonal
VIOLENCE

VOLUME 1

Edited by

Claire M. Renzetti
University of Dayton

Jeffrey L. Edleson
University of Minnesota

Los Angeles • London • New Delhi • Singapore

A SAGE Reference Publication

For information:

SAGE Publications, Inc.
2455 Teller Road
Thousand Oaks, California 91320
E-mail: order@sagepub.com

SAGE Publications Ltd.
1 Oliver's Yard
55 City Road
London EC1Y 1SP
United Kingdom

SAGE Publications India Pvt. Ltd.
B 1/I 1 Mohan Cooperative Industrial Area
Mathura Road, New Delhi 110 044
India

SAGE Publications Asia-Pacific Pte. Ltd.
33 Pekin Street #02-01
Far East Square
Singapore 048763

Printed in the United States of America.

Library of Congress Cataloging-in-Publication Data

Encyclopedia of interpersonal violence / editors, Claire M. Renzetti, Jeffrey L. Edleson.
    p. cm.
"A SAGE Reference Publication."
Includes bibliographical references and index.
ISBN 978-1-4129-1800-8 (cloth)
    1. Violence—Encyclopedias. 2. Interpersonal conflict—Encyclopedias. I. Renzetti, Claire M. II. Edleson, Jeffrey L.

HM1121.E57 2008
303.603—dc22   2008001212

This book is printed on acid-free paper.

08 09 10 11 12   10 9 8 7 6 5 4 3 2 1

Publisher:	Rolf A. Janke
Acquisitions Editor:	Art Pomponio
Assistant to the Publisher:	Michele Thompson
Developmental Editors:	Carole Maurer, Yvette Pollastrini
Reference Systems Manager:	Leticia Gutierrez
Production Editor:	Tracy Buyan
Editorial Assistant:	Eileen Gallaher
Copy Editors:	Jamie Robinson, Renee Willers
Typesetter:	C&M Digitals (P) Ltd.
Proofreaders:	Andrea Martin, Kristin Bergstad
Indexer:	Joan Shapiro
Cover Designer:	Michelle Kenny
Marketing Manager:	Amberlyn Erzinger

Contents

List of Entries

Reader's Guide

The Reader's Guide is provided to assist readers in locating articles on related topics. It classifies articles into 12 general topical categories: Children and Youth; Civil and Criminal Legal Systems; Interpersonal Violence—General; Intervention and Prevention Programs; Legislation; Organizations and Agencies; Racial/Ethnic and Cross-Cultural Issues; Research Methods and Data Collection Instruments; Sexual Violence and Abuse; Syndromes, Disorders, and Other Mental Health Issues; Theories and Theoretical Perspectives; and Violence Between Intimates/Family Violence. Entries may be listed under more than one topic.

Children and Youth

Abandonment
Animal Abuse and Child Maltreatment Occurrence
Campus Violence
Child Abductions, Family
Child Abductions, Nonfamily
Child Abuse and Disabilities
Child Aggression as Predictor of Youth and
    Adult Violence
Child Exposure to Violence, in Media
Child Exposure to Violence, Role of Schools
Child Fatalities
Child Neglect
Child Physical Abuse
Children and Adolescents Who Kill
Children Missing Involuntarily or for Benign Reasons
Children's Advocacy Center
Child Sexual Abuse
Collaborative Divorce, Benefits to Children
Community Violence, Effects on Children and Youth
Complex Trauma in Children and Adolescents
Delinquency and Violence
Divorce in Relation to Child Abuse
Divorce in Relation to Youth Violence
Failure to Protect
Failure to Thrive
Father Involvement
Fathers as Perpetrators of Child Maltreatment
Female Perpetrators of Violence, Teen Girls

Female Perpetrators of Violence Against Children
Female Slavery/Child Slavery
Feticide
Fraternities and Violence
Hazing
Health Care Response to Child Maltreatment
Health Consequences of Child Maltreatment
Incest
Infanticide
Internet, Crimes Against Children
Intimate Partner Relationship Quality and Domestic
    Violence
Maternal Responsibility for Child Physical Abuse
National AMBER Alert Program
Nonoffending Parents of Maltreated Children
Parenting Practices and Violence,
    Child Maltreatment
Parenting Practices and Violence, Youth Violence
Pedophilia
Peer Influences on Youth Violence
Punking
Runaway and Thrownaway Children
Rural Child Abuse
School Violence
School Violence, Media Coverage of
School Violence, School Shootings
Sexually Aggressive Behavior in Children
    Video Games, Violence Exposure in
Youth Violence

Civil and Criminal Legal Systems

Abolitionist Approach to Prostitution

Capital Punishment

Community Justice

Community Policing

Court-Appointed Special Advocates

Department of Homeland Security, Asylum

Department of Homeland Security, Response to Battered Immigrants and Immigrant Victims of Violence Against Women

Department of Homeland Security and Immigration Services

Domestic Violence Courts

Dual Arrest

Expert Testimony

Family Justice Centers

Hague Convention on the Civil Aspects of International Child Abduction

Hate Crimes (Bias Crimes), Criminal Justice Responses

Human Rights

Immigrant and Migrant Women and Law Enforcement Response

Insanity Defense

Investigative Interviewing of Children

Investigative Interviewing of Child Sexual Abuse Victims

Investigative Interviewing of Offenders

Legal Issues in the Treatment of Sexual and Domestic Violence

Legal System, Advocacy Efforts to Affect, Child Maltreatment

Legal System, Advocacy Efforts to Affect, Elder Abuse

Legal System, Advocacy Efforts to Affect, Intimate Partner Violence

Legal System, Advocacy Efforts to Affect, Violence Against Children

Legal System, Civil and Criminal Court Remedies for Sexual Assault/Rape

Legal System, Civil Court Remedies for Intimate Partner Violence

Legal System, Criminal Investigation of Victimization of Children

Legal System, Criminal Justice Strategies to Reduce Interpersonal Violence

Legal System, Criminal Justice System Responses to Intimate Partner Violence

Legal System and Child Protection

Mandatory Arrest/Pro-Arrest Statutes

Mandatory Reporting Laws of Child Maltreatment

Mandatory Reporting Laws of Elder Abuse

Mandatory Reporting Laws of Intimate Partner Violence

Minneapolis Domestic Violence Experiment

National Incident-Based Reporting System

National Institute of Justice

No-Drop Prosecution

Office of Juvenile Justice and Delinquency Prevention

Police, Response to Child Maltreatment

Police, Response to Domestic Violence

Police, Suicide by Cop

Police, Use of Violence/Excessive Force

Pregnancy, Criminalizing the Pregnancies of Drug-Addicted Women

Prison Violence, Sexual Assault

Prison Violence and Prison Gangs

Prison Violence by Corrections Staff

Prison Violence by Inmates

Prison Violence in Women's Facilities

Prosecutorial Practices, Child Maltreatment

Prosecutorial Practices, Elder Abuse

Prosecutorial Practices, Interpersonal Violence

Prosecutorial Practices, Intimate Partner Violence

Reasonable Efforts

Recidivism

Restorative Justice

Restraining and Protective Orders

Scottsboro Boys

Secondary Victimization by Police and Courts

Self-Defense

Self-Petitioning Process

Sex Offenders, Civil Commitment

Spouse Assault Replication Project

STOP Violence Against Women Formula Grant Program

Uniform Crime Reports

United Nations, International Law/Courts

Victim Impact Statements

Victim Witness Specialists

Interpersonal Violence—General

Alcohol and Violence
Anti-Abortion Violence
Assault
Assault, Aggravated
Assault, Simple
Assisted Suicide
Athletes/Athletics
Athletes/Athletics and Violence in Sport
Bullying
Community Violence
Contract Killings
Corporate Violence
Cyberstalking
Expressive Violence
Fear of Crime
Female Perpetrators of Interpersonal Violence
Forced Military Conscription
Gang Violence
Genocide
Gun Violence
Hate Crimes (Bias Crimes), Anti-Gay
Hate Crimes (Bias Crimes), Gender Motivated
Health Consequences of Hate Crime
Health Consequences of Incarceration
Homelessness and Violence
Homicides, Criminal
Homophobia
Homophobia and Media Representations of Gay,
   Lesbian, Bisexual, and Transgender People
Hypermasculinity
Instrumental Violence
Masculinities and Violence
Mass Murder
Media, Representations/Distortions of Crime
Media and Violence
Misogyny
Moral Panics
Neuropsychological Factors in Impulsive Aggression
   and Violent Behavior
Oppression and Violence
Patriarchy
Poverty
Prisoner Reentry
Psychophysiological Factors in Predicting Violence
Religion

Resiliency, Protective and Risk Factors
Ritualistic Abuse
Robbery
Serial Murder/Serial Killers
Sex Discrimination
Socioeconomic Status, Offending and
   Victimization by Class
Stalking
State Violence
Torture
Victimization, Predictors of
Violence Against People With Disabilities
Workplace Violence

Intervention and Prevention Programs

Abuse-Focused Therapy
Advocacy
Alcoholics Anonymous
AMEND
Batterers, Treatment Approaches and Effectiveness
Child Abuse Prevention
Child Death Review Teams
Clothesline Project
Collective Efficacy
Coordinated Community Response
Couple Counseling
Crime Victims Compensation Program
Crisis Hotlines
Culturally Sensitive Intervention
Domestic Violence Enhanced Response Team
Domestic Violence Fatality Review
Duluth Model
Early Intervention Programs
Emerge
Ethical and Legal Issues, Interviewing Children
   Reported as Abused or Neglected
Ethical and Legal Issues, Treating Elder Abuse
Faith-Based Programs
Family Group Conferencing
Family Preservation and Reunification Programs
Family Therapy and Family Violence
Father Involvement
Fathers' Rights Movement
Financial Literacy Versus Financial Abuse
Forensic Nursing

Legislation

Organizations and Agencies

Racial/Ethnic and Cross-Cultural Issues

Research Methods and Data Collection Instruments

Sexual Violence and Abuse

Syndromes, Disorders, and Other Mental Health Issues

Theories and Theoretical Perspectives

Violence Between Intimates/ Family Violence

About the General Editors

Claire M. Renzetti is Professor of Sociology at the University of Dayton. Previously, she was Professor of Sociology at St. Joseph's University in Philadelphia, where she was on the faculty for 25 years and chaired the sociology department for 10 of those years. Renzetti is also editor of the international, interdisciplinary journal *Violence Against Women*, a peer-reviewed professional journal published monthly by Sage Publications. She is coeditor of the Oxford University Press book series titled *Interpersonal Violence*, and editor of the Northeastern University Press book series titled *Gender, Crime, and Law*.

Renzetti has authored or edited 16 books as well as numerous articles in professional journals, based largely on her research on various aspects of the problem of intimate partner violence (IPV). Her groundbreaking study, published in 1992 as the monograph *Violent Betrayal: Partner Abuse in Lesbian Relationships*, was the first national empirical study of IPV in lesbian relationships. This study essentially revolutionized IPV research in that it forced researchers to think outside the box to consider violence in same-sex relationships and its implications for theorizing IPV. Renzetti's current research examines the violent victimization experiences of women who live in public housing developments. This work continues to reflect her concern with ensuring that the voices of marginalized women are heard.

Renzetti's research contributions to the study of intimate violence have been recognized by her colleagues with several awards, including four faculty merit awards for research from St. Joseph's University, which also awarded her its highest honor, the Tenglemann Award for Research and Teaching; she was the first woman to ever receive the Tenglemann Award. Her colleagues in the American Society of Criminology have also recognized her contributions to the field by bestowing on her the Outstanding Scholar Award from the Division on Women and Crime and the Major Achievement Award from the Critical Criminology Division.

Renzetti has long been active in professional organizations and in her community. She is past president of the Society for the Study of Social Problems, the second largest professional sociological association in the country; past treasurer of the Eastern Sociological Society; and past president of Alpha Kappa Delta, the international sociological honors society. She currently serves on the boards of the Artemis Center for Alternatives to Domestic Violence, the Miami Valley School, and the Dayton Art Institute, and she is involved in a number of fundraising events for nonprofits in the Dayton area, including the Food Bank of the Miami Valley, the March of Dimes, and the Dayton Visual Arts Center.

Renzetti holds a PhD in sociology from the University of Delaware, where she also received her undergraduate degree in sociology.

Jeffrey L. Edleson is Professor at the University of Minnesota School of Social Work and Director of the Minnesota Center Against Violence and Abuse (www.mincava.umn.edu). He is one of the world's leading authorities on children exposed to domestic violence and has published over 100 articles and eight books on domestic violence, groupwork, and program evaluation. Edleson is the coauthor with the late Susan Schechter of *Effective Intervention in Domestic Violence and Child Maltreatment Cases: Guidelines for Policy and Practice* (1999, National Council of Juvenile and Family Court Judges). Better known as the "Greenbook," this best-practices guide has been the subject of six federally funded and numerous other demonstration sites across the country. Edleson has also conducted intervention research and provided technical assistance to domestic violence programs and research projects across North America as well as in several other countries, including Germany, Israel, Cyprus, India, Australia, Korea, and Singapore.

He was a member of the National Academy of Sciences' Panel on Research on Violence Against Women. He has served as a consultant to the National Council of Juvenile and Family Court Judges and the U.S. Centers for Disease Control and Prevention. Edleson is an associate editor of the journal *Violence Against Women* and has served on numerous editorial boards. He is coeditor of the Oxford University Press book series titled *Interpersonal Violence* and the Sage book series titled *Violence Against Women.*

His own books include *Working With Children and Adolescents in Groups,* with Sheldon D. Rose (1987, Jossey-Bass); *Intervention for Men Who Batter: An Ecological Approach,* with Richard M. Tolman (1992, Sage Publications); *Ending the Cycle of Violence:*

Community Responses to Children of Battered Women, with Einat Peled and Peter G. Jaffe (1995, Sage Publications); *Future Interventions With Battered Women and Their Families,* with Zvi Eisikovits (1996, Sage Publications); *Evaluating Domestic Violence Programs* (1997, Domestic Abuse Project); *Domestic Violence in the Lives of Children: The Future of Research, Intervention, and Social Policy,* with Sandra Graham-Bermann (2001, APA Books); and *Parenting by Men Who Batter: New Directions in Assessment and Intervention,* with Oliver J. Williams (2007, Oxford University Press).

Edleson is a Phi Beta Kappa graduate of the University of California at Berkeley and received his master's and PhD in social work from the University of Wisconsin at Madison. He is a Licensed Independent Clinical Social Worker in Minnesota and has practiced in elementary and secondary schools and in several domestic violence agencies worldwide.

Contributors

Amir Abbassi
*Texas A&M
University–Commerce*

Jaleel Abdul-Adil
University of Illinois at Chicago

David Adams
Emerge

Patricia A. Adler
University of Colorado

Peter Adler
University of Denver

Reema S. Ali
Break the Cycle

Nicole E. Allen
*University of Illinois at
Urbana-Champaign*

Alex Alvarez
Northern Arizona University

Georgia J. Anetzberger
Cleveland State University

Sharon K. Araji
University of Alaska Anchorage

Isami Arifuku
*National Council on Crime and
Delinquency*

Phil Arkow
The Latham Foundation

Marilyn Peterson Armour
University of Texas at Austin

Karen Marlene Artichoker
Cangleska, Inc.

Frank R. Ascione
Utah State University

Emily K. Asencio
University of California, Riverside

Ronet Bachman
University of Delaware

Linda Baker
*Centre for Children & Families
in the Justice System*

Amanda Baran
*Legal Momentum: Advancing
Women's Rights*

Lisa M. Bauer
Pepperdine University

Carl C. Bell
University of Illinois at Chicago

Holly Bell
University of Texas at Austin

Larry W. Bennett
University of Illinois at Chicago

Susan H. Berg
*Hunter College School of Social
Work*

Raquel Kennedy Bergen
Saint Joseph's University

Lucy Berliner
University of Washington

Christopher Bickel
*University of California, Santa
Barbara*

James A. Black
University of Tennessee

Ashley G. Blackburn
University of North Texas

Cindy Blackstock
*First Nations Child & Family
Caring Society of Canada*

Linda K. Bledsoe
University of Louisville

Sandra L. Bloom
CommunityWorks

Rebecca M. Bolen
University of Tennessee

Jeb A. Booth
Salem State College

Denise Paquette Boots
University of Texas at Dallas

Linda Bowen
Institute for Community Peace

Bonnie Brandl
*National Clearinghouse on
Abuse in Later Life, Wisconsin
Coalition Against Domestic
Violence*

Charmaine R. Brittain
University of Denver

Christen L. Brook
*University of
Massachusetts–Lowell*

Mitchell Brown
Institute for Community Peace

Sarah K. Brown
Break the Cycle

Stephanie L. Bruhn
Nebraska State Penitentiary

Meggan M. Bucossi
*Brown Medical School and Butler
Hospital*

Leo Bulger
Minneapolis Public Schools

Frederick P. Buttell
Tulane University

Eve S. Buzawa
*University of
Massachusetts–Lowell*

Jacquelyn C. Campbell
*Johns Hopkins University School
of Nursing*

Rebecca Campbell
Michigan State University

Bonnie E. Carlson
*University at Albany, State
University of New York*

Michelle M. Carney
University of Georgia

Patrick J. Carr
Rutgers University

Ricardo Antonio Carrillo
Private Consultant

Erin A. Casey
University of Washington, Tacoma

Beth Skilken Catlett
DePaul University

Lynn S. Chancer
*Hunter College of the City
University of New York*

Mei Chao
Michigan State University

Kristen E. Cheney
University of Dayton

Michelle Chino
University of Nevada, Las Vegas

Debbie Chiodo
*CAMH Centre for Prevention
Science*

Chelsea M. Clawson
Lewis & Clark College

Caroline Clements
*University of North Carolina at
Wilmington*

Larry Cohen
Prevention Institute

Kimberly J. Cook
*University of North Carolina at
Wilmington*

Christine A. Courtois
Private Practice

Claire V. Crooks
*Centre for Addiction & Mental
Health*

Terry Cross
*National Indian Child Welfare
Association*

Chic Dabby-Chinoy
*Asian & Pacific Islander Institute
on Domestic Violence*

Fran S. Danis
University of Missouri–Columbia

Deborah Daro
Chapin Hall Center for Children

Shamita Das Dasgupta
*Manavi, Inc., & Praxis
International, Inc.*

Howard A. Davidson
American Bar Association

Mark S. Davis
Ohio State University

Tracy J. Davis
*Pennsylvania Coalition Against
Domestic Violence*

Shawndell N. Dawson
*National Network to End
Domestic Violence*

Lemyra DeBruyn
*Centers for Disease Control and
Prevention*

Michele R. Decker
Harvard School of Public Health

Christina DeJong
Michigan State University

Walter S. DeKeseredy
*University of Ontario Institute of
Technology*

Carey Anne DeOliveira
*Child and Parent Resource
Institute*

Gail Dines
Wheelock College

Aldwin Domingo
Argosy University

Alesha Dominique
Break the Cycle

Patrick G. Donnelly
University of Dayton

Joseph F. Donnermeyer
Ohio State University

George W. Dowdall
St. Joseph's University

Molly Dragiewicz
*University of Ontario Institute of
    Technology*

Howard Dubowitz
University of Maryland

Billie Lee Dunford-Jackson
*National Council of Juvenile and
    Family Court Judges*

Mary Ann Dutton
*Georgetown University Medical
    Center*

Jeffrey L. Edleson
University of Minnesota

Sue Else
*National Network to End
    Domestic Violence*

Elaine Enarson
Brandon University

Samantha Elena Erskine
Legal Momentum

Kathleen Coulborn Faller
University of Michigan

Jonathan Fast
*Wurzweiler School of Social
    Work, Yeshiva University*

Angèle Fauchier
University of New Hampshire

Jill Fertel
Break the Cycle

Susan Fineran
University of Southern Maine

Jerry Finn
University of Washington, Tacoma

Diana Fishbein
RTI International

Katherine W. Follansbee
University of Florida

Lisa A. Fontes
Union Institute & University

David A. Ford
*Indiana University–Purdue
    University Indianapolis*

Marie M. Fortune
FaithTrust Institute

Cynthia Fraser
*National Network to End
    Domestic Violence*

Jennifer J. Freyd
University of Oregon

Natasha A. Frost
Northeastern University

Juley Fulcher
Break the Cycle

Lynne Fullerton-Gleason
University of New Mexico

Stacie Robyn Furia
*University of California, Santa
    Barbara*

Shannon R. Gaskins
*National Council of Juvenile
    and Family Court Judges*

Richard J. Gelles
University of Pennsylvania

Abigail Gewirtz
University of Minnesota

Roberta E. Gibbons
University of Minnesota

Jane F. Gilgun
*University of Minnesota,
    Twin Cities*

Tameka L. Gillum
Johns Hopkins University

Lori B. Girshick
*Chandler-Gilbert Community
    College*

Rachel Evelyn Goldsmith
Mount Sinai Medical Center

Corinne Meltzer Graffunder
*U.S. Centers for Disease Control
    and Prevention*

Sandra A. Graham-Bermann
University of Michigan

Michelle Gross
University of Michigan

Debra Guckenheimer
*University of California, Santa
    Barbara*

Nancy G. Guerra
*University of California,
    Riverside*

April J. Guillen
Break the Cycle

Cuneyt Gurer
Kent State University

Liena Gurevich
Hofstra University

Neil B. Guterman
University of Chicago

Nicole Haberland
The Population Council

Susan M. Hadley
University of Minnesota

Janet O. Hagberg
Silent Witness National Initiative

Jennifer Hall-Lande
University of Minnesota

Rhonda Hallberg
Children's Aid Society of London and Middlesex

Melissa Hamilton
University of Texas at Austin

Heather Hammer
Temple University

Vanessa Handsel
University of North Carolina at Wilmington

Christine Hansen
The Miles Foundation, Inc.

Kirsten Harmon
Break the Cycle

Shelby Settles Harper
National Center on Full Faith and Credit, Pennsylvania Coalition Against Domestic Violence

Barbara J. Hart
University of Southern Maine

Michele Harway
Antioch University, Santa Barbara

Nicola Harwin
Women's Aid Federation of England

Jacquelyn Hauser
Academy on Violence and Abuse

Candace J. Heisler
Heisler and Associates

C. Terry Hendrix
Retired Publisher

Jessica P Hodge
University of Delaware

Kathryn H. Howell
University of Michigan

C. Ronald Huff
University of California, Irvine

Ray Hughes
CAMH Centre for Prevention Science

Li-Ching Hung
Mississippi State University

Peter G. Jaffe
University of Western Ontario

Shabnam Javdani
University of Illinois at Urbana-Champaign

Eric Jefferis
Kent State University

Esther J. Jenkins
Chicago State University

Robert Jensen
University of Texas at Austin

Arthur J. Jipson
University of Dayton

Byron Johnson
Baylor University

Nikki Jones
University of California, Santa Barbara

Marcus Juodis
Dalhousie University

Valli Kalei Kanuha
University of Hawaii

Jackson Katz
MVP Strategies

David Kauzlarich
Southern Illinois University, Edwardsville

Elizabeth Kelly
Baylor University

Kathleen Kendall-Tackett
University of New Hampshire

Poco Kernsmith
Wayne State University

Lloyd Klein
Kingsborough Community College

Shannon Kobes
Michigan State University

Pat Koppa
Public Health Consultants, LLC

Mary P. Koss
Mel and Enid Zuckerman College of Public Health

Sheryl Pimlott Kubiak
Michigan State University

Shanti Kulkarni
University of North Carolina at Charlotte

Traci LaLiberte
University of Minnesota

Emily Lambert
Break the Cycle

Wendy G. Lane
University of Maryland

Louanne Lawson
University of Arkansas for Medical Sciences

Lisa Lederer
PR Solutions, Inc.

Linda E. Ledray
Hennepin County Medical Center

Matthew R. Lee
Louisiana State University

Rebekah Lee
Pennsylvania Coalition Against Domestic Violence

Amy Lehrner
University of Illinois at Urbana-Champaign

Melinda S. Leidy
University of California, Riverside

Janel M. Leone
Syracuse University

Susan Lewis
National Sexual Violence Resource Center

Elizabeth Lightfoot
University of Minnesota

Terry G. Lilley
University of Delaware

Linda Loflin Pettit
AMEND

Tonya Lovelace
Pennsylvania Coalition Against Domestic Violence–WOCN

Eleanor Lyon
University of Connecticut

Shana L. Maier
Widener University

Patricia Yancey Martin
Florida State University

Rick A. Matthews
Carthage College

Christopher D. Maxwell
Michigan State University/University of Michigan

David McCollum
MD, President of the Academy on Violence and Abuse

Martha McMahon
University of Victoria

Pamela M. McMahon
Centers for Disease Control and Prevention

Beverly A. McPhail
University of Houston

Adelita M. Medina
National Latino Alliance for the Elimination of Domestic Violence

Michelle Lynn Meloy
Rutgers University

Anne Menard
National Resource Center on Domestic Violence

Jon'a F. Meyer
Rutgers University

Dan E. Miller
University of Dayton

Jody Miller
University of Missouri–St. Louis

Susan L. Miller
University of Delaware

Cindy Miller-Perrin
Pepperdine University

Angela M. Moe
Western Michigan University

Todd M. Moore
University of Tennessee

Marlene Marie Moretti
Simon Fraser University

Phoebe Morgan
Northern Arizona University

Lisa R. Muftić
University of North Texas

Wendy J. Murphy
New England School of Law

Jeremy NeVilles-Sorell
Mending the Sacred Hoop

Kirk A. B. Newring
Nebraska Department of Correctional Services

Jennifer M. Ngo
Wellesley College

Catherine Nolan
U.S. Department of Health and Human Services

Derek Nord
University of Minnesota

Jeffrey O'Brien
University of Central Florida

Patricia O'Brien
University of Illinois at Chicago

Ingrid Obsuth
Simon Fraser University

Candice L. Odgers
University of California, Irvine

Richard L. Ogle
University of North Carolina at Wilmington

William Oliver
Indiana University

Steven J. Ondersma
Wayne State University

Leslye Orloff
Legal Momentum: Immigrant Women Program

Sue Osthoff
National Clearinghouse for the Defense of Battered Women

Ana Ottman
Violence Against Women Policy Professional

Barbara Owen
California State University, Fresno

Claire S. Oxtoby
University of North Carolina at Wilmington

Rosalyn S. Park
Minnesota Advocates for Human Rights

Angela Moore Parmley
National Institute of Justice

Ellen Pence
Praxis International

Joan Pennell
North Carolina State University

Stephanie R. Penney
Simon Fraser University

Robin Perrin
Pepperdine University

Barbara Perry
University of Ontario Institute of Technology

Kathy Pezdek
Claremont Graduate University

Debby A. Phillips
Seattle University

Nickie D. Phillips
John Jay College of Criminal Justice

Nnamdi Pole
University of Michigan

Ann Marie Popp
Duquesne University

Laura F. Radel
U.S. Department of Health and Human Services

Nicole E. Rader
Mississippi State University

Allison Randall
National Network to End Domestic Violence

Jody Raphael
DePaul College of Law

Mary Gleason Rappaport
National Center for Victims of Crime

Maureen Reid
Children's Aid Society, London and Middlesex

Callie Marie Rennison
University of Missouri–St. Louis

Claire M. Renzetti
University of Dayton

Marc Riedel
Southeastern Louisiana University

Michael Robb
University of California, Riverside

Karen A. Roberto
Virginia Tech

Christine Robinson
Department of Social and Health Services

Deborah Rogow
The Population Council

Jennifer L. Root
University of Toronto

Leora Rosen
National Institute of Justice

Shannon Forbes Rushing
Southeastern Louisiana University

Ann Russo
DePaul University

Naomi Sadeh
University of Illinois at Urbana-Champaign

Michael Saini
University of Toronto

Jeff Salt
University of Illinois at Chicago

Daniel G. Saunders
University of Michigan

Frederika E. Schmitt
Millersville University

F. David Schneider
University of Texas at San Antonio

Martin D. Schwartz
Ohio University

Katreena L. Scott
University of Toronto

Alankaar Sharma
University of Minnesota

Chaitra P. Shenoy, Esq.
*Center for Survivor Agency &
    Justice*

Melanie F. Shepard
University of Minnesota Duluth

Sudha Shetty
University of Minnesota

Aron Shlonsky
University of Toronto

Sara J. Shoener
*Pennsylvania Coalition Against
    Domestic Violence*

Lynn M. Short
Analytic Systems Associates, Inc.

Toby Shulruff
*National Network to End
    Domestic Violence*

Gerald B. "Jerry" Silverman
*U.S. Department of Health and
    Human Services*

Jay G. Silverman
Harvard School of Public Health

Raghu N. Singh
Texas A&M University–Commerce

Jacqueline J. Skog
*Silent Witness Domestic Violence
    Initiative*

Mark Small
Clemson University

Carolyn Ann Smith
University at Albany

Cary Stacy Smith
Mississippi State University

Rita Smith
*National Coalition Against
    Domestic Violence*

Cindy Southworth
*National Network to End
    Domestic Violence*

Nan Stein
Wellesley College

Ted J. Stein
State University of New York

Paul Stern
*Snohomish County Prosecutor's
    Office*

Kiersten Stewart
Family Violence Prevention Fund

Gregory L. Stuart
Brown University

Richard B. Stuart
University of Washington

Erika A. Sussman
*Center for Survivor Agency and
    Justice*

Maura Doyle Tanabe
Autism Connections

Pamela B. Teaster
University of Kentucky

Jeff R. Temple
University of Texas Medical Branch

Cheryl A. Thomas
*Minnesota Advocates for Human
    Rights*

Patrick H. Tolan
University of Illinois at Chicago

Kimberly A. Tolhurst
*Battered Women's Justice
    Project/Civil Office*

Nicole Trabold
University at Buffalo

Jennifer Trotter
*University of Illinois at
    Urbana-Champaign*

Michelle J. Trotter
University of Minnesota

Carolyn Tubbs
Drexel University

Sarah Tucker
*National Network to End
    Domestic Violence*

Sarah E. Ullman
University of Illinois at Chicago

Mark S. Umbreit
University of Minnesota

Lynn Videka
*University at Albany–State
    University of New York*

Denise D. Walker
University of Washington

Froma Walsh
University of Chicago

Wendy A. Walsh
University of New Hampshire

Carole Warshaw
*National Training and TA Center
    on Domestic Violence*

Neil Websdale
Northern Arizona University

Arlene N. Weisz
Wayne State University

D. Charles Whitney
*University of California,
    Riverside*

Introduction

Interpersonal violence is behavior by people that intentionally threatens, attempts, or actually inflicts harm on other people. This violence invades both the public and private spheres of our lives, many times in unexpected and frightening ways. Interpersonal violence is a problem that individuals may experience at any point during the lifespan—indeed, even before birth. From the use of amniocentesis to identify the sex of a fetus with the intention of aborting it if it is female to the withholding of food or medication from an elderly person to punish him or her for some perceived infraction, interpersonal violence is found not only throughout the life course, but also throughout the world. It is a global problem that includes war, genocide, terrorism, and rape of women as a weapon of war.

The *Encyclopedia of Interpersonal Violence* is designed as a resource for members of the general public who are interested in learning more about various aspects of the problem of interpersonal violence. It is intended to provide accurate, research-supported information to clarify critical issues and to educate the public about different forms of interpersonal violence, their incidence and prevalence, theoretical explanations, public policy initiatives, and prevention and intervention strategies. It is also intended as a resource for students at all educational levels who are studying about interpersonal violence or who anticipate a career in one of the many fields in which professionals address aspects of interpersonal violence. Practitioners and clinicians in a wide range of fields will also find the encyclopedia helpful as a quick reference guide to definitions, statistics, theories, policies, and prevention and intervention programs.

The encyclopedia consists of two volumes, which together contain over 500 entries arranged alphabetically. The entries were written by experts on the specific topic being addressed and provide cross-references to related entries as well as suggested readings for further information on the topic. A Reader's Guide also assists readers in locating articles on specific and related topics. It is organized into 12 general topical categories that include Civil and Criminal Legal Systems; Intervention and Prevention Programs; Legislation; Research Methods and Data Collection Instruments; Syndromes, Disorders, and Other Mental Health Issues; and Theories and Theoretical Perspectives. Reflecting our concern with interpersonal violence as a problem across the lifespan as well as across cultures, entries are also listed under the topical categories of Children and Youth; Racial/Ethnic and Cross-Cultural Issues; Sexual Violence and Abuse; and Violence Between Intimates/ Family Violence. Topics not found in any of these categories are likely located in the section on Interpersonal Violence—General.

Our goal has been to make the encyclopedia as accessible and as easy to use as possible. The jargon-free style in which the articles are written further contributes to this goal. Key concepts are defined, and theoretical principles are explained clearly and succinctly. At the end of Volume 2, readers will also find appendices that provide information on current data sets, regional and national organizations specializing in various dimensions of interpersonal violence, and relevant Web sites.

The process of compiling the encyclopedia was long and, at times, arduous. In identifying headwords and potential contributors, we were joined by a capable team of advisors representing diverse fields and areas of expertise. We are indebted to our Advisory Board: C. Terry Hendrix, our long-time editor at Sage Publications who helped bring many of the key books and journals in interpersonal violence to our bookshelves; Angela Moore Parmley, U.S. Department of Justice's National Institute of Justice; Barbara Perry, University of Ontario Institute of Technology; and Patrick H. Tolan, University of Illinois at Chicago.

Once the headword list was generated, invitations were emailed to all potential contributors. This process involved nearly 1,000 emails over the course of many months, as individual accepted our invitation or declined, but recommended others. Scott Weaver, a graduate student at the time at St. Joseph's University, took on the task of sending invitations and often tracking down elusive email addresses. Scott's efficiency and good humor went a long way in alleviating much of the stress associated with this initial phase of the project.

We are also fortunate to have worked for over 2 years through over 5,000 email messages with an outstanding developmental editor, Eileen Gallaher. Eileen not only managed the day-to-day tasks associated with producing the encyclopedia but also assisted contributors with the electronic submission procedures, answered many contributors' questions, pleasantly cajoled contributors whose articles were late, and cheered us on when our energy seemed to be flagging. It has truly been a pleasure working with Eileen. She was joined by Yvette Pollastrini and then Carole Maurer in helping to take this collection of entries to a final format ready for the printing presses. Eileen, Yvette, and Carole all worked under the able leadership of Rolf Janke, the Publisher of Sage Reference.

Of course, there would be no encyclopedia without the several hundred contributors who shared their expertise and their precious time. Despite their numerous commitments, these individuals agreed to write entries—some more than one entry—for this project, a testament, we think, to their dedication to public education on the problem of interpersonal violence. We are grateful to each of them.

Jeff would like to thank his life partner, Sudha Shetty; his four sons, Nevin, Daniel, Neil, and Eli; and his staff at the Minnesota Center Against Violence and Abuse for putting up with all those hours he was distracted by communicating with authors and editors and then reading, editing, and approving submitted entries.

Finally, Claire wishes to say thank you to a very special group of friends: Brad, Bryan, Dan, Doug, Greg, and Michael. I'm grateful for your interest in and support of this project. I especially appreciate your willingness to discuss various entries with me at length and offer insightful feedback, and I look forward to your input on future projects. The mojitos are on me!

Claire M. Renzetti
Jeffrey L. Edleson

ABANDONMENT

Abandonment is generally understood in terms of infants and children being discarded by parents. Historically, women living in poverty, giving birth out of wedlock, or raped during wars were likely to dispose of their children. After World War II and the disintegration of Yugoslavia, many women walked out on the children they had conceived as a result of rape. Typically, youthful mothers without material or other support have been known to abandon their offspring in shame and desperation, at times in potentially life-threatening locations such as garbage bins, street corners, and public toilets. In the United States, abandonment of a child is a crime for which mothers can be prosecuted. To quell abandoned infant death, 45 U.S. states have passed a safe haven law (also called "Baby Moses" law) that permits parents to leave infants in designated "safe care" without fear of prosecution.

Abandoned children living in the streets without adults are found in every country. According to UN estimates in 2001, 150 million children under the age of 18 were dwelling in streets due to poverty, abuse, parental death, and deliberate abandonment. In many societies, more girls than boys are abandoned because of a strong preference for sons who can support their parents.

Emotional and economic abandonment of children by their fathers is a serious problem internationally and in the United States, where the UN estimated that 10 million single mothers were living with children under the age of 18 in 2000. In addition to children, a large number of elderly individuals of both genders are deserted each year in the United States. According to the American College of Emergency Physicians, caregivers abandoned approximately 70,000 elderly Americans in 1991, many with serious illnesses such as Alzheimer's disease. Long-term caregivers, the majority of whom are female relatives, are often overwhelmed by lack of financial and social assistance, leading to abandonment of their charges.

Wives are also abandoned by their spouses worldwide, including in the West. Many middle-aged wives who spent their youth supporting their husbands' careers are replaced by younger women. Such discarding of adult women is not considered a crime in any Western country. However, in many developing nations where women's only recourse to financial survival may be marriage, the forsaking of a wife may be a legal issue.

Desertion of wives and children has significantly grown in the wake of increased global worker mobility and many nations view it as violence against women. Following are three scenarios of wife abandonment common to immigrant communities:

- An abusive spouse might abandon his wife, and she may have no resources in the host country.
- A wife may be deceptively or forcibly transported from her home country and abandoned by her husband without any means of reentry (i.e., without passport, visa, airline ticket, or money).
- A husband might leave his wife behind in their home country and visit occasionally, with promises of bringing her back (hence the nomenclature "holiday bride"). For example, by some reports, more than 10,000 runaway immigrant grooms from India reside

1

in Canada, and 16,000 abandoned wives live in just one Indian state. The magnitude of the problem has prompted the Indian government to draft a bill to ameliorate the situation.

Shamita Das Dasgupta

See also Child Neglect; Elder Abuse; Feminist Movements to End Violence Against Women; Forced Marriages; Intimate Partner Violence

Further Readings

Thurer, S. L. (1994). *The myths of motherhood: How culture reinvents the good mother.* Boston: Houghton Mifflin.

ABOLITIONIST APPROACH TO PROSTITUTION

The abolitionist platform is clear: Prostitution is exploitation. To abolitionists, the women involved are thought of as "prostituted women" who are abused under a patriarchal society of male domination and sexual exploitation.

The results of several U.S. studies on prostitution support the view that prostitution is associated with drug abuse, HIV/AIDS risks, violence, and poor physical, emotional, and mental health outcomes for the women involved.

A strong connection has been made between drug abuse and street prostitution. Research findings suggest that some women use drugs to cope with the shame, violence, and trauma they face as prostitutes, while other women enter prostitution drug addicted and use prostitution to finance their drug habit.

Prostituted women continue to be placed at risk for contracting HIV/AIDS. Researchers cite addiction to drugs, client resistance to condom use, rape, forced prostitution by pimps/traffickers, and lack of condom use with risky intimate lovers as conditions that increase risk.

The violence experienced by prostituted women is heinous and pervasive, with researchers reporting that upwards of 70% of these women have experienced frequent and varied acts of violence. Women most commonly experience physical violence from customers, intimate lovers, pimps, and police.

Studies of psychosocial well-being and prostitution find that prostituted women typically have low self-esteem and high levels of depression and posttraumatic stress disorder.

Policies and Programs Supported by Abolitionists

Most abolitionists support policies that decriminalize prostitution for victims. They would encourage stiff penalties and/or effective interventions for pimps, who are often known as "traffickers," and customers, who are known as "johns." Community-focused programs founded by survivors or that employ survivors to intervene show promise in helping to build relationships with women on the streets. Social service programs may also help victims to address their issues and meet their needs by offering substance abuse treatment, shelter and transitional housing, case management, trauma treatment, group work, interpersonal counseling, and education and job training programs.

After the U.S. presidential signing of the Trafficking Victims Protection Reauthorization Act of 2000, federal, state, and local law enforcement joined to form task forces in various cities to address the issue of human trafficking, of which sex trafficking is a part. Professional helpers are looking to translate federal sentiments into best practices to move a woman from victim to survivor. While immediate efforts focus on rescuing and restoring victims, long-term goals include primary prevention and early intervention.

Reducing Violence Against Women

According to abolitionists, reducing violence against women requires that one see prostitution in and of itself as violence toward women. In their view, prostitution is not a choice; prostitution is often chosen for women because of their impoverished circumstances, abuses in their pasts, or blocked opportunities at conventional economic success.

Present-Day Advocates

There are several trend-setting leaders in the antiprostitution movement. These include Janice Raymond, Melissa Farley, Norma Hotaling, Vednita Carter, and Donna Hughes, among others.

Celia Williamson

See also Decriminalization of Sex Work

Further Readings

Farley, M. (2005, August 30). *Unequal*. Retrieved August 13, 2006, from http://action.web.ca/home/catw/readingroom .shtml?x=81265&AA_EX_Session=15acc93b7bb82739e1 12b283671b5d3b

Farley, M., & Barkan, H. (1998). Prostitution, violence, and posttraumatic stress disorder. *Women & Health, 27*(3), 37–49.

Farley, M., Cotton, A., Lynee, J., Zumbeck, S., Spiwak, F., Reyes, M. E., et al. (2003). Prostitution and trafficking in nine countries: An update on violence and posttraumatic stress disorder. In M. Farley (Ed.), *Prostitution, trafficking, and traumatic stress* (pp. 33–74). Binghamton, NY: Haworth Maltreatment & Trauma Press.

ABORTION, SEX-SELECTIVE

See GENDERCIDE

ABUSE-FOCUSED THERAPY

Abuse-focused therapy is an umbrella term for a range of clinical models used in treating the impacts of childhood sexual abuse and trauma. Abuse-focused therapy originated in the late 1980s as an alternative to therapies that viewed abuse survivors' trauma-specific coping strategies as evidence of intrapsychic pathology and maladaptive reactions, and trauma therapies, which narrowly focused on catharsis and flooding techniques. In contrast to these therapies, abuse-focused therapy considered posttraumatic stress reactions and other trauma-related symptoms as legitimate reactions to situations that were or are threatening and oppressive.

Initially, abuse-focused therapy was developed only for adults and children who had been victims of childhood sexual abuse. However, subsequently, abuse-focused therapy became the therapy of choice for practitioners working with adult and child victims of childhood sexual abuse, other types of abuse, and trauma. Abuse-focused therapy's popularity has been based on a manifest philosophical orientation toward (a) emphasizing clients' agency and strengths, and (b) utilizing a flexible, integrated framework of interventions for addressing biopsychosocial issues emerging throughout the course of treatment.

Philosophical Influences

Feminist ideology and humanistic philosophy inform both the practitioner–client relationship and the treatment structure in abuse-focused therapy. Feminist ideology's focused attention on the societal, local, and familial discourses about oppression, gender, and power contextualizes abuses and trauma in past, present, and ongoing beliefs about relationships. This nuanced understanding of the broader social influences surrounding abusive and traumatic events is a perspective rarely accessible to clients as they engage in the arduous process of healing. This attention to beliefs about power and gendered violence also separates the abuse and trauma from the inherent characteristics of the client, and allows for validation of the client's self-protective strategies during and after the abuse or trauma.

Influences from humanistic philosophy encourage appreciation for the various types of self- and situational knowledge that clients display as they determine the pacing and direction of their healing. The practitioner assumes that the knowledge clients used to survive the abuse or trauma is still available to them during the healing process. In addition, this philosophical perspective invites active client investment in the treatment process and outcomes in order to decrease the probability of inadvertently replicating any oppressive power dynamics that might have accompanied the trauma. Similar to feminist ideology, a humanistic orientation depathologizes clients' past and current coping strategies and invites clients' expertise on their own healing process.

Abuse-Focused Therapeutic Interventions

Abuse-focused therapies focus on a group of clinical interventions rather than on a specific intervention or technique. In addition to grounding the treatment process in feminist and humanist ideologies, practitioners integrate many of the following clinical techniques and strategies into their work: cognitive-behavioral therapy, grief/loss work, systemic concepts (i.e., roles, rules, boundaries, holism), desensitization and hypnotherapeutic practices, and understandings of traumatic stress and victimization, as well as transference and countertransference from psychoanalytical theory. The introduction and fit use of techniques is contingent on the perceived and stated needs of the client as determined by the client and the practitioner.

Most work occurs individually; however, some work may occur in group, couple, and family therapy settings.

Carolyn Tubbs

See also Child Sexual Abuse; Complex Trauma in Children and Adolescents; Trauma-Focused Therapy

Further Readings

Lanktree, C. B., & Briere, J. (1995). Outcome of therapy for sexually abused children: A repeated measures study. *Child Abuse & Neglect, 19*, 1145–1155.

McGregor, K. (2000). Abuse-focused therapy for adult survivors of child sexual abuse: A review of the literature. *Centre Report Series No. 51* (pp. 1–279). Auckland, New Zealand: Injury Prevention Research Centre, University of Auckland.

ABUSIVE BEHAVIOR INVENTORY

The Abusive Behavior Inventory is an instrument designed to measure the physical and psychological abuse of women by their male partners. The instrument was first developed by Melanie Shepard in 1984 to evaluate the Duluth Domestic Abuse Intervention Project, a highly influential program in the field of domestic violence. Items for the instrument were drawn from the program's internationally known Power and Control Wheel, which was based on the experiences of battered women. In 1992, Shepard and James Campbell published a study documenting evidence of the instrument's reliability and validity. It has subsequently been used in many domestic violence studies. The Abusive Behavior Inventory is noted for its incorporation of both physical and psychological abuse items and the use of power and control, rather than family conflict, as a framework for measuring domestic violence.

The Abusive Behavior Inventory is based upon a feminist perspective whereby battering involves the use of a range of controlling tactics, including physical, psychological, and sexual abuse, to achieve and maintain dominance in intimate relationships. The instrument is a self-report questionnaire consisting of two separately scored subscales: psychological and physical abuse. The psychological abuse subscale consists of items drawn from the subcategories of emotional abuse, isolation, intimidation, threats, use of male privilege, and economic abuse. The physical abuse subscale consists of 10 items involving physical acts (e.g., hitting and choking) and sexual abuse (e.g., forced or pressured to engage in unwanted sexual acts).

Separate versions of the Abusive Behavior Inventory were originally created for abusive men and battered women, although the male version has not been widely used. The Abusive Behavior Inventory is able to distinguish between groups of abusers/abused and nonabusers/nonabused using the reports of both men and women. On the Abusive Behavior Inventory, women's reports of being abused are considered more reliable than the reports of men about their own use of abusive behaviors.

The Abusive Behavior Inventory continues to be used as a program evaluation tool and for other research purposes, such as studying the dynamics of dating violence. The Abusive Behavior Inventory is also a useful tool for screening women for domestic violence in health care and social service settings.

Melanie F. Shepard

See also Conflict Tactics Scales; Power and Control Wheel

Further Readings

Pence, E., & Paymar, M. (1993). *Education groups for men who batter: The Duluth model.* New York: Springer.

Shepard, M., & Campbell, J. (1992). The Abusive Behavior Inventory: A measure of psychological and physical abuse. *Journal of Interpersonal Violence, 7,* 291–305.

ACADEMY ON VIOLENCE AND ABUSE

The Academy on Violence and Abuse (AVA) is a nonprofit multidisciplinary health organization with membership open to physicians, nurses, physical and occupational therapists, and many other health professionals who are involved in patient care, health education, health research, and ancillary services. AVA incorporated in 2005 in an effort to improve the health care response to patients whose health has been adversely affected by lifetime exposure to violence and abuse. Nineteen of the country's leading physicians and health care professionals on the issue of violence and abuse comprised its founding Board of Directors.

AVA's mission is to advance health education and research on the recognition, treatment, and prevention of violence and abuse.

AVA grew out of the American Medical Association's National Advisory Council on Violence and Abuse, which was first established to develop guidelines to help physicians treat patients who had suffered domestic violence. As the council explored the issue of violence and abuse it recognized that the issue, as it related to health care, was far more complex and extended well beyond domestic violence. Thus AVA was created as an independent nonprofit membership organization whose major purpose is to develop the discipline of violence and abuse as a specialized area of health care.

A 2002 Institute of Medicine (IOM) report titled "Confronting Chronic Neglect: The Education and Training of Health Professionals on Family Violence" recommended the creation of an organization like AVA to improve the infrastructure necessary to support the training of health care professionals on the health consequences of violence and abuse. The IOM report also identified deficiencies—related to violence and abuse as a health care issue—in the health care education process and practice setting thereby resulting in the failure to develop adequate training programs, measure the effectiveness of current training, provide an environment that supports addressing family violence issues, and support professionals who have a professional interest in violence and abuse as a health care issue.

AVA plans to address the issues raised by the IOM report and several others. The academy plans to develop a unique field of expertise in medicine and other health care disciplines that encompasses all categories of violence and abuse and will work to enhance the understanding of its long-term health repercussions. AVA will also advocate for research to improve our understanding of the experience of abuse and its physical, biochemical, and biopsychosocial consequences. The academy envisions that by integrating health education and research on the issue of violence and abuse into the training of all health professionals, it will promote the health of all people, protect the most vulnerable, and advance health and social policy that promotes safe families, safe workplaces, and safe communities.

*Jacquelyn Hauser, F. David Schneider,
and David McCollum*

See also Health Care Response, Prevention Strategies for Reducing Intimate Partner Violence; Health Care Response to Child Maltreatment; Health Care Response to Intimate Partner Violence; Health Consequences of Child Maltreatment; Health Consequences of Intimate Partner Violence

Further Readings

The Adverse Childhood Experiences Study. (2005, July 7). Retrieved from http://www.acestudy.org/

Cohn, F., Salmon, M. E., & Stoben, J. D. (Eds.). (2002). *Confronting chronic neglect: The education and training of health professionals on family violence.* Washington, DC: National Academies Press.

ACID ATTACKS

An acid attack is the throwing of corrosive acid on a human target. It is not a new phenomenon. Acid attacks were reported in Europe in the 19th century, and in China, India, Pakistan, Egypt, England, Italy, Jamaica, Malaysia, Nigeria, Vietnam, and the United States in the latter part of the 20th century. Most often, these attacks are by men on women, single and married, who have dared to spurn suitors, seek divorce, anger powerful community leaders, and generally transgress from their socially prescribed roles. A few men have also been victims, just as a few women have been perpetrators. Occasionally, men have attacked other men with acid to seek revenge, retaliate, or settle disputes. Acid violence has attracted international attention relatively recently with a spate of gendered attacks in Bangladesh.

Acid became the weapon of choice in violence against young women in Bangladesh, where the first case was documented in 1967. Subsequently, reported cases have been increasing: 47 in 1996, 130 in 1997, and 200 in 1998. By some reports, acid attacks increased 53% between 2000 and 2001, and nearly 300 cases were recorded per year. Such statistics are partial at best, as many families refrain from reporting acid attacks to authorities fearing further reprisals from perpetrators.

The majority of victims in Bangladesh are rural young girls and women of working and lower socioeconomic classes, ranging in age between their early teens and twenties. The weapon frequently is the sulfuric acid used in car batteries that is easily and cheaply available in local garages and stores. Commonly, perpetrators are neighbors, acquaintances, husbands, and other male relatives, who may attack a sleeping victim. The attacks might be the result of jealousy, rejection in love, rebuffed marriage proposals, or a man's failure to extort additional dowries from his wife's family. Since the motivation behind acid attacks is not only to punish women but also to permanently destroy their social and economic lives, faces are particular targets of disfigurement and blinding.

Some theorists link the upsurge in acid attacks on women in Bangladesh with forces of globalization. The main industry in Bangladesh, Western garment factories that manufacture export materials, tend to hire young women rather than men, thus placing women in the unconventional role of employed worker and men into financial dependency. This contravention of traditions challenges masculinity, which historically has been based on wage earning and protecting the family. It is thought that as men lose gender-based social power to women, their violence against women intensifies.

In the 1980s, women's nongovernmental agencies in Bangladesh, led by Naripokkho, organized to focus the national and international spotlight on acid attacks on women, which ultimately led to the founding of the Acid Survivors Foundation in 1999. Bangladeshi women's activism facilitated needed social services and medical treatment in the country for survivors, and for some survivors in Europe and the United States as well. In 1989, Bangladesh made acid violence a crime punishable by death, although very few perpetrators have been tried in courts, let alone received the death penalty. Enforcement of laws that criminalize violence against women still remains a serious problem in Bangladesh.

Shamita Das Dasgupta

See also Dowry Deaths, Bride Burning; Femicide; Feminist Movements to End Violence Against Women; Patriarchy; Torture

Further Readings

Anwary, A. (2003). Acid violence and medical care in Bangladesh: Women's activism as carework. *Gender & Society, 17,* 305–313.

Taylor, L. M. (2001). Saving face: Acid attack laws after the U.N. Convention on the Elimination of All Forms of Discrimination Against Women. *Georgia Journal of International and Comparative Law, 29,* 395–426.

ACROTOMOPHILIA

Acrotomophilia is a type of fetish from which an individual (acrotomophile) derives sexual pleasure or arousal from having intercourse with or sexually fantasizing about a person who has a body part amputated (an amputee). Acrotomophilia is a type of paraphilia, which is derived from Greek (*para* = altered, *philia* = love). Specifically, an acrotomophile is drawn to the stump(s) of the person whose limb(s) are amputated. In order to understand the topic of acrotomophilia, it is important to learn about the prevalence, development, and practice of acrotomophilia, as well as to examine related terminology.

Prevalence

The prevalence of acrotomophilia is hard to quantify and appears to be rare. Very little has been written about acrotomophilia in the scholarly literature, though there are a number of Internet sites devoted to the topic.

Development of Acrotomophilia

As theory around acrotomophilia evolves there are some suggested, but not researched, beliefs about the origins of acrotomophilia. Experts offer a range of hypotheses as to how and why acrotomophilia develops; some posit the paraphilia is developed unconsciously during childhood. Others believe the origin of the paraphilia is unknown and not necessarily linked to childhood experiences.

Practice of Acrotomophilia

Due to the stigma attached to acrotomophilia, individuals with this paraphilia tend to be secretive about their sexual preferences. While the practices of each acrotomophile vary widely, it appears that masturbatory fantasies related to amputees are most common. Some acrotomophiles seek out a person with an amputated body part and focus on their disability. Subsequently, some acrotomophiles have partners who are amputees or role-play the part of an amputee. According to case studies published in the scholarly literature, many partners with an amputated limb are not interested in the sexual attention that is based primarily on their amputated limb.

Body Integrity Identity Disorder

Related to the topic of acrotomophilia, there are individuals who wish to amputate a body part of their own, generally their limbs. These individuals are called apotemnophiles. Informally, acrotomophiles are widely referred to as "devotees," while apotemnophiles are referred to as "wannabes." In case studies published in the scholarly literature, apotemnophiles report not feeling whole with the body part they wish to amputate. Michael B. First, a researcher in the field, has identified the term *body integrity identity disorder* as an alternate and preferred term to describe apotemnophilia.

Some apotemnophiles may fantasize about being an amputee or pretend to be one to achieve sexual arousal; others may desire elective surgical amputations or pursue self-amputation. While few if any medical professionals are willing to perform voluntary amputations, apotemnophiles are left to their own resources to, in rare cases, carry out self-amputations using a variety of means. Often times, self-amputation attempts are unsuccessful in nonprofessional settings and result in emergency room visits, which, depending on the severity of the attempt, can result in a medically necessary professional amputation.

Michelle J. Trotter

See also Paraphilia

Further Readings

Elliott, C. (2000, December). A new way to be mad. *Atlantic Monthly, 286,* 72–84.

Lawrence, A. A. (2006, June). Clinical and theoretical parallels between desire for limb amputation and gender identity disorder. *Archives of Sexual Behavior, 35*(3), 263–278.

Wise, T. N., & Kalyanam, R. C. (2000). Amputee fetishism and genital mutilation: Case report and literature review. *Journal of Sex and Marital Therapy, 26,* 339–344.

Web Sites

Body Integrity Identity Disorder: http://www.biid.org/

ADOPTION AND SAFE FAMILIES ACT OF 1997

Since 1974, the U.S. Congress has enacted many laws developed to protect children affected by child abuse and neglect. One federal law is the Adoption and Safe Families Act of 1997, signed into law by President Bill Clinton on November 19, 1997. It is considered by many to be one of the strongest statements regarding child protection ever produced in the United States. The act establishes child protection as a national goal and specifies procedures for ensuring children's health and safety. The primary reasons for the initiation of the act were to ensure the health and safety of children, to promote permanent living situations for children in foster care, and to increase accountability of the child welfare system.

The law, while acknowledging the importance of family preservation and reunification in the long-term welfare of children, reaffirms that child safety must be the overriding concern of child welfare services. The act requires, for example, that the issue of child safety be specifically addressed when making decisions about service provision, placement, and permanency planning. The law also clarifies the states' responsibility to the child, explicitly noting that children should never be left in or returned to dangerous living situations. According to the act, a child may be placed in foster care either when danger to the child is imminent or when prevention attempts are unlikely to be effective. In addition, the law defines specific situations in which states should not return children to their families, such as when the parent has committed murder, manslaughter, or felony assault on the child or one of his or her other children.

The act also acknowledges that foster care should be viewed as temporary, not as a long-term solution. As such, the law establishes requirements for early permanency planning, such as a time frame for initiating termination of parental rights and timely adoption. The act specifies, for example, that services to reunify families should be time limited. States are required to initiate termination of parental rights and free children for adoption who have been waiting in foster care for 15 of the most recent 22 months. In an effort to encourage adoptions, the law also establishes various financial incentives to states that increase adoptions.

The Adoption and Safe Families Act of 1997 also requires that the child welfare system increase its accountability. The act helps to clarify that in addition to ensuring that procedural safeguards are met, services must also lead to positive results. The act requires states to establish outcome measures, for example, to document and improve child welfare service performance.

Cindy Miller-Perrin and Robin Perrin

See also Child Protective Services; Family Preservation and Reunification Programs; Foster Care; Kinship Care; Legal System and Child Protection; Legislation, Child Maltreatment

Further Readings

Myers, J. E. B. (1998). *Legal issues in child abuse and neglect practice* (2nd ed.). Thousand Oaks, CA: Sage.
National Clearinghouse on Child Abuse and Neglect Information. (2003). *Major federal legislation concerned with child protection, child welfare, and adoption.* Retrieved April 18, 2006, from http://nccanch.acf.hhs.gov

ADOPTION ASSISTANCE AND CHILD WELFARE ACT OF 1980

The Adoption Assistance and Child Welfare Act of 1980 (AACWA, Public Law 96-272) created a national framework for the present-day foster care and adoption assistance programs in the United States. The law was enacted in response to concerns, documented in several landmark studies in the late 1970s, that children were being removed from their homes unnecessarily and, once separated from parents, spent too long in foster care. *Foster care drift* was the term coined to describe this phenomenon of long-lasting though ostensibly temporary foster care.

Nearly $7 billion in federal funds in 2005 were spent to support foster care payments and adoption subsidies for eligible children in accordance with the AACWA. Federal funds match similar levels of state spending for these activities.

Prior to the AACWA, the federal government had, since 1962, supported state foster care programs through the federal welfare program Aid to Families with Dependent Children. The AACWA separated the welfare and foster care functions and created for the first time federal financial support for adoption assistance subsidies to encourage the adoption of children with special needs. Adoption subsidies had existed in some states prior to the act's passage, but in its wake all states established such programs. Foster care payments could be supported with federal funds only if a judicial determination confirmed that continuation in the child's own home would be contrary to the welfare of the child.

The AACWA institutionalized in federal law the principle of permanency planning, that the goal of foster care is to identify a permanent, stable family for the child, with his or her biological parents if that is possible, or with an adoptive family if it is not. It requires state child welfare agencies to establish individualized case plan goals for each child in foster care, and to provide periodic administrative and judicial reviews of the family's progress in meeting the requirements of the case plan. These requirements began the first significant court oversight of child welfare cases. Also of great significance is the requirement that "reasonable efforts" be made to prevent the need for foster care and to address the problems that lead to foster care placement. The law further requires that children be placed in the least restrictive, most family-like setting in which their needs can be met.

Following the passage of the AACWA, foster care caseloads declined briefly during the early 1980s. These achievements were short-lived, however, and caseloads soon began increasing once again.

Laura F. Radel

See also Adoption and Safe Families Act of 1997; Child Abuse Prevention and Treatment Act

Further Readings

Adoption Assistance and Child Welfare Act. (1980). Retrieved from http://www.ncjfcj.org/images/stories/dept/ppcd/Legislation/adptasstchildwelfareact.pdf
Fanshel, D., & Shinn, E. B. (1978). *Children in foster care.* New York: Columbia University Press.
Murray, K. O., & Gesiriech, S. (2003). *A brief legislative history of the child welfare system.* Washington, DC: Pew Commission on Children in Foster Care.

ADULT PROTECTIVE SERVICES

Adult Protective Services (APS) is the public agency generally mandated to receive reports of alleged elder abuse, neglect, and exploitation. Some version of APS (or lead elder abuse agency) exists in each state. Eligibility criteria and precise responsibilities and guidelines vary from state to state. In most jurisdictions, APS serves *vulnerable adults* (as defined by state law) age 18 and above; in others it serves *elders,* defined as persons age 60 or 65 and above, regardless of health or cognitive status, as well as vulnerable adults. There is no financial means test for eligibility, and APS services are free. While all APS programs investigate suspected elder abuse occurring in community settings, in many states APS also investigates allegations arising in facilities. In a few states, APS maintains offender registries. In some states APS workers are mandated to report criminal conduct they discover to local law enforcement.

APS was developed in the 1970s and early 1980s. Title XX of the 1974 Social Security Act authorized states to use block grant funds to protect both adults and children. By 1981 every state had some agency providing protective services to some part of the population. Federal statutes did not define the type of services, so states have developed their own definitions and services, resulting in considerable variation. Subsequent federal funding has not kept pace with the explosion of the elder population, and today APS programs are inadequately funded and often must compete with child protective services (CPS) for funding. APS funding is a fraction of that provided for CPS. The states have used other funding sources to help support APS programs.

Most APS programs are within departments of social services. Others are in departments on aging and departments of health and rehabilitation. Some units only handle calls about elder or vulnerable adults; other programs are combined APS and CPS units. There is wide variation in the educational requirements to become an APS worker. Only two states (Kansas and Utah) require that APS workers be licensed social workers.

APS usually operates during normal business hours. Reports are received 24 hours a day through either a hotline or an after-hours telephone service. In some states, workers are available to respond to emergency calls at any hour.

The core philosophy of APS is to advocate for the client's right to autonomy, support the mentally capable client's right to make decisions, and select the least restrictive option among service options. Core values also require that actions taken by APS balance the client's right to self-determination with the duty to protect. This can be a delicate balancing act when an elder with mental capacity makes what may be perceived as an unwise choice. The National Association of Protective Services Administrators has identified additional core principles as the use of community-based services rather than institutional placement, the avoidance of blaming, and the provision of inadequate or inappropriate services as being worse than no services.

APS does not function as child protective services for adults. Adults retain their civil and legal rights until a court restricts or removes them. APS cannot remove an elder involuntarily from his or her home without court authority or force a client to accept an intervention. Once the initial investigation is completed, a client can refuse specific services or the involvement of APS altogether. Nor does APS operate as a law enforcement agency. APS workers do not have arrest powers, though they can as part of their mandate sometimes obtain records for their investigations that law enforcement must seek a court order to obtain. They cannot force entry into a location and must apply for a court order if they cannot obtain permission to enter.

APS functions include receipt of reports, determination that APS eligibility criteria are met, and assessment of immediate risk to the client. The matter is investigated by attempting to interview the alleged victim (client), perpetrator, and other witnesses; observing the environment for hazards and appropriateness; assessing the elder's health and capacity; and obtaining relevant records and other information in order to attempt to substantiate the allegation. With this information APS works with the client to develop a case plan or intervention. The case plan is individualized and draws on available community resources and the client's social supports and desires. If capacity is an issue, APS workers can conduct preliminary mental health screens and refer clients for further assessment.

Local policies and statutes often address how long APS can keep a case open within the agency. APS in some states can petition a court for appointment of a guardian for a client who lacks capacity. APS then collects information and provides it to the court where a decision is made on whether a guardianship is appropriate.

Services that can be offered to a client generally include housing (emergency shelter, lock changing, cleaning, repairs, and structural modification); medical (medications, referral to medical professionals); personal needs (meals, personal care provider, transportation to appointments, cleaning services);

advocacy (applying for health care and food benefits or community programs); emergency financial support; crisis counseling; and legal interventions (referral to a legal advocacy program for court orders, money management programs, guardianship or conservatorship, involuntary mental health commitments).

APS programs also work at the community level to better serve individual clients and to improve the detection of and responses to abuse, neglect, and financial exploitation of elders. On the individual level, APS may participate in multidisciplinary and interdisciplinary teams that evaluate individual clients' situations. APS workers may do joint home visits with medical professionals to obtain both health and environmental information. They may work with law enforcement to gain entry into a home to conduct a mandated investigation or conduct joint investigations. They may work with a community-based domestic violence program to provide emergency housing and support to an older battered woman or sexual assault victim. At the community level, APS may be part of a team that examines elder fatalities to identify systemic service gaps. APS may be represented on a Domestic Violence Task Force or Community Coordinating Council, ensuring that elder abuse issues are addressed.

Bonnie Brandl and Candace J. Heisler

See also Coordinated Community Response; Domestic Violence Against Older Women; Elder Abuse; Financial Abuse, Elderly and Battered Women

Further Readings

Heisler, C., & Brandl, B. (2002). Safety planning for professionals working with elderly and clients who are victims of abuse. *Victimization of the Elderly and Disabled, 5*(4), 65–78.

Roby, J., & Sullivan, R. (2000). Adult protection service laws: A comparison of the state statutes from definitions to case closure. *Journal of Elder Abuse and Neglect, 1*(11), 17–52.

ADULT SURVIVORS OF CHILDHOOD ABUSE

Many adults are survivors of childhood physical or sexual abuse. In the first and perhaps the most rigorous prevalence study on childhood sexual abuse ever done, Diana Russell found that 38% of adult females in the San Francisco area had experienced contact sexual abuse as a child. Although the commission of sexual abuse appears to be decreasing, it is likely that approximately 30% of girls and 15% of boys are victimized. Prevalence studies of childhood physical abuse also suggest that 20% to 30% of individuals experience physical abuse in childhood. Although some children experience few effects of the abuse, most experience effects that undermine their functioning in at least one domain. For those who do not receive treatment or do not have other reparative experiences in childhood, these effects may be long term. For some, effects will be debilitating.

Types of Effects of Childhood Abuse

Perhaps the most wounded survivors of childhood abuse are found on the fringes of life, in jails or on the streets—prostitutes, drug addicts, and chronically mentally ill individuals. Survivors of childhood abuse are more likely than those not experiencing abuse to experience a wide array of problems, including physical health problems and committing acts of harm against themselves. Survivors are more likely than their nonabused counterparts to repeat a grade in school and are less likely to graduate. They also have consensual sex earlier; have more sexual relationships, sexual problems, and teenage pregnancy; and divorce more often. Survivors are at greater risk than those not abused for substance abuse, suicide attempts, committing violent acts, prostitution, adult victimization, criminality, being abusive to a child as an adult, and homelessness. Further, survivors of childhood abuse are overrepresented in health systems and are grossly overrepresented in mental health systems, as most inpatients and outpatients in mental health hospitals or agencies have a history of childhood maltreatment. Those survivors of childhood abuse with the most difficult adult trajectories may be those coming through the foster care system, as they are often poorly equipped with resources to transition safely into adulthood. The institutionalization, medical and mental health care, substance use, sexually transmitted diseases, and other problems associated with childhood abuse are a burden for society and cost billions of dollars each year.

The Brain's Response to Abuse and Terror

To understand why the effects of the abuse can be so extreme, one must have some understanding of how the brain responds to the experience of abuse. Most importantly, abuse in young children organizes the brain around the experience of the abuse. Development of the brain is dependent upon the environment. Thus the brain is taught, via the child's interaction with caregivers and the environment, how to respond to that environment. If the child experiences the environment as intermittently or chronically terrifying, the child responds in a state of heightened arousal or terror. Over time the child experiences the state of heightened arousal or terror even in nonabusive situations. The child becomes sensitized to the reaction, moving into it more and more easily. This heightened responsivity then becomes generalized to nonabusive events. The response induced by the trauma also leads to a chemical response associated with the hypothalamic-pituitary-adrenal axis that involves an increase of cortisol in the body. This chemical is critical for preparing the body to respond to the crisis. This stress response, associated with the release of cortisol, is thought to be related to some of the mental and health problems seen in many survivors of abuse.

Combined, two primary responses are prevalent in relation to trauma—a response related to a heightened anxiety related to the trauma, and a response of dissociation from the trauma. The first response is associated with increased blood pressure and heart rate, among other physiological indicators of heightened bodily responses that allow the individual to fight or flee. These features are represented symptomatically in adults primarily by heightened anxiety and associated disorders. The dissociative response, in contrast, is associated with decreased heart rate and blood pressure, among other physiological indicators representing a freeze response. These features are represented symptomatically in adults primarily by the dissociative disorders. The other obvious diagnostic category related to abuse is posttraumatic stress disorder. This disorder is represented by three groups of symptoms—hyperarousal and avoidant and intrusive symptoms. This disorder is closely associated with the same changes in the brain as discussed previously.

Treatment

Treatment for adult survivors of abuse typically consists of three phases. The first stage is a period of stabilization. This stage is particularly important for individuals who experience symptoms such as suicidality, self-injurious behaviors, or other destabilizing behaviors. During this phase of treatment it is also important for survivors struggling with relationships, those who are parenting, and any survivors experiencing heightened stress when entering treatment, to achieve stability in their lives. It is also a phase in which survivors are encouraged to create or strengthen support networks. The purpose of the first phase is to provide survivors with techniques they can use to control and manage their symptoms, as well as with coping skills and other necessary efforts to regain stability in their lives.

During the second phase, survivors process their experiences of abuse and the environments in which the abuse occurred. Multiple formal or informal techniques can be used to help survivors process the abuse events for the purpose of integrating the emotional and cognitive knowledge of the experience. It is not unusual for survivors to isolate memories of abuse from their everyday lives for fear that the memories will overwhelm them. During this phase, survivors often explore the experience of the abuse, its meaning to them when they were young, its effect on them then and now, and how it changed them. The purpose of this second phase is to reconcile the experience of abuse so that it no longer overwhelms individual functioning.

The final phase of treatment is one of integration of the abuse context with the survivor's current life. Survivors come to a better understanding of what happened to them in the past and recognize the decisions they can make about themselves today and in the future. The purpose of this phase is to help clients understand the abuse as a part of their history—often a significant part of their history—while living in the here and now with either partial or complete relief of symptoms. Even in the early 1990s, it was thought that with enough treatment, all survivors could overcome the effects of the abuse. With the developing knowledge of the effects of abuse on the brain, however, it is now being recognized that some of the effects of the abuse on the brain, such as the heightened stress response and emotional dysregulation, may lessen but may not be extinguished. Thus, some survivors in this phase may also work toward management of those symptoms that remain.

The effects of abuse on survivors can be overwhelming. The abuse can deprive them of relationships, mental health, careers, or even their lives. The abuse also deprives society of the enormous lost potential of the lives of those affected and costs society billions of dollars a year. And the damage from the abuse to the brain is just beginning to be understood. Yet what is known even at this early stage is that the damage that occurs to the brain is potentially calamitous. Thus the abuse may potentially change forever and irrevocably the life patterns of survivors, their career paths, their successes, and their potential for what they can achieve.

Rebecca M. Bolen

See also Complex Trauma in Children and Adolescents; Health Consequences of Child Maltreatment; Resiliency, Protective and Risk Factors; Self-Trauma Model

Further Readings

Briere, J. (2002). Treating adult survivors of severe childhood abuse and neglect: Further development of an integrative model. In J. E. B. Myers, L. Berliner, J. Briere, C. T. Hendrix, C. Jenny, & T. A. Reid (Eds.), *The APSAC handbook on child maltreatment* (2nd ed., pp. 205–232). Thousand Oaks, CA: Sage.

Fergusson, D. M., & Mullen, P. E. (1999). *Childhood sexual abuse: An evidence based perspective.* Thousand Oaks, CA: Sage.

Herman, J. L. (1991). *Trauma and recovery.* New York: Basic Books.

Perry, B. D., & Pollard, R. (1998). Homeostasis, stress, trauma, and adaptation: A neurodevelopmental view of childhood trauma. *Child and Adolescent Psychiatric Clinics of North America, 7*(1), 33–51.

Russell, D. E. H. (1983). The incidence and prevalence of intrafamilial and extrafamilial sexual abuse of female children. *Child Abuse & Neglect, 7*(2), 133–146.

Advocacy

Advocacy has been a core component of the movement to end domestic violence. Many of the principles of advocacy discussed here can be applied to all survivors of domestic violence, but this entry focuses on advocacy for the vast majority of these survivors—battered women. In this context, an advocate is someone who responds directly to help battered women, most often in an organizational setting. Advocacy can take many forms, but the main purpose of advocacy is to help survivors of domestic violence navigate the bureaucracy of community systems—including the criminal justice system, health care and social services, and/or religious institutions—as they attempt to acquire needed resources.

Goals of Advocacy

Safety planning is a critical goal of domestic violence advocates when working with battered women. Safety planning commonly refers to a discussion between an advocate and a battered woman about her partner's physical, mental, emotional, and/or sexual violence, as well as a plan for her to maximize her safety. Safety planning involves critical thinking on the part of the survivor with the advocate to determine which strategies will help her best find safety for herself and, if she is a mother, her children.

Another important goal of advocacy is maintaining the battered woman's agency, or autonomy. This goal is best achieved with woman-defined advocacy. Woman-defined advocacy builds on the belief that the battered woman begins safety planning after her first response to batterer-generated and life-generated risks, and continually builds on those earlier safety plans. It shows respect for the survivor, and allows her to be the decision maker, set priorities, and decide which services and resources she needs.

Restoration and the provision of resources is another goal of advocacy. Survivors of domestic violence are likely to have a wide variety of needs, including legal assistance, housing, counseling, employment, education, and child care needs. The advocate should assist survivors in acquiring resources to fill those needs in a way that ensures survivors' full participation in their restoration. It is important to note that criminal justice intervention may not always be a top priority for survivors of domestic violence. Advocacy services appear most successful when the advocacy organization provides a comprehensive response to the survivor's self-defined needs and wants.

Another goal of advocacy is the pursuit of justice for individual battered women and their families and for battered women as a group. Initially, justice for a battered woman means that she, and her family if she has one, are safe from further abuse, and that she has kept her agency or autonomy in determining the actions that promote that safety. Justice also means that the battered woman is restored and that the perpetrator has been held accountable. Restoration and accountability might be achieved through the legal system, or they might be achieved through another means within a particular community. Justice for survivors of abuse also implies that the woman's economic needs are met, and she will not be economically reliant on her batterer should she separate from him.

Seeking justice also requires advocates to seek systemic change on behalf of all battered women. Advocates seek system changes when the same injustices are experienced time and time again by battered women and their families.

Forms of Advocacy

Advocacy activities may be directed toward individual survivors or larger systems. Individual advocacy may include sharing information with the battered woman about legal options or remedies, assessing with her the risks posed by the batterer, engaging her in critical thinking and strategies to maximize safety, assisting her in identifying the array of problems arising from the violence, offering feedback on the legal and extralegal remedies she is considering, assisting her in participating in the legal system, and accompanying her to meetings and court hearings, as well as referral and follow-up.

Systemic advocacy includes a spectrum of activities directed at upgrading the process and products of community systems (including health, welfare, religious, educational, legal, employment, and neighborhood systems) to promote safety and justice for victims and the accountability of perpetrators. Coordinated community response teams, as well as other forms of community organizing, ensure accountability for the perpetrator and within the system. Systemic advocacy also promotes culturally inviting practices (i.e., practices that are relevant to battered women seeking services).

Cultural transformation advocacy seeks an end to all gender-based violence and violence that is based in sexism and the oppression of women. It seeks to remedy unequal access to justice, which is based on class, race, and gender. The means used to achieve a transformation of the larger culture might include the media; demonstrations by battered women, their families, and their supporters; neighborhood teams organized to end violence in their communities; men's engagement initiatives; monitoring of the justice system; and efforts to prevent violence.

Core Values of Advocacy

Advocacy services provided to battered women must be voluntary, which means that the advocacy is consensual and that the battered woman is there on her own behalf, instead of being compelled by a court or an agency to participate in the services. Thus the agency keeps the battered woman informed of her options and the potential impact of her decisions, so that she can make the best, informed decision for herself, and if she has a family, for her family as well.

Confidentiality is a major cornerstone in all services for battered women. Confidentiality means that the advocate or other person working with the battered woman does not communicate anything the woman shares regarding her situation, unless the battered woman specifically asks the advocate to do so. The advocate should have a full discussion of the existence of any law or programmatic policies concerning confidentiality, as well as any limits on confidentiality. If there are no laws or program policies on confidentiality, the advocate should inform the woman of this fact.

Woman-defined advocacy is a specific approach to advocacy that builds a partnership between advocates and battered women, and allows for the battered woman to define the advocacy and help she needs. Woman-defined advocacy is the acknowledgment that women experience battering in the context of their diverse lives. It includes an ongoing analysis of batterer-generated risks, or those dangers that result from the batterer's control of his partner. It is flexible, allowing for a woman to change her mind in response to new information or changes in her life circumstances. Woman-defined advocacy also considers life-generated risks. Life-generated risks might include physical and mental health, financial limitations, racism, discrimination, or other aspects of the battered woman's life over which she may have limited control. Woman-defined advocacy affords the battered woman respect as the decision maker, and allows her to set priorities and decide which services and resources she needs.

Work on behalf of battered women must be advocacy based. This means that the battered woman is allowed to speak for herself, and that the advocate creates opportunities for the battered woman to speak. In advocacy-based representation, the advocate assists the battered woman with strategic planning and other preparation and informs the battered woman of her options, but does not promote any particular option. The advocate brokers resources for the survivor, and builds bridges to ensure she has the means to acquire the resources she determines are needed.

Advocacy must also be justice seeking. Justice for the battered woman means that she, and her family if she has one, are safe from further abuse, and that she has kept her agency or autonomy in determining the actions that promote that safety. Justice also means that the battered woman is restored, the perpetrator has been held accountable, and the woman's economic needs are met.

Cultural transformation is another value of advocacy on behalf of battered women. Advocates work for a transformed society, in which there is no gender-based violence. In a transformed society, there is no unequal access to justice based on class, race, and gender.

Culturally Competent Advocacy

Cultural competence is understood as a set of cultural behaviors and attitudes integrated into the practice methods of a system, agency, or its professionals, which enables them to work effectively in cross-cultural situations. General principles of culturally competent advocacy include the following:

Advocacy services are accessible. Advocacy providers should know about the communities of color within their service area (i.e., where people live and what their communities are like), should reach out to those communities, and should be aware and strive to resolve any transportation problems that might create barriers for women of color needing services. Providers should also make the agency environment more welcoming and attractive based on the clients' cultural backgrounds. Advocates should come from the communities being served and provide services in the languages of population groups that have limited English-speaking proficiency.

Advocacy is accountable. Advocacy providers should have the ability to recognize racism, stereotyping, and systemic oppression, and the effects of such acts on the women of color they serve. Advocates should avoid stereotyping and misapplication of scientific knowledge.

Advocacy is nonracist. The organization's board of directors and staff should reflect the women in the service area. The advocacy provider should include community input at the planning and development stage of each new initiative, and should find ways for the community to take the lead.

Advocacy is respectful. Staff at service providers should understand the cultural practices that battered women say have priority over activities the organization or advocate suggests. Advocates should also use approaches and materials that honor the woman's perspective and will capture her attention.

Advocacy develops trust. Trust may not be a given, perhaps in part because of the historical foundation upon which the cultures of some advocates and battered women of color are based. When interacting with a battered woman of color, the advocate needs to acknowledge that trust must be earned, and be patient.

Shelby Settles Harper

See also Agency/Autonomy of Battered Women; Battered Women; Battered Women, Economic Independence of; Coordinated Community Response; Legal System, Advocacy Efforts to Affect, Intimate Partner Violence; Mandatory Arrest/Pro-Arrest Statutes; Restorative Justice; Restraining and Protective Orders

Further Readings

Davies, J., Lyon, E., & Monti-Catania, D. (1998). *Safety planning with battered women: Complex lives/difficult choices.* Thousand Oaks, CA: Sage.

Maicki, C. (2001). *Cultural competency and native women: A guide for non-natives who advocate for battered women and rape victims.* Rapid City, SD: Sacred Circle National Resource Center to End Violence Against Native Women.

Parker, J., Hart, B., & Stueling, J. (1992). *Seeking justice: Legal advocacy principles and practice: Section III.* Harrisburg: Pennsylvania Coalition Against Domestic Violence.

AGENCY/AUTONOMY OF BATTERED WOMEN

Agency is the power to direct one's life. It is a core principle of the battered women's movement. Historically, researchers and community actors adopted frameworks that characterized women's responses to gender-based violence as lacking in agency. This resulted in advocacy approaches and judicial responses that ignored and compromised the agency of battered women. Subsequent research illustrated that battered women are active strategists who employ an array of strategies. Thus, advocacy and interventions that recognize the complexity of battered women's lives and assist victims in their own strategic decision making foster the agency of "survivors."

Research

Survivor-centered and context-based understandings of battered women have replaced earlier characterizations of battered women as passive and psychologically weak human beings.

Learned Helplessness

In the early 1970s, Lenore Walker applied the theory of learned helplessness to battered women. This theory posited that when battered women perceive that none of their actions lead to changes in the batterer's behavior, they see their own actions as futile. She asserted that a battered woman became "psychologically paralyzed" as a result of learned helplessness, causing her to feel that she had no control over the experience, while taking the blame for its occurrence. Under Walker's theory, battered women were characterized as wholly compromised, weak, and passive. Thus, according to her research, battered women needed treatment and counseling, as opposed to community resources and institutional support.

Walker's theory was challenged by many researchers and activists. It was criticized for representing a single model of battered women's experience, which had an appearance of psychopathology. The learned helplessness account of battered women (and the "battered woman syndrome" that it created) failed to account for the deliberate, active help-seeking behaviors that women employed to resist, avoid, or escape the violence in their lives and the lives of their children.

Survivor Theory

In contrast, the survivor theory posits that battered women are active strategists, rather than passive, helpless victims. In their Texas shelter study, Edward Gondolf and Ellen Fisher explained that battered women seek assistance in proportion to the realization that they and their children are in more and more danger. Gondolf and Fisher found that the help-seeking behavior of battered women is diverse and extensive. They also found that battered women are more inclined to leave their abusive partners if they are provided with the material resources to do so. By observing various dimensions beyond the violence, including economic resources, children, and the batterer's other behavior, the empirical model demonstrated that context is critical to understanding the variability of women's help-seeking behavior and advocacy needs.

Assessment and Decision Making

The complexity of battered women's lives makes strategizing for the future much more intricate than simply "leaving" or "staying," as overly simplistic models of battering might suggest. The most dangerous time for battered women is when they attempt to separate from their abusers. When battered women leave their abusers, the risk of retaliatory violence substantially increases. Therefore, decision making requires a complex assessment of a variety of factors, not the least of which is physical safety. *Batterer-generated risks* may include physical injury, psychological harm, risks to and involving the children, financial risks, risks to or about family and friends, loss of relationship, and risks involving arrest or legal status. *Life-generated risks* are risks that are environmental or social in nature and may include risks involving finances, home location, health, inadequate responses of major social institutions, and discrimination. Many of these factors provide the context for battered women's agentic risk analysis and decision-making processes.

Implications for Advocacy and Practice

An understanding of the strategic responses of battered women has enormous implications for advocacy and policy. Many have observed that "one size fits all" approaches fail to address the variability of battered women's needs. In service-driven advocacy systems, women's needs are only met to the extent to which they reflect or coincide with the specific type of advocacy offered. In contrast, survivor-defined advocacy places the assessment and decision making in the hands of battered women, acknowledging their prior efforts to achieve autonomy and supporting their future agency. The variability in women's needs illustrates the importance of emphasizing women's active involvement in identifying their needs and how they wish to prioritize them. Such an approach requires comprehensive and individualized advocacy—comprehensive in that it offers a wide range of options to address a woman's various needs, and individualized in that the advocacy attempts to tailor responses to fit her particular circumstances as articulated by her.

Many have criticized the criminal justice system for its tendency to diminish the agency of battered women. Criminal cases are initiated and controlled by the state, as opposed to survivors, thus they may be attenuated from the needs of battered women and may in fact contradict their needs. Mandatory arrest and "no drop" prosecution policies are, by definition, not dependent upon the expressed wishes of individual survivors. Many opponents of mandatory criminal policies argue that such policies deprive women of the ability to self-direct their own lives and may in fact jeopardize their safety and agency. Others have simply argued that an exclusive focus on criminal justice strategies fails to meet the comprehensive needs of battered women.

With the expansion of the domestic violence field, professionals have come to expect survivors to avail themselves of particular remedies (e.g., protection orders, criminal charges, support groups). However, information regarding the complexity and variability of women's experiences suggests that mandating particular responses may minimize the extent to which their decision making is based upon active strategizing. Survivor-centered approaches aim to offer comprehensive services, defined and directed by battered women.

Legal scholars and practitioners have noted the important role that agency plays in crafting legal remedies for domestic violence survivors. While accounts of victimization are necessary for accessing justice, descriptions of battered women's experiences that paint a single victim profile or that fail to highlight individual women's acts of resistance lead to negative results for individual survivors. For example, many have argued that battered women's syndrome must be replaced with expert testimony that describes the contextual individual and systemic variables contributing to women's decision making, and custody cases must offer testimony that describes both the violence and the agentic steps that the battered mother had taken to keep herself and her children safe. They argue that such descriptions will not only recognize but also foster the agency of battered women in the law.

Erika A. Sussman

See also Advocacy; Battered Woman Syndrome; Learned Helplessness

Further Readings

Allen, N., Bybee, D., & Sullivan, C. (2004). Battered women's multitude of needs: Evidence supporting the need for comprehensive advocacy. *Violence Against Women, 1*(9), 1015–1035.

Davies, J. (1998). *Safety planning with battered women: Complex lives/difficult choices.* Thousand Oaks, CA: Sage.

Dutton, M. A. (1996). Battered women's strategic responses to violence: The role of context. In J. L. Edleson & Z. C. Eisikovits (Eds.), *Future interventions with battered women and their families* (pp. 105–124). Thousand Oaks, CA: Sage.

Gondolf, E., & Fisher, E. (1988). *Battered women as survivors: An alternative to treating learned helplessness.* Lexington, MA: Lexington Books.

AIDS/HIV

AIDS (acquired immune deficiency syndrome) is a fatal illness for which there is currently no known cure. HIV (human immunodeficiency virus) is the virus that causes AIDS. The disease results in the deterioration of organ functions and development of rare cancers. The symptoms initially appear in the liver or other human organs. The virus spreads throughout the human body resulting in an autoimmune problem that leaves the person unable to fight off infections or particular diseases.

The first cases in the United States were reported in 1981, although the disease originated in Africa and is believed to have been spread to the United States, Canada, and other countries by a homosexual flight attendant. Today, AIDS is found throughout the world. Approximately one third of adults and children in Africa are infected with the AIDS virus, and AIDS has also taken millions of lives in the United States and Europe. The AIDS pandemic is significant for its medical and social impacts on society. Stratification, labeling, and marginalization are some of these effects. In addition, because HIV can be transmitted through sexual contact, these impacts and effects are of particular concern for sexual assault and molestation victims and the professionals who work with these victims. This entry gives a general overview of the AIDS pandemic, focusing specifically on the modes of transmission, the sociological impact, and the U.S. government's response.

Transmission of AIDS/HIV

AIDS/HIV is transmitted several ways. The virus is primarily passed from one person to another via sexual contact. HIV is carried in blood, semen, and vaginal secretions. Men can contract AIDS/HIV through unprotected sexual contact with a male or female already infected with the virus. Married men engaging in extramarital affairs with other women or men can also transmit the virus to their wives. Vaginal intercourse is less risky than anal intercourse as a means of transmission, but the majority of heterosexual women who have contracted the virus have done so through unprotected vaginal intercourse with an infected partner. In addition, the AIDS virus can be acquired through tainted blood transfusions, although currently the risk of this form of transmission is low since all blood donors are screened and blood donations are not accepted from individuals in high-risk groups.

Another method of transmission is through contaminated needles used to inject drugs. If a drug user injects himself or herself with a used needle that has traces of blood containing HIV, he or she may become infected. Prevention of this form of transmission is the rationale underlying needle exchange programs for injection drug users. However, these programs have not gotten widespread support in the United States because some people feel that they encourage illegal drug use.

Sociological Impact

The AIDS pandemic is associated with major sociological consequences. First, the disease places a severe strain on the medical resources of every country in the world, but especially of some African and Asian countries where medical resources are already scarce. There is limited treatment for most forms of AIDS, and research has not resulted in a general vaccine or overall cure. Some drugs can bring the

virus into remission for a period of months or years. However, those drugs are expensive and often not available to many AIDS sufferers.

Recent research indicates that education efforts regarding AIDS/HIV have had some success. Such programs have prompted greater utilization of condoms and more emphasis on monogamous relationships. Nevertheless, the research also indicates that there is still a relatively high level of risk-taking behavior among some groups, particularly teens and injection drug users.

Among the general public, AIDS/HIV was originally perceived as a problem only affecting gay men. This perception changed as new cases in the gay community decreased after AIDS activist groups stressed personal responsibility in preventing AIDS and other sexually transmitted diseases (STDs). At the same time, there was an increase in cases among heterosexuals. Nevertheless, people with AIDS/HIV continue to experience stigma and discrimination and are marginalized by many in the general community. Therefore, in addition to dealing with the physical effects of the disease, infected individuals must also cope with the psychological trauma caused by stigmatization and resulting social isolation.

Government Response to the Problem

The U.S. government has been slow to respond to the AIDS epidemic. Some observers argue that this, too, is a result of the perception that the pandemic only or primarily affected gay men. In addition, conservative political and religious groups were opposed to programs that promoted safe sex, condom distribution, and needle exchanges because they felt such programs encouraged immoral and illegal behavior. Much of the funding for research and the development of effective treatments and vaccines has come from private entities, such as the Bill and Melinda Gates Foundation. The media also now devote time to exploring the AIDS problem and have played a role in raising public awareness. Much of the public has begun to understand that AIDS/HIV is a disease potentially affecting everyone around the world. The scientific community and public focus has turned to the general health threat associated with the spread of AIDS/HIV.

Lloyd Klein

See also Homophobia; Sexually Transmitted Diseases

Further Readings

Behrman, G. (2000). *The invisible people.* New York: Free Press.

Shilts, R. (2000). *And the band played on: Politics, people, and the AIDS epidemic.* New York: St. Martin's Press.

ALCOHOL AND VIOLENCE

Alcohol is a powerful psychoactive (i.e., mind-altering) substance and its use is clearly linked to violent behavior. Numerous large-scale surveys and epidemiological studies show a link between alcohol and various types of violent behavior. Individuals who drink chronically as well as individuals who binge drink are at increased risk for perpetrating violence and becoming a victim of violence themselves. Laboratory research on the role of alcohol and violent behavior has established that alcohol plays a causal role in the perpetration of violence, but only in individuals with other risk factors.

The Psychoactive Effects of Alcohol

Throughout human history, alcohol has been consumed for recreational, medicinal, and spiritual purposes. Alcohol is a central nervous system depressant, that is, alcohol decreases brain activity leading to a variety of cognitive (thought), emotional, and behavioral effects. For most drinkers these effects are nonproblematic, but for some the effects lead to severe consequences. Alcohol can lead to chronic compulsive use and physical dependence. Negative consequences can also be experienced by those who do not use in this manner. Even a single moderate dose can lead to problematic effects in some individuals and contexts.

Two alcohol-related effects relevant to violence are impaired cognitive processing (thought processes) and behavioral disinhibition (impulsivity). Both effects manifest at low doses and increase as consumption increases. Impaired cognitive processing manifests as a decreased ability to attend to environmental cues. Behavioral disinhibition is thought to occur as a result of alcohol impairing brain centers that inhibit certain processes and behaviors. Although there is some controversy, researchers believe that one or both of these mechanisms contribute to the alcohol–violence link.

The Role of Alcohol in Violent Behavior

More than any other psychoactive substance, alcohol is related to aggressive and violent behavior. This link has been established through large-scale epidemiological research conducted in the United States, Canada, and Western and Eastern Europe. These studies show that alcohol is involved in approximately 60% of all violent crime. That is, in almost two thirds of all violent crime, the perpetrator was under the influence of alcohol at the time of perpetration.

Alcohol and the Continuum of Violence

The above findings refer to a range of violent crime from simple assault to murder. Estimates of the relationship between alcohol and the degree of violence are similar for different levels of violence (e.g., for assault and murder). Importantly, this relationship is more than the relationship between alcohol and crime in general. When violent crimes are compared to nonviolent crimes, alcohol is twice as likely to be involved in the violent crime. There appears to be a unique relationship between alcohol and the perpetration of violence.

Reports of alcohol consumption prior to a violent episode are not the only place in which the alcohol–violence relationship appears. As alcohol sales increase at the national level, violent crime and homicide increase as well. This relationship has been found in numerous countries with varying base rates of consumption. In addition, as the density of alcohol establishments increases, so do violent assaults. In fact, along with poverty, density of alcohol establishments is a strong predictor of the violent crime rate in a particular geographic setting (e.g., a neighborhood or town).

Overall the findings on the relationship between alcohol use and violence are compelling. This relationship often manifests in a dose-response manner at the individual and societal levels. In addition to making general estimates of this relationship, researchers have examined the role of alcohol in specific forms of violence. Two such forms, sexual aggression and intimate partner violence, have particularly interested researchers, clinicians, and policymakers. A discussion of these forms follows.

Sexual Aggression

Sexual aggression can be defined as an attempt to coerce, threaten, or force the commission of sexual acts against an individual's will. Although many studies assessing the relationship between alcohol and sexual aggression have methodological problems, they still offer insight into the role of alcohol in the perpetration of sexual violence. Studies have shown that convicted rapists show higher levels of alcohol abuse and dependence than community samples, as well as higher rates than those convicted of nonsexual violent crimes. A number of studies have shown a relationship between intensity of alcohol use and the perpetration of sexual aggression. Specifically, as intensity increases, the severity of sexual aggression also increases. In studying the use of alcohol at the time of the offense, researchers estimate that 30% to 75% of perpetrators were using alcohol at the time of perpetration.

Because of the nature of these studies, it is difficult to know whether alcohol is directly involved in the perpetration of sexual violence, the relationship reflects a more general pattern of deviance, or the link occurs only because alcohol use and sexual aggression happen within the same contexts. There is research support for each interpretation. That is, generally deviant individuals are at risk for both alcohol use/abuse and sexual violence perpetration, a relationship exists between alcohol use and sexual aggression even after controlling for other risk factors, and alcohol use and sexual aggression often occur in similar contexts.

Intimate Partner Violence

Intimate partner violence (IPV) refers to acts of aggression directed toward an individual with whom a person is intimately involved (e.g., a spouse or partner). These acts of aggression result in short-term and long-term physical and psychological injury or, in some cases, death. A number of studies have documented a relationship between variables related to alcohol use and IPV perpetration. Heavy drinkers are up to twice as likely to perpetrate IPV than light drinkers or nondrinkers. Alcohol has been linked to IPV in studies that have controlled for factors such as age, socioeconomic status, employment, and race/ethnicity. Even after controlling for variables such as acceptance of violence, hostility, and antisocial behavior, studies have found that the relationship between alcohol and IPV remains. Drinking patterns have also been shown to predict future perpetration of domestic violence. Most importantly, however, acute alcohol consumption is related to perpetration, and alcohol intoxication at the time of perpetration is related to the severity of violence. It has been found that in over one third of fatal IPV episodes, the perpetrator was drinking at the time. The number of studies

showing these relationships leads to the compelling conclusion that alcohol is related to the perpetration of IPV. However, it is important to note that alcohol is one of a number of causes of IPV. IPV occurs in the absence of alcohol use, and most people who consume alcohol do not engage in IPV.

Even with the amount of empirical evidence establishing the relationship between IPV and alcohol, there is much controversy within the field of IPV research and treatment concerning the role of alcohol in the perpetration of IPV. This controversy is centered on the same issues mentioned for sexual aggression (i.e., general deviance predicting both issues and context). In addition, some have argued that alcohol is merely an excuse for IPV; however, empirical evidence supporting this assertion is lacking. Empirical evidence does suggest that the causes of IPV are multifactorial, and likely include cultural, contextual, and personal variables—including alcohol.

Experimental Studies of the Alcohol–Violence Link

The information discussed above comes mainly from correlational studies, which assess the strength and direction of relationships but do not assess cause and effect. Therefore, asserting a causal relationship between alcohol and violence is inappropriate based on these studies; however, experimental laboratory studies allow researchers to assess the causal role of alcohol in the perpetration of violence. The data suggest that alcohol is in fact one casual agent of aggression and violence.

Most of the studies showing evidence of a causal relationship between alcohol and violent behavior utilize an experimental procedure called the *Taylor aggression paradigm*. As part of this procedure, participants believe they are in a competition with an opponent (who is actually fictitious) where the goal is to be the fastest person to respond during the experimental task. The task involves a series of trials and the fastest respondent for a trial administers an electrical shock to his or her "opponent." In reality, winning and losing on a given trial is random. Mild shocks are administered by a computer to the participant on half the trials. On the other half, the actual participant "wins" and can administer a shock in which he or she chooses the intensity and duration. Aggression is defined as the intensity and duration of the shock administered. This method has been shown to be a highly valid measure of reactive aggression.

Numerous studies using this method show that alcohol-intoxicated participants, given provocation, apply greater intensity and duration of administered shocks compared to nonintoxicated participants and participants given a placebo. In fact, this finding is one of the most consistent and reliable findings in the psychological literature; however, not all participants manifest increased aggression. This relationship is found more often in males than females. In addition, a variety of variables moderate this relationship, including aggressive disposition, trait anger, and below average frontal lobe function. Given this, most researchers now agree that alcohol can cause aggressive behavior in certain at-risk individuals.

The current accepted view as to how alcohol causes aggression is that alcohol contributes to aggression by impairing thought processing, thus restricting individuals' processing ability such that they are only able to process highly salient (i.e., highly visible, intense) cues such as threat, provocation, or perceived loss of control. Given this, individuals are less able to process environmental and situational cues that would normally inhibit violence; therefore, aggression becomes more probable. This theory, often referred to as *alcohol myopia,* has been supported by a wealth of studies and has proven useful in improving understanding of the alcohol–violence link.

Richard L. Ogle and Denise D. Walker

See also Alcoholics Anonymous; Battered Women; Batterers; Date and Acquaintance Rape; Psychopharmacology for Violence; Substance Abuse

Further Readings

Chermack, S., & Giancola, P. (1997). The relationship between alcohol and aggression: An integrated biopsychosocial approach. *Clinical Psychology Review, 6,* 621–649.

Hoaken, P. N. S., & Stewart, S. H. (2003). Drugs of abuse and the elicitation of human aggressive behavior. *Addictive Behaviors, 28,* 1533–1554.

Lipsey, M. W., Wilson, D. B., Cohen, M. A., & Derzon, J. H. (1997). Is there a causal relationship between alcohol use and domestic violence? A synthesis of the evidence. In M. Galanter (Ed.), *Recent developments in alcoholism: Vol. 13. Alcohol and violence* (pp. 245–282). New York: Plenum Press.

Steele, C. M., & Josephs, R. A. (1990). Alcohol myopia: Its prized and dangerous effects. *American Psychologist, 45,* 921–933.

Testa, M. (2002). The impact of men's alcohol consumption on the perpetration of sexual aggression. *Clinical Psychology Review, 22,* 1239–1263.

ALCOHOLICS ANONYMOUS

Alcoholics Anonymous (AA) is an autonomous, non-professional organization with a focus on helping problem drinkers remain sober through a combination of self-help and mutual support. Founded in the United States in 1935, AA now counts more than 2 million members in over 100,000 AA groups worldwide.

The AA platform treats alcoholism as an incurable disease. Thus, AA maintains that the only way to manage the disease is through ongoing sobriety. Understanding there is no shortcut to becoming sober, nor to remaining sober, the AA philosophy encourages continued reliance on the organization and its peer group support.

A collection of articles published in a volume titled *Alcoholics Anonymous* in 1939, now generally referred to as "the Big Book," continues to be a primary source of information and guidance for AA members. This volume contains the "12 Steps" that form the plan for becoming and remaining sober. The 12 Steps provide a sequence of stages toward recovery that embody AA's main principles. Two of the earlier steps include admitting being powerless over the disease of alcoholism and acknowledging the need to rely on a higher power for guidance. While originally the higher power was assumed to be God, the definition of a higher power has been relaxed over time as AA membership has grown in numbers and expanded to include various cultural groups. Further steps require a moral inventory of one's life, including identifying personal mistakes, identifying those one has wronged, and making amends. The final steps involve a commitment to continued self-assessment, with the 12th step calling for service to assist other alcoholics with the 12-Step philosophy. The AA 12 Steps are often linked to the 12 Traditions, which provide the overarching maxims for how AA should operate at the institutional level.

The only requirement for membership is a desire to stop drinking. Peer group support is offered at regular meetings and through more individualized attention by a sponsor who acts as a member's guide. There are open meetings that families and friends may attend, and closed meetings that are just for alcoholics. Members are encouraged at meetings to publicly identify themselves as alcoholics and to tell the group their personal stories. The introduction generally follows the path of "Hi, I'm Jane, and I'm an alcoholic." Consistent with the 12 Steps, this open acknowledgment of being an alcoholic serves as an identity transformation that also reinforces membership in the group.

While lifetime sobriety is a goal of the organization, a relapse into drinking is common. The occurrence of relapse is generally not considered an offense warranting exclusion. Rather, a relapse tends to garner an increase in support by other group members and a reaffirmation of the group's goal of sobriety.

Critics complain of certain inadequacies of the AA program. Empirical studies on the efficacy of AA have been mixed, with results showing no impact or a negative impact of AA on certain groups. Others complain that AA is too heavily religious and is limited to a perspective involving a single higher (and male) authority. There is also concern that long-term membership restricts members to maintaining a deviant identity as alcoholics that may become and remain their primary identity.

Melissa Hamilton

See also Substance Abuse; 12-Step Programs

Further Readings

Alcoholics Anonymous. (2002). *Alcoholics Anonymous—Big book* (4th ed.). New York: Alcoholics Anonymous World Service. (Original work published 1939)

Bufe, C. (1991). *Alcoholics Anonymous: Cult or cure?* (2nd ed.). San Francisco: See Sharp Press.

Kownacki, R. J., & Shadish, W. R. (1999). Does Alcoholics Anonymous work? The results from a meta-analysis of controlled experiments. *Substance Use and Abuse, 34,* 1897–1916.

ALZHEIMER'S DISEASE/DEMENTIA

Dementia is a group of conditions that gradually destroys brain cells and leads to a progressive decline in mental function. Alzheimer's disease is a form of dementia. Alzheimer's disease is not a normal part of aging, and most older individuals do not contract the condition. The disease is more commonly found among persons age 85 and older. It is a progressive brain disorder that gradually destroys a person's memory and ability to learn, reason, make judgments, communicate, and carry out daily activities. As Alzheimer's disease progresses, individuals may also experience changes in personality and behavior, such as anxiety, suspiciousness, or agitation. Alzheimer's disease progresses at different rates. In early stages, areas of the brain that control memory and thinking

skills are affected. As the disease progresses, other regions of the brain die. Patients in late stages of Alzheimer's disease may need complete care.

The Impact of Dementia and Alzheimer's on Cases of Abuse

Victims

Persons with dementia, including Alzheimer's disease, may be vulnerable and, therefore, targeted by predators, who may financially exploit or abuse them. Older victims with dementia may be unaware or slow to recognize that abuse has occurred. Abusers may feel that victims are less likely to report abuse or be believed by professionals. Victims with dementia may have difficulty recounting the details of the abuse. They may be perceived as confused or recounting experiences from earlier in life. Gerontologists and experts in dementia may be able to work with law enforcement and adult protective services to gather information from a potential victim during an interview. In some cases, the case must be built without participation from the victim. Such cases should be approached like a homicide in which there is no victim to testify.

Offenders

Offenders with dementia, including Alzheimer's disease, present challenges to the justice, health care, and social service systems. In some stages, dementia and Alzheimer's disease can manifest themselves in challenging, violent actions or inappropriate sexual behavior. These individuals are no longer able to control their actions due to their medical condition. Arrest and offender counseling treatment programs will not change the behavior because its source is organic rather than a personal choice. Perpetrators with dementia still need intervention to meet medical needs, manage their behavior, and provide for personal care.

However, persons in early stages of Alzheimer's disease and other dementias retain the ability to control their actions. Often persons who were abusive throughout their lives use a diagnosis of Alzheimer's disease as an excuse to escalate their violent behavior, telling family and professionals that they cannot control their behavior and, therefore, should not be arrested or held accountable.

Whether offenders with dementia are able to control their behavior or not, the focus of intervention must be on victim safety. Victims can benefit from accurate medical information and safety planning.

Bonnie Brandl and Candace J. Heisler

See also Adult Protective Services; Elder Abuse; Risk Assessment Instruments, Elder Abuse

Further Readings

Anetzberger, G., Palmisano, B. R., Sanders, M., Bass, D., Dayton, C., Eckert, S., et al. (2000). A model intervention for elder abuse and dementia. *The Gerontologist, 40,* 492–497.
Flannery, R. B., Jr., & Raymond, B. (2003). Domestic violence and elderly dementia sufferers. *American Journal of Alzheimer's Disease and Other Dementias, 18,* 21–23.

Web Sites

Alzheimer's Association: http://www.alz.org

AMEND

AMEND, or Abusive Men Exploring New Directions, emerged in 1977 out of the Denver Commission on Human Relations to meet the community's needs for intervention with abusive men whose partners had sought shelter. Permanent AMEND offices were established throughout metro Denver in 1985 to provide group and individual counseling services to men court-ordered into and voluntarily seeking batterer intervention treatment.

Philosophy Underlying Treatment

Batterer treatment at AMEND is guided by seven basic tenets. AMEND believes

1. that the feminist conception of male violence as a means of attaining power and control explains significant amounts of the behavior of men who are violent.

2. intervention with men who batter requires a values-laden and directive approach. AMEND states that violence is a crime and affirms that violence and abuse are wrong and unethical behaviors.

3. violence and abuse are responses which people choose out of a range of potential behaviors. The victim is not responsible for violence and abuse directed at her. The perpetrator is responsible for his behaviors.

4. teaching behavioral change is the first priority of the counselor to violent men. Once an offender has stopped his abusive behaviors, he and the counselor can begin to work with the intrapsychic features of his problems.

5. intervention designed to end violent and abusive behavior permanently is a long-term process requiring 1 to 5 years.

6. ending violent and abusive behavior is a complex process requiring multimodal intervention.

7. treatment of batterers requires special skills and training.

The content of AMEND's curriculum is both attitudinal and behavioral. Counseling sessions employ a cognitive-behavioral approach and focus on identification and awareness of the problem, taking responsibility for the abuse, and building empathy, conflict resolution, and communication skills. Specific group sessions address family of origin, entitlement, victim blaming, disrespect, addictions, irrational beliefs, gender stereotypes, parenting, and more.

Victim Advocacy Services

AMEND added its advocacy services component in 1987 to provide advocacy and support to—and better ensure the safety of—the partners and children of the men in counseling. AMEND's victim advocates remain in contact with the partners of AMEND's clients *and* with its counseling staff, thus providing a vital link. Advocates may confidentially inform counselors of unreported drug and alcohol abuse and threats to victims and children. With this information counselors are assisted with focusing on clients' specific problematic behaviors. Similarly, advocates may relate critical information to the victims, alerting them to clients' successes and failures in the program and alerting them to signs of imminent danger.

AMEND also recognizes the victimization suffered by children exposed to batterers and thus collaborates with SafeHouse Denver to provide individual and group counseling to children whose fathers attend one of AMEND's counseling groups.

AMEND's advocates offer educational support groups for victims, including a support group for gay male victims of domestic violence. AMEND also collaborates with Family Tree to provide a support group for friends and family members of domestic violence victims, giving them tools they may use to assist those victims.

Linda Loflin Pettit

See also Batterers, Treatment Approaches and Effectiveness

Further Readings

Bancroft, L., & Silverman, J. (2002). *The batterer as parent.* Thousand Oaks, CA: Sage.

Evans, P. (1996). *The verbally abusive relationship.* Holbrook, MA: Adams Media.

Gondolf, E. (1984). *Men who batter.* Holmes Beach, FL: Learning Publications.

Gondolf, E. (2002). *Batterer intervention systems.* Thousand Oaks, CA: Sage.

Jones, A., & Schechter, S. (1992). *When love goes wrong.* New York: HarperCollins.

Web Sites

AMEND: http://www.amendinc.org

AMERICAN HUMANE ASSOCIATION

The American Humane Association (AHA) is the oldest national organization with the dual focus of protecting children and animals, and it provides publicity, education, advocacy, and technical assistance to local child and animal protection organizations. AHA is active in professional training and development, humane education, disaster preparedness, emergency management, and family group decision making, and it operates the National Resource Center on the Link Between Violence to People and Animals. The U.S. Department of Health and Human Services designated AHA the National Resource Center on Child Abuse and Neglect in 1987. AHA sets standards and develops training curricula for child and animal protection agencies. AHA works to create an aware and caring society by strengthening families and eliminating cruelty, abuse, neglect, and exploitation of children and animals.

Historical Background

A growing concern for animal welfare in the 19th century, propelled by an increase in the popularity of pets among a new middle class and by a romantic view of wildlife as no longer being hostile, led to worldwide efforts to prevent cruelty to animals. This movement closely followed other humanitarian reforms addressing slavery, child labor, suffrage, temperance, penal reform, and care for the mentally ill. Cruelty to animals was seen as a deviation from socially responsible behavior and a predictor of further moral degeneration; its suppression would protect potential human victims and mitigate the suffering of beasts.

Although the colonies in North America had enacted animal protection statutes as early as 1641, the founding in England in 1824 of the Society for the Prevention of Cruelty to Animals (SPCA; which acquired the prefix "Royal" in 1840) engendered the modern animal protection movement, which spread to the United States with the establishment of the American SPCA in 1866. Early prosecutions for child abuse utilizing animal protection laws inspired numerous organizations for the prevention of cruelty to children and animals.

To unify these groups, 27 local organizations met in Cleveland, Ohio, on October 9, 1877, and formed the International Humane Society. The name was changed in 1878 to the American Humane Association. The reason for the choice of "humane" is unclear, as "humane societies" had existed in England since 1774 to resuscitate drowning sailors.

AHA exposed unsanitary conditions in slaughterhouses and advocated for humane treatment of cattle, water fountains for horses, segregation of juveniles from adult offenders, abolition of corporal punishment of schoolchildren, and retirement for police and fire horses. AHA work led to the first Cruelty to Children's Act (1883) and legislation to protect child laborers. The link between violence toward animals and children was first noted in 1894.

World War I inaugurated Be Kind to Animals Week, Red Star Animal Relief to protect military horses, and campaigns to mandate humane education in school curricula. Concerns over protecting animals in the making of motion pictures led to establishment of a Hollywood Film Office in 1939 to ensure that animals in the entertainment industry receive the highest standards of care and to a 1980 agreement with the Screen Actors Guild whereby AHA awards compliant films a "no animals were harmed" certification in closing credits.

Frank R. Ascione and Phil Arkow

See also Animal Abuse and Child Maltreatment Occurrence; Animal/Pet Abuse

Further Readings

Ascione, F. R., & Arkow, P. (Eds.). (1999). *Child abuse, domestic violence, and animal abuse: Linking the circles of compassion for prevention and intervention.* West Lafayette, IN: Purdue University Press.

Web Sites

American Humane Association: http://www.american humane.org

AMERICAN PROFESSIONAL SOCIETY ON THE ABUSE OF CHILDREN

The American Professional Society on the Abuse of Children (APSAC) is a national, nonprofit, multidisciplinary, membership organization focused on enhancing the ability of professionals to respond to children and their families affected by abuse and violence. Incorporated in 1987, APSAC has over 2,000 members from the disciplines of mental health, medicine and nursing, law, law enforcement, child protective services, social work, and education. The organization is committed to providing professional education that promotes effective, culturally sensitive, multidisciplinary approaches to the identification, intervention, treatment, and prevention of child abuse and neglect. APSAC promotes research and formulates guidelines to inform professional practice, and it endeavors to educate the public about child maltreatment.

To fulfill its mission, APSAC sponsors an annual 4-day colloquium, 1-day advanced training institutes, and weeklong forensic interview clinics. The colloquium offers a variety of seminars and workshops covering all aspects of child maltreatment, including prevention; assessment; and intervention and treatment with victims, perpetrators, and families affected by physical, sexual, and psychological abuse and neglect. The Advanced Training Institutes are usually 7-hour trainings on topics such as forensic interviewing, trauma-focused cognitive-behavioral therapy, medical evaluation, children with sexual behavior problems, the expert witness, and ethics. APSAC's Forensic Interview Clinics focus on training professionals responsible for conducting investigative interviews with children in suspected abuse cases. These comprehensive clinics offer an intensive 40-hour training experience and personal interaction with leading experts in child forensic interviewing. The curriculum emphasizes state-of-the-art principles of forensically sound interviewing with a balanced review of several models.

The APSAC complements its hands-on training activities with a focused publishing program that includes a quarterly newsletter, a quarterly research journal, a series of practice guidelines, and a handbook. The *APSAC Advisor* is a quarterly newsletter featuring practical, easily accessed articles on topics that focus on particular aspects of practice, detail a common problem or current issue faced by practitioners, or review available research from a practice perspective. It also offers news of the organization, brief synopses of current research articles from a range of professional journals, a review of recent legislation and policies relating to child welfare, and a calendar of conferences of interest to the field. *Child Maltreatment: Journal of the American Professional Society on the Abuse of Children,* sponsored by APSAC and published quarterly by Sage Publications, is a respected, peer-reviewed research journal that fosters professional excellence in the field of child abuse and neglect by reporting current and at-issue scientific information and technical innovations. *Child Maltreatment* emphasizes perspectives with a rigorous scientific base that are relevant to policy, practice, and research.

APSAC's board of directors, staff, members, and many experts nationwide participated in the formulation, review, and development of the *Practice Guidelines* series. There are currently six guidelines for ethical and effective practice and others are in development. Each topic is succinctly covered in a booklet of 8 to 16 pages, and the *Practice Guidelines* now available cover investigative interviewing, psychosocial evaluation of children, descriptive terminology in child sexual abuse evaluations, photographic documentation, use of anatomical dolls in child sexual abuse assessments, and psychosocial evaluation of suspected psychological maltreatment in children and adolescents. The second edition of *The APSAC Handbook on Child Maltreatment* is an edited volume with chapters contributed by leading authorities in a variety of specialized areas. This 582-page resource provides comprehensive, interdisciplinary coverage of the causes, consequences, treatment, and prevention of child abuse and neglect. This book offers research-based applications for practice, including medical, psychological, and legal points of view about physical and sexual abuse, neglect, and psychological maltreatment.

C. Terry Hendrix

See also Child Abuse Prevention; Child Neglect; Child Physical Abuse; Child Sexual Abuse

Further Readings

Myers, J. E. B., Berliner, L., Briere, J. N., Hendrix, C. T., Reid, T. A., & Jenny, C. A. (2002). *The APSAC handbook on child maltreatment.* Thousand Oaks, CA: Sage.

Web Sites

American Professional Society on the Abuse of Children: http://www.apsac.org/

Anger Management

When applied to intimate partner violence, anger management has been controversial and sometimes misunderstood. When applied generally, the goal of anger management is to reduce overly strong anger, which may be related to a very uncomfortable or frightening sense of loss of control; health problems such as high blood pressure; and some forms of aggression. It can also help reduce anger related to passive-aggressive behavior. Anger management programs teach constructive emotional expression and point out that anger is not the problem—it is a normal feeling. Anger becomes a problem when it is expressed inappropriately through aggression or becomes a state of chronic hostility. *Aggression* is usually defined as behavior that interferes with the rights of others, and it can include emotional, symbolic, and physical abuse. Aggression is distinguished from *assertiveness,* which is the constructive expression of feelings and personal rights. Methods of anger management usually include the following: (a) relaxation to reduce physiological arousal related to anger; (b) problem solving to find rational alternatives to aggression; (c) cognitive restructuring to uncover the thoughts that lead to anger and to create constructive thoughts that reduce anger; (d) recognition of physiological cues that are early warning signs of extreme anger; and (e) time-out to remove oneself from a situation in which one's anger is escalating. Anger can also sometimes be reduced when it is recognized that hurt or fear underlie it and are being masked by anger.

Anger management has been used to prevent the occurrence or recurrence of family violence, including child abuse, elder abuse, and domestic violence, often under the heading of "cognitive therapy" or "stress management." There are several reasons why it is controversial when applied to domestic violence. Edward Gondolf and David Russell were probably the first of many authors to critique anger management for men who batter. They state that it

- "fails to account for the premeditated controlling behaviors associated with abuse,"
- "tends to diffuse the responsibility of the abuse and prolong the batterer's denial,"
- "is often misrepresented as a quick-fix that may endanger battered women,"
- "does not sufficiently address the normative reinforcements for wife abuse and violence toward women in general."

There have been proposals to prohibit the use of anger management through state legislation, and some state standards for abuser programs claim that anger management does not hold abusers accountable for their behavior.

Tolman and Saunders contend that anger management can be used effectively to end domestic violence if applied carefully and within a program that includes anti-sexist gender resocialization. Many programs are able to combine feminist and cognitive-behavioral (anger management) approaches through theory integration, for example, by seeing patriarchy as a necessary but not sufficient cause of domestic violence. For some abusers, environmental stressors and anger may be the ingredients that go beyond sexist beliefs in leading to violence. Such programs are eclectic and combine feminist models that confront male dominance, teach the benefits of gender equality for all, and expand men's gender roles, as well as teach anger management. In addition, programs increasingly recognize different types of men who batter, with an "emotionally volatile" type having impulse control problems that may not respond well to interventions that emphasize the "costs" of aggressive behavior, like arrest and divorce. These programs emphasize that they are starting with the feeling state of men who batter, helping them to accept full responsibility for generating anger-producing thoughts.

Daniel G. Saunders

See also Batterers, Treatment Approaches and Effectiveness; Social Cognitive Programs for Violence; Stress and Violence

Further Readings

American Psychological Association. (2007). *Controlling anger—Before it controls you.* Retrieved from http://www.apa.org/topics/controlanger.html

DiGiuseppe, R., & Tafrate, C. (2006). *Understanding anger disorders.* New York: Oxford University Press.

Gondolf, E., & Russell, D. (1986). The case against anger control treatment programs for batterers. *Response to the Victimization of Women, 9,* 2–5. Retrieved from http://www.biscmi.org/documents/Anger%20Control%20For%20Batterers.html

Tolman, R. M., & Saunders, D. G. (1988). The case for the cautious use of anger control with men who batter: A response to Gondolf and Russell. *Response to the victimization of women and children, 11*(2), 15–20. Retrieved March 21, 2008, from http://hdl.handle.net/2027.42/57487

ANIMAL ABUSE AND CHILD MALTREATMENT OCCURRENCE

Animal abuse and child maltreatment are empirically linked by the greater reported likelihood of perpetrating animal abuse among children who have been physically or sexually abused or who have been exposed to domestic violence. In addition, in homes where child maltreatment exists, animal/pet abuse perpetrated by adult caregivers is more likely. Since children are often strongly attached to their pets, caregivers' or siblings' threats to harm pets or actual harm of pets may be considered a form of emotional maltreatment. If abused children are removed from their homes and placed in foster care, separation from pets may increase children's emotional distress. If abused children have already engaged in animal abuse, foster care providers who have pets of their own may need to be especially watchful of these children's interactions with animals.

History of Collaboration

The animal welfare and child welfare movements share historical roots. For example, at the end of the 19th century, the New York Society for the Prevention of Cruelty to Children was established, in part, through the efforts of the American Society for the Prevention of Cruelty to Animals. In the early 20th century, some humane societies included the protection of both children and animals in their mission statements. Although separation of agencies devoted to the protection of children and the protection of animals became more common during the remainder of the 20th century, collaboration between such agencies is now reemerging. For example, in some jurisdictions, animal welfare officers investigating animal neglect or cruelty cases in homes where there are children are mandated to report suspected child maltreatment; in others, social workers investigating alleged child abuse may report that family pets have suspicious injuries (this is referred to as *cross-reporting*). One national organization, the American Humane Association, continues to include both child welfare and animal welfare in its mission and programmatic efforts.

Scholarly Study and Research Evidence

Scientific study of the relation between animal abuse and child maltreatment began in the last quarter of the 20th century. Case studies of psychiatrically distressed children and larger-scale studies of violent criminals often reported an association between perpetrating animal abuse and a history of exposure to severe physical punishment and domestic violence. The importance of the relation between animal abuse and antisocial behavior toward humans is reflected in the inclusion of animal abuse in the symptom list for conduct disorder, one of the most commonly diagnosed psychiatric problems in childhood and adolescence. The field has now progressed to the point where specialized assessment tools are available for determining the frequency and severity of animal abuse. Greater attention is also being given to the motivations and psychological mechanisms that underlie the abuse of animals.

Recent research verifies earlier clinical impressions that one symptom of abused children's distress may be violence toward animals. Pets and other animals may be physically tormented or sexually abused. In some cases, children may reenact with animals the same forms of physical or sexual abuse to which they are subjected. In one case, a veterinarian identified a human sexually transmitted infection in a dog, and the veterinarian reported the family to a child welfare agency. This led to an investigation of the family; two children were found to have the same infection, as did the father, who admitted to sexual abuse and bestiality.

Clinical and Theoretical Considerations

Evidence also exists that some abused children may become even more strongly attached to their pets, who may offer feelings of safety, nurturance, and acceptance; hence, the concern when abused children must be separated from their pets, for example, in cases of foster placement. Since child maltreatment and domestic violence often co-occur, there is a greater likelihood that children in such homes may have been exposed to animal/pet abuse perpetrated by batterers. The loss of pets through such violent adult behavior may intensify abused children's emotional distress. Child safety issues also become relevant since some children who attempt to intervene to protect pets from abuse by batterers may risk personal injury.

Current theorizing suggests that animal abuse perpetrated by children who are themselves maltreated may be due, in part, to interference with the normal development of empathy. Sensitivity to an animal's suffering requires many of the same empathic skills children need to identify with fellow humans. Children may abuse animals because they have been exposed to caregivers and other adults who model violence toward animals; social learning theory would predict that such powerful adult models are likely to be imitated by children. Other examples of maltreated children abusing animals include cases where animal phobias prompt a preemptive attack on an animal, animals are involved in aggressive or violent posttraumatic play, and animals are used to inflict self-injury. Animal abuse and child maltreatment are also linked in other insidious forms. Case studies report incidents where (a) children were coerced into engaging in bestiality for the production of pornography, (b) children were paid by an adult to torture and kill small animals so the adult could make a video record of these episodes, and (c) children who were victims of sexual abuse were photographed while being forced to abuse animals, and then threats to show parents the photos were used to coerce children into secrecy and silence about their own abuse.

Formal protocols for assessing animal abuse in the context of child maltreatment are rare. Some jurisdictions recommend or mandate cross-reporting. Greater awareness of the seriousness of animal abuse has also influenced decisions in child custody cases. For example, a parent's history of animal abuse may raise questions about the parent's ability to provide appropriate care for children.

Frank R. Ascione

See also Animal/Pet Abuse; Bestiality; Sheltering of Domestic Violence Victims' Pets

Further Readings

Ascione, F. R. (2004). Children, animal abuse, and family violence—The multiple intersections of animal abuse, child victimization, and domestic violence. In K. A. Kendall-Tackett & S. Giacomoni (Eds.), *Victimization of children and youth: Patterns of abuse, response strategies* (pp. 3.1–3.34). Kingston, NJ: Civic Research Institute.

Ascione, F. R. (2005). *Children and animals: Exploring the roots of kindness and cruelty.* West Lafayette, IN: Purdue University Press.

ANIMAL/PET ABUSE

The abuse of animals, including pets, is defined as socially unacceptable, nonaccidental behavior that causes unnecessary distress, pain, or injury to an animal, and, in some cases, the animal's death. Animal/ pet abuse includes acts of commission, for example, physical or sexual assaults, and acts of omission, for example, severe neglect of basic animal needs or the hoarding of large numbers of animals for which the owner is unable to provide minimal levels of care. Animal hoarding may be related to self-neglect in elder abuse. Certain forms of animal/pet abuse are considered felony-level crimes in 41 states. Due to the strong attachment that may exist between humans and their pets, animal/pet abuse can be considered a form of family violence. Animal/pet abuse may co-occur with other criminal activity (e.g., violent or property crimes) and be related to child maltreatment and domestic violence.

Early philosophical and psychiatric discussions suggested that animal/pet abuse in childhood might be a precursor to later violence against humans. Scientific attention to the link between animal/pet abuse and interpersonal violence increased dramatically during the last quarter of the 20th century. The

1987 revision of the American Psychiatric Association's *Diagnostic and Statistical Manual of Mental Disorders* was the first to include cruelty to animals among the symptoms of conduct disorder in childhood and adolescence. Cruelty to animals is also more prevalent in adults diagnosed with antisocial personality disorder. Elevated levels of animal/pet abuse have been reported in studies of juvenile fire setters, juvenile sex offenders, perpetrators of school shootings, and males convicted of rape, sexual homicide, and serial murder.

Animal/pet abuse in childhood and adolescence has most often been assessed using behavior problem checklists that frequently include only one item related to this behavior. Currently, a number of assessments have been introduced that focus specifically on the assessment of animal/pet abuse and include forms that can be completed by caregivers as well as self-report forms. Self-report forms are especially important since children may engage in animal abuse covertly without parental awareness. These newer assessments allow measurement of a number of important characteristics of animal/pet abuse, including the age of onset of the abuse, its frequency and severity, the types of animals/pets abused, whether the abuse was perpetrated alone or with others, and whether the perpetrator expresses empathy for the animal victim.

Veterinary professionals are aware that they may encounter animal/pet abuse in their clinics. Veterinary professional organizations are currently discussing whether or not veterinarians should be mandated to report suspected animal/pet abuse.

Frank R. Ascione

See also Animal Abuse and Child Maltreatment Occurrence; Bestiality; Sheltering of Domestic Violence Victims' Pets

Further Readings

Ascione, F. R. (2005). *Children and animals: Exploring the roots of kindness and cruelty.* West Lafayette, IN: Purdue University Press.

Munro, H. M. C., & Thrusfield, M. V. (2001). "Battered pets": Non-accidental physical injuries found in dogs and cats. *Journal of Small Animal Practice, 42,* 279–290.

Munro, H. M. C., & Thrusfield, M. V. (2001). "Battered pets": Sexual abuse. *Journal of Small Animal Practice, 42,* 333–337.

ANTI-ABORTION VIOLENCE

According to the National Abortion Federation, since 1977 there have been 7 murders, 17 attempted murders, 41 bombings, 143 arson attacks, 89 attempted arsons/bombings, and 375 invasions at health care centers where abortions are performed in the United States. Furthermore, there have been thousands of reported cases of vandalism and trespassing. Health care providers and patients have endured hundreds of physical assaults, nearly 400 recorded death threats, and close to 500 reported cases of stalking. In 1994, in one of the most extreme acts of violence, Paul Hill, a Presbyterian minister and member of an anti-abortion group, murdered Dr. John Britton and his bodyguard Lt. Col. James Barrett as they were entering the health care center where Dr. Britton provided reproductive care to women. Also injured was Dr. Britton's wife. Hill was convicted of capital murder and ultimately executed. He is now revered by many as a "martyr" to the cause of ending legal abortion and "restoring" America to its "Christian" roots.

Health care facilities for abortion patients are on the front lines of the culture war, putting patients' and workers' safety in serious jeopardy. Of course, one may question how "pro-life" ideals can inspire protesters to violate the law and, perhaps, endorse killing those who are present at these centers. Extreme anti-abortion protesters who have killed or used criminal violence to achieve their political goals espouse the view that abortion is morally equivalent to premeditated murder and should therefore be illegal. Some have advanced the belief that such "murders" should be classified as capital crimes so that abortion providers could be subjected to the death penalty.

In the United States, most extreme anti-abortion protesters who participate in, advocate for, or excuse these violent attacks adhere to a very conservative Christian fundamentalism that embraces physical punishment, retribution, and vengeance. Attempts to find "common ground" with nonviolent abortion foes or with pro-choice groups have failed largely due to the strict absolutist and authoritarian ideological stance taken by extreme anti-abortion activists.

Official nonprofit organizations that promote the recriminalization of abortion formally disavow such violence, yet some privately praise the fervor that leads people to act on those extreme views. Pro-choice organizations lobby for stricter laws regulating protesters' proximity to specific locations and people, in addition to conducting their own legislative efforts to retain legal access to abortion services. Having to promote reproductive rights *and* safety has resulted in increased need for public support by way of donations, volunteers, and public awareness campaigns. Only a small fraction of the public endorses the extreme views of the violent anti-abortion protesters, and yet 25% of the public adhere to the punitive religious views that embolden violent anti-abortion protests.

Kimberly J. Cook

See also Capital Punishment; Hate Crimes (Bias Crimes), Religiously Motivated; National Organization for Women; Religion

Further Readings

Cook, K. J. (1998). *Divided passions: Public opinions on abortion and the death penalty.* Boston: Northeastern University Press.

Cook, K. J. (1998). A passion to punish: Abortion opponents who favor the death penalty. *Justice Quarterly, 15*(2), 329–346.

Cook, K. J., & Powell, C. (2003). Christianity and punitive mentalities: A qualitative study. *Crime, Law, and Social Change, 39,* 69–89.

ANTI-RAPE AND RAPE CRISIS CENTER MOVEMENTS

In the early 1970s, the anti-rape wing of the second wave women's movement spawned the first rape crisis centers in the United States. A Washington, D.C., center published guidelines for founding a center in 1973 and, in the same year, Seattle's Rape Relief Rape Crisis Center secured the first Law Enforcement Assistance Administration funding grant. More consequentially, the National Organization for Women (NOW) established a National Task Force on rape in 1973, and by 1974, over 200 local chapters had their own task forces, many of which morphed into volunteer-run crisis hotlines and, later, permanent organizations. A U.S. Department of Justice report listed 136 rape crisis centers (RCCs) or stop rape task forces in 1975. One year later there were an estimated 400 centers; by 1979, there were 1,000, and in 1996, there were 1,200 RCCs.

Over time, RCCs changed from a small homogenous core of centers to a large, fluid, and diverse group of organizations. Many original centers folded,

surviving ones changed, and scores of new ones opened, but research indicates that centers begun before 1979 retained their more radical commitments and practices in the 1990s, confirming the influence of founding circumstances on an organization's philosophy, practices, and goals.

RCCs proliferated in conjunction with the early successes of the new women's movement. Government and the media began addressing problems that particularly affected women—abortion, birth control, and rape—and Susan Brownmiller's 1975 book, *Against Our Will,* inflamed public opinion and framed rape as a practice that materially oppresses women. Early anti-rape activists offered a political critique of rape, drawing on their own experiences and focusing on rape's harm. They viewed traditional police, medical, and court practices as detrimental to victims' well-being and labeled their unsavory practices a "second assault," a phrase that still resonates with victims and anti-rape activists.

The earliest centers demanded fundamental changes to U.S. society and, to that end, worked to improve legislation, public opinion, and mainstream organizations' policies and practices. They wanted victims to view rape as the product of gendered institutions that oppress women, not the actions of a few sex-crazed men or boys. Many early centers viewed the *mainstream* as hostile to women's welfare and created egalitarian, less authoritarian, and nonhierarchical organizations to embody their feminist ideals.

Many early centers denounced ameliorative treatment for victims, viewing it as victim blaming and accepting of the status quo—that is, the inevitability of women's being raped. They believed psychological treatment told victims the rape was their fault. They favored a political explanation of rape and political education and mobilization to eliminate rape. Yet, many early RCCs offered treatment to victims (e.g., crisis counseling) and, from the outset, monitored mainstream organizations including police, hospitals, and courts. They also did outreach to change the public's understanding of rape, a practice that continues today. "Political work" or public education is one of the most frequent activities of RCCs.

RCCs have influenced U.S. society in multiple ways. Ameliorative services for victims substantially speed up recovery. RCCs have strengthened rape statutes in nearly all U.S. states. They have pressured law enforcement, prosecutors, and hospitals to improve and coordinate their practices, and local officials and state legislators to pressure insurance companies to conduct and pay for rape exams, use uniform rape kits, and compensate victims for time lost at work. As a rule, RCCs make rape victims and community improvement top priorities, despite their services' imperfections with regard to race/ethnicity and social class, among other issues.

After initially resisting, most U.S. cities accepted the involvement of RCCs in work with victims by the mid-1980s. Communities began adopting protocols to designate specific roles for each organization and many included the RCC. In response, RCCs stopped chastising mainstream organizations publicly and worked within the system to ensure access to victims and to their staff. RCCs started mobilizing unobtrusively inside society's core institutions rather than using a confrontational approach of standing outside and allocating blame. They sacrificed some freedoms but also enhanced their odds of influencing mainstream rape workers and their employers.

RCCs see more victims than mainstream organizations do, even though they have more limited budgets and staff, and they are more responsive to victims' needs. Unlike most mainstream service providers, victims are their main concern. A woman who reports rape enters an arena where many interests are at stake; police and prosecutors view rape victims primarily as witnesses to a crime, and hospitals focus on assessing their qualifications as "real patients." Only RCCs can avoid asking rape victims to fulfill another role.

Although they have not eliminated rape, RCCs have had an impact. In the 1970s and 1980s, they pressured state officials and local organizations to eliminate victim-blaming rape laws and improve their policies and practices. Today, as in decades past, RCCs advocate for and assist victims dealing with legal and health care organizations and work to improve the public's understanding of rape. They also coordinate community organizations around the issues of staff training, protocol development, and public education. Because more interaction and coordination benefits victims, communities with an RCC to facilitate these ends are more responsive to those who have been raped.

Frederika E. Schmitt and Patricia Yancey Martin

See also Rape Crisis Centers; Rape/Sexual Assault

Further Readings

Bevacqua, M. (2000). *Rape on the public agenda: Feminism and the politics of sexual assault.* Boston: Northeastern University Press.

Brownmiller, S. (1975). *Against our will: Men, women, and rape.* New York: Simon & Schuster.

Harvey, M. (1985). *Exemplary rape crisis programs: A cross-site analysis and case studies.* Washington, DC: National Center for the Prevention and Control of Rape.

Martin, P. Y. (2005). *Rape work: Victims, gender, and emotions in organization and community context.* New York: Routledge.

Matthews, N. (1994). *Confronting rape: The feminist anti-rape movement and the state.* London: Routledge.

Schmitt, F., & Martin, P. Y. (1999). Unobtrusive mobilization by an institutionalized rape crisis center: "All we do comes from victims." *Gender & Society, 13,* 364–384.

U.S. Department of Justice. (1975). *Rape and its victims.* Washington, DC: National Institute of Law Enforcement and Criminal Justice.

ARMED FORCES, SEXUAL HARASSMENT IN

The Department of Defense (DoD) defines sexual harassment as a form of sex discrimination that involves unwelcome sexual advances, requests for sexual favors, and other verbal or physical conduct of a sexual nature when (a) submission to such conduct is made either explicitly or implicitly a term or condition of a person's job, pay, or career; (b) submission to or rejection of such conduct by a person is used as a basis for career or employment decisions affecting that person; or (c) such conduct has the purpose or effect of unreasonably interfering with an individual's work performance or creates an intimidating, hostile, or offensive working environment. While this definition mirrors those developed by litigation in the civilian community, military personnel, unlike civilians, cannot litigate sexual harassment cases against their military employers. Civilian personnel employed by the military may litigate.

History

An advisory committee to the Secretary of Defense on women's issues first mentioned sexual harassment in a 1980 report, urging that the DoD publish policy statements that define and prohibit sexual harassment, establish training programs and procedures for reporting violations, and provide for disciplinary measures for violations of that policy.

In the early 1980s, the armed services initiated the development of policies and procedures for dealing with sexual harassment complaints and programs for training military personnel on sexual harassment. The Office of the Secretary of Defense conducted the first DoD-wide survey on sexual harassment in 1988.

In 1991, sexual harassment in the military garnered media attention after widely reported incidents of alcohol abuse, destruction of private property, and sexual assault at the annual convention of the Tailhook Association sponsored by the U.S. Navy. Three investigations of the incidents ended in the resignation of high-level navy officials, but none of the alleged perpetrators was ever held accountable.

In 1995, the House Armed Services Committee conducted hearings on sexual harassment and specifically examined how to improve the military complaint system. The same year, the DoD convened a Task Force on Discrimination and Sexual Harassment and conducted its second Sexual Harassment Survey. A third survey was conducted in 2002.

In 1996, incidents of rape, sexual assault, and sexual harassment occurring at the Army's Aberdeen (Maryland) Proving Grounds were revealed. In the aftermath, several drill sergeants were convicted by courts-martial of rape or charges related to sexual harassment and the army convened a senior review panel to examine the problem of sexual harassment armywide.

Rates of Sexual Harassment

The 1995 and 2002 surveys asked questions about a wide range of unprofessional gender-related behaviors as well as behaviors defined as sexual harassment. According to the surveys, over this time period there was a general decline in unprofessional behaviors and sexual harassment. Between 1995 and 2002, the overall rate of sexual harassment declined from 45% to 24% for women and from 8% to 3% for men. The largest decline occurred for U.S. Marine Corps women, whose rate decreased from 57% to 27%. The rate of sexual assault for women declined from 6% to 3%.

Training

In the 2002 survey, 77% of women and 79% of men reported receiving sexual harassment training within the previous 12 months. Ninety percent of respondents agreed that the training provided a good understanding of what constitutes sexual harassment, and over 80% agreed that the training provided them with useful tools for dealing with sexual harassment.

The Complaint Process

There are a variety of avenues for filing a formal complaint of sexual harassment in the armed forces: (a) the chain of command of either the victim or the offender; (b) filing a formal Equal Opportunity/Sexual Harassment Complaint with the Military Equal Opportunity Office; (c) filing a complaint with the Command Inspector General, the Inspector General of the particular branch of service, or the DoD Inspector General; and (d) when applicable, filing a complaint of wrongs against the Commanding Officer through the local Office of the Staff Judge Advocate. Other channels for filing complaints may include chaplains, medical agencies, the Provost Marshal, and members of Congress. Military personnel filing complaints with members of Congress and/or the Inspector General are protected by statute (10 U.S.C. 1034 (a) (b)) relative to communications with the same (such oversight authorities) and retaliation by employers. (Civilian employees working for the DoD may use the Equal Employment Opportunity complaint system.)

Commanders have several options for dealing with military personnel who have perpetrated sexual harassment. These include counseling, a letter of admonition or reprimand, nonjudicial punishment, administrative discharge, and court-martial.

According to the 2002 survey, only 30% of women and 17% of men who experienced sexual harassment reported the situation through one of the channels listed above. For women this represented a decrease in reporting since 1995, when 38% reported harassment. Most of the reports in 2002 were made to the supervisor of the victim or offender. The most common reason for not reporting (given by 67% of women and 78% of men) was that the respondent did not regard the incident as serious enough. Thirty-two percent of women and 22% of men feared being labeled a troublemaker. Similar percentages believed that nothing would be done. Of those women who filed a complaint, 34% were satisfied with the outcome, 34% were dissatisfied, and 32% were neither satisfied nor dissatisfied. Among men, 37% were satisfied, 24% were dissatisfied, and 39% were neither satisfied nor dissatisfied.

Risk Factors and Correlates

Studies have shown that the experience of sexual harassment among military personnel is associated with psychological distress, job dissatisfaction, and a low rate of retention. Personal risk factors include female gender, younger age, lower rank, and a history of childhood abuse. Workplace characteristics associated with sexual harassment and other unprofessional gender-related behaviors include poor leadership, lack of readiness, low cohesion, and a climate that is discriminatory towards women. Studies have also shown that tolerance of sexual harassment among military members is associated with negative attitudes toward women in the military.

Leora Rosen

See also Domestic Violence in Military Families; Sexual Assault in the Military; Sexual Coercion; Sexual Harassment; Sexual Harassment in Schools; Sexual Harassment in Workplaces

Further Readings

Bastian, L. D., Lancaster, A. R., & Reist, H. E. (1996). *Department of Defense 1995 Sexual Harassment Survey.* Retrieved from http://www.defenselink.mil/prhome/docs/r96_014.pdf

Cook, P. J., Jones, A. M., Lipari, R. N., & Lancaster, A. R. (2005). *Service Academy 2005 Sexual Harassment and Assault Survey.* Retrieved from http://www.sapr.mil/contents/references/DMDC%20Academy%202005%20Survey.pdf

Lipari, R. N., & Lancaster, A. R. (2003). *Armed Forces 2002 Sexual Harassment Survey.* Retrieved from http://www.defenselink.mil/news/Feb2004/d20040227shs1.pdf

Lipari, R. N., Lancaster, A. R., & Jones, A. M. (2004). *2004 Sexual Harassment Survey of Reserve Component Members.* Retrieved http://www.sapr.mil/contents/references/2004%20Sexual%20Harassment%20Survey%200f%20Reserve%20Component%20Members.pdf

ASIAN & PACIFIC ISLANDER INSTITUTE ON DOMESTIC VIOLENCE

The Asian & Pacific Islander Institute on Domestic Violence is a national resource center and clearinghouse on gender violence in Asian and Pacific Islander (API) communities. It serves a national network of advocates, community members, organizations, service agencies, professionals, researchers, policy advocates, and activists from community and social justice organizations working to eliminate violence against Asian and Pacific Islander women. The term *Asian and Pacific Islander* includes the peoples of Central Asian, East Asian, Southeast Asian, South Asian, West Asian, Native Hawaiian, and Pacific Islander ancestry (i.e., those who trace their origins to the countries, diasporas, and/or ethnicities of the above regions).

The API Institute's focus on organizing and advocacy within and across API communities is informed by a gender-based analysis of the patriarchal roots of violence against women, embedded in additional structures of oppression based on race, ethnicity, age, sexual orientation, gender identity, type of labor performed, level of education, class position, disability, or immigration/refugee status. The API Institute also explores how subjective experiences influence help-seeking behavior and empower resistance. Its programs—Policy & Research, Community Organizing, Technical Assistance & Training—and its resource center are committed to developing and promoting pan-Asian and culturally specific community models of prevention and intervention; training and networking advocates nationally, regionally, and locally; conducting and disseminating research; and influencing public policy. Although the API Institute's analyses, reports, and policy reviews focus on the experiences and cultural contexts of immigrant or U.S.-born Asians and Pacific Islanders, much of its work is applicable to domestic violence survivors in other communities.

API's publications and training curricula analyze gender violence over the life course, cultures of patriarchy and violence against API women, and differing expressions and dynamics of domestic violence (e.g., the presence of multiple batterers from the marital family, intra-Asian cultural competency, innovative strategies, and community organizing). Research publications include fact sheets, bibliographies, directories, glossaries, and translated materials. Critical issues focus on data and analysis about domestic violence–related homicides, battered women involved in the child welfare system, and sexual violence and trafficking. Additional areas of policy analysis and trainings are custody and mediation, forced marriages, institutionalized inequality and economic development for battered women, mental health and trauma, overreliance on the criminal legal system, HIV/AIDS and domestic violence, language access for immigrant women with limited English proficiency, and intersections of race, class, and gender in advocacy and systems change. The API Institute's most notable publication, the *Lifetime Spiral of Gender Violence,* contributes to the theoretical understanding of violence against women by showing the prevalence of abuse at different stages over women's life course. It is used by advocates, counselors, trainers, and faith-based institutions nationally and internationally because it is a powerful representation of the overwhelming experiences of gender violence and accompanying disempowerment that many women, not only Asians and Pacific Islanders, face.

The API Institute is part of the Asian & Pacific Islander American Health Forum, a national policy organization advocating for the health and well-being of Asian Americans and Pacific Islanders.

Chic Dabby-Chinoy

See also Advocacy; Battered Women; Domestic Violence Among Immigrant Women; Domestic Violence in Asian and Pacific Islander Populations

Web Sites

Asian & Pacific Islander Institute on Domestic Violence: http://www.apiahf.org/apidvinstitute

ASIAN/PACIFIC ISLANDER YOUTH VIOLENCE PREVENTION CENTER

The Asian/Pacific Islander (API) Youth Violence Prevention Center (also known as the API Center) was developed by the University of Hawaii at Manoa and the National Council on Crime and Delinquency in October of 2000. Funded by the Centers for Disease Control and Prevention as one of 10 Academic Centers of Excellence in Violence Prevention, the work of the API Center has focused upon examining API youth, a relatively unknown group in relationship to violence.

The activities of the center have included conducting a risk and protective factors survey of about 700 Cambodian, Chinese, Laotian/Mien, Vietnamese, Filipino, Native Hawaiian, and Samoan youth and their parents in Oakland, California, and on the island of Oahu. Another focus has been the mobilization of API communities on violence prevention. The center

has collected and disseminated data about API youth involvement in crime and violence, their academic progress, and health issues via a semiannual newsletter, fact sheets, conference presentations, articles in academic journals, participation in community events, and press conferences, as well as through the media. The work of the center led to the Statewide Dialogue on Asian and Pacific Islander Youth Violence held at the Sacramento Convention Center on August 17, 2005, which was attended by over 350 individuals. The event was cosponsored by the California Attorney General's office and over 40 organizations.

The API Center has worked with communities in San Francisco and Richmond in California to collect data that provide portraits of the status of API youth in these communities. Lessons learned from these activities have included that aggregating data for API youth may mask many critical issues that needed to be addressed; on the surface, for API youth, crime and violence rates appear low, academic achievement seems high, and health and emotional issues are nonexistent. Disaggregating data by API ethnicity has shown that Pacific Islanders and Southeast Asian youth have had the highest crime rates after African Americans in Oakland, and the highest of all groups in San Francisco. These same groups have had among the lowest scores on standardized tests, and the highest truancy and dropout rates.

Another aspect of API youth, one that received media attention in 2005 and 2006, is their victimization in schools and in their everyday lives. This information has been captured in a survey of API youth in San Francisco in 2003, as well as in an analysis of the Healthy Kids Survey administered in the Oakland public schools every other year. Several brutal victimizations of API youth in both San Francisco and Southern California eventually led to an increase of the statute of limitations for suing perpetrators of hate crimes.

In addition to collecting data on API youth in San Francisco and Richmond, the API center has become the springboard for actively seeking services for API youth who live there.

Isami Arifuku

See also Cultural Competence; Culturally Sensitive Intervention; Prevention Programs, Community Mobilization; Prevention Programs, Youth Violence; Resiliency, Protective and Risk Factors; Youth Violence

Further Readings

National Council on Crime and Delinquency. (2003). *Culture counts: How five community-based organizations serve Asian and Pacific Islander youth.* Oakland, CA: Author.

National Council on Crime and Delinquency. (2003). *Under the microscope: Asian and Pacific Islander youth in Oakland: Needs, issues, solutions.* Oakland, CA: Author.

National Council on Crime and Delinquency. (2006). *Statewide dialogue on Asian and Pacific Islander youth violence: Dialogue proceedings, recommendations, resources.* Oakland, CA: Author.

The Services and Advocacy for Asian Youth (SAAY) Consortium. (2004). *Moving beyond exclusion: Focusing on the needs of Asian/Pacific Islander youth in San Francisco.* San Francisco: Author.

ASSAULT

In the dictionary rendition, *assault* means an attack with blows or weapons, as well as by threats, hostile words, and other ways of menacing. Although *assault* rightly can refer to all forms of physical, psychological, and verbal aggression, its use in the legal system and by criminologists is more specific.

First and foremost, assault is an unlawful action. It is a form of aggression, either real or threatened, either with or without a weapon, that the state or some other legal entity has designated as a violation of the law. Assaults that are illegal are mostly those that cause or were intended to cause bodily harm, plus threats to that effect.

Second, there are "gray areas," where aggressive actions may or may not be considered assault by law enforcement and other criminal justice agencies, the perpetrator, or the victim. For example, two acquaintances at a bar who briefly engage in a minor altercation, fueled by several rounds of alcoholic beverages, with one shoving the other to the floor after a heated debate about the relative merits of their favorite presidential candidates, is an assault, "technically speaking." However, the context of the incident—including the race, age, and other characteristics of the two parties; whether a person was injured; the degree to which the incident disturbed other patrons; the reputation of the bar with local police; and a host of other factors—will actually determine whether or not the incident "officially" is regarded as an assault crime, with arrests made by the police. Equally, if not more problematic, is assault involving members of the same household. In these cases, both the perpetrator and the victim may not consider the action unlawful or even inappropriate. Further, societal norms have shifted over the years, in part through the efforts of advocacy groups, such that actions that were once considered "private" are today viewed with much less tolerance by the general public, the police, prosecutors, and the courts. It is wise when considering any kind of data or information related to assault (and any other crime) to remember the basic distinction between *prevalence*, or the real rate at which something occurs, and *incidence*, the rate at which the same phenomenon is officially counted.

In the nomenclature of violent crime classifications, assault is considered distinctive from other forms of violence when reported in the FBI's Uniform Crime Reporting (UCR) Program, the Department of Justice's National Crime Victimization Survey (NCVS), and other types of official crime accounting systems that estimate the incidence rates for various kinds of crime. Specifically, homicide, rape or sexual assault, and robbery are counted separately as crimes of violence. As well, family violence and intimate partner violence (IPV) are regarded as different categories of crime. Even so, all of these crimes involve an attack by one person on another. Hence, assault refers to a more narrow range of interpersonal violence where physical force and threats are used by a person (or groups of persons) with the intention of causing harm to another. However, criminal codes of states vary on definitions of assault, especially in regard to whether a threat, or menacing, would be considered within the definition. Some states consider menacing or attempts to menace, which is placing another person in fear of bodily injury, as a form of assault, while other states take a stricter approach, defining a threat by the presence or use of a weapon before the action is severe enough to warrant arrest and prosecution.

Also, there are occasions when assault is considered permissible or legal, such as self-defense against an attacker or to prevent a crime from occurring against another person and even against property. Within the family, corporal punishment of children can become a controversial area with regard to what is considered legal and not legal. As well, there are cases of assault in which one party may have given another party consent, such as some forms of sexual activity.

Simple and Aggravated Assault

The UCR and the reporting systems of state agencies responsible for criminal justice statistics divide assault into two basic types, simple and aggravated. In the UCR, which is based on crimes known to the police and arrests made by the police, aggravated assault is defined as an unlawful attack by one person upon another for the purpose of inflicting aggravated bodily injury. This type of assault is accompanied by the use of a weapon or to produce death or great bodily harm. The definition is vague about the amount of injury or bodily harm, reflecting variations in the way the states legally define assault. According to the UCR, a simple assault is any assault or attempted assault that is not of an aggravated nature and does not result in serious injury to the victim.

The FBI includes aggravated assault in its index of seven major crimes used to monitor the nation's crime trends, but does not provide specific trend data on simple assault. However, the UCR does include information on the sex and age of persons arrested for both aggravated and simple assault. According to the most recent annual accounting of crime by the FBI, there were slightly over 850,000 aggravated assaults in 2004, which converts to about 291 assaults per 100,000 inhabitants. This represents a decrease of 1.5% from the previous year, and a 30.4% decline since 1995. However, preliminary data from the 2005 UCR indicated a 1.9% increase in aggravated assault. This simply may be an aberration in a long-term downward trend, or an indication that this trend has reached its end. Altogether, there were about 438,000 arrests for aggravated assault, and 1,285,000 arrests for simple assault in 2004. This represents a 9% decline in the number of assault arrests, and an 18% decrease in the rate of assault per 100,000 (from 719 in 1995 to 588 in 2004).

Based on a representative sample of the U.S. population, the NCVS asks respondents about their experiences with crime. Rates for several different kinds of crime, including one for aggravated and one for simple assault, are calculated. The NCVS screen questions reflect the generally accepted distinction, asking respondents if "anyone attacked or threatened you" with a weapon, such as a gun, knife, or objects like a baseball bat, frying pan, scissors, or stick; by throwing an object, such as a rock or bottle; by grabbing, punching, or choking; or with any "face-to-face" threat. The NCVS defines simple assault as any incident meeting two conditions: (1) an attack without a weapon, (2) which results in either no injury or an injury requiring less than 2 days of hospitalization. Aggravated assault is defined as an incident that involves either a threat with or actual assault with a weapon, or an incident, with or without a weapon, in which the victim required 2 or more days of hospitalization.

In 2004, the NCVS estimated that the rate of aggravated assault was 4.3 per 1,000 persons aged 12 and older, and for simple assault, it was 14.3. Both represent considerable decreases from 1996, when the rates were 8.8 and 26.6 per 1,000 persons, respectively. Although the data collection methodologies of the UCR and the NCVS are neither perfect nor identical, both point to a long-term decrease in assaults. Further, the downward turn in assault is part of a general statistical decline shown in the UCR and NCVS for both property and violent crime.

Consequences

Regardless of the relative strengths and weaknesses of information about assault from the FBI, the NCVS, and other data sources, and its apparent decline over the past several years, the consequences of assault are quite real to the victim. There are the physical consequences, not only in terms of the actual injury, but also the physical reaction to an assault or threatened assault. These physical symptoms include trouble sleeping and concentrating, feeling tired and sleeping more than usual, and weight gain or loss. Emotional and behavioral reactions are intimately tied to the physical symptoms, including difficulty concentrating at work or school; feeling helpless, angry, and suspicious; bad dreams and nightmares; and feeling exposed and vulnerable, both in a general manner and specifically in reference to the place or area where the assault occurred. In addition to avoiding areas where the incident occurred, assault victims may avoid other places with similar characteristics, such as places with large crowds, entertainment spots, theaters, and bars. Some assault victims may even feel a need to move to a new community or neighborhood. Altogether, the NCVS estimates that the 4.47 million assaults that occurred in 2004 resulted in an average of $196 in medical bills and other direct costs to victims, for a total bill of $876 million. This estimate likely represents the proverbial "tip of the iceberg."

Joseph F. Donnermeyer

See also Assault, Aggravated; Assault, Simple; Robbery

Further Readings

Federal Bureau of Investigation. (2005). *Uniform crime report*. Retrieved from http://www.fbi.gov/ucr/cius_04/appendices/appendix_02.html

Rosenberg, M. L., & Mercy, J. A. (1991). Assaultive violence. In M. Rosenberg & M. A. Fenley (Eds.), *Violence in America* (pp. 14–50). New York: Oxford University Press.

U.S. Department of Justice, Bureau of Justice Statistics. (2006). *National Crime Victimization Survey, 2004*. Retrieved from http://www.ojp.gov/bjs/pub/pdf/cvus.04/pdf

ASSAULT, AGGRAVATED

Aggravated assault is a form of interpersonal violence that involves either serious injury to the victim or the threat of force by means of a weapon. It is defined in various ways by state statutes and criminal justice agencies, but is usually distinguished from simple assault by the degree of injury to the victim and the seriousness of the threat. Nationwide information on aggravated assault is provided by two primary sources of information: the FBI's Uniform Crime Reporting (UCR) Program and the Bureau of Justice Statistics' National Crime Victimization Survey (NCVS).

In the UCR, aggravated assault is an unlawful attack with the intent of inflicting severe or aggravated bodily injury. The definition also adds that the attack is usually accompanied by the use of a weapon or by other methods intended to produce death or great bodily harm. Therefore, aggravated assault, as a class of crime, stands between simple assault and homicide, depending on the amount of physical injury to the victim and the means by which the attack was carried out.

The UCR provides two kinds of information on aggravated assault: (1) its incidence, based on the number of such crimes recorded or "known" by the police; and (2) the characteristics of persons arrested. A preliminary count from the 2005 UCR findings showed a 1.9% increase, or about 871,000 aggravated assaults. This increase is an interruption of an 11-year decline in aggravated assault, a downward trend also exhibited by the three other major crimes of violence reported by the UCR, namely, homicide, forcible rape, and robbery.

Rates for the incidence of aggravated assault are unequally distributed by location, and these patterns have been consistent over the years. For example, in 2004, aggravated assault rates were higher in metropolitan areas (309 per 100,000 inhabitants) than in cities outside of metropolitan areas (277) and non-metropolitan counties (158). The Southern region shows the highest aggravated assault rate at 354 per 100,000 persons, followed by the West at 305, the Midwest at 233, and the Northeast at 221. Yet, the method used to inflict bodily harm varies little by locality. Slightly over one third of all police-recorded aggravated assaults involve clubs or other blunt objects. Hands, fists, and feet are used as weapons in about one in four assaults, and in slightly less than one in five assaults firearms and knives or other cutting instruments are used.

There were slightly over 438,000 arrests for aggravated assault in 2004. This number is slightly less than the year before, and represents a 14% decrease since 1995, a decline consonant with the long-term downward trend in the incidence of aggravated assault. Regionally, it is the West, not the South, that consistently shows the highest arrest rate. For example, in 2004, the arrest rate was 213 per 100,000 persons in the West, compared to 136 in the South, 115 in the Midwest, and 114 in the Northeast. About 90% of aggravated assault arrestees are male and 14% are under the age of 18. These percentages have changed only minimally over the past decade.

The NCVS is the second source of nationwide information about aggravated assault, which it distinguishes from simple assault in a manner similar to that of the UCR. According to NCVS criteria, an aggravated assault is any incident in which the victim was either threatened with a weapon or the injury required 2 or more days of hospitalization.

According to the 2004 NCVS statistics, there were slightly over 1 million aggravated assault incidents, for a rate of 4.3 per 1,000 persons age 12 and over. The vast majority of these assaults, about 65%, were threats with a weapon only, with the remainder involving some form of injury. Consistent with the UCR statistics, the NCVS rate of reported aggravated assault has declined. For example, in 1996, the rate was 8.8 per 1,000 persons. However, in 2002 the rate was 4.3, and in 2003 it was 4.6. Hence, results over the past 3 years represent an interruption to this long-term decrease, paralleling the statistical trends found in the UCR. About 55% to 60% of aggravated assault victimizations are reported to the police.

Despite long-term fluctuations in aggravated assault rates, the pattern of victimization by various demographic characteristics of victims has not changed much. Rates for males are nearly twice as high as those for females. In 2004, for example, the overall rate was 5.8 per 1,000 males and 2.8 per 1,000 females. Similar proportions by sex were evident for those suffering injury and those who were threatened with a weapon. For both sexes, rates were at least twice as high for victims 12 to 24 years of age as for those in other age groups. Both Black males and females exhibit higher rates of aggravated assault than their White counterparts. A comparison of aggravated assault rates of Hispanic and non-Hispanic respondents in the NCVS shows somewhat inconsistent results, with rates higher for the former group during most years. However, the latter group displays higher rates for certain years. Aggravated assault rates are consistently highest for those living in urban areas, followed by rates for persons living in suburban areas. However, in the 2004 NCVS, the rate for people living in rural areas was higher than for those living in suburban areas.

According to the NCVS, the proportion of aggravated assault victimizations involving strangers ranges between 50% and 60%, depending on the reporting year. Males are much more likely to be the victims of aggravated assault by strangers than are females. Patterns are less clear by age and Black or non-Black status. Older males and females are somewhat more likely to report being victimized by strangers, but this declines for the oldest age group, namely, victims 65 years old and older. Likewise, differences in the proportion of stranger victimizations when comparing Blacks and Whites vary from year to year.

Despite its decline, aggravated assault is a costly crime. Both the UCR and NCVS statistics indicate that it is the second most frequent crime of violence, exceeded only by simple assault. Similar to all crimes of violence, its psychological, social, and economic impact on victims can be considerable.

Joseph F. Donnermeyer

See also Assault; Assault, Simple; Robbery

Further Readings

Federal Bureau of Investigation. (2005). *Crime in the United States*. Retrieved from http://www.fbi.gov/ucr/04cius
U.S. Department of Justice, Bureau of Justice Statistics. (2006). *National Crime Victimization Survey, 2004.* Retrieved from http://www.ojp.gov/bjs/pub/pdf/cvus.04/pdf

ASSAULT, SIMPLE

Simple assault is a form of interpersonal violence that involves the use of force to inflict injury or the threat of force to cause harm. The incidence of simple assault is reported in the National Crime Victimization Survey (NCVS), which is an annual survey conducted by the U.S. Census Bureau on behalf of the U.S. Department of Justice. The NCVS collects information on the crime experiences of persons, whether or not they report the incident to the police. The NCVS distinguishes simple assault from aggravated assault based on two criteria: (1) the use of deadly force, and (2) the seriousness of the injury. Hence, simple assault is an incident in which the attack did not involve the use of a weapon or in any other way was the attack considered deadly; and any injury incurred by the victim that required less than 2 days of hospitalization.

According to the NCVS, in 2004 there were an estimated 3.44 million simple assaults on persons age 12 and older. Of these, about 74% were without physical injury to the victim, with the remainder involving minor injury. The actual rate of simple assault per 1,000 persons was 14.3. Males have a higher rate (16.3) than females (12.3). Males are slightly less likely to be injured than females.

Like other crimes reported in the NCVS, the rate of simple assault has been on a steady decline. For example, the rate was 26.6 per 1,000 persons in 1996, and 20.8 in 1999. Throughout this downward trend, however, the proportion of simple assaults involving minor injury to the victim has remained relatively the same. As well, the rate of decline in simple assaults has been about the same for females and males. Finally, the percentage of simple assaults reported to the police is relatively constant, varying from 44.9% in 2004 to 37.3% in 1996. Female victims are more likely to say they reported an incident of simple assault than are males. Victims who suffered minor injuries, regardless of sex, also were more likely to report the event to the police.

There are some noticeable differences in the experience of simple assault by age, ethnicity, race, and sex. Males age 12 to 19 exhibit the highest rates of simple assault, followed by those 20 to 24 years of age, after which the rates rapidly decrease. The pattern for females is about the same; however, across all age groups, the rates are consistently lower for females.

For some years, the rate of simple assault for Black males exceeds the rate for White males, and at other times, the rate is higher for White males. The same pattern is true when comparing simple assault for White and Black females. Again, for both Blacks and Whites, rates of simple assault have declined. Finally, comparing rates by Hispanic and non-Hispanic status show few differences.

One of the larger statistical differences found in the NCVS is the percentage of simple assault victimizations involving strangers by the sex of the victim. It is far more likely that males than females will report being assaulted by a stranger. For example, the 2004 NCVS reports that nearly 54% of White males and about 48% of Black males were victimized by someone they did not know. In contrast, nearly 40% of White females and almost 30% of Black females said that their assailant was a stranger.

A second difference is in the rate of simple assaults by locality, which is broken into three groups: urban (metropolitan counties with a city of 50,000 or greater), suburban (contiguous counties economically and socially linked to the central city county), and rural (nonmetropolitan counties). Across sex, race, and Hispanic–non-Hispanic status, rates are generally the highest for respondents from urban locations. Rates for respondents from suburban counties are lower than urban rates, but higher than rates for those who live in rural areas. However, victimization rates for simple assaults are somewhat comparable for suburban and rural populations, and substantially higher for urban populations.

The FBI's Uniform Crime Reporting (UCR) Program does not include information for simple assaults within its various statistical tables summarizing "crimes known to the police." However, it does include information about the arrests of persons in the United States for simple assaults, of which there were nearly 1.3 million in 2004, for a rate of 438.6 arrests per 100,000 inhabitants. Arrest rates for simple assault, in concurrence with a downward trend in the NCVS victimization rate, have declined in recent years. For example, the arrest rate in 1995 was 496.5 per 100,000 inhabitants.

The Southern states show the highest rate of simple assault arrests, at 561.4 per 100,000 inhabitants. This rate far exceeds rates for the Midwest (428.3), Northeast (369.0), and the West (359.1). Over the years, the UCR has consistently shown the South to have the highest arrest rates for simple assault. Arrests

rates by police agencies from central cities (344.5), suburban areas (360.0), and nonmetropolitan counties (345.4) are nearly identical. The vast majority of simple assault arrests (about 75%) are of males. About one in five arrests are of persons under the age of 18.

Although simple assault may not result in serious physical injury to the victim, or involve deadly force, it remains a serious crime. For instance, according to the NCVS, the rate of simple assault in 2004 was the highest among all personal crimes, exceeding the rates for rape/sexual assault, robbery, aggravated assault, and purse snatching/pocket picking. There are more arrests made by law enforcement agencies for simple assault than for almost any other kind of crime, with the exceptions of drug abuse violations and driving under the influence, based on data from the UCR. Without a doubt, the psychological and social costs of simple assault to both the victim and society in general are significant.

Joseph F. Donnermeyer

See also Assault; Assault, Aggravated; Robbery

Further Readings

Federal Bureau of Investigation. (2005). *Crime in the United States*. Retrieved from http://www.fbi.gov/ucr/04cius
U.S. Department of Justice, Bureau of Justice Statistics. (2006). *National Crime Victimization Survey, 2004*. Retrieved from http://www.ojp.gov/bjs/pub/pdf/cvus.04/pdf

ASSISTED SUICIDE

Assisted suicide is the act of *indirectly* facilitating the death of another person per his or her request. The term is usually extended to describe physician-assisted suicide (PAS), which refers to a physician aiding a patient in taking his or her life, typically by prescribing a lethal dose of barbiturates. The physician may provide the means for suicide, while the patient is the one who actually performs the act (e.g., self-administers the medication). It is important to differentiate PAS from euthanasia, which occurs when a physician *directly* influences the death of a patient. There is significant controversy regarding whether assisted suicide constitutes interpersonal violence. Whereas some individuals have argued that assisted suicide is, in fact, one form of potentially lethal violence, others have argued that it constitutes an act of mercy for individuals enduring substantial suffering with otherwise terminal illnesses.

With the legalization of PAS in the Netherlands, Belgium, Switzerland, and recently in the state of Oregon, assisted suicide has become a contentious topic that highlights moral and ethical questions that do not have clear answers. Conservative religious groups that oppose PAS argue that it is morally wrong to take one's own life. Those from the medical community who object to PAS claim that it violates a fundamental premise of the medical profession to heal and extend human life. The potential for certain groups of people (e.g., the disabled, the elderly) to be manipulated or coerced into PAS is another argument against decriminalizing the practice. This is a particular concern with the advent of managed health care and the fear that legalizing PAS would allow it to be misused in an effort to reduce health care expenditures associated with treating terminally ill patients.

Those who support PAS assert that people should have the ability to decide when, where, and under what circumstances they die. In this way, terminally ill people who have lost self-sufficiency and independence can still maintain a sense of autonomy. It is also argued that in some cases pain cannot be relieved with conventional pain management methods, and that PAS is a compassionate way to end intolerable suffering.

The most commonly cited reasons for requesting and utilizing PAS are unbearable pain, maintaining autonomy, losing control of bodily functions, loss of dignity, and decreased quality of life, though in most cases there is a combination of factors that motivate a patient to consider PAS. Although the literature on the association between clinical depression and requests for PAS is mixed, depression is not typically endorsed as strongly as other variables when opting for PAS.

Research suggests that underlying ethical beliefs regarding PAS govern both physicians' and the general population's attitudes toward when and under what circumstances PAS is appropriate and acceptable. Presently, the American Medical Association and the U.S. Supreme Court officially oppose PAS. Opinion polls given to the public and to medical professionals reveal that about half of both groups believe that PAS is ethically acceptable under certain circumstances, although support of PAS has been substantially lower when the issue has been subjected to a formal vote.

The Oregon Death with Dignity Act (ODDA) legalized PAS for citizens of Oregon. The ODDA has many guidelines and safeguards built in to ensure that patients are fully informed and are requesting PAS voluntarily and with rational judgment that is not impaired by a psychological disorder such as depression.

Despite the fact that the ODDA has various rules to protect against its misuse, PAS remains aggressively debated among the medical community, religious groups, and the general public. It will likely continue to be a highly controversial topic, as it is deeply intertwined with moral and ethical beliefs.

Meggan M. Bucossi and Gregory L. Stuart

See also Suicidality: Nomenclature; Suicide, Risk and Protective Factors: Individual Level

Further Readings

Oregon State Public Health, Department of Human Services. (n.d.). *Physician assisted suicide.* Retrieved September 20, 2006, from http://www.oregon.gov/DHS/ph/pas/

Rurup, M., Onwuteaka-Philipsen, B., VanDerWal, G., VanDerHeide, A., & VanDerMaas, P. (2005). A "suicide pill" for older people: Attitudes of physicians, the general population, and relatives of patients who died after euthanasia or physician-assisted suicide in the Netherlands. *Death Studies, 29,* 519–534.

Werth, J., Jr. (2004). The relationship among clinical depression, suicide, and other actions that may hasten death. *Behavioral Sciences & the Law, 22,* 243–253.

Westfield, J., Sikes, C., Ansley, T., & Yi, H. (2004). Attitudes towards rational suicide. *Journal of Loss and Trauma, 9,* 359–370.

ASSOCIATION FOR THE TREATMENT OF SEXUAL ABUSERS

The Association for the Treatment of Sexual Abusers (ATSA) is a nonprofit, international, interdisciplinary organization focused specifically on the prevention of sexual abuse through effective management of sex offenders. ATSA was founded to foster research, facilitate exchange of information, further professional education, and provide for the advancement of professional standards and practices in the field of sex offender evaluation and treatment. A voluntary membership organization, the Association for the Treatment of Sexual Offenders has over 1,000 members representing a variety of fields, including psychology, psychiatry, social work, counseling, and corrections.

Formed by a small group of clinicians in Oregon, ATSA was incorporated in 1984. The mission of the organization is (a) elimination of sexual victimization, (b) protection of communities through responsible and ethical treatment of sexual offenders, (c) prevention of sexual assault through effective management of sex offenders, and (d) maintenance of high standards of professionalism and integrity within its membership.

To accomplish its mission, ATSA sponsors an annual 3-day conference plus a day of preconference clinics, publishes a professional journal, publishes practice standards and guidelines as well as a code of ethics, provides ATSA informational packages and ATSA task force reports, and supports state chapters. The ATSA Annual Research and Treatment Conference offers symposia, workshop presentations, poster sessions, discussion groups, and advanced clinics relating to issues in both victim and perpetrator research and treatment over a 3-day period. The conference format facilitates interaction with and learning from some of the most advanced practitioners in the field of sexual abuse. In addition, ATSA offers a selection of intensive half-day and full-day preconference clinics designed to provide extensive training and skills enhancement.

The official journal of the Association for the Treatment of Sexual Abusers, *Sexual Abuse: A Journal of Research and Treatment* (formerly *Annals of Sex Research*), is published quarterly by Springer. The journal provides a forum for the latest research and scholarly reviews of both clinical and theoretical aspects of sexual abuse, and it is the only professional journal to focus exclusively on articles related to sexual offending. This respected, peer-reviewed quarterly presents studies encompassing the assessment and treatment of the sexual offender and the effects of sexual abuse on victims and families.

ATSA develops and publishes ATSA Informational Packages on important aspects of assessment, treatment, and research related to sexual offenders, such as risk assessment. ATSA also develops and publishes ATSA Task Force Reports on such critical topics as children with sexual behavior problems. The ATSA Standards and Guidelines and the companion document, the ATSA Code of Ethics, are provided as a benefit of membership and are available for purchase by nonmembers.

The organization now has active state chapters in some 25 states, and the state chapters play a critical role in ATSA's efforts to meet the professional needs of its members. Each state chapter typically meets monthly to offer training and opportunities for peer networking. Some chapters also sponsor state or area conferences to provide additional training and networking opportunities.

Regular membership in ATSA requires one of the following: (a) a master's degree or above in the behavioral or social sciences and a minimum of 2,000 hours providing direct clinical services to individuals who have engaged in sexual offending behavior; (b) a master's degree or above and a minimum of 2,000 hours of research specific to issues related to sexual offending; or (c) engagement in 2,000 hours of work specifically related to sexual abuse prevention or to the management of individuals who have engaged in sexual offending behavior. Other categories of membership for those with somewhat less experience in the field include clinical associate, research associate, affiliate, and student.

C. Terry Hendrix

See also American Professional Society on the Abuse of Children; Child Sexual Abuse; Clergy Sexual Abuse; Developmentally Disabled Sex Offenders; Fathers as Perpetrators of Child Maltreatment; Female Perpetrators of Violence Against Children; Investigative Interviewing of Offenders; Pedophilia; Professional Journals on Child Maltreatment; Professional Journals on Victimization; Risk Assessment

Web Sites

Association for the Treatment of Sexual Abusers: http://atsa.com/

ATHLETES/ATHLETICS

Athletes and athletics have a prominent position in the American social world, and discussions of athletes and violence have been going on for decades. There are wide-ranging views on whether athletics promotes or controls violent and transgressive behavior among its participants and the larger society. Anecdotally, Americans are seemingly inundated with reports of athletes behaving badly, especially as this behavior relates to charges of athletes and violence. Recent examples of athletes alleged to have participated in violence include Michael Vick, Adam "Packman" Jones, Kobe Bryant, Brett Myers, Al Unser, Jr., Michael Strahan, John Daly, Patrick Roy, Mike Tyson, Jose Canseco, Mark Chumra, Jason Kidd, Lawrence Phillips, and, of course, O. J. Simpson. These names and their respective incidents roll off the tongue. And athletics draws the public attention in unique and passionate ways.

The stories are well known, and for many they serve to reinforce the notion that the United States's sporting heroes are disproportionately violent and transgressive, as well as the belief that, at the very least, athletes are privileged and arrogant and lack values, judgment, and humility. For these folks, athletics promotes violence in sports and in the larger society. They point to the exulted social status of athletics and believe that athletics serves a negative social-norming function in society promoting violence.

Still others believe that athletics and incidents of athletes behaving badly are a reflection of the problems of the larger society, with the main difference being that when an athlete commits a crime it becomes front-page news. They point to staggering numbers of violent incidents in society at large and believe focusing on only athlete-perpetrators is akin to someone not being able to see the forest for the trees. They plead for a more global focus on the causes and predictors of violence and for avoiding simplistic and minimizing explanations that dismiss a significant social phenomenon as only an athletics problem.

To date, there is no clear empirical or theoretical consensus on this issue. Limited studies have been completed focusing on athletics and violence, with inconsistent results. The current research on athletes and violence is limited with regard to the conclusions that can be drawn from it. Research results have been mixed at best and call into question longstanding assumptions about the connection between violence and sport. A range of studies that utilize qualitative and quantitative methods to compile data are needed to more clearly understand these issues.

In considering research on athletics and violence, one must examine differences between athletes' and nonathletes' perpetration of violence. Pointedly, are there unique aspects of the athletic experience that cause male athletes to be violent? Or is this a sizable social problem that is highlighted by the status and visibility of some male athletes?

Violence Defined

In looking at the connection between athletes and violence, defining these terms is important. Violence is generally defined in this context as physical assault with intent to injure. There are some who define violence more broadly and include verbal and emotional aggression as violence along with physical acts. The common thread in defining these actions as violence is the intent to harm, intimidate, or injure.

Off-Field and On-Field Violence

Off-field and on-field violence provide another area of distinction. On-field violence includes rules violations, such as physical fighting (except in boxing and martial arts competitions). Examples include bench clearing brawls in baseball, hitting with a helmet with intent to injure in football, or fighting as strategy in ice hockey. These types of rules violations occur regularly during competition. Off-field violence refers to violence perpetrated in an athlete's social or personal life. Examples include domestic violence and fighting at a party or social club. The research on these types of violence is generally anecdotal and involves more journalistic elements than empirical elements.

Types of Sports and Violence

There are different types of sports that people refer to when initiating arguments about violence and sport. There are youth sports, women's sports, revenue-producing sports, Olympic sports, professional sports, recreational sports, and more. The majority of the discourse on violence and sport involves revenue-producing sports, such as football or men's basketball at the collegiate level and the dominant men's professional sports such as football, basketball, and, to a lesser degree, NHL hockey and professional baseball.

Race, Gender, and Socioeconomic Factors

Many sociologists and others see real danger in the terminology used to describe violence in certain sports. For example, the term *athlete in revenue-producing sports* can be seen as underscoring a stereotype given the disproportionate representation of athletes of color in those sports. The concern is that some of these titles have become code for saying

Black men are the real problem. Others argue that treatment should be color-blind, and if an athlete is violent, he should have to pay for his crime. Studies in the United States and Canada have shown that an athlete's position in the most popular sports is a more consistent variable than race in gauging violent and transgressive behavior.

Men's elite and most popular sports are overwhelmingly seen as violent when compared with other men's sports and female sports. Just as there is a distinction between men's sports, there is a greater distinction between men's and women's sports. Thus, gender has a dramatic empirical impact when discussing violence and sports. Many researchers argue that the power men's sports, which vary by culture, provide us with a critical clue. They argue that males who adhere to rigid gender roles exercise themes of dominance and control on-field and off-field and feel entitled to do so.

Fan Violence in Sport

Fan violence in athletics is generally understood as contextually situated around political, historical, geographical, situational, and socioeconomic factors. The type of athletics, level of competition, perceived meaning(s) by the participating communities/countries, and unique characteristics of a particular event can impact the potential for fan violence. There are examples of fan violence from youth sports through professional sports. There are examples of rioting and looting after victories and defeats. Many argue that fan violence is best understood as a gang mentality, while others believe there are larger factors at play that inform the dynamics in a stadium.

There is a tendency to overgeneralize the connection between violence and sport. This can lead to a false understanding and negative connotation of athletics. Some researchers have argued that sports build character and instill discipline and life skills, while others see sports as promoting violence and reinforcing negative actions such as power and domination over another. Athletics is not an isolated social event that occurs in a vacuum; rather, athletics and its participants are part of the social structure.

Jeffrey O'Brien

See also Athletes/Athletics and Sexual Violence; Athletes/Athletics and Violence in Sport

Further Readings

Coakley, J. J. (1998). *Sport in society: Issues and controversies* (6th ed.). New York: McGraw-Hill.
Crossett, T. (2000). Athletic affiliation and violence towards women: Toward a structural prevention project. In J. McKay, M. Messner, & D. Sabo (Eds.), *Masculinities and sport*. Thousand Oaks, CA: Sage.
Eitzen, D. S. (1996). *Sport in contemporary society.* New York: St. Martin's Press.
Messner, M. (2002). *Taking the field: Women, men, and sports.* Minneapolis: University of Minnesota Press.

ATHLETES/ATHLETICS AND SEXUAL VIOLENCE

Since the early 1990s, increased media attention on sexual assaults involving widely known athletes has led many people to assume that male participation in college and professional sports is a key risk factor associated with rape and other forms of woman abuse. However, social scientific research has not yet found strong evidence indicating that being a professional athlete increases the likelihood of a man sexually assaulting female intimates, acquaintances, or strangers. Still, a growing body of empirical work reveals a relationship between participation in National Collegiate Athletic Association Division I sports and sexual assault. Even so, not all male members of college athletic teams are at equal risk of being sexually abusive. For example, golfers, tennis players, and figure skaters are less likely to victimize women than are basketball and football players.

Many of the same factors that affect fraternities are important with men involved in highly aggressive sports, such as football: the male bonding that leads to the objectification of women, homophobia, the tight vows of secrecy that prevent exposure, and the victim blaming that allows even public cases to be ignored. Another factor that warrants careful attention is the coach. For example, there are coaches who emphasize that the worst thing that a male athlete can do is to develop what they regard to be feminine traits.

As Martin Schwartz and Walter DeKeseredy point out in their 1997 book *Sexual Assault on the College Campus: The Role of Male Peer Support,* the training of a sports team to sacrifice everything to a group goal, and to immediately accept the complete authority of the leaders, may make some athletes unable to disagree with a group's goal, even if that goal is illegal, dangerous, or immoral. The male bonding in these groups of athletes, who work, live, and play together every day for years, can be very powerful. It starts with the peer group values on athletic teams, values that encourage athletes to treat women as objects of conquest. This group bonding can be so strong that such men are willing to take part in rape, or to observe rape, or at least to take part in a cover-up, because the alternative is to go against the group. It becomes more important to be part of the group than it is to do the right thing. This is why, many argue, so many "good" young men can take part in a gang rape, or stand and watch a woman being held down and raped in a dormitory room while she screams, or just brush off hearing about such an event the next day without even considering taking any action against it.

What makes college athletic teams special is that so many people have a strong vested interest in seeing the charges dropped or criminal behavior covered up. For example, in some cases that go to trial, jurors will acquit athletes rather than ruin the upcoming sports season. Under the best of circumstances, sports researchers argue, athletes feel that they are above the law and that the rules do not apply to them. Too often they are right. To fans, many students, professors, administrators, and some of North America's most influential sports writers, they *are* above the law.

Like most of the empirical and theoretical work on sexual assault on the college campus, the bulk of the research on athletes and sexual violence takes the view that male athletes only become abusive when they enter college. However, a few studies show that high school boys can be as violent as or more violent than college men and be in fact headed off to college looking for mechanisms that will support their violent behaviors and sexist attitudes. Still, at the time of writing this entry, only one study was published in a scientific journal that focused on the relationship between high school sports participation and sexual assaults committed by college men. A survey conducted by Forbes, Adams-Curtis, Pakalka, and White found that college men who participated in aggressive high school sports were more sexually abusive, had more sexist attitudes, were more accepting of rape myths, and were more homophobic than other men. Indeed, this study strongly suggests that many men arrive at college fully prepared to abuse women with no learning required.

Obviously, members of various male athletic teams are at high risk of committing sexual assault. However, given survey research showing that sexual abuse and other forms of woman abuse are widespread on North American college campuses, it is logical to conclude that these behaviors are not unique to athletes who participate in aggressive sports. In fact, a growing body of proabuse male peer support research shows that athletes are just one part of a larger culture that views woman abuse as a normal and legitimate way of interacting with women. Nevertheless, further research on the relationship between sports participation and sexual violence is necessary, including gathering data from larger and more representative samples of college students. Moreover, there is a need for theory construction and testing. Regardless of what new empirical and theoretical directions researchers take, there are many other groups of sexually violent men on campus and elsewhere who warrant significant scholarly, media, and political attention.

Walter S. DeKeseredy

See also Athletes/Athletics; Date and Acquaintance Rape; Male Peer Support, Theory of

Further Readings

Benedict, J. (1997). *Public heroes, private felons: Athletes and crimes against women.* Boston: Northeastern University Press.

Benedict, J. R. (1998). *Athletes and acquaintance rape.* Thousand Oaks, CA: Sage.

Forbes, G. B., Adams-Curtis, L. E., Pakalka, A. H., & White, K. B. (2006). Dating aggression, sexual coercion, and aggression-supporting attitudes among college men as a function of participation in high school sports. *Violence Against Women, 12,* 441–455.

Schwartz, M. D., & DeKeseredy, W. S. (1997). *Sexual assault on the college campus: The role of male peer support.* Thousand Oaks, CA: Sage.

ATHLETES/ATHLETICS AND VIOLENCE IN SPORT

Physical aggression, conflict, and violence have long been inherent elements of sporting endeavors, dating back to Roman and medieval contests such as gladiatorial sports, chariot races, and jousting. Current anecdotal and empirical evidence suggests a link between participating in aggressive contact sports and an increased risk of using violence both in and outside of sporting events. In high-contact sports, such as rugby or American football, rough physical exchanges are integral to the game and may contribute to a team's likelihood of winning, thereby increasing the appeal of aggressiveness. Other sports can be characterized as rule-bound fighting, such as boxing and wrestling. As inherently competitive undertakings, games and matches often inspire intense rivalry and conflict between athletic opponents that can involve physical intimidation and altercations. Athletes in sports characterized by tacit or overt support for verbal and physical intimidation during sporting contests may be at risk for having these behaviors spill over into other arenas of their lives, such as intimate relationships. The vast majority of research on violence in athletics involves male athletes, and high-contact sports such as American football, ice hockey, basketball, rugby, lacrosse, and wrestling are dominated by and nearly exclusively involve men. Therefore, this discussion will focus on violence among male participants in these sporting categories.

Violence During Sporting Events

In a widely cited attempt to categorize types of violence in sports, Michael Smith identified four levels of sports-related violence. The least extreme level is *brutal body contact,* which is the "legal" contact considered to be inherent in the game, such as tackling in American football or punching in boxing. The second level is *borderline violence,* which is contact that may breach the official rules of the sport, but which is still widely accepted and rarely criminally prosecuted or even penalized during the game itself. Examples might include side-line scuffles or throwing elbows during basketball or soccer. *Quasicriminal violence* is aggression that breaks game rules, tacit codes of conduct, and often criminal laws, and can result in serious injury, such as a vicious late hit or a sideline attack with a hockey stick. Finally, *criminal violence* is severe aggression by athletes during or after sporting events (such as postgame attacks on rival players or coaches) that results in critical injuries or death and often culminates in criminal prosecution.

The prevalence of nonsanctioned aggression during sporting contests is difficult to quantify. Evidence suggests that a majority of coaches and players view instances of verbal intimidation as a widespread problem in sports, and that over one third of coaches feel that athlete violence has reached problematic levels. Across studies, researchers estimate that aggression in the context of sports events constitutes between 10% and 15% of all violence depicted on television.

Athletes' Violence off the Playing Field

Most studies of athletes' aggression outside of sports events examine the behavior of adolescent and college-age competitors. Male participation in high-contact athletics appears to be associated with an increased risk for non-sports-related aggression, such as fighting or hurting friends or peers. Male athletes may also be at increased risk of other nonviolent antisocial behavior, such as vandalism or theft. Further, entry into aggressive sports can be associated with an increase in violent conduct among boys.

Other evidence suggests that mere participation in athletics does not, by itself, increase the likelihood of aggression, but that the characteristics and norms of particular sports teams and/or athletes themselves may ameliorate or exacerbate risk for violence. Athletes who endorse toughness as desirable; who identify with rigid, stereotypic notions of masculinity; who use alcohol excessively; and/or who have engaged in on-field violence are at greater risk of generalized aggression outside of sports events. Further, coaches who emphasize and reward extreme aggression or toughness increase the likelihood of violent behavior among their athletes. Older players and participants on more skilled, select teams are more likely to use or endorse the use of violence. These factors may be of more importance in determining risk for aggression than is membership on an athletic team.

Athletes and Violence Against Women

Extensive attention has been paid to sexual and physical violence against women by male athletes. On an anecdotal level, mass media accounts are replete with stories of professional athletes who have been accused of or charged with physical or sexual assaults against their female partners or acquaintances. Indeed, college athletes are overrepresented among defendants in sexual assault complaints filed with campus judiciary systems, and participation in "aggressive" sports such as football or wrestling is related to both self-reports of sexually aggressive behavior and to physical aggression with a female partner among some high school and college-age men. Athletic participation is also associated with increased levels of rape myth acceptance and endorsement of interpersonal violence.

Similar to more generalized violence off the playing field, however, the relationship between athletic participation and violence against women may be impacted by additional factors. The connection between athletic team membership and aggression toward women tends to diminish once factors such as attitudes, problem drinking, and perceived male support for aggression have been accounted for. Thus, binge drinking, the degree to which males endorse attributes of "traditional" masculinity (such as toughness, dominance, and sexual prowess), and norms of disrespect for women among peers may be more critical determinants of a male's risk for intimate aggression than whether or not he participates on a particular athletic team.

Theories of Violence and Sport

Although the relationship between sports and violence is likely complex, theoretical explanations for the link tend to fall along two lines. Invoking cultural spillover theory, Gordon Bloom and Michael Smith have suggested that sports can become arenas in which violence is legitimated and rewarded, increasing the likelihood that the use of violence is perceived to be acceptable and will subsequently spill over outside the sports arena into public and private settings. Violence and aggression in sports may be glorified and supported in multiple ways. Excessive roughness or intimidation during a game may increase an athlete's or team's chance of winning, reinforcing the strategic value of violence. Athletes report that extreme toughness is sometimes encouraged by coaches and modeled by teammates, and that status and perceptions of competence may be conferred on team members who are willing to use excessive force or to fight. Fans and the media may also contribute to an athletic atmosphere in which violence becomes normalized and legitimized. Research suggests that, in addition to the action and display of athletic skills, the opportunity to view violent incidents is a top reason that viewers tune into televised sports. Violent

incidents during games may get as much or more media air time than the outcome of sporting events. Taken together, these multiple reinforcers for aggressive behavior during competition may increase an athlete's sense of entitlement to the use of force or violence in other contexts.

The second explanation focuses more specifically on the role of masculinity both in athletic participation and in aggression. Sports have been identified as an arena in which boys are socialized into and can demonstrate stereotypical traits associated with masculinity, such as dominance, achievement, toughness, rejection of anything perceived to be feminine, and suppression of emotion. Participating in all-male high-contact sports can serve both to expose boys and men to hypermasculine attitudes and beliefs and to provide them with an acceptable outlet to display traditional masculinity. Although certainly not universal, athletes report that coaching and training may be infused with "masculine" injunctions to "tough it out," as well as sexist or homophobic insults comparing failure to being feminine or gay. Given the long-standing connection between adherence to traditional norms of masculinity and the risk for interpersonal violence, athletic teams that particularly reinforce narrow conceptions of masculinity, and that couple notions of masculinity with violence, may exacerbate risk for aggression among their male players.

Erin A. Casey

See also Athletes/Athletics; Athletes/Athletics and Sexual Violence; Masculinities and Violence

Further Readings

Bloom, G. A., & Smith, M. D. (1996). Hockey violence: A test of the cultural spillover theory. *Sociology of Sport Journal, 13,* 65–78.

Forbes, G. B., Adams-Curtis, L. E., Pakalka, A. H., & White, K. B. (2006). Dating aggression, sexual coercion, and aggression-supporting attitudes among college men as a function of participation in aggressive high school sports. *Violence Against Women, 12,* 441–455.

Smith, M. D. (1983). What is sports violence? A sociolegal perspective. In J. H. Goldstein (Ed.), *Sports violence* (pp. 33–45). New York: Springer.

Young, K. (2000). Sport and violence. In J. Coakley & E. Dunning (Eds.), *Handbook of sports studies* (pp. 382–407). Thousand Oaks, CA: Sage.

ATTACHMENT DISORDER

The attachment disorder diagnosis has evoked a great deal of controversy in both scientific and clinical circles. While some academics and diagnosticians would contend that the existence of the disorder itself has not even been empirically validated, other clinical groups claim ardently that they can assess and treat the devastating, almost intractable pattern of behaviors they say are indicative of an attachment disorder. The writings of the first camp, composed primarily of academics, are found almost entirely in peer-reviewed academic journals (largely inaccessible to the broader public), while the writings of the second camp, who claim to treat attachment disorders, can be easily found on the Internet, in parenting books, and through parenting support groups. Following is an overview of the conceptual origins of attachment theory, followed by a description of the formal diagnostic criteria for the reactive attachment disorder of infancy and early childhood, a description of therapeutic approaches, and, finally, a summary of the best practices for assessment and treatment.

Attachment Theory: Conceptual and Empirical Origins

John Bowlby was the original pioneer of attachment theory. He proposed that infants are biologically predisposed to stay close to their parent figures to ensure survival. The attachment system was seen as representing a balance between exploration (for growth and development) and proximity seeking (for safety and emotion regulation). Mary Ainsworth and her colleagues identified individual differences in attachment behavior patterns in infants, first through observations, and later with a structured task called the "Strange Situation." According to research, a secure infant will easily communicate to the caregiver a desire for closeness or contact when needed and is then able to go back to exploring the environment. Insecure infants either show little or no desire for closeness, contact, or interaction (insecure-avoidant pattern) or, conversely, display resistant or ambivalent behaviors when under stress (insecure-ambivalent pattern). Both of these insecure patterns can be seen as risk factors for later social development when they occur along with other risk factors. More recently, the disorganized/disoriented infant attachment category was identified. Disorganized infants showed inexplicable and bizarre patterns of behaviors in the presence of their caregivers when under attachment-related stress and did not appear to have an organized strategy for coping with the stress of the situation. Abused infants or infants whose caregivers struggle with unresolved trauma or loss are more likely to be disorganized with respect to attachment. Disorganized attachment in infancy and early childhood is associated with later emotional, relational, and psychological disturbances.

Reactive Attachment Disorder: Diagnostic Criteria

Reactive attachment disorder (RAD) of infancy or early childhood is defined in the *Diagnostic and Statistical Manual of Mental Disorders, Fourth Edition* (*DSM–IV*) as "markedly disturbed and developmentally inappropriate social relatedness in most contexts, beginning before five years of age." There is a disinhibited subtype, which is represented by indiscriminant sociability (the child lacks clear attachment behavior to the caregiver, is overly familiar and friendly to strangers, may have boundary disturbances). The other subtype of RAD is characterized by excessively withdrawn, disturbed, hypervigilant, or contradictory responses in place of attachment behaviors. There is a clear presumption that experiences of "pathogenic care" (e.g., abuse, neglect, disruption) are responsible for the social relatedness difficulties. The *DSM–IV* offers little description of other behavioral correlates of RAD. The RAD diagnosis is arguably one of the least investigated and empirically validated diagnoses in the *DSM–IV*.

Features of RAD have been observed in samples of institutionalized young children, as well as in samples of abused and maltreated infants and toddlers. What is less clear is how these children look as they develop into middle childhood and adolescence and how to assess for the presence of attachment disorders in these older age ranges. At this time researchers do not have the empirical evidence needed to validate and operationalize the presence of attachment disorders in older children. Nonetheless, frontline workers who encounter children with attachment difficulties maintain clearly that these significant difficulties in attachment persist over development.

Attachment Therapy and Other Controversial Approaches

Several popular attachment treatment centers in North America have proclaimed that they have a treatment protocol to treat children with attachment disorders; their message is that their treatments will succeed where conventional treatments have failed. Much of the popular literature and many Web sites have originated from these centers. Children referred to in this literature as having an "attachment disorder" are diagnosed as having attachment disorders due to the presence of specific and severe behavioral and interpersonal problems. The difficulty is that there are no studies proving that young children diagnosed with RAD do develop these sets of behavioral disturbances. There is no doubt that a history of very difficult and traumatic early childhood experiences can lead to behavioral and emotional problems, but whether these difficulties are attributable to an attachment disorder rather than something else (e.g., posttraumatic stress disorder, neurological disruptions) remains to be seen.

Many of the treatment centers described above utilize some variant of holding therapy as part of the treatment for attachment disorders. There are several types of holding therapies, but the approach generally involves close physical contact with a therapist, and touch and eye contact are strongly encouraged. Some practices are more intrusive and coercive than others. As summarized by Thomas O'Connor and Charles Zeanah, holding therapies run counter to the central tenets of attachment therapy (which support nonintrusive responsiveness to child cues) and can be risky and even dangerous when used inappropriately and/or with a vulnerable and traumatized child. Other controversial treatments that have been proposed have included paradoxical measures and approaches aimed at promoting unconditional compliance. In the United States there have been several reported deaths of children that are thought to be related to holding therapy and its variants. According to the American Academy of Child and Adolescent Psychiatry, coercive treatments are not recommended for children with attachment disorders.

Best Practices for Assessment and Treatment

Experts agree that the best practice for assessing attachment disorders and disturbances is to create a multimodal and comprehensive assessment protocol. Included in the assessment with a younger child should be a structured observation of attachment behaviors, ideally, using a one-way mirror and a variety of tasks such as a separation-reunion and a challenging task. The observation should be set up such that the child's behavior with a stranger can be observed in contrast with his or her behavior with the caregiver. With an older child or adolescent, social cognitions and attachment representations are largely assessed using narrative and interview methods. In addition to these direct relational assessments, questionnaire and interview methods are recommended to determine the presence of social, emotional, and behavioral concerns across different contexts and from different perspectives. A developmental history interview should include specific questions pertaining to the first 5 years of life; the presence of abuse, neglect, or other attachment-related traumas; and the presence of inhibited or undifferentiated attachment behavior patterns. Zeanah and his colleagues have created and validated a structured interview for assessing these behavior patterns in the young child.

There is some research to establish best practices for treatment when the child is an infant, toddler, or very young child. Generally, dyadic therapy, where the focus of the therapy is on enhancing interactions between caregiver and child, is seen as most appropriate for the treatment of attachment disorders in infancy and early childhood. The caregiver is supported in being a secure base for the troubled child, and responding to the child's attachment needs and signals, even when these are difficult to read and obscured by behaviors and contradictory cues. There is little empirically validated research on the treatment of attachment disorders in middle childhood and adolescence. That said, using interventions aimed at establishing a safe attachment relationship for the child when none exists, intervening in existent disturbed attachment relationships with caregivers, and providing support for stressed caregivers are generally seen as best practices for intervention with this group.

Carey Anne DeOliveira

See also Child Neglect; Child Sexual Abuse; Complex Trauma in Children and Adolescents; Nonoffending Parents of Maltreated Children

Further Readings

American Psychiatric Association. (1994). *Diagnostic and statistical manual of mental disorders* (4th ed.). Washington, DC: Author.

Boris, N., et al. & the American Academy of Child and Adolescent Psychiatry (AACAP). (2005). Practice parameter for the assessment and treatment of children and adolescents with reactive attachment disorder of infancy and early childhood. *Journal of the American Academy of Child and Adolescent Psychiatry, 44*(11), 1206–1219.

Haugaard, J. J., & Hazen, C. (2004). Recognizing and treating uncommon behavioral and emotional disorders in children and adolescents who have been severely maltreated: Reactive attachment disorder. *Child Maltreatment, 9*(2), 154–160.

O'Connor, T. G., & Zeanah, C. H. (2003). Attachment disorders: Assessment strategies and treatment approaches. *Attachment and Human Development, 5*(3), 223–244.

Zeanah, C. H., & Boris, N. W. (2000). Disturbances and disorders of attachment in early childhood. In C. H. Zeanah (Ed.), *Handbook of infant mental health* (2nd ed., pp. 353–368). New York: Guilford Press.

B

BATTERED CHILD SYNDROME

C. Henry Kempe and his colleagues provided the first comprehensive description of child physical abuse in the seminal 1962 paper titled "The Battered-Child Syndrome." According to Kempe, battered child syndrome (BCS) is the clinical evidence of injuries resulting from nonaccidental trauma in children, usually perpetrated by a parent or caretaker. In general, the explanations given for the injuries are improbable. Victims of BCS are usually very young and frequently exhibit signs of chronic neglect, such as malnutrition. Kempe illuminated the gravity of the problem by assigning physical child abuse a name and providing data on the prevalence, etiology, and consequences of child battery. Subsequently, the trauma resulting from physical child abuse became known as the battered child syndrome.

The abuse that causes BCS is often chronic in nature and directed at children under the age of 3, although the syndrome can be evident after a single incident and in children of any age. The symptoms of BCS vary considerably depending on the severity and method of abuse. Characteristic injuries include bruises, burns, fractures, and head trauma, as well as retinal damage resulting from the child being shaken. Since children are often handled by their arms and legs, injuries to the appendages are prevalent among battered children. Less frequently, children may be deliberately exposed to or made to ingest toxins. Severe abuse can lead to brain damage, disability, and death. Evidence of multiple injuries in various stages of healing is likely indicative of chronic abuse, and is often detected through radiographic investigation.

Regardless of the type of trauma sustained, a hallmark feature of BCS is that the child's injuries are incongruent in nature and severity with the alleged source of the trauma (e.g., a bruise from a "fall" shaped like a hand). A delay in seeking medical attention for the child may also signal maltreatment. Victims of chronic abuse may be malnourished, have poor hygiene, and display a general failure to thrive as a result of ongoing neglect by their parents or caretakers. Allegations of BCS generally elicit adamant denial of any wrongdoing by the perpetrator or others aware of the abuse. Thus, health care workers should pay particular attention to any inconsistencies in the medical history and document any evidence of potential abuse. If no new injuries appear while the child is hospitalized, the diagnosis of BCS may be strengthened. While doctors and other professionals can be instrumental in identifying and preventing BCS, they may also inadvertently act as barriers to intervention through a reluctance to believe that the parent or caretaker would deliberately hurt the child; such denial may prevent them from making the correct diagnosis and effectively intervening. Although traditionally defined in terms of physical symptoms, BCS has also been associated with emotional and behavioral problems in victimized children that may last long after the physical abuse has ended.

Research suggests that people with high impulsivity and poor anger regulation often perpetrate the violent acts that cause BCS during episodes of rage or frustration. The perpetrators tend to be emotionally unstable and often were victims of childhood abuse. Parents who hurt their children are more likely to be substance abusers, have low intelligence, and possess antisocial or psychopathic traits, relative to nonabusive parents. Children resulting from unwanted pregnancies are at a greater risk of being mistreated than children resulting from planned pregnancies. Research also suggests that BCS may be more common in families of lower socioeconomic status, possibly because of additional parental stress due to a lack of support and resources. It is important to note, however, that BCS impacts families from all socioeconomic backgrounds.

Once BCS is identified, securing the child's safety is of paramount importance. This generally means placing the child in protective care while both the parents and children obtain appropriate psychological and medical treatment. Frequently, criminal charges will be filed against the abuser. Intervention should include addressing any psychological, social, and behavioral factors contributing to the abuse. Success in preventing future abuse largely depends on the abusers' willingness to attend and comply with treatment. Children should be returned to the home only if and when the environment is determined to be safe; extreme caution is warranted given the potentially catastrophic consequences for the child. Providing interventions to people at risk for perpetrating violence, such as those with personal histories of abuse, unstable living situations, and/or substance abuse problems, and those who demonstrate a lack of care for their child, may be helpful in preventing BCS.

Katherine W. Follansbee and Gregory L. Stuart

See also Shaken Baby Syndrome

Further Readings

Kempe, C. H., Denver, F. N., Cincinnati, B. S., Droegemueller, W., & Silver, H. K. (1962). The battered-child syndrome. *Journal of the American Medical Association, 181,* 17–24.

Leventhal, J. M. (2003). Test of time: "The battered-child syndrome" 40 years later. *Clinical Child Psychology and Psychiatry, 8*(4), 543–545.

BATTERED WOMAN SYNDROME

The scientific evidence supporting testimony about battering and its effects continues to develop, as has the approach to expert testimony that rests upon it. Originally coined by Lenore Walker, *battered woman syndrome* (BWS) is a term used in the legal system. However, it is neither a legal defense nor a psychiatric diagnosis. Although the term *BWS* brought considerable attention to the plight of battered women, a number of factors limit its utility. Testimony about battering and its effects was introduced in the 1970s in a landmark case involving a defendant who was eventually acquitted of killing her husband. Since that time, there has been an explosion of empirically based knowledge and information about the nature of domestic violence and its effects on both adult victims and their children who witness it.

Legal definitions of BWS vary across jurisdiction. When BWS is defined as a subcategory of posttraumatic stress disorder (PTSD), it fails to explain many facets of battered women's strategic and psychological responses to violence. This leaves the judge and jury with less than adequate information on which to base their decisions. Although a substantial body of research indicates that PTSD is common following domestic violence victimization, many abused women exposed to great danger do not exhibit these symptoms.

An explanation for various questions presented to an expert witness relies on evidence concerning the ecological context of the defendant's life, including the abuser's pattern of violence over time, prior strategies used to deal with the violence, the effectiveness of those strategies including others' responses, and available resources. The victim's mental (and physical) state is important, but notably, PTSD is only one aspect of it.

Regina Schuller and her colleagues have shown that mock jurors evaluated the defendant as more psychologically unstable when an expert relied upon BWS rather than social framework testimony, thus enforcing a stereotype of the battered woman that diverges considerably from the perspective of a battered woman as one whose actions are a logical culmination of the circumstances to which she has been exposed. In sum, BWS is not adequate as a framework for understanding a battered victim's actions. Alternatively, social framework analysis focused on the circumstances of battering and its effects roots expert testimony in the continually developing scientific evidence in the field.

Mary Ann Dutton

See also Battered Women; Legal System, Criminal Justice System Responses to Intimate Partner Violence; Posttraumatic Stress Disorder

Further Readings

Dutton, M. A. (1997). Battered women's strategic response to violence: The role of context. In J. L. Edleson & Z. C. Eisikovits (Eds.), *Future interventions with battered women and their families* (pp. 105–124). Thousand Oaks, CA: Sage.

Osthoff, S., & Maguigan, H. (2005). Explaining without pathologizing. In R. Loseke, R. J. Gelles, & M. M. Cavanaugh (Eds.), *Current controversies on family violence* (pp. 225–240). Thousand Oaks, CA: Sage.

Schuller, R., Wells, E., Rzepa, S., & Klippenstine, M. A. (2004). Rethinking battered woman syndrome evidence: The impact of alternative forms of expert testimony on mock jurors' decisions. *Canadian Journal of Behavioural Science, 36*(2), 127–136.

BATTERED WOMEN

Domestic violence in the United States is a widespread and serious public health problem. The term *battered women* is still in use, but in many academic circles has been largely replaced by the more inclusive terms *intimate partner violence victims* and *intimate partner violence survivors*. This entry explores the definitions of battering as applied to women with an emphasis on heterosexual women; provides some historical perspective on the issue; cites a few of the statistical findings, causes, and effects of battering including effects on children; and ends with a brief comment on response and prevention.

Definitions

The notion of a "battered woman" derives from the criminal violation known as *battery,* or the willful or intentional touching of a person against that person's will by another person, or by an object or substance put in motion by that other person. Other terms that are currently used to refer to such activity include *domestic violence, wife abuse, spousal abuse, family violence,* and *intimate partner violence*. In many cases, the two terms *family violence* and *intimate partner violence* have taken the place of *battery,* and victimized individuals are referred to as *victims* or *survivors* rather than *battered women,* a term that in its emphasis on physical violence fails to entirely capture the various ways in which intimate partners of either gender can be manipulated and abused in heterosexual and homosexual relationships.

In 1979, psychologist Lenore Walker interviewed 1,500 women who were victims of abuse perpetrated by their spouse and noticed that they all described a similar pattern that she called the "Cycle of Violence," which begins with a positive relationship that becomes filled with tension for any variety of reasons that eventuates in a battering incident on the part of the husband in order to exert power and control. After the incident, the man feels guilty and apologizes, but continues to attribute the cause of the violence to his wife's behavior or flaws. In typical cases of what Walker described as *battered woman syndrome* (BWS), the severity of the abuse escalates over time while both partners deny the severity of the abuse and are convinced that each episode is a separate and isolated event. As the abuse escalates, the husband stops apologizing for the behavior and becomes increasingly violent while his partner becomes increasingly depressed, fatalistic, self-blaming, helpless, and hopeless, developing a sense of personal entrapment and rejecting help from others. The preexisting personality of the woman does not appear to be a major factor in the development of BWS.

In the battering relationship, the physical violence may take many forms, including pushing, shoving, slapping, punching, kicking, choking, assault with a weapon, holding, tying down, restraining, or other efforts designed to restrict the woman's freedom, or refusing to help a woman who is sick or injured. However, physical violence in such relationships is usually preceded by various forms of coercion that give way to emotional abuse and sexual abuse as a means of controlling the woman through fear and degradation. These may include the following: stalking; threats of harm to the woman, her friends and family, or her pets or property; physical, social, and financial isolation of the woman from other significant relationships; extreme jealousy and possessiveness; forcing the woman to perform sexual acts against her will; pursuing sexual activity when she is not fully conscious or refuses consent; hurting the woman physically during sex or assaulting her genitals; coercing the woman to have unprotected sex.

Historical Perspectives

The battering of women can only be fully understood within a sociopolitical context that explores the status of women's rights throughout time. Not until the mid- to late 19th century did women acquire significant legal rights in the United States, and it was not until

1920 that women in the United States could even vote. Before women achieved suffrage, married women were largely considered to be a form of marital property, while separated and divorced women were even more vulnerable to the whims of male authority figures. The battering of women, when publicly noticed, was largely attributed to the vagaries of unusually violent men or the pathology of the women involved.

It was not until the feminist movement of the 1960s and 1970s that domestic violence surfaced as an extremely common and significantly destructive social problem, not attributable to individual pathology. As a result of the women's liberation movement, battered women came to be understood as the most extreme victims of the universal and systematic oppression of women that extends far back into recorded history. Consistent with other efforts originating in the 20th century, the battering of women has become a fundamental national and international human rights issue.

As a result, it is only in the last 30 years that the system response to domestic violence has significantly changed. The first responses to victims of battering originated as the grassroots efforts of women to help and support each other through the development of domestic violence shelters and other services, including political and social advocacy. The criminal justice responses to battering, although far from perfect, have included model police protocols, significant changes in prosecution and legal defense, and judicial education. Efforts to train health care professionals, mental health care professionals, childcare workers, child protective services workers, and those in other social services are still in their formative stages.

In an effort to avoid continuing to focus on the presumed pathology of the victim and thereby denying the criminal behavior of the men involved in perpetrating acts of violence, the early originators of the domestic violence movement preferred to avoid interaction with the mental health system. However, in the last decade there has been a growing recognition that people exposed to repetitive violence are likely to suffer from a number of physical, psychological, and social consequences of that violence that must be addressed if the individual is to recover from the battering. Additionally, the impact on children of exposure to battering in the home has become a major focus of intervention and prevention efforts.

Incidence of Battering

Domestic violence is the leading cause of injury to women. Depending on the source, it is estimated that from 25% to 50% of all women in America have experienced domestic violence at some point in their lives. As a result, 4 million women in the United States experience a serious assault by a partner during a 12-month period, while at least 3 women are murdered by their intimate partner every day. Battering may start when women are still quite young. Recent surveys show that 20% of teenagers and young women have already been exposed to some form of dating violence defined as controlling, abusive, and aggressive behavior in a romantic relationship. Twenty-three percent of pregnant women seeking prenatal care are battered. In a survey of pregnant low-income women, 65% of the women experienced either verbal abuse or physical violence during their pregnancies. Thirty-two percent of all women who seek emergency room care for violence-related injuries were injured by an intimate partner. Research has shown that victimized females are 2.5 times more costly to the health care system than women who have never been the victims of abuse. Three-quarters of employed battered women were harassed at work and domestic violence is estimated to cost companies at least $73 million a year in lost productivity. Women who cohabit with same-sex partners can also become victims of battering, although the incidence of violence is substantially lower than in heterosexual relationships.

Causes of Battering

As is the case for all complex social phenomena, there is no one single cause of battering. The first—and perhaps the most important influence—is learning. The vast preponderance of violent acts in our culture are perpetrated by males and acted out against women, children, and other men. In about 95% of the cases of domestic violence, the perpetrator is male, and even in situations where women are violent, the violence tends to be less damaging and not lethal.

The dominant influence on male behavior is social expectation. Children learn the basics about how to relate to other people within the context of their own family. When they witness violence being used as a method for resolving problems, they learn violence as a fundamental intervention with other people. Boys are expected to both give and take physical violence as part of routine male conditioning. As adults, men are expected to control their violence and the amount of control that is expected has varied over time and historical period, but nonviolence has never been the social norm.

In the large Adverse Childhood Experiences (ACE) study, it was found that the greater the likelihood that children were exposed to intimate partner violence, the greater the likelihood that they were also physically, sexually, or emotionally abused. Among women, the ACE study found a strong graded relationship between the number of adverse experiences they had survived as children and their risk of becoming a battering victim. Among men, however, the study found a strong graded relationship between the number of adverse experiences they survived as children and their risk of subsequently becoming a batterer.

It has been repeatedly substantiated that children who are exposed to violence are far more likely to become violent themselves. Exposure to violence in childhood is a serious risk factor for adolescent and adult violent and criminal behavior. Over many studies, the most consistent risk factor for men becoming abusive to their own female partners is growing up in a home where their mother was beaten by their father.

Although substance abuse does not cause battering, it can play a role in exacerbating battering incidents. One fourth to one half of men who commit acts of domestic violence also have substance abuse problems. Women who abuse alcohol and/or drugs are more likely to be victims of battering, and victims of domestic violence are more likely to receive prescriptions for and become dependent upon tranquilizers, sedatives, stimulants, and painkillers and are more likely to abuse alcohol.

Poverty, homelessness, and racism are all stressors that in and of themselves do not cause violence, but alone and in combination they do put enormous stress upon families. Families that are stressed, isolated, and socially unsupported are more likely to be violent. Many women and children are made homeless as a result of domestic violence when they flee the perpetrator. The system of domestic violence shelters and services was initially created largely by and for White middle-class women. As a result, the issue of systematic oppression based not just on gender but also on race and class has not necessarily informed services for battered women. Women from lower socioeconomic classes have far fewer opportunities to leave abusive partners because they have fewer available resources to support themselves and their children.

Effects of Battering

There are immediate, short-term, and long-term effects of being battered and there are many studies connecting a wide variety of physical, psychological, social, and existential problems with domestic violence. A woman who is battered may live with constant terror and anxiety with fears of imminent doom. To others she may appear passive and lacking in energy, seemingly helpless to take charge of her own life. She may suffer from chronic depression, exhibit suicidal behavior, and develop overt posttraumatic stress disorder. She may turn to the use of drugs and alcohol to afford herself some relief, thus compounding existing problems. She is likely to feel hopeless and powerless to make any significant changes, fearing that anything she does will lead to something worse. She may be unable to relax and have difficulty sleeping. Her sleep may be interrupted by violent nightmares. However, these effects are not manifested by all battered women. Many battered women display resilience and agency and take a variety of steps to protect themselves and their children from further abuse.

The manner in which a woman will be affected by the battering will be determined by a number of interactive factors, including her previous exposure to violence as a child and adolescent; genetic, constitutional, and psychobiological factors; the presence of coexisting physical, psychological, or social problems; the presence of substance abuse; her belief systems as well as the belief systems of her family, ethnic group, or religious affiliation; and the supports that exist within the community.

The Children of Battered Women

Children exposed to domestic violence show many different responses that negatively impact their physical and mental health, their social adjustment, and their school performance. For children, the more severe the violence, the more severe their problems are likely to be. Childhood exposure to violence also has serious consequences for adult physical health as well as mental health and social adjustment. When compared to people who had safe and secure childhoods, people who had experienced four or more categories of childhood adversity—including witnessing domestic violence—had a 4- to 12-fold increase in health risks for alcoholism, drug abuse, depression, and suicide attempts; a 2- to 4-fold increase in smoking, poor self-rated health, sexual promiscuity, and sexually transmitted disease; and a 1.4- to 1.6-fold increase in physical inactivity and severe obesity. The number of categories of adverse childhood exposures showed a graded relationship to the presence of adult diseases, including ischemic heart disease, cancer, chronic lung disease, skeletal fractures, and liver disease. The seven categories of adverse childhood experiences were strongly interrelated, and persons with multiple categories of childhood exposure were likely to have multiple health risk factors later in life.

Response and Prevention

It is clear that a problem cannot be solved until it is properly recognized. In the last 30 years, public awareness of battering as a significant social problem has radically increased. Nonetheless, there is still a great deal of work to be done in educating health care and mental health care providers, social service workers, educators, criminal justice officials, and the general public about the reality of domestic violence, including the costs to society of failing to adequately address the problem. Adequate responses require that the community provide sufficient legal, health, mental health, and other community resources to protect victims and ensure that they receive the services that lead to healing and recovery. This includes sufficient resources to treat the physical, emotional, and social consequences of battering in the victim, the child witnesses, and the perpetrators. In order for these resources to be efficiently delivered, research is needed to discover those interventions that are the most effective. Ultimately, although individual suffering must be addressed, the solution to the problem of battering resides in cultural transformation so that intimate violence and all forms of interpersonal violence are no longer considered acceptable.

Sandra L. Bloom

See also Advocacy; Battered Woman Syndrome; Intimate Partner Violence; Legal System, Criminal Justice System Responses to Intimate Partner Violence; National Coalition Against Domestic Violence

Further Readings

Bergen, R. L. K., Edleson, J. L., & Renzetti, C. M. (Eds.). (2004). *Violence against women: Classic papers.* Boston: Allyn & Bacon.

Brewster, S. (2000). *To be an anchor in the storm: A guide for families and friends of abused women.* Seattle, WA: Seal Press.

Brownmiller, S. (1993). *Against our will: Men, women and rape.* New York: Random House.

Buzawa, E. S., & Buzawa, C. G. (2002). *Domestic violence: The criminal justice response.* Thousand Oaks, CA: Sage.

Campbell, J. (1998). *Empowering survivors of abuse: Health care for battered women and their children.* Thousand Oaks, CA: Sage.

Groves, B. M. (2003). *Children who see too much: Lessons from the Child Witness to Violence Project.* Boston: Beacon Press.

Kubany, E. S., McCaig, M. A., & Laconsay, J. R. (2004). *Healing the trauma of domestic violence: A workbook for women.* Oakland, CA: New Harbinger.

Web Sites

National Coalition Against Domestic Violence: http://www.ncadv.org

Battered Women, Economic Independence of

Economic independence refers to one means by which women may escape and survive abusive relationships. It is related to the ways in which money or financial assets may be used as a tool of coercive control by batterers against women. The financial status of women in terms of employment and wages, savings and investments, government subsidies, and the like is often critical to their decisions regarding abusers and abusive relationships. Women with greater financial independence are in a better position to survive, find safety, and provide for themselves and their children during and after abusive relationships. Many women feel coerced into staying in abusive relationships because they are, or have been made to be, financially dependent upon their partners. The following sections discuss the various tenets of economic (in)dependence: the role of financial abuse in battering and women's attempts to leave abusive relationships;

connections among battering, poverty, homelessness, and welfare reform; and the effects of battering on women's employment and employability.

Economic Abuse as a Dynamic of Battering

Woman battering revolves around power and coercive control that batterers exert over their victims in various ways. One of the more common ways in which power and control is accomplished involves isolating a woman from any social outlets that could legitimize and assist her with her victimization. Preventing her from attending family gatherings, meeting with friends, attending church, and/or finding or going to work, through threats, manipulation, harassment, physical force, and/or injury, are common tactics. Moreover, in many abusive relationships, the batterer controls the flow of household money and may be the sole wage earner, placing the woman at his mercy for financial support. This is particularly effective when women are already disadvantaged financially due to disability, age, immigration status, drug/alcohol addiction, or criminal record, and reliant on public subsidies (e.g., welfare, social security disability and/or income). Even in instances where women are working outside of the home, batterers may order them to turn over their paychecks or harass them at work so much that they constantly lose or quit their jobs. Likewise, violence to and destruction of household items, particularly those belonging to the victim, and marital or couple assets are common forms of abuse. Property damage is not only an expression of an abuser's control but also extremely hurtful to a woman's economic standing.

Economic abuse often continues after a woman terminates an abusive relationship as well, when the batterer uses his economic standing to continue harassing and stalking the woman as a form of separation assault. This is particularly effective in the legal system, which can be extremely time consuming and expensive, when restraining order, divorce, and child visitation, custody, and/or support proceedings go on unnecessarily for months or even years because of investigations, continuances, extensions, unnecessary pleadings, and reneging of agreements. Because of their greater economic positioning in comparison to battered women, who are less likely to afford high quality, ongoing legal representation, abusers usually stand a better chance of retaining attorneys who are willing to work on such court proceedings for a long time.

While many battered women do eventually leave their abusers, such decisions are often difficult and risky. Not only may they face their batterers' retaliation, but they are also likely to face the grave concern about how to survive financially. Many are forced to return to their abusers because of economic hardship upon separation. This is most likely the case when a woman has dependent children.

Poverty, Homelessness, and Welfare

Fleeing abusive relationships often translates into poverty and a high probability of homelessness for battered women. Many are forced to rely on welfare subsidies as their only or primary source of income, at least temporarily. In this way, there is a very strong connection among poverty, homelessness, welfare receipt, and battering. Indeed, the majority of poor and homeless women have suffered from battering; financial struggles upon leaving their abusers are paramount in their situations.

However, welfare subsidies have been substantially eroded since the mid-1990s with the passage of the Personal Responsibility and Work Opportunity Reconciliation Act (PRWORA). Provisions in the law have encouraged recipients to marry, mandated the establishment of paternity in cases where benefits are being used to support children, and placed time limits on receipt of benefits. Such provisions work in opposition to battered women's needs. While PRWORA provides an exemption from the time limits for domestic violence victims, it seems that these exemptions are not regularly made available to women. It appears that many women do not know that they may request them. Moreover, states vary in their policies regarding implementation of the exemptions, such that welfare case workers may not be required or encouraged to offer them to their clients. So while welfare is a primary option for women without alternative means of economic support, it is not always a very desirable one. Comparisons have been made between the regulation, monitoring, and coercive control of batterers and that of the welfare state. In this way, one form of economic dependency is exchanged for another.

Employment

Seeking and maintaining employment can be extremely important for battered women on several fronts. Earning wages, even if they are taken by an abusive partner, may open doors for women socially, in ways that might allow them access to helpful resources they would not otherwise have. Being employed also allows for the possibility of saving money that may be used upon leaving an abusive situation. For those who are able to maintain control of their wages, the process of leaving is often made more expedient and effective because of the economic independence provided by employment. Even in low-wage jobs, women may emotionally benefit from knowing they are employable, and thus feel more confident about their chances of financial survival upon termination of an abusive relationship. Women in higher-wage jobs may not only have the financial resources to move a far distance from their abusers; they may also, if they are highly educated and marketable, have a better chance of being able to reestablish their careers in another location. Moreover, such women may also be able to afford legal representation comparable to those of their ex-partners and thus increase their standing in postseparation court proceedings.

Regardless of the importance of employment, many battered women are not able to look for or maintain work because of the physical injuries, long-term debilitations, or psychological effects of abuse, including depression and lowered self-esteem. This in turn contributes to women's social isolation, which reinforces their partners' power and control. Retaining employment often comes at the cost of work-related harassment and stalking by the abuser, including but not limited to physical assaults immediately prior to a work shift or during work breaks, constant phone calls or email messages throughout the workday, and destruction of work-related documents. In the most dire of circumstances, women, and sometimes their coworkers, may be stalked and attacked at the workplace.

Only recently has the connection been made between woman battering and workplace violence. Employers have been slow at recognizing the specific needs of battered women in the workplace, often seeing battered women as unreliable workers and as liabilities to the organization rather than as in need of help. These women are hard pressed to meet the demands of their jobs as well as negotiate abusive relationships and the consequences thereof—medical attention, counseling, legal proceedings, and the demands of single parenthood. Employers need to weigh the women's frequent tardiness, absenteeism, sick leave, personal leave, and extended vacation requests against the importance of their maintaining

employment. Consequently, battered women may lose their jobs, be demoted, or resign due to injuries or concerns about safety. Their abusers, even when the relationship has ended, are likely to be opposed to, jealous of, and threatened by their employment. Despite the struggles involved with working, battered women who work fare better in establishing some level of financial independence, which is likely to lessen the effectiveness of their abusers' control tactics as well as increase their chances of being able to escape violence and provide for themselves over the long term.

Angela M. Moe

See also Battered Women; Battered Women: Leaving Violent Intimate Relationships; Coercive Control; Financial Abuse, Elderly and Battered Women; Power and Control Wheel

Further Readings

Browne, A., Salomon, A., & Bassuk, S. S. (1999). The impact of recent partner violence on poor women's capacity to maintain work. *Violence Against Women, 5,* 393–426.

Brush, L. D. (2000). Battering, traumatic stress, and welfare-to-work transition. *Violence Against Women, 6,* 1039–1065.

Goodman, L., Dutton, M. A., Vankos, N., & Weinfurt, K. (2005). Women's resources and use of strategies as risk and protective factors for reabuse over time. *Violence Against Women, 11*(3), 311–336.

Lloyd, S. (1997). The effects of domestic violence on women's employment. *Law and Policy, 19,* 139–167.

Moe, A. M., & Bell, M. P. (2004). Abject economics: The effects of battering on women's work and employability. *Violence Against Women, 10*(1), 29–55.

Raphael, J. (1996). *Prisoners of abuse: Domestic violence and welfare receipt.* Chicago: Taylor Institute.

Swanberg, J. E., Logan, T. K., & Macke, C. (2005). Intimate partner violence, employment, and the workplace: Consequences and future directions. *Trauma, Violence and Abuse, 6*(4), 286–312.

Zorza, J. (1991). Woman battering: A major cause of homelessness. *Clearinghouse Review, 25,* 421.

BATTERED WOMEN: LEAVING VIOLENT INTIMATE RELATIONSHIPS

People often wonder why women stay in violent relationships. Physically violent relationships are often accompanied by sexual and psychological abuse. Because these forms of abuse erode self-esteem, women lose sight of their own needs over the course of the relationship. However, through various mechanisms (e.g., social support, media that raised awareness, their own children) some abused women come to realize that the violence is not their fault and they do not deserve to be abused. Women find the strength to leave when they are able to love themselves and put themselves first.

Studies have revealed that the reasons women terminate an abusive relationship include concerns of safety for themselves and their children; personal growth, which often involves a cognitive change or turning point; and reaching a personal limit. Friends, family, counselors, and shelters have been named by women as most helpful in ending violent relationships. Many women reported that multiple types of resources were needed before they were finally able to end the relationship.

The women in these studies clearly conveyed that the decision to stay or leave the violent relationship was a highly rational choice that carefully and accurately considered the pros and cons of the situation, particularly the potentially lethal consequences of leaving. Study responses to why women stay in violent relationships clustered into two broad categories: positive and hopeful reasons on the one hand, and negative ones on the other. Positive reasons for staying included love for their partners, commitment to their wedding vows, desire to provide a two-parent home, and hope that their partners could and would change. Negative reasons for staying included lack of financial resources, housing, or childcare; emotional dependence on the abuser; fear of the repercussions of leaving, derived from the abuser's threats to take the children or kill her or the children; and feeling trapped, ashamed, or without hope of any alternatives.

The distinction between the two types of reasons cited above is critical to understanding how women come to assess their readiness to take action. "Why I stay" is a qualitatively different stage of readiness for change than "why I cannot leave." Each has implications for possible interventions.

Women often described the decision to leave the violence as "reaching a breaking point." Their responses depicted a sudden shift in how they saw their partners and themselves. Some mentioned an especially violent incident resulting in severe injuries such as a ruptured eardrum or head injuries. Reevaluating their circumstances, loving themselves, and considering their own needs were mentioned often as important precursors to ending the violence and were points of view that were previously unfamiliar to many of them.

Women also reported the realization that the violence was not going to end or that the violence was going to escalate to a point of lethality as an important decisive factor in their taking action. Finally, children were a powerful motivator for leaving as well, particularly as women became increasingly concerned that their children were being affected by witnessing the violence, mimicking it, or being abused themselves.

Women left the abusive relationship when they resolved the issues that had previously kept them feeling trapped in the relationship or when they reached the "breaking point" noted above. Additionally, the women conveyed that their leaving was greatly assisted when their friends or relatives were available to help them both logistically and emotionally.

Women indicated there were more barriers to than supports for leaving violent relationships. They noted actual criticism or fear of criticism from family and friends, withdrawal of support, violence in the family of origin that led to perceptions of intimate partner violence as the norm, weak laws, unsupportive or punitive legal personnel, and religious teachings as barriers to leaving. Lawyers, police officers, and judges were often cited as unsympathetic and harmful to women trying to leave. African American women mentioned not trusting female friends to help. Rural Caucasian women mentioned the abuser's family as supporting the violence through denial, rationalization, or active encouragement.

African American women were much more inclined to seek support from their church or family, and for them, the role of prayer and religion was especially important. They never mentioned medical care or social service providers as helpful. They had limited or negative experiences with social institutions such as shelters. White women used the legal system much more frequently. They also mentioned shelters, counseling, and legal personnel as supportive of calls for assistance in leaving the abusive relationship. They noted that shelters also share other types of information, for example, the importance of checking a potential partner's police record, the types of legal charges that can be brought, and warning signs to look for in future partners. The range of services offered by shelters seems helpful in women's decisions to leave abusive relationships, and later in helping them rebuild their lives.

Understanding the factors influencing a woman's decision to leave an abusive partner, and the barriers she faces in actually leaving, can provide important guidelines for developing social supports and facilitators for helping women leave abusive relationships.

Lynn M. Short and Pamela M. McMahon

Authors' Note: Since research to date has been done primarily with women, women's voices are reflected herein. African American and White women from urban and rural locations throughout the United States participating in focus groups or interviews in several different studies were the primary resources for this entry. Distinctions are noted only where their views differed.

See also Battered Woman Syndrome; Battered Women; Battered Women, Prevalence

Further Readings

Horton, A. L., & Johnson, B. L. (1993). Profile and strategies of women who have ended abuse. *Families in Society: The Journal of Contemporary Human Services, 74,* 481–492.

Moss, V. A., Pitula, C. R., Campbell, J. C., & Halstead, L. (1997). The experience of terminating an abusive relationship from an Anglo and African American perspective: A qualitative descriptive study. *Issues in Mental Health Nursing, 18,* 433–454.

Short, L. M., McMahon, P. M., Chervin, D. D., Shelley, G. A., Lezin, N., Sloop, K. S., et al. (2000). Survivors' identification of protective factors and early warning signs in intimate partner violence. *Violence Against Women, 6*(3), 273–287.

Ulrich, Y. C. (1991). Women's reasons for leaving abusive spouses. *Health Care for Women International, 12,* 465–473.

Wolf, M. E., Ly, U., Hobart, M. A., & Kernie, M. A. (2003). Barriers to seeking police help for intimate partner violence. *Journal of Family Violence, 18*(2), 121–129.

BATTERED WOMEN, PREVALENCE

Accurate estimation of the prevalence of domestic abuse or intimate partner violence (IPV) has been an issue from the time it was "discovered" in the 1970s and continues to be debated today. Having accurate estimates is important for several reasons, including allocation of societal resources to address the problem and assessment of whether progress is being made to ameliorate IPV. Estimating its incidence (rate during a defined period of time such as the past year) and prevalence (rate of its occurrence ever in one's lifetime) has been challenging due to continuing stigma associated with being battered or abused. This stigma makes it difficult to get accurate reports of just how common it is for women to be abused by a partner. Central to the issue of accurately measuring the extent of woman battering or IPV is how it is defined.

Definitions

Over time, researchers and advocates for battered women have tended to define battering or IPV more comprehensively. Initially, domestic violence tended to be defined as physical aggression or violence by a male partner toward a female partner. But as our understanding of domestic abuse deepened, we learned that women who were physically abused also tended to be emotionally or psychologically abused and often sexually abused as well. Thus, the extent of woman battering or IPV tends to be related in part to how broadly or narrowly it is defined. The more types of abuse that are encompassed in the definition, the higher the estimates will be.

There are other methodological issues that affect measurement of the extent of IPV that include the following:

- Sampling (the size of the group studied and how well it represents the population of people it is supposed to represent in terms of important characteristics such as age, ethnicity, education, and income)
- Data collection methods (e.g., whether people are interviewed in person or by telephone or are asked to complete a paper-and-pencil survey on their own, as well as the exact wording of questions asked; in general, more behaviorally specific questions yield higher and more accurate estimates of abuse)
- Time at risk (the past year versus over the course of a lifetime and whether estimates cover adolescence as well as adulthood or just adulthood)
- Whether threats or attempts at violence are included or only actual acts of violence
- Whether estimates are based on reports from only the female member of the couple or are based on couple agreement (this is important in that women tend to report higher rates of victimization than men report perpetrating)

Prevalence Studies of IPV

Physical Violence

There have been several national prevalence studies of physical abuse, beginning in the 1970s: the National Family Violence Surveys of 1975, 1985, and 1992; the National Violence Against Women Survey (NVAWS) conducted jointly by the National Institute of Justice and Centers for Disease Control and Prevention; the National Crime Victimization Survey (NCVS) conducted by the Bureau of Justice Statistics, which asks about criminal victimization in U.S. households; the National Survey of Families and Households; and a study of IPV conducted as part of the National Alcohol Survey.

As a group these studies yield widely varied prevalence estimates as a result of several methodological differences among them. At the high end, two studies suggest that as few as 8% and as many as 21% of American *couples,* married or cohabiting, had experienced an act of physical violence during the previous year. Regarding *individual* rates, the NVAWS reported a *lifetime* physical assault rate for women of 25%. *Past year* rates of *individual* physical victimization in the NVAWS and NCVS were 1.3% and .9%, respectively. In contrast, two other recent national surveys have reported somewhat higher rates of 1-year female victimization by male partners: 3.4% and 5.4%.

However, these studies concur that acts of less severe violence such as pushing, grabbing, or shoving occur with much greater frequency than more serious acts such as hitting with an object, choking, punching, beating up, or using a weapon. At least half of IPV victims have reported that they were abused on multiple occasions. Female victims of IPV are more likely to be injured; rates of injury are reported to be in the 25% to 50% range. According to the NCVS, about three quarters of intimate partner homicide victims are women.

Rates of IPV do not vary randomly across all women. Virtually all the national studies find similar patterns in who is most at risk of being physically abused or battered by an intimate partner. Those at higher risk tend to be younger, with the peak risk being in the late adolescence to early adulthood range; have less formal education; are poor; are separated, divorced, dating, or cohabiting versus married; live in urban areas; and are American Indian or African American. Regarding sexual orientation, few methodologically strong studies have been conducted. It appears that gay men and lesbians are as likely or more likely to be physically abused by an intimate partner than are heterosexuals.

Trends in Violence Against Women by Intimates

Criminal victimization of women by intimate partners declined between 1992 and 2001 by almost 50%, according to the Bureau of Justice Statistics. In 1993, about 1% of women experienced a nonfatal victimization by an intimate partner, compared to .5% in 2001. In contrast, female homicide by an intimate partner dropped after 1993 by about 21% after a two-decade period of relative stability. The NCVS reported that in 1998 about three quarters of intimate partner murder victims were women, up from about half in 1976.

Emotional Abuse

Emotional abuse (EA) or psychological abuse has not been as well researched as physical or sexual abuse, in part because there is no consensus on how it should be defined. Unlike physical or sexual abuse, definitions of EA often focus more on intent than specific behaviors. EA is defined here as a pattern of (recurrent) behaviors or communications that are intended to harm a woman's well-being. It appears that the most common types experienced are ridicule and other forms of verbal abuse, restriction of freedom, and jealousy. Prevalence of EA is said to be extremely high in intimate relationships, with some studies showing that a majority of those in relationships report acts of emotional or psychological abuse. However, studies of battered women have found EA to be virtually universal in such women, who report it to be extremely harmful to well-being.

Sexual Violence

Women are more likely to be raped or sexually assaulted by an intimate partner, friend, or acquaintance than by a stranger. The NVAWS reported a rate of 7.7% for lifetime rape by an intimate partner, and .2% of women reported being raped by an intimate partner in the previous 12 months. About half of these women reported the sexual assault to have occurred on multiple occasions. In the NVAWS, about a third of rape victims sustained injury.

Marital rape is a serious crime and is as "real" as rape by a stranger; in fact, it is estimated to be the most prevalent type of rape and is at least as harmful to well-being as stranger rape. Small-scale studies have reported that 9% to 14% of married women have reported rape or attempted rape by their husbands. Most of these sexually assaulted women are also physically and/or emotionally abused by their husbands. Studies of battered women have found that a third to a half reported having been raped by their husbands, oftentimes on more than one occasion.

Rates of Abuse

We are closer to being able to accurately measure the extent of abuse in intimate relationships, although there is still not a consensus on all aspects of the problem, in particular the most effective ways to measure extent of abuse and what should be considered emotional or psychological abuse. There is significant variation in rates of physical violence by male partners across well-designed national studies. However, we can conclude that substantial numbers of women are being abused by intimate partners—physically, emotionally, and sexually. As many as one in five women report having been physically abused by an intimate partner in their lifetimes, and at least 1% to 5% of women are physically assaulted each year. A substantial proportion of these physical and sexual assaults result in injury. Women who are young, poor, from certain ethnic minority groups, poorly educated, separated from their partner, and who live in urban areas are more vulnerable to being abused by a male partner. Although these forms of abuse can occur by themselves, oftentimes they co-occur.

However, recent national data suggest that rates of physical abuse may be dropping, perhaps in response to decades of research, programming, and prevention work to make the public aware of what constitutes abuse, that women do not deserved to be abused, and that assistance is available to help women escape from abusive relationships.

Bonnie E. Carlson

See also Battered Women; Intimate Partner Violence; National Crime Victimization Survey; National Family Violence Surveys; National Violence Against Women Survey

Further Readings

Bennice, J. A., & Resick, P. A. (2003). Marital rape: History, research, and practice. *Trauma, Violence, & Abuse, 4,* 228–246.

Rennison, C. (2003). *Intimate partner violence, 1993–2001* [National Crime Victimization Survey]. Washington, DC: U.S. Department of Justice, Bureau of Justice Statistics.

Schaefer, J., Caetano, R., & Clark, C. L. (1998). Rates of intimate partner violence in the United States. *American Journal of Public Health, 88,* 1702–1704.

Tjaden, P., & Thoennes, N. (2000). *Extent, nature, and consequences of intimate partner violence* (NCJ 181867) [National Violence Against Women Survey]. Washington, DC: U.S. Department of Justice, Office of Justice Programs.

Zlotnick, C., Johnson, D. M., & Kohn, R. (2006). Intimate partner violence and long-term psychosocial functioning in a national sample of American women. *Journal of Interpersonal Violence, 13,* 156–166.

BATTERED WOMEN, SHELTERS FOR

See SHELTERS, BATTERED WOMEN'S

BATTERED WOMEN AND POLICE RESPONSE

See POLICE, RESPONSE TO DOMESTIC VIOLENCE

BATTERED WOMEN'S JUSTICE PROJECT

The Battered Women's Justice Project (BWJP) is a nonprofit organization focused on improving access to justice for survivors of domestic violence. The overarching goal of the project is to promote systemic change within community organizations and governmental agencies engaged in the civil and criminal justice response to domestic violence in order to hold these institutions accountable for the goals of safety and security for battered women and their families. BWJP has three offices: the Civil Justice Office, the Criminal Justice Office, and the Defense Office.

The three offices of BWJP work both independently and on joint projects. The Civil Justice Office focuses on enhancing battered women's access to legal court options and to legal representation in civil court. The Civil Justice Office staff provides technical assistance to attorneys, advocates, court personnel, policymakers, and battered women, offering state-of-the-art advocacy and court system approaches, model protocols and practices, and policy information. Typical issues for this office include protection orders, separation violence, divorce, custody, the confidentiality of shelter records and of victim advocate communications, safety planning, welfare, immigration, and the Violence Against Women Act. The Civil Justice Office emphasizes autonomy and women-centered advocacy, as well as the importance of economic justice in securing agency, safety, and restoration for battered women and their children.

The Criminal Justice Office offers training, technical assistance, and consultation on the most promising practices of the criminal justice system in addressing domestic violence. The Criminal Justice staff provides information and analyses on effective policing, prosecuting, sentencing, and monitoring of domestic violence offenders. The Criminal Justice Office has worked extensively on issues pertaining to domestic violence and the military. This office also offers safety audits and training and consultation in cases involving battered women whose abusers are law enforcement officers.

The Defense Office, managed by the National Clearinghouse for the Defense of Battered Women, addresses issues that arise when battered women are charged with crimes. The National Clearinghouse is the only national organization that provides technical assistance, resources, and support to battered women who kill their abusers while defending themselves or their children from life-threatening violence or who are coerced by their abusers into committing a crime. The National Clearinghouse strives to prevent battered women defendants from being revictimized by the criminal justice system and has developed comprehensive resources to support attorneys, expert witnesses, advocates, and others working with battered women charged with crimes.

The three offices often coordinate both formally and informally. A prominent joint effort of the three offices has been the Coalition Advocates and Attorneys Network Meeting, a biannual conference for legal advocates and attorneys from state domestic violence coalitions. Additionally, the partnership of the three offices enables staff to provide comprehensive assistance in the many instances in which battered women and their advocates and attorneys face multiple civil and criminal issues. BWJP is a member of the Domestic Violence Resource Network.

Kimberly A. Tolhurst

See also Battered Women's Movement; Domestic Violence Resource Network; National Clearinghouse for the Defense of Battered Women

Web Sites

Battered Women's Justice Project: http://www.bwjp.org

BATTERED WOMEN'S MOVEMENT

The Battered Women's Movement (BWM) is a progressive social change and justice movement organized to eradicate the abuse of women and their children in intimate relationships. The women and men in the BWM are allied with and active in a worldwide movement for social justice and human rights. Many in the BWM are also dedicated to ending other forms of violence against women and are committed to working to end the subordination, poverty, killing, slavery, and inequality of disenfranchised people.

The BWM addresses violence against people in all types of intimate relationships. The BWM acknowledges lesbian battering, the battering of men by male partners, the battering of transgendered people, the abuse of elders by adult children, and the abuse of men by women partners. At the same time, the BWM asserts that domestic violence is rooted in male supremacy. The BWM endorses the principle that violence, abuse, and terrorism in relationships are wrong, that abusers alone are responsible for the violence, and that all abuse must stop. Most in the movement believe that sexism and all other forms of oppression are interlocking and connected and that there is no "hierarchy of oppression."

The BWM developed from several social justice movements. In the United States, it has roots in the labor movement in the 1950s and the civil rights and antiwar movements in the late 1960s and 1970s. The BWM began as an intersection between the women's liberation movement and the courageous actions of individual survivors and their allies who dared to break the silence and speak out about their horrific experiences at the hands of male partners.

Organizing against violence against women took the form of demonstrations, vigils, sit-ins, letter writing campaigns, direct actions, speak-outs, teach-ins, and lawsuits. Battered women's testimony and the advocacy of their allies began to shatter the misconceptions that were institutionalized in medicine, psychiatry, law enforcement, the media, and human services delivery. A fundamental principle of organizing in the BWM was that the voices and experiences of survivors should guide all the work. Shelter, legal, intervention, prevention, and accountability initiatives should be grounded in the expertise of survivors.

One of the first efforts of the BWM was to stop the "privatization" of domestic violence and abuse, that is, moving public discourse from discussion of domestic violence as a problem arising in the private arena of the family to identification of violence against women as state-sanctioned behavior. The BWM demanded changes in public policy to eliminate the community and social underpinnings of domestic violence.

As the movement developed, the goals generally included promoting safety, self-determination, autonomy, restoration, and healing for survivors and their children; promoting batterers ending their violence and abuse; changing community attitudes and practices that legitimate domestic violence; and advocating and organizing for social justice in order to eliminate the root causes of battering.

In the past 15 years, the BWM has focused more attention on the differential impact of violence on women experiencing multiple oppressions. Attention has increasingly been placed on the intersection of interpersonal violence inflicted on women and both community-sanctioned and state-sponsored violence, particularly for women experiencing multiple oppressions. Women suffering instrumental controls and jeopardy, not just at the hands of abusers, but also from multiple impediments constructed or tolerated by the society in which they are embedded, often find no possibility of escape from domestic violence, no reprieve from poverty, and minimal support from the community. Disenfranchised women may include women of color; Indigenous women (specifically, American Indian and Alaska Native women in the United States, and women of the First Nations in Canada); lesbians, bisexuals, or transgendered individuals; older survivors and women with physical and developmental disabilities; poor, immigrant, refugee, trafficked, or colonized women; women trapped in prostitution; women who are addicted to alcohol or other drugs; women in institutions (e.g., prisons, mental hospitals, boarding schools); women from religious minorities; and women affected by war.

In the United States, the BWM has generated and stimulated the creation of multiple types of organizations. Among the first organizations formed to address domestic violence were hotlines, networks of safe homes, and shelters. These organizations, sometimes known as battered women's shelters or domestic violence organizations, became very common. Sometimes these organizations included programs to help individuals stop their abusive behavior. Freestanding organizations designed to help batterers stop being abusive also emerged. Individuals and organizations joined together to form state coalitions and a wide variety of national organizations. Community-based, state, and national organizations sought reform in almost every institution of society. Units of government began to address domestic violence. Extensive reform of the criminal justice and civil legal systems, as well as human services systems, was achieved. Some of these organizations operate from a philosophy that male supremacy and/or privilege and social injustice are the root causes of domestic violence; some do not. Some engage in social change work, including organizing; others do not.

Believing that no reform or law change is self-implementing, the BWM and allies undertook a wide variety of training, collaboration, and partnerships with local, state, and national social and legal systems. Task forces to promote "coordinated community response" to domestic violence were formed in rural communities, small and large urban centers, states, tribes, the military, and the federal government.

Research on domestic violence began. Battered women and advocates early asserted that research institutions should shape research agendas, design, analysis, and policy implications in concert with the BWM. Universities began offering course work on domestic violence, and professional training schools in law, medicine, psychology, and social work began incorporating domestic violence into their curricula. Thousands of articles and books were written about domestic violence and more are being written. Thousands of conferences and trainings have been held. Web sites abound. As of August 2006, a search for "domestic violence" on Google generated 42.5 million references. There were many efforts that predate and exist concurrently with efforts in the United States. Shelters (refuges) in the United Kingdom and Canada predate those in the United States, and it is significant to note that one of the early shelters was formed in Copenhagen by members of the Danish women's liberation movement. There are currently movements and programs throughout the world that use various models to interrupt and eradicate violence against women in relationships.

Barbara J. Hart

See also Advocacy; Agency/Autonomy of Battered Women; Battered Women; Battered Women's Justice Project; Chiswick Women's Aid; Safe Houses; Shelters, Battered Women's; Women's Aid Federations of the United Kingdom

Further Readings

Janovicek, N. (2007). *No place to go: Local histories of the battered women's shelter movement.* Seattle: University of Washington Press.

Schechter, S. (1982). *Women and male violence: The visions and struggles of the battered women's movement.* Boston: South End Press.

Tierney, K. J. (1982). The battered woman movement and the creation of the wife beating problem. *Social Problems, 29,* 207–220.

BATTERERS

Batterers are people who inflict violent physical abuse upon a child, spouse, or other person, but the term is relatively new. Batterers are numerous but relatively invisible in American society. Usually, only the most severe batterers come to the attention of authorities. Domestic violence advocates have long argued that batterers' invisibility is one of the sources of batterers' power. Most, but not all, batterers are men. Batterers do not differ in readily observable ways from nonbatterers, but tend to differ from one another. Gender, income, substance abuse, and violence in the family of origin are the factors most often linked to battering, but batterers can never be fully distinguished from the society in which they learned to use physical and non-physical aggression to dominate others.

The term *batterer* can be applied to a broad range of individuals. A *batterer* is an individual who commits acts of physical violence and domination against an intimate partner or ex-partner. The violence is usually episodic rather than a one-time event. This entry's definition of batterer also includes a person who batters

severely on one occasion. In most of those cases, the singularity of the one physical event is surrounded by a milieu of domination and nonphysical abuse, all of which predicts a second battering event in the future. The batterer and his partner may be married or never married, living together or dating, gay or straight, young or old. A batterer may assault a lifelong partner, a first date, or a person from whom he is estranged. Batterers are present throughout our society across all social groups, although groups within our society vary in the prevalence of battering.

This entry adopts the convention of using the pronoun *he* linked to batterers, although *she* can batter too. However, when injury, fear, and goal of the violence are considered, most batterers are men and most victims of batterers are women. In U.S. households, about 85% of intimate partner crimes are committed against women. Adopting the convention here of using *he* to refer to batterers is not meant to imply that women never batter, or that they should be immune to laws against battering.

Battering is against the law in all Western democracies, but has not always been so. The earliest recorded effort to curb batterers was 202 BCE when, at the end of the Punic Wars, Roman societal and family structure changes gave women more property rights, including the right to sue husbands for unjustified beatings. However, this was not the beginning of a movement, as 500 years later, the batterer and emperor Constantine had his wife burned alive when she was of no further use to him. In 1871, Alabama became the first U.S. state to rescind the legal right of men to beat their wives. During feminism's third wave, Erin Prizzey wrote the first dedicated book on battering in 1974, *Scream Quietly or the Neighbors Will Hear,* the title emphasizing the privacy element so necessary to battering. The first intervention programs for batterers began in the late 1970s, modeled on the consciousness-raising groups of the women's movement. In 1980, California became the first state in the United States to mandate treatment for men convicted of domestic violence.

How Widespread Is Battering?

The National Family Violence Survey found that 1 in 8 women reported they had been physically assaulted in the past year, and 1 in 16 had been assaulted more than once. If limited to those who had been severely assaulted more than once in the past year, the prevalence is 2.2%. While battering using severe assault and on more than one occasion over a 12-month period are restrictive criteria, one can use these figures to estimate that *no less* than 1 in 45 paired adult males in the United States is a batterer according to the definition of repeated, severe violence. Obviously, there are a lot more batterers who use nonphysical forms of control to maintain their dominance.

Do Batterers Differ From Nonbatterers?

Since battering is often a hidden behavior, it would be useful if there were other markers of risk that would help to identify batterers among those who do not batter. An alternate way of conceptualizing battering and batterers is that there are not discrete categories but rather there is a continuum of violence. Inherent in this conceptualization, and a hallmark of the feminist perspective, is the idea that all men are capable of battering. Unfortunately, the feminist perspective does not tell us much about which men will batter. All men have grown up in a patriarchal society, but only some men batter. Other theories of domestic aggression such as social learning theory are combined with the feminist perspective to form a more complete explanation of battering and batterers.

The path to battering is complex and differs for every person. Anger, hostility, depression, relationship dissatisfaction, personality, age, stress, spouse-specific assertiveness, sex-role beliefs, and other individual-level markers have all been examined. However, there is no marker or risk factor that, when present, indicates that the risk bearer is a batterer. Likewise, there is no "smoking gun" that can be clearly identified as the cause of his violence. Battering is larger than the individual. Although individuals carry out the acts, acts of battering are incubated in a social system that has encouraged them, permitted them, and failed to sanction them when they happen.

Researchers have identified a number of risk factors for intimate partner violence (IPV) that cut across several empirical studies. Foremost among these is gender. Most representative samples of U.S. adults have found that the prevalence of IPV perpetrated by men and by women is roughly equivalent. For example, the National Family Violence Survey found that 12.4% of women reported that they had been physically violent to their spouse in the preceding 12 months

compared to 11.6% of men. When injury, fear, chronicity, and the context of aggression are considered, it is clear that battering is usually the province of men. For example, in the National Survey of Families and Households, 73% of those reporting injury in an IPV episode were women. To point out that serious IPV is more often perpetrated by men does not suggest that women are not violent, or that there are no women who batter. However, research suggests that most women's violence occurs in the context of violence against them by their male partners. Men's violence is more likely to include sexual abuse, coercive control, and stalking, while women's violence is more likely to be motivated by self-defense and fear.

In addition to gender, three other cross-cutting factors have been found to be important in discussions on batterers and IPV: substance abuse, a history of violence in the family of origin, and low income. Alcohol and drug abuse have long been linked to IPV, but the nature of the relationship is not yet clear. Early studies comparing physically aggressive couples with conflicted and satisfied couples found that chronic alcohol abuse rather than acute measures of quantity and frequency of alcohol use best distinguished between these two groups. More recent studies have suggested that the acute effects of intoxication are also linked to IPV. In one study, IPV was found eight times more likely to occur on a day when the man has used alcohol than on a nondrinking day.

In addition to the acute and chronic effects of alcohol, the frequency with which a man gets drunk is an important predictor of IPV. How often a man gets drunk has been found to be directly related to how often he batters and to the probability he will batter again after he has completed a batterer program. Drunkenness plays a special role in IPV because of its role as an instigator of fear. Drunkenness is the quintessential control tactic because people who are drunk are unpredictable, and people around them who are not drunk are usually alert to the danger and modify their behavior accordingly. When the drunken person is a man with a history of IPV while intoxicated, this fearfulness is an adaptive response. Studies have found that frequency of drunkenness almost quadruples the likelihood that victims will fear their batterer, even after these studies have controlled for the batterer's amount of alcohol used, class, race, marital status, and levels of prior abuse. Drugs other than alcohol also play an important role in battering.

The second cross-cutting risk factor in battering is a history of IPV in the family of origin. Violence in the family of origin can be either observing IPV between parent figures or experiencing violence at the hands of a parent figure. Batterers are much more likely than nonbatterers to have observed violence in their families of origin. The prevalence of parental IPV in the general population is estimated to be 13%, but for men who have been violent with their partner in the past year, the prevalence rate jumps to 35%. However, despite what many believe is a defining characteristic of batterers, only about one in three batterers in treatment report experiencing violence in their families of origin. Even though observing IPV growing up is a risk marker for battering, most batterers have to learn their violent behavior elsewhere. The visual and print media's chronic exaggeration of masculinity is one likely place to learn violence, but sports, clubs, the workplace, education, and religion also contribute.

The third identified risk factor for battering in most studies is some measure of income, employment, or social class. Batterers are more likely than nonbatterers to have low income. The average family income (in 2006 dollars) reported by male respondents in the 1985 National Family Violence Survey who did not batter was $58,371; for men who self-reported battering, income was lower by 16%, at $48,783. Regardless of which data are used, there is a visible link between income and battering.

Do Batterers Differ From One Another?

All of the risk factors discussed previously share two important features: (1) most individuals who have that risk factor do not batter; and (2) for those who do batter, most do not have that risk factor. To the careful observer, batterers often appear as different from one other as from nonbatterers. Observations of variations among batterers have led to attempts to classify or type batterers. With successful classification, additional knowledge may be gained about the dynamics of battering, and subsequently improved interventions may be developed. Studies on batterer types look at differences along three dimensions: (1) *severity* of the violence—batterers who use injury-producing violence may be different from batterers who use only moderate violence; (2) *generality* of their violence—batterers who are violent outside the family may differ from batterers who are violent only in the family; and (3) *psychopathology*—batterers who have co-occurring psychiatric, substance use, or

personality disorders may be different from batterers who do not. Most studies have found three somewhat different types of batterers.

The most common type of batterer is the *family-only* batterer. These batterers confine their aggression to their partner or children. Family-only batterers' violence is usually on the lesser end of severity, and they are less likely to have substance use or mental health issues. The second general type is called the *unstable* batterer. With somewhat elevated levels of violence severity, and more proneness to violence outside the family than the family-only type, the most salient feature of unstable batterers is the instability of their mood. Ranging from anxiety and depression problems, some of these batterers have personalities characterized by emotional lability and borderline personality features. Not surprisingly, these batterers are more likely to use alcohol or other drugs to regulate their mood. Some researchers believe that borderline personality organization and insecure attachment constitute an *abusive personality*. The third general type of batterer is *generally violent*. Often more severe in their violent behavior than the family-only or emotionally unstable batterer types, these batterers' violence toward their partners may be an extension of their general violence toward society. In some cases, these batterers may have an antisocial personality orientation.

The threefold typology is the most prominent classification system for batterers, but not the only one. Based on observations that IPV in the general population may differ from the IPV by those arrested and sent to treatment, some scientists distinguish two types of IPV: *intimate terrorism* and *situational couple violence*. Intimate terrorism is severe, chronic, injurious, instrumental, more likely perpetrated by a man, and more likely to come to the attention of the criminal justice system. There is considerable overlap between the concepts of the intimate terrorist, the abusive personality, and the unstable or generally violent batterer. More controversial is the concept of situational couple violence. Less violent and sporadic, situational couple violence is mutual pushing and shoving between partners that does not result in injury, and where neither partner fears being abused. The roles of perpetrator and victim are fluid, and in fact these terms are meaningless. These cases do not usually come to the attention of the criminal justice system.

Other researchers have looked at readiness to change as adding an important dimension to batterer typology. Since the mid-1980s, practitioners have observed variation in the extent to which batterers accept responsibility for their violence and are prepared to change their behavior. Research on and application of the stage of change model to batterer intervention programs has been under way for over a decade. This model suggests that change is not linear but cyclic, and that people making changes differ in their readiness to change; from the precontemplative or denial stage, they proceed to the contemplative stage, then to preparations for change, then into an active stage of change, and after changes have been made, to engaging in behavior to maintain those changes. While most men entering a batterer program will be in the precontemplative or contemplative stage of change, most programs provide interventions more appropriate for the action stage of change. Even men designated as family-only type batterers, usually thought of as the most change ready and treatable, are often found to have a low readiness to change.

So far, batterer typologies have not been very useful. For one thing, there is evidence that these typologies are not stable over time. For example, over time there may not be a sharp distinction between unstable and generally violent batterers, and men tend to become less "pathological." Despite well over a decade of work on batterer typologies, they remain in the province of academia rather than practice. In part this is a logistical problem. There are few criminal justice or community programs for batterers that have the resources to match batterer characteristics with differential programming, even if such differential programs were shown to be effective. Beyond the possibility of unstable typologies and logistical problems in matching, typologies present other problems. First, most courts and treatment programs do not have the diagnostic capacity, which requires personality and psychopathology assessment, to classify batterers into typologies. Second, the reliability of classification systems has not been established. Third, there are factors such as ethnicity and arrest history that confound typologies. For example, prior conviction for non-IPV crimes would be an important indicator of generally violent batterers. However, low-income African American men are more likely to have been convicted of crimes than middle-class Caucasian men.

Larry W. Bennett

See also Alcohol and Violence; Batterers, Factors Supporting Male Aggression; Batterers, Personality Characteristics of; Batterers, Treatment Approaches and Effectiveness

Further Readings

Dutton, D. G. (2002). *The abusive personality: Violence and control in intimate relationships.* New York: Guilford Press.

Fals-Stewart, W. (2003). The occurrence of partner physical aggression on days of alcohol consumption: A longitudinal diary study. *Journal of Consulting and Clinical Psychology, 71,* 41–52.

Gelles, R. J. (1999). Male offenders: Our understanding from the data. In M. Harway & J. M. O'Neil (Eds.), *What causes men's violence against women?* (pp. 36–48). Thousand Oaks, CA: Sage.

Gondolf, E. W. (1999). Characteristics of court-mandated batterers in four cities. *Violence Against Women, 5,* 1277–1293.

Holtzworth-Munroe, A., & Stuart, G. L. (1994). Typologies of male batterers: Three subtypes and the differences among them. *Psychological Bulletin, 116,* 476–497.

Hotaling, G. T., & Sugarman, D. B. (1986). An analysis of risk markers in husband to wife violence: The current state of knowledge. *Violence and Victims, 1,* 101–124.

Hutchinson, I. W. (1999). Alcohol, fear, and woman abuse. *Sex Roles, 40,* 893–920.

Johnson, M. P., & Leone, J. M. (2005). The differential effects of intimate terrorism and situational couple violence: Findings from the National Violence Against Women Survey. *Journal of Family Issues, 26,* 322–349.

Kantor, G., & Straus, M. A. (1989). Substance abuse as a precipitant of wife abuse victimizations. *American Journal of Drug and Alcohol Abuse, 15,* 173–189.

Zlotnick, C., Kohn, R., Peterson, J., & Pearlstein, T. (1998). Partner physical victimization in a national sample of American families. *Journal of Interpersonal Violence, 13,* 156–166.

BATTERERS, FACTORS SUPPORTING MALE AGGRESSION

While a large body of research is devoted to risk factors for, and the impact of, intimate partner violence (IPV) victimization among women, considerably less is known concerning perpetrators of IPV and the risk factors across the life span that may lead them to enact violent behaviors against female partners. This entry presents a brief review of factors across the life span and across social contexts (i.e., individual, family, peer, community/society) that appear to place adolescent and adult men at risk for perpetrating IPV, and also those factors that appear to protect against IPV perpetration.

Individual-Level Factors

Like IPV victimization, perpetration of physical and sexual violence against intimate partners is found across all ages, incomes, and racial/ethnic backgrounds, but research shows that certain groups are at greater risk of IPV perpetration. The highest rate of IPV perpetration is found among men ages 18 to 35. Substance use in adolescence and adulthood is consistently associated with IPV perpetration, and increases the severity of abuse and risk of injury. Depression is a mental health concern consistently found to be more prevalent in men perpetrating IPV than in the general population, but no other mental health issue or personality traits have emerged as consistently, despite numerous studies that have investigated psychopathology among IPV perpetrators. Personal beliefs and attitudes that legitimize violence against women in relationships are also consistently found to be associated with IPV perpetration.

IPV perpetrators often perpetrate other forms of violence, including nonpartner violence. Notably, high rates of child abuse perpetration are consistently demonstrated among men who physically abuse the mothers of those children, and the risk of physical abuse of children is found to rise with the severity and frequency of partner violence. Suicide and suicidal intentions also often co-occur with IPV among men; perpetration of severe IPV has been associated with reported suicide attempts among adolescents, and a review of Massachusetts IPV homicides revealed that almost one third were accompanied by a perpetrator suicide or suicide attempt. Antisocial behaviors and violence (e.g., conduct problems, police contact, aggressive delinquency, and fighting with peers) have been found to be predictive of dating violence among adolescent boys.

Family-of-Origin Factors

The greatest attention regarding sources of risk for IPV perpetration has been devoted to the family of origin. The theory of intergenerational transmission (i.e., exposure to men's partner violence in the home causes later battering behavior) has long been used to explain perpetration, but this single factor is not sufficiently explanatory, nor is it consistently supported by research findings. Rather, mixed evidence has emerged concerning the role of exposure to violence in the family on later IPV perpetration, suggesting the role of other social and developmental factors. Childhood maltreatment is one such predictor of IPV

perpetration, and has been found to relate to abuse severity among perpetrators. Additional family-level factors for IPV perpetration include low family cohesion and adaptability, dysfunctional home environment, parental substance use, harsh parental discipline practices, and low parental monitoring.

Considerably less is known concerning protective influences at the family-of-origin level. Perceptions of family connectedness have been associated with lower levels of general violence among adolescents, as well as protective of other high-risk behaviors among adolescents, including suicide attempts and substance use, suggesting its role in protecting against IPV perpetration. However, this remains untested and little is known concerning other family-level factors that may reduce IPV perpetration even in the face of known risk factors.

Relationship Factors

While relationship factors such as marital discord may play a role in IPV, the literature indicates that IPV is not relationship specific (i.e., IPV perpetrators tend to serially abuse women throughout their adulthood). Further, risk for violence is greatest after separation.

Peer Factors

Closely linked with individual attitudes and behaviors regarding IPV is the influence of peer context. Peer approval of IPV contributes to both personal attitudes sanctioning its use and actual IPV perpetration, as does hostile talk about women with peers. The actual behavior of peers also relates to IPV perpetration; peer deviance has been found to contribute to IPV perpetration in late adolescence, and adolescent and college males who report peer IPV perpetration are more likely to perpetrate IPV themselves. The potential protective role of peers regarding IPV perpetration has not been investigated.

Community and Societal Factors

Levels of social context beyond family and peers, including school- and community-level factors, have received comparatively little attention regarding their relation to IPV perpetration.

Exposure to community violence has been linked to perpetration of both community violence and IPV among adolescents. At a broader level of societal influence, exposure to violent media has also been found to influence perpetration of aggressive behaviors, via posited mechanisms of viewers learning aggressive behaviors and attitudes as well as being desensitized to this violence. A recent longitudinal analysis indicated that childhood violent television exposure predicts both spousal abuse perpetration and general aggressive behavior among adult men. Similarly, exposure to pornography has been found to be associated with sexual aggression, with batterers' use of pornography linked with women's reports of violent sexual acts from such men as well as more severe levels of violence. Community connectedness may be protective against IPV perpetration; recent evidence indicates inverse associations of community connectedness with both IPV homicide and nonlethal IPV.

Michele R. Decker and Jay G. Silverman

See also Batterers; Community Violence, Relationship to Partner Violence; Ecological Models of Violence; Male Peer Support, Theory of; Media and Violence

Further Readings

Brook, J. S., Brook, D. W., & Whiteman, M. (2007). Growing up in a violent society: Longitudinal predictors of violence in Colombian adolescents. *American Journal of Community Psychology, 40*(1–2), 82–95.

Loeber, R., et al. (2005). The prediction of violence and homicide in young men. *Journal of Consulting and Clinical Psychology, 73*(6), 1074–1088.

BATTERERS, PERSONALITY CHARACTERISTICS OF

Men who batter exhibit a variety of personality characteristics, and there is no single personality profile of the batterer. However, their personality characteristics tend to cluster into some distinct groups. This entry discusses these personality clusters and groups, the prevalence of personality disorders in men who batter, risk assessment of and interventions for men who batter, and the controversy surrounding these personality characteristic findings.

Personality Clusters and Groups

Early studies found three personality clusters: (1) schizoidal/borderline, (2) narcissistic/antisocial,

and (3) dependent/compulsive. More sophisticated studies that included measures of behaviors, beliefs, and physiological responses, along with personality, found that abusers could be placed into three major groups: (1) *family only:* those with no significant personality problems who tend to be violent only at home; these men seem to be conformists who have difficulty communicating assertively and dealing with stressful situations, and they seem to suppress their emotions more than do other abusers; (2) *antisocial:* those with strong antisocial traits who have a history of severe behavioral problems in childhood and adolescence and abuse of alcohol and other drugs; they tend to be violent inside and outside of the home, and they justify their violence and are adept at tactics of intimidation; and (3) *borderline/dysphoric:* those with borderline traits, who are emotionally "volatile," and exhibit depression and suicidal tendencies; they are the most psychologically abusive, and they have the most difficulty separating from their partners and may stalk and harass them after separation. The above differences in personality traits appear to be linked to distinct types of childhood traumas. The studies found that while the antisocial type was likely to have suffered severe physical abuse at the hands of one or both parents, the borderline type was likely to have experienced loss, rejection, and humiliation.

Research on general personality dimensions supports distinctions between "impulsive" and "instrumental" violence. Impulsive violence appears to fulfill an emotional need, such as in the borderline abuser, whereas instrumental violence is more calculated and aimed at obtaining one's way, as in the antisocial abuser. Both the borderline and antisocial abuser appear "underinhibited," in contrast to the family-only type, who appears to be "overinhibited." Some research has investigated physiological responses in the midst of couples' conflicts and linked them to personality types. One study found a *decrease* in physiological arousal among antisocial men during conflict, even when they seemed very angry. This implied that they knew how to appear intimidating and became more relaxed when their control was working. However, this study has not been replicated. Among the recent trends in research is the exploration of psychopathy, generally considered a more severe subtype of antisocial personality disorder. Psychopathic men seem to have little or no empathy for others and there is evidence that they are the most likely to reassault, even after completing treatment. This research may help in identifying an abuser type who would not benefit at all from treatment and instead may require prolonged incarceration.

Prevalence

Some studies find that the majority of men who batter have personality disorders, but prevalence rates can vary as a function of the measures and definitions being used. Some researchers suspect that the self-report nature of many personality measures leads to inflated rates. Studies rarely use more reliable, comprehensive clinical assessments that include structured clinical interviews and reports from significant others. It should be noted that *personality* disorders are distinct from *mental* disorders. There is general agreement that men who batter do not have severe mental disorders, in particular mental disorders with an organic origin such as bipolar disorder. Courts do not recognize personality disorders as factors in criminal proceedings, whereas certain mental disorder symptoms may play a role in an offender's ability to distinguish right from wrong and to understand court proceedings.

Risk Assessment and Intervention

Knowing about the personality characteristics of batterers may prove useful in risk assessment and intervention planning. For example, antisocial types are the most severely violent during the relationship and exhibit domineering and threatening behaviors. However, they do not show the strong emotional attachment of the borderline type and have a "dismissive" style of attachment, which makes it easier for them to end relationships. Borderline types, on the other hand, are more likely to emotionally abuse their partners. They seem to be at the highest risk of killing their partners and themselves after separation. Still, it is possible to become complacent about the lethality of borderline types because they often show a strong motivation to get help, express their feelings, and perpetrate relatively low rates of physical abuse.

Some types of treatments or intervention might be more successful for some personality types than others, suggesting that one size does not fit all. One experiment found that men with antisocial personality traits, compared with other men, had lower reassault rates if they completed feminist-cognitive-behavioral groups, whereas those with dependent personality traits had lower reassault rates if they completed process-psychodynamic groups. The feminist-cognitive-behavioral approach uses sex-role resocialization and the cognitive restructuring and stress management methods used in most group programs. The process-psychodynamic approach helps men to reveal and resolve childhood traumas in a safe environment. Group cohesion and leader self-disclosure are emphasized. Some researchers conclude that because the majority of abusers show narcissistic or avoidant traits, they will respond well to the commonly used cognitive-behavioral group treatment approach. Criminal justice interventions may not be very effective with the borderline type who is acting out of intense emotional needs. His "emotional survival" at the time of separation is more important to him than the consequences of arrest and jail.

Controversy

Findings on the personality characteristics of men who batter have been controversial. The findings lead some to conclude that certain personality traits, rather than cultural and social factors, are the sole cause of the violence. However, other views are possible. For example, it is possible to view the characteristics: (a) as correlated with causal factors and not causes in themselves; (b) as necessary but not sufficient causes of violence—individual level factors, such as personality, can be integrated theoretically with family factors, community factors, and sociocultural levels; and (c) as ways to understand the origins and manifestations of different forms of violence. This last view is in line with findings about different trajectories of childhood trauma leading to different forms of violence and personalities. On the other hand, some researchers who refer to an "abusive personality" mean that personality is the most important causal pathway leading from various childhood traumas to domestic violence. As research continues, a clearer picture is likely to develop on the precise role of personality traits in understanding domestic violence.

Daniel G. Saunders

See also Batterers; Batterers, Factors Supporting Male Aggression; Batterers, Treatment Approaches and Effectiveness

Further Readings

Bornstein, R. (2006). The complex relationship between dependency and domestic violence: Converging psychological factors and social forces. *American Psychologist, 61,* 595–606.

Gondolf, E. W. (1999). MCMI-III results for batterer program participants in four cities: Less "pathological" than expected. *Journal of Family Violence, 14,* 1–17.

Hamberger, L. K., & Hastings, J. (1988). Characteristics of male spouse abusers consistent with personality disorders. *Hospital and Community Psychiatry, 39,* 763–770.

Holtzworth-Munroe, A., Meehan, J. C., Herron, K., Rehman, U., & Stuart, G. L. (2000). Testing the Holtzworth-Munroe and Stuart (1994) batterer typology. *Journal of Consulting and Clinical Psychology, 68,* 1000–1019.

Holtzworth-Munroe, A., Meehan, J. C., Herron, K., Rehman, U., & Stuart, G. L. (2003). Do subtypes of maritally violent men continue to differ over time? *Journal of Consulting and Clinical Psychology, 71,* 728–740.

Langhinrichsen-Rohling, J., Huss, M. T., & Ramsey, S. (2000). The clinical utility of batterer typologies. *Journal of Family Violence, 15,* 37–54.

Saunders, D. (1996). Feminist cognitive behavioral and process-psychodynamic treatments for men who batter: Interaction of abuser traits and treatment models. *Violence and Victims, 11,* 393–414.

White, R. J., & Gondolf, E. W. (2000). Implications of personality profiles for batterer treatment. *Journal of Interpersonal Violence, 15,* 467–488.

BATTERERS, TREATMENT APPROACHES AND EFFECTIVENESS

Batterer intervention programs (BIPs) are one of several types of interventions designed to prevent the onset or continuation of intimate partner violence (IPV). Other interventions include (a) arrest, prosecution, sentencing, and probation of the offender; (b) services for victims of IPV, including counseling, crisis intervention, advocacy, children's programs, and shelter; (c) couples groups; and (d) individual counseling. Couples groups and individual counseling are less often utilized due to concerns about the safety and blaming of victims in couples treatment and concerns about reinforcing the batterer's code of secrecy in individual counseling. Nevertheless, both couples groups and individual treatment are viable interventions for other populations, and their application to batterers, with proper criteria, increases the intervention options for a very diverse group of people.

Although criminal justice actions and services for victims are not usually thought of as interventions for batterers, BIPs are now part of a larger community system of violence prevention in which criminal sanction and victim services are pivotal. Unlike mental health services, BIPs are not designed to be free-standing interventions, but a local node in a community antiviolence network.

BIPs are intended for people (usually men) arrested for domestic violence, for people who would be arrested if their actions were public, or for people who believe their aggressive behavior toward partners or ex-partners is troubling in some way. Men from this latter category of self-referred batterers are often dubbed *wife referrals* by practitioners who doubt the true motivation behind a man's self-referral to a BIP. One of the unintended consequences of BIPs is that a man's participation may support his belief that he is changing his behavior but his partner is not changing hers, therefore increasing his risk for IPV. Research suggests that self-referred batterers are more likely than court-referred batterers to drop out of the BIP and to reoffend.

BIPs usually consist of a short evaluation followed by anywhere from 3 to 12 months of weekly groups. These groups may be educational, treatment oriented, or focused on personal growth, but there are usually elements of all three in a BIP, in varying combinations. BIPs may also include other intervention elements, such as personal counseling, case management, addiction treatment, parent education, mentoring, or programming drawn from cultural and ethnic traditions. BIPs may be focused on partner violence by men or by women, by heterosexuals or by people in same-sex relationships, but groups are usually not mixed by gender or sexual orientation. BIPs are often housed in nonprofit or private agencies, and less frequently in the criminal justice system or in public institutions. The details of conducting batterer intervention programs are readily available in a number of books and papers. Most states and provinces require that BIPs meet standards, and most standards require that the staff of BIPs meet specific educational and training requirements.

The current focus is on group-based, same-sex groups for men. There are two theoretical perspectives that, although seemingly in conflict, are usually combined in practice to form what is called the standard model BIP. The original BIPs emerged from the women's movement of the 1970s and suggested that men's violence against women was socially supported as a means of maintaining male dominance of women. The function of a batterer program drawn from this tradition is to help men change their minds about male dominance through a process of psycho-education and community activism. The Domestic Abuse Intervention Program in Minnesota is the most widely known of the psycho-educational approaches, and a sizable proportion of BIPs identify their program as a Duluth model. The Duluth "power and control wheel" is ubiquitous in BIPs, regardless of theoretical orientation.

The second perspective on BIPs is based on cognitive-behavioral (CB) treatment principles. In a "CB" group, the emphasis is on learning new skills, including identifying triggers for violence, interrupting the escalation process, managing anger, and substituting prosocial behaviors for controlling behaviors. In practice, Duluth-type programs engage in CB treatment and CB group leaders are often feminists, so the distinction between CB and Duluth-type approaches is fuzzy; in fact, the thoughtful combination of these approaches forms a more complete explanation of battering and batterers. The standard model BIP in the United States at the present time is best characterized as a profeminist CB psycho-educational program.

The typical batterer program accepts both voluntary and court referrals, although since domestic violence is a crime, most programs prefer that men are referred as a condition of their prosecution or probation. Same-sex offender groups are usually the preferred modality because they allow for peer feedback and reduce the isolation and private behavior common to batterers.

Nobody knows how many BIPs there are. At this time, there is no viable national organization of BIPs, nor are BIPs registered at the federal level, so all the information about them must come from state networks or licensing bodies. Despite their growth in the past 20 years, BIPs serve far fewer batterers than programs for battered women serve victims. In Illinois, for example, researchers estimated that approximately 12,000 batterers were in BIPs at some point during 1998, which was less than a third of the number of victims served by Illinois victim service agencies during that same year.

Process, Instrumental, and Outcome Goals

The core issue addressed by this entry is the effectiveness of BIPs. Knowledge about batterer program effectiveness is important because courts now routinely refer men (and some women) convicted of domestic abuse to BIPs, suggesting a certain level of public confidence in

the effectiveness of these programs. Is that confidence justified? Another reason to puzzle over BIP effectiveness is that the victims of domestic violence often want to remain in a relationship with their partner, and are looking for help in changing their partner's violent and controlling behavior. Is that help reliable? A batterer's seeking counseling is one of the strongest predictors that a woman will leave a domestic violence shelter and return to her batterer. Consequently, victim advocates and policymakers are justifiably concerned that BIPs not hold out a promise of help that may eventually become a vehicle for injury. A third reason to be concerned about BIPs' effectiveness is that people who work with batterers are interested in outcomes so they can improve the level of program effectiveness. Is the research applicable to practice? For these people, the concern is often less about *whether* batterer programs work than *how* they work, *for whom* do they work best, and *which elements* of the program are most important. A final reason to question BIP effectiveness is that BIPs are increasingly likely to be funded by public dollars. Are these dollars well spent? Would these dollars be better spent on additional services for victims? Or, given the prevalence of substance abuse and mental illness among batterers, should public dollars be directed toward integrated programs for batterers and substance abusers or programs for mentally ill batterers? Researchers are in the early stages of answering these questions. Evaluation of BIPs using well-designed studies is relatively new, and the confidence researchers have in answering these questions is limited.

The first area to be addressed in any review of program effectiveness is: At what are they effective? BIPs have three orientations or sets of goals: (1) victim safety, (2) accountability and justice, and (3) rehabilitation. The achievement of the first goal, victim safety, is usually indicated by nonabusive behavior during and after a BIP. This is the standard indicator of BIP program effectiveness, usually measured by either victim report of IPV or criminal justice records of re-arrest.

Accountability and justice, the second possible goal for batterer programs, is usually a process or formative goal rather than an outcome goal. This goal asks to what extent batterers comply with program referrals, attend groups, and complete their probation requirements. Batterer programs, in their emphasis on accountability, are an extension of the criminal justice system. In the "New York model," a popular accountability-based approach to BIPs, proponents argue that the batterer's behavior in the program is less important than how the community responds when the batterer is noncompliant or reoffends. For advocates of this approach, the outcome to be measured is at the community level rather than at the individual level.

A final goal for BIPs is rehabilitation of and behavioral changes in the batterer, such as skill building, attitude change, and emotional development. These behavioral changes are viewed as instrumental in creating nonviolent behavior. In lieu of using more difficult measures from victims or the criminal justice system, some programs consider these instrumental variables as legitimate program outcomes. Changes in state or trait anger, misogynist attitudes, situational endorsement of violence, drug and alcohol use, gender-sensitive language, emotional expression, partner-specific assertiveness, social support, or other risk factors for abuse can be documented to measure immediate changes as a result of the program.

Goals for batterers programs can be process oriented (e.g., accountability), instrumental (e.g., attitude), or outcomes (e.g., recidivism). The fact that some of these goals are instrumental or process goals rather than outcome goals does not deter from their importance. A superior BIP evaluation would attend to all three kinds of goals. Understandably, for most evaluations of BIP effectiveness, the primary goal is recidivism: After admission to the BIP, is the batterer re-arrested, or does the batterer's partner report physical or nonphysical abuse since he started the program? As it turns out, the "batterer's partner" is usually a moving target. In a major study of over 800 batterers in four well-established BIPs in Pittsburgh, Dallas, Houston, and Denver, researchers found that 50% of the men in the study were not living with the index victim at the time of admission to the BIP, but 30 months after admission, 20% of these men had new partners, a quarter of whom had already been assaulted.

Complicating Factors

A number of issues complicate the question about whether BIPs are effective. Among these issues are the definition of what constitutes abuse, high rates of attrition from BIPs, cultural mismatching, and co-occurring problems such as substance abuse. One of the advantages of using victim reports to indicate outcome is that the victim can be asked about nonphysical forms of abuse. Nonphysical abuse, unless it involves threats, is legal, and will not come to the attention of law

enforcement authorities. Therefore, batterers who recidivate with nonphysical abuse are often not counted as program failures. Some researchers argue that nonphysical abuse and control is a qualitatively different category of behavior from physical abuse, with different risk factors. Nevertheless, much of the content of contemporary batterer intervention programs is focused on learning noncontrolling behavior. A longstanding suspicion of advocates observing BIPs is that men may learn to avoid physical abuse by substituting more economical and legal forms of control such as intimidation and isolation. Consequently, ignoring nonphysical abuse overestimates the effectiveness of batterer programs.

A second complicating factor for examining BIP effectiveness is program completion. On average, 50% of BIP participants never complete the program, regardless of whether or not a court ordered them to participate. Recidivism rates for men who drop out of BIPs are greater than for men who complete the program, so calculating recidivism based on the minority of men who complete the program results in an artificially low rate of recidivism. On the other hand, calculating recidivism based on all men referred to the program, regardless of whether they complete it or not, underestimates the impact of the program because dropouts did not get the full "dose."

The next consideration related to BIP effectiveness is the frequent mismatch between the culture of the program, including the ethnicity of the group leaders, and the culture of the participants. For example, while African American men are overrepresented in BIPs, they do not fare as well in them as do other men. Culturally focused intervention is proposed as a specialized approach for ethnically homogenous batterer groups that focus on cultural issues linked to preventing violence. At present, the effectiveness of culture-focused programs over other forms of batterer treatment has yet to be firmly established, although the same judgment could be made about any approach to batterer treatment. In general, African American and Latino men have the same reassault rate and generate the same level of victim fear as Caucasians, despite not participating in special culturally focused programs. However, there is a significant difference in the dropout rates of these ethnic groups, with African Americans dropping out twice as often as Caucasians. A clinical trial of culturally focused counseling compared to conventional batterer counseling for both racially mixed and all African American groups found no between-group differences in partner-reported violence at follow-up. However, despite the no-difference finding, that clinical trial also found that men who scored high in cultural identification were more likely to complete the all African American groups. These findings provide support for continuation of cultural-specific programming, particularly for men to whom ethnic identity is important. Culture-focused programs, while not yet superior to other groups in terms of preventing recidivism, may be superior in preventing dropout.

At least half of batterers referred to BIPs through the courts have co-occurring substance abuse or mental illness issues. Some BIPs screen out substance abusers or men with serious mental disorders, but the current standard of practice is that batterers who have co-occurring substance abuse problems should be in a BIP and in substance abuse treatment at roughly the same time, either in separate programs coordinating their services or in an integrated program addressing the issues concurrently. Integrated substance abuse and BIP intervention has been found at follow-up to be more successful than traditional serial or parallel interventions at engaging offenders in treatment, maintaining offenders in treatment, and reducing re-arrest.

Effectiveness Studies

The bottom line for BIPs is whether they prevent future episodes of physical violence as measured by partner report and/or official records. Before considering the findings of quasi-experimental and experimental studies, it is necessary to note that the science of all the studies on BIPs to date is less than satisfactory, so caution must be exercised about the conclusions drawn. Experimental studies are always challenging to conduct in the field, outside of the controls afforded a laboratory setting. BIP experiments are especially challenged in three key areas: random assignment, subject attrition, and difficulty with victim contact. Several of the studies of BIPs also lacked a control group, which makes it impossible to attribute outcomes to the program rather than a number of other potential causes, even when batterers have been randomly assigned to treatment groups. Another issue is that random assignment may break down when officials change the assignment of a batterer from one experimental condition to another. Researchers then have to decide whether to consider the men as belonging to the group to which they were assigned or the group in which they actually participated.

The second problem with BIP experiments is attrition. On average, half of the participants in BIPs do not complete the program, regardless of whether or not they were court ordered to participate. Studies have found that the "dosing" effect of keeping men in programs longer may have a direct effect on outcome, even after such studies have controlled for other differences between dropouts and completers. The number of sessions attended is an important predictor of recidivism, and successful completion of all treatment sessions reduces the likelihood of re-arrest.

The third difficulty of BIP experiments, victim contact, is an issue because of the difficulty in contacting past and current partners of batterers, as well as potential problems for victims as a result of such contact, as noted by Edward Gondolf. Victim contact is the preferred data source for recidivism in BIP research because of the poor reliability of official records compared to the reports of victims. However, victims may be coerced to participate in BIP studies by both their partner and the researcher. Any form of coercion is unethical. Also, victims are very hard to locate, and for a good reason: their safety. Coercion and inability to contact victims make using victim reports a difficult job, and for those reasons, many studies use arrest records. Arrest is a much less sensitive indicator of reoffense than victim report. For example, one study found that the proportion of arrest to victim-reported abuse was 1 in 35; that is, for every reported arrest, there were 35 assaultive actions. A second problem with arrest is figuring out what it means: Is arrest an individual marker of recidivism or a systemic marker of accountability?

Following are brief summaries of six experimental evaluations of BIPs. The studies are presented in the order they were published.

Minneapolis, Minnesota, randomly assigned 283 batterers to one of three programs (self-help vs. educational vs. combined) and one of two program intensities (weekly for 3 months vs. twice weekly for 4 months). A 6-month follow-up with 92 program completers and their partners found no significant differences between models or intensities. The main application of this study supports the contention that length of treatment is not an important consideration in BIPs.

Ontario, Canada, studied 59 men convicted of wife abuse, placed on probation, and randomly assigned either to a 10-week batterer program at a local family service agency or to probation with no batterer program. Three of the 30 men (10%) assigned to the batterer program reoffended, according to police records, compared to 8 of 26 men (31%) receiving probation only. The Ontario study provides support for the modest effectiveness of short-term BIPs.

Madison, Wisconsin, randomly assigned 218 batterers to cognitive-behavioral or process-psychodynamic group treatments. In a 18- to 54-month follow-up with program completers, there were no differences between the two treatment approaches in arrests or in victim-reported violence or fear of violence. However, men who had higher levels of dependency did better in the process-psychodynamic treatment, and men who had a more antisocial orientation did better in the cognitive-behavioral program. This study, currently being replicated, supports the suggestion that the "one size fits all" approach to BIPs may not be the best approach; matching batterers to program orientation may lead to a better fit.

Brooklyn, New York, reports the findings of a study of 376 men convicted of misdemeanor domestic violence and randomly assigned to 26 weeks of a Duluth model BIP, 8 weeks of a Duluth model BIP, or community service. At 12-month follow-up, men in the longer BIP were less likely to reoffend than men in the shorter BIP or men in the control condition, although partner report differences were not significant. A key finding of this study is its support for the value of longer-term programs over shorter-term programs.

San Diego, California, compared outcomes for U.S. Navy batterers randomly assigned to a 1-year cognitive-behavioral BIP, a 1-year couples group, a rigorous monitoring program similar to assertive probation work, or a safety planning condition approximating a control group. Men with substance abuse problems or mental disorders were excluded from the study. At 1-year follow-up, there were no differences in reoffense between the four groups. Unfortunately, the research protocol for this experiment not only excluded substance abusers and men with mental disorders but, due to the navy sample, also excluded men with prior criminal records, unmarried men, and unemployed men (i.e., most of the men who are seen in typical BIPs). While questionable as an indicator of normal batterers program effectiveness, the navy study serves as a useful indicator of the effects of assertive community intervention. The overall recidivism rate

was 30% by spouse report and 4% by arrest. These figures compare very favorably with those of other interventions. We can conclude from the navy experiment that communities that take a proactive response to domestic violence—assertive probation work, sanctions for noncompliance, victim safety monitoring, and BIPs—are more likely to reduce the incidence of repeat violence.

Broward County, Florida, randomly assigned 404 male defendants convicted of misdemeanor domestic violence to either probation and 6 months of a Duluth model BIP or probation only. At 12-month follow-up, there were no differences between the BIP participants and regular probationers on measures of attitudes toward women, beliefs about wife beating, attitudes toward treating domestic violence as a crime, beliefs about the female partner's responsibility for the violence, or estimated chance of hitting the partner in the next year, and official reports of recidivism. This study suggests that the hope of changing attitudes in BIPs may be misplaced. Another key finding of the Broward experiment is further support for the *stake in conformity* hypothesis: The men most likely to reoffend are those who have the least to lose, as measured by education, marital status, home ownership, employment, income, and length of residency.

In summary, the experimental studies of BIPs do not clearly answer the questions that have been posed about the programs' effectiveness. In addition to the San Diego navy study, there is emerging evidence that coordinated community efforts in which the batterer program plays an integral role in violence prevention are more effective than situations in which the batterer program is viewed as the singular intervention for men who batter. The advantage of longer-term interventions over shorter-term interventions has not been clearly established, despite the trend for longer BIPs. Nor has the advantage of one program type over another program type been established. Men who are more vested in society do better in BIPs than men who are at society's margins. The most concerning finding so far is that BIPs do not appear to have a clear edge over arrest and probation.

The Multisite Study

With support from the Centers for Disease Control and Prevention, researchers studied 840 batterers and their partners in four cities (Pittsburgh, Denver,

Houston, and Dallas) every 3 months for up to 4 years. Ignoring random assignment in favor of in-depth description and victim-sensitive follow-up, the research team interviewed not only initial but also subsequent partners; used funnel interviewing to increase response sensitivity; considered multiple outcomes, including a quality of life inventory for victims; analyzed numerous intervening variables such as shelter and counseling; used process measures such as program participation; collected counselor ratings; studied ethnic diversity; and conducted qualitative interviews with both batterers and victims. This study represents the most complete information about BIPs and batterer intervention systems that researchers have to date.

The researchers concluded that batterer intervention systems have a moderate effect on future violence. At 4 years after BIP intake, 11% of the men had been re-arrested for domestic violence, but according to partner report, 46% had been violent at least once. However, for participants whose partners were interviewed 4 years after the BIP intake, nearly 90% had been violence free in the past year, and three quarters of the men had not been violent at all, per partner report, for over 2½ years. These findings are supported by qualitative interviews with victims, with 85% of female partners saying they felt safe. One of the most striking findings of this study is that more than half (24%) of the 46% reoffense rate occurred during the first 6 months after intake, *the time during which the man was still in the batterer program.* This suggests that BIPs are not the short-term deterrent that some thought they might be, but may have a more far-reaching impact. The researchers also found that a small group of men, about one in five, reassault continually, including while they are in the BIP, and never desist. BIPs apparently have little effect on this group of dedicated offenders.

The best predictors of reassault in any follow-up period were drunkenness during that period and the woman's prediction of her own safety and probability of reassault. Both of these predictors are dynamic and change over time, suggesting that BIPs should pay at least as much attention to changes in the batterer while he is in the program rather than relying on static predictors at intake such as personality, mental illness, or substance abuse diagnosis. Static predictors of reassault were prior arrest for crimes other than domestic violence, severe psychopathology, and severe levels of physical abuse. These predictors, coupled with the finding that one in five men in the program were constant and undeterred offenders, suggest that there is a subset of batterers in BIPs who should not be there or, alternately, that the standard model of BIPs does not impact this subset of offenders.

Meta-Analytic Studies

Multisite studies provide a richer perspective on BIPs than the experimental studies described earlier. Nevertheless, the multisite study is quasi-experimental and, lacking random assignment, is limited in the conclusions that can be drawn from it. Meta-analysis provides an additional perspective, combining the results of all BIP studies to look for an *effect size* by program type. An effect size is an estimate of the effect of participating in a program versus not participating in a program. Two recent meta-analyses have digested the results of 24 studies on BIP effectiveness using victim report and arrest data.

The first meta-analysis of 22 BIP studies found that without treatment, the proportion of batterers who reoffend was 21% based on police reports and 35% based on victim reports. The effect size for both police and partner reports was 0.18, a small but statistically significant effect. Effects were larger for studies using quasi-experimental designs (.23 and .34) than those using experimental designs (.12 and .09). No significant differences were found between Duluth-type programs and cognitive-behavioral treatment, and the researchers pointed out that the actual differences between these two approaches are minimal. The researchers concluded that a woman is 5% less likely to be battered by a man who was arrested, sanctioned, and attended a BIP than a man who was simply arrested and sanctioned, a figure that corresponds to approximately 42,000 women a year in the United States. The 5% improvement rate for participants in BIPs was compared with other meta-analyses' findings, such as 16% improvement for treatment of aggressive adolescents and 12% for correctional treatment of adult prisoners.

The second meta-analysis was more restrictive in requirements for the analysis, including only 10 studies with a total of 19 BIP outcomes. Of the 19 outcomes, 13 were positive, but only 4 of the 13 outcomes were above the 0.5 level where the effect is considered to be of a moderate size. Like most meta-analyses, the researchers found that effect sizes from experimental studies were smaller than the effect sizes of quasi-experimental studies. They also found that studies using victim report had virtually no effect.

Current Issues

Batterer intervention programs are growing in number but still lack the necessary scientific support to be clearly established as the intervention of choice in all cases. BIPs are usually identified either as a form of cognitive-behavioral treatment or as profeminist psycho-education, but in practice BIPs do not differ that much from one other. Regardless of orientation, BIPs look to reduce violence against partners, teach new skills, and help men be more accountable for their behavior. In empirical studies, BIPs have a small, but statistically significant effect. As BIPs improve their response to attrition, cultural issues, and co-occurring disorders, they will become a better fit for participants. BIPs are a necessary but not sufficient response to intimate partner violence.

Larry W. Bennett

See also Batterers; Duluth Model; Intimate Partner Violence; Recidivism

Further Readings

Aldarondo, E., & Mederos, F. (2002). *Programs for men who batter.* Kingston, NJ: Civic Research Institute.

Babcock, J. C., Green, C. E., & Robie, C. (2004). Does batterers treatment work? A meta-analytic review of domestic violence treatment. *Clinical Psychology Review, 23,* 1023–1053.

Edleson, J. L., & Tolman, R. M. (1992). *Intervention for men who batter: An ecological approach.* Newbury Park, CA: Sage.

Feder, L., & Wilson, D. B. (2005). A meta-analytic review of court-mandated batterer intervention programs: Can courts affect abusers' behavior? *Journal of Experimental Criminology, 1,* 239–262.

Gondolf, E. W. (2002). *Batterer intervention systems: Issues, outcomes, and recommendations.* Thousand Oaks, CA: Sage.

Healey, K., Smith, C., & O'Sullivan, C. (1998). *Batterer intervention: Program approaches and criminal justice strategies.* Washington, DC: U.S. Department of Justice.

O'Leary, K. D., Heyman, R. E., & Neidig, P. H. (1999). Treatment of wife abuse: A comparison of gender-specific and conjoint approaches. *Behavior Therapy, 30,* 475–505.

Pence, E., & Paymar, M. (1993). *Education groups for men who batter: The Duluth model.* New York: Springer.

Stordeur, R. A., & Stille, R. (1989). *Ending men's violence against their partners.* Newbury Park, CA: Sage.

BESTIALITY

Bestiality is defined as sexual interaction between a human and an animal. Bestiality (sometimes referred to as *zoophilia* if the human perpetrator is emotionally attached to the animal) ranges from a human's fondling the genitals or anal area of an animal to sexually penetrative acts, for example, a human male penetrating the vagina or anus of a mammal. Pets and farm animals constitute the most common victims of bestiality. The practice of bestiality has occurred throughout recorded history and depictions of bestiality have been found in prehistoric artwork. Some forms of bestiality result in no injury to the animal, while other forms may result in severe injury to or the death of an animal (making bestiality an animal welfare concern). In some jurisdictions, bestiality is considered a crime. Since the practice of bestiality may be symptomatic of a paraphilia, bestiality can become a human mental health issue. Currently, there is debate over whether preferential bestiality (preferring animals as sex partners over humans) should be classified as a human sexual orientation.

Little is known about the etiology of bestiality or its developmental course. Most of the research on this topic is derived from surveys of self-selected individuals who practice bestiality and who consider it an acceptable or a desirable practice. One checklist of children's sexual behaviors asks about children touching animals' genital or anal areas, and caregivers of children who have been sexually abused more frequently report this behavior than caregivers of nonabused children. Both juvenile and adult sex offenders as well as serial sexual homicide perpetrators admit to bestiality more often than do nonoffenders.

Since bestiality is usually perpetrated covertly and secretively, it is difficult to study objectively, especially when children are the perpetrators. Research that does exist uses the questionnaire method, asking about current behavior or past acts of bestiality, but this research focuses on adult samples.

Bestiality is sometimes coerced. For example, an adult sex abuser may require a child to engage in sex acts with animals or a batterer may force his female partner to have sex with the family pet. Bestiality is a theme in print and video pornography and can be found on numerous Web sites. The effects of exposure to bestiality (live performances or depicted acts) have not been studied.

Debates over the acceptability of bestiality often focus on the issue of consent. Given human power over animals and animals' lack of verbal abilities, consent is difficult to establish even in cases where the animal appears to enjoy sexual interactions with humans. These debates often draw parallels between animal victims of sexual abuse and victims who are children or incapacitated adults.

Effective mental health treatments for bestiality are not specifically noted in the literature, but they may be modeled on interventions for other paraphilias.

Frank R. Ascione

See also Animal Abuse and Child Maltreatment Occurrence; Animal/Pet Abuse

Further Readings

Beetz, A. M., & Podberscek, A. L. (Eds.). (2005). *Bestiality and zoophilia: Sexual relations with animals.* West Lafayette, IN: Purdue University Press.

BETRAYAL TRAUMA

Betrayal trauma is a trauma perpetrated by a person or institution on whom the victim must depend. It involves the violation of the trust within caregiving relationships. Examples include child abuse perpetrated by relatives, teachers, or religious leaders; intimate partner violence; abusive treatment in employment settings; and political oppression. Betrayal trauma has specific psychological and cognitive consequences. A common response is dissociation, a mental process in which individuals separate themselves from conscious awareness of their present situations. Dissociation is linked to memory impairment for trauma. Betrayal trauma theory accounts for the deficits in awareness and memory for mistreatment that psychologists have observed in victims of interpersonal trauma. The terms *betrayal trauma* and *betrayal trauma theory* were first introduced by psychologist Jennifer Freyd in 1991. Since that time, at least seven research studies have demonstrated that individuals who experience betrayal trauma are more likely to report a period of amnesia for their trauma, as compared to individuals who experienced other forms of trauma such as accidents. Other investigations have demonstrated variations in experiences of betrayal trauma according to gender and age, and the impact of betrayal trauma on various aspects of physical and mental health.

Betrayal trauma theory addresses how individuals may separate instances of violation from their memory and conscious awareness in order to preserve a necessary relationship. Individuals do not need to recognize their treatment as a betrayal to experience betrayal trauma. *Betrayal blindness* is the term used to describe the deficits in awareness or memory observed in survivors of betrayal. A large body of research demonstrates that some individuals who experience memory impairment for trauma experiences later recall the trauma they endured, and there does not appear to be a link between memory accuracy and memory persistence. Although initially adaptive, dissociation and memory impairment can lead to individuals' being revictimized or becoming perpetrators themselves.

Research examining memory persistence for abuse demonstrates greater levels of memory impairment for trauma perpetrated by caregivers than for trauma perpetrated by other individuals or for noninterpersonal trauma. In addition, laboratory experiments show that individuals with higher levels of dissociation exhibit deficits in selective attention tasks, but show increased skills on divided attention tasks, as compared with people with low levels of dissociation. In particular, individuals with high levels of dissociation are less likely to remember trauma-related words, which suggests that they may be particularly adept at disregarding threatening information. Individuals with high levels of dissociation are significantly more likely to report trauma experiences in general, and betrayal trauma instances in particular, than are people with low levels of dissociation.

Child Abuse and Betrayal Trauma

Physical, sexual, or emotional abuse during childhood represents a form of betrayal trauma that often has serious negative consequences. Child abuse occurs at the same time that children are developing physically and mentally, forming attachments to their parents, and learning how to manage their emotions and relate to others. Child abuse disrupts all of these processes, and these disturbances often endure well into adulthood. For instance, rates of depression in children, adolescents, and adults are considerably higher among those who have experienced childhood abuse than among individuals who have not experienced childhood abuse. This form of betrayal trauma also is likely to occur repeatedly and in an inescapable environment.

Children who are being abused face an impossible mental and emotional conflict: They must receive care from the very adults who are hurting them. Betrayal trauma theory explains that in order to survive in such circumstances, children attempt to disregard the abusive treatment they receive. Even after they leave their homes of origin, survivors of childhood abuse may still remain unaware of their abusive treatment in order to sustain necessary relationships or to preserve an image of a positive family experience.

Other Features of Betrayal Trauma

There are several other issues related to the experience of betrayal trauma and its effects. Age of onset, severity, chronicity, and whether the perpetrator is a parent are all factors that predict levels of dissociation and delayed memories of abuse. Gender also plays a role in betrayal trauma. Women experience more betrayal traumas than men over the course of their lives, whereas men experience more nonbetrayal traumas. Female victims of child sexual abuse are more likely to experience abuse at younger ages, and to be abused by family members, than are male victims of child sexual abuse. Men are substantially more likely than women to be perpetrators of betrayal trauma. Finally, betrayal trauma is more strongly associated with physical health impairments than are other forms of trauma.

Broader Implications

Because individuals unintentionally create dissociation and/or memory impairment in order to escape their realities, these processes may later be challenging to identify and change. Furthermore, larger dynamics in society can contribute to betrayal blindness and prevent victims from confronting the betrayals they have experienced and their lasting effects. For instance, perpetrators, their families, or larger cultures may insist that victims keep silent, or may not believe victims who disclose betrayal. In addition, individuals, institutions, and larger societies may deny the prevalence of trauma and the reality of its effects in order to protect themselves from this disturbing information. Victims are likely to benefit from psychological treatment from therapists or counselors who have training in treating survivors of trauma, and societies are likely to improve from increased research, prevention, intervention, and discourse regarding different forms of trauma and their effects.

Rachel Evelyn Goldsmith

See also Dissociation; Psychological/Emotional Abuse; Sexual Abuse

Further Readings

Freyd, J. J. (1996). *Betrayal trauma: The logic of forgetting childhood abuse.* Cambridge, MA: Harvard University Press.

Freyd, J. J. (2005). *What is a betrayal trauma? What is betrayal trauma theory?* Retrieved August 12, 2006, from http://dynamic.uoregon.edu/~jjf/defineBT.html

Freyd, J. J., DePrince, A., & Zurbriggen, E. (2001). Self-reported memory for abuse depends on victim-perpetrator relationship. *Journal of Trauma and Dissociation, 2,* 5–16.

Goldberg, L. R., & Freyd, J. J. (2006). Self-reports of potentially traumatic experiences in an adult community sample: Gender differences and test-retest stabilities of the items in a Brief Betrayal Trauma Survey. *Journal of Trauma & Dissociation, 7,* 39–63.

Goldsmith, R. E., Barlow, M. R., & Freyd, J. J. (2004). Knowing and not knowing about trauma: Implications for psychotherapy. *Psychotherapy: Theory, Research, Practice, Training, 41,* 448–463.

BIOCHEMICAL FACTORS IN PREDICTING VIOLENCE

Our brains monitor our experiences through chemical reactions that lead to memories, feelings, thoughts, and other cognitive processes; thus, brain chemistry is particularly sensitive to environmental inputs and is altered accordingly. Experiences, such as learning and social interactions, trigger emotional reactions, and the chemistry of those feelings is translated into our behavioral responses. Aggressive or violent behavior is associated with the chemistry of our emotions where behavioral responses are exaggerated, inappropriate, or out of context given the social circumstances. In these cases, the individual's ability to properly evaluate the situation and regulate his or her emotional responses becomes impaired. Many who are violent are easily provoked, misinterpret the social interaction or stimulus, and overreact; it is as if survival mechanisms have gone awry. In other cases, internal stimulation is insufficient and only extreme behaviors can provide what is physically perceived to be adequate stimulation to the brain.

Neurotransmitters

Studies of biochemical mechanisms underlying violent behavior focus on the role of central neurotransmitter systems in regulating impulse control and activity levels, or arousal of the nervous system. Neurotransmitters are chemical messengers that convey "information" in the form of an electrically charged signal from neuron to neuron, and from brain structure to brain structure. In general, neurotransmitters regulate emotion, mood, hunger, thirst, sleep, and a host of other behavioral and psychological processes. The neurotransmitters dopamine, serotonin, and norepinephrine have been strongly and consistently associated with aggressive behaviors, even in the absence of a disorder.

Dopamine

The dopamine system has been implicated in displays of aggressive or violent behavior. When the dopamine system is activated, novelty seeking and self-stimulation behaviors increase. When this system goes awry, however, behavior may be activated in the absence of a reward, a threat, or some other appropriate stimulus. This "approach system" can produce dangerous asocial and disruptive behavior when it is activated in the absence of an appropriate social setting or provocation. The overproduction of dopamine has been associated with psychotic behavior, and has been linked to antisocial behavior and violence. Antipsychotic drugs that decrease dopamine levels tend to decrease fighting behaviors.

Serotonin

An abnormally low level of serotonergic activity is another significant player in influencing impulsive-aggressive behavior. Lesions that switch off areas of the brain that are dense with serotonin connections produce rage and attack behaviors. Scores of studies have found several indicators of lowered serotonin activity in studies of juveniles and adults characterized as violent or impulsive, in contrast to those who are not. Further refinements to these investigations,

however, show that serotonin is more specifically responsible for regulating impulse control than aggressive behavior. The implications are that when serotonin activity levels are relatively low, the tendency or predisposition to behave in certain ways (e.g., violently) that may be related to certain personality traits (e.g., a negative or hostile mood) is less likely to be inhibited.

Norepinephrine (Noradrenaline)

Norepinephrine (NE) is of particular interest due to its involvement in stress responses, emotions, attention, and arousal. It plays a primary role in the so-called fight-or-flight response by causing the release of stress hormones from the adrenal glands, and exciting the central and peripheral nervous systems. NE activates the fight-or-flight response by stimulating various brain structures, from the frontal cortex, to the limbic system (controlling emotions and survival functions), to the brainstem.

Significant changes in NE have been documented during preparation for, execution of, and recovery from activities that involve states of high arousal, including violent behavior. Drugs that increase NE activity are known to worsen violence in patients who are already agitated, and, conversely, because NE activity levels are suppressed by medications that are used in the treatment of violence, there are clear indications that NE's role in violence is significant.

Monoamine Oxidase

Monoamine oxidase (MAO) is an enzyme responsible for the deactivation of several neurotransmitters (e.g., dopamine, serotonin, and NE). Unusually high or low levels are believed to adversely affect social behaviors. Low MAO activity results in excessive levels of dopamine and NE, which are believed to contribute to aggression, loss of self-control, and inappropriate motivations to behave. Because MAO concentrations are particularly high in areas of the brain involved in complex thinking processes, affect and mood state, impulse control, and aggressiveness, the relationship between irregularities in its activity and possible effects on social and emotional behaviors is understandable.

For over two decades, irregularities in MAO levels have been linked with antisocial behaviors, particularly those involving psychopathy, aggression and violent behavior, sensation-seeking behavior, impulsivity, and excessive alcohol use.

Hormones

Hormones are chemicals released by glands that travel to various parts of the brain and body to exert their effects. Hormones of interest can be categorized as either "sex" or "stress" hormones; they regulate sex drive, reproductive functions, aggression, territoriality, sexual differentiation, responses to environmental stimuli, and energy levels.

Sex Hormones

The most studied hormones in relation to aggression are testosterone and other male hormones, called androgens. Studies of people with a disorder caused by exposure to high levels of androgens in prenatal and early postnatal periods (congenital adrenal hyperplasia) provide evidence for testosterone's role in aggression, in that these people are unusually aggressive. Studies have consistently found evidence for elevated testosterone levels in both male and female violent offenders relative to males and females in control groups, suggesting a role for testosterone in criminal violence and aggressive dominance.

Importantly, behaviors associated with elevated testosterone levels are substantially context dependent. In other words, high levels of testosterone are not always associated with aggression, which also depends on the person's social circumstances and characteristics. Also, these hormones not only influence dominance and aggressive behavior, but they also increase their activity *in response* to behaving that way.

There is also some evidence for the role of irregularities in sex hormone levels in female antisocial behavior. High levels of testosterone have been found among violent female inmates and delinquents relative to those considered nonviolent. Also, females exposed to high levels of androgen in the prenatal and early postnatal periods have significantly higher aggression scores than those in control groups. Unusually high testosterone levels in females may contribute to the increased incidence of a masculine appearance among female offenders and may function to reinforce aggressive tendencies under certain environmental conditions. Interestingly, giving androgens to females who are not involved in criminal behavior has been clearly associated with an increase in aggression proneness.

Stress Hormones

Certain hormones are released in response to signals from the brain and glands involved in the fight-or-flight mechanism. These hormones are sensitive to both psychosocial stressors and novel situations; thus, they are called stress hormones (e.g., ACTH, cortisol, prolactin). In general, studies report increased cortisol activity in individuals with unusually heightened reactions to challenging situations, and an increased incidence in conduct disordered behavior. These findings suggest that some people, as a result of predisposition or social experiences, have greater biological sensitivity to stress. On the other hand, low cortisol responses to stressful stimuli may reflect low levels of nervous system arousal, which characterizes people who are psychopathic, are aggressive, and/or have posttraumatic stress disorder. Consistent with that possibility is research showing low concentrations of cortisol in aggressive youth and violent adult offenders who lack anxiety. If biological responses to stressful stimuli do not occur, then the individual may be relatively insensitive to stress and may behave inappropriately.

Recent scientific advances have identified biochemical factors most consistently related to violence, although much additional work needs to be done to show cause and effect. Nevertheless, what is known is that a constellation of these factors interact in a fluid manner to influence behavior, and their effects are constantly changing as a function of age and developmental stage within a constantly changing environmental and social context.

Diana Fishbein

See also Batterers, Factors Supporting Male Aggression; Neuropsychological Factors in Impulsive Aggression and Violent Behavior; Psychophysiological Factors in Predicting Violence

Further Readings

Coccaro, E., & Murphy, D. L. (1991). *Serotonin in major psychiatric disorders.* Washington, DC: American Psychiatric Press.

Dabbs, J. M., & Hargrove, M. F. (1997). Age, testosterone, and behavior among female prison inmates. *Psychosomatic Medicine, 59,* 477–480.

Ellis, L. (1992). Monoamine oxidase and criminality: Identifying an apparent biological marker for antisocial behavior. *Journal of Research in Crime and Delinquency, 28,* 227–251.

Magnusson, D. (1988). *Individual development from an interactional perspective: A longitudinal study.* Hillsdale, NJ: Lawrence Erlbaum.

Muhlbauer, H. D. (1994). Human aggression and the role of central serotonin. *Pharmacopsychiatry, 18,* 218–221.

Niehoff, D. (1999). *The biology of violence.* New York: Free Press.

Rubinow, D. R., & Schmidt, P. J. (1996). Androgens, brain, and behavior. *American Journal of Psychiatry, 153,* 974–984.

Virkkunen, M., & Linnoila, M. (1993). Serotonin in personality disorders with habitual violence and impulsivity. In S. Hodgins (Ed.), *Mental disorder and crime* (pp. 227–243). Newbury Park, CA: Sage.

BODY INTEGRITY IDENTITY DISORDER

See ACROTOMOPHILIA

BORDERLINE PERSONALITY DISORDER

Borderline personality disorder is considered a personality disorder, which by definition consists of enduring and inflexible patterns of behavior that cause significant distress and impairment socially, occupationally, or personally. Borderline personality disorder is considered one of the most serious of the personality disorders and was historically considered the borderline between the milder mental problems (neuroses) and the more severe mental disorders (psychoses). Characteristics of borderline personality disorder include emotional instability with wide mood swings, instability in relationships, self-injurious behaviors, identity disturbance, impulsivity, and inappropriate and intense anger. This disorder has been stigmatized historically by mental health professionals, who have often considered those with the disorder manipulative, difficult to treat, resistant to treatment, or hopeless. Individuals with borderline personality disorder may require long-term therapy and may have a difficult relationship with the therapist.

Trauma

While a history of childhood abuse or other trauma has long been associated with borderline personality disorder, more recently this strong relationship has received heightened attention. Borderline personality disorder is frequently associated with childhood histories of serious sexual and/or physical abuse, extremely chaotic home environments, or both. Research on the brain has added to the understanding of borderline personality disorder. When trauma occurs in younger children, a number of different events occur in the brain, some of which lead to heightened emotional expression and hyperreactivity to abuse events. Over time, individuals react with these heightened responses to lesser and lesser stimuli, until eventually these heightened responses become generalized to stimuli not associated with the trauma. This response to trauma may be related to some of the symptoms of borderline personality disorder.

Complex Posttraumatic Stress Disorder

The most recent conceptualization of borderline personality disorder for survivors of childhood abuse is as a posttraumatic response to trauma. Complex posttraumatic stress disorder (PTSD), a recently defined diagnosis, subsumes some of the traits of PTSD and borderline personality disorder. Individuals with this disorder are likely to experience long-term emotional and relationship instability; suicidal ideation; posttraumatic symptoms such as avoidance, hyperarousal, and intrusive symptoms; and other traits associated with borderline personality disorder. Individuals with the disorder may experience remission from these severe symptoms with appropriate trauma-focused treatment. Thus, leading trauma professionals and researchers who are working to understand the brain's responses to trauma strongly recommend this more hopeful conceptualization for traumatized individuals with symptoms previously associated with borderline personality disorder.

Rebecca M. Bolen

See also Adult Survivors of Childhood Abuse; Complex Trauma in Children and Adolescents; Self-Injury; Self-Trauma Model

Further Readings

American Psychiatric Association. (2000). *Diagnostic and statistical manual of mental disorders* (4th ed., Text rev.). Washington, DC: American Psychiatric Association.

Herman, J. L. (1992). Complex PTSD: A syndrome in survivors of prolonged repeated trauma. *Journal of Traumatic Stress, 5,* 377–391.

Perry, B. D., Pollard, R. A., Blakley, T. L., Baker, W. L., & Vigilante, D. (1995). Childhood trauma, the neurobiology of adaptation, and use-dependent development of the brain: How "states" become "traits." *Infant Mental Health Journal, 16,* 271–291.

Zanarini, M. C. (2000). Childhood experiences associated with the development of borderline personality disorder. *Psychiatric Clinics of North America, 23,* 89–101.

Brief Child Abuse Potential Inventory

The Brief Child Abuse Potential Inventory (BCAP) is a 33-item measure of adult risk for maltreatment of a child. Perhaps the most important characteristic of the BCAP is that it measures risk factors associated with child maltreatment, such as emotional distress, rigidity, and social isolation, rather than asking about abusive behaviors directly. This makes it less vulnerable to socially desirable responding, and more acceptable in a variety of settings. The BCAP was developed by Steven J. Ondersma, Mark Chaffin, Sharon Mullins, and James LeBreton in 2005 to address the need for a shorter, simplified version of the 160-item Child Abuse Potential Inventory (CAP). All BCAP items are drawn from the CAP.

The BCAP was created using a development sample of $n = 1470$, and was cross-validated using an additional sample of $n = 713$. Items were selected to maximize (a) CAP variance accounted for; (b) prediction of future child protective services reports; (c) item invariance across gender, age, and ethnicity; (d) factor stability; and (e) readability and acceptability. The final measure included 33 items, 24 of which constituted the abuse risk scale and 9 of which constituted the validity scale (6 lie scale items and 3 random response items). On cross-validation, scores from the 24-item risk scale demonstrated an internal consistency estimate of .89, a stable 7-factor structure, and substantial correlations with the CAP abuse risk score ($r = .96$). The CAP risk cut-off was predicted with 93% sensitivity and 93% specificity (area under the ROC curve = .98), and the BCAP and CAP demonstrated similar patterns of external correlates.

Subsequent examination of the BCAP, utilizing a case-control design in an urban setting, has found further support for the validity of the risk scale: preliminary analyses indicate that the BCAP risk scale accurately discriminated 72.5% of a sample of at-risk ($n = 100$) and control ($n = 100$) parents. Of note, the BCAP risk scale discriminated better when applied to all protocols, rather than just to those who provided "valid" protocols according to the BCAP lie and random responding scale. More research regarding the validity and utility of these scales is needed.

The CAP is a copyrighted and proprietary measure; the BCAP is thus not available for separate purchase and cannot be disseminated independently. Those wishing to use the BCAP should purchase copies from Psytec of the full version of the CAP equivalent to the number of brief versions they would like to administer.

Steven J. Ondersma

Further Readings

Child Abuse Potential Inventory items constituting the Brief Child Abuse Potential Inventory and scoring instructions are available from Steven J. Ondersma at s.ondersma@wayne.edu

Milner, J. S. (1986). *The Child Abuse Potential Inventory manual* (2nd ed.). DeKalb, IL: Psytec.

Ondersma, S. J., Chaffin, M., Mullins, S. M., & LeBreton, J. M. (2005). The Brief Child Abuse Potential Inventory: Development and validation. *Journal of Clinical Child and Adolescent Psychology, 34,* 301–311.

Bullying

Bullying is a form of repetitive and aggressive behavior that is intended to create a feeling of fear and intimidation in the victim and to harm the physical and/or mental well-being of the victim. Typically, there is a power difference between the bully and the victim, which allows the bully to engage in the behavior with little fear of retribution from the victim. Bullying behaviors include physical assaults, physical intimidation, psychological intimidation, name calling, teasing, social isolation, and exclusion. More specifically, these behaviors can be classified into two types of bullying: direct and indirect bullying. *Direct bullying* denotes the physical attacks and threats perpetrated against the victim by the bully, while *indirect bullying* refers to the deliberate and repetitive social isolation and exclusion of the victim from the peer group. Victims of bullying can experience both types of bullying, or can be a target of either direct or indirect bullying.

Prior to the 1970s, there was very little interest in bullying behavior among researchers studying interpersonal violence. The work of Dan Olweus was responsible for generating interest in bullying behavior through his groundbreaking research on bullies and the victims in Scandinavian schools. Olweus was instrumental in shaping the definition of bullying to focus on the repetitive and deliberate nature of the behavior, the distinction between direct and indirect bullying, and the status inequality between the bully and the victim. Currently, the Revised Olweus Bully/Victim Questionnaire is the template that other researchers rely on in order to measure bullying behavior through self-report surveys.

Research on bullying among school-age children has been conducted in a variety of countries, including China, Canada, England, Finland, Ireland, Italy, Japan, Norway, Portugal, and Spain. While bullying behavior appears to be an international problem, the research suggests that the prevalence and intensity of bullying is greater in the United States than in other countries. This finding is probably linked to the overall pattern of higher rates of criminal and violent behavior in the United States.

Estimates of bullying behavior vary based on the sample utilized in the research and how bullying was measured by the survey. The National Crime Victimization Survey (NCVS) developed the School Crime Supplement (SCS) to collect data on criminal victimization, bullying, and other school-related issues. The SCS is administered from January to June every other year to a nationally representative sample of U.S. residents ages 12 through 18. According to the 2001 SCS, 8% of students reported experiencing direct bullying by their peers and 11% of students stated they experienced indirect bullying in the 6 months prior to being interviewed.

Demographic Patterns

While the estimates of the extent of the bullying problem vary, a clearer picture begins to emerge in terms of demographic and psychological profile of bullies and their victims. Boys are more likely to engage in and be victims of bullying behavior than girls. In addition, boys and girls rely on different bullying techniques to torment their victims. Boys are more likely to engage in direct forms of bullying such as physical aggression and threats, whereas girls are more likely to rely on indirect bullying techniques such as name calling and gossiping. In terms of age, bullying is inversely related to the age of the victim. As the age increases, the likelihood of being a victim of bullying decreases. While the research suggests that the age of the bully is inversely related to behavior, it also indicates that the bully might be moving toward criminal behavior instead of ceasing the antisocial behavior. Lastly, race appears to be related to bullying behavior. White students are more likely to experience bullying by their peers than either Black or Hispanic students. Like other forms of interpersonal violence, bullying tends to be intraracial.

Psychological Characteristics of the Victim

The psychological profile of bullying victims suggests that they suffer from low self-esteem, lack self-confidence, and have insufficient social skills. Due to their low self-esteem and lack of self-confidence, victims tend not to report the bullying behavior and are dependent on their peers to either report the behavior or intervene on their behalf with the bully. Therefore, the lack of social skills is a critical contributing factor in the bullying process. Victims of bullying are described by their peers as shy and socially awkward. In addition, the victims of bullying are less likely to report having a "best friend" and are more likely to report spending free time alone. Bullying victims who are successful in terminating the victimization typically rely on their friends and social network to intervene on their behalf. Victims with a limited social network will have a hard time getting the bully to cease his or her behavior. The psychological consequence of being a victim is persistent fear, reduced self-esteem, and higher levels of anxiety.

Psychological Characteristics of the Bullies

The psychological profile of the bullies suggests that like their victims, the bullies suffer from low self-esteem.

In addition, the research suggests that bullies tend to be angry, impulsive, and depressed, and possess a belief structure that supports the use of aggression to resolve problems. Bullies report being unhappy at school and have an overall negative opinion of school. Their peers reported that bullies were likely to start fights and be a disruptive influence in school.

Therefore, bullies relied on aggression to solve school-based problems and to establish their position in the school hierarchy. The long-term consequence of bullying is a pattern of antisocial behavior, which includes delinquency, gang membership, spousal abuse, and adult criminal behavior.

Peer Responses to Bullying

The ability of the bullies to torment their peers in school is linked to two factors: first, the school officials and other responsible adults are unaware of the pervasiveness of the problem, and second, the student witnesses are unsure how to handle the situation. The school officials are unaware of the severity of the bullying problem due to the fact that students fail to report the behavior to the school officials. One reason for the underreporting of bullying behavior by the students is the student's perception that the school is not responding effectively to the problem. For example, a study of middle school students in the United States found that the majority believed the teachers did nothing to stop bullying behavior. Therefore, students felt that reporting bullying would not correct the problem, but instead might generate reprisals or other negative consequences for the students. The failure by students to report the bullying behavior hinders the school's ability to effectively respond and creates the student's perception of the school as ineffective, which leads to a circular problem.

In addition to their failure to report the bullying, the student witnesses do not intervene on behalf of the victims of bullying. Instead, students respond either by acting as passive bystanders or by acting in a manner to support the bullying behavior. Research from Canada, Finland, and the United States has indicated that the majority of students would do nothing to stop bullying and would watch it take place.

Ann Marie Popp

See also Child Aggression as Predictor of Youth and Adult Violence; Child Exposure to Violence, Role of Schools; School-Based Violence Prevention Programs; School Violence

Further Readings

Bosworth, K., Espelage, D. L., & Simon, T. R. (1999). Factors associated with bullying behavior in middle school students. *Journal of Early Adolescence, 19,* 341–362.

Devoe, J. F., & Keffenberger, S. (2005). *Student reports of bullying: Results from the 2001 School Crime Supplement to the National Crime Victimization Survey* (NCES 2005-310). Washington, DC: Government Printing Office.

Elsea, M., Menesini, E., Morita, Y., O'Moore, M., Mora-Merchan, J. A., Pereira, B., et al. (2004). Friendship and loneliness among bullies and victims: Data from seven countries. *Aggressive Behavior, 30,* 71–83.

Holmes, S. R., & Brandenburg Ayres, S. J. (1998). Bullying behavior in school: A predictor of later gang involvement. *Journal of Gang Research, 5,* 1–6.

Olweus, D. (1978). *Aggression in schools: Bullies and whipping boys.* Washington, DC: Hemisphere Press.

Olweus, D. (2001). Peer harassment: A critical analysis and some important issues. In J. Juvonen & S. Graham (Eds.), *Peer harassment in school: The plight of the vulnerable and victimized* (pp. 3–20). New York: Guilford Press.

Unnever, J. D., & Cornell, D. G. (2003). The culture of bullying in middle school. *Journal of School Violence, 2,* 5–27.

C

CAMPUS VIOLENCE

College campuses had long been thought to be safe from crimes such as sexual assault and relationship violence. Such interpersonal violence simply was not on the radar of college administrators and criminal justice personnel because of underreporting to police and the private nature of these crimes. However, the myth of the "university as safe haven" quickly changed as the rape and domestic violence awareness movements gained momentum on college campuses in the 1970s and 1980s. Research, too, has added to the increased awareness of the prevalence of this violence. As research methods have become both more sophisticated and more sensitive, researchers have confirmed what advocacy groups suspected: There is a high prevalence of sexual assault, relationship violence, and stalking on campus.

The response to this violence has been witnessed at many levels. First, there has been a general increase in awareness of how a campus environment can complicate the experience of interpersonal violence. Second, the federal government has instituted grant programs aimed at the reduction of violence on campus, and has also passed laws requiring the public disclosure of crimes on campus. Third, some universities have adopted policies, protocols, and programming with the goals of discouraging campus violence and appropriately dealing with it when it does occur.

The Campus Environment and Interpersonal Violence

University students who are victims of interpersonal violence have the same responses as nonstudents who are victimized: They feel confused, hurt, and angry. They fear their perpetrator and have trouble trusting others. They can suffer from nightmares, insomnia, an inability to concentrate, and posttraumatic stress disorder. They sometimes blame themselves. They experience physical or emotional repercussions that can include sexually transmitted diseases, pregnancy, depression, and difficulty having a "normal" sex life or intimate relationship. For college students, the effects of violence may cause them to be unable to study, fall behind in or fail courses, or even drop out of school.

These reactions to interpersonal violence are common, but their severity and how they combine to affect each individual are different from person to person. On a college campus, there exist multiple unique variables that can affect a victim's response, including a shared social group, shared living quarters, financial dependence on parents, the pervasive presence of alcohol, and institutional factors.

Shared Social Group

An overwhelming majority of sexual assaults, and of course, all dating and relationship violence, occur between two people who know each other. In a campus environment, the victim and perpetrator often will share the same group of friends. Additionally, many students on campus who experience interpersonal violence share a cocurricular activity in a student group (such as band, dance, athletics, or a Pan-Hellenic group) with their perpetrator. This common network of friends and support people complicates a victim's decision whether to report the crime to police or even to tell any of her or his friends about the experience. Victims fear that they will not be believed and that they will be "dropped" by their group of friends if they accuse someone within that group of hurting them. Attending college away from their hometown and traditional support network can exacerbate this problem even further.

If they previously had a close relationship with the perpetrator, victims are often concerned that they will "ruin the perpetrator's life" if they tell anyone, especially the police. Many victims do not want to force their friends to take sides, and they fear that this is what would happen if their experience became public. When victims share a cocurricular activity with their perpetrator they are often forced to face that perpetrator every day as they pursue their interest in that group or activity. This can impact a victim's ability to classify her or his experience as "violence," because the offensive act was committed by someone that not only the victim but also many of her or his friends have interactions with on a regular basis. A shared social group is one of the many reasons why victims of interpersonal violence on campus have an astonishingly low rate of reporting the crimes against them to the police.

Shared Living Quarters

Some victims of interpersonal violence on campus share a residence hall or other living quarters with their perpetrator. This can increase their danger, fear, and confusion about the violence. If the student is a victim of relationship violence, all of the dangers associated with cohabiting with the abuser apply. More unique to colleges is the likelihood that victims of sexual assault will share living space with their perpetrator. In both cases, the victim may have concerns about seeing the perpetrator in the dining hall, the stairway, or the lounge area. Shared living quarters can increase a victim's feeling of vulnerability and can have real implications for the safety of victims of campus violence.

Financial Dependence on Parents

Most, though certainly not all, undergraduate students are financially dependent on their parents. For many students, this includes subscribing to their parents' health insurance. If students need to access medical care due to a sexual assault or injury resulting from a violent relationship, they may have concerns about a parent finding out about what happened. They may view their victimization as a failure on their own part and be concerned that they may anger, disappoint,

or be blamed by their parents. For this reason, some victims of interpersonal violence on campus do not seek medical attention nor, for cases of sexual assault, do they seek to have an evidentiary exam performed. Again, the unique circumstances of campus violence negatively affect the likelihood of reporting and prosecution of interpersonal violence.

The Pervasive Presence of Alcohol

Excessive alcohol consumption is generally considered a risk factor for perpetrating sexual assault and relationship violence. It can also be a risk factor for becoming a victim of sexual assault. Alcohol is often used by perpetrators to (a) render their victims more vulnerable through intoxication and (b) excuse their own behavior. Although many college students do not drink and, of those who do, most do not abuse alcohol, it remains true that alcohol is a complicating factor in a significant portion of campus violence.

Institutional Factors

Universities have an interest in appearing to be safe. They must recruit students, please parents, and win donations. However, the reality of campus violence can lead potential stakeholders to question the safety of the campus. Some universities unintentionally discourage reporting and help-seeking by victims. For example, they may distribute materials about self-defense and other risk-reduction measures without balancing them with a message to perpetrators regarding their sole responsibility for committing the crime. Such materials can influence victims to blame themselves because they did not stop the crime from happening, and victims who blame themselves are much less likely to make a report. In an effort to show a concern for safety, some universities have also invested in "blue lights" and safety call boxes, which does not address the fact that most sexual assaults occur in the home of either the victim or perpetrator.

Federal Law

There have been a number of federal laws enacted in the past 20 years that impact campus crime. In 1990, Congress passed the Student Right to Know and Campus Security Act, which requires schools to disclose information about crime on and around campus on an annual basis. This act was amended and renamed the Jeanne Clery Disclosure of Campus Security

Policy and Campus Crime Statistics Act in 1998. The impetus for this change was the 1986 rape and murder of Lehigh University student Jeanne Clery, and the law is commonly referred to as "The Clery Act."

The Campus Sexual Assault Victims' Bill of Rights was adopted in 1992. This law requires that universities inform victims of counseling resources and disciplinary and criminal justice options. In 1994, the Violence Against Women Act mandated the study of campus victimization and the Bureau of Justice Statistics added new questions about student victimization to the National Crime Victimization Survey. The Campus Sex Crimes Prevention Act, which requires the collection and disclosure of information about students and employees who are registered sex offenders, was passed in 2002. Finally, although Title IX is most often regarded as the law that mandates equal access to participation in athletics for girls and women, its equal protection clause also includes the right to pursue education without harassment (including assault) based on gender.

In 1999, the Office on Violence Against Women awarded the first of its Grants to Reduce Violence Against Women on Campus. This program has granted up to $10 million each year to various universities across the country to partner with community victim assistance and criminal justice agencies in an effort to prevent and respond to violence on and around campus.

University Policy, Protocol, and Programming

Many universities have responded to the growing awareness of interpersonal violence on campus by adopting policies, protocols, and programming aimed at reducing these crimes. Various universities have adopted specific policies against sexual assault, relationship violence, and/or stalking. Some have partnered with local victim assistance and criminal justice agencies to coordinate a response to campus violence, while other, usually larger universities, have developed their own centers or departments to respond to these crimes. Universities have their own disciplinary process that can be used to hold perpetrators accountable. Adjudication at the university level is separate from any pursuit of criminal charges.

Some universities have also developed educational programs, which are often facilitated by students for students. The goals of this peer-led model often include raising awareness about sexual assault, relationship violence, and stalking; educating students about the definitions of these crimes and the university's policies and protocols regarding these crimes; and suggesting how to deal with a friend who may disclose that she or he has experienced this type of crime. A handful of schools also pursue a model wherein the program facilitators seek to reduce the likelihood that a potential perpetrator might commit such a crime. This model focuses on the cultural climate that tolerates interpersonal violence and calls for men and women to work together to challenge this culture.

Roberta E. Gibbons

See also Dating Violence/Courtship Violence; Rape/Sexual Assault; Stalking

Further Readings

Fisher, B. S., Cullen, F. T., & Turner, M. G. (2000). *The sexual victimization of college women.* Washington, DC: U.S. Department of Justice, National Criminal Justice Reference Service.

Kajane, H. M., Fisher, B. S., & Cullen, F. T. (2005). *Sexual assault on campus: What colleges and universities are doing about it.* Washington, DC: U.S. Department of Justice, National Criminal Justice Reference Service.

Kilmartin, C. (2001). *Sexual assault in context: Teaching college men about gender.* Holmes Beach, FL: Learning Publications.

Koss, M. P., Gidycz, C. A., & Wisniewski, N. (1987). The scope of rape: Incidence and prevalence of sexual aggression and victimization in a national sample of higher education students. *Journal of Consulting and Clinical Psychology, 55,* 64–170.

Romeo, F. F. (2001). A recommendation for campus anti-stalking policy and procedures handbook. *College Student Journal, 35*(4), 514–516.

Schewe, P. A. (2002). *Preventing violence in relationships: Interventions across the lifespan.* Washington, DC: American Psychological Association.

Schwartz, M. D., & Dekeseredy, W. (1997). *Sexual assault on the college campus: The role of male peer support.* Thousand Oaks, CA: Sage.

CANADIAN NATIONAL SURVEY

Health and Welfare Canada sponsors the Canadian National Survey (CNS). This survey was the first nationally representative survey of Canadian university and college undergraduates about male-to-female abuse in heterosexual dating relationships. Using a broad definition and a variety of measures, principal investigators Walter DeKeseredy and Katharine Kelly designed the CNS to estimate the incidence, prevalence, sources, and consequences of intentional psychological, physical, and sexual abuse against college and university women.

Background

The CNS, fielded in the fall of 1992, was designed to measure the nature and extent of dating abuse among college or university heterosexual dating couples in Canada. The CNS measured physical and psychological abuse based on modified questions from the Conflict Tactics Scale (CTS). Further, it collected data on sexual assault using measures from a modified Sexual Experiences Survey (SES). Demographic information from respondents was also obtained.

Undergraduates were selected using a stratified, multistage sample design. The sampling frame included colleges enrolling more than 100 students, and universities enrolling 500 or more students. Of the 48 original institutions selected, 2 chose not to participate, and 17 professors also refused to participate. Once replacements for these refusals were included, individual student participation was high—99% of individuals in the 95 undergraduate classrooms participated in this voluntary, anonymous survey. The final sample consisted of 1,835 females and 1,307 males.

Estimates

CNS data collected over time reveal that, in general, males report committing less abuse than females report experiencing. The data show that while in high school, 50% of females surveyed were emotionally hurt by their partners, 9% were physically hurt, 8% were threatened with physical force to engage in sexual activity, and 15% were physically forced to engage in sexual acts. While at a college or university, 28% of females were physically abused, and 79% were psychologically abused in the preceding year. DeKeseredy and Martin Schwartz concluded that a significant number of Canadian females are victims of sexual abuse by their dating partners while at a college or university.

CNS findings also suggest that a considerable amount of female-to-male violence is motivated by self-defense. CNS data analysis identifies individuals at risk for dating abuse, including males who adhere to familial patriarchy, males who associate with friends who legitimate violence against women, males who are exposed to pornography, and those involved in a greater number of serious relationships. Other at-risk individuals include men and women who drink or use drugs frequently with their dating partners.

Advantages and Disadvantages

The CNS offers advantages to previous woman abuse surveys in Canada. It was the first nationally representative sample of college and university students in Canada. Further, it utilizes multiple measures to quantify intentional physical, psychological, and sexual abuse. And the CNS enables both prevalence and incidence estimates of dating abuse.

Obtaining a large enough sample of victims to perform reliable subgroup comparisons is a problem with CNS data, as it is with the data from many victim surveys. For example, reliable comparisons among racial/ethnic groups are not possible. A second limitation of the survey data is that the CNS uses the modified versions of the CTS and the SES, so many limitations attributed to these measures also apply to the CNS. In addition, CNS findings are not generalizable to the general population of dating females, as college and university students differ from the general population in several ways (e.g., income, race/ethnicity).

Callie Marie Rennison

See also Assault; Dating Violence/Courtship Violence; Intimate Partner Violence; Rape/Sexual Assault; School Violence

Further Readings

DeKeseredy, W. S., & Schwartz, M. D. (1998). *Woman abuse on campus: Results from the Canadian National Survey.* Thousand Oaks, CA: Sage.

Koss, M. P., Gidycz, C. A., & Wisniewski, N. (1987). The scope of rape: Incidence and prevalence of sexual aggression and victimization in a national sample of higher education students. *Journal of Consulting and Clinical Psychology, 55,* 162–170.

Straus, M., & Gelles, R. (1986). Societal change and change in family violence from 1975 to 1985 as revealed by two national surveys. *Journal of Marriage and the Family, 48,* 465–479.

CAPITAL PUNISHMENT

Capital punishment refers to the intentional killing of a person by a state or federal body of government as a penalty against that person for a crime committed against society. The United States is included in a group of less than 90 countries worldwide that continue to execute persons for ordinary crimes (as opposed to crimes such as treason or genocide). Within the international community, the United States is admonished by many of its allies and challenged under international treaties for continuing to implement the death penalty. Whereas countries such as Australia, England, Canada, and Israel have abolished capital punishment, the United States is joined by nations primarily found in the Middle East, Northern Africa, and Asia, which currently retain the death penalty. Thus, while the rest of the Western industrialized world has largely abolished this punishment, capital punishment in the United States remains an accepted punishment for specific crimes of interpersonal violence, treason, and malevolent acts against the government. Currently, 38 states and the federal government allow the death penalty.

Public Opinion Trends

The first U.S. public opinion polls on the topic of the death penalty began in 1936 following the high-profile execution of the convicted killer of Charles Lindbergh's baby. At that time, 61% of Americans favored the death penalty. This percentage continued to climb until the early 1950s, when support for capital punishment began to ebb. This decline culminated in 1966 when support levels reached an all-time low of 42%. Support gradually increased then decreased again slightly before *Furman v. Georgia* (1972), the landmark U.S. Supreme Court decision that created a national moratorium on executions. Post-*Furman,* support rose from 57% in late 1972 and peaked at a support rate of 80% in the mid-1990s. In recent years, death penalty support has decreased markedly, with 64% of Americans in a 2005 survey saying that they generally supported capital punishment.

These lower levels of support are due to growing public misgivings as reflected in jury verdicts, the actions of the courts and legislatures, and scientific opinion polls. Many Americans are concerned about new DNA testing that has exonerated condemned people, evidence of discrimination and inequality based on race or social status, and the continued possibility of executing innocent people unjustly sentenced to death. When given the choice of life without parole, public opinion for capital punishment drops dramatically. A May 2004 Gallup Poll found that approximately 50% of Americans supported the death penalty and 46% favored life without parole. Recent high-profile killers, such as Dennis Rader (BTK Serial Killer), Gary Ridgway (Green River Serial Killer), and Eric Rudolph (Olympic bomber in Atlanta), were given life sentences without parole. It is estimated that life sentences have doubled in the last 10 years, and legislation to provide "truth in sentencing" has been enacted in response to public demand. However, a majority of Americans continue to support the death penalty as the ultimate punishment for heinous acts against society, especially for cases of terrorism, child rape and murder, and serial killers.

Special Offender Populations and Capital Punishment

There have been several very important U.S. Supreme Court cases in recent years that have resulted in significant changes in the numbers and composition of death row inmates. First, and arguably receiving the most attention at home and abroad, in 2005 the Court held in *Roper v. Simmons* that the imposition of the death penalty on juveniles offended societal standards of decency. This controversial ruling immediately resulted in the commutation of more than 150 sentences of people on death row to life sentences because the crimes were committed when these people were under the age of 18. This decision was heralded by anti–death penalty groups and international human rights advocates who had condemned the United States for being one of the few countries to still execute juveniles. In contrast, some victims' rights groups criticized the holding as unjust, since some of these offenders as youngsters had committed brutal acts of violence against their victims and were unremorseful. These groups cited the fact that juries had found guilt and imposed the death penalty based on legal statutes and aggravating factors, regardless of the offenders' age.

Another major death penalty decision from the U.S. Supreme Court was handed down in 2002 and involved mentally retarded offenders. In *Atkins v. Virginia,* the Court held that mentally retarded offenders could not be executed for their crimes because they lacked the mental capacity to fully understand what they had done or why they were being executed. The court cited the great number of death-eligible states that had passed legislation to this effect as proof of societal consensus that such executions offended our evolving standards of decency. While this case was also viewed as a significant victory within the anti–death penalty movement, there are still great discrepancies across state jurisdictions as to what constitutes mental retardation. Thus, some scholars have argued that some murderers who are mentally disabled may still be executed as a result of the vagueness and inconsistency between jurisdictions.

In relation to the mentally ill, the Supreme Court has been explicit in stating that mentally incompetent murderers may not be held criminally liable for their crimes unless they can be restored to competency. In 1986, in *Ford v. Wainwright,* the Court held that there was no deterrent value in executing the mentally ill since the punishment would not deter a person lacking sound mind and body. Moreover, the Court held that the execution of a mentally ill person offended the collective conscience of society because the offender could not appreciate the reasons for the punishment or the finality of his or her own death. Thus, offenders must be held competent or brought back to mental competency prior to a death warrant being carried out.

Recent Trends in the Death Penalty

The death row population increased dramatically after 1976 when the Supreme Court, in *Gregg v. Georgia,* lifted the de jure moratorium on the death penalty. The population increased steadily between 1976 and 2001, with a peak average of 300 death sentences mandated annually in the late 1990s. Since 2001, the death row population has decreased each year. Part of this decline can be explained by the moratorium on executions in Illinois instituted by former governor George Ryan (167 cases), the ban on the execution of mentally retarded offenders per *Atkins v. Virginia* in 2002, and the commutation of sentences of offenders who committed capital crimes as juveniles per *Roper v. Simmons* in 2005 (71 cases).

In 1999, over 3,600 offenders were in prisons across the United States awaiting a death sentence, and 98 people were executed. By 2004, the death row population had decreased to 3,471 offenders and only 59 death warrants were carried out. When compared to 1999, executions in 2004 were down 40% and new death

sentences averaged less than 50%, with fewer than 130 offenders sentenced to death that year. At the end of 2005, an estimated 3,381 offenders remained housed on death rows across the United States, and approximately 125 new death sentences were imposed.

Since the reinstatement of the death penalty in 1976, the vast majority of executions have been carried out in Southern states, with 85% of all death sentences carried out in this region of the country. Beginning in 1976 and by mid-2006, Texas had the most executions with 364, followed by Virginia with 95, and then Florida with 60. California has the largest death row population, with 649 people, followed by Texas and Florida, with 409 and 388, respectively. In keeping with prior trends, of the 60 people executed in 2005, 73% had killed White victims. In contrast, no Whites were executed in the United States in 2005 for the murder of a Black person. Critics of the death penalty have pointed to the racial disparity in such statistics as a major problem in the implementation of the death penalty and have called for a moratorium until the issue of discrimination within the criminal justice system can be further addressed.

The Future of Capital Punishment

On December 2, 2005, Kenneth Boyd was executed by the state of North Carolina for the 1988 murder of his estranged wife and his father-in-law as his two sons watched. This death sentence marked the 1000th execution since the reinstatement of capital punishment in 1976. While the death penalty remains strongly favored by many Americans, especially for high-profile crimes against children or for mass killings, there is a momentum nationally that is reducing the number of death sentences and increasing skepticism about capital punishment.

The Innocence Project at the Benjamin N. Cardozo School of Law at Yeshiva University attempts to free wrongfully convicted offenders based on postconviction DNA evidence and testing. By the close of 2005, 122 inmates had been released from death row after forensic evidence and advanced testing exonerated them. These cases have helped fuel the debate in the United States about whether the death penalty should continue to be implemented. When these concerns are combined with the astronomical costs for capital trials, calls from religious organizations to abolish the death penalty, and reports of a "brutalization effect" after state-mandated executions (whereby murder rates increase after a death sentence is carried out), some academics and political commentators have argued that capital punishment may one day become extinct within the American criminal justice system. Yet the abolition of this punishment in still quite uncertain in the wake of the terrorist attacks of September 11, 2001, and of high-profile cases such as child abductions and rapes by sexual predators that evoke a definitively punitive response from the public. Clearly, the death penalty will continue to be a controversial and polarizing topic across political, religious, and criminological circles in our society for years to come.

Denise Paquette Boots

See also Human Rights; Mass Murder; Serial Murder/Serial Killers; Sex Offenders

Further Readings

Acker, J. R., Bohm, R. M., & Lanier, C. S. (2003). *America's experiment with capital punishment: Reflections on the past, present, and future of the ultimate penal sanction.* Durham, NC: Carolina Academic Press.

Atkins v. Virginia (2002). 536 U.S. 304.

Bohm, R. M. (1999). *Deathquest: An introduction to the theory and practice of capital punishment in the United States.* Cincinnati, OH: Anderson.

Coyne, R., & Entzeroth, L. (2001). *Capital punishment and the judicial process.* Durham, NC: Carolina Academic Press.

Death Penalty Information Center. (2005). *The death penalty in 2005: Year end report.* Retrieved March 31, 2006, from http://www.deathpenaltyinfo.org/YearEnd05.pdf

Del Carmen, R. V., Vollum, S., Cheeseman, K., Frantzen, D., & San Miguel, C. (2005). *The death penalty: Constitutional issues, commentaries, and case briefs.* Cincinnati, OH: LexisNexis.

Ford v. Wainwright (1986). 477 U.S. 399.

Furman v. Georgia (1972). 408 U.S. 238.

Gregg v. Georgia (1976). 428 U.S. 153.

Mandery, E. J. (2005). *Capital punishment: A balanced examination.* Boston: Jones & Bartlett.

Roper v. Simmons (2005). 543 U.S. 541.

CAREGIVERS AND VIOLENCE

Trust is the foundation for relationships between caregivers and the individuals they support. Most caregivers who provide support for persons with disabilities, older people, and children provide services in an atmosphere of mutual respect. However, there can be violence in this caregiving relationship, and most people with disabilities who experience domestic violence are abused by direct caregivers. Violence in a caregiving relationship is often perpetrated by the caregiver; it can also be directed against the caregiver by the person receiving care.

There are both formal and informal caregivers. Formal caregivers are those who are typically paid to provide a defined service in home, community, or institutional settings (e.g., nursing homes, group homes, state institutions). Some types of care they provide include medical care (e.g., medication management), home health services (e.g., bathing, dressing, eating), community-based support services (e.g., supported employment, recreation, shopping), transportation, and respite care. Informal caregivers are friends and family members who are not paid (although some do get paid under some circumstances) to provide care and/or support. These caregivers provide many of the same types of services as formal caregivers.

Risk Factors for People Who Utilize Caregiver Services

People who utilize caregiver services may have a high level of vulnerability for abuse for several reasons. Individuals who receive caregiving are often dependent on their caregivers for basic needs, including particularly personal activities, such as bathing, dressing, or toileting. This dependency may prevent a person from recognizing or reporting abuse. In circumstances involving informal care, a person requiring caregiving may also feel guilty, thus overlooking instances of violence and feeling such violence is deserved. Further, the person receiving services might believe that he or she has no other means to receive care and fear that reporting violence would result in either institutionalization or increased violence from the caregiver. People who utilize formal caregiving services may interact with multiple caregivers and may not see the same caregiver twice, thus never building a relationship of trust with the caregiver. This person may also fear increased violence and worry about losing his or her care provider agency if he or she complains. In both instances, the caregiver may control the means of reporting violence by limiting the person's access to telephones or other means of communication.

Caregiver Perpetrators

There are numerous factors associated with the perpetration of violence by caregivers to people in their care. These factors vary depending on whether the support services are provided by formal or informal caregivers. While most professional caregivers provide excellent services and support, there are some work-related issues that may increase the potential for abuse. Formal caregivers are frequently underpaid, receive little training, receive no direct supervision, and are provided little employment support. For caregivers working with individuals in their homes or in community settings, there can be intense isolation. The job duties of formal caregivers can be highly stressful. Agencies that employ caregivers experience high rates of staff turnover and have high vacancy rates, resulting in higher levels of stress in caregivers. Because of the shortage of staff in these caregiver roles, some agencies do not screen their potential employees well and risk hiring those with violent backgrounds.

Informal caregivers may also experience high levels of stress, but perhaps in different ways. Family members and friends provide caregiving support to loved ones in addition to their jobs and other life activities, sometimes resulting in exhaustion, depression, and lack of time to provide appropriate care and support. Family members typically carry significant financial burdens associated with caregiving, and many families do not have access to respite or other supportive services. However, caregiver burden is not by itself a cause of violence, and most instances of caregiver abuse are not the result primarily of caregiver burden.

Interventions for preventing caregiver perpetrated violence may differ for formal and informal caregivers. Strategies for decreasing violence by formal caregivers may include better employee screening, better pay, more direct supervision, increased training, activities to decrease isolation in providing care, and the increased professionalism of these workers. Strategies to reduce violence by informal caregivers include respite care, family caregiving support groups, behavior management training, case management services, family counseling, and domestic violence awareness education.

Caregivers Experiencing Violence

Some people with disabilities or others receiving care may have challenging behaviors that may be a result of their disabilities or other limitations. This is often termed *aggression* instead of *violence* to avoid labeling people with disabilities. However, this does not minimize the impact of the aggressive behaviors on the caregivers. Violence against caregivers happens to both formal and informal caregivers. Examples of aggressive behavior in caregiving situations may include biting, kicking, flailing, hitting, pushing, spitting, and throwing objects. Aggressive behaviors can escalate and result in serious injuries that prevent the caregiver from being able to continue in a caregiving role.

Strategies to reduce violence and aggression by people who receive services vary by individual. Typical strategies center on positive behavior supports, an approach focused on assessing the root cause of the behavior and problem solving a strengths-based solution toward eliminating the violence. An example may be changing the way the person is touched while receiving help with dressing, or providing the person with tools for communicating so that he or she does not use aggression to tell the caregiver that something is wrong.

Traci LaLiberte and Elizabeth Lightfoot

See also Elder Abuse; Family Violence, Co-Occurrence of Forms; Home Visitation Services; Violence Against People With Disabilities

Further Readings

Abramson, W., Emanuel, E., Gaylord, V., & Hayden, M. (Eds.). (2000). *Impact: Feature issue on violence against women with developmental or other disabilities, 13*(3). Retrieved from http://ici.umn.edu/products/impact/133/

National Center on Elder Abuse. (2002). *Preventing elder abuse by family caregivers.* Retrieved from http://www.elderabusecenter.org/pdf/family/caregiver.pdf

U.S. Department of Labor, Occupational Health and Safety Administration (OSHA). (2004). *Guidelines for preventing workplace violence for health care and social service workers.* Retrieved from http://www.osha.gov/Publications/osha3148.pdf

CASTRATION

Castration is the surgical removal of the testes through an incision in the scrotum; the penis is not removed. Castration has been suggested—and has been used—as a treatment for sex offenders, such as pedophiles. The testes are the major source of testosterone production in men, and testosterone is a hormone that plays a significant role in the male sex drive. Thus, the argument in favor of castration is that by reducing sexual desire, castration lowers the motivation of some sex offenders to offend, making it a useful treatment for those individuals who have tremendous difficulty resisting their sexual impulses even when punished or treated with intensive counseling. Studies that have compared recidivism among surgically castrated sex offenders with recidivism among sex offenders who have not been castrated show that the former have recidivism rates ranging from 1.3% to 5.8%, while the latter's recidivism rate may be as high as 52%.

Testosterone production may also be reduced using drugs, instead of surgery, in a treatment called chemical castration. The most common drugs used for this purpose are Depo-Provera and Depo-Lupron. Both are injected intramuscularly, usually once a week. As of 2006, eight states, including Texas (where surgical castration is also permitted), Florida, and California, allow chemical castration for sex offenders. In fact, in Florida it is a mandatory part of the sentence for certain repeat sex offenders. Nevertheless, there is disagreement over the effectiveness of castration for preventing recidivism in sex offenders as well as concern over the side effects of the drugs used for this purpose. For one thing, it is not clear what specific sex offenders may be helped by castration. Most of the studies have focused on only one type of offender, the pedophile, but there are many other sex offenders, such as the serial rapist of adult women, who have not been extensively studied in castration research. Critics of castration also point out that while it does significantly lower sexual drive, it does not completely eliminate sexual arousal or sexual function. Some of the side effects of the drugs used for chemical castration are weight gain, hypertension, mild lethargy, cold sweats, nightmares, hot flashes, and muscle aches. While there is no evidence to date that these drugs increase men's risk of cancer, the long-term effects of the drugs are still not known.

Claire M. Renzetti

See also Paraphilia; Pedophilia; Sex Offenders

Further Readings

Berlin, F. S. (2000). The etiology and treatment of sexual offending. In D. H. Fishbein (Ed.), *The science, treatment, and prevention of antisocial behaviors* (pp. 21-1–21-15). Kingston, NJ: Civic Research Institute.

Freund, K. (1980). Therapeutic sex drive reduction. *Acta Psychiatrica Scandinavia, 287,* 1–39.

Centers for Disease Control and Prevention

The Centers for Disease Control and Prevention (CDC) is one of the 13 operating divisions of the Department of Health and Human Services, the principal agency in the U.S. government for providing human services and protecting the health and safety of all Americans. Founded in 1946 to control malaria, CDC has remained at the forefront of public health efforts to prevent and control infectious and chronic diseases, injuries, workplace hazards, disabilities, and environmental health threats. Today, CDC is globally recognized for conducting research and investigations and for its action-oriented approach. CDC applies research and findings to improve people's lives and responds to health emergencies worldwide.

With a mission of promoting health and quality of life by preventing and controlling disease, injury, and disability, CDC works with partners to monitor health, detect and investigate health problems, conduct research to enhance prevention, develop and advocate sound public health policies, implement prevention strategies, promote healthy behaviors, foster safe and healthful environments, and provide leadership and training.

Committed to achieving true improvements in people's health, CDC has defined specific health impact goals to prioritize and focus its work and investments and measure progress:

Healthy People in Every Stage of Life. All people, and especially those at greater risk of health disparities, will achieve their optimal lifespan with the best possible quality of health in every stage of life.

Healthy People in Healthy Places. The places where people live, work, learn, and play will protect and promote their health and safety, especially those at greater risk of health disparities.

People Prepared for Emerging Health Threats. People in all communities will be protected from infectious, occupational, environmental, and terrorist threats.

Healthy People in a Healthy World. People around the world will live safer, healthier, and longer lives through health promotion, health protection, and health diplomacy.

To achieve the agency's health protection goals, CDC has defined six strategies to guide decisions and priorities: health impact focus; customer-centricity; public health research; leadership; global health impact; and accountability.

Realizing these goals in preventing violence CDC's National Center for Injury Prevention and Control, Division of Violence Prevention, focuses research, surveillance, communications, and programs to address priorities including the prevention of child maltreatment, intimate partner and sexual violence, youth violence, and suicide. CDC's violence prevention activities are guided by four key principles: (1) an emphasis on primary prevention, (2) a commitment to advancing the science of prevention, (3) a focus on translating scientific advances into practical application through effective programs and policy, and (4) a commitment to building on the efforts of others by addressing gaps or needs.

As the sentinel for the health of people in the United States and throughout the world, CDC strives to protect people's health and safety, provide reliable health information, and improve health through strong partnerships. By engaging with others, CDC works to achieve a vision of a better world, with safer, healthier people.

Corinne Meltzer Graffunder

See also Child Abuse Prevention; Health Consequences of Child Maltreatment; Intimate Partner Violence; Prevention Programs, Adolescent Dating Violence; Prevention Programs, Child Maltreatment; Prevention Programs, Interpersonal Violence; Prevention Programs, Youth Violence; Rape/Sexual Assault; Youth Violence

Web Sites

Centers for Disease Control and Prevention: http://www.cdc.gov

CHILD ABDUCTIONS, FAMILY

Family abduction is defined as the taking or keeping of a child by a family member in violation of a custody order, a decree, or other legitimate custodial rights, where the taking or keeping involves some element of concealment, flight, or intent to deprive a lawful custodian indefinitely of custodial privileges.

Family abducted children are both a subcategory of missing children and part of a larger type of crime and child welfare problem. Since it is possible for a child to be unlawfully removed from custody by a family member, with the child's whereabouts known, not all family abducted children are missing. For example, a child may be abducted by a noncustodial father, taken to the father's home in a different country, and kept at an address well known to the custodial mother. Even though the father refuses to return the child, the abducted child is not missing because the custodial mother knows where the child is. The most recent national incidence estimates available are 1999 estimates, according to which 203,900 children were victims of a family abduction, and 57% of these children qualified as missing.

Overall, family abducted children accounted for 9% of all missing children, and 7% of those reported to authorities as missing. Although the police were contacted regarding 60% of all family abducted children, not all of these contacts were for the purpose of locating the child. Fifty percent of the contacts were to recover the child from a known location, 42% (56,500 children) were to locate the child, 6% were for another reason, and no information was available for the remaining 2%.

The data show that family abduction is one of the few victimization perils that younger children experience to a greater extent than older children, with 44% of family abducted children under age 6, compared to 35% ages 6 to 11, and 21% ages 12 and older. Most children abducted by a family member were abducted by their father (53%), with their abductor in lawful circumstances immediately prior to the abduction (63%), and gone less than 1 month (70%). Of these, 46% were returned in less than 1 week. Only 6% of children abducted by a family member had not yet been returned at the time of data collection; however, all of these children had been located.

In addition to locating and returning family abducted children, agencies seeking to help these children must address the conflicts that produce and prolong the abduction of children by family members. The fact that the data show that fully 40% of family abductions were not reported to the police underscores the importance of agencies that can provide a response to threatened and actual family abductions over and above the important location and recovery function performed by law enforcement. Prevention efforts should focus on younger children, especially those who do not live with both biological parents. Programs that specifically promote child well-being and those that address child safety issues generally may be appropriate forums in which to raise awareness about family abduction.

Heather Hammer

See also Child Abductions, Nonfamily; Children Missing Involuntarily or for Benign Reasons; Runaway and Thrownaway Children

Further Readings

Hammer, H., Finkelhor, D., & Sedlak, A. J. (2002). *Family abducted children: National estimates and characteristics.* Office of Juvenile Justice and Delinquency Prevention Bulletin Series. Washington, DC: U.S. Department of Justice, Office of Juvenile Justice and Delinquency Prevention.

CHILD ABDUCTIONS, NONFAMILY

Although media attention tends to focus on the most sensational and tragic child kidnappings, *child abduction* is legally defined as a child being held involuntarily for a modest amount of time or moved even a short distance. In an attempt to address the variation in the severity of nonfamily abductions, the Second National Incidence Studies of Missing, Abducted, Runaway, and Thrownaway Children (NISMART-2) distinguished stereotypical kidnapping as a subcategory of nonfamily abduction.

A stereotypical kidnapping is an abduction perpetrated by a stranger or slight acquaintance and involving a child who was transported 50 or more miles, detained overnight, held for ransom or with the intent to keep the child permanently, or killed. According to the most recent national incidence estimates available, the NISMART-2 estimates for 1999, 115 children were victims of a stereotypical kidnapping nationwide, and these children account for only 19% of the 58,200 children who were identified as victims of a nonfamily abduction based on the legal definition. Among the children identified as victims of nonfamily abduction,

57% qualified as missing, and 21% were reported to authorities as missing.

Overall, nonfamily abducted children accounted for only 3% of all missing children and 2% of those reported missing to law enforcement. Although police were contacted regarding 47% of all nonfamily abducted children, less than half (44%) of these contacts were to locate a missing child; 21% were to recover a child from a known location, and 35% were for other reasons including the reporting of another related crime such as a sexual assault.

Teenage girls were by far the most frequent victims of both stereotypical kidnappings and nonfamily abductions, and nearly half of all victims were sexually assaulted by the perpetrator. Contrary to the widely held belief that strangers pose the greatest danger, less than half (45%) of all nonfamily abduction victims were abducted by a stranger or slight acquaintance. Thirty-eight percent were abducted by a friend or long-term acquaintance, and an additional 18% were abducted by neighbors, caretakers or babysitters, and others.

Whereas 99% of all nonfamily abducted children were returned home alive, the outcomes change dramatically when one looks only at the subgroup of stereotypical kidnapped children. Sadly, only 57% of these children were returned home alive, and among those returned, 32% were injured. Forty percent of the stereotypical kidnapping victims were killed, and an additional 4% were neither returned nor located.

Strategies for prevention and intervention need to recognize that acquaintances play a greater role than strangers do in abductions that occur outside the family. If parents and law enforcement assume that abductions are only or mostly committed by strangers, they may fail to provide appropriate prevention information to young people.

Heather Hammer

See also Child Abductions, Family; Children Missing Involuntarily or for Benign Reasons; Runaway and Thrownaway Children

Further Readings

Finkelhor, D., Hammer, H., & Sedlak, A. J. (2002). *Nonfamily abducted children: National estimates and characteristics.* Office of Juvenile Justice and Delinquency Prevention Bulletin Series. Washington, DC: U.S. Department of Justice, Office of Juvenile Justice and Delinquency Prevention.

Child Abuse and Disabilities

There are three ways that child abuse intersects with disability. These include children with disabilities who are maltreated, children who are maltreated and sustain injuries resulting in disability, and parents with disabilities who maltreat their children. Each area requires unique child abuse prevention and intervention strategies.

Children with disabilities are identified as having higher rates of maltreatment than children without disabilities. They are also more likely to be involved in Child Protective Services (CPS) and placed outside of their home. These higher rates of identification may be due to increased vulnerability, increased family stress due to lack of supportive services, added financial responsibilities and attitudinal barriers, and increased detection rates because of these children's involvement in other service systems. Child abuse prevention for children with disabilities includes respite care and parenting skill training for parents and personal care assistance and personal safety education for children. When children with disabilities are placed out of the home, foster parents and providers must be knowledgeable about caring for children with disabilities.

A child's disability may also be caused by abuse or neglect. As a result of intentional or unintentional acts of violence or neglect, children may acquire physical, mental/emotional, and/or cognitive conditions. Examples of such resulting conditions include shaken baby syndrome, posttraumatic stress disorder, and failure to thrive syndrome. CPS workers must be aware of the need for postmaltreatment assessments geared toward identifying acquired disabilities. Many acquired disabilities may be hidden and are initially undetected, resulting in inadequate care.

More adults with disabilities are having children, yet they have inadequate support to raise their children. When parents with disabilities maltreat their children, it is often in the form of neglect or failure to protect their children from other adults. In some instances parents with disabilities have children who also have disabilities. In these cases the parents need additional support and education about parenting their child to prevent maltreatment. Additionally, CPS workers must seek appropriate assessments of parental functioning and safety before making child removal and permanency decisions. Child abuse prevention in these families includes specialized in-home parenting classes, ongoing supports for parents, parent mentors, and creative placement options such as family foster care and open adoptions.

The intersection between disabilities and CPS needs continued attention via research, collaboration, and cross-training. Although CPS workers need not become disability experts, they do need to become competent in providing services for children with disabilities. They must know when to refer people with disabilities for assessments and services and must be able to collaborate with disability professionals and advocates. In addition CPS workers need to understand their responsibility to provide accessible services. Some CPS systems have formal relationships with disability services, and some even have specialty disability workers within the CPS system.

Traci LaLiberte and Elizabeth Lightfoot

See also Child Abuse Prevention; Child Protective Services; Violence Against People With Disabilities

Further Readings

CAN-Do! (2005, March). Retrieved April 28, 2006, from http://disability-abuse.com/

Gaylor, V., LaLiberte, T., Lightfoot, E., & Hewitt, A. (Eds.). (2006). Feature issue on children with disabilities in the child welfare system. *IMPACT, 19*(1).

Child Abuse in Immigrant Families

Immigrant families vary by ethnicity, social class, country of origin, education, immigration circumstances and status, language, religion, employment, and a host of other factors. The greater the difference between the culture of origin and the new environment, the longer lasting the culture shock from immigrating is apt to be, distorting almost every aspect of daily life and complicating efforts to obtain an accurate assessment of parenting. Immigrant families who are undocumented also live in constant fear of deportation, and refugees must cope with the aftereffects of the trauma they have suffered.

Migration has an isolating effect on many families, cutting them off from their traditional sources of support and exposing them to discrimination. Although teachers and school counselors can be key players in the prevention and detection of child abuse, children may refuse to confide in them if they perceive the schools as alien or even hostile.

There is no reason to assume higher rates of child abuse among immigrant than native-born families. However, immigrant families may be at increased risk of reports to child protection authorities due to their visibility, a tendency to punish misbehaviors in public rather than in private, misunderstandings with professionals, and parenting norms that conflict with those of the dominant culture. The more educated and acculturated a family is, the closer its child rearing norms are likely to be to those of the mainstream culture.

Immigrant parents often do not know what is expected of them but are still punished by the child protective system when they fail to comply with unwritten cultural expectations. Language and cultural barriers make it difficult for immigrant families to access resources, take advantage of services, and comply with treatment plans. Cultural competency training can help professionals in the field learn to reach out to immigrant families more effectively.

Caring immigrant parents sometimes avoid mainstream health care and opt for their traditional medicine, in the belief that this is the best way to heal their children or protect them from illness. Jurisdictions vary in how they handle instances where the family's traditional medicine has failed to improve the child's condition or has harmed the child.

Immigrant families caught in the child welfare system often fail to comprehend the system that has taken over their lives; such a system may not exist in their home countries. The problems for immigrant families in the child welfare system are exacerbated by a serious shortage of interpreters and translated material at government and private agencies. In most circumstances immigrant families have the legal right to services in their preferred language or interpreters.

The literature on child maltreatment in immigrant families is becoming increasingly fine-tuned and specific, with suggestions for working with people from particular immigrant groups, handling language difference, and collaborating with community-based agencies. Research on issues and problems concerning child abuse and immigrant families is still underdeveloped and marred by serious problems in delimiting and defining the sample, choosing concepts with cross-cultural relevance, and translating instruments.

Lisa A. Fontes

See also Child Abuse Prevention; Culturally Sensitive Intervention; Legal System and Child Protection

Further Readings

Fontes, L. A. (2005). Working with immigrant families affected by child maltreatment. In L. A. Fontes, *Child abuse and culture: Working with diverse families* (pp. 30–58). New York: Guilford Press.

Maiter, S., Alaggia, R., & Trocmé, N. (2004). Perceptions of child maltreatment by parents from the Indian subcontinent: Challenging myths about culturally based abusive parenting practices. *Child Maltreatment, 9,* 309–324.

CHILD ABUSE PREVENTION

Child abuse prevention services have three primary goals: to reduce the overall incidence of abuse and neglect; to minimize the chance that abused children will be revictimized; and to "break the cycle" of abuse by providing victims therapeutic services to overcome the negative consequences of maltreatment. Efforts to do this can be provided on a universal basis (offered to all parents or all children); targeted basis (offered only to those who present one or more risk factors associated with an elevated risk for maltreatment); or indicated basis (offered to those who have already been abused in the hopes of preventing subsequent maltreatment and remediating the negative effects of abuse).

Evolution of Prevention Services

Over the past 30 years, efforts to prevent child maltreatment in the United States have moved through three stages—public recognition of the problem, experimentation with a wide range of prevention programs that address one or more risk factors, and the evolution of systems designed to better integrate these diverse efforts.

Programmatic efforts to prevent child abuse and neglect have followed two distinct paths—interventions targeting reductions in physical abuse and neglect (including emotional neglect and attachment disorders) and interventions targeting reductions in child sexual abuse. Programs in the first group began with an emphasis on parental knowledge or parental behavior as the "cause" of maltreatment with services designed to address the cause (e.g., parent education workshops). Such programs have evolved in concert with the ecological paradigm to address the broader context in which the parent–child relationship develops. It is common for today's prevention programs to focus on parental support networks, health care access, and parent–child interaction patterns, in addition to the more traditional emphasis on parental behavior or knowledge. Further, these programs tend to focus on new parents, offering assistance when a child is born or a woman is pregnant. Subsequent prevention services are then added to this universal base in response to the specific emerging needs presented by the growing child or the evolving parent–child relationship.

In contrast to these efforts, the target population for sexual abuse prevention has been potential victims, not potential perpetrators. Three factors contributed to this pattern: the social discomfort surrounding sexuality; the difficulty in developing voluntary treatment options for offenders; and the absence of clear risk factors identifying potential perpetrators or victims. Strategies within this framework include a number of educational-based efforts, provided on a universal basis, to children on the distinction between good, bad, and questionable touching and the concept of body ownership or the rights of children to control who touches their bodies and where they are touched. As children mature, these classes cover a broader range of concepts such as appropriate dating behavior, gender stereotypes, and nonaggressive conflict resolution strategies. These educational programs also offer children and youth service options or referrals if they have been abused or are involved in an abusive peer relationship.

Today, the concept of prevention is moving away from the notion of a single response agency or targeted intervention and more toward a communitywide system of shared responsibility and mutual support. The goal of altering both the individual and context provides a programmatic and policy response more reflective of the ecological theory often cited as the most appropriate in explaining the etiology of child maltreatment.

Evidence of Success

Program evaluations and meta-analytic studies of child abuse prevention programs present a fairly positive picture. Early home visitation strategies, for example, are effective at reducing the likelihood that children will be reported as victims of child abuse and neglect or that they will need treatment for physical injuries or accidents. When the pool of relevant indicators is extended to include proximal indicators of a reduction in abuse potential or an increase in core protective factors, a number of additional strategies surface as promising. Interventions to enhance parental knowledge and skills, such as parent support groups, and strategies to protect children through child assault prevention programs also show positive results. It is important to note, however, that with this second group of strategies, a reduction in risk behaviors or change in attitude by the participants may enhance family functioning yet have little impact on aggregate rates of physical abuse and neglect.

Research Implications

Improving the quality and efficacy of prevention services requires new research in several areas. First, greater clarity is needed regarding the most accurate and appropriate way to measure prevention of child maltreatment. If maltreatment reports continue to be used as an indicator of prevention effectiveness, greater consistency is needed in how such reports are documented, including more careful identification and tracking of the type of maltreatment involved, the actual perpetrator, and the relative severity of the mistreatment.

Second, longitudinal research studies are needed that track the extent to which initial progress on various proximate outcomes is sufficiently robust to reduce subsequent maltreatment or involvement with child protective services. To the extent that prevention programs embrace the public health model and ecological theories of maltreatment, targeted outcomes for such interventions will include a dual focus on both risk and protective factors. Understanding how changes in various risk and protective factors can reduce subsequent maltreatment is essential for building better theory and enhancing program and policy effectiveness.

Finally, greater care needs to be taken to ensure that evaluative information is continuously collected and fed back into the decision-making process. Strengthening our knowledge base requires more consistent and rigorous attention to such issues as the characteristics of the target population, the rate at which programs successfully enroll and retain their population, the content of the services provided families, and the nature of the participant–provider relationship.

Deborah Daro

See also Prevention Programs, Child Maltreatment; Prevention Programs, Community Mobilization; School-Based Violence Prevention Programs

Further Readings

Daro, D., & Cohn-Donnelly, A. (2002). Charting the waves of prevention: Two steps forward, one step back. *Child Abuse & Neglect, 26,* 731–742.

Daro, D., & Cohn-Donnelly, A. (2002). Child abuse prevention: Accomplishments and challenges. In J. Myers, L. Berliner, J. Briere, T. Hendrix, C. Jenny, & T. Reid (Eds.), *APSAC handbook on child maltreatment* (2nd ed., pp. 431–448). Thousand Oaks, CA: Sage.

CHILD ABUSE PREVENTION AND TREATMENT ACT

The Child Abuse Prevention and Treatment Act (CAPTA) is the key federal statute that addresses child abuse and neglect. It is administered by the Children's Bureau, an office in the Administration for Children and Family, U.S. Department of Health and Human Services. It provides funding for states and territories to support public child protection agencies and prevention activities in communities.

Originally enacted in 1974, the statute (P.L. 93-247), was the culmination of a period of growing recognition of the prevalence of child abuse and neglect and the demand for federal action. A key stimulant to the public's awareness was the publication in 1961 in the *Journal of the American Medical Association* of a widely cited article on the battered child syndrome. Written by a physician, C. Henry Kempe, the article highlighted the negative consequences of abuse for child development and increased pressure in the medical field to champion this issue. Pressure grew in the states to take responsibility for abused children and between 1963 and 1967 every state and the District of Columbia passed some form of child abuse law, usually establishing reporting requirements for medical and service providers. By the early 1970s there were growing demands for action at the federal level. Congressional hearings brought strong attention to the issue. The hearings that led to the drafting and enactment of CAPTA were held by the Subcommittee on Children and Youth, under the leadership of Senator Walter Mondale, of the Committee on Labor and Public Welfare.

Key features of the original statute authorized funding of $85 million for 3 years to be spent over 4 years. At least 50% of the appropriated funding was to be spent on discretionary demonstration programs, at least 5% but no more than 20% for grants to states, and no more than $1 million on an in-house advisory board. The statute also defined child abuse, established requirements for state reporting laws and other requirements states had to meet to be eligible to receive these funds, and established a National Center on Child Abuse and Neglect within the Department of Health and Welfare. Since enactment, CAPTA has been amended numerous times.

The three main sections of CAPTA are Grants to States, Child Abuse Discretionary Activities, and Community-Based Child Abuse Prevention. Under the state grants program, states have wide authority to use funds for a broad range of activities in improving child protection services, including intake screening, case management, data systems, training, and collaboration with other systems. States must certify that they have in place a variety of protections and system requirements. A new program was added in 2003 to assist states in the investigation and prosecution of child abuse and neglect. The purpose of the Community-Based Prevention Program, as noted in Section 201 of CAPTA, is "to support community-based efforts to develop, operate, expand, enhance, and, where appropriate to network, initiatives aimed at the prevention of child abuse and neglect, and to support networks of coordinated resources and activities to better strengthen and support families to reduce the likelihood of child abuse and neglect."

CAPTA was reauthorized in 2003 (as P.L. 108-36) and requires reauthorization again by September 30, 2008. CAPTA programs were funded in the fiscal year 2006 budget at $95.2 million.

Gerald B. "Jerry" Silverman

See also Child Abuse Prevention; Office on Child Abuse and Neglect

Web Sites

Child Welfare Information Gateway: http://www.child welfare.gov/

CHILD AGGRESSION AS PREDICTOR OF YOUTH AND ADULT VIOLENCE

Aggression in children is a problem that garners a disproportionate amount of attention in the media and throughout society, especially when considering news accounts of school shootings and youth violence. While chronic violent offending is relatively rare in youth, and the majority of juvenile offenders desist from criminal activities in their early to mid-20s, boys, gang members, and youth of color continue to both engage and become victims of violent and antisocial behaviors in alarming numbers. Determining how child aggression develops and what the outcomes of such behaviors are is a critical topic for parents, educators, criminal justice personnel, and psychologists and psychiatrists dealing with childhood aggression in communities, classrooms, and neighborhoods. Child aggression refers to attitudes, temperament, or acts in youth under the age of 18 years old that are recognized as antisocial or problem behaviors.

The Development of Serious Offending Behaviors in Children

Patterns of serious offending commonly first emerge during the critical stage of human development known for impulsive, irrational, and immature behaviors—adolescence. The turbulence of adolescence provides a perfect opportunity to challenge one's boundaries, and the chance to display irrational, immature actions or thoughts may lead some youngsters down pathways toward aggressive, violent, and/or antisocial behaviors. For a few of these youth, this violence trajectory will continue into adulthood. Troubled youth in the criminal justice system have often reported various familial and psychopathological problems that have been linked to delinquency and adult offending. Recent longitudinal studies have also shown that youngsters in early and middle childhood frequently exhibited multiple problem behaviors across various domains that began at young ages. A commonality in many of these troubled youth, especially those seen in the criminal justice system, is that they express aggressive tendencies.

Childhood and Adolescent Psychiatric Disorders Associated With Violence

Youth with oppositional defiant disorder (ODD), conduct disorder (CD), and attention deficit-hyperactivity disorder (ADHD) have been shown in some scholarly studies to be at greater risk of aggressive or violent behaviors as adolescents or adults. ODD and CD are common disruptive disorders within the period of childhood or adolescence. These disorders are frequently diagnosed together with ADHD in youngsters with severe behavioral problems. Whereas ODD includes less serious behaviors such as defiance, anger, or annoyance of classmates or authority figures, CD involves more serious symptoms such as law-breaking behaviors (property destruction or status offenses such as curfew violations), theft, and acting aggressively toward people or animals. Youth may outgrow ODD or continue on and progress to CD at very young ages. CD is also the precursor to the more serious personality disorder in adulthood known as antisocial personality disorder (APD). Children with early onset and persistence of symptoms have been found to have poorer lifetime prognoses and to have better chances of continuance of antisocial behaviors into adulthood.

ADHD is the leading psychiatric disorder in American children, with current U.S. estimates of 10 million people having this illness. ADHD has two primary types, inattentive and hyperactive, and outcomes for children with this form of mental health disorder may vary widely depending on the severity and type of symptoms. Whereas inattentive aspects of ADHD have been found to be associated with poor academic outcomes, the impulsivity-hyperactive type has been more commonly linked with poor life course outcomes such as aggression and violence. Youth identified as ADHD have difficulty concentrating, paying attention, following instructions, and may be impulsive. This impulsivity element for hyperactive ADHD children has been linked with increased risk of aggressive behaviors over the life course and is the major focus of research looking at the link between ADHD and violence. However, it should be noted that studies investigating the relationship between these childhood disorders and later violence have produced conflicted findings depending on the sample sizes, populations, study design, and specific measurements or scales used.

In addition to these disorders common in childhood and adolescence, several other forms of mental illness have been shown to be associated with violence propensity that commonly have an onset prior to age 18. These include mood disorders such as major depressive disorder (MDD) and dysthymia, and substance use disorders (SUDs) typically involving alcohol and illicit drug use.

Research has linked mood disorders such as MDD and dysthymia with interpersonal violence, but the research on depression has been somewhat recent with regard to children and adolescents. Some studies have reported that depressed persons are most at risk of hurting themselves, especially depressed females who tend to internalize their problems. However, some scholars have argued that males with the disorder may have a form of "hidden depression" that explains their violent acts. The reason for their violent behaviors, depressive symptoms, may be easily overlooked in light of their antisocial actions. As males are prone to externalizing behaviors (or acting out), it is possible that depressive symptoms may be disguised by aggression and thus treated more as a disruptive disorder than as a mood disorder.

Finally, SUDs have the strongest link of all the psychiatric disorders with interpersonal violence. For young people, experimenting with alcohol and drugs is seen as a right of passage into adulthood, with a large majority of youngsters admitting substance use or abuse prior to leaving high school. There are dangers in using and abusing such substances, however. A large body of research indicates that comorbidity of other forms of mental health disorders and SUDs in youngsters increases the risk of aggressive behaviors. Some illicit drugs actually cause psychotic symptoms, while others have been found to make permanent chemical and physiological changes in the brain. Alcohol is one of the most common denominators in violent encounters between people, with up to half of all serious violent crimes having alcohol involved.

Together, research focusing on ODD, CD, ADHD, mood disorders, and SUDs offers promising insight into the etiology of childhood aggression as a predictor of later serious offending behaviors in adolescents and adults. Such endeavors have important public policy relevance as we develop more effective preventions, interventions, and treatments geared at helping identify young, chronic offenders before they commit seriously violent crimes against other persons.

Denise Paquette Boots

See also Children and Adolescents Who Kill; Psychiatric Illness and Violence Propensity

Further Readings

American Psychiatric Association. (2000). *Diagnostic and statistical manual of mental disorders* (4th ed., Text rev.). Washington, DC: Author.

Connor, D. F. (2002). *Aggression and antisocial behavior in children and adolescents: Research and treatment.* New York: Guilford Press.

Loeber, R., & Farrington, D. P. (Eds.). (1998). *Serious and violent juvenile offenders: Risk factors and successful interventions.* Thousand Oaks, CA: Sage.

Quinsey, V. L., Skilling, T. A., Lalumiere, M. L., & Craig, W. M. (2004). *Juvenile delinquency: Understanding the origins of individual differences.* Washington, DC: American Psychological Association.

CHILD DEATH REVIEW TEAMS

Child deaths from preventable or intentional causes have been the impetus for child death review teams (committees) worldwide. In the United States alone, an estimated 1,400 children died as a result of abuse or neglect in 2002. The majority of these children were under the age of 4. Child death reviews provide information on the underlying dynamics of child abuse and neglect cases, thereby offering the best opportunity for developing prevention interventions. By reviewing cases, the team endeavors to identify gaps or breakdowns in systems providing service to the child and family. Child death reviews can also be effective in reducing the incidence of accidental deaths involving children, and many of the reviews in the United States have now widened to include preventable deaths not caused by physical abuse or neglect. A death is considered preventable if an individual or the community could have done something that would have changed the circumstances that led to the death. Child death reviews have helped to inform policy and legislation in areas such as child physical abuse and neglect, shaken baby syndrome, abandoned infants, sudden infant death syndrome (SIDS), daycare licensing, child car seats, graduated driver's licensing, suicide prevention, smoke detectors, and fire-retardant clothing.

Background

Child death review teams date back to the late 1970s when Los Angeles, California; North Carolina; and Oregon created teams to better identify and respond to child fatalities related to abuse and neglect. For these communities and others, the awareness that the statistics they had available about child deaths offered little in the way of understanding the risk factors or circumstances that led to the death, or what could be done to prevent a death, prompted initiatives for improvement. In addition, the growing concern about the accuracy of SIDS findings led to an awareness of the need to understand how deaths were being investigated and whether services provided to children and families were adequately focused on child safety. The first review teams uncovered important indicators of maltreatment in cases that had been ruled as accidental or unintentional deaths. In 1990, a Missouri study concluded that child deaths due to maltreatment were grossly underreported and, as a result, this state became the first to enact a law requiring multidisciplinary review of child deaths involving children under the age of 15. Since that time, teams have developed in 50 states in the United States as well as nine Canadian provinces, parts of New Zealand, Australia, and South Africa. The scope of the reviews has broadened, from identifying and focusing on fatalities that are a result of maltreatment to understanding all causes of death and recommending improvements in all areas of child health and safety. Addressing system failures, particularly in abuse and neglect fatalities, is still a critical function of child death review teams.

Major Components of Child Death Reviews

Purpose and Goals

Child death reviews examine the circumstances surrounding child deaths to ensure that (a) there is accurate and unified reporting; (b) there is improved agency response to child deaths from the child protective sector; (c) there are improved criminal investigations and prosecutions; (d) there are improvements to other community services, including better communication between service sectors and better coordination of services; (e) the barriers to services are identified; (f) there are improvements to legislation or policies that protect children; and (g) there is increased public awareness of the issues related to child deaths.

Models

Each jurisdiction has its own model for reviewing deaths. Common elements of these models typically include the following: (a) having both state (or provincial) and local teams that review individual cases; (b) having a set protocol for identifying cases to be reviewed; (c) reviewing all available records, including

medical records, coroner reports, police records, child protection files and any internal agency death reviews conducted, and other sources as deemed relevant to the case; (d) having protocols for confidentiality; (e) having computerized databases for gathering and analyzing information; (f) holding child death investigation and child death review meetings; and (g) providing annual reports on state or provincial findings. Most jurisdictions have the review team's mandate written into law or government regulations.

Types of Deaths Reviewed

Each jurisdiction has its own set of criteria for flagging child death cases for review, depending on the size of the jurisdiction and the available resources. All reviews include child death as a result of homicide, suicide, neglect, or cases in which the death is unexplained. Additionally, some jurisdictions target a review of all deaths in which child protection services have been involved within a year prior to the death. Many of the reviews consider deaths of children under the age of 18; however, some only review the deaths of younger children.

Composition of the Review Team

Typically the case review team is a multidisciplinary one that includes medical examiners and health care professionals, law enforcement and prosecuting lawyers, and child protection experts. Some teams also include representatives from schools, mental health agencies, and crisis services.

Future Considerations

National studies conducted in both Canada and the United States have identified concerns with respect to child death review processes lacking uniformity across states or provinces. This lack of uniformity makes it impossible to compare programs in terms of effectiveness in preventing deaths or to identify trends and patterns of child deaths at a national level. These studies have identified the need for a national protocol for reviewing child deaths that would include (a) determining standard eligibility criteria for cases being reviewed; (b) developing criteria for gathering records and information and using standard data collection forms; (c) developing standard criteria for conducting reviews, including the composition of the review team, the purpose and scope of the reviews, the funding of review processes, and the development of standards criteria for determining whether a death will be deemed intentional, accidental, or due to abuse or neglect; and (d) annual reporting that identifies trends or patterns of child deaths at a national level. In addition, the integration of other review processes, such as domestic violence fatality reviews, could serve to strengthen prevention efforts for children given the overlap of child abuse and domestic violence.

Peter G. Jaffe and Maureen Reid

See also Child Physical Abuse; Domestic Violence Fatality Review

Further Readings

British Columbia Coroners Service Child Death Review. (2005). *Annual report.* Victoria, BC: Ministry of Public Safety & Solicitor General.

Durfee, M., Durfee, D., & West, M. (2002). Child fatality review: An international movement. *Child Abuse & Neglect, 26,* 619–636.

State Child Death Review Council. (2005). *Child deaths in California.* Sacramento: Attorney General of California.

CHILD EXPOSURE TO DOMESTIC VIOLENCE SCALE

The ways in which exposure to adult domestic violence has been measured have varied greatly from study to study, thereby prohibiting a direct comparison across studies. Most previous studies are based on parents' or other key adult informants' reports using adapted versions of established measures such as the Conflict Tactics Scales. Yet children's reports of their own experiences often differ from those of their parents. This situation points to a need for measures that gather child self-reports of exposure to violence.

Few child self-report tools have been developed. The Child Exposure to Domestic Violence (CEDV) Scale is a 42-item self-administered scale for children ages 10 to 16 years. It has been shown to be both a reliable measure and one that reflects face, content, and convergent validity. The first of three sections of the CEDV Scale includes a series of questions that specifically target the types of exposure to domestic

violence a child may have experienced. Children are asked to rate 10 different items focused on types of adult domestic violence to which they may have been exposed. Each question is answered using a 4-point Likert-type scale, with the choices being *never, sometimes, often,* and *almost always.* A second part of this first section requires a child to indicate how he or she knew of the violence occurring at home. If a child responds "never" to a particular question he or she moves onto the next question. However, if the child's response indicates exposure to such violence, the child is led by an arrow to an additional set of options that ask how he or she was exposed, including five choices: "I saw the outcome (like someone was hurt, something was broken, or the police came)," "I heard about it afterwards," "I heard it while it was happening," "I saw it from far away while it was happening," and "I saw it and was near while it was happening." After checking all applicable exposures the child is then instructed to move to the next item.

The second section of the CEDV Scale asks a series of 23 questions using the same 4-point Likert-type scale. The child is asked here to rate how often he or she intervened in violent events and about other risk factors present in his or her life. The third and final section of the CEDV Scale consists of nine questions asked to gather demographic information, including gender, age, race and ethnicity, current living situation, and family composition, and concludes with a question about favorite hobbies so as to end on a lighter note.

Jeffrey L. Edleson

See also Child Exposure to Intimate Partner Violence; Conflict Tactics Scales; Risk Assessment Instruments, Child Maltreatment

Further Readings

Edleson, J. L., Ellerton, A. L., Seagren, E. A., Schmidt, S. O., Kirchberg, S. L., & Ambrose, A. T. (2007). Assessing child exposure to adult domestic violence. *Children and Youth Services Review, 29,* 961–971.

Mohr, W. K., & Tulman, W. K. (2000). Children exposed to violence: Measurement considerations within an ecological framework. *Advances in Nursing Science, 23,* 59–68.

Web Sites

Child Exposure to Domestic Violence Scale: http://www .mincava.umn.edu/cedv

CHILD EXPOSURE TO INTIMATE PARTNER VIOLENCE

Public policymakers, practitioners, and researchers have only recently begun to understand that not only adults but also children may be affected by exposure to violence, and these professionals are now responding with new initiatives in several domains. Children are exposed to violence in many ways on a daily basis. Major research and some policy and practice responses have been developed in the following four areas of child exposure to (1) war zones, (2) media violence, (3) school and community violence, and (4) intimate partner violence. Several other entries in this encyclopedia expand on these first three forms of exposure. This entry focuses on children's exposure to intimate partner violence, including how intimate partner violence exposure is defined, what the impact of such exposure is on children, and what protective and risk factors play a role in the degree to which children are affected.

Defining Intimate Partner Violence Exposure

There are a number of issues that Ernest Jouriles and his colleagues suggest should be considered when defining child exposure to adult domestic violence. First, the types of domestic violence to which children are exposed may be defined narrowly as only physically violent incidents or more broadly as including additional forms of abuse such as verbal and emotional abuse. Second, even within the narrower band of physical violence, there is controversy about whether adult domestic violence should be defined as only severe acts of violence such as beatings, a broader group of behaviors such as slaps and shoves and psychological maltreatment, or a pattern of physically abusive acts, as suggested by Susan Osthoff. Finally, despite documented differences in the nature of male-to-female and female-to-male domestic violence, should one and not the other be included in a definition when considering children's exposure to such events?

Settling on the definition of domestic violence does not settle still other definitional questions that arise. For example, how is exposure itself defined? Is it only direct visual observation of the incident? Should definitions also include hearing the incident,

experiencing the events prior to and after the event, or other aspects of exposure?

Research on Intimate Partner Violence Exposure

It has been conservatively estimated that from 10% to 20% of American children are exposed to adult domestic violence every year. National surveys in this country and others also indicate that it is highly likely that the severity, frequency, and chronicity of violence each child experiences vary greatly.

Recent meta-analyses—statistical analyses that synthesize and average effects across studies—have shown that children exposed to domestic violence exhibit significantly more problems than children not so exposed. Researchers have the most information on behavioral and emotional functioning of children exposed to domestic violence. Generally, studies using the Child Behavior Checklist, developed by Thomas Achenbach and Craig Edelbrock, and similar measures have found that children exposed to domestic violence, when compared to nonexposed children, exhibit more aggressive and antisocial (often called *externalized* behaviors) as well as fearful and inhibited behaviors (*internalized* behaviors), show lower social competence, and have poorer academic performance. A recent meta-analysis also found that exposed children scored similarly on emotional health measures to children who were physically abused or who were both physically abused and exposed to adult domestic violence.

Another all too likely effect is a child's own increased use of violence. Social learning theory would suggest that children who are exposed to violence may also learn to use it. Several researchers have examined this link between exposure to violence and subsequent use of violence. For example, some studies have found that recent exposure to violence in the home is significantly associated with a child's violent behavior in the community. Others have suggested that children's exposure to adult domestic violence may generate attitudes justifying their own use of violence, and some studies of juvenile offenders have found that believing that aggression would enhance one's self-image significantly predicted violent offending.

A few studies have also examined longer-term problems reported retrospectively by adults or indicated in archival records. For example, a study of undergraduate students found that exposure to domestic violence as a child was associated with adult reports of depression, trauma-related symptoms, and low self-esteem among women and trauma-related symptoms alone among men. The researchers found that after accounting for the effects of being abused as a child, adult reports of their childhood exposure to domestic violence still accounted for a significant degree of their problems as adults.

Protective Factors in Children's Lives

Most people would be convinced by now that children exposed to adult domestic violence would all show evidence of greater problems than nonexposed children. In fact, the picture is not so clear. There is a growing research literature on children's resilience in the face of traumatic events. The surprise in these research findings is that many children exposed to traumatic events show no greater problems than non-exposed peers, leading Ann Masten to label such widespread resilience "ordinary magic."

Most studies of exposed children compare *groups of children* who were either exposed or not exposed to adult domestic violence. Study results report *group trends* and may or may not indicate an *individual child's* experience. Sandra Graham-Bermann, a leading researcher in this area, points out that consistent with the general trauma literature many children exposed to domestic violence show no greater problems than children not so exposed, and several studies support this claim. This does not mean that exposure is a positive experience for any child, just that some children seem to have other strengths or protective factors that buffer them from the most negative effects of exposure.

How does one explain these great variations among exposed children? Some of these children may have had greater protective social supports available to them. There are likely a number of protective assets and risk factors that affect the degree to which each child is influenced by violence exposures.

Ann Masten and her colleagues have suggested that as assets in a child's environment increase, the problems he or she experiences may actually decrease. Protective adults, including the child's mother, relatives, neighbors and teachers, older siblings, and friends, may all play protective roles in a child's life. The child's larger social environment may also play a protective role if extended family members or members of church, sports, or social clubs with which the child is affiliated act to support or aid the child during stressful periods. Harm children experience may also be moderated by how a child interprets or copes with the violence and other risks in his or her environment.

Risk Factors in Children's Lives

One risk factor that leads to variation in children's experiences is the great variation in *severity, frequency, and chronicity of violence.* Research has clearly documented the great variation of violence across families. It is likely that every child will be exposed to different levels of violence over time. Even siblings in the same household may be exposed to differing degrees of violence depending on how much time they spend at home. Increases in violence exposure may pose greater risks for children while decreases may lessen these risks.

A number of additional factors seem to play a role in children's exposure and interact with each other creating unique outcomes for different children. For example, many children exposed to domestic violence are also exposed to other adverse experiences. A study by Vincent Felitti, Robert Anda, and their colleagues found that increasing exposure to adult domestic violence in a child's life was associated with increasing levels of other "adverse childhood experiences" such as exposure to substance abuse, mental illness, incarcerated family members, and other forms of abuse or neglect. This finding points to the complexity of exposed children's lives. Problems associated with exposure have also been found to vary based on the *gender* and *age* of a child but *not* based on his or her race or ethnicity. The longer the period of time since exposure to a violent event also appears to be associated with lessening problems. Finally, *parenting* has also been identified as a key factor affecting how a child experiences exposure.

What little research there is on violent men shows that they have a direct impact on the parenting practices of women. For example, a study by George Holden and his colleagues found that battered mothers, when compared to other mothers, more often altered their parenting practices in the presence of the abusive male. Mothers reported that this change in parenting was made to minimize the men's irritability. A recent study of mothers and their children who were residing in shelters revealed that an abusive male's relationship to a child directly affected the child's well-being. Violence perpetrated by a biological father or stepfather has been found to have a greater impact on a child than the violence of nonfather figures, such as partners or ex-partners of the mother who played a minimal role in the child's life.

Conclusion

Our understanding of how children are exposed to intimate partner violence, what impact these exposures have, and how we can help children heal is slowly expanding. It is clear that children are exposed in varying ways and our responses to them should be equally varied.

Jeffrey L. Edleson

See also Child Exposure to Violence, in Media; Child Exposure to Violence, Role of Schools; Child Neglect; Community Violence, Effects on Children and Youth; Complex Trauma in Children and Adolescents; Cycle of Violence; Failure to Protect; Intergenerational Transmission of Violence; Media and Violence; Risk Assessment

Further Readings

Feerick, M. M., & Silverman, G. B. (Eds.). (2006). *Children exposed to violence.* Baltimore, MD: Brookes.

Graham-Bermann, S. A., & Edleson, J. L. (2001). *Domestic violence in the lives of children: The future of research, intervention and social policy.* Washington, DC: American Psychological Association.

Trickett, P. K., & Schellenbach, C. J. (Eds.). (1998). *Violence against children in the family and the community.* Washington, DC: American Psychological Association.

CHILD EXPOSURE TO VIOLENCE, IN MEDIA

The heart of the matter of child exposure to violence in media is threefold: (1) children are massively exposed to media from very early childhood; (2) a large fraction of mass media content contains violence; and (3) media directed toward older children and adolescents may be particularly violent, while media (particularly television) directed toward younger children, some argue, may contain "risky" violence.

Children in the 21st century increasingly inhabit a media-saturated environment, one that more than ever allows them to choose, without mediation, an extraordinarily wide array of content. Much of this content is violent. While neither positive nor harmful effects may be postulated from exposure to such content, that the media environment is a violent one is beyond dispute; moreover, a robust body of literature suggests that media violence, and particularly the sorts of violence presented in prime time television and theatrical film, is a predictor of aggression and attitudes associated with aggression.

Child Exposure to Media

Media, particularly screen media (television, computers, videogames), are virtually ubiquitous in 21st-century households. Researchers estimate that among U.S. households with children, television penetration exceeds 98%, while 80% of such households have computers, and nearly half have videogame consoles (in families of older children, this rises to 83%). Studies by the Kaiser Family Foundation show that children under age 6 and 8- to 18-year-olds are becoming increasingly media saturated, as new media technologies become layered atop one another in the home. Moreover, almost all television households are now multiset households, and even young children may have televisions in their bedrooms—18% of those under age 2, 39% of 3- to 4-year-olds, and more than two thirds of 8- to 18-year-olds. Though older children begin to supplant some of the time they devote to television to using other media, particularly computers, TV remains the dominant, consensus family medium. Two indicia of the degree of media saturation are that nearly a third of all children under age 6 live in homes where a television is on nearly all day (among kids under age 6, 1 hour and 57 minutes per day is spent using all screen media, just under 1 hour listening to music, and 40 minutes reading or being read to) and that children ages 8 to 18 average 8 hours and 33 minutes exposed to all media; allowing for "multitasking" exposure to more than one medium at a time, 8- to 18-year-olds average 6 hours, 21 minutes per day using mass media (of this, 43 minutes are spent on print media; 1 hour, 2 minutes on computers; 3 hours, 4 minutes on television; 49 minutes on videogames; and 1 hour, 11 minutes on movies on DVD or video). Among this group, half say a TV is usually on in the home, even if no one is watching.

While large majorities of parents of young children say they have rules about media use, newer media and in-bedroom televisions are frequently beyond the close scrutiny of parents. Among 8- to 18-year-olds, slightly fewer than half report any family rules governing TV watching and, of these, only an eighth report rules about which shows a child may or may not watch.

Violent Content in Media

Mass media content of course varies widely in the presence, degree, nature, and context of its violent content. Content specifically targeted to very young children contains relatively little violent content, but content targeted to older children and adolescents may in fact be more violent than that intended for adult audiences. As many content analyses have shown, screen media—television, videogames, and theatrical film—generally manifest relatively high instances of violence.

The most comprehensive analysis of television content ever undertaken, the National Television Violence Study, reported that over three TV seasons on 23 network, independent, basic cable, and premium cable channels, about 60% of all programming contained some violence, with more than half of programs depicting violence in realistic settings, and almost three quarters of violent scenes showing no remorse or penalty for commission of violent acts. The study's authors concluded that the depiction of televised violence was pervasive, glamorized, sanitized, and trivialized. Violent depictions were most prevalent on premium cable, dominated by reruns of theatrical films (90% of which contain violent content), followed by independent stations, then broadcast networks, then basic cable (public TV channels have next to none). While violence was somewhat more prevalent during prime time, when young children were less likely to be in the audience, the difference was strong only on broadcast television; on cable, daytime TV was almost as violent as prime time TV.

As noted above, parental enforcement of rules for television viewing is most likely to concern the amount of time children watch TV. Rules regulating content are less prevalent; one survey found that about a quarter of parents use TV ratings "often" to make decisions about acceptable programs, and just 7% have used the V-chip.

Large majorities of the most popular videogames and theatrical films contain content that is violent, much of it *also* glamorized, sanitized, and trivialized. In both media, industry self-regulatory ratings systems are designed to keep the most violent content away from young audiences. Such systems are variably enforced, and some research has pointed to a "forbidden fruit" effect, wherein, at least for older children, a more "mature" rating may serve to attract audiences while a "G" rating may repel them.

The Risks of Exposure to Violent Content

Older children and adolescents may be disproportionately exposed to violent media content. Programmers use violent content to attract this audience based on purchase and ratings data that indicate preferences for this content in shows watched, motion pictures attended, and videogames purchased, and economic analysis suggests these content preferences are more pronounced for adolescents and young adults than for older adults. Preferences for violent content are believed to reflect young people's seeking excitement, adventure, and risk.

While younger viewers of screen media, particularly television, are less exposed to violence than older children, researchers for the National Television Violence Study employed a cognitive developmental theory to suggest that the cartoon fantasy and slapstick humor violence to which they are exposed places them at risk, since young children are unable to distinguish fantasy from reality or to make adultlike inferences about motives and consequences. In addition, the media-effects research literature has shown that violence coupled with humor, endemic to cartoon violence, is linked with learning of aggressive behavior.

D. Charles Whitney and Michael Robb

See also Video Games, Violence Exposure in

Further Readings

Hamilton, J. T. (1998). *Channeling violence: The economic market for violent television programming.* Princeton, NJ: Princeton University Press.

National Television Violence Study. (1998). *National Television Violence Study* (Vol. 3). Thousand Oaks, CA: Sage.

Rideout, V., & Hamel, E. (2006). *The media family.* Retrieved from http://www.kff.org/entmedia/upload/7500.pdf

Roberts, D., Foehr, U., & Rideout, V. (2005). *Generation M: Media in the lives of 8–18 year-olds.* Retrieved from http://www.kff.org/entmedia/upload/Generation-M-Media-in-the-Lives-of-8-18-Year-olds-Report.pdf

Wartella, E., & Robb, M. (2007). Young children, new media. *Journal of Children and Media, 1,* 35–44.

CHILD EXPOSURE TO VIOLENCE, IN WAR ZONES

Daily images from war zones around the world illustrate the degree to which children are direct victims of war violence and exposed to the victimization of others, both in their families and in their communities.

How Many Children Are Affected

Paramijit Joshi and her colleagues suggest that measuring child exposure in war zones is very difficult. Citing UN reports, they suggest that in one decade from the mid-1980s to the mid-1990s, over 2 million children were killed in wars, 4 million were injured, and another 10 million were traumatized

How Children Are Exposed to War

Joshi and her colleagues also suggest that children experience a series of consequences from war exposure, including (a) loss of loved ones, (b) family stress and change, (c) dislocation, (d) living with distressed adults, (e) loss of traditional communities, (f) lack of educational opportunities, (g) poor physical and community environments, and (h) being socialized to use and approve of violence.

James Garbarino and his colleagues have researched this issue in a number of locations around the globe and identified four themes similar to those identified by Joshi and colleagues. First, children face many increased risks in war zones. These include dislocation, increased poverty, multiple losses, and much more. Garbarino and his colleagues suggest, in line with other resilience researchers, that efforts be made to reduce risks and also shore up both children's own abilities to cope and the social networks of family, friends, and neighbors who surround them. The second theme these researchers identify concerns not the children but the adults who care for them. War zones present adults—both in families and in communities—with great challenges in caring for their children. Adult caregivers also require support during times of war to enable them to in turn act in supportive ways for the children in their lives. The third and fourth themes concern the meaning children give to their situations. Ideology appears to motivate children in war zones. For example, if a positive and constructive framework for assigning meaning to war experiences can be created within children (for example, pitching in to help rebuild rather than destroy), Garbarino and his colleagues suggest that children may be less inclined to join in the violence around them. Related to this is the fourth and final theme of finding alternatives to violent revenge. The best revenge for children may be becoming constructive members of their community in response to the violence swirling around them.

Jeffrey L. Edleson

See also Child Exposure to Violence, in Media; Child Exposure to Violence, Role of Schools; Child Neglect; Community Violence, Effects on Children and Youth; Complex Trauma in Children and Adolescents; Cycle of Violence; Failure to Protect; Intergenerational Transmission of Violence; Media and Violence; Risk Assessment

Further Readings

Garbarino, J., Dubrow, N., Kostelny, K., & Pardo, C. (1992). *Children in danger: Coping with the consequences of community violence.* San Francisco: Jossey-Bass.

Joshi, P. T., O'Donnell, D. A., Cullins, L. M., & Lewin, S. M. (2006). Children exposed to war and terrorism. In M. M. Feerick & G. B. Silverman (Eds.), *Children exposed to violence* (pp. 53–84). Baltimore, MD: Brookes.

CHILD EXPOSURE TO VIOLENCE, ROLE OF SCHOOLS

The first societal responses to domestic violence were the creation of shelters for abused women and training other professionals in the justice system to treat this violence as a crime. After more services became available for victims and perpetrators, an increasing focus became the children living with violence. Awareness of the plight of children and development of services grew to the point that expectations began to be placed on schools as an ideal location for early intervention and prevention programs. Since educators have almost universal access to children, schools are seen as a foundation for preventing domestic violence.

The school's role can be defined under the concepts of early identification, intervention, and prevention. Early identification of children living with violence is possible by raising teachers' awareness of the impact of domestic violence on children and potential symptoms that may be seen within a school setting. Many children suffer from emotional and behavioral problems related to exposure to violence. These children may experience specific problems related to school attendance, adjustment, and achievement.

Teacher professional development regarding the impact of domestic violence on students at different ages may result in these students being identified and offered assistance. Critical skills for educators have to include handling disclosures of violence from students. Students may disclose directly by what they recount or indirectly in their play, drawings, attitudes, and/or behavior. In some cases, parents may make a disclosure during a parent–teacher meeting and seek understanding about their children's problems or assistance from school staff for referrals to other professionals. The assistance may involve counselors within the school system or community service providers. Some school districts have partnerships with domestic violence agencies and provide in-school groups or education programs.

One emerging issue that is the source of considerable debate is the appropriateness of referrals to the child protection system from schools in cases of domestic violence. School districts have developed a wide variety of policies and practices for handling disclosure and determining the extent to which mandatory reporting is triggered by incidents of children disclosing domestic violence in their home.

A more recent development in the field is the creation of school programs and curricula that address domestic violence at every grade. These developments include programs on social skills, interpersonal problem solving, gender stereotypes and equality, healthy relationships in adolescence, and dating violence. These programs are intended to be universal programs directed at all students rather than just those students experiencing domestic violence. The thinking behind these programs is that every student can benefit from this knowledge irrespective of any potential future role as a victim or perpetrator. This knowledge may assist these students in the future, as well as their friends, family members, coworkers, and neighbors, in the event they have to confront domestic violence in their environment. Ultimately, these programs may promote the shift in societal attitudes and behavior that no longer tolerates this behavior.

Peter G. Jaffe and Linda Baker

See also Child Exposure to Intimate Partner Violence; School-Based Violence Prevention Programs

Further Readings

Baker, L., Jaffe, P., Carter, S., & Ashbourne, L. (2002). *Children exposed to domestic violence: A teacher's handbook to increase understanding and improve community responses.* London, ON: Centre for Children & Families in the Justice System.

Jaffe, P., Wolfe, D. A., Crooks, C., Hughes, R., & Baker, L. (2004). The fourth R: Developing healthy relationships through school-based interventions. In P. Jaffe, L. Baker, & A. Cunningham (Eds.), *Protecting children from domestic violence: Strategies for community intervention* (pp. 200–218). New York: Guilford Press.

Rosenbluth, B., & Bradford Garcia, R. (2004). *Expect Respect curriculum.* Austin, TX: SafePlace.

Wolfe, D. A., Jaffe, P., & Crooks, C. (2006). *Adolescent risk behaviors: Why teens experiment and strategies to keep them safe.* New Haven, CT: Yale University Press.

CHILD FATALITIES

According to data from the National Center for Health Statistics, approximately 53,854 children from birth to age 19 died in the United States in 2002, a rate of 66.5 per 100,000 children. The cause of child deaths can vary from those considered "natural" (e.g., congenital anomalies, respiratory disease, sudden infant death syndrome) to those identified as "unintentional" (e.g., motor vehicle accident, drowning, fires) or "intentional" (e.g., homicides, suffocation, poisoning). Intentional child fatalities as well as many incidents involving unintentional death are considered forms of child maltreatment, as each year a significant number of child deaths are due to acts of either child physical abuse or child neglect. The prevalence of child fatalities due to various forms of child maltreatment in the

United States is presented in this entry, along with a discussion of what can be done to prevent child deaths.

Prevalence of Child Fatalities Due to Child Abuse and Neglect

The National Child Abuse and Neglect Data System (NCANDS), which produces an annual report on child maltreatment in the United States, estimates that in 2002 approximately 1,400 children died in the United States as a result of abuse and neglect. The overall rate of child fatalities for these children, from birth to 17 years old, was 2 child deaths per 100,000 children. Of these 1,400 child deaths, approximately one third resulted from child physical abuse. Physical abuse–related child deaths often result from head injury, drowning, or asphyxiation. Another 38% of child victims died as a result of child neglect (i.e., caretakers failed to provide for the children's basic needs, such as medical care or adequate supervision). Child deaths from child neglect frequently involve hazards associated with unsafe or unsupervised environments, including scald burns, plastic bag suffocation, house fires, and hypothermia. A significant percentage of child deaths are due to some combination of physical abuse and neglect, as approximately 29% of children died as a result of multiple forms of maltreatment in 2002.

The large majority (76%) of 2002 child fatalities due to child abuse and neglect were children under the age of 4 years, with 41% under the age of 1 year at the time of their deaths. Boys were at greater risk than girls, with fatality rates of 2.4 and 1.8, respectively, per 100,000 children. In terms of who was responsible for the child's death, in more than 80% of cases, the perpetrators were the child's parents, most frequently the child's mother. Additional perpetrators included other relatives (7%), unmarried partners (3%), or other individuals in the child's life, such as daycare providers, foster parents, school employees, and others (6%).

Misclassified Homicide

The number of child fatalities documented by NCANDS is certainly cause for concern, but even more alarming is the fact that such statistics are likely underestimates of the actual number of children who die at the hands of their parents. These numbers do not reflect, for example, child deaths due to maltreatment reported to other authorities, such as law enforcement agencies, hospitals, or coroners. Also excluded are homicide cases that are misclassified as accidents or medical conditions.

One example of a misclassified homicide that is sometimes masked by a medical diagnosis is sudden infant death syndrome (SIDS). SIDS is defined as the sudden unexpected and unexplained death of an infant, often occurring during sleep. SIDS is essentially a default diagnosis that describes a child who inexplicably stops breathing. Because so little is known about the condition, it is sometimes difficult to distinguish between SIDS and homicide. There is evidence that some cases attributed to SIDS are actually the result of asphyxia or deliberate smothering by a parent or caretaker.

The relationship between SIDS and child maltreatment has been somewhat controversial because there is significant disagreement concerning how frequently misdiagnoses occur. Research on the topic has uncovered several indicators that might help distinguish between SIDS and homicide, such as recurring life-threatening incidents that are poorly explained and typically witnessed by only a single caregiver, evidence of physical maltreatment, a family history of previous involvement with child protective services, and a death scene that suggests neglect. In addition, most states now require autopsies for all inexplicable infant deaths, as well as an examination of the scene of death and medical history of the child. Although in the overwhelming majority of deaths of this nature some type of medical condition or accidental suffocation is likely the cause of death, sometimes inexplicable deaths are the result of child abuse or neglect.

Child Death Review Teams

Within the past 30 years, there has been increased interest in understanding the causes of child fatalities in an effort to reduce preventable deaths in children. The establishment of child death review teams both nationally and internationally has been instrumental in this effort. The common mission of such teams is to prevent child fatalities by identifying appropriate system changes and increasing awareness about the causes of child death. Child death review began in the late 1970s in Los Angeles where the first team was formed by the Inter-Agency Council on Child Abuse and Neglect. Today, there are hundreds of child death review teams across the United States, Canada, and Australia.

Child death review teams are typically composed of community professionals that represent multiple agencies. Teams typically include representatives from a variety of disciplines, such as physicians, child welfare workers, lawyers, social workers, and mental health professionals. Although the functions of these teams vary, most evaluate cases in which a child has died (a) to identify the prevalence of deaths from child maltreatment, (b) to improve the policies and procedures of child protective services to prevent future child deaths, (c) to protect siblings of children whose causes of death are unexplained, and (d) to increase professional and public awareness of child death due to child abuse and neglect.

The American Academy of Pediatrics published a policy statement outlining recommendations for the investigation and review of unexpected deaths. One recommendation addresses the need to create state laws to establish child death review teams, and specifies that the child death review process should involve multiple groups and agencies. The policy statement also suggests that autopsies be required in all questionable deaths of children younger than 18 years. The academy also recommends that death scene investigators have special training in child abuse, child development, and SIDS. Other recommendations include the involvement of pediatricians, both as members of child death review teams and as advocates for proper investigation, and death certification in cases of child fatality. Finally, the academy recommended that data from child death review teams be used to develop initiatives to prevent child death.

Cindy Miller-Perrin

See also Child Neglect; Child Physical Abuse

Further Readings

American Academy of Pediatrics, Committees on Child Abuse and Neglect and Community Health Services. (1999). Investigation and review of unexpected infant and child deaths. *Pediatrics, 104,* 1158–1159.

Block, R. W. (2002). Child fatalities. In J. E. B. Myers, L. Berliner, J. Briere, C. T. Hendrix, C. Jenny, & T. A. Reid (Eds.), *The APSAC handbook on child maltreatment* (2nd ed., pp. 293–301). Thousand Oaks, CA: Sage.

Durfee, M., Durfee, D. T., & West, M. P. (2002). Child fatality review: An international movement. *Child Abuse & Neglect, 26,* 619–636.

National Center for Child Death Review. (2002). *United States child mortality, 2002.* Retrieved May 10, 2006, from http://www.childdeathrevieworg/nationalchildmortalitydata.htm

U.S. Department of Health and Human Services, Administration on Children, Youth and Families. (2004). *Child maltreatment 2002.* Washington, DC: Government Printing Office.

CHILD FATALITY REVIEW

See CHILD DEATH REVIEW TEAMS

CHILD NEGLECT

Child neglect is the most prevalent form of child maltreatment, and is distinct from child abuse. This entry focuses on the definition of child neglect; its incidence and prevalence, including co-occurrence of neglect with other forms of maltreatment and violence; and its precursors and consequences. The entry concludes with a brief overview of evidence-based interventions for child neglect.

Definition

Child neglect results from an act of omission of adequate care for a child by a parenting person. Neglect stands in contrast to other forms of interpersonal violence, which are acts of commission. Physical neglect consists of failing to provide shelter, food, and clothing. Education and medical neglect results from the parent's failure to access these essential services for children. In emotional neglect, the parent fails to provide basic attention to a child's emotional needs. Supervisory neglect can occur throughout a child's development and includes lack of care and attention to an infant or lack of supervision for an adolescent.

State statutes define child neglect and must meet the federal child maltreatment standard. While adhering to the basic definition provided above, states' definitions vary. For example, in some states, harsh corporeal punishment is defined as neglect. Other states discriminate between failure to provide adequate care due to financial inability and failure to provide care due to financial inability (not neglect).

What constitutes neglectful behavior is not always clear. Cultures influence standards of parenting in matters such as when a child is old enough to stay home unsupervised, and what is considered appropriate health and educational attention. Historically, only Western nations have focused on defining child neglect, but in the last decade there have been efforts to define global standards for adequate care of children.

Incidence and Prevalence

The Child Abuse Prevention and Treatment Act (CAPTA) requires states to provide data on reported child maltreatment, investigations, and investigation outcomes to the National Child Abuse and Neglect Data System (NCANDS). The latest report was for 2005. In addition, the U.S. Children's Bureau has mounted periodic National Incidence Studies (NIS). The last such study reported data from 1993 to 1994. Both studies are relevant because they employ different standards of child maltreatment. The NCANDS is based on data from child maltreatment reports; the NIS surveyed children services professionals for their observations of maltreatment of children, whether or not it was officially reported. These reports provide the basis for estimates of incidence and prevalence of child neglect.

Sixty-three percent of all children reported for maltreatment in 2005 were found to be neglected. Physical, emotional, or sexual abuse accounted for 33% of substantiated maltreatment in the same time period. Other or unclassified causes accounted for the remainder. The 2005 incidence rate for child neglect was 8.1 per 1,000 children. Thirty-five percent of child neglect victims are under 4 years of age and 22% are older than 12. Black and Hispanic families are overrepresented in all forms of reported child maltreatment. Blacks account for 24% of known neglect cases, Hispanics for 18%, and Whites for 48%. The NIS and the NCANDS studies show that incidence rates of child neglect are increasing. The NIS found that most children who are neglected are not reported to Child Protective Services. Child neglect often co-occurs with other forms of maltreatment. Child neglect can be life threatening and accounted for more than 40% of the 1,117 child fatalities due to maltreatment in 2005.

Precursors and Aftereffects of Child Neglect

Neglect is strongly associated with poverty, with unemployment, and with single-parent-headed families with more than three children. Studies have also associated neglect with a demoralized, discouraged parental worldview. Neglect typically occurs across generations; neglectful parents have often been neglected themselves and do not know how to nurture their children. Birth parents are perpetrators of child neglect in the vast majority of cases.

A constellation of factors create risk for child neglect, including the following: (a) situation factors related to lack of economic resources and to high levels of stress; (b) family factors such as conflict, spousal violence, and social isolation; (c) parent factors such as lack of parenting empathy and skills, adverse parental childhood histories, and mental health and addiction problems; and (d) child factors such as special health and mental health needs and the temperament of the child. Neglectful families are likely to have limited adaptive capacities and environmental resources. Studies of neglectful family interaction show low amounts of any interaction, and a low ratio of positive to coercive or negative interaction among family members. The newest studies suggest that early parent–child interaction has traceable effects on brain development and that poor parenting has a profoundly negative effect on the child's emotional and cognitive development.

The consequences of child neglect can be life threatening. Examples include nonorganic failure to thrive, unintentional injuries such as poisonings and drowning, and adolescent high-risk behaviors. Neglected children typically show poor school achievement, behavior and emotional regulation problems, and low self-esteem. Growing evidence suggests that neglect increases risk for adolescent and adult delinquency and relational and mental health problems.

Prevention and Treatment

Practitioners view child neglect as one of the most difficult forms of child maltreatment to change; thus, there is agreement that the emphasis should be on prevention and family supports. While a single standard of prevention and intervention does not exist, there is growing consensus on elements to reduce child neglect risk.

Successful programs contain the following elements: (a) environmental support and enrichment through social services that serve as a safety net in preventing the deleterious effects of extreme poverty (these include affordable, high-quality daycare, health care, preschool, early developmental assessment with intensive service follow-up, and after-school programs for older children and adolescents); (b) services to multiple social systems—to the child, parent, and family as needed; (c) intense emotion- and empathy-building experiences between the parent and child (neuroscience and attachment theory provide the bases for this promising component of prevention); (d) opportunities to build social relationships through neighborhood-based group services and inclusion of extended family in intervention; (e) an optimistic and strengths-based orientation; and (f) compatibility with the family's ethnic culture.

Lynn Videka

See also Child Abuse Prevention and Treatment Act; Health Consequences of Child Maltreatment; International Society for the Prevention of Child Abuse and Neglect; Legal System, Advocacy Efforts to Affect, Child Maltreatment; Office on Child Abuse and Neglect; Parenting Practices and Violence, Child Maltreatment; Prevention Programs, Child Maltreatment; Risk Assessment Instruments, Child Maltreatment

Further Readings

Caliber Associates. (2003). *Emerging practices in the prevention of child abuse and neglect.* Washington, DC: U.S. Department of Health and Human Services, Administration for Children and Families, Office on Child Abuse and Neglect. Retrieved July 27, 2007, from http://www.childwelfare.gov/preventing/programs/whatworks/report/index.cfm

Crosson-Tower, C. (2007). *Understanding child abuse and neglect* (7th ed.). Boston: Allyn & Bacon.

Gaudiosi, J. (2007). *Child maltreatment: 2005.* Washington, DC: U.S. Department of Health and Human Services, Administration for Children and Families, Children's Bureau. Retrieved July 27, 2007, from http://www.acf.hhs.gov/programs/cb/pubs/cm05/index.htm

Sedlak, A. J., & Broadhurst, D. D. (1996). *Third National Incidence Study of Child Abuse and Neglect (NIS-3).* Washington, DC: U.S. Department of Health and Human Services, Administration for Children and Families, National Center on Child Abuse and Neglect. Retrieved July 27, 2007, from http://www.childwelfare.gov/pubs/statsinfo/nis3.cfm

CHILD PHYSICAL ABUSE

Child physical abuse occurs when a child is injured due to intentional or unintentional acts by a caregiver and includes injuries from hitting, kicking, punching, biting, throwing, shaking, stabbing, choking, burning, or any other act that physically harms a child. The acts may be unintentional in that the parent may not have purposely hurt the child, but nonetheless an injury occurred. Child abuse and neglect is defined in federal law in the Child Abuse Prevention and Treatment Act or CAPTA (42 U.S.C.A. §5106g), amended by the Keeping Children and Families Safe Act of 2003, as at a minimum: "Any recent act or failure to act on the part of a parent or caretaker which results in death, serious physical or emotional harm, sexual abuse or exploitation; or an act or failure to act which presents an imminent risk of serious harm." Individual state statutory definitions of physical abuse are derived from the federal definition of child abuse and neglect and vary, but most states' definitions of physical abuse include a statement that the act resulted in some type of physical injury or mark on the child. For example, it is within a caregiver's rights to spank a child, but if this disciplinary technique leaves physical marks, it is considered physical abuse. Researchers estimate that approximately 20% of all maltreatment cases can be categorized as physical abuse. Neglect comprises about 60%, sexual abuse about 10%, and emotional maltreatment and other forms make up the balance of all maltreatment cases.

Evaluation of physical abuse should consider a careful examination of the circumstances surrounding the event, the family history, and family and community culture. More specifically, evaluation considers the following:

- What harm occurred to the child?
- What is the child's age and developmental level?
- Were the acts or behaviors based upon lack of information, or carelessness, or were they intentional?
- What were the circumstances surrounding the event and/or behaviors?
- What is the child's interpretation of the event and/or behaviors?
- What are the community and family standards and practices regarding the event?
- What is the caregiver and family history regarding similar events and risk factors?

Physical abuse can be categorized into subtypes that correspond to the type of injury experienced by the child. The major subtypes are discussed next.

Subtypes

Cutaneous Injuries

Cutaneous injuries are injuries that occur on the cutaneous areas, or skin, of the child's body. Typically these marks are bruises, abrasions, cuts, and other marks to the skin. Physical bruising is the most typical type of physical abuse injury. Sometimes, the outline of the implement that was used to create the injury can be seen on the skin. For example, a belt, switch, or hand may leave a clearly identifiable pattern on the skin. Marks caused by physical abuse are typically seen on the fleshy areas of the body, such as the buttocks, back, and thighs, while accidental injuries are typically found on bony prominences, such as knees, shins, and foreheads, as these are the body parts that first come into contact with the ground or a piece of furniture when a child falls or runs into a stationary or immovable object. Other cutaneous injuries include bite marks, circumferential marks around the ankles or wrists when a child has been tied up, and strap and switch marks.

Cutaneous injuries should be carefully assessed to distinguish them from injuries caused by accidents, naturally occurring conditions, or cultural practices. Naturally occurring cutaneous marks include Mongolian spots (grayish blue spots usually on the buttocks, backs, legs, upper arms, and shoulders), salmon patches (pink marks on the neck, eyelids, nose, or forehead of newborns), and strawberry marks (not present at birth but appearing 4–6 weeks later). Folk healing practices may also be mistaken for maltreatment. For example, a practice called "coining," which originated in Southeast Asia to treat fever and other maladies, involves rubbing the skin with a coin, which leaves long, linear bruises that may be mistaken for marks of abuse. Careful assessment of any cultural practice should consider the child's interpretation of the event, the cultural meaning behind the practice or incident, and the resulting injury.

Burns

Burn injuries are classified by the cause of the wound and include immersion, splash, electrical, object, and chemical burns. When assessing a burn, the history and story given by the caretaker provides key information to determine if the burn was accidental or intentional, but even if it was accidental, the situation should be assessed for neglect issues. Evaluation of all burns should assess who was involved in the incident, the child's developmental maturity, when the event occurred, when medical attention was sought, and the specific circumstances surrounding the event. Maltreatment should be considered when the history is incompatible with the physical findings, the developmental age of the child makes the sequence of events unlikely, and the burn is older than indicated by the historical account. Safety issues should be considered even when the burn was accidental.

Burns are typically categorized as superficial, partial thickness, or full thickness, with full thickness impacting the entire thickness of the skin and requiring more intensive treatment. The extent of the burn is also considered when determining severity, with burns covering a higher percentage of the body considered more severe. Immersion burns are the most frequently seen types of abusive burns and occur when a child's body or body part is held in scalding water, usually as some form of punishment. An immersion burn will have clear lines of demarcation, while an accidental immersion burn will present a more ragged appearance. Other types of burns include splash burns, when a hot liquid comes into contact with the skin, for example, a pot of boiling water that is knocked over; and contact burns, when a hot object touches the skin, such as a cigarette, curling iron, stove burner, or heater grate. Electrical burns most often occur when a young child mouths an electrical cord or socket.

Injuries to the Head, Eyes, Ears, Nose, and Face

Head injuries may occur on the skull, spine, neck, and the face. A subdural hematoma or hemorrhage may result from a head injury and results when bleeding occurs between areas in the brain. Shaken baby syndrome or shaken impact syndrome describes a constellation of symptoms that occur when a child is shaken, causing the child's head to experience severe acceleration, deceleration, and/or rotational force. Head injuries require a complete physical evaluation of physical symptoms including neurological functioning.

Evaluation compares the circumstances and history of the injury with the story given for how it occurred. Eye injuries can result from a blow to the eye or occur in conjunction with a head injury causing a retinal hemorrhage. Ear injuries may be caused by direct blows to the ear, grabbing, or a penetrating trauma, and may result in bruising, abrasions, and perforation of the inner ear. Nasal injuries may result from blunt trauma to the nose. A penetrating trauma can cause injury to the nasal septum. Oral injuries may be more common because of the significance of the mouth for communication and eating, which can be seen as sources of conflict by caregivers. Frenulum tears (i.e., tears to the small folds of skin that connect the lips to the gums and connect the tongue to the floor of the mouth) should generate high suspicion of abuse. Traumatic injury to the baby teeth of young children can be quite common in accidental or abusive injuries. All potentially abusive injuries should consider the history and child's developmental level.

Abusive Fractures

Abusive fractures are discerned typically by assessing the type and age of the fracture and the history given about how the fracture occurred. When abusive fractures are suspected, a full skeletal survey may be conducted to determine the presence of current or old fractures. Types of fractures include closed (a fracture with no skin wound), complicated (a broken bone also injured an internal organ), compound (the broken bone protrudes through the skin), compression (the bone collapses along the direction of the force), hairline (a minor fracture), impacted (the broken bone is wedged into the interior of another), and spiral (a slanting, diagonal fracture often caused by twisting). Organic abnormalities or genetic conditions should be ruled out before determining that a fracture is maltreatment.

Internal Injuries

Injuries to the thoracic and abdominal organs can be lethal and typically occur as the result of blunt trauma or being thrown down. Often, there is no external bruising, so diagnosis depends upon a detailed history. Abdominal injuries may include injuries to the liver, pancreas, spleen, stomach, small intestine, large intestine, or kidneys. Thoracic or chest injuries also occur as the result of blunt trauma or being thrown. Chest injuries may result in injury to the throat, rib cage, heart, or lungs. Any injury to the abdomen or chest requires immediate evaluation due to the lethality potential.

Poisoning

Poisoning occurs when a caregiver harms a child by inducing the child to take a poisonous substance or a substance taken in sufficient quantity that it becomes poisonous, and whether it is given as a punishment or for a well-intentioned reason. For example, as punishment for soiling, the caregiver may force the child to induce large quantities of water, creating an electrolyte imbalance that leads to brain swelling. Alternatively, caregivers may give a child drugs that were prescribed for themselves, such as barbiturates or antihistamines, to sedate a child whom the caregiver perceives as fussy or otherwise troublesome. Other substances that can be poisonous include table salt, hot peppers, black pepper, or laxatives. Accidental poisoning may occur when hazardous chemicals or other harmful substances are improperly stored or open and the child gets into them and ingests the poison. Supervisional neglect should be considered in those instances when chemicals or other hazardous materials are left accessible to small children.

Pediatric Condition Falsification

Formerly called Munchausen's Syndrome by Proxy, this condition has been renamed to more accurately reflect the syndrome. This abusive parenting disorder occurs when a parent purposely induces or fabricates injuries or conditions to a child that result in unnecessary and sometimes even painful tests and hospitalization. The parent conceals his or her role in inducing or faking the injuries. These conditions in and of themselves are detrimental and even dangerous to the child—for example, smothering a child to simulate sleep apnea or breathing issues, or inducing vomiting. Often, the symptoms subside when the child is separated from the perpetrating caregiver. Typically, the child's mother is the perpetrator and does this as an attention-seeking behavior. Diagnosis usually occurs after conventional treatments do not work, there are no corresponding rational reasons for their ineffectiveness, and the deceptive story surrounding the child and his or her illnesses and conditions starts to unravel.

Treatment for Physical Abuse

An understanding of the contributing factors to child physical abuse influences the selection of prevention and treatment strategies. Since contributing factors to physical abuse may be different for every person, interventions must be closely linked to a comprehensive assessment and individualized according to the risk factors identified during the assessment process. Some parents or caregivers may have totally unrealistic expectations regarding a child's crying, eating difficulties, or toilet training. In situations like these, educational and supportive approaches may be most effective. Other parents or caregivers may understand the developmental levels and needs of a child, but lack skills in self-control and managing their own anger. Parenting education will likely not reduce the risk of future maltreatment if the cause of physical abuse is lack of impulse control. Anger management or therapy to address underlying issues related to the uncontrollable rage is an appropriate intervention. Sometimes a parent's or caregiver's anger is a symptom of untreated depression or substance abuse. Even when such conditions are treated, there may be adverse effects of medication, such as increased agitation or anxiety, that are expressed as an inability to handle normal stresses of parenting. Interventions appropriate when lack of parenting skills is identified as a cause of child physical abuse include the following:

- Programs offering instruction in specific parenting skills such as discipline methods, basic child care, and infant stimulation
- Child development education
- Local support services and linkages to other parents in the community
- Increasing the parent's or caregiver's knowledge of child development and the demands of parenting
- Enhancing the parent's or caregiver's skill in coping with the stresses of infant and child care
- Enhancing parent–child bonding, emotional ties, and communication
- Increasing access to social and health services for all family members

Interventions to address anger management and lack of self-control include the following:

- Anger control training aimed at recognizing "triggers" and reducing anger-arousing behaviors
- Relaxation training that seeks to short-circuit the aggressive behavior early in its development
- Communication skills training and problem-solving strategies
- Methods for aiding the parent or caregiver not only to reduce his or her own anger level but also to help his or her child do likewise

Other interventions commonly used for physical abuse cases include the following:

- Providing food, shelter, clothing, and/or utilities to stressed or impoverished families at the same time as counseling or parent education to reduce the anxiety or stress that may lead to future maltreatment
- Addressing factors underlying physical abuse, such as substance abuse and/or domestic violence; if an assessment identifies the presence of these issues, they should be addressed as an intervention strategy to lower the risk of future abuse
- For children, specifically discussing the child's perception of the circumstances surrounding the abuse as well as the details of the abuse itself (depending on the child's level of emotional and cognitive development, children often blame themselves; they need help identifying their shame and guilt and should be told they did not cause the abuse)
- Training children in self-expression, self-control, and effective problem-solving; interventions should teach children alternative ways to express their feelings and thoughts, especially anger and anxiety

All of the interventions used to address child physical abuse should link the underlying cause of abuse to the intervention's purpose. No single intervention approach will be universally effective for all individuals.

Charmaine R. Brittain

See also Child Neglect; Child Sexual Abuse

Further Readings

Besharov, D. (1990). *Recognizing child abuse: A guide for the concerned.* New York: Macmillan.

Brittain, C. (Ed.). (2006). *Understanding the medical diagnosis of child maltreatment: A guide for nonmedical professionals.* New York: Oxford University Press.

Brittain, C., & Hunt, D. (Eds.). (2004). *Helping in Child Protective Services: A competency-based casework handbook.* New York: Oxford University Press.

Dubowitz, H., & DePanfilis, D. (2000). *Handbook for child protection practice.* Thousand Oaks, CA: Sage.

Karson, M. (2001). *Patterns of child abuse: How dysfunctional transactions are replicated in individuals, families, and the child welfare system.* Binghamton, NY: Maltreatment and Trauma Press.

Maluccio, A., Pine, B., & Tracy, E. (2002). *Social work practice with families and children.* New York: Columbia University Press.

Scannepieco, M., & Connell-Carrick, K. (2005). *Understanding child maltreatment: An ecological and developmental perspective.* New York: Oxford University Press.

U.S. Department of Health and Human Services, Administration on Children, Youth and Families, Children's Bureau, Office on Child Abuse and Neglect. *The Child Abuse and Prevention Treatment Act.* Retrieved August 6, 2007, from http://www.acf.hhs.gov/programs/cb/laws_policies/cblaws/capta03/capta_manual.pdf

CHILD PROSTITUTION

See COMMERCIAL SEXUAL EXPLOITATION OF CHILDREN

CHILD PROTECTIVE SERVICES

In the mid-1960s, C. Henry Kempe and his colleagues described the "battered child syndrome," a pattern of unexplained physical injuries, apparently inflicted by parents or caregivers. His work helped to initiate a movement in the United States to protect children from child abuse and neglect. The 1974 Child Abuse Prevention and Treatment Act (P.L. 93-247) furthered the child protection movement and provided legislation to create publicly funded child welfare agencies. Today, these agencies are most often referred to as Child Protective Services, or CPS.

CPS agencies attempt to protect children in four ways: by investigating reports of maltreatment, by providing treatment services, by coordinating the services offered by other agencies in the community to child victims and their families, and by implementing preventive services. This entry describes these complicated and intersecting roles along with several challenges facing a CPS system responsible for the monumental task of protecting children.

The Role of Child Protective Services

The 1974 Child Abuse Prevention and Treatment Act mandated reporting laws as well as procedures for investigating suspected cases of child maltreatment.

Today, various professionals (e.g., schoolteachers, medical personnel, mental health professionals) in all states are required to report suspected child maltreatment to CPS. Many state CPS agencies have adopted statewide telephone reporting systems (e.g., "hotlines") whereby professionals as well as laypersons may report children suspected of being abused or neglected.

Although all states have uniform mandatory reporting laws, there are no standard guidelines for assessment and processing of child maltreatment cases. CPS workers generally investigate reports of child maltreatment within 24 to 72 hours in order to determine whether child maltreatment has taken place. The investigation typically includes conducting interviews with the child, family members, neighbors, teachers, and medical personnel. The CPS worker must determine the degree to which the child is at risk for maltreatment, whether the home environment is safe, what factors are contributing to the family's difficulties, and whether appropriate services can alleviate the risk to the child. Caseworkers who conduct the investigations often visit the child's home to identify risk factors by assessing critical areas of individual and family functioning such as the child's age and physical and mental abilities; the caretaker's level of cooperation and physical, mental, and emotional abilities; the family's level of stress and support; and the physical condition of the home.

At the end of the investigation, CPS must assign a disposition to the case. The CPS worker must determine whether abuse or neglect occurred, whether the child is immediately at risk for abuse and/or neglect, and whether a reasonable likelihood exists that the child is at risk for abuse and/or neglect in the foreseeable future. In addition, the CPS worker also determines the need to remove the child or perpetrator from the home, the need to involve other service providers or community agencies (e.g., law enforcement, treatment providers, the courts), and the need for further agency monitoring.

In addition to its investigative function, CPS also protects children by implementing and coordinating treatment and prevention services for families. When child abuse and neglect has occurred, child protection may be implemented on either a voluntary or involuntary basis and may result in a child's remaining at home or being placed in some type of out-of-home care. A child who must be removed from the home is placed in some form of substitute living arrangement, such as foster care, kinship care, or residential treatment, until he or she can safely return home. Several factors likely influence decisions about alternate care, such as the child's age, the type of abuse experienced, and whether the child has been a victim of maltreatment in the past.

Whether or not a child is removed from the home, mandated services are implemented to address problems that threaten children's safety. Sometimes social services are offered by CPS agencies, but more often these services are contracted out to other agencies. Over the years, CPS agencies have become more focused on the investigation of abuse and the coordination of treatment, largely serving as case managers rather than service providers. Referral services generally include emergency medical services and housing, substance abuse evaluation and treatment, daycare or respite care, counseling for children and parents, parenting education and training, home visitor services, homemaker help, transportation, and self-help or volunteer programs such as Big Brothers/Big Sisters, Parents Anonymous, and Parents United.

Challenges to the Child Protective Services System

Since the inception of mandatory reporting, CPS has witnessed a staggering increase in the number of children identified as possible victims of child maltreatment. These increasing numbers, combined with funding shortages and high turnover rates among social workers, have compromised the ability of many CPS agencies to investigate all of the reports they receive and to do so in a timely fashion. In short, CPS has become overwhelmed with the scope of its charge to protect children and its capacity to respond to this complex problem.

A related challenge to the CPS system is balancing its dual roles of child protection and family preservation. In the Adoption Assistance and Child Welfare Act of 1980, child welfare policy in the United States acknowledged the sanctity of the family, and the notion that strengthening and preserving families serves the safety interests of children. CPS must balance these family preservation goals with the more immediate charge of child protection, a difficult if not impossible mandate. On the one hand, CPS investigates allegations and collects evidence of abuse, essentially serving as a policing agency. On the other hand, CPS agencies are supposed to provide sufficient support and services to preserve family units. Many question whether it is feasible to expect that CPS can be both an investigative and social service agency. Even if such lofty goals are attainable, however, one could reasonably argue that with insufficient staff and excessive caseloads, CPS has become little more than an investigative agency, all but abandoning its initial charge as a provider of social services.

Many of the system's problems can be attributed to the ways in which child welfare policy, funding, and resource allocation have evolved over the years. The growing numbers of children placed in foster care during the 1980s and early 1990s, for example, was in part due to state laws and regulations that created a process for removing abused and neglected children from their homes. Such laws and regulations said far less about how to support families or under what circumstances children should be returned to their homes. Funding guidelines have also contributed to the system's problems because they often place restrictions on service delivery. Federal funding guidelines, for instance, often influence service implementation because states receive matching dollars for some expenditures regardless of the amount spent (e.g., foster care), whereas funds for other services (e.g., treatment and prevention) are restricted to certain amounts. As public policy initiatives and resource allocation decisions evolve, reforms to improve the CPS system will also evolve. The Adoption and Safe Families Act of 1997, for example, helped to address the problems associated with thousands of children living in foster care by limiting the amount of time children spend in temporary living arrangements. Additional changes are appearing to improve child protection decision-making processes so that they more validly reflect the risks children face, with the goals of minimizing inappropriate protective interventions and maximizing efficiency.

Cindy Miller-Perrin and Robin Perrin

See also Adoption and Safe Families Act of 1997; Child Abuse Prevention and Treatment Act; Foster Care; Legal System and Child Protection; Mandatory Reporting Laws of Child Maltreatment

Further Readings

Larner, M. B., Stevenson, C. S., & Behrman, R. E. (1998). Protecting children from abuse and neglect [Special issue]. *The Future of Children, 8*(1).

Tower, C. C. (2004). *Understanding child abuse and neglect.* Boston: Allyn & Bacon.

Trotter, C. (2004). *Helping abused children and their families.* Thousand Oaks, CA: Sage.

U.S. Department of Health and Human Services, Administration on Children, Youth and Families. (2003, May 19). *Foster care and adoption statistics current reports.* Retrieved from http://www.acf.dhhs.gov/programs/cb/publications/index.htm

CHILDREN AND ADOLESCENTS WHO KILL

The terms *children* and *adolescents* refer to persons under the age of 18 years of age. Adolescence is the period of human development when puberty begins as youngsters approach adulthood, usually starting between the ages of 11 and 13. This developmental period is characterized by major physiological and physical changes in the human body and is one of emotional highs and lows. Some adolescents display abrupt and unexpected personality changes as they experiment with drugs, become increasingly independent from their families, interact more with their peers, and strive to meet social pressures of success within academic, social, and occupational settings. While many youngsters will participate in minor deviant behaviors such as underage drinking, speeding, truancy, smoking, sexual promiscuity, and less serious criminal acts, others will commit crimes such as aggravated assault, rape, arson, and even murder. When youth do commit such heinous acts, these offenses typically receive a disproportionate amount of press coverage. Of all criminal acts, homicide is the most egregious act of interpersonal violence committed within our society. A homicide is defined as the willful and purposeful killing of another human being. Thus, the topic of juvenile killers is an important issue within society.

Rates of Juvenile Homicide in the United States

The participation of youth in violent behaviors is not a new phenomenon. Rather, it is one that has had a significant historical precedent in the United States. Beginning in the 1950s and over the next 40 years, official reports of violent crime rose over 600%, with juveniles accounting for the greatest increase in these numbers. Since the mid-1970s, concerns about youth crime have brought about laws increasing the penalties for juvenile offenders who committed violent acts such as homicide. Due to public outcry for stiffer penalties, legislation has provided for a significant increase in the number of juveniles transferred into adult courts for prosecution, while simultaneously reducing judicial discretion with mandatory sentences. Beginning in the 1980s and continuing on into the mid-1990s, the United States witnessed a drastic increase in the number of both juvenile and adult violent crimes.

The record numbers of youngsters being victimized or arrested for serious violent offenses peaked in the mid-1990s and underscored the need to look at the youth violence phenomenon independently. The recognition of teen violence and aggression as a social and public health crisis, coupled with high-profile media accounts of school shootings, led the U.S. surgeon general in 2001 to call for an investigation of the issues contributing to youth violence in America. Presently, juvenile crime rates are comparable to those in the 1970s, with less than 10% of all homicides nationally committed by juveniles under the age of 18 years old.

Current Public Perceptions of Juvenile Homicide Offenders

Juvenile homicide offenders (JHOs) are perceived by much of the public to be different from youngsters in the past. They are commonly regarded as more violent, predatory, and prolific in the crimes at younger ages. Some scholars have argued that the drug war and rise of inner-city gangs have led to a new breed of juvenile killer, with minority males killing each other in record numbers in large cities throughout the United States as turf wars and retaliation murders terrorize some neighborhoods.

Dynamics Surrounding Child and Adolescent Killings

There is not a "typical" kind of juvenile homicide. Rather, when children or adolescents do kill, there are varying reasons that appear to explain the homicidal event. However, there are general observations that can be made regarding juveniles who kill. First, there tends to be a significant gender gap in young killers, with males outnumbering females in large proportions.

Some researchers have suggested that the social forces that propel boys to act aggressively do not motivate girls in the same manner. Second, it is much more common for youngsters to commit murder with peers than alone. This suggests the influence of group dynamics on youngsters' experiences of peer pressure, perceptions of their pride and stature, and efforts to impress others when in the presence of peers. Such issues rarely apply to adult homicides and are reflective of the emotional immaturity and impulsivity common during childhood and adolescence.

Third, the availability of guns has contributed to the increase in lethality when youngsters do act out violently. Critics have argued that the number of murders committed by those under the age of 18 would decrease if guns were not as readily available to them. Finally, older juveniles have a significantly greater likelihood than younger offenders of carrying out a violent attack that will result in a death. Research has shown that 16- and 17-year-olds have higher rates of homicide than any other age group of juveniles.

Parricide, or the killing of one's parents, is one particular type of juvenile homicide that is especially shocking to the public and that represents one of society's greatest taboos. Yet such killings are relatively rare phenomena, as 200 to 400 juvenile and adult children murder their parents or stepparents annually in the United States. Although juveniles receive a disproportionate amount of press when they do kill a parent, the majority of parricide offenders are adults. When a child does commit parricide, the case commonly involves years of severe emotional, sexual, and/or physical abuse from the parent who was murdered. The child kills because he or she feels that there is no way to escape or that the abuser will kill him or her. Such cases may elicit strong public support for the youngster and his or her siblings once the details of the abuse come to light. In addition, researchers have identified other types of parricide offenders who kill due to either severe mental illness or antisocial tendencies. When children do kill for money or their freedom, such as in the case of the Menendez brothers in California, the public is often fascinated and horrified, resulting in a media frenzy.

Denise Paquette Boots

See also Child Aggression as Predictor of Youth and Adult Violence; Prevention Programs, Youth Violence; Youth Violence

Further Readings

Heide, K. (1999). *Young killers: The challenge of juvenile homicide.* Thousand Oaks, CA: Sage.

U.S. Department of Health and Human Services. (2001). *Youth violence: A report of the surgeon general.* Rockville, MD: Author.

U.S. Department of Justice, Federal Bureau of Investigation. (1984–2004). *Crime in the United States.* Washington, DC: U.S. Government Printing Office.

Zimring, F. E. (1998). *American youth violence.* New York: Oxford University Press.

Children Missing Involuntarily or for Benign Reasons

Children missing involuntarily because they are lost, injured, or stranded (classified as *missing involuntary, lost, or injured,* or MILI) and those missing for benign reasons (classified as *missing benign explanation,* or MBE) constitute a substantial number of missing children who do not fall neatly into the more conventional categories. According to the most recent national incidence statistics available, children who become missing involuntarily because they are lost, injured, or stranded account for 16% of all missing children and 9% of those reported to law enforcement. Children who become missing involuntarily because they are lost, injured, or stranded are disproportionately White, male, older teenagers who disappear most frequently in wooded areas or parks and from the company of their caretakers. These cases are significant because their successful resolution often requires an immediate and well-coordinated collaborative response by law enforcement, emergency medical services, forest rangers, game wardens, and other civil authorities.

Classifying a child as missing for benign reasons is a new concept in the missing children field. Yet, children missing for benign reasons are second only to runaway and thrownaway children in the burden they place on law enforcement. Children missing for benign reasons constitute 28% of all missing children, and 43% of those reported missing. In contrast to the MILI cases where the children are either injured or at risk of harm, the benign episodes are false alarms. Common situations including unforeseeable circumstances (e.g., traffic jams), miscommunications (e.g., dad picks up the child an hour before mom planned to do so), and conflicting expectations (e.g., teenager believes she is old enough to stay out 2 hours past curfew without calling or leaving a note, and mom disagrees) can cause caretakers to become alarmed to the point of calling the police even though the child is not harmed, lost, stranded, abducted, or classified as a runaway or thrownaway child. Like the MILI children, those missing for benign reasons are disproportionately teenagers. However, most MBE children disappear from someone else's home when their caretakers are not present, or they simply fail to contact their caretakers when they are not where their caretakers expect them to be at the expected time.

Law enforcement agencies are advised to respond to every report of a missing child as if the child is in immediate danger, and this recommendation includes the dispatch of officers to the scene to make an initial decision about the type and severity of the episode. Because classifying a missing child case into a "less urgent" category will often affect the investigation, this must be done with extreme caution. Here, the challenge is to minimize the law enforcement burden by training officers how to differentiate between benign and more serious episodes accurately and efficiently, and educating the public on ways to avoid miscommunications and develop successful search strategies for resolving benign episodes without involving law enforcement. It is encouraging that the incidence of MILI and MBE episodes may have declined over the past decade, perhaps, in part, as a result of the introduction and dissemination of new communications technologies.

Heather Hammer

See also Child Abductions, Family; Child Abductions, Nonfamily; Runaway and Thrownaway Children

Further Readings

Sedlak, A. J., Finkelhor, D., & Hammer, H. (2005). *National estimates of children missing involuntarily or for benign reasons.* NISMART Bulletin. Washington, DC: U.S. Department of Justice, Office of Justice Programs, Office of Juvenile Justice and Delinquency Prevention.

Steidel, S. E. (2000). *Missing and abducted children: A law-enforcement guide to case investigation and program management.* Alexandria, VA: National Center for Missing and Exploited Children.

CHILDREN'S ADVOCACY CENTER

The term *Children's Advocacy Center* (CAC) represents a class of public and private agencies designed to serve as a hub of a coordinated community response to child maltreatment. While the model has its origins in the early efforts to create multidisciplinary child abuse investigative and/or assessment teams in communities across the nation in the 1970s and early 1980s, the specific term and core elements of the CAC model emerged from Huntsville, Alabama, in 1985. Spurred on by the explosion of child sexual abuse reports locally and across the nation in 1983, and by the resultant unexpected influx of child witnesses in the courtroom, the district attorney, Bud Cramer (later a U.S. Congressman), encouraged a broad community task force to look for a better way to handle these cases. Fanning out across the country they found examples of promising multidisciplinary investigative teams. Deciding to create a child-centered team in Huntsville, they added a key essential component of their new model, the "Children's Advocacy Center," a place that was neutral ground for all the agencies and disciplines involved and was designed specifically for the children.

Within a few years the model had spread and an increasing number of communities around the country were building a coordinated response to child abuse around their unique CAC. By 1987 many of these communities had organized into the National Network of Child Advocacy Centers (changing their name to the National Children's Alliance in 1998) and soon established membership standards. CACs now exist in the largest urban areas in the nation and in remote locations throughout rural America. Some are free-standing nonprofit organizations, like the National Children's Advocacy Center in Huntsville, Alabama, while other CACs are part of hospitals or large multi-service community nonprofit organizations and others are housed in government agencies.

By 2006 membership requirements had evolved in a 10-part set of accreditation standards. These standards require all centers to share 33 essential components, including a "child-friendly" facility that provides complete separation of victims and alleged offenders and where children can be interviewed while being observed by team members; a functioning multidisciplinary team with written agreements and protocols that provides for routine involvement in cases and regular sharing of information; regular case review meetings involving representatives from, at least, law enforcement, child protection, prosecution, mental health, medicine, and victim advocacy; a capacity to perform or secure through referral specialized medical exams; delivery of or referral to mental health services; victim advocacy services, all delivered with cultural competence and diversity; and the organizational capacity to maintain operational stability. Centers seeking accreditation must demonstrate compliance with each of these standards and other related "rated" subcomponents.

Charles Wilson

See also Health Care Response to Child Maltreatment; Legal System, Advocacy Efforts to Affect, Child Maltreatment; Police, Response to Child Maltreatment; Prosecutorial Practices, Child Maltreatment

Web Sites

National Children's Alliance: http://www.nca-online.org

Child Sexual Abuse

Child sexual abuse is the use of a child for sexual gratification by an older or more powerful person. This involves touching as well nontouching behaviors, and includes, but is not limited to, penetration of a child's vagina, mouth, or anus by penis, other body parts, or inanimate objects; simulated intercourse; genital touching; touching of other body parts such as breasts, nipples, and buttocks; exhibitionism (exposing sexual body parts, sometimes called "flashing"); voyeurism (sexualizing other people who are in states of undress or engaged in sexual activities without their knowledge, sometimes called "peeping"); deep, sexualized kissing; exposure to age-inappropriate sexual activity or material; and use of a child in pornography or prostitution.

The World Health Organization defines child sexual abuse as involvement of a child in sexual activity that he or she does not fully comprehend, is unable to give informed consent to, or is not developmentally prepared for and cannot consent to, or that violates the laws or social taboos of society. Child sexual abuse is evidenced by an activity between a child and an adult or another child who by age or development is in a relationship of responsibility, trust, or power, the activity being intended to gratify or satisfy the needs of the other person. This may include but is not limited to the inducement or coercion of a child to engage in any unlawful sexual activity; the exploitative use of a child in prostitution or other unlawful sexual practices; and the exploitative use of children in pornographic performances and materials.

While there are variations in how countries, researchers, and academic disciplines define child sexual abuse, the core definition involves the abuse of power, power differentials, the inability of children to give informed consent, and sexual gratification or stimulation of perpetrators. The term *children* generally refers to those under the age of 18.

Perpetrators

Most sexual abuse is committed by people children know, such as family members, friends of the family, neighbors, and trusted professionals including clergy, teachers, and childcare workers. People who think they can tell that someone is a sexual abuser by looking at him or her are often shocked when they learn that someone they know, respect, care about, and may love has abused children sexually.

Perpetrators can be adults, teenagers, or children, and they can be women and men, boys and girls. Although males are more likely to abuse children sexually than females, it is important not to be blinded by assumptions about who abuses children sexually.

Types of Abuse

There are several different types of child sexual abuse. Incest is sexual abuse that members of families commit. Family members may be mothers, fathers, sisters, brothers, aunts, uncles, grandparents, or cousins. Child molestation is sex abuse committed by people the children know or by strangers. Strangers can be individuals who abuse children in public places such as parks, apartment houses, or neighborhoods or they can pay adults to use children sexually as child prostitutes.

Individuals who use child pornography or who make, buy, and/or sell child pornography also participate in the sexual abuse of children. Finally, people called sex traffickers, who buy and sell children for the purpose of using them as prostitutes, also participate in the sexual abuse of children.

A widely held belief that sex with a child virgin will cure sexually transmitted diseases, including HIV/AIDS, has contributed to the numbers of children sexually abused worldwide.

Prevalence and Incidence

There is wide variation in figures for incidence and prevalence of child sexual abuse. These variations are due to inconsistencies in how child sexual abuse is defined and measured, how questions are asked, and the reliability of data collection techniques. It is clear that child sexual abuse is a major social problem that is international in scope and affects the quality of life of girls and boys, their families, and communities.

Studies at the national, state, and local levels conducted in the United States over the past 25 years have indicated a child abuse prevalence level of between 2% and 62% for girls, and 1% and 16% for boys. With regard to incidence rates, the Third National Incidence Study of Child Abuse and Neglect (NIS-3) provides the most extensive results and reports incidence rates of 6.8 per 1,000 for females and 2.3 per 1,000 for males. These figures, however, only account for incidents that are reported to police and child protection services. Most incidents of child sexual abuse are not reported. In fact, one of the major reasons for underreporting is that abused children often do not disclose to anyone the abuse they have experienced. Another national survey on victimization of children and youth reports an incidence rate of 82 per 1,000 children having experienced a sexual victimization in a given year.

Internationally, findings from different studies report a prevalence rate of 20% for females and 5% to 10% for males. The World Health Organization reports that 8% of male and 25% of female children up to the age of 18 years' experience sexual abuse of some kind. Though most of the available empirical data on child sexual abuse prevalence and incidence originates from the developed countries, information from developing nations is now gradually increasing and reports similar trends.

Studies from different countries across continents have reported prevalence rates of 16.7% for females and 10.5% for males in China, 12% for females and 4.5% for males in Australia, 16% for females and 7% for males in Denmark, 12.8% for females and 4.3% for males in Canada, 26% for females and 20% for males in Nicaragua, and 53.2% for females and 60% for males in South Africa.

Nongovernment and voluntary sector organizations have begun to report on prevalence of child sexual abuse in their respective social, cultural, and geographic contexts. Although these reports may not always be based on randomly selected participants and may not pass the test of academic scrutiny in terms of research methodologies used, they provide valuable information that is indicative of the magnitude of sexual abuse of children within their contexts. Such studies have reported a prevalence of 39% for females and 48% for males in India. Girls are reported to have a higher rate of victimization than boys. As noted earlier, these figures may underestimate the incidence and prevalence because of social taboos associated with child sexual abuse.

Effects

The traumatic impact of sexual abuse on a child is an important and well-documented area of concern. The effects can be long term, short term, or both, and can impact the child physically and/or psychologically. However, the impact of sexual abuse is not uniform, and varies widely from child to child. The available evidence through different studies conducted across the world suggests that negative effects during childhood can continue into adulthood. Some of the more common effects of child sexual abuse found in victims are posttraumatic stress disorder; mood, anxiety, and substance disorders; low self-esteem; depression; and unhappiness.

Some children develop sexual behavior issues, including sexual preoccupation and sexual behaviors beyond what is commonly thought of as age and developmentally appropriate. Child sexual abuse has also been found to be associated with sexual identity confusion, sexual dysfunction, and sexual risk-taking behavior in later life. In terms of parenting, evidence suggests an association between child sexual abuse and teenage pregnancy and parents' anxiety that their intimate behaviors with their children may be inappropriate (or perceived by others as inappropriate). Child sexual abuse is also associated with failure to develop and maintain healthy interpersonal relationships and with suicidal behavior.

Resilience of Children

Child sexual abuse hurts children. There is little question about this. On the other hand, being sexually abused affects some children more deeply than others. Available research and theory suggest that the impact of child sexual abuse on children's development and functioning varies according to two major factors. The first is the other risks and adversities children have experienced. The second is the capacities that child survivors have and that others in their lives have to help them cope with, adapt to, and overcome the effects of harsh life events, such as child sexual abuse. Children who have resources that help them overcome the effects of child sexual abuse and other adversities are said to be resilient. For children to be resilient, however, knowledgeable and empathic adults must be available to them over the long term.

Children who have many resources in their lives that help them cope with the effects of child sexual abuse will recover quite well, although there are likely to be some effects, which can vary from child to child. Children with few resources in their lives are at much greater risk to have negative outcomes resulting from being sexually abused.

Children who have many resources but also many adversities are likely to be able to cope with, adapt to, and overcome the effects of child sexual abuse, but they may require long-term interventions such as individual, group, and family therapy. Children with few resources and many other adversities are likely to have the most difficulty coming to terms with being sexually abused.

It is important to keep in mind that the impact of child sexual abuse also varies according to the severity of the abuse and the relationship of perpetrators and children. Children who have a one-time incident of sexual abuse by a stranger are likely to be less affected than children whose close family members sexually abuse them over a period of time. Of course, how children experience the abuse—what abuse means to them—is the major factor on how severe the outcomes are.

Understanding the effects of child sexual abuse requires flexible thinking on the part of parents, professionals, and survivors. We must take into consideration the resources available to children to help them cope, the other adversities they have experienced, and the severity of the abuse as they experience it.

Blaming the Victims

Social customs and ideologies often blame child victims for their own sexual abuse. Questions such as "Why didn't you tell?" "What did you do to provoke the abuse?" "How could you let it go on for so long?" are automatic for many people when a child discloses sexual abuse. Such responses direct attention away from perpetrators who are the persons responsible.

The shame and stigma associated with being sexually abused silences survivors and allows perpetrators to continue their sexually abusive behaviors. In some cultures, child victims are forced to marry perpetrators, killed, or expelled from their families and forced to live on the streets. The shame attached to being sexually victimized becomes a matter of family honor.

Only in the last 30 years has there been a large-scale outcry about child sexual abuse in some countries. This has resulted in more awareness and understanding of child sexual abuse. As a result, there now are more resources than ever before for survivors and their families and more policies and programs intended to prevent child sexual abuse. Much more, however, needs to be done.

In many developing countries, the movement against child sexual abuse is still in its beginning stages, and even the existence of child sexual abuse remains unacknowledged by the general public and professionals alike.

Child sexual abuse is a major social problem of worldwide proportions, and most survivors suffer in silence out of fear of being stigmatized and blamed for their own abuse.

Holding Perpetrators Solely Responsible

Perpetrators have sole responsibility for child sexual abuse. Typically, they are older, are stronger, and can overcome the children's resistance or take advantage of children's socialization to obey older children. Many children say, "He was big. I was little. I had to do what he said."

Perpetrators have many excuses and justifications, such as "My wife won't give me sex. I have to get it from somewhere" or "She loved me, and I loved her. This is love and not child sexual abuse." Sometimes they have no excuses at all. What they care about is their own self-centered satisfaction: "Sex with children makes me feel good." Some distance themselves from what they are doing and depersonalize the children: "I thought of the children as 'things,' as 'objects.' Certainly, they weren't children."

Almost all perpetrators are trusted and even loved members of families and communities. They are fathers, mothers, stepfathers, aunts, uncles, brothers, sisters, cousins, babysitters, social workers, physicians, teachers, youth workers, or others who come in contact with children. They look like everyman. It is not possible to look at someone and say that person is a child sexual abuser.

Resources for Children

Resources that help children cope with child sexual abuse fall into the general category of quality of attachments to others. Children who have secure attachments to others are more likely to trust that if they tell someone about being sexually abused, they will be believed, will be comforted, and will be helped to understand what happened to them. The adults who love them and care for them, however, must understand child sexual abuse and respond to children's distress in constructive ways.

Children who believe they have no one to turn to may become confused about what happened and may think they somehow are at fault. It is up to adults to create a sense of safety for children so that they believe if they tell someone about being sexually abused they will be comforted and helped to cope with the effects.

Children's recovery is greatly enhanced when perpetrators take responsibility for their behaviors, turn themselves in to law enforcement, enter treatment, make sincere apologies to child survivors and others they have harmed, and take to heart what survivors tell them about the impact of their sexually abusive behaviors.

They may have to live with the fact that those whom they have hurt want nothing more to do with them, but in some cases, with careful work with professionals, healthy reconciliation happens.

Children can and do recover from child sexual abuse. Sensitive, responsive caregivers are key to recovery, even when perpetrators do not take responsibility for their behaviors. While few risks and many resources increase the likelihood of recovery, child survivors benefit from competent professional intervention that includes work with their parents and other family members. Over time, the negative impact of the abuse can lessen, but recovery means that survivors have integrated the fact of being a survivor into their self-concepts and they are able to live full lives, pursuing their own dreams.

Jane F. Gilgun and Alankaar Sharma

See also Adult Survivors of Childhood Abuse; Clergy Sexual Abuse; Commercial Sexual Exploitation of Children; Incest; Resiliency, Protective and Risk Factors; Sex Offenders

Further Readings

Bolen, R. M. (2001). *Child sexual abuse: Its scope and our failure.* New York: Kluwer Academic/Plenum Press.

Briere, J. N., & Elliott, D. M. (1994). Immediate and long-term impacts of child sexual abuse. *The Future of Children, 4,* 54–69.

Finkelhor, D. (1994). Current information on the scope and nature of child sexual abuse. *The Future of Children* 4(2), 31–53.

Gilgun, J. F. (2005). Evidence-based practice, descriptive research, and the resilience-schema-gender-brain (RSGB) assessment. *British Journal of Social Work, 35*(6), 843–862.

Gilgun, J. F. (2006). Children and adolescents with problematic sexual behaviors: Lessons from research on resilience. In R. Longo & D. Prescott (Eds.), *Current perspectives on working with sexually aggressive youth and youth with sexual behavior problems* (pp. 383–394). Holyoke, MA: Neari Press.

Gilgun, J. F., Jones, D., & Rice, K. (2005). Emotional expressiveness as an indicator of progress in treatment. In M. C. Calder (Ed.), *Emerging approaches to work with children and young people who sexually abuse* (pp. 231–244). Dorset, UK: Russell House.

Save the Children. (2006). *Abuse among child domestic workers: A research study in West Bengal.* Calcutta, India: Save the Children Fund.

CHILD SEXUAL ABUSE ACCOMMODATION SYNDROME

The child sexual abuse accommodation syndrome (CSAAS), identified by Roland C. Summit in 1983, describes a common disclosure pattern for victims of child sexual assault (CSA). The syndrome was developed on the basis of clinical observations of victims made by Summit and other treatment professionals. According to Summit, secondary trauma results when the child's allegations of sexual abuse are met with anger and disbelief by trusted adults (e.g., parents, clinicians). Summit's aim in documenting the disclosure process was to increase understanding of CSA among treatment professionals, and to encourage validation and therapeutic intervention for victims.

The CSAAS has five components: (1) secrecy; (2) helplessness; (3) entrapment and accommodation; (4) delayed, unconvincing disclosure; and (5) retraction. The first two components are implicit vulnerabilities of children exploited by perpetrators of CSA; the latter three are chronological stages in the CSA disclosure process. Children's submissiveness allows them to be easily coerced by adults. Threats such as retaliation and dissolution of the family (particularly when a parent is the perpetrator), as well as blaming the child, are methods used to elicit secrecy and compliance, and signal to the child that what is happening is inappropriate. Contrary to popular belief, the majority of CSA is perpetrated by a trusted adult such as a parent, relative, or close family friend, which may magnify the child's feelings of helplessness. According to Summit, the psychological survival of the child depends largely on his or her ability to adjust or accommodate to the ongoing abuse. For example, children may cope with the abuse by taking responsibility for it. This coping mechanism may be a less traumatic alternative to accepting that they were abused by someone they rely on for care and protection. It may also provide the child with some feeling of control over the abuse, including an ability to end it (e.g., the child may think, "If I act differently the abuse will stop"). As a result of the child's fear and sense of helplessness, disclosure generally occurs long after the abuse and is characterized by indecisiveness and hesitation. This delayed, unconvincing disclosure can make the allegation appear fabricated, and the child may be further victimized by the disbelief and anger from adults who learn of the abuse. In response, the child's accusation may be spontaneously retracted in an effort to repair the damage caused by the disclosure, or because the child is pressured to withdraw his or her claim.

It is critical for the long-term psychological health of victims that their experiences be validated and their innocence acknowledged. However, due to the confounding pattern of disclosure, the veracity of legitimate allegations is frequently disputed. Consequently, Summit developed the CSAAS with the goal of increasing awareness among treatment professionals as to why that pattern exists. Of note, the CSAAS was developed on the basis of legitimate sexual abuse; therefore, it cannot be used as a diagnostic tool to identify victims of CSA. Furthermore, there has been a general lack of empirical study of the CSAAS, and the few existing studies have yielded equivocal results. Thus, testimony regarding the CSAAS is controversial and is often inadmissible in court. Future research on this topic is clearly warranted.

Katherine W. Follansbee and Gregory L. Stuart

See also Child Sexual Abuse; Incest; Pedophilia

Further Readings

Summit, R. C. (1983). The child sexual abuse accommodation syndrome. *Child Abuse & Neglect, 7,* 177–193.
Summit, R. C. (1992). Abuse of the child sexual abuse accommodation syndrome. *Journal of Child Sexual Abuse, 1*(4), 153–163.

CHISWICK WOMEN'S AID

Chiswick Women's Aid was one of the first refuges for women and children fleeing domestic violence to be established in the world. Thirty-five years ago, "wife battering" was seen as a private matter, a hidden and largely ignored problem. A woman and her children living with a violent and abusive man could expect no protection from the law and little help from welfare services. When Chiswick Women's Aid was set up, in England in 1972, most women living with a violent man had a stark choice: stay with him, or become homeless and see their children taken into care.

The organization had its origins, like many of the other women's aid services across the United Kingdom, in a group of women meeting in a women's center to discuss and take action on issues affecting women. As women arrived fleeing violent men, Chiswick, like women's centers elsewhere, became a refuge, and by the end of 1972, a building had been secured in Chiswick just for that purpose. The women's aid refuge movement was born.

A key figure in the development of the movement was Erin Pizzey, a charismatic figure in the Chiswick Women's Aid group with connections to the media. The publicity created by Pizzey over the next few years helped propel the issue of battered women into the spotlight. By the end of 1972, women's aid refuges were opening across the United Kingdom, in short-life houses on peppercorn rents from local councils, or in empty houses squatted by determined activists and survivors.

Chiswick Women's Aid itself took over the Palm Court Hotel in Richmond in 1975 as a massive publicity campaign to highlight the fact that refuge houses were full to overflowing with desperate women and children, not least because a key principle at that time was that women's aid refuges always had an open door. Fifty women and children squatted the hotel, led by Anne Ashby, another key figure in Chiswick Women's Aid.

By 1974, there were over 35 refuges in England alone, which then came together to form the National Women's Aid Federation, to campaign for better protection under the law, for public awareness and education, and for funding for vital services. The National Women's Aid Federation (later the Women's Aid Federation of England) became the main coordinating body and national voice for the movement. Later the underlying ethos of Chiswick Women's Aid changed and it became Chiswick Family Rescue. In the early 1980s, Erin Pizzey left the organization, and after 1983 the management changed again, reverting to a feminist analysis of domestic abuse. In 1992 Chiswick Family Rescue again changed its name to Refuge.

Nicola Harwin

See also Shelters, Battered Women's; Women's Aid Federations of the United Kingdom

Further Readings

Dobash, R. E., & Dobash, R. (1992). *Women, violence and social change.* London: Routledge.
Hague, G., & Malos, E. (2005). *Domestic violence: Action for change* (3rd ed.). Cheltenham, UK: New Clarion Press.
Pizzey, E. (1974). *Scream quietly or the neighbors will hear.* Harmondsworth, UK: Pelican.

CIVIL RESTRAINING ORDERS

See RESTRAINING AND PROTECTIVE ORDERS

CIVIL RIGHTS/DISCRIMINATION

Early leaders in the battered women's movement consciously defined battering within a larger framework of gender subordination. Domestic violence and sexual assault were linked to discrimination against women in other contexts, including discrimination and harassment in the workplace, wage inequity, gender role stereotypes, and lack of social supports and respect for mothering and childcare. More generally, leaders articulated a "civil right" to be free from violence.

As a theoretical and political-organizing framework, this civil rights perspective has been extremely important, particularly in the early reforms of the 1960s and the 1970s. As a matter of actual legal remedies, on the other hand, litigants and advocates have had limited success in defining acts of domestic violence or sexual assault, and the response (or lack thereof) of the police to such violence, as a civil rights violation.

Civil rights may be considered in four different contexts: (1) the civil rights remedy passed in 1994 as part of the Violence Against Women Act ultimately held to be unconstitutional by the Supreme Court; (2) cases seeking to challenge inadequate response by the police to domestic violence as civil rights violations; (3) state and federal statutes protecting victims of domestic and sexual violence from discrimination in housing and employment; and (4) the intersectionality of violence against women with issues of race, disability, age, immigration status, and sexual orientation, and the need to ensure that supports and services for victims appropriately respond to the differing needs of these overlapping communities.

Civil Rights Remedy in the Violence Against Women Act and *United States v. Morrison*

The Violence Against Women Act (VAWA) passed in 1994 was the first federal attempt to address comprehensively the challenges faced by victims of domestic and sexual violence. VAWA addressed the problem of domestic violence and sexual assault from many perspectives, such as increasing funding available for services to survivors, improving law enforcement response to domestic and sexual violence, mandating research on violence against women, and facilitating nationwide enforcement of protective orders. VAWA also created a new legal right—the *civil rights remedy*—that permitted an individual victim of gender-based violence to sue the perpetrator of the violence in federal court. The civil rights remedy was modeled on other civil rights legislation, such as prohibitions on discrimination on the basis of race or sex in the employment and housing contexts.

The VAWA civil rights remedy gave important new legal rights to victims by permitting them to sue a perpetrator of gender-based violence for compensation. Victims could bring a case in civil court; they were not dependent on a criminal justice system that had often proved unresponsive to domestic violence and sexual assault. Since the injury was framed in a discrimination context, plaintiffs could present circumstantial evidence of discrimination (such as gender-based epithets or gender-based bias) to support their claim. This kind of evidence would likely have been ruled irrelevant in traditional personal injury claims. Additionally, the VAWA civil rights remedy was available even in states that still had prohibitions on marital rape prosecutions or on personal injury claims between spouses.

The civil rights remedy also had immense symbolic importance. It reframed gender-based violence as a public concern, implicating fundamental civil rights that the government had a duty to protect, rather than a private family matter into which government intrusion was inappropriate. It recognized that gender-based violence, like segregated schools, poll taxes, and employment discrimination, limited the ability of individuals to participate fully in the political process and our democracy. The civil rights remedy consciously fit into a tradition of civil rights laws that had been used to transform society's understanding of systemic deprivations of individual rights.

When passed, the civil rights remedy was hailed as a significant advance of women's rights. But defendants who were sued under VAWA soon challenged the civil rights remedy, claiming that Congress lacked authority to pass the legislation. The Supreme Court considered the constitutionality of the civil rights remedy in *United States v. Morrison.* In a 5–4 decision, the Court held that it was unconstitutional. The decision did not challenge the assertion that violence against women was a significant problem, but it held that it was a "local" problem that should be addressed by the states and local governments. California, Illinois, New York City, and Westchester County, New York, have since passed civil rights remedies modeled on the VAWA provisions.

Challenges to Inadequate Police Response to Domestic Violence

Victims of domestic violence have sought to frame inadequate police enforcement of protective orders or response to domestic violence complaints as civil rights violations. Recent decisions have made it difficult to win such claims.

Victims have argued that the police violate constitutional equal protection guarantees by treating domestic violence crimes differently from other crimes. To succeed in an equal protection claim, victims must establish that the police had a general policy or custom of providing less protection to victims of domestic violence than to victims of other comparable crimes. Most courts require evidence of statistical difference in addition to the plaintiff's own experience. This kind of evidence can be difficult to obtain. Generally, a plaintiff also must present evidence that the police actually *intended* to discriminate. This can be very difficult to prove.

Victims have also argued that police inaction violates their right to "due process" under the law. However, in 1989, in *DeShaney v. Winnebago County Department of Social Services,* the Supreme Court ruled that the government does not have a general duty to protect citizens. Rather, to make out a claim, a victim must show that the police actually took actions that increased the danger to her. And in 2005, in *Castle Rock v. Gonzales,* the Supreme Court ruled that victims cannot sue the police for failing to enforce a protective order, even if the police failed to comply with a mandatory arrest law. After these holdings, advocates suggested a need to reform mandatory arrest laws, expand tort liability for such situations, and increase police training initiatives to better address victims' needs.

Civil Rights Statutes Protecting Victims' Rights in Employment and Housing

Victims of domestic violence or sexual assault often face discrimination in employment and housing. Advocates have sought to challenge discriminatory firing and evictions using federal and state civil rights laws that make it illegal to discriminate on the basis of sex, typically arguing that the laws should apply because the vast majority of victims are women or because the tendency to punish the victim of such crimes often comes from gender-based stereotypes. There have been some significant successes, mostly in the housing context.

Additionally, federal, state, and local legislatures have passed laws that explicitly protect victims of domestic violence (and in some cases sexual assault and stalking) from employment and housing discrimination. The 2005 reauthorization of VAWA includes specific protections making clear that it is illegal to discriminate against individuals living in public housing, using federally funded vouchers ("Section 8 vouchers"), or living in certain subsidized housing ("project-based Section 8") because they are victims of domestic violence, dating violence, or stalking, or to evict them because of the criminal acts against them. Additionally, civil rights laws in a rapidly growing number of states and localities specifically protect victims from housing discrimination (e.g., Washington, Rhode Island, and North Carolina) or employment discrimination (e.g., Illinois, New York City). Other jurisdictions have narrower protections that make it illegal, for example, to evict a victim because she called the police or to fire a victim because she took time off to obtain a protective order. These laws help promote the economic security and independence of victims.

Intersectionality of Violence Against Women and Other Civil Rights Issues

Domestic violence and sexual assault are primarily crimes against women, and the women's movement has been active in defining such violence as part of a larger pattern of gender subordination. For individual women, however, the violence they experience may be shaped by other dimensions of their identity, such as race, class, sexual orientation, immigration status, age, or disability. In an influential article, Kimberle Crenshaw raised awareness of the necessity of considering these overlapping identities, a concept that she called *intersectionality,* by showing how traditional feminist and traditional antiracism discourses tended to marginalize the particular experiences of women of color.

Crenshaw's article sparked a growing focus on ensuring that the antiviolence movement is responsive to these overlapping identities. For example, the battered women's movement has traditionally sought to utilize the criminal justice system as a primary means of addressing domestic violence. Many victims, however, may be reluctant to seek refuge from the criminal justice system. Women of color might perceive it as a tool of racist oppression; undocumented persons might perceive it as jeopardizing their ability to remain in the country. Thus, programs and policies seeking to serve battered women must be sensitive to these concerns. The most recent reauthorization of

VAWA requires that grantees providing victim services collaborate with representatives of racial, ethnic, and other underserved communities and that culturally specific community-based organizations are eligible to receive funding for providing victim services.

Deborah Widiss

See also Feminist Theories of Interpersonal Violence; Intersectionality; Legal System, Civil Court Remedies for Intimate Partner Violence; Sex Discrimination; Violence Against Women Act

Further Readings

Crenshaw, K. (1991). Mapping the margins: Intersectionality, identity politics, and violence against women of color. *Stanford Law Review, 43,* 1241–1299.
Goldscheid, J. (2005). The civil rights remedy of the 1994 Violence Against Women Act: Struck down but not ruled out. *Family Law Quarterly, 39,* 157–180.
Legal Momentum. (2006). *Employment and housing rights for victims of domestic violence.* Retrieved from http://www.legalmomentum.org/ehrvdv
Martin, E. J., & Bettinger-Lopez, C. (2005, October–November). *Castle Rock v. Gonzales* and the future of police protection for victims of domestic violence. *Domestic Violence Report,* 11–15.
Schneider, E. M. (2000). *Battered women and feminist lawmaking.* New Haven, CT: Yale University Press.

CLERGY SEXUAL ABUSE

Clergy function as religious leaders in a wide variety of religious traditions. In order for them to be effective leaders and counselors, they must be trustworthy. Specifically this means they must not take advantage of the vulnerabilities of those they serve by crossing sexual and emotional boundaries. If they do betray this trust, they do damage to individuals, congregations, and their entire faith community. Although this is not a new phenomenon (the historical record is extensive), it has only begun to surface in public awareness since the mid-1980s. Sexual abuse by clergy is a major crisis for both individuals and institutions.

It is a violation of professional ethics for any person in a pastoral role of leadership or pastoral counseling (clergy or lay) to engage in sexual contact or sexualized behavior with a congregant, client, employee, student, or other person (adult, teen, or child) while within the professional (pastoral or supervisory) relationship. It is wrong because sexual activity *in this context* is exploitative and abusive.

In the mid-1980s in the United States, persons who had been victimized by their clergy began to disclose their experiences, which resulted in panic and disbelief at every level of religious institutions. Every tradition was and continues to be confronted with the fact of abusive leaders who take advantage of the vulnerability of their followers, whether these followers are children, teens, or adults. Often in response to civil litigation, slowly denominations, movements, and organizations with responsibility for oversight of clergy began to respond. Every religious institution continues to struggle to find effective means to prevent sexual abuse by its clergy and to screen, supervise, and if necessary, suspend abusive religious leaders.

Although ministerial violations of boundaries involving sexualization of a relationship can take place in the staff supervisory or mentor relationship, instances of pastoral misconduct are most likely to occur in the ministerial relationship or the counseling relationship. When an individual congregant seeks guidance, instruction, or counsel from a clergyperson or spiritual leader and the minister sexualizes this relationship, it is similar to the violation of the therapeutic relationship by a therapist or the violation of a teaching relationship by the teacher. When a child or teenager is the object of the sexual contact or sexualization, the situation is one of pedophilia or child sexual abuse, which is by definition not only unethical and abusive but criminal.

When clergy and pastoral counselors cross sexual boundaries with congregants or clients, the pastoral relationship and the trust necessary to that relationship are lost. Congregants and clients seek the help of a clergyperson assuming that they will be safe to address their concerns. Consequently, they make themselves vulnerable, but also they become an easy target for a clergyperson who has no respect for boundaries or the well-being of the congregant or client.

Sexual boundary crossings that constitute sexual contact or sexualization of a pastoral relationship include but are not limited to sexual comments or suggestions (jokes, innuendoes, invitations, etc.), touching, fondling, seduction, kissing, intercourse, molestation, and rape. There may be only one incident or a series of incidents or an ongoing intimate relationship over time. Neither the nature of the boundary crossing nor

the duration necessarily determines the negative impact or damage to the congregant. What may appear to an outsider to be a "minor" incident may have major consequences for the recipient and should not be minimized.

Sexual boundary crossing by clergy in pastoral relationships is an instance of unethical professional behavior that is often minimized or ignored. It is not "just an affair," although it may involve an ongoing sexual relationship with a client or congregant. It is not merely adultery, although adultery may be a consequence if the clergyperson or congregant or client is in a marital relationship. It is not just an instance of bad judgment by the minister or counselor. It is often a recurring pattern of misuse of the pastoral role by clergy who seem to neither comprehend nor care about the damaging effects their behavior may have on the congregant or client.

Although in reported cases most clergy offenders are adult heterosexual males and most victims are adult heterosexual females, it is clear that neither gender nor sexual orientation excludes anyone from the risk of offending (clergy) or from the possibility of being taken advantage of (congregants or clients) in the pastoral relationship.

Sexual abuse by clergy violates professional ethics in the following ways:

It is a violation of role. The expectations of the pastoral role include making available certain resources, talents, knowledge, and expertise to serve the best interests of the congregant. Sexual contact or sexualization of the pastoral relationship is not included in the clergyperson's role.

It is a misuse of authority and power. Inherent in the pastoral role is a degree of authority and power with which the clergyperson provides leadership to a congregation. This power is intended to be used to benefit individuals and congregations. But it can easily be misused, as is the case when a minister or counselor (intentionally or unintentionally) uses his or her authority to initiate or pursue sexual contact with a congregant. Even if the congregant sexualizes the relationship, it is still the clergyperson's responsibility to maintain the boundaries of the pastoral relationship in the best interests of the congregant.

It is taking advantage of vulnerability. The congregant is by definition vulnerable to the clergyperson; he or she has fewer resources and less power than the clergyperson in the pastoral relationship. If the clergyperson takes advantage of this vulnerability to gain sexual access to the congregant, then he or she violates the mandate to protect the vulnerable from harm. (For Jews and Christians, the protection of the vulnerable is an expectation that derives from the Jewish and Christian traditions of a hospitality code.)

It is an absence of meaningful consent. Meaningful consent to sexual activity requires a context of choice and equality; meaningful consent requires the absence of fear or the most subtle coercion. There is always an imbalance of power and thus inequality between the clergyperson and those whom he or she serves in a pastoral relationship. Even if the clergyperson and congregant see themselves as "consenting adults," the difference in role precludes the possibility of meaningful consent.

The violation of pastoral boundaries when a religious leader sexualizes a pastoral relationship is a common problem in all religious traditions (Buddhist, Christian, Jewish, Native American, Muslim, etc.). The unethical and exploitative misconduct of a few undercuts the integrity of all as it destroys the trust necessary for a healthy and meaningful pastoral relationship. The impact on laypeople who are members of these various traditions is usually painful and can be long term. It is the responsibility of the church, synagogue, or other religious organization or group to protect its members and provide a safe place for religious practice.

Marie M. Fortune

Author's Note: This entry is adapted from "Sexual Abuse and Exploitation by Clergy and Spiritual Leaders," by M. M. Fortune, 2004, in M. D. Smith (Ed.), *The Encyclopedia of Rape*, Westport, CT: Greenwood.

See also Child Sexual Abuse; Pedophilia; Sexual Abuse

Further Readings

Fortune, M. M. (1988). *Is nothing sacred? The story of a pastor, the women he sexually abused, and the congregation he nearly destroyed.* Cleveland, OH: Pilgrim Press.

Fortune, M. M. (2005). *Sexual violence: The sin revisited.* Cleveland, OH: Pilgrim Press.

CLOTHESLINE PROJECT

The Clothesline Project is a public display of shirts created by survivors of intimate partner violence, where each shirt is decorated to tell the story of the woman's experience. Displays of the Clothesline Project are generally held to provide public education on violence against women and to create a public forum for survivors of intimate partner violence to share their experiences through creating a shirt, in a healing and supportive space.

The Clothesline Project was started by a coalition of women on Cape Cod in Massachusetts. These women were looking for a way to visually represent the statistics of violence against women and turn them into a vehicle for public education. Rachel Carey-Harper is credited with the concept of using shirts on a clothesline as the way to depict the violence women have endured. The concept was chosen because hanging laundry on a clothesline was always perceived as women's work and hanging up clothes has traditionally been a way neighborhood women exchanged information. The first Clothesline Project consisted of 31 shirts displayed in October 1990 as part of a "Take Back the Night" Rally in Hyannis, Massachusetts. Due to the success of this initial project in educating the public, the Clothesline Project has been replicated by communities throughout the United States and Canada and in some countries in Europe and Africa.

The purpose of the Clothesline Project is twofold: (1) to represent violence against women visually in a way that can be used as a tool in educating individuals and communities about this violence, and (2) to give survivors of violence a way to speak out about the violence they have endured in a way that is supportive and healing.

Generally, a Clothesline Project is produced by asking survivors of intimate partner violence, or loved ones of a woman who has been killed, to express their feelings about their abuse by decorating a shirt. Some Clothesline Projects color code the shirts to represent the various forms of violence against women. These decorated shirts are then hung on a clothesline in public spaces for others to view, often as a part of other violence against women awareness and public education activities.

Jennifer L. Witt

See also Prevention Programs, Community Mobilization; Public Education

Further Readings

The Clothesline Project. (n.d.). *History of the clothesline project*. Retrieved February 19, 2007, from http://www.clotheslineproject.org/History.html

Gregory, J., Lewton, A., Schmidt, S., & Smith, D. (2002). Body politics with feeling: The power of the Clothesline Project. *New Political Science, 24*(3), 433–448.

COERCED SEXUAL INITIATION

Coerced sexual initiation is generally defined as the use of persistent coercive strategies (i.e., psychological and emotional manipulation, verbal persuasion, or physical tactics) to initiate sexual contact. Only the tactics and strategies used to initiate sexual contact are specified in this definition, as it does not apply to a sexually coercive experience in its entirety. However, definitions of sexual coercion vary considerably in the existing literature, contributing to the difficulty inherent in defining coerced sexual initiation. For example, in some studies, sexual coercion is defined broadly and includes the use of alcohol or drugs to decrease the victim's inhibitions to obtain sexual contact. In other studies, the use of physical force to coerce sexual contact is included in the definition of sexual coercion. Conversely, some studies focusing on sexually coercive behavior narrow the definition by excluding the use of physical *force* to obtain sexual contact, but still include physical tactics such as continual attempts to sexually arouse the victim and removal of clothing. Although coerced sexual initiation can lead to rape, the less severe tactics (e.g., verbal persuasion) are not currently included in the legal definition of rape. As defined by the Department of Justice, rape is the use of physical force or threats of physical force to obtain sexual intercourse *without the consent* of the victim, though specific definitions vary among state statutes. Sexual coercion differs from rape in that victims are coerced into consenting to sexual contact when they may not have initially agreed. It should be noted that consensual sexual experiences include many of the behaviors that are also considered coercive, such as removal of clothing, continued kissing, and genital touching, thus highlighting the crucial importance of the context in which these behaviors occur.

Verbal sexual coercion can be negative or positive and typically is used persistently until the desired outcome is achieved or the victim leaves the situation. Negative verbal sexual coercion can take the form of threats to terminate the relationship, threats to obtain sex from someone else, swearing, or attempts to gain sympathy from the victim. Forms of positive verbal persuasion include using compliments (e.g., "I love you so much," "You are so sexy") or promises of a committed relationship to elicit sexual contact. Repeated requests, nagging, and pleas for sex are considered to be neutral verbal persuasion and are most common in established relationships. Emotional persuasion such as threats to end the relationship, or eliciting feelings of guilt in a partner, are more common in romantically established relationships in which the victim may feel sexually obligated to the perpetrator than in relationships between acquaintances or friends.

Physical coercion is the use of sexual contact in an attempt to arouse the victim (e.g., continued kissing, touching, or removal of clothing) and change the victim's mind about furthering the sexual encounter. This tactic is more often employed in coercive experiences between acquaintances or friends than in committed relationships. In some cases, physically aggressive behaviors such as holding the victim down, threats of physical harm, or blocking the victim's ability to leave are included in the definition of physically coercive tactics.

Research shows that alcohol and drugs may facilitate coerced sexual initiation by decreasing sexual inhibition and impairing the judgment of the victim. Perpetrators may encourage intoxication in a deliberate attempt to coerce sexual contact or may take advantage of someone who is already intoxicated and thus has a diminished capacity to resist the coercion. Furthermore, alcohol and drugs may contribute to coerced sexual initiation by decreasing the perpetrator's ability to pick up on the victim's cues communicating that he or she should stop.

The most frequently reported tactics of coerced sexual initiation are physical arousal and verbal persuasion, though in many cases a combination of tactics is used to coerce sexual contact. In general, men report using tactics of coerced sexual initiation more often than women do. According to female victims' reports, men are more likely to use physical force, while women typically report using less "exploitative" tactics such as sexual arousal and verbal persuasion to coerce sexual contact. The literature generally suggests that women are more likely than men to be victims of sexually coercive tactics. However, at present, gender differences in coercive initiation of sex are difficult to assess, as there is a relative lack of research focusing on female perpetration and male victimization. Interestingly, it has been shown that women's use of aggression and coercion in sexual experiences is not perceived in the same negative way as men's use of the same tactics. It is possible that female perpetrators and male victims are less attuned to recognizing coercive tactics when they are used and/or that the consequences of women's use of these tactics are less severe.

Research indicates that reasons for compliance with coerced sexual initiation can be extrinsic, such as wanting the perpetrator to stop requesting sexual contact, avoiding the potential for further aggression, or preserving the relationship. Acquiescence can also be due to intrinsic motivations such as a sense of obligation to the perpetrator, feelings of guilt, low self-esteem, or permissive attitudes regarding sex. Extrinsic motivations for compliance to coercion are more commonly reported than intrinsic motivations.

While coerced sexual initiation is generally not considered as serious as rape, both men and women report negative outcomes resulting from victimization, including increased tension in or termination of a romantic relationship or friendship with the perpetrator, psychological distress, and guilt associated with blaming oneself for what happened. Moreover, the high rates of depression, trauma symptoms, shame, and anger associated with sexual assault victimization in general may also be consequences of coerced sexual initiation.

Meggan M. Bucossi and Gregory L. Stuart

See also Date and Acquaintance Rape; Intimate Partner Violence; Legislation, Rape/Sexual Assault; Marital Rape/Wife Rape; Rape/Sexual Assault; Sexual Abuse; Sexual Coercion

Further Readings

Abbey, A., BeShears, R., Clinton-Sherrod, A., & McAuslan, P. (2004). Similarities and differences in women's sexual assault experiences based on tactics used by the perpetrator. *Psychology of Women Quarterly, 28,* 323–332.

Anderson, P., & Sorensen, W. (1999). Male and female differences in reports of women's heterosexual initiation and aggression. *Archives of Sexual Behavior, 28,* 243–253.

DeGue, S., & DiLillo, D. (2005). "You would if you loved me": Toward an improved conceptual and etiological understanding of nonphysical male sexual coercion. *Aggression and Violent Behavior, 10,* 513–532.

Livingston, J., Buddie, A., Testa, M., & VanZile-Tamsen, C. (2004). The role of sexual precedence in verbal sexual coercion. *Psychology of Women Quarterly, 28,* 287–297.

Oswald, D., & Russell, B. (2006). Perceptions of sexual coercion in heterosexual dating relationships: The role of aggressor gender and tactics. *Journal of Sex Research, 43,* 87–95.

Struckman-Johnson, C., Struckman-Johnson, D., & Anderson, P. (2003). Tactics of sexual coercion: When men and women won't take no for an answer. *Journal of Sex Research, 40,* 76–86.

Tyler, K., Hoyt, D., & Whitbeck, L. (1998). Coercive sexual strategies. *Violence and Victims, 13,* 47–61.

COERCIVE CONTROL

Coercive control involves the use of abusive behaviors to gain and maintain power and control over an intimate partner. These tactics are used frequently in daily interactions in an attempt to control the behaviors of the partner. Physical and sexual violence, or the potential for it, are typically used only occasionally to reinforce and add power to the emotional abuse. This is achieved by instilling fear in the survivor of the abuse and escalating the abuse when the emotional tactics are not achieving the desired goals.

The concept of coercive control was initially introduced by the Duluth Domestic Abuse Intervention Project in the form of the *power and control wheel.* This model identifies eight categories of emotional and psychological behaviors, including (1) intimidation, including threatening looks and gestures; (2) emotional abuse, such as criticism and humiliation; (3) isolation, which involves limiting contact with others; (4) minimizing or denying the abuse or blaming the survivor for the perpetrator's abusive behavior; (5) using the children, including threatening to take or hurt children or involving them in the abuse; (6) using social privilege, such as patriarchy, racism, homophobia, or other forms of oppression; (7) coercion and threats; and (8) economic abuse, involving controlling or limiting access to resources.

Although physical violence is more overt and obviously objectionable, some research indicates that intimate partner violence survivors report that the behaviors involved in coercive control are more emotionally harmful than physical violence. These sometimes subtle behaviors are more difficult to detect and prove, and may appear to be more forgivable to those who do not understand the dynamics and motivations of coercive control.

Although legal definitions of intimate partner violence focus almost exclusively on physical forms of violence, most definitions make the distinction that intimate partner violence involves more than a one-time incident of violence. Coercive control is central to the definition of intimate partner violence.

This concept has also been used in the development of Johnson's and others' typologies of violence, which are useful in determining appropriate intervention. For example, intimate terrorism is defined as a relationship in which one partner is the primary aggressor and is both violent and controlling. Some research has indicated that in heterosexual relationships, the male is most often the primary aggressor. Other forms of violent relationships include mutual violent control, in which both partners are physically violent and use coercive control; common couple violence, in which both partners use violence but not coercive control; and violent resistance, in which physical violence is perpetrated by the partner who has historically been the victim. This violence is perpetrated in response to the violence and controlling behavior of the primary aggressor.

Poco Kernsmith

See also Duluth Model; Intimate Partner Violence; Intimate Terrorism; Power and Control Wheel

Further Readings

Johnson, M. P. (2001). Conflict and control: Symmetry and asymmetry in intimate partner violence. In A. Booth & A. C. Crouter (Eds.), *Couples in conflict* (pp. 95–104). Mahwah, NJ: Lawrence Erlbaum.

Osthoff, S. (2002). But Gertrude, I beg to differ, a hit is not a hit is not a hit. *Violence Against Women, 8,* 1521–1544.

Pence, E., & Paymar, M. (1983). *Education groups for men who batter: The Duluth model.* New York: Springer.

Collaborative Divorce, Benefits to Children

There has long been concern about the detrimental impact of divorce on children. Although the research is inconsistent, there is evidence that children whose parents divorce may exhibit a wide range of poor adjustment outcomes compared to children whose families stay intact. The variability in research findings may largely be accounted for by the role of conflict. That is, it may not be *divorce* that is bad for children, but conflict between parents, which is associated with poorer outcomes for children across all developmental stages, regardless of whether or not parents separate.

What Is Collaborative Divorce?

In recognition of the negative impact of interparental conflict, the collaborative divorce movement arose in Minneapolis in 1991 to encourage a new type of divorce process. Collaborative divorce (also known as collaborative family law) is a philosophy that emphasizes win–win solutions. It is associated with particular alternative dispute resolution strategies such as mediation, four-way settlement conferences (involving both parties and their lawyers), and parental education. Collaborative divorce may infer a preference for shared parenting plans, although it is not synonymous with joint custody. Finally, collaborative family law approaches dictate a nontraditional role for family lawyers. In this context, lawyers coach their clients in communication and negotiation, and may help contain some of the adversity and hostility by helping clients focus on the best interests of the children. In some jurisdictions, family law practitioners sign agreements to confirm their commitment to collaborative practices and to avoid litigation at all costs. Indeed, a disqualification clause stipulates that the counsel could not represent their clients should matters progress to litigation. A related approach known as cooperative law includes emphasis on the same alternative dispute resolution strategies, but without the signed agreement to avoid litigation.

Benefits of Collaborative Divorce

There is no doubt that when collaborative divorce works the way it was intended, children benefit greatly. Their adjustment tends to be better across a wide range of psychosocial and academic outcomes, and they maintain better relationships with both parents. These benefits are likely conferred in a number of ways. When parents are able to maintain a degree of civility and protect their children from overt hostility, children are prevented from the anxiety-provoking scenes that are characteristic of high-conflict divorce. Furthermore, they are able to benefit from the involvement of both parents in their lives without feeling torn by loyalty conflicts. In addition, collaborative divorce approaches tend to exact less of a toll (both emotionally and financially) on parents than a more adversarial process, thus leaving them with more resources to direct toward the well-being of their children.

Cautions About Collaborative Divorce

It recent years, clinicians and researchers have raised concerns about the overuse of collaborative divorce. Clearly, the collaboration, trust, and communication required between the divorcing parties for the approach to be successful cannot be attained by all parents. Of particular concern are high-conflict families and/or families who have experienced violence. In high-conflict cases, the trust and communication required for collaborative solutions are notably absent, and mental health and personality issues may preclude cooperation, in which case ongoing attempts at mediation and conferencing may simply prolong the conflict. In these cases the goal may be management of the conflict rather than resolution per se. In family violence cases, power and control may continue to be exerted by a perpetrator of violence during attempts at collaborative solutions. In addition, victims of violence may feel coerced into accepting arrangements that compromise their safety in an attempt to appear collaborative and cooperative. Thus, while collaborative divorce may be the best process for most families, there is a critical need for differentiated pathways for higher-needs families.

Claire V. Crooks

See also Divorce and Intimate Partner Violence

Further Readings

Emery, R. E. (1999). *Marriage, divorce, and children's adjustment.* Thousand Oaks, CA: Sage.

Johnston, J. R. (1999). High-conflict divorce. *The Future of Children, 4,* 165–182.

Lande, J., & Herman, G. (2004). Fitting the forum to the family fuss: Choosing mediation, collaborative law, or cooperative law for negotiating divorce cases. *Family Court Review, 42*(2), 280–291.

Wallerstein, J. S., Lewis, J. M., & Blakeslee, S. (2000). *The unexpected legacy of divorce: A twenty-five-year landmark study.* New York: Hyperion.

COLLECTIVE EFFICACY

Coined by Robert Sampson, Stephen Raudenbush, and Felton Earls, *collective efficacy* refers to mutual trust among neighbors combined with a willingness to act on behalf of the common good, specifically to supervise children and maintain public order. In communities where collective efficacy is high, neighbors interact with one another, residents can count on their neighbors for various types of social support such as childcare, people intervene to prevent teenagers from engaging in delinquent acts, and neighborhood leaders struggle to obtain funding from governments and local businesses to help improve neighborhood conditions.

Inspired in large part by a deep-rooted commitment to developing a rich sociological understanding of the impact of community characteristics on crime, especially acts of interpersonal violence in impoverished inner-city communities, these social scientists have conducted pathbreaking studies showing that collective efficacy mediates the effects of neighborhood poverty on violations of legal and social norms.

Research in the late 1990s showed that in Chicago neighborhoods where concentrated poverty was high, collective efficacy was low, which is why, it was hypothesized, these neighborhoods had higher rates of crime. The data showed that collective efficacy—not race or poverty—was the greatest single predictor of violent crime. However, collective efficacy does not completely mediate the relationship between a community's structural characteristics and crime. For example, research has controlled for collective efficacy and still shown that concentrated disadvantage exerts independent effects on violent crime. Therefore, although it is necessary to develop community-based, informal crime prevention strategies, such approaches should not be viewed as substitutes for economic strategies and public spending. To nourish a community, and to develop one that is rich in collective efficacy, jobs and effective social programs are necessary.

Several key issues should be addressed in future theoretical work on collective efficacy. For example, it can take different shapes and forms, and definitions of the "common good" of a neighborhood may vary among residents in different contexts or situations. If social cohesion and trust are considered, for instance, many poor urban public housing residents may feel that the police are oppressive and are more likely to target them and their neighbors for wrongdoing than those in more affluent areas. So, in addition to counting on their neighbors to help them care for their children, they may be able to rely on them to hide from the police if they are being investigated for criminal activity.

Similarly, an exploratory qualitative study of separation/divorce sexual assault in rural Ohio revealed that what is perceived as the common good may actually be behaviors and discourses that threaten the health and well-being of women seeking freedom from abusive male partners. For example, if one considers social cohesion, many of the women interviewed (67%, $n = 29$) for this study reported a variety of ways in which their ex-partners' male peers (some of whom were police officers) perpetuated and legitimated sexual assault. Moreover, in rural sections of Ohio and other states, such as Kentucky, research has shown that there is widespread acceptance of woman abuse and community norms prohibiting victims from publicly talking about their experiences and from seeking social support.

Another issue is that many poor neighborhood residents, like a sizable portion of middle- and upper-class people, are reluctant to deal with crime and disorder themselves. This does not mean, however, that they are unwilling to act on behalf of the common good or that they are unwilling to contribute to making their communities safer. Rather, many people prefer formal means of social control and will call the police if they directly observe or suspect crime in their community. Thus, future research on collective efficacy should ask survey respondents questions about the likelihood of their neighbors seeking the assistance of the police or other authorities.

Measures of social cohesion and trust need to be elaborated to address other important issues such as the following:

- The type of people in the neighborhood who can be trusted
- The people to whom respondents are most closely tied
- The reasons why people in a neighborhood do not get along
- The specific types of values that are shared or not shared by people in the neighborhood

Less than a handful of studies have applied collective efficacy theory to woman abuse in intimate, heterosexual relationships. Moreover, almost all studies of collective efficacy and crime use quantitative techniques, such as analyses of census data. However, many rural social problems are not easy to study using such methods, which is perhaps one of the key reasons why so few researchers focus on crime in these settings.

Despite these concerns, theoretical and empirical work on collective efficacy has had a major influence on criminology and will continue to do so in the future. Further, research has shown that informal methods of social control are highly effective means of making communities safer.

Walter S. DeKeseredy

See also Community Violence; Poverty

Further Readings

DeKeseredy, W. S., Schwartz, M. D., Alvi, S., & Tomaszewski, E. A. (2003). Perceived collective efficacy and women's victimization in public housing. *Criminal Justice: The International Journal of Policy and Practice, 3,* 5–28.

Sampson, R. J., Raudenbush, S. W., & Earls, F. (1997). Neighborhoods and violent crime: A multilevel study of collective efficacy. *Science, 277,* 918–924.

Sampson, R. J., Raudenbush, S. W., & Earls, F. (1998). *Neighborhood collective efficacy: Does it help reduce violence?* Washington, DC: U.S. Department of Justice.

St. Jean, P. K. B. (1998). *Elaborating collective efficacy as it relates to neighborhood safety.* Unpublished manuscript, Department of Sociology, University of Chicago.

COMMERCIAL SEXUAL EXPLOITATION OF CHILDREN

An estimated 2 million children are said to be involved in the multibillion dollar global sex trade. Child sexual exploitation worldwide consists of two activities: participation of children in the sex trade industry and child pornography. Both involve violence and harm to children, in addition to other hazards, including early pregnancy and risk of sexually transmitted diseases, primarily AIDS.

Surveys of adult women in prostitution in North America demonstrate that the majority of women became regularly involved in the sex trade industry as teens. For this reason, the entire sex trade industry can be said to be based on child sexual exploitation.

Children in Prostitution

In developed countries, teens enter the sex trade industry, which depends on young girls free of AIDS infection, in various ways. Forced to leave home early, some sell sex to earn money for survival. The overwhelming majority of girls in prostitution state they were sexually molested as children and, as a result, they may have come to view their bodies as valuable commodities. Pimps and procurers have a way of targeting these needy girls. After providing material support, they will coerce them to earn money in the sex trade in exchange. Frequently, the pimp or manager keeps the girls in the industry against their will through violence and threats of violence. All too often, alcohol and drug addiction results from attempts to ameliorate their pain through disassociation. And the girls are certainly subject to violence from some of their customers.

In underdeveloped countries, it is not uncommon for poor families to sell their girls to managers in the sex trade, and some youth have been raised to see the industry as a viable means of earning money for their families. Escape from brothel owners, who employ violence to control the teens, is difficult. However, research has documented that this practice also occurs in poor communities in North America, where some families view their young girls as money-making commodities.

Estimates of the number of youth involved in prostitution are only guesses; one report estimates that there are 300,000 girls involved in the United States alone. Experts have found that 60% to 70% of all homeless youth in the United States regularly sell sex to meet their survival needs.

Sex Tourism

Although most exploitation of children takes place after they are integrated into the adult sex trade, there are locales worldwide that have developed as destinations for those seeking sexual experiences with children. The customers are not only pedophiles, who are said to organize tours abroad for this purpose, but also other adults who may believe that the sexual use of children in a particular country's culture is acceptable, that the youth have freely chosen prostitution, or are more sexually experienced at earlier ages; they may excuse their behavior as benevolent since the youth so clearly need the money. Thailand, Sri Lanka, the Philippines, Cambodia, and India are believed to be among the main centers of child sex tourism. Most of the countries with child sex tourism have passed laws making the trade illegal, but without enforcement these laws have not had an impact. In addition, collusion of police, hotels, and travel agencies with traffickers makes this practice difficult to root out.

Trafficking of Children

Given the large market for children in the sex trade, many young people will unfortunately be trafficked into prostitution. Sometimes children are abducted, but more typically traffickers promise young women they will have work in the other country as waitresses or domestic servants, when they are in fact being sold to brothels in their own country or in other countries where they will be held by force. The United Nations believes the number of children trafficked annually is 1.2 million. Trafficking can involve individual recruiters, but international trafficking is said to be highly organized, often involving sophisticated criminal gangs who forge passports and arrange for travel. Despite the passage of laws criminalizing and punishing trafficking, finding and prosecuting the perpetrators of these practices have proven difficult.

Until recently, girls in prostitution in developed countries were viewed as delinquents. However, documentation of the practice of trafficking of children has modified views, and many jurisdictions have passed new laws making clear that there are no "child prostitutes," but rather victims of sexual exploitation. New laws seriously criminalizing both the arranging and engaging in sex with minors signal a new interest in eliminating this kind of sexual exploitation; however, the girls' use of fake IDs makes prosecution difficult.

Child Pornography

Distribution of images of minor children engaged in sexually explicit conduct is another aspect of sexual exploitation of children. Because there is thought to be a direct linkage between the pictures and child molestation, possession of such images is always a crime.

The only way to produce child pornography is to molest a child. Experts believe that child pornography exists primarily for the consumption of pedophiles and that it is generated as a record of sexual abuse, exchanged rather than sold. Needy children involved in child pornography are often seduced by the pedophile whose caring attitude and gifts or favors work to keep the child in the relationship. The pedophile is also thought to use the images to lower inhibitions of the child, and pictures taken of the child can also be used to blackmail the child into silence.

Statistics are scarce about this clandestine activity, but one network that was broken up had 180 members spread over 49 countries, with 750,000 pornographic images. Clearly, the Internet has facilitated the dissemination and exchange of child pornography.

Jody Raphael

See also Abolitionist Approach to Prostitution; Adult Survivors of Child Abuse; Child Sexual Abuse; Incest; Trafficking, Human

Further Readings

Finkelhor, D. (1984). *Child sexual abuse.* New York: Free Press.

Finkelhor, D. (1990). *Missing, abducted, runaway, and thrownaway children in America: First report: Numbers and characteristics, national incidence studies.* Darby, PA: Diane Publishing.

Kitzinger, J. (2004). *Framing abuse: Media influence and public understanding of sexual violence against children.* New York: Pluto Press.

COMMON COUPLE VIOLENCE

See SITUATIONAL COUPLE VIOLENCE

COMMUNITY JUSTICE

Community justice is the label given to restorative social and criminal justice–based efforts to respond to the harm that problems such as bias, prejudice, and criminality cause in a community. Consistent with peacemaking and progressive sociological and criminological approaches, this focus leads to a concentration on education, prevention, and interdiction efforts through the prism of consequences for all members of the public. The simple goal of community justice is to make social life better for everyone in the community (which can be defined as a city, neighborhood, district, or policing jurisdiction) through social change.

The core components of a community justice approach include a focus on change and rehabilitation through advocacy and efforts to shape local and national policy, restitution to victims and communities when applicable, education and programming, efforts to support strong families and individuals, respect for diversity and inclusion, and collaborative relationships between various stakeholders in the area. Decision making is structured to be democratic and shared among the identified stakeholders and activists. Key issues, strategies, and organizational goals for those involved in community justice are varied and depend upon the individual members and the group (e.g., Homelessness Outreach and Prevention Projects, the Anti-Bias Project, Take Back the Night).

Community justice efforts are often created and led by individuals concerned with local civil and civic rights at the national level (e.g., the National Center for Community Justice, Southern Poverty Law Center, Anti-Defamation League) and by neighborhood and grassroots local organizations. These activists are concerned with giving members of the community who have been disenfranchised a voice in the nature of their communities, as well as with establishing the priorities of law enforcement and crime prevention in their communities. Community justice efforts have historically been advocated by individuals and organizations of faith and conscience.

Community justice brings the justice system, advocates, and the community together in partnership efforts to solve problems, reduce crime, and build public confidence in the agencies of the criminal justice system, most notably in the area of policing, as well as advance the strength of the community through bonds of involvement and activism. Community advancement and solidarity formation through social and civic engagement are essential ingredients to community justice. For example, when offenders are given a community-based penalty, the court can order that the offender returns to court on a regular basis for analysis, treatment, and counseling. The intention is to increase oversight by the judge, magistrates, probation officers, and appointed others to increase the responsibility of offenders and encourage them to comply with the conditions of their sentences. This oversight is meant to cause a change in offenders in which they realize the harm that they have caused the community. It also gives the court the opportunity to support the offenders as they face challenges and adapt to the conditions of their sentences. Several different efforts have grown out of these attempts to change the punitive nature of the criminal justice system, for example, community-centered courts that provide a sense of place to legal proceedings, victim–offender forms of mediation, meaningful offender counseling that examines the full sense of well-being and social location, as well as community-oriented policing models where officers are involved members of the neighborhoods they patrol.

Arthur J. Jipson

See also Community Policing; Restorative Justice; Take Back the Night; Victim–Offender Mediation and Dialogue

Further Readings

Harris, M. K. (2004). An expansive, transformative view of restorative justice. *Contemporary Justice Review, 7,* 117–141.

Jesilow, P., & Parsons, D. (2000). Community policing as peacemaking. *Policing & Society, 10,* 163–183.

Lanni, A. (2005). The future of community justice. *Harvard Civil Rights-Civil Liberties Law Review, 40,* 359–405.

Rodriguez, N. (2007). Restorative justice at work: Examining the impact of restorative justice resolutions on juvenile recidivism. *Crime & Delinquency, 53,* 355–379.

Wozniak, J. F. (2002). Toward a theoretical model of peacemaking criminology: An essay in honor of Richard Quinney. *Crime & Delinquency, 48,* 204–231.

COMMUNITY POLICING

As gatekeepers to the criminal justice system, police are typically the first responders to intimate partner violence (IPV) incidents and thus shape formal responses to domestic violence. Historically, victims of IPV received little to no support within the criminal justice system. Domestic violence was considered a private matter, a problem that most often occurred within people's homes. Consequently, police were reluctant to intervene, and often no legal actions were taken against offenders. This began to change in the 1970s, however, as the women's movement and other advocacy groups brought the issue of domestic violence to the public's attention. In addition to lobbying for the mobilization of community resources to provide assistance to victims of IPV, such as emergency shelters and counseling, advocates also lobbied for the increased use and severity of criminal sanctions against offenders of such crimes. As a result of these efforts, IPV was no longer considered a private matter existing outside the domain of the criminal justice system.

During this same period, the public, along with various advocacy groups, began to criticize other law enforcement practices, such as police use of excessive force and racial discrimination. Furthermore, police and community interaction was minimal, which subsequently led to increased citizen dissatisfaction of current policing strategies and a reluctance to rely on police to address social problems. A new philosophy, termed *community policing,* was created to transform traditional policing methods and facilitate greater trust between citizens and police. Rather than rely on traditional reactive policing strategies that exacerbated the gulf between citizens and police, community policing stressed partnerships with community members in order to increase personal contact and better address and prevent neighborhood problems. As a result of these reforms, policing strategies for handling domestic violence also changed.

Comparison of Traditional and Community Policing Strategies

Traditional policing strategies consist of reactive measures for controlling crime, with the goal of either catching a criminal after a crime occurred or deterring future crimes through police presence in the community. This focus consisted primarily of two tactics: (1) police responding to service calls placed by citizens, and (2) random vehicle patrols through business and residential districts. Because officers spent most of their time responding to calls or patrolling in their vehicles, the traditional approach thwarted development of positive relationships between officers and community members, particularly those who were not in crisis. In line with crime control strategies, police concentrated their efforts on "real" crime fighting, thus relegating IPV to nuisance calls in which police prioritized the separation of the disputants or tried to mediate the quarrels; arrest of batterers was uncommon since police were not trained to classify IPV situations as criminal matters.

Community policing focuses on proactive strategies and exists simultaneously with a change in police response to IPV. In general, community policing efforts focus on preventing and resolving issues within the community before larger problems develop. Officers forge relationships with citizens to encourage greater respect of law enforcement, which ultimately leads to increased participation in community crime control. For example, officers may hold meetings with residents in order to address concerns and find ways to resolve problems together within their community. As such, it is important for these officers to work with the same community so that residents will get to know them and be more willing to cooperate with policing efforts. Typically, officers no longer rely solely on patrol vehicles; instead, officers utilize more foot and/or bike patrols. These new techniques encourage further interaction between community members and police officers, thus increasing the familiarity and level of trust between the two groups. In fact, although previous studies have shown that community policing has little or no impact on crime rates, the research does reveal that community policing has a positive impact on citizen attitudes toward the police and patrol officer attitudes toward their job.

Another proactive strategy entails collecting and analyzing data to find the nature and scope of various problems within the community. To do so, police again need to collaborate with community residents. Furthermore, law enforcement must collaborate with community organizations such as schools, churches, and other citizen groups in order to implement and assess effective preventive strategies. In sum, community policing altered the ways in which law enforcement utilized community support networks to combat crime and deal with other important issues.

Community Policing Strategies for Intimate Partner Violence

Because community policing models emphasize activities that are absent from the more traditional methods of policing, community policing models have altered the strategies utilized by law enforcement for tackling issues such as domestic violence. One significant change is how police interact with both victims and offenders involved in IPV. Because officers under community policing are assigned to a specific jurisdiction, they become familiar with the residents of that community. As a result of this familiarity, victims of domestic violence are more willing to assist officers during domestic violence incidents. For instance, victims are

more willing to divulge personal information and report such crimes to police due to the increased level of trust between the two groups. Offenders, too, may exhibit greater cooperation with law enforcement officers because of the ongoing shared knowledge of residents and community officers.

In addition to the increased level of trust, participants in domestic violence are less likely to manipulate the criminal justice system because officers are familiar with the particular situations and households. For example, offenders are more likely to comply with court-mandated interventions because they are more likely to be shamed by the officers and the general community if they are noncompliant. Likewise, research has shown that community policing officers are more effective in monitoring court-mandated interventions such as civil protection orders, temporary restraining orders, and participation in treatment programs.

Another community policing strategy strives to develop collaborative partnerships with community organizations in order to provide resources and other support networks to victims of IPV. With the understanding that police cannot combat domestic violence alone, the community policing approach encourages the help of community leaders, organizations, and individual citizens. Through these collaborative partnerships, police can ensure that victims have the necessary resources to handle domestic violence within their homes. For example, policing goes beyond arrest as officers typically work with community organizations to provide ongoing safety and emergency shelter and offer resource referrals and financial or medical services to victims of such crimes.

In summary, by expanding the role of police officers to include a community-oriented approach that facilitates greater communication and connection between officers and citizens, the ability of police to respond more efficaciously to IPV is possible. Community police officers have a stronger connection to a range of residents, and this familiarity means that when managing a crime such as IPV, officers have a greater contextual knowledge of the situation and what problems need better monitoring, and victims and offenders experience more responsive law enforcement.

Jessica P Hodge and Susan L. Miller

See also Community Justice; Intimate Partner Violence; Police, Response to Domestic Violence

Further Readings

Giacomazzi, A. L., & Smithey, M. (2001). Community policing and violence against women: Lessons learned from a multiagency collaborative. *Police Quarterly, 4,* 99–122.

Laszlo, A. T., & Rinehart, T. A. (2002). Collaborative problem-solving partnerships: Advancing community policing philosophy to domestic violence victim services. *International Review of Victimology, 9,* 197–209.

Long, J., Wells, W., & De Leon-Granados, W. (2002). Implementation issues in a community and police partnership in law enforcement space: Lessons from a case study of a community policing approach to domestic violence. *Police Practice & Research, 3,* 231–246.

Miller, S. L. (1999). *Gender and community policing: Walking the talk.* Boston: Northeastern University Press.

Novak, K. J., Frank, J., Smith, B. W., & Engel, R. S. (2002). Revisiting the decision to arrest: Comparing beat and community officers. *Crime & Delinquency, 48,* 70–98.

Robinson, A. L., & Chandek, M. S. (2000). Philosophy into practice? Community policing units and domestic violence victim participation. *Policing: An International Journal of Police Strategies & Management, 23,* 280–302.

Sudderth, L. K. (2006). An uneasy alliance: Law enforcement and domestic violence victim advocates in a rural area. *Feminist Criminology, 1,* 329–353.

COMMUNITY VIOLENCE

Community violence is broadly understood to include any violence that takes place in the public arena. Though most definitions of community violence refer to experiencing or witnessing interpersonal violence, such as gang violence, homicides, fighting, robbing, or looting, community violence can also include systematic or institutional violence perpetrated against a group of people or community with public manifestations that can be social, political, or economic. The probability of experiencing or witnessing community violence is greater for people, especially children and adolescents, in low-income communities and communities of color, than for their counterparts in more affluent communities and White communities.

The effects of community violence are myriad and pervasive, taking a toll on the quality of life, psyche, and safety of individuals, families, neighborhoods, and institutions within the given geographic area experiencing the violence. Negative consequences include, but are not limited to, increased levels of aggression, post-traumatic stress disorder (PTSD), depressive symptoms, and antisocial behavior; a reduced sense of control, efficacy, and school or workplace performance; neighborhood deterioration and weakened social bonds and control; and diminished public will and trust.

One practice model promotes the notion that effective violence prevention addresses the causes of structural violence as well as the causes of interpersonal violence at the community level. In both cases, the model asserts, community residents should be at the forefront of efforts to make their communities safe. While outsiders can stimulate action, the real impetus for change emerges when communities own the identification of problems and solutions that lead to prevention.

This work fits within a broader theoretical frame of collective efficacy (social cohesion and communal engagement needed to act on behalf of the common good) and community organizing and mobilization (intended to rebuild neighborhood cohesion and public will and trust). Both are protective factors against crime and violence, and research has demonstrated that collective efficacy can be mobilized to protect communities and promote better outcomes for children, families, and neighborhoods. The model takes this notion one step further. It posits that the development of collective efficacy is the only route for poor, disadvantaged communities to promote and sustain healthy community and individual outcomes, as it provides a venue for organized efforts to prevent interpersonal violence and collective action against structural violence.

Research indicates that there is a developmental trajectory for building collective efficacy and reducing and preventing community violence. Efficacy builds up over time as communities achieve success in addressing issues and take on more and more complex issues. Many factors are involved in collective efficacy. The extent to which communities possess characteristics associated with efficacy determines the speed with which they can be organized on behalf of a social good. Community organizing and achieving efficacy should be engaged as long-term processes whose aims are to transform the way a community works. Transformation takes the shape of changed laws, policies, and programs as well as changed behavior on the part of community members and those from outside the community whose work takes them there.

Linda Bowen and Mitchell Brown

See also Collective Efficacy

Further Readings

Bowen, L. K., Gwiasda, V., & Brown, M. (2004). Engaging community residents to prevent violence. *Journal of Interpersonal Violence, 19*(3), 356–367.

Gibson, C. L., Zhao, J., Lovrich, N. P., & Gaffney, M. J. (2002). Social integration, individual perceptions of collective efficacy, and fear of crime in three cities. *Justice Quarterly, 19,* 537–565.

Overstreet, S. (2000). Exposure to community violence: Defining the problem and understanding the consequences. *Journal of Child and Family Studies, 9,* 7–25.

Sampson, R. J. (2004). Neighborhood and community: Collective efficacy and community safety. *New Economy, 11,* 106–113.

Sampson, R. J., Raudenbush, S. W., & Earles, F. (1997). Neighborhoods and violent crime: A multilevel study of collective efficacy. *Science, 277,* 918–925.

Schieman, S. (2005). Residential stability and the social impact of neighborhood disadvantage: A study of gender and race contingent effects. *Social Forces, 83,* 1031–1065.

Smock, K. (2004). *Democracy in action: Community organizing and urban change.* New York: Columbia University Press.

COMMUNITY VIOLENCE, EFFECTS ON CHILDREN AND YOUTH

Parallel with the increase in homicides and violent crime that began in the mid-1980s was a growing concern over youth's exposure to community violence. Distinguished from family violence by its location—violence that occurs outside of the home—*community violence* is a relatively broad term that refers to witnessing of violence, but also frequently includes personal victimization and knowing of others who have been victimized. Community violence exposure (CVE) may affect children's socioemotional development, beliefs about the world, school performance, and mental health. Children exposed to community violence are often at greater risk for a number of clinical and adjustment problems, most notably posttraumatic stress disorder (PTSD), depression, and aggression.

Prevalence

Estimates of the number of children exposed to community violence fluctuate with the amount of violence in the larger community, the sample on which the estimate is based, and the manner in which CVE is measured. Most studies in this area have been done with children and adolescents who, because of location or income, are at risk for CVE. Measures that combine relatively minor (e.g., seeing a dead body, a drug deal, a fight) and lethal and potentially lethal events (shootings, stabbings, killings), plus victimization and hearing about violence, find that 90% of these children have CVE. Focusing on more lethal and near lethal events, research finds that 25% to 70% of children in high-violence neighborhoods have seen a shooting. Children's CVE often occurs in a cumulative manner from witnessing to victimization to perpetration. Children who perpetrate community violence frequently have been victimized by and witnessed violent events. Community violence is often characterized by its chronic nature: children frequently have experienced multiple acts and different types of violence.

Most research on CVE has been done with African American children who reside in high-violence areas. Studies with more representative populations find that White and Latino youth are also at risk for CVE, but that African American children are exposed to more violence and more serious violence.

Effects

Children traumatized by community violence may display a range of disorders and maladaptive behaviors. Most research on CVE among children and youth has focused on PTSD symptoms and externalizing behaviors (acting out, aggression, delinquency). First used to describe the reactions of soldiers during war, PTSD occurs in response to an extreme stressor and is characterized by specific behaviors in the categories of reexperiencing the event, avoidance of reminders and psychic numbing, and increased arousal that last for at least a month. In particular, traumatized children are likely to engage in repetitive play and reenactments of the event, display subdued behavior and affect with less interest in previously enjoyed activities, and have sleep disturbances. Children often have trauma-specific fears and worry about a recurrence of the event. These children may be pessimistic about their future (not believe that they will live very long) and have difficulty forming close personal relationships. In addition to PTSD, these children are at risk for depression and substance abuse.

In addition to the above internalizing symptoms children affected by community violence are more likely to display externalizing behaviors, characterized by anger, aggression, acting out and delinquency, and substance use. This aggression may be a result of modeling, or beliefs about the efficacy and acceptability of force and violence in one's relationships that comes from existence in a violent milieu. Some research has found that children exposed to chronic violence, which is characteristic of community violence, display more externalizing than internalizing symptoms or may display such symptoms in the absence of depression and anxiety-related reactions. As children often know the victims of community violence, they frequently experience grief, in addition to trauma symptoms, which further complicates their recovery. When the victim is a relative or close family friend, the entire family may be traumatized, seriously undermining its ability to support the child's recovery and healing.

Specific behaviors displayed by children traumatized by CVE depend on their developmental level. For example, very young children may show regressive behaviors such as extreme anxiety when separated from the caregiver, bedwetting, and decreased verbalization. School-age children may report more fights and academic difficulties, while teenagers' symptoms include more risk taking and self-destructive behavior. If not addressed, trauma symptoms can impact the child's development, resulting in diminished life chances over the lifespan. Intrusive images, trouble concentrating, or fatigue from sleep disturbances can lead to difficulty with learning and school performance, which has long-term implications for achievement and success. Aggressive behaviors and difficulties getting along with others may negatively impact the traumatized child's ability to form positive and supportive relationships, which, in turn, may be replaced by involvement with more deviant peers, a primary factor in subsequent engagement in antisocial activities.

Moderators

Several individual and event-related characteristics affect the strength of the relationship between CVE and any potential consequences. While boys are more likely to experience community violence, girls seem to be more affected by their exposure. In comparison to boys, violence-exposed girls report more PTSD-related symptoms. However, recent research has not found clear gender differences in externalizing behaviors, with violence-exposed girls at similar risk as boys for aggression and acting out.

Several characteristics of the incident may affect the impact of CVE. Children in the greatest physical danger and in closest physical proximity to the incident frequently have the most severe reactions. In addition, children are most distressed by incidents involving those with whom they have close personal relationships. Some research has shown that children are *only* affected by those incidents that involve known others.

Like adults, children who dissociate during the event may be most likely to develop PTSD, which has been related to the development of additional symptoms. For example, children with PTSD are most likely to also be depressed and to use substances. Such results suggest that PTSD functions as a pathway between traumatic exposure and additional negative outcomes, indicating the importance of addressing the trauma early on to avoid the occurrence of PTSD.

There is wide variation in the impact of CVE. While violence-exposed children are more likely to be distressed than their nonexposed counterparts, the majority of children experiencing CVE do not report severe symptoms. Many factors may account for this, including the operation of the moderators described above and other individual, familial, and community level variables. Children who are exposed to both community violence and family violence are more at risk for negative consequences. Also, a child's personal competency, social support from friends and family, and warm parental relationships serve some protective functions, but only when violence exposure and threat are not extreme.

Esther J. Jenkins and Carl C. Bell

See also Community Violence; National Child Traumatic Stress Network; Posttraumatic Stress Disorder; Resiliency, Protective and Risk Factors

Further Readings

Buka, S. L., Stichick, T. L., Birdthistle, S. M., & Earls, F. J. (2001). Youth exposure to violence: Prevalence, risks and consequences. *American Journal of Orthopsychiatry, 71,* 298–310.
Jenkins, E. J., & Bell, C. C. (1997). Exposure and response to community violence among African American children and adolescents. In J. Osofsky (Ed.), *Children in a violent society* (pp. 9–31). New York: Guilford Press.

National Child Traumatic Stress Network and National
Center for PTSD. (2006). *Psychological first aid: Field
operations guide* (2nd ed.). Retrieved from
http://www.nctsn.org and http://www.ncptsd.va.gov
Ozer, E. J., Richards, M., & Kliewer, W. (Eds.). (2004).
Protective factors in the relationship between community
violence exposure and adjustment in youth [Special
section]. *Journal of Clinical Child and Adolescent
Psychology, 33*(3).

COMMUNITY VIOLENCE, RELATIONSHIP TO PARTNER VIOLENCE

Community violence broadly understood is any violence that takes place in the community, but it has only been recently understood to include intimate partner violence. In the public domain, the stress and strain of living and witnessing community violence produces a decreased sense of civic control and increased levels of aggression, and contributes to the loss of collective efficacy. Community and intimate partner violence are particularly pernicious in terms of how they affect children. In private spheres, violence has direct and indirect effects on children. Children in homes experiencing partner violence are significantly more likely to become victims of physical abuse or neglect than are children in homes that are not violent. Indirectly, children who live in violent homes have a dampened ability to relate to the public world and are more likely to become victims of partner and other forms of violence as adults.

Approaches to preventing partner violence and child maltreatment tend to focus on individual rather than community change. Some consider these approaches to be shortsighted, ultimately producing suboptimal program efforts, as violence in the home and violence in the community are intricately connected, with spillover effects from each to the other. Community residents tend to treat violence in the home as private, though they may recognize the connection between the actions of those who commit violence in the streets and those who are violent or witness violence in their homes. Residents are often reluctant to intervene directly in instances of violence within the private domain, though they have become increasingly engaged in efforts to end violence in their communities.

There is growing interest in examining a broader approach to preventing partner violence by engaging community residents. One practice model, the Institute for Community Peace (ICP), believes that residents should be at the forefront of efforts to prevent not only public violence, but also violence that occurs in the home. It has found that gains in community safety are not sustainable unless there is also peace in the home. While building community capacity to understand the root causes of violence, ICP learned that residents were awakened to the prevalence of intimate partner violence and eventually engaged this form of violence as part of a comprehensive strategy for community peace.

Another practice model, Close to Home, in Dorchester, Massachusetts, takes a more direct approach to involving the community to prevent intimate partner violence. Close to Home is a resident-driven domestic violence prevention and community organizing campaign that seeks to prevent domestic violence by educating, supporting, and developing leadership from the existing network of friends, family, and neighbors. The program strategically engages the strengths of social networks and values and trusts community members' ability to develop safe, meaningful, and effective responses to domestic violence in their own neighborhoods. It works to mobilize the neighborhood's civic life through dialogue and problem solving to address domestic violence as a priority community issue. Both programs acknowledge the need for changes in norms, values, and action by community residents and the broader society to foster peace in homes and communities.

Mitchell Brown and Linda Bowen

See also Community Violence, Effects on Children and Youth; Intimate Partner Violence; Prevention Programs, Community Approaches to Intimate Partner Violence; Prevention Programs, Interpersonal Violence

Further Readings

Cole, D. (1999). *No equal justice: Race and class in the American criminal justice system.* New York: The New Press.
Hambien, J., & Goguen, C. (n.d.). *Community violence: National Center for PTSD fact sheet.* Retrieved from http://www.ncptsd.va.gov/ncmain/ncdocs/fact_shts/fs_comm_violence.html

Lynch, M., & Cicchetti, D. (1998). An ecological-transactional analysis of children and contexts: The longitudinal interplay among child maltreatment, community violence, and children's symptomatology. *Development and Psychopathology, 10,* 235–257.

National Center for Injury Prevention and Control, Centers for Disease Control. (2006). *Understanding intimate partner violence.* Retrieved from http://www.cdc.gov/ncipc/dvp/ipv_factsheet.pdf

Overstreet, S. (2000). Exposure to community violence: Defining the problem and understanding the consequences. *Journal of Child and Family Studies, 9,* 7–25.

COMPASSION FATIGUE

See VICARIOUS TRAUMATIZATION

COMPLEX TRAUMA IN CHILDREN AND ADOLESCENTS

Complex trauma may be best thought of as an imprecise label that refers to children in clinical settings who present with a history that includes severe or prolonged exposure to multiple traumas and/or other adverse events and a clinical presentation of serious emotional and behavioral problems and/or conditions that extend across functioning domains. From a clinical perspective it is less important how these children are labeled than it is to help them with their problems and needs. In selecting treatment approaches, the focus should be on matching interventions that are supported by theory or empirical evidence for improving outcomes to the problems or conditions that bring the children and their families into the clinical setting.

Exposure to Trauma

It is now well established that children and adolescents are exposed to potentially traumatic events (PTEs) at significant rates, that most children have some distress following exposure to a PTE, that a nontrivial percentage of exposed children develop significant emotional and behavioral problems related to PTEs, and that exposure increases risk for a variety of subsequent problems.

Prevalence rates of exposure vary between studies due to a number of factors, including the type of PTE exposure assessed, the specificity of the screening questions, whether children are asked the questions directly, whether the design is retrospective, and the nature of the sample. For example, studies using multiple, behaviorally descriptive questions typically yield higher rates for sexual and physical abuse than those using a single, general gate question. Studies employing samples of children residing in inner-city areas report much higher rates of exposure to serious community violence than do other groups. Until quite recently, studies tended to focus on one or a few types of potentially traumatic events, making it difficult to ascertain the cumulative burden of exposure. More recent studies that have screened for multiple traumas find that it is common for children who are exposed to one type of trauma to be exposed to others, with a substantial percentage having been exposed to four or more traumas.

In terms of impact, studies also vary for similar reasons, including what outcomes are assessed; how outcomes are measured; whether the design is prospective or cross-sectional; and whether self-report, parent report, official report, or a combination of sources for outcomes is used. The degree and nature of impact tends to differ based on the source of the information. In general children report higher levels of posttraumatic stress, anxiety, and depression than caregivers. Overall, the results converge in finding that a significant percentage of exposed youth develop a posttraumatic stress response such as posttraumatic stress disorder (PTSD) and have higher rates of emotional and behavioral problems than nonexposed children. Predictors for negative outcomes include severity (e.g., sexual penetration, injury), perception of life threat, and duration. Prior exposure to trauma increases the likelihood of negative impact for a particular event, and a history of more traumas is associated with worse outcomes.

Definitions

There is currently no consensus definition of the term *complex trauma.* In part this is due to the use of the term *trauma* to describe both PTEs and their impact. In terms of defining the events, an unresolved question is what events are included. PTE was originally defined, as described in the *Diagnostic and Statistical Manual* of Mental Disorders, Third Edition (DSM–III), as an event outside ordinary human experience that was associated with a threat to life and limb. Now that it is known that even conservatively defined traumas are relatively common, rareness is no longer a relevant criterion. The objective threat criterion was abandoned as it became widely accepted that such often nonviolent experiences as child sexual abuse were subjectively experienced as threatening. Direct exposure is no longer considered necessary, as individuals who know someone who died violently or offspring of trauma-exposed individuals can develop PTSD.

More recently, however, the definition of trauma has expanded further. For example, children with serious illnesses such as cancer have been studied for posttrauma reactions. Some commentators have characterized insecure attachment and neglect as forms of trauma. Others have argued that historical experiences of oppression or subjugation of a group constitute a form of trauma history for all current members of the group (e.g., Native Americans or African Americans). This departure from defining trauma as an event or series of events experienced directly or indirectly by the individual to including a whole range of adverse conditions that might negatively affect children or groups makes it difficult to arrive at a definition of trauma or complex trauma.

Broadening the definition of trauma raises questions about what constitutes trauma as distinguished from other types of adversities that negatively affect children's growth and development. Many children exposed to trauma, however it is defined, have also been exposed to other adverse life events (e.g., poverty, homelessness, parental divorce, parental substance abuse, mental illness, and/or imprisonment) and have complicating circumstances (e.g., being an undocumented immigrant, a non-English-speaker, and/or developmentally disabled). Co-occurrence of trauma and adversity is common and cumulative burden is associated with more severe outcomes.

This suggests that complex trauma might best be defined by the presence of severe and pervasive psychological distress and impairment in a child who has a history of trauma. In almost all cases where children exposed to trauma have significant persisting psychological and functional problems there will be a constellation of historical and contemporaneous variables that include multiple trauma exposures and other adversities.

Treatment

In terms of treatment effectiveness, the evidence for children exposed to trauma is highly consistent with research on child psychotherapy in general. What is most relevant to treatment planning is the nature and severity of the problems, not the source. Key principles are matching interventions with theoretical and empirical support to identified problem areas, systematically applying the interventions, and focusing on skill acquisition.

Trauma-focused cognitive-behavioral therapy is the best researched trauma-specific intervention, with multiple randomized clinical trials. It has been shown to reduce PTSD symptoms, anxiety, and depression and moderate trauma-related behavioral reactions in sexually abused children, community violence–exposed youth, and children exposed to multiple traumas.

A variety of other interventions that target other outcomes have been applied to children with trauma histories and shown to have empirical support. Parent–child psychotherapy, a dynamically informed, attachment-based intervention for mothers who have been exposed to domestic violence and their young children, has produced very promising results in a randomized trial. An efficacious version of parent behavior management, parent–child interaction therapy, has been shown to be effective for children exposed to physical abuse, neglect, and domestic violence in reducing behavior problems, in improving the parent–child relationship, and in cases of physical abuse, in reducing referrals to Child Protective Services. Abuse-focused cognitive-behavioral therapy for physically abusive families similarly reduces child behavior problems and violent family behavior. There is emerging evidence on the application to adolescents of an intervention called dialectical behavior therapy that was originally designed for self-harming adults, most of whom had trauma histories. Although clinical trials of youth given other proven treatments have not always collected data on trauma exposure, it is likely that many of the youth have significant trauma histories and benefit by the treatment that the intervention targets (e.g., multisystemic therapy, functional family therapy for delinquents).

Lucy Berliner

See also Adult Survivors of Childhood Abuse; Child Exposure to Intimate Partner Violence; Trauma-Focused Therapy

Further Readings

Turner, H. A., Finkelhor, D., & Ormrod, R. (2006). The effect of lifetime victimization on the mental health of children and adolescents. *Social Science and Medicine, 62,* 13–27.

CONFLICT TACTICS SCALES

The Conflict Tactics Scale (CTS) and the Revised Conflict Tactics Scale (CTS2) are the best known and most widely used quantitative techniques used to obtain estimates of violence in intimate relationships. Murray Straus developed the CTS in the 1970s and the original or a modified version appears in over 150 scientific journal articles and at least 15 North American books. The CTS generally consists of eighteen items that measure three different ways of handling interpersonal conflict in intimate relationships: reasoning, verbal aggression (referred to by some researchers as psychological abuse), and physical violence. The items are ranked on a continuum from least to most severe, with the first ten describing nonviolent tactics and the last eight describing violent strategies. The last five items make up what Straus and his colleagues refer to as the "severe violence index."

The CTS used to measure violence that occurred in the past year is usually introduced to respondents as follows:

> No matter how well a couple gets along, there are times when they disagree on major decisions, get annoyed about something the other person does, or just have spats or fights because they're in a bad mood or tired or for some other reason. They also use many different ways of trying to settle their differences. I'm going to read a list of some things that you and your partner might have done when you had a dispute, and would first like you to tell me for each one how often you did it in the past year.

The CTS is commonly recognized as a reliable method of capturing data on violence in intimate relationships. Moreover, many social scientists contend that CTS data are the best available when it comes to estimating the extent of intimate heterosexual violence in the population at large. Still, scores of researchers criticize the CTS for the following reasons:

- Since the CTS rank orders behaviors in a linear fashion, it incorrectly assumes that psychological abuse and the first three violence items (e.g., slaps) are less injurious than those in the severe violence index. This is problematic because emotional abuse is often more painful than physical violence, and a slap can often draw blood or break teeth.
- The CTS misses many types of abuse, such as scratches, burns, and sexual assault.
- The CTS simply counts the raw number of violent acts committed and thus cannot tell us why people use violence. Even though CTS data almost always show that men and women are equally violent, the fact is that they use violence for different reasons, with women using violence primarily to defend themselves and men using violence mainly to control their partners.
- The CTS only situates violence in the context of settling conflicts or disputes. Hence, it ignores assaults that "come out of the blue" and control-instigated assaults that are not rooted in conflicts or disputes.
- The CTS overlooks broader social psychological and social forces (e.g., patriarchy) that motivate people to assault their partners.

These and other critiques have been widely voiced for close to 20 years. Still, few researchers who use the CTS seem aware of them. However, in the mid-1990s, Straus and his colleagues developed the CTS2 to address some of the criticisms. For example, it includes more physical and psychological abuse items, as well as seven types of sexual assault. Further, to help researchers determine the difference between behaviors that cause physical injury and those that do not, the CTS2 includes several injury or physical outcome measures, such as "I needed to see a doctor because of a fight with my partner."

The CTS2 contains 39 questions and is deemed by many researchers to be much better than the CTS. Nevertheless, the CTS2 still situates abuse in the context of settling disputes or conflicts, and it provides no data on the contexts, meanings, and motives of violence. This is a major problem because fathers' rights groups and others critical of woman abuse research use sexually symmetrical CTS2 data to support their claim that men and women are equally violent. This has devastating effects on abused women and their struggles for effective social support services.

Both versions of the CTS have serious pitfalls, but this does not mean that social scientists should not use them. For example, researchers such as Daniel Saunders, Walter DeKeseredy, Martin Schwartz, and Shahid Alvi show that one key problem can be avoided by adding questions about motives, meanings, and contexts in different sections of the CTS or CTS2. Further, using supplementary open- and closed-ended questions provides respondents with more opportunities to disclose abusive experiences than they have by only completing the CTS or CTS2. For example, many people may not report incidents for several reasons, such as embarrassment, fear of reprisal, shame, or reluctance to recall traumatic memories. However, if respondents are asked again later by an interviewer or asked to complete self-report supplementary questions, some silent or forgetful participants will reveal in this second round having been assaulted or abusive.

The CTS and CTS2 have strengths and limitations, and researchers devote a substantial amount of time and effort to either attacking or defending their scientific value. Such debates will never end. Still, the CTS and CTS2 can help elicit rich data on intimate violence if researchers use one or the other, as well as supplementary measures of violence and questions about the specific context, meanings, and motives of respondents.

Walter S. DeKeseredy

See also Incidence; Measurement, Interpersonal Violence; Prevalence, Measuring

Further Readings

DeKeseredy, W. S., Saunders, D. G., Schwartz, M. D., & Alvi, S. (1997). The meanings and motives for women's use of violence in Canadian college dating relationships. *Sociological Spectrum, 17,* 199–222.

DeKeseredy, W. S., & Schwartz, M. D. (1998). *Measuring the extent of woman abuse in intimate heterosexual relationships: A critique of the Conflict Tactics Scales.* Retrieved from http://www.vaw.umn.edu/documents/vawnet/ctscritique/ctscritique.html

Straus, M. A. (1979). Measuring intrafamily conflict and violence: The Conflict Tactics (CT) Scales. *Journal of Marriage and the Family, 41,* 75–88.

Straus, M. A., Hamby, S. L., Boney-McCoy, S., & Sugarman, D. B. (1996). The revised Conflict Tactics Scales (CTS2): Development and preliminary psychometric data. *Journal of Family Issues, 17,* 283–316.

CONTRACT KILLINGS

A contract killing is a unique type of homicide in which one person enters into an agreement with another to have him or her kill a third person for monetary or other gain. Absent reliable baseline data, and given the paucity of research on contract killings, a reliable profile of offender and victim characteristics and offense circumstances has yet to be established. Although contract killings occur with far less frequency than other types of homicides, anecdotal evidence from news articles, case studies, novels, and historical works suggests that such killings have been a persistent part of the landscape of American lethal violence since the beginning of the country.

Several distinctive patterns of contract killing have emerged over time, including entrepreneurs, professionals/independents, and amateurs. Perhaps the most interesting change has occurred in recent decades, as contract killings have become more personalized and amateurish, been less embedded in organized underworld criminal organizations, and less frequently involved professionals. Along with this change have been variations in the motives of solicitors and "hit men" from ideological, economic, and protective ones to those that are more personal and intimate.

Contract killings involve distinctive relationships between a solicitor, a contract killer, and a victim that are different from those found in other types of homicides. Exploratory studies suggest that the emerging personalized contract killings differ from other types of homicides in important respects. Among their more interesting features are a greater proportion of females as solicitors, their taking place in suburban and small town areas as well as highly urbanized areas, the middle-class backgrounds of participants, the killings' lack of connection to the organized criminal underworld, and the participants, both solicitors and killers, usually being White.

The process of conceiving the use of a contract killer, entering into and negotiating a contract, planning and executing the killing, and dealing with the aftermath involves various stages that begin when the solicitor decides that this is the only solution to a problem perceived as otherwise insurmountable. Next, a killer must be found and convinced to participate in the murderous scheme. Then, a contract is negotiated between the solicitor and killer, the details (e.g., choice of weapons, time, location, payment) of which will vary from incident to incident, depending on the degree of professionalism of the participants. That is followed by various specifics related to planning for and executing the killing and deciding on how the final payment is to be collected.

It is important to note that a number of would-be contract killings are never completed because the solicitor is put in touch with an undercover law enforcement officer posing as a killer for hire.

James A. Black

See also Homicides, Criminal; Honor Killing/Crime

Further Readings

Black, J. A. (2000). Murder for hire: An exploratory study of participant relationships. In P. H. Blackman, V. L. Leggett, B. Olson, & J. P. Jarvis (Eds.), *The varieties of homicide and its research: Proceedings of the 1999 annual meeting of the Homicide Research Working Group*. Washington, DC: Federal Bureau of Investigation.

Black, J. A., & Cravens, N. M. (2001). Contracts to kill as scripted behavior. In P. H. Blackman, V. L. Leggett, & J. P. Jarvis (Eds.), *The diversity of homicide: Proceedings of the 2000 annual meeting of the Homicide Research Working Group*. Washington, DC: Federal Bureau of Investigation.

Mouzos, J., & Venditto, J. (2003). *Contract killings in Australia*. Canberra: Australian Institute of Criminology.

COORDINATED COMMUNITY RESPONSE

Coordinated community response (CCR) refers to communitywide efforts to bring together relevant stakeholders to address complex social problems (e.g., intimate partner violence, sexual assault, child abuse, substance abuse). Efforts to coordinate responses to social problems developed out of an awareness that (a) many stakeholders (such as parents, friends, neighbors, social service agencies, law enforcement, educators, religious leaders, employers, government officials) interact with those affected by social problems and have a potential role to play in addressing such problems and that, (b) unless these stakeholders work together in a coordinated way, there will be gaps and duplication in the community response. Importantly,

a coordinated effort emphasizes that it is the entire community, rather than isolated agencies or stakeholders, which is responsible for responding to social issues. While coordinated efforts exist in response to a wide variety of social problems, the phrase *coordinated community response* was coined regarding the response to intimate partner violence.

Attempts to coordinate the community response to intimate partner violence have become widespread in the United States and elsewhere. Goals for these efforts usually include victim safety, batterer accountability, and community education and prevention. While many CCRs initially focused on reforming policies and protocols in the criminal justice system (e.g., police, prosecutors, judges, probation), there is increasing recognition that stakeholders in other arenas must be included in such efforts (e.g., health care, education, human service and social services systems, all levels of government, religious organizations, and businesses).

To date, there have been few examinations of the efficacy of CCRs, but early evaluations and anecdotal evidence suggest that where these efforts exist, greater strides are being made toward addressing the complex issues that arise when responding to intimate partner violence. For example, one study found that when police action was coordinated with other systems, perpetrators were less likely to reoffend. In fact, this study found that arrest alone—in the absence of coordination—increased perpetrators' use of violence against women. Similarly, another study found that batterers who were arrested but not mandated to attend batterers' intervention were more likely to recidivate than those arrested *and* mandated to attend treatment.

The development of a CCR to domestic violence has taken three forms: (1) free-standing organizations responsible for encouraging cooperation and institutional change (e.g., the Domestic Abuse Intervention Project, or DAIP, in Duluth), (2) programs within existing organizations that are responsible for encouraging coordination and institutional change (e.g., new policies and protocols within a prosecutor's office), and (3) domestic violence coordinating councils (i.e., free-standing committees formed to lead the coordinating effort). While there is no empirical evidence determining which of these three strategies is most effective in facilitating a CCR, domestic violence coordinating councils have become very popular and are increasingly formed as a way to meet the collaboration requirement to receive federal and state funding.

Importantly, coordinating councils are not uniformly effective; these councils must foster an inclusive climate that incorporates input and active participation from the wide array of stakeholders who have a role to play in the community response to domestic violence. Further, it is essential that the dual goals of survivor safety and batterer accountability are central in coordinated efforts. Finally, it is important that coordination is not viewed as an end unto itself. That is, the goal is not simply coordination across stakeholders, but coordination that increases survivor safety and batterer accountability.

Nicole E. Allen and Amy Lehrner

See also Battered Women's Justice Project; Domestic Violence Courts; Duluth Model; Health Care Response to Intimate Partner Violence; Intimate Partner, Violence; Legal System, Advocacy Efforts to Affect, Intimate Partner Violence; Police, Response to Domestic Violence

Further Readings

Allen, N. E. (2005). A multilevel analysis of community coordinating councils. *American Journal of Community Psychology, 35*(1/2), 49–63.

Allen, N. E. (2006). An examination of the effectiveness of domestic violence coordinating councils. *Violence Against Women, 12*, 46–67.

Burt, M. R., Newmark, L. C., Jacobs, L. K., & Harrell, A. V. (1998). *Evaluation of the STOP Formula Grants under the Violence Against Women Act of 1994* [Urban Institute report]. Washington, DC: Urban Institute.

Clark, S. J., Burt, M. R., Schulte, M. M., & Maguire, K. (1996). *Coordinated community responses to domestic violence in six communities: Beyond the justice system.* Final Report to the U.S. Department of Health and Human Services by the Urban Institute. Washington, DC: Urban Institute.

Edleson, J. L. (1991). Coordinated community responses. In M. Steinman (Ed.), *Woman battering: Policy responses* (pp. 203–220). Cincinnati, OH: Anderson Press.

Gamache, D., & Asmus, M. (1999). Enhancing networking among service providers. In M. F. Shepard & E. Pence (Eds.), *Coordinating community responses to domestic violence: Lessons from Duluth and beyond* (pp. 65–88). Thousand Oaks, CA: Sage.

Murphy, C. M., Musser, P. H., & Maton, K. I. (1998). Coordinated community intervention for domestic abusers: Intervention system involvement and criminal recidivism. *Journal of Family Violence, 13*(3), 263–284.

Pence, E. L. (1999). Some thoughts on philosophy. In M. F. Shepard & E. Pence (Eds.), *Coordinating community responses to domestic violence: Lessons from Duluth and beyond* (pp. 25–40). Thousand Oaks, CA: Sage.

Shepard, M. F., & Pence, E. (Eds.). (1999). *Coordinating community responses to domestic violence: Lessons from Duluth and beyond.* Thousand Oaks, CA: Sage.

Steinman, M. (1990). Lowering recidivism among men who batter women. *Journal of Police Science and Administration, 17*, 124–132.

Syers, M., & Edelson, J. L. (1992). The combined effects of coordinated criminal justice intervention in woman abuse. *Journal of Interpersonal Violence, 7*, 490–502.

CORPORATE VIOLENCE

Scholars of corporate violence study the ways in which corporations—not simply individual actors within a corporation—engage in activities that are harmful or socially injurious. Sometimes these acts are illegal; other times they are not. In other words, it is not only illegal corporate activity that is capable of causing harm.

Acts of corporate violence may include the harms caused by corporate action or inaction. Corporate actions that are violent may be intentional or unintentional, and corporate inaction includes all the things corporations fail to do that cause harm. Corporate violence, then, may include a wide array of activities and/or failures to act.

Victims of Corporate Violence

There are several categories of victims of corporate violence, such as individuals, groups of individuals (e.g., employees and consumers), and the natural environment. Several case studies conducted by scholars of corporate violence illustrate the harms caused to these categories of victims.

One case that illustrates violence against workers is the Imperial Food Products fire in Hamlet, North Carolina. In this instance, 25 workers died in a fire at the Imperial Foods processing plant when plant managers locked the fire escapes to prevent employees from stealing chicken nuggets. Other forms of violence against workers can result when companies do not follow Occupational Safety and Health Administration (OSHA) laws, thus failing to protect workers.

For example, with the deaths of several miners in recent years, attention has been given to the subject of unsafe working conditions. However, those who study corporate violence have noted that there is a long history of some corporations in the mining industry failing to adequately protect workers (e.g., "black lung" disease, collapsing mines, fires and explosions). Finally, some corporations have been accused of conspiring with paramilitary death squads in economically undeveloped countries to prevent unionization through acts of violence directed toward union organizers and/or employees.

Consumers have also been victimized by corporate violence, which has been documented in a substantial body of research. One example is the crash of ValuJet Flight 592 in 1996 where 105 passengers (and 5 crew members) were killed as a result of ValuJet's failure to follow Federal Aviation Administration (FAA) regulations. Other groups of consumers who may have been victims of corporate violence include those killed or injured because of fires in Ford Pinto cars resulting from design flaws, women who were harmed by the Dalkon Shield (an IUD birth control device known to be the cause of uterine infections, blood poisoning, and the deaths of 12 women), children born with birth defects because their mothers had taken thalidomide (a drug used to offset morning sickness), those who have died or have serious illnesses caused by the effects of products sold by major tobacco companies, and those involved in accidents linked to unsafe tires.

While consumers and workers are easy to identify as victims, violence to the environment and its subsequent harmful effects on humans have not always been easily recognized as corporate violence. Recently, however, researchers have begun exploring the ways in which corporate violence to the environment is a significant threat to the natural habitat as well as to large groups of people.

One of the most widely publicized cases of corporate violence to the environment was Love Canal. Between 1942 and 1953, the Hooker Chemical Company dumped toxic chemicals in Love Canal, near Niagara Falls, New York. The toxic site was sold to the community for a dollar, and local officials decided to build a school there. Schoolchildren, as well as the families living near Love Canal, were exposed to toxic waste. The results were increased health problems in the community, including significantly higher rates of miscarriages of pregnancies, increased rates of birth defects, and chromosomal abnormalities in the children born to mothers exposed to the toxins.

Another significant environmental disaster was the 1989 *Exxon Valdez* oil spill where nearly 250,000 barrels of oil were spilled when the *Valdez* oil tanker ran aground on a reef off the coast of Alaska. The spill covered nearly 1,000 miles of Alaskan coastline, and the environmental impact of the *Valdez* oil spill was devastating: tens of thousands of birds and coastal mammals were killed, significant damage was done to the fish population, and hundreds of millions of dollars were spent to clean it up.

Other examples of corporate violence against the environment include the toxic waste dumped by the nuclear weapons industry, asthma and other respiratory illnesses caused by air pollution, and the environmental and human damage caused by the chemical herbicide known as Agent Orange used during the Vietnam War. In recent years, some multinational corporations have moved production plants to countries that do not have many laws regulating pollution, and the environmental damage has been significant.

Differences Between Corporate Violence and Interpersonal Violence

While the harms caused by corporate violence and interpersonal violence may have similar consequences, David Friedrichs has argued that corporate violence is different from other forms of interpersonal violence in at least four distinct ways. These differences may be summarized as follows: first, corporate violence is indirect in that one person is not directly assaulting another; second, corporate violence, by its very nature, is collective; third, the effects of corporate violence are usually difficult to link to the policy or policies that created them; fourth, corporate violence is motivated by a desire to maximize profits while reducing costs. Examples that illustrate each of these differences can be found in the extant literature on corporate violence.

The indirect and collaborative nature of corporate violence can easily be seen in that the managers and other people of power within the corporation do not have direct contact with the victims of corporate violence. As such, it is easy for corporate managers to view the victims in abstract terms (i.e., to view them as "units" or "costs" rather than people). Oftentimes, the moral accountability for decisions that are made within the corporation to move forward with the production and distribution of a dangerous product is diffused among several people (i.e., it is someone else's responsibility). For example, Kermit Vandivier has documented the ways in which groups of B. F. Goodrich managers and engineers attempted to hide design flaws in the aircraft brakes they were creating, because of time constraints in getting the brakes to their customers. At each turn, managers and engineers displaced any personal responsibility for the consequences that were likely from the design flaws, and were ready to release a defective and potentially harmful product into the market.

In addition, it is difficult to uncover specific policies that lead to corporate violence. When corporate violence occurs, it is often difficult to link the harms caused to specific policies and/or individuals making the corporation responsible. In some cases, "whistle-blowers" will come forward and shed light on the misconduct of a corporation. Oftentimes, however, it is not until great harm is caused and someone in the media or a governmental agency conducts an investigation that the policies are uncovered.

Finally, the motivation for corporate violence is not malevolence directed toward the victim, but rather the desire to maximize profits while reducing costs. Indeed, many forms of corporate violence could be eliminated or drastically reduced if corporations reduced profits by spending extra money to reduce pollution, recall unsafe products, and provide safe working conditions for employees. However, this is not likely to happen since there are strong corporate mandates to externalize—or pass on to someone else—the costs associated with making profits.

Rick A. Matthews

See also State Violence

Further Readings

Aulette, J. R., & Michalowski, R. J. (1993). Fire in Hamlet: A case study of state-corporate crime. In K. Tunnell (Ed.), *Political crime in contemporary America* (pp. 171–206). New York: Garland.

Bakan, J. (2004). *The corporation: The pathological pursuit of profit and power.* New York: Simon & Schuster.

Derber, C. (2004). *The wilding of America: Money, mayhem and the new American dream* (3rd ed.). New York: Worth.

Ermann, D., & Lundman, R. (Eds.). (2002). *Corporate and governmental deviance: Problems of organizational behavior in contemporary society.* New York: Oxford University Press.

Friedrichs, D. O. (2004). *Trusted criminals: White collar crime in contemporary society.* Belmont, CA: Wadsworth/Thompson.

Kauzlarich, D., & Kramer, R. C. (1998). *Crimes of the American nuclear state: At home and abroad.* Boston: Northeastern University Press.

Matthews, R. A., & Kauzlarich, D. (2000). The crash of ValuJet flight 592: A case study in state-corporate crime. *Sociological Focus, 3,* 281–298.

COUPLE COUNSELING

Couple counseling focuses on interpersonal relationships, with problems related to the couple relationship becoming the central focus of treatment. Its use with couples involved in intimate partner violence (IPV) is controversial.

Why Couple Counseling?

Sustaining a couple relationship is a difficult endeavor because of the myriad adjustments that couples must make when beginning their life together. The realities of being in a couple relationship often conflict with the romanticism of fairy tales and movies. The first year is likely to be the most difficult year of the relationship as new couples adjust to being together. Even when couples come from similar backgrounds, the daily living habits they have developed in their family of origin may contribute to tension. They may have different expectations of the relationship and different values. These differences may be accentuated in cross-cultural couples. When the challenges of being in a relationship accumulate (in particular, when facing IPV), some couples seek professional help and consult a couple counselor.

Couple counseling is a type of short-term psychotherapy that focuses on interpersonal relationships, with problems related to the couple relationship becoming the central focus of treatment. There are many approaches to couple counseling, and its effectiveness varies as a function of the form of intervention.

Behavioral marital therapy, emotionally focused therapy, and integrative behavioral couple therapy have received the most research support. Cognitive-behavioral marital therapy, strategic therapy, and insight-oriented marital therapy are also somewhat effective, as are programs such as marital and premarital enrichment programs. Couple counseling has also been shown to be helpful in the treatment of mental health disorders co-occurring with relationship distress (for example, depression, agoraphobia, obsessive-compulsive disorders, and substance abuse). Key to success in all of these approaches is interrupting cycles of negative emotion and rebuilding emotional connections.

The research is clear that not all couples do equally well in counseling. Most important, from the perspective of IPV, there is disagreement as to whether couple counseling is even appropriate for couples experiencing physical aggression.

Couple Counseling for Couples Experiencing IPV

One of the advantages of couple counseling for those experiencing IPV is that it may be possible for the counselor to get more accurate information about the violence when the couple presents together. When the partners are interviewed apart, the aggressor is likely to underrepresent the severity of the violence. Having both members of the couple in the counseling room at the same time also allows the two of them to get the same information at the same time about what is acceptable behavior, what constitutes violence, and how the counseling will proceed. Working together as a couple allows the individuals to postpone discussions about volatile or controversial issues until the next counseling session, thus decreasing the likelihood of escalating arguments at home. Proponents of couple counseling for those experiencing IPV contend that interrupting cycles of negative emotion and negative communication in counseling leads to a decrease in violence because it changes the patterns of interaction that lead to physical aggression in these couples. Because bidirectional violence is present in some of these couples, both partners can learn to control their use of physical aggression better when learning how to do this at the same time.

Arguments Against Couple Counseling

Opponents of couple counseling argue that it is never appropriate to work with a couple together once IPV has been identified until all evidence of physical aggression has been absent for some time (6 months to 1 year is the typical time frame stated). They give a number of reasons why it is inappropriate, ineffective, and, in some cases, dangerous to do couple counseling when IPV is present. The most important limitation to using couple counseling is that by its very nature it communicates that it is the system (the relationship) that is faulty, rather than the behaviors of the individual members that are problematic. What this subtly communicates is that both partners are responsible for the violence. However, there is a great deal of evidence that IPV is a disorder of the abuser and attributing coresponsibility to the victim could in fact exacerbate the cycle of violence. Abusers chronically blame others for the unfortunate things that happen to them. Attributing coresponsibility to the victim could be interpreted by the aggressor as confirming his or her basic belief that the victim is in fact wholly responsible for the violence. Moreover, since victims tend to blame themselves for the violence, attribution of coresponsibility could contribute to the victim's belief system that it is indeed his or her fault.

Opponents of couple counseling cite research that it is not effective in stopping abusive behavior since the individual's abusive behaviors are unrelated to the behaviors of the partner, whether the behaviors are conflict engaging, conflict lessening, or conflict avoidant. Thus, focusing on the problems in the relationship would not be effective in stopping abusive behavior. Focusing on relational issues in a couple when violence continues could instead increase the danger to the victim.

Opponents of couple counseling recommend instead that the aggressor be referred to a treatment group for abusers—perhaps one incorporating anger management in a psychotherapy group—until such a time as the violence has come under clear control. The victim may receive supportive counseling during this time either in individual counseling or in a group modality.

Common Beliefs About Couple Counseling

Proponents and opponents of couple counseling for those experiencing IPV agree that when the victim of physical aggression is afraid of the partner, when risk of lethality exists, or when one member of the couple wants to end the relationship, couple counseling is not appropriate. All also agree that it is appropriate and even desirable to do couple counseling to resolve underlying relational issues after the violence has ceased.

Michele Harway

See also Anger Management; Marriage Education and Violence; Social Cognitive Programs for Violence

Further Readings

Geffner, R., & Rosenbaum, A. (Eds.). (2002). *Domestic violence offenders: Current interventions, research, and implications for policies and standards.* Binghamton, NY: Haworth Maltreatment & Trauma Press.

Harway, M., & Hansen, M. (2004). *Spouse abuse: Assessing and treating battered women, batterers and their children* (2nd ed.). Sarasota, FL: Professional Resource Press.

Holtzworth-Munroe, A., Clements, K., & Farris, C. (2005). Working with couples who have experienced physical aggression. In M. Harway (Ed.), *Handbook of couples therapy* (pp. 289–312). Hoboken, NJ: Wiley.

COURT-APPOINTED SPECIAL ADVOCATES

In every state in the United States (but not in every court) there are programs in which trained, volunteer, court-appointed special advocates (CASAs) serve to protect a child before the court. There are more than 50,000 advocates serving in some 1,000 state, county, or local program offices nationwide. CASA programs across the country are known by several different names, including Guardian ad Litem (GAL), Child Advocates, and Voices for Children. Since the inception of CASAs, volunteers have helped over 1,000,000 abused and neglected children by providing judges with objective, unbiased recommendations to support the best interests of each child.

The movement began in 1977 when a Seattle Superior Court Judge named David Soukup was concerned about trying to make decisions on behalf of abused and neglected children without sufficient information. He conceived the idea of appointing community volunteers to speak up for the best interests of these children in court. Fifty citizens responded to his request for volunteers, and the CASA movement was born. So successful was the Seattle program that soon other judges across the country began using citizen advocates. In 1990, the U.S. Congress encouraged the expansion of CASA programs with the passage of the Victims of Child Abuse Act.

The National Court Appointed Special Advocate Association now provides leadership, training, technical assistance, and grants to CASA programs across the nation. It also stages an annual conference and promotes CASA programs through public awareness efforts. The National Association is a 501(c)3 nonprofit organization that offers consultation and resources to start new CASA programs and provides continuing assistance to established programs.

The role of local CASA programs is to recruit, train, and support volunteers in their work with abused and neglected children. The national organization provides and continuously improves a core volunteer training curriculum, conducts national campaigns to help recruit volunteers and raise awareness about child abuse, and provides pass-through funding to local and state CASA/GAL programs. Grant funding comes primarily from the Department of Justice but also from private corporations and foundations. State organizations provide additional support to local programs and try to develop new CASA programs within the state. The state organizations also work to promote increased awareness of CASA work and the needs of children who are abused and neglected in the state.

Local (usually county or city) CASA programs work to prevent abused, neglected, and abandoned children from becoming lost in the Juvenile Dependency system, and aim to find them safe, permanent homes as soon as possible. To accomplish these goals, each volunteer is matched with a child and is expected to fulfill the advocate role by (a) meeting with the child once per week for at least an hour; (b) gathering information from all interested parties, such as attorneys, social workers, teachers, caregivers, therapists, and so on; (c) being alert to any unmet needs of the child and advocating those needs be met; (d) writing a report to the juvenile or family court judge for each hearing concerning the child to give the judge the information the advocate has gathered, what the advocate believes to be in the child's best interest, and what the child would like to have happen; (e) attending all court hearings regarding the child (usually once every 6 months, sometimes more frequently); and (f) monitoring the case by doing all of the above until the child is placed in a safe, permanent, nurturing home. Generally, volunteers receive at least 30 hours of expert training in skills relevant to accomplishing their tasks as well as ongoing mentoring.

As court-appointed advocates, CASA volunteers are unique in providing information often not available to the court. A CASA's objective, unbiased recommendation to support the best interest of the child is an invaluable aid to judges, and judges do value the information these trusted advocates present.

C. Terry Hendrix

See also Abandonment; American Professional Society on the Abuse of Children; Child Neglect; Child Physical Abuse; Child Sexual Abuse; Complex Trauma in Children and Adolescents; Failure to Protect; Failure to Thrive; Family Preservation and Reunification Programs; Fathers as Perpetrators of Child Maltreatment; Female Perpetrators of Violence Against Children; Foster Care; Legal System and Child Protection; Legislation, Child Maltreatment; Professional Journals on Child Maltreatment; Professional Journals on Victimization; Prosecutorial Practices, Child Maltreatment; Runaway and Thrownaway Children

Web Sites

National Court Appointed Special Advocate (CASA) Association: http://www.nationalcasa.org

CRIME VICTIMS COMPENSATION PROGRAM

Victims of violent crimes suffer serious psychological, social, and economic injuries resulting from the crime that may continue long after their physical injuries have healed. In recognition of the financial consequences of crime victimization, the Crime Victims Compensation program is designed to reimburse crime victims for expenses incurred as a consequence of the crime.

The Office for Victims of Crime (OVC) in the U.S. Department of Justice administers the federal Crime Victims Compensation (CVC) program. CVC is funded through fines and penalties paid by federal criminal offenders. Federal regulations require each state to offer CVC to victims of "compensable crimes," including crimes involving sexual assault, child abuse, and domestic violence.

OVC reimburses state programs for 60% of all eligible payments from the previous year. Each state may add its own funds to its program. Eligible expenses include medical bills, mental health counseling, loss of wages, funeral expenses, and relocation expenses for battered women. Other expenses that may be covered are eyeglasses, dental services, prosthetic devices, crime scene clean-up, replacement costs for clothing and bedding held as evidence, and annuities for child victims for loss of support. States are also required to pay the full out-of-pocket cost of sexual assault medical forensic examinations to receive STOP Violence Against Women Formula Grant funds even if the victim did not report the crime to law enforcement. Expenses not covered by most programs include theft and property loss.

Laws governing compensation vary from state to state, with each state responsible for establishing limits on awards, guidelines, and procedures for applying for benefits. Victims must report the crime to the police, cooperate with law enforcement and prosecutors, and apply for compensation within a stated period to be eligible for compensation, whether or not the offender is caught or convicted. Victims must also show that they did not contribute to the crime. Maximum awards generally range from $10,000 to $25,000, though compensation is paid only when other financial resources, such as private insurance and offender restitution, do not cover the total loss associated with the crime.

Victims must present evidence of their losses, which may include police reports and investigative files, medical or funeral bills, employer's reports for lost wages, prosecutor's reports, presentence reports, and insurance reports. Law enforcement officers and victim advocates provide information about CVC to victims. Information can also be found through the state attorney general's office.

Fran S. Danis

See also Office for Victims of Crime; Victims of Crime Act; Victims' Rights Movement

Further Readings

Danis, F. S. (2003). Domestic violence and crime victim compensation: A research agenda. *Violence Against Women, 9,* 374–390.

Office for Victims of Crime. (1999). *Victims of Crime Act crime victims' fund.* Washington, DC: U.S. Department of Justice, Office of Justice Programs.

CRISIS HOTLINES

Crisis hotlines are dedicated telephone numbers available for persons who need immediate assistance. Hotlines may provide services to individuals experiencing specific problems or address a variety of emotional and/or health related issues. Hotlines are often the first link persons in crisis have with formal services.

In the late 1960s, the first crisis hotlines were organized around suicide prevention. Since then, hotlines have been established for rape crisis, domestic violence, teen dating violence, teen runaways, missing and abducted children, and the reporting of abuse of children, elders, or persons with disabilities.

Crisis telephone hotlines are answered 24 hours, 7 days a week. Hotlines are sponsored by community-based organizations, state and national organizations, and governmental agencies. While most hotlines target the general population, some hotlines specialize in providing services to specific populations. For example, a community-based program serving the Latino community may offer a hotline in which the services are offered in Spanish. For persons with hearing disabilities, crisis hotlines are accessible through relay services in the United States (by calling 711), and many hotlines also have TTY capacity (the ability to receive text telephone calls).

When an individual calls a crisis hotline, he or she is provided emotional support, information about the problem he or she is facing, potential short- and long-term options, and referrals to appropriate service providers. Because people respond to a crisis in different ways, the overall goal of crisis hotline services is to help callers reduce their crisis responses long enough to identify their next steps. Information on the dynamics of abuse and sexual assault, safety planning, options such as protective orders or criminal justice system involvement, and referrals for counseling services are all provided over the telephone. Rape crisis and domestic violence hotlines may send an advocate to meet a caller in need of hospital-based advocacy services or help a caller gain immediate admittance to an emergency shelter. Because of the sensitive nature of the calls, information that a caller reveals over a hotline is confidential. Callers also have the option to remain anonymous.

Hotlines receive calls from persons directly experiencing violence or they may receive calls from relatives, friends, neighbors, and coworkers seeking information on ways they can assist someone. Other service providers may also call the hotline with referrals for individuals they have been seeing.

Crisis hotlines are answered by paid staff or trained volunteers. Staff and volunteers receive training in crisis intervention theory and information on specific issues such as domestic violence, sexual assault, child abuse, teen dating violence, elder abuse, and the role of other community resources such as law enforcement, hospitals, and agencies addressing child and elder maltreatment. Hotline workers also receive training for specific skills in active listening, crisis intervention strategies, and call documentation. Records are kept about the time and date of the call, specific problems addressed, any referrals made, and whether follow-up is necessary. Identifying information such as names and addresses are not kept to respect the confidentiality of callers.

Hotline telephone numbers are widely publicized. The numbers for local, state, and national hotlines are often located in the emergency numbers pages of local telephone books. Hotline numbers are also available over the Internet. To protect hotline workers, the physical addresses of hotlines are often kept confidential.

Fran S. Danis

See also National Domestic Violence Hotline

Web Sites

The Childhelp National Child Abuse Hotline: http://www
    .childhelp.org/home
National Domestic Violence Hotline: http://www.ndvh.org/
National Teen Dating Abuse Hotline: http://loveisrespect.org/
The Rape, Abuse & Incest National Network:
    http://www.rainn.org/

CULTURAL COMPETENCE

Cultural competence refers to the set of attitudes, practices, and policies that enables a person or agency to work well with people from differing cultural groups. Other related terms that have been used are *cultural sensitivity, transcultural skills, diversity competence,* and *multicultural expertise.*

Until the early 1990s literature on cultural competence in interpersonal violence was virtually unknown, although there were a few limited studies on particular problems (e.g., rape, battering) among members of specific groups. The literature began to grow in the 1990s, but many areas remain underexplored. There is a particular dearth of information on the effectiveness of cultural competency training and culturally competent approaches to interpersonal violence.

Discussions of cultural competence can be divided broadly into two groups. The first takes a *cultural literacy approach*. In this approach, information is provided about working with people from a specific culture on issues of interpersonal violence in general, or on a particular problem of interpersonal violence. Cultural literacy approaches emphasize learning about the history, values, and practices of members of particular cultural groups, so work can be adapted to them. While the cultural literacy approach is helpful, it can also be misleading since not everyone from a single culture behaves the same way or shares the same values, and the culture itself evolves and changes every day.

The second broad group of discussions takes a *multicultural approach*. The multicultural approach describes ways to be as fair, supportive, and effective as possible to individuals and families from a variety of cultural groups. Rather than offering information or guidelines about people from a specific group, the multicultural approach takes the position that there are ways to address interpersonal violence that "fit" a variety of cultures. Multicultural approaches emphasize openness, flexibility, and a respectful curiosity toward the people with whom one is working.

Individual Cultural Competence

Cultural competence is often described as a direction in which to head rather than as a plateau to be reached. Individual cultural competence includes skills such as building rapport, conducting assessments, and interviewing people from diverse backgrounds. Cultural competence also includes attitudes such as respect toward all people, an appreciation of the diversity of solutions to common problems, and openness. Other components of cultural competence include a willingness to engage in introspection and be humbled by the limits of one's own experience and knowledge, a developed sense of the role of power in social relations, and willingness to advocate for members of oppressed groups encountered within one's professional role. Linguistic competence is a subset of cultural competence and refers to providing services in the language preferred by the consumers of those services.

Culturally competent practice in interpersonal violence includes fair assessments, so that given problems are neither over- nor underreported among members of specific cultural groups. Culturally competent intervention ensures a fit between the professionals' practices and the cultures of the people who are experiencing the intervention. Common practices that have been developed by and used with members of the dominant culture may need to be adjusted so they can fit better with people from particular cultural groups. In addition, culturally competent interventions include practices that are indigenous to the cultures in question and build upon existing strengths.

Culturally Competent Policies

Culturally competent policies are those that make it most likely that people from diverse cultural groups will benefit from the services offered and not be overpenalized by punitive interventions. Culturally competent policies also work to support the hiring of professionals who are well suited to working with members of a variety of cultural groups. Sometimes this implies matching for ethnicity or race, whereas at other times it implies language competence or comfort with minority religious values.

Culturally Competent Agencies

Just as individuals vary in their cultural competence, so do organizations. In organizations, cultural competence refers to meeting the needs of stakeholders outside the agency such as clients, as well as meeting the needs of diverse members of the organization, such as employees. At one extreme are *monocultural organizations,* which are primarily Eurocentric and ethnocentric and which do not take cultural diversity into account. In the middle are *nondiscriminatory organizations,* which have inconsistent policies and practices regarding multicultural issues and where changes that are implemented to promote diversity are often superficial. On the far end of the spectrum are *multicultural organizations,* which see diversity as an asset; their commitment to diversity is infused throughout the organization.

A diverse staff (in terms of training, age, gender, class, religion, race, ethnicity, sexual orientation, and ability) improves the likelihood of cultural competence and enhances an agency's ability to generate creative approaches to diverse client experiences. Diverse staff communicates an openness toward culture that may be key to working in ethnic minority communities.

Culturally Competent Research

Research within the field of interpersonal violence is often seen as ethnocentric and lacking cultural competence, resulting in an overemphasis on problems and an underemphasis on solutions in members of minority and oppressed groups. Culturally competent research in interpersonal violence not only conforms to the highest ethical principles within the professions, but also integrates extra sensitivity in the design, execution, and dissemination of studies, to take cultural variations into account. Such research makes sure the key concepts are relevant to the cultures being studied, that groups are labeled in ways that make sense, and that the results will be used to enhance the well-being of the cultures studied. Common errors, such as the confounding of ethnicity and social class, or the collapsing of subgroups into larger groups with limited validity, are avoided.

Culturally competent theory in interpersonal violence is based on principles that are either universal or especially relevant to the cultures in question, not theories that are imposed by theorists who lack knowledge of the culture being discussed. Discussions of cultural competence in the various areas of interpersonal violence such as child abuse, rape, intimate partner violence, and youth violence have developed largely independently of one another. These problems frequently are interrelated and co-occur within individuals, families, and communities; thus achieving cultural competence in the field of interpersonal violence will most likely require a knitting together of the diverse approaches generated in each of these areas and others.

Lisa A. Fontes

See also Culturally Sensitive Intervention

Further Readings

Fontes, L. A. (2005). *Child abuse and culture: Working with diverse families.* New York: Guilford Press.
Incite! Women of Color Against Violence. (2006). *Color of violence.* Cambridge, MA: South End Press.
Lewis, A. D. (1999). *Cultural diversity in sexual abuse treatment: Issues and approaches.* Brandon, VT: Safe Society Press.
Sokoloff, N. J. (2005). *Domestic violence at the margins: Readings on race, class, gender and culture.* New Brunswick, NJ: Rutgers University Press.

CULTURAL DEFENSE

A cultural defense is an affirmative defense used by defendants to explain their behavior and the inability to conform their behavior to the law. This rationale is used by defendants to argue that the beliefs of their culture dictate their actions and therefore make them less culpable when committing a crime. In their most discussed form, cultural defenses have been used by immigrant defendants in cases involving the commission of violent crimes, specifically those involving acts of domestic violence. Typically the argument presented is that the woman acted in a way that the defendant's culture views as morally wrong and this same culture has taught him to correct the woman's wrongs through the use of violence.

Cultural defenses attempt to get at the question of whether or not the defendant had the requisite state of mind, *mens rea,* at the time of committing the crime in order for him or her to be found criminally liable. The *mens rea* required to find a defendant guilty varies depending on the specific crime. A defendant using a cultural defense may argue that his culture caused him to misinterpret the victim's actions or words. For example, in rape cases, defendants have argued that their culture caused them to interpret a victim's protests as consent and that they did not possess the state of mind required to be found guilty of rape. In other cases, defendants have asserted that their cultural background influenced their mental state at the time of the crime and, therefore, they were incapable of forming the intent necessary to commit the crime.

The debate over the validity of the cultural defense centers on the extent to which a person's cultural background should be taken into account when explaining behavior. Critics of the cultural defense argue that it condones violence against women and children by excusing a defendant's actions on the basis of his or her cultural background. In the end, it protects the perpetrators of violence and leaves vulnerable a group of victims the criminal legal system is supposed to protect. Proponents of the cultural defense assert that the U.S. legal system historically has been racist and prosecuted and punished people of color in disproportionately large numbers. This discrimination is perpetuated when the system ignores the fact that individuals from different cultures have different values and beliefs than those of dominant White American culture. Others argue for a compromised version of cultural defense that allows courts to take culture into account in deliberations and sentencing, while at the same time arguing for a complex vision of culture that is not static or one dimensional. Under this theory, views about a defendant's culture should not be reduced to stereotypes and should take a critical approach to understanding traditional systems of oppression.

Tracy J. Davis

See also Cultural Retaliatory Homicide

Further Readings

Tunick, M. (2004). "Can culture excuse crime?": Evaluating the inability thesis. *Punishment & Society, 6,* 395–409.

Volpp, L. (1994). (Mis)identifying culture: Asian women and the "cultural defense." *Harvard Women's Law Journal, 17,* 57–101.

CULTURALLY SENSITIVE INTERVENTION

This entry briefly identifies the major issues surrounding a specific form of batterer intervention program (BIP), namely Afrocentric or culturally sensitive intervention with African Americans. For the purposes of this discussion, Afrocentric and culturally sensitive interventions are those that acknowledge the intersection of gender and race, adopt a constructivist perspective in learning about the different cultural views of clients, and account for different cultural pathways regarding courtship and marriage. Importantly, culturally sensitive interventions do not sanction violence against women, but acknowledge that the cultural backgrounds of the participants may create different pathways to violence. Although culturally sensitive programs for batterers exist, two important issues have yet to be addressed: (1) a lack

of any systematic evaluations of the models being used, comparing their effectiveness with the model that is being institutionalized through state standards, and (2) the adoption of state program standards without empirical evidence that the model being adopted works for minority batterers.

Batterer Intervention Programming Effectiveness

Recently, more rigorous evaluation studies of BIPs have indicated mixed success. Importantly, however, an issue inadequately addressed in the evaluation literature is the appropriateness of these programs for ethnic/racial minorities. Although there is no empirical research investigating the differential effect of the standard cognitive-behavioral treatment program on outcomes for Caucasian and African American batterers, some authors have argued that the lack of cultural competence among treatment programs has a severe negative impact on African American participants. In brief, survey research has documented the absence of culturally sensitive intervention approaches among treatment providers nationally. This absence of culturally sensitive intervention approaches is a concern, given both the high rate of violence occurring in African American relationships and the high attrition rate among African American men in batterer treatment programs.

Few studies of BIPs have evaluated the effect of different types of intervention efforts on batterers of different ethnic/racial backgrounds. Consequently, the mixed findings on BIP effectiveness may be attributable either to (a) the fact that batterers are not a homogenous group or (b) the fact that minority batterers may have responded differently to the standardized intervention model being evaluated. Such conclusions seem plausible, as the limited data available on this issue suggest a possible need for a specialized response to African American men arrested, convicted, and sentenced to a BIP for domestic violence. Importantly, this should not be misconstrued as a suggestion that there is a lack of culturally sensitive BIPs available, as many culturally sensitive intervention programs for violent men have been created.

State Program Standards

States have legislated standards for treatment providers in an effort to create uniformity in BIPs. In fact, by January 2006, 43 states had instituted such standards. Among the many aspects of batterer intervention addressed by these standards is the formalizing of program structure and length. As a result, most treatment programs nationally, regardless of theoretical perspective, offer a feminist informed, cognitive-behavioral, group treatment approach for batterers. In short, these programs incorporate a patriarchal analysis of male–female intimate relationships and attempt to help participants modify their beliefs about intimate relationships and develop new skills for nonviolent conflict resolution. The impact of this trend on culturally specialized programming is not entirely clear. The unintended consequence of this legislation for treatment programs seeking to create culturally sensitive approaches for batterers of color is that they must now seek to create such services within the constraints of current state guidelines. Specifically, treatment providers must figure out how to provide specialized, culturally sensitive intervention services to diverse groups of batterers, while, at the same time, adhering to state standards that set basic uniform guidelines.

Frederick P. Buttell and Michelle M. Carney

See also Batterers; Batterers, Factors Supporting Male Aggression; Batterers, Treatment Approaches and Effectiveness

Further Readings

Almeida, R., Woods, R., Messineo, T., & Font, R. (1998). Cultural context model. In M. McGoldrick (Ed.), *Re-visioning family therapy: Race, culture, and gender in clinical practice* (pp. 404–432). New York: Guilford Press.

Babcock, J. C., Green, C. E., & Robie, C. (2004). Does batterers' treatment work? A meta-analytic review of domestic violence treatment. *Clinical Psychology Review, 23,* 1023–1053.

Buttell, F., & Carney, M. (2006). A large sample evaluation of a court mandated batterer intervention program: Investigating differential program effect for African-American and Caucasian men. *Research on Social Work Practice, 16,* 121–131.

Holtzworth-Munroe, A., Meehan, J., Herron, K., Rehman, U., & Stuart, G. (2000). Testing the Holtzworth-Munroe & Stuart (1994) batterer typology. *Journal of Consulting and Clinical Psychology, 68,* 1000–1019.

CULTURAL RETALIATORY HOMICIDE

Homicide, the killing of one person by another, can have many motivations. Retaliation, which is simply getting even with another person for some real or perceived wrong, has long been a motivation for committing homicides. Some experts argue that culture, defined as knowledge, beliefs, and values shared by members of society, can help explain higher rates of retaliatory homicides among certain segments of society.

As early as the 1930s, criminologist Thorsten Sellin argued, in a monograph titled *Culture Conflict and Crime,* that the beliefs and values people immigrating to America brought with them often clash with those of mainstream American society. To illustrate his theory, Sellin discussed an actual case of an immigrant who killed a young man accused of dishonoring his daughter. The immigrant, who had responded in the way he had been socialized to respond in the old country, was surprised when arrested for murdering the young man. Marvin E. Wolfgang, a former student of Sellin's, and Italian legal scholar Franco Ferracuti delved further into the role of culture in homicide by identifying what they termed a *subculture of violence.* Examining homicide rates among African Americans, which were six times higher than rates for Whites, Wolfgang and Ferracuti suggested that the Black subculture in fact values violence as a means of punishing those who violate subcultural norms. Noteworthy is their theory that members of this subculture of violence interpret stimuli such as a jostle, a derogatory remark, or the presence of a weapon in the hands of others differently from the way those in the dominant culture interpret them.

Subsequently, those attempting to confirm the subculture of violence theory discovered that the South and West experienced significantly higher rates of retaliatory homicides. Several studies have confirmed that in these regions a "culture of honor" exists in which insults are perceived by males much more negatively than by their counterparts in other regions, prompting violent and sometimes lethal responses.

Some of the most interesting and insightful findings were made by Elijah Anderson, an ethnographer who conducted research in Philadelphia neighborhoods. Anderson found that there exists among low-status African American young men a "code of the streets," which dictates how they respond to shows of disrespect and personal attacks by other males.

Failing to respond violently to such displays is interpreted by others as weakness and makes the man vulnerable to further victimization. So ingrained is the code in certain neighborhoods that even family members and neighbors give lip service to such retaliatory violence. Preliminary quantitative research has confirmed some of Anderson's qualitative findings.

Recent research attaches greatest importance to the role of structural disadvantage in explaining how culture spawns retaliatory homicide in certain neighborhoods. As persuasive as the evidence is for cultural retaliatory homicide, there remains disagreement on appropriate data and methods of analysis. Legal scholars contend that as important as culture may be in shaping individual behavior, it is not yet an acceptable defense for committing retaliatory homicide.

Mark S. Davis

See also Honor Killing/Crime; Subcultures of Violence

Further Readings

Anderson, E. (1999). *Code of the street: Decency, violence, and the moral life of the inner city.* New York: Norton.

Kubin, C. E., & Weitzer, R. (2003). Retaliatory homicide: Concentrated disadvantage and neighborhood crime. *Social Problems, 50,* 157–180.

Nisbett, R. E., & Cohen, D. (1996). *Culture of honor.* Boulder, CO: Westview Press.

Sellin, T. (1938). *Culture conflict and crime.* New York: Social Science Research Council.

Wolfgang, M. E., & Ferracuti, F. (1967). *The subculture of violence.* London: Tavistock.

Custody, Contact, and Visitation: Relationship to Domestic Violence

Domestic violence harms children, and usually escalates, or less commonly only begins, after their parents' separation. It is involved in at least 50% to 70% of contested custody cases. Many batterers lack empathy for their children and may put their own needs before those of their children. They may also use the court process and visitation to continue the abuse, and 11% of them abduct their children.

While less is known about abusive mothers, 30% to 60% of fathers who abuse their female partners also abuse their children, and abusive fathers sexually molest their daughters at least 6 times as often as nonabusive fathers. Abused gay and lesbian parents face similar issues, plus bias from courts and helping agencies.

Contested custody cases are very costly, averaging $90,000 per abuse family and causing 27% of battered women to file for bankruptcy. Custody courts can help children by supporting protective parents to protect themselves and their children from abusive parents.

Custody and Visitation Standards

In intact families, the parents are presumed to share custody of the minor children, although a few states presume that mothers should have custody of children born out of wedlock. If parents separate and cannot reach a suitable custody agreement, courts determine physical custody (with whom the child will live, visitation arrangements, and whether children may relocate) and legal custody (who may make the major religious, educational, and medical decisions). Physical and legal custody can be shared or sole. Custody is decided based on a best interest of the child (BIOC) standard, whose criteria are codified or listed in case law. The standard is criticized as being too subjective. Appellate courts reverse custody decisions when the trial court abused its discretion, a difficult standard to meet.

Batterers' families often fight for custody, particularly when the batterer is denied access. To win, they must meet a higher standard than the BIOC one, often the same unfitness or unavailability standard required for the child protection system to remove a child from parents. Grandparent visitation laws have been struck down in some states, but also require a higher standard than the BIOC criteria provide. When parents are not in the picture, the custody battles of nonparents are typically decided on a BIOC standard.

Domestic Violence Ramifications

Many states' laws encourage parents to have shared or joint legal or physical custody; some use shared parental rights language instead of *custody* and *visitation.* While most cooperative parents can coparent reasonably well, shared parenting increases the tension and abuse in families with violent members. At least 32 states have added "friendly parent" provisions (FPPs) to their BIOC laws that favor giving custody to the parent who will encourage the child to have a better relationship with the other parent. Although written to encourage cooperation, FPPs discourage victims from raising abuse allegations lest they be labeled "unfriendly" and lose custody, and FPPs reward abusers who reframe their partners' protective behaviors as "unfriendly" by depriving victims of custody. Batterers may use FPPs, shared parenting, and unsupervised visitation to increase and prolong their hostility and control, and facilitate further abuse.

Laws Discourage Giving Abusers Custody

Spurred by battered women's advocates, the findings of court gender bias studies in the 1980s and 1990s, and *the model code,* every state enacted gender-neutral statutes, enabling or requiring judges to consider domestic violence in their custody determinations. These laws often specifically encourage protecting victims and giving batterers restricted, supervised visitation. At least 24 states have enacted a rebuttable presumption that it is not in the BIOC to award custody to an abusive parent. Federal laws and uniform codes now permit courts to consider domestic violence in interstate custody disputes to protect victims, and require police and courts to honor and enforce custody and protective provisions issued in courts of other states, including those in protective orders.

Laws Are Not Always Implemented, Disadvantaging Victims

Although domestic violence is a BIOC factor or presumption in every state, states and judges vary in how much weight to give it. Some minimize its importance, particularly in states with FPPs, a joint custody preference or a harsh relocation standard. Others use BIOC factors like stability to disadvantage abused victims particularly when they move often or are homeless. Protective judges are thwarted from protecting victims by the paucity of supervised visitation programs. Supervision by family members may be as dangerous as unsupervised visitation.

Practices in the criminal justice system often leave victims with no record of the criminal abuse they have endured. Police may wrongfully arrest the victim, prosecutors may never charge the batterer, or courts may ultimately dispose of cases without any record of conviction. Protective orders entered by agreement of both parties may not be admissible in other cases.

In addition, mental health professionals (MHPs), who influence custody determinations in their roles as guardians ad litem, mediators, custody evaluators, and expert witnesses, often lack adequate training in domestic violence. Most were schooled in a family systems dynamic perspective, which minimizes domestic violence, assumes both parents cause it, and favors shared custody. Some advocate FPPs or more punitive, discredited theories like parental alienation syndrome to deny custody and even visitation to protective parents. Custody evaluators often give psychological tests that bias abuse victims, failing to correct for the abuse. Most courts follow the advice of MHPs, even when it is at odds with the state's custody laws.

These practices result in many protective parents losing custody.

Visitation Problems

A child who has been abused by a parent may refuse to see the abuser, or a protective parent may refuse to allow the abuser to see the child. Rarely do mothers make deliberately false allegations of incest or domestic violence in custody cases, although courts may believe such allegations are rampant. Some courts jail protective parents or, more rarely, the children when abusers are denied access, often with the encouragement of MHPs. Children forced to visit occasionally run away, abuse themselves, or even commit suicide. Some protective parents have fled with their children hoping to protect them, only to find that they face contempt or abduction charges. Some adult children are speaking out about these injustices, and a few judges are reconsidering their approach.

New Proposed Child Custody Standard

After meeting for 10 years, the prestigious American Law Institute has proposed granting custody by the "approximation rule," whereby each parent would presumptively receive roughly the same percentage of time spent with the child prior to the separation. The approximation rule would streamline most custody disputes, and maximize stability for children. But it is still too early to see if it will be adopted. Many MHPs oppose it, some fearful it will eliminate their jobs.

Victims able to file costly appeals win custody reversals 40% of the time.

Joan Zorza

See also Child Exposure to Intimate Partner Violence; Parental Alienation Syndrome

Further Readings

American Psychological Association. (1996). *Violence and the family: Report of the American Psychological Association Presidential Task Force on Violence and the Family.* Washington, DC: Author.

Bancroft, L., & Silverman, J. G. (2002). *The batterer as parent: Addressing the impact of domestic violence on family dynamics.* Thousand Oaks, CA: Sage.

Jaffe, P. G., Lemon, N. K. D., & Poisson, S. E. (2003). *Child custody and domestic violence: A call for safety and accountability.* Thousand Oaks, CA: Sage.

Myers, J. E. B. (1997). *A mother's nightmare: Incest. A practical legal guide for parents and professionals.* Thousand Oaks, CA: Sage.

National Council of Juvenile & Family Court Judges. (1994). *Model code on domestic and family violence.* Reno, NV: Author.

Zorza, J., & Rosen, L. (Eds.). (2005). *Violence against women* [Special issue on child custody and domestic violence], *11*(8).

CYBERSTALKING

The term *cyberstalking* is used to describe stalking behaviors that (a) involve repeated threats and/or harassment, (b) use electronic mail or other information technology-based communication, or (c) would cause a reasonable person to be afraid or concerned for his or her safety. Cyberstalkers most commonly harass their victims through email, but may also use Web sites, chat rooms, discussion forums, and open publishing Web sites (e.g., blogs and online journals). Cyberstalking may involve direct harassment of a victim or may use indirect means such as email to employers or postings in online newsgroups. Cyberstalking may be part of a systemic pattern of online harassment and may include sending repeated email or instant messages that may or may not directly threaten the recipient; flooding a victim's email box with unwanted mail; sending the victim files with a virus; using a victim's email address to subscribe her or him to multiple listservs or to purchase books, magazines, or other services in her or his name; sending misinformation and false messages to chat rooms, Usenet groups, listservs, or places of the victim's employment; stealing a person's online identity to post false information; sending a victim's demographic information and/or picture to sexually oriented or pornographic sites; or seeking and compiling various information that a victim may have posted on newsgroups with the intent to locate personal information and then use this information to harass, threaten, and intimidate the victim, either online or in the real world.

Reasons for Cyberstalking

Stalking has been viewed by some theorists as aberrant behavior involving obsessive behavior or personality disorder. Feminists, however, view stalking and cyberstalking as related to sexism, a means to gain power and control over a victim. Others believe stalking has a long history among the general public and is rooted in the romantic tradition in which a reluctant female must be wooed from "no" to "yes" by a persistent suitor. In any case, cyberstalking is an extension of the traditional stalking methods of following, making telephone calls, and writing letters. As with stalking in the physical world, cyberstalking can result from an attempt to initiate a relationship, to repair a relationship, or to threaten and traumatize a person. Recent research, however, found differences between real-world and cyberstalking. Cyberstalking is more likely to involve strangers and to take place over a shorter period of time than real-world stalking. In addition, cyberstalkers are more likely not to know their victims, to have multiple victims, and to have no history of criminality, substance abuse, or restraining orders.

The Internet medium itself may contribute to cyberstalking. The online environment can promote a false sense of intimacy and misunderstanding of intentions. People may feel in proximity to each other when they are online despite the actual physical distance involved. In addition, emotionally intensified interactions often develop in online communication. The limited nonverbal, historical, and contextual information available in online contexts may enable potential cyberstalkers to develop idealized perceptions of those with whom they communicate online and to misjudge the intentions of the messages they receive. In addition, the relative anonymity, the lack of social status cues, and the propensity for disinhibited behavior in the online environment may promote greater risk taking and asocial behavior by a greater number of people. The availability of free email and Web site space, as well as the anonymity provided by some chat rooms and newsgroups, has contributed to the increase of cyberstalking as a form of harassment. Finally, the ease of using a search engine to find someone's alias, real name, or email address contributes to cyberstalking.

Extent of Cyberstalking

There is no comprehensive national study of the extent of cyberstalking, but estimates have been made based on local research studies, reports of abuse to Internet Service Providers, FBI crime statistics, and reports to Web sites that provide online assistance to victims of violence. Cyberstalking has been described by the Department of Justice as a serious and growing problem. Cyberstalking can be just as threatening as stalking in the real world, and can lead to mental anguish and stress reactions including paranoia, panic attacks, chronic sleep disturbances, weight fluctuations, persistent nausea, increased usage of alcohol or cigarettes, headaches, depression, physical harm, and even homicide. Cyberstalking may occur in combination with real-world stalking, and research indicates that this occurs in approximately one in five cases of reported stalking or cyberstalking. Research suggests that the majority of cyberstalkers are men and their victims are women. There have been reports, however, of women cyberstalking men and of same-sex cyberstalking. Studies are very difficult to compare due to differences in the definition of cyberstalking and research methods employed. Several studies have used surveys of college students to estimate the extent of cyberstalking since almost 100% of this group is online and they are the age at which stalking is most likely to occur. College samples estimate that between 13% and 25% of women have experienced cyberstalking or online harassment. Estimates from Internet safety groups such as Working to Halt Online Abuse, SafetyEd, and CyberAngels reveal an increasing number of cyberstalking reports, with 50 to 500 requests per day for help from victims of cyberstalking. It is likely that research underestimates the true extent of cyberstalking since many cases go unreported and the number of people online is increasing each year.

Legal Issues

Both federal and state laws have addressed some forms of cyberstalking. Federal law makes it a crime to cross state lines to injure, harass, or intimidate a person. Certain forms of cyberstalking may be prosecuted under federal communications laws (47 U.S.C. 223). Section 113, which was signed into law by President George W. Bush on January 5, 2006, amends 47 U.S.C. 223 to prohibit anyone from using a telephone or a telecommunications device "without disclosing his identity and with intent to annoy, abuse, threaten, or harass any person." It includes "any device or software that can be used to originate telecommunications or other types of communications that are transmitted, in whole or in part, by the Internet." While this law may cover some aspects of cyberstalking, it does not cover harassment in which no explicit threat has been made or harassment in which messages are sent to third parties. In addition, Title 42 of the Civil Rights Act has been interpreted to prohibit sexual harassment in work environments. Conduct producing a hostile environment is specifically included in this statute. Sexual harassment via email may therefore be prosecuted under this statute.

Currently all but four states (Idaho, Nebraska, New Jersey, and Utah) have laws prohibiting harassing conduct of adult victims through the Internet, email, or other electronic means. Laws vary by state in terms of specificity, prohibited behavior, and consequences. For example, in Massachusetts, a perpetrator must have intent to cause "imminent fear," while in Arizona the standard is that the victim is "seriously alarmed" or "annoyed." In some states, such as New York, cyberstalking is part of the general stalking or harassment laws, while other states, such as North Carolina, have a separate section under special computer crime legislation. The patchwork of laws and recent definition of the problem make prosecution of cyberstalking confusing and more difficult for law enforcement.

Survival in Cyberspace

Socialization for survival in cyberspace was not part of the normal growing-up experience of most people. For their safety, people who use the Internet, especially those who have been victims of violence or are emotionally vulnerable, need education about the kinds of victimization that can occur online, how best to prevent it, and what to do if victimization occurs. They need information about password protection, encryption software, blocking and filtering software, anonymous remailers, alternate email receiving sites, chat room and newsgroup safety, the potential for misinformation, how privacy may be lost, how to deal with online harassment, policies and laws regulating interactions in cyberspace, and where to get help if victimization occurs. Several Web sites are currently dedicated to providing education and assistance regarding cyberstalking.

Jerry Finn

See also Stalking

Further Readings

Finn, J., & Banach, M. (2000). Victimization online: The downside of seeking services for women on the Internet. *Cyberpsychology and Behavior, 3*(2), 776–785.

Fisher, B. S., Cullen, F. T., & Turner, M. G. (2002). Being pursued: Stalking victimization in a national study of college women. *Criminology & Public Policy, 1*(2), 257–308.

Lee, R. (1998, Spring). Romantic and electronic stalking in a college context. *The College of William and Mary Journal of Women and the Law*, pp. 373–409.

U.S. Department of Justice. (1999). *Cyber stalking: A new challenge for law enforcement and industry—A report from the attorney general to the vice president.* Washington, DC: Author. Retrieved April 16, 2006, from http://www.usdoj.gov/criminal/cybercrime/cyberstalking.htm

Valtek, H. A. (2002). *A guide to the maze of cyberstalking laws.* Retrieved April 16, 2006, from http://www.gigalaw.com/articles/2002-all/valtek-2002-07-all.html

Working to Halt Online Abuse (WHO@). (2006). *Online harassment statistics.* Retrieved April 16, 2006, from http://www.haltabuse.org/resources/stats/offline.shtml

Web Sites

CyberAngels: http://www.cyberangels.org
SafetyEd International: http://www.safetyed.org
Working to Halt Online Abuse (WHO@): http://www.haltabuse.org

CYCLE OF VIOLENCE

There are two cycles of violence often referred to in the literature on interpersonal violence. One is the "intergenerational transmission of violence" and the other is the cycle of intimate violence that escalates to violence and then subsides only to escalate again. This entry focuses on the cycle of escalation and de-escalation during violent incidents between intimates.

The best known proponent of a cycle of violence model is Lenore Walker, whose landmark 1979 book titled *The Battered Woman* devoted an entire chapter to a "cycle theory of violence." In this chapter, Walker suggested there are three phases that couples move through in this cycle of violence: (1) tension building, (2) acute battering incident, and finally (3) kindness or contrite loving behavior. She also suggested that the full cycle varies greatly and that treatment may be more successful in one phase than in another.

Tension-Building Phase

Walker suggested that a series of "minor battering incidents" occurs during this phase. As these so-called minor incidents occur battered women react through a variety of coping mechanisms, including working harder to please the batterer and managing children toward the same goal, denying the seriousness of the violence, and making other efforts to restore stability to the home. As these battering incidents accumulate, Walker noted, the batterer increasingly escalates his battering behavior and this increasingly overwhelms the battered woman's ability to cope with it.

Acute Battering Incident

A period of increasingly escalating tension will eventually lead to a severe violent incident in which, Walker wrote, "an uncontrollable discharge" of tensions takes place. The cycle of violence theory suggests that this phase is the shortest of the three and both the batterer and the battered recognize that this violence is significantly different from the violence in the earlier, tension-building phase. Walker also noted that occasionally a battered woman will "provoke" an acute incident in order to get past the tension that has been building to the inevitable severe event.

Kindness and Contrite Loving Behavior

The final phase in Walker's cycle of violence theory is a period of calm following an acute violent incident. She suggested that it immediately follows the acute incident and is seen as a relief by both parties involved. The battered woman will often seek help during or immediately after an acute incident and this is when, Walker suggested, many battered women come into contact with service providers. The batterer is also likely to seek help during this period and he is often on his best behavior, promising to make changes so he is not violent again and aiming his affection and behaviors in a way to win back his partner's affection and loyalty. His positive behavior often creates confusion for his victim. Walker also suggested that this phase is usually longer than the one immediately prior to it but shorter than the first, tension-building phase. Sometimes this phase can be extremely brief, and others have suggested that chronic batterers stop trying to make up for their behavior, thus eliminating this phase over time.

Critiques

The cycle of violence, learned helplessness, and battered woman's syndrome, all originally promoted by Walker, have been heavily criticized and are discussed elsewhere in this encyclopedia. Many, including Walker, have argued that the cycle of violence is not automatic and does not always follow a predictable script by moving from one phase to another. Walker's use of the term *minor battering incidents* and suggestion that battered women learn helplessness as part of the cycle are problematic in the view of many. How does one define "minor" incidents? A slap or a shove can have severe consequences if one looks at it in context. Terms like *learned helplessness* have been countered by the use of the term *survivors* of violence and a greater focus on women's strategies to resist violent behavior.

Jeffrey L. Edleson

See also Battered Woman Syndrome; Intergenerational Transmission of Violence; Learned Helplessness

Further Readings

Stith, S. M., Rosen, K. H., Middleton, K. A., Busch, A. L., Lundeberg, K., & Carleton, R. P. (2000). The intergenerational transmission of spouse abuse: A meta-analysis. *Journal of Marriage and the Family, 62,* 640–654.

Walker, L. E. (1979). *The battered woman.* New York: Harper & Row.

Widom, C. S. (1989). Does violence beget violence? A critical examination of the literature. *Psychological Bulletin, 106,* 3–28.

Danger Assessment Instrument

The Danger Assessment (DA) instrument is designed to assess the likelihood of lethality or near lethality occurring in a case of intimate partner violence (IPV). The most important risk factor for intimate partner homicide (IPH) is prior domestic violence. Even though abused women are fairly good assessors of their own risk of reassault, they often underestimate the risk of homicide. In a major multi-city case control study of intimate partner femicide (IPF), only about half (46%) of victims accurately predicted that her husband, boyfriend, or ex-partner was capable of killing her.

Original Development

The DA was developed in consultation on item wording and content validity from battered women, advocates, law enforcement officials, and other clinical experts on battering. The initial DA items were developed from Jacqueline C. Campbell's research reviewing police IPH records as well as reviews of other studies of IPH or serious injury from IPV.

The DA first assesses severity and frequency of battering by asking an abused woman to mark on a calendar the approximate days when physically abusive incidents occurred, ranking their severity on a scale of 1 to 5. Using a calendar increases accurate recall in general and the DA calendar helps raise the woman's consciousness and reduce the normal minimization of IPV. In one study, 38% of 97 abused women initially reporting no increase in severity and frequency of violence in the past year changed their response to "yes" after filling out the calendar portion.

The second part of the original DA was a 15-item yes/no dichotomous response format of risk factors associated with IPH. Both portions of the DA take approximately 20 minutes to complete. The woman can complete the DA by herself or with professionals from the health care, criminal justice, or victim advocate systems. The original DA was scored by counting the "yes" responses, with more "yeses" indicating more danger.

The original DA has published psychometric support in eight studies with internal consistency acceptable (.70–.80) and two studies of test-retest reliability of 0.89 and 0.94. Discriminant group validity was supported by significant differences in DA mean scores among contrasting groups of women, the lowest among nonabused women and the highest in women in the emergency department. Convergent construct validity was supported with moderate to strong correlations between the DA and validated instruments (e.g., Conflict Tactics Scales) measuring severity and frequency of IPV. All of the studies testing the DA have had substantial proportions (33% to 77%) of women of color, primarily African American and Hispanic, with psychometric properties at least as strong among minority ethnicity women. Additionally, three independent predictive validity studies in the United States and one in Taiwan were published that at least partially support the DA's ability to predict IPV reassault.

Revision

The most important validation is based on data from the 11-city case-control study designed to identify risk factors for IPF and to test the DA. Consecutive police or medical examiner records of IPF from 1994 to 2000 were examined for victim–perpetrator relationship. Cases were eligible if they involved a victim aged 18 or older, a current or ex-intimate partner perpetrator, and were designated as "closed" by the police. Records were abstracted for data specific to the homicide and for potential proxy informants (i.e., mother, sister, brother, or friend) knowledgeable about the victim's relationship with the perpetrator. A knowledgeable proxy was located in 68% (373 out of 545) of the cases, and 83% (310 out of 373) agreed to participate.

A sample of 194 *attempted femicides* was identified through district attorneys, law enforcement, community domestic violence advocacy, or trauma centers in each city. Attempted femicide was defined as nonfatal gunshot or stab wound to the head, neck, or torso; strangulation or near drowning with loss of consciousness; or severe injuries inflicted that easily could have led to death of a female current or former IP of the perpetrator. The attempted femicide cases allowed direct interviews with victims rather than proxies, but yielded lower location rates (56%), since many women had moved from the attempted murder site. Once located, 90% of the attempted femicide victims (n = 215) agreed to participate (n = 194).

The control group of abused women was identified by stratified random-digit dialing for English- and Spanish-speaking women ages 18 to 50 years involved "romantically or sexually" in a relationship during the past 2 years in the same 11 cities. A total of 3,637 (76.6%) women of 4,746 meeting inclusion criteria consented to participate. Four hundred twenty-seven (8.5%) had been physically abused or threatened with a weapon by a current or recent intimate partner in the past 2 years, but never seriously enough to qualify as an attempted femicide.

The interview for all participants included the DA along with demographic and relationship characteristics including type, frequency, and severity of any violence, psychological abuse, and harassment. Safety protocols were carefully followed.

Victims and perpetrators of femicides and attempted femicides were similar in social and demographic characteristics except for a larger proportion of African American perpetrators of attempted femicides (64.1% vs. 48.9%). In multivariate analysis, the only significant demographic difference between the femicide and attempted femicide cases and the abused controls was more unemployment among the more lethal perpetrators.

The DA was revised based on the findings by adding four items—abuser unemployment, a child of the victim not the offspring of the abusive partner, abuser stalking, and the victim leaving her abuser—plus rewording of the child abuse item to read "Does he threaten to harm your children?" and the division of "threaten to kill you" and "perceive him as capable of killing you" into two items to separately assess victim perception. An item on the "prior arrest of the abusive partner for IPV" was substituted for one on the abuser "being violent outside of the home," since arrest for IPV was more predictive in the multivariate analysis. With these revisions, there is a total of 20 items.

Validation of Revised 20-Item DA

The adjusted odds ratios from the multivariate analyses of the femicide cases in comparison to the controls (abused women) were used to develop a weighted scoring algorithm identifying four levels of danger. The levels of danger and DA scores are (1) variable danger (0–7), (2) increased danger (8–13), (3) severe danger (14–17), and (4) extreme danger (18+). The language used to label the levels of danger was chosen in consultation with survivors and advocates for its meaning to abused women and to convey that even at the lowest level (variable danger), the risk of lethal violence is never negligible and can change quickly.

In a comparison of the mean scores on the revised 20-item DA of the three study groups, it was found that the femicides and attempted femicides had similar mean and median scores on the revised DA, which were more than twice as high as that of the abused control group (p < .001).

The ability of the revised DA to correctly identify the attempted femicide cases, an independent sample, was tested through plots of receiver operating characteristic (ROC) curves. ROC curves represent the sensitivity and specificity of a measure at each successive unit. Estimates of the area under the ROC curve (AUC) are compared to the average value under random prediction methods (.500).

The AUC for the ROC curve comparing attempted femicides to the abused controls was .916 (p < .001; 95% CI .892 to .941). Sensitivity of the revised DA for identifying attempted femicides ranged from .545 for the *extreme danger* level to .987 if *increased danger* is used to designate high-risk status. The sum of sensitivity and specificity is maximized if the *severe danger* level is the threshold for high-risk designation (sensitivity = .750; specificity = .863). Sensitivity and specificity were acceptable with higher values for the revised DA than victim perception of risk of lethal or near lethal violence (sensitivity = .622; specificity = .770).

Future Directions

Although limited by restrictions of an urban sample and retrospective data, the ROC curve analysis is strongly supportive of the predictive accuracy of the revised DA, far better than the .70 AUC considered acceptable in risk assessment instruments. Further testing of the DA is needed, especially independent evaluations, prospective studies, and meta-analyses, as with all of the current IPV risk assessment strategies. The DA also needs to be psychometrically evaluated with various ethnic groups and rural and immigrant populations for cultural and linguistic appropriateness. The DA is only the first step in a process of safety planning or "risk management." Protocols addressing issues such as confidentiality and communication of results and training for assessors need to be developed in each system where it is used. The science in the field is as yet young, but supports the use of the DA with IPV victims as they make important decisions about their safety in collaboration with domestic violence advocates, health care professionals, and/or criminal justice practitioners—with both practitioner expertise and the woman's perception of risk taken into account. The DA can help women come to a more realistic appraisal of their risk as well as improve the predictive accuracy of those who are trying to help them.

Jacqueline C. Campbell

See also Femicide; Gun Violence; Marital Rape/Wife Rape; Pregnancy, Violence Against Women During; Risk Assessment Instruments, Intimate Partner Violence

Further Readings

Block, C. R. (2003). How can practitioners help an abused woman lower her risk of death? *NIJ Journal, 250,* 5–7.

Campbell, J. C. (2002). Safety planning based on lethality assessment for partners of batterers in treatment. *Journal of Aggression, Maltreatment, and Trauma, 5*(2), 129–143.

Campbell, J. C. (2004). Helping women understand their risk in situations of intimate partner violence. *Journal of Interpersonal Violence, 19*(12), 1464–1477.

Campbell, J. C. (2005). Assessing dangerousness in domestic violence cases: History, challenges, and opportunities. *Criminology and Public Policy, 4,* 653–672.

Campbell, J. C. (2007). *Assessing dangerousness: Violence by batterers and child abusers.* New York: Springer.

Dutton, D. G., & Kropp, P. R. (2000). A review of domestic violence risk instruments. *Trauma, Violence & Abuse, 1,* 171–181.

Heckert, D. A., & Gondolf, E. W. (2004). Battered women's perceptions of risk versus risk factors and instruments in predicting repeat reassault. *Journal of Interpersonal Violence, 19,* 778–800.

Weisz, A., Tolman, R., & Saunders, D. G. (2000). Assessing the risk of severe domestic violence. *Journal of Interpersonal Violence, 15*(1), 75–90.

Web Sites

Danger Assessment: http://www.dangerassessment.com

DATE AND ACQUAINTANCE RAPE

Endemic to college campuses in North America and elsewhere, date and acquaintance rapes are the most common threats to female students' safety. Many researchers, rather than restricting their focus to forced sexual intercourse, now define date and acquaintance rape as involving a wide range of unwanted sexual acts stemming from physical force, threats of physical force, verbal coercion, and emotional coercion. Contrary to popular belief, an alarmingly high number of women experience these harms on an annual basis, as shown by surveys conducted in the late 20th and early 21st centuries. For example, the Canadian National Survey on Woman Abuse in University and College Dating Relationships found that 28% of the female participants stated that a male dating partner sexually assaulted them in the past year, while 11% of the males reported having sexually victimized a female dating partner during the same time period. The U.S. National College Women Sexual Victimization Survey estimated that 9 of 10 women knew the male perpetrator who raped them. Of course, the types of assaults uncovered by these and other widely cited studies begin to occur well before women reach college age, as documented by several North American surveys.

Even though a broad spectrum of college students is affected by sexual assault, the problem appears to be of little concern to many students, faculty, and administrators. Date and acquaintance rapes are often dismissed as "boys will be boys," or as some sort of exaggeration by the woman or something she was "asking for." There are a number of reasons for this, including ideologies of gender inequality.

Researchers have gathered quantitative data on these crimes. Most studies use some rendition of the Sexual Experiences Survey (SES). Developed by Mary Koss and Cheryl Oros in 1982, the SES consists of 12 yes/no items that can be examined in their totality for one measure of sexual abuse or can be divided into four types of sexual abuse:

- *Sexual contact*, which includes unwanted sex play (fondling, kissing, or petting) arising from menacing verbal pressure, misuse of authority, threats of harm, or actual physical force
- *Sexual coercion*, which includes unwanted sexual intercourse arising from the use of menacing verbal pressure or the misuse of authority
- *Attempted rape*, which includes attempted unwanted sexual intercourse arising from the use of or threats of force from the use of drugs or alcohol
- *Rape*, which includes unwanted sexual intercourse arising from the use of or threats of force and other unwanted sex acts (anal or oral intercourse or penetration by objects other than the penis) arising from the use of or threat of force or from the use of drugs or alcohol

Social scientists have also identified various risk factors, including male peer support, alcohol and drug consumption, men's adherence to the ideology of familial patriarchy, and experiencing sexual abuse prior to coming to college. However, theoretical developments in this field have not kept pace with the empirical literature. Theories attempt to explain what many people define as deviant or criminal behaviors. In response to calls for theory integration in explaining male-to-female victimization, Alberto Godenzi, Martin Schwartz, and Walter DeKeseredy have offered a relatively new theory of conformity. This social bond/male peer support theory asserts that since so many college men sexually abuse their female dating partners and acquaintances, it is college men who *do not* victimize women who are the deviants and whose bond to the dominant social order is weak or broken.

Most of the safety measures implemented by campus officials to lower date and acquaintance rape have often served to perpetuate the widespread but outdated view that women are most likely to be victimized by strangers. If the problem is defined as stranger rapists wandering around the campus, then curbing sexual assault is mostly a matter of architectural design. For this reason, the typical measures taken across North America include increased lighting, changed landscaping (e.g., removing trees), the provision of escort services, the monitoring of public places, and the installation of alarms and security phones. The main problem with these initiatives is that women are most likely to be sexually assaulted by male intimates in private places, such as houses or apartments.

In addition, because alcohol use is a major correlate of date and acquaintance rape, many colleges throughout North America have shut down student pubs, prohibited campus parties that involve alcohol consumption, and banned alcohol from dormitories and campus apartments. Further, some schools have begun to deal with the fact that many students drink off campus by extending their alcohol codes to include violations by students in off-campus environments. This may not have much more effect than on-campus bans because bar owners and bartenders may not report their patrons to campus officials for fear of losing business.

No matter what alcohol policies are developed and implemented, many sober people sexually assault women. Programs that focus on eliminating alcohol use by themselves do little, if anything, to address the broader social forces that perpetuate and legitimate sexual assault. A man may stop drinking, but this does not mean that he will no longer be exposed to sexist media, other patriarchal institutions, and pro-abuse male peer groups. For this and other reasons, scholars, practitioners, and activists are increasingly calling for prevention and control initiatives that target macro-level and social psychological factors that motivate men to victimize women.

Walter S. DeKeseredy

See also Athletes/Athletics and Sexual Violence; Male Peer Support, Theory of; Peer Influences on Youth Violence

Further Readings

DeKeseredy, W. S., & Schwartz, M. D. (1993). Male peer support and woman abuse: An expansion of DeKeseredy's model. *Sociological Spectrum, 13,* 393–413.
Fisher, B. S., Sloan, J. J., Cullen, F. T., & Lu, C. (1998). Crime in the ivory tower: The level and sources of student victimization. *Criminology, 36,* 671–710.

Godenzi, A., Schwartz, M. D., & DeKeseredy, W. S. (2001). Toward a gendered social bond/male peer support theory of university woman abuse. *Critical Criminology, 10,* 1–16.

Koss, M. P., & Oros, C. (1982). Sexual Experiences Survey: A research instrument investigating sexual aggression and victimization. *Journal of Consulting and Clinical Psychology, 50,* 455–457.

Schwartz, M. D., & DeKeseredy, W. S. (1997). *Sexual assault on the college campus: The role of male peer support.* Thousand Oaks, CA: Sage.

Schwartz, M. D., & Pitts, V. (1995). Toward a feminist routine activities approach to explaining sexual assault. *Justice Quarterly, 12,* 10–31.

Dating Violence/ Courtship Violence

Dating or courtship violence is a pattern of actual or threatened acts of physical, sexual, and/or emotional abuse perpetrated by an individual against a current or former dating partner. Abuse may include insults, coercion, intimidation, sexual harassment, and threats. The effects of dating violence can last a lifetime, particularly for those who are victims of the abuse in their teens and young adult years.

Occurrence

Dating violence occurs in the intimate relationships of persons in a range of ages, from the preteen years through adulthood. Dating violence can occur in heterosexual and homosexual relationships. Statistics indicate that a majority of reported cases of teen dating violence involve male-on-female violence. One in five teenage girls is a victim of dating violence. The highest rates of intimate violence affect women aged 16 to 24 years. Forty percent of teenage girls 14 to 17 years old report knowing someone their age who has been hurt or beaten by a boyfriend. Fifty percent of dating violence victims report the violence to someone else; of these, 88% report the violence to a friend and 20% to criminal justice authorities.

Teen Dating Violence and Adult Intimate Partner Violence

Teen or young adult dating violence mirrors adult intimate partner violence in several ways. For example, teen dating violence covers the same continuum of different types of abuse as adult intimate partner violence. Also similar to adult intimate partner violence, research shows that ending an abusive relationship is the most dangerous time for the victim. However, teen dating violence is different from adult intimate partner violence in two key ways. First, for teens, who are just starting to develop thoughts on dating and love, recognizing that their partner is controlling or abusive is challenging. Second, once they recognize the abuse, teenagers are less likely to disclose the abuse to anyone due to fear that disclosure may lead to backlash by their peers and/or legal guardians.

Barriers
Confidentiality

Most state laws require teens to obtain parental consent to services and mandate agencies and certain professionals to report any abuse that comes to their attention. Therefore, many teenagers are hesitant to share what is happening in their relationship with service providers, such as teachers and doctors. Teens may not want their parents to know about the relationship or about the abuse. They fear that their parents will call the police or medical professionals for assistance in ending the relationship. Although mandatory reporting laws may not apply to lawyers, seeking legal help may be difficult since attorneys may not be able to represent minors who are not emancipated from their legal guardians.

Shelters and Safety Planning

Many shelters are not equipped to handle teenage victims of dating violence. Therefore, teenagers face different roadblocks in their safety planning than adult intimate partner violence survivors. Safety planning may need to incorporate teachers, school administrators, family members, and friends.

Protection Orders for Teens

Protection orders usually only cover adult relationships. Nineteen states and the District of Columbia extend protection orders to teenagers. In some states, such as California, teenagers can petition the civil court for a protection order with the consent of a parent or legal guardian.

Adult Misconceptions

Research shows that adults often minimize the seriousness of dating violence. They generally fail to recognize the severity of the abuse. Adding to this problem is the fact that teenagers themselves sometimes mislabel the abuse as "passionate love."

Self-Blaming and Peer Pressure

Some teens may blame themselves for the abuse. They may feel that others are judging them and the relationship. Gay and lesbian teens may not be able to tell others about their relationship for fear of "outing" themselves and the consequences that would entail. And some teenagers may stay in a relationship due to peer pressure.

Chaitra P. Shenoy

See also Cycle of Violence; Date and Acquaintance Rape; Intimate Partner Violence; Restraining and Protective Orders

Further Readings

Dating Violence Resource Center. (2002). *Teen dating violence fact sheet.* Retrieved April 27, 2006, from http://www.ncvc.org/ncvc/AGP.Net/Components/document Viewer/Download.aspxnz?DocumentID=38057

Green, C., & Mohlenrich, L. M. (2005). *Dating violence: Can teens access protection orders?* Retrieved April 27, 2006, from http://www.ncvc.org/ncvc/main.aspx?dbName =DocumentViewer&DocumentID=42052

National Resource Center on Domestic Violence. (2004). *Teen dating violence: Overview.* Retrieved April 27, 2006, from http://www.vawnet.org/NRCDVPublications/TAPE/Packets/NRC_TDV.pdf

DEATH PENALTY

See CAPITAL PUNISHMENT

DECRIMINALIZATION OF SEX WORK

From this perspective, the act of selling sex for money is not inherently harmful to women. Advocates for sex workers' rights view consensual sexual activity among adults for money as an occupational choice of individual sex workers who decide to sell sex for money. *Sex work* is a term consciously used by advocates to identify sex for money as legitimate work. To these activists, there is no difference between a woman who chooses to sell her vagina for intercourse and one who sells her hands for dishwashing, her body for modeling, or her brain for calculating.

These advocates posit that to believe that all women in prostitution are exploited is to reject a fundamental feminist principle of valuing and accepting the existence of multiple realities in women's lives. Further, dismissing the claims of sex workers that they are not exploited and are choosing sex work denies their reality, is maternalistic, and serves to silence their voice.

Sex work disturbs the sensibilities of society and is therefore deemed a crime. When prostitution is made a crime, sex workers are oppressed and prevented from exercising their right to self-determination and denied the basic human right to control their own body. Feminists agree that women should control the decision to have an abortion, because each woman's body is her own, but in the same breath will not assign ownership and decision making to a woman who chooses to sell her body for money.

In recent years sex worker rights advocates have argued and lobbied for decriminalization of sex work and for protection of sex workers under a free and democratic society. Their argument is rooted in the American ideal of free choice and free enterprise denied under a society that stigmatizes sex workers and asserts political control over an often misinterpreted and largely misunderstood issue.

Advocates put forth several reasons why sex work among consenting adults is demonized by society. At the core of their argument is the fundamental belief about women and male ownership of a woman's sexuality through marriage or commitment. Sex workers challenge the very system built to maintain this status quo. Because prostitution is one of the few work experiences where women dominate the field financially and challenge beliefs about gender and sexuality, it remains stigmatized and unaccepted. Indeed it is this stigma, labeling, and demonizing by society that creates a perspective and societal milieu that pushes sex work underground where it can be dangerous and psychologically and physically harmful to women.

Policies and Programs Supported by Sex Worker Rights Advocates

Legalization of prostitution is not popular among sex worker advocates because it typically means state control over a woman's activities. To them, legalization may involve new taxes, restrictions, and regulations on when, where, and how to work; mandated licenses and registration; and a host of other costs designed to be financially coercive. Advocates for sex worker rights support the decriminalization of all aspects of adult prostitution, including those who purchase or manage the women involved.

Sex worker advocates acknowledge that although sex work may be a temporary job for some women, all sex workers need proper health care and prevention, awareness, and interventions to keep them safe, healthy, and prosperous. Thus, these advocates support and operate harm reduction programs designed to reduce and/or prevent violence, HIV, and poor health outcomes and to promote health, safety, and overall well-being. Sex worker advocates conduct outreach, operate clinics, and provide needed social services. Beyond direct service with sex workers, advocates engage in local, national, and international advocacy to facilitate discussion; promote sex worker decriminalization; and push for more sex work–friendly agendas in their own communities as well as in other parts of the world.

Reducing Violence Against Women by Decriminalizing Prostitution

Preventing violence against women in sex work is at the forefront of the sex worker rights agenda. However, attempting to rescue women who are not victims is viewed as demeaning and disrespectful to these women. Advocates acknowledge that street-based prostitution, the bottom rung of sex work, is fraught with violence, risks of HIV, poor mental health outcomes, and drug addiction.

While street-based prostitution is estimated to occupy upwards of 30% of all prostitution, most published research is focused on street prostitution and generalized to the experiences of all women in prostitution. Critics argue that this is an unfair and biased reporting of the experience of prostitution.

Advocates believe that violence against women in sex work would be reduced if such work were a legitimate profession in which sex workers were afforded all of the protections of society that women in other professions have. The example of the sexually harassed secretary, who without the protections of workplace policies and the support of society would have to suffer continued victimization at the hands of her employers and other male employees, serves as a case in point. The secretary who is victimized has access to formal complaints and protections under the law.

Decriminalizing sex work is, in the minds of these advocates, the best way to respond to violence against this population of women. Decriminalizing prostitution removes the fear that women have to report the violence inflicted on them to authorities.

Advocates for the Cause

The following are among the trendsetting leaders in the movement regarding sex workers' rights: Robin Few, Margo St. James, Carol Leigh, and Norma Almovodar. Some of the most notable U.S.-led movements have come from Call Off Your Old Tired Ethics (COYOTE), International Sex Worker Foundation for Art, Culture, and Education (IASFACE), St. James Infirmary, and the Sex Workers Outreach Project (SWOP).

Celia Williamson

See also Abolitionist Approach to Prostitution; Prostitution

Further Readings

Jenness, V. (1990). From sex as sin to sex as work: COYOTE and the reorganization of prostitution as a social problem. *Social Problems, 37,* 403–420.

Kinnell, H. (2002). *Why feminists should rethink on sex workers' rights.* UK Network of Sex Work Projects. Retrieved from http://www.nswp.org/pdf/kinnell-feminists.pdf

Pheterson, G. (1990). The category "prostitute" under scientific inquiry. *Journal of Sex Research, 27*(3), 397–405.

Prostitutes Education Network. (2006). *International Committee for Prostitutes' Rights: Human rights.* Retrieved August 10, 2006, from http://www.bayswan.org/ICPRChart.html

Prostitutes Education Network. (2006). *Prostitution in the United States—The statistics.* Retrieved August 10, 2006, from http://www.bayswan.org/stats.html

Scott, M. S. (2006). *Street prostitution.* Retrieved August 15, 2006, from http://www.popcenter.org/Problems/problem-street_prostitution.htm

Simmons, M. (1999). Theorizing prostitution: The question of agency. In B. M. Dank & R. Refinetti (Eds.), *Sex work and sex workers* (pp. 125–148). New Brunswick, NJ: Transaction.

Sloan, L., & Wahab, S. (2000). Feminist voices on sex work: Implications for social work. *Affilia, 15*(4), 457–479.

Vanwesenbeeck, I. (2001). Another decade of social scientific work on sex work: A review of research 1999–2000. *Annual Review of Sex Research, 12,* 242–289.

Delinquency and Dating Violence

A history of delinquency, aggression, or conduct problems is linked to dating violence—defined as physical, sexual, or psychological violence within a dating relationship. However, research on family violence and other kinds of violence and antisocial behavior has been generally conducted separately, and examination of links between these phenomena, especially for teenagers, is relatively new.

Initially, focus on violence between intimate partners was placed exclusively on violence between married partners since it was believed that dating violence, particularly among teenagers, was rare or inconsequential. In the last decade it has become clear that it is neither, as national studies have established more accurate estimates of prevalence and correlates. Since violence between married partners has been linked consistently to patterns of antisocial behavior, investigation of overlap between delinquency, aggression, and dating violence is of interest, especially since both partner violence and antisocial behavior are most prevalent during adolescence and early adulthood.

Prevalence of Dating Violence

Estimates of teen dating violence vary widely. Data gathered in the context of criminal victimization by the National Crime Victimization Survey (NCVS) show low estimates in general, and much higher estimates of victimization reported by teenage females (12.4%) compared to teenage males (1.2%). Other national studies of high school students gathered in the context of a survey of general behaviors, such as the Youth Risk Behavior Survey conducted in 2003 by the Centers for Disease Control and Prevention, have suggested higher and more gender-equivalent estimates, with about 1 in 11 students having reported physical victimization in the past year. Another national estimate of adolescents in high school indicated that almost one third of respondents report experiencing some lifetime dating violence, including psychological

and physical violence, again with similar rates for males and females. Other studies of dating violence have reported even higher prevalence rates of some violence in a current dating relationship. Differences in estimates across studies are due to many factors, including different samples, varying confidentiality of responses, time frames, and instrumentation. The most widely used measure to survey partner violence is the Conflict Tactics Scales developed by Murray Straus, which assess the occurrence and frequency of a range of violent behaviors during arguments, ranging from hitting to injuring with a weapon.

Despite earlier focus on male violence perpetration, surveys that include both genders have found that young women and young men indicate similar rates of violence perpetrated and received, and also indicate they are involved in mutual or reciprocal violence. Both men and women display clinically significant levels of relationship violence, that is, at levels that are more typically seen in shelters or court-mandated treatment, although much violence does not fall into that category. It appears that young women are more likely than men to suffer serious harm and to experience sexual violence.

Risk Factors

Many studies have indicated that a history of aggression and antisocial behavior during childhood or adolescence is a risk factor for adult male partner violence perpetration. Longitudinal studies conducted in different contexts and countries also have indicated that delinquency and conduct problems in childhood and adolescence prospectively predict young adult partner violence in both genders (i.e., having experienced conduct problems in youth significantly increases individuals' risk of being in a relationship where dating violence occurs). In general, delinquency and conduct problems are measured by youth or parent report, and not arrest. The much smaller amount of research on teenagers also has suggested that people of both sexes who display violence toward their dating partners are more aggressive than their peers, as well as more likely to display other risk behaviors, including engaging in sex, attempting suicide, and heavy drinking.

Since there is overlap between dating violence and antisocial behavior, it is important to understand the similarities and differences in the risk profiles of adolescents who engage in one or the other or both behaviors. As is the case with adult partner violence, many variables appear to be linked to dating violence, including personal, contextual, and interpersonal variables of those experiencing violence as well as of the perpetrators. Individual risk factors that cross both sets of behaviors include poor parenting; socioeconomic disadvantage; and, importantly, a history of violence in the family of origin, including physical child abuse and witnessing parental violence. Psychological risk factors are less studied, but also include personality characteristics such as reactivity, impulsivity, and negative emotionality, which may have a genetic basis but could also arise from or be exacerbated by lack of warmth and bonding in early family relationships.

Some studies have tried to elucidate developmental pathways that might link risk factors like experiencing family violence to delinquency, violence, and dating violence. A learning theory approach suggests that early coercive, hostile relationship patterns in the family are learned and carry through into individuals' relationships with their peers and dating partners. Another hypothesis is that exposure to violence in the family leads to failure in adolescents' ability to regulate emotions, especially anger and anxiety, and also difficulties in forming rewarding relationships with others. In addition, adolescents who have been exposed to violence are hypothesized to gravitate toward an aggressive deviant peer group, including opposite sex peers who share similar characteristics and are also ill equipped to negotiate developmentally appropriate intimate relationships.

In the few longitudinal studies that have been conducted, early family risk such as ineffective parenting or exposure to family violence predicted early adolescent antisocial behavior, which then predicted dating violence. Other studies have found that experiences of family violence predict later dating violence, without an intervening history of conduct problems or aggression outside the family. Thus, these behaviors do not completely share an underlying propensity. It appears that dating violence and aggressive behavior are partly overlapping phenomena but are also distinct, and that a history of conduct problems is not a necessary prelude to being in violent dating relationships. Some studies have indicated that having both problems is linked with higher levels of cumulative risk. Both females and males seem to display continuity in aggressive and antisocial behavior at young ages. There is also some evidence of pathways that may differ by gender: Males engaging in partner violence may have more undercontrolled personality histories, whereas females engaging in partner violence may experience more depressive symptoms, and may age out of dating violence at higher rates. Inconsistent and incomplete findings result from the few tests of these hypotheses.

Prevention and Intervention

The continued investigation of theoretically and clinically informed risk factors for dating violence in teenagers should inform prevention and intervention programs. Some researchers feel intervention is premature in view of the still emerging state of research on at-risk teenagers. However, dating violence interventions for high-risk teens, including those who have been victims of child maltreatment or who have witnessed domestic violence between parents, show promising results in modifying teens' cognitions and norms about the acceptability of violence. There is no strong justification for focusing on males exclusively since patterns for males and females are more similar than different. Given the links between delinquency and dating violence, successful delinquency interventions could also modify trajectories toward dating violence, particularly if the target was broader antisocial, aggressive behaviors that included violence to dating partners. It is of special concern that antisocial teens and teens in violent dating relationships also frequently become young parents, thus perpetuating intergenerational transmission of antisocial behavior and relationship conflict.

Carolyn Ann Smith

See also Dating Violence/Courtship Violence; Delinquency and Violence; Intergenerational Transmission of Violence; Prevention Programs, Adolescent Dating Violence

Further Readings

Avery-Leaf, S., Cascardi, M., O'Leary, K. D., & Cano, A. (1997). Efficacy of a dating violence prevention program on attitudes justifying aggression. *Journal of Adolescent Health, 21,* 11–17.

Centers for Disease Control and Prevention. (2006). *Physical dating violence among high school students—United States, 2003.* Retrieved from http://www.cdc.gov/mmwr/preview/mmwrhtml/mm5519a3.htm

Ehrensaft, M. K., Cohen, P., Brown, J., Emailes, E., Chen, H., & Johnson, J. G. (2003). Intergenerational transmission of partner violence: A 20-year prospective study. *Journal of Consulting and Clinical Psychology, 4,* 741–753.

Giordano, P. C., Millhollin, T. J., & Cernkovich, S. A. (1999). Delinquency, identity, and women's involvement in relationship violence. *Criminology, 37*(1), 17–36.

Halpern, C. T., Oslak, S. G., Young, M. L., Martin, S. L., & Kupper, L. L. (2001). Partner violence among adolescents in opposite-sex romantic relationships: Findings from the National Longitudinal Study of Adolescent Health. *American Journal of Public Health, 91*(10), 1679–1685.

Hickman, L. J., Jaycock, L. H., & Aronoff, J. (2004). Dating violence among adolescents: Prevalence, gender distribution and prevention program effectiveness. *Trauma, Violence and Abuse, 5,* 123–142.

Lewis, S. F., & Fremouw, W. (2003). Dating violence: A critical review of the literature. *Clinical Psychology Review, 21,* 105–127.

O'Keefe, M. (1998). Factors mediating the link between witnessing interparental violence and dating violence. *Journal of Family Violence, 13,* 39–57.

Simons, R. L., Lin, K.-H., & Gordon, L. C. (1998). Socialization in the family of origin and male dating violence: A prospective study. *Journal of Marriage and the Family, 60,* 467–478.

Straus, M. A. (1990). Measuring intrafamily conflict and violence. The Conflict Tactics (CT) Scales. In M. A. Straus & R. J. Gelles (Eds.), *Physical violence in American families: Risk factors and adaptations to violence in 8,145 families* (pp. 403–424). New Brunswick, NJ: Transaction Press.

DELINQUENCY AND VIOLENCE

Delinquency is commonly associated with violent behavior. Chances are that when people are asked what they commonly perceive as delinquent behavior, youth violence will not be far from their minds. Although the specter of youth violence has fueled fears about crime generally, and moral panics erupt every so often about so-called superpredators or youth gangs, the vast majority of delinquent behavior is nonviolent. Delinquent behavior generally peaks at around age 16, yet the peak for violent crime comes a little later in the life course. This is not to say that young people under the age of 18 do not commit violent acts—they do—but they do so in fewer numbers than is commonly perceived. This entry discusses not only the extent of violent delinquency in the United States but also the explanations for and public responses to violent delinquency.

The Extent of Violent Delinquency in the United States

Delinquency is an illegal act committed by a minor, and what is known about delinquency has been gleaned from a number of different sources. The first source of data on delinquency is the annual arrest data collated by the Federal Bureau of Investigation (FBI) from most law enforcement agencies in the United States. Recent arrest data show that law enforcement agencies made an estimated 2.14 million juvenile arrests in 2005. In terms of juvenile arrests for violent behavior, there were 95,300 made for violent index crimes—murder, rape, robbery, and aggravated assault—and a further 247,900 arrests made for other assaults. What this means is that in real terms only 4.4% of juvenile arrests were for serious violent offenses, and a further 11.5% were for simple assaults or assaults where no weapon was used.

There are advantages and disadvantages to using official sources of data. The advantage is that one can get a sense of the trends in arrests over time because the data are collated annually. So in terms of violent delinquency the trends of the past two decades illustrate that arrests for serious violent crime peaked in the early 1990s, with the juvenile arrest rate for murder peaking in 1991 at 13.1 per 100,000. Since then, juvenile arrests for violence have decreased markedly, the arrest rate for murder being 3.8 per 100,000 in 2005. There have been similar declines in arrests for other serious violent offenses. For instance, between 1996 and 2005, juvenile arrests for rape declined 25%, while there were declines of 34% and 20% for robbery and aggravated assault, respectively. In terms of arrest then, one can conclude from the available data that violent delinquency has decreased from its high water mark in the early 1990s, though there is a perception that the United States is poised for another increase. While arrest statistics give one a general idea of the trends in violent delinquency, there are a number of drawbacks with respect to relying solely on official data. In the first place the data only count the total number of arrests, which does not account for an individual being arrested multiple times in a year, nor for an individual arrested once, but charged with multiple offenses. More importantly, official data do not count those who committed illegal acts but who were never arrested.

Self-reports are a second set of data that researchers commonly rely upon for a sense of the extent of violence among minors. Self-report studies are designed to capture the so-called hidden figure of crime, that is, those acts committed but never officially recorded, and they do this by simply asking individuals to self-disclose delinquent acts. Generally, self-report studies have shown delinquency to be more widespread than official statistics would have one believe. There are several notable self-report studies that illustrate the prevalence of violent behavior among young people. For example, Monitoring the Future is an ongoing national sample of 12th graders that is conducted annually by the University of Michigan, and it calculates a violence index, based on how respondents answer five questions about violent behavior. The violence index has remained remarkably stable over time, and it shows that approximately 30% of 12th graders surveyed have engaged in at least one of the five violent acts specified, which range from hitting a teacher to injuring a person badly enough that he or she required medical attention. The latter category, called assault with injury, had an average prevalence of about 12% over the 10-year period from 1988 to 1998. That this prevalence rate is high reveals the disjuncture between official and self-report data, but it is also indicative of the fact that the subjects interviewed had an average age of 18, which is just about the peak age for violent offending. Other self-report studies use different questions to assess the prevalence rate for violence among minors, but their results reveal similar prevalence rates. The National Youth Survey reports an average of 9% prevalence in serious violent delinquency-aggravated assault, gang fights, robbery, and rape among 17-year-olds interviewed in the 1976 and 1982 waves of that longitudinal study.

The self-report studies demonstrate how the arrest data underestimate the prevalence of violence among minors, but as with official statistics, there are drawbacks to relying solely on self-reports. In the first place, there are differences between self-report studies in the questions that they use to ascertain prevalence levels and, in some cases, the questions used focus on trivial offenses. There is also the possibility that respondents may exaggerate their involvement, thus inflating the prevalence levels.

The third variant of data that is used to assess violent delinquency is victimization data, specifically those data reported in the National Crime Victimization Survey (NCVS). The NCVS is collected annually from a large sample of households, and it asks people to report victim experiences. Routinely, the results from the NCVS show that individuals do not report about half of all violent crime, and this holds true for minors as well as adults.

Taken together, these three sources of data illustrate that while only a small amount of delinquent behavior is violent, a large proportion of youth admit to engaging in violent behavior. It is known from studies of desistance that the vast majority of offenders will eventually cease engaging in illegal behavior, but because the peak age for committing violent offenses occurs in the mid- to late teens, it follows that violent delinquency garners a great deal of attention from scholars and policymakers. The former group has proffered a variety of explanations as to why minors engage in violence, while the latter group has come up with ways to prevent and/or reduce juvenile violence.

Explanations for Violent Delinquency

Explanations for the causes of youth violence are plentiful, and this entry concentrates on three broad types of argument: those that advocate structural, cultural, or psychological lines of reasoning. The first category of explanation examines how structural factors are largely what drive youth violence. So, for example, some scholars see violent delinquency as being due to demographics, in that when there is a large generation of teenagers, there will be more crime. However, the simple demographic model has come under criticism in that it failed to predict the steady decreases in youth violence that have occurred from the mid-1990s into the present at the same time as the teenage population has increased. A more widely accepted structural argument concerning violent delinquency is one that views it as an epidemic. This explanation holds that violence behaves in ways similar to disease, and can spread rapidly when a certain mix of factors is in place. So, for example, the much vaunted high water mark of youth violence in the United States in the late 1980s and early 1990s was due to the structural factors that sustained this epidemic, such as the increased availability of guns and the instability of urban drug markets, and levels of youth violence have decreased as the contributory conditions have changed. A final variant of structural explanations examines the ecological and structural context in which much youth violence occurs. Scholars in this tradition point to the fact that youth violence is concentrated in certain types of neighborhoods, characterized by concentrated disadvantage, low social controls, and low levels of collective efficacy. It is the combination of these ecological factors that allows youth violence to flourish, though not all young people exposed to these conditions commit violent acts. In sum, structural explanations focus more on the aggregate than on the individual, which contrasts with cultural explanations of violent delinquency.

Cultural explanations of youth violence hold that young people engage in violent acts because they are conforming to the norms of their group. Such cultural analyses are used to explain the presence and activities of youth gangs and the violence that is often associated with them. Though there are several variants of the cultural approach, the most widespread are those that argue for a subculture of violence, and those that view violence as part of a wider cultural adaptation to a marginal status. The subculture of violence theory argues that cultural norms and values, particularly among lower class people, call for the use of violence in certain social situations, and violence is thus normative for people socialized into this culture. The cultural adaptation approach is a variation on the subculture of violence explanation and holds that many people adapt to a marginal social position by imbuing a tough reputation and the maintenance of respect with an elevated status. One must maintain one's reputation by violent means if necessary, and similarly, any disrespect must be met with violence or the threat thereof. This so-called street code then explains how high levels of violence endure in many low status neighborhoods. Subcultural explanations of violent delinquency, and of gang violence especially, have proven popular and controversial in equal measure. The chief criticism of the cultural approach is that it overstates the normative nature of violent behavior and overestimates the extent of immersion in an oppositional culture on the part of subjects.

Psychological explanations form a third major approach commonly used to account for youth violence. Psychological explanations focus on the individual and explain youth violence as being due to an excess of risk factors for violent behavior over protective factors that inhibit such acting out. Common risk factors that can predispose individuals to violence are exposure to violence, being a victim of violence, and

displaying early antisocial behavior. Several scholars in the psychological camp argue that violence is an adaptation to risk factors, which can cause future problems for the individual but which also is an alternative to depression or other self-destructive behaviors. A frequent criticism of psychological explanations is that they underplay the fundamentally situated and group nature of much violent delinquency.

Public Policy Responses

Violent delinquency is an area of periodic controversy, and public policy responses tend to reflect this fact in that they have been mainly reactive and punitive in the recent past. As levels of violent delinquency rose to their high point in the early 1990s, the most widespread policy response became the waiver system, in which cases involving minors are waived from the jurisdiction of juvenile to adult courts. All states have juvenile waiver laws for certain serious violent crimes, usually homicide and robbery, and this has resulted in a more punitive approach being taken toward violent delinquents. Trying juveniles as adults and incarcerating them in the adult prison system has not been effective in reducing recidivism, though advocates argue that the deterrent effect has been instrumental in reducing rates of violent delinquency.

A second type of delinquency intervention program that has been linked with some success is the intensive parole and probation programs that formed the mainstay of the so-called Boston model. In this approach, authorities singled out the youth most likely to be violent, who were either on probation or being paroled from juvenile detention, and they aggressively monitored them and attempted to build upon their prosocial attachments in terms of education and employment. The program, which entailed multiagency cooperation, claimed success in that there were no youth homicides in Boston over an 18-month period. Though the Boston model has been imitated elsewhere, the successes have not been as spectacular.

There are other approaches that are reactive but less punitive, such as the use of restorative justice approaches, including shaming circles. These programs are designed as alternatives to the conventional juvenile justice system and require that the juvenile offender encounter the people that she or he has wronged and, in many cases, make reparation and restitution to them. Though restorative justice is more commonly used for nonviolent crimes, it is increasingly being employed in cases of violent delinquency, with mostly positive results in terms of recidivism and victim satisfaction.

Though it is uncertain as to whether the punitive turn has had the desired effects with regard to reducing violent delinquency, being tough on young violent offenders is still the predominant policy response in the United States.

Patrick J. Carr

See also Community Violence, Effects on Children and Youth; Gang Violence; Moral Panics; Prevention Programs, Youth Violence; Restorative Justice; Subculture of Violence; Youth Violence

Further Readings

Butts, J. A., & Snyder, H. N. (2007, Spring). Where are the juvenile crime trends headed? *Juvenile and Family Justice Today,* pp. 16–21.

Cook, P. J., & Laub, J. H. (1998). The unprecedented epidemic in youth violence. In M. Tonry & M. H. Moore (Eds.), *Youth violence* (pp. 27–64). Chicago: University of Chicago Press.

Cook, P. J., & Laub, J. H. (2002). After the epidemic: Recent trends in youth violence in the United States. In M. Tonry (Ed.), *Crime and justice: A review of research* (pp. 1–29). Chicago: University of Chicago Press.

Satcher, D. (2001). *Youth violence: A report of the surgeon general.* Washington, DC: U.S. Department of Health and Human Services.

DEPARTMENT OF HOMELAND SECURITY, ASYLUM

Every year, thousands of people come to the United States seeking asylum. Asylum is given to those individuals fleeing persecution on account of their race, religion, national origin, political opinion, or membership in a particular social group. A person seeking asylum must do so within a year of his or her arrival in the United States. Those granted asylum must stay in that status for 1 year before they are allowed to file for lawful permanent residency status. Although the standard asylum seekers must meet is governed by the law defining *refugee,* asylum status differs from refugee status in that people seeking asylum file applications from within the United States or at the border, while refugees are identified and file for refugee status while outside of the United States. However, in both categories applicants must prove that they qualify under one of the previously listed categories of persecution.

There are two pathways to asylum: affirmative and defensive. The affirmative process is when an applicant seeks asylum by filing his or her own application with the United States Citizenship and Immigration Services (USCIS). The asylum seeker affirmatively initiates contact with the Department of Homeland Security (DHS). The asylum seeker has not been picked up by DHS and placed in immigration removal (formerly deportation) proceedings before an immigration judge. The defensive process involves applicants who are in removal proceedings. These applicants must request asylum before an immigration judge during these proceedings.

Affirmative Process

Applicants fill out a USCIS application form, attach relevant supporting material/documents, and send it to the USCIS Service Center that has jurisdiction over their place of residence. Asylum applicants may also include applications for their spouse and/or children in their applications. Once the Service Center has received the forms, it will send the applicant a notice acknowledging receipt of the application. Applicants then go through a security check. After the applicant passes the background check, interviews are scheduled with an asylum officer. If an applicant is applying for others as well (e.g., his or her spouse and/or children), then the others must also attend the interview. In this interview, the applicant must prove that he or she meets the definition of *refugee.* To do so the applicant must prove that he or she was persecuted on account of race, religion, nationality, political opinion, or membership in a particular social group. After the asylum officer has a chance to review and discuss the interview with supervisory officers, the applicant returns to the asylum office to receive a decision. If asylum is approved, the applicant receives a final approval letter. If asylum is denied, the applicant will either be referred to an immigration court for removal or receive a notice of intent to deny asylum. The decision on whether to send an applicant to immigration court depends on what his or her immigration status is at the time asylum is denied.

Defensive Process

Immigration judges hear asylum applications in the context of "defensive" asylum proceedings where applicants request asylum as a defense against removal from the United States. Immigration judges hear such cases in courtroom-like proceedings. The immigration judge hears both the applicant's side and the government's side of the case, and then makes a determination of eligibility for asylum. If the applicant is not found eligible for asylum, the immigration judge determines whether the applicant is eligible for any other forms of relief from removal. If the immigration judge determines that there is no other relief available, the individual is ordered removed from the United States.

If applicants are denied asylum after having filed either an affirmative or defensive asylum application, they are entitled to have their denial reviewed by the Board of Immigration Appeals (BIA), the immigration appeals court. If their claim is denied by the BIA, the asylum applicant can appeal the case to a United States Circuit Court of Appeals for what is usually a final decision. The appeals process can be lengthy and very costly, so most asylum seekers do not pursue this path. Additionally, people seeking asylum have no legal right to an attorney. Many of those denied often cannot afford the expensive legal representation it can take to have an asylum application granted. Furthermore, asylum offices do not provide interpreters for applicants. Many applicants speak little to no English, may not be able to understand American accents, may have difficulty getting their thoughts across in English, and may not be able to afford or find proper interpreters. Worthy asylum seekers, who genuinely fear returning to their countries of origin, may be unable to access asylum because they lack access to interpreters and/or legal representation.

Asylum seekers can also come to the United States across borders or through various other ports-of-entry. If they are undocumented, many stopped by immigration officials may be subject to *expedited removal*—a method of removing people without allowing them the opportunity to plead their case in court. However, some people subject to expedited removal are genuine asylum seekers fleeing persecution. Because of the circumstances of their flight from their homes, they may have arrived in the United States with no documents or with fraudulent documents.

Any person subject to expedited removal who raises a claim for asylum—or expresses fear of removal—will be given the opportunity to explain his or her fears. Immigration officers are required to ask people about their fears. This requirement was created based on an understanding that unless asked, many asylum seekers may be afraid to reveal details about the persecution they have suffered.

Leslye Orloff and Amanda Baran

See also Department of Homeland Security and Immigration Services; Refugee/Asylee

Web Sites

Department of Homeland Security: http://www.dhs.gov
U.S. Citizenship and Immigration Service: http://www.uscis.gov

DEPARTMENT OF HOMELAND SECURITY, RESPONSE TO BATTERED IMMIGRANTS AND IMMIGRANT VICTIMS OF VIOLENCE AGAINST WOMEN

In 1986, Congress enacted the Immigration Marriage Fraud Amendments (IMFA) to deter marriage-related immigration fraud. In an effort to ensure that lawful permanent resident status was granted only to immigrant spouses in valid marriages to U.S. citizens, IMFA required that immigrant spouses who obtained permanent residence based on a marriage to a U.S. citizen or lawful permanent resident fulfill a 2-year conditional residence requirement before being granted lawful permanent residence. The law required a joint petition to be filed 90 days before the expiration of the 2-year conditional resident status period, possibly followed by a joint interview with a Department of Homeland Security (DHS) official.

For immigrant victims of domestic violence, the joint filing requirement proved difficult. Immigrant women who were being abused remained in dangerous and abusive relationships in order to fulfill the joint filing requirement. In 1990, Congress enacted the first piece of federal legislation designed to help immigrant domestic violence victims—the *battered spouse waiver.* The waiver allowed battered immigrants to file an application for the purpose of removing the conditions on their permanent residence without the knowledge or assistance of the abusive spouse.

A range of additional legal remedies now exists to aid battered immigrants and immigrant victims of violence against women. The Violence Against Women Act (VAWA) of 1994, which was amended and expanded through VAWA II in 2000 and VAWA III in 2005, contains several provisions designed to prevent abusers from using immigration as a tool to control their victims. The VAWA self-petition is an important form of relief that service providers, health care providers, and justice system personnel and counselors need to be familiar with so that they can educate immigrant victims who qualify about the forms of access to legal immigration status that have been created to help immigrant victims of violence against women. The VAWA self-petition enables a battered immigrant to obtain lawful permanent resident status without the help, knowledge, or cooperation of her U.S. citizen or lawful permanent resident abusive spouse or parent. The filing of this self-petition can occur at any time and, due to the changes in 2000, can even occur after a divorce if the petition is filed within 2 years of the divorce and if the divorce was related to the abuse. Approval of a VAWA self-petition provides the immigrant victim access to work authorization, protection from deportation, and ultimately access to legal permanent residency status, which is a required precursor to applying for U.S. citizenship status. VAWA 2005 extended the benefits of VAWA self-petitions to abused parents of U.S. citizen adult sons and daughters.

Changes to VAWA in 2000 created additional remedies for survivors of violence. Congress created two new nonimmigrant visas to help battered victims and immigrant victims of sexual assault, trafficking, and other violent crimes. The first nonimmigrant visa is the U-visa, also known as a crime victims' visa. An applicant must prove that she has been a victim of a certain type of serious crime, has suffered substantial physical or mental abuse as a result of the crime, has information about the crime, and can provide a certification from a law enforcement official, prosecutor, judge, or other government official (e.g., the Equal Employment Opportunity Commission, or EEOC) that the victim has been, is, or is likely to be helpful in investigating or prosecuting criminal activity. The other type of nonimmigrant visa is the T-visa. An applicant must prove that she has been a victim of a severe form of trafficking and has either complied with any reasonable request for assistance in the investigation or prosecution of trafficking or has not yet turned 15 years old. Both applications require law enforcement involvement, but only the U-visa requires a law enforcement letter or affidavit. If either the U-visa or the T-visa is approved, the applicant may be eligible to apply for lawful permanent resident status under certain circumstances.

Self-Petitions Under the Violence Against Women Act

VAWA of 1994 created a way for victims to obtain lawful permanent residency without depending on their abusive husbands or parents to apply for such residency. This form of relief is known as a VAWA self-petition. If an immigrant woman is or was married, and her husband has abused her or her child, she may qualify for this relief. Unmarried children under the age of 21 who are being or were abused by a parent who is a citizen or a lawful permanent resident are also eligible for VAWA relief. Those who were abused while under the age of 21 may file a VAWA self-petition while they are still minors, or their nonabusive parents may file for them. Children have until the age of 25 to file a VAWA self-petition so long as they were abused when they were under 21 years of age. VAWA relief is only available to women and children whose abusive husbands or parents are U.S. citizens or lawful permanent residents. Nonabusive immigrant parents whose citizen or lawful permanent resident spouse has abused the immigrant parent's natural or adopted child or stepchild can also file a VAWA self-petition so that they can come forward without fear of deportation to protect their child. The nonabusive immigrant parent can qualify for a VAWA self-petition without regard to the immigration or citizenship status of the abused child.

A victim may be eligible for a self-petition if she is

1. married to a U.S. citizen or a lawful permanent resident, or

2. was divorced less than 2 years ago from a U.S. citizen or lawful permanent resident spouse, or

3. the child of a U.S. citizen or lawful permanent resident.

Additionally, a victim

4. must live in the United States, or

5. if living abroad,
   a. must have been abused in the United States, or
   b. her abusive spouse or parent must either be an employee of the U.S. government or a member of the U.S. armed forces.

Furthermore,

6. a victim or her child must have been physically or sexually abused or suffered extreme cruelty perpetrated by her citizen or lawful permanent resident husband or parent.

If a victim qualifies for a self-petition she will be able to obtain a "green card" (permanent residence in the United States) without her abuser's help or knowledge.

Crime Victims' Visas

In October of 2000, Congress created an immigration remedy that expanded the categories of victims covered by VAWA. This remedy, the U-visa, offers legal immigration status to immigrant victims of domestic violence, sexual assault, trafficking, and other violent crimes. This visa is especially helpful to victims abused by intimate partners who are not spouses, or by spouses or parents who are not citizens or lawful permanent residents. It also helps those victims whose abusers are employers, other family members, or strangers. The immigration status of the abuser is not a factor in the U-visa case. The abuser or crime perpetrator can be undocumented, a diplomat, a person with a legal work visa, a citizen, or a permanent resident.

To qualify for a U-visa a victim must prove

1. substantial physical or emotional abuse from criminal activity,

2. possession of information about the criminal activity,

3. that the criminal activity occurred in the United States or otherwise violates U.S. law.

In addition, a victim must obtain a certification from law enforcement stating that she has been, is likely to be, or is being helpful to an investigation or prosecution of criminal activity. The certification must come from a federal, state, or local law enforcement official, prosecutor, judge, or EEOC officer investigating or prosecuting the criminal activity.

A victim must have been the victim of at least one of the following criminal activities: rape, torture, trafficking in persons, incest, domestic violence, sexual assault, prostitution, female genital mutilation, being held hostage, peonage, involuntary servitude, slave trade, kidnapping, abduction, false imprisonment,

blackmail, extortion, manslaughter, murder, felonious assault, witness tampering, obstruction of justice, perjury or attempt, conspiracy, or solicitation to commit any of these crimes. A victim must be willing to cooperate in the investigation or prosecution of criminal activity committed against her. Usually this will require a victim to make a police report and a willingness to speak with law enforcement about the crime.

A victim may apply for the U-visa as soon as she gets the needed certification and can gather the proof of the substantial physical or emotional abuse she has suffered. The goal of the U-visa protections is to encourage immigrant victims to come forward and cooperate in criminal investigations as well as prosecutions. U-visas are available even if the criminal case has not yet been filed, if prosecutors decide not to file the criminal case, if the perpetrator cannot be found, if a case is filed and the applicant is not needed as a witness, or if the abuser is not ultimately convicted of the crime. Applicants' children can also receive U-visas.

Leslye Orloff and Amanda Baran

See also Department of Homeland Security and Immigration Services; Domestic Violence Among Immigrant Women; Immigrant and Migrant Women; Violence Against Women Act

Further Readings

Bui, H. N. (2004). *In the adopted land: Abused immigrant women and the criminal justice system.* Westport, CT: Praeger.

Raj, A., Santana, M. C., & Orloff, L. E. (Eds.). (2007). Gender-based violence against immigrant women in the United States [Special issue]. *Violence Against Women, 13*(5).

Raj, A., & Silverman, J. G. (2002). Intimate partner violence against immigrant women: The roles of immigrant culture, context, and legal status. *Violence Against Women, 8*, 367–398.

DEPARTMENT OF HOMELAND SECURITY AND IMMIGRATION SERVICES

On November 25, 2002, President George W. Bush signed the Homeland Security Act of 2002 into law. This law transferred the Immigration and Naturalization

Service's (INS's) functions to the new Department of Homeland Security (DHS). DHS then created three separate bureaus: United States Citizenship and Immigration Services (USCIS), United States Immigration and Customs Enforcement (ICE), and United States Customs and Border Protection (CBP). As of March 1, 2003, the former Immigration and Naturalization Service was dismantled, and its functions delegated to DHS.

USCIS is the immigration services branch of DHS. It processes applications for immigration benefits filed by immigrants filing affirmative applications for immigration benefits. These include family-based petitions, employment-based petitions, asylum and refugee processing, document issuance and renewal, and other special status programs. Immigrants come into contact with USCIS regularly. For example, those who have had family-based petitions filed on their behalf, or who are filing family-based petitions for others, route their paperwork through this branch. Those filing applications for lawful permanent residency and refugees and asylees have their paperwork processed by this branch. Most notably, immigrants who are or have been victims of violence send their applications (VAWA self-petitions, U-visa applications, and T-visa applications) to a specialized unit within the Vermont Service Center. This unit is staffed by adjudicators who have been trained on the different aspects of violence and how it operates in intimate and nonintimate relationships. Sending these sensitive types of applications to a well-trained group of adjudicators makes the immigration process more efficient, impartial, and safer for victims.

ICE is the enforcement and investigative branch of DHS. Among its duties are operating detention centers, putting immigrants into removal proceedings, investigating immigration crimes, and investigating human trafficking and smuggling. Immigrant victims can come into contact with ICE in a variety of ways. ICE officers regularly identify women who are trafficked for commercial sex or labor purposes through their investigations and sting operations. Sometimes ICE officers acting on "tips" from abusers will arrest undocumented immigrant women who are eligible for or have pending VAWA self-petitions and U-visa applications. To stop these practices, Section 384 of the Illegal Immigration Reform and Immigrant Responsibility Act of 1996 prohibits an adverse determination of an immigrant victim's deportability from being made using information gathered solely from an abuser. Additionally, immigrants seeking asylum, or who have VAWA, U-visa, or T-visa immigration relief available to them, can be detained at U.S. ports of entry by ICE after they have passed through immigration inspection. Some of these victims are removed expeditiously, without any opportunity to plead their case before a judge, in a practice known as *expedited removal.*

CBP patrols and secures the U.S. land and ocean borders. Its articulated mission is to enforce all applicable U.S. laws and keep terrorists and their weapons from entering the United States while welcoming all legitimate travelers and trade. CBP officers are the immigration inspectors who examine the documents of visitors to the United States through a program called US-VISIT. For many immigrants seeking asylum or who have VAWA, U-visa, or T-visa immigration relief available to them, CBP is the first point of contact they have with the immigration system.

Leslye Orloff and Amanda Baran

See also Department of Homeland Security, Asylum; Department of Homeland Security, Response to Battered Immigrants and Immigrant Victims of Violence Against Women; Immigrant and Migrant Women; Refugee/Asylee

Further Readings

U.S. Customs and Border Patrol. (n.d.). *CBP: Securing America's borders.* Washington, DC: Author. Retrieved from http://www.cbp.gov/xp/cgov/border_security/antiterror_initiatives/border_sec_initiatives_lp.xml

U.S. Department of Homeland Security. (2007). *DHS US-VISIT program.* Retrieved from http://www.dhs.gov/dhspublic/interapp/content_multi_image/content_multi_image_0006.xml

DEPRESSION

Depression is a common aftereffect of abuse and violence. The Commonwealth Fund Adolescent Health Survey found that physically and sexually abused girls were five times more likely to report depressive symptoms than nonabused girls. In a primary-care sample, 65% of sexually abused women reported feeling blue or depressed compared with 35% of nonabused women. And in a study of chronic pain in primary-care patients, women with a history of child or domestic abuse were significantly more likely to be depressed than a matched group of nonabused women. Unfortunately, depression can lead to poor health in abuse survivors.

Immune Dysfunction in Depression

For several years, researchers considered depression to be primarily immunosuppressive. More recent studies indicate that depression causes an immune dysfunction, meaning that some aspects of immunity are suppressed, while others are elevated. For example, depressed people have fewer lymphocytes, making them more vulnerable to infection. However, depressed people also have elevated levels of inflammation—and this increases the risk of disease.

How Depression Influences Health

A number of significant health problems have been associated with depression, including coronary heart disease, chronic pain syndromes, premature aging, impaired wound healing, and Alzheimer's disease. The National Comorbidity Study found that childhood physical abuse, sexual abuse, and neglect increased the risk of cardiovascular disease ninefold. In this study, however, it was trauma history, rather than depression, that accounted for the increased risk of cardiovascular disease.

Although these findings are still preliminary, depression is something that must be identified and treated in abuse survivors to effect a positive impact on their health.

Kathleen Kendall-Tackett

See also Adult Survivors of Childhood Abuse; Health Consequences of Child Maltreatment; Health Consequences of Intimate Partner Violence

Further Readings

Batten, S. V., Aslan, M., Maciejewski, P. K., & Mazure, C. M. (2004). Childhood maltreatment as a risk factor for adult cardiovascular disease and depression. *Journal of Clinical Psychiatry, 65,* 249–254.

Campbell, J. C., & Kendall-Tackett, K. A. (2005). Intimate partner violence: Implications for women's physical and mental health. In K. A. Kendall-Tackett (Ed.), *Handbook of women, stress and trauma* (pp. 123–140). New York: Taylor & Francis.

Hulme, P. A. (2000). Symptomatology and health care utilization of women primary care patients who experienced childhood sexual abuse. *Child Abuse & Neglect, 24,* 1471–1484.

Kendall-Tackett, K. A. (2003). *Treating the lifetime health effects of childhood victimization.* Kingston, NJ: Civic Research Institute.

Kendall-Tackett, K. A., Marshall, R., & Ness, K. E. (2003). Chronic pain syndromes and violence against women. *Women and Therapy, 26,* 45–56.

Kiecolt-Glaser, J. K., & Glaser, R. (2002). Depression and immune function: Central pathways to morbidity and mortality. *Journal of Psychosomatic Research, 53,* 873–876.

Kop, W. J., & Gottdiener, J. S. (2005). The role of immune system parameters in the relationship between depression and coronary artery disease. *Psychosomatic Medicine, 67,* S37–S41.

DEVELOPMENTALLY DISABLED SEX OFFENDERS

The term *developmental disability* (DD) when applied to sex offenders is largely synonymous with the terms *intellectual disability, mental retardation,* and *learning disability.* These descriptors are used to refer to sex offenders who have IQ scores below 70 and who display concurrent deficits in adaptive behavior. There are particular challenges in the service delivery, assessment, and treatment of sex offenders with DD.

It wasn't too long ago that this group was labeled "feebleminded imbeciles" and thought to be untreatable. As such, little attempt was made to provide them with even basic human rights, let alone understand their abilities, disabilities, or behavior. Through a change in professional and societal views, the knowledge base regarding sexual offenders with DD has grown extensively in the last 25 years. Clinical efforts initially worked on adapting the approaches used with mainstream offenders, often with limited success.

In the past 10 years, the clinical and research focus has moved to the development and evaluation of specific assessment and intervention approaches for individuals with DD. This approach has yielded a plethora of theoretical, clinical, and ethical advancements in the treatment of sex offenders with DD.

When working with individuals with DD it is important to identify their strengths and developmental challenges in order to provide successful assessment and intervention. Individuals with DD display a range of information-processing deficits. These may include difficulties with attention, memory, and language comprehension. Cognitive and language deficits should be comprehensively assessed and incorporated into individualized assessment and treatment strategies. This may limit the use of complex language and self-report questionnaires and increase the need for multimodal presentation of information (i.e., pictorial or visual presentation). In addition, a comprehensive assessment should include information regarding personal history, social history, psychiatric history, offending history, coping strategies, and cognitions.

A range of treatment approaches have been utilized with DD sexual offenders. There is very little research evidence for the efficacy of psychopharmacology approaches. Behavioral approaches have been used to teach self-control techniques, improve social/sexual skills, and decrease inappropriate arousal. Cognitive-behavioral approaches have received the most empirical validation. These approaches apply behavioral methods in conjunction with challenging cognitive distortions regarding the offense (e.g., minimization or denial). This work is tailored from the relapse prevention literature and has been developed specifically for DD offenders. There is some evidence that treatment programs of greater than 1 year duration are better at reducing recidivism than shorter programs.

A range of etiological models have been developed to help explain sexual offending in this population. They include impulsivity models, sexual abuse theories, deviant sexual interests and arousal patterns, lack of sexual knowledge, and poor social skills.

Jeff Salt

See also Sex Offenders

Further Readings

Lindsay, W. R., Michie, A., Whitefield, E., Martin, V., & Grieve, A. (2006). Response patterns on the Questionnaire on Attitudes Consistent with Sexual Offending in groups of sex offenders with intellectual disabilities. *Journal of Applied Research in Intellectual Disabilities, 19,* 47–53.
Lindsay, W. R., Taylor, J. L., & Sturmey, P. (2004). *Offenders with developmental disabilities.* Chichester, UK: Wiley.

DIMINISHED CAPACITY DEFENSES

See INSANITY DEFENSE

DISABILITY AND PORNOGRAPHY

Pornography is any medium that depicts erotic behavior for the sake of sexual arousal. This controversial subject is most often associated with magazines and movies but also includes books, art, cartoons, and other media. With the advent of Internet-based media and commerce, the pornography industry has expanded into cyberspace, thus allowing for greater product accessibility while maintaining relative user anonymity.

One of the many genres of pornography is pornography depicting people with disabilities. This genre, which spans nearly every media type, displays people with a wide range of disabilities engaged in sexual acts alone or with others. Most often, in this type of pornography people with physical disabilities play characters with disabilities, those with amputated limbs, who use wheelchairs, or who have vision impairment; however, people without disabilities have also been cast to play characters with disabilities. Overall, women with disabilities are more prevalent in the industry than men.

With respect to interpersonal violence, a critical feminist perspective views pornography as degrading, oppressive, and exploitive for women, as they are objectified for the sake of sexual arousal of pornography consumers, who are mostly men. This male-centered objectification ultimately promotes inequality and subjugation, which are seen not only as forms of violence but also as pathways to other types of abuses such as physical and emotional abuse. When considering women with disabilities in pornography, this critical view is expanded, as women with disabilities are perceived to be more vulnerable and therefore in greater danger of sexual abuse, exploitation, and subjugation.

Other feminist perspectives view disability pornography differently. Many sex-positive feminists tend to believe that everyone should have freedom to make their own sexual choices, including accepting a broad array of human sexuality, which includes pornography. In this view, pornography is but an avenue for individuals to freely display their sexuality, both in creating it and in using it. From this perspective, people with disabilities participating in the pornography industry are exerting their sexual freedom by displaying their sexuality in ways they choose. Therefore, pornography tends not to be viewed as a violent act toward women with disabilities, as they, like all others participating, are displaying their sexual power and freedom.

Third-wave feminism tends to view pornography more pluralistically, as it may have both beneficial and damaging effects at the same time. For example, women with disabilities who participate in pornography may benefit others by reducing the social stigma where people with disabilities are viewed as asexual, unattractive beings. Conversely, by participating in pornography, women with disabilities may promote the emotional and physical abuse of women with and without disabilities. This feminist view differs from others, as it does not present a dichotomy, where pornography is either good or bad. Instead, it acknowledges that those participating in its creation may interpret the pros and cons differently, thus leaving the interpretation to the participant women.

Disability, Sexual Abuse, and Pornography

Exploring the topic of disability and pornography from the various feminist perspectives allows for a broad discussion; however, those with disabilities and the practitioners working in the field tend to be more focused on pornography's impact on sexual abuse. In fact, it is widely accepted that the presentation of pornography to people with disabilities, without their informed consent, is a form of sexual abuse. Those most vulnerable to such abuses tend to include people with intellectual and/or developmental disabilities (ID/DD). This higher risk can be attributed to a variety of factors, including communication difficulties, lack of understanding about the event or its legality, desire for acceptance, power differentials, and/or fear. Similarly, as identified in the literature, pornography usage by people with disabilities, particularly those with ID/DD, may be an indicator of sexual abuse.

Derek Nord

See also Acrotomophilia; Sexual Abuse

Further Readings

Benjamin, J. (1983). Master and slave: The fantasy of erotic domination. In A. Snitow, C. Stansell, & S. Thompson (Eds.), *Powers of desire: The politics of sexuality* (pp. 460–467). New York: Monthly Review Press.

Dworkin, A. (1990). *Pornography: Men possessing women.* New York: Dutton.

Elman, A. R. (1997). Disability pornography: The fetishization of women's vulnerabilities. *Violence Against Women, 3*(3), 257–270.

Heywood, L., & Drake, J. (Eds.). (1997). *Third wave agenda: Being feminist, doing feminism.* Minneapolis: University of Minnesota Press.

MacKinnon, C. A., & Dworkin, A. (1997). *In harm's way: The pornography civil rights hearings.* Cambridge, MA: Harvard University Press.

McElroy, W. (1995). *XXX: A woman's right to pornography.* New York: St. Martin's Press.

Queen, C. (1996). *Real live nude girl: Chronicles of sex-positive culture.* Pittsburgh, PA: Cleis Press.

Sobey, D. (1994). *Violence and abuse in the lives of people with disabilities.* Baltimore, MD: Paul H. Brookes.

Waxman-Fiduccia, B. F. (1999). Sexual imagery of physically disabled women: Erotic? Perverse? Sexist? *Sexuality and Disability, 17*(3), 277–282.

DISSOCIATION

Dissociation is a neurophysiological process by which individuals become disconnected from their behavioral, affective, cognitive, or sensory reality. This process occurs for some individuals when they are in a terrifying situation and have no perceived means of escape. This is one of two primary neurophysiological processes that occur when individuals are confronted with a terrifying situation and is associated with a "freeze" response. The other process is better known as the fight-or-flight response. The dissociative response is more typical of females, and the fight-or-flight response is more typical of males. Certain individuals appear to have a greater genetic predisposition to dissociate under terrifying conditions. Children are especially prone to dissociation.

Dissociative experiences encompass a continuum of internal states, ranging from the most basic daydreaming on one end of the continuum to dissociative identity disorder (formerly multiple personality disorder) on the other. Dissociative experiences so problematic as to be considered maladaptive are labeled dissociative disorders. These experiences can be isolated or repetitive. In dissociative fugue, individuals suddenly and unexpectedly travel away from home and assume a new identity without being able to recall their previous identity. In dissociative amnesia, individuals cannot recall essential information about themselves, often of a traumatic nature. Depersonalization disorder occurs when individuals' sense of their own reality is temporarily lost or distorted, as when individuals experience themselves as being in a dream or outside their body.

Dissociative Identity Disorder

Dissociative identity disorder is the most serious dissociative disorder. When children respond to repeated terrifying experiences by dissociating, they find it progressively easier to move into a dissociative state. Over repeated episodes of abuse, this state may develop its own unique knowledge or history of the abuse as well as its own sensory, affective, and behavioral realities. When these four realities converge within a single state, individuals typically experience this state as a unique identity or personality that is capable of taking control over behavior. Individuals may or may not be aware of this personality state. Once individuals are able to develop a single personality state, they also become capable of developing multiple personality states. Thus, most individuals with dissociative identity disorder have more than one personality state. Although treatment for individuals with the disorder is typically long term, the disorder can be resolved over time with appropriate therapeutic attention to the incipient traumas. Successful treatment can culminate with complete integration of personality states or with multiple personality states that have learned to coexist in harmony with the individual.

Rebecca M. Bolen

See also Adult Survivors of Childhood Abuse; Child Exposure to Intimate Partner Violence; Complex Trauma in Children and Adolescents

Further Readings

American Psychiatric Association. (2000). *Diagnostic and statistical manual of mental disorders* (4th ed., Text rev.). Washington, DC: Author.

Silberg, J. L. (2000). Fifteen years of dissociation in maltreated children: Where do we go from here? *Child Maltreatment, 5,* 119–136.

DIVORCE AND INTIMATE PARTNER VIOLENCE

Intimate partner violence (IPV) has consistently been shown to be a strong predictor of relationship dissolution. Research generally finds that a majority of victimized women leave their abusive partner within 2 years of marriage. One research group found that couples with a history of IPV were twice as likely as couples with no history of IPV to be separated after 2 years. Consistent with existing literature, this study also found that severe violence was more strongly related to relationship dissolution than was moderate violence. Similar to nonviolent divorces, the process of leaving a violent relationship may be characterized by self-doubt and a decision to return to the partner. The literature suggests that a majority of people who ultimately leave their violent partner will reunite with the aggressive partner at least once. Reasons victimized women give for returning to the relationship often relate to the perpetrator apologizing, expressing remorse, and promising to change.

In addition to being a determinant of relationship separation, IPV has also been found to be a consequence of or exacerbated by separation. Indeed, victimized women frequently endorse fear of retaliation and increased violence as major reasons for remaining in abusive relationships. This fear may be warranted; separation is predictive of continued violence and increases the frequency and severity of violence. Moreover, many nonviolent relationships become violent at the time of separation. At the extreme, separation has been identified as a risk factor for lethal violence, including being killed by an intimate partner. Recent estimates suggest that, compared to married women, separated women are five times more likely to be murdered.

Barriers to Leaving a Violent Relationship

In addition to the threat of continued violence, several other factors have been associated with the decision to stay in or leave a violent relationship. Women with more financial independence (e.g., personal income, employment) are more likely to leave a violent relationship than economically disadvantaged women. Additionally, women who are less invested in the relationship (e.g., in terms of resources, time, love for their partner) and who exhibit fewer positive feelings toward their violent partner are more likely to leave their abuser. The size and quality of women's social support network is positively related to leaving and not returning to a violent relationship. The receipt of psychological abuse has also been implicated as a barrier to leaving a physically violent relationship. Psychologically abused partners may lose feelings of self-worth and assertiveness, possibly making it even more difficult for them to leave the relationship.

The decision to leave a violent relationship is considerably more complicated when children are involved. In addition to coping with the stressors of single parenthood (e.g., income, employment, child care), women separating in the context of victimization are at an increased risk of being revictimized during visitations and frequently worry about the safety of their children. Violent partners often use custody threats and threats to abduct or otherwise harm the children as a form of manipulation.

Based on the aforementioned difficulties with leaving a violent relationship and on the finding that women often separate from abusive partners, the focus should not be on why individuals stay in abusive relationships, but rather on what gives them the ability to leave.

Postseparation Psychological Well-Being

It is generally assumed that psychological distress improves after leaving a violent relationship. While mental health tends to improve over time, research suggests that problems such as depression, anxiety, and posttraumatic stress disorder persist for months after exiting a violent relationship. This is likely the result of a combination of the lingering effects of the erstwhile abuse, the continued threat of physical and psychological aggression, and the stressors associated with leaving any relationship, albeit a violent one. This has important implications for how mental health workers treat individuals who have left or are contemplating leaving an abusive relationship. Treatment should usually persist well after the violent relationship has ended. In addition to helping abused individuals

process and cope with their erstwhile abusive relationship, mental health workers should also assist with newly acquired situational stressors (e.g., child care, finances).

Cultural Influences

A person's decision to stay or leave a violent relationship is likely influenced by that person's cultural and religious beliefs. For example, studies have shown that Hispanic women tend to more strictly interpret gender roles and have a strong belief in the sanctity of marriage, suggesting they may have less of an inclination to leave a violent relationship. In addition, Asian women and men may be less likely to seek help from community resources for fear of bringing shame to their family. Although religion can be an instrumental resource for women coping with IPV and divorce, there is some evidence that clergy, while not excusing the violence, may encourage victimized women to avoid divorce and remain in a violent relationship. Of course, religious and cultural influences vary across individuals, and thus the above findings should not be overgeneralized. An individualized, tailored assessment of these factors should be carefully undertaken for each person.

It should be noted that much of what is known about IPV and divorce is limited to studies of victimized women and studies of relationship separation (i.e., not divorce per se). Thus, additional research is needed on divorce and victimized men and on how relationship status (e.g., married, cohabiting) influences the dissolution of violent relationships.

Jeff R. Temple and Gregory L. Stuart

See also Battered Women, Leaving Violent Intimate Relationships; Custody, Contact, and Visitation: Relationship to Domestic Violence; Divorce in Relation to Child Abuse; Intimate Partner Relationship Quality and Domestic Violence

Further Readings

Anderson, D. K., & Saunders, D. G. (2003). Leaving an abusive partner: An empirical review of predictors, the process of leaving, and psychological well-being. *Trauma, Violence, & Abuse, 4,* 163–191.
Bradbury, T., & Lawrence, E. (1999). Physical aggression and the longitudinal course of newlywed marriage.

In X. Arriaga & S. Oskamp (Eds.), *Violence in intimate relationships* (pp. 181–202). Thousand Oaks, CA: Sage.

Walker, R., Logan, T. K., Jordan, C. E., & Campbell, J. C. (2004). An integrative review of separation in the context of victimization: Consequences and implications for women. *Trauma, Violence, & Abuse, 5,* 143–193.

Divorce in Relation to Child Abuse

For many child welfare professionals, the connection of child abuse and divorce brings to mind false allegations. A recent study in Australia examined the "myth of abuse in divorce" and found that there is reason to believe that allegations made from families experiencing marital breakup may actually have a high incident of truth. Much depends on the child welfare system's process of investigating, as well as the knowledge and understanding of professionals involved with the family.

The Myth

The classic child abuse allegation coming from a parent in a divorce action involves children spending time with one parent, and when returned to the other parent, an allegation of abuse being made. In a study of child abuse reports involving emergency room staff, the participants were asked what reports they considered false. Eighty percent believed that if a divorce was involved and the allegation was against the "other" parent, then the information should be considered suspect. Many times this was reinforced by the reporting parent asking for a record of the medical visit. Child welfare systems tend to abrogate these reports by insisting that a follow-up be done with either a medical doctor or a therapist. Basically these systems are looking for a second professional opinion on the validity of the allegation.

Current Research

The Australian study examined close to 200 divorce actions with child abuse allegations. The study found that only 9% were actually false allegations. A larger percentage were allegations that were not able to be proved to the extent of the legal standard; however, there was shared opinion among professionals that the abuse did happen. Further findings from the study showed that the separation of courts involved in marriage dissolution and the child welfare courts presented a problem in communicating issues relating to children's welfare.

What research has been done in this area has not linked the underlying reasons for divorce and the incidents of child abuse. Anecdotal evidence shows that if family violence is part of the reason for marriage dissolution, the incidents of child abuse may be very high. Family violence research has a history of segmenting the violence into categories, thus not showing overlaps or correlations. One study did find evidence that child abuse may persist even after the parents physically separated. This may be due to underlying violence in the family system.

The Children as Victims

Children who experience marital dissolution often become much more vulnerable. They struggle with security and abandonment issues following the breakdown of their family structure. This may lead to their being vulnerable to abuse. These children often seek security and acceptance from their parents, and if they are victims of parental child abuse they may be very reluctant to disclose. Furthermore, disclosure that leads to the child welfare system's intervention can result in blame being put on the reporting child. Thus the child ends up being even more alienated from the abusing parent.

Timothy Brett Zuel

See also Child Abuse Prevention; Collaborative Divorce, Benefits to Children; Divorce in Relation to Youth Violence; Family Therapy and Family Violence

Further Readings

Brown, T., Frederico, M., Hewitt, L., & Sheehan, R. (2001). The child abuse and divorce myth. *Child Abuse Review, 10,* 113–124.

Humphreys, C. (1997). Child sexual abuse allegations in the context of divorce: Issues for mothers. *British Journal of Social Work, 27,* 529–544.

Johnson, J., & Campbell, J. (1993). Parent–child relationships in domestic violence families. *Family and Conciliation Courts Review, 31,* 282–312.

Schuman, D. C. (1986). False accusations of physical and sexual abuse. *Bulletin of the American Academy of Psychiatry and the Law, 14*(5), 6–20.

DIVORCE IN RELATION TO YOUTH VIOLENCE

Divorce is a permanent marital breakup that has both short- and long-term links to youth violence. Research does not universally support this relationship directly, and may be related to measurement of single-parent families rather than divorce specifically. Divorce has been identified as a significant risk factor for adolescent violence, albeit not the only one. Short-term effects have been likened to experiencing an accident where the effects are immediate. Long-term effects have been viewed as a disintegration of the family, one that begins before divorce and persists long after. The relation of divorce to youth violence also appears at both the individual and neighborhood levels. Violence includes a range of behaviors, from very serious behaviors such as murder and rape to fighting and bullying, and can also include suicide as an act of violence against oneself.

At the individual level, youth whose parents divorce are subject to the loss of a parent, experienced as a negative life event, that is a stressor linked to violence, the effects of which can be seen often in the short term, for example, fighting or even suicide. In some cases, this is exacerbated by marital conflict leading to the divorce. Long term, divorce can also lower supervision and interrupt the formation of attachments or positive connections between parents and children, which inhibits the internalization of prosocial norms. In addition, divorce can lead to numerous transitions in the child's life, such as adjusting to stepparents and moving, which have been linked to delinquency and violence. This, in turn, can lead to greater peer influence. However, the continued involvement of the displaced parent has been shown to decrease delinquent youth outcomes. Theories that contribute to these areas include general strain theory, social control theory, and social learning/differential association theory.

Divorce rates have also been linked to youth violence. Youth from neighborhoods with higher levels of single-parent families commit a higher number of violent acts. This association has remained when research has assessed the influence of other important variables and for crimes measured through official police reports as well as those self-reported by adolescents. These findings may be related to high numbers of youth who have experienced the circumstances indicated above and live in an area characterized by a cumulative lack of supervision and heightened peer influence. Research on neighborhood effects on violence often uses a social disorganization or underclass theoretical framework. Another potential link to violence comes from an increased use of guns in the commission of crimes in disadvantaged neighborhoods, those often characterized by high divorce rates, which increases the likelihood of a violent result.

Gender is also important to consider when examining the relationship between divorce and youth violence, yet little research focuses on gender specifically. Although males are consistently more outwardly violent than females, recent research shows divorce may have a greater influence on females' violent offending than on males' offending. Recent findings show divorce increases the likelihood of female perpetration of dating violence more than it does male perpetration of dating violence.

Jeb A. Booth

See also Delinquency and Dating Violence; Divorce and Intimate Partner Violence; Divorce in Relation to Child Abuse; Parenting Practices and Violence, Youth Violence

Further Readings

Banyard, V. L., Cross, C., & Modecki, K. L. (2006). Interpersonal violence in adolescence: Ecological correlates of self-reported perpetration. *Journal of Interpersonal Violence, 21,* 1314–1332.

Knoester, C., & Haynie, D. L. (2005). Community context, social integration into family, and youth violence. *Journal of Marriage and the Family, 67,* 767–780.

McMahon, J., & Clay-Warner, J. (2002). Child abuse and future criminality: The role of social service placement, family disorganization, and gender. *Journal of Interpersonal Violence, 17,* 1002–1019.

Rebellon, C. J. (2002). Reconsidering the broken homes/delinquency relationship and exploring its mediating mechanism(s). *Criminology, 40,* 103–136.

Sampson, R. J., & Groves, W. B. (1989). Community structure and crime: Testing social disorganization theory. *American Journal of Sociology, 94,* 774–802.

Simons, R. L., Lin, K.-H., Gordon, L. C., Conger, R. D., & Lorenz, F. O. (1999). Explaining the higher incidence of adjustment problems among children of divorce compared with those in two-parent families. *Journal of Marriage and the Family, 6,* 1020–1033.

DOMESTIC VIOLENCE, TRAUMA, AND MENTAL HEALTH

Domestic violence can have a range of mental health consequences. According to the Domestic Violence & Mental Health Policy Initiative's training manual *Access to Advocacy,* women experience poorer physical and mental health as a result of abuse. Advocates confirm this, with many noting that the number of clients—women and children—with trauma-related, mental health needs has been increasing. Likewise, over half of women seen in a range of mental health settings either currently are experiencing or have experienced abuse by an intimate partner. Nonclinical studies examining the prevalence of intimate partner violence in the general population also reveal multiple associated mental and physical health effects.

Although for many women symptoms abate with increased safety and social support, for others this is not the case. And, while many abuse survivors do not develop psychiatric conditions, a number of studies have shown that women who have been victimized by an intimate partner are at significantly higher risk for depression, anxiety, posttraumatic stress disorder (PTSD), somatization, medical problems, substance abuse, and suicide attempts, whether or not they have suffered physical injury. Researchers have found that nearly 50% of survivors of domestic violence experience depression, over 60% experience PTSD, and nearly 20% experience feelings associated with suicidality. Domestic violence also increases women's risk for substance abuse. Abusive partners frequently coerce women into using drugs or alcohol, and substance abuse is a common method of relieving pain and coping with anxiety and depression. Substance abuse, itself, puts women at greater risk for victimization.

For many women, abuse by an adult partner is their first experience of victimization; for others, domestic violence occurs in the context of other lifetime trauma. A number of studies have begun to explore the link between histories of physical and sexual abuse in childhood and experiencing partner abuse as an adult. Women who are sexually abused as children or who witness their mothers being abused appear to be at greater risk for victimization in adolescence and adulthood. Additionally, studies of battered women in both clinical and shelter settings are finding increased rates of childhood abuse and childhood exposure to domestic violence. For women who have experienced multiple forms of victimization (e.g., childhood abuse; sexual assault; historical, cultural, or refugee trauma), adult partner abuse puts them at even greater risk for developing posttraumatic mental health conditions.

The development of mental health symptoms in the context of domestic violence is influenced by a number of factors in addition to the severity and duration of the abuse. For example, low-income women have the highest risk of being physically and/or sexually victimized throughout their lives. These experiences, however, do not occur in isolation; a body of clinical literature describes the retraumatizing effects of more subtle forms of social and cultural victimization (e.g., microtraumatization due to gender, race, ethnicity, sexual orientation, disability, and/or socioeconomic status). Thus, although intimate partner violence is itself associated with a wide range of psychological consequences, women living in disenfranchised communities face multiple sources of stress in addition to violence, including social discrimination, poorer health status, and reduced access to critical resources.

Domestic Violence, Lifetime Victimization, and Mental Illness

While most survivors of domestic abuse do not develop long-lasting psychiatric disabilities, women living with mental illness often have histories of abuse. Studies across a variety of mental health settings have found significant rates of lifetime abuse among people living with mental illness, with those in inpatient facilities reporting the highest rates (53% to 83%). Researchers have found similar rates of adult victimization by acquaintances, strangers, family members, and intimate partners among people with psychiatric disabilities.

Domestic violence presents particular risks for individuals with mental illness. Exposure to ongoing abuse can exacerbate symptoms and impede recovery, making it more difficult to access resources and increasing abusers' control over their lives. Stigma associated with mental illness and lack of clinical training about domestic violence reinforce abusers' abilities to manipulate mental health issues to control their partners; undermine them in custody battles; and discredit them with friends, family, and the courts. For example, abusers may commit or threaten to commit their partners to psychiatric institutions. They may force women to take overdoses, which are then presented as suicide attempts, or they may withhold medications. They may also assert that accusations of abuse are simply delusions, lying outright about their partners' behaviors or rationalizing their own (e.g., by claiming their partner "needed to be restrained"). Poverty, homelessness, institutionalization, unsafe living conditions, and dependence on caregivers exacerbate these risks, leaving individuals with psychiatric disabilities vulnerable to victimization by a range of perpetrators—within families, on the streets, in institutional and residential settings, and by intimate or dating partners. Domestic violence, itself, is often a precipitant to homelessness.

Despite these concerns, the mental health system has not systematically responded to these issues, and there have been systematic efforts to build community partnerships with domestic violence and mental health consumer advocacy programs to address the mental health effects of domestic violence and other lifetime trauma. Because of this lack of collaboration between sectors, many women and children are left without a safe way to address these concerns. In addition, many providers are left without resources to support them in doing this work.

Implications of Trauma Theory for Working With Survivors of Domestic Violence

More recently, trauma theory has begun to be viewed as a potential framework for bridging clinical and advocacy perspectives. The emergence of trauma theory over the past three decades has created a significant shift in the ways mental health symptoms are conceptualized and in our understanding of the role abuse and violence play in the development of psychological distress and mental health conditions. Trauma theory, which arose out of observations of the experiences of survivors of civilian and combat trauma, views symptoms as survival strategies—adaptations to potentially life-shattering situations that are made when real protection is unavailable and normal coping mechanisms are overwhelmed. Trauma theory helps destigmatize the mental health consequences of domestic violence by recognizing the role of external events in generating symptoms, normalizing human responses to traumas such as interpersonal violence, and creating a framework for understanding the ways in which the biological, emotional, cognitive, and interpersonal effects of chronic abuse can lead to future difficulties in a person's life.

It also affords a more balanced approach to treatment—one that focuses on resilience and strengths as well as psychological harm. Lastly, a trauma framework fosters an awareness of the impact of this work on providers, and emphasizes the importance of provider self-care, along with administrative, consultative, and peer support.

Although trauma models are not a substitute for advocacy-based approaches that help survivors achieve freedom and safety and work to end domestic violence, trauma theory can greatly inform and enhance advocacy work by increasing understanding of the psychological consequences of abuse and how trauma affects both domestic violence survivors and the providers and programs that serve them. Trauma models offer guidance on creating services that are sensitive to the experiences of survivors of chronic abuse and that incorporate an understanding of how those experiences can affect individuals' ability to regulate emotions, process information, and attend to their surroundings. The models also provide tools for responding skillfully and empathically to individuals for whom trust is a critical issue, without having one's own reactions interfere. Trauma-informed service environments provide emotional as well as physical safety and are consistent with advocacy models in their focus on empowerment, collaboration, and choice. They are also designed to ensure that services themselves are not retraumatizing to survivors and provide strategies for attending to the effects that bearing witness to another's painful experiences has on advocates as well.

Adapting trauma theory to create more comprehensive and attuned advocacy models holds promise for creating services that are more responsive to survivors' experiences and needs. While existing trauma models need to be adapted and reframed to address the particular issues faced by survivors of domestic violence, ongoing dialogue will be necessary to address the applicability of these models for a diverse range of communities and to develop alternate models for healing that may be more community based. Whether it is finding ways for domestic violence programs to enhance their ability to respond to trauma-related mental health issues, or ensuring that those women and children with greater needs are able to access culturally relevant, trauma-specific mental health care, issues of philosophy, resources, training, and collaboration are highly important. Developing the capacity to respond more effectively to trauma and mental health issues will require thoughtful consideration of these issues.

Carole Warshaw

See also Health Consequences of Intimate Partner Violence; Intimate Partner Violence; Mental Illness; Posttraumatic Stress Disorder

Further Readings

Golding, J. M. (1999). Intimate partner violence as a risk factor for mental disorders: A meta-analysis. *Journal of Family Violence, 14*(2), 99–132.

Harris, M., & Fallot, R. (2001). *Using trauma theory to design service systems.* San Francisco: Jossey-Bass.

Warshaw, C. (2001). Women and violence. In N. Stotland & D. Stewart (Eds.), *Psychological aspects of women's health care: The interface between psychiatry and obstetrics and gynecology* (pp. 477–548). Washington, DC: American Psychiatric Press.

Warshaw, C., Pease, T., Markham, D. W., Sajdak, L., & Gibson, J. (2007). *Access to advocacy: Serving women with psychiatric disabilities in domestic violence settings.* Chicago: Domestic Violence & Mental Health Policy Initiative.

DOMESTIC VIOLENCE AGAINST OLDER WOMEN

The term *domestic violence in late life* refers to abuse of an elder by someone in a trusted, ongoing relationship. It may manifest as a continuation of longstanding abuse, as violence that starts only in old age, or as violence that begins with a new relationship in later years. Although reports of domestic violence decrease with age, the problem does not dissipate. National age-aggregated data suggest that between 2% and 10% of substantiated cases of violence in late life involved a spouse or intimate partner.

Most victims of domestic violence are female; their abusers use a pattern of coercive tactics, such as isolation, threats, intimidation, manipulation, and violence, to gain and maintain power over them. Domestic violence against older women is associated with the younger old ages, race and ethnicity, lower income, poorer education, and being employed in a service-sector job. Older women are likely to experience violence for a long time, and the severity and frequency of the violence tends to increase over time. Older battered women suffer physical and psychological health problems, such as injuries, chronic illness, and even death at the hands of their partners.

Older women face unique personal and family issues and community obstacles that influence their decision to leave violent relationships. For example, potential informants of domestic violence, including family members, friends, neighbors, and community workers, more easily accept the isolation that may occur in late life. Women who have not worked outside the home, and who are now past the age of retirement, are much more likely to be financially dependent on their abusers. Moreover, older women become resigned to living in situations of longstanding abuse and may be unable to realize that there are choices. With declining physical health, older women may be more dependent on their partners for care than is typical of younger women. Conversely, older women whose husbands are dependent on them for physical care may be even more reluctant to leave an abusive relationship. In addition, most domestic violence shelters are oriented toward younger women; older women may not feel comfortable participating in services and programs dominated by younger women. Usually, older women have fewer housing and employment options available to them should they decide to leave the relationship. They also may encounter ageism from law enforcement, courts, and others who do not fully understand their plight or who suggest they go to divorce court instead of seeking arrest or protective orders. Finally, because governmental policies have yet to focus specific attention on the issue of abuse of older women, few mechanisms are in place to encourage older women to exit a violent relationship.

Karen A. Roberto

See also Elder Abuse; Intimate Partner Violence

Further Readings

National Center for Elder Abuse. (2006, February). *Late life domestic violence: What the aging network needs to know.* Retrieved May 4, 2006, from http://www.elderabusecenter .org/pdf/publication/nceaissuebrief.DVforagingnetwork.pdf

Teaster, B. P., Roberto, K. A., & Dugar, T. A. (2006). Intimate partner violence of rural aging women. *Family Relations, 55,* 636–648.

DOMESTIC VIOLENCE AMONG IMMIGRANT WOMEN

Victims of domestic violence face a variety of complex legal and personal issues that can be further exacerbated by the pressures of immigration and cultural concerns. Battered immigrant women often feel isolated from their communities, both domestically and internationally. Moreover, foreign-born women are frequently uninformed about, unfamiliar with, or simply confused about their legal rights and the social services available to them in the United States. Unfortunately, too often both governmental and nongovernmental agencies that help to redress domestic violence are not prepared to meet the diverse needs of battered immigrant women. Many lack language accessibility, lack cultural sensitivity, and have insufficient information regarding the legal rights of battered immigrants.

Numerous factors influence a battered immigrant's response to domestic violence. Some of these factors are as follows:

- Immigration-related abuse/fear of deportation
- Economic abuse
- Concerns over loss of custody of her children
- Language barriers
- Cultural barriers

Immigration-Related Abuse/Fear of Deportation

Immigration-related abuse plays upon the fact that the abuser may control whether or not his spouse attains legal immigration status in this country, whether any temporary legal immigration status she has may become permanent, and how long it may take her to become a naturalized citizen. The fear induced by immigration-related abuse makes it extremely difficult for a victim to leave her abuser, obtain a protection order, call the police for help, or participate in the abuser's prosecution.

Fear of deportation is the principal barrier to immigrant victims' seeking any type of aid after experiencing abuse. This fear affects both immigrant victims of domestic violence who have legal permission to live and work in the United States and those that are undocumented. As a result, many battered immigrants believe that they have no legal right to protection from their abuser. The threat of being turned over to the immigration authorities and subsequently placed in removal proceedings deters a battered immigrant woman from seeking help from police stations, shelters, counseling programs, and the courts.

Economic Abuse

Immigrant women residing with their abusers list "lack of money" as the main reason for remaining in abusive relationships. Research has found that over two thirds of battered immigrant women who stayed with their abusers reported a lack of money as the primary reason for not leaving their home. Economic abuse includes forcing the woman to work without documentation, preventing her from working, refusing to give her money, and refusing to pay her child support.

Concerns Over Loss of Custody of Children

Many battered immigrant women are the primary caretakers of their children and are concerned that if they leave their abusers, it will have a negative impact on their children. An immigrant woman may believe her abuser when he tells her that if she leaves him, he will receive custody of the children because he has secure immigration status and she does not. When an immigrant woman comes from a country that traditionally awards custody and control over children to their fathers, as a matter of law, she often believes her abuser's threats that if she leaves him he will obtain custody of the children. This belief that they will lose custody to their abusers is heightened when victims are unfamiliar with the U.S. legal system, specifically the laws that require courts to look at domestic violence in custody cases and to protect victims regardless of their immigration status.

Language Barriers

Immigrant women who are unable to communicate effectively in the dominant language of the country in which they reside can face numerous barriers when trying to access help. Many have problems talking with police—police often believe abusers at the scene of a crime because only the abusers speak English. They can face barriers when trying to participate and understand court proceedings or when being involved in the legal system in any capacity. Furthermore, shelters, victim service programs, and legal service offices may not have employees who can speak an immigrant woman's native language and may not provide interpreters. According to the Department of Justice, failure to ensure that limited English proficient (LEP) persons can participate in or benefit from federally assisted programs might be a violation of the Civil Rights Act of 1964, Title IV and the Title VI regulations against national and origin discrimination 67 Federal Regulation 41455, 21(2002). Additionally, if a battered immigrant woman needs to seek work, her ability to speak English can affect the types of employment she can obtain. These linguistic limitations can seriously harm a woman's ability to respond to domestic violence.

Cultural Barriers

Like many victims of domestic violence, immigrant victims often look to their community for support. An immigrant woman can face unique challenges from her cultural community as she begins to explore addressing her abuser's domestic violence. Her cultural or religious community may put a high value on marriage, so much so that she fears being held responsible for breaking up her family if she tries to escape. Many systems that are designed to help victims may seem inaccessible because they are not sensitive to a victim's cultural needs. A shelter may not allow an immigrant victim to cook certain foods that would make her and her children feel more at home in a strange environment. Cultural considerations are essential when assisting immigrant victims, as they can help assuage feelings of isolation and ostracization from a victim's cultural community.

Leslye Orloff and Amanda Baran

See also Department of Homeland Security, Asylum; Department of Homeland Security, Response to Battered Immigrants and Immigrant Victims of Violence Against Women; Immigrant and Migrant Women; Legal Momentum; Office on Violence Against Women; Violence Against Women Act

Further Readings

Dutton, M. A. (1996). Battered women's strategic response to violence: The role of context. In J. L. Edelson & Z. C. Eisikovits (Eds.), *Future interventions with battered women and their families* (pp. 105–124). Thousand Oaks, CA: Sage.

Dutton, M. A., Orloff, L., & Hass, G. (2002). Offering a helping hand. *American University Journal of Gender, Social Policy, & the Law, 10*(1), 95–183.

Lai, T. A. (1986). Asian women restricting the violence. In M. C. Burns (Ed.), *The speaking profits us: Violence in the lives of women of color* (pp. 10–11). Seattle, WA: Center for the Prevention of Sexual and Domestic Violence.

Orloff, L., & Sullivan, K. (Eds.). (2004). *Breaking barriers: A complete guide to legal rights and resources for battered immigrants.* Washington, DC: Legal Momentum.

DOMESTIC VIOLENCE COURTS

The number of domestic violence cases in the United States has increased exponentially since the 1980s when the first mandatory arrest laws were put in place. Responses to domestic violence cases by traditionally organized courts were often fragmented. It was sometimes the case that a single family could be involved in several courts in one judicial system simultaneously with conflicting court orders being the result. Consequently, many jurisdictions across the country developed specialized criminal courts to hear these cases. These courts are generally referred to as *domestic violence courts* and often have judges and staff specially trained to work with victims and perpetrators of domestic violence. Major benefits of these courts include the ability to address domestic violence cases in a more holistic and efficient manner; the provision of more consistent services to victims, perpetrators, and other affected family members, including dependent children; and the development of strong ties to other public and community-based agencies that respond to domestic violence (i.e., the development of a coordinated community response to domestic violence).

Major values underlying the organization of domestic violence courts include a focus on (a) safety for both adult and child victims, (b) providing up-to-date information on case status and services to victims, (c) holding domestic violence offenders accountable, (d) increasing coordination and information sharing among community service providers for both victims and offenders, and (d) more effectively using court systems to help limit domestic violence.

Five primary components of domestic violence courts have been addressed in the literature. They are (1) case assignment, (2) screening for related cases, (3) intake units and case processing, (4) service provision, and (5) monitoring. At least three models of specialized domestic violence courts, however, have been developed, and they address these components differently. One model focuses on civil protection orders. Protection order petitions and protection order violation hearings make up a large proportion of domestic violence caseloads. As a result, some jurisdictions have created specialized civil protection order dockets. There is some variation in terms of the number of judges a jurisdiction dedicates to the docket and whether the court also handles protection order enforcement. This model is also rather limited in that victims often have myriad other legal issues that need to be addressed. Nevertheless, evaluators of this model point out that it promotes victim safety and, as one element of a coordinated community response, can link victims to appropriate services and other justice system remedies.

A second model is the specialized domestic violence court that focuses on criminal cases. Again, there is variation across jurisdictions, with some of these courts processing only misdemeanors, others only felonies, and still others both misdemeanors and felonies. Advocates of this model emphasize its ability to hold offenders accountable by imposing sanctions and monitoring offenders' compliance. However, critics of the model point out that some victims prefer civil, rather than criminal, remedies and that unless this type of court is part of a coordinated community response effort, victims are not likely to consistently avail themselves of civil remedies such as protection orders or other available services.

A third court model attempts to provide a comprehensive response to domestic violence cases by handling criminal matters as well as protection orders, child custody disputes, child support petitions, and divorce petitions. Such courts are often called *integrated domestic violence courts* because they provide a menu of needed services to family members, including adult victims and their children as well as perpetrators, all in one location. Variations on this model include the unified family court, in which one judge addresses all legal issues posed by a single family, civil as well as criminal; and coordinated courts, in which criminal domestic violence cases and related civil issues are addressed by the same court division, but on separate dockets.

Opposition to domestic violence courts has been expressed by judges, defense attorneys, and prosecutors. These objections include an increased workload and, from defense attorneys in particular, a concern that such courts may be biased against the accused. Representatives of communities of color have also expressed opposition due to the perception that specialized domestic violence courts are part of a "get tough" approach to crime, which typically targets men of color. Because specialized domestic violence courts are relatively new, evaluations of their success are still underway. Indeed, some observers have pointed out that measuring the success of domestic violence courts depends largely on how "success" or "effectiveness" is defined (e.g., speed of disposition, victim satisfaction, reduced recidivism on the part of offenders). However, jurisdictions seeking to establish domestic violence courts need to ensure that all offices and agencies that deal with any aspect of domestic violence cases are educated about the purposes and goals of such courts and have the opportunity to provide meaningful input into the process.

Claire M. Renzetti and Jeffrey L. Edleson

See also Coordinated Community Response; Legal System, Civil Court Remedies for Intimate Partner Violence; Legal System, Criminal Justice System Responses to Intimate Partner Violence; Mandatory Arrest/Pro-Arrest Statutes; No-Drop Prosecution; Prosecutorial Practices, Intimate Partner Violence; Restraining and Protective Orders

Further Readings

Helling, J. (n.d.). *Specialized criminal domestic violence courts.* Retrieved October 21, 2007, from http://www .vaw.umn.edu

Little, K. (2003). Specialized courts and domestic violence. *Issues of Democracy.* Retrieved October 21, 2007, from http://usinfo.state.gove/journals/itdhr/0503/ijde/littel.htm

Sacks, E. (2002). *Creating a domestic violence court: Guidelines and best practice*s. Retrieved October 21, 2007, from http://www.endabuse.org

Domestic Violence Enhanced Response Team

Police often have been frustrated that after they have intervened at a home where domestic violence has occurred, other parts of the criminal justice and social service system seldom followed through. In 1987, the City of Colorado Springs was one of several communities around the country selected by the National Institute of Justice to replicate an earlier experiment in Minneapolis where police responded to domestic violence incidents with one of several alternative actions, one being the then novel idea of arresting the perpetrator. Out of this early start grew a series of community initiatives that have drawn in an ever-widening group of collaborative agencies.

The Domestic Violence Enhanced Response Team (DVERT) is an interdisciplinary group of professionals from 11 agencies who are located in a common space and coordinate their agencies' response to cases of domestic violence. Agencies contributing staff include probation, a battered women's program, two police and one sheriff's department, the Humane Society, and legal services. The Team has been expanded to include professionals working with children exposed to violence, including local child protective services and the court-appointed special advocates (CASA) program.

The team maintains several levels of intervention. Referrals are received from a variety of sources, and the first level of intervention involves a confidential intake conducted by a victim advocate who is assigned to work with the victim from beginning to end. Cases moving beyond intake are also assigned a law enforcement detective who works with the victim and the advocate to ensure the victim's safety over time. Another level of intervention involves problem-oriented policing, in which officers visit the victim's home to provide additional information and support in the community. Finally, the DVERT coordinates a variety of community resources in support of the adult and child victims' safety.

Jeffrey L. Edleson

See also Coordinated Community Response; Family Justice Centers

Web Sites

Domestic Violence Enhanced Response Team: http://www.dvert.org

Domestic Violence Fatality Review

In the United States, approximately 1,600 women are murdered each year by their current or former partners. Domestic violence deaths often display predictable patterns and causes. Many experts in the field believe that many of these homicides are preventable. When a woman is murdered by a partner, the public often wants to know why the woman was not protected and the homicide not prevented. A recent and increasingly popular approach to preventing these tragedies is the formation of domestic violence death (fatality) review committees (DVDRCs). The effort of a DVDRC is comparable to that seen in the airline industry in reducing aviation disasters or in the medical profession in learning from deaths occurring in hospitals under questionable circumstances. DVDRCs are interdisciplinary teams of domestic violence experts who are dedicated to understanding how and why domestic violence deaths occur through a detailed examination of individual cases. Each committee utilizes the benefit of hindsight to recommend what could have been done in their community to prevent each fatality, with the goal of preventing future deaths. There is emerging evidence supporting the utility of DVDRCs in assisting the overall effort of reducing domestic violence fatalities and domestic violence, in general, through the implementation of their recommendations.

History

One of the first publicly documented fatality reviews, known as "The Charan Investigation," was conducted in 1990 in San Francisco, California. The investigation was driven by the Commission on the Status of Women at the request of the San Francisco Domestic Violence Consortium. Joseph Charan murdered his wife and committed suicide in front of numerous schoolchildren and teachers. The killing occurred 12 days after

Mr. Charan received a suspended sentence for felony domestic assault and malicious mischief. Relatively soon after the official report was released in 1991, Santa Clara County in California started one of the first regularly operating DVDRCs (1994). At the end of 1994, jurisdictions in two states had committees conducting regular reviews. In 1998, nine states had jurisdictions with DVDRCs. By 2003, 27 states and the District of Columbia had committees operating or planning to operate at county or state levels, and 18 of these states had passed legislation or given directives on making the formation of DVDRCs and consistent reviews a mandatory practice. In September of 2002, the Ontario government publicized the formation of Canada's first DVDRC through the Office of the Chief Coroner, making fatality reviews an international practice. Another important development in the field came in 2004 with the launch of the National Domestic Violence Fatality Review Initiative. The purpose of the initiative is to provide technical assistance with reviews by providing a clearinghouse, a resource center, and several other unique services.

Structure, Mandate, and Process

DVDRCs vary in their compositions, directives, and procedures, largely due to the amount of funding they receive (many operate on a volunteer basis). Most are comprised of coroners, medical and mental health professionals who specialize in domestic abuse, criminologists, prosecutors, judges, shelter staff and women's advocates, law enforcement staff, and representatives from child protection services. The typical cases teams are charged with identifying and reviewing include intimate partner (a) homicide, (b) homicide-suicide, (c) attempted homicide followed by suicide, (d) attempted-homicide followed by related accidental death (e.g., the perpetrator was killed in a car accident during a police pursuit), and (e) attempted homicide followed by related homicide (e.g., the perpetrator was killed in a police shooting). Reviewed cases may include those involving multiple deaths (e.g., familicide) or the deaths of any individuals connected to incidents of domestic violence, such as third-party interveners, friends, neighbors, coworkers, new partners, extended family members, and children. DVDRCs operate under the philosophy that the perpetrators are ultimately responsible for the deaths and do not assign blame to individuals or agencies involved in the cases under examination. Generally, a fatality review is the process by which a DVDRC uses multiagency data

and interviews with families, friends, neighbors, and others to document, analyze, and report on the history of the victim, perpetrator, their relationship, and their family. Teams also track risk factors associated with lethal intimate partner violence in each case to aid in enhancing the predictability of the tragedies. They examine the effects of all interventions that took place before the deaths, consider changes in relevant prevention and intervention systems to address gaps in service delivery, and develop recommendations for coordinated community plans. Broadly, recommendations stemming from reviews address (a) increasing awareness and education of domestic violence; (b) enhancing assessment and intervention practices with victims and perpetrators; (c) improving training and policy development within target agencies; (d) increasing resource development for victims, abusers, and their families; (e) advancing coordination of services among agencies servicing at-risk families; (f) legislative reform; and (g) increasing and improving prevention programs for those at risk of becoming victims and perpetrators. DVDRCs report their findings and recommendations annually to enhance public, professional, and policymaker understanding of domestic violence death.

Current and Future Directions

To date, there has not been a systematic evaluation of the DVDRC initiative. Based on the annual reports of individual committees, there would seem to be a high level of community engagement and collaboration inherent in the process. Individual communities and states often refer to their DVDRC as a rationale for new practices or legislation. For example, in Ontario, Canada, there has been a broad-based initiative to educate friends, family, and neighbors about lethal domestic violence, in light of all the common warning signs overlooked in many homicides. Some jurisdictions monitor specific recommendations such as the Santa Clara committee highlight of the fact that there were no deaths in the 5,337 domestic violence cases referred to the district attorney's office for prosecution in 2004. It was also noted that 2004 was the third year in a row their community had been without police-assisted suicides (i.e., "suicide-by-cop"). Many committees report that in their view, fatality reviews save lives. We can expect more empirical studies to test this hypothesis in the future.

Peter G. Jaffe and Marcus Juodis

See also Danger Assessment Instrument; Familicide;
   Femicide; Intimate Partner Violence; National Domestic
   Violence Fatality Review Initiative

Further Readings

Ontario Domestic Violence Death Review Committee.
   (2006). *Annual report to the chief coroner.* Toronto, ON:
   Ministry of the Attorney General. Retrieved from
   http://www.mpss.jus.gov.on.ca/english/publications/
   comm_safety/DVDRC_2005.pdf
Santa Clara County Domestic Violence Council. (2004).
   Death review committee final report. San Jose, CA:
   County Government Center. Retrieved from http://www
   .growing.com/nonviolent/council/pubs/dvc_intro.htm
Websdale, N. (1999). *Understanding domestic homicide.*
   Boston: Northeastern University Press.
Websdale, N. (2003). Reviewing domestic violence deaths.
   National Institute of Justice Journal, 250, 26–31.
Websdale, N., Town, M., & Johnson, B. (1999). Domestic
   violence fatality reviews: From a culture of blame to a culture
   of safety. *Juvenile and Family Court Journal, 50,* 61–74.

Web Sites

National Domestic Violence Fatality Review Initiative:
   http://www.ndvfri.org

DOMESTIC VIOLENCE IN ASIAN AND PACIFIC ISLANDER POPULATIONS

Asians and Pacific Islanders are people who trace
their origins and/or ancestry to the countries or dias-
poric communities of the region and identify as
Central, East, South, Southeast, or West Asians;
Native Hawaiians; and Pacific Islanders.

In community-based studies compiled by the Asian
Pacific Islander Institute on Domestic Violence in San
Francisco, 41% to 60% of Asian women reported
experiencing physical and/or sexual violence during
their lifetime. This is higher than the prevalence rate
found in the National Violence Against Women
Survey for other Asian and Pacific Islander (API)
women or any other group.

Domestic violence in API communities has some
distinct patterns, forms, and dynamics of abuse, warranting distinct approaches to prevention and intervention. The similarities between all battered women's
experiences are not enumerated in this entry. Some
dynamics occur in one ethnic group, and some are
common to many, thus cautioning against stereotyping or universalizing API cultures. Gender violence
is experienced in the context of gender oppression
as well as oppressions based on race, ethnicity, age,
sexual orientation, gender identity, type of labor
performed, level of education, class position, disability, and/or immigration or refugee status.
Domestic violence in the lives of API women may
involve physical abuse, multiple batteries, push and
pull factors, sexual abuse, abuse of mothers, same-
sex violence, immigration-related abuse, and isolating sociocultural barriers and victim-blaming
community norms,

Physical abuse can include culturally specific
forms such as abuse by multiple perpetrators, severe
isolation compounded by immigration, abandonment,
hyperexploitation of women's (including elderly
women's) household labor, withholding health care,
and the mistreatment of widows. Domestic homicides
include murder by an intimate or family member,
honor killings, contract killings, dowry (bride price)
related deaths, targeting a woman's family members
in the home country, and/or being driven by the marital family to suicide (abetted suicide).

Multiple batterers in the home can include members of a woman's family of origin, members of her
partner's family of origin, or her partner's ex- or
new wives. The implications of multiple batterers
include greater or more severe injuries; family
collusion and increased impunity; legal remedies
requiring protection orders against several individuals; deeply internalized victim blaming and devalu-
ation by survivors; diminished credibility afforded
to battered women by systems, families, and communities; and uncomprehending systems that respond
inadequately.

Push and pull factors are experienced by many API
battered women: "push" factors, such as being pushed
out of the relationship by a partner (e.g., "Leave the
house, I'm divorcing you after 3 months of marriage, I
can always find another wife"; "I don't want you and
these children around"), may be more frequently experienced than "pull" factors (e.g., "Come back to me, I
won't do it again") back into the relationship. These
factors affect how women's agency is understood—
about "decisions" to stay or leave; how often, if at all,
women return to their abusive partners; if they leave
with or without their children; and how dangers

connected to postseparation violence and the loss of children and financial support are assessed.

Sexual abuse includes excessive restriction and monitoring of women's sexuality and sexual activity; blaming women for rape, incest, or coerced sex; and keeping women ignorant about sex, sexual health, and anatomy. Asian women are disproportionately victims of sex trafficking, entering servile marriages through international marriage bureaus and forced marriages (as opposed to arranged marriages). Refugees and immigrants may have been raped in war zones, refugee camps, police custody, and on unsafe immigration routes, and/or because of their status as cultural or religious minorities in their home countries. In addition to marital rape, there can be extreme sexual neglect; being forced to watch and imitate pornography; and coerced unprotected sex resulting in sexually transmitted diseases or unwanted pregnancies.

Abuse of mothers increases the vulnerability related to mothering. This may start with pregnancy, as the abuse includes forcing women to undergo abortions and to endure multiple pregnancies to have sons in the family. Loss of children is a constant threat to mothers and may result from the mother's deportation, needing to send children to paternal grandparents in the home country, kidnapping, manipulative reporting of the mother as a child abuser or batterer, and individual and family abusers seeking custody because of prevailing cultural beliefs that children belong to their father and the stigmatization of divorced mothers. Batterers have increasingly manipulated social service, child protection, immigration, and criminal and civil legal systems to their advantage, most effectively around women's status as mothers.

Same-sex domestic violence in API couples carries greater threats associated with outing a partner in communities where homosexuality is severely ostracized.

Immigration-related abuse includes threats of deportation, taking away children, making false declarations to the U.S. Immigration and Customs Enforcement agency about the victim, withholding passports and important documents, and/or not proceeding with applications that regularize the victim's immigration status. Permanent abandonment in the home country immediately after marriage is increasing, as (untraceable) husbands return alone to the United States on the pretext of filing papers.

Isolating sociocultural barriers and victim-blaming community norms concern particularly noncitizens and those with limited English proficiency who may face language, economic, racial, cultural, religious, professional, and/or identity-based barriers to social and legal services. Warranted fears about their immigrant status include that they or their abusers could be deported. Living away from natal families adds to their isolation. Community reinforcements that keep gender violence in place utilize victim blaming, silencing, and shaming, and rejecting battered women who speak up. The nexus of public disclosure and shame is strong in API communities, as are covert and overt support for batterers and a lack of sanctions and accountability. Barriers and community attitudes are exploited by batterers and incorporated into their abuse.

Oppression of victims and resistance to oppression by victims are constantly in conflict. Hence, in addition to daily acts of private and public resistance by abused API women and their children, nationally, API advocates have established over 90 community-based organizations, with new ones emerging regularly for API survivors of violence.

Chic Dabby-Chinoy

See also Asian & Pacific Islander Institute on Domestic Violence

Further Readings

Tjaden, P., & Thoennes, N. (2000, July). *Extent, nature and consequences of intimate partner violence: Research report.* Washington, DC: National Institute of Justice and the Centers for Disease Control and Prevention.

DOMESTIC VIOLENCE IN MILITARY FAMILIES

The Department of Defense defines domestic violence as an assault, battery, threat to injure or kill, other acts of violence, and emotional maltreatment committed by a spouse against another spouse. The definition recognizes only "spouse abuse." The definition does not reference violence between unmarried intimate partners of military personnel. Relationships between girlfriends or boyfriends, engaged individuals, former spouses, or individuals who share a child in common are excluded by the definition. The definition differs substantially from standards contained in state and federal statutes.

Reports have shown that the victim seeking services from the military departments is predominantly the female civilian spouse of active duty personnel. Victims normally have children and more than half have been married approximately two years. Spousal abuse as substantiated by the military departments is predominantly perpetrated by male active duty personnel. An increasing number of military families reside off the installation, which impacts the response of civilian and military authorities to incidents of domestic violence.

Policy and Program Development

Programs, policies, and procedures to address spousal abuse and child maltreatment in military families have existed in the U.S. Armed Forces since the enactment of the Child Abuse Prevention and Treatment Act of 1974. Child advocacy programs were mandated within the military departments by the act. The military effort was initially fragmented among the services in the late 1970s. The General Accounting Office (GAO) issued a report, *Military Child Advocacy Programs—Victims of Neglect,* criticizing the inconsistency and recommending centralized efforts at the Department of Defense level, including a single policy for collection of incidence data, increased staffing and education, and training of military personnel in the child abuse area. A series of regulations, instructions, directives, and orders mandated the development of the Office of Family Policy and Family Advocacy Program. Subsequently, each service adopted policies and programs.

The parallel development of policies to address child maltreatment and spouse abuse resulted in mandatory reporting to military authorities of maltreatment, neglect, or abuse occurring on a military installation, involving service members, and reported to military and civilian personnel, including health care professionals, to be codified.

The passing decades have produced changes in military and civilian communities' response to domestic violence. The civilian community has supported shelters, criminal statutes, and treatment and training programs, culminating in the enactment of the Violence Against Women Act (VAWA) and its reauthorizations. The Department of Defense issued a zero tolerance memorandum declaring that domestic violence will not be condoned or tolerated among the ranks. The message has not been clear or consistent throughout the armed forces, however.

Intimate partner violence in the U.S. Armed Forces attracted significant public attention following tragic events at Fort Campbell, Kentucky, in 1998 and Fort Bragg, North Carolina, in 2002. The homicides in Fort Campbell, Kentucky, fostered the establishment of the Department of Defense Domestic Violence Task Force (DTFDV). The mission of the DTFDV was to conduct a broad, thorough investigation of the nature of domestic violence within the military community and the systems' response, and to develop policy and program recommendations for change. The annual reports of the DTFDV contained nearly 200 recommendations for consideration of the Department of Defense.

The homicides in Fort Bragg, North Carolina, precipitated the enactment of the Armed Forces Domestic Security Act. The act enables the service and enforcement of civilian orders of protection on military installations. In addition, the Department of Defense was authorized to create a privacy policy for victims of domestic violence and enhance the victim advocate program within the services.

The Department of Defense established the Family Violence Policy Office to implement the recommendations of the DTFDV in 2003. The Department of Defense issued 16 interim directive-type memoranda. Funding was provided to the policy office to contract victim advocates and conduct training for military command, first responders, chaplains, and personnel.

In 2006, the Department of Defense established a privacy policy for victims of domestic violence, *Restricted Reporting Policy for Incidents of Domestic Abuse.* Victims choose unrestricted or restricted reporting following an incident of domestic violence. Nonrestricted reporting follows the current channels of reporting (including chaplain, command, Family Advocacy Program, victim advocates, and others), resulting in notification of the command of an alleged perpetrator and law enforcement. Restricted reporting enables a victim to receive victim advocacy services and medical treatment without notification of the command or law enforcement. Adult victims of domestic violence who choose the restricted reporting option may report only to health care professionals, victim advocates, or supervisors of victim advocates.

A report by the General Accounting Office, *Military Personnel: Progress Made in Implementing Recommendations to Reduce Domestic Violence, but Further Management Action Needed,* outlined the limitations of data collection within the services, criticized the failure of the Department of Defense to fully implement the DTFDV recommendations, and defined the limitations of the directive-type memorandums.

The Department of Defense subsequently issued the instruction *Domestic Abuse Involving Department of Defense Military and Certain Affiliated Personnel*. The instruction includes previously issued directive-type memoranda outlining the role of the command, law enforcement, judge advocate, victim advocate, medical personnel, chaplain, and Family Advocacy Program staff. The directive supports the development of a coordinated community response to domestic violence within the armed forces.

Risk Factors

The military community or culture encompasses risk factors that enhance the vulnerability of victims of domestic violence, including, but not limited to, geographical isolation from family and friends; social isolation within the military community; residential mobility; financial insecurity; economic dependence; and fear of adverse career impact. Military training affords a perpetrator an opportunity to develop and enhance techniques. Deployments impact the prevalence and severity of incidents. Combat stress and posttraumatic stress disorder may influence risk and prevalence of domestic violence in the armed forces.

Prevalence

The prevalence of domestic violence within the armed forces is difficult to ascertain due to the lack of standardized data, uniform interpretation of data, and failure to implement databases authorized by Congress. Recidivism and reoffense data remain unreliable.

Department of Defense estimates suggest that domestic violence in the military rose during the 1990s. The rate escalated from 19 cases per 1,000 individuals in 1990 to 26 per 1,000 in 1996. Reporting practices were altered in 1997, which resulted in a decrease. Although substantiated reports decreased, the levels of moderate to severe violence increased.

The Department of Defense estimates indicate a slow decline in the number of cases of substantiated domestic violence since 2000. In 2004, the rate was 14 per 1,000, entailing 16,400 reported cases with 9,450 substantiated incidents. The army consistently shows the highest rate of domestic violence, followed by the marines, navy, and air force.

The GAO reports that the failure to fully implement the domestic violence component of the Defense Incident-Based Reporting System, personnel shortages, installations not reporting command disciplinary actions, law enforcement systems not yet operational, and ineffective communication of standards preclude a comprehensive analysis of Department of Defense data or a comparative analysis of military and civilian communities.

Christine Hansen

See also Armed Forces, Sexual Harassment in; Military, Family Advocacy Programs; Violence Against Women Act

Further Readings

Defense Task Force on Domestic Violence. (2001). *Initial report*. Arlington, VA: U.S. Department of Defense.

Defense Task Force on Domestic Violence. (2002). *Second annual report*. Arlington, VA: U.S. Department of Defense.

Defense Task Force on Domestic Violence. (2003). *Third annual report*. Arlington, VA: U.S. Department of Defense.

Hansen, C. (2001). A considerable service: An advocate's introduction to domestic violence and the military. *Domestic Violence Report, 6*(4), 49–50, 60–64.

The Miles Foundation, Inc., & Survivors in Service United (SISU). (2007). *Choices and challenges: A guide to surviving intimate partner violence in the U.S. Armed Forces*. Newtown, CT: The Miles Foundation.

Rosen, L., & Hansen, C. (Eds.). (2003). Violence against women associated with the military: Part I. Intimate partner violence. *Violence Against Women* [Special issue], *9*(9).

DOMESTIC VIOLENCE MOVEMENT

See BATTERED WOMEN'S MOVEMENT

DOMESTIC VIOLENCE RESOURCE NETWORK

In 1993, federal funds from the U.S. Department of Health and Human Services (DHHS) were provided to establish and provide ongoing support to the Domestic Violence Resource Network (DVRN). This network of national resource centers was designed to inform, coordinate, and strengthen public and private efforts to end domestic violence by providing guidance and expertise in key areas of practice and policy. The DVRN includes the following:

- *National Resource Center on Domestic Violence (NRCDV)*—provides a source of comprehensive information, training, and technical assistance in support of effective domestic violence intervention and prevention
- *Battered Women's Justice Project (BWJP)*—provides legal training, technical assistance, and other resources on domestic violence related to civil court access and representation, criminal justice response, and battered women's self-defense issues
- *National Health Resource Center on Domestic Violence*—works to guide the development of a multidisciplinary and comprehensive health care response to domestic violence
- *Resource Center on Domestic Violence: Child Protection and Custody*—focuses on domestic violence issues arising within the context of child custody cases and within child protection agencies
- *Sacred Circle National Resource Center to End Violence Against Native Women*—addresses violence against Native women in the context of the unique historical, jurisdictional, and cultural realities facing American Indians and Alaskan Natives

The constituency of the resource centers is broad, not limited to grantees of DHHS. To ensure maximum impact, however, each of the resource centers targets its training and technical assistance. Utilizing toll-free numbers, Web sites, newsletters, teleconferences, training workshops, and national and regional conferences and workgroups, each resource center provides the following:

- Materials and publications on a range of domestic violence issues
- Support for the development and replication of model programs, legislation, and practices
- Technical assistance, training, and referrals to assist advocates, programs, allied professionals, government agencies, and communities to meet local, state, and national needs

The technical assistance and training provided through the DVRN is both reactive and proactive, not only responding to requests from the field but also anticipating the need for information and guidance around emerging policy and practice issues.

In 2006, the DVRN was expanded to include other DHHS-funded national domestic violence initiatives with which the resource centers have forged strong partnerships. This expanded DVRN now includes the National Domestic Violence Hotline; the National Training Center on Domestic Violence, Mental Health and Trauma; and three multicultural institutes—Alianza: The National Latino Alliance for the Elimination of Domestic Violence, the Institute on Domestic Violence in African American Communities, and the Asian Pacific Islander Institute on Domestic Violence.

Members of the DVRN have worked collaboratively to ensure that training and technical assistance available throughout the country are complementary, comprehensive, advocacy based, and informed by the entire network.

Anne Menard

See also Asian & Pacific Islander Institute on Domestic Violence; Battered Women's Justice Project; National Latino Alliance for the Elimination of Domestic Violence; National Resource Center on Domestic Violence; Sacred Circle National Resource Center to End Violence Against Native Women

Web Sites

Alianza: The National Latino Alliance for the Elimination of Domestic Violence: http://www.dvalianza.org

Asian & Pacific Islander Institute on Domestic Violence: http://www.apiahf.org/apidvinstitute

Battered Women's Justice Project: http://www.bwjp.org

Institute on Domestic Violence in African American Communities: http://www.dvinstitute.org

National Domestic Violence Hotline: http://www.ndvh.org

National Health Resource Center on Domestic Violence: http://www.endabuse.org/health

National Resource Center on Domestic Violence: http://www.nrcdv.org

National Training Center on Domestic Violence, Mental Health and Trauma: http://www.dvmhpi.org

Resource Center on Domestic Violence: Child Protection and Custody: http://www.ncjfcj.org/fvd

Sacred Circle National Resource Center to End Violence Against Native Women. http://www.sacred-circle.com

DOWRY DEATHS, BRIDE BURNING

Anthropologists and sociologists have provided information on several forms of dowry-related violence against women in various countries, including some in Africa, Asia, and the Middle East. However, it is only in India that some unique and historically significant examples of burning women alive have been reported. Studies indicate that there are countless ways of killing people; burning them alive has been rather uncommon and torturous. Examples of lethal violence against women in India through fire, therefore, are suggestive of peculiar socioreligious background. Although there seems to be little consensus on dates of origin as well as number of cases involved in fire-related deaths of Hindu women, recent studies have identified data and case histories of such female victims in India.

Background: The Sati Practice

The word *sati*, or *suttee*, as Westerners have often spelled it, describes an ancient ritual according to which a Hindu wife follows her husband to his death by ascending his cremation pyre with him or ascending one of her own shortly afterward; it also refers to a woman cremated in this way. The customary rite involved the cocremation of the living wife with the dead husband. The practice was traditionally based upon a belief in the karma principle (implying fatalism and predestination) of Hindu marriage, which as a sacrament demands that a widow kill herself so that her soul may join that of her deceased husband. It was also based upon the dharma principle, implying duty and sacrifice on the part of the wife. However, a husband usually accepts the death of his wife with indifference, as if his own soul did not have to join that of his late wife. This double standard reflects an aspect of the male domination and control exercised by Hindu husbands. The woman who became sati was generally hailed and accorded a heroic status by the community, as not every widow was provided the opportunity to become sati. A husband who had multiple wives might have stated in a will his choice of his favorite wife to be the sati. Although the sati practice was not usually based on dowry considerations, it has been suggested that women may have been burnt alive because of possible disputes over dowry.

Dowry-Related Burning

The practice of dowry in India involves giving of gifts by a bride's family during the marriage to the son-in-law and his family, either in cash or in kind. Dowry is generally displayed socially, although it may sometimes be given in secrecy. The gift giving continues on different occasions through the first few years of marriage. The practice may have been present in Indian society for a long time, though now it seems to have developed into a form of commerce in many arranged marriages in India. Many married women have been reported to be emotionally abused, physically tortured, murdered, or driven to commit suicide because of persistent demands for dowry. About 5,000 deaths a year were reported by the government in the 1980s and 1990s. Many of these reports suggest that husbands (and their families) often blame the burnt victims for having committed suicide or been involved in accidental deaths (for example, while cooking). Women who survive the fire are too afraid to come forward to tell their full stories. This form of violence is likely to be far more serious than what government and the media actually report. However, systematic research on the topic hardly exists.

Explanation

The sociodemographic and other risk factors for lethal violence against women in the traditional aspect of Indian society, particularly in the rural areas, are numerous. Women in those orthodox settings are generally uneducated, ignorant of their own rights, chronically dependent on their husbands' families, and denied a right to build a social support network outside those families. That may make them vulnerable to violence and control. They also do not have access to protection from law enforcement agencies and are under pressure to keep their marriages going. Husbands, on the other hand, may have options for remarriages and fresh chances for dowries, making them and their families aggressive whenever deficiencies are noticed in wives and their dowry history. In addition, women who survive burning attempts might face a continued oppression with a difficult recovery and become further victimized even through their own families and communities.

Prevention

In 1982, Indira Ghandi, the Prime Minister of India, spoke of her frustration at the situation of dowry deaths by saying, "We have got a lot of laws, but it is not so easy to implement them." However, it seems that tough laws against incidents, or the so-called accidents, of women burning enacted under her leadership have started to have preventive implications. Demands for dowry as well as connected homicidal or suicidal attempts are now federal offenses, requiring the police to intervene. Law enforcement agencies throughout India have been setting up offices and shelters to help victims of bride burning. Women's rights groups as well as popular media have been actively involved in educational and news programs trying to raise levels of awareness about injustices and violence experienced by female victims. However, studies show that demands for dowry have been on the rise, now more than in the past through under-the-table "gifts" arranged by marriage mediators. In addition, reported rates of dowry deaths have not been declining in India. Systematic research is needed to investigate all aspects of dowry-related issues and specific mitigating strategies for prevention of violence against women in the future.

Raghu N. Singh

See also Forced Marriages; Religion; Ritualistic Abuse

Further Readings

Bumiller, E. (1990). *May you be the mother of one hundred sons: A journey among the women of India.* New York: Fawcett Columbine.

Hawley, J. S. (Ed.). (1994). *Sati: The blessing and the curse: The burning of wives in India.* New York: Oxford University Press.

Kumari, R. (1989). *Brides are not for burning: Dowry victims in India.* New York: Advent.

Narashimhan, S. (1990). *Sati: Widow burning in India.* New York: Doubleday.

Prasad, D. (1994). Dowry-related violence: A content analysis of news in selected newspapers. *Journal of Comparative Family Studies, 25,* 71–89.

DUAL ARREST

Dual arrest refers to the practice of arresting both parties involved in a domestic violence incident at the same time. This practice has increased as mandatory and preferred arrest policies have been implemented, and occurs when police cannot, or choose not to, determine the primary aggressor in a domestic violence incident. Police may choose dual arrest if both parties show evidence of having been injured, or when they only have the word of both parties, each stating that the other was the aggressor. Thus, the decision of guilt is left to the court system. It is unknown if dual arrest is a result of strict adherence to the word of mandatory or preferred arrest policies, a backlash to the policies, or indicative of bias or prejudice that leads to over-enforcement.

Dual arrest rates vary widely across states, comprising between 11% and 50% of arrests, since the implementation of mandatory arrest. Police departments argue that dual arrests must occur because police officers have a responsibility to arrest when there is any evidence that a crime has been committed. Additionally, police officers report wanting both parties to be mandated into counseling for the relationship. Research indicates that decisions to arrest are frequently based on officers' attitudes and moral judgments that determine their perceptions of blame, justifications for violence, and believability of the accounts of the incidents.

The picture of males arrested in a dual arrest is significantly different from that of dually arrested women, using research based on heterosexual couples. Males are significantly less likely than females to have been a domestic violence victim in the preceding 2 years. They are also more likely to have a history of domestic violence arrests than are females. This supports the belief that most women arrested for domestic violence are acting in self-defense or retaliation from prior abuse.

When women are arrested for domestic violence, it is often in the context of dual arrest. Alcohol or other drug use is significantly more likely to be involved in dual arrest cases than single arrest cases. Women are typically charged with minor offenses, such as disorderly conduct or breach of peace, in these incidents. The arrests rarely result in prosecution, with only half the prosecutions of single arrest cases. These findings support the perspective that many of these women are arrested unjustifiably or due to violent behavior that is a response to ongoing victimization by a partner. This is not to say that women are never the primary aggressor, or that they never initiate violence. However, with the high consequences of arrest, such as emotional ramifications, financial burdens, and social stigma, as well as cost for the legal system, police should take seriously their role in determining the primary aggressor when making decisions to arrest.

Poco Kernsmith

See also Legal Issues in the Treatment of Sexual and
Domestic Violence; Legal System, Criminal Justice
System Responses to Intimate Partner Violence; Police,
Response to Domestic Violence

Further Readings

Feder, L., & Henning, K. (2005). A comparison of male and
female dually arrested domestic violence offenders.
Violence and Victims, 20, 153–171.

Martin, M. E. (1997). Double your trouble: Dual arrest in
family violence. *Journal of Family Violence, 12*, 139–157.

DULUTH MODEL

The Duluth model offers a method for communities to use in coordinating their responses to domestic violence. It is an interagency approach that brings the justice and human service interventions together around the primary goal of protecting victims from ongoing abuse. It was conceived and implemented in a small working-class city in northern Minnesota from 1980 to 1981. The original Minnesota organizers were activists in the battered women's movement. They selected Duluth as the best Minnesota city in which to try to bring criminal and civil justice agencies together to work in a coordinated way to respond to domestic abuse cases involving battering. By battering they meant an ongoing pattern of abuse used by an offender against a current or former intimate partner. Eleven agencies formed the initial collaborative initiative. These included 911, police, sheriff's and prosecutors' offices, probation, the criminal and civil court benches, the local battered women's shelter, three mental health agencies, and a newly created coordinating organization called the Domestic Abuse Intervention Project (DAIP). The initiative's activist, reform-oriented origins shaped its development and popularity among reformers in other communities. Over the next three decades this continuously evolving initiative became the most replicated woman abuse intervention model in the country.

The Duluth model engages legal systems and human service agencies to create a distinctive form of organized public response to domestic violence. It is characterized by the following:

- clearly identifiable and largely shared assumptions and theories about the source of battering and the effective means to deter it
- empirically tested intervention strategies that build safety and accountability into all elements of the infrastructure of processing cases of violence
- well-defined methods of interagency cooperation guided by advocacy programs

The Duluth model holds that public intervention in domestic violence cases should include several key elements. It must protect victims of ongoing abuse (battering). It must hold perpetrators and intervening practitioners accountable for victim safety. It must offer offenders an opportunity to change (including punishment if it enhances victim safety), and it must ensure due process for offenders through the intervention process. The focus of intervention is on stopping the violence, not on fixing or ending interpersonal relationships.

The Duluth model asserts the following:

- The primary responsibility of placing controls on abusers belongs to the community and the individual abuser, *not* the victim of abuse.
- Battering is a form of domestic violence that entails a patterned use of coercion or intimidation, including violence and other related forms of abuse that may be legal or illegal. To be successful, initiatives must distinguish between and respond differently to domestic violence cases that constitute battering and cases that do not, and the intervention must be adjusted for the severity of the violence.
- Intervention must account for the economic, cultural, and personal histories of the individuals who become abuse cases in the system.
- Both victims and offenders are members of the community; while they must each act to change the conditions of their lives, the community must treat both with respect and dignity, recognizing the social causes of their personal circumstances.

The Duluth model offers four primary strategic principles of interagency intervention:

First, change will be required at the basic infrastructure levels of the multiple agencies involved in case processing. Workers must be coordinated in ways that enhance their capacity to protect victims and must comply fully with interagency agreements. Participating agencies must work cooperatively on examining, adjusting, and standardizing practices by making changes in eight core methods of coordinating workers' actions on a case. This involves (1) identifying each agency's mission, purpose, and specific function or task at each point of intervention in these cases; (2) crafting policies guiding each point of intervention; (3) providing administrative tools that guide individual practitioners in carrying out their duties (e.g., 911 computer screens, specially crafted police report formats, domestic violence–appropriate presentence investigation formats; education and counseling curricula designed for abusers); (4) creating a system that links practitioners to each other so that each practitioner is positioned to act in ways that assists subsequent interveners in their interventions; (5) adopting interagency systems of accountability, including an interagency tracking and information-sharing system; periodic evaluations of aspects of the model; bimonthly interagency meetings to identify, analyze, and resolve systemic problems in the handling of cases; and accountability clauses in written policies; (6) establishing a cooperative plan to seek appropriate resources; (7) reaching agreements on operative assumptions, theories, and concepts to be embedded in written policies and administrative practices; and (8) developing and delivering training across agencies on policies, procedures, and concepts.

Second, the overall strategy must be victim-safety centered. There is an important role for independent victim advocacy services and rehabilitation programming for offenders. Small independent monitoring and coordinating organizations should be set up to coordinate work groups, operate the tracking system, and help coordinate periodic evaluations and research projects. Victim advocacy organizations should be central in all aspects of designing intervention strategies.

Third, agencies must participate as collaborating partners. Each agency agrees to identify, analyze, and find solutions to any ways in which their practices might compromise the collective intervention goals. Small ad hoc problem-solving groups, training committees, evaluation projects, and regular meetings are used to coordinate initiatives. These working groups are typically facilitated by DAIP staff but, when appropriate, may be led by another participating agency.

Fourth, abusers must be consistently held accountable for their use of violence. Effective intervention requires a clear and consistent response by police and the courts to initial and repeated acts of abuse. These include the following: (a) mandatory arrest for primary aggressors; (b) emergency housing, education groups, and advocacy for victims; (c) evidence-based prosecution of cases; (d) jail sentences in which offenders receive increasingly harsh penalties for repeated acts of aggression; (e) the use of court-ordered educational groups for batterers; and (f) the use of a coordinating organization (DAIP) to track offenders, ensuring that repeat offenders or those in noncompliance do not fall through the cracks and that victim-safety is central to the response.

The Duluth model has been widely successful in offering greater victim protection and reducing repeat acts of violence in many different communities. But it has not been successful everywhere. Its success appears to depend on skills, leadership, and follow-through from the victim advocacy groups and key intervening agencies.

Martha McMahon and Ellen Pence

See also Coordinated Community Response; Power and Control Wheel

Further Readings

Shepard, M. E., & Pence, E. (Eds.). (1999). *Coordinating community responses to domestic violence.* Thousand Oaks, CA: Sage.

Web Sites

Duluth model: http://www.duluth-model.org

E

EARLY INTERVENTION PROGRAMS

Early childhood intervention programs aim to positively impact developmental outcomes for at-risk children by targeting and enhancing skill sets related to school achievement, social competence, and mental and physical health. Research shows that social, emotional, cognitive, behavioral, and health problems that appear early in childhood generally worsen over time in the absence of intervention. Furthermore, these problems are related to school failure, substance abuse, and aggression later in the child's life. Children whose backgrounds include low socioeconomic status, low maternal education and verbal ability, minority status, parental histories of substance abuse and mental illness, or a parental native language other than English appear to be particularly susceptible to these problems. Relative to their more advantaged counterparts, at-risk children are likely to have been exposed to and victimized by more violence, which has been shown to be predictive of a range of emotional and behavioral problems. Moreover, at-risk children are likely to already suffer from language delays stemming from a lack of access to developmentally appropriate books and learning tools, a chaotic home environment, and parents who may have low education and verbal ability themselves. Early intervention programs are predicated on the hypothesis that decreasing risk factors (e.g., early behavioral problems, language delays) while increasing protective factors (e.g., child social competence, parenting skills) in at-risk children and their families may prevent chronic distress and facilitate healthy child development.

Head Start

Head Start, an early intervention program funded by the U.S. Department of Health and Human Services, is perhaps the best known, as well as the most comprehensive program currently available for at-risk families. Participants include children from birth to age 5 and their families whose household incomes fall below the poverty line. Head Start provides services through a variety of modalities, including center-based, home-based, and "mixed" programs in urban and rural communities across the country. The program intervenes directly with both the children and their parents, training each in relevant skills, while providing access to medical care and other social services.

Head Start promotes cognitive and social development for preschool-age children. Classrooms provide a stimulating and supportive learning environment in which children can hone their language, prereading, and cognitive skills in preparation for school. This may be the first socialization experience for these children in which they have an opportunity to practice social skills such as negotiation, emotion regulation, and communication. This is critically important given the evidence that children who can make and keep friends and navigate social situations effectively are more likely to be academically successful and less likely to become aggressive and use substances than children who fail to achieve social competence. Head Start also recognizes the substantial impact that physical health has on a child's developmental course; consequently, children in the program receive routine medical and dental health screenings, and are taught good nutrition and health maintenance practices.

209

Head Start maintains a commitment to working in conjunction with parents in order to cultivate a nurturing, supportive, and safe home environment that will be conducive to long-term developmental success. This is accomplished by addressing parental risk factors, including mental health problems and substance abuse, while teaching parents developmentally appropriate parenting skills. Indeed, Head Start parents report using less corporal punishment and experiencing less domestic violence than at-risk families not enrolled in Head Start. Furthermore, Head Start parents report reading more frequently with their children. Early parent–child reading is thought to be an important literacy experience for several reasons: It teaches children that books tell stories and that stories follow a logical sequence; it teaches that real life objects can be represented by words; it allows children to build their vocabularies; it is a correlate of language and cognitive development; and it serves as a bonding experience for parents and children. Head Start also encourages parents to further their own education, which, in turn, may help to promote the value of education in a household.

Efficacy of Early Intervention Programs

According to available data, Head Start children make gains during the course of program enrollment compared to their at-risk counterparts who do not receive intervention. It appears that center-based and combined programs produce the largest impact for children, while home-based programs elicit the greatest change in parenting skills. Outcomes for parents and children seem to depend in part on both the quality and the quantity of the intervention. While Head Start has demonstrated short-term improvement in child and family functioning to varying degrees, it is unclear whether the program reliably elicits long-term change in at-risk families.

Other two-generation early intervention programs (targeting at-risk children and their parents) have produced equivocal results. For instance, the Infant Health and Development Program recruited low-birth-weight infants and their families and provided a comprehensive intervention including home, center-based, and group support components, until the children turned 3. At the end of the program, those children receiving the intervention demonstrated greater cognitive and behavioral gains than their counterparts; however, those gains had faded by age 7. Another early intervention program, Even Start, aims to improve school achievement in at-risk children by providing literacy-focused education to children and parents from low-literacy homes. The findings thus far suggest that children and parents receiving interventions do not achieve greater literacy ability than those not receiving the interventions.

Across early intervention programs, outcome studies tend to compare subsets of at-risk children, making it less clear how disadvantaged children receiving interventions ultimately fare compared to children whose families have greater financial resources. Furthermore, research indicates that the families at the greatest risk for poor outcomes are also the most likely to be noncompliant with program procedures and to leave the program prematurely; this suggests that the children who would potentially benefit the most from such interventions are also the least likely to profit from the experience. More research on the efficacy of early intervention programs is clearly warranted, with a particular emphasis on means of enrolling and retaining the most vulnerable families, as well as collecting data on long-term outcomes.

Katherine W. Follansbee and Gregory L. Stuart

See also Child Exposure to Violence, Role of Schools; School-Based Violence Prevention Programs

Further Readings

Love, L. M., et al. (2005). The effectiveness of Early Head Start for 3-year-old children and their parents: Lessons for policy and programs. *Developmental Psychology, 41,* 885–901.

Magnuson, K. A., & Waldfogel, J. (2005). Preschool child care and parents' use of physical discipline. *Infant and Child Development, 14,* 177–198.

Raikes, H., Green, B. L., Atwater, J., Kisker, E., Constantine, J., & Chazan-Cohen, R. (2006). Involvement in Early Head Start home visiting services: Demographic predictors and relations to child and parent outcomes. *Early Childhood Research Quarterly, 21,* 2–24.

Raikes, H., et al. (2006). Mother-child bookreading in low-income families: Correlates and outcomes during the first three years of life. *Child Development, 77,* 924–953.

EARLY WARNING SIGNS OF INTIMATE PARTNER VIOLENCE

Research has indicated that it is very difficult to leave a violent relationship and that survivors undergo an agonizing process to achieve safety for themselves and their children. Understanding early warning signs and characteristics of intimate partner violence (IPV) perpetrators are critical factors in developing educational messages to help women avoid engaging in relationships with abusers.

National studies with urban, suburban, and rural African American, Hispanic, and White women found the following early warning signs: whirlwind romances involving attempts to quickly and completely involve the woman, extreme charm and flattery, excessive gestures to please her family, jealousy, and early efforts to control and isolate her from her social support system. Other early warning signs include abuse in his home of origin, his abusive behavior toward other women, blaming others for his failures and misbehavior, and alcohol and drug abuse. Additional factors found to be associated with perpetration of partner violence include lower socioeconomic status, deficits in interpersonal skills, and acceptance of the use of violence within relationships. As for the survivors of IPV, studies have found that women with histories of child abuse are more likely to experience IPV as adults.

Numerous national, state, and community domestic violence programs, colleges, and other organizations working with IPV victims and perpetrators have posted Web pages that support the empirical findings and are based on the experience of many IPV survivors. The following points are synthesized from several of these Web sites. They describe a potentially violent partner as someone who

- is jealous and possessive, won't allow the woman to have friends, and puts down people who are important to her;
- checks up on the woman or makes her check in with him;
- gets too serious about the relationship too fast;
- won't accept breaking up;
- exhibits controlling behavior by being very bossy, giving orders, making all the decisions; tells the woman what she should or shouldn't wear, doesn't take her opinion seriously;
- yells, swears, manipulates, spreads false and degrading rumors, or tries to make the woman feel guilty;
- threatens, criticizes, or humiliates; makes the woman feel stupid, incapable, lazy, ugly, worthless, helpless, crazy, or trapped;
- owns or uses weapons;
- is frightening and causes worry about reactions to things said or done;

- has unpredictable mood swings, has a history of fighting, is cruel to animals or children, loses his temper quickly, or brags about mistreating others;
- thinks detructive displays of emotion are signs of love;
- pressures the woman for sex, is forceful or threatening about sex; thinks women or girls are sex objects;
- drinks too much or uses drugs; pressures the woman to take drugs or blames the alcohol and drugs for his behavior;
- blames the woman when he mistreats her; says she provoked him, pressed his buttons, made him do it, led him on;
- has a history of bad relationships and blames the other person for all the problems or feelings (e.g., saying, "Girls just don't understand me");
- does not accept responsibility for his actions;
- believes in stereotypical gender roles for males and females; believes one person should be in control and have all the power in a relationship and the other person should be passive and submissive;
- accepts or defends the use of violence by others;
- has been warned against by the woman's family and friends, who may have told her they were worried for her safety.

One Web site cautions that it is important to get to know someone for a long time before getting serious with him, because abusers can be polite and charming for several months at a time to convince their dates that they are acceptable partners.

It has been speculated in the literature that extreme charm and flattery foster a sense of trust on the part of unsuspecting victims and may groom them for succumbing to forceful control later in the relationship. Additionally, early attempts to control behavior may be construed in a positive fashion given the context of flattery. Flattery combined with early forms of control may make women more vulnerable to escalating attempts to control a large number of areas of their lives.

Statistics indicate that one in three teenagers have experienced violence in a dating relationship. Young people initiating dating relationships need to be better prepared for the likelihood of encountering an abusive partner. Although the information summarized here is easily available, additional prevention and intervention programs and targeted messages that reach the right audiences at the right times are needed.

Lynn M. Short and Pamela M. McMahon

See also Battered Women: Leaving Violent Intimate Relationships; Dating Violence/Courtship Violence; Prevention Programs, Adolescent Dating Violence; Prevention Programs, Interpersonal Violence

Further Readings

Advocates for Youth. (2006). *Dating violence warning signs.* Retrieved from http://www.advocatesforyouth.org/youth/health/relationships/violence.htm

Alabama Coalition Against Domestic Violence. (2006). *Early warning signs that your date may eventually become abusive.* Retrieved from http://www.acadv.org/dating.html

Bauer, H. M., Rodriguez, M. A., & Perez-Stable, E. J. (2000). Prevalence and determinants of intimate partner abuse among public hospital primary care patients. *Journal of General Internal Medicine, 15,* 811–817.

The Haven of RCS Domestic Violence Center. (2006). *Early warning signs of teen dating violence.* Retrieved from http://www.computerbob.com/abuse/teen_dating_ violence.php

Health First. (2006). *Twenty-three warning signs of abusive relationships.* Retrieved from http://www.health-first.org

Holtzworth-Munroe, A., Bates, L., Smutzler, N., & Sandin, E. (1997). A brief review of the research on husband violence. Part I: Maritally violent versus nonviolent men. *Aggression and Violent Behavior, 2,* 65–99.

Holtzworth-Munroe, A., Smutzler, N., & Bates, L. (1997). A brief review of the research on husband violence. Part III: Sociodemographic factors, relationship factors, and differing consequences of husband and wife violence. *Aggression and Violent Behavior, 2,* 285–307.

National Youth Violence Prevention Resource Center. (2006). *Know the early warning signs that you're in a dating situation or relationship that could have the potential to become violent.* Retrieved from http://www.safeyouth.org/scripts/teens/dating.asp

Short, L. M., et al. (2000). Survivors' identification of protective factors and early warning signs in intimate partner violence. *Violence Against Women, 6,* 273–287.

Women's Rural Advocacy Program. (2006). *Characteristics of men who batter: Twelve ways to tell whether your man may turn into an abuser.* Retrieved from http://www.letswrap.com/index02.htm

Ecological Models of Violence

Ecological models focus on multiple levels of influence and result in a comprehensive understanding of human behavior. Research has shown that violence permeates every level of our environment and society, from effects on the individual and family to violence in neighborhoods, communities, and the broader culture. Until recently, researchers investigated unique forms of violence and outcomes, such as child abuse or intimate partner violence, out of the context of the multiple traumas that individuals frequently encounter. Investigators have begun studying exposure to multiple forms of violence and the exponential effects of these experiences on individuals' health and well-being. Researchers know, for example, that child abuse and intimate partner violence overlap in approximately 40% of cases and that siblings in child-abusing families are at risk for abuse themselves. Studies show that interadult violence is replicated in the earliest of social relationships, those of siblings. Further, in cases of childhood sexual abuse, research has shown that violent revictimization in adulthood is high. In addition, researchers know that violence is more likely to occur in certain contexts. For example, children who are the victims of violence are generally more likely to live in urban and poor neighborhoods. Further, by the time the average child graduates from elementary school he or she will have witnessed thousands of murders and tens of thousands of vicarious acts of violence on television, and poor children report the highest exposure.

Thus, it is clear that violence can and does impact individuals at any age, in any environment, and often co-occurs in various forms. However, the broad range of potential influences on violence exposure and perpetration is difficult to organize and assess. One way of capturing the complex array of violent acts and interactive effects is with an ecological model that illustrates influences that occur at different levels of an individual's environment.

Defining an Ecological Schema

In 1968 Edgar Auerswald first described the use of an ecological approach to understanding family processes by connecting families to the broader community in which they were embedded. Around the same time, Roger Barker described the influence of physical surroundings and social settings on individual behavior. It was Uri Bronfenbrenner, however, who in 1979 first proposed a four-level ecological schema used to illustrate the complex layers of factors found to influence and explain variations in individual behavior. He organized factors as existing within the individual and the family at the *microsystem* level, which is posited to be surrounded by the *mesosystem*, or the interrelationships between such places as the school and home or the various components of the microsystem. These systems are nested within the *exosystem,* which consists of the community setting in which the family is embedded. Finally, these three systems are encompassed by the *macrosystem,* which is the most distal to the individual and made up of the broader culture's norms, rules, expectations, and values. Insofar as these levels are nested, they are considered to have transactional qualities—that is, factors at one level can influence, shape, or constrain factors at another level.

Adding the Temporal Dimension to the Ecology

Time, or the *chronosystem,* is a dimension that was added to the model by Bronfenbrenner in 1986. Here, the developmental influence of the related risk and protective factors found at each contextual level can be tracked over the course of an individual's life.

The ecological model has been used to explain processes related to single problems, such as substance abuse or child maltreatment. When applied to violence, this model allows us to examine the issues of multiple victimizations and continuity, as it allows us to identify those individuals whose early exposure to violence and maltreatment puts them at risk for revictimization or perpetration in childhood and

beyond. Further, by using this model, we can account for what contributes to discontinuous effects; for example, where some children either show no negative effects early on but develop serious problems later in life—the so-called sleeper effects—or show initial problems and recover, only to exhibit negative outcomes at a later date.

The Ecological Model of Violence

Using ecological systems theory, as well as concepts from the field of developmental psychopathology, a comprehensive model can be adapted to account for the varied, intertwined, and transactional forces that shape the lives of individuals who either are responsible for or have been exposed to violence and maltreatment. The model is shown in Figure 1.

Example of Ecological Effects on Children Exposed to Family Violence

To illustrate, a father may have been exposed to violence between his parents when he was growing up. His own child witnesses similar abuse of his mother by his father. This young child may be at risk for later antisociality or delinquency. However, the probability of a delinquent outcome can be reduced or enhanced depending on the availability of resources for the

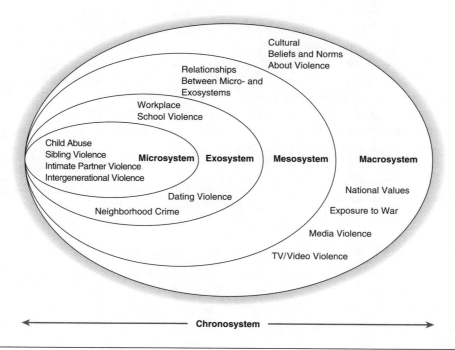

Figure 1   Ecosytem

family or community. The child's young age is an individual-level risk factor that may be countervailed at the contextual level of the family (e.g., having a parent who is not depressed, living in a family with few children, and/or having an empathic mother). Given such protective factors, the child can learn other ways of handling conflict or, perhaps, can get enough attention, information, and support to better cope with the violence.

However, if the immediate environmental context situates the family in a poor neighborhood with few resources and high exposure to community violence, then the buffering effects provided by the mother's positive parenting may be diminished or eliminated. In this case, the child may not have access to programs in the school or community; the mother may not be able to use a battered women's shelter; the child may witness additional acts of violence in the community—some, perhaps, committed against him or his friends. Community resources and initiatives that can provide help for such children are influenced by the broader culture's beliefs in, and support for, efforts to reduce such violence. These resources at the broadest social level, or lack thereof, can constrain the range of available options for the family in a given neighborhood. Thus, despite the protective features of the home, the risk elements at play in the community may overwhelm the child, who may begin to use violent tactics in interpersonal situations. When such violence is reinforced by role modeling in television and other media, the expectation that violence is an appropriate response to challenges or stress may be enhanced. Difficulties in social relationships, violence in dating relationships, or delinquency and eventual incarceration may follow.

The model also can be used to explain resilient coping in those whose exposure to violence is mitigated by protective features at all levels of the environment and does not lead to unhealthy outcomes. Thus, the model can offer a detailed and complex picture of ways in which features of the individual, family, neighborhood, community, and culture can contribute to more healthy trajectories for those exposed to violence.

Utility of the Ecological Model

The ecological model permits appreciation of how multiple forms of violence in the life of an individual may add up, coalesce, and interact. With this information we can identify individuals whose early exposure to violence and maltreatment may lead them into trouble in

adolescence and adulthood. Ideally, interventions can be designed for each level of the ecological system to reduce the salience of violence in the culture, in the media, in schools and neighborhoods, and finally, in the family.

Testing Ecological Models in Research

There is a need to continue to refine the study of violence as a serious developmental risk to children, particularly with studies that address violence early in the life of the child. In addition, studies should assess factors that serve to protect some children from the deleterious consequences of exposure to violence. Yet, there is no study that puts all forms of violence and related risk and protective factors together in accounting for the mental health, physical development, and social competence of young children. However, the national research bodies have called for precisely this type of study. If undertaken all at once, such a study would be prohibitively expensive and involve a large sample followed over time. Still, the issue is to capture as much of the salient environment as possible in trying to understand and explain the contributions of particular stressors to children's adjustment.

As difficult as it may be to measure the presence of the broadest cultural risk factors, such as the acceptance of an atmosphere of violence, this is the kind of research challenge that needs attention if we are to continue exploring why some children are more seriously affected by violence than others. Further, studies that take the qualities of the immediate neighborhood and broader social context into account can shift focus from the individual to extrafamilial contributing factors. This information can be used to situate the family in a particular ecological niche with certain contextualized features of risk and protection.

Sandra Graham-Bermann and Michelle Gross

See also Resiliency, Protective and Risk Factors; Risk Assessment

Further Readings

Auerswald, E. H. (1968). Interdisciplinary versus ecological approach. *Family Process, 7*(2), 202–215.
Barker, R. (1968). *Ecological psychology: Concepts and methods for studying the environment of human behavior.* Stanford, CA: Stanford University Press.

Bronfenbrenner, U. (1979). *The ecology of human development: Experiments by design and nature.* Cambridge, MA: Harvard University Press.

Bronfenbrenner, U., & Evans, G. W. (2000). Developmental science in the 21st century: Emerging questions, theoretical models, research designs, and empirical findings. *Social Development, 9*(1), 115–125.

ELDER ABUSE

Elder abuse is harm or risk of harm to older adults by trusted other persons. This definition includes the failure of caregivers to protect vulnerable elders from harm or provide them with goods and services, like food or medical care, to meet basic needs. Elder abuse may be intentional or unintentional. It can assume various forms, such as physical, psychological, sexual, or financial abuse, neglect, or abandonment. The effects of these forms may be injury, suffering, loss, or rights violation. Research suggests that abused elders die three times sooner than nonabused elders.

Elder abuse is a major aspect of interpersonal violence. Former U.S. Surgeon General Louis Sullivan declared it to be a public health concern and criminal justice issue. All states and territories have laws authorizing the use of adult protective services to investigate and respond to elder abuse situations. They also have criminal codes to punish the perpetrators in some instances.

History of Problem Recognition

Elder abuse existed prior to modern times. However, it usually was not considered to be a social problem. For example, in early America some Indian tribes forced older members to work until exhaustion, and Hudson Bay Eskimos moved, leaving elderly members behind when there was not enough food for everyone. Among colonists, families sometimes cast out older dependent kin when they were unable or unwilling to provide care. In addition, conflict over property could result in family scorn or worse for older people.

Recognition of elder abuse as a problem began in the 1950s, when many younger family members moved from their hometowns in search of better jobs and other opportunities, leaving older kin behind. Communities became concerned about the possible neglect and exploitation of those who were mentally impaired and living alone, outside of institutions. Adult protective services was created and spread nationwide to address these concerns.

Public recognition of other elder abuse forms was sparked during the mid-1970s to early 1980s. This began with professional writings on a "battered old person syndrome" by geriatrician Robert Butler in 1975 and testimony on "battered parents" by sociologist Suzanne Steinmetz before the U.S. House Science and Technology Committee, which was exploring overlooked aspects of family violence in 1978. Recognition of most other elder abuse forms emerged from pioneering research on the topic. Although often methodologically flawed, these early studies served to characterize the problem, contrast it with child abuse, and speculate on its etiology and scope.

Nature and Scope of the Problem

Elder abuse research has not advanced as rapidly or far as research on most other aspects of interpersonal violence. Reasons for this include funding deficits, few investigators, weak theory, and methodological ambiguities. However limited, existing research does provide a beginning understanding of elder abuse as a complex problem that occurs across settings and affects a large number and diversity of older adults.

Theory and Risk Factors

Various theories have been advanced to explain elder abuse. Most were borrowed from the family abuse literature used to understand either child abuse or partner abuse. Those from child abuse, such as role theory and situational theory, see elder abuse as arising out of inadequate caregiving. Those from partner abuse, like conflict theory and feminist theory, see elder abuse as an issue of power, control, and inequities. None of these theories considers the impact of the aging process. None alone seems sufficient to explain elder abuse in all of its forms and contexts. None has been rigorously tested.

More inquiry has gone into discovering risk factors for elder abuse. Risk factors are characteristics of victims, perpetrators, or environments that indicate the possibility of abuse occurrence. Existing research suggests that elder abuse risk factors may vary by form and have greater potency in combination. Moreover, characteristics of the perpetrator tend to be more predictive of abuse occurrence than those of either the victim or the environment. Perpetrator risk factors include pathology (e.g., alcoholism, mental illness) and financial or housing dependence on the victim. Victim risk factors include reduced functional capacity and problem behaviors, such as those originating out of dementia, like aggressiveness and wandering. Finally, environmental risk factors include social isolation and the victim and perpetrator sharing living quarters.

Prevalence, Incidence, and Reporting

National prevalence studies have been conducted on child abuse and partner abuse. This is not true for elder abuse, despite repeated calls for them and their importance for program planning and public policy purposes. Localized studies in Ohio, Maryland, New Jersey, and Massachusetts suggest an elder abuse prevalence rate of 1% to 10%. Lower figures usually relate to general populations of older adults, higher ones to frail or disabled elders served by health or social service agencies. Variation in prevalence rates also can be attributed to differences in elder abuse definitions and forms used during the investigations. Applying prevalence rates to the current population of older Americans indicates that there may be as many as 5 million victims annually.

A national elder abuse incidence study was conducted by the National Center on Elder Abuse. It concluded that 450,000 abuse victims age 60 and over were seen by adult protective services and agencies serving older people in 1996. The most commonly encountered elder abuse form was neglect, followed by psychological abuse, financial abuse, and physical abuse. Only 1 in 5 of the situations were reported to adult protective services, although mandatory elder abuse reporting exists in all but a handful of states. As low as this reporting ratio seems, it is higher than estimates emerging out of prevalence studies (i.e., 1 in 14). An analysis of 2004 elder abuse reports to adult protective services nationwide identified a rate of 833 for every 100,000 older adults.

Victim and Perpetrator Profiles

Research findings and reports to adult protective services indicate that the typical elder abuse victim is female, age 75 or older, and living in her own home. She has experienced more than one abuse form and multiple occurrences of the problem. Usually her perpetrator is an adult child, spouse, or other family member. Typically the perpetrator is female as well. Profile specifics, however, vary by abuse form. For instance, physical abuse victims tend to be younger and more functionally independent. Neglect victims tend to be older and functionally impaired.

Cultural Variation

There is some evidence of elder abuse variation by cultural grouping. For example, Korean American elders tend to attach a narrower meaning to elder abuse and show less willingness to seek help in addressing it than do Caucasian American or African American elders. Japanese Americans are more likely to seek help from family in elder abuse situations than are European Americans, Hispanics, or African Americans.

Problem Response

Five major systems have responsibility for intervening in elder abuse situations: (1) The lead system is adult protective services. It is authorized by law to receive and investigate elder abuse reports and then to determine the need for protective services to correct or discontinue the situation. (2) Law enforcement acts to address violations of law and represents first responders in many crisis situations. (3) Health care offers emergency and ongoing treatment for the effects of elder abuse. It also is the system best positioned to detect and report the problem. (4) Aging Network represents the vast group of supportive and clinical services for older adults created out of the Older Americans Act, and it can help victims manage at home without an abusive caregiver as well as provide support for older adults who are socially isolated and at risk of elder abuse. (5) Domestic violence programs work to ensure safety for victims of domestic violence, including those in later life. They also attempt to hold perpetrators accountable for their violent behavior.

In an effort to provide a coordinated response to elder abuse situations, many communities have formed multidisciplinary teams with representatives from these systems. Multidisciplinary teams are used for problem identification and treatment recommendation. They provide a more holistic perspective than any single system can offer and ensure that no system has the sole responsibility for handling challenging elder abuse situations.

Georgia J. Anetzberger

See also Adult Protective Services; Legislation, Elder Abuse; Risk Assessment Instruments, Elder Abuse

Further Readings

Anetzberger, G. J. (Ed.). (2005). *The clinical management of elder abuse.* Binghamton, NY: Haworth Press.

Lachs, M. S., Williams, C. S., O'Brien, S., Pillemer, K. A., & Charlson, M. E. (1998). The mortality of elder mistreatment. *Journal of the American Medical Association, 280*(5), 428–432.

National Center of Elder Abuse. (1998, September). *The National Elder Abuse Incidence Study: Final report.* Available at http://www.elderabusecenter.org

National Research Council. (2003). *Elder mistreatment: Abuse, neglect, and exploitation in an aging America.* Washington, DC: National Academies Press.

Pillemer, K. A., & Wolf, R. A. (Eds.). (1986). *Elder abuse: Conflict in the family.* Dover, MA: Auburn House.

Tatara, T. (Ed.). (1999). *Understanding elder abuse in minority populations.* Philadelphia: Brunner/Mazel.

Teaster, P. B., Dugar, T. A., Mendiondo, M. S., & Otto, J. M. (2005, May 12). *The 2004 survey of state adult protective services: Abuse of adults 60 years of age and older.* Available at http://www.elderabusecenter.org

EMERGE

Emerge is an international training and resource center on domestic violence. Founded in 1977 in Boston, it was the world's first batterer intervention program. The initial emphasis of the battered women's movement in the United States and globally had been on calling attention to domestic violence, redefining it as a crime against women, and promoting safety and justice for women. But many victim advocates argued that men must join women in this effort, not only to communicate that violence against women is a human rights issue of equal importance to men, but also to play a unique role in educating and confronting men who abuse women. Emerge was established at the behest of women who had founded the first battered women's programs in Boston. Hotline staff at Transition House and Respond were receiving an increasing number of calls from batterers. Since it was not their mission to work with abusive men, staff from these programs publicized a request for men to establish a program for abusers. Nearly all of the 10 men who founded Emerge were friends or relatives of workers at local battered women's programs. While most were social workers or counselors, the others included a teacher, a community organizer, a lawyer, and a cab driver.

Emerge has remained on the cutting edge of change in terms of its innovative intervention model for abusers, its annual trainings and consultations to hundreds of other agencies and institutions, and its efforts to influence public policy on the local, state, and national levels. Emerge has pioneered culturally specific interventions for abusers, beginning with the establishment of groups for Latino men in 1985, African American men in 1990, and Vietnamese and Cambodian men in 1993. During the 1990s Emerge also created specialized groups for lesbians as well as gay men. All of these culturally specific programs have been accompanied by specialized outreach and education collaborations.

In 1986, Emerge created groups for teen offenders, and together with Transition House, founded the Dating Violence Intervention Project. Emerge subsequently established the Responsible Fatherhood Program, a parenting education program geared to abusive men. These groups seek to help men rebuild trust with children who have witnessed their violence, and to become more responsible coparents.

Emerge has continuously sought to help create more coordinated and effective criminal justice responses to domestic violence. With federal funding, Emerge has provided national trainings on domestic violence danger assessment and safety planning since 1998, and developed danger assessment tools. Emerge has also helped to create innovative collaborations with social service programs, religious centers, child welfare agencies, and health care providers to better address and to prevent domestic violence.

David Adams

See also Batterers; Batterers, Personality Characteristics of; Batterers, Treatment Approaches and Effectiveness; Parenting Practices and Violence, Domestic Violence; Prevention Programs, Community Mobilization

Further Readings

Adams, D., & Cayouette, S. (2002.) Emerge: A group model for abusers. In E. Aldarondo & F. Mederos (Eds.), *Programs for men who batter: Intervention and prevention strategies in a diverse society* (pp. 1–31). Kingston, NY: Civic Research Institute.

Domestic violence danger assessment and safety planning [Interactive training DVD]. Available at http://www .emergedv.com

Schechter, S. (1982). *Women and male violence: The visions and struggles of the battered women's movement.* Boston: South End Press.

END VIOLENCE AGAINST WOMEN INTERNATIONAL

In January 2003, Joanne Archambault founded End Violence Against Women International (EVAWI), a nonprofit 501(c)(3) organization whose stated mission is to "provide effective, victim centered, multidisciplinary training and expert consultation regarding crimes of sexual assault and domestic violence." To achieve this goal, EVAWI conducts international conferences and regional training seminars to educate the general public, law enforcement, community organizations, and others working in the field of domestic violence and sexual assault on best practices for responding to these crimes and ensuring thorough, evidence-based investigations are performed to hold offenders accountable.

The organization's stated goals are to (a) counter crimes of sexual assault and domestic violence by ensuring a coordinated, competent, and effective response by all members of Domestic Violence Councils and Sexual Assault Response Teams and other community stake holders; (b) increase reporting of sexual assault and domestic violence by providing members of a multidisciplinary response team with information that will enable them to effectively respond to domestic violence and sexual assault; (c) identify, support, and disseminate best practices that foster men taking responsibility for ending violence against women; and (d) conduct and disseminate evidence-based research on domestic violence and the sexual assault of women by strangers and nonstrangers.

The Making a Difference project was recently started by EVAWI, in coordination with Canadian professionals, with the stated purpose of "challenging the legal process in both the U.S. and Canada to more effectively prosecute sexual offenders." According to EVAWI, research unequivocally shows that a majority of sexual assault cases are committed by a person the victim knows. However, authorities are less likely to prosecute cases involving incidents of sexual assault if there is a relationship between the victim and the accused, there is no sign of physical injury, and the suspect is not otherwise associated with criminal activity. The project is working to address this problem by "facilitating reform in the U.S. and Canadian legal systems to challenge the status quo and more effectively prosecute incidents of adult sexual assault."

The organization's multidisciplinary focus is reflected in the diversity of its staff and Board of Directors. EVAWI's founder, Joanne Archambault, spent nearly 23 years working for the San Diego Police Department before retiring in 2002. During her last 10 years with the department she supervised the Sex Crimes Unit, coauthored the San Diego County Sexual Assault Response Team (SART) resource pamphlet, and produced a video on SART that is used as a popular training aid for professionals. The organization's board of directors is comprised of sexual assault and domestic violence experts, law enforcement officials, attorneys, advocates, and health professionals who are committed to addressing national and international issues relating to domestic violence and sexual assault, with a particular focus on the role of law enforcement.

April J. Guillen and Chelsea M. Clawson

See also Legislation, Rape/Sexual Assault

Further Readings

Ryan, V. M. (2004). Intoxicating encounters: Allocating responsibility in the law of rape. *California Western Law Review, 40*(2), 407, 411.

Web Sites

End Violence Against Women International: http://www .evawintl.org

EPIDEMIOLOGY, DEFINED

Epidemiology is the quantitative study of the distribution or frequency of, and the determinants or factors associated with, a particular issue affecting the public. These issues of interest range from diseases, to accidents, to behaviors such as violence. Stated concisely, epidemiology is interested in counting and describing events.

In epidemiology, events of interest are generally counted, or quantified, in terms of *incidence* and/or *prevalence*. Incidence refers to the number of *separate events* that affect individuals within a group during a specific time. For example, an incidence of completed rape takes the form of 3 per 1,000 women in a given year, meaning 3 completed rapes were measured per 1,000 women in the population during that year. This is not the same as prevalence, which identifies the total number of *persons* within a group who experience an event during a specific time period. The corresponding prevalence rate may take the form of 2 completed rapes per 1,000 women during that year, meaning 2 women were victims of completed rape (some were victims more than one time) over the specified period.

Epidemiology is concerned with more than counting. It also identifies characteristics of affected individuals, event characteristics, and environmental characteristics. This descriptive task generally takes the form of addressing questions such as these: Who is influenced? What happens during the event? Where does the event occur? When does the event take place? Extending the above example, answers to these sorts of questions include that, in general, younger females are more likely to experience a completed rape. The rape generally does not involve a weapon, the victims tend not to sustain injuries beyond the rape, and the perpetrator is most often someone they know. Finally, completed rapes tend to occur in or near the victim's home during evening hours.

Given an understanding of the extent and nature of the problem of interest, epidemiology approaches the issue analytically by addressing two additional important questions. First, how did the event take place? And second, why did the event take place? Answering these critical questions generally involves analytic comparisons between groups in the population to determine critical risk factors. Though very important, identifying risk factors is not the same as establishing causation. For example, epidemiological work demonstrates that poor women are more likely to be victims of completed rape. This does not mean that being poor is a *cause* of rape. Instead, it merely demonstrates that there is an increased risk of victimization among poor women. To establish a causal relationship, additional analyses are necessary.

Ultimately, findings from epidemiological research can be used to inform the public about the nature and extent of a problem. In addition, using this knowledge, policies designed to reduce frequency of the problem of interest may be implemented. Further, results from epidemiological analyses can be used to evaluate interventions designed to minimize, and eventually eradicate, the problem of interest.

Callie Marie Rennison

See also Epidemiology, Perpetration Patterns by Age, Gender, Ethnicity, Socioeconomic Status; Epidemiology, Victimization Patterns by Age, Gender, Ethnicity, Socioeconomic Status; Incidence; Prevalence; Prevalence, Measuring

Further Readings

Berkman, L. (2000). *Social epidemiology.* New York: Oxford University Press.
Bhopal, R. (2002). *Concepts of epidemiology.* New York: Oxford University Press.
Gordis, L. (2004). *Epidemiology* (3rd ed.). Philadelphia: Saunders.
Rothman, K. (2002). *Epidemiology: An introduction.* New York: Oxford University Press.
Rothman, K., & Greenland, S. (1998). *Modern epidemiology.* Philadelphia: Lippincott Williams & Wilkins.

EPIDEMIOLOGY, INTERNATIONAL PATTERNS

Epidemiology is the quantitative study of the distribution or frequency of, and the determinants or factors associated with, a particular issue affecting the public. For example, an interpersonal violence epidemiologist may study the nature and extent of homicide across nations. In epidemiology, investigated events are generally counted, or quantified, in terms of *incidence* and *prevalence*. However, the field is concerned with more than counting; it also identifies characteristics of affected individuals, event characteristics, and environmental characteristics. In addition, researchers investigate other important aspects, including *how* did the event take place? And *why* did the event take place?

Epidemiological research is challenging in a single setting, but it is exponentially more challenging across nations. To put it directly, one must ensure that the violence of interest is counted in the same way across jurisdictions. This is especially difficult because how violence is counted is contingent on how it is defined, legitimated, and sanctioned from nation to nation. These affect how policing agencies measure, collect, and verify violent acts in each locale. Even data collected from sources other than police agencies are problematic. Data from victimization surveys are influenced by a nation's political and cultural milieu in that they affect how respondents recognize, view, and report victimization experiences. A further complication arises when considering that all of these factors have fluctuated over time within countries.

Even given investigative difficulties including differing definitions, measures, and data collection, this cross-national research is worth the effort since all nations are affected by interpersonal violence.

Official Police Data

International interpersonal violence research primarily relies on two types of data: official police data and victimization surveys. Both types of data are essential because neither is capable of providing all the information about the extent and nature of interpersonal violence. Together they can provide a more complete picture.

There are several sources of official police data in the world. Most data are generated by large international organizations such as the United Nations. Other data come from sources such as Amnesty International and the International Red Cross. In this entry, the most widely used sources of police data on interpersonal violence are reviewed. A widely used data source comes from the United Nations Surveys of Crime Trends and Operation of Criminal Justice Systems. This collection, initiated in 1977, is based on a compilation of a wide range of official crime and criminal justice statistics taken from multiple waves of questionnaire distribution. The surveys are administered to national officials by the United Nations Statistical Office and cover topics such as crimes reported to the police; arrests, prosecutions, and convictions; the extent and types of formal punishments; and criminal justice system resources (e.g., personnel, budgets). The number of nations participating in this effort has varied over time, and depending upon which survey is being administered. Participating nations have ranged from a low of about 65 nations to a high of approximately 100 nations. Most recently, the ninth survey was fielded, which generated statistics from 2003 to 2004.

A second widely cited official police data source is the International Criminological Police Organization, also known as Interpol. Interpol cross-national data collection began in 1950 and is ongoing. Interpol data are published biennially. At present, police agencies from more than 180 member countries supply data on a wide range of topics, including murder, sex offenses, white-collar crime, child pornography, and weapons smuggling. The Comparative Crime Data File (CCDF) is a collection of statistics on crime compiled by Dane Archer and Rosemary Gartner and is found in their 1984 publication *Violence and Crime in Cross-National Perspective*. This collection includes information on crimes such as murder, homicide, assault, robbery, rape, and property theft. Like the other data, CCDF data are gathered by nations that volunteer information. However, information is also gathered through available documentation. Statistics from over 100 countries are included in this data collection, which goes through 1982. And finally, the World Health Organization compiles what is generally considered the most complete and reliable source of death and homicide data across nations. These data are gathered from national public health organizations and published volumes.

Official police data are limited in well-documented ways. These shortcomings include reflecting only crime known to law enforcement agencies and variation in definitions of crime across nations. Further, because reporting of violence to the police and police recording of incidents differs from nation to nation, one cannot be certain whether international differences in these statistics reflect actual crime differences or merely crime reporting and recording differences. Because of these limitations, it is generally agreed that comparisons of interpersonal violence across data sets—especially for nonlethal violence like rape, assault, and robbery—are problematic. And it has been demonstrated that comparisons between individual nations are also inappropriate. However, international crime data do offer information on homicide that researchers view as reliable, especially when the findings are corrected for identified definitional differences.

Victimization Survey Data

In an effort to correct for some of the limitations of official police records, and to allow for the comparison of crime rates across nations independent of the idiosyncrasies of police records, the International Crime Victimization Survey (ICVS) series was created. These standardized questionnaires, which have been fielded four times now, with the most recent being in 1990, are distributed in several countries. The first wave of ICVS surveys was fielded in 1989. The fourth, and most recent wave, was fielded in 47 nations during 2000. Nations in the sample include industrialized nations, developing nations, and nations in transition. Industrialized countries were surveyed nationwide using random-digit-dialing, while developing and transitional nation surveys were restricted to face-to-face interviews in urban areas (primarily capital cities). Because of these differences, researchers discourage the comparison of victimization statistics of developed and developing countries. The ICVS series queries respondents about several forms of personal violence, including robbery, sexual assault, and nonsexual assault. Sexual assault questions are asked only of female respondents.

The ICVS series offers useful information on global interpersonal violence; however, data from this series are limited in certain ways. Most obviously, the ICVS series cannot offer information on homicide, the most severe of all interpersonal violence, as ICVS data are based on self-reported experiences of victimization. In addition, cultural and political differences among nations may affect a respondent's willingness or ability to disclose victimization. In addition, like all retrospective surveys, respondents' answers are based on the accurate memory of events, and the details of those events, that occurred during the previous 12 months. Information on offenders is limited and reflects the victim's perception. Though the ICVS is a large survey, sample sizes from each country are relatively small, ranging from about 1,000 to 6,000 interviews, with corresponding variation in sampling error. Finally, response rates among nations range from less than 40% to almost 90%.

Interpersonal Violence Data

Though many things conspire to make comparisons of interpersonal violence across nations difficult, there are several general findings that emerge from the data. Findings show that in the aggregate, the risk of being victimized by interpersonal violent crime is about one in five. Findings also demonstrate great variation in personal violent victimization rates from nation to nation. Data suggest that the level of development of a nation is related to the rate of violence its inhabitants experience. More developed nations tend to be characterized by the lowest rates of violence, transitional countries tend to have higher violence rates, and developing nations the highest rates of violence. While this is generally true, it is also important to recognize that there is a great deal of variation in rates of violence among nations of each type of development. For several types of violence, victimization rates are higher in Latin America and in sub-Saharan Africa. Not surprisingly, data suggest that where people are economically deprived, violence rates are generally higher. This is especially the case among younger persons, who tend to be victimized at higher rates than others.

However, individual risk of victimization is not randomly distributed among nations or persons. Gender differences in interpersonal violence are found throughout the world. The rates of lethal and nonlethal victimization are higher for males than for females. International data suggest that developed Western countries are characterized by the highest rates of assault against males. In contrast, victimization against females is highest in Latin America, Africa, and new world countries. Though lower than male rates in general, there is great variation in female victimization rates. For instance, in nations with widespread poverty, and in countries where women have low social status, women are victimized at higher rates.

Homicide

Homicide, the most severe form of interpersonal violence, varies across nations. Research suggests an inverse relationship between a nation's development level and its homicide rates. In other words, homicide rates tend to be higher in developing nations, and lower in developed nations. Again, though, there is great variation within groups of developed and developing nations. Among the developed nations, the United States has the highest rate of homicide. Substantially lower homicide rates characterize other developed nations, such as New Zealand, Germany, Canada, Switzerland, and Japan. The homicide rate in the United States is comparable to rates found in Eastern European nations such as Poland, Slovakia, and the Czech Republic. Homicide rates greater than those of the United States are found in nations such as Mexico, South Africa, Colombia, and Lithuania.

Homicide risk is not randomly distributed among individuals in the populations. In general, relationships among risk factors found in the United States are applicable to those in other nations. For instance, males are more likely to become a victim of homicide than are females, regardless of the nation considered. Further, younger people—teens and those in their 20s—are victims of homicide at higher rates than older people. This is the case again regardless of the nation under consideration.

Homicide rates are thought to be related to several factors aside from development. Most hotly debated is the relationship between firearm availability and homicide rates. It is thought that where firearms, especially illegal firearms, are readily available, homicide rates are higher.

Nonlethal Violence

The nonlethal forms of interpersonal violence most often examined include robbery, nonsexual assault, and physical assault. It has been demonstrated that the homicide rate is not a valid proxy for nonlethal violence (or vice versa). Indeed, though the homicide rate in the United States sets it apart from other developed nations, the nonlethal victimization rate in the United States is much more like that of similarly developed nations. For example, nonlethal violent victimization rates in the United States are generally similar to those found in Sweden.

Robbery

Robbery rates differ greatly among nations. Like homicide rates, robbery rates are lowest in developed nations and higher in developing nations. Also like homicide rates, there is considerable variation in robbery rates among developed nations, as well as among developing nations. Further, the differences in these rates change from year to year and depending upon the data considered. In general, however, it appears that among developed nations, Canada and the Netherlands tend to have higher robbery rates than do nations such as the United States, Scotland, and Australia.

Nonsexual Assault

Nonsexual assault rates tend to be higher in developing nations than in developed nations. However, assault rates are not generally lower in the industrialized countries of the world than in the urban areas of east and central Europe. The relationship between assault and gender is contingent on the nation considered. In the United States, Canada, and Australia, assault rates are generally higher than robbery rates. This is not the case in other industrialized countries where assault and robbery occur at similar rates. In developed nations, males are more likely to be a victim of assault than are females. In developing nations, males and females experience assault at similar rates. This is especially the case where assault is very prevalent.

Sexual Assault

Like much interpersonal violence data, data on sexual assault suggest that it is more frequent in developing nations than in developed nations. However, there is considerable variation among developed countries with regard to sexual assault rates. For instance, data suggest that females in the United States, Australia, and England are at greater risk than are females in Japan, Northern Ireland, Poland, and Portugal. In developing nations, the highest rates of sexual assault have been recorded in the areas of Northern Africa and Latin America and the lowest rates of sexual assault have been measured in Asian nations.

Callie Marie Rennison

See also Assault; Homicides, Criminal; Rape/Sexual Assault

Further Readings

Basch, P. (1999). *Textbook of international health*. New York: Oxford University Press.
Koop, C. E., Pearson, C. E., & Schwarz, M. R. (2002). *Critical issues in global health*. San Francisco: Jossey-Bass.

EPIDEMIOLOGY, PERPETRATION PATTERNS BY AGE, GENDER, ETHNICITY, SOCIOECONOMIC STATUS

Epidemiological data on perpetration of interpersonal violence are useful in understanding the extent of the problem and whether perpetration rates vary by age, gender, ethnicity, and socioeconomic status. However, perpetration rates do not provide a complete picture of interpersonal violence rates, largely because they are almost exclusively based on arrest records or self-report surveys. Arrest records rely on accurate reporting of violent incidents and uniform arrest policies across demographic groups and community settings. Yet, many violent acts are not reported, and arrest policies may vary considerably by gender, ethnicity, and community setting. For instance, an overrepresentation of a particular ethnic group in perpetration of a specific type of interpersonal violence could reflect a true difference in perpetration or a bias in arrest of individuals from that ethnic group. Self-report surveys, although less likely to reflect underreporting or bias than arrest data, are also limited by characteristics of the sample selected, the lack of a regular survey methodology (such as a national interpersonal violence perpetration survey), and possible inaccuracies in self-report. Accordingly, it is important to supplement perpetration data with other sources of information, such as victimization surveys, in order to provide the best estimate of actual rates.

There are also many different types of interpersonal violence and an assortment of agencies tasked with reporting perpetration rates for one or more types of interpersonal violence. There is no single repository of perpetration data for all types of interpersonal violence. In the United States, the most comprehensive source of information on arrests for certain interpersonal violence criminal offense categories is the Uniform Crime Reporting (UCR) Program, administered by the Federal Bureau of Investigation (FBI) since 1930 and based on monthly reports from nearly 17,000 state and local agencies. Four types of offenses that would be considered interpersonal violence are reported: murder and non-negligent manslaughter, forcible rape, robbery, and aggravated assault. Offense data are provided separately for males and females and by age group, but data on ethnicity are limited to race, and data on socioeconomic status of offenders are not provided. However, studies that have examined the geographic distribution of interpersonal violence, particularly UCR offenses, suggest that crime rates are higher in lower-income and inner-city communities.

The UCR must be supplemented by other sources of information for forms of interpersonal violence perpetration not specifically addressed. Two additional types of interpersonal violence of major concern (and linked to age of victims) are child maltreatment and elder abuse. Most child maltreatment perpetration data

in the United States are provided annually by the Department of Health and Human Services, Administration for Children and Families (ACF). However, data for elder abuse (and other types of interpersonal violence, such as violence in the workplace and intimate partner violence perpetration) often rely on surveys or estimates from various sources of information that are not always available annually or for the most recent year.

Murder and Non-Negligent Manslaughter

The UCR defines murder and non-negligent manslaughter as one human being killing another in a manner that is willful and non-negligent. Incidents that fall into this category in the UCR are determined by police investigation rather than by medical examiners and/or a judge or jury. For 2004, the UCR reported a total of 15,935 incidents of murder and non-negligent manslaughter in the United States. Of these, approximately 13% were perpetrated by youth 13 to 19 years old, 17% were perpetrated by younger adults 20 to 24 years old, and 17% were committed by individuals 25 to 34 years old. Rates decline steadily after age 35. There are also significant gender and ethnicity differences in perpetration rates. In 2004, 64% of these crimes were perpetrated by males, 7% were perpetrated by females, and the remaining 29% were classified as perpetrated by individuals of "unknown" gender. Looking at ethnic/racial breakdowns reported in the UCR, Whites committed approximately 51% of all incidents of murder and non-negligent manslaughter, Blacks committed 47% of these crimes, and American Indians/Alaskan Natives and Asians or Pacific Islanders each committed 1%. Whites committed more murder and non-negligent manslaughter in terms of numbers of offenses than other ethnic groups, but Blacks were overrepresented relative to their percentage in the overall U.S. population.

Forcible Rape

The UCR defines the crime of forcible rape as the forcible carnal knowledge of a female against her will. Attempts to commit forcible rape are also included in this category. In 2004, there were a total of 18,489 instances of forcible rape reported. The age breakdown of perpetration was as follows: 25% of rapes were committed by youth ages 13 to 19; 19% by those 20 to 24; 23% by those 25 to 34; and 33%, by those 35 and older. Males perpetrated 98.5% of forcible rapes in 2004, with female perpetrators accounting for the additional 1.5%. Approximately 66% of forcible rapes in 2004 were committed by Whites, 32% by Blacks, 1% by American Indians or Alaskan Natives, and an additional 1% by Asians or Pacific Islanders. Again, the UCR does not provide data on the socioeconomic status of perpetrators of crime.

Robbery

The UCR defines robbery as the use of force or threat of force for theft or attempted theft of anything of value directly from the care, custody, or control of another person. In 2004, there were 78,494 instances of robbery. The age breakdown of perpetration was as follows: 37% of the robberies were committed by youth ages 13 to 19; 22% by those 20 to 24; 20% by those 25 to 34; and 21% by those 35 and older. These statistics suggest that a disproportionately high percentage of adolescents is responsible for robbery. Males accounted for 89% of all robberies in 2004, with females committing the remaining 11%. Whites were responsible for approximately 45% of robberies in 2004, while Blacks were responsible for 53%. American Indians or Alaskan Natives perpetrated less than 1% of robberies in 2004, as did Asians or Pacific Islanders.

Aggravated Assault

The UCR defines aggravated assault as an unlawful attack with the intent of inflicting bodily injury. In 2004, there were 312,911 incidents of aggravated assault. The age breakdown of perpetration was as follows: 20% of aggravated assaults were committed by youth ages 13 to 19; 19% by those 20 to 24; 26% by those 25 to 34; and 45% by those 35 and older. Approximately 89% of all aggravated assaults in 2004 were perpetrated by men, and 11% by women. Whites accounted for approximately 65% of all aggravated assaults, while Blacks accounted for approximately 33%. American Indians or Alaskan Natives and Asians or Pacific Islanders accounted for approximately 1% of aggravated assaults, respectively.

Child Maltreatment

For 2004, the ACF reported a total of 872,000 instances of childhood maltreatment in the United States. This figure includes neglect (62.4%), physical abuse (17.6%), sexual abuse (9.7%), and psychological maltreatment (7.0%), and an additional category of "other," which includes such forms of maltreatment as abandonment, threats of harm, and/or congenital drug abuse (3.3%). Approximately 84% of perpetrators of child maltreatment were parents of the victim, and 6.5% were nonparental caregivers. Approximately 5% of perpetrators were under 20 years old. The majority of acts of child maltreatment were perpetrated by those in the 20 to 39 age group, with 35% of perpetrators between the ages of 20 and 29, and 37.5% between the ages of 30 and 39. The remaining 22% of child maltreatment perpetrators were over 40 years old. Male perpetrators accounted for 42% of child maltreatment cases in 2004, and female perpetrators accounted for 58%. Breakdowns of perpetration by ethnicity and socioeconomic status were not recorded; however, there is evidence to suggest that financial problems may lead to child maltreatment, indicating a link with socioeconomic status.

Elder Abuse

The National Committee for the Prevention of Elder Abuse (NCPEA) defines elder abuse as any form of mistreatment resulting in a harm or loss to an older person. NCPEA has identified six categories of elder abuse: physical abuse, sexual abuse, domestic violence, psychological abuse, financial abuse, and neglect. Based on estimates, it is generally believed that 4% to 6% of the elderly in the United States are abused each year. In addition to being underreported, elder abuse is considered a relatively new phenomenon, and data collection regarding this type of crime is in the early stages. As with child maltreatment, perpetrators of elder abuse are likely to be persons known to the victim. Most often they are the adult children of victims, although there are cases in which other relatives (including spouses) and/or caregivers commit elder abuse. The NCPEA reports that perpetrators of elder abuse are likely to be unmarried, live with their victim, and be unemployed. Many perpetrators of elder abuse engage in some form of substance abuse. Perpetration does not vary by gender.

Emily K. Asencio and Nancy G. Guerra

See also Assault, Aggravated; Child Neglect; Elder Abuse;
  Homicides, Criminal; Intimate Partner Violence;
  Workplace Violence

Further Readings

Federal Bureau of Investigation. (2004). *Crime in the United States*. Retrieved from http://www.fbi.gov/ucr/ucr.htm

National Committee for the Prevention of Elder Abuse. (2003). *What is elder abuse?* Retrieved from http://www.preventelderabuse.org/index.html

U.S. Department of Health and Human Services, Administration for Children and Families. (2004). *Child maltreatment 2004*. Retrieved from http://www .acf.hhs.gov/programs/cb/pubs/cm04/index.htm

EPIDEMIOLOGY, VICTIMIZATION PATTERNS BY AGE, GENDER, ETHNICITY, SOCIOECONOMIC STATUS

In trying to determine the extent of the interpersonal violence problem, it is important to supplement self-report and arrest data on perpetration with information on victimization. Hospital emergency room and police data have been used to estimate victimization through surveillance systems that collect data on intentional injuries from national samples. Because victims may fail to report interpersonal violence victimization, particularly when injuries are minor and do not require medical attention or when there is fear of retaliation, large-scale national surveys can provide an additional perspective on victimization rates.

In the United States, the most widely referenced assessment of interpersonal violence victimization is the National Crime Victimization Survey (NCVS), administered since 1972 by the Bureau of Justice Statistics. Yearly data are obtained from a representative sample of 42,000 households comprising approximately 76,000 respondents. Survey data are used to estimate the number of victimizations and rate per 1,000 persons or households for the interpersonal violence offenses of rape/sexual assault, robbery, and assault. Assault information is further broken down by the relationship between the victim and the perpetrator. Victimization estimates are categorized by gender, ethnicity, and annual family income. A number of federal agencies such as the Centers for Disease Control and Prevention (CDC) use these surveys combined with other sources of information—for example, Uniform Crime Reporting Program data on homicides and Department of Health and Human Services data on child maltreatment—to develop summary profiles of victimization patterns for different types of interpersonal violence in the United States. Building on these multiple sources of information, patterns of interpersonal violence victimization data for 2003–2004 can be examined for several types of interpersonal violence, including homicide, rape/sexual assault, robbery, assault/intimate partner violence, and child maltreatment.

Homicide

Homicide victimization rates in the United States have been found to be several times higher than rates in all other industrialized countries. A recent international collaborative effort compared homicide rates of 11 industrialized nations. U.S. rates averaged about 8.5 per 100,000, with rates from all other countries at or below 2.3 per 100,000. Homicide rates for children and young adults are particularly high. According to the CDC, homicide is the second leading cause of death for male and female adolescents and young adults ages 15 to 24, and the fourth leading cause of death for boys and girls ages 5 to 9. Interestingly, looking at homicide rates for very young children ages 1 to 4, homicide is the fourth leading cause of death for boys but the third leading cause of death for girls. This pattern reverses in early adulthood, with homicide being the third leading cause of death for males and the fifth leading cause of death for females. In addition, of significant concern is the fact that for Blacks, homicide is the first leading cause of death for individuals ages 15 to 34, the second leading cause of death for children ages 1 to 4, and the third leading cause of death for children ages 5 to 14. The risk of homicide victimization is higher in poor, urban areas. The reasons for such elevated homicide rates in the United States compared to other countries and for younger Blacks within the United States likely include a combination of risk factors. These include easy availability of firearms, escalation of gun and drug markets, poverty, income disparities, and patterns of racism and discrimination that disproportionately affect young Blacks in the United States.

Rape/Sexual Assault

Sexual violence is a serious problem that affects millions of individuals in the United States and worldwide. According to a recent national survey of violence and threats of violence against men and women in the United States conducted by Patricia Tjaden and colleagues, 17% of women and 3% of men reported experiencing an attempted or completed rape at some time in their lives. Young people and females are at particular risk of victimization—78% of victims of rape/sexual assault are female and 22% are male. More than half of all rapes of females (54%) occur before age 18, with 22% of rapes occurring before age 12. Although sexual violence against males is less prevalent, it occurs at even younger ages, with 75% of all male rapes occurring before age 18 and 48% occurring before age 12. For both males and females, the perpetrator of sexual violence is almost exclusively male. Information from the NCVS shows that victimization rates for rape/sexual assault do not vary between Whites and Blacks, although reported victimization is lowest among Hispanics. The NCVS also reports that rape/sexual assault victimization is associated with lower socioeconomic status. Low income individuals reported rates three times as high as rates reported by high income individuals.

Robbery

The NCVS estimates the robbery victimization rate overall to be 2.5 per 1,000 persons. Males, young people, and Blacks are at particular risk. Males are almost twice as likely as females to be the victims of robbery, with rates at 3.2 per 1,000 for males and 1.9 per 1,000 for females. Individuals under age 24 are more than four times as likely to be victims of robbery as individuals age 35 and above. What is striking is the fact that victimization rates are quite high for all youth and young adults, with rates for the 12 to 15 age group at 5.2 per 1,000 and for the 20 to 24 age group at 6.4 per 1,000. Robbery victimization rates are also highest for Blacks, with a rate of 5.9 per 1,000. The highest risk group for robbery victimization is young Black males (ages 12–15), with a rate of 20.8 per 1,000. Although lower socioeconomic status is also associated with increased victimization risk, individuals in the lowest income strata report robbery victimization rates that are less than half of those reported by the young Black male group. The reasons for such an elevated robbery victimization rate for this particular demographic group likely are similar to patterns seen in homicide victimization, including the particular economic and social circumstances experienced by young Black males in the United States.

Assault/Intimate Partner Violence

Assault victimization typically is broken down into simple and aggravated categories, with aggravated assault defined as an unlawful attack with the intent of inflicting bodily injury. Assault is often further broken down according to the relationship between victims, with assaults in the context of intimate partner violence defined as attacks that occur between partners in dating or marital relationships (although there are other specific types of intimate partner violence, including stalking, rape, and homicide). Across all contexts, most assaults fall within the category of simple assault. For instance, the NCVS reports an overall assault rate of 19.3 per 1,000 persons, with 14.6 per 1,000 classified as simple assaults and 4.6 per 1,000 classified as aggravated assaults. Consistent with most other types of victimization, risk is greatest for males, young people, and ethnic minorities. NCVS reports an overall assault rate of 23 per 1,000 for males and 15.7 per 1,000 for females. However, within the context of intimate partner violence, assault victims are more likely to be female than male. Indeed, information from multiple sources suggests that females are approximately 1.5 times as likely as males to be victims of intimate partner assaults. Assault victimization rates are also highest in the younger age groups, with rates declining steadily with age. Looking at ethnicity and race, assault victimization is highest for Blacks, with an overall rate of 22.3 per 1,000 persons, followed by Hispanics with a rate of 20.8 per 1,000 and Whites with a rate of 18.4 per 1,000. Aggravated assault rates are highest for young Black males and females. For Black males, the rate is highest for the 16 to 19 age group at 26.5 per 1,000, followed by a rate of 10.2 per 1,000 for the 20 to 24 age group. In contrast, rates for Black females are also high, but rates are lower for the younger 16 to 19 age group at 10.6 per 1,000 and increase for the 20 to 24 age group at 26.9 per 1,000.

Child Maltreatment

Victimization rates for child maltreatment are reported by agencies tasked with gathering data on child welfare rather than by victimization surveys of children. In the United States, the Administration for Children and Families (ACF) reported a total of 872,000 incidents of childhood maltreatment in 2004. However, these figures may reflect underreporting of the problem, particularly in the case of less visible forms of maltreatment, including psychological abuse. The majority of child maltreatment reports involve neglect (62.4%), followed by physical abuse (17.6%), sexual abuse (9.7%), and psychological maltreatment (7.0%). States also submit reports to the National Child Abuse and Neglect Data System (NCANDS). For 2003, NCANDS reported that victimization was approximately evenly split by gender, although slightly more cases were reported involving females (51.7%) than males (48.3%). Risk was also greatest for the youngest age group, with rates as high as 16.4 per 1,000 for children from birth to 3 decreasing steadily to 5.9 per 1,000 for young people ages 16 to 17. Victimization rates were highest for Black, Pacific Islander, American Indian, and Alaskan Native children, averaging 21.0 per 1,000; in the mid-range for White and Hispanic children, averaging 10.5 per 1,000; and lowest for Asian children at 2.7 per 1,000.

Jennifer K. Williams and Nancy G. Guerra

See also Assault, Aggravated; Child Physical Abuse; Date and Acquaintance Rape; Epidemiology, International Patterns; Intimate Partner Violence

Further Readings

Tjaden, P., & Thoennes, N. (2000). *Intimate partner violence: Fact sheet.* Retrieved from http://cdc.gov/ncicp
Trends in the well-being of America's children and youth: 2003. Retrieved from http://aspe.hhs.gov/hsp/03trends

Ethical and Legal Issues, Interviewing Children Reported as Abused or Neglected

When a child may be a victim of severe abuse or neglect, there is a dual imperative: to provide services to ameliorate suffering and to punish the offender. To simultaneously achieve both goals may not be possible, resulting in an ethical dilemma regarding the obligations of professionals. One of the ways of reducing this dilemma is for professionals to work as a team, where joint decision making and collaborative work may produce the best results for child victims. This entry not only addresses the ethical conflict and professional codes involved with interviewing child victims but also describes forensic interviews and discusses the role of child advocacy centers.

Ethical Dilemma

Social work and legal ethics may be in conflict when the matter at hand is interviewing child victims, because of different goals of the social service and criminal justice systems. In 2004, approximately 3 million children were reported to child abuse and neglect hotlines across the United States. Approximately 87,000 children were determined to be victims of abuse or neglect. When a report suggests serious injury due to physical abuse, sexual abuse, or severe neglect, some states require that a district attorney decide whether a prosecutor or child protective services worker will oversee the investigation. Legal and ethical implications follow from this decision, because social workers, unless they are working for a prosecutor as a forensic specialist, and law enforcement personnel have different objectives. Social workers are concerned mainly with providing services to ameliorate the effects of victimization and to rehabilitate families; law enforcement personnel and forensic social workers are concerned with acquiring information to aid in the apprehension and punishment of offenders.

Professional Ethics

The ethical codes that guide the practice of social workers and attorneys create an obligation for each to serve their clients. When an attorney is serving a prosecutorial function, the attorney's client is his or her governmental employer. The attorney is charged with protecting the public by enabling the apprehension and prosecution of criminals. For social workers the question "Who is the client?" is not as easily answered. Whether employed in the private or public sector, social workers have an ethical obligation to their clients, to the agency that employs them, and, for some in the private sector, to a unit of government that financially supports the services they provide. For a social worker, conflict may result because public policy requires a worker to temporarily set aside his or her concern for providing treatment-focused services in favor of the state's interest in prosecuting offenders. As acknowledged in Ethical Standard 1.01 of the Code of Ethics of the National Association of Social Workers:

Social workers' primary responsibility is to promote the well-being of clients. In general, clients' interests are primary. However, social workers' responsibility to the larger society or specific legal obligations may on limited occasions supersede the loyalty owed clients, and clients should be so advised.

Forensic Interviews

In the 1960s, when laws mandating reporting of child abuse and neglect were being drafted, an issue under discussion was whether an investigation should be conducted by social workers or police. The decision favoring social workers was the result of the profession's rehabilitative mission, and the notion that child abuse and neglect involving family members should not be treated in the criminal justice system. In recent years there has been a shift away from the original view to one that favors criminal prosecutions. Joint social worker–police investigations are becoming common; and legislation that requires child protective agencies to report to the police or to a prosecutor's office serious cases of abuse or neglect has been enacted in the majority of states. This shift has led to a growth in forensic social work.

A forensic social worker applies the principles and practices of social work for the purpose of law, whereas a clinical social worker applies the same principles for the purpose of diagnosis and treatment. For the clinical social worker, activities such as interviewing, assessment, and evaluation are framed by knowledge of child development and theories of clinical intervention. For the forensic worker, these activities are undertaken with knowledge of the legal framework that surrounds particular areas of practice and applicable legal principles, including (a) legislation, such as that addressing child abuse and neglect; (b) the legal processes involved in prosecuting cases of child abuse or neglect; (c) the structure and functioning of the social service and court systems in the practitioner's state; (d) the roles played by the parties to a court proceeding, such as judges, attorneys, and advocates for children; and (e) an understanding of what evidence is admissible and how evidence is used in court.

Interest in forensic social work was spurred, in part, by the role that social workers played in the criminal prosecution of teachers and administrators charged with sexually abusing children in daycare settings. For example, in August 1983, the mother of a child at the McMartin preschool reported to the police that she thought that her son might have been abused. Before the investigation was completed, prosecutors alleged that school officials and teachers had molested hundreds of children over the course of 5 years. There were no convictions. Douglas J. Besharov, in a discussion of the McMartin case, pointed out that jurors expressed concern that the children's statements had been undermined by investigative and prosecutorial missteps that created doubt for the jurors as to whether the children had actually gone through the horrible things they described or whether they imagined them following prompting by adult interviewers. The McMartin case and several other similar cases have raised the specter that children were coerced into giving false testimony and have served to heighten a concern with developing new ways to interview children.

Child Advocacy Centers

Research has shown that a child's testimony can be coerced by inappropriate interviewing techniques. These findings, coupled with the prosecutorial mishaps just discussed, gave rise to a movement to establish procedures to coordinate the investigation, prosecution, and treatment of child sex abuse victims. A number of states have established child advocacy centers.

Common characteristics of child advocacy centers are that they (a) are neutral, child-friendly facilities where trained forensic staff interview children in a manner that is neutral, whose purpose is fact finding, and where interviews are coordinated to avoid duplicative efforts; (b) provide for the audio- or videotaping of interviews; (c) have policies and procedures that support culturally competent practice so that staff are able to appreciate, understand, and interact with members of diverse populations within the local community; (d) have protocols that allow professionals to collaborate in conducting joint interviews and in preparing evaluations; (e) have multidisciplinary review teams that meet regularly to review case progress and whose members include mental health, law enforcement, and medical personnel, representatives from the office of the prosecuting attorney, and from state or local social services, and a victim's advocate; and (f) have the capacity to provide crisis intervention services, make referrals for medical examinations and mental health therapy, and have methods established for follow-up of referred cases.

Ted J. Stein

See also Child Neglect; Child Physical Abuse; Child Protective Services; Children's Advocacy Center; Child Sexual Abuse; Legal System, Criminal Investigation of Victimization of Children

Further Readings

Administration for Children and Family Services. (2006). *Investigation dispositions of child maltreatment: 2004.* Washington, DC: U.S. Department of Health and Human Services.

Besharov, D. J. (1986). Child abuse: Arrest and prosecution decision making. *American Criminal Law Review, 24,* 315–327.

Ceci, S. J., & Friedman, R. D. (2000). The suggestibility of children: Scientific research and legal implications. *Cornell Law Review, 86,* 39–71.

Doris, J., Mazur, R., & Thomas, M. (1995). Training in child protective services: A commentary on the Amicus Brief of Bruck and Ceci. *Psychology, Public Policy and Law, 1,* 479–491.

National Association of Social Workers. (n.d.). *Code of Ethics of the National Association of Social Workers.* Retrieved from http://www.socialworkers.org/pubs/code/code.asp

Stein, T. J. (in press). *Child welfare and the law* (3rd ed.). Washington, DC: Child Welfare League of America.

Warren, A. R., & Marsil, D. F. (2002). Why children's suggestibility remains a serious concern. *Law and Contemporary Problems, 65,* 127–147.

ETHICAL AND LEGAL ISSUES, TREATING ELDER ABUSE

Elder abuse is a complex and multifaceted problem often requiring the collaboration of professionals from a variety of disciplines. When professionals with varying roles, responsibilities, and ethical guidelines work together, ethical and legal issues related to those professional differences are bound to arise. In elder abuse practice, three key ethical and legal issues that may come into conflict are (1) the legal duty to report certain suspected conduct to law enforcement and/or protective services versus victim autonomy and safety; (2) the victim's right to self-determination versus protection and safety; and (3) when intervening, selecting the least restrictive alternative versus protection and safety.

Duty to Report Versus Victim Autonomy and Safety

Most states mandate that some professionals or the entire community report cases of elder abuse to social services and/or law enforcement. In enacting elder abuse reporting laws, legislators were guided by the belief that older individuals, like children, are in need of protection and assistance, are physically or cognitively frail and more vulnerable, are at risk for abuse, and may be unable to report for themselves. As a result, professionals and others should be required to contact social services and/or law enforcement.

The duty to report can create ethical dilemmas for some professionals. Many older individuals are healthy, active members of the community. They are capable of making their own decisions about their lives, including whether they want professional intervention when they are being harmed. Some victims are at greater risk of being seriously harmed or killed by an abuser if they leave or get help from professionals. Older victims may have thoughtful reasons for not wanting professionals to report abuse and may accurately understand that they are at greater risk following a report.

Some professionals also are concerned about the breach of confidentiality and trust that can occur if a report is made. Health care providers and advocates are concerned that an older individual may decline to accept or stop using their services if a report about abuse is made to adult protective services.

Victim's Right to Self-Determination Versus Protection and Safety

Weighing the victim's rights to make personal decisions against the potential risk of harm or death is a difficult task in any case of abuse. These competing principles may be even more complicated in elder abuse cases. On the one hand, most elder abusers use a pattern of coercive tactics to gain and maintain power and control over the victim. These abusers set the rules for the relationship (such as when dinner will be served, and who can come and go from the home) and deny older victims their right to make decisions in their own lives. Well-meaning professionals who see elder abuse cases may make decisions for victims with capacity because they believe the victim is older and may have dementia or because of discomfort or anxiety with the victim's choices. They may believe that the older victim is unable to make wise choices and needs assistance making these choices. For example, a case management plan may outline specific steps the professional believes a victim must take to live free from the abuser overriding the victim's right to consider alternatives and then decide what if any actions are desired.

In elder abuse cases, one of the challenges with using an empowerment model is that some older victims may not be able to make their own decisions due to dementia or other cognitive challenges. Often the risks of serious harm or death are heightened due to the advanced age and health status of some victims. Professionals may assess that if an older victim remains in the current situation he or she will die or be seriously harmed. These professionals may feel a moral and ethical obligation to step in and make decisions for the older victim to keep him or her alive. Self-determination may be seen as less important or critical to decision making. Desires of the older victim may not be considered, even if they could be incorporated into an intervention. The ethical and legal dilemma is differentiating situations when decisions must be made for an older victim from situations in which professionals use their authority unnecessarily or without attempting to create interventions that incorporate victim desires to the extent possible.

Least Restrictive Alternative Versus Protection and Safety

A guiding principle in the elder abuse and health care fields is to use the least restrictive alternative for older individuals. For example, if an older individual needs some care, ideally services can be brought into the home. If that option does not provide enough support, then the older victim may be moved to assisted living, and finally, only if necessary, to a nursing home.

In elder abuse cases, professionals can disagree on what is the least restrictive intervention needed to achieve protection and safety. For example, adult protective services workers may listen to an older victim who wants to remain at home and insist that no action be taken that results in a move. Health care providers working with that same individual may assess the situation and determine that the older patient must be moved to a facility or he or she will die. One of the legal and ethical challenges facing any interdisciplinary team is wrestling with these complex situations

and developing a plan that focuses on the older victim's safety and needs with the least loss of independence to him or her and harmonizes these competing considerations.

Multiple or interdisciplinary responses to elder abuse cases are often the most effective responses. When professionals work together, ethical and legal challenges often arise. Preplanning among team members to develop a process for discussion and decision making in these tough cases can be useful to ensure that victims' needs are addressed and teams continue to work together cohesively.

Candace J. Heisler and Bonnie Brandl

See also Domestic Violence Against Older Women; Elder Abuse; Legal System, Advocacy Efforts to Affect, Elder Abuse

Further Readings

Brandl, B., Dyer, C., Heisler, C., Otto, J., Stiegel, L., & Thomas, R. (2006). *Elder abuse detection and intervention: A collaborative approach.* New York: Springer.
Heisler, C., & Brandl, B. (2002). Safety planning for professionals working with elderly and clients who are victims of abuse. *Victimization of the Elderly and Disabled, 5*(4), 65–78.

ETHNIC CLEANSING

See CULTURAL RETALIATORY HOMICIDE; GENOCIDE

EXPERT TESTIMONY

Expert testimony is the endpoint of a process involving an expert witness who engages in consultation with an attorney or legal team, reviews case materials, and usually performs an evaluation of an individual who is party to a legal matter. Expert testimony concerning battering can be offered in both civil and criminal cases, including divorce and custody, personal injury, and criminal cases such as homicide and assault, as well as other matters.

Expert testimony in these cases is used to explain battered women's common experiences and the impact of repeated abuse. It is offered to show the judge and jury the context of a battered woman's actions. This process of using social science research to provide a social and psychological context to understand and evaluate issues in a legal case has been referred to as *social framework testimony*.

An expert witness typically describes the clinical, empirical, and theoretical literature in the field of domestic violence—both in cases involving an evaluation of an individual party to the case (case-specific testimony) and in cases involving no such evaluation (general testimony)—to educate the judge and jury about battering and its effects relevant to the case. Relevant topic areas often include the dynamics of battering relationships, danger assessment or risk factors related to serious or lethal violence, women's perception of danger in abusive relationships, patterns of coercion in intimate partner violence, battered women's coping behaviors, effects of exposure to intimate partner violence on children, factors that increase vulnerability to partner violence and its effects, the role of substance abuse in intimate partner violence, intimate partner violence within specific groups (e.g., immigrants, lesbians, elderly, ethnic minorities), and traumatic stress and other health, social, and economic consequences of violence exposure.

When an expert has performed an evaluation of an individual (e.g., a victim, an alleged perpetrator, or child witnesses of partner violence), the expert's testimony also extends to questions that are unique to the specific case under consideration. With rare exception, an opinion about an individual requires an in-person evaluation. The expert evaluation is based on a theoretical and empirical framework that forms the foundation of the expert's analysis. For example, in a criminal self-defense case, a defendant must demonstrate that his or her behavior was based on a reasonable perception of serious bodily harm, although specific statutory language varies across jurisdictions. An expert's task is to consider what information is necessary to formulate an explanation of and support a conclusion about relevant questions.

Direct testimony by the retaining attorney is presented in a question and answer format that communicates the conclusion of an evaluation and the basis for it. A cross-examination by the opposing counsel typically challenges the expert's statements regarding the

foundation and/or the conclusions of his or her testimony. An experienced and well-trained expert understands both the strengths and the weaknesses in his or her evaluation and becomes an advocate for that opinion rather than for a party in the matter.

Mary Ann Dutton

See also Battered Women; Legal System, Civil and Criminal Court Remedies for Intimate Partner Violence; Legal System, Criminal Justice System Responses to Intimate Partner Violence

Further Readings

Dutton, M. A. (1998). Suicide prevention. In L. VandeCreek, S. Knapp, & T. L. Jackson (Eds.), *Innovations in clinical practice: A source book* (Vol. 16, pp. 293–311). Sarasota, FL: Professional Resource Press/Professional Resource Exchange.
Schuller, R. A. (1992). Battered woman syndrome evidence in the courtroom. *Law and Human Behavior, 16*(3), 273–291.

EXPRESSIVE VIOLENCE

Aggression has been classified in a variety of ways. It is important to differentiate between the types of abuse perpetrated, because they may differ in their etiology, course, potential harmfulness, and amenability to intervention. Expressive violence (also known as hostile, impulsive, and reactive aggression) is affect driven. It is triggered by emotional reactions that are disproportionate to the situational factors that elicit them. The triggers may stimulate feelings of hurt and/or fear that are transformed into anger. Expressive violence may be physical or verbal, expressed directly toward an intimate partner; indirectly toward objects, pets, or other people; or even self-directed. The abuse tends to be brief and explosive. Following the violent outburst, expressive aggressors often experience genuine remorse as the tension that fueled the abuse abates, and they are often apologetic. Victims may be harmed by the assault, but expressive aggressors typically stop the abuse at the sign of distress by the victim. While the physical injuries are rarely severe, victims often suffer emotional trauma, and the intimidation they feel depreciates the quality of their relationship with the abuser. Because their remorse is real, expressive aggressors are often motivated to seek and to benefit from intervention.

Expressive violence may be viewed on a continuum, with expressive aggression at one end, predatory violence at the other, and instrumental aggression in between. Expressive violence differs markedly from predatory abuse, which is normally far more destructive. Although a particular act of expressive violence may be easily distinguishable from predatory abuse, it may be harder to differentiate an act of expressive violence from instrumental or goal-oriented violence, as some acts of aggression may be both expressive and instrumental in nature. Of note, some have characterized this continuum of aggression as simply ranging from expressive through instrumental abuse.

Expressive aggressors may respond disproportionately and counterproductively to mislabeled provocations. Learning to label one's experience in problem-solving terms, and thereby to balance one's responses with the intensity of the triggering events, is a core component of the process of developmental socialization. Children who were not exposed to appropriate models or who experienced trauma that exceeded their resources for resilience may not have learned the adaptive coping skills that are needed to weigh the meaning of social offenses and to plan a constructive, problem-solving response. Even when developmental experience does support adaptive functioning, emotional problems such as depression, severe anxiety, fatigue or stress, and use of alcohol and certain drugs can overwhelm coping resources.

When intervening with expressive aggressors, it may be helpful to direct attention to reducing the emotional and situational pressures and/or substance abuse that may weaken the aggressor's ability to manage triggering situations constructively. Helping the aggressor develop prosocial problem-solving skills and the ability to self-manage emotional surges may also prove beneficial. If the aggressor and victim are intimate partners who wish to continue their relationship, both could participate in developing routines that improve the quality of their interaction while building in safeguards, such as time-outs, that protect the victim from future abuse.

Gregory L. Stuart and Richard B. Stuart

See also Instrumental Violence; Intimate Terrorism; Situational Couple Violence; Violent Resistance

Further Readings

Fava, M. (1998). Depression with anger attacks. *Journal of Clinical Psychiatry, 18*(Supplement 59), 18–22.

Haller, J., & Kruk, M. R. (2006). Normal and abnormal aggression: Human disorders and novel laboratory models. *Neuroscience and Biobehavioral Reviews, 30,* 292–303.

Stuart, R. B. (2005). Treatment for partner abuse: Time for a paradigm shift. *Professional Psychology: Research and Practice, 36,* 254–263.

FAILURE TO PROTECT

Failure to protect is a form of child neglect. Historically it has been difficult to define, and many times it is not even included in state statutes on child maltreatment. It may appear as some form of child endangerment in statutes, and inconsistencies exist across the United States. As Randy Magen has suggested, it implies that the neglecting parent has failed to protect a child when it was possible to do so. While this may sometimes be the case, the term is very controversial when applied to parents who are also victims themselves, such as in the case of battered women. As viewed by advocates of domestic violence, this term is a key charge by which child protective services find mothers who are victims of domestic violence neglectful under state law, by failing to protect or endangering their children through exposure to domestic violence against them. The consequence of such a finding can lead to children being removed from the home and placed in foster care.

Effective Intervention in Domestic Violence and Child Maltreatment Cases: Guidelines for Policy and Practice, a document published by the National Council of Juvenile and Family Court Judges, and commonly called the Greenbook, states,

A major issue of contention between child protection workers and domestic violence advocates is the perceived blaming of mothers for "failing to protect" their children from the violence a male perpetrator commits against adults and children in the family. Finding nonabusive mothers responsible for the failure to

protect in cases of domestic violence may result from the system's inability to hold the actual perpetrator of violence accountable. (p. 66)

There is evidence that this rationale for removal of children has been used by public child protective service agencies. In a federal court case in New York City, Judge Jack B. Weinstein found that the children of Sharwline Nicholson and others were removed from the home solely on the grounds that the mothers were victims of domestic violence and that such grounds were violations of the Constitution. In his opinion, the judge stated: "the consistent policy applied by ACS [the New York City child welfare agency] is to remove children of abused mothers in violation of their rights solely because the mother has been abused. No legislatively appropriate policy, no compelling state interest, justifies these removals." The New York City Department was ordered to cease this practice when no other form of neglect or abuse was found.

A major problem in determining how prevalent this practice is around the country is that the term *failure to protect* is not defined in most state statutes as a form of neglect, nor is it a term against which states collect information and report a finding of neglect. It is not known whether the New York City experience is typical or not, in which jurisdictions it may be regularly used, and how many children are placed in foster care for this reason alone.

State child abuse and neglect statutes typically contain nonspecific language under which conditions children exposed to domestic violence could be removed, providing child protective service agencies with considerable discretion. For example, the Ohio statute (Section 2151.03 Ohio Revised Code) defines, in part, a child as neglected "who lacks proper parental care because of the faults or habits of the child's parents, guardian, or custodian." In another example, the Michigan statute (MCL 722.622) defines one form of neglect as "placing a child at unreasonable risk to the child's health or welfare by failure to intervene to eliminate that risk when that person is able to do so and has, or should have, knowledge of the risk." These examples of language, which are typical of many state statutes, do not use the term *failure to protect* per se but are broad enough to justify such action if agencies permit findings on these grounds. It should also be noted that state reports to the federal government of the number of cases of abuse and neglect do not include a category of neglect that indicates the prevalence of findings of failure to protect due to domestic violence.

The National Council of Juvenile and Family Court Judges' Greenbook provides a policy recommendation for practice that would be an important step toward not blaming victims of domestic violence. The recommendation addresses how petitions presented to the court should be drafted to make clear the actual source of risk to a child and how a battered mother may actually not be failing to protect. "The juvenile court should insist that a petition alleging 'failure to protect' on the part of the battered mother also allege efforts that the mother made to protect the children; the ways in which the mother failed to protect, and the reasons why; and should identify any perpetrator who may have prevented or impeded her from carrying out her parental duties" (p. 109).

Gerald B. "Jerry" Silverman

See also Child Abuse Prevention and Treatment Act; Child Exposure to Intimate Partner Violence; Child Neglect; Greenbook, The; National Council of Juvenile and Family Court Judges; Office on Child Abuse and Neglect

Further Readings

Magen, R. H. (1999). In the best interests of battered women: Reconceptualizing allegations of failure to protect. *Child Maltreatment, 4,* 127–135.

National Council of Juvenile and Family Court Judges. (1999). *Effective intervention in domestic violence and child maltreatment cases: Guidelines for policy and practice.* Reno, NV: Author.

Nicholson v. Williams, 820 N.E. 2d 840 (N.Y. 2004). Retrieved from http://f11.findlaw.com/news.findlaw .com/hdocs/docs/nyc/nchlsnwllms030102drft.pdf

Web Sites

Child Welfare Information Gateway: http://www .childwelfare.gov/
The Greenbook: http://www.thegreenbook.info/

Failure to Thrive

Failure to thrive (FTT) refers to a child's poor physical growth. The term has mostly been applied to infants and toddlers. An approach to FTT requires an understanding of children's growth patterns, nutritional needs, diet and feeding behavior, possible medical contributors, and the psychosocial context.

Diagnosis

It is not always straightforward establishing whether a child's growth is adequate. Most important is to consider the child's growth trend, rather than his or her growth at a single point in time. By carefully plotting a child's weight for age, height for age, weight for height, and head circumference for age on the CDC (2000) growth charts, one can compare a child's growth to the growth rates in a large sample of healthy children. FTT is generally diagnosed when the child's weight for age or the weight for height falls below the fifth percentile. Height (or length) is affected later due to more protracted or severe problems, resulting in stunting. The head circumference (reflecting brain growth) is usually involved only late and under the worst circumstances.

The diagnosis of FTT is complicated by several circumstances. For example, prematurely born babies need to be plotted on special charts. Similarly, genetics plays a role, and so the average parental height should be considered in evaluating a short child. Fetal conditions may impede growth resulting in babies being born small for their gestational age; with time and depending on the cause, many of these infants will catch up. It is therefore important that a physician knowledgeable about growth evaluate whether the trend is really problematic.

Contributors

There are many conditions and circumstances that can contribute to FTT. Traditionally these have been separated into "organic" and "nonorganic." Organic refers to medical conditions such as cyanotic heart disease or

Down's syndrome. Nonorganic refers to psychosocial factors that may be at different levels: child (e.g., temperament), parent (e.g., a depressed mother), family (e.g., stress), community/society (e.g., inadequate food or poverty). Sometimes, there are both organic and nonorganic contributors. Many of these nonorganic factors directly or indirectly result in an inadequate food intake.

Evaluation

Ideally, a comprehensive and interdisciplinary evaluation is conducted by a pediatrician, nutritionist or dietician, and social worker. A thorough medical history and examination generally help detect whether there are organic contributors. Assessment of the child's behavior and development is also important. Limited medical tests are needed to confirm concerns raised by the evaluation. Basic screening for anemia, lead poisoning, and a urinary infection may be done. A detailed evaluation of the child's diet is essential as is an evaluation of the feeding or eating behavior. Direct observation of a parent feeding an infant can be valuable. A social worker can help clarify the parent–child relationship, and how the family, parent, and child are functioning.

Addressing Failure to Thrive

The approach needs to be tailored to the severity and the specific contributors to the FTT. Helping ensure an adequate diet is critical, but attention to other problems underpinning the FTT is also important. Most children with FTT (and their families) can be helped as outpatients. If the problem is severe or persistent, hospitalization may be needed. The FTT should be carefully monitored to ensure good progress. If growth continues to falter and there is a persistent inability to meet the child's nutritional needs, child protective services can help with in-home and other community services, and their ability to closely monitor the situation.

Howard Dubowitz

See also Child Sexual Abuse

Further Readings

Kessler, D. B., & Dawson, P. (1999). *Failure to thrive and pediatric undernutrition: A transdisciplinary approach.* Baltimore, MD: Paul H. Brookes.

FAITH-BASED PROGRAMS

A faith-based program is a social service or advocacy organization that explicitly affirms a particular religious or spiritual affiliation as part of its mission. Historically, these organizations (e.g., the Salvation Army, Catholic Social Services, Jewish Family Services) have provided a significant proportion of social services to communities. They have been a stable provider because of their historic links to various religious traditions with strong values regarding the responsibility to provide for those in need due to crisis, poverty, violence, and so on. In many communities they have operated side-by-side with government-sponsored programs addressing the same problems. Some have also provided leadership in social change efforts by addressing institutional inequities.

The advantage of utilizing faith-based programs to help provide services to the community is that they are often well established, trusted, and effective and have a strong volunteer base. In addition, they have provided faith-based support and counseling within the context of particular religious and cultural traditions (e.g., a domestic violence program sponsored by a local mosque or a Christian shelter for battered women).

The challenge within a democracy like the United States that affirms a separation of church and state comes with the possibility of the use of public funds by faith-based organizations. Historically these organizations have been supported only by private funds.

In order for a faith-based agency to receive government funding, (a) it must freely serve anyone who seeks its services, regardless of religious affiliation (or nonaffiliation); (b) it must not require participation in any religious activities in order to receive services; and (c) it must not proselytize.

For faith-based organizations, the receipt of government funding can limit their traditional program, so they may have to revise their offerings. For those who are comfortable with the limitations, federal funding can provide significant support.

Marie M. Fortune

See also Religion; Social Support Networks

Further Readings

Adams, C. J., & Fortune, M. M. (Eds.). (1995). *Violence against women and children: A Christian theological sourcebook.* New York: Continuum.

Ellison, C. G., Trinitapoli, J. A., Anderson, K. L., & Johnson, B. R. (2007). Race/ethnicity, religious involvement, and domestic violence. *Violence Against Women, 13*, 1094–1112.

FALSE MEMORY

The use of the term *false memory* by psychologists can be traced to a symposium at the 1992 meeting of the American Psychological Society titled "Remembering 'Repressed' Abuse." Elizabeth Loftus served as the symposium discussant and presented her research on planting in adults false childhood memories of having been lost in a mall. She drew generalizations from this research to the real-world issue of assessing whether memories for incidents of childhood sexual abuse may be suggestively planted and thus be "false memories." This symposium was followed by a lead article on this topic in the *American Psychologist* in 1993. The False Memory Syndrome Foundation, which coined the phrase *false memory syndrome,* was also founded in 1992. In both the symposium and the subsequent article, the use of the term *false memory* was specifically intended to refer to memory for an entirely new event that in fact never occurred.

There have been several published literature reviews that have examined what types of research studies are being conducted under the term *false memory.* Although PsycINFO searches of the empirical publications using the subject heading "false memory" reveal several hundred publications since 1992, few researchers have studied false memories by studying the planting of memories for an entirely new event that was never experienced by an individual. The large majority of empirical studies published under the descriptor "false memories" have utilized what is called the Deese, Roediger, and McDermott paradigm. In this task, participants are presented a list of related words to study (e.g., *sandal, foot, toe, slipper*) in which at least one prototypical word (e.g., *shoe*) is not presented. When asked later to recall or recognize words in the presented list, participants frequently mis-remembered the related-but-not-presented word (e.g., *shoe*). Prior to the early 1990s these would be called intrusion errors, commission errors, or false alarms. However, in the wake of the false memory research bandwagon, these errors have been labeled "false memories." Although numerous researchers have cautioned against generalizing from the Deese, Roediger,

and McDermott paradigm to contested memories for abuse, this caution is frequently ignored. Thus, the term *false memories* has come to refer to two very different research literatures that probably do not relate to the same memory processes.

By specifically examining the few studies that have investigated false memory as defined by the planting of an entirely new event in memory, one can see that several factors affect the probability of this occurring. False events are more likely to be planted in memory if an individual imagines him- or herself performing the event and if the suggestion is instantiated by presenting a picture of the individual (a) performing the false event, or even (b) in the context in which the false event is suggested to have occurred. However, in several recent studies, Kathy Pezdek has reported that false memories are less likely to be planted for implausible than for plausible events, and whereas imagining a plausible false event increases individuals' belief that the event occurred to them, imagining an implausible event does not have this effect.

How does a suggested false event become planted in memory? If a suggested false event is judged to be true, then (a) generic information about the event as well as (b) specific details from related episodes of the event that the individual may have experienced are "transported" in memory and used to construct a memory for the false event. The degree of detail in the constructed false memory will be affected by the degree of relevant information already available in memory.

Controversy about the accuracy for abuse memories has been widely covered in the media. Within this controversy the term *false memory* has often been presented as the opposite of *recovered memory,* as in references to false versus recovered memories. However, this is confusing rhetoric; memories can be false and recovered, true and recovered, false and always-remembered, and true and always-remembered. In fact, Jennifer Freyd has reported that recovered memories are no more likely to be false than always-remembered memories.

Kathy Pezdek and Jennifer J. Freyd

See also Repressed Memory

Further Readings

DePrince, A. P., Allard, C. B., Oh, H., & Freyd, J. (2004). What's in a name for memory errors? Implications and ethical issues arising from the use of the term "false memory" for errors in memory details. *Ethics & Behavior, 14,* 201–233.

Freyd, J. J. (1998). Science in the memory debate. *Ethics & Behavior, 8,* 101–113.

Loftus, E. F. (1993). The reality of repressed memories. *American Psychologist, 48,* 518–537.

Pezdek, K., & Banks, W. P. (Eds.). (1996). *The recovered memory/false memory debate.* San Diego, CA: Academic Press.

Pezdek, K., & Lam, S. (2007). What research paradigms have cognitive psychologists used to study "false memory," and what are the implications of these choices? *Consciousness & Cognition, 16,* 2–17.

FAMILICIDE

The word *familicide* refers to various forms of mass killing within familial or kinship networks or among those connected through bonds of sexual intimacy. The term is usually reserved for those killings that occur in a relatively short time period, often within 24 hours. However, it is conceivable that someone could kill a significant number of family members over a period of years and that such acts might be construed as a form of familicide. Compared with other forms of homicide, including those involving family members, familicides are relatively rare events. In part because of their rarity and in part because they offend common understandings of what families are supposed to be like, familicides attract considerable media attention. However, there is relatively little substantive research on this phenomenon.

Researchers recognize that perpetrators of familicide may or may not subsequently commit suicide. There is no agreed upon number of victims that a perpetrator must kill for the act to constitute a familicide. Indeed there is a great deal of variation in those forms of familial or kinship mass killings that potentially qualify as familicides. A few examples help illustrate this point.

One form involves a parent, nearly always the father, killing the entire family and then killing himself. For example, on January 12, 1999, Terry M. Jones of Anderson, Indiana, killed his wife and two children then committed suicide. He allegedly did so because he thought his wife was having an affair on the Internet. In this case the perpetrator had a previous conviction for domestic violence against his wife.

The historical record contains very few cases of women killing their families and then killing themselves. One such example is a familicide in Cadillac, Michigan, perpetrated by Mrs. Daniel Cooper who shot and killed her husband and six of her seven children before taking her own life. According to newspaper accounts, Mrs. Cooper had been "mentally unsound" for more than a year prior to the killings.

The concepts of familicide and homicide–suicide are sometimes used interchangeably. Some writers use the term *familicide* to describe, for example, a case where a parent kills his or her children and then commits suicide. Others might use the term *homicide-suicide* to describe the same killings. Some criminologists reserve the word *familicide* for only those mass killings in which all the children are killed. Others still use the term if only a proportion of the children are murdered. These inconsistencies speak to the range and complexity of some of the various forms of mass killing that occur within familial or kinship networks. At this point it is safe to say that the word *familicide* is usually used to describe mass killings where perpetrators kill a significant proportion of family members, to the extent that the family, as a unit or network, is no longer recognizable.

There is also some overlap between familicides and other forms of mass killing. Clearly, the term *familicide* includes cases where a perpetrator kills his current or ex-wife or partner, most or all of their children, and other relatives. However, it sometimes happens that the killing of kin accompanies the murder of community members, bystanders, or other persons significant to the perpetrator. The following examples illustrate this overlap.

On September 25, 1982, in Wilkes-Barre, Pennsylvania, George Banks killed five of his own children and four women with whom he had had intimate relationships. At the same time, relatives of these women and a passerby also were killed by Banks. In a comparable case, Mark Barton, angered by losing money through day trading on the Internet, murdered his wife and two children before opening fire at two Atlanta brokerage houses killing nine people and wounding twelve more before committing suicide.

The research into familicide is in its infancy and dwells mostly on male offenders. Margo Wilson and Martin Daly identify two types of male familicidal offenders. The "angry" perpetrator has various grievances against his female partner, many apparently associated with his perception of her sexual infidelity or her desire to exit their intimate relationship. In these cases the perpetrator may have battered his female intimate on one or more occasions prior to the familicide. The second type of familicidal offender they term *despondent*. This man is more likely to suffer depression, much less likely to have battered his partner prior to the familicide, and much more likely to commit suicide after killing his family members. However, as Wilson and Daly acknowledge, the validity and usefulness of this taxonomy have not yet been established. In both types of cases they note the common strand of male entitlement in taking the lives of family members. Specifically, they point out that the reason the killer gives for his actions is that his wife and children belong to him, and that he feels entitled to make decisions about their fates.

Charles Ewing does not emphasize the anger/despondency typology proposed by Wilson and Daly. Instead he focuses on the notion of "control" or control that is ebbing. At one point he notes that the typical family killer usually is afraid of losing control not only of his wife and/or family, but also of the aspects of his life that matter most to him and of becoming a failure.

Neil Websdale

See also Mass Murder; Maternal Homicide

Further Readings

Ewing, C. P. (1997). *Fatal families: The dynamics of intrafamilial homicide.* Thousand Oaks, CA: Sage.

Insane mother kills seven: She first took them to a show, then shot them and herself. (1908, June 14). *New York Times,* p. 16.

Jealous over Internet, man kills family, self. (1999, January 16). *Herald Bulletin* (Anderson, IN).

Wilson, M., & Daly, M. (1998). Lethal and nonlethal violence against wives and the evolutionary psychology of male sexual proprietariness. In R. E. Dobash & R. P. Dobash (Eds.), *Rethinking violence against women* (pp. 199–230). Thousand Oaks, CA: Sage.

FAMILY GROUP CONFERENCING

Family group conferencing (FGC) is an inclusive and informal process of making and implementing a plan that safeguards children, young persons, and adults.

At the center of the planning is the "family group," encompassing the immediate family as well as their relatives, friends, and other informal ties. Supporting the process are the involved community organizations and public agencies. The model's origins, legalization, process, dissemination, and outcomes all reflect a culturally based approach to resolving interpersonal violence and other relationship concerns.

FGC's deliberative processes are rooted in South Pacific practices and evident in many Native cultures. In 1989, the model was first legislated in New Zealand following protests by its Indigenous peoples against Eurocentric approaches to child welfare and youth justice. The legislation emphasized the family group's responsibility for their young relatives, children's safety and rights, the family's culture, and community–government partnerships.

The New Zealand model of FGC has six key features that emphasize the centrality of the family group. First, the conference is organized by an independent FGC coordinator who is not the family's worker. This decreases role confusion and keeps the coordinator focused on creating a safe and effective process. Second, the coordinator invites and prepares the participants. This makes it possible to explain the purpose and process, assess for safety, and develop sound conference arrangements. Third, the conference begins with a welcome, overview of the process, and information sharing. Fourth, the family group has its private time in which to develop a plan without the service providers present. Fifth, the service providers are invited back to review and approve the plan and authorize agency resources. And sixth, the plan is implemented, and the family group can be reconvened to address emerging issues.

Today, FGC has been adopted in countries from all continents and utilized in diverse cultures to address such issues as child protection, youth and adult offending, school bullying, domestic violence, mental health, and disabilities. As an imported model, it has been variously renamed and its practices reshaped. Nevertheless, FGC remains distinct from court procedures because of its informality, from mediation because of its group approach, and from family therapy because of its decision-making focus.

The available studies report promising results. In general, FGC is carried out without violence and leads to mutually agreed-upon plans. The plans keep children and youth connected with their family group and cultural heritage without endangering them in the home, school, or community. Widening the circle of support and participation in the process helps in healing the emotional harm caused by interpersonal violence and creating lasting solutions.

Joan Pennell

See also Peacemaking Circles; Restorative Justice

Further Readings

Hudson, J., Morris, A., Maxwell, G., & Galaway, B. (Eds.). (1996). *Family group conferences: Perspectives on policy and practice.* Monsey, NY: Willow Tree Press.
Pennell, J., & Anderson, G. (Eds.). (2005). *Widening the circle: The practice and evaluation of family group conferencing with children, youths, and their families.* Washington, DC: NASW Press.
Strang, H., & Braithwaite, J. (Eds.). (2002). *Restorative justice and family violence.* New York: Cambridge University Press.

FAMILY HOMICIDES

Family homicides refer to murders by one family member of another. Some terms, such as *parricides,* also sometimes refer to murders of a king or other ruler who resembles a father figure. Family homicides include feticide, filicide, fratricide, infanticide, matricide, parricide, patricide, sororicide, and uxoricide. Each of these forms of murder is defined below.

Feticide refers to killing of a fetus and may or may not be by a family member.

Filicide is the killing of one's own son or daughter.

Fratricide is the killing of one's brother.

Infanticide is the killing of an infant and may or may not be by a family member.

Matricide refers to the killing of one's mother.

Parricide is the killing of one's parents or other close relative.

Patricide is the killing of one's father.

Sororicide is the killing of one's sister.

Uxoricide is the killing of one's wife.

Jeffrey L. Edleson

See also Familicide; Femicide; Feticide; Filicide; Homicides, Criminal; Infanticide; Maternal Homicide

Further Readings

Heide, K. H., & Petee, T. A. (2007). Parricide: An empirical analysis of 24 years of U.S. data. *Journal of Interpersonal Violence, 22,* 1382–1399.

FAMILY JUSTICE CENTERS

Family justice centers (FJCs) reflect recent innovations that bring together several emerging trends over the last two decades in responding to domestic violence victims and their families. Victims of domestic violence and their children are often forced to travel from agency to agency in order to access the help they need to achieve safety in their lives. As a result, two emerging trends—greater community coordination and co-location of staff from multiple agencies—have driven the innovation that has resulted in FJCs. FJCs were established in the United States to respond to this fragmentation by co-locating a variety of services in one facility so that battered mothers and their children would find much of the help they need coordinated in just one location. The Web site for one of the earliest FJCs, the FJC in San Diego, states, "The premise was simple: Victims will have an easier time receiving needed services if all the necessary help is located under one roof." Co-location also offered the opportunity to coordinate services so that one agency was not countering the work of another.

The origins of current FJCs can be found in early coordination efforts of the San Diego City Attorney's Office, domestic violence programs, and others in the early 1990s. In 1989, then Deputy City Attorney Casey Gwinn proposed a one-stop location for battered women to receive help. The proposal was not approved, but his office pursued the idea by developing closer working relationships with domestic violence programs and others who were concerned about the fragmentation and often ineffectiveness of services for families experiencing domestic violence. In 1998 the San Diego Police Department joined the effort, and in 2001 the City of San Diego approved the creation of the first FJC. It officially opened in April 2002 with 20 agencies and over 100 professionals co-located in the San Diego Family Justice Center.

As the San Diego FJC Web site states, "Before the San Diego Family Justice Center opened, the criminal justice system made it difficult for victims to seek help; it unintentionally wore them down. Victims were required to travel from location to location to seek services that were scattered throughout the county. They had to tell their story over and over again. Needless to say, the criminal justice system made it easy for victims to become frustrated and ultimately give up." It continues,

> A collaborative effort provides more support to victims and children involved in domestic violence through improved case management and a more fluid exchange of information and resources. The entire process of reporting a domestic violence incident is much less overwhelming for the victims and children involved. This collaboration also dramatically improves the quality of police investigations and ultimately increases convictions of domestic violence perpetrators. The combination of this extensive counseling for perpetrators in conjunction with the empowerment and education of victims and children works in a synergistic fashion to reduce the rates of child abuse and domestic violence recidivism in San Diego.

Soon after San Diego's long efforts formally emerged as the FJC, the U.S. government decided in 2003 to fund the replication of the FJCs in communities across the United States. Four hundred communities expressed interest in the President's Family Justice Center Initiative and 15 were funded to develop centers. All of these centers were opened and operating by 2007. In addition, there are many other similarly configured sets of co-located services in other communities that have not received federal funding. Recently, all of these community-based FJCs have come together to form the National Family Justice Center Alliance.

Jeffrey L. Edleson

See also Coordinated Community Response; Domestic Violence Enhanced Response Team; Prosecutorial Practices, Intimate Partner Violence

Web Sites

President's Family Justice Center Initiative: http://family justicecenter.org/

San Diego Family Justice Center: http://sandiegofamily justicecenter.org/

FAMILY PRESERVATION AND REUNIFICATION PROGRAMS

Child welfare policy in the United States is based on the assumption that strengthening and preserving families serves the long-term welfare and safety interests of children. Family preservation and reunification programs are short-term and intensive interventions intended to help parents whose children are in imminent danger of abuse or neglect. They attempt to stabilize a crisis, teach families new problem solving skills, and break the cycle of family dysfunction. Their primary goal is to remove the risk of harm so that the child does not have to be permanently removed from the home. This entry discusses the history of family preservation programs and the services provided by them, as well as debates about the effectiveness of such programs.

History of Family Preservation

Historically, the child welfare system has struggled to reconcile the sometimes competing goals of child protection and family unity. With the passage of the Adoption Assistance and Child Welfare Act of 1980 (P.L. 96-272), the goal of family preservation became the guiding principle. The 1980 act, sometimes referred to as the "Reunification Act," requires that states, as a condition of receiving federal child welfare funding, make every "reasonable effort" to rehabilitate abusive parents and keep families together.

The Family Preservation and Support Services Act of 1993 (P.L. 103-66) and the 1997 Adoption and Safe Families Act (P.L. 105-89) changed and clarified a number of policies established in the Reunification Act, subtly moving federal policy away from preservation as the overriding concern. Although family unity remains an important long-term goal, the 1997 law explicitly established child safety as a "paramount concern" and encouraged expedited permanency decisions for abused children.

Social Services Provided

Family preservation and reunification programs are based on the assumption that parents whose children have been removed from the home, or who face the possibility that their children could be removed, will be open to receiving services and learning new behaviors. Specific programs vary by state, but typical services provided include behavioral training for parents (including appropriate and inappropriate discipline techniques), child development issues, conflict resolution, and various other household issues related to family stress, neglect, and abuse (e.g., budgeting, housekeeping). States may also coordinate referrals on any of a number of other needs, including medical or psychological treatment, emergency financial assistance, housing information and assistance, daycare assistance, and substance abuse treatment.

The oldest and most thoroughly researched family preservation program is Homebuilders, which began in Washington State in 1974 and has now been implemented in various locals across the country. The Homebuilder model calls for small caseloads (typically two to three families per caseworker), intensive home-based services (10–20 hours per week for 4–6 weeks), and 24-hour-per-day availability of caseworkers. Like other preservation and reunification services, Homebuilders is based on the assumption that families in the midst of a crisis are amenable to change. In addition to child protection and family preservation, the goals of Homebuilders include providing social support; improved family functioning, school, and job performance; improved living conditions; and increased adult and child self-esteem.

Debate About Family Preservation Programs

There is considerable debate about whether family preservation programs are effective in successfully rehabilitating abusive parents. Proponents of the family preservation model maintain that children can be safely left in their homes *if* their communities offer vulnerable families the social services and training they need. Other defenders of family preservation assert that needy families need to be protected from the strong arm of the state. The real problem facing abusive families, they argue, is lack of resources. In less serious cases of abuse, where poor, young, stressed, and needy parents are likely to benefit from social services, family reunification should be the goal, and supportive intervention should be the means to achieving that end.

Critics maintain that family preservation is "single minded." While acknowledging the sanctity of the family unit, they argue that family preservation and unification goals too often put children at risk. Several highly publicized child deaths in recent years serve as a reminder of the potential dangers of reuniting children with parents who have a history of abuse. An overcommitment to reunifying families also sometimes leaves children in temporary settings for a long time, which is rarely in the best interests of the child.

At the center of the debate is the question of whether preservation services effectively strengthen families or prevent abuse. Initial evaluations of Homebuilders and other programs produced positive results, leading to considerable enthusiasm in the 1980s and 1990s. However, more methodologically rigorous experimental designs, which randomly assign families into experimental and control groups, have been disappointing. The most influential study, funded by the Department of Health and Human Services (DHHS), evaluated preservation programs in four states (Kentucky, New Jersey, Tennessee, and Pennsylvania). Three of the states had implemented the Homebuilders model. Researchers examined a variety of outcome variables, including foster care placement rates and improvement in family functioning, and found no differences between the experimental and control groups. This research is compelling because it focused on four independent evaluations in four different states.

Defenders of preservation programs maintain that several methodological problems make the results less than definitive. These methodological problems include a smaller than desirable sample size, marginal differences between the experimental and control groups (i.e., even the control group families received some services), and problems with the specific programs selected for the study (e.g., none of the programs strictly adhered to the Homebuilders model). It is also worth noting that the authors of the DHHS report did not interpret their findings to mean preservation services should be abandoned. Instead, they interpreted the results as a challenge to work harder to find programs that are effective.

Robin Perrin and Cindy Miller-Perrin

See also Adoption and Safe Families Act of 1997; Adoption Assistance and Child Welfare Act of 1980; Home Visitation Services

Further Readings

Gelles, R. (2005). Protecting children is more important than preserving families. In D. R. Loseke, R. J. Gelles, & M. M. Cavanaugh (Eds.), *Current controversies on family violence* (2nd ed., pp. 329–340). Thousand Oaks, CA: Sage.

U.S. Department of Health and Human Services. (2002). *Evaluation of family preservation and reunification programs: Final report.* Retrieved February 1, 2006, from http://aspe.hhs.gov/hsp/evalfampres94/final/

FAMILY THERAPY AND FAMILY VIOLENCE

Family therapy is a unique mental health discipline whose primary focus is to improve relationship problems, as well as offer relationally based treatment for mental health concerns. In short, its primary orientation to individual, couple, family, and organizational concerns is systemic, or one that focuses on the nature and quality of relationships in which problems reside. Therefore, the core assumption that problems cannot exist outside the context of relationship facilitates working with more than one person in a family, relationship, or community and references this logic when formulating interventions. Rules, roles, and boundaries are key concepts informing family therapists' ways of thinking about relational concerns, and communication, adaptability, cohesion, and flexibility are key markers of relational health. Given these unique aspects, in the field of family and interpersonal violence, family therapy has met with mixed outcomes as it has progressed through three "moments" in reference to family violence.

First Moment

In the first moment, as an emergent field at the time that family violence was being named and acknowledged, family therapy engaged the issue from a purely systemic perspective and emphasized relational mutuality, dysfunctional family roles, and poor communication patterns. In the case of childhood sexual abuse, a systemic perspective focused on the unconscious maintenance of the family's emotional and relational equilibrium (even though it was unhealthy) through behavioral contributions of the perpetrator, child, nonoffending parent, and siblings. Similarly, sustaining relational stability motivated battered women's decisions to continue relationships with abusive partners. Treatment focused on conjoint sessions attended by all members of the immediate family in the case of childhood sexual abuse, and attendance by husband and wife in couple therapy. Further victimization of abused and battered family members was implicit in this intervention structure in that the presence of the perpetrator encouraged further denial of the abuse. Critics, primarily feminists, challenged this descriptive, yet neutralized, systemic ideology and structure as unacknowledged support of institutionalized patriarchy, overt victim blaming, and dangerous to women and children.

Second Moment

As a result of feminists' challenges in the 1980s, the second moment of family therapy's conceptualization and treatment of family violence evidenced a more informed position on the institutionalized oppression of women and mental health's role in endorsing its continued acceptance. Feminist-informed family therapists questioned unacknowledged endorsements of prescribed male and female roles in the family (male—intellectual, decision maker, breadwinner; female—emotional, mothering, nurturer) that contributed to violent and abusive behavior. Family therapists reexamined longstanding beliefs about mother blaming, male superiority, emotionally unavailable men and needy women, secrets, boundaries, and accountability. Similar types of feminist critiques occurred in other mental health disciplines, and therapeutic interventions shifted away from privileging male voices over female voices. For family therapy, this shift was marked by clinical models overtly assessing culpability, and emphasizing physical and emotional safety for victims. Pragmatically, this shift signaled a move from conjoint family or couples therapy to extended individual and group work for perpetrators, victims, and other family members. Placing an abused child or battered woman in clinical situations where he or she could be revictimized or coerced was understood as unethical. For example, conjoint therapy for couples with ongoing or past violence was such a sensitive topic that many family therapists were uncomfortable discussing it and referred violent couples.

Third Moment

Currently, the third moment of family therapy's attempt to deal with family violence has indicated a more balanced position that incorporates moments one and two. In the cases of child physical and sexual abuse, the field continues to take strong positions on accountability and safety. Therefore, assessing for abuse and inappropriate boundaries between immediate and extended family members occurs early in treatment. Interestingly, though, once family therapists have facilitated the process of acknowledging and addressing abuse, they are also the key mental health professionals involved in family reunification, a process of helping the family to rebuild itself in ways that encourage communication, safety, accountability, and development of appropriate social supports.

The work of John Gottman and Neil Jacobson, Michael Johnson, and Sandra Stith, Karen Rosen, Eric McCollum, and Cynthia Thomsen has been instrumental in convincing family therapists that the therapeutic constellation is a less critical factor in intervening in intimate partner violence than the type of batterer involved. Research by Gottman and Jacobson and by Johnson has called for mental health providers to consider the distinct profiles of male batterers and their implications for intervention. Specifically, men who become verbally and behaviorally more aggressive and physiologically less excitable in violent episodes are considered inappropriate candidates for conjoint therapy. In addition, men who use violence as their primary relational strategy with both men and women are also considered high risk. Stith, Rosen, McCollum, and Thomsen, following this logic, found that men who used violence episodically to control specific situations with their partners could engage in couples therapy to rebuild their relationships and reduce violence.

The third moment of family therapy's interface with family violence has also evidenced the impact of postmodern/poststructuralistic philosophy. Generally, postmodernism emphasizes the value of understanding life as socially constructed realities rather than objective, immutable realities. As such, the mutability of victims' and perpetrators' histories and futures with violence becomes the context for creating change and providing hope. Dialogic, or language-focused therapies, such as narrative therapy and collaborative language systems, provide alternate relationally focused clinical approaches to abuse-focused therapies and traditional batterers programs. Three examples, one dealing with childhood physical and sexual abuse and two with intimate partner violence, follow.

Just therapy, a systemic clinical model steeped in narrative therapy and social justice ideas, originated from the work of a multicultural clinical staff in New Zealand. The model utilizes a holistic approach that partners therapy and social services, with respect for community context and ways of knowing, to work with child abuse. In addition to bringing community, therapeutic, and social service resources to the safety and protection of children, and accountability of perpetrators, it also uniquely deals with macro-level issues, such as the effects of public policy on negative outcomes of child protection and family reunification.

Similarly, Rhea Almeida and Tracy Durkin have also integrated couples therapy with community supports to address intimate partner violence in low-income communities. Their work has successfully focused on establishing accountability and support for abusive men through the involvement of community mentors and increased social support. Abused women also are encouraged to gain support and empowerment within the traditions of their community. On a more individual and familial level, Alan Jenkins and Tod Augusta-Scott employ an "invitations to responsibility" model to acknowledge batterers' duality around desiring intimate relationships and yet utilizing control and abuse as primary behaviors within them. This model differs from the historical psychoeducational/confrontational model of batterers treatment in that it combines elements of cognitive-behavioral therapy, solution-oriented therapy, and client-directed therapy with accountability. Its intent is to remove opportunities for defensiveness about abusive behavior that impede responsibility taking.

Carolyn Tubbs

See also Family Group Conferencing; Family Justice Centers; Family Preservation and Reunification Programs; Intensive Family Preservation Services; Spirituality and Family Therapy

Further Readings

Almeida, R. V., & Durkin, T. (1999). The cultural context model: Therapy for couples with domestic violence. *Journal of Marital and Family Therapy, 25,* 313–324.

Augusta-Scott, T., & Dankwort, J. (2002). Partner abuse intervention: Lessons from education and narrative therapy approaches. *Journal of Interpersonal Violence, 17,* 783–805.

Jacobson, N., & Gottman, J. (1998). *When men batter women: New insights into ending abusive relationships.* New York: Simon & Schuster.

Jenkins, A. (1990). *Invitations to responsibility: The therapeutic engagement of men who are violent and abusive.* Adelaide, Australia: Dulwich Centre.

Stith, S. M., Rosen, K. H., McCollum, E. E., & Thomsen, C. J. (2004). Treating intimate partner violence within intact couple relationships: Outcome of a multi-couple versus individual couple therapy. *Journal of Marital and Family Therapy, 30,* 305–318.

FAMILY VIOLENCE, CO-OCCURRENCE OF FORMS

Many families experience multiple forms of violence both concurrently and sequentially. Parallel assessments, for example, of adult domestic violence, child maltreatment, sibling abuse, and elder abuse offer an opportunity to determine how these types of violence interact with each other and with other family problems. Such an understanding is vital for the development of more integrated and coordinated social policies and interventions.

Common Risk and Protective Factors

An ecological or integrated framework suggests that individuals who commit or who are victims of violence face a number of common personal, socioeconomic, and environmental challenges. Common risk markers found among perpetrators of child maltreatment and adult domestic violence include poor impulse control and a lack of empathy for others, often stemming from their own early exposure to violence or victimization as children. Living in poverty and resource-poor communities and associating with peers who support the use of violence are also common risk markers in studies of all forms of violence among family members. Such environments can create a state of stress and uncertainty that encompasses all aspects of daily living, making it difficult to approach child rearing or relationship building in a measured and nonviolent manner. Although it is not universal, it is often the case that those engaged in violent behaviors have a history of poor performance in other domains, such as school, social relationships, and the workplace, failures that further isolate them

from formal and informal systems that might modify their behaviors.

In addition to sharing common risk factors, at-risk individuals also share a variety of personal, familial, and cultural conditions that serve to minimize levels of family violence. Adults who have a strong sense of self and feel rewarded in their personal and work relationships are better able to manage the inevitable setbacks and disappointments in life without resorting to violent coping strategies. Strong family and friendship ties that reinforce respect for the opinions and needs of others also reduce the likelihood for violence. Communities with strong educational systems, employment opportunities, and a range of recreational and supportive services provide families and individuals ready access to the types of assistance that can bolster an individual's resistance to violence.

Over and above these shared risk and protective factors, a more coordinated examination of family violence is justified by the frequent co-occurrence of these problems within individual families. Most community mental health, child welfare, and juvenile court caseloads include a large proportion of clients who struggle with myriad problems. Within the context of violence, a number of reviews document the co-occurrence of child maltreatment in families where adult domestic violence is also occurring. Over 30 studies of the link between these two forms of violence show a 40% median co-occurrence of child maltreatment and adult domestic violence in the families studied. Similarly, children involved in mistreating their siblings often have experienced or observed violence by their parents. Adult children who physically or emotionally abuse their elder parents may do so, in part, because of how they were cared for as children.

One challenge in building on these commonalities in advancing practice and policy reforms is the tendency for those working in these domains to become more focused on their specific concerns, resource requirements, and professional training. In the absence of direct communication and shared learning, the efforts on each issue run the risk of becoming more self-contained and competitive. While recognizing the uniqueness of each form of violence and the reality that there is no perfect correlation among the causal patterns, impacts, and response systems associated with each form of violence, meaningful progress on each issue might best be realized by advancing coordinating reforms that cut across one or more of these problems.

Common Intervention Issues

The co-occurrence and common causal characteristics of different forms of family violence have significant implications for how assessments are conducted and services delivered. Recognition of these commonalities is reflected in the establishment of dual assessment tools, more diversified case planning, and more formalized interagency agreement. Although far from universal, these types of treatment reforms are generating a number of opportunities for those working in various areas of family violence to learn from each other and to more accurately recognize indicators of multiple acts of violence. Recognizing the complex causal patterns surrounding various forms of family violence, a growing number of therapeutic interventions targeting these families seek change on multiple, ecological levels. Improvement is sought in how individuals view themselves, interact with other family members, and function within a broader social context.

Efforts to prevent various forms of family violence also share a common set of concerns. In addition to seeking change within individuals, prevention advocates for adult domestic violence, child abuse, and elder abuse pay attention to altering the cultural values and assumptions that enable and, in some cases, justify violent interactions among family members. Acceptance of corporal punishment and gender inequality as well as a general unwillingness to support actions that challenge the supremacy of parental rights or family privacy in determining appropriate behaviors between adults, or between adults and children, raise formidable barriers for creating prevention systems that can significantly reduce levels of violence. Progress in overcoming these barriers, however, is being made, as reflected in the development of universal education efforts with children and widespread public education and awareness efforts. In addition, prevention programs adopting a developmental perspective place greater emphasis on engaging families in supportive programs early in the parenting process or as relationships are formed, offering families an opportunity to establish stronger positive communication patterns and appropriate boundaries.

Deborah Daro

See also Community Violence, Effects on Children and Youth; Cycle of Violence; Intergenerational Transmission of Violence; Intimate Partner Relationship Quality and Domestic Violence

Further Readings

Daro, D., Edleson, J., & Pinderhughes, H. (Eds.). (2004). Child abuse, youth violence and adult domestic violence [Special issue]. *Journal of Interpersonal Violence, 19*(3).

Edelson, J. (1999). Children's witnessing of adult domestic violence. *Journal of Interpersonal Violence, 14*(8), 839–870.

National Research Council. (1993). *Understanding and preventing violence* (A. J. Reiss & J. A. Roth, Eds.). Washington, DC: National Academy Press.

FAMILY VIOLENCE OPTION

The Family Violence Option (FVO) was enacted in 1996 as part of federal welfare legislation titled the Personal Responsibility and Work Opportunity Reconciliation Act (PRWORA). PRWORA replaced the prior Aid to Families with Dependent Children program with the Temporary Assistance to Needy Families (TANF) program. The FVO is an optional program that states may adopt that aims to meet the needs of domestic violence victims accessing the welfare system. The FVO allows states to waive TANF work requirements temporarily for renewable 6-month periods if those requirements interfere with a violence survivor's safety.

The effort to include protections for domestic violence victims in welfare policy grew out of an increasing recognition of the relationship between domestic violence and public assistance. Research has shown that 20% to 30% of women enrolled in welfare are currently in violent relationships. Domestic violence victims often are economically dependent on their abusers, and abusers frequently undermine victims' efforts to gain or maintain employment. TANF requirements can put victims at further risk by requiring their cooperation in paternity establishment and child support enforcement or by compromising victims' safety when their benefits are reduced or eliminated because of failure to meet requirements. The FVO permits victims of domestic violence to receive temporary waivers or exemptions from these TANF requirements while they receive assistance in dealing with the abusive relationships and obtaining employment.

The FVO outlines that adopting states should screen for domestic violence, provide supportive services and/or referrals, and waive certain programmatic requirements if the requirements might make it more difficult for the victim to escape violence or further endanger or unfairly penalize the victim. Some examples of requirements that can be waived by a state FVO program are the 60-month time limits for welfare recipients, mandatory child support cooperation, and residency conditions. How exactly states implement these policies varies widely from state to state. Federal legislation outlines the standard that must be met in order for an applicant to receive a FVO waiver. The standard looks at whether or not compliance with TANF requirements would make it more difficult for individuals receiving benefits to escape domestic violence or unfairly penalize them. Some states have adopted their own standard for granting FVO waivers. The federal definition of *victim of domestic violence* is one who has been battered or subject to extreme cruelty. It is not restricted to violence perpetrated by a family, household member, or intimate partner. Not all states use the federal definition of domestic violence.

Tracy J. Davis

See also Battered Women, Economic Independence of

Further Readings

Legal Momentum. (2004). *Family violence option: State by state summary.* Washington, DC: Author.

Lein, L., Jacquet, S., Lewis, C., Cole, P., & Williams, B. (2001). With the best of intentions: Family violence option and abused women's needs. *Violence Against Women, 7,* 193–210.

Stern, N. (2003). Battered by the system: How advocates against domestic violence have improved victims' access to child support and TANF. *Hastings Women's Law Journal, 14,* 47–68.

Family Violence Prevention and Services Act

The Family Violence Prevention and Services Act (FVPSA, pronounced phip-SAH) is a U.S. government program administered by the Family and Youth Services Bureau of the Department of Health and Human Services. FVPSA provides key funding for emergency services for domestic violence victims and their children, to state coalitions to provide technical assistance to local programs, and to support a national network of resource centers on the topic. FVPSA was first authorized in 1984 and most recently reauthorized and expanded in the Keeping Children and Families Safe Act of 2003.

Prevention, Public Awareness, and Cooperation

In a recent fact sheet, the National Coalition Against Domestic Violence reported that the FVPSA funds provide the "primary Federal mechanism for encouraging state, Tribal and local support to implement, maintain and expand programs and projects to prevent family violence and increase public awareness of domestic violence issues." One of ten FVPSA dollars is spent to support state-level coalitions that provide technical assistance to domestic violence programs and help develop coordinated community efforts with other institutions, such as the police, criminal justice agencies, social services, and health care systems.

Emergency Services

There are over 2,000 emergency service programs in the United States that rely on FVPSA funds to support their work. They include shelters and safe houses for battered women and their children and nonresidential services to these same families, such as crisis hotlines, counseling, and information and referral services.

Funding

FVPSA plays a major role in supporting both prevention of domestic violence and our social responses to adult victims of domestic violence and their children. Funding for services envisioned for children in FVPSA have yet to be enacted as a result of only partial funding by Congress. Each year Congress has authorized $175 million to support FVPSA programs, but has actually appropriated only about 70% of this figure, or about $125 million (for example, in 2006 Congress appropriated $124.7 million). Still, this amount is one of the key federal sources of funding for a variety of prevention and emergency services for both adults and children.

Jeffrey L. Edleson

See also Domestic Violence Resource Network; National Network to End Domestic Violence; National Resource Center on Domestic Violence

Further Readings

National Coalition Against Domestic Violence. (2007). *Family Violence Prevention and Services Act (FVPSA).* Retrieved from http://www.ncadv.org/files/2008fvpsa.pdf

Web Sites

National Coalition Against Domestic Violence: http://www.ncadv.org/

FAMILY VIOLENCE PREVENTION FUND

Since 1980, the Family Violence Prevention Fund (FVPF) has been pioneering innovative programs to help end domestic and sexual violence. FVPF President Esta Soler first established the organization with a federal grant in 1980. Today, with offices in San Francisco, Boston, and Washington, D.C., and partners around the world, it is a national and international leader on violence against women and children, the source of numerous trailblazing prevention and intervention campaigns, and a major force in shaping public policies that prevent violence and help victims in the United States and worldwide.

The FVPF was instrumental in enacting the landmark Violence Against Women Act, and is well known for its outreach to men and youth and its community-based violence prevention programs. It has helped transform the way health care providers, police, judges, employers, and others address violence against women and children. FVPF model programs, policies, and publications have been distributed to, and replicated in, every state and an increasing number of countries.

Programs

Because sometimes the only messages boys get are the wrong ones, in 2003 the FVPF and the Advertising Council launched a campaign to encourage men to teach boys that violence against women is wrong. Coaching Boys Into Men includes television, radio, and print public service announcements, and numerous resources.

Supported by distinguished CEOs, professional athletes, entertainers, coaches, and others, the FVPF's Founding Fathers campaign is mobilizing men to teach the next generation to treat women and girls with honor and respect, and to teach boys that violence does not equal strength. It gives men tools to make change in their homes, communities, and workplaces.

The FVPF's highly successful Health Care Initiative is teaching providers to inquire about whether their patients have been exposed to violence, and to offer help to patients who need it. The FVPF is the nation's Health Resource Center on Domestic Violence—the only federally funded clearinghouse helping health care providers improve their response to family and sexual violence.

The FVPF's National Judicial Institute is providing judges with guidelines, education, and materials to ensure that their courtrooms provide real help to victims of family violence.

Its Children's Initiative is working with domestic violence and batterer intervention programs, child welfare agencies, and community organizers to build collaborations that promote safe and healthy families.

Its Workplace Project is a historic collaboration with employers and unions, and offers an online resource kit offering sample workplace domestic violence policies, education and training materials, case studies, resources, and more.

Its Immigrant Women Campaign is expanding services for immigrant victims of violence and mobilizing Americans to press for more humane asylum policies.

Its International Partnerships in China, India, Mexico, and Russia are addressing all forms of violence, including human trafficking.

The FVPF is supported by the Annie E. Casey, Hewlett, Hilton, MacArthur, Packard and Waitt Family Foundations, among others. The Ford Foundation made it one of the few organizations it endows.

The FVPF has won awards from the Sara Lee Foundation and the State Justice Institute, and been named one of *Worth* magazine's 100 Best Charities, among many other honors.

Lisa Lederer

See also Child Exposure to Intimate Partner Violence; Date and Acquaintance Rape; Dating Violence/Courtship Violence; Domestic Violence Among Immigrant Women;

Health Care Response to Intimate Partner Violence; Health Consequences of Intimate Partner Violence; Legal System, Criminal Justice System Responses to Intimate Partner Violence; Prevention Programs, Interpersonal Violence

Web Sites

Family Violence Prevention Fund: http://www.endabuse.org

FATHER INVOLVEMENT

Father involvement has been an area of study since the 1970s, with the majority of research completed after the mid-1980s. The term *father involvement* encompasses the number of hours fathers spend directly interacting with their children and being accessible to their children, as well as fathers' investment in the parental role and associated responsibilities. In general, higher levels of father involvement are associated with better outcomes for children. Exceptions include involvement of antisocial fathers and involvement of fathers where there are high levels of interparental conflict, both of which are associated with negative outcomes for children. Fathers are less likely to be involved with their children when they are unemployed, when they have a conflict-laden relationship with their children's mothers, and when they do not reside in the same home as their children. Age is also a predictor of involvement, with young fathers less likely to maintain involvement with their children, and older fathers showing particularly high levels of involvement. There appear to be more similarities than differences in fathers' roles and in the predictors of father involvement across cultural, racial, and ethnic groups; however, there are still relatively few studies in this area. Even fewer studies have explored fathering in gay, bisexual, or transgender men.

The following sections provide a brief review of the definition of father involvement, the history and politics of father involvement, the benefits to children of having an involved father, and the predictors of father involvement.

Definition

The most widely accepted definition of father involvement is Michael Lamb's tripartite division of such involvement into engagement, accessibility, and responsibility. Engagement, also called interaction, refers to direct, one-on-one interactions with the child (e.g., time spent playing with the child). Accessibility refers to times when a parent is available for interaction with the child, but is not presently engaged in direct interaction (e.g., when the parent is gardening while a child is playing in the yard). Responsibility refers to taking ultimate responsibility for ensuring the child's welfare (e.g., ensuring that the child has clothes). A variety of measures have been used to track fathers' engagement, accessibility, and responsibility, including time diaries, time estimates, activity frequency measure, relative engagement measures, and measures of fathers' investment in the parental role. Recently, some scholars have started to purposefully use the term *father involvement* to denote only positive involvement with a child, rather than involvement in its original, content-free sense.

History

Social constructions of the role of fathers in child development have varied over history. During the 17th and 18th centuries, fathers were characterized as moral guides and teachers to their children. With industrialization, fathers' role as breadwinner was stressed. Social disruption brought on by war and economic hardship during the 1930s and 1940s and the rise in popularity of psychoanalytic theories led to an emphasis on fathers as sex-role models for their sons. Finally, since the mid-1970s, emphasis has been placed on fathers as nurturing parents, actively involved in the day-to-day care of their children.

As the socially constructed role of fathers has changed, so has the relative amount of time that fathers spend with children. Averaging across studies prior to 1980, it is estimated that in U.S. families, fathers' engagement was about one third of mothers' and their accessibility was about one half that of mothers. In the mid-1980s and 1990s, fathers' relative engagement and accessibility rose to 43% and 66%, respectively. Research conducted on fathers' involvement since 1990 suggests still greater increases in the relative and absolute engagement of fathers with children. Similar trends have been documented in Canada, Finland, Norway, and the Netherlands, and are likely in other industrialized nations. Changes over time in the amount of responsibility that fathers take for ensuring their children's care have been measured less often and less consistently, and comparisons across time yield inconsistent findings.

Political Context

In the past two decades, fathering has become an important political issue in the United States, and to a somewhat lesser extent, in most other industrialized countries. Political focus on fathers, particularly father absence, has led to government funding for fathering initiatives, shifts in family law toward joint custody of children, support for implementing paternal work leave for child care, and a proliferation of fathering information, support, and intervention programs. Political mobilization around fathering in the United States is distinguished from similar movements in other industrialized nations by the strong moral and religious presence in much of the political rhetoric. Although some fathering rights groups and activists promote parental equity, a proportion of fathering involvement organizations in the United States are connected to socially conservative efforts to promote (heterosexual) marriage, reduce divorce, and reestablish men as the authority in the family.

Benefits

Higher levels of father involvement have been associated with better outcomes for children, such as greater cognitive development, academic achievement, social competence, and with more adaptive and resilient emotional functioning. Children with involved fathers are also less likely to have negative outcomes such as school dropout and delinquency. The benefits of father involvement extend to the mother–child relationship, with associations to higher maternal sensitivity to their children and greater maternal emotional availability, patience, and flexibility. Relationships between father involvement and positive outcomes have been found regardless of the methods used to assess these variables and after accounting for the influence of differing levels of mother involvement.

There are at least two exceptions to the generally positive relationship between father involvement and positive child outcomes. First, high levels of interparental conflict are detrimental to children, and some research suggests that ongoing exposure to such conflict is a more important predictor of negative child outcomes than is father absence. Second, when fathers engage in high levels of antisocial behavior, rates of problem behaviors in children increase with higher levels of father involvement.

Among nonresident fathers, paying child support and having a close relationship predict positive child outcomes more strongly than frequency or duration of father–child contact. These results are similar to those from studies of resident fathers in suggesting that both the amount and the quality of involvement should be considered.

Predictors

Residence

Fathers who are living with their children typically have much higher rates of involvement than fathers who are not. Nonresident fathers tend to be more involved during the preschool years and become increasingly less involved as children age.

Employment

Mothers' and fathers' employment both increase father involvement. Fathers' involvement is consistently higher in two-parent families when mothers are working outside the home than when mothers are not employed. Father involvement is also higher when men are employed, and when they have higher education and income levels. Unemployed fathers are more likely to leave or limit their involvement with their families than employed fathers, and are less likely to take on parenting responsibilities. Fathers' employment status appears to be particularly important to predicting men's involvement when they are not living with their children. Specifically, when fathers are able to contribute financially, they are more likely to remain involved with their children. It is theorized that societal emphasis on the importance of fathers as breadwinners largely explains the relationship between fathers' employment and their involvement with their children.

Relationship With Children's Mother

Harmonious mother–father relationships are related to higher rates of father involvement, and conflict-laden relationships are associated with lower rates of father involvement. Conflict between mothers and fathers is a particularly strong predictor of low father involvement when parents do not live together.

Skills and Self-Confidence

Men with greater knowledge of parenting and men who feel competent to perform caregiving tasks tend to have higher levels of involvement with their children.

Age

Men who become fathers when they are adolescents have the lowest rates of contact with their children. Older fathers (i.e., men who become fathers later than the norm) have the highest rates of involvement with their children and have been shown to be particularly responsive, affectionate, and likely to take on responsibilities for childcare tasks.

Characteristics of the Child

Fathers spend more time with younger children than older children and with firstborn children than with later-born children. There is some research to suggest that fathers are also more involved with children who are more difficult to care for, such as children who were born prematurely or who have difficult temperaments. Earlier studies found that father involvement was higher for boys than girls, but more recent studies have found no effect for child gender.

Other Predictors

A number of other variables have been investigated as potential predictors of fathers' involvement, with inconsistent results. These variables include fathers' gender-role orientation, egalitarian gender-role attitudes, men's perception of their own fathers, role salience, maternal gatekeeping, and fathers' level of stress.

Katreena L. Scott and Jennifer L. Root

See also Fathers' Rights Movement

Further Readings

Gavanas, A. (2004). *Fatherhood politics in the United States.* Urbana: University of Illinois Press.

Jaffee, S. R., Moffitt, T. E., Caspi, A., & Taylor, A. (2003). Life with (or without) father: The benefits of living with two biological parents depends on the father's antisocial behavior. *Child Development, 74,* 109–126.

Lamb, M. E. (2004). *The role of fathers in child development* (4th ed.). New York: Wiley.

FATHERS AS PERPETRATORS OF CHILD MALTREATMENT

National incidence studies of child abuse and neglect find that fathers (i.e., biological fathers, stepfathers, and father surrogates) are perpetrators of a significant proportion of child maltreatment. In two-parent families, fathers are perpetrators in the majority of child physical abuse and about half of emotional maltreatment cases. Fathers are particularly overrepresented as perpetrators of severe, injurious forms of abuse. Child sexual abuse is most often perpetrated by nonparental adults; however, when a parent is implicated, it is much more likely to be a father than a mother. Fathers are generally less likely than mothers to be implicated in cases of child neglect.

Although fathers are often perpetrators of child maltreatment, there still is little research on their characteristics and intervention needs. Interest in this area began in the early 1990s with recognition of the overlap of men's abuse of their intimate partners and of their children, and has expanded slowly. As a result, the following information represents the beginning of an understanding of the characteristics of and risks posed by father perpetrators.

Characteristics of Father Perpetrators

There is ongoing debate on whether risk factors for the perpetration of maltreatment differ in fathers and mothers. Clinical descriptions of the characteristics of maltreating fathers tend to portray these men as emotionally distant, harsh, authority figures in the family rather than as distressed, overwhelmed parents lacking skills and knowledge. Rigid expectations for children, poor family cohesion, lack of accountability for past behavior, and the absence of a biological relationship between father and children are important risk factors for men's perpetration of child abuse and neglect. Personal distress, which is an important risk factor for mothers, seems to play a less important role in predicting maltreatment in fathers. For both mothers and fathers, victimization in their family of origin and past investigations for child abuse or neglect are strong predictors of subsequent child maltreatment. Other major risk factors for both include poverty, younger age, and problematic use of alcohol and drugs.

The influence of a father's relationship with his children and the children's mother is another emerging area of study as it relates to risk for child maltreatment. Father absence contributes to child poverty, reduced parental resources, and increased child exposure to nonbiologically related father surrogates, all of which are associated with higher rates of child maltreatment. However, father absence, by itself, does not lead to maltreatment, and sometimes having a father involved is a greater risk for children than is their mother's single parenthood. In particular, involvement of fathers who are antisocial, mentally ill, addicted to substances, and/or violent toward the children's mothers likely increases children's risk of being maltreated.

Finally, fathers who are present in the lives of their children may convey risk or protection to their children, depending on how they support and relate to children's mothers. A higher level of support from fathers is related to reduced maternal harshness and to greater responsiveness of both parents to children's needs. In contrast, interparental conflict is related to higher rates of coercive parenting by both fathers and mothers.

Prevention and Treatment Initiatives

Until recently, fathers were seldom included in child maltreatment prevention and intervention initiatives. Neglect of fathers has been attributed to cultural views of the preeminence of mothers in caring for and protecting children, policies and practices that failed to encourage father involvement, reluctance of professionals to work with fathers, and lack of training on working with men.

There are a variety of current initiatives to involve fathers in efforts to prevent and intervene in child maltreatment. First, there are attempts to involve fathers in already established programs for at-risk children and families, such as Head Start, home-visiting services, and community-based parenting education and support programs. These programs have traditionally served mothers and children, but many are now aiming to either involve fathers as part of regular intervention or adapt services specifically for men. To date, such initiatives have been only modestly successful at engaging fathers.

Prevention initiatives focusing directly on fathers have shown greater promise. Examples include fathering support groups, programs for fathers at key transition points (e.g., new fathers, fathers of children going into adolescence), and intensive support services to fathers in fragile, at-risk families. These programs are often profiled by national fathering organizations such as Fathers Direct, Fathering Involvement Research Alliance, Dads and Daughters, and the National Fatherhood Initiative.

A third way that father-perpetrated child maltreatment is being addressed is through intervention programs for men who have been violent toward their intimate partners. Many batterer intervention programs now include four to six sessions aimed at educating men on the effects of exposure to violence on children, on the importance of promoting safety for children, and on repairing father–child relations.

Finally, there have been efforts within child welfare services to better engage fathers. Major reports on child welfare practice have emphasized the importance of locating children's biological fathers, involving fathers in child protection monitoring efforts, utilizing the strengths of fathers to support healthy child and family functioning, and providing intervention when fathers are perpetrators of abuse. A few treatment programs targeting the intervention needs of maltreating fathers have also been developed and are available in an increasingly large number of communities.

Little research has been done on the potential of any of these prevention or treatment programs to reduce child maltreatment.

Katreena L. Scott and Jennifer L. Root

See also Child Physical Abuse; Intergenerational Transmission of Violence; Maternal Responsibility for Child Physical Abuse; Nonoffending Parents of Maltreated Children; Parenting Practices and Violence, Child Maltreatment

Further Readings

Coohey, C., & Zhang, Y. (2005). The role of men in chronic supervisory neglect. *Child Maltreatment, 11,* 27–33.

Dubowitz, H. (2006). Where's Dad? A need to understand father's role in child maltreatment. *Child Abuse & Neglect, 30,* 461–465.

Guterman, N. B., & Lee, Y. (2005). The role of fathers in risk for physical child abuse and neglect: Possible pathways and unanswered questions. *Child Maltreatment, 10,* 136–149.

Scalera, M. B. (2001). *An assessment of child welfare practices regarding fathers.* Retrieved from http://www.nfpn.org/tools/articles/fathers.php

Scott, K. L., & Crooks, C. V. (2006). Intervention for abusive fathers: Promising practices in court and community responses. *Juvenile and Family Court Journal, 57*(3), 29–44.

Fathers' Rights Movement

The fathers' rights movement advocates for fathers who feel deprived of their parental rights and subjected to systematic bias as men after divorce or separation. The term *fathers' rights* is relevant to interpersonal violence primarily in custody and visitation cases involving domestic violence.

The fathers' rights movement emerged in the 1970s as a loose social movement with a network of interest groups primarily active in Western countries. Established to campaign for equal treatment for men by the courts on issues such as child custody after divorce, child support, and paternity determinations, this network is also part of the broader men's rights movement. While there is no written history of the movement, it is generally viewed as stemming from changes in both the law and societal attitudes. These changes include the introduction of no-fault divorce in 1969 and the attendant rise in divorce rates; the increasing entry of women into the workforce, upturning traditional gender roles; and the increasing social acceptance of single parents and their increased proportion of all families.

Fathers' rights activists typically believe that the application of the law in family courts is biased against men. Because mothers have historically been seen as the primary caregivers for their children, they have often been granted custody of their children, causing some fathers to feel marginalized. Thus, one longstanding goal of fathers' rights groups is obtaining "shared parenting," asking that courts uphold a rebuttable presumption of joint custody after divorce or separation. Under a shared parenting arrangement, children would be required to live with each parent for the same amount of time, unless there were valid reasons not to do so.

Fathers' rights advocates claim that women often falsify allegations of domestic violence to gain advantage in family law cases, and misuse protection orders to remove men from their homes or deny them contact with their children. Attorneys and advocates for abused women note that while it is not uncommon for family court proceedings to be accompanied by allegations of domestic violence and the use of protection orders, this is largely representative of the prevalence of domestic violence in our society, and of the fact that domestic violence often increases (or begins) at the time of separation or divorce. Many battered women seek protection orders as a last resort, after being subjected to continuous violence, because the orders can provide an effective means to gaining safety from the batterer.

While many mothers are awarded custody, there are many contested custody cases. In these contested cases, fathers often seek and win joint or full custody of the children. One way that a mother might lose custody is through the father's use of a theory called parental alienation syndrome (PAS). Fathers' rights groups see PAS as occurring when the mother has "poisoned" the minds of their children toward the other parent by brainwashing them into reporting abuse. When this legal tactic is used, the mother often loses custody or is forced to accept joint custody based on the father's allegations of PAS.

While the fathers' rights movement presents PAS as a credible theory, it is recognized as deeply flawed, based on extreme gender bias, and rooted in a disbelief of women and children who report abuse. Neither the American Psychological Association nor the American Psychiatric Association recognizes PAS as a credible theory, and the National Council of Juvenile and Family Court Judges has rejected the theory and recommended that it not be used when considering custody matters.

Women's rights groups and profeminist men argue that fathers' rights groups want to entrench patriarchy and undo the advances made by women in society. Those opposed to the fathers' rights movement believe that the bias fathers' rights members speak of in family courts either does not exist or is such that single mothers in particular are not advantaged as a class to the extent stated, especially in the face of sexism and male privilege and power.

Ana Ottman and Rebekah Lee

See also Custody, Contact, and Visitation: Relationship to Domestic Violence; Father Involvement; Parental Alienation Syndrome

Further Readings

Dominus, S. (2005, May 8). The fathers' crusade. *New York Times Magazine,* pp. 26–33, 50, 56–58.

Flood, M. (2004). Backlash: Angry men's movements. In S. E. Rossi (Ed.), *The battle and backlash rage on: Why feminism cannot be obsolete* (pp. 261–278). Philadelphia: Xlibris Press.

FEAR OF CRIME

Fear of crime is one of the most lasting outcomes of a crime-ridden society. Individuals who have been victims of crime often fear that they may be victimized again. Individuals who have never been victimized may also fear crime since they are reminded of crime and victimization through the media, they hear about the victimization experiences of others, and they are told to be concerned about crime and victimization from politicians and law enforcement officials. Both victims and nonvictims alike often fear strangers in public spaces. This is especially true of women, who are much more likely to be victimized by a known assailant in the private sphere. The consequence of fear of crime involves taking a variety of behavioral measures to stay safe, potentially causing changes in lifestyle, stress, and additional fear for self or others.

Criminologists have studied fear of crime for over 30 years. Much of the early literature focused on defining and measuring fear of crime, debating if fear of crime was an emotive or cognitive response to potential victimization. Although definitional and measurement issues clearly still concern fear of crime researchers, the majority of researchers now focus on understanding the causes and consequences of fear of crime.

Causes

A person's gender, race, class, and age may influence his or her fear of crime level. Although men, non-White individuals, younger individuals, and lower-class individuals are most likely to be victims of a crime, they may not be the individuals found to be most fearful. For example, a person's gender is a strong predictor of fear of crime, with women reporting more fear of crime than men. This has led to the study of the "gender-fear paradox," since women are less likely than men to be the victim of a crime, even though they report substantially more fear of crime. With regard to age, elderly individuals are often found to have higher levels of fear of crime than younger people. However, age-based fear of crime is increased by other factors, such as living alone or having a low income. In terms of social class, low-income individuals are most likely to report fear of crime. Finally, the connection between a person's race and fear of crime is complicated since it is not only individuals' race that determines their fear of crime, but also the racial composition of the neighborhood in which they live.

Two other causes of fear of crime include victimization experiences and neighborhood conditions. Direct and indirect victimization experiences may both impact fear of crime. In this area of research, study results have been mixed, with some studies suggesting that direct victimization experiences cause individuals to fear the possibility of experiencing victimization in the future, while other studies suggest that being a nonvictim makes individuals more likely to experience fear of crime. This issue is further complicated in studying indirect victimization, where individuals experience victimization vicariously by hearing stories of others' victimization. The possibility that what happened to someone on the news, to a family member, or to a next door neighbor might happen to oneself is sometimes sufficient to make an individual afraid of crime. In terms of neighborhood conditions, social disorganization or perception of the environment as unsafe greatly impacts fear of crime. Physical incivilities in neighborhoods include things such as trash on the street, broken windows in buildings, or graffiti. Social incivilities include gangs of teenagers hanging out on neighborhood street corners or open drug sales in a neighborhood. Both physical and social incivilities are found to increase fear of crime.

Consequences

Another important facet of fear of crime involves the consequences of fear of crime in individuals' daily lives. The primary way that individuals cope with fear of crime is by engaging in constrained behaviors (the behaviors individuals take to keep themselves safe from potential victimization). There are two forms of constrained behaviors: protective behaviors (proactive measures, such as owning a gun, locking doors, or having an alarm system) and avoidance behaviors (reactive measures, such as avoiding going places alone, avoiding going places at night, or avoiding certain areas of a city). Most research suggests that individuals engage in a variety of protective and avoidance measures to reduce potential criminal victimization. The research findings on the impact of these behaviors in reducing fear of crime are mixed, with some studies arguing that constrained behaviors produce more fear of crime and others arguing fear subsides as a result of these behaviors. In addition, some researchers suggest that engaging in constrained behaviors, especially avoidance behaviors, can restrict mobility, decrease freedom, and minimize autonomy.

In some cases, fear of crime may be more of a problem than crime itself. Those most likely to fear crime include women, the elderly, White individuals in non-White neighborhoods, and lower-income individuals. Further, individuals who live in socially disorganized neighborhoods or those who have experienced direct or indirect victimization show increased levels of fear as well. The consequences of fear of crime are the increased behaviors taken to protect from potential crime occurring. These behaviors can greatly restrict individuals' mobility and can actually increase their fear of crime. Future research on this topic may help alleviate fear of crime and promote greater understanding of victimization experiences.

Nicole E. Rader

See also Media, Representations/Distortions of Crime; Victimology

Further Readings

Hale, C. (1996). Fear of crime: A review of the literature. *International Review of Victimology, 4,* 79–159.

Mesch, G. (2000). Perceptions of risk, lifestyle activities, and fear of crime. *Deviant Behavior, 21,* 67–72.

Reid, L. W., Roberts, J. T., & Hilliard, H. M. (1998). Fear of crime and collective action: An analysis of coping strategies. *Sociological Inquiry, 68,* 312–328.

Rountree, P. W. (1998). A reexamination of the crime-fear linkage. *Journal of Research in Crime and Delinquency, 35,* 341–377.

FEMALE GENITAL MUTILATION

Female genital mutilation (FGM), also sometimes called female genital cutting or female circumcision, is practiced in more than 25 African countries, as well as several countries in western Asia and in various ethnic minority communities in other Asian countries. The practice takes one of three forms. The mildest form of FGM is called *Sunna* and involves cutting the hood of the clitoris. It is the form of FGM considered most analogous to male circumcision, but traditionally *Sunna* has not been widely practiced. More common is infibulation, which is the most extreme form of FGM. Infibulation is the removal of the clitoris, labia minora, and most of the labia majora. The vagina is then stitched closed, except that a tiny opening is left for the passage of urine and menstrual blood. The most commonly practiced form of FGM is excision. In excision, the clitoris and all or part of the labia minora are removed.

Although FGM is sometimes performed on infants, it is more typically considered a rite of passage for young girls between the ages of 6 and 14. Traditionally, the practice has been accompanied by much fanfare to celebrate the girl's entry into womanhood and to mark her as marriageable. The underlying rationale for FGM is to ensure a girl's purity. In most societies that practice FGM, it is widely believed that females have a naturally insatiable sex drive. By removing their genitalia, the societies are protecting girls from sexual temptation. In fact, the uncut are usually considered "unclean" and, therefore, unmarriageable, so they are consequently unfit to fulfill their culture's most valued roles for women: wife and mother. To refuse to have one's daughters cut is essentially economic suicide in many practicing societies, since no respectable men will associate with uncut girls.

Historically, FGM received little attention in Western countries. Beginning in the 1970s, however, feminist researchers began publicizing information about the practice in order to raise awareness about its detrimental effects on women and girls and to pressure governments of practicing countries to outlaw it. Because the cutting is usually done by an elder village woman or traditional birth attendant using various nonsurgical and unsterilized instruments (e.g., a razor, a knife, a piece of broken glass, a flattened nail) without the benefit of anesthetics, the practice is not only extremely painful, but also has many serious health complications. These include shock, hemorrhage, septicemia, and tetanus, and the practice also can result in death. At the very least, those who have been cut are unlikely to ever experience sexual pleasure. FGM makes sexual intercourse quite painful, and also increases the incidence of serious complications during childbirth, raising the probability of maternal and infant mortality.

Western feminists, joined by groups of African women and men, have organized campaigns to eliminate FGM, primarily by educating parents about the dangers of the practice and by lobbying governments to enact legislation prohibiting it. Only a few African governments, such as that of Kenya, have passed such laws, but research indicates that they are weakly enforced and that many parents continue to adhere to traditional beliefs, so they have the cutting done in secret rather than with the customary public celebration. Several Western countries, including the United States, Canada, France, and Great Britain, have enacted laws prohibiting FGM, in response to recent cases involving African immigrants importing the practice to their new countries of residence. Nevertheless, some immigrant parents try to save enough money to send their daughters back to their home country for the cutting ritual. In Canada, the threat of FGM in an individual's home country is grounds for granting the individual trying to escape the practice refugee status. The courts in the United States have been reluctant to follow Canada's lead, but some have granted asylum to women fleeing FGM.

Despite the serious complications from FGM, resistance to eliminating it has come not just from parents who do not wish to jeopardize their daughters' marriageability, but also from individuals who resent what they perceive as "outsiders" imposing Western values and trying to destroy the Indigenous culture. Women themselves have also been resistant to change since the practice serves as a source of power and status for them. Efforts to eliminate FGM, therefore, need to be sensitive to local cultural concerns and should simultaneously implement policies and programs to provide women with other avenues of power and status in their societies.

Claire M. Renzetti

See also Cultural Competence; End Violence Against Women International; Foot Binding; Human Rights; United Nations Conventions and Declarations

Further Readings

Barker-Benfield, J. (1976). *The horrors of the half-known life*. New York: Harper & Row.

Lightfoot-Klein, H. (1989). *Prisoners of ritual: An odyssey into female genital circumcision in Africa*. New York: Harrington Park Press.

Wilson, T. D. (2002). Pharonic circumcision under patriarchy and breast augmentation under phallocentric capitalism: Similarities and differences. *Violence Against Women, 8*, 495–521.

FEMALE PERPETRATORS OF INTERPERSONAL VIOLENCE

Women's and girls' involvement in interpersonal violence has received increased attention over the last few decades. During this time, girls' arrests for violent offenses increased more rapidly and decreased more slowly than arrests of boys for similar offenses, and the number of women incarcerated for violent offenses increased exponentially. This entry discusses explanations, hypotheses, and recent scholarship regarding women and girls as perpetrators of interpersonal violence.

The earliest criminological explanations for women's and girls' involvement, or lack of involvement, in interpersonal violence rested on researchers' essentialist understandings of inherent biological or psychological characteristics of women and girls. For example, early theorists concerned with the delinquent, deviant, or criminal behavior of White ethnic and immigrant populations argued that, in general, women and girls were "naturally" constrained from engaging in all forms of crime, including violence. The pseudoscientific arguments of the late 19th and early 20th centuries also contained a racialized and, at times, racist dimension. In *The Female Offender* (1895), for example, Cesare Lombroso, a founding father of criminal anthropology, argued that only "savage" women are capable of violent crimes, and he cited the Hottentot, a Negro woman, and a Red Indian woman as examples of "savages." According to Lombroso, "civilized" White women did not engage in violent crimes because it was inconsistent with their feminine nature.

Serious, critical investigations into women's and girls' participation in interpersonal violence did not appear until after the 1970s. This scholarship was ushered in by Freda Adler's liberation hypothesis, which posited that as women become more like men in social status and position, women's participation in traditional male crimes, including violent crimes, would also increase. While the liberation hypothesis was soundly discounted on empirical grounds—there was statistically no "new violent female offender" to explain—Adler's suggestion that there may be led criminologists to more critically examine patterns and trends in women's offending. The evidence produced by this burst of feminist scholarship and research on gender and crime offers a more complicated explanation for girls' and women's involvement in interpersonal violence. This research strongly suggests that external pressures or "push–pull" factors, such as economic marginalization, victimization, or addiction, help explain women's and girls' arrests for violent offenses in general and, specifically, why those who are arrested for violent offenses are more likely to be poor and non-White.

Recent scholarship critically considers how varying structural positions of girls and women produce interracial and intragender differences in arrests and sentencing for aggressive and violent offenses. The work of feminist criminologists reveals that girls' and women's troubles, and not changing attitudes or opportunities, structure girls' and women's involvement in interpersonal violence as well as their subsequent arrests and detention. Researchers who use a race, gender, and class framework or an intersectionality in their analysis argue that some girls and women experience what feminist criminologist Meda Chesney-Lind refers to as "multiple marginality" as a result of their position in race and class hierarchies. Interracial differences in arrests thus reflect a double standard in criminal justice system responses to girls' and women's offending. For example, young Black women are more likely to serve time in detention facilities, while young White women are more likely to be placed in private mental health facilities. Recent research on girls' and women's arrests for aggressive or violent offenses strongly suggests that these increases reflect policy changes, such as the introduction of zero-tolerance policies in public schools, and not girls' increasingly violent behavior. Such research dispels the myth of a new violent female offender.

Qualitative and ethnographic research on women's and girls' involvement in interpersonal violence shifts attention away from the violent female offender to the structural, cultural, and situational contexts in which women and girls encounter violence in their everyday lives. The few studies that have examined girls' involvement in interpersonal violence in these settings reveal similarities and differences in girls' and boys' involvement in interpersonal violence. These studies reveal that when girls and women are involved in interpersonal violence, their experiences are shaped by normal group processes and gendered patterns of situated interaction, including processes and patterns that similarly affect boys and men. These studies also reveal distinct gendered patterns in interpersonal violence. For example, women and girls are more likely to engage in physical fights with their hands and fists; when a weapon is used, often in self-defense, women and girls are more likely to use piercing weapons (e.g., knives or razor blades) instead of guns.

Recent quantitative and qualitative scholarship illuminates how worsening structural conditions; changes in criminal justice policies; intersections of race, gender, and class; and, at times, the toxic cultural conditions in which girls and boys come of age in distressed urban areas shape women's and girls' involvement in interpersonal violence and subsequent entrance into the juvenile or criminal justice system for aggressive or violent behavior. Today's women and girls are not necessarily "more violent" than women and girls at the turn of the 20th century. The structural and cultural conditions in which girls are coming of age, however, shape women's and girls' experiences with interpersonal violence in new and complicated ways.

Nikki Jones

See also Female Perpetrators of Violence, Teen Girls

Further Readings

Baskin, D., & Sommers, I. (1998). *Casualties of community disorder.* Boulder, CO: Westview Press.

Chesney-Lind, M. (1997). *The female offender.* Thousand Oaks, CA: Sage.

Chesney-Lind, M., & Shelden, R. G. (1992). *Girls, delinquency, and juvenile justice.* Pacific Grove, CA: Brooks/Cole.

Jones, N. (2004). "It's not where you live, it's how you live": How young women negotiate conflict and violence in the inner city. *Annals of the American Academy of Political and Social Science, 595,* 49–62.

Lombroso, C., & Ferrero, G. (1895). *The female offender*. London: Fisher Unwin.

Miller, J. (2000). *One of the guys: Girls, gangs, and gender*. New York: Oxford University Press.

Miller, J., & Mullins, C. (2006). Stuck up, telling lies, and talking too much: The gendered context of young women's violence. In K. Heimer & C. Kruttschnitt (Eds.), *Gender and crime: Patterns of victimization and offending* (pp. 41–66). New York: New York University Press.

Ness, C. D. (2004). Why girls fight: Female youth violence in the inner city. *Annals of the American Academy of Political and Social Science, 595*, 32–48.

Steffensmeier, D., & Allan, E. (1996). Gender and crime: Toward a gendered theory of female offending. *Annual Review of Sociology, 22*, 459–487.

FEMALE PERPETRATORS OF INTIMATE PARTNER VIOLENCE

Despite the reported increase in arrests of women for use of violence against their current or former intimate partners, research suggests that two findings are crucial to use in interpreting what these arrest increases actually mean: first, women's violence is more self-defensive than aggressive; and second, changes in law enforcement strategies are significantly responsible for changes in domestic violence arrest patterns. Moreover, one of the key questions that needs to be addressed when exploring intimate partner violence (IPV) and the criminal justice system is: Within intimate relationships in which women use violence and are arrested, are they batterers? Recent scholarship explores this issue, demonstrating that while some women use violence and are aggressive, most women are *not* the aggressors in the relationships and do not exert the power and control that seem inextricably connected to batterers. Understanding the context in which IPV occurs, rather than simply relying on arrest statistics or surveys to explore the issue, offers the most help in determining the motivation and consequences of women's use of violence.

Measurement issues confound the problem. Most studies rely on the Conflict Tactics Scales (CTS) and the revised version, the CTS2, which are empirical measures of IPV developed by Murray Straus and his colleagues to explore family violence. These scales are used in national surveys of households of married or cohabitating heterosexual couples. Despite improvements in measurement, these quantitative surveys rely on respondents checking boxes that indicate various levels of violence use without distinguishing between the meaning and motivation of the acts; tallies from these surveys provide the false impression that IPV is committed by women at rates equal to or higher than those of men. For example, in one study that uses the CTS, researchers found that 61% of the sample in which respondents reported "mutual violence" actually showed something very different: that women respond to men's acts of violence in self-defensive ways. Self-report data also raise reliability issues in that men underreport their use of violence, while women underreport their victimization by men. CTS measures also exclude complete information on injury and sexual assault; other studies show that women are six times more likely than men to need medical care for their injuries and that 4% of murdered men are killed by their current or former partner, compared to about one third of murdered women. Findings from the National Violence Against Women Survey (NVAWS) revealed that 7.7% of female respondents were raped by their intimate partners, yet the category of "sexual coercion" is excluded from the original CTS, the basis for a huge number of studies that claim mutual violence. Finally, violence perpetrated by ex-partners and ex-spouses is also excluded; the National Crime Victimization Survey statistics show that rates of IPV perpetration against women by their former intimates are eight times higher than rates of perpetration against married women.

Despite the research findings presented by scholars and federal agencies within the Department of Justice, men's rights groups (such as the Men's Defense Association, Men's Activism, and the National Coalition of Free Men) routinely point to numerous investigations and empirical studies demonstrating that women are as physically aggressive as or more aggressive than men in their relationships. Members of the National Coalition of Free Men even filed suit against the state of Minnesota, demanding the end of state funding for domestic violence programs on gender discrimination grounds. However, these assertions are proved faulty upon greater scrutiny of the empirical studies.

One early study by James Makepeace that explored the context of IPV found that, when questioned for motivation, women were twice as likely as men to list self-defense as a motive for inflicting violence, whereas the men were three times more likely than women to indicate that their motive was to intimidate. Likewise, using items from a modified CTS, Christian Molidar and Richard Tolman's work on dating violence found that when incidents of violence are placed into context, a different gendered pattern emerges, one that shows boys' accounts of their girlfriends' violence might really be classified as acts of self-defense. A recent 3-year study conducted by Susan Miller observed three treatment groups for women arrested on domestic violence charges. Only 5% of the women used violence in aggressive ways; these women were in one group. Another group included women who used violence when they were frustrated in situations with their abusive partners or ex-partners and the arresting incident reminded them of past abusive situations (30%). The largest group was comprised of women who described their use of violence as self-defensive (65%). From the detailed descriptions on the probation reports and in the treatment groups, it is clear that the majority of the arrested women were not batterers, but were arrested as a result of new enforcement strategies that were designed to protect women, not create additional hardships for them. These data mirror findings reported elsewhere.

The issue of women's use of violence is further complicated by changes in domestic violence arrest policies. Pro-arrest and mandatory arrest policies were designed and have been supported as ways of responding uniformly to a problem that had suffered from years of police inaction and a trivialization of IPV. Police now respond "by the book," meaning that police make an arrest if the law is broken. Unless they have been trained to distinguish between primary aggressor action and self-defensive action, the result is that arrests occur regardless of the history of abuse in the relationship or the meaning or motivation underlying the use of violence. Ironically, one of the results of this gender-neutral approach has been the arrest of many battered women for the use of self-defensive violence against their battering partners, and the court-ordered funneling of these women into batterer treatment programs. For example, in a study of 39 women arrested for domestic violence, Kevin Hamberger and his colleagues found that 36 of the women were identified at treatment program intake as victims of battering, not batterers, and had been arrested for using violence that was self-defensive in nature. Often, women arrested for IPV are offered treatment rather than a challenge of their arrest on self-defensive grounds. For victims who fought back, and who are desperate to prevent the personal, family, employment, and/or financial crises posed by a conviction, the treatment programs are an attractive option. However, these women remain under supervision by probation departments, and violations of probation could result in harsher penalties when it comes to custody issues or jail time. Threats of jeopardizing probation status are used by abusers to intimidate their victims.

By taking individual acts of violence out of these contexts, researchers and policymakers run the risk of furthering the harm done to battered women by discounting the abuse that is inflicted on them by their male partners and by labeling victims as offenders. The differentiation of self-defensive acts of violence from acts of violence reflective of a larger pattern of abuse is necessary for the criminal justice system to become more equitable and better able to protect victims of IPV.

Susan L. Miller and Terry G. Lilley

See also Female Perpetrators of Interpersonal Violence; Measurement, Interpersonal Violence

Further Readings

Anderson, K. L., & Umberson, D. (2001). Gendering violence: Masculinity and power in men's accounts of domestic violence. *Gender & Society, 15,* 358–380.

Dasgupta, S. D. (2002). A framework for understanding women's use of nonlethal violence in intimate heterosexual relationships. *Violence Against Women, 8,* 1368–1393.

Hamberger, L. K., & Arnold, J. (1990). The impact of mandatory arrest on domestic violence perpetrator counseling sessions. *Family Violence Bulletin, 6,* 10–12.

Makepeace, J. M. (1986). Gender differences in courtship violence victimization. *Family Relations, 35,* 383–388.

Miller, S. L. (2005). *Victims as offenders: The paradox of women's violence in relationships.* New Brunswick, NJ: Rutgers University Press.

Molidar, C., & Tolman, R. (1998). Gender and contextual factors in adolescent dating violence. *Violence Against Women, 4,* 180–194.

FEMALE PERPETRATORS OF VIOLENCE, TEEN GIRLS

Until recently, research on aggression and violence has focused primarily on boys. This is understandable given that boys engage in more serious acts of violence and inflict more physical injury on others at every stage of development than girls. However, over the past several decades, juvenile justice statistics have documented an unprecedented increase in the rate of violent crime perpetrated by girls. This entry summarizes trends in aggressive and violent behavior among adolescent girls, discusses sex differences in aggressive behavior, highlights key risk and protective factors, and notes pressing research questions.

Recent Trends

The rate of violent crime, particularly serious violent acts such as homicide, is consistently higher in males than in females. For example, in Canada, the violent crime rate for girls is one third of the rate for boys. Nevertheless, this rate more than doubled for girls (+127%) from 1988 to 1998, compared to a much smaller increase for boys (+65%). Moreover, there was a modest increase in violent crime rates for girls from 1996 to 2002, while rates for boys slightly decreased. In each case, the increase in girls' violent crime reflected less serious acts such as common assault. These findings parallel statistics reported in the United States: The growth in person offenses over the last two decades has been greater for adolescent females (157%) than for males (71%). Outside North America, the picture is much the same: In the United Kingdom, between 1981 and 1999, there was a 23% decrease in juvenile male offenders and an 8% increase in female offenders.

In sum, juvenile justice statistics across several countries consistently reveal a trend toward greater involvement of girls in the perpetration of aggressive and violent acts. This trend also appears in girls' reports about their own behavior: According to the 2001 U.S. Surgeon General's report, the gap between boys and girls in self-reported engagement in serious aggression has shrunk by approximately 50%. These trends signal the need to fast track research on aggression in girls and develop appropriate interventions.

Sex Differences in Aggressive Behavior

The vast majority of research focuses on physical aggression and violence. Recently researchers have turned their attention to other forms of aggression, including relational aggression that involves attempts to harm others through social exclusion and public humiliation. Over the past decade, research has shown that girls engage in equal levels of relational aggression but less physical aggression than do boys. It is possible to detect relational aggression as early as preschool, and children who engage in it are more likely to suffer peer rejection and are at greater risk for deviant peer affiliation.

How serious is relational aggression? Studies show that girls suffer more than boys do when they are the targets of relational aggression, and victims show higher rates of depression, loneliness, and low self-esteem. In some contexts, social aggression may be a prelude to or co-occur with physical aggression. In their research, Marlene Marie Moretti, Ingrid Obsuth, Candice L. Odgers, and Stephanie R. Penney found a high correlation between relational and physical acts of aggression among high-risk adolescent girls. Anecdotally, these girls reported that their peer groups were often highly relationally aggressive, with rampant rumors of sexual impropriety and fast-changing loyalties that eventually escalated to acts of physical aggression. Girls differed in how well they fared in these complex social interactions. Some emerged at the top of the social ladder and were admired but feared by their peers. Others found themselves more frequently in the victim role.

The increased focus on alternative forms of aggression has prompted proposals to add female-specific symptom criteria to research and clinical protocols assessing aggression and antisocial behavior. Yet, to date, there are no empirical findings to support the inclusion of sex-specific criteria. Research is required that comprehensively maps the construct of aggression by including traditional and contemporary indicators to determine whether aggression is truly gendered.

A Gender-Sensitive Perspective on Risk and Resilience

Gender-Specific Risk Factors and Developmental Trajectories

As more research is devoted to the topic of female aggression, a key question is whether female-specific theories of aggressive and violent behavior are required. To date there is no comprehensive theory of the development of antisocial or aggressive behavior that is *specific* to females. Many studies using normative samples show that the majority of the known risk factors for aggression in boys, such as parental criminality, family conflict/violence, physical maltreatment, sensation seeking, low IQ, and poor self-esteem, also increase risk for girls. However, some studies comparing risk and normative samples, and studies focused only on high-risk samples, suggest that certain risk factors have a greater effect on risk in girls. For example, some research has shown that girls who experience physical abuse and family breakdown are at much higher risk for aggression than girls not exposed to these risks. Yet some studies have shown that these risk factors are unrelated to violence in boys. Other research has suggested that cumulative social risk factors differentiate early versus later onset of aggression problems in girls, while biological factors differentiate early versus later onset aggression in boys.

Such findings have given rise to a new perspective on the problem of aggression in girls, one that focuses on the importance of relational contexts in female development and adjustment. Moretti, Obsuth, Odgers, and Penney's findings concur with this view, showing that girls at high risk for aggression are more likely than boys to have a history of early removal from their biological parents; more frequent care outside their parental home; and greater likelihood of being relinquished by their parents to government care. Although very high rates of maltreatment of both girls and boys have been found, girls report higher rates of physical maltreatment by their mothers and higher rates of sexual abuse than do boys.

The fact that similar findings have emerged across both normative and high-risk samples suggests that these results are not merely artifacts of extreme populations and may bear relevance to understanding girls' development and aggression more generally. This research was recently summarized by Miriam Ehrensaft, who concluded that (a) disrupted relationships are more likely to give rise to aggression and antisocial behavior in girls than boys, (b) aggression is more likely to be expressed within close relationships by girls than boys, and (c) the long-term impact of aggression on development is more likely to extend to relationship domains for girls than boys. Longitudinal research is required with samples of girls at high risk, to understand fully the links among relational contexts, risk and developmental pathways, and consequences of aggressive behavior.

Protective Factors

Relational factors (e.g., positive family, peer, and romantic partner relationships) and social supports appear to be important in reducing vulnerability to risk for aggressive behavior, and perhaps particularly so for girls. The protective benefit of positive social relationships may extend outside the family. For example, research shows that having a boyfriend who is at least moderately prosocial during adolescence can be a protective factor for highly aggressive and antisocial girls. More research is needed to identify key protective factors, particularly those that buffer girls growing up in adverse environments—as is the typical case for girls within high-risk clinical and forensic samples.

Developmental Trajectories

Findings are mixed on whether developmental trajectories are comparable for girls and boys. Terrie Moffitt and colleagues have argued that the distinction between early onset life-course persistent and adolescent time-limited trajectories applies similarly to girls and boys. Others have questioned the applicability of this distinction to females because aggressive and antisocial behavior in girls more often emerges in adolescence and carries the same poor prognosis as early onset aggression and antisocial behavior in boys.

Developmental Consequences

Even with the onset of aggressive behavior delayed until adolescence, girls involved in aggression are more likely to leave school early, achieve limited occupational success, and rely on social assistance to support themselves and their children. If they become romantically involved with older delinquent boys, they are particularly at risk for poor adjustment. As they transition to adulthood, girls involved in aggressive and antisocial behavior are likely to experience a wide range of psychiatric and social adjustment problems, including early sexual involvement and pregnancy and higher rates of divorce and child custody loss.

The physical health costs associated with antisocial behavior are just beginning to be realized. There is reason to believe that the interplay between mental and physical health may be particularly critical for females. While normative samples are providing insights into the relationships between developmental trajectories of antisocial behavior and mental and physical health outcomes, virtually nothing is known about this relationship among adolescent girls and young women at the highest level of risk.

Cultural and Social Marginalization

A disproportionate number of non-Caucasian girls from impoverished backgrounds are incarcerated: African American girls in the United States and Aboriginal girls in Canada are unquestionably overrepresented in the juvenile justice system. Research on social and cultural marginalization of ethnocultural minority girls and problems of aggressive and antisocial behavior is extremely limited. Understanding how protective factors influence adjustment is critical, especially with regard to girls of minority status who also frequently grow up in impoverished inner-city neighborhoods.

Future Research

Why study the causes, concomitants, and consequences of aggressive and antisocial behavior in girls? Beyond the opportunity to generate new knowledge to enhance the social, physical, and mental well-being of girls, the potential for cost-saving is extraordinarily high. The presence of severe behavioral problems in conjunction with other mental health problems, such as depression, substantially inflates health service costs, totaling as much as $13,000 per child for outpatient services in a 6-month period. Beyond mental health costs, forensic services for youth with serious aggressive and antisocial behavior consume substantial public funds. A recent estimate in the United Kingdom puts the cost of incarceration at £4,645 (US$ 9,145) *per month*. These estimates do not include other social costs incurred by victims, or projected lifetime costs that result from lower educational achievement, poor vocational adjustment, and early parenthood. Importantly, these estimates fail to include the costs of increased risk in children of mothers with a history of severe behavior problems. The lack of knowledge and the high cost of health and forensic services associated with serious aggressive and antisocial behavior calls for an investment in research on aggressive and antisocial behavior in girls.

Marlene Marie Moretti, Ingrid Obsuth,
Candice L. Odgers, and Stephanie R. Penney

See also Bullying; Delinquency and Violence; Parenting Practices and Violence; Youth Violence; Sexual Abuse; Youth Violence

Further Readings

Ehrensaft, M. K. (2005). Interpersonal relationships and sex differences in the development of conduct problems. *Clinical Child and Family Psychology Review, 8*(1), 39–63.

Kim-Cohen, J., Moffitt, T. E., & Caspi, A. (2004). Genetic and environmental processes in young children's resilience and vulnerability to socioeconomic deprivation. *Child Development, 75*(3), 651–668.

Moffitt, T., Caspi, A., & Rutter, M., & Silva, P. (2001). *Sex differences in antisocial behavior: Conduct disorder, delinquency, and violence in the Dunedin longitudinal study.* New York: Cambridge University Press.

Moretti, M. M., Obsuth, I., Odgers, C., & Reebye, P. (2006). Exposure to maternal versus paternal partner violence, PTSD, and aggression in adolescent girls and boys. *Aggressive Behavior, 32*(4), 385–395.

Moretti, M. M., Odgers, C., & Jackson, M. (2004). *Girls and aggression: Contributing factors and intervention principles.* New York: Kluwer-Plenum.

Pepler, D., Madsen, K. C., & Webster, C. (2005). *The development and treatment of girlhood aggression.* Mahwah, NJ: Lawrence Erlbaum.

FEMALE PERPETRATORS OF VIOLENCE AGAINST CHILDREN

Across most cultures and societies women are viewed as having the defined role as nurturing caregivers for children. The idea of women as violence perpetrators is so counter to the expected norms in society that social scientists have done little research in the area. The last decade has seen a focused attempt by both state and federal governments to gather statistics on violence toward children. Thus the figures are showing that in fact women are perpetrators of violence in substantial numbers. Concrete research into understanding who these women are and how to help them is just beginning to emerge.

Violence Against Children

Child violence is most often described in terms of child abuse. Child abuse is further delineated into physical abuse, sexual abuse, emotional/psychological abuse, and neglect. Violence against children is most often associated with physical abuse or with sexual abuse. Extreme neglect may also be viewed as a benign form of violence, especially if it results in a child death. Gender information on the identified perpetrator is not always collected, making it difficult to gather an accurate picture. Furthermore, children who are victims of female-perpetrated violence tend not to disclose to the degree they would if the perpetrator was male. This is especially true for male victims of female-perpetrated sexual abuse.

Physical Abuse

Physical abuse of children is most often defined as a nonaccidental injury to a child. Such an injury usually results in bruising or physical impairment. Physical abuse can include kicking, biting, burning, or physically striking a child. U.S. data on child abuse for 2005 show that approximately 17% (150,000) of substantiated reports of child abuse were identified as physical abuse. Of these, 40% (60,000) had the child's mother identified as the sole perpetrator. The incidence of women's involvement in physical violence rises to close to 70% when one adds all occurrences involving other female perpetrators who acted alone or with others.

Sexual Abuse

Sexual abuse perpetrated by women has been a little understood phenomenon as well as scantily researched. Studies in the 1990s reported estimates of women perpetrators to be from as low as 5% of all known child sex abuse cases to as high as 60%. Several well-regarded researchers in the late 1990s confirmed that the actual numbers were close to 25% of all sex abuse cases of children, irrespective of child gender. The U.S. data from 2005 show that of all child abuse types, 9.3% (84,000) were identified as sex abuse. If current research holds on the numbers of

female perpetrators, then in 2005 there were approximately 21,000 occurrences of sexual abuse of children committed by women.

Other Forms of Violence

Besides physical and sexual abuse, children are exposed to situations of profound neglect leading to mortality as well as other rare forms of perverse parenting. Of the 1,371 deaths of children reported through child welfare agencies in the United States in 2005, 72% of the deaths were caused by some form of neglect. Approximately 58% of the perpetrators were women, and of these 45% were under the age of 30. A rare form of mental illness called *Munchausen syndrome by proxy* also may cause serious harm, if not death, to children. This disorder is characterized by a deliberate attempt to make a child ill or a repeated attempt to fabricate a child's having a serious illness. In most cases the mother has been identified as the primary perpetrator.

Causes of Female-Perpetrated Violence Against Children

Research is scarce on the causation of female-perpetrated violence against children. Perhaps the statistics reflect the cultural norm of women as caregivers, and by default women and children end up spending most of their time together. Furthermore, child violence statistics tend to reflect that responsibility for the violence belongs to primary caregivers. Studies that have examined this cohort of violent women have come up with the following findings:

- Many women who perpetrate violence on children have come from a violent childhood themselves. They may believe that violence toward children is appropriate.
- These women tend to be under 30 years of age.
- In most cases of sole female violence, the women were single parents. This may attest to the added stress of child-rearing responsibilities not being shared.
- Substance abuse and mental health issues are common among these women.

In cases of sexual abuse, women's profiles are similar to their profiles in other forms of violence, with these added exceptions:

- Women sexual perpetrators rarely coerce their victims. This is probably due to the fact they are often in a very trusting position with the child victim.
- Compared to men, women start sexual abuse much older, usually in adulthood.
- Women tend to use fewer threats to silence their victims. They also rarely deny their actions when confronted.

In cases of Munchausen syndrome by proxy, the perpetrators have an unusual need for attention that they express through having an "ill" child or a child with special needs. The attention they receive from the medical professionals is more important to them than the needs of their child. These perpetrators become even more dangerous if they realize that someone suspects them of acting deliberately. They tend to have a vast health care knowledge and change medical providers often so as to avoid detection.

Though it is difficult to generalize the profiles of women who perpetrate violence on children, it is beginning to be understood that overall these women use violence to satisfy a need for power and control through their actions against children.

Social Issues With Women as Violent Perpetrators

As stated at the beginning of this entry, most societies find it very difficult to label women as violent perpetrators of children—especially in the area of sexual abuse, where the abuse is often defined as penile penetration. A woman is rarely labeled as a perpetrator in rape. This speaks more to the society's definition of rape than the woman's role as the person responsible for the sexual assault. In a recent study of females convicted of sexual abuse, over 50% of them stated they derived sadistic pleasure from inflicting pain on their victims. Nonetheless, in this society women are consistently seen as victims of violence not perpetrators.

Victims of female violence have a more difficult time disclosing their abuse. A survey of 127 known victims of sexual assault by females found that 86% of them were not believed at their first disclosure. Very young children who have been physically abused are unable to be verbal about their perpetrator. It is left up to investigators to re-create the child's recent past, and in most cases there is a bias to examine exposure to males. Another issue for victims is that professionals

do not expect abuse from women, thus the victims tend to have longer exposure to the abuse, feel more victimized and powerless, and feel betrayed by those in their lives who are supposed to protect them.

The criminal and judicial systems tend to have a bias in favor of females accused of perpetrating violence. Studies show that women who are convicted of violence toward children are given more lenient sentencing than male perpetrators. The rules of evidence in sexual assault are difficult to follow since female sexually perpetrated abuse may not leave concrete DNA samples.

Violence by women against children is starting to be uncovered, and the incidence might be much larger than previously thought. Intervention techniques for these violent women will be different from those currently utilized for men. Furthermore, victims of female abuse have unique experiences that require sensitive practitioners.

Timothy Brett Zuel

See also Abusive Behavior Inventory; Battered Child Syndrome; Child Fatalities; Female Perpetrators of Interpersonal Violence; Infanticide; Victim Precipitation Theories

Further Readings

Boroughs, D. S. (2004). Female sexual abusers of children. *Children and Youth Services Review, 26,* 481–487.
Finkelhor, D., & Russell, D. (1984). Women as perpetrators. In D. Finkelhor (Ed.), *Child sexual abuse: New theory and research* (pp. 171–187). New York: Free Press
Lasher, L. J. (2004). *Munchausen by proxy: MBP basics.* Retrieved December 16, 2006, from http://www.mbpexpert.com/definition.html
Trickett, P., & Schellenbach, C. (1998). *Violence against children in the family and community.* Washington, DC: American Psychological Association.

FEMALE SLAVERY/CHILD SLAVERY

Slavery exists today despite international and domestic laws prohibiting ownership of a person or compulsory labor. Article 1 of the Slavery Convention of 1926 defines slavery as the "status or condition of a person over whom any or all of the powers attaching to the right of ownership are exercised." In 1930, the International Labour Organization Convention (No. 29) expanded the definition of slavery to include compulsory labor. Article 2.1 of the Slavery Convention prohibits "work or service which is exacted from any person under the menace of any penalty and for which the said person has not offered himself voluntarily." Slaves are under the control of other people and lack the ability to exercise their free will or earn compensation for the work they produce.

Slavery persists for many reasons, including poverty, a lack of opportunity for education or employment, and warfare. Additionally, in some countries there is a social acquiescence in the exploitation of women and children. Modern forms of slavery are prevalent in Southeast Asia, Africa, and Latin America, and can include forced labor, debt bondage, trafficking of persons for sexual slavery or other purposes, and child soldiers.

Child Slavery

The exploitation of children is a phenomenon that exists throughout the world. The International Labour Organization estimates that 120 million children under the age of 15 are employed full time and are often uncompensated for their work. Such full-time employment prevents children from attending school and often exposes them to hazardous conditions.

Domestic slavery is common in many countries because of the economic disparities created by a growing middle class and increased rural poverty. Young girls from rural communities are sold by their families to middlemen in exchange for a purchasing price and, in some cases, a monthly stipend. These families are destitute and easily convinced their children will have a better life in an urban center with the opportunity to attend school and obtain employment in the home of a wealthier family. However, once the children reach their employer's home they are forced to work long hours, and as they tend to the household duties, are often the first to rise and last to sleep. They are not given the opportunity to attend school and are often exposed to severe abuse by employers who view them as property. Sexual abuse is especially prevalent because domestic servants are hidden from public view in the privacy of an employer's home. Domestic servants may be as young as 5 years old and are unable to defend themselves against the verbal, physical, and sexual abuse of their employers.

Another common form of child slavery in developing countries occurs in the manufacturing sector, with women and young children working in factories and sweatshops under grueling conditions. The global demand for textiles, apparel, footwear, and cheap labor continues to perpetuate this slavery. Employers circumvent local labor laws by housing underaged employees in homes or small shops. Children are often forced to work under threat of physical abuse and are compensated little to nothing for their work.

Debt Bondage

The practice of debt bondage is a financial agreement whereby a debtor pledges to provide his or her personal services, or the services of someone under his or her control, as security for a debt. Children are often bonded by their families in exchange for a loan they have taken from a creditor or employer. Others are born into a bonded family, a practice that is common in India, Nepal, and Pakistan.

In India, destitute parents needing money to pay for food or other expenses, such as expenses arising from an illness in the family, can offer their child in exchange for a loan. The creditor or employer forces the child to work as repayment. The child can work and save to purchase his or her freedom or work until his or her family repays the loan. However, high interest rates are attached to these loans by the creditor or employer so that the child is unable to earn enough to purchase his or her freedom and the family's low wages, which forced them to seek a high interest rate loan in the first place, make repaying the loan impossible. As a result, the child may pass the family debt on to a younger sibling or his or her own child.

In Pakistan and other rural and agricultural countries, children may be born into a bonded family. This type of debt bondage usually stems from a sharecropping arrangement where families seek loans to pay for seeds, fertilizer, and the other supplies they need to buy before they can earn the income from their first harvest. This type of arrangement promotes violence on multiple levels, where a landowner is physically or verbally abusive toward the children as well as the parents. In some cases, children must witness abuse directed at their parents by the landowner. These loans are also offered with a high interest rate and perpetuate generations of debt bondage.

Trafficking and Sexual Slavery

The trafficking of women and girls for sexual slavery is a global problem. Statistics on the number of women involved and their countries of origin are nearly impossible to obtain because human trafficking is an illegal and underground business that often involves organized crime. The United Nations Development Fund for Women estimates that 700,000 to 2 million women and girls are trafficked each year. From 1990 to 1997, more than 200,000 Bangladeshi women were victims of trafficking and 5,000 to 7,000 Nepali women and girls were illegally trafficked into India. In Belgium, 10% to 15% of foreign prostitutes were trafficked from other countries and sold into prostitution rings. Increased concerns about the transmission of HIV/AIDS have made young girls the primary target of traffickers for the global sex industry.

Traffickers utilize several techniques to capture women and children. They often lure women with the prospect of well-paying jobs as domestic servants, waitresses, or factory workers. They also lure women by telling them they will be mail-order brides for eligible suitors or have modeling careers abroad. Traffickers also resort to kidnapping young women and girls or purchasing them from their families, with the promise of greater opportunity for employment and a better life. However, this promise is not kept in most circumstances and the young women and girls are forced into lives of sexual slavery.

During confinement many women and girls experience violence, including rape, physical and verbal abuse, and threats to harm their family if they refuse to engage in forced sexual activity. There is generally no hope of escape for these victims, because many of them are in a foreign country without travel documents, are meagerly compensated for the services they perform and cannot earn enough to repay their purchase price, or have no one to help them, since they are too ashamed to tell their families they are prostitutes. Young girls who are forced into sexual slavery experience severe physical and psychological trauma that often causes irreparable harm.

Child Soldiers

In 2006, the United Nations estimated that nearly 250,000 children worldwide were actively involved in armed conflict. The majority of these children are located in the war-torn countries of Africa, such as Uganda, Liberia, and Sierra Leone. Children are abducted, trained as soldiers, and forced to engage in combat that is hazardous to their well-being. They are often captured during combat after their parents are killed, and are threatened with violence if they refuse to fight. In cases where a child soldier unsuccessfully attempts to escape, the child is executed as punishment and as an example for potential deserters. The youngest children are often placed on the front lines of a war because they are less demanding, eat less, and are more easily manipulated than adults. Moreover, they are often sent into battle high on drugs to give them courage. Child soldiers become slaves of the military forces that control them because they engage in combat to avoid abuse or are used as slave labor for carrying military supplies. The lives of child soldiers can be mentally and emotionally traumatizing because they are forced to experience war, death, and murder at a young age.

April J. Guillen

See also Commercial Sexual Exploitation of Children; Sex Tourism; Trafficking, Human

Further Readings

Bales, K. (1999). *Disposable people: New slavery in the global economy.* Berkeley: University of California Press.

Blagbrough, J., & Glynn, E. (1999). *Child domestic workers: Characteristics of the modern slave and approaches to ending such exploitation.* Thousand Oaks, CA: Sage.

Estacio, E., & Marks, D. (2005). *Child labour and the International Labour Organization's Convention 182: A critical perspective.* London: City University.

International Labour Organization Convention. *C29 Forced Labour Convention, 1930.* Retrieved July 25, 2007, from http://www.ilo.org/ilolex/english/convdisp1.htm

Office of the United Nations High Commissioner for Human Rights. *Slavery Convention.* Retrieved July 25, 2007, from http://www.ohchr.org/english/law/slavery.htm

FEMICIDE

Femicide is the murder of women. It is one of the top five causes of premature death in the United States for young women from 20 to 49 years old.

Intimate Partner Femicide

U.S. women are murdered by an intimate partner (IP) (husband, boyfriend) or former partner approximately nine times more often than by strangers. According to recent research, between 40% and 50% of women killed by a known perpetrator are killed by an IP, compared to 5.5% of men killed by an intimate partner. African American women die at the hands of men almost three times as often as do White women, with Native American and Hispanic women also having higher rates of IP femicide. In New York City, immigrant women were found to be more at risk for IP femicide than those born in the United States. Also important are IP attempted femicides, with approximately eight such near fatal incidents occurring for every actual femicide.

The vast majority (67% to 80%) of IP homicides involve physical abuse of the female by the male partner or ex-partner before the murder, no matter which partner is killed. Thus, prior domestic violence against the female partner is the number one risk factor for IP homicide. During the last 20 years of the 20th century, IP homicides decreased by almost 50% in the United States, with rates decreasing far more for male victims (67.8%) than female victims (30.1%). The rates have since stabilized. The decreases in IP homicides occurred during the same time period as national social programs and legal interventions to reduce intimate partner violence, and in states where the laws and resources (shelters and crisis hotlines) were the most available, there were the greatest decreases in women killing male intimate partners. Increases in women's resources, decreases in marriage rates, domestic violence policies such as pro-arrest mandates, as well as decreases in gun accessibility are all associated with the decreases in IP homicides.

A recent national case control study found the following factors most strongly associated with increased IP femicide risks *over and above prior domestic violence:* perpetrator access to a gun, estrangement, perpetrator unemployment, perpetrator highly controlling, perpetrator threatens to kill partners, prior threats or use of weapons against their partners, biological child of female partner not the perpetrator's, and forced sex.

Protective factors were the victim and perpetrator never living together and prior arrest for domestic violence.

Femicide-Suicide

Recent research has found that in about a third of the cases of IP femicide, or about 400 cases per year, the male partner kills himself (and sometimes his children) after killing his partner. Only about 1 case of IP homicide-suicide per year involves a female killing a male partner. The major risk factors, including prior domestic violence, are the same as for IP femicide cases without suicide, with an additional factor of prior threats or attempted suicide by the perpetrator. Suicidal perpetrators are more likely to be married and employed and less likely to use illicit drugs than those perpetrators who do not kill themselves. These differences suggest that men who kill their partners and then kill themselves may appear to be somewhat less dangerous than other batterers seen in domestic violence systems. Even so, the femicide-suicide perpetrators and the perpetrators who do not commit suicide engendered a similar amount of fear in their partners (with 53% and 49%, respectively, thinking their partner was capable of killing them).

Same-Sex Intimate Partner Homicide

According to the research, the proportion of IP homicide committed by same-sex partners is six times greater for gay men than lesbians. From the nine female perpetrated cases of IP femicide and attempted femicide in the large multicity study described above, prior physical violence, controlling behaviors, jealousy, alcohol and drugs, and ending the relationship were consistently reported antecedents to the murder. These findings support that power and control are central to models of IP femicide, whether it is perpetrated by a man or a woman.

Maternal Mortality and Intimate Partner Femicide

The national homicide database does not indicate whether a woman was pregnant or had recently had a baby when she was killed. However, a review of the national mortality surveillance system data by the Centers for Disease Control and Prevention has demonstrated that homicide is the second leading cause of injury-related maternal mortality and pregnancy-associated death in the United States, causing 2 maternal deaths for every 100,000 live births. In several major urban areas, homicide is the leading cause of maternal mortality, causing as many as 20% of maternal deaths. Although the national data do not allow the identification of the perpetrator in these maternal mortality homicides, it may be that the majority of the homicides were committed by an IP and preceded by domestic violence against the woman. Abuse during pregnancy was associated with a threefold increase in risk of IP-completed or -attempted femicide in the multicity femicide study. These findings lend support to the proposal that health care settings, including prenatal care, need to assess for domestic violence and intervene to help those at risk.

Prevention Strategies

Even though femicide has decreased, IP violence ends with femicide all too frequently. Many studies have identified characteristics of IP femicide that distinguish it from other forms of homicide, but there is still a lack of systematic research studies on several issues, especially femicide-suicides, maternal mortality femicide, and ethnic-specific issues. Although research to date suggests that the disproportionate risk related to ethnic/racial minority status is primarily a reflection of poverty, discrimination, and unemployment and their negative consequences, which result in a lack of access to resources that could prevent IP homicide, the research is not conclusive.

It is clear that the most important strategies to prevent IP femicide are the reduction of IP violence and the identification of cases at most risk for IP femicide, with interventions targeted especially to the immediate 3 months after an abused woman leaves her batterer. Addressing perpetrators' access to guns is particularly important. Where shelters, legal advocates, health care professionals, and police are trained to intervene collaboratively in cases of domestic violence, and where communities are aware of IP violence and femicide, women and children are more likely to survive the violence in their lives.

Jacquelyn C. Campbell

See also Danger Assessment Instrument; Domestic Violence Fatality Review; Intimate Partner Violence; Maternal Homicide

Further Readings

Brock, K. (2005). *When men murder women: An analysis of 2003 homicide data.* Violence Policy Center. Retrieved from http://www.vpc.org

Campbell, J. C. (2007). *Assessing dangerousness: Violence by batterers and child abusers.* New York: Springer.

Campbell, J. C., Glass, N. E., Sharps, P. W., Laughon, K., & Bloom, T. (2007). Intimate partner homicide: Review and implications for research and policy. *Violence, Trauma & Abuse, 8*(3), 246–269.

Campbell, J. C., Webster, D., Koziol-McLain, J., Block, C., Campbell, D., Curry, M. A., et al. (2003). Risk factors for femicide in abusive relationships: Results from a multi-site case control study. *American Journal of Public Health, 93*(7), 1089–1097.

Dobash, R. E., Dobash, R. P., Cavanagh, K., & Lewis, R. (2004). Not an ordinary killer—Just an ordinary guy. When men murder an intimate woman partner. *Violence Against Women, 10,* 577–605.

Dugan, L., Nagin, D., & Rosenfeld, R. (2003). Do domestic violence services save lives? *National Institute of Justice Journal, 250,* 20–25.

Fox, J. A., & Zawitz, M. W. (2004). *Homicide trends in the US.* U.S. Department of Justice. Retrieved from http://www.ojp.usdoj/bjs/

Frye, V., Hosein, V., Waltermaurer, E., Blaney, S., & Wilt, S. (2005). Femicide in New York City, 1990 to 1999. *Homicide Studies, 9,* 204–228.

Koziol-McLain, J., et al. (2006). Risk factors for femicide-suicide in abusive relationships: Results from a multi-site case control study. *Violence and Victims, 21,* 3–21.

Vigdor, E. R., & Mercy, J. A. (2006). Do laws restricting access to firearms by domestic violence offenders prevent intimate partner homicide? *Evaluation Review, 30,* 313–346.

Websdale, N. (1999). *Understanding domestic homicide.* Boston: Northeastern University Press.

FEMINIST MOVEMENTS TO END VIOLENCE AGAINST WOMEN

Women's resistance to men's violence against women seems to be a constant through known history. The terms of that resistance have changed, and yet are often bound up with ideas around gender, sexuality, class, race, colonialism, and other historical systems of oppression. Collective efforts in the United States to address men's violence against women consistently occur within the context of social and political movements addressing systemic inequality, oppression, and violence, including the antislavery movement, women's rights movements, Black women's club and antilynching movements, and anticolonial, socialist, and labor movements, among others. This entry focuses on the feminist movements aimed at ending violence against women.

Social and Political Movements

The issue of violence against women gained prominence in the United States within the context of contemporary feminist movements of the 1970s and their connections with the Black nationalist, civil rights, La Raza, lesbian and gay, American Indian, antiwar, and other social movements of the 20th century. The explicit naming of violence against women as a tool of social power and control serves as yet another rupture in public consciousness about the personal and social realities of the gender-specific violence in women's lives. Feminist movements struggle to challenge and change a mainstream discourse that mostly constructs this violence as individual women's problems to be borne in silence and shame, except in the cases of interracial rape involving men of color and White women. In the latter case, the socially constructed myth of the "stranger" and often Black rapist of "innocent" White womanhood circulates and is responsible for justifying the lynching and incarceration of African American as well as Latino, poor, and/or working class men.

Feminist movements since the late 1960s have created contexts for women to understand their experiences of men's mistreatment, abuse, harassment, and violence in an effort to challenge and ultimately end violence against women. Many women participate in consciousness-raising groups, direct action groups, and other forums to name, analyze, and strategize to end this violence. They politicize their experiences by linking them to gender-based subordination with its connection to interlocking systems of oppression. Feminist movements provide validation, support, and recognition of women's stories, develop analyses and theories based on these stories, and collectively engage in political action to change everything—from individual selves to the culture to the social, legal, and religious institutions, to the entire world.

Forms of Violence

As a result of this movement, thousands of women (and increasingly men) have testified to the many forms of interpersonal, public, and state violence in the lives of women, men, and children across race, class, sexual orientation, ethnicity, religion, and other social groups and identities as well as contexts. The forms of violence include physical, sexual, emotional, verbal, and economic violence, among others, and occur in intrafamilial, intimate, and interpersonal relationships on the street, in the workplace, and in educational, medical, prison, and military institutions—as well as in contexts of war, colonial and imperial domination, and through globalized markets and industries (including prostitution and pornography, among others). Most feminist antiviolence work has focused on men's gender-based violence against women, although feminists continually negotiate and conflict with one another over the limits of focusing on men's violence as if men were always/already the perpetrators and women always/already the victims. Some groups in the United States, particularly incest survivor and child sexual abuse groups and lesbian, gay, bisexual, transgender, and queer (LGBTQ) groups, tend to include women as perpetrators of violence as well as men as victims of interpersonal and familial violence. Other groups have increasingly recognized the realities of violence against men that may be motivated by gender, sexuality, race, and other systems of domination (e.g., antigay violence, gang violence, rape in prison, lynching, militarized torture). In addition, increasingly, feminists who struggle to address the realities of structural violence and violence stemming from interlocking systems of oppression and privilege that cannot be reduced to patriarchal violence continue to expand and make complex their analysis of violence and what would need to change to end it.

Organizations, Initiatives, and Projects

Thousands of organizations, initiatives, and projects have developed to address the endemic violence in women's lives. These draw from many different perspectives, approaches, and strategies and focus on individual, community, institutional, and/or international change. In general, they provide validation, critical analysis, resources, activism and advocacy, and more; they include survivor groups, direct action organizations, rape crisis centers, domestic violence agencies and shelters, prison rights and prison abolitionist groups, human rights organizations, and grassroots community organizing and community accountability initiatives. Feminist activism against violence has taken a variety of forms—including direct action protests, civil disobedience, demonstrations and vigils, speakouts, Take Back the Night marches, spoken word performances, art exhibits and installations, newsletters and zines, safe home networks and legal defense organizations, civil and criminal court cases, legislative and judicial reform, and social and institutional change. Some individuals and groups publicly confront their perpetrators in efforts to create community accountability, while others press criminal charges, and/or file civil suits (a method successfully used by some adult incest survivors against their fathers).

The contemporary movement's approaches to the violence in women's lives have taken multiple perspectives. In the United States, the most mainstream sources of the broadly based movement to end violence have become more integrated into the hegemonic system. Some organizations that began as feminist political action and advocacy groups have become more institutionalized in ideology, structure, and connection with the welfare, criminal justice, and health care systems. Many citywide and state organizations have become dependent on governmental and foundation funding. Collectives have thus, in some cases, turned into organizations with hierarchies of paid staff whose credentials are increasingly dependent upon professional degrees and who decreasingly possess firsthand knowledge of violence and a connection to grassroots activism in the community. Many rape crisis and advocacy organizations and domestic violence agencies are modeled on traditional social services and work closely with the criminal justice system, efforts to end sexual harassment have morphed into policy offices in educational and/or corporate institutions, and the feminist challenge to endemic child sexual abuse is now oriented toward traditional counseling and therapy rather than politics. Because of their ties to state and national government and foundation funding, policies, and institutions, they are less connected to more politicized feminist analysis and politics in their approaches and strategies. A major result of these changes is that the movement has become oriented to managing the violence in women's lives, rather than committed to ending the violence and the social systems of inequality that perpetuate it.

Mainstream organizations tend to approach the violence in women's lives with a monolithic framework that emphasizes the commonalities in gender-based violence against women and often marginalizes and/or overlooks differences in race, class, sexual orientation, and social, historical, and/or political context. In many ways these organizational initiatives look less like social movement organizations and more like social service agencies. Political analysis and strategy has been supplanted by a focus on interpersonal and familial violence. These groups approach differences in women's (and men's) experiences in terms of individual cultural and/or personal differences between women and the need for specialized services for "other" women (i.e., women who are not White, middle class, heterosexual, U.S. citizens).

In part, in response to these universalizing approaches, women of color, lesbians, women in the sex trade, and disabled women, among others, continue to develop their own initiatives based on a recognition of how race, ethnicity, religion, and/or sexual orientation shape the experience and response to this violence. These initiatives tend to situate their strategies and actions within the particular cultural and social contexts in which the violence takes place. They are as focused on a critical analysis of the social and institutional responses to the violence, including barriers to service and/or justice given these contexts, as on the inequalities underlying these responses. In addition, they consider the particular cultural and/or religious and/or spiritual identities and beliefs of women in their communities. For instance, there are a number of faith-based organizations and networks that have been generated by Muslim, Jewish, and Christian communities, as well as ones focused on South Asian, Latino/a, Asian American, African American, and LGBTQ communities.

A critical mass of feminist antiviolence initiatives—often led by women of color, poor women, queer women, women in the sex trade, formerly incarcerated women, women with disabilities—focus on social and structural forms of violence. These groups often critique the mainstream focus on individual experience and identity, with its preference for psychology and social service, and reorient the movement to address how race, class, globalization, militarism, and colonialism shape the pervasiveness and context of the violence and the forms of resistance needed to address it. The work of Incite! Women of Color Against Violence focuses on the intersections of interpersonal and state violence. Critically challenging the overreliance of the mainstream movement on the criminal justice system, Incite! initiates ideas, gatherings, and actions to generate ideas around community accountability to end violence against women and to create discussions and collaborations between antiviolence activists and those focused on addressing the prison industrial complex. An increasing number of antiviolence projects are bringing attention to state violence against women, including police harassment and brutality, sexual abuse of women in prison, and Immigration and Naturalization Service violence against migrant and immigrant women in the United States and along the U.S.–Mexico border.

Men who identify themselves as allies and/or profeminists have been consistently involved in contemporary feminist antiviolence movements. There are organizations, activist projects, newsletters, and educational initiatives that focus on men's responsibility for the perpetuation of men's violence against women, on men's privilege and the need for accountability, and on the social construction of masculinities and the relationship to sexual and other forms of violence. In addition, profeminist men have sought to research and explore systems of privilege and their own implication for the perpetuation of privilege and power, as well as violence.

Mass Media

Another major focus of feminist movements to end violence has been on the contributions of the mass media in perpetuating violence and the apathy and victim blaming that is so endemic to social and institutional responses to violence. There are a variety of critical media projects addressing the pervasive violence in the mass industries of advertising, popular culture, and pornography. In this arena, feminists educate the public about the connection between the media and pervasive violence in women's lives. Many argue that the media and popular culture are responsible for cultural ideas that justify, normalize, minimize, and deny the significance of the many forms of violence against women. They see the ideology of the media as creating a context of apathy, denial, and victim blaming, and seek to find ways to hold the media accountable. The strategies include creating campaigns against particular advertisements, media literacy campaigns to create critical consciousness, and alternative media that offer alternative images, stories, and counternarratives.

International Initiatives

U.S. feminist efforts to address and end violence against women are intricately tied to initiatives around the world. There have been a number of international

tribunals on the specific issue of violence against women. Activists from around the world have used the United Nations Conferences in Mexico, Copenhagen, Nairobi, and Beijing and other international women's forums and gatherings to exchange information, ideas, and strategies. Each of these gatherings has had a central and vital focus on violence in women's lives. The violence connected to war and militarism continues to be a major source of international solidarity and action addressing violence against women in the contexts of war and imperialism. The international and transnational efforts toward connection and solidarity across nations and contexts are also fraught with tension and their own set of problems given a world in part shaped by imperialist domination and global power inequalities.

Ann Russo

See also Advocacy; Battered Women's Movement; Rape Culture

Further Readings

Buchwald, E., Fletcher, P. R., & Roth, M. (Eds.). (2005). *Transforming a rape culture* (Rev. ed.). Minneapolis, MN: Milkweed Editions.

Delacoste, F., & Newman, F. (1982). *Fight back! Feminist resistance to male violence.* Minneapolis, MN: Cleis Press.

Incite! Women of Color Against Violence. (2006). *Color of violence: The Incite! anthology.* Cambridge, MA: South End Press.

Kivel, P. (1992). *Men's work: How to stop the violence that tears our lives apart.* Center City, MN: Hazelden.

Matthews, N. A. (1994). *Confronting rape: The feminist antirape movement and the state.* New York: Routledge.

Morales, A. L. (1998). *Medicine stories: History, culture, and the politics of integrity.* Cambridge, MA: South End Press.

Ristock, J. L. (2002). *No more secrets: Violence in lesbian relationships.* New York: Routledge.

Russo, A. (2001). *Taking back our lives: A call to action in the feminist movement.* New York: Routledge.

Schechter, S. (1983). *Women and male violence: The visions and struggles of the battered women's movement.* Cambridge, MA: South End Press.

Waller, M. R., & Rycenga, J. (Eds.). (2001). *Frontline feminisms: Women, war, and resistance.* New York: Routledge.

FEMINIST THEORIES OF INTERPERSONAL VIOLENCE

There are various feminist theories of interpersonal violence (e.g., socialist feminism, standpoint feminism, multicultural feminism), but despite this diversity there is a set of assumptions that feminist theories share. First, feminist theorists see *gender*—that is, the socially constructed expectations, attitudes, and behaviors associated with females and males, typically organized dichotomously as *femininity* and *masculinity*—as a central organizing component of social life. This means that in studying any form of behavior, including violence, one must consider in what ways the behavior is gendered; in other words, one must study how gender influences the frequency of the behavior and how it is expressed. Furthermore, instead of conceptualizing gender as natural and dichotomous, feminist theorists see gender as a process that is shaped by and that shapes social action, opportunities, and experiences.

In making the argument that gender shapes and is shaped by social action, opportunities, and experiences, feminists are not claiming that the genders or gender relations are equal or symmetrical. Instead, a second assumption of feminist theories is that on both the structural and the interpersonal levels, one gender is valued over another, a phenomenon called *sexism*. In American society and many others, male voices and experiences have historically been privileged over female voices and experiences. At the same time, however, not all men are equally privileged, nor are all women disadvantaged equally. A third assumption of feminist theorists, then, is that gender intersects with other demographic factors, including social class, race and ethnicity, age, and sexual orientation, to influence advantage and disadvantage, behavior, opportunities, and experiences.

In theorizing violence, feminists reject traditional legalistic definitions that focus almost exclusively on forms of physical assault, such as beating, kicking, threatening with a weapon, or using a weapon against another person. Feminist theorists consider such definitions too narrow. Instead, feminist theorists adopt a broader definition of violence that includes sexual, psychological, and economic violence as well as physical violence. At the same time, feminist theorists

emphasize victims' perceptions and experiences along with the consequences of particular actions, instead of relying on purely legalistic criteria. For example, someone could be injured or harmed by behavior that does not involve physical assault, such as stalking or being constantly berated or insulted. Feminist theorists, therefore, define violence as any act—physical, sexual, or verbal—that is experienced by an individual as a threat, invasion, or assault and that has the effect of harming or degrading that individual or depriving her or him of the ability to control various aspects of daily life, including contact with others.

Early Feminist Theories of Interpersonal Violence

One early feminist perspective on interpersonal violence, the *liberation hypothesis,* was developed during the 1970s. Historically, women's rates of violent crime had been significantly lower than men's violent crime rates. During the 1970s, several reports indicated that women's rates of violent offending were not only increasing, but were increasing faster than those of men. Some theorists argued that these changes were the result of the women's liberation movement, which was giving women not only more legitimate opportunities, but also more illegitimate opportunities, including opportunities to engage in violent behavior. Careful reanalyses of crime data, however, showed that women's violent offending had not changed significantly and that the women who were being arrested for violent offenses could hardly be characterized as "liberated."

Most early feminist theorizing on interpersonal violence focused not on women's violent offending, but rather on men's violent victimization of women. Feminists pointed out that men's violence against women—for example, sexual assault, battering, incest, sexual harassment—had historically been overlooked by crime theorists. Feminists emphasized that women's victimization at the hands of men, especially men they knew and with whom they had intimate relationships, was more widespread than commonly thought. This violence, they argued, was a direct outgrowth of gender inequality, a means by which men preserve and reinforce their dominance and women's subordination in a patriarchal society. Men in patriarchal societies have greater access to resources and, therefore, greater power than women. Gender norms justify this inequality and bestow on men a sense of entitlement to women's bodies, services, and deference. Indeed, research with male perpetrators has documented their sense of entitlement as well as their motives for using violence to punish and control women.

More Recent Feminist Theorizing on Interpersonal Violence

Although rates of male violence against women are high, relatively few men actually violently victimize women. Recent feminist theorizing on interpersonal violence, then, has addressed the question of why some men find violent behavior, against women, children, and other men, rewarding. Feminist theorists are also examining women's use of violence in intimate relationships and other social contexts.

One theoretical model that has emerged from this research conceptualizes gender as something men and women *do* in response to contextualized norms of masculinity and femininity. This perspective rejects the notion of gender as a static social role. Instead, it sees gender as flexible, changing over time and from situation to situation, as males and females decide or choose how they will establish their masculinity or femininity, respectively, in a given set of circumstances. Such choices, of course, are constrained by structural conditions and learned normative expectations, as well as by a person's social class, race/ethnicity, sexual orientation, and age. But rather than producing a single, homogenous gender role for males and another for females, these conditions produce a multitude of masculinities and femininities, each influenced by the social positioning of the individual.

Violence, then, may be a means of doing gender in certain situations. For example, in studying the characteristics of typical hate crime perpetrators and their victims along with the characteristics of the crimes themselves, criminologist Barbara Perry argues that committing such crimes is a way of accomplishing a specific type of masculinity, hegemonic masculinity, which is White, Christian, able-bodied, and heterosexual. Similarly, criminologist Jody Miller, who has studied girl gang members, maintains that while girls sometimes behave in ways they think of as "masculine," such as fighting, at other times they embrace a feminine identity, as girlfriends of male gang

members or as mothers of young children. Moreover, while crime may be a way of "doing gender," gender may also be used to accomplish crime, such as when a woman capitalizes on her femininity in order to manipulate a robbery target into a situation that makes the crime easier to complete.

Feminist theorists also examine the ways in which violent victimization may be a pathway to criminal offending, including violent offending, especially for girls and women. Recent research indicates that girls who were sexually abused as children are significantly more likely than nonabused girls and than both abused and nonabused boys to be arrested for violent offenses. This pattern appears to hold in adulthood as well.

There are various other feminist theoretical approaches to understanding interpersonal violence. However, it should be clear that all feminist theories place gender at the center of the analysis and examine how gender intersects with other social locating factors to influence specific behavioral outcomes.

Claire M. Renzetti

See also Female Perpetrators of Interpersonal Violence

Further Readings

Miller, J. (1998). Up it up: Gender and the accomplishment of street robbery. *Criminology, 36,* 37–66.

Miller, J. (2002). The strengths and limits of "doing gender" for understanding street crime. *Theoretical Criminology, 6,* 433–460.

Perry, B. (2001). *In the name of hate: Understanding hate crime.* New York: Routledge.

Renzetti, C. M. (2004). Feminist theories of violent behavior. In M. A. Zahn, H. H. Brownstein, & S. L. Jackson (Eds.), *Violence: From theory to research* (pp. 131–143). Cincinnati, OH: LexisNexis.

FETICIDE

Feticide has been deemed the act or occurrence of terminating the life of a fetus, generally with the use of force and intention of harm against the mother. Feticide is particularly deemed as such when causing the termination of the life of the fetus is accomplished unlawfully. The term further includes the act of a purposefully caused miscarriage.

When reviewing the history of feticide the primary court case referenced is *Keeler v. Superior Court of Amador County*. This 1970 case involved the husband of a woman who was at the time 35 weeks pregnant with a fetus not fathered by the husband. The husband assaulted his wife after verbally indicating that his intent was to rid her body of the fetus. The fetus was delivered by cesarean section, without life, and found to have a fractured skull. The husband was charged with murder by use of section 187 in California law. The California Supreme Court found that by definition this law did not apply to the unborn child, and at the time feticide was not a criminal act in that state, as a fetus was not recognized as a human being until after birth.

It was after this ruling that many states began enacting feticide laws. Initially, the primary purpose of these laws was to guard the fetus from a third party, such as in the assault involving the aforementioned case of *Keeler v. Superior Court of Amador County*. Feticide laws essentially provided the fetus a separate defense from the mother and rights that had not been previously afforded.

It was in the late 1980s that the purpose of the feticide laws began to shift and, instead of separating mother from fetus for the purpose of providing a separate defense, the laws began to set mother and fetus in opposition to each other. Many of these laws increased the rights of the fetus while decreasing the rights of the mother.

Many states have feticide statutes that deal specifically with feticide, while others cover unlawful fetal death under general homicide statutes. The requirements determining whether a fetal death will be deemed a feticide or a homicide vary among jurisdictions. In either case, it is the terminology chosen by each jurisdiction to define the death as unlawful that must be considered. Some states' laws do not apply to the fetus at all stages, and many laws take into consideration the viability of the fetus. Other states require that the attacker be aware that the woman was pregnant at the time of the attack. Because the variation in definition from state to state is considerable, it is necessary to view the law of each jurisdiction individually.

Shannon Forbes Rushing

See also Femicide; Filicide; Homicides, Criminal; Infanticide

Further Readings

Faludi, S. (1991). *Backlash: The undeclared war against American women.* New York: Crown.
Garner, B. (Ed.). (2004). *Black's law dictionary* (8th ed.). St. Paul, MN: West.
Keeler v. Superior Court of Amador County, 87 Cal. Rptr. 481, 470 P. 2d 617 (1970).

FILICIDE

Filicide refers to the purposeful killing of a child, son or daughter, by his or her own parent. In addition, filicide identifies the parent who has killed his or her own child. A mother killing her own child can be further classified as maternal filicide. A father killing his own child can be further classified as paternal filicide.

In some cultures, and over a range of periods in history, the practice of killing one's child has for various reasons been deemed an acceptable practice. During ancient Roman times, a father was guaranteed the right by law to kill his children. This right was recognized as *patria potestas*. In countries such as China and India, a preference for male children historically has been accepted, thereby creating a culturally accepted killing of female infants. In other societies it has been acknowledged as a culturally customary event to kill newborns found to have birth defects.

Modern reasons for killing one's own child include, but are not limited to, monetary considerations, power, apprehension, and rejection. Due to economic issues, some cultures still deem it acceptable to kill one's child as a form of controlling family size.

The practice of child murder is not frequent. However, children are killed by their own parents more often than by other perpetrators, such as strangers. Children are considered to be most at risk during the first 24 hours after birth. A filicide during this time period is also termed *neonaticide*. It is in this time frame that most child murders occur, and babies, regardless of their sex, are most frequently killed by their mothers. Paternal filicide at this age is uncommon. It is estimated that more than 90% of male and female infants, 1 week old or younger, are killed by their mothers.

Child murders involving paternal filicide sometimes involve murder and suicide. The children are generally older than in maternal filicides, and involve child abuse that has turned fatal. Instances involving both children and spouse being killed are termed *familicide*. This practice is nearly exclusive to male perpetrators.

The ability to determine the actual number of filicides has been questioned, and there is disagreement as to whether the official number is too low. This is because some of the victims' deaths may have been incorrectly classified, for example, where they have been attributed to natural causes such as sudden infant death syndrome.

Shannon Forbes Rushing and Marc Riedel

See also Familicide; Femicide; Feticide; Homicides, Criminal; Infanticide

Further Readings

Garner, B. (Ed.). (2004). *Black's law dictionary* (8th ed.). St. Paul, MN: West.

Kunz, J., & Bahr, S. J. (1996). A profile of parental homicide against children. *Journal of Family Violence, 11*, 347–362.

Pitt, S., & Bale, E. (1995). Neonaticide, infanticide, and filicide: A review of the literature. *Bulletin of the American Academy of Psychiatry and the Law, 23*, 375–386.

Riedel, M., & Welsh, W. N. (in press). *Criminal violence: Patterns, causes, and prevention* (2nd ed.). Los Angeles: Roxbury.

Stanton, J., & Simpson, A. (2002). Filicide: A review. *International Journal of Law and Psychiatry, 25*, 1–14.

FINANCIAL ABUSE, ELDERLY AND BATTERED WOMEN

Financial exploitation in this context is generally defined as illegal or improper use of an older individual's financial resources, which may include money, property, or other assets. While scams and identity theft in which strangers target older individuals do occur, in most cases of financial exploitation, the perpetrator is someone known to the victim, such as a family member, caregiver, or friend. In some cases, financial resources are stolen from older individuals without their knowledge. In other cases, threats, intimidation, and violence are used as methods to steal resources. In some instances, undue influence is used for financial exploitation. In domestic violence,

an abuser uses financial exploitation as a tactic to gain and maintain power and control and deny a victim resources needed for health and well-being or to leave and start anew. If an older victim has assets, the abuser may engage in acts of economic sabotage to reduce his or her independence and may bankrupt the victim if he or she rejects the abusive relationship. Finally, guardianships, conservatorships, or powers of attorney for an older individual may be misused to benefit the exploiter.

Indicators of financial exploitation can include but are not limited to the following:

- The older individual is kept unaware of assets, bank accounts, income, and net worth.
- Possessions, documents, or credit cards are missing.
- The exploiter isolates the older individual from friends, family, activities, and information.
- Bills are unpaid.
- The caregiver refuses to spend the older individual's money on that individual.
- The older individual has given many expensive gifts to the caregiver.
- Checks are made out to cash, often in whole dollar amounts.
- The caregiver convinces an older individual to sign a blank check for one purpose and then misuses the check or steals the money.

Some exploiters use undue influence to steal from an older adult. Undue influence is the substitution of one person's will for the true desires of another. Undue influence occurs when one person uses his or her role and power to deceptively exploit the trust, dependency, and fear of another. The power is used to gain psychological control over the decision making of a weaker person. Unlike common persuasion and sales techniques, fraud, duress, threats, and other deceits are often components of undue influence. Victims may or may not have capacity.

Anyone can be a victim of undue influence, and anyone can experience circumstances that may increase his or her susceptibility. Individuals with medical conditions, cognitive challenges, or mental health issues, or who are grieving, are isolated, or lack financial expertise, may be particularly vulnerable. Exploiters can also be anyone, including family members, caregivers, fiduciaries, opportunists, and career criminals. Undue influence is seldom itself a crime, but it is a method to commit financial exploitation.

In some cases, an older victim will have a guardian or attorney in fact under a power of attorney. The older individual will have voluntarily given or legally relinquished some or all decision-making power due to cognitive or physical needs to a surrogate decision maker. In some cases, the surrogate exploits the older individual by stealing from him or her, by misusing the victim's resources, and by not providing for the older person. While powers of attorney and guardianship documents bestow considerable legal authority, they are not legal licenses to steal.

The impact of financial exploitation on older victims can be significant. Its impact can be as significant as that of physical abuse. Often older victims lose the assets they have worked a lifetime to accumulate. They may be forced to leave their homes and live in poverty. Due to their age, many older victims may not be able to join the work force and may never financially recover. Some older victims experience a significant decline in their health or have committed suicide after being financially exploited.

Financial abuse usually occurs along with other forms of elder abuse. Physical abuse may be used to force the older victim to hand over assets. Neglect may be used to weaken an older victim to the point that he or she cannot resist what the abuser demands or as a threat to gain compliance with the perpetrator's demands. Psychological and emotional abuse may be used to convince older victims that they cannot live independently without the abuser and to discourage them from reporting.

Financial exploitation is often a crime. Victims can report their exploitation to law enforcement. If a case is criminally prosecuted, in addition to incarceration, a court can order victim restitution. Victim compensation funds may be able to provide emergency financial assistance as well.

Victims can also work with adult protective services and the aging network to learn about housing and potential benefit programs to help them if they are unable to recover the lost assets. If the financial exploitation is part of a pattern of power and control, a domestic violence program may be able to assist civil attorneys who can file lawsuits and protective orders to recover assets, separate the parties, demand accountings of expenses, and seek damages. In some cases, they can get orders setting aside property transfers. Professionals who misuse client assets also can be subjected to professional discipline.

Bonnie Brandl and Candace J. Heisler

See also Adult Protective Services; Domestic Violence Against Older Women; Elder Abuse; Ethical and Legal Issues, Treating Elder Abuse

Further Readings

Brandl, B., Heisler, C., & Stiegel, L. (2006). The parallels between undue influence, domestic violence, stalking and sexual assault. *Journal of Elder Abuse and Neglect, 17,* 37–54.

Brandl, B., Heisler, C., & Stiegel, L. (2006). *Undue influence: The criminal justice response* [CD]. Available at http://www.ncall.us/resources.html#OTHERPUBS or call (608) 255–0539 or (608) 255–3560 TTY to order.

Hafemeister, T. (2003). Financial abuse of the elderly in domestic settings. In R. Bonnie & R. Wallace (Eds.), *Elder mistreatment: Abuse, neglect, and exploitation in an aging America* (pp. 382–445). Washington, DC: National Academy Press.

FINANCIAL LITERACY VERSUS FINANCIAL ABUSE

Financial literacy is commonly defined as skills and knowledge that enable individuals to manage their finances, reach financial goals, build assets, and engage the mainstream economy. Financial education is an important tool that sets individuals on the path toward economic security and financial independence.

The power of financial education when coupled with comprehensive advocacy support can serve as a solid foundation for domestic violence survivors who are seeking safety and autonomy. Access to economic resources that help meet basic human needs is a safety predicator for many who experience abuse.

The financial impact of domestic violence is far reaching and devastating. Financial abuse is a tactic commonly used by abusive partners for controlling relationships by preventing their victims from accessing money, financial resources, or any means of financial security (such as employment). Financial abuse occurs in relationships marred by inequality, verbal abuse, emotional manipulation, violence, rape, and fear. Many people in abusive relationships have been denied access to resources, skills development, practical experience, or any encouragement to stand on their own and live financially independent lives. Whether they remain in or leave an abusive relationship many survivors are challenged by dire circumstances, including homelessness, unemployment, years of financial debt, and sometimes bankruptcy.

Across the country, local community programs and coalitions have adopted financial literacy education programs to economically empower survivors while advocating to eliminate economic barriers survivors encounter when struggling to be safe. Financial literacy is a tool that can be used to help domestic violence survivors move toward long-term financial stability. Many survivor-centered financial education programs are attached to initiatives that focus on helping survivors with budgeting, saving, building credit, managing debt, purchasing a vehicle, preparing to purchase a home, or starting their own businesses. Survivor-centered financial education programs focus not only on financial abuse that occurs within the larger context of an abusive relationship, but they also provide key strategies for helping survivors manage or end financial responsibilities shared with an abusive partner.

When approaching financial education with a domestic violence survivor, it is important to adopt a philosophical acknowledgment that many political, social, and cultural beliefs influence views about how money is discussed, used, and valued, and these beliefs may define "financial security" for each individual. This framework also recognizes that financial education is not the only predictor of financial security or success.

Financial literacy and resource access must also be considered within the context of oppression. The financial impact of oppression continues to result in denied accessibility of resources for many individuals within this country. Domestic violence survivors who are gaining additional information, skills, and resources to engage with the economic mainstream also need to be prepared to navigate oppressive barriers and discrimination.

Domestic violence programs are serving as a resource for learning personal financial management, but without the assumption that all survivors of violence lack the information or skills they need to make informed decisions about their financial lives or safety.

Shawndell N. Dawson

See also Agency/Autonomy of Battered Women; Financial Abuse, Elderly and Battered Women

Further Readings

Correria, A. (2000). *Strategies to expand battered women's economic opportunities.* Washington, DC: National Resource Center on Domestic Violence.

FIREARMS

See GUN VIOLENCE

FOOT BINDING

Foot binding was practiced in China on young girls, usually at age 4 to 6, for about 1,000 years, from the 10th to the 20th centuries. The toes on each foot, except for the big toes, were broken—bent under and into the sole—then wrapped with the heel as tightly as possible with a piece of cloth that had been soaked in warm water or animal blood along with certain herbs. Every few days, the binding would be changed and the feet rewrapped so that they could be squeezed into progressively smaller shoes. The goal was to shrink the feet as much as possible, with the most desirable foot being only about 3 inches long. The practice caused a number of serious problems. For example, the feet usually would bleed and often became infected. The binding also typically cut off circulation to the feet and flesh as well as toes would fall off. The process was extremely painful, and most women were physically crippled by it, making walking difficult and, for some, impossible. As they aged, women with bound feet were at high risk of falling and incurring injuries from such falls, and they also had greater difficulty squatting and standing up after sitting.

Several justifications were offered for foot binding. One was simply that in Chinese culture, tiny feet were considered feminine. A woman with unbound (i.e., natural) feet was considered sexually unattractive, more masculine than feminine. Future mothers-in-law would inspect the feet of their sons' fiancés to ensure the young women did not have natural or "clown" feet. Foot binding was also a way to ensure that women remained chaste and faithful to their spouses in a culture that believed women were naturally lustful and lascivious. Inheritance was also important in Chinese society and was distributed along patrilineal lines.

Consequently, men wished to ensure the legitimacy of their heirs. A woman whose feet were bound literally could not "run around" on her husband. Finally, a woman with bound feet was a status symbol for men. An immobile woman could not engage in physical labor, so she was completely dependent on her husband for financial support. Having a wife with bound feet was a testament to a man's wealth and privilege, signifying his financial ability to afford such a spouse. One might expect, then, that foot binding was limited to the upper classes in China. However, although the practice originated with the nobility, it was often copied by the less privileged who aspired to higher status.

With the advent of the Qing Dynasty in China in the mid-1600s, an effort was made by the Manchu emperor to eliminate foot binding. A tax was imposed on parents whose daughters had bound feet, and the practice was outlawed in certain regions. Nevertheless, the practice continued to be passed on from mothers to daughters for nearly another 400 years, since most people clung to the belief that bound feet were beautiful and beauty ensured a good and lasting marriage. In a society in which all roles other than wife and mother—or prostitute—are closed to women, women often would do whatever they deemed necessary for the personal and economic security of their daughters. It was under the leadership of Sun Yat-Sen in 1911 that foot binding was officially eliminated in China, although it continued in isolated rural areas for several more years.

Claire M. Renzetti

See also Female Genital Mutilation

Further Readings

Blake, C. F. (1994). Footbinding in neo-Confucian China and the appropriation of female labor. *Signs, 19,* 676–712.
Dworkin, A. (1983). Gynocide: Chinese footbinding. In L. Richardson & V. Taylor (Eds.), *Feminist frontiers* (pp. 178–186). Reading, MA: Addison-Wesley.

FORCED MARRIAGES

Forced marriage is defined as a marital union where at least one of the intended spouses refuses to participate but is intimidated into marrying. The issue drew the attention of women's advocates, law enforcement, and policymakers internationally when Britain attempted to criminalize it in 2005. While the bill was abandoned, it inspired debates and concerns. Opponents of forced marriage have been careful to distinguish it from arranged marriage, which is customary in many Asian, Middle Eastern, African, and South American cultures. Historically, forced marriage was practiced in the West among aristocrats, royalty, and religious sects. "Shotgun weddings" occurred in the United States until the mid-20th century and were a way of forcing recalcitrant men to accept responsibility for women they had impregnated. Between 1890 and 1950, U.S. prosecutors often charged men with rape to persuade them to marry their sexual partners.

Although men can certainly be forced into marriages, the overwhelming majority of victims worldwide are girls and women. However, homosexual men or men who wish to marry outside their religion, caste, class, or ethnicity may be compelled to wed women selected by their families. There are no comprehensive statistics on how many females are forced into marriages each year, let alone an estimation of victimized men. The UK Forced Marriage Unit reports that out of approximately 300 victims it assists annually, 15% are men. Boys and young men may also be forced into marriage due to religious, political, and cultural dicta. For example, many adolescent boys are married off in Iran to avoid military service.

Arranged, child, early, and forced marriages and violence against women are closely linked. Fathers and brothers often exchange their young daughters and sisters for bride-price to increase family fortunes, swap them to confirm desirable matches for men in the family, offer them to repay debts and negotiate peace with feuding parties, or surrender them in lieu of monetary penalties for social miscreancy. In countries such as Kyrgyzstan and Ethiopia, young women are routinely abducted by men who want to marry them and are held captive until they consent. After a night spent with a man, a woman may have no other option but to marry him since her reputation is sullied. Many of the abductions are planned in conjunction with the girls' parents. The average age range of women forced into marriage globally is 13 to 30 years. Nonetheless, marriages of girls as young as 8 and 9 are frequently arranged with men in their 40s and 50s.

In traditional societies, girls are socialized to be obedient to their parents and are made cognizant early on that their families' respectability and happiness rest on their conduct. Thus, they may see no alternative but to submit to their families' wishes regarding marriage. Parents threatening to commit suicide may also subdue uncooperative daughters. For females who are considered parental or paternal property, forced marriage may be the norm, as most could not realistically resist the emotional and physical coercion and survive. The few who defy face the risk of life-threatening violence, alienation from family and community, ruined reputation, and the prospect of lifelong penury. Women are starved, imprisoned, beaten, maimed, and murdered by their own relatives to extract their acquiescence and to restore family status if they renounce their marriages. Between 1996 and 2005, 45 Turkish immigrant women in Germany were killed to save their families' "honor" because they had rejected their husbands after forced marriages. The toll women pay for forced marriages includes low education, lack of earning opportunities, early pregnancy, exposure to HIV, rape trauma, and risk of suicide.

Forced marriages are present in immigrant communities that have migrated to the West from traditional societies. Second-generation young women in particular may be deceived into returning to their parents' home-countries and are married off under duress. At times, parents subject their daughters to physical and psychological abuse and withhold travel documents to ensure compliance. The dynamics of immigrant forced marriages are somewhat distinct.

Many immigrant communities in the West believe that their cultures will be engulfed by the dominant host society unless actively maintained. Endogamy is consequently viewed as a means of extending traditional cultures. Furthermore, parents unused to dating and hypervigilant of their daughters' virginity may become alarmed at the personal and sexual autonomy girls reared in the West seek. Many experience it as disintegration of family cohesion and erosion of paternal authority that would eventually lead to social anomie. Since marriage in traditional societies is considered an alliance between families, the focus on individuals in Western-style romantic marriages is deemed selfish and inconsiderate. Arranged marriages thus are thought to not only preserve the traditional form of family alliance but also save children from their own foolishness.

By several United Nations charters, such as the Universal Declaration of Human Rights, the Convention on the Rights of the Child, the Declaration on Elimination of Discrimination Against Women, and the Convention on the Elimination of All Forms of Discrimination Against Women, forced marriage is a violation of human and women's rights. In accordance, Syria, Belgium, and Norway have already passed laws, while the United Kingdom, Holland, Germany, and Austria are reflecting on pertinent legislation. A few British provinces are deliberating ways to sanction clerics who solemnize forced weddings. Still, these laws are powerless to protect offshore marriages of immigrant children.

A few Middle Eastern and African countries have approached the issue innovatively. The highest religious leader in Saudi Arabia has issued a fatwa against forced marriage, declaring it un-Islamic. In Sierra Leone, prosecutors are pursuing forced marriage as a crime against humanity, relating it to the 1991–2002 civil war when large numbers of women were abducted, forced to marry, and forced to bear children by the rebel forces. Other nations, such as Cameroon and Iran, have responded to the problem by increasing the minimum age of marriage for girls.

Shamita Das Dasgupta

See also Abandonment; Acid Attacks; Battered Women; Honor Killing/Crime; Marital Rape/Wife Rape

Further Readings

An-Nai'im, A. (2000). *Forced marriage.* Retrieved on August 12, 2006, from http://www.soas.ac.uk/honourcrimes/FMpaperAnNai'im.htm

LaFraniere, S. (2005, November 27). Forced to marry before puberty, African girls pay lasting price. *New York Times.* Retrieved on August 12, 2006, from http://www.nytimes.com/2005/11/27/international/africa/27malawi.html

FORCED MILITARY CONSCRIPTION

Forced military conscription describes the recruitment of civilians into an armed group through the use of physical force. State military conscription, in which a country legally requires its citizens to serve in its military, has existed for centuries. Popularly known as "the draft" in Western countries, conscription became the model for maintaining a large standing army in Europe in the 19th century. Although many countries around the world have required all able-bodied men (and sometimes women, as is the case in Israel) to serve in the military, a number of countries eliminated the requirement in the 20th century as a result of moral arguments opposed to the practice: Many have argued against it as an instance of structural violence, in which state institutions do harm to individuals and populations. Military conscription was abolished in favor of voluntary recruitment in Great Britain in 1960 and the United States in 1973.

Military conscription becomes a form of interpersonal violence when it involves forcible abduction of individuals who are then ordered to complete military training and participate in combat against their will. This practice has been documented recently in Burma and Turkey. In Burma, local leaders are required to send a certain number of residents for military training, for which they must pay. In more extreme cases, reports state that adolescent males have been tied with ropes by military recruitment personnel and taken to remote military training camps. Family members seeking their release are told to pay bribes to have their relatives released. Witnesses in Turkey have reported similar incidents, as well as cruel treatment of trainees and imprisonment of conscientious objectors.

With the decrease in interstate warfare and the increase in intrastate or civil wars, forced military conscription by paramilitary groups has risen in the past few decades. Civilians caught between rebel factions are ordered to join militia to avoid being killed. Through a range of controlling tactics, civilians are trained in warfare and forced to engage in armed conflict. This practice often involves the abduction of children because they are typically less able to resist, physically and psychologically. The most grievous example comes from northern Uganda, where the rebel Lord's Resistance Army (LRA) has been abducting children and forcing them to fight against government troops since 1992. It is estimated that the LRA has forcibly conscripted as many as 30,000 children. If children are caught trying to escape, other abducted children are forced to kill them as part of their socialization into the LRA fighting force.

Aside from the brutality employed in forcible military conscription, many experts consider both state and paramilitary forced conscription to be forms of involuntary servitude and thus human rights violations.

Despite protests, forcible conscription continues to be a prevalent tactic of military recruitment.

Kristen E. Cheney

See also Child Abductions, Nonfamily; Children and Adolescents Who Kill

Further Readings

Cheney, K. E. (2005). "Our children have only known war": Children's experiences and the uses of childhood in northern Uganda. *Children's Geographies, 3*(1), 23–45.

Flynn, G. Q. (2002). *Conscription and democracy: The draft in France, Great Britain, and the United States.* Westport, CT: Greenwood Press.

Steinberg, D. L. (2002). *Burma: The State of Myanmar.* Washington, DC: Georgetown University Press.

FORENSIC NURSING

Forensic nursing is the nursing care of crime victims and people who are accused or convicted of committing crimes. The term *forensic nurse* came into use in 1992 after a group of about 70 sexual assault nurses met in Minneapolis and started the International Association of Forensic Nursing. Forensic nursing is defined as the application of the medicolegal aspects of health care in the scientific investigation of trauma and/or death related issues. Forensic nursing practice is as old as the interface between the legal and health care systems and has been considered a subspecialty of nursing since 1995.

Forensic Nursing Practice

Clinical forensic nurses do many of the same things other nurses do: conduct health interviews, perform physical assessments, conduct medical tests, collect specimens, help people manage crises, document information, and prevent problems. Unlike other nurses, however, forensic nurses are involved with the patient specifically because there is an interface between the health care and legal systems, and that influences what the nurses do. For instance, a forensic nurse may collect specimens, an ordinary nursing function. Specimen collection becomes a forensic function when the specimens come from a suspect in a reported sexual assault. In the same way, forensic psychiatric nurses may use the familiar tools to evaluate mental status, but the information may be used in court rather than in a discharge planning conference.

Forensic nurse researchers add to the body of scientific knowledge that supports forensic nursing practice, education, and administration. The National Institute of Nursing Research has funded over 40 violence-related research studies since 2001, most focusing on sexual violence or interpersonal violence. Forensic nurse education is provided in 32 master's and post-master's certificate programs nationwide, 13 of which are offered exclusively online. Forensic nurse administrators manage Sexual Assault Nurse Examiner programs in every state in the United States, some of which also incorporate services to victims of domestic violence.

The Forensic Nursing Workplace

Forensic nurses work in hospitals and clinics, just like other nurses do. The difference is that the hospital might be in a prison, or the clinic might be in a jail. Forensic nurses who are death investigators go to crime scenes. Forensic psychiatric nurses work in mental health facilities and advocacy organizations. Sexual assault nurse examiners work in hospital emergency departments and freestanding clinics.

Forensic nursing is a role rather than a job description, so forensic nursing principles are useful in any setting. If, for example, a nurse is focused on intimate partner violence and its effect on women and children, he or she might work in a prenatal or pediatric clinic. Legal nurse consultants help both the prosecution and defense in their search for truth and justice; they often own their own businesses and may have additional training as attorneys or paralegals.

Louanne Lawson

See also Elder Abuse; Expert Testimony; Intimate Partner Violence; Rape/Sexual Assault

Further Readings

Benak, L. (2006). Forensic nursing: A global response to crime, violence and trauma. *On the Edge, 12*(4), 9–10.

Lynch, V. A. (1993). Forensic aspects of health care: New roles, new responsibilities. *Journal of Psychosocial Nursing, 31,* 5–6.

FOSTER CARE

Foster care is a social service providing temporary care to children whose homes are unsafe because of child maltreatment or parent or caregiver incapacity. When the substitute caregiver is related to the child, foster care may be referred to as kinship care. Typically, the term *foster care* includes only children in the legal custody of the state or county child welfare agency, while *kinship care* may refer to any child in a relative's care, whether or not the state or the relative has legal custody.

If a child welfare agency has placed a child in foster care, it must justify to the dependency court that the child would be at imminent risk of harm in the home from which he or she was removed. The state is required to make "reasonable efforts" to prevent the need for foster care, to reunify the family, and to find permanent family alternatives for children who cannot return home. Rules about circumstances that make foster care placement justifiable, as well as criteria for licensing and monitoring foster homes, are established through state laws and regulations. In most states, a parent may also place a child in foster care voluntarily. Federal law provides a national framework regarding the care of dependent children in foster care.

The foster care system has its roots in colonial period practices in which impoverished or orphaned children were indentured to families who could care for them and teach them a trade. Systems of indenture were later replaced by orphan asylums and then succeeded in the late 1800s by systems of "placing out" impoverished children from urban slums to host families in the countryside. These systems evolved with changing societal standards regarding appropriate living conditions for children and accepted practices related to child labor, as well as with the professionalization of the social work field. Over time, the focus of foster care shifted from orphans and destitute children to maltreatment of children by parents and caregivers.

Foster Care Settings and Foster Parents

Nearly half of children in foster care in the United States live in nonrelative family foster homes and another quarter live in foster care with relatives. The use of relatives as foster parents varies widely by state. About one in ten foster children live in institutions and a similar proportion live in group homes.

Foster parents are usually recruited, licensed, and trained by state or county child welfare agencies. They are paid a stipend as reimbursement for the child's room and board, but are not salaried employees. Foster care payment rates vary with the child's age and needs for specialized care. Foster parents tend to be older than biological parents and about 40% are employed full time outside the home. While the median level of experience of foster parents is about 3 years, there is a great deal of turnover in the population of foster parents, and state and local agencies face difficulties recruiting and retaining them.

Children in Foster Care

At the end of 2004, there were 518,000 children in foster care in the United States and 800,000 had spent some time that year in foster care. The number of children in foster care in the United States has risen nearly every year since national data collection began in the 1960s. Foster care is intended as a short-term service for families in crisis, although some children experience extended foster care stays. The median length of stay of children in foster care during 2004 was 18 months, and the median age at the time of entry to foster care was 8.3 years. Approximately half of children in foster care have a case goal of reunification with the parent or principal caretaker. Another fifth have adoption as their case goal, with the remaining children having case goals such as guardianship, long-term foster care, or emancipation.

Most children who enter foster care do so after a state child protection agency verifies or "substantiates" a report of child abuse or neglect, although relatively few substantiated maltreatment reports result in children's placement in foster care. The National Survey of Child and Adolescent Well-being (NSCAW), a nationally representative, longitudinal study of children in foster care and children investigated by child protective services, reveals that of children in foster care for 1 year, 60% had entered foster care primarily as a result of child neglect. Ten percent of children in foster care had experienced physical abuse as their most serious type of maltreatment, and 8% were victims of sexual abuse. Approximately 8% of children in foster care had not experienced abuse or neglect, but had been referred for reasons such as their own mental health needs or domestic violence in their families. Parental mental illness, substance abuse, and other serious impairments are associated with many children's foster care placements.

Rates of entry into foster care are highest for infants. The rates drop dramatically for 1-year-old children, and the risk of entry continues to decrease until children reach adolescence, at which point the risk rises again. Entry rates are higher for African American children than for White or Hispanic children. Children living in poor and urban communities are also much more likely to enter foster care than children living in other environments.

Many children in foster care have physical, emotional, and behavioral issues that warrant specialized treatment. The NSCAW study found that, on average, children in foster care scored somewhat below national norms on a variety of developmental measures. Of particular concern was that one third of children in foster care for a year demonstrated significant cognitive and/or behavioral problems.

Laura F. Radel

See also Adoption and Safe Families Act of 1997; Adoption Assistance and Child Welfare Act of 1980; Kinship Care

Further Readings

Mallon, G. P., & Hess, P. M. (Eds.). (2005). *Child welfare for the 21st century.* New York: Columbia University Press.

NSCAW Research Group. (2005). *National Survey of Child and Adolescent Well-Being research brief no. 1: Who are the children in foster care?* Retrieved July 7, 2006, from http://www.ndacan.cornell.edu/NDACAN/Publications/NSCAW_Research_Brief_1.pdf

NSCAW Research Group. (2005). *National Survey of Child and Adolescent Well-Being research brief no. 2: Foster children's caregivers and caregiving environments.* Retrieved July 7, 2006, from http://www.ndacan.cornell.edu/NDACAN/Publications/NSCAW_Research_Brief_2.pdf

Fraternities and Violence

There are two very distinct literatures on violence as related to fraternities, with only the smallest overlap. One literature, on hazing, touches lightly on predominantly White (PW) fraternities and is mainly concerned with violence in hazing in historically Black (HB) fraternities. The other literature is almost completely focused on PW fraternities and deals with sexually predatory and aggressive practices. In neither case is the empirical support in the literature particularly strong.

Sexual Aggression

Sexual aggression and date rape are discussed here only in the context of PW fraternities, as there has been little research on these behaviors in HB fraternities. Often, people studying fraternities have felt that these organizations have provided a sort of subculture that insulates their members from the general norms or rules of the entire campus. Over the years, studies have shown that fraternities promote conformity, and earlier work showed that fraternity members were more likely to be accepting of racial prejudice and hate crimes. A preoccupation with loyalty, a very strong concern with masculinity, and the abuse of alcohol can easily lead to either individual or group violence. A historic indifference by most college administrations to violence against women has provided a lack of deterrence that allows such behavior to continue. If fraternity men think that they can get away with violence against women, it is because on most campuses, most of the time, they can.

Most of the citations in the literature have been to the earlier ethnographic studies of Patricia Martin and Robert Hummer or Peggy Sanday, or to an array of surveys on rape supportive attitudes, which did not find as clear an association between PW fraternity membership and self-reported sexual aggression as more recent empirical studies have found. For example, in a meta-analysis of a variety of empirical studies, researchers found a significant but modest relationship between fraternity membership and admitted sexual aggression. One reason why the effect is only modest may be that researchers lumped all fraternity members together into one pool, while in truth some fraternities may be more sexually aggressive than others. Further, fraternities are rarely monolithic entities where all members think alike; some members may be much more sexually aggressive than others, especially where they are more influenced by male peer support networks. Thus, those who live in the on-campus houses of the most predatory chapters may be the most influenced by male peer support and perhaps be the most aggressive. Male peer support further sustains hypermasculinity, group secrecy that promotes a lack of deterrence, and a culture of alcohol abuse that

has repeatedly been associated with sexual aggression. Research indicates that bedroom wall pictures show that fraternity men engage more in the sexual objectification of women.

Physical Hazing

Hazing is rarely recognized as a criminal act, although virtually all states have laws against it. It has a long history on American campuses, particularly in the 19th century, but more recently it seems to have been limited mainly to fraternities and sororities. Hazing might include relatively lesser forms of degradation (marching around campus, singing songs on the campus green, wearing beanies), or it might include any uncomfortable activity that a young person could think up for the pledge: for example, spanking with paddles as often as daily for months or a year, forced drinking of large quantities of alcohol, eating disgusting foods designed to induce vomiting, being left outdoors in winter overnight wearing only underwear, not being allowed to sleep for days. Both fraternities and sororities practice mental forms of hazing, which are commonly dismissed as pranks, but which have occasionally left pledges so affected that they develop such symptoms as speech impediments.

To deal with abuses, physical hazing is banned today by all fraternity national organizations and central offices, such as the National Pan-Hellenic Council, the coordinating body for the eight historically African American fraternities and sororities, which has banned hazing in any form whatsoever. Spurred by the potential liability from lawsuits by harmed students, universities have also instituted strong antihazing rules. However, the net effect has been to hide the extent of current hazing; anywhere it continues it has been driven off campus and underground, where critics claim that it is getting more physically abusive beyond the control of campus officials and alumni.

There are strong pressures to keep hazing alive. Students often have not bought into the antihazing prohibitions. Alumni may be strong advocates of hazing and a problem in preventing university action. Pledges volunteer for hazing, not unlike some street gangs where those who join without major pain and stress are given much less prestige as members than those who are beaten. This has been particularly true in some HB chapters, where it may be a badge of masculinity, self-esteem, and pride to have undergone painful hazing.

Virtually all of the literature on hazing suggests that although PW fraternities are now only using humiliation techniques, some HB fraternities still engage in serious beatings of pledges and branding of members. In PW fraternities, pressure from national chapters seems to have cut back or ended beatings in the past 20 to 30 years, although a lack of alcohol and beatings has not meant an end to deaths or injuries in PW hazing.

Martin D. Schwartz

See also Alcohol and Violence; Hazing; Male Peer Support, Theory of; Rape Culture; Rape/Sexual Assault

Further Readings

Jones, R. L. (1994). *Black haze: Violence, sacrifice and manhood in black Greek-letter fraternities.* Albany: State University of New York Press.

Murnen, S. K., & Kohlman, M. H. (2007). Athletic participation, fraternity membership, and sexual aggression among college men: A meta-analytic review. *Sex Roles, 57,* 145–157.

Ruffins, P. (1997). Fratricide: Are African American fraternities beating themselves to death? *Black Issues in Higher Education, 14*(8), 18–25.

Sanday, P. R. (2007). *Fraternity gang rape: Brotherhood and privilege on campus* (2nd ed.). New York: New York University Press.

Schwartz, M. D., & DeKeseredy, W. S. (1997). *Sexual assault on the college campus: The role of male peer support.* Thousand Oaks, CA: Sage.

FRATRICIDE

See FAMILY HOMICIDES

FULL FAITH AND CREDIT MANDATE

The Full Faith and Credit (FF&C) mandate requires states to honor and enforce (or give FF&C to) the orders of protection and to stop stalking issued by other states. The FF&C clause of the U.S. Constitution (article IV, § 1) and the statute, 28 U.S.C.

§ 1738, require every state to honor and enforce the public records and judicial decisions of other states as if they had issued them themselves. Thus a marriage certificate, driver's license, or divorce decree granted in one state will be honored by every other state unless the responding party was not afforded due process, particularly if the party was not notified of the action or given the right to contest it in court. States also need not give FF&C when the official action or court decision is against public policy, which is why states refused to give FF&C to polygamous marriages when they were legal in Utah.

A state may also opt through the principle of comity to enforce judgments of another state or country, even when it is not required to do so by the FF&C mandate. Comity is based on the same need for finality of legal proceedings as is FF&C, and also the legal principles of res judicata and issue preclusion, which prevent the same parties from relitigating the same case or claim previously decided by a court.

Need for FF&C

Some of the most violent and coercive batterers and stalkers drive their victims away, often forcing them to seek safety in other states. Many other battered victims travel temporarily across state lines for work or health care or to see family, shop, or vacation. Since abusers generally escalate their violence when their victims leave them or show any independence, victims of domestic violence need immediate police protection in the new state if their abusers threaten them. Yet most cannot obtain new orders of protection in a new state unless there is abuse in that state, and even then there are often long delays and difficulties in serving the abusers with court papers, assuming the victim has access to the courts in the new state. Furthermore, states may not be able to order sufficient protection when the abuser does not reside in the new state. Some abusers keep forcing their victims to flee to ever new states. The clear solution for victims who already have an order of protection from one state is for other states to honor and enforce the previously enacted order, without requiring them to go to court to register the order.

History

Traditionally U.S. court decisions held that because judicial determinations (such as injunctions and child custody or support orders) were not final judgments and could be modified, they were not entitled to FF&C. Orders of protection and restraining orders to stop domestic violence and stalking are injunctions, which were seen to fall under this exception. Ex parte orders (those that courts give in an emergency before the respondent is given notice or a chance to contest the order) were particularly seen as not entitled to FF&C because they gave the respondent no due process.

The U.S. Supreme Court reversed this train of decisions in *Baker v. General Motors Corporation,* which held that equitable decrees (which include injunctions such as protective orders) are entitled to FF&C, even though they may not be final and may be modified in the state that issued them. Also supporting this new trend, orders of protection are not concerned with competing orders and are not against public policy.

New Hampshire, West Virginia, Kentucky, and Oregon voluntarily chose to provide comity to some protective orders of other states, but they were the exception and the procedures were generally cumbersome, were little known, and did not cover all orders.

Model for Custody Cases

Until recently child custody orders were not given FF&C because (a) they could always be modified and (b) two or more states could issue conflicting orders. Moving the child to another state was usually grounds for modifying a custody order. This actually encouraged someone who lost custody to abduct the child and shop for a more favorable forum in a new state in the hope of winning custody there. To prevent child abductions and forum shopping, the National Conference of Commissioners of State Laws (NCCUSL), which drafts model legislation for states to adopt, drafted an act to determine when a state must (a) decline custody cases and (b) agree to honor and enforce the custody orders of other states. Because some states were slow in adopting the model legislation or changed it, Congress enacted a law to accomplish the same goals. The federal law was slightly different, and, as federal law, it preempted inconsistent parts of any state's law. It also spurred the remaining states to enact consistent legislation. Congress took a similar approach so that states would have to give FF&C to the child support orders of other states.

Violence Against Women Act

Knowing that FF&C for preexisting protective orders would solve many of these problems, Congress provided language in the Violence Against Women Act (VAWA) I requiring states to give FF&C for orders of protection and/or to stop stalking that were issued by other states, similar to what it did for child custody and child support orders. The FF&C mandate for protective orders was enacted in 1994 and codified at 18 U.S.C. §§ 2265–2266, and covers protective provisions issued as part of other types of actions, such as divorce, paternity, and custody and juvenile cases.

The mandate also includes orders issued to Native Americans by tribal courts. Few tribes had domestic violence and stalking laws when VAWA was first enacted, but many have since enacted such laws.

Another part of VAWA also provided that no state may charge for a protective order if the state receives federal money under that part of the act. Every state accepts this money and certifies that it does not charge for orders of protection. Some states or counties still charge for orders, or order the respondent to pay on the theory that the orders are free to victims.

Police in some states are supposed to give FF&C to any order of protection or to stop stalking that is in effect if the respondent was given notice and an opportunity to be heard, and to honor and enforce it without requiring that the victim first have the order registered in the new state. This is true for ex parte orders as well.

Limitations

VAWA I included language for FF&C for all protective orders except those that violated due process, namely (a) orders when no notice or opportunity to be heard had been afforded to the respondent, including ex parte orders, and (b) mutual orders unless the respondent had filed a pleading, the original petitioner had been given notice and opportunity to be heard, and the court had made findings that both parties were legally entitled to be given orders. The exception for mutual orders given to respondents is because many courts automatically enter them or encourage the parties to agree to them, even though they usually deny the petitioning party's due process rights and are more dangerous to victims than no order at all. Congress made clear it did not mean to exempt the part of mutual orders given to the petitioner if notice and opportunity had been given to the respondent, but only the part of such orders given to the respondent without due process.

Many states in their domestic violence statutes prohibit mutual orders or strongly discourage their use, often including similar due process guarantees. Some also require the court to decide if one party was the primary aggressor, the one who caused most of the domestic terror (but not necessarily the one who started the abuse), and not issue an order to that party even if some abuse had been mutual.

Although VAWA I excluded coverage for child custody and child support provisions in protective orders, VAWA II and III made clear that the FF&C mandate included child custody and child support provisions in protective orders.

Complications

In 2002 NCCUSL issued another model act for states to give FF&C to other states' protective orders. Although federal law makes clear that protective provisions in other types of civil and criminal cases are covered by law, and that child custody and child support provisions in protective orders are covered, NCCUSL's Uniform Interstate Enforcement of Domestic-Violence Protection Orders Act is inconsistent with many of these federal provisions. Almost a third of states have enacted this act, thwarting some domestic violence and stalking victims from receiving the full protection in other states that Congress intended them to get.

Joan Zorza

See also Violence Against Women Act

Further Readings

Baker v. General Motors Corporation, 522 U.S. 222 (1998).

Goelman, D. M. (2004). Shelter from the storm: Using jurisdictional statutes to protect victims of domestic violence after the Violence Against Women Act of 2000. *Columbia Journal of Gender and Law, 13,* 101–168.

Klein, C. F. (1995). Full faith and credit: Interstate enforcement of protection orders under the Violence Against Women Act of 1994. *Family Law Quarterly, 29,* 253–271.

Sack, E. J. (2004). Domestic violence across state lines: The Full Faith and Credit clause, congressional power, and interstate enforcement of protection orders. *Northwestern University Law Review, 98,* 827–906.

Uniform Interstate Enforcement of Domestic-Violence Protection Orders Act. Retrieved from http://www.nccusl.org/Update/ActSearchResults.asp

VAWA I, eventually enacted in 1994 as part of the Crime Bill, Pub. L. No. 103-322108 Stat. 1796. 18 U.S.C. §§ 2265–2266.

Gang Rape

Gang rape is a serious and greatly understudied form of rape. Gang rape is also sometimes referred to as group rape. Both terms refer to a rape or sexual assault committed by more than one perpetrator against one victim. Most research on gang rape has focused on cases reported to police or incidents in college populations. In general, research has shown that gang rape is less common than rape committed by one offender against one victim, yet more serious in terms of the number and severity of sexual acts suffered by victims.

Prevalence, Reporting, and Risk Factors

Research has shown estimated rates of gang rape range from under 2% in student populations to up to 26% in police-reported cases. However, according to the *Sourcebook of Criminal Justice Statistics*, there were 28,350 rapes/sexual assaults in 2005 that involved multiple offenders. That year there were 94,347 forcible rapes known to the police; therefore, approximately 30% of rapes in 2005 were gang or group rapes. Less than one third of rapes overall are reported to police, according to the National Crime Victimization Survey, and only 5% or fewer rapes of college students are reported to police. It is likely that gang rapes are also underreported to police, but data on this issue are lacking. Past studies of students and police-reported cases have shown that there is a preponderance of young offenders and victims in gang rapes, and greater levels of violence by offenders and substance use involved in gang rapes. Evidence is mixed about the demographic characteristics of offenders and victims in gang rapes, but some data suggest that victims and offenders in these incidents may more likely be of lower socioeconomic status. Although researchers and journalists have documented gang rape cases occurring in the context of fraternities and sports teams, no statistical evidence exists to show that these contexts pose greater risk of gang rape than other situations.

Comparisons of Gang and Individual Rapes

A few studies have compared gang and individual (e.g., single-offender) rapes, and most research shows that victims experience more completed rape and a greater number of other forced sexual acts in gang rape attacks. Studies have shown either no differences or higher levels of physical injuries for victims of gang rapes. Research on police-reported stranger rapes has found more alcohol and drug involvement, fewer weapons, more attacks at night, and less victim resistance in gang rapes. On the other hand, some research with college students has shown no difference in substance use involvement, but more victim resistance and more offender violence, including weapons, in gang rapes. A recent study of sexual assault victims recruited from the community showed that gang rapes are more likely than single-offender rapes to occur outdoors, be committed by stranger assailants, and involve more offender violence and weapons and greater physical injury to victims. These offenses are also more likely to involve substance use and victim resistance.

287

Postassault Functioning

Few studies have examined measures of postassault victim functioning. It is unclear whether gang rape victims are more likely than single-offender victims to tell others about their assaults. However, when they do disclose, research shows that gang rape victims are more likely to seek help from police, medical, and rape crisis services than single-offender victims. They also are more likely to contemplate or attempt suicide, have greater likelihood of having posttraumatic stress disorder, and are more likely to seek therapy after the assault than single-offender rape victims. Some research suggests that gang rape victims have greater histories of other traumatic events and child sexual abuse in their lives than single-offender rape victims.

Social Networks

A recent media-recruited community sample of over 1,000 sexual assault survivors in a large metropolitan area showed that 17.9% of sexual assaults were committed by two or more offenders. Although the gang rape victims in the sample did not differ from individual rape victims in their frequency of contact with social networks, they did perceive themselves to be getting along more poorly with others. In addition, even though the gang rape victims reported getting the same degree of positive social reactions from others whom they told about the assault, they also received more negative social reactions to sexual assault disclosure than individual rape victims received. This is important because other research shows that negative social reactions (e.g., being blamed) relate to more posttraumatic stress disorder in sexual assault victims. It is possible that gang rape victims may have poorer relationships or ability to elicit social support from their social networks and/or face greater stigma from others following assault.

Implications

Although cases of gang rape have been reported in the media and in research, this form of sexual assault is understudied. Unfortunately, statistics on the incidence and prevalence of gang rape from representative community samples are lacking. More research attention and intervention are needed to address this serious crime. A small body of existing research comparing gang to single-offender rapes does suggest that gang rapes are more violent and appear to have more serious consequences for victims. Treatment and intervention efforts are needed for victims of gang rape to address this high-risk subgroup of rape victims.

Sarah E. Ullman

See also Rape Culture; Rape/Sexual Assault; Rape Trauma Syndrome

Further Readings

Bachman, R., & Saltzman, L. E. (1995). *Violence against women: Estimates from the redesigned survey.* Washington, DC: U.S. Department of Justice, Bureau of Justice Statistics.

Gidycz, C., & Koss, M. P. (1990). A comparison of group and individual sexual assault victims. *Psychology of Women Quarterly, 14,* 325–342.

O'Sullivan, C. S. (1991). Acquaintance gang rape on campus. In A. Parrot & C. Bechhofer (Eds.), *Acquaintance rape: The hidden crime* (pp. 140–156). New York: Wiley.

Ullman, S. E. (1999). A comparison of gang and individual rape incidents. *Violence and Victims, 14,* 123–133.

Ullman, S. E. (2005, November). *Comparing gang and individual rapes in a community sample of urban women.* Paper presented at the annual meeting of the American Society of Criminology, Toronto.

Web Sites

Sourcebook of Criminal Justice Statistics online: http://www.albany.edu/sourcebook

GANG VIOLENCE

The problems posed by gangs in many communities have received increasing attention in the United States and, more recently, in some European nations as well. What is called delinquent behavior when the gang member is a minor and criminal behavior when the gang member is an adult has been the subject of more scholarly and public attention during the past few decades. According to the most recent National Youth Gang Center (NYGC) survey of law enforcement agencies, 21,500 gangs with 731,500 members have been officially reported in the United States. Since the NYGC surveys began in 1996, every city whose population exceeded 250,000 has reported the presence of gangs. A number of cross-sectional and longitudinal studies have demonstrated that membership in a gang is associated with a significant *enhancement effect*—that is, belonging to a gang enhances the chances that an individual will commit delinquent or criminal offenses, including serious, violent offenses, and that the individual will engage in more delinquent or criminal behavior while in the gang than either before joining the gang or after leaving the gang.

In analyzing gang-related violent crime, it is important to define that term. Two major definitions are employed by law enforcement agencies in classifying crimes that they believe may be gang related. The first, utilized by more than half of all law enforcement agencies, defines gang-related crime as crime that involves a gang member as a perpetrator or as a victim. The second, utilized by about one third of all law enforcement agencies, is a more restrictive definition that requires that the crime be determined to be gang motivated (committed for the purpose of furthering the gang's interests and activities). If such motivation can be proved, the convicted offender may be subject to "sentence enhancements" (additional time to be served), since many states have integrated these "add-on" sentences in their sentencing statutes with the intention of deterring gang-motivated criminal behavior. Using the more restrictive "gang-motivated" definition significantly reduces the number of crimes that are classified as gang related.

One important, although not sufficient, indicator of gang violence is gang-related homicides. Although homicide data are generally accurately reported, determining whether they are gang related depends on many factors. It is thought that the number of gang-related homicides is likely to be underestimated. Nonetheless, in a recent year, more than 1,300 homicides committed in 132 U.S. cities with populations of at least 100,000 were classified as gang related, in that they involved a gang member. The two cities with the most chronic gang problems, Los Angeles and Chicago, accounted for more than half of those homicides. Also, about one in every five homicides committed in those cities involved a gang member, and they were most likely to occur in areas with greater populations, chronic gang presence, and a larger number of gang members. Major factors that contribute to these gang-related homicides and other gang-related violent crime include the increasing access to and use of highly lethal weapons by gang members, along with the retaliation and status concerns of gang members.

Popular perceptions notwithstanding, research consistently shows that only a small percentage of gang-related crime is violent in nature, most gang members' behavior is neither violent nor related to drug sales, and most violent criminals are not gang members. For example, homicides generally constitute less than 5% of all serious gang-related offenses in Los Angeles and less than 1% of *all* gang-related offenses in that city, which has one of the most chronic gang problems in the United States. Furthermore, during the late 1990s (as opposed to the preceding decade), juvenile arrests for violent felony offenses *declined* by 34%, while reports of gang membership were up significantly. Such divergence between the reported growth of gangs and the concomitant *decline* in juvenile felony arrests provides further evidence against the popular assumption of an automatic connection between gangs and serious crime.

Another popular assumption—that drug trafficking–related violence generally involves gang members—is also not borne out by research. Drug selling and violence are not causally related within gangs and, historically, gang-related violence preceded the more recent advent of drug sales as a significant source of income for gang members. Moreover, recent fears about large increases in violence by female gangs have not been borne out by empirical research. Females, both those in gangs and those not in gangs, are generally less violent than are males, although research does show that female gang members are more violent than those who are not in gangs.

Most gang members' behavior, including their criminal behavior, is in fact quite diverse. This has been termed *cafeteria-style* criminal/delinquent behavior. Nonetheless, the stereotype of the "violent gang" is often perpetuated by inaccurate media portrayals. When violent crime *is* gang related, it is most often gang *member* violence, rather than an organized, collective gang activity. Occasionally, violent conflict does take place *between* rival gangs and can involve many individuals at the same time. Sometimes, the level of violence to which a gang member is exposed can even be a catalyst that precipitates his or her leaving the gang. While popular opinion holds that one cannot ever leave the gang, research shows that although this can be a challenging process, it can and does occur successfully and exposure to violence is often cited as a significant factor influencing the decision to leave the gang.

Finally, a major factor that is currently contributing to gang-related violence in U.S. communities—and is likely to worsen—is the return of gang members from prison to the communities from which they came. In the most recent National Youth Gang Center Survey, 63% of jurisdictions reported that they had experienced the return of gang members from confinement and two thirds of those jurisdictions indicated that those gang members were significantly involved in violent crime. The challenge of "prisoner reentry" is a major one, with more than half a million ex-prisoners—many of whom are gang members—returning to society each year, mostly without having benefited from any significant rehabilitation services. Gang affiliation in prison has an independent effect on prison violence, and the connection that exists between gang members in prison and those in the community has been well documented. The "revolving door" of conviction, incarceration, release, rearrest, and reincarceration provides a steady and fresh supply of experienced gang members that exacerbates efforts to control gang-related crime and violence in the community, and incidents that occur in either the prison or the community can have rapid and serious repercussions in the other location due to the close ties that exist between gang members inside and those outside the prison walls.

C. Ronald Huff

See also Delinquency and Dating Violence; Peer Influences on Youth Violence; Prison Violence and Prison Gangs; Youth Violence

Further Readings

Decker, S. H. (1996). Collective and normative features of gang violence. *Justice Quarterly, 13,* 243–264.

Decker, S. H., & Lauritsen, J. L. (2002). Leaving the gang. In C. R. Huff (Ed.), *Gangs in America* (3rd ed., pp. 51–67). Thousand Oaks, CA: Sage.

Decker, S. H., & Weerman, F. M. (Eds.). (2005). *European street gangs and troublesome youth groups.* New York: AltaMira Press.

Egley, A., Jr., Howell, J. C., & Major, A. K. (2006). *National Youth Gang Survey, 1999–2001.* Washington, DC: Office of Juvenile Justice and Delinquency Prevention.

Esbensen, F.-A., & Huizinga, D. (1993). Gangs, drugs, and delinquency in a survey of urban youth. *Criminology, 31,* 565–589.

Huff, C. R. (1998). *Comparing the criminal behavior of youth gangs and at-risk youths.* Washington, DC: National Institute of Justice.

Klein, M. W. (1995). *The American street gang.* New York: Oxford University Press.

Miller, J. (2002). The girls in the gang: What we've learned from two decades of research. In C. R. Huff (Ed.), *Gangs in America* (3rd ed., pp. 175–197). Thousand Oaks, CA: Sage.

Thornberry, T. P., Krohn, M. D., Lizotte, A. J., Smith, C. A., & Tobin, K. (2003). *Gangs and delinquency in developmental perspective.* New York: Cambridge University Press.

GENDERCIDE

Gendercide is the practice of killing a child, or letting a child die by not taking care of him or her, because of his or her gender. Sex-selective abortion, or feticide, refers to a particular method of gendercide in which a fetus is aborted after determining, usually through an ultrasound or amniocentesis procedure, that the fetus is of an undesired or unwanted gender. Gendercide, in any form or manner, is denounced by researchers as "morally deplorable," "uncivilized," and a grim example of violence against children.

The prevalence of sex-selective feticide and infanticide, directed mainly at females, is not necessarily based on an individual's or particular family's decision. Instead, it is a social phenomenon rationalized through traditions and sociocultural values. Historical evidence of these practices, including selective neglect of female children, has been found in cultures around the globe. Many patriarchal societies have historically tended to recognize that raising daughters is less financially beneficial than raising sons. These societies have assumed that sons will provide their parents a sense of security and continuation of the family lineage. Through this lens, daughters are viewed more as liabilities than assets.

Anthropologists refer to many examples of female infanticide in the pre-Christian Mediterranean, Middle Eastern, African, and Asian cultures. Countries like China, India, Bangladesh, and Nepal have continued this traditional practice. The governments in these countries have declared these practices illegal. However, the enforcement of abortion laws based on fetus determination has generally been poor in all these countries. For example, media reports from all parts of India claim that female feticide cases have totaled millions during the past several years and are on the rise even among the educated middle-class people due to an increasing awareness of overpopulation and a high cost of raising children.

There are numerous official as well as unofficial reports in China and India stating that the female infanticide practices have caused a decline in the ratio of females to males. That demographic imbalance is likely to affect marriage and family relations in years to come.

Studies indicate denial among populations of the realities of violence against women. Studies are not available that identify short-range as well as long-range consequences of female feticide and infanticide.

Raghu N. Singh

See also Feticide; Infanticide

Further Readings

Freed, R. S. (1989). Beliefs and practices resulting in female deaths and fewer females than males in India. *Population and Environment, 10,* 144–161.

Jones, A. (Ed.). (2004). *Genocide and gendercide.* Nashville, TN: Vanderbilt University Press.

Warren, M. A. (1985). *Gendercide: The implications of sex selection.* Totowa, NJ: Rowman & Allanheld.

GENOCIDE

Genocide has emerged as one of the most important problems facing the international community. It stands alone in terms of the human suffering, loss, and death it engenders as well as the destruction of homes, property, and even cultures. Research suggests that during the 20th century, genocide and related crimes have killed more than four times as many people as all the international and civil wars combined. During the second half of the last century the pace and lethality of genocidal crimes increased dramatically and the world was witness to genocides in such places as Cambodia, Bosnia, and Rwanda. The new century is not starting out well if the genocide in the Darfur region of the Sudan is any indication. Since 2003 the Sudanese government has organized militia groups known as the Janjaweed to kill, terrorize, and displace thousands of members of non-Arabic tribes in the Darfur.

The term *genocide* was originally coined by Polish lawyer Raphael Lemkin in 1944. He created it from the ancient Greek word *genos* (race, tribe) and the Latin *cide* (killing). The word, therefore, is intended to describe the destruction of a group of people. While this might seem fairly clear, a great deal of confusion surrounds the meaning of the word *genocide*. One reason for this problem is that it is often difficult to distinguish between genocide and other forms of atrocities such as war crimes and human rights violations. Genocide, it is important to point out, is usually perpetrated during the middle of an ongoing conflict such as a civil war, and it is often hard to distinguish between massacres that are considered war crimes and others that might be part of a genocide. Unfortunately, international law defines these crimes broadly, with a great deal of conceptual overlap and ambiguity. Torture and medical experimentation, for example, are specifically listed as war crimes, yet both also occur frequently during genocides. During the Holocaust, for example, many infamous experiments were performed on unwilling victims. Do we consider these to be war crimes or genocide? In the same vein, do we merely perceive genocide as a type of human rights violation, or do we see it as a distinct and separate type of phenomenon? Additionally, because it is such a powerful and emotion-laden word, *genocide* has also often been used by social commentators and activists to describe such things as integration, bisexuality, urban sprawl, and family planning, which often serves to further muddy the waters regarding the nature of genocide.

These definitional difficulties do not mean, however, that genocide cannot be accurately defined. According to the United Nations (UN) Genocide Convention of 1948, genocide is defined as follows:

> Any of the following acts committed with intent to destroy, in whole or in part, a national, ethnical, racial or religious group, such as: (a) Killing members of the group; (b) Causing serious bodily or mental harm to members of the group; (c) Deliberately inflicting on the group conditions of life calculated to bring about its physical destruction in whole or in part; (d) Imposing measures intended to prevent births within the group; (e) Forcibly transferring children of the group to another group.

This definition makes clear that genocide is about destroying entire populations. Mass killings and massacres, as horrible as they are, do not rise to the level of genocide unless they are part of a larger program intended to destroy a group. In other words, genocide is a systematic attempt to exterminate an entire population group. According to the UN definition, genocide is also more than just murder, and can include a variety of policies and behaviors, many of which are not immediately lethal. Forcing sterilization, imposing measures intended to prevent births within a group, and sending children to boarding schools where they are forbidden to speak their language or practice their beliefs are all potentially genocidal. Although these practices do not involve overt acts of violence against individuals, they are, nonetheless, considered genocide because their intent is to destroy a group. While the individuals are left alive, the ties that bind them together as a people are obliterated.

According to the convention document, genocide can only occur against national, ethnic, racial, or religious groups. This means that destroying other types of collectives does not count as genocide. Political parties, for example, are a type of group that is excluded from the official UN definition of genocide because it was suggested that they did not have the same permanence and stability as the listed groups. This is a problem since many examples of mass crimes may have all the hallmarks of genocide, but may not be defined as such because the targeted group does not fit into one of the listed categories.

Defining genocide is one thing, trying to explain such violence is quite another. Genocide is a group's attempt to achieve a specific goal or goals. The group may consider their plans rational, but theirs is a flawed rationality since the decision-making process is typically influenced by various nationalistic and racial ideologies, historic perceptions of injustice and persecution, a desire for revenge, and a host of other emotive issues. Genocides are therefore not completely objective and rational because old hatreds and prejudices often guide the thinking processes of leaders intent on gaining or achieving some ambition.

Generally speaking, a number of motivations have been identified as providing the rationale for genocide. Helen Fein, a leading scholar of genocide, suggests four types of genocide in terms of motivation: (1) developmental, (2) despotic, (3) ideological, and (4) retributive.

Developmental genocides are those in which the targeted groups are seen as an impediment to the colonization and/or exploitation of a given geographic area. This happens most often against Indigenous peoples who may be perceived as being in the way of progress. In Central and South America, for example, many Native peoples have been subjected to genocide as various nations have attempted to remove them from land found to be rich in oil and valuable minerals.

Despotic genocides, on the other hand, involve situations in which a government uses genocide as a weapon against rivals for political power. The violence of the Stalinist Soviet Union fits into this category since Stalin and his henchmen tried to eliminate members of various political, economic, and national groups because they were perceived to be a threat to the consolidation of power.

Ideological genocide refers to the attempted destruction of a population because of a belief system. The Nazis and the Khmer Rouge of Cambodia, for example, perpetrated their excesses in the name of building a better society. The Nazis saw themselves as revolutionaries who would create a new Germany of wealth, prosperity, and order based on notions of racial hygiene and purity, and they attempted to eliminate from the nation everyone who was seen as an obstacle to achieving this new social order. Similarly, the Khmer Rouge wanted to return Cambodia to a historic and mythic era of greatness when the ethnic Khmer empire ruled the region. The Khmer Rouge attempted to achieve this through the destruction of all corrupting and oppositional influences within Cambodian society.

The last category of Fein's typology concerns *retributive* genocides. These are perpetrated by one group against another engaged in a struggle for political and social power. The Rwandan genocide is illustrative of this type since the Hutu government instigated the genocide against the Tutsi population partially because it was trying to maintain power during a civil war.

Fein's typology of genocide indicates that genocides are perpetrated for ostensibly rational, if reprehensible, reasons. Ultimately, genocide occurs because governmental officials decide that it is the solution to a real or perceived problem and is the preferred method to achieve a variety of political, economic, and/or social goals. While it may appear to be completely unjustified and irrational to outsiders and the larger world community, to those officials advocating the destructive policies of genocide, it makes perfect sense.

Alex Alvarez

See also Community Violence; Human Rights; Mass Murder; Oppression and Violence; United Nations, International Law/Courts; United Nations Conventions and Declarations

Further Readings

Alvarez, A. (2001). *Governments, citizens, and genocide: A comparative and interdisciplinary approach.* Bloomington: Indiana University Press.

Apsel, J. (Ed.). (2005). *Darfur: Genocide before our eyes.* New York: Institute for the Study of Genocide.

Churchill, W. (1997). *A little matter of genocide: Holocaust and denial in the Americas 1492 to the present.* San Francisco: City Lights Books.

Fein, H. (1993). *Genocide: A sociological perspective.* Thousand Oaks, CA: Sage.

LeBlanc, L. J. (1991). *The United States and the Genocide Convention.* Durham, NC: Duke University Press.

Power, S. (2002). *A problem from hell: America and the age of genocide.* New York: Basic Books.

Reisman, W. M., & Antoniou, C. T. (Eds.). (1994). *The laws of war: A comprehensive collection of primary documents on international law governing armed conflict.* New York: Vintage Books.

Totten, S., Parsons, W. S., & Charny, I. W. (Eds.). (1997). *Century of genocide: Eyewitness accounts and critical views.* New York: Routledge.

Valentino, B. A. (2004). *Final solutions: Mass killing and genocide in the 20th century.* Ithaca, NY: Cornell University Press.

Weitz, E. D. (2003). *A century of genocide: Utopias of race and nation.* Princeton, NJ: Princeton University Press.

GEOGRAPHIC PATTERNS

Criminologists, law enforcement officials, and city planners have long been interested in the relationship between geography and crime. Some of the earliest empirical studies of crime were conducted in the 1830s and 1840s by Andre Michel Guerry and Adolphe Quételet, who plotted recorded crimes on maps and showed considerable variation in the numbers of crimes across geographic areas. As part of the Chicago ecological school of the 1920s and 1930s, Clifford Shaw and Henry McKay examined rates of delinquency in reference to the concentric zones in urban areas. The development of social area analysis and factor analytic techniques in the 1950s and 1960s renewed interest in the relationship between space and crime. These methods demonstrated a strong relationship between the population characteristics and crime rates in areas. The related fields of environmental criminology and the geography of crime emerged in the 1970s and 1980s, demonstrating the multidisciplinary nature of the subject. These fields seek to explain the spatial distribution of offenses and the spatial distribution of offenders. While many of these developments have focused on an understanding and explanation of spatial variations in interpersonal crime per se, they also have contributed to crime prevention and control efforts.

Understanding Spatial Variations

Research on geography and interpersonal violence examines variations in violence across very broad geographical areas down to relatively small areas. It has demonstrated significant regional variations within countries, variation within regions, within cities, and within neighborhoods. Many of the studies of the relationship between geography and crime rely on official data provided by law enforcement officials such as the Federal Bureau of Investigation's Uniform Crime Reporting (UCR) Program. Since many crimes of violence are not reported to the police, these findings must be viewed cautiously. Other studies use data generated by self-report studies, including the Department of Justice National Crime Victimization Survey (NCVS).

Throughout the 20th century, homicide rates showed a consistent regional variation. The South has had the highest rate of homicides, followed by the West, then the Midwest. The Northeast has consistently had the lowest homicide rate. Rates of sexual assault and other assaults also vary across regions. Based on the recent self-report studies of the NCVS, the Northeast has the lowest rate of sexual assaults. The Midwest has the next lowest rate of sexual assaults, and the South and the West report the highest rates.

Within regions, there is considerable variation in violent crime rates across areas. Data from the UCR and the NCVS show that urban areas have higher rates of violent offenses than suburban areas, which are higher than rural areas. The 2005 NCVS reported a violent victimization rate for persons age 12 and over of 29.8 per 1,000 urban residents, 18.6 for suburban residents, and 16.4 for rural residents. This overall pattern was similar for rapes and sexual assaults (1.5 per 1,000 for urban areas, 0.7 for suburban areas, and 0.1 for rural areas) as well as robberies (4.7, 1.9, 1.4, respectively) and other assaults (23.6, 16.0, 14.9, respectively).

Crime is not evenly distributed across city neighborhoods. Many neighborhoods in the same city have much higher crime rates than others. In most cities, the majority of violent offenses occur in a small percentage of the city's neighborhoods. For example, William J. Wilson pointed out that over half of the murders and aggravated assaults in Chicago occurred in 7 of the city's 24 police districts. Areas that have higher rates of violent offenses tend to have higher rates of poverty, residential mobility, and ethnic heterogeneity. Extremely deprived areas have much higher rates of violent crime than areas with moderate or low levels of disadvantage.

Even within neighborhoods, crime is not evenly distributed across all spaces. Recent research has begun to use a "micro" approach that focuses on specific places within neighborhoods. These may be particular buildings or addresses, blocks or street segments. One study found that 14% of all crimes against persons were concentrated in 56 hot spots that comprised only 4% of all street segments or intersections in the city.

Research on the geography of crime also shows that most violent criminals tend to commit their crimes close to home and most crime victims are victimized near their homes. Numerous studies of murder, robbery, and rape show that offenders commit a high percentage of offenses within a short distance of their homes. The average violent offender travels 1.5 miles to the location of the crime. About 25% of all murder offenders commit their offense within two blocks of their home. Spontaneous offenses tend to occur in places where offenders spend the majority of their time (i.e., close to home). Offenders choose to commit premeditated offenses in areas that they know well, again, areas closer to home.

Recent research suggests that about 25% of all violent victimizations occur in the victim's home. Fifty percent of violent victimizations occur within 1 mile of the victim's home, and over 75% occur within 5 miles of the victim's home. The NCVS report shows that 38% of rapes and sexual assaults occurred in the victim's home and another 23% occurred within 1 mile of the victim's home. Thirty-three percent of assaults occurred inside or near the victim's home and another 17% occurred within a mile of the victim's home.

Explanation of Spatial Variations

Social scientists have tried to explain these variations in crime across physical space from a number of different perspectives, including the social disorganization and routine activities approaches. Social disorganization is defined as the inability of a community to achieve the common goals of its residents and maintain effective controls. The social disorganization approach, rooted in the early works of Clifford Shaw and Henry McKay on juvenile delinquency, suggests

that crime is higher in communities characterized by low socioeconomic status, high rates of transiency, racial heterogeneity, and family disruption. It is not these demographic characteristics themselves that directly lead to high rates of crime. Rather, these characteristics are related to low levels of neighborhood friendship networks, low levels of membership in local organizations, and high levels of unsupervised youth. These are the factors that contribute to higher levels of crime in some neighborhoods.

The routine activities approach, again based on the human ecological model, seeks to explain crimes involving direct contact between a victim and offender. It suggests that there must be a convergence in time and space of three essential components of crime: an offender motivated to commit a crime, a suitable target, and the absence of guardians capable of preventing the crime. The convergence of these factors depends on the structure of everyday routine interactions. The nature of these everyday activities determines the location of potential victims and the pool of personal contacts they will have, including contacts with potential offenders.

Crime Prevention and Control

Law enforcement officials have a particular interest in the geography of crime. Knowledge of the relationship between physical space and crime provides police with important information that affects their allocation of resources and criminal investigations. Simple mapping techniques that plot known offenses allow police to target certain hot spots for special attention. Geographic profiling assists law enforcement in investigations. When serial violent offenders are suspected, the locations of crime sites are entered into a computer and analyzed to determine the area where the offender is most likely to reside.

The relationship between space and crime is also of interest to groups concerned with crime prevention, including urban planners and architects. Drawing from the concepts of the social disorganization and routine activities approaches, some researchers suggest that buildings and areas can be designed to reduce crime. Jane Jacobs suggests that buildings should be oriented toward the street to encourage surveillance by residents and that there should be a clear separation between public and private spaces. Oscar Newman's defensible space concept suggests the use of real or symbolic barriers to divide neighborhoods into manageable areas. The barriers, either gates or clearly marked entrances to areas, may reduce access to the area by outsiders. Gated communities, suburban cul-de-sacs, and inner-city street closings all serve to reduce the likelihood of potential offenders entering the area and becoming familiar with the area. Reducing the number of outsiders coming into the community may also increase the territoriality of residents, who will be more likely to notice and be more watchful of any strangers who do enter the area. Offenders would be deterred by the increased likelihood of being observed and few escape routes if they were observed. Crime would be lower in areas with these designs, because the physical layout of the areas and the heightened social organization of residents would make potential offenders less likely to enter areas to commit their crimes.

The work of Jane Jacobs and Oscar Newman contributed to the growth of C. Ray Jeffery's urban and architectural design perspective, Crime Prevention Through Environmental Design (CPTED). This approach focuses on reducing crime through design principles that include providing natural surveillance of areas, territorial reinforcement, access control, and target hardening. Implementing CPTED has resulted in significant decreases in criminal activity in some communities.

Patrick G. Donnelly

See also Legal System, Criminal Justice Strategies to Reduce Interpersonal Violence; National Crime Victimization Survey; Uniform Crime Reports

Further Readings

Brantingham, P., & Brantingham, P. (1984). *Patterns in crime.* New York: Macmillan.

Evans, D. J., & Herbert, D. T. (1989). *The geography of crime.* New York: Routledge.

GREENBOOK, THE

The "Greenbook" is so named because its cover is green. Its real title is *Effective Intervention in Domestic Violence and Child Maltreatment Cases: Guidelines for Policy and Practice,* and it was published in 1999 by the National Council of Juvenile and Family Court Judges (NCJFCJ) after an 18-month development process.

A growing body of research in the 1980s and 1990s showed (1) that there was a co-occurrence of child maltreatment and adult-to-adult domestic violence in up to half of the families studied, and (2) that even when children were not themselves maltreated, many were exposed to violence by one parent against another. The Greenbook was developed as a result of this growing research and the frustration of service providers that their responses to battered mothers and their children were fragmented. The Family Violence Department of NCJFCJ convened a national group of experts from child welfare systems, domestic violence organizations, and juvenile courts to discuss this issue and establish national best-practice guidelines. The Greenbook contains 67 such recommendations on how to better serve families with the coordinated responses of these three social service and justice systems. The recommendations are grouped into five chapters focused on overarching principles and each of the three systems. The committee that developed the Greenbook struggled with many difficult issues, including defining terms, the sharing of confidential information, and mandating services among others. In the end, the committee found common ground in a shared language that sought safety, stability, and well-being for all victims in a family, and accountability for perpetrators of violence.

The Greenbook drew the interest of the federal government and after its publication the government developed a Greenbook Initiative that provided funding to support six demonstration sites in five states, technical assistance providers, and a national cross-site evaluation. A unique aspect of the federal initiative was that it drew support from across multiple government agencies, including the Office on Violence Against Women, the National Institute of Justice, the Office of Juvenile Justice and Delinquency Programs, the Office on Victims of Crime, the Centers for Disease Control and Prevention, and several units of the Department of Health and Human Services, including the Children's Bureau and the Office of the Assistant Secretary of Planning and Evaluation. In addition to the federally funded demonstration sites many other communities around the United States have adopted the recommendations found in the Greenbook.

The results of the national cross-site evaluations comparing the six federally funded demonstration sites are becoming available and show positive outcomes as well as some mixed results. There have been increases in collaboration and changes in agency policies and practices, yet some of these changes appear transitory or partial.

Jeffrey L. Edleson

See also Child Exposure to Intimate Partner Violence; Failure to Protect; National Council of Juvenile and Family Court Judges; Office on Violence Against Women

Further Readings

National Council of Juvenile and Family Court Judges. (1999). *Effective intervention in domestic violence and child maltreatment cases: Guidelines for policy and practice.* Reno, NV: Author.

Web Sites

The Greenbook: http://www.thegreenbook.info/

GUN CONTROL

Gun violence has become an epidemic in the United States and concerns about reducing gun violence have created a number of policy choices at the state and federal level. Federal authorities have encouraged local governments to create programs such as Project Safe Neighborhood (PSN) and Project Exile, which focus on reducing gun violence in many U.S. cities. However, these programs are only a portion of the gun control initiative. Gun control policy is also related to the social and historical foundations of the problem, political ideologies, and gun control legislation.

The debate on gun control laws and policies in the United States demonstrates a struggle that has been ongoing in both politics and policy process for decades. Gun control and regulations of gun ownership have played a significant role in gaining public support during elections. Debate on gun control policies has become a highly salient issue, especially at times when gun violence has appeared in schools or other public places. Social science research on gun control can be divided into three main categories that present the scientific and political debate on the issue.

History, Culture, and Gun Control

The first group of research studies focuses on gun control from a historical viewpoint and mainly explains the role of guns in American society throughout history. This type of research also considers gun ownership as a cultural phenomenon and claims that gun ownership is at the center of traditional American life. Discussions on the role of guns in American traditional life are also connected to the origins of the Second Amendment of the U.S. Constitution, which guarantees citizens the right to bear arms. Advocates of gun ownership claim that the Constitution gives citizens of the United States the right to own a gun and that the right is protected. On the other hand, advocates of gun control arguments highlight the relationship between gun ownership and gun violence and claim that it is not against the spirit of the Constitution to make guns unreachable to criminals. Advocates of gun control also argue that the Constitution is a "living and changing" document; that is, any part of it can be discarded at will, and that rights are never absolute. They argue that at the time the Constitution was drafted citizens were arms of the government, so they needed weapons to protect their government. Gun control advocates argue that the states, the federal government, and the people have all changed over time.

Another argument centers on the differences in beliefs about gun control among cultures and demographic regions. Gary Kleck's study of the cultural foundations of gun control indicates that gun control support is more a product of culture conflict than response to crime. The findings of his study suggest that high crime rates and prior victimization do not increase support for gun control among the general urban population. Gun control opinion was found to be related to membership in groups whose cultures have certain opinions concerning guns, hunting, modernism versus traditionalism, change orientation versus status quo, and internationalism versus localism. On the other hand, the research shows that regional origins, gender, and affiliation with a religion are unrelated to gun control opinions. Research also shows that support is stronger in cities with more police and fewer gun owners per capita.

Gun Control and Politics and Legislation

The second type of research puts gun control at the center of the political arena. Political debate about gun control and the ideological foundations of that debate, interest group participation, and party politics are some of the major issues studied under this type of research. This research suggests that the American political process muddies the gun control debate. The interaction of different political actors makes the issue even more complicated, which later results in poorly crafted and ineffective policy that accomplishes nothing more than conflict that feeds back into the policy debate.

A significant amount of research has been conducted to examine the legislative aspects of gun control and measure the effectiveness of gun control laws. Political debates on gun control are also related to the legislative side of the gun control issue. Liberals and conservatives differ from each other when they look at gun control as a policy option. Liberals argue that gun availability causes violence and insist that gun control is both justified and necessary to prevent such violence. Conservatives, on the other hand, think that it is unfair to disarm responsible citizens because of irresponsible criminals. Conservative ideology supports the idea that almost all gun violence is perpetrated by a very small group of criminals using illegal guns, while the vast majority of firearms are never used illegally. From the conservative perspective, outlawing guns to prevent violence would be like outlawing speech or printing presses in order to prevent libel.

In terms of legislative process, conservatives oppose passage of new legislation for gun control and support the enforcement of existing laws and programs that provide sentence enhancements for crimes committed with guns. Both gun control supporters and Second Amendment advocates agree that prosecutors should be given the discretion to be able to increase sentences for crimes committed with guns. From a deterrence perspective, sentence enhancement should reduce gun violence by incapacitating gun criminals through longer sentences. Such a policy does not affect the ability of law-abiding adults to keep guns for self-defense or recreation.

The social science literature presents contradictory findings about the application of sentence enhancement laws and their effects on reducing firearm-related crimes. However, a large number of studies show that sentence enhancement laws are not significant in deterring firearm-related crimes, and in many cases those laws are used as a plea-bargaining tool.

Most recently, the federal government began an initiative called Project Safe Neighborhood (PSN) to reduce gun violence by increasing enforcement and prosecution of gun laws. PSN is a coordinated effort to stop gun violence in communities through enhanced, directed resources and more effective prosecutions of gun crime. Prosecutors are expected to apply the maximum sentence for gun crimes in their jurisdictions. With a budget of $550 million, PSN aims to enhance penalties for gun crime by diverting those who have committed federal firearm offenses into federal court, where prison sentences are typically more severe than in most state systems.

Criminal Justice Interventions and Policy Perspectives

The third category of research basically approaches gun control from a policy perspective and includes criminal justice interventions, the outcomes of gun violence reduction programs, and criminological research that seeks to explain the relationship between firearms and violent crimes. The main concern among these researchers is whether gun ownership increases or decreases crime rates. On one side of the spectrum, scholars who take the "more guns, less crime" approach argue that gun ownership increases deterrence by allowing people to defend themselves. Classical criminological theory underlies this approach, with the principle that people will be deterred from crime if the pain associated with punishment outweighs the pleasure associated with crime. There is research that indicates that allowing citizens to carry concealed weapons deters violent crimes without increasing accidental deaths. However, at the other end of the spectrum, researchers focus on the idea that the availability of guns and increased number of gun owners are two of the most important causes of violent crimes. Supporters of this approach criticize the way the government and the media emphasize the costs of gun ownership over the benefits, despite the fact that the best evidence shows that the benefits clearly outweigh the costs.

The theoretical and policy implications of the assumption that the objective of gun ownership is to enhance the security of gun owners and their associates have also been explored by researchers. Gun ownership may be one possible way to reduce crime; however, alternative ways to achieve this objective, such as better police control, education, and socioeconomic justice, should be considered before drawing the conclusion that gun ownership reduces crime.

The various segments of the gun control debate are interconnected and are not necessarily mutually exclusive. Any historical explanation can be related with the political, policy level, and legislative aspects of the gun control debate. However, looking at the gun control issue at different levels of analysis helps us to clarify one of the most controversial social and political debates in American history.

Cuneyt Gurer

See also Gun Control, Legislation; Gun Violence

Further Readings

Correa, H. (2001). An analytic approach to the study of gun control policies. *Socio-Economic Planning Sciences, 35,* 253–262.

Egendorf, L. K. (2005). *Guns and violence: Current controversies.* Farmington Hills, MI: Greenhaven Press.

Kleck, G. (1996). Crime, culture conflict and the sources of support for gun control. *American Behavioral Scientist, 39,* 387–404.

Lott, J. R. (2003). *The bias against guns: Why almost everything you heard about gun control is wrong.* Washington, DC: Regnery.

Vizzard, W. J. (1995). The impact of agenda conflict on policy formulation and implementation: The case of gun control. *Public Administration Review, 55,* 341–347.

GUN CONTROL, LEGISLATION

Political debate about gun control has a direct influence on the legislative aspect of gun control policies in the United States. How liberal and conservative parties think about gun control determines their approach to gun legislation. Therefore, liberals who support strict control policies emphasize the necessity of new laws and restrictions on gun ownership, whereas conservatives argue that the Second Amendment of the Constitution gives citizens the right to bear arms and, instead of new laws with more severe restrictions on gun ownership, they support enforcement of existing laws.

In democratic societies, legislative proposals gain popular support and are passed into law for two basic reasons. The first reason has been labeled the *instrumentalist explanation* and suggests that laws are passed because their supporters believe that they will help solve social problems. The second reason, the *conflict perspective,* suggests that laws are instruments of power used by conflicting social groups to gain or preserve some advantage of wealth, prestige, or influence.

Gun control legislation represents both instrumentalist and conflict perspectives where legislative proposals to require restrictions on gun ownership, assuming such laws will affect violent crime rates, face significant opposition from interest groups and political parties that support policies other than legislative restrictions. For example, in 1994, during the Clinton administration, the federal government enacted legislation banning certain semiautomatic weapons and large capacity ammunition magazines. Even though this law only included a small portion of the group of weapons that ban advocates proposed, it was a product of a highly competitive legislative process. The main source of opposition to the ban was the National Rifle Association (NRA), a third-party interest group. In 2001, the Bush administration designed a nationwide program that proposed enhanced sentences for gun crimes and increased law enforcement capacities. Enhanced sentences were considered to have a deterrent effect on gun crimes and found bipartisan support because they did not affect gun ownership by law-abiding citizens.

Aside from the political aspect of the legislative process, it is also worth mentioning the instrumental aspect of the laws, which suggests that those laws are believed to help solve gun-related problems. Research on the impact of gun laws to reduce gun crimes provides little evidence about their effectiveness, suggesting that gun laws are not really effective tools in reducing gun violence. Sentence enhancement for gun crimes, a common feature of the federal programs, and their effect on violent crime and reduction of gun use also do not show promising results in research evaluating their effectiveness. For example, one recent study explored the effects of sentence enhancement laws on reduction of violence in Detroit, Jacksonville, Tampa, and Miami and concluded that there was little evidence that sentence enhancement laws are successful in reducing violent crime. However, in a similar study conducted in two Pennsylvania cities, Philadelphia and Pittsburgh, there was evidence that sentencing laws substantially reduced the number of homicides.

In summary, two characteristics of gun control legislation have been documented: the instrumentalist approach that aims to find a solution to the problem of gun violence, and the conflict approach that represents the law as a product of power in the political process. In either case, in order to have effective gun control policies, social programs, effective law enforcement strategies, and targeted problem-solving instruments are necessary in addition to legislation.

Cuneyt Gurer

See also Gun Control; Gun Violence

Further Readings

Hahn, R. A., Bilukha, O., Crosby, A., Fullilove, M. T., Liberman, A., Moscicki, E., et al. (Task Force on Community Preventive Services). (2005). Firearms laws and the reduction of violence: A systematic review. *American Journal of Preventive Medicine, 28*(2S1), 40–71.

Kleck, G. (1996). Crime, culture conflict and the sources of support for gun control. *American Behavioral Scientist, 39,* 387–404.

McDowall, D., Loftin, C., & Wiersema, B. (1992). A comparative study of the preventive effects of mandatory sentencing laws for gun crimes. *Journal of Criminal Law and Criminology, 83,* 378–394.

GUN VIOLENCE

Guns and violence are integrally related. A discussion about guns that does not mention their role in violence, or a discussion of violence without regard to guns, misses part of the whole picture. Understanding the nature of gun violence requires looking at the issue from different levels of analysis and different political approaches. Examining varying levels of analysis allows us to consider the issue of how individuals, society, and state institutions see the problem. An examination of different political approaches will highlight the issue of the political debate around gun control and violence. This entry begins with gun violence statistics and then discusses gun violence with regard to individuals, society, and governmental interventions.

Gun Violence Statistics

Between 1999 and 2003, there were 140,795 gun-related violent deaths in the United States, accounting for 57.8% of all violence-related deaths within the same period. During this time frame, firearm-related homicide was the leading cause of violence-related deaths in the United States for individuals between the ages 15 and 34.

According to Federal Bureau of Investigation (FBI) statistics, 68% of the homicides that occurred in 2005 were committed with firearms. Of those, 75% involved handguns, and the remaining 25% involved shotguns, rifles, and unknown gun types. The number of murders committed with a firearm increased from 8,890 to 10,100—nearly 14%—between 2001 and 2005.

The proportion of gun involvement in violent offenses remains well above the average of other industrialized countries. Most gun violence scholars agree that gun violence is an "epidemic" for the United States; however, the causes and solutions are debated widely. The primary form of the debate on how to reduce gun violence involves policy options regarding gun availability. On one side of the debate, it is claimed that gun violence is related to easy access to guns in American society. Conversely, others argue that the ability to legally possess guns decreases violence because the legal carriers of the weapons are able to protect themselves from violent offenders; therefore, they actually have a deterrent effect.

In addition to the high proportion of fatal incidents of violence, the National Crime Victimization Survey (NCVS), which is a national victimization survey of about 134,000 persons age 12 and older, reveals that a substantial number of nonfatal violent crimes were also committed with a firearm. While the proportion of nonfatal violent incidents that involved the use of a firearm fell to 6% by 2004, a substantial increase to approximately 9% was observed in 2005.

It is estimated that 49% of U.S. households have guns, which amounts to 47.6 million households. Half of the weapons in these households are owned specifically for self-defense. Nevertheless, guns are involved in approximately 70% of homicides and 60% of suicides in the United States. Death by firearm is the second leading cause of injury death. In the United States, gun mortality is more than twice that of the next highest of the industrialized countries. It costs as much as $100 billion each year, and it disproportionately affects young people, as it is the second leading cause of death among youth ages 10 to 19.

Individuals and Gun Violence

Violent behavior, in general, can be considered a way of communicating where such action is either accepted or tolerated. In this context, Deanna L. Wilkinson and Jeffrey Fagan have argued that the presence of firearms presents a unique contingency that shapes decision-making patterns of individuals. The presence of firearms influences decisions both in social interactions with the potential for becoming disputes and within disputes that have already begun. From an individual point of view, gun use has become a means of status and identity formation for members of inner-city neighborhoods in the United States. Therefore, gun violence can be thought of as an ultimate tool to form and sustain positive social identities within the neighborhood. For some, firearms represent toughness, power, dominance, self-defense, and protection for those living in a violent subculture.

Society and Gun Violence

Violence in the society and the availability of guns present risk factors. Some studies indicate that television programs and video games cause further violence. Research also indicates that adolescents who are exposed to higher levels of community violence also engage in higher levels of violent activity, associate with more deviant peers, and adhere more strongly to an aggressive cognitive style. Families are important determinants of both violent victimization and perpetration. Neighborhood disadvantage also plays a significant role in violence outcomes.

Federal Government/State Intervention in Gun Violence

Gun violence in the United States has created a huge and ongoing debate on gun control laws and policies, which has resulted in a struggle both in politics and policy processes for decades. In politics, gun control and regulation of gun ownership have played a significant role in gaining public support during elections. Debate on gun control policies has become a highly salient issue, especially at times when gun violence occurs in schools or other public places. As gun violence grew in the United States, gun control became an important topic for the federal government to address in various ways. It has been argued, in fact, that American policy processes promote a complicated debate on the gun issue and that the debate on gun control is a product of the American political process, rather than America's romance with guns.

One policy option shared by both gun control supporters and Second Amendment advocates is enhanced prison penalties for gun crimes, which has found widespread support from all sides of the U.S. gun policy debate. From a deterrence perspective, sentence enhancements ought to reduce gun violence by incapacitating gun criminals through longer sentences. Sentence enhancements give prosecutors discretion to be able to increase sentences for gun crimes. However, others have found that sentence enhancement laws have not produced a significant deterrent effect for firearm-related crimes and, in many cases, those charges are used as a plea-bargaining tool.

Most recently, the federal government proposed Project Safe Neighborhood (PSN) to reduce gun violence by increasing enforcement and prosecution of gun laws. Under this initiative, prosecutors are expected to argue for the maximum sentence for gun crime charges in their jurisdictions. PSN is a coordinated effort to stop gun violence in communities through enhanced, directed resources and more effective prosecution of gun crimes.

Criminologist Lawrence Sherman examined gun violence programs and research on gun violence in the United States from an epidemiological perspective. He concludes that most gun crimes would still occur even if every convicted felon in the United States were shipped to Australia, rather than just barred from legal gun ownership. By making this argument, Sherman illustrates that a policy of using prior felony conviction to determine which people are unsafe to have guns is too simplistic. Rather, gun crime rates might be better reduced by adopting an epidemiologically based perspective. An individual's decision to use a gun in crime cannot adequately be predicted simply by previous criminal history, and alternative strategies to restricting sales to "safe people" are needed to substantially reduce gun violence. Taking such an epidemiologic approach would involve such tactics as increasing gun patrols that focus on high-risk times and geographically concentrated violent places.

Gun violence is a substantial and pervasive problem that has been difficult to solve in the United States. While some strategies have shown promise for reducing gun violence in targeted communities, large-scale changes in policies have been less successful at addressing the gun violence issue. While the debate continues on the most appropriate policy response to gun violence, few would argue that individuals in the United States continue to be killed by firearms at an unacceptable rate.

Eric Jefferis and Cuneyt Gurer

See also Gang Violence; Gun Control; Gun Control, Legislation; Homicides, Criminal

Further Readings

Behrman, R. E. (2002). Children, youth, and gun violence. *The Future of Children, 12*(2). Retrieved from http://www.futureofchildren.org/pubs-inf02825/pubs-info_show.htm?doc_id=154414

Egendorf, L. (2005). *Guns and violence.* Farmington Hills, MI: Greenhaven Press.

Federal Bureau of Investigation. (2005). *Crime in the United States, 2005.* Retrieved August 24, 2007, from www.fbi.com

National Center for Injury Prevention and Control. (2008). *WISQARS (Web-based Injury Query and Reporting System).* Retrieved from http://www.cdc.gov/ncipc/wisqars/default.htm

Sherman, L. W. (2000). Reducing gun violence: What works, what doesn't, what's promising. In *Perspectives on crime and justice: 1999–2000* [Lecture series]. Washington, DC: U.S. Department of Justice, National Institute of Justice.

Vizzard, W. J. (1995). The impact of agenda conflict on policy formulation and implementation: The case of gun control. *Public Administration Review, 55,* 341–347.

Wilkinson, D. L., & Fagan, J. (2001). What we know about gun use among adolescents. *Clinical Child and Family Psychology Review, 4*(2), 109–132.

Zimring, F., & Hawkins, G. (1997). *Crime is not the problem: Lethal violence in America.* New York: Oxford University Press.

Hague Convention on the Civil Aspects of International Child Abduction

The Hague Convention on the Civil Aspects of International Child Abduction was completed in 1980 in the Netherlands. Countries that agree to the Hague Convention are expected to help quickly return abducted children to their country of habitual residence, where other issues, such as custody, can be resolved by local jurisdictions.

Under the Hague Convention, the "left behind" parent files a petition for the return of the child. This parent must prove that the removal was wrongful by showing there was a breach of custody rights and that those rights were being exercised at the time of the removal. Courts first decide where the child's habitual residence is located, for this determination settles which country's court has jurisdiction over custody and other issues related to the child. If the court decides that the habitual residence of the child is in the other country, the parent who has taken the child—called the *removing parent, taker,* or *abducting parent*—can use one of the six defenses in order to stop the return of his or her child to the country of habitual residence. These include the following: (a) the left behind parent consented or acquiesced to the removal of the child by, for example, sending belongings or even forcibly excluding the child and his or her mother from the habitual residence; (b) the child has reached an age of maturity at which his or her own wishes to stay with

the taking parent can be considered; (c) at least 1 year has passed from the date of removal and the child is well settled into a new residence; (d) the left behind parent was not exercising his or her custody rights; (e) returning the child would create a grave risk of physical or psychological harm to the child; or (f) the return of the child would violate his or her human rights, for example, where there are inadequate protections in place in the other country to safeguard the child from an abusive parent. If the court decides that one or more of these situations exist then the order for return of the child most often will not be granted and any further court proceedings will take place in the same country where the petition was heard, that is, in the country to where the child was taken.

When the Hague Convention was completed, it mainly focused on helping the left behind parent because at that time research showed that the typical abductor was the male noncustodial parent who had taken the child to a country where the mother did not have any access to the child. However, recent surveys have shown that 68% of taking parents are now mothers and that many are victims of adult domestic violence fleeing for their safety. Furthermore, other studies have shown that female parents are more likely to abduct when they were the victims of abuse, while male parents are more likely to abduct when they are the abuser. As the Hague Convention now stands, battered mothers may be drawn into Hague proceedings as a respondent to a petition accusing them of child abduction when they were attempting to protect their children and themselves from gravely dangerous adult partners.

Although a few courts have refused to order the return of children when the mother was fleeing her abuser, many courts fail to find or classify this situation as a defense to wrongful removal and the child is ordered to be returned to the country of the left behind parent. Even though the orders do not mandate that mothers return with their children, when the return is ordered, often the mother will follow her children back to the country of the abuser. This may place the battered mother and children back into physical danger. The Hague Convention may be ill equipped to deal with domestic violence today because there is no defense for women fleeing domestic violence with their children. Some judges have recognized children's exposure to violence as a grave risk and refused to return children. One formal solution would be to change Hague Convention–implementing legislation in each nation, such as International Child Abduction Remedies in the United States, so that it recognizes what the social science literature has found, that child exposure to adult domestic violence may pose a grave risk to a child's physical and mental health.

Sudha Shetty and Jeffrey L. Edleson

See also Child Abductions, Family; Child Exposure to Intimate Partner Violence; United Nations, International Law/Courts

Further Readings

Shetty, S., & Edleson, J. L. (2005). Adult domestic violence in cases of international parental child abduction. *Violence Against Women, 11,* 115–138.

Web Sites

The Hague Domestic Violence Project: http://www .haguedv.org

HARVARD SCHOOL OF PUBLIC HEALTH COLLEGE ALCOHOL STUDY

The Harvard School of Public Health College Alcohol Study (CAS) conducted four large surveys of American college students in the spring semesters of 1993, 1997, 1999, and 2001. Over 80 publications based on CAS data explore the role of alcohol in college life, including its role in interpersonal violence. Among its most important findings about interpersonal violence is that 1 in 20 college women reported experiencing rape in the 7 or so months since the beginning of the school year, with most of the rapes (72%) occurring when the woman was too intoxicated to give consent.

Questions about rape are included in the 1997 and later surveys. Women were asked to respond to three questions about whether (since the beginning of the school year) they had sexual intercourse against their wishes because they had been forced or threatened, or when they were so intoxicated that they were unable to consent to sex. The items conform to the legal definition of rape in many states and have been used in other studies. Several factors were associated with the risk of rape, most importantly the level of binge drinking at the college, being underage, residing in a sorority house, having engaged in binge drinking in high school, and using illicit drugs. Women who attend colleges with high rates of binge drinking (rates of 50% or more) were significantly more likely to be raped while intoxicated than women who attend schools with low rates of binge drinking (where 35% or fewer students engage in binge drinking).

The findings suggest that substance abuse prevention (for both potential perpetrators and victims) should place a significant role in rape prevention. While the perpetrator is always responsible legally and morally for rape, identifying the factors that place women at increased vulnerability to rape (such as binge drinking) remain important. The CAS data identified binge drinking and its overall rate on campus as such a factor. Far from being an innocent rite of passage, college binge drinking is a risk factor in violence against women. Men need to know what constitutes rape, and that intoxication is a stop sign for sex.

Binge drinking has been the focus of the CAS since its inception. The CAS defines it as five or more drinks in a row for men and four or more drinks for women, at least once in the 2 weeks before the survey was completed. Roughly two in five college students meet that definition, with one in five a frequent binge drinker with three or more episodes during the 2 weeks. These results remained largely stable from 1993 to 2001, despite increased attention to this issue by colleges. One in three colleges had 50% or more of students defined as binge drinkers.

The methods used in the CAS distinguish it from other attempts to measure excessive drinking by college students. The CAS was funded by the Robert Wood Johnson Foundation. A representative sample of 179 four-year colleges was selected, with probability proportionate to enrollment sampling. Each of the 140 institutions that initially participated in the study provided the CAS with a list of full-time students, from which a random sample was drawn. Institutions were located in 40 states and the District of Columbia and represented a cross-section of American higher education. The principal investigator of CAS, Henry Wechsler of the Harvard School of Public Health, designed a 20-page questionnaire based on his own previous college studies and other large-scale surveys. Questionnaires were mailed to students in the spring semester of each year, with four separate mailings as well as a drawing for a cash award designed to increase participation. An initial response rate of 69% was achieved, with over 17,000 students completing the questionnaire in the first survey year.

Binge drinking is associated with higher risks of alcohol-related problems for the individual drinker, including missing classes, getting behind in schoolwork, doing something one regrets, and arguing with friends. Binge drinkers have higher rates of engaging in unplanned sexual activity, not using protection during sex, and getting hurt or injured. Almost half of the frequent binge drinkers surveyed had experienced five or more different alcohol-related problems since the beginning of the school year.

In addition to the effects of binge drinking, the CAS also explored secondhand binge effects, problems that affect nonbingeing students who live in residence halls or a fraternity or sorority house. Nonbingeing students at schools with higher rates of binge drinking are more likely than students at schools with lower rates to have experienced secondhand binge effects as the result of others' drinking, such as experiencing an unwanted sexual advance or being pushed, hit, or assaulted.

The CAS helped call attention to binge drinking and associated problems such as intoxicated rape and has led to considerable research and prevention efforts. A special task force on college drinking was created by the National Institute of Alcohol Abuse and Alcoholism. Its 2002 report used CAS and other data to present a snapshot of the problems associated with binge drinking, including 1,400 student deaths, over 70,000 sexual assaults or date rapes, and 600,000 assaults each year. The report urges colleges to change the culture of college binge drinking, and provides information about prevention efforts that have been proved to be effective among college students and the general population, as well as programs that hold promise for changing behavior.

George W. Dowdall

See also Alcohol and Violence; Rape/Sexual Assault; Substance Abuse

Further Readings

Dowdall, G. W., & Wechsler, H. (2002). Studying college alcohol use: Widening the lens, sharpening the focus. *Journal of Studies on Alcohol, Supplement, 14,* 14–22.

Kuo, M., Dowdall, G. W., Koss, M. P., & Wechsler, H. (2004). Correlates of rape while intoxicated in a national sample of college women. *Journal of Studies on Alcohol, 65,* 37–45.

Task Force of the National Advisory Council on Alcohol Abuse and Alcoholism. (2002). *A call to action: Changing the culture of drinking at U.S. colleges.* Rockville, MD: National Institute of Alcohol Abuse and Alcoholism.

Wechsler, H., Davenport, A., Dowdall, G., Moeykens, B., & Castillo, S. (1994). Health and behavioral consequences of binge drinking in college: A national survey of students at 140 colleges. *Journal of the American Medical Association, 272,* 1672–1677.

Wechsler, H., Dowdall, G., Davenport, A., & Rimm, E. (1995). A gender-specific measure of binge drinking among college students. *American Journal of Public Health, 85,* 982–985.

Wechsler, H. W., & Wuethrich, B. (2002). *Dying to drink: Confronting binge drinking on college campuses.* New York: Rodale.

HATE CRIMES (BIAS CRIMES), ANTI-GAY

Identifying a crime that is motivated by hate is important because this type of violence sends a message to an entire group of people beyond the immediate victim of the crime. Such victims are targeted because of who they are, and the message is that their group is inferior, wrong, and unworthy. Still, there is much disagreement as to whether these crimes should be treated differently from other crimes and how to determine bias motivation on the part of the offenders.

The U.S. Congress defined a hate crime as a crime in which "the defendant's conduct was motivated by hatred, bias, or prejudice, based on the actual or perceived race, color, religion, national origin, ethnicity, gender, sexual orientation, or gender identity of another individual or group of individuals" in HR 4797 in 1992, and added disability status in 1994.

These hate crime categories are used by the Federal Bureau of Investigation (FBI) in collecting crime statistics, but they are not the categories used in the federal hate crime law passed in 1968. The federal law only protects those who were victims of hate crimes because of their religion, race, or national origin.

Types of Anti-Gay Hate Crimes Data Collection

Congress passed the Hate Crime Statistics Act of 1990 after rising anti-gay violence in the 1980s. This was the first federal civil rights law to include sexual orientation as a class. However, collecting accurate anti-gay hate crimes statistics is a challenge. The first impediment is that many lesbians and gay men will not take the risk to "out" themselves as gay to medical or legal personnel; hence, there is an incalculable underreporting factor. The second impediment is that there are three main sources of anti-gay hate crimes report sources, each of which has its own limitations.

One source of information on hate crimes is the FBI. In 2003, the FBI reported 1,239 hate crimes (17% of the total number) based on actual or perceived sexual orientation of the victims. However, such reporting is voluntary and over a third of law enforcement jurisdictions do not report to the FBI. Furthermore, some jurisdictions that do not report show up as having "0" hate crimes, which leads to faulty numbers. Due to lack of training, personnel may believe the FBI is not interested in minor hate crimes, such as hate graffiti or vandalism, and so do not report them. Differing local definitions of hate crimes and political pressure around reporting hate crimes may contribute to inconsistent numbers. In addition, some persons in law enforcement are reluctant to assess the motive of the offender and feel it is outside of their purview.

A second source, the National Crime Victimization Survey (NCVS), is based on interviews of 77,600 nationally representative persons interviewed biannually about their experiences with crime. The NCVS reported an annual average of 210,000 hate crime victimizations between July 2000 and December 2003. Of these, 1 in 6 incidents were based on the sexual orientation of the victim. The NCVS requires corroborating evidence of derogatory language used by the offender, hate symbols left by the offender, or police confirmation that a hate crime occurred.

A third source, the National Coalition of Anti-Violence Programs (NCAVP), collects annual data from NCAVP member organizations around the country. The NCAVP's *2004 Report on Anti-Lesbian, Gay, Transgender & Bisexual Violence* stated that 1,792 incidents of bias had been reported to them involving 2,131 victims. The NCAVP is comprised of over 20 antiviolence organizations that serve lesbian, gay, bisexual, and transgender (LGBT) victims of bias, domestic violence, and other forms of violence affecting the LGBT community. The NCAVP data are dependent on victims knowing about their organizations and calling to make self-reports.

Anti-Gay Activism

Significantly, there was a wave of anti-gay hate crimes across the country in 2005 that included vandalism, murder, graffiti, and assaults. The increased sense that homophobia can be freely expressed resulted from a number of factors, such as the debate over who is entitled to marriage rights, the possibility of a constitutional amendment defining marriage as between one man and one woman, and the 11 states that passed constitutional amendments prohibiting same-sex marriages in 2004.

This negative climate, however, has a 30-year history. Since the late 1970s when Anita Bryant founded the first national anti-gay organization, Save Our Children, the conservative religious Right has unified under anti-gay themes. The rhetoric has shifted over time, from references to "diseased perverts" to stopping "special rights" to promoting "family values," but the political organizing has effectively supported the platform for hate crimes. Fred Phelps of the Westboro Baptist Church, with his godhatesfags Web site, is the extreme version of the religious Right. Paul Cameron, whose "research" has been discredited by both the American Sociological Association and the American Psychological Association but is touted by anti-gay groups, provides "data" that gays and lesbians are physically and mentally diseased. The gains of gays and lesbians such as civil unions in Vermont and marriage in Massachusetts, and the U.S. Supreme Court's striking down sodomy laws in 2003, have further served to unite anti-gay activists.

Legal Response to Hate Crimes

High-visibility hate crime murder victims, such as Matthew Shepard in Wyoming in 1998 and Billy Jack Gaither in Alabama in 1999, bring the debate about gay rights to national prominence. In 2000, the U.S. Supreme Court ruled that the Boy Scouts could discriminate against gay scoutmasters. In 2004, the Massachusetts Supreme Court ruled that gay and lesbian couples could legally marry. The alternation of victory and defeat takes place on the field of civil rights where real people live and where some suffer from hate crimes because of who they are and their associated group membership. Introduced into the House of Representatives in September 2005, the Local Law Enforcement Enhancement Act adds the categories of sexual orientation and gender identity to federal hate crimes legislation. It remains to be seen whether this bill will be passed and whether hate crimes legislation has any impact on lessening anti-gay hate crimes as long as some in society oppose the right to safely be gay or lesbian.

Lori B. Girshick

See also Homophobia; Homophobia and Media Representations of Gay, Lesbian, Bisexual, and Transgender People; Legislation, Hate Crimes

Further Readings

Harlow, C. W. (2005). *Hate crime reported by victims and police.* Washington, DC: U.S. Department of Justice, Office of Justice Programs.

Patton, C. (2005). *2004 Report on anti-lesbian, gay, transgender & bisexual violence.* New York: National Coalition of Anti-Violence Programs.

HATE CRIMES (BIAS CRIMES), CRIMINAL JUSTICE RESPONSES

In 1990, President George H. W. Bush signed into law the federal Hate Crime Statistics Act (HCSA), which mandated that the attorney general's office collect data on hate crime, that is, crime motivated by the victim's race, religion, ethnicity, or sexual orientation. An array of other criminal justice responses—not just legislative ones—has also been implemented across the United States as a means of either preventing or responding to bias-motivated violence.

As is typical of governmental decrees, the HCSA provides a legalistic definition of hate crime: "crimes that manifest evidence of prejudice based on race,

religion, sexual orientation or ethnicity." For the most part, states that subsequently (or previously) introduced hate crime legislation have followed suit, adopting a similar definitional style. All states except Utah currently have some form of hate crime statute. What differs across the nation is the breadth of protected classes. Indeed, there is considerable variation in the victim populations addressed by state hate crime statutes. The common categories are reduced to race, religion, and ethnicity. Sexual orientation and gender, for example, appear in only a handful of statutes, as does country of origin. Minnesota, for instance, records hate crime motivated by the victim's race, religion, national origin, sex, age, disability, and sexual orientation. In New Jersey, however, criminal violations of persons or property are designated as hate crimes when the victim's race, color, creed, ethnicity, or religion was a motivating factor. Oregon hate crime protections are extended to victims violated because of perceived race, color, religion, national origin, sexual orientation, marital status, political affiliation or beliefs, membership or activity in or on behalf of a labor organization or against a labor organization, physical or mental handicap, age, economic or social status, or citizenship of the victim.

What these otherwise diverse statutes do share is an emphasis on the legal definition of *crime*. That is, the term *hate crime* assumes the commission of a criminal offense, a violation of an existing criminal code. The hate crime designation may only be applied when a *predicate offense* or underlying crime is committed as a result of bias or prejudice. For the most part, these statutes apply only to index offenses. However, some states specify a different, often narrower range of relevant offenses, such as harassment, vandalism, and assault.

Moreover, the nature of hate crime legislation is itself disparate. At the federal level, hate crime may be confronted through the Hate Crime Statistics Act, the Hate Crime Sentencing Enhancement Act, the Violence Against Women Act, the Hate Crimes Prevention Act, the Church Arsons Prevention Act, or the Civil Rights Act. At the state level, some jurisdictions account for institutional vandalism, some require hate crime data collection, some provide for police hate crime training, and most allow for penalty enhancement for bias-motivated crime. The latter refers to the provision for increasing the penalty associated with an offense if it is deemed motivated by bias. In some states, the bias must be the sole motivation; in others, it must only be motivated "in part" by animus. In addition, most states also have an array of civil rights statutes that might be invoked to protect vulnerable groups from victimization or to provide redress. In fact, these were the precursors to hate crime legislation. Until the 1990s, they were often the only means by which bias-motivated crimes could be addressed.

However, it is not enough to simply legislate against hate crime. It is debatable, first of all, whether it has anything more than symbolic impact. Moreover, in order for it to have any impact, it must be enforceable. To date, there is a limited tendency for police to designate hate crimes, or for prosecutors to follow up even where charges are laid. Consequently the criminal justice response to serving the needs of victims must be varied and broad, to include not just legislation, but such things as the establishment of victims' bills of rights such as that developed by the International Association of Chiefs of Police in 1983, or the array of services known as victim-witness programs. These programs serve the general needs of victims, but may have particular relevance for hate crime victims.

Victims who come in contact with the criminal justice system may find themselves in a quandary in that those to whom they turn for help may be unwilling or unable to respond to their victimization effectively. The experience of victimization is traumatic for all people; however, it can be even more so for those whose racial, sexual, or ethnic identity, for example, leaves them vulnerable. Hate crime victims may fear the risk of secondary victimization. Some criminal justice personnel have themselves been perpetrators of bias-motivated violence.

Criminal justice agencies that are representative of the communities they serve will almost invariably be more aware of the particular problems of these communities. However, minority groups are dramatically underrepresented as service providers in the criminal justice system. As the United States has become even more diverse, police agencies, in particular, have begun to recognize the need to recruit those from minority communities. These recruits bring with them an understanding of their clientele, as well as slightly different approaches to their jobs. Latino/a police officers, for example, may bring insights into the specificity of domestic violence among Latinos/as; women may bring dialogic rather than aggressive tactics into emotional confrontations; people with disabilities may bring attention to the barriers implied by the physical environment. In other words, hiring those who are different is a way to celebrate and take advantage of diversity.

Nonetheless, hiring and promoting diversity within criminal justice agencies is no guarantee that those agencies will necessarily be more sensitive to cultural diversity and more effective in responding to hate crimes. There are gay men who are racist, women who are homophobic, Latinos/as who are classist. Prejudice cuts across difference. Consequently, regardless of the makeup of criminal justice agencies, cultural awareness training has also grown in importance as a means of sensitizing professionals to the experiences, values, and needs of the communities they serve. The Anti-Defamation League, for example, regularly provides police training on hate groups, on the impacts of hate crime, and even on how to identify a hate crime.

Additionally, criminal justice practitioners must be made aware that different communities may in fact experience the trauma of victimization in different ways. Awareness and knowledge of how hate crimes affect diverse communities allows criminal justice actors to implement services that are appropriate to localized dynamics. For example, communities experiencing high rates of victimization of women may implement nighttime transportation services, or short- and long-term shelter programs. These would not be an appropriate response, however, where the paramount problem is violence against gay men and lesbians. In those cases, the creation of media and educational campaigns against homophobia or of a local gay and lesbian advocacy panel may be the most effective intervention. Ultimately, the key to effective delivery of victim services is sensitivity to the cultural needs of the victim's community, in a way that empowers victims and potential victims.

Barbara Perry

See also Hate Crimes (Bias Crimes), Anti-Gay; Hate Crimes (Bias Crimes), Gender Motivated; Hate Crimes (Bias Crimes), Racially Motivated; Hate Crimes (Bias Crimes), Religiously Motivated; Victimology; Victims' Rights Movement

Further Readings

Jacobs, J., & Potter, K. (2000). *Hate crimes: Criminal law and identity politics.* New York: Oxford University Press.

Jenness, V., & Broad, K. (1998). *Hate crimes: New social movements and the politics of violence.* New York: Aldine de Gruyter.

Lawrence, F. (2002). *Punishing hate: Bias crimes under American law.* Cambridge, MA: Harvard University Press.

Perry, B. (2004). *Hate and bias crime: A reader.* New York: Routledge.

HATE CRIMES (BIAS CRIMES), GENDER MOTIVATED

Gender bias hate crimes are a subset of the larger category of hate crimes, that is, crimes committed due to an offender's bias or prejudice toward a victim's real or perceived group membership. Specifically in the case of gender-motivated bias crimes, the bias is a result of prejudice or hostility due to the victim's gender. Although hate crime laws' categorization of gender as a protected status can include anyone based on his or her gender, male or female, in practice "gender" is a proxy for girls and women. Protection for transgendered individuals, when it is offered under hate crime statutes, is usually provided by the categories of "gender expression" or "transgender."

Violence against women fits the hate crime paradigm when women are selected as victims due to their gender (the discriminatory selection model) or due to the perpetrator's hatred of women (the animus model). In either case, women are targeted because they are women, that is, not *who* they are, but *what* they are. Many crimes committed against women fit these models, such as sexual assault, domestic violence, and other assaults in which men are the primary perpetrators and women the primary victims. Violence against women most likely to be designated a gender bias hate crime is sexual or physical assault by a serial male offender; certain cases of domestic violence in which a pattern of a man's repeated violence against consecutive women can be established; or the murder of women because they are women, termed *femicide*.

One incident of violence against women that is frequently held up as the hallmark of a gender-biased hate crime is known as the Montreal Massacre. The crime occurred in Montreal, Canada, on December 6, 1989, at the University of Montreal. A 25-year-old man, Marc Lépine, entered the university's school of engineering and separated the women from the men, ordering the men out of the classroom. While screaming of his hatred for feminists he opened fire, killing 14 young women and wounding another 9 women and 4 men, before killing himself. A suicide note blamed his educational and personal failures on women. Additionally, a hit list of prominent Canadian women holding nontraditional jobs was found on his body. This tragedy was almost unanimously held to be a gender-motivated hate crime, which opened the door for viewing other violence against women in the same way.

One benefit of viewing violence against women as gender-bias hate crimes is that prosecutors can seek additional punishment if a bias motivation can be proved in states with penalty enhancement measures. Another benefit is being able to connect the dots between individual incidents of violence against women, creating a picture of institutionalized sexism, prejudice, and misogyny directed toward women as a group that often erupts into violence. When violence against women is identified as political and institutional, rather than personal, then solutions will be addressed at that level.

Policy History

In lobbying for the federal Hate Crimes Statistics Act (HCSA) in 1988, which was adopted in 1990, a hate crime coalition of racial/ethnic, religious, and sexual orientation groups lobbied for the national collection of data on hate crimes directed toward their constituencies. Then-president of the National Organization for Women, Molly Yard, advocated for the inclusion of the category of gender. Yard argued that violence against women fit the hate crimes paradigm, that is, many times women are targeted for victimization because they are women.

The hate crime coalition refused to add gender as a status category under the HCSA for a number of reasons, including (a) fear that its inclusion would delay the passage of the bill; (b) concern about opening the gates for admission of additional categories, such as age and disability; (c) concern that the prevalence of violence against women would overwhelm data collection efforts; and (d) a belief that gender did not fit the hate crime paradigm since many women know their attackers. In contrast, the gender category was often added at the state level, mostly because the legitimacy of women as a historically oppressed group requiring special protections under the law had become an established part of the legal canon.

Gender as a Controversial Category

Therefore, gender has increasingly become a part of the hate crime policy template, although gender's fit within the hate crime paradigm remains controversial. At least 20 states currently include gender as a status category in their hate crime statutes, although that inclusion may be more symbolic than practical.

Opponents of inclusion of violence against women as a hate crime note that many women know their attackers and special laws already exist that address violence against women, such as sexual assault and domestic violence statutes. Also acting against the inclusion of gender into hate crime categories is its prevalence and the fact that women constitute half the population. These two factors combine to make violence against women look essentially random and unrelated, rather than targeted. Anecdotally, many people believe men hurt or kill women because they love them, not because they hate them. Additionally, crimes are less likely to be categorized as hate crimes if there are multiple or mixed motives, which tend to muddy the hate crime waters. A perpetrator often has multiple motives when committing a violent offense against a woman, making a hate crime charge less likely.

Supporters of the perspective that violence against women constitutes a hate crime note that similar to established patterns in hate crimes, women are often called names during the assault that specifically target their gender, and the larger community of women is often affected by the violence committed against one woman. For example, when a woman is sexually assaulted in a neighborhood, fear ripples through the community of women who fear they could be targeted next. Although women may change where they go, they cannot change what they are—women. When a rapist is looking for a victim, he often lies in wait, not for the next *person* to cross his path, but the next *woman*.

Beverly A. McPhail

See also Femicide; Hate Crimes (Bias Crimes), Criminal Justice Responses

Further Readings

Angelari, M. (1994). Hate crime statutes: A promising tool for fighting violence against women. *Journal of Gender & the Law, 2,* 63–105.
Copeland, L., & Wolfe, L. (1991). *Violence against women as bias motivated hate crime: Defining the issues.* Washington, DC: Center for Women Policy Studies.
Jenness, V. (1999). Managing differences and making legislation: Social movements and the radicalization, sexualization, and gendering of federal hate crime law in the U.S., 1985–1998. *Social Problems, 46,* 548–571.
Jenness, V., & Broad, K. (1994). Antiviolence activism and the (in)visibility of gender in the gay/lesbian and women's movements. *Gender & Society, 8,* 402–423.
McPhail, B. A. (2002). Gender-bias hate crimes. *Trauma, Violence, & Abuse, 3,* 125–143.
McPhail, B. A., & DiNitto, D. (2005). Prosecutorial perspectives on gender-bias hate crimes. *Violence Against Women, 11,* 1162–1185.
Weisburd, S. B., & Levin, B. (1994). "On the basis of sex": Recognizing gender-based bias crimes. *Stanford Law & Policy Review, 5,* 21–47.

HATE CRIMES (BIAS CRIMES), LEGISLATION

See LEGISLATION, HATE CRIMES

HATE CRIMES (BIAS CRIMES), RACIALLY MOTIVATED

To date, hate crime literature has tended to be very broad and nonspecific in its focus. That is, little scholarship devotes attention to specific categories of victims. Extant literature has tended to discuss hate crime in generic terms, as if it was experienced in the same ways by women, by Jews, by gay men, by Latinos/as, or by lesbians. Even racial violence is collapsed into one broad category, as if all racial and ethnic groups experienced it the same way. Consequently, there is not a very clear picture of the specific dynamics and consequences that may be associated with victimization on the basis of different racial identities.

Anti-White Violence

Interestingly, U.S. data sources report high numbers of anti-White violence—although Whites remain underrepresented as victims. For example, the Uniform Crime Reporting (UCR) Program hate crime data consistently report approximately 1,000 incidents motivated by anti-White bias—or 10% of all victimizations, and 20% of all racially motivated victimizations. However, scholars have made virtually no attempt to understand the dynamics of anti-White victimization, or the dynamics of reporting by White victims. It may be that White victims are more likely to report their victimization, seeing it as an affront to the racial order. Or, in fact, it might be a form of ethnic bias—anti-Italian, or anti-Polish—that does not fit neatly into the limited Hispanic/non-Hispanic ethnic categories in the UCR. Scholars have hardly acknowledged, let alone explored, this apparent anomaly.

Anti-Black Violence

Not surprisingly, in the United States, the limited data available suggest that African Americans are the most frequent victims of racial violence. UCR data, for example, regularly reveal that African Americans make up approximately two thirds of all victims of racially motivated violence. Thus, the history of discrimination and intolerance against Black Americans persists in the form of normative violent practices: verbal taunts, assaults, vandalism, church arsons, police brutality. While certainly not as dramatic as the thousands of lynchings in the late 19th and early 20th centuries, hate crime continues to be an everyday expectation for African Americans. And many of the same stereotypes—for example, Black male predator, lazy cheaters—continue to inform the hostility that predisposes offenders to assault blacks.

Anti–Native American Violence

Native Americans are also overrepresented as victims of racially motivated violence. History is replete with stories of the genocidal attempts to remove the American Indians from their land. However, scholarly attention to the historical and contemporary victimization of American Indians as nations has unfortunately blinded us to the corresponding victimization of American Indians as individual members of those many nations. The UCR indicates that in 2004, there were 83 incidents in which Native Americans were victims of hate crime, representing less than 1% of all offenses, and just over 1% of all those motivated by race. However, even these data must be taken with a grain of salt, since the UCR is fraught with limitations, especially with respect to underreporting. This may be particularly relevant in the case of Native Americans, thereby explaining the low rates of

victimization recorded in UCR statistics. Some recent work has begun to shed light on the specific experiences of American Indians and the ways in which the genocidal history of colonialism continues to inform hate crime perpetrated against them.

Anti-Hispanic Violence

Nearly as little is known about Latino/a victims of racially motivated crime. While this population has a staggeringly high rate of victimization in general, little effort has been made to tease out the effect of racial animus in this context. Moreover, anti-Hispanic victimization is often inseparable from anti-immigrant violence, given the elision between race, ethnicity, and immigration. As is the case with Native Americans, there is no uniform collection of data on violence against Hispanics. A recent National Council of La Raza report offers some insights here, but even that is limited. It is a one-time-only report that does not systematically replicate its inquiry on an annual basis.

Anti-Asian Violence

In contrast to anti-Black and anti-Hispanic hate crime, anti-Asian violence accounts for a relatively small proportion of all racially motivated hate crime. However, it does represent a growing proportion. Many sources suggest that it constitutes the most dramatically and rapidly growing type of racial violence. The 2002 National Asian Pacific American Legal Consortium yearly audit seems to confirm what anecdotal evidence and intuitive observations have suggested: riding a wave of anti-immigrant sentiments, anti-Asian violence was consistently on the rise throughout the 1990s. Decreases in the early years of the 21st century are attributed more to failures to investigate and fear of reporting than to significant changes in victimization. Moreover, the audit suggests that anti-Asian hate crime remains very violent.

It is interesting to note that a substantial number of suspected offenders involved in violence against Asian Americans are African American or Hispanic. In 1995, these two groups accounted for nearly 45% of offenders. However, neither the dynamics of White-on-Asian violence nor Asian conflicts with other groups have been systematically examined. In the aftermath of the September 11, 2001, attacks in the United States, it is more important than ever to study and understand the animus that underlies anti-Asian violence.

Since the terrorist attacks on September 11, anti-Asian violence has taken a dramatically different form, and racial and ethnic minorities associated with Islam in most Western countries have experienced increased negative attention from the media, police, and security forces, and indeed from agitated citizenry. There has been a concomitant increase in all such countries in the extent of anti-Muslim or "Islamophobic" hate crime, racial vilification, and discrimination. This has been exacerbated by subsequent terrorist events, notably in Bali in October 2002 and October 2005, Madrid in March 2004, and London in July 2005.

Evidence of retaliatory anti-Muslim violence abounds. Within the first week after the September 11 attacks, there were at least seven homicides that appeared to have been racially motivated, reactionary violence. Most major U.S. cities experienced a rash of hate crime, ranging in seriousness from verbal abuse to graffiti and vandalism to arson and murder. By September 18, 2001, the FBI was investigating more than 40 possible hate crimes thought to be related to the terrorist attacks; by October 3, they were investigating more than 90. The number had risen to 145 by October 11. The Muslim Public Affairs Council of Southern California reported 800 cases nationwide by mid-October, and the American-Arab Anti-Discrimination Committee had recorded over 1,100 such offenses by mid-November. The slogans that accompanied the violence reveal a strong sense of the illegitimacy of Arab residence in the United States along with a similarly strong desire for revenge.

While the recent wave of anti-Muslim violence clearly was motivated by anger and outrage at the 9/11 terrorist attacks, it is also informed by a broader history and culture that supports anti-Muslim, anti-Arab, and anti–Middle East sentiments. Many Americans have long been hostile to what they perceive as Islamic fundamentalism, which in turn is increasingly associated with terrorism in the American psyche. Especially in the aftermath of the September 11 attacks on New York City and Washington, D.C., Americans have come to associate the fundamentalism of Islam with fundamentalist violence, believing Muslims will do anything they deem to be the "will of Allah." Consequently, Muslims are suspected of being foreign and domestic terrorists, and thus "worthy" victims of hate crime.

Anti-Immigrant Violence

"Immigrant bashing" has also become a part of the daily reality of those who have reached new shores in search of promised freedom and opportunity. In this context, racially motivated violence may be a response to the violation of concrete, geographical boundaries. Hostility toward those perceived as "foreign" is apparent in acts ranging from vandalism and graffiti to brutal assaults worldwide. Inspired by political and media constructions of immigrants as the root of all problems, native-born Americans and native-born Europeans express their opinions in hateful words and deeds.

In the United States, unfortunately, there are no concrete data on anti-immigrant violence. Violence against a Korean shop owner, for example, is classified and recorded as anti-Asian violence. However, the connection between the perpetrator's tendency to equate ethnicity with immigrant status is apparent in the verbal assaults that often accompany physical assaults. When East Indians or Haitians are told to "go back where you belong," the assumption is clear: regardless of whether they are first-, second- or third-generation, those who are "different" are perpetual foreigners who do not belong. It is likely, therefore, that a significant proportion of the more than 500 anti-Asian and nearly 1,000 anti-Hispanic hate crimes recorded by the FBI in 2000 were motivated by anti-immigrant sentiments. Perhaps even some of the more than 3,000 anti-Black hate crimes were motivated by the perception that the victims were Nigerian, or Haitian, or South African, for example. The data sources are simply too limited to allow researchers to tease out the complicated relationship between race and immigration status.

Barbara Perry

See also Hate Crimes (Bias Crimes), Criminal Justice Responses; Hate Crimes (Bias Crimes), Religiously Motivated; Victimology; Victims' Rights Movement

Further Readings

Bowling, B. (1998). *Violent racism: Victimization, policing and social context.* Oxford, UK: Oxford University Press.

Gerstenfeld, P. (2004). *Hate crimes: Causes, control and controversies.* Thousand Oaks, CA: Sage.

Perry, B. (2001). *In the name of hate: Understanding hate crime.* New York: Routledge.

Perry, B. (Ed.). (2004). *Hate and bias crime: A reader.* New York: Routledge.

HATE CRIMES (BIAS CRIMES), RELIGIOUSLY MOTIVATED

Hate crimes are acts of violence, intolerance, and bigotry, intended to hurt and intimidate someone because of his or her race, ethnicity, national origin, religion, sexual orientation, or disability. Religiously motivated hate crimes are an integral part of interpersonal violence in the United States. In 2000, there were 9,721 reported cases of single-bias incidents. Of these, 18.8% were determined to be religiously motivated. The violence perpetrated in a hate crime, including a religiously based motive, affects not only that individual and his or her family, but also the community with similar religious characteristics as the victim.

Federal and State Legislation

During the 1960s, the federal government passed several statutes to protect individuals from discrimination due to race, ethnicity, national origin, or religious prejudice. Prior to the passage of hate crime legislation, the police classified incidents of religious intimidation and harassment under the headings of "suspicious circumstances" or "malicious mischief."

Due to rising public pressure, Congress passed the Hate Crimes Statistics Act (HSCA) in 1990. The Act requires the Department of Justice (DOJ) to collect data from law enforcement agencies on crimes that manifest prejudice based on race, religion, sexual orientation, or ethnicity. Every year, the Bureau of Justice Statistics, a branch of the DOJ, must publish a summary of the findings. The HSCA has brought distinct awareness to hate crimes, strongly encouraging law enforcement to provide bias training. In 1996, Congress passed the Church Arson Prevention Act, which criminalizes any intentional destruction, damage, or defacement to religious property primarily due to the fact that it is religious property. Furthermore, the act punishes those who interfere with an individual's free exercise of religious beliefs.

On the state level, 45 states have enacted statutes that give broader protections against hate crimes, and all of them protect individuals from religiously motivated crimes.

Crime Reporting

On the federal level, the Federal Bureau of Investigation (FBI) and Bureau of Alcohol, Tobacco and Firearms are the law enforcement agencies authorized to conduct investigations into federal hate crimes and assist local police with hate crime investigations. For example, in a recent hate crimes case in Alabama, local law enforcement teamed with FBI agents to investigate several church arsons.

The FBI's Uniform Crime Reporting Program is the only national data collection program. The FBI has encouraged local jurisdictions to report incidents of crimes, including hate crimes, using the National Incident-Based Reporting System, but participation by police departments in reporting systems is voluntary, so not all jurisdictions participate. Furthermore, studies show that the law enforcement agencies that participate in these reporting systems sometimes deflate their hate crime statistics. The most frequent form of religiously motivated hate crime, according to these reports, is intimidation tactics, followed by the destruction of property.

Examples of Incidents of Religiously Motivated Hate Crimes

Violence Against Muslims

Several cities saw an increase in anti-Muslim violence following the September 11, 2001, terrorist attacks. In 2001, there were 481 anti-Islamic hate crimes reported to the FBI, an increase of 1,700%, most thought to be related to September 11. Many Muslim women who wear traditional head scarves, or *hijabs,* were afraid to travel alone during the immediate post-9/11 period, concerned that they would be subject to anti-Muslim slurs, harassment, and even physical violence.

Violence Against Jews

Historically, anti-Semitism, or hatred, prejudice, and discrimination toward Jews, has fueled religiously motivated bias crimes against this population. Jewish synagogues and areas where large congregations of Jewish immigrants and families live have been targets of anti-Semitic attacks, including verbal taunts and slurs, and swastika spray paintings. Recently, teenagers who are self-identifed Nazis were arrested in New York for beating a group of girls who they believed were Jewish.

Community Education

Several federal departments fund various organizations to develop programs and provide training seminars and technical assistance to individuals and local agencies regarding hate crimes. There needs to be a strong community response to religiously motivated hate crimes, in order to avoid the polarization of groups and the targeted group's isolation and escalation of hate-motivated violence in the name of self-defense.

There are several national organizations that tackle religious prejudice and hate. For example, the Anti-Defamation League, an organization whose mission is to "stop the defamation of Jewish people and to secure justice and fair treatment for all," develops curriculum and teaching tools for educators to utilize with their students. The Council on American-Islamic Relations works to address the understanding of Islam by encouraging dialogue and educating the community about civil liberties. Other groups, such as the Southern Poverty Law Center and American Civil Liberties Union, do community education through litigation and policy advocacy.

Chaitra P. Shenoy

See also Community Violence; Hate Crimes (Bias Crimes), Criminal Justice Responses; Hate Crimes (Bias Crimes), Racially Motivated; Health Consequences of Hate Crime

Further Readings

Anti-Defamation League. (2007, January). *Education.* Retrieved July 17, 2007, from http://rac.org/advocacy/issues/issuehcp

Human Rights Watch. (2002, November). *We are not the enemy.* Retrieved April 10, 2006, from http://www.hrw.org/reports/2002/usahate/

National Criminal Justice Service. (2003, August). *Hate crime: A summary.* Retrieved March 16, 2006, from http://www.policyalmanac.org/crime/archive/hate_crime.shtml

HAZING

Hazing is characterized by tests of loyalty for social group membership that can involve physical or emotional abuse of the candidates. Hazing has been reported in diverse social contexts, such as academic fraternities and sororities, sports teams, military and paramilitary forces, and street gangs. Research has shown that the methods of hazing vary among different social groups. Athletic groups (e.g., football teams) employ physical challenges (e.g., degrading positions

and tasks, exposure to the elements, excessive physical activity) and physical abuse as their preferred hazing methods; these methods are extended in the physical endurance and abuse associated with military and gang initiations. In contrast, fraternities and sororities often employ violations of social rules and norms (e.g., wearing humiliating dress and attire, complete or partial nudity) as their preferred hazing methods. In particular, excessive alcohol consumption has been widely used in fraternity and sorority hazing and accounts for a significant proportion of hazing-related deaths.

Hazing has a dual purpose of promoting loyalty to a social group through shared hardship of the candidates and of reinforcing the established social structure within the social group. The procedures used to enforce hazing legitimize the positions earned by the group members within a social group. For example, a president of a fraternity has to take charge of recruiting new pledges and delegating the responsibilities of hazing the candidates to other fraternity members. Receiving group membership provides a justification for candidates' efforts and the hardship they experienced during the hazing experience. Victims of hazing are often reluctant to report the physical or emotional abuse they suffer because of the shame involved in the experience or because they would forfeit membership in the social group by speaking out. Furthermore, the secretive nature of hazing leads to a lack of awareness of it by authority figures (e.g., college administrators, athletic coaches, police) who have the influence to disrupt hazing activities.

Some suggested methods to prevent hazing include using alternative group-building activities (e.g., fundraising, mentoring, communal field trips), clarification and strict enforcement of antihazing policies by authority figures, and providing an immediate and detailed investigation of any reports of hazing.

Aldwin Domingo

See also Attachment Disorder; Campus Violence; Fraternities and Violence

Further Readings

Hollmann, B. B. (2002). Hazing: Hidden campus crime. *New Directions for Student Services, 99,* 11–23.

Keating, C. F., Pomerantz, J., Pommer, S. D., Ritt, S. J. H., Miller, L. M., & McCormick, J. (2005). Going to college and unpacking hazing: A functional approach to decrypting initiation practices among undergraduates. *Group Dynamics: Theory, Research, Practice, 9,* 104–126.

HEALTH CARE RESPONSE, PREVENTION STRATEGIES FOR REDUCING INTERPERSONAL VIOLENCE

Prevention is a systematic process that promotes safe, healthy environments and behaviors and reduces the likelihood or frequency of an incident, injury, or condition from occurring. There are three types of prevention: primary, secondary, and tertiary. *Primary* prevention is taking action before a problem arises. *Secondary* prevention is the early detection of the problem, relying on physical changes, symptoms, or abnormal tests to determine action. It focuses on responses that take place shortly after the condition has developed or has been recognized. *Tertiary* prevention slows or prevents deterioration from a condition, focusing on treatment of and rehabilitation from the consequences of the condition. These are usually long-term responses to ameliorate or prevent further negative effects.

Primary prevention strategies can target the individual, relationship, community, or societal levels. *Individual* strategies address personal or biological factors. *Relationship* strategies focus on relations with others. *Community* strategies target the policies and practices of communities and social environments, such as schools, workplaces, and neighborhoods. *Societal* strategies focus on the macro level, addressing norms, beliefs, or policies. For example, tobacco control used this continuum to frame its work to reduce smoking. Prohibiting smoking in public places changed societal norms. To date, most public health and health care efforts to prevent interpersonal violence have focused on the first two areas (individual and relationship).

Prevention Strategies for the Prenatal and Birth Period

During this time period, primary prevention efforts focus on the individual level, largely with home visits. In addition to violence reduction and child abuse prevention, prenatal and early childhood home visitation has been used for a wide range of health and non-health goals. Home visitation programs are common in Europe, where they are most often made available to all childbearing families, regardless of estimated risk of child-related health or social problems. In the United States, home visitation programs are commonly targeted to specific population groups that are at high risk for problems. These include low-income groups; minorities; youth; less-educated groups; first-time mothers; substance abusers; children at risk for abuse or neglect; and low birth weight, premature, disabled, or developmentally compromised infants. Visitation programs include, but are not limited to, one or more of the following components: training of parent(s) on prenatal and infant care, training on parenting, child abuse and neglect prevention, developmental interaction with infants or toddlers, family planning assistance, development of problem-solving skills and life skills, educational and work opportunities, and linkage with community services. In addition to home visits, programs can include daycare; parent group meetings for support, instruction, or both; advocacy; transportation; and other services. When such services are provided in addition to home visitation, the program is considered multicomponent.

The evaluations of home visitation programs demonstrate that women's prenatal health-related behaviors improve, child abuse and neglect rates are reduced, maternal welfare dependence is reduced, successive pregnancies are spaced, and maternal criminal behavior as well as behavior problems related to drug and alcohol abuse are also reduced. Early home visits have also impacted antisocial behavior and the use of substances by teens.

In 2003, the Centers for Disease Control and Prevention (CDC) reviewed the scientific evidence concerning the effectiveness of early childhood home visitation in preventing violence by the visited child against others or self (i.e., suicidal behavior), violence against the child (i.e., maltreatment, which is defined as abuse or neglect), violence by the visited parent, and intimate partner violence. They concluded that there was insufficient evidence to determine the effectiveness of early childhood home visitation in preventing violence by visited children and between adults. However, this is difficult research to do. Home visitation programs in the United States are diverse, differing in focus, curricula, duration, visitor qualifications, and target populations. Although no single optimal, effective, and cost-effective approach could be defined for the multiplicity of possible outcomes, settings, and target populations, the CDC stated that the findings were robust, suggesting that programs can be effective. Health professionals and policymakers are encouraged to carefully consider the attributes and characteristics of the particular home visitation program to be implemented.

Secondary prevention efforts can occur during routine prenatal care visits when women are assessed for factors that might complicate the pregnancy or impact a healthy outcome. In addition to screening for health problems like anemia, diabetes, or poor weight gain, providers have the opportunity to assess for violence. This is encouraged by the American College of Obstetrics and Gynecology. Screening is recommended for a number of symptoms and problems that have been identified as potential indicators of abuse such as preterm labor, poor weight gain, and depression.

Strategies for Infants and Children

During the infancy and childhood years, parents are encouraged to bring children into a health care office for well-child visits. This time is used to give immunizations preventing childhood diseases and to assess biomedical health, behavior, development, and family functioning, as well as to provide parent education through age-appropriate counseling, referred to as *anticipatory guidance.* Anticipatory guidance has been part of the well-child check for years and has been integrated into state-supported efforts such as Bright Futures or Child and Teen Check-ups. This is a primary prevention approach that includes topics such as nutrition, sleep, toileting, discipline, childcare, screening for lead exposure, and safety in the home regarding poisons and medications. When a problem is identified, the child and parent are referred for additional assistance.

Recent efforts have summarized the components of anticipatory guidance to prevent violence throughout the child's life—infancy, toddler, school age, adolescence—and guidance for the parents of adolescents. These components are all included in the program Connected Kids: Safe, Strong, and Secure, which is a complete package of parent and adolescent educational brochures, a clinical guide for pediatricians, and a Web site with supporting literature and supporting training materials from the Internet.

Anticipatory guidance can have several positive outcomes. Used strategically, it can be effective in leading to behavioral change, particularly if the counseling addresses issues of concern to the parent. Verbal counseling accompanied by personalized written information seems to be effective. Supportive materials need to be compelling and written to match the educational level of the parent.

Anticipatory guidance is encouraged by professional medical organizations that focus on the health of children (American Academy of Pediatrics and the American Academy of Family Physicians), but how to best translate the directive into practice is far from simple. Clinics often delegate some of the assessment to a nurse, incorporate questions in the office visit grid, or, with the advent of the electronic medical record, include smart texts with the guidance appropriate to the age of the child. Studies show that anticipatory guidance is provided inadequately in many practices and the format is not always useful to the parent. There are many topics to cover and topics are not equally relevant; priorities need to be set.

Linking prevention strategies to risk and protective factors improves the chance of effectiveness. For example, one of the most consistent risk factors for intimate partner violence (IPV) as an adult is exposure to it as a child. Therefore, secondary and tertiary prevention efforts with victims and perpetrators, such as referrals to shelters and domestic violence support groups for victims, and using the court and batterers programs for perpetrators, may actually be primary prevention for exposed children. In 1998, the American Academy of Pediatrics encouraged physicians to inquire about IPV, since witnessing the abuse between adults in the home is associated with physical and mental health problems in the child. IPV is generally not a mandatory report in most states unless the child is being hurt.

In the realm of secondary and tertiary prevention, watching for signs of child abuse and neglect has been the responsibility of physicians since the mid-1960s. As mandated reporters, physicians are required by law to report a family to the local children's protective services when there is a concern about abuse or neglect.

Strategies for Adolescents

Relationship health falls on a spectrum that includes healthy, unhealthy, and abusive relationships. Primary prevention focused on the relationship level can be done individually or with a curriculum in a classroom or group setting. This means educating teens about their dating or peer relationships before abuse or violence happens.

Guidelines for Adolescent Preventive Services, developed by the American Medical Association, outlines areas of anticipatory guidance and health assessments that providers should address with teens in the health care setting. Violence prevention recommendations include counseling teens about resolving personal conflicts without violence and avoiding the use of weapons and weapon safety. As previously discussed, the implementation of these recommendations is a challenge.

On the community level, prevention efforts for teens have resulted in a number of curricula on "healthy relationships." Some examples are the Family Violence Prevention Fund's *Expect Respect: Working with Men and Boys,* which focuses on educating males about dating violence; the CDC's sexual violence prevention program, *Beginning the Dialogue,* which identifies concepts and strategies that may be used as a foundation for planning, implementing, and evaluating sexual violence prevention activities in a community; and the CDC's *Choose Respect,* which focuses on healthy teen relationships.

Strategies for Adults

To date, there has been no deliberate approach for discussing relationship health with adult patients in the health care setting. To achieve this, providers must understand the elements of healthy, unhealthy, and abusive relationships, and also have the skills, comfort level, tools, and time to initiate and follow through on conversations about relationship health. At this point, few health systems or professional health organizations have developed an approach to this issue. Promotion of positive relationship health should lessen individual, financial, and social costs of both intimate partner and employee abuse and violence. However, this requires sustained efforts on the part of health systems, with commitment from leadership, the designation of internal champions, and the implementation and ongoing evaluations of policies and practice.

Most efforts in the health care setting are secondary or tertiary prevention in nature. A number of screening tools and guidelines are available to assist providers in inquiring about IPV during the health care encounter in order to identify individuals in abusive relationships so that they can be referred before long-term consequences begin. Tertiary prevention seeks to identify victims and to limit the disability from the violence by caring for their health issues, both physical and mental, and linking them with resources to address the abuse.

Strategies for Seniors

Assessing elders for the evidence of abuse or neglect by their caregivers has been encouraged for a number of years. U.S. physicians are mandated by law to report cases where they suspect the abuse or neglect of an elderly person or vulnerable adult to local adult protective services. The "vulnerable adult" is defined in law and refers to an adult who is physically or mentally incapacitated, so that he or she is unable to make decisions for him- or herself. Efforts to identify older victims of IPV are a more recent development. Meeting the needs of these victims requires the collaboration of domestic violence advocacy and services for the elderly. Identifying elder abuse or older victims of IPV can be both secondary and tertiary prevention. Screening questions and tools are available. Efforts are needed to raise the awareness of physicians so that they understand the signs and symptoms associated with abuse and neglect, take the time to create privacy, and then routinely inquire about abuse when the signs and symptoms are present. Once abuse is identified, then the individual needs to be linked with services.

Community-Focused Efforts

Over the years, public awareness campaigns have addressed interpersonal violence. Messages communicate the norms of nonviolence in relationships and in the family and publicize available community resources for violence and abuse. Outlets for these campaigns have occurred through the media, slogans on buses, billboards, and educational literature distributed at various community locations. Examples include education about shaken baby syndrome or child abuse; about what is appropriate and inappropriate in dating relationships or intimate relationships; and about financial exploitation.

There are many opportunities to prevent interpersonal violence across the lifespan at the individual, relationship, and community levels within the realm of health. These approaches include primary, secondary, and tertiary prevention. The Institute of Medicine, in its report *Confronting Chronic Neglect,* concludes that additional effort is needed to enhance the education of physicians throughout their careers so that they have the skills to do a better job in identifying and assisting victims of interpersonal violence.

On the relationship and community levels, continued efforts by public health and health systems are needed.

Therese Zink and Pat Koppa

See also Health Care Response to Child Maltreatment; Health Care Response to Intimate Partner Violence; Health Consequences of Child Maltreatment; Health Consequences of Intimate Partner Violence; Home Visitation Services; Prevention Programs, Adolescent Dating Violence; Prevention Programs, Child Maltreatment; Prevention Programs, Community Mobilization; Prevention Programs, Definitions; Prevention Programs, Interpersonal Violence

Further Readings

American Medical Association. (1997). *Guidelines for adolescent preventive services.* Retrieved November 25, 2006, from http://www.ama-assn.org/ama/upload/mm/39/gapsmono.pdf

Centers for Disease Control and Prevention. (2003). *First reports evaluating the effectiveness of strategies for preventing violence—Early childhood home visitation: Findings from the Task Force on Community Preventive Services.* Retrieved November 4, 2006, from http://www.cdc.gov/mmwr/preview/mmwrhtml/rr5214a1.htm

Centers for Disease Control and Prevention, National Center for Injury Prevention and Control. (2006). *Choose respect.* Retrieved November 25, 2006, from http://www.chooserespect.org/scripts/about/aboutcr.asp

Institute of Medicine. (2002). *Confronting chronic neglect: The education and training of health professionals on family violence.* Washington, DC: National Academy Press.

Page-Glascoe, F., Oberklaid, F., Dworkin, P. H., & Trimm, F. (1998). *Brief approaches to educating patients and parents in primary care.* Retrieved November 6, 2006, from http://pediatrics.aappublications.org/cgi/reprint/101/6/e10

Salber, P. R., & Taliaferro, E. (2006). *The physician's guide to intimate partner violence and abuse: A reference for health care professionals.* Volcano, CA: Volcano Press.

Web Sites

Connected Kids: Safe, Strong, and Secure: http://www.aap.org/ConnectedKids/

HEALTH CARE RESPONSE TO CHILD MALTREATMENT

The health care system has the potential to address child maltreatment in a number of different ways, including primary, secondary, and tertiary prevention programs and services.

Primary prevention programs and services aim to prevent maltreatment from occurring in the first place. Home visitation programs staffed by health care professionals such as nurses have been well studied, and at least one has demonstrated some effectiveness in preventing child abuse and neglect. More recently, prevention programs based in the hospital and primary care setting have been developed. Programs to prevent abusive head trauma typically teach parents not to shake babies, and offer methods other than shaking for dealing with new baby frustrations. Less structured, but similar interventions may occur in primary care settings, and may include printed handouts from organizations such as the American Academy of Pediatrics, the National Exchange Club, and others.

Secondary prevention includes interventions that target families already at high risk for maltreatment, such as those with substance abuse, intimate partner violence, depression, other mental health problems, and/or lack of social support. Parents and caregivers with these risk factors can be identified through screening during their own primary or pregnancy-related health care, or during child health care visits. Brief screening questionnaires for substance abuse, intimate partner violence, and depression have been developed and validated for a variety of populations and health care settings.

The purpose of tertiary prevention is to ameliorate the short- and long-term adverse effects of maltreatment once the abuse or neglect has occurred. The health care system spends more resources on tertiary prevention than on primary or secondary prevention. Components of tertiary prevention may include diagnosis and acute treatment; long-term medical, rehabilitative, and mental health services; reporting to child protective service and law enforcement agencies; and providing court testimony.

Health care professionals play a significant role in identifying children with suspected maltreatment, and in providing further medical evaluation and treatment.

Children who have been maltreated may present to their primary health care providers, to a hospital emergency department, or to subspecialists such as orthopedic surgeons, gastroenterologists, pulmonologists, neurologists, and neurosurgeons. Therefore, all health care professionals who treat children must be aware of the possibility of maltreatment, and the need to distinguish abuse from other injuries. Specialists in the field of child maltreatment are available in many, but not all, jurisdictions to assist in the identification, evaluation, and reporting of maltreatment.

Medical care for children with suspected abuse may include treatment of presenting injuries, as well as identification and treatment of occult (masked) injuries, such as fractures, head/brain injuries, and abdominal injuries. Because caregivers of maltreated children may provide a misleading or absent history of injury, such injuries may be missed unless they are screened for using x-rays and/or laboratory tests. Identification of occult injuries may also solidify a diagnosis of abuse when a child presents with injuries that are suspicious for, but not diagnostic of, maltreatment. Medical treatment will vary according to the type and extent of injuries present. Injuries such as bruises may require no medical intervention. Minor burns and fractures may require emergency department care. Other, more severe injuries such as burns, fractures, brain injuries, and injuries to internal organs may demand hospitalization, surgery, and/or intensive care management.

All health care professionals in the United States are required by law to report children with suspected maltreatment to child protective service agencies. Doing so allows for further investigation into the circumstances surrounding the alleged abuse or neglect, and intervention, when necessary, to ensure the safety of the maltreated child. Health care professionals may also be required to report suspected physical and sexual abuse to law enforcement for investigation of possible criminal activity. Professionals in health care may be subpoenaed to testify in criminal and/or civil legal proceedings.

Abused and neglected children may have chronic medical and mental health care needs as a result of maltreatment. Children with significant brain, skin, and/or abdominal injuries may require extensive physical, occupational, speech, and other therapy to aid in functional recovery. These services may be provided to inpatients in acute care and rehabilitation hospitals. Outpatient rehabilitation services may also be needed.

Finally, health professionals play an important role in addressing the mental health care needs of children who have been abused or neglected. While some providers will refer children to mental health services, others, such as psychiatrists, psychologists, social workers, and licensed therapists, will be directly responsible for providing mental health treatment services.

Wendy G. Lane

See also Child Abuse Prevention; Child Neglect; Child Physical Abuse; Child Sexual Abuse; Health Consequences of Child Maltreatment

Further Readings

Dias, M., Smith, K., deGuehery, K., Mazur, P., Li, V., & Shaffer, M. L. (2005). Preventing abusive head trauma among infants and young children: A hospital-based parent education program. *Pediatrics, 115*, e470–e477.

Dubowitz, H. (2002). Preventing child neglect and physical abuse: A role for pediatricians. *Pediatrics in Review, 23*(6), 191–196.

Ewing, J. A. (1984). Detecting alcoholism: The CAGE Questionnaire. *Journal of the American Medical Association, 252*(14), 1905–1907.

Feldhaus, K. M., Koziol-McLain, J., Amsbury, H. L., Norton, I. M., Lowenstein, S. R., & Abbott, J. T. (1997). Accuracy of 3 brief screening questions for detecting partner violence in the emergency department. *Journal of the American Medical Association, 277*(17), 1357–1361.

Olds, D. L., et al. (1997). Long-term effects of home visitation on maternal life course and child abuse and neglect. *Journal of the American Medical Association, 278*(8), 637–643.

Reece, R. M. (Ed.). (2000). *Treatment of child abuse: Common ground for mental health, medical, and legal practitioners.* Baltimore, MD: Johns Hopkins University Press.

Whooley, M. A., Avins, A. L., Miranda, J., & Browner, W. S. (1997). Case-finding instruments for depression. Two questions are as good as many. *Journal of General Internal Medicine, 12*, 439–445.

HEALTH CARE RESPONSE TO INTIMATE PARTNER VIOLENCE

Studies show that intimate partner violence (IPV) affects the physical and mental health of victims and the children who witness it. Because IPV is widespread and the consequences, acute and chronic, are serious, health care organizations have encouraged providers to identify patients experiencing IPV and refer them to local resources. To date a number of screening tools have been validated, but research is limited on how provider identification impacts the health and quality of life of IPV victims. Several best practice guidelines have been developed to guide providers in the identification and management of IPV. Research demonstrates that training alone is insufficient to ensure that providers screen for IPV. Rather, systemwide approaches that incorporate prompts about screening, formal training with tool kits, referral resources and routine consultation, and timely feedback with providers on the initiative or program have been the most successful.

Health Impact

IPV victims use more health care resources than persons who are not abused. Health care costs for victims are almost 50% higher than those of nonvictims. Much of this is nonemergent care. In the primary care office, 11% to 22% of women are currently experiencing physical violence by an intimate partner. In fact, almost half (47%) of the victims who were murdered by their intimate partners were seen in the health care setting for general health or mental health issues during the year prior to their deaths. In addition to injuries, studies show that chronic health conditions, such as migraine headaches, chronic pain, and irritable bowel syndrome are common among victims of IPV. A recent study by the Harvard School of Public Health demonstrates that physical violence compromises a woman's health during pregnancy, her likelihood of carrying a child to term, and the fetal development and health of her newborn. Mental health diagnoses such as depression, substance abuse, anxiety, and posttraumatic stress disorder occur up to four times more often in victims compared to persons who are not abused.

Health Care Response

Since 1992 professional health care organizations, such as the American Medical Association (AMA), American Academy of Family Physicians, American College of Obstetrics and Gynecology (ACOG), American College of Physicians, and American Nurses

Association, have encouraged health providers to identify and treat IPV victims. Recognizing the impact of witnessing IPV on children, the American Academy of Pediatrics encouraged pediatricians to screen during well-child visits and when children presented with symptoms or problems often associated with IPV exposure (e.g., behavior problems, depression, and chronic pain complaints). In 1992, the Joint Commission on Healthcare Organization Accreditation introduced standards that hospitals and their associated clinics must adhere to regarding the identification and management of patients living with IPV as part of accreditation.

The AMA, ACOG, the Family Violence Prevention Fund, and others have developed best practice guidelines that endorse screening all women for IPV during well-woman exams and when women present with "red flag" signs and symptoms, such as injuries, chronic conditions, depression, or pregnancy concerns. Always keeping in mind victim privacy and confidentiality, providers are encouraged to respond by (a) validating the victim's experience, (b) affirming no one deserves to be abused, (c) assessing support and safety, (d) sharing IPV resources, and (e) scheduling follow-up appointments.

Recognizing that an intimate relationship is abusive and attaining behavior change is a process, and health providers are encouraged to respect the victim's timeline and decisions in coping with the abusive relationship. In most states, it is not mandatory to report IPV to authorities, unless a weapon is used or severe injury occurs.

Current Research

Evidence-based reviews neither support nor negate the value of these efforts in the health care setting, but call for further research as much evidence is anecdotal in nature. Rebuttals to these reviews encourage efforts to identify signs of IPV in patients, due to the prevalence and impact of IPV, in order to produce comprehensive and quality care. Failing to identify signs of IPV means the provider may miss an important dimension of the patient's situation and associated stressors that are contributing to the patient's health condition. For example, treating migraines without identifying IPV may result in a reduced benefit to the overall health and function of a patient. Conversely, treating headaches and discussing safety and available options would be more comprehensive.

Qualitative research shows that victims want to be asked about IPV, even if they do not disclose immediately. Victims report wanting hope and knowing that support and options are available. A number of validated screening tools exist. Recent work by Harriet MacMillan demonstrates that women prefer self-completed (computer, audiotape, or written) to face-to-face questioning about IPV. All formats identify similar rates of IPV.

Research on what types of interventions impact the health and welfare of victims is limited. Studies show that discussing safety behaviors with a nurse helped women adopt more of the behaviors. Victims also need help with obtaining orders of protection, which decrease the occurrences of abusive incidents. Postshelter advocacy and counseling have been found to improve women's scores on quality of life, social supports, depression, and self-esteem as well as to elevate self-worth scores for children. Onsite advocacy services improve provider screening and referral rates.

Specialized Training for Health Care Providers

Despite the encouragement of professional organizations, less than 10% of health providers routinely inquire about IPV. Training alone does not increase screening rates. However, specialized training based on models for behavior change with built-in reinforcement, such as feedback on screening, chart prompts, newsletters, and periodic updates on patient outcomes, improves rates of inquiry. Systemwide approaches, like those instituted at WomanKind in Minnesota and Kaiser Permanente in California with specialized training and victim interventions, have brought about improved outcomes and comprehensive system change. Support from system administration and health leaders, who make IPV management a priority, allocate resources, ensure training of staff, and deliver necessary health system supports, is essential for success. Collaboration with local advocacy services is also imperative.

Future Opportunities

With more research, there are many opportunities to improve the care of victims within the health care setting. IPV impacts the physical and mental health of victims, perpetrators, and children. More research on how to assist all members of the family and identifying and implementing public health prevention efforts are important goals for future work.

Therese Zink and Susan M. Hadley

See also Health Care Response, Prevention Strategies for Reducing Interpersonal Violence; Health Consequences of Intimate Partner Violence; Intimate Partner Violence

Further Readings

AMA Council on Scientific Affairs. (2005, June). *Report 7 of the Council on Scientific Affairs (A-05): Diagnosis and management of family violence.* Chicago: American Medical Association.

American College of Obstetrics and Gynecology (ACOG). (1999). *Domestic violence: Educational bulletin.* Washington, DC: Author.

American College of Physicians. (1986, March 3). *Domestic violence.* Position paper presented to the American College of Physicians, Philadelphia.

Committee on Child Abuse and Neglect, American Academy of Pediatrics. (1998). The role of pediatricians in recognizing and intervening on behalf of abused women. *Pediatrics, 101,* 1091–1092.

Flitcraft, A. H., Hadley, S. M., Hendricks-Matthews, M. K., McLeer, S. V., & Warshaw, C. (1992). *American Medical Association diagnostic and treatment guidelines for domestic violence.* Chicago: American Medical Association.

Institute of Medicine. (2002). *Confronting chronic neglect: The education and training of health professionals on family violence.* Washington, DC: National Academy Press.

MacMillan, H. L., et al. (2006). Approaches to screening for intimate partner violence in health care settings. *Journal of the American Medical Association, 296*(5), 530–536.

Nelson, H. D., Nygren, P., McInerney, Y., & Klein, J. (2004). Screening women and elderly adults for family and intimate partner violence: A review of the evidence for the U.S. preventive services task force. *Annals of Internal Medicine, 140,* 382–386.

Ramsay, J., Richardson, J., Carter, Y., Davidson, L., & Feder, G. (2002). Should health professionals screen women for domestic violence? Systematic review. *British Medical Journal, 325,* 314–318.

Silverman, J. G., Decker, M. R., Reed, E., & Raj, A. (2006). Intimate partner violence victimization prior to and during pregnancy among women residing in 26 U.S. states: Associations with maternal and neonatal health. *American Journal of Obstetrics and Gynecology, 195*(1), 140–148.

Wathen, C., & MacMillan, H. (2003). Interventions for violence against women: Scientific review. *Journal of the American Medical Association, 289*(5), 589–600.

Health Consequences of Child Maltreatment

Men and women who have experienced interpersonal violence often have poorer health than their nonabused counterparts—and these effects last long after the abuse has ended. Moreover, abuse survivors are significantly more likely to have a number of serious illnesses and to die prematurely compared to nonabused people. They often experience increased rates of cardiovascular disease, diabetes, and metabolic syndrome, the precursor to type 2 diabetes. Using an adult HMO sample, the Adverse Childhood Experiences (ACE) study found that men and women who had experienced four or more types of ACE were significantly more likely to have ischemic heart disease, cancer, stroke, skeletal fractures, chronic obstructive pulmonary disease, chronic bronchitis, and hepatitis. The types of adverse experiences included childhood maltreatment (physical abuse, sexual abuse, and neglect), parental mental illness, parental substance abuse, and parental criminal activity. The researchers counted each type (not incident) of ACE that a person experienced as "one."

Given these rates of illness, it is not surprising that abuse survivors see doctors more often and have higher patterns of health care use. In an HMO sample, 22% of child sexual abuse survivors had visited a doctor 10 or more times a year, compared with 6% of the nonabused control group. High health care use was also noted in a study of women who had been battered or raped as adults.

In addition to office visits, health care use can include hospitalizations and surgery. Women who have experienced child or domestic abuse were also more likely to have had repeated surgeries. Severity of the abuse experience was the most powerful predictor of number of physician visits and outpatient costs.

One factor that might be driving the higher patterns of health care use among adult survivors is the increased likelihood of one or more chronic pain syndromes. Chronic pain is a major form of disability, accounting for an estimated $125 billion each year in health care costs, and it is common among victims of violence. In one study, pain was the most commonly occurring symptom in a community sample of child sexual abuse survivors.

Of the functional chronic pain syndromes, irritable bowel syndrome has been studied the most with regard to past abuse. In samples of patients in treatment for irritable bowel, abuse survivors comprise 50% to 70%. Abuse survivors can also suffer from chronic pain in other parts of the body. Abuse has been related to chronic or recurring headaches, pelvic pain, back pain, or more generalized pain syndromes. These findings apply to both survivors of childhood abuse and those abused as adults. Patients with these conditions often have marked physiological abnormalities in brain structure and function that are apparent using technology such as positron emission tomography (PET) scans, computed tomography (CT) scans, and magnetic resonance imaging (MRI) of the brain.

Why Maltreatment as Children Makes Adults Sick

While researchers have documented that abuse survivors are more prone to physical illness, they know substantially less about why this occurs. However, researchers have identified five possible pathways by which victimization is likely to influence health in abuse survivors—physiological changes, behavior, cognitive beliefs, social relationships, and emotional health. Adult survivors can be influenced by any or all of these, and the five types influence each other. Indeed, they form a complex matrix of interrelationships, all of which influence health.

Physiological Changes

Traumatic events change the way the body functions. The body becomes "threat sensitized" and more vulnerable to stress reactions and depression when faced with subsequent stressors. There is also evidence that survivors' pain threshold is lowered, making them more vulnerable to chronic pain syndromes. The more severe the abusive experience, the more dramatic the physiologic changes.

Behavior

Traumatic events increase the risk of participation in harmful activities that include smoking, eating disorders and obesity, substance abuse, and unsafe sexual practices. Sleep disturbances are also common in abuse survivors, and this compromises every aspect of health.

Cognitive Beliefs

What one thinks about oneself and others can have a measurable impact on one's immune system and cardiovascular health. Shame and low self-esteem and self-efficacy all have deleterious effects on health. Hostile or mistrusting beliefs about others can also have a negative impact on health, and influence the next category: quality of social relationships.

Social Relationships

Abuse survivors have higher rates of unstable relationships, divorce, and revictimization at the hands of intimate partners. Marital strife, for example, increases the risk of heart disease in women. But positive and supportive relationships buffer stress and even increase longevity. In short, one's social relationships can either enhance health or make it substantially worse. And abuse survivors often have troubled relationships.

Emotional Health

A person's emotional health also influences his or her physical health. Psychological stress, depression, and posttraumatic stress disorder increase inflammation by increasing levels of proinflammatory cytokines. Elevated inflammation increases the risk of diseases such as cardiovascular disease, metabolic syndrome, and even Alzheimer's disease.

Recognizing the complexity of the forces that are related to the health of abuse survivors, researchers and health care professionals can strive for an approach that addresses all five of these pathways. Health outcomes are unlikely to improve if such professionals continue in the current mind-set of treating mental health and physical health aftereffects separately. Recognizing, and addressing, all these underlying factors can help health care professionals improve the health of adult survivors of childhood abuse.

Kathleen Kendall-Tackett

See also Depression; Incest

Further Readings

Arnold, R. P., Rogers, D., & Cook, D. A. G. (1990). Medical problems of adults who were sexually abused in childhood. *British Medical Journal, 300,* 705–708.

Batten, S. V., Aslan, M., Maciejewski, P. K., & Mazure, C. M. (2004). Childhood maltreatment as a risk factor for adult cardiovascular disease and depression. *Journal of Clinical Psychiatry, 65,* 249–254.

Bremner, J. D. (2005). The neurobiology of childhood sexual abuse in women with post-traumatic stress disorder. In K. A. Kendall-Tackett (Ed.), *The handbook of women, stress and trauma* (pp. 181–206). New York: Taylor & Francis.

Felitti, V. J. (1991). Long-term medical consequences of incest, rape, and molestation. *Southern Medical Journal, 84,* 328–331.

Felitti, V. J., et al. (2001). Relationship of childhood abuse and household dysfunction to many of the leading causes of death in adults. In K. Franey, R. Geffner, & R. Falconer (Eds.), *The cost of child maltreatment: Who pays? We all do* (pp. 53–69). San Diego, CA: Family Violence and Sexual Assault Institute.

Kendall-Tackett, K. A. (2003). *Treating the lifetime health effects of childhood victimization.* Kingston, NJ: Civic Research Institute.

Kendall-Tackett, K. A. (2007). Cardiovascular disease and metabolic syndrome as sequelae of violence against women: A psychoneuroimmunology approach. *Trauma, Violence and Abuse, 8*(2), 117–126.

Kendall-Tackett, K. A., & Marshall, R. (1999). Victimization and diabetes: An exploratory study. *Child Abuse & Neglect, 23,* 593–596.

Kendall-Tackett, K. A., Marshall, R., & Ness, K. E. (2000). Victimization, healthcare use, and health maintenance. *Family Violence & Sexual Assault Bulletin, 16,* 18–21.

Kendall-Tackett, K. A., Marshall, R., & Ness, K. E. (2003). Chronic pain syndromes and violence against women. *Women and Therapy, 26,* 45–56.

Koss, M. P., Koss, P. G., & Woodruff, M. S. (1991). Deleterious effects of criminal victimization on women's health and medical utilization. *Archives of Internal Medicine, 151,* 342–347.

Leserman, J., Drossman, D. A., Li, Z., Toomey, T. C., Nachman, G., & Glogau, L. (1996). Sexual and physical abuse history in gastroenterology practice: How types of abuse impact health status. *Psychosomatic Medicine, 58,* 4–15.

Okifuji, A., Turk, D. C., & Kalauokalani, D. (1999). Clinical outcome and economic evaluation of multidisciplinary pain centers. In A. R. Block, E. F. Kremer, &

E. Fernandez (Eds.), *Handbook of pain syndromes* (pp. 77–97). Mahwah, NJ: Lawrence Erlbaum.

Teegen, F. (1999). Childhood sexual abuse and long-term sequelae. In A. Maercker, M. Schutzwohl, & Z. Solomon (Eds.), *Posttraumatic stress disorder: A lifespan developmental perspective* (pp. 97–112). Seattle, WA: Hogrefe & Huber.

HEALTH CONSEQUENCES OF HATE CRIME

Hate crimes are generally defined as crimes motivated by bias or prejudice against the victim's real or perceived race, ethnicity, religion, sexual orientation, gender, or disability. Hate crime legislation varies by state according to the victim characteristics protected, as well as by requirements for data collection and law enforcement training. According to the Federal Bureau of Investigation, hate crimes comprise less than 1% of all reported crimes. However, hate crimes are believed to be underreported, and the National Crime Victimization Survey reported over 200,000 hate crime victimizations from mid-2000 through December 2003. Since hate crimes are perceived by many as qualitatively different from nonhate crimes, it is logical to expect unique physical and emotional responses to victimization experiences.

The health effects of hate crimes may be felt by both the individual victim and the broader community. Proponents of hate crime legislation argue that the harm extends beyond the individual victim to members of the group that share the victim's real or perceived characteristics. However, there has been a dearth of research on the effects of hate crime on communities at large. Additionally, early researchers focused on the physical harm experienced by victims of hate crimes, which has been characterized as excessively brutal. Media coverage of high-profile cases—such as the murder in 1998 of Matthew Shepard, a gay university student in Wyoming who was severely beaten and died from his injuries, and James Byrd, an African American man in Texas who was dragged to his death the same year—highlights the extreme cruelty inflicted on some hate crime victims.

Some researchers have found that hate crime victims suffer more severe physical injuries than those who are the victims of nonhate crimes. A study in the 1990s by Jack Levin and Jack McDevitt on hate crime assaults in Boston found that a higher percentage of hate crime victims than nonhate crime victims required medical treatment. Similarly, a 2005 study of National Incident-Based Reporting System data on hate crime assaults found that hate crime victims were more likely to be seriously injured than nonhate crime victims. However, not all studies confirm that hate crime victims suffer more severe physical injuries than nonhate crime victims, and the vast majority of reported hate crimes are low-level offenses, such as harassment and intimidation, in which no injuries are sustained.

In addition to examining the physical effects of hate crime victimization, researchers have explored the psychological effects of victimization, finding some indication that hate crime victims report higher levels of psychological harm. Studies have found that hate crime victims report feeling more nervous, having trouble concentrating, and feeling more angry than nonhate crime victims. A victim survey conducted by researchers at Northeastern University measured psychological and behavioral responses of victims of both hate- and nonhate-motivated incidents of aggravated assault. The researchers found that hate crime victims suffered more severe and longer-lasting psychological effects than victims of nonhate crimes, but there was little difference between the victims' behavioral responses. Hate crime victims reported psychological effects, such as having trouble concentrating at work, experiencing intrusive thoughts about the crime, feeling depressed or sad, and feeling more nervous than usual. However, there was no difference between hate and nonhate crime victims' behavioral responses, such as avoidance, relocating, attempted suicide, or taking self-defense classes.

Overall, more research is needed to investigate the physical and psychological health consequences of hate crimes. In general, there is little research to support the contention that hate crime victims suffer more severe injuries than nonhate crime victims. However, some research bears out that hate crime victims may in fact experience greater psychological harm.

Nickie D. Phillips

See also Hate Crimes (Bias Crimes), Anti-Gay; Hate Crimes (Bias Crimes), Criminal Justice Responses; Hate Crimes (Bias Crimes), Gender Motivated

Further Readings

Garcia, L., McDevitt, J., Gu, J., & Balboni, J. (2002). *Psychological and behavioral effects of bias and nonbias motivated assault.* Washington, DC: National Institute of Justice.

Garofalo, J. (1997). Hate crime victimization in the United States. In R. Davis, A. Lurigio, & W. Skogan (Eds.), *Victims of crime* (2nd ed., pp. 134–145). Thousand Oaks, CA: Sage.

Harlow, C. W. (2005). *Hate crime reported by victims and police.* Washington, DC: U.S. Department of Justice, Bureau of Justice Statistics.

Herek, G., & Berrill, K. (1992). *Hate crimes: Confronting violence against lesbians and gay men.* Newbury Park, CA: Sage.

Herek, G., Cogan, J., & Gillis, J. (2002). Victim experiences in hate crimes based on sexual orientation. *Journal of Social Issues, 58,* 319–399.

Lawrence, F. (1999). *Punishing hate: Bias crimes under American law.* Cambridge, MA: Harvard University Press.

HEALTH CONSEQUENCES OF INCARCERATION

Prisons and jails hold not only those responsible for inflicting interpersonal violence, but also those who have chronic histories of physical and/or sexual abuse. Individuals most likely to be imprisoned are often impoverished with little access to physical and/or mental health care prior to incarceration. As such, the rates of infectious communicable diseases in the penal institutions are far greater than in the general population, resulting in a vulnerability that can negatively affect individuals' physical health. Similarly, conditions of confinement may exacerbate or contribute to the high rates of mental health disorders among the incarcerated. Although accreditation standards exist for the delivery of health care services within jails and prisons, privatization of those services and movement toward managed care may affect the quality and quantity of services available.

Prisoners have a much greater prevalence of active tuberculosis, hepatitis C, and HIV/AIDS than the general population. Due to the crowded conditions, they may pass on their infection to other prisoners and staff. In addition, a higher prevalence of sexually transmitted infections (STIs) means that unprotected sex during incarceration threatens health through the transmission of STIs, including HIV/AIDS.

Recently, the Bureau of Justice Statistics reported that 55% of men and 73% of women in state prisons have a diagnosable mental health disorder. Certainly the loss of social supports and separation from family can contribute to symptom intensity. However, other conditions of confinement, such as threats to physical safety, sexual assaults and harassment by staff and other inmates, overcrowded conditions, and segregation also erode mental health, leading to decompensation. Although therapeutic services, such as medications and therapy, are available, only about one third of those who need treatment receive it.

Due to their being a relatively small proportion (8% to 10%) of the incarcerated, women often receive inadequate health care. This is particularly problematic because health care needs are complicated by the high rates of physical and sexual abuse women experience. Personnel delivering gynecological care may be insensitive to the possibility that an exam might trigger a reexperiencing of a traumatic event. In addition, pregnancy is a particularly high-risk situation, both medically and psychologically. Obstetrical visits and delivery take place in community hospitals. Women are escorted and observed by guards during delivery, and are sometimes shackled. Except in a few instances, mothers are returned to the institution without their infants.

The National Commission on Correctional Health Care requires institutions seeking accreditation to comply with standards for health services. These standards include thorough screening for infectious diseases and communicable illnesses at intake. In addition, mental health screening, assessment, and treatment are essential. Many states have retained private health care providers or correctional health maintenance organizations. Medical malpractice lawsuits brought by inmates against states and prison health care providers have been largely unsuccessful.

Sheryl Pimlott Kubiak

See also AIDS/HIV; Mental Illness; Prison Violence, Sexual Assault; Prison Violence by Corrections Staff; Prison Violence by Inmates; Sexually Transmitted Diseases

Further Readings

Amnesty International. (2000). *Pregnant and imprisoned in the United States.* New York: Author.

Hammett, T. M. (2006). HIV in prisons. *Criminology and Public Policy, 5,* 109–112.

Treadwell, H. M., & Nottingham, J. H. (Eds.). (2005). Public health consequences of imprisonment [Special issue]. *American Journal of Public Health, 95*(10).

HEALTH CONSEQUENCES OF INTIMATE PARTNER VIOLENCE

The negative health effects of intimate partner violence (IPV) are diverse and epidemic. IPV, which is often interchangeably called domestic violence, spousal abuse, family violence, or wife beating, can significantly degrade the physical, sexual, reproductive, and mental health status of IPV survivors. Survivors of IPV have been shown to need more emergency room visits, physician visits, and prescriptions filled than individuals who have not experienced IPV. Not only does IPV cause immediate injury, but its effects also culminate over time and manifest as an array of health problems that prevail far after the abuse has ended. The complexity and duration of the negative health effects of IPV cause it to be difficult to identify, diagnose, and treat by medical professionals who have not been properly trained. The public health community has accordingly recognized IPV as a public health priority and has begun addressing its health consequences through position papers, changes in health care delivery, community partnerships, and medical trainings.

Long-Term Health Consequences of Physical Violence

In addition to the immediate injury that often results from physical violence, such as lacerations, bruises, broken bones, and concussions, victims of IPV also often suffer from related long-term physical health problems. The effects of ongoing or consistent abuse are cumulative and proportionate to the duration and severity of abuse. Consequently, routine violence has been shown to increase the likelihood of recurring physical ailments such as arthritis and chronic pain syndrome. When the

violence is more focused around the head and neck, it can lead to neurological difficulties such as headaches, vision and hearing impairment, and an inability to concentrate.

Health Consequences of Sexual Violence

In addition to physical violence, the definition of IPV also often includes sexual assault by an intimate partner. The term *sexual abuse* refers to any sexual action that is committed to establish, maintain, or exploit an imbalance of power. This abuse includes but is not limited to the use or threat of physical violence for sex, degrading or cruel sex acts, and sex with the intention of emotional manipulation. While the immediate and chronic health consequences of sexual abuse include many of the effects of physical abuse, these consequences also encompass a set of problems characteristic to this type of violence.

Victims of sexual abuse are often not permitted to negotiate safer sex practices, and therefore are at a higher risk for unwanted pregnancies and sexually transmitted diseases. Possible cumulative effects of sexual violence include vaginal and anal tearing, gynecological infections, urinary tract infections, pelvic inflammatory disease, bladder infections, chronic pelvic pain, and cervical cancer.

Health Consequences of Psychological Violence

Psychological abuse and emotional abuse are also strong predictors of poor physical and mental health. Survivors of IPV are more likely to suffer from depression, posttraumatic stress disorder, insomnia, and panic attacks. A lack of agency, constant fear of safety for oneself and loved ones, verbal abuse, and psychological intimidation are only a few contributing causes of a survivor's mental health ailments.

In addition to mental health problems, psychological abuse can also result in physical problems caused by emotional strain, often called psychosomatic effects. These effects can manifest themselves as gastrointestinal problems, such as irritable bowel syndrome, stomach ulcers, constipation, diarrhea, and chronic stomach pain. Survivors of IPV are also more likely to experience high blood pressure and poor heart health. Additionally, stress caused by violence most likely reduces immune system response, increasing the potential to contract communicable diseases.

Survivors of violence may also employ coping behaviors that are physically harmful in an effort to reduce psychological suffering. Individuals who have experienced IPV are more likely to have an eating disorder, abuse drugs, drink alcohol, and smoke cigarettes. The most detrimental health effect rooted in the psychological suffering caused by IPV is the increased likelihood to have thoughts of suicide and to commit suicide.

Health Care and Intimate Partner Violence

In addition to health problems caused directly by IPV, survivors of abuse also face difficulties in receiving effective health care. Batterers often employ controlling and isolating behavior that limits the people, institutions, and services with whom their partner has the ability to interact. In an effort to conceal the violence or to exert control in the relationship, perpetrators of IPV may not allow victims to seek prescriptive or preventive medical care. Thus survivors of IPV are less likely to visit medical professionals to treat injuries that have already occurred or to participate in regular health screenings such as pap smears and mammograms.

When survivors of IPV do receive screening and treatment from medical professionals, they may not receive care that is tailored to their experiences. Survivors are often reluctant to disclose experiences of abuse in hospitals because they fear for their safety, are embarrassed, or do not identify their abuse as a cause of their deteriorating health. Additionally, questions regarding abuse are typically not a routine part of screenings administered in medical settings. Therefore, the complexity of causes and effects of this type of violence may evade medical professionals who have not been appropriately trained to accurately and comprehensively identify, diagnose, and treat the health consequences of abuse.

Public Health Response to Intimate Partner Violence

In response to the far-reaching and distinctive health consequences of IPV, the United States' public health community has been acknowledging domestic violence as a public health priority since the 1980s. In 1985, U.S. Surgeon General C. Everett Koop publicly recognized domestic violence as a pressing public health issue. In the following 15 years, a number of leading national health organizations issued position papers identifying violence against women, family violence, or domestic violence as a public health priority. These health organizations include the American College of Obstetrics and Gynecology, the American Nurses Association, the American Medical Association, the American Public Health Association, the American Academy of Family Physicians, the American Academy of Pediatrics, the American Psychological Association, and the American Academy of Nurse Practitioners.

In 2006 the World Health Organization (WHO) released the results of its multicountry study on the health effects of domestic violence. Through this investigation that interviewed over 24,000 women in urban and rural areas of 10 countries, WHO asserted that IPV is the most common type of violence in women's lives and must be viewed as a key global health priority.

Sara J. Shoener

See also Depression; Health Care Response, Prevention Strategies for Reducing Interpersonal Violence; Health Care Response to Intimate Partner Violence; Intimate Partner Violence; Posttraumatic Stress Disorder; Self-Injury

Further Readings

Campbell, J. C. (Ed.). (1998). *Empowering survivors of abuse: Health care for battered women and their children.* Thousand Oaks, CA: Sage.

Chamberlain, L. (2006). *Making the connection: Domestic violence and public health.* San Francisco, CA: Family Violence Prevention Fund.

Coker, A., Smith, P., Bethea, L., King, M., & McKeown, R. (2000). Physical health consequences of physical and psychological intimate partner violence. *Archives of Family Medicine, 9*(5), 451–457.

Garcia-Moreno, C., Jansen, A. F. M. H., Ellsberg, M., Heise, L., & Watts, C. (2005). *WHO Multi-country Study on Women's Health and Domestic Violence Against Women: Initial results on prevalence, health outcomes, and women's responses.* Geneva: World Health Organization.

Morewitz, S. J. (2004). *Domestic violence and maternal and child health.* New York: Kluwer Academic/Plenum.

HELP-SEEKING BEHAVIORS OF ABUSED WOMEN

Help-seeking refers to the process of an individual seeking assistance from informal and formal sources of support. Informal sources of support include family members, friends, coworkers, neighbors, employers, and faith-based leaders, whereas formal support refers to agencies within larger systems (e.g., criminal justice, human service, social service, and child protective systems). Regarding intimate partner violence (IPV), in particular, evidence suggests that survivors seek assistance from *both* informal and formal sources of support to meet a variety of needs; however, survivors are more likely to seek informal support. Survivors reported telling family and/or friends about the violence before telling formal sources like police. Informal assistance sought from family and friends is often important in helping the survivor cope with violence-associated stress or to become safer.

While the decision of whether and from whom to seek assistance is a complicated one, survivors of IPV engage in *active* help-seeking. Early theorizing about battered women and learned helplessness implied that survivors of IPV were unlikely to seek assistance. Others proposed that it was, in fact, the learned helplessness of the community that hindered survivors' safety. Survivor theory provided an alternative that suggested that women's help-seeking efforts are largely unmet by the community.

Indeed, IPV survivors face frequent barriers in their efforts to seek help from both formal and informal sources. Survivors seeking assistance from their informal network do not experience wholly positive or supportive reactions; rather, evidence suggests that survivors of IPV sometimes experience negative reactions from family and friends. Reactions perceived to be negative include victim blaming, making demands on the survivor (e.g., that she leave the relationship or move on with her life), withholding or removing tangible aid or emotional support, and jeopardizing the survivor's safety. Research on negative reactions to sexual assault victims suggests such reactions are strongly related to overall health and well-being (e.g., increased rates of depression, posttraumatic stress disorder, somatic symptoms) and have implications for recovery and future help-seeking.

IPV survivors may also face barriers in their efforts to engage formal helping sources. Historically, the community response to IPV against women has been characterized by inadequate services, as well as a lack of coordination across the systems involved in responding to domestic violence cases. IPV survivors have experienced revictimization by the formal systems designed to help them (e.g., the human service system) and to hold batterers accountable (e.g., the criminal justice system). Fortunately, with the current emphasis on creating a coordinated community response to violence against women and changes in federal and state laws, the community response is changing and, ideally, becoming more responsive to the needs of survivors.

Importantly, IPV survivors are not a monolithic group with regard to their help-seeking behavior. Survivors have varied wants and needs, including, for example, housing, financial assistance, emotional support, education, support for their children, and legal assistance. IPV survivors present a wide variety of diverse needs, and it is essential to tailor interventions to their stated priorities. Specifically, it is important for those responding to survivors' help-seeking not to impose their own "helping" agenda but to assist in the ways survivors indicate would be helpful.

Survivors' help-seeking behavior is shaped by many sources of diversity including, for example, personal preferences, geographic locale (rural, urban, and suburban), culture, race and ethnicity, available resources, age, religious preferences, immigration status, and previous experiences (with abuse and with the helping response). For example, African American IPV survivors may be less likely to seek assistance from the police because of past historical mistreatment by the justice system. This suggests that survivors' help-seeking behavior must be understood at multiple levels and that every effort should be made to respect and support survivors' help-seeking decisions.

Finally, help-seeking is not a one-time, singular event, but a complex process that involves decision making that changes over time as it is shaped by an individual's environment. Generally speaking, evidence suggests a progression in battered women's active help-seeking from the first violent incidents to escalating forms of abuse. After the first abusive incidents survivors may blame themselves and try to change their own behavior. But as the abuse escalates, survivors increasingly hold the batterer responsible, realize the hope for changing him is futile, and begin to plan for life without him or look for additional ways to cope. Work is currently underway to develop a better understanding of battered women's help-seeking processes. One theory suggests this process involves three stages: (1) recognizing and defining the problem, (2) making the decision to seek help, and (3) selecting a helpsource (e.g., friends, police). Additional research is needed to understand if these three stages adequately represent help-seeking among survivors of IPV.

Nicole E. Allen and Jennifer Trotter

See also Advocacy; Agency/Autonomy of Battered Women; Battered Woman Syndrome; Battered Women; Battered Women: Leaving Violent Intimate Relationships; Shelters, Battered Women's

Further Readings

Allen, N. E., Bybee, D., & Sullivan, C. M. (2004). Battered women's multitude of needs: Evidence supporting the need for comprehensive advocacy. *Violence Against Women, 10*(9), 1015–1035.

Bowker, L. H. (1984). Coping with wife abuse: Personal and social networks. In A. R. Roberts (Ed.), *Battered women and their families: Intervention strategies and treatment programs* (pp. 168–191). New York: Springer.

Campbell, R., Ahrens, C. E., Sefl, T., Wasco, S. M., & Barnes, H. E. (2001). Social reactions to rape victims: Healing and hurtful effects on psychological and physical health outcomes. *Violence & Victims, 16*(3), 287–302.

Golding, J. M., Siegel, J. M., Sorenson, S. B., Burnam, M. A., & Stein, J. A. (1989). Social support sources following sexual assault. *Journal of Community Psychology, 17,* 92–107.

Gondolf, E. W. (1988). The survivor theory. In E. W. Gondolf & E. R. Fisher (Eds.), *Battered women as survivors* (pp. 11–25). Lexington, MA: Lexington Books.

Goodkind, J. R., Gillum, T. L., Bybee, D. I., & Sullivan, C. M. (2003). The impact of family and friends' reactions on the well-being of women with abusive partners. *Violence Against Women, 9*(3), 347–373.

Hart, B. J. (1995). *Coordinated community approaches to domestic violence.* Paper presented at the Strategic Planning Workshop on Violence Against Women, National Institute of Justice, Washington, DC. Retrieved from http://www.mincava.umn.edu

Liang, B., Goodman, L., Tummala-Narra, P., & Weintraub, S. (2005). A theoretical framework for understanding help-seeking processes among survivors of intimate partner violence. *American Journal of Community Psychology, 36*(1/2), 71–96.

McEvoy, A., Brookings, J. B., & Brown, C. E. (1983, February). Responses to battered women: Problems and strategies. *Social Casework: The Journal of Contemporary Social Work,* pp. 92–96.

Richie, B. E., & Kanuha, V. (1997). Battered women of color in public health care systems: Racism, sexism and violence. In M. Baca Zinn, P. Hondagneu-Sotelo, & M. A. Messner (Eds.), *Through the prism of difference: Readings on sex and gender* (pp. 121–129). Boston: Allyn & Bacon.

Sullivan, C. M. (1991, August). Battered women as active helpseekers. *Violence Update,* pp. 1, 8.

Sullivan, C. M. (1997). Societal collusion and culpability in intimate male violence: The impact of community response toward women with abusive partners. In A. P. Cardarelli (Ed.), *Violence between intimate partners: Patterns, causes, and effects.* Boston: Allyn & Bacon.

Sullivan, C. M. (2000). A model for effectively advocating for women with abusive partners. In J. P. Vincent & E. N. Jouriles (Eds.), *Domestic violence: Guidelines for research-informed practice* (pp. 126–143). London: Jessica Kingsley.

Tan, C., Basta, J., Sullivan, C. M., & Davidson, W. S. (1995). The role of social support in the lives of women exiting domestic violence shelters. *Journal of Interpersonal Violence, 10*(4), 437–451.

Trotter, J. L. (2005). *The good, the bad, and the ugly: Domestic violence survivors' experiences with their informal social networks.* Unpublished master's thesis, University of Illinois, Urbana-Champaign.

Walker, L. E. (1979). *The battered woman.* New York: Harper & Row.

HIGH-TECH VIOLENCE AGAINST WOMEN

High-tech violence against women refers to the use of technology by abusers to stalk, monitor, or impersonate their victims in order to perpetrate sexual, domestic, or other violence against women. This high-tech violence might include an abuser intercepting phone calls via listening devices, intercepting electronic communications through spyware or hacking, or tracking a victim's movements through her location, the Internet, and camera technologies.

Technology makes an abuser's traditional power and control tactics increasingly easy to perpetrate, enabling abusers to monitor their victims more closely and efficiently. Phone, surveillance, and computer technologies are increasingly effective and available, and provide a wide array of dangerous tools for abusers to use to harass, intimidate, impersonate, and stalk their current and former intimate partners.

While perpetrators have misused technology since its inception, community awareness of high-tech harassment increased in the mid-1990s, when Internet users began reporting online harassment and threats. The term *cyberstalking* is often used to describe this type of behavior. However, the term *cyber* commonly connotes computer and/or Internet crimes, and, it is important to note that high-tech abusers use a wide variety of technologies beyond the Internet, including global positioning satellite (GPS) devices, camera and video imaging technologies, and the full range of telephone technology (e.g., cell phones, telecommunication devices for the deaf [TDDs], and faxes).

Technologies Used

Communications, location, surveillance, and information technologies are routinely used by abusers to monitor victims. Some abusers install global positioning systems to stalk their victim's real-time location, while others use telephones to leave hundreds of threatening messages. Other stalkers use technologies like caller identification (Caller ID) to monitor who a victim calls, and to locate her after she has fled. Still others use services available on the Internet to alter the number displayed on a victim's Caller ID screen, making it appear as though the phone call is coming from the victim's mother or best friend.

Abusers continue to identify and adapt common household technologies to stalk and harass their victims. Some abusers use baby monitors, while others purchase imaging devices marketed as home protection or "nanny cams" to view or listen to a victim's activities at home or elsewhere. Abusers hide wired and wireless cameras and other recording devices in everything from audio speakers to clock radios and potted plants in order to do remote real-time or asynchronous monitoring.

Monitoring a victim's computer use is another tactic used by abusers. They not only use low-technology monitoring options such as viewing the Web site browser history or intercepting email, but also are increasingly using more sophisticated spy software and hardware (spyware) for surveillance.

Spyware is a powerful stalking tool. An abuser does not need to have physical access to the victim's computer to install or run the software. The abuser can send an email with an attached greeting card, computer game, or other ruse in order to entice the victim to open the attachment. Once opened, the attachment automatically installs spyware on the victim's computer, in stealth mode without notification or consent. Spyware programs can automatically record every word typed, every Web site visited, and every document printed and even turn on Web cameras that may be connected to the computer. The spyware program can regularly transmit this information to the abuser.

Strategies for Change

Given the array of techniques used by abusers, strategies for change concentrate on education and policy change. The varied language and content of state and other jurisdictional laws often present a challenge for those attempting to hold perpetrators accountable, especially because these crimes can easily occur across jurisdictional lines. While some states include the use of electronic surveillance in their stalking statutes, others must rely on creative interpretation of older laws to address these crimes. On the U.S. federal level, the Violence Against Women Act of 2005 was one of the first pieces of U.S. federal legislation to explicitly and comprehensively address high-tech violence against women.

In addition to policy solutions, other efforts have focused on providing survivors of interpersonal violence with strategies to limit the amount of their personally identifying information available to others. For example, court systems, newspapers, and government agencies are publishing victim information on the Internet. Thus, survivors and advocates must regularly ask agencies to seal or restrict access to files to protect survivor safety. Address confidentiality programs, offered by many U.S. states, are one example of mechanisms created to ensure a victim's address remains confidential regardless of whether that victim votes, buys property, goes to court, or engages in other public activities.

To enhance their safety and reduce the opportunities a stalker has to access their computers, survivors are using public computers at libraries and computer technology centers. More anonymous computer terminals allow survivors to set up free email accounts on Internet-based services, select new alphanumeric passwords, choose not to be listed in the public directories provided by these services, and not have that Internet use linked back to their residence.

Additionally, advocates and survivors are taking advantage of the many wireless phone donation programs to equip survivors with phones that are not part of a shared or family phone plan purchased by the abuser. This allows the survivor to have access to a phone in an emergency, and also to receive private calls or arrange escape plans without that information becoming available to an abuser through billing records and phone logs.

The Future

As quickly as new technologies emerge, abusers find ways to manipulate them in order to spy on their victims. While the use of technology to stalk was once the exception, it has now become prevalent. Anecdotal and empirical evidence indicates that traditional modes of stalking have been greatly enhanced with the newest technologies, but significant research is needed to fully understand the parameters and types of technology used in stalking. Carefully crafted study that never compromises victim safety or confidentiality is needed to better document what survivors are experiencing and to inform the systemic change needed to address and prevent high-tech violence against women.

Cindy Southworth, Sarah Tucker, Cynthia Fraser, and Toby Shulruff

See also Batterers; Cyberstalking; Legal System, Advocacy Efforts to Affect, Intimate Partner Violence; Stalking; Violence Against Women Act

Further Readings

Safety Net: The National Safe & Strategic Technology Project. (2004). *Technology safety planning with survivors.* Retrieved May 5, 2006, from http://nnedv.org/SafetyNet/tspEnglish.pdf

Southworth, C., Dawson, S., Fraser, C., & Tucker, S. (2005, June). A high-tech twist on abuse: Technology, intimate partner stalking, and advocacy. *Violence Against Women Online Resources.* Retrieved May 5, 2006, from http://www.vawnet.org

Southworth, C., Finn, J., Dawson, S., Fraser, C., & Tucker, S. (2007). Intimate partner violence, technology and stalking. *Violence Against Women, 13*(8), 842–856.

Homelessness and Violence

Homelessness is a widespread problem in the United States that has increased in recent years due to a lack of affordable housing in many urban and suburban areas throughout the country, as well as natural disasters such as Hurricane Katrina and, most recently, the subprime mortgage crisis that is causing a substantial increase in home foreclosures. Individuals who are homeless make up a particularly vulnerable population because they lack the protection that private shelter typically affords.

Since the turn of the 21st century, organizations that monitor homelessness have reported increasing rates of violent crimes against homeless people. Between 2002 and 2004, for example, the number of violent deaths of homeless people rose by 67% and the number of nonlethal violent attacks on homeless people increased 281%. Typically, these violent assaults are beatings of homeless people sleeping on the street, under bridges, or at campsites.

Perpetrators of violent attacks on the homeless are primarily young White males, although available data indicate that perpetrators range in age from 11 years to 65 years old. Victims, too, are from all age groups, from infants as young as 4 months old to the elderly. The data show, however, that most victims are men; in 2004, for instance, there were 296 homeless male victims identified as violence victims, compared with 44 homeless female victims. Nevertheless, women are more vulnerable to specific types of violent crime, such as rape and sexual assault.

Violence is also more likely to be a cause of homelessness for women than for men. Research indicates that a large percentage of homeless women—in one study, in fact, 92%—have experienced severe physical and/or sexual assault at some point in their lives, often as children in the homes of their parents. A majority of homeless women have been victims of intimate partner violence (IPV) as adults, with as many as one third of homeless women reporting IPV victimization as ongoing or recent. In studies of urban homelessness, more than half of cities show IPV to be a primary causal factor in homelessness. Domestic violence service providers also report that battered women and their children may be forced to return to abusive households because they have no other alternative for housing; their only option would be homelessness.

Claire M. Renzetti

See also Assault; Battered Women, Economic Independence of; Transitional Housing Programs

Further Readings

Correia, A., & Rubin, J. (2001). *Housing and battered women.* Applied Research Forum, National Online Resource Center on Violence Against Women, Minneapolis, MN. Retrieved October 17, 2007, from http://www.vawnet.org

Golden, S. (1992). *The women outside: Meanings and myths of homelessness.* Berkeley: University of California Press.

National Coalition for the Homeless. (2005). *Hate, violence and death on Main Street USA: A report on hate crimes and violence against people experiencing homelessness in 2004.* Retrieved October 20, 2007, from http://nationalhomeless.org/civilrights/hatecrimes.html

HOME VISITATION SERVICES

Home visitation services represent one of the dominant early prevention strategies targeting physical child abuse and neglect in the United States and in a growing number of other nations. As the name implies, home visitation services provide services to families directly in their homes, most typically during the perinatal and early childhood phases of the children's lives. Home visitation programs are varied in the specific activities and strategies employed, and seek to promote an array of positive family and child developmental outcomes, including the early prevention of physical child abuse and neglect. Typically home visitation programs initiate services very early in the life of a child, often at birth or even shortly before birth. With regard to physical child abuse and neglect prevention, families are usually engaged in services prior to any identified abuse and/or neglect (unlike child protective services), and therefore home visitation services are most appropriately categorized as a primary or secondary (and sometimes universal or selective) prevention strategy. As no maltreatment has yet been identified, home visitation services identify families via universal service systems, such as the health care system, and are therefore designed to be nonstigmatizing and voluntary.

Service activities focus on ways of strengthening families that promote positive parenting patterns and child developmental trajectories and, in so doing, aim to reduce risk for future physical child abuse and/or neglect. Most typically, direct services focus on ways of supporting the development of a healthy parent–child attachment through parenting guidance, education, and skill development. As well, home visitors often focus efforts on helping families with information and support around infant health, home safety, and environmental challenges, and home visitors often link families up with needed resources and supports in the local community. Services are typically available during the first few years of each child's life, and taper off as families' risks and stated goals are addressed over time. Depending upon the program type, home visitors may be nurses, social workers, or paraprofessionals with intensive training in the role.

Emergence

Although home visitation services have emerged rather rapidly over the last several decades, the idea and practice of providing services directly in the homes of at-risk families is far from new. Home health visiting services date at least as far back as Florence Nightingale's pioneering work in the 1860s in Britain, and it was a home visitor who was responsible for finding little Mary Ellen in a New York City tenement in 1874, leading to the establishment of the world's first child protection organization, the New York Society for the Prevention of Cruelty to Children.

The most recent impetus for the rapid emergence and expansion of home visitation services targeting positive child developmental outcomes, including child maltreatment risk reduction, rests on the convergence of at least three interrelated threads of developing scientific evidence. The first is the growing evidence base pointing out the uniquely important period of early childhood in shaping later life functioning, including findings on the rapid and "building block" development of neurobiological systems, the establishment of primary psychosocial competencies, and, importantly, the development of primary emotional attachments with caregivers. The second is the evidence pointing out the inordinate risk children face for physical child abuse and neglect during their earliest years of life, particularly in their most devastating and sometimes fatal forms. Finally, there is the growing evidence base on home visitation services themselves, which continues to indicate that, in the right circumstances and under careful scientific scrutiny, early home visitation services can indeed serve as an effective vehicle to avert child abuse and neglect before it occurs.

Evidence

A series of carefully executed studies have reported reductions in physical child abuse and neglect risk as a result of home visitation, although the evidence base is far from uniform, underscoring a need to carefully design and implement such services with quality evaluations and with a close fit to the problem and family need. Nonetheless, a series of careful reviews of the evidence base have pointed out that home visitation services, when delivered properly, have been linked to a modest but discernable reduction of risk for future physical child abuse and neglect. Policymakers have increasingly turned to home visitation services not only as a preventive mechanism for child maltreatment and problems stemming from child maltreatment (such as juvenile delinquency and crime, and later life mental health and school problems); the appeal of home visitation services also stems from their potential to yield significant cost savings to the public, as some reports have suggested that home visitation, when successful in averting child maltreatment, can also avert much greater public costs associated with an array of publicly funded systems of child welfare, criminal justice, education, and health care.

Two notable home visitation program initiatives explicitly targeting child maltreatment prevention in the United States are the Nurse Family Partnership program developed and studied by David Olds and colleagues of the University of Colorado Health Sciences Center, and the Healthy Families America initiative of Prevent Child Abuse America that supports the development of programs based on the Healthy Start program model, originally established in Hawaii. Especially noteworthy are findings reported by Olds and colleagues indicating not only some reduction in physical child abuse and neglect associated with home visitation services, but also improvements in a wide array of maternal outcomes in select subgroups of mothers and developmental outcomes that are still noticeable when the children have reached 15 years of age. These and other promising findings have added momentum to the expansion of home visitation programs in the United States and internationally.

While not a panacea, home visitation services targeting child abuse and neglect prevention have demonstrated they can successfully engage and support large proportions of families who may benefit, and can prevent significant proportions of physical child abuse and neglect. As of this writing, early home visitation services remain the dominant and most promising child maltreatment prevention strategy on the horizon.

Neil B. Guterman

See also Child Abuse Prevention; Prevention Programs, Child Maltreatment; Prevention Programs, Definitions

Further Readings

Guterman, N. B. (2000). *Stopping child maltreatment before it starts: Emerging horizons in early home visitation services*. Thousand Oaks, CA: Sage.

Wasik, B., Bryant, D. M., & Lyons, C. M. (2001). *Home visiting: Procedures for helping families*. Thousand Oaks, CA: Sage.

HOMICIDES, CRIMINAL

There is a great deal of confusion in the use of the terms *homicide* and *murder,* partly because criminologists and lawyers tend not to use the terms in the same way. Legally, homicide is the killing of one person by another, and homicide is divided into justifiable and criminal homicides. A justifiable homicide is the killing of another in self-defense when faced with the danger of serious bodily injury. This includes killing of combatants during war, legal executions, and homicides by police in the course of carrying out their duties. A civilian justifiable homicide is the killing of another when faced with death or to prevent the death of another.

Criminal homicides consist of murder and manslaughter. The Model Penal Code, used by many states, defines criminal homicide as the act of purposely, knowingly, recklessly, or negligently causing the death of another human being. Murder is defined as the killing of another human being with malice aforethought, while manslaughter is killing without malice aforethought. The term *malice aforethought* is applied to murders that resulted from the intentional infliction of serious bodily harm, from outrageously reckless conduct, or, in some states, from a felony such as robbery. Manslaughter is defined as murder committed in the heat of passion or the responsibility for another's death through reckless conduct, such as driving a car with defective brakes in a large city.

Most of the research on criminal homicides focuses on murders, and criminologists tend to use the term *homicide* to include murder. As a rule, their research on homicide does not include justifiable homicides or negligent manslaughters. Criminologists tend to use the terms *homicide, criminal homicide,* and *murder* interchangeably.

Data

According to nationwide Federal Bureau of Investigation (FBI) statistics for 2004, there were 16,137 murders and non-negligent manslaughters in the United States, a rate of 5.5 per 100,000 inhabitants. Criminal homicide is a male crime. According to 2004 data, 77.8% of homicide victims and 64.4% of offenders were males. Females were more frequently victims (21.9%) than offenders (7.1%), a fact reflected in their higher level of victimization in intimate partner murders.

With respect to race, the murder victimization rate for Blacks was 18.2 per 100,000, which is more than five times higher than the rate for Whites (3.2 per 100,000). The Uniform Crime Reporting (UCR) Program does request information from police departments on whether murder victims and offenders are of Hispanic origin; however, there is typically a large amount of information missing from the reports regarding this variable. California, though, is the largest state and does report homicide rates for Hispanics. For 2004, the homicide rate for Hispanics in California was intermediate (8.1 per 100,000), that is, between the rates for Whites (2.6) and for Blacks (31.6).

The highest homicide victimization rates are for those 18 to 24 years old. The rate for that age group was 14.3 per 100,000. The next highest rate is for victims ages 25 to 34, which was 11.1 per 100,000. The rates for the remaining age groups were less than 5 per 100,000.

With respect to the relationship between victim and offender prior to the offense, the largest proportion (25.9%) were simply classified by police and the FBI as homicides in which the "offender was known to the victim." A little less than 1 in 10 murders (9.4%) involved intimate partner relationships; other family relationships were involved in 7.6% of murders.

Strangers accounted for 12.9% of murder victims, but there was no victim–offender relationship information on 44.1% of the murders.

Not surprisingly, over half (51%) of the murders in 2004 were committed with handguns. If the 14% attributed to other types of firearms is included, 65% of murders involved the use of firearms of one type or another. The remaining 34% involved other types of weapons such as knives, blunt objects, hands, or feet. The three most frequent motives for homicide were brawls and arguments (30.5%), followed by robbery (7.0%) and drug-related motives (3.9%).

One recent development has been the decline in homicide rates, as shown in Figure 1.

Beginning in 1991, there was a downturn in homicide rates, which continued through 2004. In 1991, the homicide rate was 9.8 per 100,000 population; by 2004, the homicide rate was 5.3 per 100,000, a 34.8% decrease. Among the explanations offered for the decline in homicides are the following:

- The growth of homicide during the 1980s was largely due to the increase in the 15-to-24 age group. The decline beginning about 1992 was partly accounted for by a decline in the 15-to-24 age group.
- Beginning about 1993, there has been a decline in handgun homicide among both Whites and Latinos, but the greatest decline has been among Black youth.

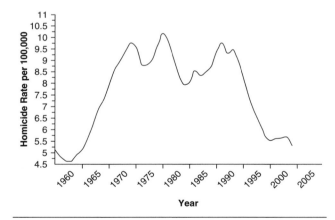

Figure 1   Homicide Rates in the United States: 1960–2004

Sources: Federal Bureau of Investigation. (2006). *Crime in the United States.* Retrieved from http://www.fbi.gov/ucr; Bureau of Justice Statistics. (2006). *Sourcebook of Criminal Justice Statistics.* Retrieved from http://www.albany.edu/sourcebook

- Drug markets may have matured and stabilized, and other dispute resolution mechanisms may have emerged.
- Economic expansion has increased the number of legitimate job opportunities and increased the amount of interaction between legal and illegal opportunities to earn money.

Arrest Clearances

It is obvious that in the event of any crime, including homicide, an offender should be arrested. The FBI's crime reporting program specifies that a law enforcement agency has cleared a particular offense when at least one person is arrested, charged with the commission of an offense, and turned over to the court for prosecution. Arrest clearances are extremely important to individual officers and law enforcement agencies as measures of performance and to the public for several reasons:

- Regardless of the goals of criminal justice, the process begins with the arrest of offenders. Without arrests, there is neither further processing of offenders nor reduction of crime.
- If offenders are not arrested they are free to offend again, which increases the risk of victimization.
- Failure to arrest offenders further traumatizes victims' families and contributes to an increase in the fear of violent victimization.
- Because clearances are a performance measure, failure to arrest undermines the morale of law enforcement personnel and agencies.
- When there are no arrests, there is no information on offenders, which limits research on offenders because of incomplete or biased data.

The problem is that for violent crimes in general, and homicide in particular, arrest clearances have been falling since at least 1960, as Figure 2 indicates. Arrest clearances are reported annually as the percentage of crimes for which one or more persons have been arrested. The percentage of homicides cleared by arrest in 1960 was 92.3%. Figure 2 shows that it declined almost linearly from year to year through 2004, when arrest clearances for homicide were 62.6%. Put another way, of the 16,137 homicides in 2004, no one was arrested for 37.4%, or 6,035 events.

Interest in arrest clearances has increased, but the available body of research distinguishes cleared homicides from uncleared homicides on only a few characteristics. In other words, for characteristics such as gender and race/ethnicity, some studies show differences between cleared and uncleared homicides and other studies do not.

However, there is agreement that homicides involving very young victims are more likely to be cleared than homicides involving older victims. The higher clearance rate for murders of small children is probably a consequence of low homicide rates and very high surveillance. A number of authors have noted that the rate of homicide of children between about 6 and 12 years of age is extremely low. This age group is also under more surveillance by agents such as parents and schools than are other age groups.

Homicides involving weapons other than firearms are more frequently cleared by arrest. The reason for this is that firearms provide the opportunity for individuals to kill at a greater distance and minimize the amount of evidence left at the scene.

Drug-related homicides are less likely than non-drug-related homicides to be cleared by arrest. While many of these offenses involve business-related conflicts, they also raise the possibility that third parties refuse to cooperate with the police for fear of being targeted.

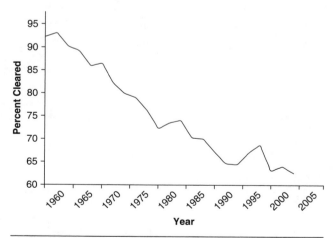

Figure 2   Arrest Clearances for Homicide: 1960–2004

Sources: Federal Bureau of Investigation. (2006). *Crime in the United States.* Retrieved from http://www.fbi.gov/ucr; Bureau of Justice Statistics. (2006). *Sourcebook of Criminal Justice Statistics.* Retrieved from http://www.albany.edu/sourcebook

Finally, the research is consistent in showing that nonstranger homicides (those committed by family, friends, acquaintances) are cleared more frequently than stranger homicides. One of the most easily cleared offenses involves intimate partners. For example, a physically abused wife decides she will no longer be beaten and kills her husband. When she realizes what she has done, she calls the police, awaits their arrival, and freely confesses.

Law enforcement has begun to come to terms with the declining clearance rates for homicide by an increasing use of cold case squads. There are two reasons that cold case squads are useful in clearing homicides. First, homicides have no statute of limitations and, second, conventional wisdom holds that homicides that have not developed significant leads or witness participation within 72 hours after the event are unlikely to be cleared. The statute of limitations for a crime refers to the time period following the crime during which an offender can be prosecuted. Unless there are some special legal provisions, most crimes cannot be prosecuted after a certain statutory time has passed. Homicide has no statute of limitations.

While cold case squads vary in size and organization throughout the United States, one of their major values is that they have access to technology, investigative methods, and resources not available one or two decades ago. DNA analysis is probably the best known. However, there have been advances in fingerprint technology that include systems for lifting prints from leather and cloth as well as systems that use lasers.

Marc Riedel

See also Expressive Violence; Familicide; Femicide; Gun Violence; Maternal Homicide; Serial Murder/Serial Killers

Further Readings

Blumstein, A., & Wallman, J. (Eds.). (2000). *The crime drop in America.* Cambridge, UK: Cambridge University Press.

Riedel, M., & Jarvis, J. (1998). The decline of arrest clearances for criminal homicide: Causes, correlates, and third parties. *Criminal Justice Policy Review, 9,* 279–305.

Riedel, M., & Welsh, W. N. (in press). *Criminal violence: Patterns, causes, and prevention* (2nd ed.). Los Angeles: Roxbury.

Turner, R., & Kosa, R. (2003). *Cold case squads: Leaving no stone unturned.* Washington, DC: Bureau of Justice Assistance.

Wellford, C., & Cronin, J. (1999). *An analysis of variables affecting the clearance of homicides: A multi-state study.* Washington, DC: Justice Research and Statistics Association.

HOMOPHOBIA

Homophobia is usually defined as the irrational fear and hatred of gay men and lesbians. It combines the words *homosexual* and *phobia*; hence it refers to fear or panic regarding people who are sexually attracted to a person of the same sex. Many people contend that the word *heterosexism* is a more accurate concept, since fear or panic is not the problem as much as the power and privileging of heterosexual people over gay men, lesbians, and bisexual people. Heterosexism assumes that people are heterosexual and asserts that heterosexuality is normal, natural, and right.

Homophobia is also related to sexism in that the denigration of the feminine is central to both. Males who are even slightly effeminate are seen as traitors to male dominance. Females who do not "stay in their place" are also targets of homophobia. An outspoken woman or a woman who does not accept subordinate status may be *lesbian baited*—that is, called a lesbian whether or not she is one. The purpose of this is to silence her or to encourage her to change her behavior.

An additional confusion is the erroneous connection between sexual orientation and gender identity. Sexual orientation refers to the object of a person's romantic or intimate desire. Gender identity is an individual's sense of being male identified, female identified, neither, or both. A common mistake is to assume every transgendered person is gay and to confuse a gender issue (which is related to sense of self) with sexual orientation (which is related to desire).

Internalized Homophobia

Young children in elementary schools are exposed to societal homophobia on the playground when the words *faggot, gay,* and *dyke* are used in a derogatory way to tease and humiliate other kids. The expression *that's so gay* is also used as an insult. Hence, individuals grow up surrounded by homophobia in schools, in the media, in families, in peer groups, in religious sermons, and in legislation. One of the consequences of this frequent exposure is internalized homophobia, that is, the belief by homosexuals themselves that homosexuality is wrong, perverted, and "less than" to be gay or lesbian. The suicide rate for young gay people is three times the national rate for teens in general. Low self-esteem, higher rates of alcohol and drug use, and mental health problems are serious problems in the gay and lesbian communities as a result of individuals feeling they need to be secretive about being gay or lesbian.

Heterosexism

Heterosexist prejudice is seen throughout the institutions of society. On the cultural level, traditional gender roles of masculinity and femininity, definition of the family, religious views condemning same-sex sexuality as a sin, lesbian baiting, and anti-gay jokes all enforce anti-gay prejudice. Lack of civil rights protections in employment and housing, in access to the rights of marriage, and in the military policy of "Don't Ask, Don't Tell" are institutional-level discriminations. These and other limitations form a constant message that the gay or lesbian person does not deserve the same rights or access to resources that heterosexuals have available to them.

Legal Protection and Hate Crimes

As of January 2008, 13 states and the District of Columbia banned discrimination based on sexual orientation and gender identity/expression. Seven states had legislation banning discrimination based on sexual orientation. There is no federal level anti-discrimination protection.

Hate crimes, which are on the increase against gay people and gender-variant folks, are "message crimes" in that they go beyond the crime against the person who is targeted to send a message to the group that the individual is a member of. For this reason, taking a stand against hate crimes is important, so as to say that it is not okay to target this group and that it is a serious offense. Of 45 states with hate crime legislation, 12 states and the District of Columbia cover sexual orientation and gender identity, 20 states include sexual orientation, and 13 states include neither sexual orientation and gender identity (as of April 2008).

The Local Law Enforcement Hate Crimes Prevention Act of 2007, also known as the Matthew Shepard Act, would have added sexual orientation and gender identity to existing hate crimes legislation. It passed the House in 2007, but when introduced into the Senate as an amendment to the Senate Defense Authorization Bill, it was stripped of the gender identity provision. It passed, but 6 weeks later it was dropped. The last federal hate crime act was passed in 1968 and does not include sexual orientation, gender, gender identity, or disability.

Coming Out

Due to the repression and secrecy of being gay or lesbian many people are *closeted,* that is, they do not tell others that they are gay or lesbian. This means they cannot live full and free lives and need to pick and choose to whom and when they reveal their sexual orientation. To come out as gay or lesbian entails taking risks of losing friends and family, jobs, and safety. Coming out is a personal decision with political consequences because it brings the person in opposition to a power structure that has placed him or her in a subordinate position. One strategy of the political movement for gay and lesbian rights is advocating that all gay and lesbian people come out. This may break down stereotypes and myths as others realize gays and lesbians are in every type of group, class, occupation, and so forth.

Advances in Gay and Lesbian Rights

Homosexuality as a mental illness was removed from the American Psychiatric Association's *Diagnostic and Statistical Manual of Mental Disorders* in 1973. However, there are still some mental health professionals who treat homosexuality as a mental illness. Generally referred to as *reparative therapy* or *conversion therapy,* its practitioners believe homosexuality is wrong, is a choice, and is caused by environmental factors. These therapists tend to come out of a religious perspective and usually incorporate prayer and religious worship in the treatment. The American Psychiatric Association opposes reparative therapy, as it can cause serious psychological harm and there is no empirical evidence that the treatment works.

The gay rights movement for equality and social acceptance formally dates back to June 27, 1969, when lesbians, gay men, and gender-variant people stood up to police harassment during a raid at the Stonewall Bar in New York City. There has been a flurry of activism since then, from gay pride parades and events to countless educational forums and trainings, National Coming Out Days, marches on Washington, the formation of national organizations such as the Human Rights Campaign, lobbying for legislation, efforts toward full acceptance of gays serving in the military, advocacy for full marriage rights and benefits, and more. *Lawrence v. Texas* was a milestone for gay and lesbian people when, in June 2003, the U.S. Supreme Court struck down existing sodomy laws and affirmed the constitutional right to privacy.

Homophobia and heterosexism are hurtful in that they lock people into rigid gender roles and expectations. People are unable to be their authentic selves and contribute their full potential to society. Homophobia silences and stigmatizes people, including gay, lesbian, bisexual, and transgender people and nonconforming heterosexuals, because they are different.

Lori B. Girshick

See also Hate Crimes (Bias Crimes), Anti-Gay; Homophobia and Media Representations of Gay, Lesbian, Bisexual, and Transgender People; Legislation, Hate Crimes

Further Readings

Blumenfeld, W. (Ed.). (1992). *Homophobia: How we all pay the price.* Boston: Beacon Press.

Lorde, A. (1984). *Sister outsider.* Trumansburg, NY: Crossing Press.

Pharr, S. (1988). *Homophobia: A weapon of sexism.* Little Rock, AR: Chardon.

HOMOPHOBIA AND MEDIA REPRESENTATIONS OF GAY, LESBIAN, BISEXUAL, AND TRANSGENDER PEOPLE

In a culture of homophobia (an irrational fear of gay, lesbian, bisexual, and transgender [GLBT] people), GLBT people often face a heightened risk of violence and violence specific to their sexual identities. Media representations of GLBT people have contributed to this culture of homophobia and elevated risk of vio-

lence. Historically, GLBT people have been made invisible, marginalized, demonized, or portrayed as unrealistic stereotypes by the media. These depictions have contributed to a culture that considers GLBT people to be deviant, abnormal, and/or pathological, and normalize the violence perpetrated against GLBT people. Homophobia also is internalized by GLBT people themselves and encourages self-hatred and shame. These feelings can be used by abusers against GLBT victims to control and further isolate them from the rest of society and their support systems.

From the 1890s to the 1930s, GLBT people and representations of them were rarely present in the media. When present, GLBT characters or themes were the object of ridicule and laughter. The characters' non-heterosexual identities were rarely named explicitly by their portrayers and only were hinted at through negative and degrading stereotypes. Following the 1930s, the media industry came under the scrutiny of the U.S. government, resulting in strict censorship guidelines that included a ban on overtly homosexual characters. In the 1960s and 1970s, the GLBT and feminist movements gained momentum and challenged dominant perceptions of gender and sexuality. GLBT people became more visible in mainstream media, but with this added visibility came the increased risk of violence. During the 1980s, news media finally began to cover the GLBT stories that should reach the level of national attention. However, many of the television, film, and news portrayals of GLBT people continued to represent the population as dangerous, psychotic, and violent.

In recent years, there has been an increase in the presence of GLBT people and characters in the media. This includes an increase in news coverage of violent crimes, also known as hate crimes, committed against people based on their GLBT identity or perceived GLBT identity. In 2004, there were over 1,400 reported incidents of hate crimes based on sexual orientation. Some GLBT critics continue to criticize mainstream media for their distillation of GLBT people and culture. This muted coverage continues to perpetuate homophobic perceptions of GLBT people as unnatural and amoral. Such coverage contributes to a larger homophobic culture that serves to rationalize a dislike for GLBT people and the acts of violence committed against them.

Tracy J. Davis

See also Hate Crimes (Bias Crimes), Criminal Justice Responses; Media, Representations/Distortions of Crime; Media and Sexuality; Media and Violence

Further Readings

Castañeda, L., & Campbell, S. (Eds.). (2005). *News and sexuality: Media portraits of diversity.* Thousand Oaks, CA: Sage.

Gross, L. (2002). *Up from invisibility: Lesbians, gay men, and the media in America.* New York: Columbia University Press.

Leventhal, B., & Lundy, S. (Eds.). (1999). *Same-sex domestic violence: Strategies for change.* Thousand Oaks, CA: Sage.

Russo, V. (1987). *The celluloid closet: Homosexuality in the movies.* New York: HarperCollins.

Honor Killing/Crime

Honor killing and honor crime are violent acts against women and girls (beating, battering, or killing, for example) that are rationalized by a notion that an individual's or family's honor has been threatened because of the actual or perceived sexual misconduct of the female.

Honor killing of a woman or girl by her father, brother, or other male relative may occur because of a suspicion that she engaged in sexual activities before or outside marriage and thus has dishonored the family. Even when rape of a woman or girl has occurred this may be seen as a violation of the honor of the family for which the female must be killed. Wives' adultery and daughters' voluntary and involuntary premarital sexual activity, including rape, are seen as extreme violations of the codes of behavior, and thus may result in the death of the female through this so-called honor killing. Honor killing and honor crime are based on the shame that a loss of control of the woman or girl brings to the family and to the male heads of the family.

Because any suspicion of sexual activity or suspicion that a girl or woman was touched by another in a sexual manner is enough to raise questions about the family's honor, strict control of women and girls within the home and outside the home is therefore seen as justified. Women are restricted in their activities in the community, religion, and politics. These institutions, in turn, support the control of females. Thus, the existence of honor killing is useful for maintaining male dominance. Submissiveness may be seen as a sign of sexual purity, and a woman's or girl's attempts to assert her rights can be seen as a violation of the family's honor that needs to be redressed. Rules of honor and threats against females who "violate" such rules reinforce the control of women and have a powerful impact on their lives. Honor killings and crimes serve to keep women and girls from "stepping out of line." The manner in which such behaviors silence women and kill their spirit have led some to label honor killings/crimes more broadly as *femicide*.

Under patriarchy, male dominance is based on the authority of the father or male head of the household or family. Women's safety and sexuality are seen as property. Honor killing and crimes have been discussed mostly in reference to experiences of women in traditional societies in the Middle East, Southwest Asia, India, China, and Latin America. However, comparative research has shown that validating violence against women as a "crime of honor" occurs around the globe and not only in more traditional societies. Battering of female intimate partners has at times been tolerated or even sanctioned by many societies around the world, including in the United States, as a means of controlling female behavior. In the United States, some men have been exonerated for killing wives who have been found having sexual relations with others, and such behaviors have been called "crimes of passion." Permitting or requiring (in some communities) such killing is the extreme expression of the notion that males must control "their" women.

Linda M. Williams

See also Femicide; Hymen Replacement Surgery; Patriarchy; Rape/Sexual Assault

Further Readings

Baker, N., Gregware, P., & Cassidy, M. (1999). Family killing fields: Honor rationales in the murder of women. *Violence Against Women, 5,* 164–184.

Haj, S. (1992). Palestinian women and patriarchal relations. *Signs, 17,* 761–771.

Shalhoub-Kevorkian, N. (2003). Reexamining femicide: Breaking the silence and crossing "scientific" borders. *Signs, 28,* 581–608.

Human Rights

Human rights are the basic rights that all people are entitled to by virtue of being human. Most importantly, human rights are inalienable, indivisible, and interdependent. Human rights are inalienable in that they inherently belong to each person and cannot be taken away from him or her. They are indivisible in that all human rights are equally important and as crucial as other rights. Finally, human rights are interdependent as a complete framework of interconnected and related rights.

There are fundamental legal guarantees that enable individuals and groups to live in dignity and that safeguard all people against violations of fundamental freedoms and human dignity. Human rights are defined and set forth in international, regional, and national laws and policies. The obligation to respect and protect human rights falls upon states and their actors. Violations of human rights occur when illegal acts of violence are committed by state or private actors that the government cannot or fails to control.

Interpersonal violence is often employed as a part of many human rights violations. This entry discusses the philanthropic, religious, and legal foundations of human rights. It also describes various human rights violations where interpersonal violence is used.

History of Human Rights

Recognition of the importance of human rights began early in history through philosophical and religious teachings. Aristotle postulated a natural moral order that transcends sociohistorical context to apply universally to everyone. The Roman Stoics similarly advanced a natural and universal code that counseled living in harmony with the divine order. In the 17th century, philosopher John Locke presented the concept that, long before and irrespective of state acknowledgment, all people possessed natural rights. These natural rights to life, liberty, and property stemmed from natural law, under which all people owed a duty of self-preservation to God. The 18th-century philosopher Immanuel Kant posited that morally autonomous and rational people will act according to a self-imposed categorical imperative. This categorical imperative denotes the moral autonomy and equality of all rational beings and forms the basis for laws established by such individuals. These rights-based philosophies were complementary to the religious ideologies of human worth.

Many religions, including Buddhism, Christianity, Confucianism, Hinduism, Islam, and Judaism, have principles relating to the responsibility or duty toward others, as well as on human dignity. Tenets of human rights can be found in various religious teachings. For example, the Bible quotes Jesus as saying, "Do to others as you would have them do to you" (Luke 6:31). The Babylonian Talmud, Shabbat 31a, says, "What is hateful to you do not do to your neighbor." Chaitanya, a Hindu philosopher, believed that the only caste was that of humanity. The Qur'an also recognizes one common humanity: "God knows best about your belief, and you are equal to one another, as far as belief is concerned" (4:25).

Beginning in the 13th century, countries began adopting legal instruments to protect certain rights and limit the government's power. The Magna Carta (1215) represented an early effort to establish restrictions on the English government's authority and set forth important concepts of due process. Other instruments soon followed that protected the rights to be free from arbitrary arrest and imprisonment and to freedom of speech and prohibited cruel or unusual punishments. For example, the 1776 Declaration of Independence asserted the equality of all men and their inalienable rights, including "Life, Liberty and the Pursuit of Happiness." The French Declaration of Rights of Man and Citizen (1789) established the rights to liberty, security, and due process, to possess property, and to have freedom of expression, as well as equality before the law.

Following World War I, countries sought to achieve greater international cooperation by creating the League of Nations in 1919. This organization addressed specific human rights, such as the rights of minorities, labor standards, slavery, and the treatment of former colonies, but it lacked the same human rights emphasis found later in the United Nations. The League of Nations' activities ceased after it failed to prevent World War II. The United Nations (UN) was the international community's subsequent undertaking to form an international body to promote international peace, security, and cooperation and better interstate relations, as well as respect for human rights and fundamental freedoms. On October 24, 1945, the UN Charter entered into force. According to the charter, member states are to promote human rights and fundamental freedoms without discrimination based on race, sex, language, or religion. Of the 193 nations in the world, 192 have ratified the charter and become member states of the United Nations.

On December 10, 1948, the UN adopted the Universal Declaration of Human Rights (UDHR). The

UDHR sets forth comprehensive human rights and fundamental freedoms in 30 articles and was the first international document to recognize that all people have human rights regardless of who they are or where they live. In 1966, the UN General Assembly adopted the International Covenant on Civil and Political Rights (ICCPR) and the International Covenant on Economic, Social and Cultural Rights (ICESCR). Together, the UDHR, ICESCR, and the ICCPR and its two accompanying protocols constitute the International Bill of Human Rights. Four other conventions, together with the International Bill of Human Rights, comprise the core human rights treaties. These instruments include the Convention on the Elimination of All Forms of Discrimination Against Women; the Convention on the Elimination of All Forms of Racial Discrimination; the Convention on the Rights of the Child; the Convention Against Torture and Other Cruel, Unusual, Degrading Treatment or Punishment; and the International Convention on the Protection of the Rights of All Migrant Workers and Members of Their Families. Other thematic documents followed, and today there are over 60 international human rights instruments promulgated by the UN that contain many protections against forms of interpersonal violence.

Human Rights Protections Against Interpersonal Violence

When the state fails to prevent, stop, or punish acts of interpersonal violence, it is a violation of human rights. Certain populations are more vulnerable to acts of interpersonal violence. They may not be guaranteed equal and effective protection of the law. For example, migrant workers and immigrant women have the right to effective protection from violence, physical injury, threats, and intimidation, yet they may be reluctant to seek protection from the law because of their immigration status. The universality of human rights guarantees that all people are entitled to protection of their human rights.

Right to Equality and Freedom From Discrimination

When people experience violence based on a specific characteristic, such as race, color, sex, language, religion, political or other opinion, national origin, property, or birth or other status, which impairs or nullifies their enjoyment of rights and freedoms, it is a violation of their rights to equality and freedom from discrimination.

One of the most pervasive causes of violence is racial discrimination. Colonialism and slavery illustrate the widespread discrimination that perpetuated massive human rights violations against entire populations. Human beings were enslaved, killed, tortured, and subject to numerous other forms of violence. Today, racism, racial discrimination, xenophobia, and related intolerance emerge as genocide, economic disparities, marginalization, and social inequities. Apartheid in South Africa is another example where legalized racism enabled White rule to dominate and terrorize Africans, Asians, and people of mixed descent for years. Today, in the context of post–September 11, discrimination is manifested in the hate crimes perpetrated against immigrants, refugees, and religious minorities.

All people are born equal and are entitled to equal protection before the law. For instance, when a state punishes strangers who rape, but not those who commit date or marital rape, it is failing to provide all women with equal protection of the law. The right to equality, however, may require legitimate preferential treatment, such as affirmative action, to rectify discrimination. Human rights law recognizes that everyone is equal and entitled to human rights without discrimination and provides that governments should condemn and seek to eliminate all forms of discrimination.

Right to Life

The violence that claims a life can take the form of suicide, war-related death, or homicide. According to a 2002 report of the World Health Organization, violence is one of the leading causes of death for individuals 15 to 44 years old and kills more than 1.6 million people per year.

Human rights law protects the right not to be arbitrarily deprived of life. This right is so fundamental that it may not be suspended, even during times of emergency. While the right to life is protected in many human rights documents, it is not an absolute right. For example, violence may be justified when used in self-defense or to protect another person. Killings are expected during wartime, but certain groups, such as those who do not participate in the hostilities, wounded or sick combatants, and prisoners of war, are protected.

In addition, there are still countries that impose the death penalty. The ICCPR does not directly prohibit the death penalty, but it places limitations on its application. For example, it prohibits the execution of juveniles under 18 years of age and pregnant women. The death penalty may only be executed under a final judgment issued by a competent court for the most serious crimes, and those sentenced to death are entitled to seek pardon or commutation of their sentences. Increasingly, full respect for the right to life is being realized around the world through the abolition of the death penalty. Fifty-seven countries have ratified the Second Optional Protocol to the ICCPR aimed at the abolition of the death penalty, signaling their commitment to end this form of punishment. There is a growing movement toward abolition of the death penalty, as seen by policies of the European Union, which requires abolition by all member states, and U.S. state moratoria suspending the use of capital punishment.

Right to Liberty and Security

Everyone has the right to liberty and to be free from arbitrary arrest and detention. Some scholars and states have posited a broad interpretation of the right to liberty and security to include freedom from torture and violence. Constitutional protections against violence can be found under the right to security of the person. The Bill of Rights of the Constitution of South Africa (1996) states that, "everyone has the right to freedom and security of the person, which includes the right . . . to be free from all forms of violence from either public or private sources; not to be tortured in any way; and not to be treated or punished in a cruel, inhuman or degrading way" (Art. 12(1)). International and domestic authorities have recognized that violence against women constitutes a violation of this right. The Committee on the Elimination of All Forms of Discrimination Against Women has stated that gender-based violence transgresses several rights, including those of liberty and security of person. Officials in Australia and Canada have also found that violations of the right to security of person encompass crimes of sexual violence.

Freedom From Slavery

Violence and coercion are used to enslave people for exploitative purposes. It is the abusive means and conditions under which the person is forced to work that constitute slavery. Typically, slavery exists when a person is forced to work under threat, is controlled or owned by another person, is treated as property, and has his or her freedom of movement restricted. It is estimated that more than 12 million people are living in situations of forced labor. While transatlantic slavery and the slave trade have been long abolished, modern forms of slavery still exist. Some examples of slavery today include forced recruitment into combat, enforced prostitution, worst forms of child labor, slavery through descent, trafficking in persons, and early and forced marriage. Another example is debt bondage, in which humans are sold or deceived into entering situations where they are forced to repay debts through labor and are subject to threats and physical and sexual violence. The debts, which are heavily inflated and accrue continuously, are unreasonable and the labor highly undervalued. Thus, the debtor is in effect enslaved, never knowing when he or she will repay the loan.

Everyone is entitled to live a life free from slavery and forced labor, a right that may never be suspended or limited.

Freedom From Torture or Cruel, Inhuman, or Degrading Treatment or Punishment

Torture is the physical or mental severe pain or suffering used to elicit a confession or information, as punishment or intimidation, or for any reason based on discrimination. Torture is done or instigated by a public official or someone acting in an official capacity, or else carried out with that person's consent or acquiescence. Violent acts that constitute torture vary, but include severe beatings, electroshocks, sexual violence, mutilation, and simulating suffocation. Torture does not include the pain or suffering that arises from lawful punishment. Cruel, inhuman, or degrading treatment or punishment includes acts that may not rise to the level of torture, but still violate a person's rights.

Torture includes not only the acts that occur in the public sphere, but also acts committed by private actors when the government knows and fails to prevent such acts. For example, domestic violence is perpetrated using violent acts, such as battering, acid burning, "honor" killings, sexual assault, and psychological abuse. Domestic violence is torture when the government has not provided effective protection and the violence is of the type and severity to constitute torture.

Every person is entitled to be free from this type of violence. Freedom from torture, and cruel, inhuman, or degrading treatment or punishment is a right that may not be suspended or limited, even in emergencies. Torture is a human rights violation and a crime under international human rights law.

Freedom of Assembly and Association; Freedom of Opinion and Expression; Freedom of Belief and Religion; Right to Participate in Government

Although each of these freedoms and rights is separate, violations of one are often similar to or carried out in connection with another. States and those acting on their behalf use attacks, intimidation, and harassment of individuals and groups to repress these rights.

Everyone has the right to establish and operate groups without state interference. Organizing over an issue is a critical means of impacting policies and representatives. For example, trade unions are an important tool for advocating for labor rights in the workplace. These rights are denied when governments and private actors use intimidation and harassment to shut down activities or associations. Members may be harassed individually or collectively. Likewise, the right to peaceful assembly is also impaired when officials use violent means to end such activities. The right does not extend to violent assemblies, however, and authorities may use force commensurate to the threat as a last resort to reduce harm. States sometimes use informal and violent means of censorship, such as personal attacks, to halt or penalize publication. This is a violation of the right to freedom of expression. People have the right to access information and to express their ideas as a move toward democracy and public participation. Freedom of expression must be balanced against other human rights, and there are restrictions on some expressions, such as hate speech, fighting words, or inciting to violence. Religious intolerance is manifested through abuses such as forced conversions, violent repression of worshipers, death sentences, summary executions, arrests, attacks, and destruction of religious property. Everyone has the right to freedom of thought, conscience, and religion, and this encompasses the right to nonreligious beliefs, such as nontheistic or atheistic beliefs. This right may never be suspended or limited. Finally, governments and opposition parties violate the right to participate in government when they use violence to intimidate or stop people from voting or running in elections.

Right to an Adequate Standard of Living

The right to an adequate standard of living comprises several rights, such as the rights to food, water, social services, clothing, and housing. Sometimes, the violation of one of these rights can indirectly lead to violence. For example, adequate housing is an important right that provides safety, shelter, privacy, and personal and communal space. When a person is deprived of adequate housing, it increases his or her susceptibility to violence. For example, domestic violence, rape, or harassment can occur inside the home before, during, or following an eviction. Other factors that increase vulnerability to violence in inadequate housing include age, ethnicity, migrant status, armed conflict, poverty, disabilities, and HIV/AIDS.

Embedded within the right to an adequate standard of living is the right to health. While this generally addresses the issues of provision of health services, prevention and treatment of diseases, and hygiene and infant mortality, it also encompasses the treatment of injuries that result from violence. These include not only physical harm, such as bodily injuries, but also psychological or mental harm. It is important to note that the ICESCR provides for the "highest attainable standard" of health, a benchmark that can vary depending on whether it is in relation to an individual country or a global consensus.

Conclusion

All people are entitled to human rights and fundamental freedoms. Human rights are universal, and they belong to every person regardless of who that person is or where the person lives. Early tenets of human rights can be found in many philosophies and most major religions. Interpersonal violence violates the enjoyment of many rights, including the rights to life, liberty, security, equality, an adequate standard of living, and participation in government, as well as freedoms from discrimination, slavery and torture and of association, expression, and belief. International, regional, and national laws promote and protect human rights, but equal protection and adequate implementation of the law is also required for human beings to fully enjoy their human rights and fundamental freedoms.

Rosalyn S. Park and Cheryl A. Thomas

See also United Nations, International Law/Courts; United Nations Conventions and Declarations

Further Readings

Fagan, A. (2008). Human rights. In J. Fieser & B. Dowden (Eds.), *The Internet encyclopedia of philosophy*. Retrieved from http://www.iep.utm.edu/h/hum-rts.htm

Human Rights Education Associates. (n.d). *Study guides: Freedom of assembly and association*. Retrieved from http://www.hrea.org/learn/guides/freedom-of-association.html

Human Rights Education Associates. (n.d). *Study guides: Freedom of expression*. Retrieved from http://www.hrea.org/learn/guides/freedom-of-expression.html

Human Rights Education Associates. (n.d). *Study guides: Housing*. Retrieved from http://www.hrea.org/learn/guides/housing.html

Human Rights Education Associates. (n.d.). *Study guides: The right to life*. Retrieved from http://www.hrea.org/learn/guides/life.html

Human Rights Education Associates. (n.d.). *Study guides: Slavery and forced labor*. Retrieved from http://www.hrea.org/learn/guides/slavery.html

Human Rights Education Associates. (n.d.). *Study guides: Torture, inhuman or degrading treatment*. Retrieved from http://www.hrea.org/learn/guides/torture.html

Krug, E. G., Dahlberg, L. L., Mercy, J. A., Zwi, A. B., & Lozano, R. (Eds.). (2002). *World report on violence and health*. Geneva: World Health Organization.

University of Minnesota Human Rights Center. (2003). *Study guide: The right to means for adequate health*. Retrieved from http://www1.umn.edu/humanrts/edumat/studyguides/righttohealth.html

Web Sites

Minnesota Advocates for Human Rights: http://www.stopvaw.org

HYMEN REPLACEMENT SURGERY

Hymen replacement surgery is a procedure by which a doctor, using dissolvable stitches, reattaches to a woman's vaginal wall the skin membrane—called the hymen—that once covered the opening to the vagina. The medical term for the procedure is *hymenoplasty,* but it is also known as *hymen restoration surgery, hymen reconstruction,* and *revirgination.* The latter term is used because an intact hymen was—and still is in some cultures—considered to be proof of a woman's sexual purity. Intercourse will tear the membrane, causing pain and bleeding. If there was no evidence of blood following first intercourse by a newly married couple, the woman was assumed not to be a virgin, which called into question the paternity of a child born within the first 9 months of the marriage, brought disgrace to the woman and her family, and could even result in her death if the culture imposed such a penalty on women for "sexual immorality."

Today, the procedure is a growing part of the cosmetic surgery "industry" in the United States, Great Britain, and other Western industrialized countries, with some long-married women having the procedure done as a "gift" to their husbands. In addition, the procedure is popular in the Middle East and Latin America, particularly among Muslims and Catholics, whose religious traditions teach that a woman's virginity prior to marriage is sacred.

Supporters of the procedure maintain that it protects women, particularly in cultures that punish sexual impurity with extraordinary penalties such as death. Supporters also point out that wider availability of the procedure performed by cosmetic surgeons prevents women in such cultures from resorting to "back alley" procedures that can result in serious injury or infection. Critics, however, liken the procedure to female genital mutilation and argue that it reinforces the primacy of female virginity over all else. Moreover, since hymen repair, unlike other types of reconstruction, is not taught in medical residencies, surgeons performing the procedure may not be properly trained. Critics of the procedure also include Catholic and Muslim religious groups, who point out that hymen reconstruction does not alleviate the sin of sex before marriage, but rather is the sin of deceit because the woman who has the surgery is still not a "genuine" virgin.

Claire M. Renzetti

See also Female Genital Mutilation; Honor Killing/Crime

Further Readings

Boodman, S. G. (2007, March 6). Cosmetic surgery's new frontier. *Washington Post*. Retrieved September 20, 2007, from http://www.washingtonpost.com

Chozick, A. (2005, December 15). Virgin territory: U.S. women seek a second first time. *Wall Street Journal*. Retrieved September 20, 2007, from http://www.cosmeticgyn.net/media_wsj_hymenoplasty.htm

HYPERMASCULINITY

Gender roles have some generally acknowledged boundaries that tend to shift over time. Social acceptance of masculinity and femininity is expressed through everyday behavior, fashions, and ascribed or achieved qualities associated with each gender group. The distinction between heterosexuals and homosexuals or bisexuals is generally made based on how blatantly the latter individuals deviate from the expectations of mainstream individuals. Some individuals can pass for heterosexual, while others embrace a homosexual identity. In the case of masculinity, males and females can overemphasize masculine values to a point where such behavior defines their personality and everyday behavior. In addition, this overexaggeration of male traits can be generalized into patterns that result in the stereotyping of individuals based upon their outward appearance.

Hypermasculinity is the exaggeration of male stereotypical behavior. Those who are hypermasculine embrace male physical and/or behavioral stereotypes that define the primary nature of their everyday interaction with others. Body hair, strength, aggression, and outward appearance are expressed as male traits. Oppressed groups can focus on these traits as their way of fighting control by other individuals or competing interests. The dominant traits become associated with the person or group identity.

Hypermasculinity and Violence

Hypermasculinity is based on behavioral choices. The ascribed male behavior is thought to focus on strength and assertiveness. Males are more often associated with violence and killing than are females. Some individuals claim that there is a genetic or biological source to hypermasculinity. For example, it has been argued that having an extra Y chromosome, known as XYY chromosome syndrome, produces hypermasculine behavior and a greater likelihood of assertiveness because the additional Y chromosome is responsible for overproduction of the male hormone testosterone. However, there is little to no empirical support for this position. Others locate the source of hypermasculinity in culture and socialization. For instance, boys are taught to be aggressive and are rewarded for such behavior, whereas girls learn more nurturing roles.

Thus hypermasculine behavior may be partially explained by the creation of social stereotypes. Social stereotypes are created in many different ways, such as when individuals overemphasize their own gender characteristics. Males may strive for the development of a more muscular appearance or think that a beard makes them more masculine. In addition, such outward appearances will reinforce their assertiveness toward others. This assertiveness can lead to violence against women, child abuse and molestation, and a greater likelihood of embracing violence as a way of life.

Hypermasculinity has also been associated with the ambiguity of gender roles in contemporary society. Traditional gender roles accepted by men and women often converge when women compete alongside men in the workplace and everyday life. Hypermasculinity may emerge when men feel they must be more masculine as women embrace the aggressive behavior more commonly associated with males. In addition, hyperfemininity is often referred to as the flip side of this problem, wherein women overemphasize their emotional tendencies and physical appearance for the sake of control over men. Both conditions create an imbalance within relationships that can produce misunderstandings between the sexes.

Consequences

The consequences of hypermasculinity include the occurrence of males overemphasizing their physical strength and aggressiveness in interpersonal relationships. The utilization of strength in dominating interaction results in strained relationships between males and females. Lack of emotional understanding and physical dominance can ultimately weaken men's interpersonal relationships. Men exhibiting hypermasculinity and boys growing into hypermasculine roles will seek out ultimate fighting, wrestling, and other contact sports that embody their perceived hypermasculine gender identities. The message is that force or violence is instrumental in dealing with the many aspects of social life. In one example, exaggeration of these traits can be seen in prison inmates who embrace hypermasculine values for everyday survival in a captive situation. Violence is a notable constant in how relationships are formed and sustained in such an environment.

Lloyd Klein

See also Child Physical Abuse; Coercive Control; Community Violence; Fraternities and Violence; Media and Violence; Socialization

Further Readings

Kindlon, D., & Thompson, M. (2000). *Raising Cain: Protecting the emotional life of boys.* New York: Ballantine.

West, J. (2007). *The death of the grown-up: How America's arrested development is bringing down Western civilization.* New York: St. Martin's Press.

I

IMMIGRANT AND MIGRANT WOMEN

Immigrant women migrate to the United States for a variety of reasons. Many come here voluntarily to better their lives, to reunite with their family members, to attend school or look for jobs. Others come involuntarily, as victims of human trafficking, fleeing persecution, sexual assault or domestic abuse, economic, social, or political upheavals in their home countries. Some immigrant women have obtained legal permission from immigration authorities to be in the United States and are "documented." Others may have no immigration documents. Many undocumented immigrant women may qualify to receive legal immigration status but be unaware of their eligibility, particularly when they have been victims of domestic violence, sexual assault, or trafficking and the information they do have has been controlled and provided by the perpetrator of the crimes against them. Immigrant women represent a broad cross-section of society. They are mothers, daughters, students, workers, caretakers, and professionals. They may have a great deal of formal education or they may not have any at all. Some speak English fluently, while others speak hesitantly, or only speak the language of their home country or community. Their experiences are rich and varied.

For many immigrant women, access to legal immigration status is intimately connected with their roles as wives and mothers. In general, men immigrate in search of better employment and educational opportunities, while women immigrate based on family ties. Sixty-nine percent of women attain lawful permanent residency through family relationships. Women are 38% more likely than men to attain legal permanent residency through family-based visas. Less than 4% of women enter the United States on employment visas.

Once women from other countries reach the United States, their families and communities expect these women to become protectors of culture and responsible for maintaining and passing on customs of their home country to children, oftentimes remaining obedient and subservient to male family members. By contrast, in the United States, expectations of acculturation encourage immigrant women to strive for independence and equality. Cultural clashes, the stress of immigration, a history of traumatic experiences, and the extent of access to resources in this country can have a significant effect on how an immigrant woman responds to family or sexual violence.

For many immigrant women, their legal immigration status is tied to a spouse, to other family members, or to a job. If any of these relationships turns abusive, the immigrant woman can become trapped in the abusive relationship—say, tied to an abusive spouse or a harassing employer—by the abuser's control over her immigration status.

In 1994's landmark Violence Against Women Act (VAWA), Congress recognized that violence against women affects immigrant women in unique ways and created a special procedure for victims to use in applying for legal immigration status that is not tied to the citizenship or immigration status of their abusive spouses or parents (VAWA self-petitioning). Today, over 30,000 immigrant women and their children have attained legal immigration status as VAWA self-petitioners. In 2000 VAWA expanded immigration protections to cover immigrant victims of domestic violence, sexual assault, trafficking, and many other crimes by creating the crime victim U-visa. This new legal immigration visa helps immigrant victims whose abusers were not their spouses, were undocumented immigrants, were strangers, or were employers. These are all victims for whom the VAWA self-petition was not an option. The U-visa allows victims of mostly violent and kidnapping-related crimes to petition for a visa if they participated in an investigation or prosecution of the perpetrator. This visa helps many immigrant women and children obtain protection from deportation and legal work authorization. It also helps law enforcement and the criminal justice system bring perpetrators to justice. All VAWA self-petition, U-visa, and trafficking victim visa cases are filed with and adjudicated by the specially trained VAWA Unit of the Vermont Service Center, Department of Homeland Security.

Migrant worker is defined in Article 2 of the International Convention on the Protection of the Rights of All Migrant Workers and Members of Their Families as "a person who is to be engaged, is engaged or has been engaged in a remunerated activity in a State of which he or she is not a national." The Convention points to specific categories of workers such as "frontier worker," "seasonal worker," "project-tied worker," and "specified-employment worker."

Women make up a large number of migrant workers, seasonal and farm workers, in the United States. Migrant women leave economically depressed countries in Asia, Latin America, Eastern Europe, and Africa for countries in Western Europe and the United States in order to find jobs and send money back to their families, sometimes not seeing family members for years at a time. In fact, many countries' economies depend on the labor of women working abroad. Migrant women are extremely susceptible to exploitation. Migrant women are often extremely isolated by geography, repeated relocation, language, and culture. When migrant women work for the same companies as their husbands, employers pay the husband for the wife's labor and the migrant farm worker wife has little access to money. Migrant women working in agricultural fields, food-processing plants, and other factories are particularly susceptible to sexual harassment, sexual assault, and rape by employers and coworkers.

Many women in developing countries (source countries) who are looking for jobs in the United States and Western Europe (destination countries) are often approached by people promising high-paying employment opportunities. These people, their eventual traffickers, facilitate the women's entries into destination countries, confiscate their papers, and force them to perform work for little or no wages. The work ranges from working on farms to working in sweatshops or performing commercial sex acts like prostitution or exotic dancing.

Many women do not speak out or seek help because they fear retribution or loss of their jobs, thus cutting off the flow of money back home. Similarly, since many migrant women are undocumented, they fear that speaking out will attract law enforcement attention that could turn into reporting to immigration authorities and deportation.

Leslye Orloff

See also Department of Homeland Security, Asylum; Department of Homeland Security, Response to Battered Immigrants and Immigrant Victims of Violence Against Women; Department of Homeland Security and Immigration Services; Domestic Violence Among Immigrant Women; Immigrant and Migrant Women and Law Enforcement Response; Legal Momentum; Office on Violence Against Women; Sexual Harassment; Violence Against Women Act

Further Readings

International Convention on the Protection of the Rights of All Migrant Workers and Members of Their Families. (1990). Retrieved from http://www.ohchr.org/english/law/cmw.htm

Orloff, L. E. (2001). Lifesaving welfare safety net access for battered immigrant women and their children: Accomplishments and next steps. *William and Mary Journal on Women and the Law, 3,* 597–658.

Orloff, L. E., & Kaguyutan, J. E. (2002). Offering a helping hand. *American University Journal of Gender, Social Policy, & the Law, 8*(2), 231–282.

Orloff, L. E., & Sullivan, K. (Eds.). (2004). *Breaking barriers: A complete guide to legal rights and resources for battered immigrants.* Available at http://www.legalmomentum.org

Tamayo, W. R. (2007, November). *Sexual harassment and assault in the workplace: A basic guide for attorneys in obtaining relief for victims under federal employment law.* Presentation delivered to the Legal Momentum Immigrant Women Program Conference, Washington, DC.

IMMIGRANT AND MIGRANT WOMEN AND LAW ENFORCEMENT RESPONSE

Immigrant and migrant women who are caught in abusive relationships and/or victims of sexual assault, trafficking, or other violent crime must often turn to law enforcement for assistance. Many times, law enforcement officers are the first responders to incidents involving violence—be they at the home or in public. An immigrant or migrant woman's willingness to reach out to law enforcement is shaped by many factors, including her experiences with law enforcement and the criminal justice system in her home country; her past experiences with law enforcement in the United States; and her facility with the English language, fear of deportation, and fear of retribution by her abuser, his family members, or her cultural community.

Immigrant and migrant victims may have tried to call police back in their home countries or previously in the United States, but felt that the police did not take their concerns seriously. In many countries, violence in the home is still seen as a private, not public, matter. Additionally, many immigrant women often turn to other women for support. If other women in the community have reached out to law enforcement, but have had bad experiences, it is less likely that a woman will turn to police for help.

In many communities law enforcement officials have not made their services language accessible to non–English-speaking victims, despite Title VI of the Federal Civil Rights Act requirements. Many times, immigrant and migrant victims are unable to communicate with police when they arrive at the scene of the crime. The abuser or other crime perpetrator will control the conversation if he speaks English, and police will oftentimes take his word. This can lead to the victim's instead of the abuser's arrest, despite physical evidence that the abuser is the perpetrator and primary aggressor. When police are not bilingual and do not access interpreters at the crime scene to facilitate communication with a non–English-speaking victim, they increase the risk that they will arrest the victim rather than the perpetrator. The victim's arrest can increase danger to her from the perpetrator, who evades being held accountable by the criminal justice system and whose power and control over his victim is enhanced. Furthermore, the victim's arrest can cut her off from immigration relief available to her under the Violence Against Women Act.

Of all the reasons immigrant women do not call the police, fear of deportation is the primary one. If the victim is undocumented, she may fear that if she calls for help she will be turned in to immigration authorities and be deported. Abusers of immigrant women, traffickers, and other crime perpetrators use threats of deportation to keep immigrant victims from calling the police, from obtaining protection orders, and from telling anyone about the abuse. Sometimes, the victim's immigration status and/or options for legal immigration status are tied to her abusive spouse, parent, or employer under U.S. immigration laws. The victim may fear that if she reaches out to police, her abuser may not help her or her children file for and obtain legal immigration status.

Violence against immigrant and migrant women can take forms other than intimate partner violence. Women may have been trafficked for labor or commercial sex purposes. Trafficking for either purpose involves extreme isolation of women from the outside world, so that control over many aspects of their lives belongs to the trafficker. Traffickers tell their victims to fear law enforcement and that police will discover they are undocumented immigrants, will catch them, and will send them back to their home countries. Trafficking victims' extreme isolation keeps them hidden from the outside world. As a result they rarely come in contact with police. Law enforcement raids of trafficking rings may be the first time a trafficked victim has ever had contact with law enforcement. Being introduced to the police in such a violent way can reinforce everything the trafficker has told the victim about law enforcement. Since the passage of the Trafficking Victims Protection Act in 2000, federal and state law enforcement have undertaken significant efforts to reach out to and identify trafficked victims. However, close collaborations between law enforcement and victim advocates are needed as early as possible to ensure trafficking victims protection and access to the services and support they need.

The Violence Against Women Act of 2000 created a crime victim visa (U-visa) for which the Department of Homeland Security published implementing regulations that took effect on October 17, 2007. In order to qualify for a U-visa a crime victim must have suffered substantial physical or emotional abuse as a result of criminal activity and must be helpful, have been helpful, or be willing to be helpful in an investigation or prosecution of criminal activity. To file, a victim must obtain a certification from a government (usually law enforcement) official. The U-visa provides an important opportunity for advocates and law enforcement to work together to improve law enforcement response to calls for help from immigrant victims. Advocates for victims should work with local law enforcement to ensure that as wide a range of supervisors as possible are authorized by the law enforcement agency to sign U-visa certifications. By becoming involved in U-visa certification, law enforcement agencies can work more effectively to help immigrant and migrant victims and to bring the perpetrators of crimes against them to justice, while giving immigrant and migrant women an incentive to reach out to law enforcement.

Leslye Orloff

See also Department of Homeland Security, Response to Battered Immigrants and Immigrant Victims of Violence Against Women; Department of Homeland Security and Immigration Services; Domestic Violence Among Immigrant Women; Immigrant and Migrant Women; Legal Momentum; Office on Violence Against Women; Violence Against Women Act

Further Readings

Ammar, N., Orloff, L. E., Dutton, M. A., & Aguilar-Hass, G. (2005). Calls to the police and police response: A case study of Latina immigrant women in the USA. *International Journal of Police Science and Management, 7*(4), 230–244.

Department of Homeland Security. (2007). *New classifications for victims of criminal activity; Eligibility for "U" nonimmigrant status.* Retrieved from http://www.dhs.gov/xlibrary/assets/uscis_u_nonimmigrant_status_interimrule_2007-09.pdf

Orloff, L. E., Dutton, M. A., Aguilar-Hass, G., & Ammar, N. (2003). Battered immigrant women's willingness to call the police for help. *UCLA Women's Law Journal, 13*(1), 43–100.

Sreeharsha, K., & Orloff, L. E. (2007, November). *Human trafficking and the T visa.* Presentation delivered to the Legal Momentum Immigrant Women Program Conference, Washington, DC.

Web Sites

Limited English Proficiency: A Federal Interactive Website: http://www.LEP.gov

Immigration and Naturalization Service

See Department of Homeland Security and Immigration Services

Incest

Sexual abuse accounts for 12% of the 1 million substantiated cases of child abuse and neglect annually. Approximately 20% of adult women and 5% to 10% of men were sexually abused as children. The peak age of vulnerability to sexual abuse is between 7 and 13 years of age. Girls are approximately three times more likely to be sexually abused than boys.

Incest is a subtype of child sexual abuse, referring to sexual abuse that occurs within the family. Research estimates that for girls, 33% to 50% of perpetrators are family members, whereas for boys, only 10% to 20% are. The most common perpetrators of intrafamilial abuse of girls are fathers, stepfathers, uncles, cousins, brothers, and grandfathers. The vast majority of perpetrators are male, but mothers and other female relatives can also abuse. Fathers' involvement in early caretaking may make them less likely to sexually abuse their daughters.

Unique legal issues occur when a child is abused within the family. The nonabusing parent may have to choose between the child and the abuser. A separation or divorce may ensue, including a custody dispute. False allegations of abuse in custody cases appear to be fairly rare. In one study of 9,000 divorces, only 2% ($N = 180$) had allegations of sexual abuse. Of those 180 cases, less than 1% of the total number were determined to be false reports. Further, professionals who regularly evaluate children report that preschoolers make the smallest percentage of false allegations.

Many factors contribute to severity of the abuse experience. Abuse by a nonblood relative is not automatically less severe than abuse by a blood relative, especially if the victim is emotionally close to the perpetrator. For example, a girl might be seriously affected by a stepfather's abuse, even though he is not related to her by blood. Other factors that make the experience severe include sexual penetration (oral, vaginal, or anal), use of force, long duration and frequent contact, and lack of support from a nonabusive parent. Many of these factors relate to each other, and are related to whether the abuse occurs within or outside of the family. For example, abuse that occurs within the family may start earlier, go on for a longer time, and include increasingly more serious sexual acts.

There is a range of symptoms that occur among sexually abused children and adults. Severity of the experience is often, but not always, related to the severity of the symptoms. Symptoms of abuse that occur among preschoolers include anxiety, nightmares, and inappropriate sexual behavior. Among school-age children, symptoms include fear, mental illness, aggression, nightmares, school problems, hyperactivity, and regressive behavior. For adolescents, symptoms include depression; withdrawn, suicidal, or self-injurious behaviors; physical complaints; illegal acts; running away; and substance abuse.

Long-Term Effects

The effects of child sexual abuse can continue well into adulthood. Symptoms adult survivors manifest are often "logical extensions" of dysfunctional coping mechanisms developed during childhood. While these dysfunctional behaviors may have helped the child cope with ongoing abuse, they have a negative impact on adult functioning. Incest and child sexual abuse can affect men and women physiologically, and can influence their behavior, beliefs about themselves and others, social relationships, and emotional health. These effects are described below.

Traumatic events, including incest, can alter the way the body handles stress. After experiencing a severe or overwhelming stressor, the victim's body becomes "threat sensitized," which causes it to be over-responsive to current stressors. This can manifest as higher resting heart rate, chronic activation of the sympathetic nervous system, and the presence of chronic pain.

Incest can also shape how survivors see themselves and the world. They may come to view the world as a dangerous place, and respond to others with mistrust and hostility. They may also blame themselves for what happened to them, increasing their risk of revictimization as adults. They are also at higher risk for substance abuse, high-risk sexual practices, smoking, and eating disorders.

Among adult survivors, depression is the most commonly reported symptom. Incest survivors have a four-time greater lifetime risk for depression than others. Incest survivors are also at risk for developing posttraumatic stress disorder. Even if they do not meet full criteria for posttraumatic stress disorder, they may have symptoms that are troubling and may cause difficulties in other areas of their lives (e.g., sleep difficulties).

Also common among incest survivors are problems in relationships such as parent–child relations, relations with partners (including increased risk for revictimization), and relations with others that affect the availability of effective social support for these survivors.

Men and women vary in their reactions to incest and sexual abuse, and not everyone who has been sexually abused will have the problems listed above. There are effective treatments for incest survivors. Indeed, those who have experienced incest or child sexual abuse may use their experiences as an impetus to become better parents, and even to help others who have had similar experiences.

Kathleen Kendall-Tackett

See also Child Sexual Abuse; Depression; Health Consequences of Child Maltreatment

Further Readings

Arata, C. M. (2000). From child victim to adult victim: A model for predicting sexual revictimization. *Child Maltreatment, 5,* 28–38.

Kendall-Tackett, K. A. (2003). *Treating the lifetime health effects of childhood victimization.* Kingston, NJ: Civic Research Institute.

Kendall-Tackett, K. A. (2004). *Breastfeeding and the sexual abuse survivor.* Lactation Consultant Series 2, Unit 9. Schaumburg, IL: La Leche League International.

Kendall-Tackett, K. A., & Marshall, R. (1998). Sexual victimization of children: Incest and child sexual abuse. In R. K. Bergen (Ed.), *Issues in intimate violence* (pp. 47–63). Thousand Oaks, CA: Sage.

Kendall-Tackett, K. A., Williams, L. M., & Finkelhor, D. (1993). The effects of sexual abuse on children: A review and synthesis of recent empirical studies. *Psychological Bulletin, 113,* 164–180.

McMillen, C., Zuravin, S., & Rideout, G. (1995). Perceived benefit from child sexual abuse. *Journal of Consulting and Clinical Psychology, 63,* 1037–1043.

Reece, R. M. (2000). *Treatment of child abuse: Common ground for mental health, medical, and legal practitioners.* Baltimore, MD: Johns Hopkins University Press.

INCIDENCE

Incidence is defined as the frequency with which offenders commit crime. More specifically, it is the number of times a criminal behavior is observed during a particular time frame. Incidence tends to be unevenly distributed and skewed, which means most individuals will report very little, if any, criminal activity, while a small number of individuals will report high levels of criminal activity. In addition, incidence is influenced by demographic characteristics. Certain groups have higher incidence rates than other groups; for example, gender is an important variable, with males having higher incidence of criminal behavior than females. To control for such factors, incidence is usually reported as a rate.

Incidence can be measured using official crime data such as those provided by the FBI's Uniform Crime Reporting (UCR) Program or by self-report surveys. In official crime data, incidence is measured as the average number of offenses per offender, which is calculated by dividing the number of offenses reported by the number of offenders arrested during a specified time period. In self-report surveys, the respondent reports the number of times he or she has engaged in a particular criminal behavior in a given period of time. Incidence is more commonly measured by self-report surveys due to the methodological problems associated with official crime data.

The measurement of incidence using official crime data is influenced by two critical problems. First is the underreporting of crime. The National Crime Victimization Survey estimates that only 50% of all crime is reported. The underreporting of crime generates an underestimation of the number of offenses and adversely impacts incidence. Second is the low clearance rate for most types of crimes. The UCR estimates a clearance rate of 20% for serious felonies. The low clearance rate causes an overestimation of incidence per offender, since many of the offenders are not apprehended.

When incidence is measured using a self-report study, three problems can impact the accuracy of the measure. The first problem with self-report studies is the veracity of the respondent: Only to the extent that the respondent answers the survey honestly will the respondent's measured incidence rate be an accurate representation of his or her true incidence rate. The next two problems focus on the quality of the respondent's memory. The respondent can suffer from memory decay, which is a problem where the respondent does not recall the details of his or her behavior such as how often he or she has engaged in the behavior. This is especially problematic when the respondent engages in the behavior frequently and incidents blur together. Typically, memory decay causes self-report surveys to underestimate incidence. The other problem with the respondent's memory is telescoping, which is when the respondent reports a behavior that occurred prior to the time period covered by the survey. Telescoping causes an overestimation of incidence.

Ann Marie Popp

See also Prevalence

Further Readings

Pepper, J. V., & Petrie, C. V. (2003). *Measurement problems in criminal justice research: Workshop summary.* Washington, DC: National Academies Press.

Tracey, P. E., Jr. (1990). Prevalence, incidence, rates and other descriptive measures. In K. L. Kempf (Ed.), *Measurement issues in criminology* (pp. 51–78). New York: Springer-Verlag.

INFANTICIDE

Infanticide refers to the killing of an infant, typically up to 1 year of age, though some sources classify as infanticides the killings of children up to 2 or 5 years of age. Both men and women commit infanticides, which differ in many ways from the killings of older children and adults. Infanticides include neonaticides, in which a newborn is killed on the day of his or her birth, and some filicides (i.e., the killing of a child by a parent). Though relatively uncommon, infanticide is an important form of interpersonal violence.

Infanticide in History

Historically, newborns and infants were killed because the societies into which they were born felt it was an acceptable way to deal with unwanted children or those who threatened the survival of the larger family unit, band, or tribe. Infants who were perceived as unhealthy were more likely than their sound counterparts to be slain immediately or shortly after their births in order to devote scarce resources to ensure the survival of the social group. In some societies, female infants were often slaughtered, a trend that has continued into the modern era. Other children met their untimely ends when they were sacrificed to the gods, when their paternity was uncertain or undesirable, or when their parents simply did not want the burden of another child. Historically, infanticide was a common response to the stresses of rearing children.

Due to the dangerous environments in which they were raised, some children in history were killed through what would now be considered neglect or lack of supervision by their caregivers. Overlaying of infants by mothers (or others) who rolled over onto and suffocated their infants while sleeping, for example, was so common that laws were passed to outlaw the practice of adults sharing their beds with youngsters. Infants were scalded or burned to death when their parents were absent or were unintentionally killed during quarrels between the adults in their homes so frequently that the incidents were not considered especially newsworthy.

In days of old, superstition and beliefs in the paranormal played a unique role in the abuse and ultimate deaths of defective or unusual children. A child whose appearance was strange (e.g., due to deformity or disability) or whose behavior displeased his or her parents (e.g., crying too much) was sometimes labeled a changeling (i.e., a fairy child who had been switched at birth with a human infant). Popular belief held that only through continual abuse of a changeling could human parents hope that the fairies would come to rescue their own child and return the human one to its rightful family. No fairy ever returned a stolen child, of course, meaning that the so-called changelings were literally abused to death through beatings, burning, and other forms of torment. Similarly, in some tribal societies, infants believed to be witches were violently destroyed.

Contemporary Infanticides

The motivations behind and methods of contemporary infanticides differ greatly from those of the past. Especially in the United States, killings motivated by necessity are very rare and superstition plays a minuscule role in the deaths of modern infants. Overlayings are now so unusual that many individuals have never even heard of the phenomenon.

Infanticides are far less common now than in the past. In Victorian England, infanticides were the most common form of killing and the crime was routinely committed in other European nations, in the United States, and around the world. Recent estimates from the FBI's Uniform Crime Reporting Program, on the other hand, show that between 175 and 225 children under the age of 1 year are killed each year in the United States. This means that around 1% of killings in this country are infanticides. This rate may be misleading, however, given the difficulty in ascertaining the cause of death in some cases. The risk of a child being the victim of a homicide drops dramatically for school-age children and remains low until the teen years.

Types of and Motivations Behind Infanticides

Infanticides are committed by both men and women and the crime typically involves a victim who is in the real or temporary care of the killer. Infanticidal women seem to eschew weapons and tend to suffocate or drown their victims, while men tend to strangle or use weapons against their victims (e.g., stabbing or bludgeoning). Though routinely used in the killings of older children, especially teenagers, firearms are rarely involved in infanticides. Those who kill infants are often young, typically in their teens or early twenties. The vast majority of infanticides are committed by parents, stepparents (including parents' paramours), or other family members. Infanticide is one of the few violent offenses that is not dominated by male offenders; when women kill, they tend to kill intimates and children.

Infants are more likely than older children and adults to be beaten to death and to be killed in their own homes, which is sometimes attributed to their inability to escape from abusive situations by running away or seeking help from outsiders. Deaths due to head injuries are quite common among infants, occurring at a far higher rate than among older children or adults. The proportion of deaths due to neglect, of course, declines rapidly with age of the victim—while the majority of neonaticides are due to exposure or neglect, very few deaths of older children can be attributed to neglect. Victims of infanticides are more likely than older homicide victims to be White.

Unlike the killing of older children and adults, infanticides tend to be the unintended consequences of abuse or neglect or of unrestrained discipline that goes too far. Some research has linked infanticide to overly aggressive attempts by parents to quiet crying children or to correct children who have soiled themselves. A sizable proportion of infanticides involve killers with a history of mental illness and/or who suffer from postpartum psychopathology.

Infanticide Typologies

Several scholars have posited typologies of those who commit infanticide. Despite minor variations between the models, most acknowledge that infanticides result from (a) mistreatment of unwanted children; (b) overzealous discipline or abuse directed against otherwise wanted children; (c) emotional responses by adults such as retaliation, revenge, or jealousy; or (d) mental illness, including postpartum psychopathology.

Some infanticides are termed *altruistic* because the killer, often suffering from mental illness, believes he or she is helping the victim avoid some greater imagined terror, such as being seized by the devil or suffering from some nonexistent malady or disease; a sizable proportion of altruistic infanticides are followed by suicide attempts by the killer. Though postpartum depression and psychosis in perpetrators of infanticides are relatively rare, their role in infanticides is the subject of a great deal of discussion and research.

Neonaticides differ from other infanticides in that they usually follow denied or concealed pregnancies and typically are committed by females who are afraid to tell the adults in their lives about an unwanted pregnancy. Males, even the fathers of the infants, are seldom involved in neonaticides. Many neonaticides occur during the process of hiding or disposing of a live-born infant to prevent discovery of the pregnancy and birth by parents or others. Due to the unique phenomenon of neonaticide, the first day of an infant's life is considered the most dangerous in terms of risk of being a homicide victim.

Prevention of Infanticide

In order to prevent infanticide, society must address each of the many causes of infant death. Some scholars have advocated for better monitoring of those who are pregnant and new mothers for signs of postpartum psychopathology, combined with educational campaigns aimed at increasing awareness of the devastating

condition. Support programs aimed at helping families cope with the stresses of parenting have certainly reduced the number of abuse-related infanticides. The ability of medical and social service professionals to detect the abuse of unwanted children can also reduce the number of fatalities. Neonaticides may be prevented by a variety of programs aimed at reducing the stigma of unwanted pregnancies and creating situations conducive to disclosure of such pregnancies. Unfortunately, there is no single solution to the problem of infanticide.

Jon'a F. Meyer

See also Child Fatalities; Child Neglect; Child Physical Abuse; Homicides, Criminal; Parenting Practices and Violence, Child Maltreatment

Further Readings

Crittenden, P. M., & Craig, S. E. (1990). Developmental trends in the nature of child homicide. *Journal of Interpersonal Violence, 5,* 202–216.

Goetting, A. (1995). *Homicide in families and other special populations.* New York: Springer.

Haffter, C. (1968). The changeling: History and psychodynamics of attitudes to handicapped children in European folklore. *Journal of the History of the Behavioral Sciences, 4,* 55–61.

Mann, C. R. (1996). *When women kill.* Albany: State University of New York Press.

Meyer, C. L., & Oberman, M. (2001). *Mothers who kill their children: Understanding the acts of moms from Susan Smith to the "prom mom."* New York: New York University Press.

Moseley, K. L. (1986). The history of infanticide in Western society. *Issues in Law and Medicine, 1,* 345–361.

Pitt, S., & Bale, E. (1995). Neonaticide, infanticide, and filicide: A review of the literature. *Bulletin of the American Academy of Psychiatry and the Law, 23,* 375–386.

INSANITY DEFENSE

The insanity defense is an affirmative defense to a criminal charge. Affirmative defenses are those in which the defendant tries to limit or completely eliminate criminal liability by offering an excuse or justification for the act. (Self-defense and duress are also affirmative defenses.) In the insanity defense's traditional form, the defendant enters a plea of "not guilty by reason of insanity" (NGRI). Defendants who plead NGRI do not deny having committed the offense, but rather argue that at the time the crime was committed, they were unable to form the necessary intent and therefore should not be held legally responsible for their acts. The insanity defense has evolved over time, and jurisdictions have adopted different standards or tests. Four states—Montana, Idaho, Utah, and Kansas—do not permit insanity as a defense.

Insanity is a legal concept, not a psychological or psychiatric one. The American legal tradition recognizes two elements to any criminal offense: the *actus reus* (criminal act) and the *mens rea* (guilty mind). The inclusion of the second element, mens rea, requires that the prosecution establish culpability (or blameworthiness) by demonstrating that the accused not only committed the offense, but also intended to commit the offense. Although proving the defendant committed the act often supersedes the need to literally prove the intent (it is generally accepted that most acts are intended), the mens rea requirement opens up the opportunity for the defense to launch a diminished capacity or insanity defense in response to a criminal charge.

The traditional insanity defense, the M'Naughten Rule, which was adopted from the English Common Law, states that a defendant's criminal conduct can be excused if "at the time of the committing of the act, the party accused was labouring under such a defect of reason, arising from a disease of the mind, as not to know the nature and quality of the act he was doing, or, if he did know it, that he did not know what he was doing was wrong." The M'Naughten Rule established a cognitive test that was supplemented in some jurisdictions by an "irresistible impulse" test (a test of whether the defendant could control his or her conduct). Appellate court decisions established the Durham Rule, which required that the act be a "product" of the mental defect or illness, and the Brawner Rule, which endorsed the American Legal Institute's (ALI's) Model Penal Code definition of insanity. The ALI expanded the cognitively based M'Naughten Rule to allow for an insanity defense based on either the defendant's capacity to appreciate the wrongfulness of his or her conduct or his or her capacity to conform his or her conduct to the law.

The most substantial insanity defense reform followed John Hinckley, Jr.'s 1982 NGRI acquittal for his 1981 attempt to assassinate then-president Ronald Reagan. At the time of Hinckley's acquittal, the insanity defense was based on the ALI's standard and included both a cognitive and a volitional prong. A defendant's NGRI plea would succeed if the defendant could demonstrate an inability to appreciate the wrongfulness of his or her conduct or lacked the ability to control the conduct. The public outrage that followed Hinckley's acquittal led to swift legislative action culminating in the 1984 passage of the Insanity Defense Reform Act (IDRA). The IDRA was a sweeping reform of the insanity defense that eliminated the volitional component, shifted the burden of proof from the prosecution to the defense, and increased the evidentiary standard from "preponderance of the evidence" to "clear and convincing evidence." Following IDRA reforms at the federal level, states began to revisit their insanity defense statutes, with many states reverting to a purely cognitive test. States have also revised their penal codes to allow for a diminished capacity defense (a defense that, if successful, might result in conviction on a lesser charge rather than a finding of not guilty) or a guilty but mentally ill verdict (a verdict that recognizes the mental illness without negating the defendant's responsibility for the offense).

High-profile insanity defense pleas and acquittals have led to public outcries against the use of the insanity defense; however, contrary to popular misconceptions, the most comprehensive study of the insanity defense suggested that the defense is infrequently used and, when used, is rarely successful.

Natasha A. Frost

See also Biochemical Factors in Predicting Violence; Mental Illness

Further Readings

Model Penal Code (1985). § 4.01(1).

Murdock, D. (Executive Producer). (2002, October 17). *Frontline: A crime of insanity* [Television broadcast]. New York and Washington, DC: Public Broadcasting Service.

Steadman, H. J., McGreevey, M. A., Morrissey, J. P., Callahan, L. A., Robbins, P. C., & Cirincione, C. (1993). *Before and after Hinckley: Evaluating insanity defense reform.* New York: Guilford Press.

Institute on Domestic Violence in the African American Community

The Institute on Domestic Violence in the African American Community (IDVAAC) is a national policy and practitioner training center established to address domestic violence in the African American community. The formal mission of IDVAAC is as follows: To provide an interdisciplinary vehicle and forum by which scholars, practitioners, and observers of family violence in the African American community will have the continual opportunity to articulate their perspective on family violence through research findings, the examination of service delivery and intervention mechanisms, and the identification of appropriate and effective responses to prevent and reduce family violence in the African American community.

IDVAAC's goals include the following:

- Creating a community of African American scholars and practitioners devoted to working in the area of violence prevention in the African American community
- Raising consciousness of the impact of violence in the African American community by gathering and disseminating information
- Identifying community needs and recommending best practices

IDVAAC was conceived in 1993 when a group of four African American practitioners and researchers found themselves to be the only African Americans attending the First National Conference on Domestic Violence and informally gathered to discuss their concerns about the lack of emphasis on domestic violence in the African American community. Following the initial discussion in 1993, the group engaged in efforts to establish a formal organization by securing operating funds from the Administration for Children and Families, U.S. Department of Health and Human Services.

IDVAAC is housed in the School of Social Work at the University of Minnesota–St. Paul and is administered by Oliver J. Williams and a Steering Committee comprised of 10 women and men who have professional backgrounds in the areas of service delivery, violence prevention advocacy, and academic research. A major contribution of IDVAAC to the field of domestic violence has been the rejection of domestic violence intervention strategies that have been designed from a "one size fits all" perspective. As such, IDVAAC has led the way in promoting the view that effective prevention and intervention aimed toward the reduction of domestic violence among African Americans must be informed by culturally competent service delivery. That is, domestic violence interventions targeted to African Americans must take into consideration the experiences and realities that influence motives for and justifications leading to domestic violence, and how African American victims of domestic violence experience and make sense of their victimization.

Over the course of its existence, IDVAAC has sought to enhance awareness of domestic violence in the African American community and the competency of practitioners to address domestic violence among African Americans by hosting national forums that have featured practitioners and researchers recognized for their innovative approaches in the areas of domestic violence prevention and intervention. Selected forum topics have included Partner Abuse in the Black Community: Culturally Specific Prevention and Treatment Models, African American Children and Domestic Violence, Substance Abuse and Domestic Violence in the African American Community, Welfare Reform, Domestic Violence and the African American Community, Domestic Violence and the Hip Hop Generation, and Mobilizing the African American Community to End Domestic Violence.

In recent years IDVAAC has secured a combination of public and private funding to address a variety of issues, including assessing community stakeholders' perspectives on the causes and prevention of domestic violence in the African American community, conducting national training institutes on the intersection of prisoner reentry and domestic violence, and examining factors that hinder and promote the use of supervised visitation in minority communities. Additionally, IDVAAC has embarked on a project to more broadly disseminate its work by hosting a series of Webcasts pertaining to cultural competency and prisoner reentry and domestic violence.

William Oliver

See also Cultural Competence; Culturally Sensitive Intervention

Web Sites

Institute on Domestic Violence in the African American Community: http://www.dvinstitute.org

INSTRUMENTAL VIOLENCE

Instrumental violence is goal-oriented aggression or violence that occurs as a by-product of an individual's attempting to achieve a superordinate goal. Early 20th-century theorist Edward Thorndike's law of effect is useful in understanding the nature of instrumental abuse, as it is based on the observation that many behaviors appear to be efforts to obtain some desired results or avoid the occurrence of other unwelcome outcomes. Such goal-oriented behaviors are labeled "instrumental" because they appear to be deliberate attempts to achieve specific results.

Instrumental behaviors are common in interactions between two people, occurring whenever one person attempts to influence the other to act or refrain from acting in specific ways. In this sense, these behaviors lie at the core of reciprocal exchanges. However, when the tactics of influence are covert, overly harsh, and entirely one-way, behaviors that might have shaped and sustained relationships can become abusive and destroy intimacy.

The primary motivation for instrumental abuse appears to be manipulating another person to comply with a demand for access to some asset (e.g., money, power). As with all coercive behavior, the force behind instrumental aggression is threatened or actual delivery of some feared consequence. This could be threatened or actual violence toward the other or objects valued by the other, refusal to engage in interactions desired by the other, or forms of withdrawal including ending the relationship. Physical harm may be a product of instrumental abuse.

In theory, instrumental abuse may fall on a continuum between maliciously destructive predatory abuse, in which the primary aim is to injure the other person, and affective abuse, in which the goal is essentially self-protection or the expression of emotion, albeit through aggression. It should be noted that some have conceptualized this continuum as simply ranging from expressive to instrumental abuse. In certain cases, it may be difficult to determine whether a specific act of violence is instrumental or expressive, as some behaviors may share the characteristics of both.

It has been argued that instrumental abusers are inherently narcissistic; have a weak, albeit not absent, sense of empathy; and have at least mild psychopathic tendencies. This description stems from the willingness of instrumental abusers to exploit others in pursuit of some personal gain. Intervention outcomes are likely to be inversely proportional to the presence of these antisocial tendencies. For treatment to succeed, abusers must be helped to develop a sense of morality and an appreciation of the centrality of reciprocity to well-functioning social relationships. These are among the more difficult challenges faced by therapists.

Gregory L. Stuart and Richard B. Stuart

See also Intimate Terrorism; Situational Couple Violence

Further Readings

Haller, J., & Kruk, M. R. (2006). Normal and abnormal aggression: Human disorders and novel laboratory models. *Neuroscience and Biobehavioral Reviews, 30,* 292–303.

Stuart, R. B. (2005). Treatment for partner abuse: Time for a paradigm shift. *Professional Psychology: Research and Practice, 36,* 254–263.

INTENSIVE FAMILY PRESERVATION SERVICES

Intensive Family Preservation Services (IFPS) are services designed to prevent a child's placement out of the home, most commonly into the foster care system. Families are typically identified by child protective services systems because of suspected or confirmed child abuse and/or neglect, and referred to IFPS in an effort to reduce risk of future maltreatment to such a degree that a child will be able to remain at home safely. When successful, IFPS prevents the need to protectively remove a child from home and place him or her into the foster care system to avert further maltreatment.

Although a variety of family supportive services have been around for many years, IFPS emerged as a distinct strategy most noticeably in the 1970s and 1980s with a growing recognition of the importance of primary attachments for children's well-being; the need to strive for more stable permanent settings for developing children; and the growing recognition that foster care placement was often expensive, unstable, and even in some instances unsafe. Several promising service models that were tested in Alameda, California, and in Oregon in the late 1970s suggested that if families received intensive supportive services, the need to place a child out of the home to avert further mal-treatment could be averted. The passage of the federal Adoption Assistance and Child Welfare Act (P.L. 96–272) in 1980 required states to document "reasonable efforts" to maintain children in their own homes prior to their placement into foster care, which spurred the national expansion of IFPS. Since that time, a growing number of service models and accompanying evidence have shed light on IFPS and the capacity of the services to avert the placement of children in foster care.

Most commonly, IFPS are provided directly in the child's home by a trained IFPS social worker. IFPS is intensive in that services provided in the home are often provided on a short-term but frequent basis (several times per week is common), with workers handling only a few cases at a time and available around the clock for crisis needs. Services typically consist of crisis intervention support, guidance around parenting techniques, activities to link families up with needed community resources and supports, and sometimes modest material assistance to purchase essential goods for the family. One of the strengths of IFPS is that such programs have been carefully studied, providing evidence guiding their development. At present, a number of studies examining the overall effectiveness of IFPS in reducing out-of-home placement rates have failed to find program effects, while others have reported significant preventive trends and improvement in family functioning. While the evidence base is increasingly identifying which families are most likely to most benefit from IFPS, further research is necessary to reliably guide the advancement of IFPS so that the services can fulfill their promise to prevent children's being placed away from home as a protective option.

Neil B. Guterman

See also Child Abuse Prevention; Family Preservation and Reunification Programs; Foster Care; Kinship Care

Further Readings

Berry, M., & Ginsberg, L. (Eds.). (1997). *Family at risk: Issues and trends in family preservation services.* Columbia: University of South Carolina Press.

Biegel, D. E., & Wells, K. (Eds.). (1991). *Family preservation services: Research and evaluation.* Newbury Park, CA: Sage.

INTERGENERATIONAL TRANSMISSION OF VIOLENCE

The notion that family violence persists across generations is pervasive among clinicians, researchers, and the general public. Although many people expect consistent intergenerational transmission of violence (ITV), many scholars have questioned the supposed inevitability of transmission. Phenomena such as partner violence and child abuse clearly lead to myriad negative outcomes for many victims, including subsequent victimization due to involvement in relationships with violent partners, as well as perpetration of violence toward others, including partners and children. Estimates of the likelihood of ITV across generations vary widely, and researchers have found several risk and protective factors that alter the rates of transmission. Ultimately, the majority of people exposed to family violence during childhood are *not* involved in partner violence or child abuse as adults.

Transmission of family violence across generations may occur via several mechanisms. Social learning theory indicates that children learn to be perpetrators and/or victims of violence through exposure to their parents' expressions of violence. According to attachment theory, child abuse leads to insecure attachment between parents and children; changes in the child's internal working model result in later relationship difficulties and inadequate care for one's own children. Another possible explanation is that family violence during childhood results in increased stress and negative life events; during adulthood, high stress and limited resources lead people to use violence. Assortative mating suggests that people select mates similar to themselves, increasing the risk of becoming involved in partner violence for people who are already predisposed. Some researchers point to features with genetic components shared by parents and children that predispose both to family violence, such as antisocial traits, alcoholism, and impulsivity. Some traits shared by parents and children may not be passed genetically but instead may be learned during childhood, such as violence approval, poor emotion regulation, deficits in social information processing, and hostile attributions about interpersonal relationships.

ITV research typically employs one of three methodologies, with inclusion of control samples varying among studies. First, many researchers examine the rates of violence in the childhoods of adults currently involved in family violence as perpetrators or victims. Alternatively, researchers begin with a sample of adults who experienced violence in their families of origin, then investigate rates of family violence during adulthood. Less commonly, researchers take a sample of children with varying family violence histories and follow them into adulthood. This latter prospective approach avoids reliance on retrospective recall of participants, which can be prone to error and bias. However, prospective studies are costly in terms of money, time, and researcher effort. Typically, retrospective studies result in higher estimates of transmission rates than prospective studies. Use of self-report measures produces much higher rates of violence than reliance on substantiation by government agencies, which can result in large variations in transmission rates.

Joan Kaufman and Edward Zigler illustrated how the same transmission data can be presented in different ways, resulting in substantially different estimates of transmission. For example, using parents' abuse histories as the starting point, a 1979 study by Rosemary Hunter and Nancy Kilstrom found an 18% rate of transmission; that is, of parents with an abuse history, only 18% abused their own infants. If current abuse had been the starting point instead, these same data would have shown a 90% transmission rate because 9 of the 10 parents currently abusing their infants had been maltreated as children.

Transmission of Partner Violence

Sandra Stith and colleagues conducted a meta-analysis of marital ITV, combining the results of 39 separate studies. They found an average correlation of $r = .18$ between witnessing partner violence as a child and perpetrating partner violence as an adult; this link was stronger for men ($r = .21$) than women ($r = .11$), indicating that boys who witness partner violence are more likely than girls to become perpetrators. There was a small correlation ($r = .14$) between witnessing partner violence and becoming the victim of partner violence as an adult; this link was stronger for women ($r = .18$) than men ($r = .09$), suggesting that girls who witness partner violence are more likely than boys to become victims. Although not included in that meta-analysis, evidence from other studies is mixed as to whether adults resemble their same-sex parent more

than their opposite-sex parent in terms of violence perpetration and victimization. Because the base rate of violence is higher in dating relationships than in marriages, the transmission rate may be somewhat higher as well, but there have been no meta-analyses to date that compare dating and married couples. Among the factors that can increase likelihood of partner ITV are antisocial behavior, receipt of harsh parenting during childhood, experiencing abuse as a child, depression, substance abuse, attitudes condoning violence, and general relationship conflict.

Transmission of Child Physical Abuse

Kaufman and Zigler estimated that one third of abused children grow up to become abusive parents. Subsequent studies have found both higher and lower rates ranging from less than 10% to more than 40%, depending on factors such as study samples, methodology, and definitions of abuse and violence. Regardless of exact rates, the bulk of the literature is clear that having a history of child abuse consistently increases the likelihood of later perpetration of child abuse, but the majority of people abused as children do not go on to maltreat their own children. Researchers have looked for factors that cause some parents to break the cycle of violence and others to continue the cycle. Several protective factors have been found to decrease the likelihood of violence transmission, such as stable relationships, nonviolent partners, receipt of emotional support, involvement in psychotherapy, and stable home environments. Risk factors that increase the likelihood of violence transmission include young parental age, mental illness including depression and posttraumatic stress disorder, substance abuse, child illness or disability, poor parenting, financial stress, and other forms of violence in the home. In addition, children who experience more severe abuse, more frequent acts, and more injuries are more likely to go on to abuse their own children.

Transmission of Child Sexual Abuse

Because most perpetrators of sexual abuse are men, transmission studies have focused on men as perpetrators and women as mothers of sexually abused children. The largest longitudinal study following sexually abused boys into adulthood found that less than 12% became perpetrators of sexual abuse against children (most of the victims were outside their families). Looking retrospectively at known child sexual abusers, studies have found an average of 28% were sexually abused as children. One of the largest risk factors that appears to increase risk of transmission is exposure to other forms of family violence. In terms of female victims, there is a higher rate of sexual abuse among children of sexually abused mothers than those of nonabused mothers. Contact with the mother's abuser appears to increase children's risk of being sexually abused, indicating that in many families, the same person may be responsible for transmission across generations.

Multiple Forms of Family Violence

The 2000 meta-analysis by Stith and colleagues found that witnessing partner violence and experiencing child abuse in the family of origin had similar impacts on subsequent adult partner violence. In terms of child physical abuse and sexual abuse, extant research indicates that all forms of family violence do appear to lead to some increase in child maltreatment in the next generation. The extent of the increased risk is modest, however, and there are numerous factors that can increase and decrease the likelihood of ITV.

Transmission Over Time

Although a history of family violence is one of the greatest risk factors for perpetration and victimization as an adult, intergenerational transmission is far from certain. The majority of people exposed to violence as children later break the cycle of violence. It should also be noted that the rates of violence found to date may not hold true for future cohorts; as the rates of family violence decline over time, the rates of ITV may also change in future generations.

Angèle Fauchier

See also Adult Survivors of Childhood Abuse; Cycle of Violence; Family Violence, Co-Occurrence of Forms

Further Readings

Belsky, J., & Pensky, E. (1988). Developmental history, personality, and family relationships: Toward an emergent family system. In R. A. Hinde & J. Stevenson-Hinde (Eds.), *Relationships within families: Mutual influences* (pp. 193–217). Oxford, UK: Clarendon.

Kaufman, J., & Zigler, E. (1987). Do abused children become abusive parents? *American Journal of Orthopsychiatry, 57,* 186–192.

Salter, D., et al. (2003). Development of sexually abusive behaviour in sexually victimized males: A longitudinal study. *The Lancet, 361,* 471–476.

Stith, S. M., Rosen, K. H., Middleton, K. A., Busch, A. L., Lundeberg, K., & Carleton, R. P. (2000). The intergenerational transmission of spouse abuse: A meta-analysis. *Journal of Marriage and the Family, 62,* 640–654.

Widom, C. S. (1989). Does violence beget violence? A critical examination of the literature. *Psychological Bulletin, 106,* 3–28.

INTERMITTENT EXPLOSIVE DISORDER

Intermittent explosive disorder (IED) is a little studied psychological disorder characterized by repeated violent outbursts against people or objects, which is caused by a failure to resist aggressive impulses. The violent or aggressive reaction is disproportionate to the stimulus that provokes it, and outbursts occur repeatedly. IED is considered by some to be a cause of interpersonal violence from road rage to intimate partner violence. Others consider IED's diagnostic and definitional criteria to be too vague or too broad, calling into question its legitimacy and utility as a diagnosable psychological disorder.

The *Diagnostic and Statistical Manual of Mental Disorders, Fourth Edition (DSM–IV)* places IED within the larger category of impulse disorders. Impulse disorders are characterized by the failure to resist impulses despite the potential for negative consequences. The diagnostic criteria for IED are vague and include any violent or aggressive outbursts that are repetitive, out of proportion to the situation, and not accounted for by other psychological disorders, drug use, or biological disorders. Due in part to its expansive diagnostic criteria, research on IED is very limited and some psychologists question its legitimacy. Despite the dearth of scholarly consensus and evidence about IED, it has been used successfully as a defense in court cases. Defendants have attempted to use it in court in response to charges as serious as homicide, primarily in cases related to road rage or intimate partner violence.

The available research is marked by a small number of studies, research definitions that differ from the

DSM diagnostic criteria, and small sample sizes. Studies claim that IED is more common in men than women by a ratio of about three to one, and that it generally manifests in adolescence. Characteristics of IED described in the literature include an irresistible violent impulse followed by pleasure or relief derived from acting on the impulse, followed by remorse for the violent outburst or its consequences. The violent outbursts last less than 30 minutes. Often, the aggression is aimed at intimate partners. It may be either a grossly disproportionate response to provocation or unprovoked. Some scholars recommend treatment using drugs that are used to treat other impulse disorders. Others recommend cognitive-behavioral therapy or a combination of the two.

Critics have noted that the diagnostic criteria for IED are so vague that they could include nonpathological and instrumental violence. The criteria include no minimum number of outbursts beyond repetition, and no time period in which the outbursts must occur. This means that virtually all violence that is not specifically identified as caused by another psychological disorder, biological problem, or drug use could ostensibly be termed IED. Common abusive behaviors could fall under the diagnostic criteria for IED, and scholars caution against pathologizing violence against intimate partners. Current research on IED fails to rule out social and cultural influences on violent and aggressive behavior within and outside of the family.

Molly Dragiewicz

See also Intimate Partner Violence

Further Readings

American Psychiatric Association. (1994). *Diagnostic and statistical manual of mental disorders* (4th ed.). Washington, DC: Author.

INTERNATIONAL SEX INDUSTRY

In recent years, there have been a number of significant shifts in the organization of the commercial sex industry, each relevant to women's experience of violence within prostitution. Internationally, the last decades of the 20th century witnessed a tremendous growth in what is known as "sex tourism"—the development and expansion of industries providing sexual services, catering primarily to Western and Japanese men who travel to economically undeveloped countries for business or leisure activities. In conjunction with the development and expansion of sex tourism has been a rise in trafficking of individuals for prostitution and the widespread involvement of children in the sex tourism industry.

A common thread in the organization and control of the global sex industry is that it emerges from and is sustained by gender, race, and class inequalities, as well as power imbalances resulting from colonial and imperialist relations across nations. The current scope and nature of the global sex industry is unprecedented. It is also associated with widespread exploitation, human rights abuses, and violence.

International organizations define trafficking as all acts and attempted acts involved in the recruitment, transportation within or across borders, purchase, sale, transfer, receipt, or harboring of a person (a) involving the use of deception, coercion, or debt bondage or (b) for the purpose of placing or holding such person, whether for pay or not, in involuntary servitude, in forced or bonded labor, or in slavery-like conditions, in a community other than the one in which such person lived at the time of the original deception, coercion, or debt bondage. According to the U.S. government, between 50,000 and 100,000 women are trafficked into the United States annually, and more than half a million women are trafficked worldwide every year. However, given the illicit nature of the industry, many suspect the numbers are probably much higher.

Several factors are responsible for the growth of this phenomenon. In addition to the evolution of sex tourism, broader global economic patterns in the late 20th century have encouraged women from developing countries to migrate abroad in search of economic opportunities to better themselves and their families. There are currently an estimated 60 million female migrants around the globe, and they constitute fully half of the world's migrant population. While migration itself is distinct from trafficking, and trafficking from prostitution, they are interconnected in that the growth in women's migration has made trafficking, including sexual trafficking, particularly easy to achieve. This is largely because the trafficking of girls and women often follows the same routes as legitimate migration, increasing traffickers' ability to deceive women, and to transport and control them without detection.

Trafficking is a global activity, and nearly every country in the world serves as a source, transit, and/or receiving country. Trafficking is found in Latin America and the Caribbean, in Africa, and to and from North America, the Middle East, Europe, and Australia. However, it is believed to be highest in two regions of the world: within Asia and from Asia to other parts of the world, and from Eastern Europe and the former Soviet Union to Western Europe and other destination countries. The intersections of race, class, and gender inequalities often dictate these routes: ethnic minority women and women from poor countries are routed to meet the desires of more privileged men.

Traffickers generate gross earnings of an estimated US$7 billion annually. Trafficking today is well organized and is often controlled by organized crime groups. Recruiting agents can include employment agencies, brokers, "marriage" agents, and acquaintances, as well as family friends or relatives. Often ads are placed in newspapers that describe well-paying job opportunities overseas in the service industries, including domestic work, dancing, and work as waitresses and hostesses. Researcher Donna Hughes estimates that about 20% of women are recruited for trafficking through false advertising. Recruitment methods usually involve deceit or debt bondage, but can also involve violence.

Women often are deceived about the nature or conditions of the work for which they are migrating. Regardless of whether they know they are migrating for sex work, women are often unprepared for the working conditions they discover. For example, often trafficking generates a system of debt bondage. With transnational prostitution, this occurs when women borrow money for the cost of travel, visas, false documents, and employment location. They are then charged exorbitant interest and required to work off the debt before accumulating their own earnings. It is not uncommon for women's debt to be sold from one employer to another, and for the new employer to then add the women's purchase price to their debt. Women's passports are routinely confiscated as security on the "loan," and this gives the women's debtors further control over their movement.

Women's status as illegal immigrants makes them vulnerable to exploitation and coercion in these markets; this is exacerbated when women are trafficked or migrate to foreign nations in which they do not speak the language and thus cannot communicate their experiences or easily seek assistance. Evidence consistently shows that the organization of the sex industry, including the transnational sex industry, results in widespread patterns of violence, coercion, and exploitation, as well as discriminatory law enforcement. Women who are trafficked, as well as women who voluntarily migrate for sex work, often find themselves working in slavery-like conditions in which their mobility is restricted and they are not given the right to control the conditions of their work. As a consequence of illegal confinement and forced labor, women are subject to a range of abuses, including physical and sexual assault, as well as exposure to HIV and other sexually transmitted diseases. Health care is minimal, and women who contract diseases are often simply discarded.

Advocates argue that strict migration laws, in conjunction with legal statutes governing the sex industry, allow this system to flourish and increase sex workers' dependence on outside agents. Despite the United Nations convention prohibiting trafficking for prostitution, the countries into which women are trafficked routinely give precedence to their status as illegal aliens engaged in illicit work, rather than to their status as victims of trafficking or forced prostitution. Brokers, managers, traffickers, recruiters, and middlemen, as well as legitimate businesses such as hotels and travel agencies, continue to profit from the industry, while sex workers face distinct disadvantages that undermine their ability to control their labor, and make them dependent on the individuals and organizations who exploit them. In addition, these women are victims of police corruption, bribery schemes, and government collusion, all of which are well documented. Around the world, sex workers are detained and imprisoned and subjected to cruel and degrading treatment and suffer violence by the state or by private individuals with the state's support, but there are no international conventions or antitrafficking organizations that explicitly support sex workers' human rights.

Jody Miller

See also Commercial Sexual Exploitation of Children; Prostitution; Sex Tourism; Trafficking, Human

Further Readings

Coomaraswamy, R. (2001). *Integration of the human rights of women and the gender perspective: Addendum mission to Bangladesh, Nepal and India on the issue of trafficking of women and girls.* Geneva: United Nations Economic and Social Council.

Doezema, J. (1998). Forced to choose: Beyond the voluntary v. forced prostitution dichotomy. In K. Kempadoo & J. Doezema (Eds.), *Global sex workers: Rights, resistance, and redefinition* (pp. 34–50). New York: Routledge.

Farr, K. (2004). *Sex trafficking: The global market in women and children.* New York: Worth.

Hughes, D. M. (2001, January). The "Natasha" trade: Transnational sex trafficking. *National Institute of Justice Journal,* pp. 8–15.

Kempadoo, K., & Doezema, J. (Eds.). (1998). *Global sex workers: Rights, resistance, and redefinition.* New York: Routledge.

Lim, L. L. (Ed.). (1998). *The sex sector: The economic and social bases of prostitution in Southeast Asia.* Geneva: International Labor Organization.

Miller, J. (2002). Violence and coercion in Sri Lanka's commercial sex industry: Intersections of gender, sexuality, culture and the law. *Violence Against Women, 8,* 1045–1074.

Truong, T. (1990). *Sex, money and morality: Prostitution and tourism in Southeast Asia.* London: Zed Books.

INTERNATIONAL SOCIETY FOR THE PREVENTION OF CHILD ABUSE AND NEGLECT

Henry Kempe, a Denver pediatrician who coined the term *the battered child,* founded the International Society for Prevention of Child Abuse and Neglect (ISPCAN) in 1977. Initially conceived by an international group of 18 professionals meeting at the Bellagio Conference and Study Center (Italy) in 1975, the association was formally established following the First International Congress on Child Abuse and Neglect in Geneva in 1976.

ISPCAN's initial objectives included establishing an international professional journal and holding biannual international congresses. These vehicles were designed to facilitate the transfer of knowledge and to build relationships among the growing number of professionals addressing this problem worldwide.

Today, ISPCAN has over 1,800 individual members working in over 180 countries. Although initially supported through the volunteer efforts of its members, ISPCAN now operates under the direction of a professional staff based in the United States.

ISPCAN's annual revenue of some \$2 million comes from membership fees, royalties, conference and training fees, and philanthropic donations. Although its services have expanded, ISPCAN's core mission remains unchanged—to support those working to protect children from all forms of maltreatment (e.g., from physical abuse, sexual abuse, and neglect; from child prostitution and child labor; from becoming children of war).

ISPCAN's most visible product is its well-known and influential monthly journal, *Child Abuse & Neglect: The International Journal,* which publishes high-quality research from a variety of disciplines and relates this research to practice reforms. More recently, ISPCAN has added a quarterly newsletter (*The Link*) and biannual reports on the scope and public policy response to child abuse worldwide (*World Perspective on Child Abuse*) to its publication portfolio. ISPCAN also maintains an active listserv to improve member-to-member direct communication.

Since 1976, ISPCAN has convened 16 international congresses, rotating venues around the world to ensure accessibility to the greatest cross-section of individuals and organizations. ISPCAN also sponsors regional conferences, expanding educational opportunities for those working in African, Arab, Asian, South American, and Eastern European countries.

Beginning in 2000, ISPCAN increased its developing country training program to include an explicit emphasis on local capacity building. ISPCAN's International Training Project, in partnership with local professionals, supports multiyear training projects in 12 developing countries to improve knowledge and foster interdisciplinary professional networks.

ISPCAN's unique identity and strength has rested on its commitment to establishing a multidisciplinary and multicultural understanding of child abuse. Publications and training efforts are grounded in empirical research and in promoting those practices that have been rigorously tested and evaluated. Its increased influence in the field is reflected not only in its expanding membership base but also in its collaborative efforts with over a dozen national professional societies and major international associations including the United Nations, UNICEF, and the World Health Organization.

Deborah Daro

See also Human Rights; International Sex Industry; Professional Journals on Child Maltreatment; United Nations Conventions and Declarations

Further Readings

Cohn Donnelly, A. (Ed.). (2002). *An international movement to end child abuse: The story of ISPCAN.* Chicago: The International Society for the Prevention of Child Abuse and Neglect.

Web Sites

International Society for the Prevention of Child Abuse and Neglect: http://www.ispcan.org

INTERNATIONAL SOCIETY FOR TRAUMATIC STRESS STUDIES

The International Society for Traumatic Stress Studies (ISTSS) was formed in 1985 as the Society for Traumatic Stress Studies with the purpose of advancing knowledge about traumatic stress and promoting effective methods for preventing and ameliorating its negative consequences. In 1990 the name was changed to reflect the sincere intentions of the society to be international in scope. The society has sought to accomplish its goals by recognizing achievement in knowledge production and disseminating the knowledge through face-to-face contact with colleagues and by other methods. The society has a newsletter, *StressPoints,* and its official journal is the peer-reviewed *Journal of Traumatic Stress,* the leading academic journal for traumatic stress research.

The ISTSS was born in the aftermath of the Vietnam War and the increasing recognition of the persisting psychological effects of war on veterans. This coincided with the emergence of awareness that rape victims also suffered serious aftereffects. An early organizing force for those concerned with trauma survivors was the acknowledgment in the mental health professions that there are specific trauma consequences. This occurred in 1980 through the incorporation of posttraumatic stress disorder into the American Psychiatric Association's *Diagnostic and Statistical Manual of Mental Disorders.* At that time there was no field of traumatic stress and no organization that provided a forum for professionals

or was dedicated to advancing the accumulating knowledge.

Researchers and activists came together to create the society, which has become the premier professional association focused on knowledge development and dissemination related to traumatic stress. From the beginning the society extended its focus to encompass the range of trauma experiences, including those of rape victims, violent crime victims, police officers and emergency workers, combat veterans, families of victims, victims and families of intrafamilial abuse, and natural and humanmade disasters. Very soon thereafter the experiences of children were also incorporated into the society's concerns.

Over the years, the ISTSS has reflected the maturation of the field of traumatic stress studies. Interest has extended far beyond posttraumatic stress disorder. The society exerts scientific and clinical leadership on relevant issues, including the definition of trauma, general population epidemiology of trauma consequences, risk and protective factors for trauma impact, the biology of trauma responses, and effective interventions to counter the deleterious effects of trauma. The society's annual meeting, committees and task forces, and publications serve as primary vehicles for disseminating new knowledge as well as grappling with the complex issues that have arisen as the field has evolved. In addition, the ISTSS acts to promote social policy that advances the interests of trauma survivors.

Lucy Berliner

See also Posttraumatic Stress Disorder; Rape Trauma Syndrome

Web Sites

International Society for Traumatic Stress Studies: http://www.istss.org/

INTERNET, CRIMES AGAINST CHILDREN

The expansion of access by children to the Internet, and the wide availability of chat rooms, email, online messaging, webcams, and bulletin boards, have unfortunately led to the possibility that child predators can use this technology to come into contact with unsuspecting children. Each year more and more children are using online technologies and so the possibility of crimes against them using these technologies increases.

A 1999 survey of Internet crimes against children conducted by the Crimes Against Children Research Center at the University of New Hampshire found that 1 in 5 children reported being approached or solicited for sex and 1 in 33 were exposed to aggressive sex solicitation over the Internet in the 12 months prior to the survey. One quarter of the children reported that in the preceding year they had unwanted exposure to pictures containing nudity or sex acts.

Internet crimes against children can take many forms. A report by the U.S. Department of Justice's Office for Victims of Crime suggests that Internet crimes against children can take the following forms: (a) using online contacts to entice children into meeting with the purpose of sexually abusing the child; (b) using the Internet to produce, manufacture, and distribute child pornography; (c) using the Internet to expose a child to pornography; and (d) enticing a child into travel for the purpose of sexually abusing him or her.

There are several unique aspects of this crime that make it different from other crimes. First, there does not need to be physical contact or even a meeting between the perpetrator and victim. A crime could be committed over the Internet, for example, when a child is exposed to pornography by a perpetrator. Second, such a crime may continue for years even without the child being aware of it, for example, photos or videos of the child may be posted on the Internet. Third, these crimes have no boundaries and can occur across state and national jurisdictions. Finally, some children may not disclose or even be aware that they are victims.

National organizations responding to this issue include the National Center for Missing and Exploited Children (NCMEC) that operates the NetSmartz Workshop program, the Internet Crimes Against Children (ICAC) Task Forces nationwide, and several government agencies. NCMEC's efforts are covered elsewhere in this encyclopedia. The ICAC's Web site states that it was "created to help State and local law enforcement agencies enhance their investigative response to offenders who use the Internet, online communication systems, or other computer technology to sexually exploit children." According to the ICAC, there are now 46 regional ICAC task forces.

Jeffrey L. Edleson

See also Child Sexual Abuse; High-Tech Violence Against Women; Internet, Pornography; Internet-Based

Interventions; National Center for Missing and Exploited Children; Office for Victims of Crime; Office of Juvenile Justice and Delinquency Prevention

Further Readings

U.S. Department of Justice, Office of Justice Programs, Office for Victims of Crime (OVC). (2001). *Internet crimes against children* [OVC bulletin]. Retrieved from http://www.ojp.usdoj.gov/ovc/publications/bulletins/internet_2_2001/welcome.html

Web Sites

Internet Crimes Against Children Task Force: http://www.icactraining.org/
NetSmartz Workshop: http://www.netsmartz.org/

INTERNET, PORNOGRAPHY

The history of the pornography industry is inextricably linked to the development of communication technology. From the printing press to the Internet, pornography helped both popularize and mainstream technological innovations by providing men (the vast majority of pornography consumers) expanded opportunities and venues to view sexually explicit material.

One of the best examples of how pornography facilitated the growth of a new technology is the videocassette recorder (VCR). Pornography consumers were willing to pay high prices for a VCR and tapes in the early days of the technology before costs came down. Studies suggest that pornography tapes constituted over half of all sales of prerecorded tapes in the late 1970s, and that by 1983 there were more than 13,000 pornographic videos on the market. The power of pornography is seen in the fact that Sony's decision to refuse to license its Betamax technology to pornographers allowed VHS to monopolize the market by the early 1980s.

Pornography's profitability also drove innovation in Internet technology, as the pornographers pioneered streaming audio and visual, flash and chat, the click-through ad banner, the pop-up window, high-speed internet connections, security improvements, and a la carte pay services. While the pornography business can thank the Internet for its massive growth over the last few years, the Internet industry owes an even bigger debt to the pornographers.

The Internet is attractive to pornographers for several reasons. Start-up and distribution costs are low, and the Internet affords consumers easy and constant access in relatively private settings. In addition, the rapid growth of Internet pornography has meant that the laws restricting Internet content and access cannot keep up with the demand.

While statistics are difficult to collect on Internet pornography use, studies suggest the Internet generates $2.5 billion of the $57-billion-a-year global pornography industry. With 4.2 billion Web sites and 372 million pornography pages, there are 72 million visitors to porn Web sites annually, and 25% (68 million) of total search engine requests are for pornographic materials.

Internet pornography includes heterosexual, gay, lesbian, and transsexual material, with the vast majority being heterosexual aimed at a male audience, running the gamut from softcore (nudity with limited sexual activity, not including penetration) to hardcore (graphic images of actual, not simulated, sexual activity, including oral, vaginal, and anal penetration, sometimes by more than one man at a time). Constant accessibility means that pornography can be viewed in multiple locations, such as work, school, and Internet cafes as well as the home. Since the pornography "pops up" even when uninvited, it seamlessly flows into daily life and is increasingly part of the cultural landscape. This accessibility has also led to an increase in addictive behavior among consumers, with studies showing that almost 20% of male Internet pornography users report negative financial, legal, occupational, relationship, and personal repercussions from their activities.

The single largest public concern with Internet pornography has been children's easy access to the material. Many researchers have argued that children's viewing of Internet pornography constitutes a form of child abuse and requires immediate legislation. While there are few studies on the effects of Internet pornography, past research suggests that this increase in pornography consumption is implicated in greater levels of male violence against women and children.

Gail Dines and Robert Jensen

See also Decriminalization of Sex Work; International Sex Industry; Pornography

Further Readings

Coopersmith, J. (1998). Pornography and progress. *Icon, 4,* 94–125.

Dines, G. (2004). Unmasking the pornography industry: From fantasy to reality. In R. Morgan (Ed.), *Sisterhood is forever: The women's anthology for the new millennium* (pp. 306–314). New York: Simon & Schuster.

Lane, F. S. (2000). *Obscene profits: The entrepreneurs of pornography in the cyber age.* New York: Routledge.

Morrison, J. (2004). The distracted porn consumer: You never knew your online customers so well. *Adult Video News On-Line.* Retrieved June 1, 2004, from http://www.adultvideonews.com

INTERNET, VIOLENCE AGAINST WOMEN

See HIGH-TECH VIOLENCE AGAINST WOMEN

INTERNET-BASED INTERVENTIONS

Psychotherapeutic, counseling, and supportive services have been available on the Internet for victims of interpersonal violence since the late 1990s. Services include education, information and referral, problem solving, supportive counseling, and psychotherapy. For example, Safe Horizon offers education through an online domestic violence shelter tour as well as a link to email for help. Rape, Abuse and Incest National Network provides chat-based online intervention for rape crisis and support. Services are offered online by professionals and trained volunteers of domestic violence organizations, rape and sexual abuse crisis centers, child abuse agencies, and a variety of private nonprofit agencies as well as by private practice professionals. Service delivery may use asynchronous email, real-time chat-based communication, or Internet-based audio/visual communications. In addition, a large variety of self-help groups for support of victims and others faced with interpersonal violence are also offered on the Internet.

Advantages and Concerns

Scholars and practitioners have debated the advantages and potential harm of online services. The benefits of online therapy over in-person therapy include easier access to therapy, more privacy, and lower cost. Online therapy is convenient, since services may be available at any time from any place. They offer a stable source of support in an increasingly mobile society. Online services may be more likely to be used by those faced with concerns that are often stigmatized, such as domestic violence and rape, since they can be accessed anonymously and without in-person contact. In addition, services are available to those who might not otherwise seek services due to time constraints, geographic distance, caregiving responsibilities, lack of transportation, physical or social isolation, and/or physical or psychological disabilities. Online therapy may be more effective with some people since it uses a medium that promotes more open and disinhibited communication due to the perceived anonymity and safety of online communications. In addition, online services may offer a source of culturally relevant information and services when they are not available in the local community. Finally, although costs vary greatly, online therapy may be less expensive, since more consumers can be served in a shorter time with fewer overhead costs.

A number of ethical and legal concerns are associated with online services. The effectiveness of online therapy has not been established. There is very limited empirically validated evidence related to the outcomes of online service delivery. Therapists trained in face-to-face counseling rely on many visual cues in their assessment and intervention. A therapist's skills in assessment and providing empathy may not directly transfer to the online world. Since visual and verbal cues are unavailable online, assessment is more difficult online. Misunderstandings are more likely in text-based communications and cannot be immediately addressed in asynchronous modalities. In addition, development of trust may be impaired, since it is difficult to know the true identity of the consumer or the practitioner in a strictly online environment. Another concern is that providing privacy, security, and confidentiality of online communications requires both technological safeguards from practitioners and education of consumers in safeguarding their own computers. Furthermore, a number of ethical requirements, such as duty to warn vulnerable third parties, to make appropriate referrals, to be available and intervene in emergencies, and to consult with previous service providers, may be difficult in online relationships. Finally, practitioners and consumers face unclear legal and liability standards surrounding the jurisdiction and practice of online therapy.

A number of organizations have developed ethical and practice standards related to online therapy. The National Board for Certified Counselors has adopted ethical codes for the practice of e-therapy. The American Psychological Association (APA) has issued the *APA Statement on Services by Telephone, Teleconferencing, and Internet*. In addition, the International Society for Mental Health Online has adopted *Suggested Principles for the Online Provision of Mental Health Services*. The National Association of Social Workers (NASW) has not adopted a specific statement on the ethics of online practice. The NASW has adopted a policy statement about technology and social work that emphasizes the importance of using technology in social work directed by the values and ethics that are essential principles of the profession. There is general agreement in these codes of ethics that all ethical standards of face-to-face practice must be met in online therapy.

Research

Increased consumer use of the Internet to meet health and mental health needs is taking place in the context of very limited research about the effectiveness of online therapy. The research literature suggests that online therapy can be an effective treatment modality. Studies are limited in scope, sample size, duration, level of therapist experience, and outcome measures. Studies suggest that a therapeutic relationship can be established through text-based communications. In addition, a relatively small number of empirical studies comparing online treatment with face-to-face therapy or wait-list control groups have examined the effectiveness of online therapy with a variety of populations and social problems. These studies generally find online therapy to be as effective as face-to-face interventions or more effective than wait-list control groups with a variety of diagnostic categories, including anxiety, depression, eating disorders, panic disorder, substance abuse, caregiver stress, pediatric pain, cigarette addiction, grief, posttraumatic stress disorder, and recurrent headache. Studies have not yet evaluated online services for victims of violence. Further research is needed to better determine for whom and under what circumstances online therapy is effective.

As more people use the Internet, human service professionals working in interpersonal violence intervention will need to determine to what extent they will engage in online therapeutic and supportive services. For those who do offer online services, it will require creating secure systems, training workers in online communication, creating policies regarding what services may be offered online by whom, developing policies for handling both expected and unsolicited email, creating record keeping procedures for online communications, developing new forms of supervision, and evaluating the impact of online services. The future will likely see the development of new models of service delivery that include 24-hour access, a geographically distributed workforce, and new ways to link service recipients with information and supportive resources. Finally, services will need to be expanded to accommodate the tremendous increase in those seeking services as a result of online access.

Jerry Finn

See also Prevention Programs, Interpersonal Violence; Risk Assessment; Social Support Networks

Further Readings

Barak, A. (2001). *Online therapy outcome studies.* Retrieved from http://www.ismho.org/issues/cswf.htm

Barak, A. (2004). Internet counseling. In C. E. Spielberger (Ed.), *Encyclopedia of applied psychology* (pp. 369–378). San Diego, CA: Academic Press.

Finn, J., & Banach, M. (2002). Risk management in online human services practice. *Journal of Technology and Human Services, 20*(1/2), 133–154.

Grohol, J. M. (2000). *The insider's guide to mental health resources online.* New York: Guilford Press.

Mallen, M. J., Vogel, D. L., Rochlen, A. B., & Day, S. X. (2005). Online counseling: Reviewing the literature from a counseling psychology framework. *Counseling Psychologist, 33,* 819–871.

Rochlen, A. B., Zack, J. S., & Speyer, C. (2004). Online therapy: Review of relevant definitions, debates, and current empirical support. *Journal of Clinical Psychology, 60,* 269–283.

Seuler, J. (2000). Psychotherapy in cyberspace: A 5-dimension model of online and computer-mediated psychotherapy. *Cyberpsychology and Behavior, 3,* 151–160.

Waldron, V., Lavitt, M., & Kelley, D. (2000). The nature and prevention of harm in technology-mediated self-help settings: Three exemplars. *Journal of Technology in Human Services, 17*(1,2,3), 267–294.

Zack, J. S. (2004). Technology of online counseling. In R. Kraus, J. Zack, & G. Stricker (Eds.), *Online counseling: A handbook for mental health professionals* (pp. 93–121). San Diego, CA: Elsevier Academic Press.

Web Sites

Rape, Abuse and Incest National Network: http://www.rainn.org

Safe Horizon: http://www.safehorizon.org

INTERSECTIONALITY

Intersectionality is an analytic tool through which all social relations are structured, viewed, and acted upon. The concept of intersectionality specifically as applied to violence against women is often attributed to critical race scholar Kimberle Williams Crenshaw. As an African American feminist, Crenshaw was the first to make a link between the ways the social construction of political identities such as ethnicity and gender often submerge the complex "intersections" within and between such categories. Crenshaw and others also have asserted that the notion of intersectionality sheds light upon the ways social problems are constructed because such issues occur within historical, political, and cultural contexts that cannot be extricated from or analyzed without accounting for social variables such as socioeconomic class, sexuality, age, religious affiliation, and nationality.

Specifically with regard to domestic and sexual violence, Crenshaw has argued that without a more complex analysis of the interconnections among various forms of domination and oppression, the structural dimensions of intimate violence as well as those who are both victims and victimizers cannot be well understood.

The Race-ing of Violence Against Women

Growing out of the modern-day women's movement, feminist theorizing about violence against girls and women initially attributed the violence to gendered power relationships built upon and maintained through socially proscribed patriarchal constructions of family life, domesticity, marriage, and intimacy. Some feminist historians have suggested, however, that both the second wave of American feminism and the violence against women movement have been strongly defined by and through the race, class, and political perspectives of its main proponents—White, middle-class women. Late activist and scholar Susan Schechter, who wrote the first account of the American battered women's movement, suggested that the norms, organizing methods, and leadership of early feminist strategists set the tone for most of the prevailing domestic violence policies and practices that are now considered "mainstream" in the United States.

The notion of intersectionality first emerged as a critique of this predominantly White feminist and particularly U.S.-based analysis of sexual and domestic violence. Intersectionality as a complementary theoretical framework to explain violence against women focuses on two major points. First, while liberal and radical feminism have placed sex and gender inequality as the central if not sole cause of the structural domination of women in society, women of color and lesbians understand misogyny as co-constructed with racial and class stratification, heterosexism, xenophobia, and other systems of oppression. Crenshaw and others have argued that the social contexts in which race, class, gender, nationality, age, sexuality, and other social-political classifications combine to create institutions of domination are not merely additive in nature, but uniquely structured as an amalgam of power, supremacy, and social control.

The second basis of intersectionality is a critique of White feminism's claim that domestic and sexual abuse affects all women equally (i.e., all women could be raped or battered regardless of race, class, or sexuality). The predominant analysis of gender violence as a crime "against *all* women" suggests that whether you are the immigrant wife of a rural factory worker or the daughter of a wealthy East Coast industrialist your experience as a victim of intimate violence—including how such systems as the police, courts, social services, or medical facilities respond to you—is structured primarily or solely by your sex and gender, and not mediated by sex and gender in combination with socioeconomic class, age, sexuality, nationality, and other factors.

The Gender-ing of Ethnic Analyses of Violence

Feminists of color have argued both that White feminists' understanding of violence has excluded race as it intersects with gender and that the focus of communities of color on ending racism is not only dominated by the perceptions and leadership of men of color, but has precluded any analysis of how racism *and* sexism

disproportionately affect women of color. Therefore, any attempts to interrogate violence by men of color against women (whether female victims are White or non-White) are perceived either as a betrayal of racial/ethnic identity as envisioned by ethnic male solidarity or as duplicity with White feminism (which is equated with Whiteness). Battered and raped women of color thus are forced to choose between racial/ethnic loyalty and their safety as defined in a feminist/White analysis of violence.

This conundrum is similarly structured for other women victims of violence who must traverse the multiple spaces of their various identities. Battered lesbians must rely upon either the politically defined but protective boundaries of lesbian identity/community or the expected safety of often heterosexist antiviolence interventions such as shelters. Immigrant rape survivors may remain silent in their ethnic communities for fear of subjecting themselves and/or their families to regressive immigration policies or instead may consent to Western medical evidentiary exams established by well-meaning sexual assault health care providers who are nonetheless ill prepared to deal with non-English-speaking victims. Proponents of intersectionality theory suggest that violence against women exists within a historical and political structure that implicates all forms of domination. Therefore, sex and gender oppression is not necessarily primary in such theorists' analysis of intimate violence but contextualized along with racism, classism, heterosexism, xenophobia, and other institutionalized misuses of power.

In summary, intersectionality as an underlying assumption, operating principle, and organizing theory in understanding and responding to violence against women requires us to stand at multiple locations, to hold many and sometimes conflicting analyses, and to listen for distinct voices within the chorus of each victim's story.

Valli Kalei Kanuha

See also Anti-Rape and Rape Crisis Center Movements; Battered Women's Movement; Cultural Competence; Feminist Theories of Interpersonal Violence

Further Readings

Crenshaw, K. W. (1994). Mapping the margins: Intersectionality, identity politics and violence against women of color. In M. A. Fineman & B. Mykitiuk (Eds.),

The public nature of private violence (pp. 93–120). New York: Random House.

Kanuha, V. (1996). Domestic violence, racism, and the battered women's movement in the United States. In J. Edleson & Z. Eisikovits (Eds.), *Future interventions with battered women and their families* (pp. 34–50). Thousand Oaks, CA: Sage.

Richie, B. E. (2000). A black feminist reflection on the antiviolence movement. *Signs, 25*(4), 1133–1137.

Schechter, S. (1982). *Women and male violence: The visions and struggles of the battered women's movement.* Boston: South End Press.

Intimate Partner Relationship Quality and Domestic Violence

Relationships in which one or both partners are violent are often characterized by dissolution and low relationship quality. Indeed, across a variety of samples, studies comparing violent and nonviolent couples generally find that individuals in violent relationships report less satisfaction with their relationships and exhibit more negative behaviors during relationship problem discussions. In a study of newlywed couples, one research team found that whereas violent and nonviolent couples did not differ shortly after marriage, violent relationships were over two times more likely to fail over a 4-year period. In this study, marital failure was defined as evidence of relationship distress and/or a change in marital status. Also of note, in this study wives in aggressive marriages were considerably more likely to be maritally distressed than wives in nonviolent marriages; however, husbands in aggressive relationships were only slightly more likely to be maritally distressed than husbands in nonviolent relationships. The association between partner violence and relationship dissatisfaction is further supported when considering divorce as a proxy for marital quality. Several studies have shown that partner violence is a very strong predictor of divorce.

Importantly, there appears to be a dose-response association between violence and relationship quality. Research suggests that as the frequency and severity of intimate partner violence increase, the quality of the relationship decreases. For example, even after controlling for initial relationship variables, research found that while moderately violent relationships are slightly more likely to end in divorce than nonviolent relationships, severely violent relationships are twice as likely to end in divorce.

Perceived relationship quality has also been shown to be associated with partner violence. For example, in studying nonaggressive, mildly aggressive, and severely aggressive men, one research team found that a 20% increase in relationship discord increased the odds of being mildly aggressive by 101% and being severely aggressive by 183%. Although cross-sectional data support this relationship, longitudinal research suggests that it is more likely that the violence itself predicts low relationship satisfaction than that relationship discord predicts the onset of partner violence. However, there is some evidence that relationship dissatisfaction predicts psychological abuse, which, in turn, predicts the future onset of partner violence.

Complex Relationship

Despite the apparent simplicity of the notion that violence negatively affects the quality of relationships, the actual association is more complex. Not all violent relationships are characterized by relationship discord. In fact, some studies have found that a substantial number of couples with a history of intimate partner violence are not distressed. Studies of newlywed couples have shown that approximately one third report a history of intimate partner violence, even though most report high relationship satisfaction. It should be noted, however, that intimate partner violence among these newlywed couples is typically relatively mild in severity. There is also some evidence that a number of nonnewlywed couples who report being satisfied with their marriage also report the occurrence of physical aggression. Thus, it may be that the severity of the violence and/or additional factors predicts the quality of abusive relationships, as opposed to a direct relationship between violence and relationship quality. This notion is supported by previous research findings on the interplay of factors such as relationship status, substance use, life stressors, negative communication, and day-to-day interactions among partners that may determine the impact of violence on relationship quality. Finally, it may be that positive aspects of the relationship counteract the impact of the abuse.

Early Intervention

Although not all violent couples are distressed and not all distressed couples are violent, it is clear from existing literature that, in general, intimate partner violence is inversely related to relationship quality and positively related to relationship dissolution. This association seems especially strong in relationships characterized by severe violence. Additionally, research has shown that compared to their nonviolent counterparts, premarital and newlywed couples experiencing violence report similar relationship satisfaction initially, but become less satisfied over time. This finding suggests that intervention (e.g., counseling, education) early on in the relationship may reduce the occurrence of violence and improve the quality of the marriage.

Jeff R. Temple and Gregory L. Stuart

See also Divorce and Intimate Partner Violence

Further Readings

Heyman, R. E., O'Leary, K. D., & Jouriles, E. N. (1995). Alcohol and aggressive personality styles: Potentiators of serious physical aggression against wives? *Journal of Family Psychology, 9,* 44–57.

Holtzworth-Munroe, A., Smutzler, N., & Bates, L. (1997). A brief review of the research on husband violence. Part III: Sociodemographic factors, relationship factors, and differing consequences of husband and wife violence. *Aggression and Violent Behavior, 2,* 285–307.

Katz, J., Kuffel, S. W., & Coblentz, A. (2002). Are there gender differences in sustaining dating violence? An examination of frequency, severity, and relationship satisfaction. *Journal of Family Violence, 17,* 247–271.

Lawrence, E., & Bradbury, T. N. (2001). Physical aggression and marital dysfunction: A longitudinal analysis. *Journal of Family Psychology, 15,* 135–154.

O'Leary, K. D., Barlilng, J., Arias, I., Rosenbaum, A., Malone, J., & Tyree, A. (1989). Prevalence and stability of marital aggression between spouses. A longitudinal analysis. *Journal of Consulting and Clinical Psychology, 57,* 263–268.

Pan, H., Neidig, P. H., & O'Leary, K. D. (1994). Predicting mild and severe husband to wife aggression. *Journal of Consulting and Clinical Psychology, 62,* 975–981.

INTIMATE PARTNER VIOLENCE

Intimate partner violence (IPV), also called domestic violence or wife abuse, was first identified as a social problem by feminist advocates and scholars in the 1970s. Before that time, abuse of women in the context of intimate relationships and families was a largely hidden problem, although there is much evidence that it is not a new problem. Since that time much has been learned about the complex nature of IPV, although it is still not a well-understood problem. In the beginning, it was married women who were the target of concern, based on the assumption that there was something about the institution of marriage itself that led some men to feel entitled to assert control over their wives through physical violence. Over time, however, both researchers and advocates for women have learned that women in all types of intimate relationships—dating, cohabiting, married, as well as separated and divorced—experience violence at the hands of their partners.

Definitions

IPV is predominantly violence against women by men and consists of physical, emotional, sexual, or psychological abuse or violence committed by intimate partners or acquaintances, including persons who are current or former spouses, cohabiting partners, boyfriends, and dates. Regardless of how it is socially or legally defined, women's experiences of violent victimization are dominated by victimization by people they know, generally men they know well.

Physical Violence

Physical violence is defined to include fatal and nonfatal physical assault, such as acts of physical aggression intended to harm an intimate partner, including pushing, grabbing, and shoving; kicking, biting, and hitting (with fists or objects); beating up and choking; and threatening or using a knife or gun.

Sexual Assault

Legal definitions of rape and sexual assault differ from state to state, although their common element is the lack of victim consent to sexual acts. Although many states have ceased to use the term *rape* in their criminal codes, rape is generally understood to mean forced or coerced vaginal, anal, or oral penetration; sexual abuse involves either less serious threats or engaging in other sexual acts with a person who cannot give consent.

Emotional Abuse

Emotional abuse, also referred to as psychological abuse or maltreatment, can be defined as acts intended to denigrate, isolate, or dominate an intimate partner.

Emotional abuse might include verbal attacks (including harassment, insults, criticism, ridicule, name calling, discounting and discrediting); isolating the victim from social ties or controlling contact with others; denying access to resources, including finances and transportation; extreme jealousy and possessiveness, monitoring of behavior, and accusations of infidelity; threats to harm the victim's family, children, or friends; threats of abandonment or infidelity; or damage or destruction of possessions. Common to many definitions of emotional abuse are attempts to control victims by limiting resources and social contacts, creation of emotional dependence, and attempts to make the victim doubt her self-worth, competence, and value.

Prevalence

Estimating rates of partner violence is difficult for many reasons, including historical stigma, victim underreporting due to fear of retaliation from their perpetrators and other safety concerns, and lack of agreement about definitions. There have been several major national survey studies of IPV. The 1985 National Family Violence survey found that partner violence was reported by 116 of every 1,000 women. The National Crime Victimization Survey (NCVS), an ongoing general victimization survey begun in 1972, concluded that around 5 million victimizations are experienced by females over age 12 each year; of the victimizations involving single offenders, 29% were perpetrated by intimates, 9% by other relatives, 40% by someone known to the victims but not an intimate or relative, and only 24% by strangers. The National Violence Against Women Survey (NVAWS) conducted during 1995 and 1996 examined IPV rates in a sample of 8,000 U.S. women 18 years and older. This study concluded that 1.3% of women experienced violence by an intimate partner in the preceding year, with 22% reporting physical assaults by an intimate partner at some time over the course of their lives. The differences in these studies' results are likely due to differences in the contexts in which victimization questions were asked, populations sampled, and number and type of screening questions asked. Despite differences in the overall rate estimates, the results of these studies indicate that partner violence is a prevalent problem and that women are at higher risk of assault from someone known to them than by strangers. It should also be noted that IPV is estimated to occur at approximately the same rates among gay men and lesbians in intimate relationships.

Risk Factors

There is a strong consensus among experts that there is no single cause or risk factor for IPV. Instead, there are numerous risk factors that affect perpetrators and victims, in relationships and family systems, and within communities and society.

Perpetrator

Individual risk factors affecting perpetrators have been studied extensively. Age is among the best documented risk factors for physical and sexual violence for both victims and perpetrators; younger men are at greater risk of perpetrating IPV. Substance abuse, especially alcohol use and abuse, has also been found to be associated with both partner violence and sexual assault. One third to two thirds of sexual assaults are said to be alcohol related. Low income is a risk factor for both occurrence and continuation of IPV; the lower the income, the more likely men are to perpetrate IPV. Unemployment of the abusive male partner has also been found to elevate risk for IPV.

Numerous perpetrator personality characteristics or traits have been studied as antecedents of physical or sexual abuse, although it is clear that there is not a single male personality type that is prone to sexual or physical violence. A 1998 review of research concluded that the following are personality risk markers for male partner abuse: emotional dependence and insecurity; low self-esteem, empathy, and impulse control; poor communication and social skills; aggressive, narcissistic, and antisocial personality types; and anxiety and depression. Some researchers have attempted to identify different types of batterers. These studies have concluded that while there may be several different types of abusive men, there are at least two types (one type that is violent only toward intimates and another that is more generally violent toward others) that may require different interventions. Because emotional or psychological abuse typically precedes as well as accompanies physical abuse, emotional abuse should also be considered a risk factor for physical abuse. A history of violence in the family of origin has been extensively researched, with most researchers concluding that exposure to violence between one's parents or being the recipient of violent punishment is a risk factor for violence toward intimates as an adult, although not all studies have supported this conclusion.

Victim

Numerous experts have found that earlier victimization, especially childhood physical and sexual abuse and witnessing violence between parents, increases risk for sexual assault and partner violence. Many of the same risk factors for male perpetration of IPV also apply to female victimization. For example, younger women are more likely to be abused, and alcohol and drug abuse have been found to increase the risk of becoming a victim of IPV, and especially of sexual assault. One study concluded that substance abuse appears to be both a cause and an effect of IPV, affecting young women and women of color in particular. Abuse of alcohol or drugs, which may have origins in childhood victimization and the ongoing distress it causes, appears to be associated with the kind of lifestyle and male relationships that increase women's risks for victimization, also making it more difficult for women to terminate abusive relationships. Poverty status is also a risk factor for victimization, and economic dependency on the abuser can be a barrier to a woman's being able to terminate an abusive relationship.

Social isolation is associated with IPV. Although it can be a consequence of abuse, it may also serve as a risk factor for women's victimization. It is plausible that women with greater social support are less likely to be physically or sexually assaulted, and thus social support may be protective. Some research suggests that social isolation both precedes and follows partner violence. Much anecdotal information suggests that abusive men often attempt to control their partners by cutting them off from meaningful social contact. In addition, isolated women and families may be less closely monitored by others, allowing abuse to occur more easily.

Relationship Type

Relationship status is a risk factor. Among intimates, separated and cohabiting couples are at higher risk for partner violence than are married or dating couples.

Community

Two factors at the community level have been found to increase risk for IPV. First, rates of IPV are highest in urban areas. In addition, a lack of services for victims or perpetrators increases the risk of staying in abusive relationships and/or being unable to address the consequences of physical or sexual abuse. Although services for abuse have increased over the past three decades, some victims are dissatisfied with the help they have received from community agencies, and research continues to be conducted on how to provide services to victims and offenders that are effective in ameliorating abuse and its effects.

Culture and Society

Sociocultural risk factors establish a broad context that has made many forms of IPV socially acceptable in the context of historical patriarchy. Many agree that sexism in American society and gender-role stereotyping are risk factors for victimization of women. For example, rates of marital violence are highest in states where there is the most economic, educational, political, and legal inequality. In addition, there is still stigma associated with identifying oneself as an abused woman or rape victim. Although victims may be less likely to be held responsible for being abused, many feel criticized and misunderstood for not leaving abusive relationships sooner than they do.

Race and ethnicity have been studied as possible risk factors for IPV, although research findings are inconclusive. Some studies show that, compared with White women, African American women experience higher rates of physical violence, whereas others find higher rates for Whites compared with Hispanic women or find no racial/ethnic differences. Many of these studies have not taken into consideration the effects of socioeconomic status, which is correlated with race and ethnicity, so they may overestimate the effect of race on violent victimization. The highest rates of rape have been found among Native American women, with Latinas reporting the lowest rates. As is the case with domestic violence, however, most research on race and sexual assault has not controlled for the effects of socioeconomic factors such as income that may help to explain ethnic differences in sexual assault rates.

Consequences

A wide variety of different types of consequences of IPV can occur. Offenders and children in families where abuse is occurring experience adverse consequences as well as victims. Victims of IPV may experience consequences in several domains. One obvious effect is physical injury. The NVAWS found that 36% of rape victims and 42% of physical assault victims reported injuries, most commonly scratches, welts, and bruises. However, injuries are not the most common type of health effect to occur. A large body of research in health care has documented that abused women tend to have poorer health and report more symptoms of all kinds compared to nonabused women. These include gastrointestinal disorders, chronic pain, fatigue, dizziness, appetite problems, and gynecological problems such as sexually transmitted diseases. Emotional distress is also common in the aftermath of IPV, including depression, suicide attempts, posttraumatic stress, fear and anxiety, and, in some studies, drug and alcohol abuse. The likelihood of symptoms is related to abuse severity. Many victims also blame themselves for the abuse and experience guilt or shame. Although for some women psychological symptoms subside when the abuse stops, others continue to experience emotional distress long after the abuse has ended.

A question often asked is why abused women remain in abusive relationships. Although many women do leave—as many as two out of five within 2 to 5 years according to some research—others remain in abusive relationships due to practical barriers to leaving such as the inability to economically support oneself and one's children or lack of safe, affordable housing. Emotional attachments and dependency on the abusive partner and lack of social support also entrap some victims.

Perpetrators, too, can experience adverse consequences of abusing their partners. These include, increasingly, criminal justice sanctions such as arrest and incarceration and either temporary or permanent loss of their female partner and children. This, in turn, can lead to loss of self-esteem and self-respect. Finally, injuries or even death can occur at the hands of the victim.

Children can also be affected in negative ways, manifesting problems of various types and in all areas of development. These include fear, insecurity, and confusion; "externalizing behavior problems" such as anger, aggression and other acting-out behavior problems, and noncompliance; learning violence as a way of approaching problems; withdrawal, passivity, depression, and other "internalizing problems"; and injury, as they attempt to intervene in a violent argument to protect their mother.

Intervention

Although concerns about intervention initially focused on victims, it was quickly realized that offenders need services to stop their abuse. Most communities now have domestic violence programs as well as services for perpetrators. In contrast to the common stereotype of abused women as helpless, two large-scale studies have shown most abused women as seeking help and doing so repeatedly before seeking shelter, which for many survivors may be a last resort. Most abused women who seek help go first to family and friends and are quite satisfied with the substantial assistance they receive from such supporters.

The most commonly used formal services tend to be criminal justice (law enforcement, lawyers), social service agencies, medical services, crisis counseling, mental health services, clergy, and support and women's groups. Women's programs are generally evaluated highly, despite not being used as frequently as many other types of services. Counselors who are knowledgeable about abuse and understand the situation in which abused women find themselves have been perceived as most helpful. Other helpful responses include listening and taking the woman seriously, believing her story, and helping her see her strengths.

Also important is prevention education targeted at young people. Such work is often organized by domestic violence programs and other types of social agencies or educational institutions committed to educating students about IPV in the hopes of preventing future generations of victims and perpetrators.

IPV has been recognized as a serious and complex social problem for which communities have a responsibility to intervene and ameliorate. As a result of work by advocates and researchers, women are less likely to be blamed for their victimization and more likely to be perceived as deserving assistance. At the same time, abusers are increasingly likely to be held accountable for their abusive behaviors while also being perceived as needing assistance to change their problematic behaviors.

Bonnie E. Carlson

See also Battered Women; Batterers, Personality Characteristics of; National Crime Victimization Survey; National Family Violence Survey; National Violence Against Women Survey; Prevalence; Risk Assessment Instruments, Intimate Partner Violence; Substance Abuse

Further Readings

Barnett, O. W. (2001). Why battered women do not leave. Part 1: External inhibiting factors within society. *Trauma, Violence, & Abuse, 1,* 343–372.

Barnett, O. W. (2001). Why battered women do not leave. Part 2: External inhibiting factors—social support and internal inhibiting factors. *Trauma, Violence, & Abuse, 2,* 3–35.

Jasinski, J. L., & Williams, L. M. (Eds.). (1998). *Partner violence: A comprehensive review of 20 years of research.* Thousand Oaks, CA: Sage.

Tjaden, P., & Thoennes, N. (2000). *Extent, nature, and consequences of intimate partner violence.* Washington, DC: U.S. Department of Justice, Office of Justice Programs.

INTIMATE TERRORISM

Abusive behavior within violent relationships is heterogeneous and likely differs with respect to etiology, course, mutuality, and severity. This has resulted in researchers and clinicians postulating various subtypes or categories of violent relationships. For example, while some violent relationships are characterized by both partners perpetrating infrequent use of less severe forms of violence, others are characterized by one-sided battering with the goal of physically and psychologically subduing the victim. The method of intervention and the processes underlying these two scenarios likely differ substantially. Thus, understanding the characteristics of specific types of violence may be crucial for effective intervention in which treatment can be adapted to the needs of each group.

Michael Johnson and his colleagues reviewed qualitative and quantitative research and posited that couple violence in families takes one of two distinct forms—situational couple violence (previously labeled common couple violence) or intimate terrorism (previously labeled patriarchal terrorism). The motivation to control one's partner is the primary variable distinguishing these two groups. Unlike those experiencing situational couple violence, whose aggression is likely a response to a specific event or stressor, intimate terrorists' desire to control results in continuous destructive abuse that takes many forms.

Intimate terrorists go to extreme measures to dominate their partners through intimidation created by threatened and actual violence, forced isolation from others, and economic or other types of dependency. The purpose of these dehumanizing and harmful acts is to force their victims into submission and powerlessness through the loss of identity and self-esteem. Their aggression, which is commonly fueled by a desire to increase control and/or a desire to manifest their control over their partner, often escalates in intensity in an effort to extract more convincing signs of obedience. Intimate terrorists, who typically believe in patriarchy, often maintain that it is their right to control "their" women whom they regard as "property." In the spectrum of domestic violence, intimate terrorists are the most extreme, engaging in highly destructive predatory practices.

Johnson has argued that violence perpetrated by intimate terrorists is frequent, severe, and potentially injurious in nature, primarily initiated by the male partner, and rarely involves violence in self-defense by the victim. Fortunately, intimate terrorism is less prevalent than situational couple violence. His research has demonstrated that, relative to those experiencing situational couple violence, women experiencing intimate terrorism report greater frequency of violence, physical injury, time off from work, psychological distress, and use of certain drugs. Johnson noted that violence research conducted in shelter and clinical populations typically identifies relationships characterized by intimate terrorism, whereas research conducted with community samples generally reveals relationships characterized by situational couple violence.

Given Johnson's typology, as well as the intimate partner violence classification systems developed by others, it is apparent that the underlying processes and goals of violence perpetration vary by offender or couple. Although some perpetrators may use violence to control their victim (intimate terrorism), others may use violence in response to a stressful situation due to a lack of alternative adaptive coping mechanisms (situational couple violence). Thus, a one-size-fits-all conceptualization and treatment approach would likely be less effective than individually tailored treatments. For example, couple counseling is likely to be dangerous and contraindicated for those experiencing intimate terrorism, but may be appropriate for some couples experiencing situational couple violence. Despite the potentially useful treatment implications of Johnson's typology, other classification systems should also be considered when developing treatment programs for violent perpetrators. Researchers have found support for a different set of subtypes of offenders and, in particular, there is evidence from Johnson and others that there are likely more than two subtypes of partner violence perpetrators.

Gregory L. Stuart, Jeff R. Temple,
and Richard B. Stuart

See also Expressive Violence; Instrumental Violence; Situational Couple Violence

Further Readings

Holtzworth-Munroe, A., & Stuart, G. L. (1994). Typologies of male batterers: Three subtypes and the differences among them. *Psychological Bulletin, 116,* 476–497.

Johnson, M. P. (1995). Patriarchal terrorism and common couple violence: Two forms of violence against women. *Journal of Marriage and the Family, 57,* 283–294.

Johnson, M. P., & Leone, J. M. (2005). The differential effects of intimate terrorism and situational couple violence: Findings from the National Violence Against Women Survey. *Journal of Family Issues, 26,* 322–349.

Leone, J. M., Johnson, M. P., Cohan, C. L., & Lloyd, S. E. (2004). Consequences of male partner violence for low-income minority women. *Journal of Marriage and the Family, 66,* 472–490.

Stuart, R. B. (2005). Treatment for partner abuse: Time for a paradigm shift. *Professional Psychology: Research and Practice, 36,* 254–263.

INVESTIGATIVE INTERVIEWING OF CHILDREN

Investigative interviewing of children has unique characteristics as an assessment technique. First, its goal is to elicit accurate information from children about specific upsetting events. These events include directly experienced child abuse and trauma, as well as witnessed startling or traumatic events. Second, investigative interviewers use methods of inquiry as open-ended as possible to obtain a narrative from children about the events in question. Finally, in most states, investigative interviews are conducted by mandated professionals—law enforcement officers and child protection caseworkers.

Historical Context of Investigative Interviewing

Investigative interviewing evolved in response to reports made to child protection agencies of child sexual abuse. Reports of physical abuse and physical neglect, as a rule, are resolved by examining the child's condition and/or the child's environment. In cases of physical abuse, a medical professional determines whether the type, pattern, and explanation of the child's injuries indicate they are inflicted or perhaps accidental. Physical neglect generally is investigated by examining the child's living situation to determine if shelter, food, and supervision are adequate, and the child's person to see if the child's height, weight, and general physical health are within normal limits.

Sexual abuse, in contrast, usually doesn't result in definitive physical evidence, and when there is genital or anal injury, it quickly resolves, typically before the child is taken for a medical exam. Consequently, professionals must rely on other means for determining whether sexual abuse has occurred. Because offenders and even nonoffending family members commonly deny sexual abuse, the child's statements and behavior constitute the best source of information about the likelihood of sexual abuse. In recent years, the investigative interviewing methods developed for sexual abuse have been applied to cases involving physical abuse and cases where children witness a traumatic event, such as domestic violence and homicide.

Rationale for Special Investigative Interview Techniques

Fact gathering is a practice employed in all child maltreatment cases. Children's reports of sexual abuse, however, have been challenged in terms of their accuracy. One reason for such challenges is that, for most people, it is difficult to contemplate an adult engaging in sexual abuse of a child. However, the most vigorous challengers of children's accounts have been those accused of sexual abuse and their advocates. Moreover, research has demonstrated that preschool children are more suggestible than older children and that all children can be overly compliant with authority figures and adults; these child characteristics could lead to an inaccurate report.

Concerns about children's accuracy also have led to scrutiny of the interview techniques of the fact-gathering professionals as a possible source of false accusations of sexual abuse. This scrutiny has influenced the types of questions and other interview techniques that professionals use when conducting investigative interviews.

Specific Strategies Employed in Investigative Interviewing

In this section, guidelines for investigative interviews will be described: number of interviews, interview phasing, demonstrative communication aids, and understanding the scope of abuse. Dozens of protocols have been developed. These guidelines will focus on commonalities among protocols.

Number of Interviews

Most children receive a single interview, but prevailing professional opinion is that additional interviews should be conducted if needed to resolve the question of sexual abuse. The use of a single interview is driven largely by the volume of reports and consequent pressure on scarce investigative resources. The single interview practice also derives from concerns that interviewers unwittingly could program children to provide a false account over several interviews.

Phases of the Interview

Investigative interviews are intended to have phases, at minimum a beginning, a middle, and an end. Presently there are interview protocols advising three to nine phases. In actuality, interviewers may find it difficult to follow a phased approach because interviewers are also admonished to follow the child's lead.

The Beginning Phase

In the beginning phase, the interviewer explains his or her role in a way the child can understand and may set rules and expectations for the interview, such as telling the truth during the interview and not guessing at answers to questions. The interviewer also attempts, by various means, to develop rapport with the child and ascertain the child's ability to describe past events, knowledge of his or her environment, and capacity to communicate.

Transition to the Abuse-Related Phase

The transition from the beginning phase to the middle or abuse-related phase of the interview is sometimes challenging. If the alleged abuse is recent, the interviewer may say, "Now that we've gotten to know each other, tell me why you came to talk to me," or "I understand something may have happened to you. Tell me about it as best you can." If the alleged abuse is more remote and/or less salient, the interviewer will need to employ more closed-ended questions.

The Abuse-Related Phase

During the abuse-related phase, the interviewer attempts to gather information to help determine if the child has been sexually abused, or if there is some other explanation for the report. The level of concern about sexual abuse will vary based upon information in the report. This information usually will guide the interviewer's inquiry.

Despite reliance on background information, the goal of the abuse-related phase of the interview is to gather information from the child, not to ask the child to affirm information already known. Best practice is to use probes and questions as open-ended as possible—for example, "Tell me all about what happened to you"—and use follow-up prompts such as "Anything else?" and "Then what happened?" If the interviewer must use more closed-ended questions, such as "Did you get hurt?" or "Has someone touched you?" the interviewer will have less confidence in information the child provides. Furthermore, if the child provides an affirmative response to such closed-ended questions, the interviewer should follow up with an open-ended probe; for example, "Tell me everything you can remember about the touching, from the beginning, to the middle, to the end."

After the interviewer has gained as much information as seems possible using open-ended probes, the interviewer asks follow-up questions to gather details, so that "who," "what," "when," and "where" information is ascertained. The interviewer will also want to gather sensorimotor details about the sexual acts. The purpose of gathering details is twofold; detail will help the interviewer decide about the likelihood of sexual abuse, and detail should furnish information the prosecutor needs to make criminal charging decisions.

The Closure Phase

When the interviewer thinks all information related to the abuse has been gathered, he or she commences the closure phase, perhaps by saying, "I think we're about done." Closure may include letting the child know what will happen next, calming the child if the child is upset, and praising or thanking the child for participation in the interview.

Demonstrative Communication

Because children may lack verbal communication skills or may be reluctant or distressed when asked to respond verbally, the interviewer may employ demonstrative communication modes. These can include drawing pictures, demonstrating with a dollhouse, writing responses, or employing body maps—for instance, anatomical dolls, anatomical drawings, or a "gingerbread" body outline. When these communication modes are employed, the interviewer is not interpreting play, but rather asking the child to demonstrate acts by saying, for example, "Show me with the dolls what happened to you," or "Can you mark on the man drawing the part or parts that Mr. Jones used to hurt you?"

Scope of the Abuse

Many children experience multiple acts of abuse. In such circumstances, interviewers try to determine approximate duration and frequency. Because of difficulties providing precise numbers, interviewers are advised to ask young children, "Did the abuse happen one time or more than one time?" With older children, interviewers may say, "Tell me how often he abused you," or "Did he abuse you about once a week, once a month, or how often?" Because most children have difficulty describing every event in detail, a good practice is to ask, "Tell me about the last time the abuse happened." The interviewer might also ask about the most memorable instance and the first time. In addition, interviewers probe to see if the child knows if the offender has abused other children and whether anyone else has sexually abused the child. Finally, some protocols call for queries about other types of maltreatment and parental problems such as substance abuse, domestic violence, and criminal activity.

The Role of Mandated Professionals

State child protection and criminal statutes mandate to child protection workers and law enforcement primary responsibility for investigating sexual and other types of abuse. Consequently these professionals usually conduct investigatory interviews. In some jurisdictions, however, Children's Advocacy Center forensic interviewers or mental health professionals also conduct investigative interviews.

Many states also require child protection and law enforcement professionals to do joint investigations of sexual abuse. How these joint endeavors are structured varies by jurisdiction, but these professionals have different roles. Child safety and well-being are primary mandates of child protective services (CPS). Investigating crimes, including sex crimes and other serious maltreatment, is the mandate of law enforcement. Differences in mandates can make joint investigation challenging.

Because both CPS and law enforcement may lack specific training in interviewing and assessment, investigative interviewing guidelines have added importance. Their potential lack of expertise is a rationale for scripting investigative interviews.

Protocols and Nondisclosure

Investigative interview protocols propose ideal interviews. In reality, many children cannot provide a narrative and need to be asked a fair number of closed-ended questions. In addition, protocols emphasize techniques that guard against eliciting fictitious reports of abuse. Research indicates about 60% of children thought to have been sexually abused make disclosures during investigative interviews. Little guidance is available for assisting children who do not readily disclose, although research from a variety of sources indicates nondisclosure of actual abuse is a larger problem than fictitious reports.

Kathleen Coulborn Faller

See also Child Protective Services; Child Sexual Abuse; Investigative Interviewing of Child Sexual Abuse Victims

Further Readings

American Professional Society on the Abuse of Children. (1997). *Guidelines for psychosocial evaluation of suspected sexual abuse in children* (2nd ed.). Available at http://www.APSAC.org

American Professional Society on the Abuse of Children. (2002). *Guidelines on investigative interviewing in cases of alleged child abuse.* Available at http://www .APSAC.org

Bourg, W., Broderick, R., Flagor, R., Kelly, D., Ervin, D., & Butler, J. (1999). *A child interviewer's guidebook.* Thousand Oaks, CA: Sage.

Davies, D., Cole, J., Albertella, G., McCulloch, L., Allen, K., & Kekevian, L. (1996). A model for conducting forensic interviews with child victims of abuse. *Child Maltreatment, 1*(2), 189–199.

Faller, K. C. (2003). *Understanding and assessing child sexual maltreatment* (2nd ed.). Thousand Oaks, CA: Sage.

Poole, D., & Lamb, M. (1998). *Investigative interviews of children.* Washington, DC: American Psychological Association.

INVESTIGATIVE INTERVIEWING OF CHILD SEXUAL ABUSE VICTIMS

Child sexual abuse is a complex problem that is difficult to investigate because unlike cases of physical abuse or neglect, it is typically not determined from a medical examination or through the interviewing of eyewitnesses. The interview with the child complainant is a critical component in any criminal or child protection sexual abuse investigation. The investigator must be skilled at interviewing techniques that maximize details without leading the child. Investigative interviewing protocols (also termed frameworks) guide the interviewer through the steps and stages of the interview process and are designed to obtain detailed statements from children while minimizing suggestibility. Interviewers must have knowledge in the area of child development, especially with respect to memory and language, and an understanding of the dynamics involved in sexual abuse.

Historical Context

The focus on child sexual abuse awareness in the 1980s resulted in a significant increase in the number of disclosures investigated by child protection and police authorities. As these cases moved through the child protection and criminal justice systems, the debate flourished with respect to the reliability of children to report sexual abuse and whether or not they were highly suggestible. In the late 1980s there were several high-profile sexual abuse prosecutions involving preschool-age children that highlighted the problems that result from interviewer bias, suggestive interviewing techniques, and the use of interview aids such as anatomically correct dolls. The notion that children do not lie about being sexually abused was challenged, raising questions about the reliability of children's memory and conditions that could influence children to make a false statement. Research studies revealed that children are highly suggestible if they are young and subjected to repeated coercive questioning by adults. This led to the development of interview protocols that addressed concerns related not only to children's suggestibility, but also to their memory and language skills. It is now understood that children can remember as accurately as adults, but they typically recall fewer details. The goal of an investigative interview is to obtain as much factual information as possible given the child's age, stage of development, and functioning.

Interview Context

Child sexual abuse is a criminal act that is seldom witnessed by others. Children often find it difficult to disclose sexual abuse for a number of reasons, including the shame they feel, the belief they are to blame, the fear of rejection from others, the need to protect the abuser or other family members, and the difficulty they have describing the abuse, as well as because they have been warned not to tell. These issues can impact the timing of the disclosure and the quality of the details. For example, it is not uncommon for a child to disclose fewer details at the outset of an investigation than during subsequent interviews, during therapy, or at a trial. Conversely, recantation can be influenced by postdisclosure factors such as the reactions of family members, the abuser, and child protection systems.

Child sexual abuse investigations are done for two purposes: to determine if a crime has occurred and if a child is in need of protection. Joint police and child protection investigations are the preferred practice and typically conducted by a child protection worker and police officer. In some jurisdictions, Child Advocacy Center forensic interviewers conduct the investigative interview.

Investigative Interviewing Protocols

Investigative interview protocols are designed to address suggestibility. Prior to the interview being conducted, investigators should have considered all the possible reasons for why the report has been made (alternative hypotheses) and gathered as much background information as possible to inform the interview. It is common practice to videotape child interviews, thereby allowing for an evaluation of the interviewer's skills as well as the details provided by the child.

Number of Interviews, Physical Setting, and Support Persons

Concerns about suggestibility from repeated questioning have led investigators to limit the number of interviews conducted with a child, often to a single interview. A primary interviewer is determined prior to the commencement of the interview to avoid having the child respond to two interviewers. The physical setting of the interview is also considered important, with many jurisdictions having designated interview rooms that are equipped with video cameras and free of distractions such as toys or electronics that might make it hard to focus the child on the interview. The preferred practice is to interview the child without a support person present. If a support person is necessary, that person should be situated behind the child and in the full view of the video camera.

Steps in the Investigative Interview Process

Introductions and initial rapport building set the stage for the interview and orient the child to the interviewer's job. Typically a "truth and lies ceremony" comes next, as courts in some jurisdictions require that the child demonstrates an understanding of the difference between a truth and a lie. This is followed by ground rules that help explain the child's right to say "I don't know," "I don't remember," or "I don't understand" and encourage the child to correct the interviewer as necessary. Further rapport building occurs through asking the child to recall an event in his or her life and include as much detail as possible about that event. This exercise is an important element of an interview because it helps the interviewers to know the quantity and quality of details a child can give about a nontraumatic event. It also gives the child practice in answering open-ended questions (questions that don't include the answer) and helps the interviewer better understand the child's language and cognitive abilities. The interviewer should have determined in advance how to introduce the topic of the abuse allegation in the least suggestive manner as possible. In the event the child discloses abuse, the interviewer encourages the child to provide as much detail as possible about the abuse by asking open-ended questions and allowing for a free narrative. Once the child has given as many details as possible, questioning and clarification of the information provided can be more focused. The most reliable information comes from the child's free narrative (where the child talks uninterrupted) and answers to nonleading questions (questions that do not suggest answers). The closure of the interview is designed to answer any

questions the child may have about what will happen and to end on a neutral topic.

Maureen Reid and Rhonda Hallberg

See also Child Protection Services; Child Sexual Abuse; Investigative Interviewing of Children

Further Readings

American Professional Society on the Abuse of Children. (1997). *Guidelines for psychosocial evaluation of suspected sexual abuse in children* (2nd ed.). Available at http://www.APSAC.org

American Professional Society on the Abuse of Children. (2002). *Guidelines on investigative interviewing in cases of alleged child abuse*. Available at http://www.APSAC.org

Ceci, S., & Bruck, M. (1999). *Jeopardy in the courtroom*. Washington, DC: American Psychological Association.

Pool, D., & Lamb, M. (1998). *Investigative interviews of children*. Washington, DC: American Psychological Association.

INVESTIGATIVE INTERVIEWING OF OFFENDERS

The investigative interviewing of offenders is, arguably, the most important aspect of a criminal investigation. It allows law enforcement the opportunity to gather information from people who have or may have knowledge needed in the investigation. Interviewing and interrogating are often confused with each other, though major differences exist. *Interviewing* may be defined as the process of obtaining information from individuals who might possess information about a particular offense, as part of the process of investigation. *Interrogation,* on the other hand, is where information acquired through the investigation is matched to a specific suspect in order to secure a confession.

To succeed in interviewing potential suspects, a person needs a number of advantageous personal characteristics. For instance, an interviewer needs to control the interview in a surreptitious fashion, that is, control the events taking place during the interview in a manner that could lead to the gleaning of new information. Establishing rapport, asking good questions, and listening carefully are elements needed for a successful interview.

An effective interviewer must be both knowledgeable and skilled in psychology, acting, and sales ability. Persuasiveness and perseverance are mandatory for success. The interviewer must appear friendly, the type of person who is easy to talk with. The interviewer can accomplish this by using vocal inflection and modulation as an actor does, with emphasis placed on his or her body language; that is, the interviewer looks, talks, and acts like a "nice" person. The interviewer needs the ability to exhibit empathy, sympathy, anger, fear, and joy at various times (even if he or she does not feel the emotion). For the interview to be successful, the interviewer must be knowledgeable regarding the facts of the case, as well as the individuals involved. If the interviewer is shoddy in his or her preparation, a criminal could escape unscathed. If the interview is to be conducted with a witness other than the victim, the interviewer should find out as much as possible about the witness before the interview takes place. The interviewer should know the victim's background, lifestyle, and the nature of the injury or loss—as much information as possible in order to solve the crime. In terms of questioning potential suspects, the interviewer should have as much personal information about the individual as possible.

A good interviewer must be able to ferret out useful information from the witnesses and/or suspects of the crime. For instance, information may still be affected by other factors that influence all witnesses, such as age, physical characteristics, and emotions. A skilled interviewer would probably interview a talkative witness at the beginning of an investigation, and then compare it with stories given by other witnesses later.

Prior to 1936, interviewers could do almost anything they pleased concerning the extraction of an admission of guilt from a suspect. However, the Supreme Court, in its first decision regarding investigative interviewing, ruled in *Brown v. Mississippi* that a confession gained due to the police exhibiting barbaric behavior toward the accused could not be considered freely given. In the 1960s, in a 5–4 decision, the U.S. Supreme Court wrote in *Miranda v. Arizona* that certain procedures had to be followed by officers when conducting an in-custody interrogation of a suspect. The court specified that prior to interrogation, the suspect must be told that he or she has the right to remain silent, that anything he or she said could and would be used in court against him or her, and the right to consult with an attorney prior to answering any questions and to have an attorney present during interrogation, as well as the right to

counsel, so if the suspect could not afford an attorney, the court would appoint one.

The questions an interviewer asks should not be complex; rather, they should be short, direct, and confined to one topic. Deception is often difficult to detect, but a skilled interviewer/interrogator can spot verbal and nonverbal cues that can be examined to determine whether a suspect is telling the truth or is being deceptive. Moreover, what works in one interview may not work in another, so a fair measure of common sense is needed when using a specific approach.

The emotional approach may be used if the interrogator hopes to appeal to the suspect's sense of respect, ethics, and/or righteousness. Using sympathy allows the suspect a way out of his or her dilemma, and is used often because it is effective, primarily because the suspect has the opportunity to keep his or her respect. When the interrogator is unsure regarding a suspect's guilt, an indirect approach is often helpful, but only if the examiner has all of the facts. The "Mutt and Jeff" or "good guy/bad guy" approach to interrogation (a staple for crime shows on television) works in some cases. When there is more than one suspect, one may be used against the other, both of whom state they are telling the truth during separate interrogations.

A skilled interviewer realizes that the physical circumstances under which the interview takes place can be critical to the value of the information obtained. Although the comfort of the witness is important, the interviewer should strive to maintain his or her psychological advantage over the interviewee; that is, make sure that the time and place of interview works for the police, not the witness or accused. In addition, possibly the most important feature of a successful interviewer/interrogator is his or her ability to listen. While the interviewer's level of education, training, and experience are all important factors, they are meaningless if the interrogator is a poor listener. What makes for an effective listener? Paying attention to spoken language and body language. Nonverbal language, like facial expression, silence, body positioning, and eye movements, sends messages and a successful interrogator can hear them. These unconscious modes of communication may confirm, obscure, or contradict what is being said.

Cary Stacy Smith and Li-Ching Hung

See also Police, Response to Child Maltreatment; Police, Response to Domestic Violence

Further Readings

Hall, D. (1993). *Survey of criminal law.* New York: Delmar.

Milne, R., & Bull, R. (1999). *Investigative interviewing: Psychology and practice.* New York: Wiley.

Yeschke, C. (2002). *The art of investigative interviewing* (2nd ed.). Burlington, MA: Butterworth-Heinemann.

Zulawski, D. E., & Wicklander, D. E. (2001). *Practical aspects of interview and interrogation* (2nd ed.). Ottawa, ON: CRC Press.

KIDNAPPING

See CHILD ABDUCTIONS, NONFAMILY

KINSHIP CARE

Kinship care refers to the placement of children within the child welfare system with family members or others who have a significant relationship with the children. This term was created when the child welfare system began to formalize family foster care. Historically, families have been the primary source of caring for children when the custodial parent was unable to be the primary caregiver. When biological relatives were unavailable, many communities had informal systems in place to care for children that involved religious community members, neighbors, or friends.

Historical Perspective

Prior to the advent of formal, government run child welfare systems, communities and families responded to children in need. This response was true both in cities and in rural communities as well as in indigenous communities throughout the United States. In many incidents, an informal system through religious organizations was created to care for children in need. Government was much less involved in families' lives, and the responsibility for children tended to rest within the community. In late 19th century America,

the need for assistance in dealing with abandoned or orphaned children was growing, and pressure was put on both state and federal government to create solutions for their care. A formal child welfare system began to be created through the actions of individual states, initially with little federal government involvement. This historical legacy still holds true today, with differing processes and regulations ascribed to foster care dependent on state parameters.

Informal care networks were in place due to the absence of a government system. In addition, many cultures have an inherent value of multiple primary caregivers for children. In Native American languages, it is very common to have the same word for mother refer to aunts. The same can be said for father and uncle. Within these cultures, the creation of a government run foster care system that utilized trained strangers may have actually created harm and dislocation for these communities. Many in the Native American communities and the African American communities feel they have been victimized by the government run foster care structure.

The last 30 years of the 20th century brought the formalized foster care debate to the forefront. Native Americans along with other minority communities began to speak out about their children being placed in foster homes of other races and cultures. In 1978, the U.S. government passed the Indian Child Welfare Act in which one of the principal tenets was that Native American children must be placed with their family or with their tribal communities. Child welfare practice began to also focus on children of color, and it became standard social work practice to place minority children in minority homes. This philosophy carried through to adoptive homes selection and resulted in large numbers of children of color waiting for minority homes for both foster care and adoption.

The U.S. Congress addressed the "waiting children" issue in 1997, bypassing legislation making identification of race in placing children in the child welfare system against the law. This legislation does not affect those Native American children covered under the Indian Child Welfare Act, where family and tribal home placements are required. Congress further legislated in the 1990s the need for child welfare systems to find and assess family and kin for child placements. Thus, states began to create processes for relative and kinship searching for the children in the child welfare system as well as strategies for licensure.

Current Practices in Government

Since the child welfare system is a joint regulation between the federal and state government, kinship foster care's structure is unique to each locality. By the very nature of the label foster care, kin placements are usually licensed (assessed and/or regulated) in some fashion and often paid. Some states have a separate process for kinship foster care with differing license requirements and separate payment schemes. Some states offer no separate payment and require families caring for children to apply for a "relative only" welfare payment. Still others have incorporated the kinship foster care into their state run foster care system with the same licensing requirements and the same payment schemes as any other foster care situation.

States With Separate Schemes

States with separate processes and payment schemes tend to have capped budgetary restraints with these relative care payments. These systems usually run out of payment monies prior to the end of a budget cycle. These systems tend to have less regulation when it comes to licensing of homes; therefore, designated kin do not need to adhere to the higher standard of foster care.

States With Little Involvement

These states place children with relatives without a separate foster care payment. The relative is usually allowed to apply for the state's welfare payment system. There are usually no licensing requirements for relatives in these situations. Children may be placed in less than ideal conditions, and the state may never be aware of the issues due to the lack of regulation.

States With Foster Care Licensing

These states do not treat relative and kin homes differently from regular nonrelated homes. The relative foster home must be licensed, and payments are the same as any other home. It is a highly regulated system; however, children are usually at less risk for further abuse in families since the regulation may eliminate suspect environments. The disadvantage is that some relatives may not be able to obtain a foster care license and, therefore, are not allowed to care for their children.

Current Child Welfare Practice

The profession of child welfare has begun to focus on the importance of relative and kin placements for children in the system. The federal government audits child welfare systems and has begun to track the percentage of relative placements. Research has supported that children's well-being is enhanced by placing them with family. Natural cultural systems are now respected as being capable of child caring. Family group conferencing arose out of the relative placement debate within the indigenous communities of Australia. Through a family gathering when children are put into the system, the child's family decides who and how the children will be cared for.

Timothy Brett Zuel

See also Adoption and Safe Families Act of 1997; American Humane Association; Child Protective Services; Culturally Sensitive Intervention; Family Group Conferencing; Foster Care

Further Readings

Berrick, J. D., Barth, R. P., & Needell, B. (1994). A comparison of kinship foster homes and foster family homes: Implications for kinship foster care as family preservation. *Children and Youth Services Review, 16*(1–2), 33–63.

Chipman, R., Wells, S. J., & Johnson, M. A. (2002). The meaning of quality in kinship foster care: Caregiver, child, and worker perspectives. *Families in Society, 83*(5), 508–520.

Gibbs, P., & Muller, U. (2000). Kinship foster care: Moving to the mainstream: Controversy, policy, and outcomes. *Adoption Quarterly, 4*(2), 57–87.

LEARNED HELPLESSNESS

Learned helplessness is the acquisition of the belief that attempting to escape from a negative situation is futile due to a previous situation in which escape was not possible. It is learning that nothing an individual does will affect what will happen to him or her, and, therefore, the individual does nothing to escape from the situation. Symptoms of learned helplessness include passivity, anxiety, depression, increased health problems, lower self-esteem, lack of motivation, and a general disinterest in life.

Learned helplessness has been used to explain the sense of loss of control that is reported by some victims of repeated instances of interpersonal violence. The battered woman who is abused repeatedly and unpredictably may begin to believe that her actions are futile in preventing violence. Similarly, children may develop beliefs of learned helplessness when abuse is administered in ways that are not contingent on their actions.

In a classic learned helplessness study, Seligman and Maier placed dogs in one of three conditions. Dogs in the escape group received shocks that they were able to terminate by pressing a panel with their nose. Each dog in this condition was paired with (yoked to) a dog in the inescapable condition. Dogs in the inescapable condition received the same shocks as the escape group, but they were unable to terminate the shocks. Rather, the shocks would end only when the "yoked" dog in the first group pressed the panel. Dogs in the control condition did not receive any shocks. Twenty-four hours later the dogs were placed in a shuttle box. In this new situation, the dogs had to learn to jump over the barrier during a period of darkness to escape being shocked. The escape group and the control group quickly learned how to avoid the shocks. However, 6 of the 8 dogs in the inescapable group made no effort to escape the shocks. Since the escape group and the yoked group both received the same shocks, the researchers concluded that it was the uncontrollable nature of the shocks that caused the helplessness rather than the trauma of being shocked. The dogs in the inescapable condition initially learned that they did not have any control over the situation; this lack of control later impaired their ability to learn how to control a subsequent situation.

Researchers have found that in situations in which there is no contingency between responses and outcomes, some individuals learn that control is not possible and therefore stop trying to control the situation. Researchers suggest that the perception of lack of control in one situation is not necessarily sufficient for learned helplessness to be displayed in another situation. According to the revised learned helplessness theory, how an individual explains the causes (explanatory theory) of the initial lack of control influences the likelihood of learned helplessness. The cause may be due to something about the person (internal) or due to something about the situation (external). The cause may be a factor that remains stable across time, or it may change over time. The cause may occur in a variety of situations (global), or it may be limited to a specific situation. Individuals who make global and stable attributions are more likely to view future events as uncontrollable. Individuals who rely heavily on stable, global, and internal attributions are more likely to experience depressive episodes when negative events occur.

Motivational and cognitive deficits associated with learned helplessness may create a self-perpetuating cycle of helplessness. Individuals who believe that their responses will have no impact on the outcomes are less likely to initiate new responses (ones that have the potential to end the helplessness). Cognitive deficits may prevent an individual from understanding that if the situation changes, a change in contingency will also take place.

Lisa M. Bauer

See also Battered Women: Leaving Violent Intimate
    Relationships; Learned Optimism; Sibling Abuse

Further Readings

Palker-Corell, A., & Marcus, D. K. (2004). Partner abuse, learned helplessness, and trauma symptoms. *Journal of Social & Clinical Psychology, 23,* 445–465.

Peterson, C., & Seligman, M. E. P. (1983). Learned helplessness and victimization. *Journal of Social Issues, 2,* 103–116.

Seligman, M. E. P., & Maier, S. F. (1967). Failure to escape traumatic shock. *Journal of Experimental Psychology, 74,* 1–9.

Walker, L. E. (1979). *The battered woman.* New York: Harper and Row.

LEARNED OPTIMISM

Learned optimism is the acquisition of a set of cognitive beliefs that allow situations to be interpreted in a positive manner. According to Martin Seligman, individuals interpret situations in terms of permanence, pervasiveness, and personalization. An event can remain stable across time (permanent) or change over time (temporary). The cause of the event may occur in a variety of situations (global), or it may be specific to the current event. Personalization refers to the focus of the blame. It can either be the individual's fault (internal) or due to someone else or to circumstances (external). People who exhibit optimism are likely to interpret positive events (successes) as permanent, global, and internal whereas negative events (or failures) are likely to be interpreted as temporary, specific, and

external. Pessimists, on the other hand, believe that the causes of negative events are permanent, global, and internal. The difference between optimists and pessimists lies within how a situation is interpreted.

Research suggests that individuals with a pessimistic explanatory style who experience negative events are more likely to become depressed than individuals with a more optimistic style. Research also suggests that optimists are more resilient, more successful at work and at school, and are in better physical health than pessimists. Thus, according to this theory, changing one's outlook on life could significantly impact one's life.

According to Seligman, individuals can learn how to interpret negative events in an optimistic explanatory style, thereby permanently improving the quality of their lives. With this approach, an individual can learn to be an optimist by learning a set of cognitive skills that should be implemented when a setback occurs and the cost of failure is low. Seligman suggests that individuals be taught how to see the connection between adversity (a situation), beliefs (how the situation is interpreted), and consequences (behavior). He states that if individuals can change their maladaptive beliefs, then their ability to cope and their behavior will change. The most effective way to change beliefs is through disputation. Here, an individual examines the support for his or her belief, the alternatives, the implications, and the usefulness of his or her beliefs. This examination allows an individual to change his or her normal pessimistic reaction to a reaction that motivates the individual to master the challenges of life. New experiences can then be interpreted through these cognitive skills.

Seligman believes that an optimistic explanatory style is important in everyday events. Research has shown that learned optimism reduces depression and can lead to increases in productivity, achievement, health, marital satisfaction, and political victories.

Lisa M. Bauer

See also Learned Helplessness

Further Readings

Gillham, J. E. (Ed.). (2000). *The science of optimism and hope: Research essays in honor of Martin E. P. Seligman.* Philadelphia: Templeton Foundation Press.

Seligman, M. E. P. (1990). *Learned optimism: How to change your mind and your life.* New York: Vintage Books.

LEGAL ISSUES IN THE TREATMENT OF SEXUAL AND DOMESTIC VIOLENCE

There are two key legal issues related to the treatment of sexual and domestic violence: privacy and record keeping. This entry addresses privacy rights and laws, including the Health Insurance Portability and Accountability Act (HIPAA); disclosures in the legal process; releases; informed consent; and privacy rights for children. This entry also discusses issues and concerns associated with providers' record keeping, including the safety of others, mandatory reporting laws, providers serving as witnesses, family law proceedings, and professional liability.

Privacy

Privacy rights exist as a matter of constitutional, statutory, and/or common law. Privacy laws can vary from state to state and from state law to federal law. Some jurisdictions offer more privacy protection to treatment providers with certain levels of education, training, and licensure. All jurisdictions offer at least some protection.

Confidentiality as an aspect of privacy law refers to the promise made to a victim by a treatment provider and the corresponding duty of nondisclosure. Privilege as an aspect of privacy law refers to the rule of evidence that insulates information from disclosure in litigation. Confidential information is not always protected by a rule of privilege. Privileges can be created by statute, constitution, or common law.

The extent to which privileges and privacy rights provide resistance to compel disclosure of treatment information in litigation is affected by the authority of the requestor to seek disclosure as balanced against the weight of the privacy interest. Examples of information covered by privacy rights and privilege laws include a patient's or client's name and address, HIV status, drug and alcohol treatment records, sexually transmitted diseases, medical and psychological treatment records, sexual history, sexual orientation and other personal matters, and communications to certain individuals such as a medical or psychological treatment provider, a spouse, a religious counselor, an attorney, or a sexual assault or domestic violence counselor.

Privacy and Health Insurance Portability and Accountability Act

The HIPAA imposes certain federal restrictions on the gathering and release of treatment-related information. HIPAA applies only to health plans, health care clearinghouses, and health providers that transmit information electronically. State laws can provide more privacy protections than HIPAA, but not less. In general, treatment-related information cannot be used or disclosed without informed consent from the patient or client. Psychotherapy notes are entitled to additional protections and cannot be used or disclosed without explicit authorization from the patient or client.

Privacy and the Legal Process

Treatment-related information can be subject to disclosure in the legal process, though not all types of legal proceedings afford litigants the same weight of authority to seek or compel disclosure. Most courts recognize that people who seek mental health care are not less credible as witnesses in court proceedings than people who never seek mental health care. Still, cultural biases and historical stereotypes related to the credibility of women and mental health treatment in particular can foster a disproportionate willingness on the part of judges to allow disclosure of victims' treatment records in litigation.

Certain types of litigation justify board disclosure of treatment records. For example, in civil litigation where the patient or client has filed a lawsuit to recover compensation for injuries reflected in treatment records, disclosure is usually necessary because emotional or psychological injuries are relevant and admissible. Treatment records can assist the court in developing a full understanding of the value of the patient's or client's harm.

Civil cases usually occur between private persons, and parties to the litigation can conduct discovery by issuing subpoenas or summonses not only to each other, but also to nonparties, such as victims and treatment providers. Subpoenas or summonses can be used to uncover not only relevant evidence, but also evidence that might lead to the discovery of relevant evidence.

Criminal cases, by contrast, are initiated by the government against an individual for the purpose of punishing and deterring public wrongdoing. Discovery occurs only between the government or prosecutor and the accused or defendant. The crime victim is a witness for the prosecution, not a party to the case. Defendants in criminal litigation generally cannot send subpoenas or summonses to conduct discovery against victims, witnesses, and other nonparties.

Because the power to issue pretrial subpoenas or summonses in criminal cases is far more limited than in civil cases, a treatment provider who receives a subpoena or summons should make an initial determination as to whether the litigation is criminal or civil in nature. If a subpoena or summons is issued without lawful authority, the treatment provider need not comply, but should notify the court and seek legal advice to determine whether redress against the issuing party is appropriate.

Even when issued in a civil case by a party with lawful authority, a subpoena or summons is generally considered insufficient to justify privileged or confidential material, such as treatment-related information, because a subpoena or summons does not necessarily require the approval of a judge. Without the approval of a judge, there was no need for a due process hearing to balance the privacy rights of the patient or client against the authority of the requestor to seek disclosure.

A court order signed by a judge is generally a stronger form of process than a subpoena or summons, and it usually indicates that a due process hearing was held after which a decision was made that disclosure was necessary. If a court order is issued without a due process hearing, it may be appropriate for the treatment provider or patient or client to ascertain whether proper legal standards were met before the court order was issued.

The holder of private information generally has a legal and ethical obligation to resist unlawful efforts to compel disclosure. Failure to abide this obligation can expose the holder to liability and ethical or licensing sanctions.

When treatment-related information must be released in connection with a legal proceeding, providers can assess whether the request is overbroad or unduly burdensome. For example, unless the treatment itself is a key issue in dispute, it would likely be deemed overbroad if a court order sought disclosure of "any and all treatment records related to Jane Doe" because this language contains no time or subject matter limitations.

Because process notes and whole treatment files are not verbatim transcripts, they can be unclear, misleading, and unhelpful to the interests of justice if information is taken out of context or assumptions are made about the meaning of certain words and phrases. Treatment providers can offer as an alternative the option of a prepared summary of treatment-related information responsive to a particular litigation need.

Treatment providers can take steps to redact irrelevant information related to the patient or client and third parties such as family members and friends. Treatment providers can request that all material be returned to the care provider at the conclusion of the legal proceeding and that no copies be retained in the litigation or court files. Privacy rights may survive the death of the patient or client depending on the jurisdiction.

Privacy and Releases

It may be appropriate to disclose treatment-related information if a signed release is received from the patient or client. A signed release may be considered inadequate if it is not reasonably clear regarding the nature of information to be divulged or if it is not signed near in time to the moment of disclosure. Prior to disclosure, a treatment provider should ascertain that at the time the release is signed, the patient or client (a) has proper legal capacity, (b) is not under duress or subject to coercion at the time the release is signed, and (c) has been made aware of the likely consequences of disclosure. In some jurisdictions, the care provider can resist disclosure even after a release is signed if revealing certain information would prove harmful to the patient or client.

Privacy and Informed Consent

Treatment providers are required to inform patients or clients of the nature and extent of treatment offered and the limits and likely consequences thereof at the outset of care. This information should be sufficient to enable the patient or client to make a reasoned decision about treatment.

Treatment providers are required to inform patients or clients of the nature and extent of privacy protections at the outset of care. This information includes advising the patient or client regarding the limits of confidentiality and the policies and procedures employed by the caregiver in the event disclosure becomes necessary or a request for disclosure is received.

Treatment providers should advise victims at the outset of care that disclosure of information shared during the treatment process can lead to a waiver of privacy rights.

Treatment providers can inform patients or clients involved in litigation that they have a right to refuse to answer probing irrelevant questions asked of them during the investigative or litigation process.

Privacy and Children

Privacy rights for children vary from state to state. In general, children's privacy rights are not entitled to much legal protection, but their rights become stronger as they age toward majority.

Record Keeping

Treatment providers should maintain records sufficient to ensure that the proper standard of care has been met. The primary purpose of record keeping is to record the reflections of the caregiver as a measure of progress in treatment.

Policies and procedures regarding note-taking should be reduced to writing and explicitly address concerns regarding privacy rights, note-taking, and document destruction. For example, a policy can allow for minimal note-taking and swift destruction of certain documents (subject to regulations that may require maintenance of files that establish dates of treatment and other statistically significant information).

Record-keeping policies enable caregivers to respond in summary fashion to requests for disclosure of entire files. For example, if a court order seeks disclosure of "any and all treatment records related to Jane Doe," a treatment provider with a written policy that allows for prompt destruction of records can respond that "files indicate Jane Doe was treated for sexual violence, but treatment records no longer exist as they were destroyed pursuant to standard document destruction policy."

Treatment providers serving as expert witnesses or involved in forensic work, such as sexual assault nurse examiner and sexual assault response team nurses, may use note-taking standards that differ from those employed in direct care and treatment services. Forensic witnesses may record more direct quotes and fewer reflective observations because the purpose of forensic work is not to provide care and treatment, but rather to prepare evidence for use in a legal proceeding.

Safety

Treatment providers should notify law enforcement officials when a patient or client credibly threatens to harm him- or herself or another or faces a risk of serious harm by another. Failure to do so can result in civil liability.

Treatment providers can offer supportive and corroborative information for a patient or client seeking a protective order or other legal intervention. Disclosures of treatment information for these purposes can lead to the public disclosure of treatment information and a determination that privacy rights have been waived.

Mandatory Reporting

In many jurisdictions, treatment providers are obligated to report incidents of sexual and domestic violence to law enforcement officials. Some laws require only statistical information, while others require identifying information. Failure to comply with mandatory reporting laws can lead to civil and criminal liability.

Treatment providers are obligated to report incidents of child abuse and neglect, which includes experiencing and witnessing domestic and sexual violence. In some jurisdictions, treatment providers are obligated to report incidents of elder abuse, which includes elder victims of domestic and sexual violence. Mandatory reporting laws can also include abuse and neglect of disabled and mentally ill individuals and other vulnerable persons in institutional settings and in trust relationships.

Treatment Providers as Witnesses

Treatment providers can serve as witnesses in legal proceedings. Rules regarding the testimony of treatment providers vary according to the type of litigation and the issues legitimately in dispute. In general, a treatment provider must be approved by a court as a qualified expert in a certain field before testimony will be allowed. A provider who has personal knowledge about an issue in dispute can also be a fact witness for which no expert qualifications are necessary.

Family Law

Family law proceedings generally deal with matters of divorce, custody, and visitation. Unlike civil and criminal cases, family court vests much discretion in a single judge. When children are not involved, issues of violence in the marriage may be relevant. Treatment providers can offer testimony regarding the nature and impact of such violence on the issues in dispute. When children are involved, a judge may appoint a guardian ad litem to give general guidance or to specifically investigate certain matters in dispute. For example, a judge can require a guardian to investigate allegations of sexual abuse.

A guardian ad litem may issue a report effectively determining whether allegations of sexual or domestic violence are credible and what impact if any the violence should have on issues in dispute. A guardian can seek assistance in making such determinations from a treatment provider. The judge usually, but not always, follows the opinions and recommendations of the guardian ad litem.

Unlike in civil and criminal cases, a family court judge can apply more flexible standards of evidence admissibility: a treatment provider can usually offer live testimony, an affidavit, and/or a narrative summary report.

Professional Liability

Treatment providers can face professional liability for substandard care in the treatment of sexual and domestic violence victims. Liability can extend to non-licensed volunteer counselors and licensed caregivers employed or volunteering at hospitals and crisis centers, although in many jurisdictions, nonprofit entities and employees or volunteers are either immune from suit or the amount recoverable is capped at a minimal sum.

Wendy J. Murphy

See also Anti-Rape and Rape Crisis Center Movements; Battered Woman Syndrome; Domestic Violence, Trauma, and Mental Health; Expert Testimony; Family Therapy and Family Violence; Feminist Theories of Interpersonal Violence; Investigative Interviewing of Children; Legal System, Criminal Justice System Responses to Intimate Partner Violence; Legal System and Child Protection; Mandatory Reporting Laws of Intimate Partner Violence; Mental Illness; Rape Culture; Rape/Sexual Assault; Rape Trauma Syndrome; Sexual Abuse; Trauma-Focused Therapy; Victims' Rights Movement

Further Readings

American Psychological Association. (2002). *HIPAA for psychologists.* Washington, DC: Author.
Goldman, J., Hudson, R., Hudson, Z., & Sawires, P. (2000). *Health privacy principles for protecting victims of domestic violence.* San Francisco: Family Violence Prevention Fund.
Murphy, W. (1998). Minimizing the likelihood of discovery of victims' counseling records and other personal information in criminal cases: Massachusetts gives a nod to a constitutional right to confidentiality. *New England Law Review, 32*(4). Available at http://www.nesl.edu/lawrev/
Schulhofer, S. (1998). *Unwanted sex: The culture of intimidation and the failure of law.* Cambridge, MA: Harvard University Press.
Summary of New Federal Medical Privacy Protections for Victims of Domestic Violence. (n.d.). Retrieved from http://endabuse.org/programs/display.php3?DocID=56
U.S. Department of Health and Human Services. (2002, August 14). Standards for privacy of individually identifiable health information: Final rule. 45 CFR Parts 160 and 164. *Federal Register,* vol. 67, no. 157 §§ 164.501, 164.502 (g)(1), 164.524 (Regulation Text, Unofficial Version, December 28, 2000, as amended May 31, 2002, August 14, 2002, February 20, 2003, and April 17, 2003). Retrieved April 18, 2006, from http://www.hhs.gov/ocr/combinedregtext.pdf

LEGAL MOMENTUM

Legal Momentum is the oldest nonprofit organization in the United States dedicated to advancing the rights of women and girls by using the power of the law and creating innovative public policy. Founded in 1970 as NOW Legal Defense and Education Fund and renamed in 2004, a principal focus of Legal Momentum's work is eliminating all forms of violence against women: sexual assault, domestic violence, dating violence, and stalking.

Legal Momentum helped drive passage of the historic Violence Against Women Act (VAWA) and leads the efforts to reauthorize this critical legislation. Legal Momentum created and chairs the National Task Force to End Sexual and Domestic Violence Against Women that was instrumental in the drafting and passage of VAWA in 1994 and its 2000 and 2005 re-authorizations. VAWA has secured nearly $9 billion for services for survivors, including immigrant victims, improved law enforcement and prosecution, judicial education, prevention education, and research.

Legal Momentum's Immigrant Women Program (IWP) advocates for legal protections, social services, and economic justice for battered immigrant women while reforming laws, policies, and practices that may harm them. IWP leads a national advocacy campaign that secures access to legal immigration status, benefits, and legal services for thousands of victims of violence against women and foreign fiancées. It conducts trainings for attorneys, advocates, police, prosecutors, and judges to build skills and knowledge that are critical to immigrant women receiving legally correct, culturally competent assistance from professionals in their communities. IWP also paves the way for immigrant women to acquire legal work authorization, housing, child and/or spousal support, and college loans to enhance economic security so that they can escape abusive homes and employers.

Legal Momentum works to ensure that welfare policies recognize and respond to the special needs of domestic violence victims. Women are much more likely to be poor than men are, and a significant percentage of impoverished and homeless women are battered. Their poverty may force women on to the welfare rolls, where federal antidiscrimination laws do apply. Staff attorneys work to ensure that welfare recipients are also protected from violence.

Legal Momentum's staff attorneys focus on employment and housing rights for victims of gender-based violence. Legal Momentum uses targeted litigation, legislative advocacy, and training to protect victims from employment and housing discrimination and help employers and landlords understand how they can assist survivors and promote safety. Legal Momentum has won landmark court decisions holding that employers may not fire domestic violence victims for taking time from work to seek court protection and landlords may not evict victims of domestic violence for "allowing" violence on the premises.

Legal Momentum's National Judicial Education Program (NJEP) promotes gender fairness in judicial decision making and courtroom interaction across the spectrum of civil, criminal, family, and juvenile law. NJEP has available extensive educational materials for judges, prosecutors, law enforcement, forensic sexual assault examiners, advocates, and the community. These written materials, videos, DVDs, and Web-based curricula provide the legal, social science, and medical knowledge necessary to conduct fair rape trials, counter societal myths about nonstranger rape, and respond to the co-occurrence of domestic violence and sexual assault.

Samantha Elena Erskine

See also Battered Women; Dating Violence/Courtship Violence; Immigrant and Migrant Women; Rape/Sexual Assault; Stalking; Violence Against Women Act

Web Sites

Legal Momentum: http://www.legalmomentum.org/

LEGAL SYSTEM, ADVOCACY EFFORTS TO AFFECT, CHILD MALTREATMENT

There are two major types of legal advocacy efforts to affect changes in the legal process related to child maltreatment. The first involves individual, generally court-appointed, legal representation of individual children who are alleged to be victims of child abuse or neglect. The second is the filing (in state or federal court) of child welfare system impact litigation, also known as class action lawsuits. In the former, lawyers will often identify problems faced not only by their current client but also by others they have represented, and they may attempt through motions, briefs, and arguments to convince judges to handle current and future cases in specific ways that will improve the outcomes for their clients, hear and resolve cases more quickly, or involve an exercise of the judge's inherent authority over public agencies responsible for providing services to their child clients (e.g., schools, mental health agencies) to help facilitate delivery of the resources their clients need. Through class actions, attorneys may look, for example, to the federal courts to rectify what they perceive is a large-scale deprivation of the constitutional rights of their child clients and/or their families. In both state and federal court class actions, the lawyers are generally seeking an injunction against unlawful actions and/or a court's declaration (finding) that the law requires, for example, that the child welfare agency or local juvenile court take certain actions. Sometimes, these class action suits also seek financial compensation (damages) for the harm done to their clients by the allegedly unlawful actions of child welfare agencies or others. Many of these cases are settled through agreements known as consent decrees, where there is a commitment by child welfare agencies or others to improve practice and service delivery in certain specified ways and by specified dates. The court will often appoint a monitor and/or review panel to oversee the successful implementation of these decrees.

Individual Case Advocacy

In most states, but not all, when a case involving an abused or neglected child goes to court the child must have an attorney appointed to represent him or her. In some states, the court will appoint a lay (nonlawyer) advocate for the child, who may have the title of guardian ad litem or court-appointed special advocate (CASA). The increasing complexity of the legal or judicial process, the frequent failures of child welfare agencies and other government programs to provide services to children they are legally required to provide, and the ability that only a lawyer has to understand and utilize legal mechanisms to improve the lives of their child clients all point out the critical importance of first-rate legal advocacy. There has been a requirement for many years, as the result of federal law, that juvenile courts only appoint lawyers for children who have received, before any of these appointments are made, appropriate training. The American Bar Association has approved standards of practice for lawyers appointed to represent abused and neglected children that address what should be included in such training, and there are other excellent resources available, in print and online, to help guide attorneys in achieving quality representation of their child clients. One major barrier to quality legal representation of abused and neglected children is where an attorney is responsible for a caseload of too many open court cases and thus has difficulty giving each child and family the individualized attention they need and deserve. It is not unusual for some lawyers to have over 200 or 300 open cases, each awaiting some additional court hearings, child placement changes, permanency plans to be implemented, and so on. If a lawyer is personally responsible for more than 100 children at any given time, effective case representation becomes extraordinarily difficult, if not impossible.

There is widespread agreement on what knowledge an attorney representing an abused or neglected child should have. This knowledge includes the following: an understanding of the causes and consequences of child maltreatment; the different types of and evidence required to prove abuse or neglect, including physical abuse factors, sexual abuse diagnosis, emotional maltreatment, physical and medical neglect, and educational neglect; the short- and long-term mental health aspects of these cases, including evaluations, psychological testing, and the psychiatric commitment process; physical, cognitive, language, social, and emotional child development issues, including the impact on children of attachment, separation, and loss problems; family dynamics in child maltreatment; cultural context issues; the federal and state law framework for child protection; the civil child protection court process and collateral court proceedings that may involve their child client; legal permanency issues; educational and medical care advocacy; confidentiality, privacy, and information sharing; child clients in court, including testimonial competence; rules of evidence regularly applied in child maltreatment cases; nonadversarial case resolution; appellate law and practice; understanding the roles of the other attorneys, CASAs, and case workers; legal ethics in child maltreatment cases; and trial advocacy skills. Representing a child well involves complex, multidisciplinary case components that require the attorney to not only be well versed in the law, but also to understand the roles and responsibilities of personnel in child welfare agencies, schools, mental health programs, and other government programs and services.

Class Action Advocacy

For several decades, individuals and organizations have brought class action lawsuits in which one party or a group of parties sues as representatives of a larger class of individuals. Class action lawsuits have had a major impact on the operation of state and local child protection systems. These lawsuits have often been used as tools to address failures by child welfare agencies to provide adequate services to children and parents and to achieve systemic reform that might otherwise have required legislation or many individual lawsuits. In the 10 years from 1995 to 2005 alone, there was child welfare class action litigation in 32 states, with consent decrees or settlement agreements in 30. The consent decrees in these lawsuits, once approved by the court, in effect become a contract, binding the child welfare agency and the attorneys acting on behalf of the class members to its terms, and they are fully enforceable by the court. The substance of each consent decree describes specific actions defendants must take to resolve the identified problems and the plaintiffs' responsibilities to ensure the provisions in the decree are implemented. These decrees, in decreasing order of frequency, have addressed the following: child placement issues such as recruitment, retention, licensing and training of foster parents, relative placements, and group homes;

protective service issues such as reporting, investigating, and intake; requirements that defendants ensure the provision of certain services to children and their families such as medical, dental, and mental health examinations, parent–child or sibling visitation, and independent living training; requirements that defendants address issues concerning caseworkers such as adequate staffing, maximum caseloads, and enhanced training and supervision; case planning issues such as enhancing numbers of children achieving permanency and/or identified case goals; requirements for some sort of new resource development such as the creation of universal information systems or quality assurance reviews; adoption reform issues; and reforms to the judicial system in civil child protection cases. Most of the class action consent decrees that have been active within the past 10 to 15 years have addressed state failures to properly license and train foster parents; place children in adequate and safe foster and group homes; properly report, investigate, and address abuse and neglect incidents; provide needed medical, dental, and mental health services to foster children; ensure adequate parent–child or sibling visitation; ensure social workers have manageable caseloads, training, and supervision; and provide children and families with adequate case planning and review.

Advocacy Efforts Within Organizations and Agencies

There is an additional form of advocacy for abused and neglected children that does not involve litigation. This advocacy is work done by governmental and nongovernmental agencies and organizations to improve services to children and families and the agency and court process through which such services are provided. Some child welfare agency advocacy efforts are led by ombudsmen, individuals and offices located either independent of or within the service delivery agency. Their role is to solicit, receive, and investigate complaints related to services and interventions for abused and neglected children. Following these investigations, the ombudsman may issue public reports that address and present recommendations for overcoming systemic barriers and other problems that impede prompt and effective delivery of services to maltreated children and their families. Some state legislatures have oversight committees that have similar roles in examining child protection system functions. Many

private nongovernmental agencies and programs are actively involved in addressing systemic improvements for abused and neglected children. These include such well-established and effective organizations as the Child Welfare League of America and the Children's Defense Fund. Many professional organizations have entities that address child protection system reform, such as the Center on Children and the Law within the American Bar Association. Some systemic criticism and highlights of needed reform also come from organizations that have been established specifically to identify and recommend how to address shortcomings in child protection agency activities. These include the National Coalition for Child Protection Reform, Center for the Study of Social Policy, Justice for Children, and First Star.

Howard A. Davidson

See also Court-Appointed Special Advocates; Legal System, Advocacy Efforts to Affect, Violence Against Children; Legal System, Civil Court Remedies for Intimate Partner Violence; Legal System and Child Protection; Legislation, Child Maltreatment

Further Readings

American Bar Association. (1996). *Standards of practice for lawyers who represent children in abuse and neglect cases.* Available at http://www.abanet.org/

Haralambie, A. M. (1993). *The child's attorney: A guide to representing children in custody, adoption, and protection cases.* Chicago: Section of Family Law, American Bar Association.

Peters, J. K. (2001). *Representing children in child protective proceedings: Ethical and practical dimensions* (2nd ed.). Newark, NJ: LexisNexis.

Renne, J. (2004). *Legal ethics in child welfare cases.* Washington, DC: ABA Center on Children and the Law.

Ventrell, M., & Duquette, D. (Eds.). (2005). *Child welfare law and practice: Representing children, parents, and state agencies in abuse, neglect, and dependency cases.* Denver, CO: Bradford.

LEGAL SYSTEM, ADVOCACY EFFORTS TO AFFECT, ELDER ABUSE

Legal advocacy is commonly divided into individual advocacy and systems advocacy within both the criminal and civil system. Within the legal system, individual advocacy means working with a client one-on-one to assist the client to understand or prepare for a legal proceeding. Individual advocacy might also entail making calls on behalf of the client, attending court hearings or proceedings with the client, or assisting the client with any needed information or referrals before, during, and after legal proceedings. Systems advocacy entails working on behalf of a group of clients within the legal system to advocate for systems change and/or to encourage the legal system to develop practices and procedures that might assist a group of clients when they use the legal system.

Individual Advocacy

Civil Legal System

Individual advocacy for the elderly within the civil legal system may include assisting with the preparation and filing of an order of protection; giving information about possible benefits such as housing, welfare, disability needs, consumer needs, and health care needs; and advocating for and assisting an individual client as needed and appropriate. It may also include providing the following:

- information regarding confidentiality of records within a domestic violence program, social services agencies, and the legal system;
- information around issues of personal protection such as health care and financial powers of attorney, protection of personal assets and finances, protection of privacy in health care and other settings;
- information about issues such as a power of attorney for health care, finances, and general welfare;
- information about the role of a guardian in legal cases;
- information specific to an underserved population, such as issues impacting refugees, and documented and/or undocumented immigrants, or information about tribal laws; and
- information about and assistance with accessing interpreters, translators, guardians, court-appointed advocates, and attorneys.

In addition, individual advocacy may include accompanying the elderly client to any hearing, deposition, or court matter.

Criminal Legal System

As with individual advocacy in the civil legal system, individual advocacy in the criminal legal system may include accompanying an elderly client to any hearing, deposition, or legal proceeding and advocating for and assisting an individual client as needed and appropriate. It may also include providing the following:

- information about the criminal justice system including when and how an arrest can be made by law enforcement, when and how a charge can be issued by a prosecutor, types of crimes that might apply to a specific fact situation, and crimes or penalty enhancers specific to the elderly;
- information about assistance in a criminal case, such as victim or witness personnel;
- information about victims' rights;
- information regarding specific crimes to which the elderly may be especially vulnerable, such as stalking, strangulation, sexual assault, and financial abuse;
- information about elder and vulnerable adult abuse reporting laws and requirements;
- information and assistance if abuse is alleged to have occurred in a facility or entity; and
- information about and assistance with accessing interpreters, translators, advocates, and defense attorneys.

Systems Advocacy

Civil Legal System

Systems advocacy for the elderly within the civil legal system may include, as appropriate, advocating to create, modify, or implement laws, policies, and practices that reflect the needs of elder abuse victims such as the following:

- restraining orders that address types of abuse unique to the elderly (e.g., financial abuse);
- filings by caretakers and guardians that address the needs of competent and incompetent adults and those with disabilities;
- guardianship laws that address the need to protect the elderly and vulnerable (e.g., how to make a guardian respond to abuse or remove an abusive guardian); and
- laws that require collaboration and networking among or between systems for the elderly, with an emphasis on elder abuse issues.

In addition, systems advocacy also may provide cross-trainings on issues that impact the elderly and may advocate for accessibility in legal physical settings and in documents and forms, languages and devices, and resources or assistance needed for and by those with disabilities.

Criminal Legal System

Systems advocacy for the elderly within the criminal legal system may include, as appropriate, advocating to create, modify, or implement laws, policies, and practices to address issues such as the impact of undue influence, abuse in institutions and facilities, and financial abuse by family members, guardians, and caretakers. As with systems advocacy in the civil legal system, systems advocacy in the criminal legal system may provide cross-trainings to all players in the system, which includes presentations by those with expertise in elder abuse and in-person or video clips reflecting real-life experiences of elder abuse. It may also include advocating for accessibility in legal physical settings and in documents and forms, languages and devices, and resources or assistance needed for those with disabilities, as well as advocating for and providing funding for the hiring of victim assistance personnel who are trained in elder abuse. In addition, systems advocacy within the criminal legal system may entail creating, monitoring, and taking positions on all proposed laws, practices, and policies that impact elderly, disabled, and vulnerable adults so as to educate those with decision-making power. Writing and submitting articles to local and state law publications on elder abuse, including articles on laws, policies, and practices that address such abuse so as to educate and create allies within communities, may also be a component of systems advocacy in the criminal legal system.

Preparation

Individual Advocacy

Preparation for individual advocacy with the elderly should include the following: learning about the power and control wheel for tactics used against the elderly; arranging for the best time of day to talk to the client and whether any special assistance is needed such as a translator, interpreter, or hearing-aid device; and allowing for extra time to move and to talk more slowly and for the slow unfolding of a story.

In addition, one should come to advocacy with an attitude that reflects respect for the elderly client's life experiences and should not presume that all elderly clients need special assistance, but should find out what special assistance is needed.

Systems Advocacy

Preparation for systems advocacy on behalf of the elderly should include learning who the players are within one's state and local legal systems who deal with issues impacting the elderly and then cultivate a relationship with these systems and players. In addition, one may prepare by creating opportunities to meet and discuss, both individually and collectively, the needs of older individuals and persons with disabilities and by providing a forum for the expertise of many, such as printed media, videos, fundraisers, and trainings.

Bonnie Brandl and Candace J. Heisler

See also Advocacy; Coordinated Community Response; Elder Abuse

Further Readings

DiMotto, J. M. (2000, September). Accommodating the elderly in court. *Wisconsin Laywer,* 34–36.

Heisler, C. (1999). Domestic violence among the elderly: A blueprint for the criminal justice system. *Wisconsin Coalition Against Domestic Violence Newsletter, 18*(4), 9–13.

Meuer, T. (2000, September). Using restraining orders to protect elder victims. *Wisconsin Lawyer,* 38–80.

LEGAL SYSTEM, ADVOCACY EFFORTS TO AFFECT, INTIMATE PARTNER VIOLENCE

Although intimate partner violence was once considered a private issue, in recent decades advocacy groups shifted the issue out of the home and into the public arena. As public awareness grew, so did the perception of domestic violence as an unacceptable problem requiring societal reform for resolution. Partnerships between governments and organizations substantially increased the resources for battered women. However, the governmental–nongovernmental partnerships also resulted in unforeseen consequences. This entry discusses the historical perspective of domestic violence advocacy efforts, the benefits and drawbacks of both the criminal justice system and the civil justice system in addressing intimate partner violence, and federal funding for domestic violence advocacy efforts.

Historical Perspective

For much of history, the United States has refrained from interfering in domestic violence situations. During the colonial period, intimate partner violence was justified by the belief that women were property for men to discipline and control. In the late 19th century, states were no longer explicitly condoning violence. In fact, the first state laws specifically making wife beating illegal were passed in 1871, though proliferation of laws to all states and enforcement of those laws lagged very far behind. The courts instead adopted the philosophy that domestic violence was a private issue to be dealt with in the household, and the court's inactivity allowed husbands to continue beating their wives with little to no retribution.

The feminist movement gave women the opportunity to share their experiences freely. Through these interactions, it became clear that domestic violence was far more pervasive than initially believed, that resources for battered women were severely inadequate, and that the American public was largely unaware of the issue.

By sharing their collective stories, women began viewing partner violence as more than just a personal issue and as both social and political issues as well. The philosophy emerged that domestic violence was in large part a consequence of society's systematic subordination of women. Lack of economic and social opportunities made women vulnerable to abuse. Advocates tied domestic violence prevention directly to the eradication of women's subordination and the increase of women's social and economic empowerment.

Now that domestic violence was no longer dismissed as a private matter but instead commanded attention as an issue requiring significant societal reform, advocates created an action plan focusing on three urgent tasks: securing resources and shelters for battered women, raising public awareness of the issue,

and creating legal protections for protecting women's safety. As a result, the next few decades brought about an explosion of resources and awareness surrounding domestic violence.

A systematic response to eradicating domestic violence did not emerge until the late 1960s and early 1970s. The first battered women's shelter opened in St. Paul, Minnesota, in 1973. Service organizations dedicated to aiding battered women were characterized by a desire to empower staff members. Organizations tended to emphasize egalitarian and participatory organizational models, encouraging equal involvement in decision-making processes and equal salary distribution. Today, more than 2,000 shelters providing services to battered women are in operation across the United States.

The Criminal Justice System

The pervasive scope of domestic violence prevented grassroots organizations from eradicating domestic violence without the aid of the state. By pushing domestic violence into the public domain and demanding that it be treated as other violent crimes, advocates called upon the justice system to address the issue as part of the criminal system. In redefining domestic violence from a private matter to an offense against the state, the public began to take the issue more seriously, but other problems arose.

The criminal justice approach has had drawbacks. Domestic violence is a pattern of behavior that takes place within an intimate relationship. The pattern often includes repeated physical violence, intimidation, threats, economic abuse, emotional abuse, controlling behavior, irrational jealousy, stalking, harassment at work or at school, and threats to harm the victims' children, family members, friends, or pets. The American criminal justice system, on the other hand, is designed to address single incidents of criminal behavior. In fact, principles of criminal justice demand that such incidents be considered in a vacuum, independent of past behavior of the defendant and independent of the prior relationship between the defendant and victim. Such a system makes responding to the pattern of behavior typical of domestic violence difficult. Moreover, the criminal justice approach often leads to victim blaming. A system that thinks in terms of a single criminal act has difficulty comprehending a victim who does not immediately remove her- or himself from a situation where she or he is likely to be victimized again. A system that is designed to deal with street violence among strangers is not adequately structured to respond to violence in families and intimate relationships.

The criminal justice approach has also resulted in dual arrests—police arresting both parties when called on a domestic dispute. The concept of dual arrest was fueled by an unwillingness of police officers to view domestic violence as a crime as well as poor legal definitions of domestic violence. Once the criminal and civil laws on domestic violence were created, years of struggle began to try to force the system to work, including mandatory arrest laws, mandatory police and judicial training, and definitions and redefinitions of primary or predominant aggressor.

The Civil Justice System

One major drawback of the criminal justice system is the disempowering effect that it can have on survivors of domestic violence. In the criminal system, the parties to the case are the government and the defendant. The victim of the crime is relegated to the role of witness. The decisions to arrest, charge, prosecute, dismiss, divert, or punish the case (and the batterer) are all within the purview of state actors. Although the victim may be consulted about her or his preferences, the choice is ultimately out of the hands of the victim. Combined with the historical resistance of the police and courts to treat domestic violence as a serious crime, the state's sole control often meant that the state response was negligible or nonexistent.

To empower the survivor of domestic violence and provide her or him with control over the justice process, civil remedies were created. The civil protective order provided an opportunity for a survivor to file a case and retain control over much of the advancement of the case. The civil system moves at a faster pace than the criminal system, thus allowing a more immediate response. It allows a survivor to speak to a judge, tell the story, and have a judge determine whether the violence occurred. It also provides the remedy of a written court order issued by a judge that restricts the ability of the abuser to continue the abuse. The issuance of the order may in itself be empowering for the survivor. However, it serves the additional purpose of encouraging police, prosecutors, and judges to take the case more seriously if

violence recurs. It also puts the survivor in a position to bring a contempt case against the abuser if the order is violated, regardless of whether the police or prosecutors file charges.

The process by which civil protective orders came to be the remedy they are today was a gradual process of statutory and systemic changes advocated by nongovernmental organizations. This advocacy expanded the remedies available in protective orders to include a range of essential provisions critical to reducing opportunities for continued violence, including child custody provisions and ordering an abuser to move out of a joint home. Systems were put in place to ensure immediate access to a judge on a pro se basis to obtain emergency protection orders in place until a hearing could be scheduled. Increasingly, nongovernmental organizations train court-based lay advocates who assist victims in explaining rights and options to survivors and help guide them through the process. Advocacy has also ensured that filing for a protective order is free and that judges often receive training on domestic violence.

Federal Funding

Despite the good intentions of grassroots advocates, financial limits to their reach seemed insurmountable. The government, however, could provide a financial investment in addressing domestic violence. The first major step toward government involvement occurred in 1984 with the passage of the federal Family Violence Prevention and Services Act. This legislation earmarked federal funding for domestic violence programs and served as a precursor to the further-reaching Violence Against Women Act of 1994 (VAWA). VAWA was reauthorized and expanded in 2000 and reauthorized and expanded once again in 2005, reflecting the evolution of the movement from a grassroots feminist campaign to a mainstream political movement. Today, funding of domestic violence services and systems commonly comes from local and state governments, as well as the federal government. Moreover, the support of the government has encouraged corporate support of services as well.

Although governmental involvement allowed for an increase in funding and resources, some believe it also diluted the feminist orientation originally associated with the movement, which centered primarily on empowering individuals and ensuring equality of power within organizations. To accommodate the growth of domestic violence programs, domestic violence resource centers faced growing pressure to develop more hierarchical organizational structures. Changes in hiring standards brought more social workers and lawyers into the fold, rather than the grassroots, community organizers who had traditionally been chosen. This change in hiring led to a growth in psychotherapy, legal services, and employment counseling, while political activism moved toward the periphery.

Juley Fulcher and Teresa Yeh

See also Advocacy; Intimate Partner Violence; Legal System, Civil Court Remedies for Intimate Partner Violence; Legal System, Criminal Justice System Responses to Intimate Partner Violence; Police, Response to Domestic Violence; Restraining and Protective Orders; Violence Against Women Act

Further Readings

Fulcher, J. (2002). Domestic violence and the rights of women in Japan and the United States. *Human Rights, 29*(3), 16–17.

Goodman, L., & Epstein, D. (2007). *New strategies for empowering battered women: A survivor-centered approach to the advocacy, mental health and justice systems.* Washington, DC: American Psychological Association Press.

LEGAL SYSTEM, ADVOCACY EFFORTS TO AFFECT, VIOLENCE AGAINST CHILDREN

Since children under age 18 frequently must appear in court as witnesses in criminal cases because of their victimization either within or outside of their home, it is important to examine how they interact with the criminal justice system process. For many years, pursuant to federal law, there has been, for example, authority for federal court judges (in federal prosecutions involving crimes against children) to protect the best interests of the child victim or witness. Federal judges or magistrates have authority to appoint a special guardian ad litem for the child during these criminal proceedings. These guardians ad litem are specifically empowered by law to attend all depositions and hearings and the trial of the case; make recommendations to the court concerning the welfare of the child; access all reports, evaluations, and records related to the case (but not privileged attorney work products) to effectively advocate on behalf of the child; and to marshal and coordinate the delivery of resources and special services to their child client. Several states have similar legislation, giving the child victim a legal representative who can, for example, make recommendations to the court, based on the preferences and best interests of the child; help make decisions and/or recommendations regarding the child's testimony and special protections the child may require during his or her testimony; meet with the child and offer him or her consistent support; and attend hearings and possibly even participate in examining or calling witnesses on the child's behalf. These federal and state provisions of law are consistent with international guidelines for child victims or witnesses that, subsequent to their drafting, have been endorsed by the United Nations. These include treating child victims or witnesses with respect and protecting their dignity; treating them fairly and without discrimination; helping the courts focus on the child's best interests; helping ensure prompt aid to children who are traumatized as a result of their victimization; making sure there is due consideration of their right to participate in the case, to express their personal views, and to have those views reflected upon by the judge and prosecutor; protecting the child from undue interference in their lives or invasions of their privacy; having them examined/questioned only by well-trained people and in child-sensitive environments; keeping them and their families informed on the court process and its outcomes; helping ensure speedy case resolutions and reduction of necessary interviews of the child; helping prevent intimidation and threats that may impede a child's testimony; and addressing the child's needed medical, social, mental health, and legal needs.

Legal Issues That Arise When Aiding Victimized Children

One of the first issues that is likely to come up for those working with victimized children, especially because many are victimized by abuse within their own homes, is the issue of mandatory reporting. All

50 states, the District of Columbia, and the U.S. territories have laws that designate specific professions and groups as mandatory reporters of known or suspected child maltreatment. The legal definitions of mandatory reporter, abuse, and neglect, as well as the circumstances under which one must report (e.g., known abuse, suspected abuse, reasonable grounds to suspect, intrafamilial abuse only, or extrafamilial abuse), vary from state to state. Most states designate health care workers, school personnel, childcare providers, social workers, law enforcement officers, and mental health professionals as mandated reporters. Certain states specify additional categories, such as substance abuse or domestic violence counselors, and some states require all citizens to report. State laws related to the obligations of mandatory reporters can be searched at the Child Welfare Information Gateway Web site. Teenagers under the age of 18 are still children under the law, and thus mandatory reporting requirements still apply. Of course, a dilemma that arises for many professionals who work with child victims of crime is the concern that reporting abuse against a child's wishes can destroy the trust they are working to establish and may prevent that child from ever trusting or opening up about his or her victimization to another adult. All professionals who work with child victims of crime must know and follow their state's laws related to mandatory child abuse and neglect reporting. The intent of such laws is to ensure intervention in all known or suspected cases of abuse in order to stop the abuse, prevent the situation from worsening, and help the victim recover. Another legal issue when working with child victims of crime is parental consent and involvement. Laws related to when, for example, a child can consent to his or her own medical or mental health treatment related to their victimization are complex. When working with child victims of crime, it is important to know what the law says regarding parental consent, notification, and involvement when related to that child's needed services, treatment, and other interventions.

Law-Related Child Victim Interviewing Issues

In the 1980s, as cases involving disclosures of child sexual abuse made by young children became more frequent, there arose a need for social workers, police officers, and others to learn interviewing skills that could better help ensure accuracy in those disclosures and help those children be better witnesses in court, when necessary. Victim-sensitive interviewing began to emerge as a critical special skill, and in 1994, the American Bar Association published the *Handbook on Questioning Children: A Linguistic Perspective* to help child victim interviewers learn how children acquire and understand language used in the context of such case investigations. Interviewers must understand basic principles of child questioning for forensic purposes, to be able to look for problems in questioning or in the answers children provide, to understand language-related explanations for inconsistencies in children's testimonies, and so on. The development of Children's Advocacy Centers has provided, throughout the country, community-based central facilities for interviewing children suspected of being abuse victims and offers a setting for professionals from various agencies (police, child protective services, prosecutor, medical) to do multidisciplinary collaborative work in such cases. The child interviews in such settings are often videotaped, in part to avoid children having to be subjected to multiple repetitive questioning and to maintain evidence that the child's interview was not contaminated by improperly suggestive questions or other techniques that could negate the effective use of their prior disclosures in court. Building on all this knowledge, a special skill set for forensic interviewers was developed, with training throughout the country available to help ensure that the interview procedures themselves would not jeopardize successful prosecutions of a child's offender. Such groups as the National Center for the Prosecution of Child Abuse, part of the National District Attorneys Association, have engaged in a nationwide effort to bring high-quality forensic interviewing skills to as many professionals as possible through a program called Finding Words.

Finding Words and other similar programs not only focus on improving interviewer skills, but also on better preparing the child for the in-court experience. Court schools are local programs that also seek to do the latter.

The goal of many prosecutors of crimes against children, however, remains avoiding whenever possible the traditional in-court testimony of young children where their testimony may be severely traumatic. Over the past 25 years, the U.S. Supreme Court in a series of cases has clarified the parameters for use of alternatives to a child's in-court face-to-face testimony in the presence of the accused. Through admission of out-of-court hearsay disclosures of the child victim, video-recorded interviews or special closed-circuit television live testimony that avoids the child testifying in the close physical proximity to the defendant, prosecutors have been given a set of tools in their arsenal to use in aiding child victims or witnesses, subject to following the rules set forth in the Supreme Court's decisions and state or federal statutes. Laws and practices also provide, in many states, authority for changing the layout of the courtroom during child testimony, judicially controlled procedures for examination of child witnesses, allowing children to have support persons accompany them to the courtroom during their testimony, permissible use of anatomically detailed dolls and other testimonial aids, and closing the courtroom from the public during child testimony.

Howard A. Davidson

See also Children's Advocacy Center; Ethical and Legal Issues, Interviewing Children Reported as Abused or Neglected; Mandatory Reporting Laws of Child Maltreatment

Further Readings

American Bar Association. (2002). *The child witness in criminal cases: A product of the Task Force on Child Witnesses of the American Bar Association Criminal Justice Section*. Washington, DC: American Bar Association, Criminal Justice Section.

Finkelhor, D., Cross, T. P., & Cantor, E. N. (2005, December). How the justice system responds to juvenile victims: A comprehensive model. *Crimes Against Children Series* (Bulletin No. NCJ 210951). Available at http://www.ojp.usdoj.gov/ojjdp

International Bureau for Children's Rights. (2003). *guidelines on justice for child victims and witnesses of crime*. Retrieved from http://www.ibcr.org/ Publications/VICWIT/2003_IBCR_Guidelines_ En-Fr-Sp.pdf

United Nations Office on Drugs and Crime. (2006). *United Nations guidelines on justice in matters involving child victims and witnesses of crime: A child-friendly version*. Retrieved from http://www.ibcr.org/Publications/VICWIT/ 2007_Child-Friendly_Guidelines_En.pdf

Walker, A. G. (1999). *Handbook on questioning children: A linguistic perspective* (2nd ed.). Washington, DC: ABA Center on Children and the Law.

Web Sites

Child Welfare Information Gateway: http://www.childwelfare .gov/systemwide/laws_policies/state/index.cfm

Legal System, Civil and Criminal Court Remedies for Sexual Assault/Rape

In the United States, the legal definitions of sexual assault and rape vary from state to state. However, it is generally accepted that sexual assault involves sexual conduct of an involuntary nature. Rape, a form of sexual assault, involves the nonconsensual use of another person's sexual organs. Both are considered serious crimes, and in both cases, convictions lead to serious consequences.

Survivors of sexual assault have two legal options for recourse: criminal prosecution and civil litigation. Criminal cases are prosecuted by the state with the sexual assault survivor serving as a witness for the state. In civil cases, the survivor brings a lawsuit against the perpetrator, usually with the aid of a private attorney. This entry discusses both criminal and civil court recourses, along with civil protection orders, mutual filing of suits, and the difficulties involved in prosecuting sexual assault and rape cases.

Criminal Court Remedies

Criminal laws exist to impose social control and to serve as a deterrent to behavior that threatens societal well-being. Therefore, in criminal cases, the perpetrator is charged with committing a crime against the state. Society at large is the victim of the perpetrator's actions, and thus criminal prosecution is led by the state and not the survivor.

The criminal process begins when a sexual assault is reported to the authorities. Once a police report is filed, a warrant can be issued for the perpetrator's arrest. If the perpetrator is apprehended, a prosecutor for the state must then determine whether there is enough evidence to prosecute. If the case is brought to trial, the survivor becomes a state witness and may be called to testify during the trial. Since the survivor is a witness and not a client, she or he has no direct control over whether or how the case is prosecuted.

However, since the survivor's testimony is usually the state's most valuable piece of evidence and crucial to the success of the prosecution, criminal prosecutors rarely pursue a case without the survivor's cooperation. If convicted of criminal charges, the perpetrator could face a variety of punishments, including but not limited to prison time, a fine, or probation.

The Federal Rules of Evidence and most states mandate that a survivor's prior sexual history, reputation for sexual activity, and sexual behavior be inadmissible during the trial. A few exceptions exist, such as when the survivor has had previous sexual contact with the perpetrator. In these instances, the survivor may be questioned about her or his past relationship with the perpetrator.

Civil Court Remedies

Civil law refers to the part of the law that deals with relations between private individuals and between individuals and organizations. Civil suits are becoming an increasingly commonplace legal remedy. In civil proceedings, survivors can be awarded financial compensation from the perpetrator or the perpetrator's insurer for physical and mental harm endured. A broad range of financial reparations is available, including but not limited to coverage of medical expenses and therapy, payment of lost wages or lost potential income, damages to property during the assault, and even punishment for a perpetrator's malicious actions.

Civil litigation is valuable not only because it allows for financial recompense, but also because it can prove to be an empowering experience for the survivor. Unlike criminal cases, civil suits allow for the survivor to be the decision maker and to take control of her or his own case. The survivor is the client, so the attorney representing the client is bound by the client's wishes in deciding how to proceed with the case. The sense of empowerment often achieved with civil suits can serve as a form of therapy for the survivor, who is able to take back the control that was lost during the assault.

Civil Protection Orders

In addition to financial recompense, survivors also may be able to file for a civil protective order (PO) to protect themselves from further harm by the perpetrator. POs are court orders for the perpetrator to stay away from and have no contact with the victim. Historically, POs have been limited to survivors of domestic violence, and, as such, only sexual assault survivors victimized by intimate partners were eligible. However, an increasing number of states have passed laws granting access to POs to sexual assault survivors in situations that fall outside of domestic violence. POs can be invaluable in cases where the survivor has continuing proximity to the perpetrator, such as when the perpetrator is a neighbor, classmate, or coworker. Although civil POs are granted through the civil court system, violation of a PO is a crime and is prosecuted through the criminal court system.

Mutual Filing of Criminal and Civil Suits

Civil litigation and criminal prosecution are regarded independently. Regardless of whether criminal charges have been brought or even dismissed, survivors are still entitled to file suit against their perpetrators in civil court. Similarly, survivors who do choose to pursue a civil case against their perpetrator may still be involved in state prosecution of criminal charges.

In criminal courts, the prosecutor must prove beyond a reasonable doubt that the perpetrator is guilty of sexual assault. The perpetrator has the benefit of a legal right to counsel and stringent rules of evidence designed to protect the accused. On the other hand, the burden of proof is lower in civil courts. In civil suits, a survivor must prove liability by a preponderance of evidence, meaning she or he must prove that a 51% probability exists that the perpetrator was responsible. Since the burden of proof is significantly lower in a civil case, failure to prosecute or convict a perpetrator in a criminal case should not deter a survivor from pursuing a subsequent civil case against the perpetrator where the burden of proof may be easier to meet.

Difficulties in Prosecution

Although sexual assault is one of the most serious of violent crimes, criminal prosecution of sexual assault offenders is particularly difficult. In fact, out of all the violent crimes in the United States, rape is the least reported and prosecuted and results in the fewest convictions.

This difficulty in prosecuting sexual assault and rape cases is a result of several factors. Not only is it a challenge to prove rape under most states' laws, but also there are rarely other witnesses to corroborate a survivor's account. It is common for these cases to have a lack of physical evidence, both because survivors often are reluctant to report the crime immediately and because this type of violence may not leave observable injuries. Furthermore, sexist stereotypes and common law work together to create a situation in which both judges and jurors tend to question the survivor and her or his behavior rather than the actions of the perpetrator.

Juley Fulcher and Teresa Yeh

See also Rape/Sexual Assault; Rape Shield Laws; Restraining and Protective Orders; Sexual Abuse

Further Readings

Berman, J. (2004). Domestic sexual assault: A new opportunity for court response. *Juvenile and Family Court Journal, 55*(3), 23–34.

Hunter, S., Burns-Smith, G., & Walsh, C. (2001). *Equal justice? Not yet for victims of sexual assault.* Madison, WI: Connecticut Sexual Assault Crisis Services.

Perry, A. L. (1998). Insurance company liability for sexual assault. *Sexual Assault Report, 1*(6), 85–86, 96.

Perry, A. L. (2003). Evidentiary decisions in sexual assault cases. *Sexual Assault Report, 7*(1), 5–6.

Prendinger, S. (2000). *Court preparation for crime victims.* Denver: Colorado Coalition Against Sexual Assault.

Suffolk University Law School. (2004). *Beyond prosecution: Sexual assault victims' rights in theory and practice.* Boston: Author.

LEGAL SYSTEM, CIVIL COURT REMEDIES FOR INTIMATE PARTNER VIOLENCE

Over the course of the past 3 decades, state legislatures have enacted civil laws that address violence against women. Unlike criminal legal remedies, which are guided by the state and focus upon the offender, civil remedies are controlled by the survivor and are intended to serve the survivor's particular needs. Civil legal remedies now exist for a wide range of issues faced by survivors. Civil legal remedies seek to prevent future abuse, enhance victim physical safety, minimize the coercive power of perpetrators over victims,

offer the resources necessary for survivors to live independently of the perpetrator, provide restitution to victims for losses resulting from the violence, prevent discrimination, enhance access to justice, and facilitate survivors' ability to self-direct their lives.

Shortcomings of the Criminal Justice System

Since the beginning of the violence against women movement, advocates have agitated for the enactment and enforcement of criminal legal responses to domestic violence, sexual assault, and stalking. Faced with a history of state nonintervention in private affairs, they organized to encourage the criminal justice system to respond to domestic violence with the same level of commitment as other crimes. These efforts resulted in a groundswell of change aimed at increasing arrests and prosecution of batterers and rapists, including mandatory arrest and no-drop policies, as well as enhanced penalties for these crimes. However, although the criminal justice system has provided critical assistance for many survivors of domestic violence, fostering batterer accountability, it has often failed to meet the varied, complex, and comprehensive needs of battered women and their children.

The criminal justice system has led to dangerous outcomes for many battered women, particularly women of color. Battered women are often arrested when they act to defend themselves, when a police officer makes a dual arrest, or as a result of false accusations by batterers who attempt to manipulate the system against their partners. Many victims are charged with failure to protect their children, based solely upon their victimization. The collateral consequences of criminal intervention are wide reaching and include deportation (for immigrant women), loss of child custody, and barriers to employment and housing. All of these harms reflect a loss of agency for women and the communities in which they live.

Even when these harms do not occur, the nature of criminal justice remedies prevents battered women from directing the process. Because mandatory criminal legal interventions are controlled by the state, battered women are left without the ability to determine their own course based upon their individual needs. Indeed, studies have shown that the main reason for battered women's lack of satisfaction with the criminal justice system rests with their lack of control over the process.

Agency and the Material Needs of Survivors

A woman-centered advocacy model suggests that survivors must be actively involved in identifying their particular needs and crafting strategies that address those needs. Survivors of domestic and sexual violence have a wide variety of needs, which depend upon their particular circumstances and extend far beyond the remedies offered by the criminal justice system. Examples of these needs include the following: housing, education, employment, transportation, health care, social support, financial assistance, and material goods and services.

Access to material resources is a critical factor in the short- and long-term safety of battered women and their children. Research has shown that the best predictors of whether a survivor will be free from intimate partner violence include access to childcare, access to transportation, and access to an independent source of income. Perpetrators of domestic and sexual violence inflict enormous economic harms upon their victims. The civil legal system offers survivors of domestic and sexual violence an array of tools for recouping the damages resulting from past harms and for garnering resources needed for future safety and restoration.

Types of Civil Legal Remedies

The following are civil legal remedies available to survivors.

Civil Protection Orders

The grandparent of legal provisions, the civil protection order (also known as a protective order or a restraining order), is the most common form of civil legal relief accessed by survivors. It is also the most immediate and perhaps most accessible relief available to survivors of domestic violence. Available in every state and territory, civil protection orders provide abused persons in statutorily defined relationships with the ability to petition the court for injunctive relief. Examples of relief include orders for temporary custody of children-in-common, temporary child support, eviction of the perpetrator from the residence of the abused, restitution of medical expenses and property damages incurred as a result of the abuse, stay-away orders that direct the abuser to stay a specified distance from the victim and the locations she frequents, no-contact orders that direct the abuser to refrain from

contacting the petitioner and/or direct others to contact the petitioner on his behalf, and catch-all provisions that enable the judge to order relief geared toward future safety. Unlike criminal cases, civil protection order cases are filed and litigated by the petitioner as opposed to the state. If the respondent violates a protection order, the petitioner can file for civil or criminal contempt; some criminal codes include violation of a protection order as a misdemeanor criminal offense.

Child Custody

Survivors of domestic and sexual violence who share a child in common with the abuser often face substantial hurdles in accessing legal custody of their children. After separation, batterers often use custodial access as a mechanism for maintaining control over their partner. In response to the dangers that battering parents pose to women and children, state legislatures have developed statutory provisions requiring courts to include domestic violence as a factor in custody and visitation determinations. Many state statutes contain a rebuttable presumption against awarding custody to the abusive parent. In addition, many state custody statutes require that the court make findings of abuse and include language explaining how the custody or visitation arrangement ordered by the court is tailored to address the particular safety of the abused parent and the children.

Torts

Criminal conduct may give rise to civil tort claims, which offer survivors a mechanism for obtaining economic compensation or punitive damages for past harms. Tort cases can be brought against the perpetrator for his abuse. Common tort claims include assault, battery, intentional or reckless infliction of emotional distress, false imprisonment, and wrongful death. Tort cases may also be brought against third parties (e.g., employers, landlords, retailers, police officers) for playing a causative or collusive role in the abuse either through their acts or their omissions.

Immigration

Battered women who are immigrants face unique challenges. Perpetrators of domestic and sexual violence often use their partner's immigration status to entrap them and to facilitate their coercive control. The Violence Against Women Act (VAWA) provides immigrant victims with several mechanisms for obtaining legal status without having to rely upon their abusive partners. VAWA immigration remedies include the following: self-petitioning, VAWA cancellation, battered spouse waivers, U-visas, T-visas, and asylum.

Other

Additional civil claims may lie in housing law, employment law, privacy law, consumer law, and civil rights law, to name only a few. The potential civil legal remedies are as varied and expansive as the prior harms and future needs of individual battered women and sexual assault survivors.

Erika A. Sussman

See also Agency/Autonomy of Battered Women; Mandatory Reporting Laws of Intimate Partner Violence; Restraining and Protective Orders; Violence Against Women Act

Further Readings

Allen, N. E., Bybee, D. I., & Sullivan, C. M. (2004). Battered women's multitude of needs: Evidence supporting the need for comprehensive advocacy. *Violence Against Women, 10,* 1015–1035.

Hotaling, G. T., & Buzawa, E. S. (2006, January). Victim satisfaction with criminal justice case processing in a model court setting. *NIJ Journal, 253.*

Lehrman, F. L. (1997). *Domestic violence practice and procedure.* Minneapolis, MN: West Group.

Ms. Foundation for Women. (2003). *Safety and justice for all: Safety program: Examining the relationship between the women's anti-violence movement and the criminal legal system.* New York: Author.

National Advisory Council on Violence Against Women and the Violence Against Women Office. (n.d.). Enhancing the response of the justice system: Civil remedies. In *Toolkit to End Violence Against Women.* Retrieved from http://toolkit.ncjrs.org/vawo_3.html

LEGAL SYSTEM, CRIMINAL INVESTIGATION OF VICTIMIZATION OF CHILDREN

The criminal investigation of crimes against children is unique compared to the criminal investigation of crimes against other age groups. It is unique because of the wide range of crimes against children, the different systems that are involved, and the impact of the legal system on children. Given the vulnerable position of children, it is essential that the legal system hold offenders accountable while not retraumatizing child victims. Because juveniles are among the most victimized age group in the population, it is critical to understand how the legal system responds to the victimization of children.

Types of Victimization

There is a wide range of types of victimizations that children experience. Children may be victims of conventional crime (e.g., assault, property crime, theft), victims of witnessing domestic violence, custodial abductions, or victims of child maltreatment (e.g., physical abuse, sexual abuse, neglect, emotional abuse). Moreover, victimized children may come into contact with the criminal justice system because they have been arrested for criminal delinquent behavior or picked up for running away or truancy. Large percentages of children arrested for such crimes have histories of victimization that may contribute to the delinquent behavior. Not only do children experience a wide range of victimizations, but also children experience rates of victimization that are substantially higher than adults.

Legal System

The legal response to the wide array of crimes that child victims experience is complicated because there are two distinct systems that can be involved: the criminal justice system and the child protection system. The criminal justice system investigates conventional crimes, while the child protection system investigates child maltreatment by perpetrators in a caretaking responsibility. Little data are available about the criminal investigations for all the types of victimizations. For example, the percentage of arrests or prosecutions that involve child victims is not known. Furthermore, many crimes against children are not reported. Therefore, the information that is available from the criminal justice system describes only a fragment of the crimes committed against children. Conventional crimes, as well as some types of physical and sexual abuse, are referred to the criminal justice system. Police make an arrest in a minority of juvenile victim crimes, and arrests are more common when the crime involves a weapon or a serious offense. Many of the offenders who victimize juveniles are other juveniles. Generally, there are special institutions to handle juvenile offenders. One type of victimization, however, that has received greater emphasis in the legal system is sexual assaults against children.

Prosecution of Sexual Assaults Against Children

The prosecution of sexual assaults against children is similar to prosecution of other crimes. After prosecutors receive a referral they evaluate whether a crime has been committed and whether they can prove it beyond a reasonable doubt. Prosecutors may decline a case because of lack of evidence. A case may be reopened later if evidence is obtained or a witness is able to testify. Some declined cases are closed and go no further in criminal court. Other cases may go to civil court. Even after a prosecutor accepts a case, a case may be dismissed or dropped. If a case is carried forward, defendants decide whether to plead guilty or go to trial.

Although there are similarities, there are many differences in the prosecution of sexual assaults against children and other crimes. First, the referral process is different. Two agencies can make referrals to the legal system: the police and child protection services. The extent to which these agencies are involved may further complicate the investigation process. The complicated process has led to the development of comprehensive multidisciplinary agencies, such as Children's Advocacy Centers. Second, the prosecution of sex crimes against children may be difficult because of the lack of evidence. For example, often it is the word of the child victim versus that of the defendant. A successful prosecution also depends on the family's commitment to prosecution and the capacity of the child to withstand the stress of a criminal trial.

Third, there have been a number of concerns raised about the impact of the legal system on the child victim. Concerns include the length of the legal process, the stress of retelling a horrible event, the impact on the family, especially if the defendant is a family member, and the embarrassment of the nature of what happened. These issues may have a potential negative impact on a child's well-being and make the criminal investigation too much for a child to endure. Defense strategies such as challenging the child's credibility, memory, suggestibility, and delays in reporting may

make it particularly uncomfortable for children. Not all children, however, have a negative experience. Furthermore, there have been a number of innovations in how the legal system responds to the criminal investigation of the victimization of children.

Innovations in the Legal System

Because dramatic developmental differences exist for children, it is necessary to consider a child's age when thinking about the legal system's response to child victimization. First, because childhood is a time for development—emotional, cognitive, and biological—the same event may impact children in different ways depending on a child's age.

Specific services, such as victim advocates, court school, special prosecution units, and vertical prosecution, are now in place in many jurisdictions and seem to have a positive impact in reducing child trauma sometimes associated with involvement in the legal system. Victim advocacy programs help to prepare victims, witnesses, and families for the court process. Court school programs often include role-playing to talk through the legal process and tours of the courtroom. Special prosecution units have dedicated people to work on specific types of cases. Vertical prosecution means that one prosecutor handles a case at all stages of the criminal justice process.

Disposition Rates

Only a minority of sexual assaults against children are criminally prosecuted. Thus, the legal system does not come in contact with the vast majority of these types of crimes. Those cases that are prosecuted generally result in conviction, usually by a guilty plea. Child sexual abuse cases are less likely to have charges filed than felonies overall and other violent crimes, but the rate is similar to the rate for rape and sexual assault. Guilty pleas and trial rates for child sexual abuse cases are generally similar to these comparison categories. In some cases, a child has to testify during the criminal court proceedings.

In addition to the criminal prosecution of the perpetrator, the legal system (typically dependency courts) may be involved when a child victim of maltreatment has to be removed from her or his home. Again, this involvement impacts only a minority of cases.

Policy Issues

Child victims usually have access to services that compensate them for the costs associated with being a victim of crime, such as medical care, counseling, and replacing stolen items. It is not known to what extent child victims make use of such services. It is also important to consider what impact the legal system might have on child victims. Three impacts are particularly important: child interviews, therapeutic services, and family disruption. First, a child victim most likely will need to be interviewed—and this need may continue, especially if the case goes to trial. A number of forensic interviewing programs now exist to enhance this process. Second, a child victim of a crime most likely would benefit from receiving therapeutic services. Third, depending on the nature of the crime, sometimes criminal investigation results in family disruption. All of the special nuances of criminal investigation should be weighed.

Future Directions

There is much to learn about the criminal investigation of crimes against children. This field is a relatively new area of research; only within the past decade has there been concentrated research in this area. Future efforts should consider why some cases are criminally prosecuted and the majority of cases are not prosecuted. Although there have been a number of innovations to help reduce the trauma that children sometimes experience with legal system involvement, there is a need to better understand the impact of such innovations. There is also a need to better understand the time it takes to reach a resolution in the criminal prosecution of child abuse.

Wendy A. Walsh

See also Child Sexual Abuse; Legal System, Civil and Criminal Court Remedies for Sexual Assault/Rape; Legal System and Child Protection; Legislation, Child Maltreatment; Police, Response to Child Maltreatment

Further Readings

Cross, T. P., Walsh, W. A., Simone, M., & Jones, L. M. (2003). Prosecution of analysis of child abuse: A meta-analysis of rates of criminal justice decisions. *Trauma, Violence, & Abuse, 4,* 323–340.

Finkelhor, D., Cross, T., & Cantor, E. (2005). The justice system for juvenile victims: A comprehensive model of case flow. *Trauma, Violence, & Abuse, 6,* 1–20.

Goodman, G. S., Quas, J. A., Bulkley, J., & Shapiro, C. (1999). Innovations for child witnesses: A national survey. *Psychology, Public Policy, and Law, 5,* 255–281.

Jones, L. M., Cross, T. P., Walsh, W. A., & Simone, M. (2005). Criminal investigation of child abuse: The research behind "best practices." *Trauma, Violence, & Abuse, 6*(3), 254–268.

LEGAL SYSTEM, CRIMINAL JUSTICE STRATEGIES TO REDUCE INTERPERSONAL VIOLENCE

Violence is an intentional aggressive action against another person that can present as a physical attack, sexual assault, or psychological abuse. Some forms of violence also include nonactions in the form of neglect. Interpersonal violence is usually described in one of two ways: as community violence or as family violence. Several unique acts of violence fall under each of these headings. Interpersonal violence negatively affects our society by leaving emotional and psychological wounds on families and communities and draining our community and financial resources. The costs of medical care, counseling, and lost wages from missed work due to violent acts are astronomical. Although the criminal justice system cannot address every issue involved to eradicate interpersonal violence, there are criminal justice strategies in place to assist victims and to hold perpetrators accountable for their actions.

Community Violence

Community violence entails violent acts between strangers or acquaintances that emulate a victim–offender relationship. It may describe an assault committed by a neighbor against someone else in the community or a random act of violence involving two strangers. Community violence takes many forms, which include various types of violence in a multitude of settings. Particularly, interpersonal violence occurring at colleges and schools has recently increased at an alarming rate.

Campus Violence

Traditionally, colleges, schools, and other institutions were not held liable for acts of violence committed on their property. However, there has been an increase in the number of civil actions against colleges and universities as a result of their failure to take the necessary precautions to ensure the safety of their students. As a result of these suits, there has been a major shift toward strengthening security in educational institutions. These institutions now have a greater sense of responsibility to ensure the safety of their students, faculty, and staff. Currently, legislation such as the federal Students Right-to-Know and Campus Security Act mandate that colleges and universities publish reports regarding their campus crime rates so that students and their families can make their own determination regarding the safety of the school.

One form of interpersonal violence in a school setting is hazing. Hazing is a form of initiation or testing for new recruits who are interested in joining a particular campus organization, most notably fraternities, sororities, and athletic teams. The hazing practices often involve physical assault and/or psychological abuse against the interested pledge to test his or her loyalty and dedication to the group as well as his or her stamina. Most states recognize certain types of hazing behavior as a crime, although the definition of criminal hazing varies by state. Currently, there are 44 states that have enacted statutes in an effort to decrease the occurrence of violent acts of hazing.

Hate Crimes

Interpersonal violence includes hate crimes. Hate crimes are violent acts that are committed because of a victim's religion, ethnicity, sexual orientation, disability, race or ethnicity, or a combination of these factors. Hate crimes can be committed through physical attacks against the victim, malicious destruction of property, and harassment—to give a few examples. Unfortunately, there is a severe amount of intolerance embedded in our society that is exemplified by the increasing number of hate crimes committed each year. In response, 43 states and the District of Columbia have enacted criminal penalties for committing such crimes. Furthermore, several of these states now mandate enhanced penalties for hate crime offenders. These enhancements often include a victim–offender restitution program, which aims to deter offenders from committing acts of violence in the future. In addition, many states require hate crime offenders to complete a diversity awareness program as part of their sentence. Other states have implemented training for court personnel, law enforcement, and even school district officials in identifying, reporting, and prosecuting hate crimes. Organizations and agencies are also being penalized in many states for failing to report hate or bias crimes. All of these measures demonstrate an effort to decrease incidents of hate crimes.

Family Violence

Family violence includes acts of child abuse, child neglect and maltreatment, violent acts between intimate partners, and elder abuse.

Elder Abuse

Elder abuse is an intentional or negligent act, most often committed by a caregiver, which causes harm or serious risk of harm to a vulnerable adult. Elder abuse, like other forms of family abuse, is often underreported. Currently, a national database to track the exact number of elder abuse cases does not exist. However, based on various surveys and samples, estimates of the frequency of elder abuse are recorded and criminal sanctions are in place for persons found guilty of elder abuse. The exact penalties vary from state to state; however, most states have legislation that determines the penalty according to the type and severity of abuse. The charges and penalties may range from simple assault to manslaughter or murder. Studies show that elders are usually abused by members of their family, particularly at the hands of a spouse.

Intimate Partner Violence

As previously mentioned, intimate partner violence is a form of family violence. Intimate partner violence includes both a single act of physical or emotional maltreatment by one intimate partner against the other and a pattern of repeated abuse. In addition, it includes conduct by one partner intended to assert or maintain control and power over the other through the use or threat of physical harm, financial control, and emotional manipulation.

Intimate partner violence has recently received some much needed recognition, and as a result, there is now an increased understanding of the detrimental effects on children who witness violence. In most states, courts have established programs that help identify victims of intimate partner violence and refer them to other service organizations. These services often include counseling, medical care, and safety and financial planning. At the same time, some states are initiating services specifically tailored for the batterer and have implemented criminal justice strategies to address intimate partner violence. The victim may pursue assault or criminal charges against the abuser. If found guilty, these state programs have joined forces with facilities that offer rehabilitation services for batterers, such as anger management classes and batterer counseling. Completion of these programs is often incorporated into the abuser's sentencing and terms of probation in an effort to decrease the likelihood of future incidents of violence. In addition, all states offer some type of civil restraining order that requires the batterer to refrain from abusing or threatening to abuse the victim along with various other terms of relief. In most jurisdictions, violation of the terms of the order may cause the offender to face criminal liability, including jail time.

Most states have implemented a collaborative effort between the criminal and civil courts, law personnel, and counseling professionals to effectively address interpersonal violence within the community.

Shannon R. Gaskins

See also Campus Violence; Community Justice; Elder Abuse; Financial Abuse, Elderly and Battered Women; Hate Crimes (Bias Crimes), Criminal Justice Responses; Hazing; Intimate Partner Violence; Legal System, Civil Court Remedies for Intimate Partner Violence; Legal System, Criminal Justice System Responses to Intimate Partner Violence; Legislation, Elder Abuse; Legislation, Hate Crimes; Legislation, Intimate Partner Violence

Further Readings

Boucher, J. (2005). Hazing and higher education: State laws, liability, and institutional implications. *Stop hazing: Educating to eliminate hazing.* Retrieved October 25, 2006, from http://www.stophazing.org/devtheory_files/devtheory7.htm

Lees, M., Deen, M., & Parker, L. (2000). Why do young people join gangs? *Research Review: Gang Violence and Prevention.* Retrieved October 23, 2006, from http://focusas.com/Gangs.html

Magellan Assist. (2005). *Interpersonal violence on college campuses.* Retrieved October 23, 2006, from https://www.magellanassist.com/mem/library/default.asp?TopicId=370&CategoryId=0&ArticleId=18

National Center on Elder Abuse. (2005). *Elder abuse prevalence and incidence.* Retrieved October 25, 2006, from http://www.ncea.aoa.gov/ncearoot/Main_Site/index.aspx

National Criminal Justice Reference Service. (2006). *In the spotlight: Family violence.* Retrieved October 24, 2006, from http://www.ncjrs.gov/spotlight/family_violence/Summary.html

LEGAL SYSTEM, CRIMINAL JUSTICE SYSTEM RESPONSES TO INTIMATE PARTNER VIOLENCE

The criminalization of intimate partner violence reflects both society's intolerance for domestic violence and a belief that holding batterers legally accountable will protect women from physical abuse. As early as 1641, the Massachusetts Bay Colony legislated against wife-beating in its *Body of Liberties.* However, absent organized police and public prosecutors, there was no criminal justice system as we recognize it today. If law was to be enforced, it was through private prosecution, with either the victim or her representatives arguing her case before a magistrate. The growth of organized police, public prosecution, and corrections in the 19th century allowed for the systematization of law and practice to control intimate partner violence. In recent decades, there has been a substantial increase in the number of laws against domestic violence, with rising expectations for vigorous application of law enforcement and criminal justice.

All states in the United States have criminal laws meant to control intimate partner violence. The laws classify crimes as either misdemeanors or felonies. Misdemeanors are less serious offenses typically carrying sentences of up to a year in jail, relatively small fines, and probation. Most incidents of domestic violence are classified as misdemeanors, such as battery, criminal recklessness, or disorderly conduct. Felonies are more serious offenses that have harsher penalties. Felony crimes range from battery with serious injury through rape and murder. Unless specifically excluded, as in the case of rape, any number of criminal laws, both misdemeanors and felonies, may apply to intimate partner violence.

In the United States, the Violence Against Women Act (VAWA) of 1994 is the most important federal law applicable to domestic violence. Where previously offenders might have escaped the reach of criminal law simply by leaving the jurisdiction where it occurred, VAWA carries provisions allowing federal jurisdiction over crimes associated with interstate domestic violence, such as crossing a state line with the intent to commit violence against an intimate partner or to violate a protective order. VAWA also ensures that one state will recognize and enforce protective orders issued by another state. A significant effect of VAWA for state law is its having forced states to bring their laws into line with federal law with respect to intimate partner crimes and relationships, thus fostering consistency in law and criminal justice nationwide.

Systems of criminal justice are expected to enforce laws against domestic violence. There is no one criminal justice system. In the United States, in addition to the federal justice system, there are at least as many systems as there are states, counties, territories, and Indian lands. Their common feature is a structure with four major parts: police or law enforcement, prosecution, courts, and corrections. Together the parts should function as a coordinated system committed to enforcing criminal laws. The police conduct street-level law enforcement and investigations with authority to arrest suspects. Prosecutors manage cases within the system, acting as gatekeepers in tracking cases toward final adjudication or alternative outcomes, such as dismissal or diversion. A prosecutor argues the state's case against a criminal in plea negotiations or in court. On behalf of the courts, judges oversee trials and determine the guilt or innocence of defendants in non-jury trials. Finally, defendants found guilty of a crime are processed by corrections agencies—probation or jails and prisons. What distinguishes the system in one jurisdiction from another are the differences in the set of laws to be enforced, the policies governing enforcement, and their levels of commitment to enforce domestic violence laws.

Whether or not criminal law is brought to bear on cases of domestic violence is a matter of local policy and practice as shaped by police, prosecutorial, and judicial discretion. Until recently, discretionary practices often failed to address domestic violence as a crime worthy of criminal justice. During the 1970s, domestic violence victim advocates challenged the unresponsiveness of police, in particular, for lack of action on victim complaints. Police were not alone among criminal justice practitioners in failing victims. Even where victims brought charges to prosecutors, independent of the police, they found state attorneys unwilling to file charges and judges unwilling to sign warrants for the arrest of domestic abusers.

The thrust of criminal justice as applied to intimate partner violence changed dramatically in the 1980s with the convergence of feminist advocacy, a law-and-order political climate, and one particularly influential criminological experiment on the protective impacts of on-scene arrest for domestic violence. The Minneapolis Domestic Violence Experiment found that arrest, in comparison to police advising suspects or sending them away from the victim for a few hours, was effective in reducing the chance of further violence, even without subsequent prosecution. Additional research funded by the National Institute of Justice in recent decades further demonstrates that criminal justice interventions against domestic violence are likely to reduce the chance of a victim being abused again by the same offender. It is not certain, however, that one specific criminal justice intervention is more effective than another in preventing habitual abuse.

Effective criminal justice is presumed to serve as a general deterrent to crime. That is, a man who is predisposed to beating his wife should be less inclined to do so if he knows that a system of criminal justice will identify and punish him. It should also serve to deter men who have already experienced criminal processing for beating an intimate partner from doing so again. Researchers today are looking beyond traditional expectations for deterrence through criminal justice in order to evaluate how different types of offenders respond to criminal sanctions, how mandated rehabilitative counseling for batterers alters their continuing violence, how criminal justice might facilitate victims' efforts to protect themselves against further violence, and how the criminal justice system can strengthen coordinated community responses to intimate partner violence.

David A. Ford

See also Domestic Violence Courts; Legislation, Intimate Partner Violence; Minneapolis Domestic Violence Experiment; Police, Response to Domestic Violence; Prosecutorial Practices, Intimate Partner Violence; Violence Against Women Act

Further Readings

Buzawa, E. S., & Buzawa, C. G. (2002). *Domestic violence: The criminal justice response* (3rd ed.). Thousand Oaks, CA: Sage.

Sherman, L. W., & Berk, R. A. (1984). The specific deterrent effects of arrest for domestic assault. *American Sociological Review, 49,* 261–272.

Steinberg, A. (1989). *The transformation of criminal justice, Philadelphia, 1800–1880.* Chapel Hill: University of North Carolina Press.

LEGAL SYSTEM AND CHILD PROTECTION

There are two separate components in the legal system's approach to addressing child protection issues. The first, dating far back in the American legal system, is the criminalization of behavior by any adult who inflicts serious harm on a child, whether a parent, caretaker, or other. As law evolved, special labels, such as child endangerment, and special enhanced penalties for crimes committed against children, such as for sexual molestation, became part of the legal framework. The other component is a structure under civil law for child protective government agency and judicial interventions for parental abuse or neglect of children. This component is largely a 20th century development. As public child protective services agencies emerged in the second half of the century, a juvenile court structure for child protection intervention (which actually dates back to the early part of the century) became more sophisticated and complex.

The Criminal Law

When conduct of a parent or legal guardian of a child rises to the level of child abuse or neglect constituting a violation of the criminal law, there is authority on the part of prosecutors to bring criminal charges against that adult. However, most child maltreatment in the home, even when clearly in violation of criminal law, does not result in criminal charges against the child's caretaker. Rather, such charges are generally reserved for the most serious of intrafamilial offenses. These include serious inflicted physical harm to children, as well as sexual abuse. If a parent's severe omissions or gross negligence in care of a child (e.g., leaving very young children unattended) results in severe harm to a child or in his or her death, criminal charges will also be more likely under criminal child endangerment or other similar laws. In recent years, special criminal laws for causing the death of a child by the infliction of child abuse have been enacted. In criminal child maltreatment cases, judges who hear these proceedings do not have authority to remove children from parental care or from the family home, but they do frequently exercise authority to separate the adult from the child by imposing upon the defendant child access-related conditions of bail, pretrial release, or—after conviction—probation. The criminal court can also, upon the adult's conviction, order restitution to be paid on behalf of the child, restitution that could, for example, include payment for the costs of a child's treatment.

Civil Child Protection Laws

In every state, judges have authority under special laws to intervene in the lives of families due to parental abuse or neglect of their children. It is important to note that most substantiated cases of child abuse or neglect never result in a caseworker filing such cases in court, since the majority of child protective services interventions with families involve voluntary provision of home-based services to reduce the risk of further child maltreatment—and no civil court intervention is seen as necessary. The most common reason why these court cases are initiated is the need for a caseworker to obtain judicial authority for removal of a child from the home. These court actions may have unusual names—such as dependency, care and protection, child in need of care or assistance cases—or simply abuse or neglect proceedings. The authority of judges or other judicial hearing officers in these cases includes issuance of orders to have a child removed from or returned to the home based on safety and other considerations, as well as a common but not universal authority to order parents into treatment or require them—if they have been resistant—to appropriately participate in child protective-related services provided to them. Either through a separate civil court proceeding initiated after a judge finds a child abused or neglected or as a later disposition in the abuse or neglect civil child protection case, judges have authority in extreme cases to terminate all parental rights. In the last 25 years, these abuse or neglect and termination of parental rights cases have become more complicated, involving multiple special hearings and judicial requirements for certain factual findings at various case stages and increased participation at hearings by a wider group of participants, including attorneys for children, parents, and the child protection agency; nonlawyer volunteer guardians ad litem or court-appointed special advocates (CASAs); foster parents; relatives; and others.

Other Court Proceedings Related to Child Protection

In addition to criminal cases resulting from child maltreatment and civil child protective court interventions, there are additional judicial proceedings where child maltreatment issues may be addressed. The first is in the domestic relations, or family, court, where abuse or neglect allegations may arise for the first time in the context of a divorce or other proceeding brought by one of the child's parents. Domestic relations judges are occasionally called upon to resolve cases where, for example, a parent seeks a change in custody or a restriction or prohibition on visitation by the other parent due to allegations of child sexual abuse in that other home. The second additional court environment where child maltreatment allegations may arise is the domestic violence court. In many cases heard in these courts, there are children adversely impacted by the violence occurring between the adults, and the court's issuance of orders of protection, requirements placed upon batterers, and other actions taken by the judge may need to include special protections and services for the affected child. The third judicial forum where child maltreatment cases may be addressed is in juvenile court delinquency or juvenile status offender proceedings. When a child is arrested or otherwise brought before the court for a criminal act or for running away from home or school truancy, the court may be apprised of facts that suggest a critical underlying problem facing the child is abuse or neglect in the home. It would not be unusual in such cases for a civil child protective proceeding to then be initiated. Finally, child maltreatment issues may also arise in mental health proceedings brought in court by a parent or other person seeking to have a child, who presents a danger to him- or herself or others, committed to a psychiatric facility.

Stages of the Legal Process in Civil Child Protection Cases

These cases often are commenced by a petition filed by a child protective services agency caseworker, or his or her attorney, seeking a judge's order to have a child removed from the home. In rare situations, a caseworker may seek, even earlier, a judge's order to help him or her overcome parental resistance to completion of an investigation of reported abuse or neglect. For example, a court order may be sought to ensure access to the child for interviewing, medical examination, or other purposes or for entry into the family home. Even if the court issues orders to aid completion of the child protective investigation, that does not mean a full child maltreatment civil protection case must be initiated since the result of the completed investigation may not warrant the degree of family intrusion found in judicial proceedings. If the judge authorizes removal of a child from home, even that act may not mandate a full child protective judicial proceeding. For example, a court order may have been sought because young children were left at home without parental supervision, but later the parent's explanation, and voluntary services offered to help prevent a reoccurrence of the situation, may negate any necessity to pursue further judicial action. If, however, there is a court-ordered emergency removal, then typically within 24 to 72 hours of that order (unless the child is returned home) there must be a court hearing (sometimes referred to as the shelter care or initial hearing) at which the parent is present, the issue of continued placement is revisited, and an attorney is appointed for the parent if he or she cannot afford one, as well as an attorney, guardian ad litem, CASA, or some combination appointed for the child. At this, the judge will often hear preliminary evidence related to the child's alleged maltreatment, but this is not a trial or adjudicatory hearing—which comes later.

If the case is not dismissed at the shelter care or initial hearing, in many courts representatives of the child welfare agency, parent, and child will be asked to explore whether there can be an agreement (stipulation) as to the facts and possible resolution of the case. In some courts, there is a mediation program, family group conferencing process, or other mechanism to attempt resolution in a nonadversarial manner. If such efforts fail or are not part of the court's array of services, then the next phase of the case may include the filing of various legal motions and other activities geared toward sharing key information that led to court proceedings. This phase is often called the discovery process and typically involves attorney access to child protective services case records and other information vital for each of the parties (agency, parent, and child) to prepare for the trial of the abuse or neglect allegations. The trial is known as the adjudication (or adjudicatory) hearing. The rules of evidence strictly control witness testimony and the introduction in court of any material related to the allegations. The government child protection agency will have the burden of proving that the allegations in its petition are true. If the court concludes the child was abused or neglected, then the next phase will be the disposition hearing. At this, the court will review the child welfare case plan and specially prepared reports to the court, hear additional testimony, and then decide among several possible courses of action, ranging from having the child at home subject to ongoing child welfare agency protective case supervision, to (in some states) the ability of the judge to permanently terminate parental rights. The most common dispositional actions, if the child remains in foster care or other out-of-home placement, is to continue monitoring the agency's implementation of the family's case plan by setting periodic review hearings (often at 3- to 6-month intervals) to help move as quickly as possible toward a safe and permanent placement for the child.

At and after the disposition hearing, judges have authority to order the child left with or returned to his or her parent, kept in the current placement, or placed elsewhere (e.g., with a relative). Federal law requires states receiving federal financial support for foster care placements to have judges hold one additional type of special hearing, known as the permanency hearing. At such hearing (which is supposed to be held no later than 12 months from the date the child enters foster care), the judge is required to make a case determination with one of the following options: the child's return home immediately or at some date soon; permanent placement with a relative, foster parent, or other nonrelative; permanent legal guardianship; another specified permanent legal arrangement; or termination of parental rights to then permit the child to be adopted.

Howard A. Davidson

See also Adoption and Safe Families Act of 1997; Adoption Assistance and Child Welfare Act of 1980; Domestic Violence Courts; Legal System, Advocacy Efforts to Affect, Child Maltreatment; Legislation, Child Maltreatment; National Council of Juvenile and Family Court Judges

Further Readings

Hardin, M. (2005). *How to work with your court: A guide for child welfare agency administrators* (2nd ed.). Washington, DC: ABA Center on Children and the Law.

Jones, W. G. (2006). *Working with the courts in child protection* (3rd ed.). Washington, DC: U.S. Department of Health and Human Services, Children's Bureau.

National Council of Juvenile and Family Court Judges. (1995). *Resource guidelines: Improving court practice in abuse and neglect cases.* Reno, NV: Author.

LEGISLATION, CHILD MALTREATMENT

Both federal and state laws govern responses by child protective services agencies and the courts to reported cases of abuse and neglect. In many ways, the emergence of state law reform over the past 30-plus years in the field of child maltreatment intervention has been based upon requirements for state law, policy, and practice contained in federal law, beginning with the Child Abuse Prevention and Treatment Act of 1974. However, much of the initial state legislation related to abuse or neglect of children dates back to the 1960s, after the development by the U.S. Department of Health and Human Services of a model child abuse reporting law that states were urged to replicate. Thus, early legislative areas of focus, and the area of much continued reform today, included a listing of those who must report suspected abuse or neglect of a child, how abuse and neglect is defined for purposes of these reporting laws, the required responses to such reports by government child protective services agencies or the police, immunity and privacy protections for those reporting abuse and neglect, and the confidentiality of reported abuse and neglect information and records. Following federal enactment of the Adoption Assistance and Child Welfare Act of 1980 (and subsequent amendments in 1997), state legislatures expanded their laws to mirror issues raised in federal law, including a wider range of requisite court hearings in abuse or neglect cases, expansion and clearer definitions of grounds for the termination of parental rights, and requirements of child welfare agencies to take steps to prevent unnecessary removal of children from their homes, or to speed family reunification.

Common Topics of Child Maltreatment Legislation

In addition to mandatory reporting laws, state legislation addresses both the confidentiality of child protective services agency records and the need for disclosure or sharing of that information in certain situations (e.g., to aid in multidisciplinary case collaboration or in the event of a child maltreatment related death where public information disclosure may be mandated). The central recordkeeping practices of child protective services agencies, enabling them to access and use these databases when confronted later with new reports of child maltreatment that might involve the same child, family, or alleged perpetrator (frequently referred to as central registries), have been the subject of much legislation, as has the use of that information for other purposes, such as background screening of applicants for childcare work, foster care licenses, adoption, or other situations. More recently, state laws also have addressed when child protective services agency personnel must or can access criminal history (arrest and conviction) information on those adults seeking to become foster or adoptive parents or for use in aiding in the investigation of a report of child maltreatment or the conducting of a safety assessment related to the adults present in the child's home.

Reporting laws, however, also continue to be modified frequently. For example, the listing of those professionals who must report suspected abuse or neglect of a child has continued to expand. Members of the clergy in many states are now mandated reporters, although states vary on whether information received in a confessional situation would be covered. A few states specifically mandate reporting by attorneys, despite the fact that they may have learned of suspected abuse or neglect in the context of a privileged attorney–client relationship. Recognizing the links between child maltreatment and animal cruelty, some state laws now mandate reporting of suspected child maltreatment by animal control or humane officers who may learn such information in the course of their

animal protection work. Another issue that is more common than this mandate in child maltreatment statutes is the requirement for cross-reporting to the police or a criminal prosecutor, most typically with reports of serious child maltreatment initially made to child protective services agencies. State legislatures continue to revise definitions of child maltreatment: in many states, expanding the scope of what is considered abuse or neglect of a child (e.g., when children are exposed to severe or repetitive domestic violence that risks subjecting the children to emotional harm or situations involving parental substance abuse), while in fewer states, actually contracting the scope of child abuse or neglect interventions by limiting interventions to serious or recent maltreatment situations. State laws also frequently include criminal penalties for failure to report child maltreatment, and some have penalties for deliberately and falsely reporting abuse or neglect. State criminal laws continue to be regularly modified to enhance penalties for child maltreatment related crimes, to revise the statutes of limitation that have in the past precluded both civil and criminal interventions in cases where child maltreatment occurred many years earlier, and for placing those who commit abuse-related crimes against children on special offender registries.

Finally, many state laws have directly focused on implementation of specific provisions of the 1974 federal child abuse and neglect legislation, addressing such topics as the requirement that a trained attorney or guardian ad litem be appointed for the child in every civil child protective court action; the mandatory referrals to child protective services of children born exposed to illegal drugs or cases of withholding medically indicated treatment from disabled infants with life-threatening conditions; the provisions for prompt expungement from central registries of publicly accessible information or use of the registry entry for employment or background checks if the report of child maltreatment is unsubstantiated; the protections of parental rights in the conduct of child maltreatment investigations by child protective services agencies, including early notification of parents of the reasons for the child protection investigation; and the creation and maintenance of citizens groups (citizen review panels) to provide oversight and review of child protective service agency operations. Within the next few years, the Child Abuse Prevention and Treatment Act will likely be amended once again, as it has every 3 to 5 years since 1974, and this revision may lead to additional state law or practice requirements that may result in new areas of state legislative change.

Child Welfare Legislative Reforms

Based upon the 1974 federal child abuse act, the 1980 federal child welfare act, and the 1997 federal Adoption and Safe Families Act that amended the 1980 legislation, states have also passed many new laws related to the work of the child welfare system, more broadly, in its response to aiding the families of abused and neglected children. Other legislative changes have been prodded by the federal Child and Family Services Reviews conducted by the U.S. Department of Health and Human Services, which have noted some profound shortcomings in state and local practice related to the safety, permanency, and well-being of abused or neglected children in foster care. Some legislative changes have been needed because of changes in child welfare agency practice and policy, such as the increasing use of kinship care or relative placement as an alternative to foster care with a stranger or the advocacy for infant "safe haven" laws that negate parental criminal responsibility if a parent leaves his or her newborn in a safe environment with the intent of not resuming care. Because of the importance of other child welfare best practices, state laws frequently address such topics as case planning requirements and parental participation in the development of case plans; concurrent planning by agencies for child permanency; reasonable efforts to preserve or reunify families (and when those efforts need not be made) and to achieve legal permanency for children; criminal background checks on prospective foster and adoptive parents and how the results may impact upon related agency decisions; and laws establishing both timelines and decision criteria for certain important child-related court hearings, such as the permanency hearing mandated by the Adoption and Safe Families Act. Another area where there continues to be legislative activity relates to the involvement in court proceedings of the child, parents, foster parents, relatives, and other interested adults, including having their voices more effectively heard in court and ensuring that they be given effective opportunities to actively participate at all hearings. Finally, certain issues related to child and youth permanency remain the topic of much legislation, such as subsidized permanent guardianship (expanding upon subsidized adoption laws) and laws related to improving outcomes for older youth who are in the process of transitioning to adulthood from foster care.

Howard A. Davidson

See also Adoption and Safe Families Act of 1997; Adoption Assistance and Child Welfare Act of 1980; Child Abuse Prevention and Treatment Act; Mandatory Reporting Laws of Child Maltreatment; Office on Child Abuse and Neglect

Further Readings

Adoption Assistance and Child Welfare Act and Adoption and Safe Families Act, 42 U.S. Code Sections 620 and 670.

Baker, D. R. (2001). *Making sense of the ASFA regulations: A roadmap for effective implementation.* Washington, DC: ABA Center on Children and the Law.

Child Abuse Prevention and Treatment Act, 42 U.S. Code Section 5101.

Web Sites

Child Welfare Information Gateway, State Statutes Search: http://www.childwelfare.gov/systemwide/laws_policies/state/index.cfm

LEGISLATION, ELDER ABUSE

Elder abuse is a global term referring to the abuse, neglect, and exploitation of adults who are approximately 60 years of age and older. The National Center on Elder Abuse (NCEA) contends that between 500,000 and 5 million older Americans are abused each year. Adult Protective Services (APS) is typically the agency of first report for abuse of elders over 60 years of age in each state in the United States. According to the most recent survey of APS agencies, self-neglect was the most common category of investigated reports (29.4%), followed by caregiver neglect (26.1%) and financial exploitation (18.5%). Researchers estimate that as many as 1 in 14 instances of elder abuse go unreported. From 1996 to 2006, reports of the abuse of older adults increased by approximately 80%. This increase in 10 years' time highlights the growing need for understanding elder abuse legislation.

History

States' provision of protective services for adults emerged from government's concern for adults who could not manage their own affairs. Protective services were funded in 1975 under Title XX of the Social Security Act, which required funding protective services for all adults 18 years of age and older without regard to income. The legislation placed an emphasis on persons found in situations that included abuse, neglect, and exploitation. Under the Title XX federal mandate, states created APS units in their local social service agencies, either through statute or regulation. Programs included mandatory reporting laws, modeled after child abuse reporting legislation, as well as involuntary interventions, such as emergency orders, and civil commitments.

Congressional involvement in elder abuse prevention spans more than 25 years. From 1978 through 1990, the House Select Committee on Aging held hearings on the problem of elder abuse. The hearings prompted a number of reports documenting the scope of the problem, including *Elder Abuse: An Examination of a Hidden Problem* (House Select Committee on Aging) and *Elder Abuse: A National Disgrace* (Rep. Claude Pepper). In 1990, the Subcommittee on Health and Long-Term Care of the House Select Committee on Aging issued *Elder Abuse: A Decade of Shame and Inaction.*

In an effort to combat elder abuse in nursing homes, the ombudsman program was created in 1972 as a Public Health Service demonstration project. Demonstration projects were carried out in seven states, which were transferred to the Administration on Aging in 1974. In 1978, the U.S. Congress amended the Older Americans Act (OAA; 42 U.S.C. §3001 et seq., as amended), requiring that each state develop a long-term care ombudsman program. Additional statutory requirements for the program were added, with existing requirements strengthened in subsequent OAA amendments.

In 1987, the federal government described elder abuse, neglect, and exploitation in amendments to the OAA under Title VII. Included were definitions of elder abuse in addition to funding for a National Center on Elder Abuse (NCEA) and for elder abuse and awareness activities for states. Subsequent re-authorizations of the Older Americans Act have increased dollars for the NCEA and for states' elder abuse and awareness efforts, which are carried out by a variety of state-level entities.

Other pieces of legislation, such as the Violence Against Women Act (1994), have provisions for addressing elder abuse, although its focus is primarily on a younger adult population.

The Elder Justice Act

After piecemeal policymaking on elder abuse, Senator John Breaux (D) of Louisiana emerged as a champion for federal legislation on the issue. Named the Chairman of the Senate Special Committee on Aging in 2001, in 2002, Breaux, along with Orin Hatch (R, Utah), first introduced the Elder Justice Act in the Senate. Although the act failed to pass with its first and second years of introduction in Congress, it was reintroduced for a third time on November 16, 2005. With Senator Breaux retiring from office, Senator Hatch introduced the Elder Justice Act (EJA), federal legislation proposed to increase the detection, prevention, and prosecution of elder abuse. The bill was introduced by Representative Peter King (R, New York), chairperson of the House Committee on Homeland Security, in March 2006. The Elder Justice Coalition, a nonpartisan coalition of national, regional, state, and local advocacy groups and concerned citizens, is working to promote public support for the act.

The EJA contains at least six major provisions. First, it establishes an Elder Justice Resource Center, a repository of national data collection, maintenance, and dissemination of information related to elder justice. Second, the EJA includes provision for a steady flow of grants to eligible entities for abuse detection, prevention, and intervention as well as for Centers of Excellence. The national Centers of Excellence are conceived to specialize in research, clinical practice, and training. Third, the act provides for the creation of stationary and mobile forensic centers to promote forensic expertise, particularly for professionals in forensic pathology and geriatrics. Fourth, the act contains language that enables safer long-term care facilities by incentivizing the reporting of elder abuse and training of and criminal background checks for staff. Fifth, technical assistance is provided to law enforcement in order to increase the prosecution of elder abuse. Finally, consistent funding to APS is included via grants to state and local offices.

Pamela B. Teaster

See also Adult Protective Services; Elder Abuse

Further Readings

Fulmer, T. (Ed.). (2002). *Journal of Elder Abuse and Neglect,* *14*(2/3).

The Library of Congress Thomas. (2006, May). *The Elder Justice Act.* Retrieved May 19, 2006, from http://thomas.loc.gov/

National Center for Elder Abuse. (2006, February). *Information about laws related to elder abuse.* Retrieved May 19, 2006, from http://www.ncea.aoa.gov/ncearoot/ Main_Site/index.aspx

National Long Term Care Ombudsman Resource Center. (2001). About the Long-term Ombudsman Resource Center. Retrieved May 19, 2006, from http://www .ltcombudsman.org/ombpublic/49_151_940.CFM

Teaster, P. B., Dugar, T. D., Otto, J. M., Mendiondo, M. S., Abner, E. L., & Cecil, K. A. (2006). *The 2004 survey of state Adult Protective Services: Abuse of adults 60 years of age and older. Report to the National Center on Elder Abuse, Administration on Aging.* Washington, DC: National Center on Elder Abuse.

Web Sites

Elder Justice Coalition: http://www.elderjusticecoalition .com/index.htm

LEGISLATION, HATE CRIMES

Hate crime legislation takes into consideration the factor of the crime victim being targeted specifically because he or she is a member of a protected group in addition to the actual criminal act against him or her. Hence, the victim has been singled out in a way that sends a message to other members of the group based on the hatred of or prejudice against the group.

Definitions

The Federal Bureau of Investigation (FBI) defines a hate crime as a criminal offense committed against a person, property, or a group that is motivated in whole or in part by the offender's bias against a race, ethnicity, national origin, religion, disability, or sexual orientation. This definition forms the basis of the Hate Crimes Statistics Act of 1990. However, the FBI has no federal jurisdiction to investigate hate crimes in which the motivation is sexual orientation and can only investigate crimes based on disability bias as it relates to housing rights. The FBI's involvement in civil rights investigations is rooted in the 1964 Civil Rights Act, a response to the need to investigate and prosecute crimes against those working for equal rights for Black Americans.

Although the basic premise of bias is the same, state and federal hate crime legislation differs in terms of which groups are included as protected classes and under what circumstances. The federal hate crime law, passed in 1969, for instance, covers only race, color, religion, and national origin and applies only if the crime occurs when the victim is attending public school or is at work or participating in one of four federally protected activities (18 USC § 245). Individual state laws vary widely.

Pros and Cons of Hate Crime Legislation

People who oppose hate crime legislation argue that the crimes to which it applies to are already illegal under existing law. Opponents also tend to argue that a crime is a crime, and hate crime victims should not be accorded special treatment, since all crime victims suffer. However, hate crimes apply to particularly vulnerable groups, groups that have been targeted in the past and are in need of extra protection. As "message crimes," the sentence enhancements of hate crime legislation send a warning to perpetrators that singling out these group members is unacceptable. Perpetrators of bias crimes choose to commit these acts precisely because of the characteristics of their particular targets. In that case, the penalty speaks specifically to the offenders' motivations, a factor that is taken into account in other cases, such as the differing degrees of a murder conviction.

Some feel that hate crime legislation grants special rights to protected groups or is politically motivated to grant equal treatment to these groups in society. Hate crimes are perpetrated by individuals who have underlying fears of others who are different. These crimes are often attempts to prevent the equal rights of other citizens. In that sense, the legislation does work to contribute to the social and political equality of all people regardless of group membership—equality that offenders try to delay or deny. Protected groups may need this legislation until equal rights are truly in effect and individuals are no longer targeted because of who they are.

The criticism that hate crime legislation punishes free speech has also been raised. However, the legislation only applies when a criminal act has been committed and then only in certain circumstances. Preaching hatred is constitutionally protected speech under the First Amendment, and hate crimes legislation does not punish anyone for holding biased views or speaking about them.

Hate Crime Statistics

The Hate Crime Statistics Act of 1990 authorizes the Justice Department to collect data on hate crimes and publish annual findings. The act covers crimes based on prejudice concerning race, religion, sexual orientation, ethnicity, and disability. There are some significant challenges with collecting data on hate crimes. One is that hate crime victims often do not report the crimes to the police. Coming from groups that face societal stigma and discrimination, these crime victims often distrust police and courts or fear retribution if they come forward. Another significant issue is that reporting these data to the FBI is voluntary. Consequently, hate crimes are underreported. The most recent estimate by the Bureau of Justice Statistics is that hate crimes have been underestimated by as much as 16 to 23 times for the past 15 years.

Based on data from two data sources, the FBI and the National Crime Victimization Survey (NCVS), the Bureau of Justice Statistics reported in 2005 that between July 2000 and December 2003 there was an annual average of 210,000 hate crime victimizations. Hate crimes tend to be serious violent crimes. Most (84%) of the hate crimes were crimes of rape, sexual assault, robbery, or assault. Approximately 44% of the crimes were reported to police.

Existing Legislation

As of 2004, four states had no hate crimes legislation, two states had legislation that does not specify categories, 15 states had laws that did not include the categories of sexual orientation or gender identity, 21 states included sexual orientation, and eight states included both sexual orientation and gender identity as protected classes.

In 1994, U.S. Congress passed the Hate Crimes Sentencing Enhancement Act, which applies to attacks and vandalism in national parks and on other federal property. The protected categories include race, color, religion, national origin, ethnicity, gender, disability, or sexual orientation.

Proposed Legislation

Hate crimes legislation was introduced into the U.S. Congress in 1997 and has been called various names, such as the Hate Crimes Prevention Act, the Children's Safety Act, and the Local Law Enforcement Hate Crimes Prevention Act. These acts (or as amendments to other acts) sometimes passed, but they would be stripped out of the acts before final votes. Hate crimes legislation was introduced into both houses of Congress in May 2005. Called the Local Law Enforcement Enhancement Act, this law expands federal protection to sexual orientation, gender, gender identity, and disability. Most recently, in 2007, the Local Law Enforcement Hate Crimes Prevention Act, renamed the Matthew Shepard Act, passed in the House of Representatives. It was added as an amendment to the Senate Defense reauthorization bill. However, in September 2007, Senate Democrats said they lacked the votes to pass the two together, and before the bill went forward the amendment was removed. Advocates for the lesbian, gay, bisexual, and transgender community are lobbying hard for this bill because they believe it provides needed protection for those targeted based on their sexual orientation or gender identity, the third largest category of hate crimes.

Lori B. Girshick

See also Hate Crimes (Bias Crimes), Anti-Gay; Hate Crimes (Bias Crimes), Criminal Justice Responses; Hate Crimes (Bias Crimes), Gender Motivated; Hate Crimes (Bias Crimes), Racially Motivated; Hate Crimes (Bias Crimes), Religiously Motivated; Homophobia

Further Readings

Harlow, C. W. (2005). *Hate crime reported by victims and police.* Washington, DC: U.S. Department of Justice, Bureau of Justice Statistics.

Legislation, Intimate Partner Violence

Historians suggest that the temperance laws of the late 1800s may actually be the first laws created to help address intimate partner violence, known more commonly as domestic violence. Spurred on by the belief that men's drinking of alcohol increased violence against women and girls, women activists fought to outlaw alcohol consumption and were successful with the creation of the 18th amendment in 1919. Although the amendment was ultimately repealed, calls to end wife beating were integral parts of almost every major women's movement in the late 1800s and early 1900s. By the end of the 20th century, women's advocacy efforts resulted in state legislatures recognizing domestic violence as a crime and the passage of the first comprehensive national legislation to address domestic violence.

State and Local Legislation

Most laws outlawing domestic violence developed at the state and local levels. Massachusetts and Alabama were the first states to outlaw wife beating in 1871. However, it was not until a century later, in the 1970s, that domestic violence emerged as a serious issue worthy of a public response in state legislators' minds. This shift occurred largely as a result of a strong women's movement and a burgeoning battered women's movement. States tended to focus their legislative efforts on outlawing types of assault, only some of which were ever actually labeled domestic violence. State efforts also focused on including intimate relationships as covered by the scope of existing laws. It is difficult to definitively catalog when every state actually passed a law outlawing domestic violence, though all states now have some criminal sanction against violence against an intimate partner.

States and localities also have passed laws creating protective or stay away orders that require abusers to stay away from their victims for a certain period of time. Focused in the civil courts typically, protective order statutes now exist in all 50 states as well as in the District of Columbia. Created in the mid-1970s largely because criminal courts were not applying existing criminal statutes to domestic situations, protective orders can be effective in preventing further victimization, and their violation is now often viewed as a criminal matter.

The early 1990s saw the recognition of stalking as a serious crime, usually involving intimate partners. California first enacted a law prohibiting stalking in 1990, and since, every other state has created a similar statute. Stalking is repeated harassment and threatening behavior and, like domestic violence, is defined differently by different states.

Although rape within the marital context was not historically recognized, marital rape was finally criminalized in all 50 states by 1993. However, marital rape statutes in many states still grant some exemptions from prosecuting husbands for rape.

Federal Legislation
Family Violence Prevention and Services Act

The first federal legislation to support services for victims of domestic violence was created in the mid-1980s. Known as the Family Violence Prevention and Services Act, it was created in 1984 and remains the only federal funding source dedicated solely to the funding of domestic violence shelters and programs.

Violence Against Women Act of 1994

In 1990, the first more comprehensive legislation to address domestic violence or intimate partner violence was introduced in the U.S. Congress. The U.S. Senate held several hearings and reported bills out of committee over the next few years. The trial of O. J. Simpson, the former football star and television announcer who was accused of killing his wife and a friend, brought new attention to the issue in 1993 and 1994. With the help of outspoken advocates across the country, the Violence Against Women Act (VAWA) was finally signed into law in September of 1994 as a part of the Violent Crime Control and Law Enforcement Act of 1994.

Because VAWA was included as part of a crime bill, most of its provisions focused on the criminal justice response to violence against women. Specifically, it included

- new penalties for gender-related violence;
- new grant programs encouraging states to address domestic violence and sexual assault including law enforcement and prosecution grants (STOP grants), grants to encourage arrest, rural domestic violence and child abuse enforcement grants, creation of a national domestic violence hotline; and
- Full Faith and Credit provisions allowing for protection orders from one state to be recognized in another state.

Although not many felt this act completely addressed the needs of victims of domestic violence, almost all involved believed it was a vital first step in the nation's efforts to treat domestic violence as a serious problem.

Violence Against Women Act of 2000

Because the authorization for the original VAWA provisions expired in 2000, Congress took up the reauthorization of this landmark legislation in 1998 and completed its efforts in the fall of 2000 with the passage of the Violence Against Women Act of 2000. The House version of the bill, known as H.R. 1248, passed on September 26 by a vote of 415–3. During the course of final negotiations, VAWA 2000 was merged with the Trafficking Victims Protection Act and several smaller bills and then passed the Senate in early October by a vote of 95–0. President Clinton signed the final legislation, The Victims of Trafficking and Violence Protection Act, into law on October 28, 2000.

Despite early efforts by advocates and congressional allies to create a more comprehensive bill, the final version of VAWA reauthorization included a continuation of already existing programs with a few improvements, additions, and funding increases. The following new programs were created:

Civil Legal Assistance—A separate grant program for civil legal services to give victims legal help with protection orders, family court matters, housing, immigration, and administrative matters.

Transitional Housing—A program providing grants to aid individuals who need housing as a result of fleeing a situation of domestic violence.

Supervised Visitation Centers—A pilot project to provide grants to state and local law enforcement to provide supervised visitation exchange for the children of victims of domestic violence, child abuse, and sexual assault.

Battered Immigrant Women—Legislation addressing the needs of battered immigrant women was probably the most significant addition to the original VAWA. This section removed onerous requirements for immigrant women to receive VAWA protections, allowed battered immigrant women to obtain lawful permanent residence without leaving the country, restored access to VAWA protections for immigrants regardless of how they entered the country, and created a new type of visa for victims of serious crimes. Although many of these provisions were included in the original VAWA, immigration legislation in 1996 stripped many of them away, creating the need to add them to VAWA 2000.

Dating Violence—The definition of dating violence was changed to allow grants to go to programs that addressed intimate partner violence between people who were dating but not necessarily married.

Services for Disabled and Older Women—Funds were authorized to provide grants to train law enforcement and develop policies to address the needs of older and disabled victims of domestic and sexual violence.

The Violence Against Women Act Reauthorization of 2005

VAWA was reauthorized in 2005 and while continuing existing programs, it also expanded in four critical areas: sexual assault, children and youth, health, and prevention. In addition, a new emphasis was placed within all of the programs on addressing the needs of communities of color and Native American women living on and off tribal lands. Mainly grant programs, these new provisions were created to address areas of need beyond immediate crisis and criminal justice responses. Although most agreed that the first VAWA must address the immediate safety needs of battered women and their children, the new VAWA was able to expand to reach out to populations that were not currently being served and to reach younger victims, those both witnessing and experiencing violence. The new VAWA also saw increases in authorized spending, reaching close to $1 billion a year.

The new provisions in VAWA 2005 included the following:

Services for youth who are experiencing dating violence. Most existing programs had only served adult victims, including those with young children in shelter settings. VAWA 2005 recognized that younger women, who actually experience the highest rates of violence, were not being served because they often would not reach out to a shelter, and those who interacted with youth often were not trained to recognize the warning signs of physical and sexual abuse.

Prevention programs. New programs focused on stopping violence before it starts were also included.

Specifically, programs working with children exposed to domestic violence, new moms and young families, and boys and men addressed some of the newer thinking on how to reach those most at risk for becoming both victims and perpetrators of violence.

Health care. Reaching out to health care providers became a new priority in VAWA. Based on research demonstrating the overwhelming health effects of violence and abuse, health and behavioral health professionals became a new target audience for training. In addition, health care providers are uniquely positioned to address violence early on, before many women or their families might turn to law enforcement or shelters.

Sexual assault services. VAWA in 2005 also created for the first time a direct federal funding source for rape crisis centers throughout the nation. Previously, only rape prevention and education programs had been funded through the Centers for Disease Control and Prevention.

The unanimous passage of VAWA in the winter of 2005 and the noncontroversial signing of it by President George W. Bush marked a major milestone in the movement to end violence against women. What had once been controversial or seen as only a "radical feminist issue" had now become mainstream with a truly national consensus forming. Domestic violence and sexual assault were viewed as wrong, no longer a private family matter but rather a public problem in need of public solutions.

Kiersten Stewart

See also Family Violence Prevention and Services Act; Legal System, Criminal Justice Strategies to Reduce Interpersonal Violence; Office on Violence Against Women; Prevention Programs, Interpersonal Violence; Violence Against Women Act

Further Readings

Dugan, L. (2003). Domestic violence legislation: Exploring impacts on domestic violence and the likelihood that police are informed and arrest. *Criminology & Public Policy, 2*(2), 283–312.

Klein, A. (2004). *The criminal justice response to domestic violence.* Belmont, CA: Wadsworth/Thomson Learning.

Siskin, A. (2001). *Violence Against Women Act: History, federal funding, and reauthorizing legislation.* Washington, DC: Congressional Research Service.

LEGISLATION, RAPE/SEXUAL ASSAULT

There have been many reforms to the laws governing rape and sexual assault in recent decades. Prior to the 1970s, the definition of rape was quite narrow; the law only recognized an assault as rape in limited circumstances and restricted those who could be considered victims of rape. Further, evidentiary requirements placed a much higher burden on rape victims than other victims of crime. Unlike other crime victims, rape victims were required to corroborate their testimonies and their past sexual history was often introduced into evidence to rebut charges of rape. The issue of resistance was a dominant theme in rape cases with victims having the burden of proving not only that their attackers penetrated them forcibly and against their will, but also that they fought back sufficiently. The change from the pre-1970s rape statutes and the modern rape statutes that are in place today is largely due to feminists' activism and urge for legislative change during the 1970s. Today, rape law has expanded its scope to include different sexual crimes and a broader definition of rape and recognizes that men can be raped. Most states have eliminated the corroboration and resistance requirements in exchange for a lack of consent, and rape shield laws have been enacted to protect victims from having their sexual history introduced in court unnecessarily.

An Evolution in Defining Rape and Sexual Assault

Prior to the 1970s, the definition of rape and its scope was rather constricted. The law only recognized a sexual assault as rape when there was some forced penetration of the vagina by the penis, and only assaults by a male perpetrator and a female victim were included within the legal definition of rape. Further, in pre-1970s rape laws, all states exempted a husband from being prosecuted for raping his wife. The popular belief was that a husband could not rape his wife, stemming from older laws classifying a wife as her husband's property to do with as he wished.

To address the realities of assault victims, modern laws embrace a broader definition of rape. Today, rape is generally defined as sexual penetration by force without consent. Thus, unwanted anal penetration is also included within the definition of rape, and the law now recognizes rape by foreign objects besides the penis, such as bottles, baseball bats, and broomsticks. Further, sexual assault crimes have expanded to include sexual acts besides penetration, such as unwanted fondling, touching, or oral sex. In an attempt to remedy some of the widespread preconceptions and prejudices about rape, many states have also enacted new terminology that replaces *rape* with words such as *sexual assault, sexual battery,* or *criminal sexual conduct.*

Modern rape laws also now protect a wider spectrum of individuals. Today, perpetrators and victims of rape can be either gender, and the law recognizes that rape can occur between people of the same sex. The law in every state has changed to include spousal abuse as a crime. Similarly, state laws have removed the marital rape exception, meaning that rape laws apply regardless of whether the victim and the perpetrator are married or have been married before, though sometimes the standard of proving lack of consent is higher.

Corroboration Requirement

Prior to the 1970s, to prevail in a rape case, the law required that evidence be presented to corroborate (or substantiate) the female victim's testimony about the alleged rape. The rationale was based on the widely held belief that women often falsely reported being raped as a form of retaliation against a man. Another rationale for the requirement was based on the belief that disproving a false charge in a rape case was more difficult than in other crimes. The corroboration requirement, however, proved to be a huge obstacle for many rape victims because rape often occurs in private, so obtaining corroborating evidence was often incredibly difficult. Many reformers and activists felt that this requirement was responsible for the low rate of rape convictions. Further, critics of the requirement considered it to be sexually discriminatory, arguing that the corroboration requirement only applied to rape cases, a crime largely committed against women, and not to other crimes such as assault and robbery where the victim's word was held to be sufficient evidence for a conviction. In response to this overwhelming criticism, most states have eliminated the corroboration requirement.

Resistance Requirement

In order for the intercourse to constitute rape, the law used to require that the perpetrator used some amount of physical force against the victim and that the victim resisted to the utmost through physical resistance or struggle. The degree of a woman's resistance and the resultant injuries used to be the deciding factor as to whether a rape occurred. However, today the law has changed so it is no longer necessary that a perpetrator use physical force against the victim in order for the intercourse to constitute rape. In some states, the amount of force necessary to constitute rape is only the amount of force needed for the penis to enter the vagina (which essentially eliminates the force requirement). Under today's rape statutes, the victim is not required to physically struggle or resist the unwanted sexual advances. Society has recognized that there are some situations in which a victim feels that by physically resisting or struggling with the perpetrator, she or he may put her- or himself in danger of death or serious bodily harm. The victim may feel so afraid of the perpetrator that she or he submits to the perpetrator's will. Even though the perpetrator may not have used excessive force and the victim did not physically fight back, the assault would still constitute rape since the victim did not consent to the sexual act.

Consent

Under the law today, resistance by the victim and use of force by the perpetrator have become less important determining factors, and the issue of consent has become the primary focus of the law. In determining whether a rape has been committed, the question is now whether a reasonable person should have known that the victim was not consenting to the sexual act. Consent is defined as positive cooperation in act or attitude pursuant to an exercise of free will. The person must act freely and voluntarily and have knowledge of the nature of the act or transaction involved. The only real consent is established by asking for and discussing sexual contact prior to the act. Just because someone did not verbally say no does not mean that she or he automatically consented to the act. Furthermore, it is rape if the victim was incapacitated and thus unable to say no to the sexual act or resist the perpetrator's advances. If the victim was incapacitated, she or he is not legally able to consent to the sexual act, so any act of sexual intercourse would be rape under the law.

Rape Shield Laws

Rape shield laws represent another area of reform. Historically, courts would admit into evidence the victim's sexual past because it was deemed to be relevant in determining issues of consent and credibility. Courts believed that an "unchaste" woman would be more prone to consent to intercourse and that these women were more inclined to lie because of these experiences. Many victims felt embarrassed in revealing such personal information and reported feeling as if they themselves were on trial. As a result, victims were less likely to press charges in order to avoid the ordeal altogether. Even when a woman did press charges, once her sexual past was introduced into evidence, the perpetrator was often acquitted. Reformers sought to change this practice by criticizing the underlying rationale behind the requirement, arguing that there was no evidentiary basis to support the conclusion that a woman's sexual past served as a probative link to her credibility or consent. In response, the U.S. Congress and nearly every state have enacted laws designed to restrict the admissibility of a victim's sexual past as evidence. Today, there are very restrictive laws that prohibit the introduction of a victim's sexual history except as constitutionally required or if the information is relevant in the interest of justice.

Many activists and reformers sought to change early rape and sexual assault laws in an effort to improve the treatment of victims in the criminal justice system while simultaneously working to dismantle myths and preconceived notions about how and why rape occurs. The hope was that better treatment would encourage reporting and would lead to more rape convictions. In response to overwhelming criticism, legislators enacted rape and sexual assault laws to better protect victims of sexual assault and hold perpetrators accountable. Research shows that as a result of rape law reform, society's views on rape tend to be more refined and more sympathetic toward rape victims than ever before.

*Juley Fulcher, Alesha Dominique,
and Emily Lambert*

See also Legal System, Civil and Criminal Court Remedies for Sexual Assault/Rape; Rape Shield Laws; Rape/Sexual Assault; Sex Offenders; Sexual Abuse; Sexual Assault Response Team; Sexual Coercion; Statutory Rape

Further Readings

Berger, R. J., Searles, P., & Neuman, W. L. (1988). The dimensions of rape reform legislation. *Law & Society Review, 22,* 329–355.

Cuklanz, L. (1996). *Rape on trial: How the mass media construct legal reform and social change.* Philadelphia: University of Pennsylvania Press.

Curcio, A. (2004). The Georgia roundtable discussion model: Another way to approach reforming rape laws. *Georgia State University Law Review, 20,* 565–615.

Futter, S., & Mebane, W. R. (2001). The effects of rape law reform on rape case processing. *Berkeley Women's Law Journal, 16,* 72–131.

Horney, J., & Spohn, C. C. (1996). The impact of rape law reform on the processing of simple and aggravated rape cases. *Journal of Criminal Law and Criminology, 86,* 861–884.

Mail Order Brides

In industrialized nations including the United States, some men desire to locate women from outside their own country for the purpose of marriage. In the past, listings of women interested in such a marriage primarily came through correspondence by mail and through pen pal clubs, giving them the name *mail order brides*. Today, there are hundreds of different services available to men who seek a bride from another country, including the use of the Internet, magazines, and brochures with photos and descriptions of women.

The extent to which such marriages succeed and are fulfilling to both partners is unknown. Physical, sexual, and psychological abuse of mail order brides has been reported. The circumstances surrounding these marriages present risk for violence against women, and there is a growing body of research on this topic. Risk factors include that the women have little opportunity to assess the character of the men they are marrying and men are not screened by agencies for prior abuse history or failed international marriages. Many of the men possess characteristics that may be associated with a greater likelihood of partner violence. Some seek marriage to women from outside the United States due to dissatisfaction with North American women who they view as too aggressive, demanding, and liberal. Men seeking mail order brides frequently report a desire for a more submissive, traditional wife. Women may be at increased risk for partner violence especially when they speak little or no English; have no social support system in their new communities; have no personal finances to leave an abusive husband; lack formal education, training, or marketable work skills to be independent; and are unaware of their rights in the United States in regard to reporting domestic violence and to special provisions available to abused immigrant women to help them avoid revocation of visas if they divorce.

Today, the largest number of mail order brides available to men in the United States comes from Southeast Asia, including the Philippines; Russia; and other countries of the former Soviet Union. Women seek a better life in the United States and often are from countries where war or other hardships have led to lower life expectancies for males and a reduction in the number of marriageable or desirable men.

Customarily men pay for contact information for women they find interesting and initiate correspondence with them either via the Internet or mail. A lucrative and mostly unregulated international marriage agency business has developed to provide services such as translating correspondence between clients who do not speak a common language and arranging excursions where a man is introduced to a number of women interested in marriage and immigration to the United States. Men may pay $3,000 to $10,000 for such arrangements. There is also evidence that listings of women seeking marriage to men in other countries are used by traffickers who contact the women, arrange travel to a foreign destination ostensibly for the purpose of marriage, and then take their papers and force them into prostitution.

Linda M. Williams and Christen L. Brook

See also Trafficking, Human; Department of Homeland
Security and Immigration Services; Domestic Violence
Among Immigrant Women

Further Readings

Belleau, M. (2003). Mail-order brides in a global world.
Albany Law Review, 67(2), 595–607.
Chun, C. (1996). The mail-order bride industry: The
perpetuation of transnational economic inequalities and
stereotypes. *University of Pennsylvania Journal of
International Economic Law, 17,* 1155–1183.
Raj, A., & Silverman, J. (2002). Violence against immigrant
women. *Violence Against Women, 8*(3), 367–398.

MALE PEER SUPPORT, THEORY OF

Woman abuse has many determinants or sources.
Still, one of the most significant risk factors is male
peer support, which is defined as attachments to male
peers and as the resources they provide that perpetuate and legitimate woman abuse. Approximately 20
years ago, Walter DeKeseredy developed the first
male peer support model of woman abuse in college
dating, and it is heavily informed by social support
theory. Social support theory is generally used to
explain the role of social support in health maintenance and disease prevention. However, DeKeseredy
reconceptualized it to apply to woman abuse.

Male peer support theory argues that many men experience various types of stress in dating relationships,
ranging from sexual problems to challenges to their male
authority. Some men try to deal with these problems
themselves, while others turn to their male friends for
advice, guidance, and various other kinds of social support. The resources provided by these peers may encourage and justify woman abuse under certain conditions.
Further, male peer support can influence men to victimize their dating partners regardless of stress.

There is some support for this model. For example,
based on analyses of self-report survey data gathered
from a convenience sample of 333 Canadian male
undergraduates, DeKeseredy found that social ties
with physically, sexually, and/or psychologically abusive peers are strongly related to abuse among men who
experience high levels of dating life-events stress. This
finding supports a basic sociological argument promoted by differential association theorists and other
scholars: that the victimization of women is behavior

that is socially learned from interaction with others.
Nevertheless, the model does not account for other
explanatory variables; therefore, in 1993, DeKeseredy
and Martin Schwartz developed the modified male
peer support model of woman abuse in college dating.

In addition to addressing the importance of factors
identified above, the modified model focuses on the
contributions of the ideology of familial and courtship
patriarchy, alcohol consumption, membership in formal
groups (e.g., fraternities), and the absence of deterrence.
Although it is better than the original, the modified perspective also has several limitations. Perhaps the most
important one is that although each of the individual elements has been tested empirically, there has not yet been
a test of the entire model. In fact, given its complexity,
it may very well be that it has more value as a heuristic
or teaching model than as a predictive one.

Since the late 1990s, researchers and theorists have
continued to modify male peer support theory and
have constructed integrated versions that attempt to
explain woman abuse in public housing, sexual and
physical assaults in dating, variations in woman abuse
across different marital status categories, and separation and divorce sexual assault.

Walter S. DeKeseredy

See also Date and Acquaintance Rape; Peer Influences on
Youth Violence; Rape/Sexual Assault

Further Readings

DeKeseredy, W. S., & Schwartz, M. D. (2002). Theorizing
public housing woman abuse as a function of economic
exclusion and male peer support. *Women's Health and
Urban Life, 1,* 26–45.
Godenzi, A., Schwartz, M. D., & DeKeseredy, W. S. (2001).
Toward a gendered social bond/male peer support theory of
university woman abuse. *Critical Criminology, 10,* 1–16.
Schwartz, M. D., & DeKeseredy, W. S. (1997). *Sexual
assault on the college campus: The role of male peer
support.* Thousand Oaks, CA: Sage.

MANDATORY ARREST/ PRO-ARREST STATUTES

Mandatory arrest and pro-arrest statutes are state laws
that direct how government agencies respond to
domestic violence. There are three types: mandatory

laws, preferred laws, and discretionary laws. States with mandatory laws require police compliance with their provisions, states with preferred laws indicate a preference for arrest, and states with discretionary laws leave the decision making to the individual police departments. This entry discusses the growing role of arrest in domestic violence, the impact of mandatory and pro-arrest statutes, and the advantages and disadvantages of these statutes on victims.

The Growing Role of Arrest

Since the early 1980s, there has been an increased policy preference toward the use of arrest when responding to domestic violence, coupled with a growing desire to limit police discretion in domestic violence incidents. The new pro-arrest consensus emerged when the traditional policy of nonintervention lost credibility and when earlier reform efforts such as crisis intervention lost adherents. Further, there was growing political pressure by women's groups, a surge of lawsuits brought against police departments for negligence and failure to provide equal protection to female victims in domestic violence situations, and the research findings of the Minneapolis Domestic Violence Experiment.

It had long been known that arresting certain domestic violence offenders was both proper and essential. Arrest provided the only method by which police could ensure separation of the couple and prevent subsequent violence, at least until the offender was released. Although the impact of arrest on domestic violence offenders was uncertain, at a minimum it was believed essential to the creation of a formal societal boundary defining acceptable behavior.

As a result, there has been an almost unprecedented wave of statutory changes since the 1970s, culminating in legislation in all 50 states, an effect that has irrevocably altered this position. These laws seek to expand police powers and govern practice when responding to domestic violence calls and enforcing suspected violations of restraining orders. State statutes provide the outside parameters within which the police must operate in their particular state.

State statutes vary considerably in their requirements. However, they all expressly purport to make profound structural changes in how government agencies respond to domestic violence. They enhance police powers, grant new criminal sanctions to prosecutors and the judiciary, increase the availability and enforcement of civil restraining orders, educate the public about the problem and the effects of violence in the family, and provide state and federal funding through the Violence Against Women Act for police, prosecutors, courts, and victim services.

In the calendar year of 2000, there were statutory provisions in 22 states and the District of Columbia for mandatory arrest, 6 states for preferred arrest, and 22 states for discretionary arrest in cases of domestic violence. Thirty-three states mandate arrest when there is probable cause to believe there has been a violation of a restraining order.

Arrest requirements in states with mandatory arrest statutes vary based on the circumstances, including elapsed time and seriousness of injury, as well as the relationships encompassed. Although some states have mandatory arrest provisions that apply to all crimes of domestic violence, others limit their provisions to felonies or limit their provisions to offenses committed within a specified timeframe.

In states with discretionary arrest provisions, there is variation in the arrest powers granted to officers. Although they typically allow police the authority to make warrantless arrests with probable cause to believe that a domestic violence offense has been committed, states vary in their limitations. These limitations include specifying the types of domestic violence offenses (such as felonies only), the time period during which the offense must have been committed, and the requirement of physical injury.

However, many departments within discretionary or preferred arrest states have mandatory or more restrictive arrest policies than required by state statute. Therefore, the interrelationship between state law, departmental policy, and actual police practices is the source of considerable investigation by researchers.

Impact

The implementation of legislative and policy mandates was intended to influence and change police behavior. This expectation has been supported by research on domestic violence legislation that has resulted in increased rates of arrest, prosecution, and conviction as well as improved responsiveness toward victims with the imposition of mandatory arrest requirements.

Research indicates that the implementation of mandatory and preferred arrest laws and/or policies is clearly associated with higher arrest rates. Arrest rates from data collected in the 1970s and 1980s were generally increasing. For example, in one analysis of 2000 National Incident-Based Reporting System data, it was reported that the overall arrest rate for assault and intimidation was well in excess of 30%: 49% for intimate partner violence cases and 44% for other domestic violence cases.

Advantages for Victims

Although possibly unintended, the current effect of such legislation has been to give primary responsibility—and power—for the suppression of ongoing domestic violence to the criminal justice system. This approach provides several potential benefits for victims. First, the criminalization of domestic violence confirms the status of domestic violence victims as victims of crime rather than as guilty participants in a battling relationship. The legal identification and label of *victim* (although many would prefer the term *survivor*) was also believed to increase victims' confidence in asserting their legal rights and as a possible vehicle for a victim to gain access to support services.

Second, by placing the burden of an arrest fully on police, it is also believed that there will be less pressure on already traumatized victims. When the police aggressively respond by arresting an offender, the victim might be greatly relieved because both the immediate source of the terror and the responsibility for coercive actions taken against the offender have been removed.

Third, such a policy fulfilled some victims' needs for retribution or punishment. The underlying rationale of retribution is that, given similar factors, victims of interpersonal violence deserve the same societal reaction as victims of stranger violence. Although many researchers discredit the legitimacy of retribution, it is a well-recognized goal of criminal justice intervention—institutionalizing retribution and obviating the need for vigilantism.

Fourth, many victims want batterers arrested in order to mandate their treatment by the courts. Their preferred outcome is to maintain the relationship without violence.

Disadvantages for Victims

The primary goal of all mandatory arrest policies is to prevent further violence and to protect victims. However, its implementation may further disempower victims and possibly work against their best interests. In many cases, the goals of assisting and empowering domestic violence victims are not as straightforward as in other settings. Even among violent crimes, victims of domestic violence may differ from other victims if only based on their intimate knowledge of and relationship to the offender. The victim's goals are similarly diverse. Some may wish to salvage a flawed relationship in which aggressive behavior is now customary, whereas other victims may have already terminated contact with the offender.

Jurisdictions with mandatory arrest policies cannot incorporate the complexity of these victim needs and preferences into policies and practices. However, some consider this concern irrelevant because the goal of the criminal justice system is to address the offender's behavior rather than the victim's preferences and needs. This concern is justified by pointing out that when victims successfully leave an abusive relationship, the batterer simply targets a new victim. Without the offender's identification by the criminal justice system, potential victims as well as police will be unaware of the threat this individual poses.

In addition, it has been argued that although victims have preferences, they may not be capable of judging what is in their best interests and that professionals should make these decisions. For many racial and ethnic minorities, the risks of arrest may outweigh potential benefits. Rates of domestic violence are the highest among racial and ethnic minorities and the poor in general, and thus arrest rates will disproportionately increase among these subpopulations.

There has also been an increase in the arrest of an ongoing victim of abuse in jurisdictions with a preferred or mandatory arrest policy. In some cases, dual arrests may be a result of insufficient police training in identifying the primary aggressor. Alternatively, such arrests may constitute a mechanism to further punish women. With the inability or refusal of police to distinguish victims from offenders accepted as the first explanation for the existence of high dual arrest rates, states, beginning with Washington in 1985, enacted primary or predominant aggressor laws. Currently 24 states have such laws.

Eve S. Buzawa

See also Legal System, Advocacy Efforts to Affect, Intimate Partner Violence; Legal System, Criminal Justice System Responses to Intimate Partner Violence; Legislation, Intimate Partner Violence; Police, Response to Domestic Violence

Further Readings

Buzawa, E. S., & Buzawa, C. (2003). *Domestic violence: The criminal justice response.* Thousand Oaks, CA: Sage.

Hirschel, J. D., Buzawa, E. S., Pattavina, A., Faggiani, D., & Reuland, M. (2007, May). *Explaining the prevalence, context and consequences of dual arrest in intimate partner cases* (NJC No. 218355). Retrieved from http://www.ncjrs.gov/App/Search/SearchResults.aspx?txtKeywordSearch=hirschel+buzawa&fromSearch=1

Sherman, L. W., & Berk, R. A. (1984). The specific deterrent effects of arrest for domestic assault. *American Sociological Review, 49,* 261–272.

MANDATORY REPORTING LAWS OF CHILD MALTREATMENT

Every U.S. state has laws mandating that professionals, and in some states laypersons, report cases of suspected child abuse and neglect. It is the responsibility of Child Protective Services (CPS) to respond to these reports by investigating their validity, assessing the risk to the child, and developing a course of action to both protect the child and strengthen the family. Initially, these mandatory reporting laws focused only on medical personnel, but the list of professionals required to report has grown in recent years, as has the list of abusive behaviors they must report. Mandatory reporting legislation has been instrumental in drawing attention to the problem of child maltreatment and has been heralded as a triumph in protecting children. Such laws, however, are also associated with a number of unintended consequences. In this entry, the history of child maltreatment mandatory reporting laws is discussed, as are the characteristics of mandatory reporting and its impact.

History of Child Maltreatment Mandatory Reporting Laws

Following the publication of R. S. Kempe's work identifying the battered child syndrome in 1962, the U.S. Children's Bureau adopted the first laws mandating that physicians report any known cases of child abuse and neglect. Between 1963 and 1967, all jurisdictions in the United States passed statutes requiring certain professionals to report suspected cases of child maltreatment. Over time, research about the problem of child maltreatment mounted, leading to broader definitions and greater awareness that a number of different professionals were in a position to identify and report abuse. The Child Abuse Prevention and Treatment Act of 1974 (P.L. 93-247) provided federal child protection funds for states that changed existing mandatory reporting laws to conform to federal standards. By the mid-1980s, doctors, nurses, social workers, mental health professionals, and teachers and other school staff were all required to report suspected physical, sexual, or emotional child abuse.

Currently, reports of child maltreatment are made either to states' local child protective services agencies, law enforcement agencies, or central state registries. Most states require reporters to contact appropriate agencies immediately after suspicion is raised, and many states also require a written report to follow within a specific time period, usually 24 to 48 hours. To encourage reporting and to reduce legal impediments to reporting, all states provide for some type of immunity from civil or criminal action to mandated reporters who make a report in good faith with the intention of protecting a child. In addition, other provisions protect reporters such as exceptions to required confidentiality in situations of suspected maltreatment and the requirement that only a reasonable suspicion is necessary to make a report. There is also the possibility of legal penalties for professionals who fail to report suspected cases of child maltreatment.

Characteristics of Mandated Reports

Each year the National Child Abuse and Neglect Data System collects annual data on child abuse and neglect reports accepted by CPS. In 2003, CPS agencies received approximately 3 million referrals of abuse or neglect. The agencies accepted approximately two thirds of these referrals for investigation or assessment. Of these accepted reports, 57% came from professionals such as educational personnel (16%), legal or law enforcement personnel (16%), social service personnel (12%), medical personnel (8%), and others (5%). The remaining 43% of reports came from nonprofessional sources including anonymous reports (9%), parents (7%), other relatives (8%), friends or neighbors (6%), alleged victims or perpetrators (1%), and other sources (12%).

Of the referrals that received investigation or assessment in 2003, more than one quarter were ultimately substantiated, meaning that CPS determined that there was sufficient evidence to conclude that at least one child was a victim of child abuse or neglect. Of these substantiated cases, the most common form of maltreatment was neglect (60%), followed by physical (20%), sexual (10%), and psychological (5%) abuse.

Impact of Mandatory Reporting Laws

Most experts agree that mandatory reporting laws have had a significant impact on the identification of child abuse and neglect. Between 1976 and 1993, for example, the number of children officially reported for child maltreatment increased dramatically and reached the 3 million mark in 1993, representing a 347% increase from 1976. The number of reports began to level off or decline in the mid-1990s and have since become relatively stable.

Although mandatory reporting laws have clearly succeeded in increasing rates of reporting and the identification of child maltreatment, they have also been associated with a number of unanticipated outcomes. One unintended consequence of these laws, for example, is the overburdening of the CPS system. When mandatory reporting laws were first enacted in the 1960s, child maltreatment was thought to be a relatively rare occurrence. Reports of child abuse and neglect have provided evidence to the contrary, and the dramatic rise in reports has overwhelmed CPS agencies whose resources are unable to meet the needs of children and families. CPS agencies have lacked the capacity to respond appropriately to reports of child maltreatment and as a result have been forced to make accommodations in an effort to manage caseloads. Out of necessity, many agencies have narrowed their definitions of abuse to address only the most severe reports, resulting in the provision of services to only a limited number of children and families in need.

Another unanticipated impact associated with mandatory reporting laws is that they might place people in the helping professions in a difficult position, essentially forcing them to violate the confidences of their clients. Professionals who want to help may fear that reporting the suspected abuse will cause the family or child more harm than good. They may be concerned that the child will be unnecessarily removed from the home or that there will be reprisals against the child. Professionals who are familiar with the child protection system, furthermore, are likely well aware of its shortcomings. They may realize that a particular allegation is unlikely to be substantiated or that a family is unlikely to receive the services it needs. Knowing the CPS system is overburdened, they may see themselves as better equipped to help needy families. In the end, professionals might reasonably conclude that it is better to maintain confidentiality and continue to work with these clients than to violate the client's trust and risk disruption of treatment. In addition, mandated professionals may have quite reasonable concerns about the potential for negative personal consequences, perhaps fearing that they could be sued, accused of false allegations, or forced to appear in court. The combined effects of these factors are that many professionals who are required to report suspected abuse choose not to do so. In the second National Incidence Study, for example, only half of the maltreatment cases known to community professionals were officially reported to CPS.

Despite problems associated with mandatory reporting, the consensus among legal scholars and others involved in child protection has been that mandatory reporting laws are essential to child protection. Given the concerns about CPS and many professionals' corresponding reluctance to report cases, however, more and more experts are calling for modifications in mandatory reporting laws. One possible solution would be to create an alternative, less adversarial response to less severe cases of child maltreatment. This approach would remove the reporting obligation from mental health professionals who encounter minor cases of abuse that appear not to present a serious threat to a child's safety. Such families could be diverted to a different department within CPS or to a separate agency, be handled on a voluntary basis, and/or be offered services that might stop their problems from escalating without a costly CPS investigation. Of course, this change would make mandated professionals responsible for determining what is or is not a severe case, a responsibility that also creates a less than perfect system with potential difficulties (e.g., successfully distinguishing among various degrees of risk via a telephone call). Recent efforts to develop risk-assessment tools and preliminary investigations of states using the triage approach, however, appear promising.

Cindy Miller-Perrin and Robin Perrin

See also Child Abuse Prevention and Treatment Act; Child Protective Services; Legal System and Child Protection; Legislation, Child Maltreatment

Further Readings

Larner, M. B., Stevenson, C. S., & Behrman, R. E. (1998). Protecting children from abuse and neglect [Special issue]. *The Future of Children, 8*(1).

Sedlak, A. J. (1990). *Technical amendment to the study findings: National incidence and prevalence of child abuse and neglect: 1988.* Rockville, MD: Westat.

U.S. Department of Health and Human Services, Administration on Children, Youth and Families. (2005). *Child maltreatment 2003.* Washington, DC: Government Printing Office.

Zellman, G. L., & Fair, C. C. (2002). Preventing and reporting abuse. In J. E. B. Myers, L. Berliner, J. Briere, C. T. Hendrix, C. Jenny, & T. A. Reid (Eds.), *The APSAC handbook on child maltreatment* (2nd ed., pp. 449–475). Thousand Oaks, CA: Sage.

MANDATORY REPORTING LAWS OF ELDER ABUSE

Many states have enacted reporting laws mandating the reporting of violence, including gunshots, injuries, and child abuse to law enforcement and/or social services. A few states have enacted domestic violence reporting laws. All states and the District of Columbia have enacted elder abuse reporting laws. In most cases, reporting is mandated; in a handful of states, laws encourage or permit reporting.

There is considerable variation in who is a mandated reporter and what conduct is reportable. In some states, everyone is a mandated reporter of elder abuse; in others, only certain professionals (typically law enforcement officials, health care and mental health providers, social workers, staff of Adult Protective Services [APS], Long Term Care Ombudsman, and aging services programs), persons providing care services to the elderly, attorneys, guardians, educators, and employees of financial institutions are mandated. Reportable conduct usually includes abuse, neglect, and financial exploitation. In some states, self-neglect is not reportable conduct. In some states, abandonment and abduction are also included as reportable conduct.

Reports are usually made to APS. In some jurisdictions and situations, reports are made to law enforcement instead of APS or in addition to APS. In most jurisdictions, failure of a mandated reporter to report is a crime. In many states, persons who report in good faith are immune from criminal and civil liability. Generally, the name of the reporting party is confidential and is not disclosed except pursuant to a court's order.

Elder abuse reporting laws have been largely modeled on child abuse reporting laws. Little analysis was given to whether the analogy is appropriate. The primary motivation for enacting them was to assist in detection. Mandatory reporting has resulted in more investigations than voluntary reporting. Relying on victims and their family members to report was seen as ineffective.

Benefits of mandatory reporting include enhancing safety by linking victims with services that provide information and referrals. Supporters of mandatory reporting argue that many victims are unable to report due to physical or cognitive deficits, isolation, or the inability to recognize what has occurred. Mandatory reporting offers an opportunity to train reporters on abuse issues, including the dynamics and effects of abuse. Reporting may lead to greater abuser accountability, potentially enhancing victim safety. Mandatory reporting increases the number of documented cases, increasing understanding of elder abuse prevalence and incidence.

However, elder abuse reporting laws are controversial and have been criticized. Older individuals may fear loss of control if outsiders are involved, loss of independence and isolation if a caregiver is removed, and fear of angering family members for involving outsiders. They may fear not being believed if they do report. Family members may be unwilling to report because of family privacy, love and affection, fear, uncertainty of how to handle a situation, or a desire not to get involved. They may be unaware of elder abuse and protective services. Some professionals are concerned that an older person will not return for help if he or she knows a report will be made and the professional relationship will be harmed. Investigations are involuntary and can be intrusive, resulting in an outcome the older person does not desire.

Opponents of mandatory reporting believe adult victims should have the right to decide if they want help and from whom. In jurisdictions using age-only criteria (not impairment or vulnerability), laws have been challenged as ageist and as approaches that infantilize adults. Laws do not take into account that adults retain their rights to make decisions for themselves and their ability to control confidential information provided as part of a professional relationship. Mandatory reporting removes from the victim the decision whether to ask for help and from which agency. Elder abuse laws largely override confidentiality even without a finding of incapacity.

Current laws generally do not address victim safety in the context of mandatory reporting. Specifically, there is no requirement that reporters provide safety planning or a referral or assistance to the subject of the report. Reports do not require that the reporter ask about or include in the report information about victim safety concerns. Statutes generally do not require that the mandated reporter notify an older person that a report will be filed with appropriate authorities.

Even when the older adult lacks capacity, reporting laws may be unable to deliver what they have promised. Mandatory reporting is only successful if supportive services with qualified staff and necessary resources exist. Unfortunately, APS is generally underfunded and understaffed in most areas of the country. Reporting does not guarantee a successful APS intervention. APS programs face increasing caseloads and dwindling resources. Investigations may be undertaken with inadequate funding or training, substantiation criteria may be subjective and inconsistent, available services vary widely, and funding levels do not ensure that adequate resources are available to address or improve an elder's situation. In addition, there are few quality treatment programs for perpetrators. The Governmental Accountability Office has concluded that public and professional awareness, interagency coordination, and adequate in-home and respite care services are more effective responses to elder abuse than the existing mandatory reporting laws.

Community-based advocates who are mandatory reporters face ethical and practice dilemmas. They must balance legal duties with client autonomy and safety considerations. They should confirm if state statutes on client confidentiality apply and which have priority over the other. Discussions of safety planning should include reporting situations. Cross training with APS and other mandated reporters on victim safety issues should be considered. Forging professional contacts and relationships with APS and developing

memoranda of understanding regarding mandatory elder abuse reporting situations may become critical.

Candace J. Heisler and Bonnie Brandl

See also Adult Protective Services; Coordinated Community Response; Elder Abuse

Further Readings

Brandl, B. (2005). *Mandatory reporting of elder abuse: Implications for domestic violence advocates.* Madison, WI: National Clearinghouse on Abuse in Later Life, A Project of the Wisconsin Coalition Against Domestic Violence. Retrieved from http://www.ncall.us/docs/Mandatory_Reporting_EA.pdf

Daly, J. M., Jogerst, G. J., Brinig, M. F., & Dawson, J. D. (2003). Mandatory reporting: Relationship of APS statute language on state reported elder abuse. *Journal of Elder Abuse and Neglect, 15*(2), 1–21.

Web Sites

National Adult Protective Services Association: http://www.apsnetwork.org/Abuse/index.html

National Center on Elder Abuse: http://www.elderabusecenter.org

MANDATORY REPORTING LAWS OF INTIMATE PARTNER VIOLENCE

Mandatory reporting laws for intimate partner violence aim to provide additional protection for victims by requiring persons other than the victim to report the crime or suspected crime. In the United States, only five states (Alabama, Louisiana, South Carolina, Washington, and Wyoming) do not mandate some form of reporting for various types of violence. Mandatory reporting laws specific to intimate partner violence have been enacted in five states (California, Colorado, Kentucky, New Hampshire, and Rhode Island).

Laws relating to intimate partner violence, including mandatory reporting, have generally been seen as substantively different from the broader case of violence against persons along two major issues: the nature of the relationship between victim and perpetrator and the autonomy of the adult victim. The historical stance that violence between intimates should be treated differently is reflected in legal decisions such as in an 1824 Mississippi case finding that under certain circumstances a man would not be subject to prosecution if he physically disciplined his wife. The second issue has its roots in the feminist movement and challenges mandatory reporting for victims who are autonomous adults.

State statutes vary widely on what must be reported and by whom. California and Colorado laws include intimate partner violence in requiring that health care providers report to law enforcement if they know or reasonably suspect that a patient's physical injury was caused by a firearm or by assaultive or abusive acts. Kentucky's law requires reporting to a state social service agency by any persons, not just by health care providers who have reasonable cause to suspect intimate partner violence. New Hampshire law mandates reporting by health care providers similar to that required in California and Colorado, unless the patient is also a victim of sexual assault or abuse or if the patient is over 18 and objects to the release of this information to the police. These exclusions from reporting do not apply if a gunshot wound is being treated. In Rhode Island, health care providers must report intimate partner violence for data collection purposes only without any patient identifying information.

The goal of mandatory reporting law is to provide additional protection to victims of intimate partner violence, but questions remain concerning the effectiveness of such laws and possible unintended effects on victims that will need to be resolved through continuing research and surveillance.

Linda K. Bledsoe

See also Health Care Response to Intimate Partner Violence; Legal System, Advocacy Efforts to Affect, Intimate Partner Violence

Further Readings

Bledsoe, L. K., Yankeelov, P. A., Barbee, A. P., & Antle, B. (2004). Understanding the impact of intimate partner violence mandatory reporting law. *Violence Against Women, 10,* 534–560.
Houry, D., Sachs, C. J., Feldhaus, K. M., & Linden, J. (2002). Violence inflicted injuries: Reporting laws in the fifty states. *Annals of Emergency Medicine, 39,* 56–60.
Hyman, A. (1997, November). *Mandatory reporting of domestic violence by health care providers: A policy paper.* San Francisco: Family Violence Prevention Fund. Retrieved May 9, 2006, from http://www.endabuse.org/health/mandatoryreporting/policypaper.pdf

MARITAL RAPE/WIFE RAPE

Marital rape is a serious form of intimate partner violence that is experienced by approximately 10% to 14% of married women. Rape by one's intimate partner may be one of the most common forms of sexual violence. In their Canadian study, Melanie Randall and Lori Haskell found that 30% of the adult women who were victims of sexual assault had been assaulted by their intimate partners.

The definitions of wife rape vary within the United States; however, it is commonly defined as unwanted intercourse or penetration (oral, anal, or vaginal) that occurs when a woman is forced, threatened with force, or unable to give her consent. Most studies of rape in marriage have focused on couples who were legally married, separated, divorced, or cohabiting. Cohabiting couples have generally been included in research on wife rape because it is believed that the dynamics of violence between long-term cohabiting couples are similar to married couples.

Rape in marriage occurs regardless of one's age, race, ethnicity, religion, social class, or geographic location; however, there are some risk factors. It is believed that men who rape their partners are often domineering individuals who feel a sense of entitlement to sex with their partners. This sense of entitlement does not necessarily end when a couple is separated or divorced. Women may be particularly vulnerable to rape by their partners when this sense of entitlement is challenged, such as when women are ill or have recently been discharged from the hospital. Pregnancy may be a factor that also places women at higher risk for sexual abuse by their partners.

One of the most significant risk factors is physical abuse. Research with clinical samples of battered women or those who are seeking help for the violence indicate that between 20% and 70% of them have been sexually assaulted at least once by their partner. However, not all women who are raped by their partners are battered women. In the first major study of wife rape, Diana Russell found that 4% of women who had been raped by their partners had not been battered. In their classic work, David Finkelhor and Kersti Yllo found that 40% of the women who experienced marital rape experienced force-only rape—that is, their husbands used the amount of force necessary to coerce their wives into having sex, but battering did not characterize these relationships. Some women also experience what has been called sadistic or obsessive rape, which often includes physical violence, forms of torture, the use of pornography, and/or what women define as perverse sexual acts. Women who are raped by their partners often experience multiple forms of violence, and the violence may vary over the course of the relationship with their abusers.

There are serious physical, gynecological, and emotional consequences associated with women's experiences of marital rape. Women commonly report experiencing broken bones, lacerations, knife wounds, torn muscles, and black eyes. Marital rape survivors also report gynecological consequences, including anal and vaginal tearing, miscarriages, bladder infections, urinary tract infections, and increased contraction of sexually transmitted diseases. Women who are raped by their partners also are at increased risk for unwanted pregnancy, often as a result of their partners' refusal to use contraception and/or their refusal to allow their wives to use contraception.

The emotional consequences of marital rape can be severe. Although historically marital rape may have been portrayed as a marital tiff, the psychological consequences are often severe and long-lasting. Similar to other survivors of rape, women who are raped by their husbands frequently suffer from depression, intense fear, posttraumatic stress disorder, and sleeping disorders. These consequences may be short-term or last for extended periods of time. Raquel Bergen's research found that some women report sexual dysfunction, sleeping disorders, and depression years after the violence ends. Women who are raped by their partners often suffer emotionally because of the bond of trust and love that has been violated given that their assailant is their partner.

It is evident that rape in marriage is a serious and prevalent form of intimate violence. Future research should address the issue of prevention and how marital rape might best be eliminated.

Raquel Kennedy Bergen

See also Marital Rape/Wife Rape, Marital Exemptions in Rape Statutes; National Clearinghouse on Marital and Date Rape

Further Readings

Bennice, J. A., & Resick, P. A. (2003). Marital rape: History, research and practice. *Trauma, Violence and Abuse, 4,* 228–246.

Bergen, R. K. (1996). *Wife rape: Understanding the response of survivors and service providers.* Thousand Oaks, CA: Sage.

Campbell, J. C., & Soeken, D. (1999). Forced sex and intimate partner violence: Effects on women's risk and women's health. *Health Care for Women International, 10,* 335–346.

Finkelhor, D., & Yllo, K. (1985). *License to rape.* New York: Holt, Rinehart, & Winston.

Mahoney, P., & Williams, L. M. (1998). Sexual assault in marriage: Prevalence, consequences and treatment of wife rape. In J. L. Jasinski & L. M. Williams (Eds.), *Partner violence: A comprehensive review of 20 years of research* (pp. 113–163). Thousand Oaks, CA: Sage.

Randall, M., & Haskell, L. (1995). Sexual violence in women's lives. *Violence Against Women, 1,* 6–31.

Riggs, D., Kilpatrick, D. G., & Resnick, H. (1992). Long-term psychological distress associated with marital rape and aggravated assault: A comparison to other crime victims. *Journal of Family Violence, 7,* 283–295.

Russell, D. (1990). *Rape in marriage.* New York: Macmillan.

MARITAL RAPE/WIFE RAPE, MARITAL EXEMPTIONS IN RAPE STATUTES

Although rape in marriage is a prevalent form of violence against women, the criminalization of forced sex with one's wife is a relatively recent occurrence. According to Laura X of the National Clearinghouse on Marital and Date Rape, on July 5, 1993, marital rape became a law under at least one section of the sexual offense code in every state, the District of Columbia, and on federal lands. This development is important because historically married men were exempt from charges of raping their spouses. Some researchers, such as David Finkelhor and Kersti Yllo, have argued that men were provided with a license to rape their wives. Historically, legal definitions of rape included forcible intercourse with a woman not the wife of a man. The origin of this exemption is grounded in English Common Law and in the words of Chief Justice Hale who decreed that with marriage women gave their irrevocable consent to sex.

This marital rape exemption went largely unchallenged until the 1970s when women in the anti-rape movement argued for its elimination on the grounds that the existing rape laws did not provide all women with equal protection from rape. Changes occurred slowly. In 1978, John Rideout became the first man to be criminally prosecuted for raping his wife while they still lived together. In the case of *People v. Liberta* in 1984, New York became the first state to have its marital rape exemption legally overturned on the grounds that it provided unequal protection to married women.

Today, marital rape is a crime in every state under at least one section of the sexual offense codes. However, there is considerable variation in states' rape legislation and how men are prosecuted for raping their wives. According to the National Clearinghouse on Marital and Date Rape, there are currently 20 states with no exemptions; in these states, rape by one's husband is treated as seriously as rape by another perpetrator. However, in 30 states, rape by one's spouse is treated as a lesser crime. In most states, husbands may be exempt from charges of rape if the crime is not reported to the police quickly or if additional force was not used in the assault. In many states, consent from one's wife is assumed unless she is resisting. In addition, a woman's consent may be assumed when she is legally unable to give consent (or resist), such as if she is asleep or physically or mentally incapacitated.

Although much progress has been made in changing the legislation so that all women are protected equally under the law, there are still many states that treat rape in marriage as a lesser crime.

Raquel Kennedy Bergen

See also Marital Rape/Wife Rape; National Clearinghouse on Marital and Date Rape

Further Readings

Bergen, R. K. (with Barnhill, E.). (2006, February). *Marital rape: New research and directions.* Retrieved from http://new.vawnet.org/Assoc_Files_VAWnet/AR_Marital RapeRevised.pdf

Eskow, L. R. (1996). The ultimate weapon: Demythologizing spousal rape and reconceptualizing its prosecution. *Stanford Law Review, 48,* 677–709.

Finkelhor, D., & Yllo, K. (1985). *License to rape: Sexual abuse of wives.* New York: Holt, Rinehart, and Winston.

Russell, D. E. H. (1990). *Rape in marriage.* New York: Macmillan Press.

X, L. (1999). Accomplishing the impossible: An advocate's notes from the successful campaign to make marital and date rape a crime in all 50 U.S. states and other countries. *Violence Against Women, 5,* 1064–1081.

MARRIAGE EDUCATION AND VIOLENCE

Marriage education gained prominence in the United States during the 1950s and 1960s when divorce rates began to increase, cohabitation and out-of-wedlock childbearing became more common, and the social costs associated with disrupted marriages were increasingly documented. Marriage and relationship education was designed to help individuals and couples develop the attitudes, skills, and behaviors needed to achieve satisfying and stable marriages. Early programs grew out of studies on middle- and upper-income White couples, were offered to these populations, and although they did address issues such as conflict resolution and communication and negotiation skills, they failed to direct focused attention to issues of violence in marital relationships. After years of relative obscurity, marriage and relationship education has been catapulted into the limelight as a focus of public policy attention and debate. The origins of this increased national attention trace back to 1996 when welfare reform identified the promotion of marriage and the formation and maintenance of two-parent families as a governmental goal. Since this time, substantial federal funding has been earmarked for marriage education primarily with low-income individuals and families. The high rate of domestic violence among young, low-income welfare recipients has been well documented. As a result, scholars and practitioners currently are grappling with the challenges of offering relationship and marriage education to low-income populations and, more specifically, with the necessity of having and implementing a policy for dealing with domestic violence issues in marriage education programs.

Historical Roots

Marriage and relationship education developed largely from the work of religious institutions. In the early 1950s, many religious organizations began to offer structured education for marrying couples. And soon thereafter, secular groups began to offer similar programs. Historically, the marriage and relationship education approach has been preventive and most typically addresses relationship choices, challenges, and skills before problems become ingrained and damaging. Thus, marriage education programs are distinguished from couple therapy and offer a complementary approach whereby relationship professionals' expertise can be shared with couples. The primary audience for such programs generally has been middle- and upper-income White couples in committed relationships. Marriage education generally employs a variety of teaching methods that include a combination of lecture material and experiential exercises designed to teach relationship skills such as listening and speaking clearly and positively, managing anger, negotiating disagreements, and increasing positive and respectful interactions.

Program Evaluation

The marriage education programs that are generally agreed to be the strongest are evidence-based—that is, they are grounded in the findings of research. Several of the best known and highly regarded programs (e.g., The Prevention and Relationship Enhancement Program, Relationship Enhancement, and the Couple Communication Program) are empirically based. Moreover, the majority of couples who attend marriage and relationship education report high satisfaction with their programs. At the same time, however, the systematic evaluation of such programs is limited. For instance, randomized clinical trials are rare, and very few studies measure impact on marital stability over time.

Marriage Education and Welfare Reform

In 1996, the U.S. Congress passed the Personal Responsibility and Work Opportunity Reconciliation Act, which led, in turn, to the creation of the Temporary Assistance to Needy Families program. This legislation explicitly established the promotion of marriage, the formation and maintenance of two-parent families, and the reduction of out-of-wedlock childbearing as policy goals. Thus, in 2001, the federal government for the first time began to fund marriage education programs around the country, making these services available to more economically and racially diverse populations. This change has raised a set of questions about the challenges of offering marriage education that was designed for relatively small numbers of White middle- and upper-income couples to the very different target population of welfare reform and marriage promotion policies: young, poor, and unmarried couples. One particular question centers on the suitability of marriage education for couples with a history of or at high risk for domestic violence. This question has prompted considerable policy debate, especially in light of research indicating that up to 60% of women receiving welfare have been abused at some point in their lives.

Scholars and practitioners working in the fields of marriage education or promotion and domestic violence historically have interacted only infrequently and, perhaps as a result, view each other's motivations and agendas with some skepticism. Many in the domestic violence community are concerned that implementation of federally funded marriage education programs may threaten the lives and safety of women and their children if women in abusive relationships will be encouraged to marry or stay married to their abusive partners. From their perspective, proponents of marriage education or promotion express concern that domestic violence advocates do not acknowledge the importance of strengthening marriage and ignore the idea that most people aspire to a healthy marriage for themselves and their children.

Currently, alliances are being created between marriage educators and domestic violence programs. For instance, all federally funded marriage education programs are now required to consult with domestic violence experts in developing their curricula. In addition, scholars and practitioners have emphasized that there are substantial cultural, economic, and racial differences in attitudes about marriage and domestic violence. Therefore, efforts are being made to more fully understand these differences and to use this expanded knowledge to develop culturally relevant and sensitive programs.

Beth Skilken Catlett

See also Divorce and Intimate Partner Violence; Early Warning Signs of Intimate Partner Violence; Faith-Based Programs; Intimate Partner Relationship Quality and Domestic Violence; Intimate Partner Violence

Further Readings

Catlett, B. S., & Artis, J. E. (2004). Critiquing the case for marriage promotion: How the promarriage movement misrepresents domestic violence research. *Violence Against Women, 10,* 1226–1244.

Halford, W. K. (2004). The future of couple relationship education: Suggestions on how it can make a difference. *Family Relations, 53,* 559–566.

Ooms, T., & Wilson, P. (2004). The challenges of offering relationship and marriage education to low-income populations. *Family Relations, 53,* 440–447.

Roberts, P. (2006, September). Building bridges between the healthy marriage, responsible fatherhood, and domestic violence movements: Issues, concerns, and recommendations. *Center for Law and Social Policy Couples and Marriage Series* (Issue Brief No. 7). Retrieved April 16, 2007, from http://www.clasp.org/publications/buildingbridges_brief7.pdf

MASCULINITIES AND VIOLENCE

Masculinities refer to the culturally constructed social norms for behavior, comportment, and characteristics assigned to men and boys. Scholars talk about multiple masculinities instead of a singular masculinity because the category varies according to context, culture, geographic location, and historical period. Masculinities are relevant to interpersonal violence because the research indicates that establishing and defending a masculine sense of self is fundamentally important to many men's use of violence. Much of men's violence is perpetrated in response to threats to the man's sense of masculinity. This response is true of violence against strangers, acquaintances, and intimates. It is especially important to distinguish between sex and gender when studying human behavior such as violence because this distinction has implications for the prevention of violence as well as for effective interventions.

In the most simplified terms, sex refers to biological sex, as conventionally determined by the appearance of genitalia at birth. Sex is commonly thought of as a binary system, although this understanding is a conceptual oversimplification that excludes intersex and transgendered people. Intersex babies are born with nonstandard genitals that do not identify them accurately and immediately as male or female. Transgender individuals perform a gender that is different from the one they were assigned at birth, with or without having surgery or taking hormones to facilitate the performance. Gender refers to the culturally specific set of characteristics and behaviors associated with biological sex in a given culture. Male and female are sex categories, and masculine and feminine are gender categories.

Gender is a continuum of attributes ranging from feminine traits, those traditionally associated with women and girls, to masculine traits, those stereotypically associated with men and boys. Gender is often essentialized. In other words, femininity and masculinity are thought of as the natural expression of a person's biological identity. However, gender varies significantly across time and geography, and it is therefore recognizable as culturally constructed, or shaped by the culture in which it is produced. This construction does not mean that there are no biological differences between women and men, only that the differences that exist are small in comparison with the social factors that magnify their significance.

Masculinity is normative for men, meaning that men are expected to display more of the traits that are associated with masculinity than femininity. Some stereotypically masculine traits include toughness, power, strength, stoicism, leadership, rationality, and virility. Pressure to conform to these stereotypes has negative implications for men and can promote behavior that puts men at greater risk of violence perpetration and victimization than women. For example, men are more likely to drink to excess and drive recklessly, behavior that can put them at disproportionate risk of causing or experiencing injury or death. Since gender is often essentialized, some people think of stereotypically masculine characteristics as biologically determined in men. However, social scientists point to variation in gender performance as evidence that culture shapes and magnifies the manifestation of sex differences.

There are formal and informal social sanctions for men who fail to display appropriately gendered behavior. For example, sexist and homophobic taunts are often directed at men and boys who do not perform their masculine role in accordance with hegemonic expectations. Violence against gay men and transgender people are examples of severe forms of social punishment for violating gender norms.

Due to the importance of physical power and prowess to the social construction of masculinities, displays of violence and aggression are a viable option for men who feel it is necessary to assert or reestablish their masculinity. Since women are held to an opposite set of gender norms, women do not receive an equivalent social reward for violence and aggression. Men can and do use violence to demonstrate and reinforce their masculinity. Women do not use violence and aggression to affirm their femininity. Disparate social expectations for women and men's violence are one of the reasons that men are more violent than women.

Although men's greater violence is often thought of as biologically determined, gender categories regiment human behavior in nearly every area of our lives, from the way we walk, talk, and act to the way we dress. In addition, social variables are easier to change than biological variables, so most violence prevention efforts focus on behavior that it is possible to change rather than biological factors, which may be impossible to alter.

Many of the biological differences that do exist, for example, men's generally greater upper body strength, are reinforced by gender norms that enhance these differences and emphasize their social importance. For example, men are encouraged to participate in sports and activities that help to emphasize this sex difference, while women are discouraged from developing muscles that are too large. Sex and gender differences such as this have implications for the causes and outcomes of violence that are more and less direct.

In common usage, sex and gender are often conflated, and the terms are sometimes used interchangeably. Unfortunately, this interchanging can make for unclear writing, with readers unable to discern whether an author is really talking about sex (biological) or gender (social) differences. Scholars in the social sciences, humanities, public health, and law sometimes draw distinctions between sex and gender to ensure that their scholarship accurately represents biological and cultural contributions to phenomena. For example, medical researchers attempt to discern between gendered cultural factors, such as men's reluctance to visit doctors, and biological factors, such as hormones, when investigating medical problems and treatments. This distinction is necessary in order to adequately understand the etiology of social and health problems as well as to make appropriate and effective recommendations for prevention and intervention.

Molly Dragiewicz

See also Battered Women's Movement; Batterers, Factors Supporting Male Aggression; Male Peer Support, Theory of; Patriarchy; Sex Discrimination

Further Readings

Bograd, M. (1990). Why we need gender to understand human violence. *Journal of Interpersonal Violence, 5,* 132–135.

Connell, R. W. (2005). *Masculinities.* Berkeley: University of California Press.

Gilligan, J. (2001). *Preventing violence.* New York: Thames & Hudson.

Kimmel, M. S., Hearn, J. R., & Connell, R. W. (Eds.). (2004). *Handbook of studies on men and masculinities.* Thousand Oaks, CA: Sage.

MASS MURDER

Mass murder is the killing of multiple people at one location in a relatively short period of time. It is commonly believed that the mass murderer is an individual who kills randomly after experiencing a mental breakdown or psychotic episode. Research, however, does not support this belief. Studies of mass murderers indicate that their motivations typically stem from some wrong they perceive has been unjustly inflicted upon them. Their hatred of the supposed wrongdoer festers over time until some incident prompts them to act out against the wrongdoer and/or others who belong to the wrongdoer's group (e.g., women, coworkers). Consequently, criminologists delineate two types of mass murders. One type involves the killing of specific individuals whom the offender believes has wronged him or her. For example, in one recent mass murder, two students at Columbine High School in Colorado shot classmates whom they felt had ignored or mistreated them. The second type of mass murder involves killing individuals who have not had personal contact or a relationship with the offender, but who belong to a group the offender has come to hate. For example, in 1989, at the University of Montreal, a man who had been rejected from the school's engineering program went into an engineering class, ordered all the men to leave, and then shot the women, killing 14 and wounding 13 because he believed that the need to admit more women to the program had led to his rejection. The research also shows that mass murderers usually think about committing murder for some time before they actually act and prepare for the crime (e.g., by stockpiling weapons), although they may not plan the exact time and location of the killings.

The mass murderer may kill multiple people at different locations over a period of days rather than in one location in a short time. This type of mass murder is usually referred to as *spree murder*. The characteristics of mass murderers and spree murderers, however, are largely indistinguishable. Most are White males, who are impulsive, alienated, depressed, and frustrated, largely because of their perception of having been unjustly wronged. They appear to be fascinated by guns and have the weapons at their disposal. The way they kill is very public, and they appear to be concerned about their own lives in the process. In fact, most commit suicide or die at the hands of police at or near the crime scene. An important exception to this general portrait, though, is felony-related and gang-related mass murders. In these types of murders, the offenders are usually young non-White men, who do not commit suicide and who are not killed by police at or near the crime scene.

Although mass murders are rare relative to other types of violent offenses, data show that they have increased in the United States in recent years. During the decade of the 1950s, for instance, there were only four mass murders. Throughout the 1960s, there were seven mass murders. However, from the mid-1970s to 1991, there were 269 cases that resulted in the deaths of 1,447 people. From 2000 to 2002 alone, there were 567 cases. This dramatic increase in only half a century is alarming, but criminologists disagree over why it has occurred. In contrast, mass murder is relatively rare outside the United States, leading some criminologists to argue that the relative ease of acquiring guns in the United States is, in large part, responsible for the relatively high rate of mass murders in this country.

Claire M. Renzetti

See also Gang Violence; Homicides, Criminal; Serial Murder/Serial Killers

Further Readings

Fox, J., & Levin, J. (2001). *The will to kill: Making sense of senseless murder.* Boston: Allyn & Bacon.
Fox, J., & Levin, J. (2005). *Extreme killing: Understanding serial and mass murder.* Thousand Oaks, CA: Sage.
Holmes, R. M., & Holmes, S. J. (1992). Understanding mass murder: A starting point. *Federal Probation, 56,* 53–61.

MASS RAPE

Mass rape is the use of rape as a war strategy. In a military conflict, armies and paramilitaries plan systematic sexual assaults against women in enemy communities with the goal of demoralizing and terrorizing the enemy and driving them from their home regions. Mass rape as a war strategy is not new; there are numerous historical accounts dating back to ancient societies that include graphic descriptions of the systematic rape, enslavement, and sexual torture of enemy women as a state-supported warfare tactic. However, mass rape began to garner more public attention in 1993 as a result of two significant events. One event was the issuance of a report by the Japanese government admitting to the sexual enslavement of "foreign" women during World War II. Euphemistically called "comfort women," these women were coerced into prostitution to provide sexual services for Imperial Army military personnel. It is estimated that 100,000–300,000 women were enslaved, most of whom were from South Korea, but others were from Indonesia, China, Taiwan, the Philippines, and the Netherlands.

Also in 1993, media reports began to document the systematic rape, sexual enslavement, torture, and murder of Bosnian Muslim women and children by Serbian military forces in the former Yugoslavia. Although estimates vary, a commonly cited figure is that approximately 20,000 Muslim women were raped by Serbian soldiers. When mass rape is used as a warfare strategy, it often takes the form of *rape-and-kill* in which the victims are murdered following the sexual assault as if they themselves were enemy combatants. But in Bosnia, it appeared that mass rape was one of the strategies used in the Serbian ethnic cleansing campaign. That is, Bosnian men were murdered, but the women were raped for the purpose of impregnating them so that they would produce offspring with desirable genetic material.

Since 1993, human rights workers and other investigators have documented extensive state-supported violence against women, including gang rape by police and military personnel, in many countries including Haiti, Honduras, El Salvador, Iran, Rwanda, Kosovo, East Timor, Myanmar, and the Sudan. According to a recent UN report, however, the sexual violence in the Congo is among the worst in the world. There it has been reported that in some villages as many as 70% of the women residents have been brutally raped by raiding militias, whose only goal appears to be sexual assault and terror. The assailants sometimes rape the women with objects, such as bayonets and chunks of wood, causing severe internal injuries to the women's reproductive and digestive systems.

Physicians and others in the Congo who have been interviewed regarding the mass rapes have been at a loss to explain why they occur. However, other observers argue that such atrocities occur because the assailants behave with impunity. Their actions are often secretly endorsed by military or government officials, or because their victims are women and women are highly devalued in many societies, their actions are not regarded as being as serious as other types of war crimes.

In 1994, the UN General Assembly adopted the Declaration on the Elimination of Violence Against Women, which calls on governments to condemn all forms of violence against women and to punish acts of violence against women, whether these acts are perpetrated by the state or by private individuals. The declaration also urges all member nations to ratify the Convention on the Elimination of All Forms of Discrimination Against Women, which includes provisions that in their effect impose sanctions for violence against women. (The United States remains the only industrialized country in the world that has not ratified this convention.) Nevertheless, despite these measures, mass rape and other forms of sexual abuse continue to be used by combatants as a warfare strategy.

Claire M. Renzetti

See also Rape/Sexual Assault; State Violence; United Nations Conventions and Declarations

Further Readings

Allen, B. (1996). *Rape warfare: The hidden genocide in Bosnia-Herzegovina.* Minneapolis: University of Minnesota Press.

Barstow, A. L. (Ed.). (2001). *War's dirty secret: Rape, prostitution, and other crimes against women.* Cleveland: Pilgrim Press.

Brownmiller, S. (1975). *Against our will.* New York: Simon & Schuster.

Gettelman, J. (2007, October 7). Rape epidemic raises trauma of Congo war. *New York Times,* pp. 1A, 11A.

Schellstede, S. C. (Ed.). (2000). *Comfort women speak: Testimony by sex slaves of the Japanese military.* New York: Holmes & Meier.

Stigilmayer, A. (Ed.). (1994). *Mass rape: The war against women in Bosnia-Herzegovina.* Lincoln: University of Nebraska Press.

MATERNAL HOMICIDE

What is most striking about child homicide are the very high rates during the first few months of life and that the offender is the mother of the child. Figure 1 shows rates by age of children from birth to age 18. Two data sources were used from 1996 to 2000: state homicide rates from California and national rates from the FBI.

Figure 1 shows that homicide rates among newborns are the second highest in the 18-year lifespan. The newborn rate is not exceeded until about age 15 in California and about age 16 nationally. What is also

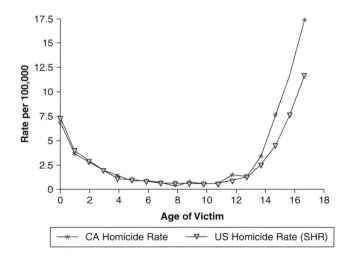

Figure 1   Age-Specific Homicide Rates: California and United States, 1996–2000

Sources: California Department of Justice, Criminal Justice Statistics Center, Homicide file; U.S. Department of Justice; Federal Bureau of Investigation Uniform Crime Reports.

noteworthy is that the homicide rates in Figure 1 drop sharply and remain low between age 6 and age 12; this period has the lowest homicide rates in the human lifespan and reflect the high level of surveillance of children during that period by parents, schools, and other agencies.

Figure 2 gives the rates adjusted by age for Black, White, and Hispanic children in California from 1987 through 2002.

As Figure 2 indicates, the curves for race and ethnic groups follow the same general form as Figure 1. However, the rates for Black victims are much higher in the first few years of life compared to Whites and Hispanics. One research study found the relative risk for Black infant homicides was over 3 times higher than for Whites. There are two lines of reasoning that suggests the high rates among Blacks reflect social and economic hardships frequently of a single parent unprepared for child raising.

First, the evidence is generally clear that there is little distinction among genders in the killing of infants; both male and female infants are killed at about the same rates. Second, Hispanic rates are low because research indicates fewer homes with Hispanic fathers absent—even among immigrants. This difference suggests social and economic factors are operative.

The available research suggests that over 90% of homicides during the first week of life are committed by the mother. Thereafter, fathers, other family members, and people outside the family gradually play a more important role as offenders.

There seem to be two general classes of causes of maternal homicide. There are a number of maternal homicides occurring among young women who become unexpectedly pregnant. The case of the "prom mom" in New Jersey, who concealed her pregnancy until she delivered the child in the toilet at her senior prom, killed it, wrapped in trash bags, threw it in the dumpster, and returned to the prom.

Young women who fall in the category of the unexpectedly pregnant go to great lengths to conceal their pregnancy. The expectant mother is fearful and concerned about what her parents and friends will think; overwhelmed by guilt and shame, she denies the pregnancy until she is faced with the newborn child. Such cases may be the result of dissociative disorders; the latter are an inability to recall important information, usually of a traumatic or stressful nature. Confronted with the undeniable fact of a newborn infant, rather than acknowledging what happened, she disposes of the baby as quickly as possible.

Second, although the latter explains a limited number of neonaticides, a more frequent reason is that the mother either does not know or is not prepared to take care of a newborn child. A study of over 34 million death certificates found that half the homicides by the mother occurred by the fourth month. Important risk factors were a second or subsequent infant born to a mother less than 17 years old, no prenatal care, and less than 12 years of education.

Marc Riedel

See also Feticide; Filicide; Homicides, Criminal; Infanticide

Further Readings

Boudreaux, M. C., Lord, W. C., & Jarvis, J. P. (2001). Behavioral perspectives on child homicides: The role of access, vulnerability, and routine activities theory. *Trauma, Violence, & Abuse, 2,* 56–78.

Kunz, J., & Bahr, S. J. (1996). A profile of parental homicide against children. *Journal of Family Violence, 11,* 347–362.

Overpeck, M. D., Brenner, R. A., Trumble, A. C., Trifiletti, L. B., & Berendes, H. W. (1998). Risk factors for infant homicide in the United States. *The New England Journal of Medicine, 339,* 1211–1216.

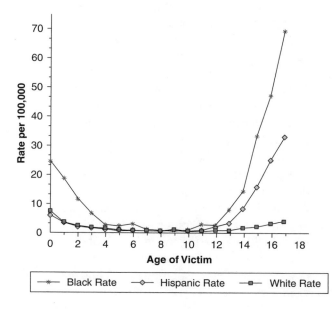

Figure 2   Victim Race/Ethnicity by Age

Source: California Department of Justice, Criminal Justice Statistics Center, Homicide file.

Riedel, M. (2003). Homicide in Los Angeles County: A study of racial and ethnic victimization. In D. Hawkins (Ed.), *Violent crime: Assessing race and ethnic differences* (pp. 44–66). New York: Cambridge University Press.

MATERNAL RESPONSIBILITY FOR CHILD PHYSICAL ABUSE

Maternal child physical abuse is a subset of child abuse that nevertheless is considered a separate phenomenon, requiring specific explanations distinct from the explanations of paternal, caretaker, and other forms of child abuse. According to domestic, as well as cross-national studies, mothers bear responsibility for approximately half of the identified cases of parental child abuse involving physical injuries. The high rates of violence against their own children invite questions in view of generally low representation of women as compared to men as the perpetrators of other forms of physical violence. As with most forms of interpersonal violence and abuse, maternal violence against children is associated with poverty; however, material deprivation and social class are intervening rather than causal factors. Younger mothers and mothers with multiple children who had their first child at a young age, especially teenage mothers, are overrepresented among abusers.

One of the explanations provided by researchers is an opportunity thesis that concentrates on the physical proximity of women (but not men) to children as caretakers. However, in the 1990s, Leslie Margolin discovered that, when compared to women, men abuse their children out of proportion to the hours spent in caregiving, putting the opportunity theory in question.

Another set of theories explaining maternal child abuse, as well as homicide, comes out of the strain tradition in sociology and criminology. Strain theory combines the structure of opportunities with the psychological effects of continuous stress experienced by mothers involved in what Sharon Hays describes as intensive mothering. The social isolation of the nuclear family unit and labor-intensive, high-pressure mothering, when combined with additional external stress factors such as, for example, poverty, cause some mothers to lash out at the easiest and immediately available target—the child.

The contemporary nuclear family is perceived by some as a microcosm that generates internal strains and tensions through its hermetical character. Often parental abuse, maternal abuse in particular, is seen as stemming from the microprocesses of family interaction and psychological problems of the family's individual members who become part of the ecology of a family.

Feminist psychoanalytic theories of maternal ambivalence concentrate on the integration of inherently conflicting emotions toward the child that accompany motherhood and mothering. This set of psychodynamic explanations posits that violence toward a child results when the delicate balance of loving and resentful emotions toward a child is compromised, either due to the lack of emotional maturity of the mother or due to externally induced stress.

One of the strangest and rarest forms of child physical abuse by mothers is Munchausen Syndrome by Proxy. In that form of abuse, a mother causes a medical condition in her child and then presents the child for medical examination while making ostensibly heroic efforts to alleviate the symptoms. Often the request for intrusive medical tests and proceedings by the mother to treat a manufactured condition is construed as a form of physical abuse in itself. As the name suggests, Munchausen Syndrome by Proxy is considered to be a psychiatric condition, but there are a few known instances in which cases of this form of abuse were successfully prosecuted under the criminal statutes.

In the past 30 years, maternal child abuse has been increasingly recognized as a problem properly falling within the purview of the criminal justice system. However, only a handful of mothers are prosecuted to the full extent of the original criminal charges. Most cases of maternal physical abuse are still resolved through the family courts with supervision, suspension, or withdrawal of custodial rights as outcomes. There has also been a trend to prosecute on charges of child abuse new mothers who have abused drugs and alcohol prenatally.

Most remedies proposed for dealing with maternal child abuse involve psychological counseling, parenting classes, and amelioration of stressful conditions associated with mothering. As indicated above, there is also a tendency to rely on the deterrent effect of criminal prosecutions. Feminist writings on child abuse urge reconsideration of intensive mothering as a cultural practice and easing the stresses and burdens placed on women by instituting free comprehensive child care.

Liena Gurevich

See also Child Physical Abuse; Fathers as Perpetrators of Child Maltreatment; Munchausen Syndrome by Proxy; Poverty; Prosecutorial Practices, Child Maltreatment; Stress and Violence

Further Readings

Bools, C., Neale, B., & Meadow, R. (1994). Munchausen Syndrome by Proxy: A study in psychopathology. *Child Abuse and Neglect, 18,* 773–788.

Dowdy, E. R., & Prabha Unnithan, N. (1997). Child homicide and the economic stress hypothesis: A research note. *Homicide Studies, 1,* 281–290.

Margolin, L. (1992). Beyond maternal blame: Physical child abuse as a phenomenon of gender. *Journal of Family Issues, 13,* 410–423.

Roberts, D. E. (1991). Punishing drug addicts who have babies: Women of color, equality, and the right of privacy. *Harvard Law Review, 101,* 1419–1482.

Straus, M., & Kaufman Kantor, G. (1987). Stress and child abuse. In R. E. Helfer & R. S. Kempe (Eds.), *The battered child* (pp. 42–59). Chicago: University of Chicago Press.

Wauchope, B., & Straus, M. (1990). Physical punishment and physical abuse of American children: Incidence rates by age, gender and occupational class. In M. Straus & R. J. Gelles (Eds.), *Physical violence in American families: Risk factors and adaptation to violence in 8,145 families* (pp. 133–148). New Brunswick, NJ: Transaction.

MATRICIDE

See FAMILY HOMICIDES

MEASUREMENT, INTERPERSONAL VIOLENCE

There are many different definitions of interpersonal violence. For example, some include inflicting verbal or emotional harm as violence, while others do not. Some specify that intent to cause harm by the perpetrator be present, while others do not. The National Academy of Sciences defines interpersonal violence as any behavior by an individual that intentionally threatens, attempts, or inflicts physical harm on others.

It is also helpful to classify acts of interpersonal violence into subtypes. One distinction is between *instrumental* and *expressive* acts of violence. Instrumental acts of violence are those in which violence is a means to an end, such as an armed robbery. The threat of force or actual use of force in cases of robbery is used to help accomplish the robbery, but it is not an end in and of itself. Expressive acts of violence, on the other hand, are those in which the motivations are expressive of some emotional state, such as anger or jealousy. In these cases, the violence serves to fulfill some internal or intrinsic desire. As the name implies, the violence is expressing something. Acts of interpersonal violence can also be categorized into different crime types, such as homicide, rape, robbery, and assault.

Acts of interpersonal violence are often private and hidden, such as violence that occurs in the home. As such, estimating the magnitude of interpersonal violence is difficult. For many reasons, including the stigma attached to some types of violence such as rape and intimate partner (e.g., spouse or boyfriend or girlfriend) violence, the fear of perpetrators retaliating, and numerous other safety concerns, estimating incidence rates of interpersonal violence has always been difficult. Scholars, policymakers, and activists alike typically rely on a number of different sources of data for information on the nature and scope of interpersonal violence, but each has its own strengths and weaknesses.

Reports to Police

The most enduring source of statistical information about violent crime in the United States is the Uniform Crime Reporting (UCR) program compiled by the Federal Bureau of Investigation (FBI). The UCR has collected information about criminal incidents of violence that have been reported to the police since 1930. These data rely on voluntary participation in the program by state, county, and city law enforcement agencies across the United States.

For the crime of homicide, information about both the victim and the offender (e.g., the gender and race of both, the relationship between the victim and offender, the weapon utilized) is obtained in a separate reporting program called the Supplementary Homicide Reports. Unfortunately, such detailed information is not collected for other crimes in the UCR. To remedy this problem, in 1988 the FBI implemented a change in its collection of crime information that includes more characteristics of the incident and is appropriately called the National Incident-Based Reporting System (NIBRS).

NIBRS data are very specific and include many more offenses and many details of an incident for which local agencies must report, including the characteristics of the victim such as age, gender, race, ethnicity, and resident status and characteristics of lost property. In all, NIBRS categorizes each incident and arrest in one of 22 basic crime categories that span 46 separate offenses. A total of 53 data elements about the victim, property, and the offender are collected under NIBRS. Not surprisingly, it takes a great deal of time and money to make this change and fill out this paper work at the local police department level. Consequently, only about half of all states currently use the NIBRS format for collecting information about reported crimes.

Both the UCR and the NIBRS data collection methods are problematic when estimating incidence rates of violence primarily because if victimizations are not reported to police, they are never counted in either data collection effort in the first place. This condition is particularly problematic for certain types of violence, such as rape and violence that occurs between intimates such as spouses and boyfriends and girlfriends. A large percentage of these victimizations are never reported to police. In fact, based on comparisons with national survey data, it is estimated that only about 40%–50% of crimes become known to police.

Random Sample Surveys

Because of this weakness in police reports, random sample surveys of the population have begun to be used as the social science tool of choice for uncovering incidents of violent victimization. However, as can be imagined, surveys employing diverse methodologies and different definitions of violence have resulted in tremendously diverse estimates. Taking violence against women as an example, survey estimates of how many women experience violence by an intimate partner annually range from 9.3 per 1,000 women to 116 per 1,000 women. Further, the methodological differences across survey methodologies often prevent a direct comparison of estimates across studies.

Without going into too much detail, to estimate incidence rates of the general population, surveys must be based on probability sampling theory, meaning that respondents in a survey must be randomly selected. This theory means that every person in the population of interest has an equal probability of being selected, ensuring that a sample will be representative of the population to which one wishes to make a generalization.

Because of space limitations, this entry reviews only two surveys used to measure various types of interpersonal violence. The first was designed to more accurately measure crime victimization and is sponsored by the Bureau of Justice Statistics of the U.S. Department of Justice. It is called the National Crime Victimization Survey (NCVS). Instead of focusing on victimizations, the second survey is designed to measure the offending behavior of adolescents, and is called the National Youth Survey (NYS).

The NCVS interviews over 65,000 individuals ages 12 or older annually and is the second largest ongoing survey sponsored by the U.S. government. It measures both violent and property crime victimizations. But asking respondents to recall incidents of victimization is a tricky business. After several changes and redesigns, the NCVS currently uses the following screening questions:

1. Other than any incidents already mentioned, has anyone attacked or threatened you in any of these ways: (a) with any weapon—for instance, a gun or knife; (b) with anything like a baseball bat, frying pan, scissors, or a stick; (c) by something thrown, such as a rock or bottle; (d) include any grabbing, punching, or choking; (e) any rape, attempted rape, or other type of sexual attack; (f) any face to face threats; and/or (g) any attack or threat or use of force by anyone at all? Please mention it even if you are not certain it was a crime.

2. Incidents involving forced or unwanted sexual acts are often difficult to talk about. Have you been forced or coerced to engage in unwanted sexual activity by (a) someone you didn't know before, (b) a casual acquaintance, and/or (c) someone you know well? If respondents reply affirmatively to one of these latter questions, interviewers next ask, "Do you mean forced or coerced sexual intercourse?" to determine whether the incident should be recorded as rape or as another type of sexual attack.

3. People often don't think of incidents committed by someone they know. Did you have something stolen from you, or were you attacked or threatened by (a) someone at work or school, (b) a neighbor or friend, (c) a relative or family member, and/or (d) any other person you have met or known?

Notice that these screening questions rely on very behavior-specific wording instead of asking directly about victimizations using crime jargon such as "Have you ever been robbed?" This wording is important. A great deal of survey research has demonstrated that asking questions using behaviors instead of terms uncovers a significantly greater number of victimizations, particularly when victims may not self-identify as crime victims. Asking people about their experiences in this way uncovers many more victimizations than those reported only to police.

Relying on police reports to estimate who is most likely to perpetrate acts of violence suffers the same problems as using these data to estimate who is most likely to be victimized. Are offenders who are arrested for violent offending actually representative of all offenders? The quick answer is no. In fact, early self-report surveys of offending behavior in the 1940s revealed that a relatively large number of committed offenses were not detected by the police. For example, although police report data at the time indicated offenders were more likely to be minorities from low socioeconomic backgrounds, self-report data revealed that a great number of self-reported offenses in surveys were being reported by people from relatively privileged backgrounds, but these offenses rarely came to the attention of the police. If they did, they rarely resulted in an arrest. Based on these early studies, researchers interested in offending behavior, like those interested in victimization, began to rely on survey methodology instead of police reports.

One of the most thorough contemporary surveys to measure offending behavior is the National Youth Survey (NYS), which was first collected in 1976 from a national probability sample of 11- to 17-year-olds. These youth were interviewed many times during the following years, with the last interview collected in 1995. The questions used to measure the violent offending behavior in the NYS are also behaviorally specific instead of relying on the use of crime categories and labels. For example, respondents are asked if they had carried a hidden weapon other than a plain pocket knife, attacked someone with the idea of seriously hurting or killing him or her, been involved in a gang fight, and/or tried to take something from someone with the use of force or with the threat of force.

In sum, there is a great deal of evidence that documents the large gap between the true extent of victimization and offending and the amount of crime known to police. The major sources of this gap are the inability of police to observe all criminal activity and the reluctance of crime victims and witnesses to report crime to the police. In addition, there is a great deal of variability in estimates of violent victimization and offending across survey methodologies. Generally, surveys that employ behaviorally specific questions with many cues about various types of offenders, including intimates and other known offenders, are more valid than those that do not.

Ronet Bachman

See also Incidence; National Crime Victimization Survey; National Family Violence Surveys; National Incident-Based Reporting System; National Violence Against Women Survey; Prevalence; Uniform Crime Reports

Further Readings

Alvarez, A., & Bachman, R. (2008). *Violence: The enduring problem.* Thousand Oaks, CA: Sage.

Reiss, A. J., & Roth, J. A. (1993). *Understanding and preventing violence.* Washington, DC: National Academy Press.

Media, Representations/ Distortions of Crime

Journalists of varying stripes are sometimes accused of misrepresentations and distortions in their coverage of crime. One major criticism has been that news coverage frequently reflects biases in reporters' and editors' own worldviews. Another involves concerns about journalistic philosophy—in particular, the still widespread belief that the press can and should be objective—that may lead, intentionally or not, to distortions in the way that news is presented to the public.

Media Stereotyping

The media have often been accused of circulating stereotypes through news coverage. For example, as Columbia journalism professor Helen Benedict has shown, news coverage of violence against women has often been sexist, portraying victims as either innocent virgins or promiscuous vamps. This portrayal can have troubling consequences for women attempting to prosecute cases of assault and may lead to blaming victims for the assaults they suffered. For example, in the well-known 1983 New Bedford, Massachusetts, gang rape case—on which the award-winning film *The Accused* was based—the character of media coverage of the victim as a single welfare-mother may have contributed to some people wondering, "Why wasn't she home with her kids?"

In the New Bedford case, too, even further hostility toward the victim resulted from local reporters repetitively referring to the defendants as the "Portuguese rapists." Since New Bedford, Massachusetts, has a long history of anti-Portuguese discrimination, these media references fanned defensive community reactions and also inflamed blaming-the-victim attitudes directed at the young woman who had been assaulted.

Not only ethnic but racial biases also surfaced in the well-known 1989 New York City "Central Park jogger" case when activists objected to local newspapers' mistakenly coining the term *wilding* and to some journalists' Darwinistic usage of "wolfpack" language to characterize a crime journalists assumed to be a gang rape.

The national media followed suit in assuming that the Central Park jogger was attacked by a group of youth. Yet in 2001, many years after the conviction of several minority and working class youth who served lengthy prison sentences, these young men's sentences were commuted. In that year, a DNA match confirmed convicted rapist Mathias Reyes' confession that he alone had brutally assaulted the young woman in Central Park. Apparently, biased race and class-based assumptions had led journalists, in conjunction with criminal justice officials at that time, to a rush of judgment. Thus, unless monitored, media biases and distortions can have worrisome consequences for the legal system and for public policy.

Beliefs in Objectivity

Many journalists, particularly in what have been called mainstream news outlets (as opposed to alternative newspapers, television stations, and other new forms of media), are committed to the concept of objectivity. They try to highlight two sides to every story and to hold to principles of value detachment. Yet many scholars and media critics assert that this common journalistic philosophy obscures what are actually unequal social relations; for example, as a result, an individual and a corporation may appear to have analogous power in a given news story. According to sociologist Todd Gitlin, such practices can even contribute to the decline of social movements, as he asserts happened through the media's destructive effects on Students for a Democratic Society in the Vietnam era.

Lynn S. Chancer

See also Media and Sexuality; Media and Violence

Further Readings

Benedict, H. (1992). *Virgin or vamp? How the press covers sex crimes.* New York: Oxford University Press.
Chancer, L. (1987). New Bedford, Massachusetts, March 6, 1983-March 22, 1984: The "before" and "after" of a group rape. *Gender & Society, 1,* 239–260.
Chancer, L. (1996). O.J. Simpson and the trial of the century? Uncovering paradoxes in media coverage. In G. Barak (Ed.), *Representing O.J.: Murder, criminal justice, and mass culture.* New York: Harrow and Heston.
Gitlin, T. (1980). *The whole world is watching: Mass media in the making and the unmaking of the New Left.* Berkeley: University of California Press.
Hall, S., Critcher, C., Jefferson, T., Clarke, J., & Roberts, B. (1978). *Policing the crisis: Mugging, the state, and law and order.* London: Macmillan.

MEDIA AND SEXUALITY

The production of media with the inclusion of sexuality is focused on a product that seeks to attract a diverse audience. Nudity and physical sexual activity are incorporated as part of the entertainment experience. Television and movies, as a form of visual media, reach this goal through a focus on needs and gratification. The needs and gratification approach is aimed at giving the audience what they desire as a form of reinforcement. Sexuality would be a good basic impulse reinforced through this process. Sexual content serves to attract and hold audience attention through reinforcement with conspicuous imagery. The utilization of sexuality in motion pictures, and to a more limited extent on commercial television, is now more prevalent with changes in social acceptance of such material. There is a social link between the expansion of sexuality in media and the social values of a given time and place. Cultural change is not widespread, and some places or communities will be more receptive than others to sexual content.

Historical Connections

The connection between media and sexuality must be understood within a historical perspective. Motion pictures produced during the 1930s through the 1960s were largely governed by the Hays Code. Will Hays was appointed the head of a commission designed to ensure that motion pictures maintained basic family values. Content was screened for offensive language, explicit images, and adult content. Films had to focus on clean content without any hint or entendre of sexual activity or sexual intention. The advent of the 1960s featured such films as *The Graduate* and *Easy Rider.* Success of these and similar films led to the message that sexuality was a potent element in attracting larger audiences. Such was the case when movies were criticized for excessive violence. The motion picture studios showed that films needed to utilize sexuality to maintain a consistent audience. Television media followed the same pattern. Development of the television media from the 1940s to 1960s relied on nationally televised programs reflecting middle-class families and their contrived everyday lives. *Leave It to Beaver, I Love Lucy,* and *Father Knows Best* were some of the programs concerned with nuclear family structures and a seeming disinterest in sexual expression. This theme changed when the innocence of the 1950s was replaced by a coming of age during the 1960s. Television dramas and family comedies incorporated sexual images and more powerful themes. Married couples no longer slept in single beds or chose to disrobe to a certain degree. As time went on, partial nudity became more permissible.

Changing Social Standards

The connection between media and sexuality is reflected by a constantly changing social landscape. Nudity and blatant sexuality became a mainstay on cable television. Films and television programs could be shown uncensored for language or nudity because such fare was provided on a paid subscription basis. *The Sopranos* on HBO would be one such case. The explanation is that consenting adults voluntarily chose to watch such programming. But there are still some contradictions. Janet Jackson's "wardrobe malfunction" is still the subject of heavy fines levied by the Federal Communications Commission. However, both daytime and nighttime television historically contain partial nudity or explicit or double-entendre language (e.g., *Jerry Springer* as a daytime show and such programs as *NYPD Blue* or *Three's Company*). The same concerns can be expressed for the depiction of sexuality on daytime serials (otherwise known as soap operas).

Sociological Expression of Sexual Content

One can argue that sexuality is a mediated factor in the expression of social values. The depiction or expression of sexuality is influenced by accepted mores or social expectations. One can now utilize words such as *pregnant* on network television today versus when *I Love Lucy* was produced during the early 1950s. In particular, society sets fluid standards for when such content is appropriate. There is a vast difference between network programming after approximately 10 p.m. and family-oriented programs earlier in the evening. Adult situations or language are shown later in the evening to avoid objections from families with younger children. In addition, there is a nationwide concern with the expression of community values. *Miller v. CA* (1972) served as an important U.S. Supreme Court case focusing on pornography, adult materials, and media content. The Court focused on community values as a basic criterion defining appropriate sexual or other content within local media. On the basis of this case, there were lawsuits against the publication of *Hustler* magazine in some parts of the country, the screening of *Deep Throat* in other areas, and community petitions requesting the removal of the Playboy Cable Channel in some parts of the United States. As a result of a failure to reconcile acceptable criteria delineating the relationship between media and sexual content, the courts and media producers are aiming toward safer programming and tighter "over air" (as opposed to cable) restrictions.

Lloyd Klein

See also Media and Violence; Sexual Ethics; Socialization

Further Readings

Arthur, J. (2004). *Television and sexuality: Regulation and politics of taste.* New York: Open University Press.
Key, W. B. (1974). *Subliminal seduction: Ad media's manipulation of a not so innocent America.* New York: Signet.

MEDIA AND VIOLENCE

How the media represent crime, and particularly crimes involving violence, has been the subject of innumerable scholarly and popular treatments. Ray Surette and

Gregg Barak are among the many criminologists in the United States who have noted how journalists, nationally and internationally, believe that crime stories sell. This belief is even more the case when crimes involve heinous acts of brutality. Thus, a hefty proportion of all news is devoted to crime news; among all crime news, cases involving violence comprise well over two thirds of all news stories. Indeed, in a study that used Lexis/Nexis to identify the top 10 crime cases in U.S. newspapers between 1985 and 1995, eight of these incidents involved violence, that is, murders, rapes, and assaults. This entry focuses on how journalists select which of all violent crime cases they will cover in myriad news outlets, including politicized and celebrity violent crimes, and briefly discusses other approaches to studying media and violence.

Selection Criteria: The Novel and the Routine

In a classic study on the social construction of news, sociologist Gaye Tuchman argued that journalists are interested in cases that involve both routine and novel events. Covering violent crimes that have been committed is a regular feature of crime news, but what is literally new also affects journalists' selection criteria: Some cases are perceived as more circumstantially unusual than others, providing news pegs that are used to justify high levels of coverage. For example, in one sense, it has been routine for journalists to cover serial killers; the history of this coverage goes back to Victorian times and to the notoriety of cases such as that of Jack the Ripper. However, more recently, some cases have elicited more intensive coverage than others. The serial killings committed by Jeffrey Dahmer in Wisconsin attracted an unusual amount of notoriety. Here, the news hook may well have been that this particular serial killer targeted gay male rather than female victims. Analogously, the case of Eileen Wuornos in Florida may have elicited especially high levels of media coverage because this story had two unusual features. Wuornos had worked as a prostitute and allegedly murdered a number of her customers. Consequently, in this case, too, not only were men the victims, but the perpetrator was a woman. These angles may have made covering these serial killers both routine and novel by Tuchman's usage. Moreover, once media saturation of this crime occurred, not only did newspaper and television coverage ensue, but also

popular cultural representations in other mass media—for example, television movies—followed suit.

Coverage of Politicized and Celebrity Violent Crimes

Some violent crimes may attract media attention because they are perceived as having symbolic political implications. Reporters in New York City in 1989 stated that their intensive coverage of the now well-known "Central Park jogger" rape case ensued from this horribly violent crime having occurred in a landmark New York City location. Yet *The New York Times* later reported that over 20 rapes had taken place during the same week that the young female jogger in Central Park was attacked and beaten nearly to her death. Why did only this one case garner ongoing local and national coverage? Cynical observers argued that, whether or not journalists admitted it, the case reflected sociological biases. Rather than the news peg being location, critics at the time protested that high-profile coverage was due to the Central Park jogger being a White investment banker allegedly attacked by a group of working class minority youth; in most of the other cases, victims were young women of color. Consequently, debate took place, even in the media itself, about whether violent crimes that receive coverage in the media reflected journalists' own racial, class, and gender-related biases.

Through the 1980s and 1990s, a number of other violent crimes received national and even international attention as they became symbolic not only of individual but also of broader social problems. In 1991, in Los Angeles, media attention to the Rodney King case simultaneously gave voice to an individual who had been beaten by members of the Los Angeles Police Department (LAPD) and to collective concerns many young minority males felt about racial profiling and police brutality. That same year, a trio of cases involved charges of violence brought against people well known on the basis of their family connections or sports-based celebrity. In 1991, rape charges against William Kennedy Smith and Mike Tyson brought the issue of date rape to mass cultural consciousness. (Although both rape cases went to trial, only Tyson was convicted in February 1992.) Finally, in 1994, football star and movie celebrity O. J. Simpson was accused of and later tried for, but acquitted of, the murders of his ex-wife, Nicole Brown Simpson, and her friend, Ron Goldman. The Simpson case became symbolic of two social causes. Parties sympathetic to the prosecution believed that the Simpson case symbolized domestic violence in particular and the cause of violence against women in general. On the other hand, parties sympathetic to the defense believed that Simpson had been the victim of racial biases on the part of the LAPD. Although journalists dubbed this case "the trial of the century" as though it were unique, a more convincing interpretation is that the enormous coverage given the Simpson case was the culmination of a decade when high-profile violent crime cases involving issues of gender, race, class, and celebrity were preoccupying cultural attentions. These cases may have become a way of talking politics in the American context and may have been selected not only for their routine and novelty, but also because they provided mass-mediated vehicles of public debate.

Other Approaches to Studying Media and Violence

Other work in the area of media and violence has focused on reception studies. This approach involves studying how diverse audiences—of different ages as well as genders, races, and classes—interpret images of violent crimes presented to them in multiple media. Still other approaches to the study of media and violence have focused on narrative analysis of trials and on in-depth case studies of particular instances.

Lynn S. Chancer

See also Media, Representations/Distortions of Crime; Media and Sexuality

Further Readings

Barak, G. (Ed.). (1999). *Representing O.J.: Media, criminal justice, and mass culture.* New York: Harrow and Heston.

Chancer, L. (2005). *High-profile crimes: When legal cases become social causes.* Chicago: University of Chicago Press.

Gans, H. J. (1979). *Deciding what's news.* New York: Vintage.

Surette, R. (1998). *Media, crime and criminal justice: Images and realities.* Belmont, CA: Wadsworth.

Tuchman, G. (1978). *Making news: A study in the construction of reality.* New York: Free Press.

MEDIATION

Mediation is the process where a neutral third party assists disputing parties in a confidential, nonhostile way to reach an agreement that is satisfactory to both parties. Ideally, it also empowers the parties with a model that can be used to resolve further disputes. Mediation can be used for any dispute, but is probably most often used for divorce, custody and visitation, child support, property settlement, and restorative justice.

Although all forms of alternate dispute resolution use a neutral third party, mediation differs from conciliation because reconciling the parties is not a goal, and it differs from arbitration because the arbitrator makes a decision usually based on legal principles after hearing the evidence, with resolution the goal and not achieving a satisfactory solution. Mediators often do not know the laws, since satisfaction is a primary goal. All three methods have the potential to resolve conflicts with less bitterness and expense than litigating the dispute.

Does Mediation Work?

Over 90% of cases resolve regardless of whether courts use any type of alternative dispute resolution. Short-term gains from mediation's success over litigation vanish within 2 years, with both groups returning to court equally often with further disputes. The cost savings are far less or nonexistent than litigating a case, particularly when the parties pay the mediation costs.

Judges prefer mediation since it resolves many cases without their involvement. Most mediators find their work highly gratifying. Where it works, parties are often pleased to resolve disputes quickly, amicably, and with less cost.

Men like mediation far more than women do, and victims of domestic violence are less likely to be satisfied or save money than nonabused parties, although studies have failed to find physical abuse increases more after mediation than litigation. Many states and courts permit domestic violence victims to opt out of mediation, and many require mediators to screen out cases where there is domestic violence or to do it in ways to protect the victim, for example, where the parties do not meet together (often called shuttle mediation as the mediator shuttles between the parties) or even mediate over the telephone or through videoconferencing.

Problems With Mediation

Mediation is often conducted before discovery is completed so that the parties may not know the true value of an estate being divided or how to determine child support fairly, particularly if mediation includes alimony and property division.

Court mediators often make recommendations to the court about unsettled cases. This practice breaches the confidentiality promised and may result in unfairness, especially for the 85% to 90% of people who are unrepresented in family court in the United States.

In many states it is harder to modify an agreement of the parties than a court-ordered decision. Courts might honor a statement in the agreement that the parties intend their agreement to be modifiable upon the same standard as a court-ordered decision, although this is a two-edged sword and might encourage abusers to return to court.

How Mediation Disadvantages Abuse Victims

Mediators May Minimize Abuse

Few mediators understand domestic violence and most minimize its seriousness. Most are mental health professionals who believe all dynamics within the family are the result of both parties' behavior, so they fail to see abuse as a crime, blaming both parties. Many assume abuse ends once the parties have resolved their dispute or as a result of learning the new skills imparted on them through mediation. Although domestic violence is involved in 50% to 80% of divorce cases, mediators required to screen out domestic violence cases do so in about 5% of the cases, believing they are competent to handle the rest fairly. Victims may not feel believed and may feel unsupported when the abuse is not validated.

Mediators assume that increasing communication is better for the parties and the children. However, this increase may permit the batterer to use the communication to verbally intimidate, demean, disparage, or abuse the victim or to pressure reconciliation.

Mediators also often have a strong shared or joint custody bias and often need to impose shared parenting to reach seemingly fair agreements since custody

generally outweighs all other aspects of the marital estate to be divided, particularly when mediation excludes property division. Batterers typically get more custody and less supervised visitation when cases are mediated, increasing the danger for children and abused parents.

Batterers May Not Mediate Fairly

Many batterers have no intention of mediating fairly. They may push to optimize their situation and often to punish their victims. Being charming and more powerful, they often manipulate the mediator and turn their desires into a likely end product, making their victim seem unreasonable for rejecting them.

Even if batterers get all of their demands, they may have no intention of abiding by the agreement. When the agreement breaks down and returns to court, usually as a contempt or modification, the court often sends the case back to mediation, and the mediator, using the failed agreement as a starting point, negotiates a new agreement, often more favorable to the abuser than the prior one. This ratchet wheel effect continues with each successive breakdown, with courts and mediators oblivious to the pattern or realizing they colluded in increasing the power differential, unfairness, and danger.

Further disadvantaging victims, mediation often assumes equal bargaining power and ability to articulate one's needs and desires. Some victims are so overwhelmed or afraid that they cannot step back to think what they need, or even if they know, dare to articulate it or why they or the children need these protections.

Mediation Impedes Healing

Because mediation focuses on forgetting the past and looking to the future and blames both parties for past behaviors, it silences victims and reinforces the abusers' messages that their partners are to blame. Failing to hold the abuser accountable for the abuse, mediation may reinforce to the whole family, including the children, that abuse is acceptable, works, and will be rewarded. The result is that mediation impedes the ability of everyone in the family from healing and moving beyond.

Possible Challenges to Mediation

Victims not permitted to opt out of mediation can object using one or more of the following four strategies: (1) They can go to mediation, get a written agreement that nothing further will be reported to the court about what happened in mediation, and then state they have nothing further to say, that the mediation failed, and walk out. If what happened is reported to the court, they should demand that the judge withdraw from the case and report the mediator for malpractice. (2) If the court sends them more than once to mediation on the same issue(s), they should object that they are being denied their constitutional right to access to court. (3) If they have a lawyer and their lawyer is not permitted to attend and advise them in the mediation process, they can object on the grounds that this denial violates their Sixth Amendment rights. (4) Someone objecting to mediation as violating their religious or philosophical beliefs can try arguing that it violates their First Amendment religious rights. They must be able to convince the court of their sincerity in objecting to mediation as a violation of their beliefs and that these beliefs are religious in nature. But it is irrelevant if others in their religion do not hold this view, only that they personally and sincerely hold it.

Joan Zorza

See also Custody, Contact, and Visitation: Relationship to Domestic Violence; Restorative Justice

Further Readings

Bruch, C. S. (1988). And how are the children? The effects of ideology and mediation on child custody law and children's well-being in the United States. *International Journal of Law and the Family, 2,* 106–126.

Bryan, P. E. (1992). Killing us softly: Divorce mediation and the politics of power. *Buffalo Law Review, 40*(2), 441–523.

Grillo, T. (1991). The mediation alternative: Process dangers for women. *Yale Law Journal, 100,* 1545–1610.

Murphy, J. C., & Runinson, R. (2005). Domestic violence and mediation: Responding to the challenges of crafting effective screens. *Family Law Quarterly, 39*(1), 53–85.

Treuthart, M. P., & Woods, L. (1990). *Mediation—A guide for advocates and attorneys representing battered women.* New York: Legal Momentum.

Zorza, J. (2004). What is wrong with mediation. *Domestic Violence Report, 9*(6), 81, 91–94.

MEGAN'S LAW

See SEX OFFENDER REGISTRATION LAWS

MENDING THE SACRED HOOP

Over a hundred years ago Black Elk had a vision of a time when Indian people would heal from the devastating effects of European migration. In his vision, the Sacred Hoop, which had been broken, would be mended in seven generations. In 1990, a small group of Indian people from Minnesota, Wisconsin, and South Dakota began meeting to discuss the issues of violence in Native communities. This group was referred to as the Inter-Tribal Council to End Violence, which led to the creation of Mending the Sacred Hoop (MSH). This name was chosen for the organization to acknowledge the colonized history that has devastated the tribal communities and created the conditions in which Native women are brutalized.

There were various projects during these formative years, and in 1993, MSH established its core project of domestic violence systems advocacy and intervention in northern Minnesota. As MSH endured, it expanded to include training other communities across the country on its intervention efforts. In 1995, as part of the passage of the Violence Against Women Act (VAWA), MSH received a federal STOP Violence Against Indian Women grant that furthered its training and technical assistance and created Mending the Sacred Hoop Technical Assistance Project (MSH-TA). Through this grant, experienced Native trainers were identified and recruited to develop trainings and serve as resources for tribal communities addressing violence against American Indian and Alaskan Native women. The 14 STOP Violence Against Indian Women grantees, a handful of trainers or faculty, and a few MSH-TA staff set a vision and philosophy of a national scope that MSH continues to operate today.

The vision was to create a movement across Native communities and not to centralize expertise and resources in one place. At the time, MSH-TA was the only national organization addressing violence against women. Being a program based in Ojibwe country and northern Minnesota, it recognized its limitations in knowing all the complexities that are unique to each tribe or geographical area and knew the vulnerabilities of creating a dependency on one organization when, at the time, VAWA's funding was only committed until the year 2000. MSH's goal over 4 years was to build networks and expand the pool of trainers employing the concept, "Nin Gikenoo Amadimin," which means, "We Teach Each Other," so if the funding should cease there would be enough of a foundation that the work would continue on local and regional levels. Today there are five national Native technical assistance providers providing training and resources to well over 100 tribes funded through the Office on Violence Against Women.

In the upcoming years, MSH will continue with its local organizing and will branch out statewide, and on a national level, it will assist tribes in developing their own responses to violence against women in program development, grant management, the implementation of batterer's intervention programs, and creating a national network of Native batterer's intervention programs. From local criminal and civil court intervention efforts, to national collaborations with Native and non-Native organizations, MSH continues to raise the issues in Native communities and the experiences of Native women. MSH truly believes the health, survival, and sovereignty of Native people are directly connected to the safety and well-being of Native women.

Jeremy NeVilles-Sorell

See also Sacred Circle National Resource Center to End Violence Against Native Women; Tribal Issues; Violence Against Women Act

Web Sites

Mending the Sacred Hoop Technical Assistance Project: http://www.msh-ta.org

MENTAL ILLNESS

In the United States, mental health problems have come to the forefront of the public consciousness through large-scale public information campaigns, grassroots mental health movements, and more formal education on the specifics of various conditions. Mental illness is broadly defined here as clinical levels of psychiatric disorders that negatively impact one's social, academic, and/or occupational functioning. The clear need to develop an official classification system for mental disorders led the American Psychiatric Association (APA) to develop the first manual of mental disorders in 1952, known as the *Diagnostic and Statistical Manual of Mental Disorders* (*DSM*). With over 400 mental disorders defined and diagnosed, the *DSM* is the current guide

for clinicians, academics, and practitioners in the United States. Although public acceptance and understanding of mental illness is increasing, there is still considerable social stigmatization, stereotyping, and fear of persons with serious mental health problems. Of particular concern to the public are delusional, psychopathic, or antisocial persons who may become violent.

Deinstitutionalization and Public Fears of the Mentally Unstable

Although about half of all Americans will have a *DSM* disorder in their lifetimes, the vast majority of these diagnoses are not associated with aggressive behaviors. Estimates from the National Institute of Mental Health (NIMH) project that less than one out of five Americans receives the help needed for their mental problems. Research in the 1920s through the 1950s showed that mental patients actually had similar arrest rates as that of the general population. With the rise of deinstitutionalization in the 1960s or the release of mental patients from hospitals into community-based treatment, studies began reporting that mentally ill persons were responsible for a disproportionate number of violent crimes. Although many of these studies were later criticized for methodological weaknesses, they helped to fuel public fears about the release of mentally unstable persons into the community.

Numerous studies have reported on public perceptions that mental disorders and violence are invariably related. Individuals with severe mental illness are commonly regarded as dangerous, unpredictable, and at times, predatory. Yet according to a 2001 report by the U.S. Surgeon General, the danger that the majority of individuals with mental illness pose is actually quite small. Although an abundance of research has come forward to support these statements, the same literature does indicate that specific types of mental illness may play a role in the development of violent offending in childhood and adulthood.

Childhood or Adolescent Mental Disorders Linked With Violence

Although most children are unruly, disruptive, or recalcitrant at times in their growth, such behaviors become problematic when they regularly interfere with their function across a number of domains, including family, school, and peers. Numerous studies have documented a link between early and persistent aggressive behaviors in childhood and adolescence and subsequent later aggression. The number of juvenile offenders entering the criminal justice system with multiple mental health problems has also raised important questions about what role mental health might play in the development of violent behaviors.

There is compelling evidence of a relationship between various childhood disruptive disorders such as oppositional defiant disorder and conduct disorders and later serious offending. In addition, other disorders such as attention-deficit/hyperactivity disorder, depression, and substance abuse disorders have also been associated with aggression in youngsters. Depressed children, especially boys, may be filled with feelings of hostility, irritability, and aggression much more than are similar adults. Depression in children and adolescents has also been linked to violent behaviors such as suicide ideation and attempts, delinquency in adolescence, and homicidal ideation in adulthood. Research has suggested that boys with depression who also use or abuse substances become significantly more aggressive against others than do females, who tended to hurt themselves more. Youths with comorbid, or co-occurring, mental disorders have been shown to have a greater risk of violence later in life. Although there has been increasing attention to these types of juvenile mental health problems, the complexity surrounding childhood disorders and human development makes this a controversial topic. The media attention given to high profile school shootings and senseless acts of cruelty by youths has only reinforced public fears about juvenile predators.

Other Mental Disorders Linked With Violence

Besides these disorders, antisocial personality disorder (APD), schizophrenia, and substance abuse disorders (SUDs) have also been empirically linked to violent behaviors. Arguably the most controversial and feared adult mental health disorder is APD, which is typically preceded by oppositional defiant or conduct disorders earlier in childhood and adolescence. These individuals possess personality traits including a lack of conscience, low frustration thresholds, impulsivity, sadistic tendencies, and reckless abandon for others in their behaviors. There has been considerable

controversy over the years concerning the symptomology of antisocial personalities, with current debates focused on the reliability of the diagnostic criteria and possible overdiagnosis in criminal populations. Despite these concerns, APD is one of the most commonly linked diagnoses with serious and aggressive criminal behaviors, especially in males.

Schizophrenia includes symptoms such as psychotic delusions, hallucinations, disorganized thinking, purposeful and repetitive behaviors, and social withdrawal. The onset of this disorder typically occurs in late adolescence and into young adulthood for most individuals. Gender appears to influence the typical age of onset, with females developing the disorder later in life than males. In contrast to public perception, a review of the empirical relationship between schizophrenia and violent behaviors indicates a weak association at best. As adult schizophrenics may withdraw from others and be severely limited in functioning, it is more likely that psychotics will hurt themselves before committing violence against others.

Although not absolute, the most impressive body of scientific evidence shows a link between SUDs and violence, especially with respect to alcohol. This relationship has been much more tentative and indirect with marijuana use and violence. Overall, SUDs have been consistently identified as the most commonly associated mental disorder co-occurring with violent behaviors. The use of alcohol or illicit drugs has been shown to dramatically increase the likelihood of interpersonal violence when combined with certain mental disorders.

Denise Paquette Boots

See also Alcohol and Violence; Psychiatric Illness and Violence Propensity

Further Readings

American Psychiatric Association. (2000). *Diagnostic and statistical manual of mental disorders.* Washington, DC: Author.

Loeber, R., Farrington, D. P., Stouthamer-Loeber, M., & Van Kammen, W. B. (1998). *Antisocial behavior and mental health problems.* Mahwah, NJ: Lawrence Erlbaum.

Meadows, R. J., & Kuehnel, J. (2005). *Evil minds: Understanding and responding to violent predators.* Upper Saddle River, NJ: Pearson/Prentice Hall.

Monahan, J., & Steadman, H. J. (Eds.). (1994). *Violence and mental disorder: Developments and risk assessment.* Chicago: University of Chicago Press.

MENTORS IN VIOLENCE PREVENTION

The Mentors in Violence Prevention (MVP) model is an approach to gender violence and bullying prevention that was created in 1993 at Northeastern University's Center for the Study of Sport in Society. With initial funding from the U.S. Department of Education, the multiracial MVP program was designed to train college and high school male student-athletes and other student leaders to use their status to speak out against rape, battering, sexual harassment, gay-bashing, and all forms of sexist abuse and violence. A female component was later added with the complementary principle of training female student-athletes and others to be leaders on these issues.

The MVP model utilizes a creative bystander approach to gender violence prevention. It focuses on men not as perpetrators or potential perpetrators, but as empowered bystanders who can confront abusive peers—and support abused ones. It focuses on women not as victims or potential targets of harassment, rape, or abuse, but as empowered bystanders who can support abused peers—and confront abusive ones. In this model, a bystander is defined as a family member, friend, classmate, teammate, or coworker—anyone who is embedded in a family, social, or professional relationship with someone who might be abusive or be experiencing abuse.

The heart of the model is interactive discussion in single- and mixed-gender workshops using real-life scenarios that speak to the experiences of young men and women in college, high school, and other areas of social life. The chief curricular innovation of MVP is a training tool called the Playbook, which consists of realistic scenarios depicting abusive male (and sometimes female) behavior. The Playbook transports participants into scenarios as witnesses to actual or potential abuse, then challenges them to consider a number of concrete options for intervention before, during, or after an incident. Many people mistakenly believe they have only two options in cases of violence: intervene physically and possibly expose themselves to personal harm or do nothing. As a result, they often choose to do nothing.

But intervening physically or doing nothing are not the only possible choices. The MVP model provides bystanders with numerous options, most of which carry no risk of personal injury. With more options to choose from, people are more likely to respond and not be passive and silent—and hence complicit—in violence or abuse by others.

By the late 1990s, MVP had become the most widely utilized gender violence prevention program in college and professional athletics. Numerous Division I, II, and III athletic programs regularly participate in MVP trainings. The National Collegiate Athletic Association uses MVP materials in its Life Skills program. In 1997, MVP became the first gender violence prevention program in the history of the U.S. Marine Corps, and trainings have also been held with Army, Navy, and Air Force personnel. Although it began in the sports culture, by the mid-1990s, MVP had moved from a near-exclusive focus on the athletic world to general populations of college and high school students and to other institutional settings.

Jackson Katz

See also Athletes/Athletics and Sexual Violence; Prevention Programs, Interpersonal Violence

Web Sites

Jackson Katz's Web site: http://www.jacksonkatz.com
Mentors in Violence Prevention: http://www.sportinsociety .org/vpd/mvp.php

MILITARY, FAMILY ADVOCACY PROGRAMS

The Department of Defense was mandated within the Child Abuse Prevention and Treatment Act of 1974 to establish policy and practice to address domestic violence and child maltreatment. The department issued a directive, DD 6400.1, to establish practices relative to prevention, response, intervention, and treatment. The department and the services established programs collectively referenced as the Family Advocacy Program (FAP) within the Office of Family Policy.

The FAP is a command support program responsible for ensuring victim safety, access to support and advocacy services, and appropriate intervention and treatment for abusers. FAP coordinates activities among command, law enforcement, medical personnel, family centers, and victim advocates.

FAP provides a wide array of services including training for command and personnel, identification of domestic violence and child maltreatment, intervention services for victims and abusers, support services to victims, and treatment for abusers. The dual responsibility for safety and support services for victims conflicts with ensuring that abusers receive appropriate intervention services and treatment. Essentially, FAP handles the case from receipt of the initial report through case closure.

FAP staff include clinically licensed professionals trained in family violence. Victim advocates authorized by the U.S. Congress supplement the staff and response to family violence. Victim advocates navigate the system and coordinate services for victims within the military community.

Mandatory reporting of domestic violence and child maltreatment to FAP is required of active duty military personnel, health care providers, and others. FAP is mandated to coordinate the military community response to such reports. FAP may also engage civilian organizations and agencies in such efforts.

Christine Hansen

See also Armed Forces, Sexual Harassment in; Domestic Violence in Military Families

Further Readings

Army Community Service Program. (1995, September 1). *The Army Family Advocacy Program.* Washington, DC: Department of the Army.

Department of Defense. (1992). *The Family Advocacy Program.* Arlington, VA: Author.

Department of Defense. (2007). *Domestic abuse involving Department of Defense military and certain affiliated personnel.* Arlington, VA: Author.

Department of the Air Force. (1994, July 22). *Family advocacy.* Washington, DC: Author.

Secretary of the Navy. (1995, September 1). *Family Advocacy Program.* Washington, DC: Department of the Navy.

U.S. Marine Corps. (1994, July 1). *Marine Corps Family Advocacy Program standing operating procedures.* Washington, DC: Author.

MINNEAPOLIS DOMESTIC VIOLENCE EXPERIMENT

Published by Lawrence Sherman and Richard Berk in 1984, the Minneapolis Domestic Violence Experiment was the first to attempt to assign police responses randomly after domestic violence incidents. The findings suggested that arrest did reduce recidivism (the relapse into abusive and/or criminal behavior), and the findings were widely distributed. The researchers found, according to victims' and official reports, that arrest for misdemeanor domestic violence was significantly more effective than other police actions in reducing repeated violence during a 6-month follow-up period. The study received a great deal of attention and seemed to influence public policies.

Background

From the beginning of the modern battered women's movement in the 1970s through the mid-1980s, most supporters of battered women emphasized the lack of police responsiveness to their needs and advocated for more active police intervention. Newspapers often publicized incidents in which battered women were unprotected after calling the police. In most jurisdictions prior to the mid- to late 1980s, mediation and advice were standard police responses to domestic violence, and arrest was rare. When police officers intervened, they usually talked to the batterer, urged him to walk around the block to calm down, and then allowed him to return home. Such an approach often led to resumed violence after the perpetrator returned.

Methods

The study included 314 misdemeanor domestic violence incidents that were handled by police in Minneapolis in 1981 and 1982. Misdemeanor domestic violence crimes differ from felonies, which usually involve serious injuries or use of a weapon.

Volunteer officers agreed to arrest, mediate, or separate couples after an incident according to instructions on the top page of a randomly organized color-coded pad of paper. Then the researchers followed the cases by looking for official reports of subsequent incidents and by interviewing the victims twice weekly for 6 months. The employment of victims' as well as official reports to measure subsequent violence was extremely important because victims could report on incidents that were not officially documented.

Results

The arrest treatment showed a significantly smaller recidivism level over a 6-month period than the recidivism level for perpetrators who were ordered to leave. The victim interviews indicated a significantly lower recidivism rate for those who were arrested versus those who received advice.

After publication of these findings, there were criticisms related to selection of cases, low level of participation by police officers, and lack of complete adherence to the randomized police responses. In addition, since violence can be cyclical, a 6-month follow-up period is not long enough to demonstrate a deterrent effect on batterers with long cycles.

Impact

In the late 1980s and in the 1990s, the percentage of police departments using arrest as their preferred or mandated policy increased greatly. It is unclear whether the change was due to the impact of the study and its replications (Spouse Assault Replication Project), to the influence of some successful lawsuits against police departments, or to the influence of advocates. A debate about effectiveness has accompanied the spread of preferred arrest policies, and there are philosophical disagreements about whether mandatory arrest promotes victim empowerment.

Arlene N. Weisz

See also Police, Response to Domestic Violence; Spouse Assault Replication Project

Further Readings

Sherman, L. W., & Berk, R. A. (1984). The specific deterrent effects of arrest for domestic assault. *American Sociological Review, 49,* 261–272.

MISOGYNY

Misogyny is the hatred of women. Misogyny also refers to contempt for the qualities that are associated with femininity, whether exhibited by women or by men. Misogyny is synonymous with sexism. It is relevant to interpersonal violence because antipathy toward women shapes the forms, meanings, and motives for violence as well as the responses to it. Misogyny also influences the dynamics of interpersonal relationships and the structure of social institutions in patriarchal cultures. Although the relevance of misogyny may be most readily apparent in the dynamics of woman abuse, it has also been linked by the research to additional forms of violence.

By men's own accounts, misogyny is an important ingredient in much of their violence. The dehumanization of victims is one part of the perpetration of violence, and misogyny contributes to the dehumanization of women and gay men, increasing their risk of experiencing particular types of violence. Likewise, misogyny is one of the motives for violence for many men, shaping the forms of the violence they choose as well as their selection of targets.

The Cultural Context of Misogyny

Misogyny exists in the context of patriarchal cultures that place men's experiences, power, and values at the center of community and family life. In addition to contributing to men's power in the family and society, patriarchy establishes masculinity as the normative gender. Masculine characteristics are considered to be universal and natural under patriarchy. Conversely, femininity is defined in opposition to masculinity. Accordingly, femininity is often considered unnatural, perverse, weak, derivative, or inferior in comparison to masculinity. Each masculine characteristic is the antithesis of a feminine characteristic. Misogyny ensures that these opposites are not equal but are instead differently valued in polarized dichotomies of masculine and feminine.

Misogyny, Gender, and Violence

As a result of the binary and oppositional nature of gender construction, men are encouraged to establish and perform their masculinity as antagonistic to femininity. Masculinity is established by demonstrating that one is not feminine and not gay. This demonstration is not necessarily an intentional process. Just as racism and heterosexism may appear to some to be just how things are or a logical response to real differences between groups, misogyny is often internalized and taken for granted, although sometimes it is blatant and articulated. As with other forms of prejudice, misogyny is manifested in ways of thinking that incorporate stereotypes as well as in violent behavior. The link between misogyny and violence comes from the association of masculinity with power and force. Since the ability to do violence is considered to be an important part of masculinity in many cultures, some men use violence to solidify their status when their masculinity is challenged.

Misogyny and Violence Against Women

Men's violence against women is the most visible connection between misogyny and interpersonal violence. Serial killers, rapists, and men who batter women in intimate relationships frequently use their contempt for women to account for their violence. In recounting their perpetration of violence, some men refer to their prerogative to control and discipline the women with whom they are associated. Other violent men talk about a generalized hatred of all women that motivates their violence. Some violent perpetrators describe their violence against women as justified by mistreatment by one woman in their past.

Feminist scholars identify the virgin–whore dichotomy as one manifestation of misogyny. The virgin–whore dualism divides women into good and bad categories based on their adherence to normative gender roles. Women who are perceived to transgress gender roles, especially the sexual double standard, are placed in the bad category. When this happens, they are often considered to be "bad victims" in court. For example, women who are sexually active outside of marriage may be seen as unrapeable since violating the gender order destroys their virtue. Women sometimes face a higher standard of credibility in the courts because it is assumed that women are dishonest and likely to make false reports against men.

Misogyny and Violence Against Children

Violence against female and male children is also shaped by misogyny. In addition to child rape and murder by people outside the family, some men use violence against children as part of the abuse they inflict on their wives, ex-wives, or girlfriends. Battered women report that abusers' threats to take or harm the children are a factor in their fear of leaving abusive relationships.

Even when the perpetrator of violence is another child, as in the Jonesboro, Arkansas, middle school shooting, misogyny may be a factor. Although media reports of the Jonesboro shooting talked about the violence in sex-neutral terms, the older shooter told classmates he was out for revenge against a girl who rejected him. The students and teacher who were killed in the Jonesboro shooting were all female, and the girl who broke up with the older shooter was one of the students he shot and injured. Other perpetrators of school shootings have commented that their violence was a way to prove their masculinity and gain some power in a social world that derided them as inadequately masculine, citing homophobic and sexist taunts as part of their motivation.

Misogyny and Violence Against Men

Research on violent men has also found misogyny to be a significant factor in the etiology of violence against other men. Most often cited by perpetrators are challenges to their masculinity or the perception that they are at risk of rape or another form of feminization. Perpetrators of violence in prison, violence against strangers, and violence against acquaintances and intimates have all been linked to this manifestation of misogyny.

Molly Dragiewicz

See also Battered Women's Movement; Feminist Movements to End Violence Against Women; Sex Discrimination

Further Readings

Brownmiller, S. (1975). *Against our will: Men, women and rape.* New York: Bantam Books.
Frye, M. (1983). *The politics of reality: Essays in feminist theory.* Berkeley, CA: The Crossing Press.

Gilligan, J. (2001). *Preventing violence.* New York: Thames and Hudson.

Johnson, A. G. (1997). *The gender knot: Unraveling our patriarchal legacy.* Philadelphia: Temple University Press.

Walby, S. (1990). *Theorizing patriarchy.* Oxford, UK: Blackwell.

MORAL PANICS

The term *moral panic* is most often attributed to British sociologist Stanley Cohen, who in a 1972 book, *Folk Devils and Moral Panics,* defined it as a condition, episode, person, or group of persons that come to be seen as a threat to societal values and interests. In recent years, moral panic has been defined more broadly as any exaggerated fear or overreaction to social deviance. Moral panics are often traced to media attention and are fueled by politicians, law enforcement, or advocates or activists. Phenomena related to interpersonal violence that have been described as examples of moral panics include, but are not limited to, satanic ritual abuse, abuse in daycare centers, missing children, crack babies, sex offenders, and school shootings.

Among British sociologists, moral panics are likely to be interpreted as an expression of outrage by those in power over a threat perceived to challenge core societal values. Cohen, for example, describes media reaction to the violence between two British youth gangs during the 1960s that sparked a moral panic in Great Britain about the societal threat posed by British youth. Among American sociologists, moral panics are more typically understood within the context of a social constructionist perspective of social problems. From this perspective, social problems only come to be defined as such after claims-makers mobilize enough resources (e.g., media attention, money, political clout) to bring the social condition they deem egregious or harmful before the public eye. Because social problems compete for societal recognition and resources, claims-makers will invariably err on the side of exaggeration and overreaction. The concept of moral panics is important because it draws our attention to the rhetorical strategies employed by claims-makers in their attempt to garner attention for a particular cause.

Some moral panics fade from the public eye seemingly as quickly as they arise. For example, during the 1980s and early 1990s thousands of adult survivors of satanic ritual abuse supposedly recovered memories of ritual abuse, torture, pornography, forced prostitution, and child sacrifices at the hands of Satanists. By the late 1990s, however, with claims of an active satanic conspiracy largely discredited, the moral panic associated with satanic ritual abuse quickly subsided.

One should be careful not to focus exclusively on largely imagined fears such as satanic ritual abuse because such limited application may contribute to the misunderstanding that the term *moral panic* is synonymous with *false* or *imagined.* To describe a threat as a moral panic, however, is not necessarily to suggest that the threat is completely unfounded or that no public concern is warranted. Rather, moral panic merely refers to phenomena that generate fear out of proportion with the actual threat.

Robin Perrin

See also Media, Representations/Distortions of Crime; Ritualistic Abuse; School Violence, Media Coverage of; Sex Offender Registration Laws

Further Readings

Cohen, S. (2002). *Folk devils and moral panics* (3rd ed.). New York: Routledge. (Original work published 1972)

Goode, E., & Ben-Yehuda, N. (1994). *Moral panics: The social construction of deviance.* Cambridge, MA: Blackwell.

MUNCHAUSEN SYNDROME BY PROXY

Munchausen Syndrome by Proxy (MSBP) is a form of child abuse that occurs when a caregiver, usually the mother, fabricates or induces illness in a child. The caretaker repeatedly presents the child to a physician or hospital with a variety of symptoms including bleeding, vomiting, diarrhea, fever, lethargy, apnea, and seizures. The child victims are usually under the age of 3 years, but may be older; older children may become convinced by the caregiver that they have an illness or they may passively or actively participate with the caregiver in deceiving health professionals. The caregiver may falsely claim a child has experienced serious symptoms such as seizures, may contaminate test results to indicate illness, and/or may physically harm the child to produce symptoms.

Because the victim is a child, MSBP is considered a form of child abuse. The child victim may undergo repeated invasive and painful tests and examinations, be given unnecessary medications with negative side effects, or even be subjected to exploratory surgical procedures. Physicians dealing with young children rely heavily on the medical history provided by the caregiver, and in MSBP cases the caregiver misrepresents, exaggerates, or creates symptoms and incidences the child is not experiencing or has not naturally experienced. The caregiver may also have taken the child to several different physicians or hospitals that she does not include in her medical history for the child. The situation is further complicated by the fact that the caregiver is often intelligent, appears devoted to the child, may have had some medical training or experience, and is generally very cooperative with the medical personnel.

MSBP has been referred to by various names, including factitious illness by proxy, fictitious disorder by proxy, Meadow's syndrome, and chronic nonaccidental poisoning. More recently, especially in the United Kingdom and Australia, it is being labeled fabricated or induced illness by caregivers (FIIC). This naming is due to some extent to the fact that MSBP has never been listed in the *Diagnostic and Statistical Manual of Mental Disorders* of the American Psychiatric Association as a clinical diagnosable disorder but Factitious Disorder by Proxy is listed in the current edition of the manual as a topic or classification for further study.

There continue to be significant differences of opinion on whether FIIC or MSBP exists, but there is considerable evidence that there are caregivers who do fabricate or induce illnesses in their children. There is video surveillance that has shown parents harming their children and then presenting the children as having unexplained medical conditions and who agree to unneeded medical procedures. In the literature, there are numerous documented cases in several countries where illnesses in children have been fabricated or induced by caregivers.

Incidence data on MSBP or FIIC is somewhat sketchy, but cases seem to be relatively rare. A rather thorough national survey in the United Kingdom in the mid-1990s (with every pediatrician in the United Kingdom being asked every month for 18 months if he or she had diagnosed a case) suggested that only about 50 new cases a year were diagnosed. An estimated 600 cases occurred in the United States in 1996, and in 2001, 18 cases per annum were reported in New Zealand. But however relatively rare FIIC may be, it has serious consequences for the child victims, including death, and makes it critical for practitioners to be able to identify the condition and take appropriate action to protect the child and obtain treatment for the perpetrator.

A major impediment to the diagnosis of MSBP or FIIC is the unwillingness or failure of professionals to consider the possibility that a parent could do something so detrimental to his or her child. However, once the diagnosis is suspected, it may require a multidisciplinary team that includes a child protective services worker, law enforcement officer, psychologist or psychiatrist, prosecutor, hospital social worker, and the child's medical team to reach a firm diagnosis. The process requires a thorough review of present and past medical records, careful monitoring of the patient (with or without video surveillance) when any family member is present, and possibly separation of the child from the suspected parent. If the diagnosis is confirmed, the team undertakes the immediate steps necessary to ensure the child's safety.

C. Terry Hendrix

See also Child Fatalities; Child Physical Abuse; Child Protection Services; Ethical and Legal Issues, Interviewing Children Reported as Abused or Neglected; Female Perpetrators of Violence Against Children; Foster Care; Health Care Response to Child Maltreatment; Health Consequences of Child Maltreatment; Kinship Care; Legal System and Child Protection

NATIONAL AMBER ALERT PROGRAM

The AMBER Alert program is an emergency response system established to enable the public to aid in the search for children who are believed to have been abducted and to be in imminent danger. Following the 1996 abduction and murder of 9-year-old Amber Hagerman, the Dallas–Fort Worth police and local broadcasters established the first operational AMBER Alert system in 1997. Between 1997 and 2003, local, regional, and statewide voluntary collaborative arrangements between police, transportation authorities, and broadcast media were launched in 41 states.

With the passage of the PROTECT Act in 2003, AMBER Alert formally became a national program overseen by the U.S. Department of Justice (DOJ) and coordinated by the Assistant Attorney General. Named in part as a tribute to Amber Hagerman, the acronym AMBER in AMBER Alert actually stands for America's Missing: Broadcast Emergency Response. The National Center for Missing and Exploited Children (NCMEC) provides links to the AMBER Alert plans and the public contact representatives for all 50 states. In May 2005, the wireless communication industry and the NCMEC launched a wireless AMBER Alert initiative that allows wireless phone subscribers to opt to receive AMBER alerts on their cellular phones.

Although there are no mandated AMBER Alert criteria, the DOJ has established advisory criteria for the issuance of an alert. These criteria include (a) that law enforcement officials reasonably believe the child has been abducted and is in imminent danger, (b) that the child be age 17 or younger, (c) that there be enough information regarding the abduction that the public could reasonably aid in the recovery of the child, and (d) that the crime be entered and flagged as an abduction in the National Crime Information Center database. When a potential child abduction meets the criteria, police notify broadcast media and transportation authorities who in turn issue emergency alerts over the radio and television airwaves and post notices on electronic highway message boards (traditionally used to alert drivers of accidents, hazards, or road construction ahead). The alerts issued include pertinent information that might aid in the rapid recovery of the child (typically a description of the child and of any vehicle involved in the abduction).

Neither the DOJ nor the NCMEC provide official data on the total number of AMBER alerts issued to date (estimates range from 200 to 250 alerts issued per year), but the agencies do provide data on the successes of the initiative. As of June 2006, the NCMEC Web site attributed 278 successful child recoveries to AMBER Alert systems. According to a mandated annual report to Congress, more than 80% of the successful AMBER recoveries have occurred since the program became a coordinated national effort.

The National AMBER Alert program was passed as part of the PROTECT Act, formally named the Prosecutorial Remedies and Other Tools to End the Exploitation of Children Today Act (Public Law 108-21) signed into law on April 30, 2003, by President George W. Bush. Billed as a comprehensive package of initiatives to protect children, the PROTECT Act included provisions designed to prevent child abuse, abduction, and exploitation. The PROTECT Act also included provisions that expanded prosecutorial powers extending wiretapping authority and curtailing judicial discretion through limiting downward sentencing departures.

Natasha A. Frost

See also Child Abductions, Family; Child Abductions, Nonfamily

Further Readings

Office of Juvenile Justice and Delinquency Prevention. (2004). *When your child is missing: A family survival guide*. Washington, DC: U.S. Department of Justice. Retrieved from http://www.ncjrs.gov/html/ojjdp/204958/index.html

U.S. Department of Justice. (2004, October). *Report to the White House on AMBER Alert*. Washington, DC: Author. Retrieved from http://www.amberalert.gov/newsroom/pdfs/04_amber_report.pdf

Web Sites

National Center for Missing and Exploited Children: http://www.missingkids.com

NATIONAL CENTER FOR MISSING AND EXPLOITED CHILDREN

The National Center for Missing and Exploited Children (NCMEC) was established after several high-profile child abductions and murders made it clear there was a need for coordinated responses when children went missing. It was established in 1984 and officially opened by President Ronald Reagan. NCMEC is best known as the people who put missing children's pictures on milk cartons and in mailings to millions of homes. But it does much more than sending out pictures of missing children.

NCMEC's Web site lists its mission to "help prevent child abduction and sexual exploitation; help find missing children; and assist victims of child abduction and sexual exploitation, their families, and the professionals who serve them." The organization achieves this mission in a number of ways. First and foremost NCMEC acts as an international clearinghouse of information and a first stop for parents, family members, and professionals worried about or looking for missing children. There are a multitude of published educational and training materials available online for parents and guardians, law enforcement officers, childcare providers, attorneys, and the media. They provide training and technical assistance nationally on this topic and operate the CyberTipline that allows, according to the Web site, the reporting of child sexual exploitation "including child pornography, online enticement of children for sex acts, molestation of children outside the family, sex tourism of children, child victims of prostitution, and unsolicited obscene material sent to a child," using both online and toll-free telephone reporting systems. NCMEC also takes part in the national AMBER Alert system by helping rapidly validate and distribute alerts about missing or abducted children through a variety of law enforcement outlets.

NCMEC also houses an international division that, among other tasks, assists the U.S. State Department with children being abducted into the United States from other countries. In 2006 alone, NCMEC's international division was working on 1,850 international abduction cases.

As the Internet has expanded its reach to more and more children, NCMEC has become more involved in helping to protect children from becoming victims of crimes by predators initially contacting children online. As this aspect of their program has evolved, they have created a separate NetSmartz Workshop. NetSmartz's Web site states that it is "an interactive, educational safety resource from the National Center for Missing & Exploited Children (NCMEC) and Boys & Girls Clubs of America (BGCA) for children aged 5 to 17, parents, guardians, educators, and law enforcement that uses age-appropriate, 3-D activities to teach children how to stay safer on the Internet."

Jeffrey L. Edleson

See also Child Abductions, Family; Hague Convention on the Civil Aspects of International Child Abduction; Internet, Crimes Against Children; National AMBER Alert Program

Web Sites

National Center for Missing and Exploited Children: http://www.missingkids.com/

NetSmartz Workshop: http://www.netsmartz.org

NATIONAL CENTER FOR VICTIMS OF CRIME

The National Center for Victims of Crime is the nation's leading resource and advocacy organization for crime victims and victim service providers. Founded in 1985 by the children of Sunny von Bulow, the victim of a murder attempt that left her in a decades-long diabetic coma, the National Center works with local, state, and federal partners to help individuals, families, and communities who have been harmed by crime.

The National Center provides direct services and resources to victims of crime across the country through its victim helpline (1-800-FYI-CALL), which helps victims—in 150 languages—understand the impact of crime, access victim compensation, develop safety plans, navigate the criminal justice and social service systems, learn their legal rights and options, and find the most appropriate local services. Victims of crime also receive direct assistance via e-mail at gethelp@ncvc.org and through the national center's *Get Help* bulletins on a wide range of victim-related issues available at www.ncvc.org. The organization also operates the Victim Services Referral Database, a unique resource that gives victims access to detailed information about the services of nearly 10,000 victim-service agencies throughout the country. Victims may also receive referrals to attorneys through the National Crime Victim Bar Association, an affiliate of the national center and the nation's only organization of attorneys dedicated to helping crime victims seek justice through the civil justice system.

The National Center for Victims of Crime fosters cutting-edge thinking about the impact of and response to crime and has published several landmark reports including *Rape in America,* a groundbreaking national study on rape conducted in partnership with the Medical University of South Carolina; *Our Vulnerable Teenagers,* released jointly with the National Council on Crime and Delinquency, which analyzed existing, but largely unnoticed, research and data on the alarming crime experiences of teenagers; and *Repairing the Harm,* which highlighted major shortcomings in the nation's victim compensation system.

The National Center for Victims of Crime advocates for laws and public policies that secure resources, rights, and protections for crime victims and is the nation's leading proponent of a new vision of justice for crime victims called *Parallel Justice,* a framework for responding to crime with two separate, but complimentary paths to justice—one for victims and one for offenders.

The center's Stalking Resource Center, the only national technical assistance center focused solely on stalking, works to raise public awareness about stalking and helps communities across the country develop multidisciplinary responses to this insidious crime. Since its inception in 2000, the center has provided training to tens of thousands of victim service providers and criminal justice practitioners throughout the United States. In addition, the center's Teen Victim Initiative focuses on building the nation's capacity to support teenage victims of crime, one of the largest groups of underserved victims.

Through its Training Institute and national conferences, the National Center for Victims of Crime provides trainings and technical assistance to victim service providers, counselors, attorneys, and allied professionals serving victims of crime and publishes a wide array of resources, including *NETWORKS,* the National Center's flagship magazine.

Mary Gleason Rappaport

See also Rape/Sexual Assault; Stalking; Victimology; Victims' Rights Movement; Victim-Witness Advocacy Programs

Web Sites

National Center for Victims of Crime: http://www.ncvc.org

NATIONAL CENTER ON CHILD ABUSE AND NEGLECT

See OFFICE ON CHILD ABUSE AND NEGLECT

NATIONAL CHILDREN'S ALLIANCE AND CHILDREN'S ADVOCACY CENTERS

National Children's Alliance (NCA) is a nationwide 501(c)3 nonprofit membership organization formed in 2000 from a network of children's advocacy centers.

NCA's mission is to promote and support communities in providing a coordinated response to victims of severe child abuse; it also provides services to children's advocacy centers, multidisciplinary teams, and professionals across the country.

In 1985, the first children's advocacy center opened in Huntsville, Alabama. This program was initiated by a prosecutor seeking a safe, competent, and reliable service for interviewing children suspected of having been sexually abused. The Huntsville organization soon expanded its services and was renamed the National Children's Advocacy Center. The Huntsville model became popular and gained national support from the U.S. Department of Justice, resulting in a national network of children's advocacy centers.

Children's Advocacy Centers (CACs) offer a comprehensive approach to services for abused children and their families, with programs designed by professionals and volunteers to meet the needs of their own communities. CACs emphasize coordination of investigation and intervention services by bringing together professionals from child protective services, law enforcement, and health and mental health services as a multidisciplinary team to create a child-focused approach to child abuse cases. The goal is to ensure that children are not revictimized by the systems designed to protect them.

What makes the CAC model so effective is the multidisciplinary community response to child abuse that enables law enforcement, prosecutors, child protective services, and the medical and mental health professionals to work together as a team to investigate and prosecute cases of child abuse. CAC programs strive to minimize trauma, break the cycle of abuse, and provide communities with increased rates of prosecution of perpetrators. In many cases, the child suspected of having been abused may be examined and interviewed only once with the interdisciplinary team members conducting or observing the process; this approach prevents the possible trauma of the victim being interviewed and examined several times by the various agencies and professionals concerned with the victimization.

The NCA is an umbrella organization that provides a standard setting, education, and accreditation for the CACs throughout the country. To be accredited, CACs must offer all forms of assessment services with the exception of perpetrator interviews and examinations, and they may also provide mental health facilities. CACs may be based in any number of community institutions such as hospitals, or they may be housed in their own buildings. Whatever the setting, CACs make every effort to provide a child-friendly environment and appropriate facilities for the multidisciplinary team to function effectively.

Many professionals in the field of child abuse believe that more than any other professional group, the NCA and the more than 400 component CACs are building a national model for coordinated and competent child abuse interventions and services—one that is fully committed to the multidisciplinary team approach that is essential for all competent professional work regarding child abuse.

C. Terry Hendrix

See also Child Protective Services; Court-Appointed Special Advocates; Ethical and Legal Issues, Interviewing Children Reported as Abused or Neglected; Family Preservation and Reunification Programs; Family Therapy and Family Violence; Investigative Interviewing of Child Sexual Abuse Victims; Legal System and Child Protection; Legislation, Child Maltreatment; Nonoffending Parents of Maltreated Children; Police, Response to Child Maltreatment; Secondary Victimization by Police and Courts

Web Sites

National Children's Alliance: http://www.nca-online.org/

NATIONAL CHILD TRAUMATIC STRESS NETWORK

The National Child Traumatic Stress Network (NCTSN) is a group of 70 treatment and research centers across the United States providing or developing services for traumatized children and their families. All 70 centers receive or have received grant funding from the Center for Mental Health Services, Substance Abuse and Mental Health Services Administration, U.S. Department of Health and Human Services. The NCTSN was created through the Donald J. Cohen National Child Traumatic Stress Initiative (NCTSI), passed by Congress in 2001, to recognize the devastating impact of trauma on children, youth, and their families. The mission of the initiative is "to raise the standard of care, and increase access to services for traumatized children, families and communities throughout the United States." The initiative recognizes the pioneering work of Donald J. Cohen, a national leader in the field of child traumatic stress, Sterling Professor of Child Psychiatry, Psychology and Pediatrics at Yale University, and Director of the Yale Child Study Center until his death in 2001 at the age of 61.

The NCTSN aims to provide leadership and knowledge in the area of childhood traumatic stress through public information and awareness efforts, nationwide training, and the development, adaptation, and dissemination of evidence-based interventions for childhood traumatic stress. The NCTSN integrates cultural and developmental knowledge in developing and disseminating interventions toward the development of a comprehensive continuum of care for all traumatized children and their families. The NCTSI emphasizes collaboration between network centers, across multiple child-serving systems, and between providers and consumers of trauma-focused mental health services.

Centers in the NCTSN provide services for children traumatized by natural disasters, terrorism, community and intimate partner violence, homelessness, and related severe stressors. Across the United States, 45 centers are currently funded by the NCTSI, as Category 1, 2, or 3 grantees. The National Center for Childhood Traumatic Stress (NCCTS), the sole Category 1 grantee, is a collaboration of the University of California, Los Angeles, and Duke University. The NCCTS works closely with the Substance Abuse and Mental Health Services Administration to provide administrative leadership and coordination activities to the network, to deliver technical assistance to NCTSN grantees, to develop and provide national training and education on childhood traumatic stress, and to oversee resource development and dissemination efforts.

Treatment and Services Adaptation Centers (nine Category 2 grantees) provide national expertise in childhood traumatic stress by developing and evaluating interventions for specific types of traumatic stress across different populations and service systems. These centers provide support to 35 Community Treatment and Services Centers in adapting, implementing, and disseminating promising and model practices across a broad range of communities and service systems. Community Treatment and Services Centers provide direct services in community settings and child-serving systems to a broad range of children affected by traumatic events. Centers collaborate within and across network categories to advance knowledge of trauma-informed service provision and clinical, policy, training, and fiscal issues in relation to childhood traumatic stress.

Abigail Gewirtz

See also Child Exposure to Intimate Partner Violence; Child Exposure to Violence, in War Zones; Child Exposure to Violence, Role of Schools; Child Physical Abuse; Child Sexual Abuse; Community Violence, Effects on Children and Youth; Complex Trauma in Children and Adolescents

Further Readings

Gray, A., & Szekely, A. (2006, November). *Thinking broadly: Financing strategies for child traumatic stress initiatives.* Los Angeles: National Child Traumatic Stress Network. Retrieved from http://www.financeproject.org/publications/ThinkingBroadlyCTS.pdf

Martin, A. (2002). Donald J. Cohen, M.D. 1940–2001. *American Journal of Psychiatry, 159,* 1829. Retrieved from http://ajp.psychiatryonline.org/cgi/reprint/159/11/1829.pdf

United States Department of Health and Human Services. (2001). *HHS awards $10 million for Child Traumatic Stress Initiative* [Press release]. Retrieved from http://www.hhs.gov/news/press/2001pres/20011003a.html

Web Sites

National Child Traumatic Stress Network: http://www.nctsnet.org

NATIONAL CLEARINGHOUSE FOR THE DEFENSE OF BATTERED WOMEN

The National Clearinghouse for the Defense of Battered Women was founded in 1987 to work for justice for battered women charged with crimes where a history of abuse is relevant to the woman's legal claim or defense. A nonprofit organization located in Philadelphia, Pennsylvania, the National Clearinghouse provides technical assistance and other resources to battered women defendants, defense attorneys, battered women's advocates, and expert witnesses across the nation. Most frequently, the organization assists battered women who have defended themselves and/or their children against their batterer's violence and who have been charged with assault or homicide. The National Clearinghouse works with battered women who have been coerced into criminal activity, women charged with a crime for allegedly "failing to protect" their children from their batterer's violence, and women charged with kidnapping or custodial interference for fleeing to protect themselves and/or their children.

The first and only national organization to focus exclusively on battered women defendants, the National Clearinghouse maintains a comprehensive resource bank of information regarding battered women's legal defense issues, provides direct support to battered women in prison, coordinates a national network of advocates working with battered women defendants, and provides education and information regarding the unique experiences of battered women defendants to members of the criminal justice and advocacy communities and to the general public.

In all of its activities, the National Clearinghouse strives to change the attitudes and institutions that create and support the extreme levels of oppression battered women experience when they find themselves in conflict with the law. The organization's educational and policy efforts are designed to change beliefs and behaviors of individuals, increase positive outcomes in individual cases, and facilitate short- and long-term changes at the institutional level. Because these activities cannot be done by one organization alone, the National Clearinghouse has organized an ever-growing network of people and organizations committed to justice for battered women who end up in conflict with the law.

Recognized for its quality services and national leadership role, the National Clearinghouse was one of five organizations chosen in 1993 to receive funds from the U.S. Department of Health and Human Services (DHHS) as part of the Battered Women's Justice Project (BWJP). Through a number of continuation grants from DHHS, the National Clearinghouse continues to be an active partner in BWJP and in the Domestic Violence Resource Network, a coalition of the DHHS-funded special resource centers on domestic violence.

The National Clearinghouse remains committed to its organizational mission "to secure justice for battered women charged with crimes related to their battering and prevent further victimization of arrested, convicted, or incarcerated battered women." Since it opened its doors nearly 20 years ago, the National Clearinghouse has brought hope to hundreds of battered women and their families by providing them and their defense teams with direct assistance, information, and support; by helping their voices and stories be heard; and by advocating steadfastly on their behalf when they cannot take a seat at the table.

Sue Osthoff

See also Battered Women's Justice Project; Domestic Violence Resource Network

Further Readings

Dutton, M. A. (1996). Impact of evidence concerning battering and its effects in criminal trials involving battered women. In *The validity and use of evidence concerning battering and its effects in criminal trials* (section 1). Washington, DC: U.S. Department of Justice, National Institute of Justice, U.S. Department of Health and Human Services, & National Institute of Mental Health. Retrieved from http://www.ncjrs.org/pdffiles/batter.pdf

Maguigan, H. (1991). Battered women and self-defense: Myths and misconceptions in current reform proposals. *University of Pennsylvania Law Review, 140,* 379–486.

National Clearinghouse for the Defense of Battered Women. (2006). *Our mission.* Retrieved from http://www.ncdbw .org/mission.htm

Osthoff, S. (2001). When victims become defendants: Battered women charged with crimes. In C. M. Renzetti & L. Goodstein (Eds.), *Women, crime and criminal justice* (pp. 232–242). Los Angeles: Roxbury.

Osthoff, S., & Maguigan, H. (2004). Explaining without pathologizing: Testimony on battering and its effects. In D. R. Loseke, R. J. Gelles, & M. M. Cavanaugh (Eds.), *Current controversies on family violence* (2nd ed., pp. 225–240). Thousand Oaks, CA: Sage.

NATIONAL CLEARINGHOUSE ON MARITAL AND DATE RAPE

The National Clearinghouse on Marital and Date Rape (NCMDR) was founded in 1980 as a project of the Women's History Research Center (WHRC) in order to document rape laws in the United States that entitled men to rape their wives and dates. It was a network of academic researchers; law interns; health, mental health, and religious professionals; prosecutors; defense attorneys; judges; and activists from the anti-rape and battered women's movements and especially of victims or survivors. Laura X, the founder and director, as an individual, campaigned successfully for the repeal of date and marital rape exemptions from prosecution, which were in the laws of 45 states, in federal and military law, in laws of Guam, as well as in the laws of 20 other countries, from 1978 through June 1993 for the United States, and until 2004 elsewhere, when she retired and closed NCMDR.

When Laura X started collecting materials in 1968 for what would become in 1970 the Women's History Library of the WHRC, one goal was to create an activists-shared archive for materials growing out of the emerging women's liberation movement. Operating out of her Berkeley, California, home, the formerly battered woman and University of California, Berkeley, alumna, harbored battered women and rape survivors who were in desperate straits because there were still no community services available to them. From this refuge, Laura printed interviews with survivors in her own publication *SPAZM* (the only national women's liberation newsletter from April to December 1969) as well as printed "Anatomy of a Rape" on July 23 in the newspaper she copublished in 1970 (*It Ain't Me, Babe,* the first newspaper of the women's liberation movement). She published the first rape bibliography and an entire reel of microfilm on rape by 1974 as part of the WHRC Women and Law collection. This research was used for several subsequent best-selling books on rape.

In 1975, Laura X learned from prominent feminist Diana Russell that rape was still legal within marriage in most places in the United States. That same year, she worked to publicize the words of the judge who presided in the trial of Judy Hartwell, a battered woman who had killed her husband. The judge in the case validated Hartwell's right to say no and to defend herself, even though marital rape was not yet a crime.

In December 1978, Laura X assisted a rape crisis center involved in the trial of John Rideout in Salem, Oregon, which was the first time in the United States a husband was tried for raping his wife while they were living together. This electrified and polarized the country. Rideout was acquitted, a verdict which motivated Laura to lead the successful campaign to make marital rape a crime in California.

From 1980, 44 state-by-state campaigns included research; newspaper and magazine articles; well over 300 high school, college, and law school campuses; TV and radio appearances; and activist involvement in court cases. Articles appeared in *USA Today,* the *Wall Street Journal,* and the *New York Times.* Television appearances included *60 Minutes, Donahue, Sally Jessy Rafael, Geraldo, The Today Show,* and *Mark Wahlberg.* NCMDR also assisted the Montel Williams and Oprah shows.

Major court decisions that used NCMDR work include the following: *Smith* in Florida, 1981; *Morrison* in New Jersey, 1982; *Rider* in Florida, 1984; *Liberta* in New York, 1984; *Warren* in Georgia, 1985; and *Bobbitt* in Virginia, 1994. In the precedent-setting *Liberta* decision, by Judge Sol Wachtler of New York's highest court, the exemption for husbands from rape prosecution when they raped their wives was struck down as an unconstitutional denial of equal protection, privacy, and bodily integrity.

After helping the New York County Lawyers Association produce the first forum on marital rape in February of 1980, NCMDR provided seminars for the Academy of Criminal Justice Sciences, the National Coalition Against Domestic Violence, the National Coalition Against Sexual Assault, the National Conference of Women and the Law, the Association of Women in Psychology, and local agencies around the country and Canada. In 1983 and 1984, NCMDR coproduced the world's first conferences on marital rape in St. Louis, Missouri, and Des Moines, Iowa. Laura X served with Surgeon General C. Everett Koop on his 1985 National Task Force on Violence as a Public Health Issue.

NCMDR published on an ongoing basis the State Law Chart, a reference summary of marital rape exemptions for each state, and a prosecution statistics chart, as well as pamphlets on the Rideout trial and wives who were forced to kill their rapists in self-defense. This research was used by most law article and book authors on the topic.

NCMDR also expanded its activities to the international level with campaigns in Ireland, Puerto Rico, Costa Rica, Mexico, and China (the UN Women's Conference in Beijing in 1995), including a successful legislative reversal of a Mexico Supreme Court decision in 1997, which allowed marital rape as the "undue exercise of a right" upon a spouse.

NCMDR's highest reward came at the 1995 UN Women's Rights Conference in Beijing, when all voting delegates, many of them men, supported wives' rights to enjoy intimacy, only if by mutual consent.

Laura X

See also Date and Acquaintance Rape; Legal System, Advocacy Efforts to Affect, Intimate Partner Violence; Legal System, Civil and Criminal Court Remedies for Sexual Assault/Rape; Legislation, Intimate Partner Violence; Marital Rape/Wife Rape; Marital Rape/Wife Rape, Marital Exemptions in Rape Statutes; National Clearinghouse for the Defense of Battered Women; National Coalition Against Domestic Violence; Rape/Sexual Assault; United Nations Conventions and Declarations

Further Readings

Drucker, D. (1979, Spring). The common law does not support a marital exception for forcible rape. *Women's Rights Law Reporter, 5*(2–3), 181–200.

Faison, S. (1995, September 11). Women's meeting agrees on right to say no to sex: A spousal prerogative. *New York Times*, p. A1. Available at http://tiny.cc/SXE4A

Harmes, R. (1999). Marital rape: A selected bibliography. *Violence Against Women, 5*, 1082–1083. Retrieved from http://vaw.sagepub.com/content/vol5/issue9/

People v. Liberta. (1984). 64 N. Y. 2d 152, 474 N.E.2d 567, 485 N.Y.S.2d 207. Retrieved April 7, 2008, from http://bulk.resource.org/courts.gov/c/F2/839/839.F2d.77.87-2199.185.html

X, L. (1994). A brief series of anecdotes about the backlash experienced by those of us working on marital and date rape. *Journal of Sex Research, 31*(2), 151–153.

X, L. (1999). Accomplishing the impossible: An advocate's notes from the successful campaign to make marital and date rape a crime in all 50 U.S.states and other countries. *Violence Against Women, 5*, 1064–1081. Retrieved from http://vaw.sagepub.com/content/vol5/issue9/

X, L., & Peterson, E. (1995, December 10). When husbands rape: Cases of "'soul murder" [Opinion]. *New York Times*. Retrieved from http://query.nytimes.com/gst/fullpage.html?res=9C03E7DF1639F933A25751C1A963958260&scp=9&sq=%22soul+murder%22&st=nyt

Web Sites

National Clearinghouse on Marital and Date Rape: http://www.ncmdr.org

NATIONAL COALITION AGAINST DOMESTIC VIOLENCE

The National Coalition Against Domestic Violence (NCADV) was formed in 1978 when over 100 battered women's advocates from all parts of the nation attended the U.S. Commission on Civil Rights hearing on wife battering in Washington, D.C. They came hoping to address common problems usually faced in isolation.

From its beginnings, the organization was led by survivors of domestic violence, women of color, and lesbians who were actively working in local communities to address this new and emerging issue. There was no such thing as a shelter for battered women in 1970. In the 30-plus years since that time, over 2,000 local programs have been established to end violence in the family and to make communities safer.

The women who were NCADV's first leaders came together to create an organization that would establish a national voice, create public awareness, provide technical assistance to developing programs, provide continuing education for advocates, and build a strong and active network to provide services in cities and towns across the United States. They were committed to developing an organization that acted on their belief that for women to be safe women had to be empowered and in leadership positions.

NCADV leadership also believed that major social change had to occur to end violence in the family. Domestic violence was not an individual issue, but a cultural one. NCADV leaders felt they had to address and end all forms of oppression, believing that oppressions are the root of violence. NCADV chose consensus, rather than Robert's Rules of Order, as its formal decision-making process, believing that in order for the best decision to be made all voices and life experiences at the table must be included and supported.

Caucuses were established to give an organizational place of power and voice to groups traditionally silenced by the majority. The caucuses that have been established are Battered/Formerly Battered Women; Women of Color; Jewish Women; Rural; Child and Youth Advocacy; Rainbow Pride; and Queer People of Color.

Beginning in 1980, NCADV has sponsored a biennial conference attended by 900–1,200 advocates from all over the United States, including some international participants. The NCADV conference continues to be a unique and critical learning experience for advocates working in the domestic violence movement.

As NCADV listened to battered women and learned from their experiences, its efforts have expanded to include working with the police, prosecutors, judges, health professionals, and child protective services. Men who are not abusive will be an important addition to allies in NCADV's goal to make every home a safe home.

NCADV programs based in the main office in Denver, Colorado, include Cosmetic and Reconstructive Surgery, Financial Education, Remember My Name, National Directory of Programs, and Information and Referral. Based in Washington, D.C., the NCADV Public Policy Office works to impact public policy and legislation.

Rita Smith

See also Advocacy; Battered Women

Web Sites

National Coalition Against Domestic Violence: http://www.ncadv.org

NATIONAL COUNCIL OF JUVENILE AND FAMILY COURT JUDGES

The National Council of Juvenile and Family Court Judges (NCJFCJ), the nation's oldest and largest judicial membership organization, originated in 1937 in Chicago, Illinois. It maintained its headquarters there until 1969, when it relocated to Reno, Nevada, and became part of the University of Nevada, Reno, community. NCJFCJ is a nonprofit, 501(C)(3) corporation, which relies on funding from federal and state grants, private foundations, and donations from members and others. Membership in the organization is open to all judges and judicial officers whose work involves juvenile and family justice, and associate membership is available to professionals working in related fields.

NCJFCJ pursues a mission to improve courts and systems practice and raise awareness of the core issues that touch the lives of many of our nation's families and children. A leader in continuing educational opportunities, research, and policy development in issues pertaining to juvenile and family justice, NCJFCJ provides practice-based resources to jurisdictions and communities nationwide. The organization seeks to improve the standards, practices, and effectiveness of the nation's juvenile and family courts while acknowledging and upholding victims' rights, the safety of all family members, and the safety of the community.

NCJFCJ accomplishes its work through four departments whose efforts support and extend its mission. The Family Violence Department and the Permanency Planning for Children Department focus on issues of domestic violence and child dependency. Both departments engage in numerous ongoing projects that explore and implement best practices and effective strategies for judges who hear cases on these matters and for other involved professionals. The Juvenile and Family Law Department presents educational opportunities on a wide range of topics, including child abuse and neglect, custody and visitation, juvenile delinquency, minority issues, victims' issues, substance abuse, and court management issues.

Each year, NCJFCJ educates more than 20,000 judges and juvenile justice, child welfare, and family law professionals. Judges and court professionals also rely on NCJFCJ's wide-ranging, in-depth technical assistance and numerous publications. In addition, NCJFCJ and the University of Nevada, Reno, work together to provide the nation's only advanced degrees in judicial studies.

In 1973, NCJFCJ established a research division, the National Center for Juvenile Justice (NCJJ), which is the country's only nonprofit research organization concentrating solely on the juvenile justice system and the prevention of juvenile delinquency child abuse and neglect. Located in Pittsburgh, Pennsylvania, NCJJ maintains the National Juvenile Court Data Archive, which contains more than 20 million automated delinquency and status offense case records from courts nationwide.

NCJFCJ's membership of nearly 1,700 judges, commissioners, court masters, and other juvenile and family law professionals represents all 50 states and several territories and foreign countries. Its reach, however, extends beyond its membership. Through the availability of educational opportunities and technical assistance for judges and other professionals around the country and the world, NCJFCJ continues to play a leadership role in improving both the practice of juvenile and family justice and outcomes for families using these court systems.

Billie Lee Dunford-Jackson

See also Adoption and Safe Families Act of 1997; Child Exposure to Intimate Partner Violence; Coordinated Community Response; Custody, Contact, and Visitation: Relationship to Domestic Violence; Full Faith and Credit Mandate

Further Readings

Family violence issue [Special issue]. (2003). *Juvenile and Family Court Journal, 54*(4).
National Council of Juvenile and Family Court Judges. (1990). *Family violence: Improving court practice: Recommendations from the National Council of Juvenile*

and Family Court Judges: Family violence project. Reno, NV: Author. Available at http://www.ncjfcj.org

National Council of Juvenile and Family Court Judges. (1998). *Resource guidelines: Improving court practice in child abuse & neglect cases*. Reno, NV: Author. Available at http://www.ncjfcj.org

National Council of Juvenile and Family Court Judges. (2000). *Passport to safety: Full faith and credit, a judge's benchbook*. Reno, NV: Author. Available at http://www.ncjfcj.org

National Council of Juvenile and Family Court Judges. (2004). Building a better collaboration: Facilitating change in the court and child welfare system. *NCJFCJ Technical Assistance Bulletin, 8*(2).

National Council of Juvenile and Family Court Judges. (2004). *Navigating custody & visitation evaluations in cases with domestic violence: A judge's guide*. Reno, NV: Author. Available at http://www.ncjfcj.org

National Council of Juvenile and Family Court Judges. (2005). *A guide for effective issuance and enforcement of protection orders*. Reno, NV: Author. Available at http://www.ncjfcj.org

Schechter, S., & Edleson, J. L. (1999). *Effective intervention in domestic violence & child maltreatment cases: Guidelines for policy and practice*. Available at http://www.thegreenbook.info

Web Sites

National Council of Juvenile and Family Court Judges: http://www.ncjfcj.org/

NATIONAL CRIME PREVENTION COUNCIL

The National Crime Prevention Council (NCPC) is arguably the best known and best funded private non-profit organization devoted to the reduction of crime and the promotion of personal and community safety in the United States today. Through their publications, conferences, the McGruff campaign, and other activities, NCPC's impact extends worldwide, influencing mass media safety campaigns and crime prevention programs in thousands of communities in several dozen countries.

The roots of NCPC go back to the 1970s when there were a number of federal, state, and local initiatives to address issues of crime in a so-called proactive as opposed to reactive manner. Public concern about crime and safety had risen to alarming levels. Through funds available from the now-defunct Law Enforcement Assistance Administration, various local, state, and regional associations of crime prevention police officers had begun, and programs such as Neighborhood Watch were widely promoted.

In the late 1970s, a coalition of state and national organizations, both public and private, founded the National Citizens' Crime Prevention Campaign. They teamed up with the Advertising Council, which had a long history of developing information campaigns utilizing volunteer talent from private sector marketing and advertising firms on a variety of public service topics, including the World War II slogan, "Loose Lips Sink Ships," which is still in use today; the creation of Smokey the Bear, who reminds viewers that "Only You Can Prevent Forest Fires"; and the recent "I Am an American" campaign to promote awareness of America's race and ethnic diversity.

In support of crime prevention, the Advertising Council and an advertising firm based in New York City developed a public service announcement for television that featured a dog wearing a trench coat and encouraging viewers to "Take a Bite Out of Crime." In 1982, the dog was given the name McGruff, and he remains one of the most recognizable social marketing icons. That same year, the NCPC was officially founded. Nearly 3 decades later, it continues to promote safety and security in America's communities through partnerships with the Advertising Council, the U.S. Department of Justice, a network of local and national crime prevention groups known as the Crime Prevention Coalition of America, and numerous corporate and foundation supporters.

Over the years, NCPC has sponsored or cosponsored a number of important nationwide safety initiatives, including the designation of October as "National Crime Prevention Month," the National Night Out campaign, an annual national conference on crime prevention, and an incredible array of educational materials covering nearly every issue related to safety and security. NCPC continuously updates old materials and develops information on new safety issues, which recently have included involvement in the AMBER Alert campaign, identity theft, and homeland security. They have developed an extensive set of materials specifically focused on violence prevention, especially for teenagers. However, almost all their resources are either directly or indirectly relevant to issues of interpersonal violence. Through it all, McGruff the crime dog is the one constant woven into all of NCPC's initiatives and educational materials.

Joseph F. Donnermeyer

See also National AMBER Alert Program; Prevention
Programs, Community Mobilization; Prevention
Programs, Interpersonal Violence

Web Sites

National Crime Prevention Council: http://www.ncpc.org/

NATIONAL CRIME VICTIMIZATION SURVEY

The National Crime Victimization Survey (NCVS) represents an unofficial measure of crime in the United States that focuses on surveying individuals about their experience as crime victims. The NCVS attempts to measure the frequency, characteristics, and consequences of criminal victimization for persons ages 12 and older.

The first NCVS (previously known as the National Crime Survey) was undertaken in 1972. Currently conducted by the Bureau of the Census, the NCVS surveys a representative sample of about 42,000 U.S. households, representing about 76,000 persons, about their victimization experiences during the previous 6 months. Once added to the sample, a household is queried every 6 months for a 3-year period. If initial screening questions uncover potential crime victimization, the survey is then designed to record various aspects of the criminal events, including victim demographic information, victim–offender relationships, the impact of alcohol or weapon use, the extent of injury, whether the police were contacted, and, if not, reasons for not reporting.

The NCVS focuses on the crimes of assault, sexual assault, robbery, theft, residential burglary, motor vehicle theft, and vandalism. A major purpose of the NCVS is to provide a better understanding of unreported crime, which is often referred to as the "dark figure of crime." Thus, the NCVS serves as a significant tool in showing disparities between unreported crime and official statistics. The discrepancies are particularly high for crimes of violence, where the NCVS reports significantly higher incidences of interpersonal violence than official measures of crime (e.g., police reports or arrest records). Recent NCVS statistics show that 36% of rapes and sexual assaults are reported to police, while 45% of simple assaults are reported. Crimes of violence are often not reported to

police because people feel the police will not do anything, they are embarrassed, or they fear retribution.

The results are particularly valuable in understanding the risk and impact of criminal victimization on various subpopulations, including women, the elderly, various racial and ethnic groups, the poor, and city-dwellers. The NCVS is also useful in offering information to understand trends in the crimes on which it reports over time.

Critics point to some more significant deficiencies in the NCVS as a method of calculating crime statistics. First, the NCVS does not report on a wide variety of crimes, including those involving businesses or the homeless or victimless crimes. A second criticism is that, as a survey method, the NCVS is subject to the common problems of surveys in criminal justice in which participants may have erroneous recollections about past events. A third issue is that the survey method tends to underestimate certain crimes where the victim knows the offender. To address these concerns, a redesign in 1997 was intended to improve the NCVS as a survey tool.

Melissa Hamilton

See also Incidence; National Family Violence Surveys; Uniform Crime Reports; Victimology

Further Readings

U.S. Department of Justice, Bureau of Justice Statistics. (2005). *Criminal victimization, 2004.* Washington, DC: Author.

NATIONAL DOMESTIC VIOLENCE FATALITY REVIEW INITIATIVE

The National Domestic Violence Fatality Review Initiative (NDVFRI) is headquartered at Baylor University in Waco, Texas. The NDVFRI was created with a grant from the Office on Violence Against Women in the U.S. Department of Justice. It provides technical assistance, evaluative reviews, and serves as a clearinghouse for information and other resources for states that conduct domestic violence fatality reviews.

Domestic violence fatality review refers to the deliberative process of identification and review of deaths, both homicide and suicide, caused by domestic violence. Fatality reviews examine the systemic interventions into known incidents of domestic violence occurring in the family of the deceased prior to the death for consideration of altered systemic response to avert future domestic violence deaths or for development of recommendations for coordinated community prevention and intervention initiatives to eradicate domestic violence. This deliberative process can be formal or informal and can provide basic demographic information or very detailed data on victims and perpetrators. The goals of domestic violence fatality review include prevention of future deaths and injuries due to domestic violence by examining deaths that have occurred through a lens of preventive accountability. Error recognition, responsibility, honesty, and systemic improvement should be the focus rather than denial, blame, and personalizing the review. By bringing diverse individuals to the table, fatality review teams are able to examine these deaths in much greater detail than one would otherwise expect.

A fatality review can offer more insight into the cause of death, leading to a solution to eliminate or decrease homicides, such as domestic violence deaths, elder abuse, and child abuse. The team, inclusive rather than exclusive, may comprise an attorney general or prosecutor, public defenders, media, researchers, child protective services, mental health workers, medical examiners, victim advocates, faith-based personnel, social workers, and any other interested community members.

A fatality review team, regardless of the focus, will examine all or some of the following reports: police department homicide logs; past investigation calls; newspaper reports; crime scene investigations; prior protective orders; civil court data; criminal histories; child protective agency data and prior abuse histories; psychological evaluations; medical examiners' reports; workplace information; medical histories; shelter data; school data; parole information; statements from neighbors, friends, family, and witnesses; and state statutes on domestic violence.

Fatality review team members will often incorporate what they have learned into their daily jobs, increasing awareness among those they encounter on a day-to-day basis. Multiagency cooperation also allows for a better understanding of the day-to-day case load and frustrations and celebrations each person encounters. The annual reports set forth by fatality review teams garner public attention and hopefully lead to increased reform.

Greater collaboration and understanding can lead to more funding, increased public awareness, and policy changes that reduce domestic violence–related deaths.

In addition to providing technical assistance to state fatality review teams, the NDVFRI also helps

identify gaps in the delivery of services to domestic violence victims, perpetrators, and their families and assist agencies and service providers in rectifying these problems. The objectives of the NDVFRI are to prevent domestic violence and increase the safety of domestic violence victims.

Byron Johnson and Elizabeth Kelly

See also Child Death Review Teams; Danger Assessment Instrument; Domestic Violence Fatality Review; Femicide

Web Sites

National Domestic Violence Fatality Review Initiative: http://www.ndvfri.org/

NATIONAL DOMESTIC VIOLENCE HOTLINE

The National Domestic Violence Hotline (NDVH) was established in February 1996 from funding allocated in the Violence Against Women Act. NDVH is a national toll-free hotline that provides 24-hour crisis intervention and information and referral services. NDVH was developed and established as a program of the Texas Council on Family Violence, one of the largest and most established state coalitions in the country. NDVH operates on a budget with a combination of federal, state, and private funding sources. In 2006, NDVH fielded on average about 17,000 calls a month. In addition to providing callers with immediate crisis intervention and general information about domestic violence and the dynamics of abuse, the hotline maintains an extensive database of the available domestic violence services and other social services in communities across the nation.

Though many local domestic violence shelters maintain their own hotlines, NDVH with enhanced technical and financial resources is able to provide consistent, coordinated, and responsive services to callers throughout the country. As a result, NDVH has been successfully used to enhance national outreach campaigns, public service announcements, and media presentations about domestic violence. For example, the hotline's number has been published on the back of stamp packages, women's clothing labels, and during television shows that feature domestic violence content. In fact, NDVH's Web site provides a variety of downloadable outreach materials that include numerous posters, information cards, and radio and TV public service announcements.

NDVH receives calls from survivors of domestic violence and from those who have not yet named their experiences as abuse. They receive many calls from friends and family members who are concerned that someone they care about is being abused and from professional helpers, such as police officers, physicians, nurses, and social workers, who are seeking information about how to respond to situations of domestic violence. They also receive calls from batterers and from batterer treatment providers. NDVH staff and volunteers answer calls in both English and Spanish, and interpreter services are utilized for over 140 languages. NDVH provides advocacy services to survivors of abuse in the deaf community through a TTY line and is currently implementing increased outreach to the persons who are deaf, deaf and blind, and hard of hearing using technology that is replacing TTY use. The deaf community is rapidly increasing in their use of personal handheld communication devices, which are widely available, well supported, portable, and require no special equipment, so in the fall of 2006, NDVH piloted interactions with the deaf community via instant messaging, live chats with an advocate on the NDVH Web site, and video conferencing to facilitate sign language interactivity.

Hotline advocates use active listening, safety planning, information sharing, and empowerment techniques to assist callers with their immediate concerns. NDVH is also using technology to better achieve its service mission. The hotline has recently upgraded computerized systems to improve its community resource database and allow for more sophisticated tracking of service requests and resource gaps. The NDVH Web site receives 30,000 (roughly 14,000 unique visitors) visits per month.

Shanti Kulkarni

See also Battered Women; Battered Women: Leaving Violent Intimate Relationships; Violence Against Women Act

Further Readings

Bell, H., & Kulkarni, S. (2005, October). *Assessing the service needs of survivors of intimate partner violence.* Austin, TX: Institute on Domestic Violence and Sexual Assault. Retrieved from http://www.utexas.edu/research/cswr/projects/pj0240rept.pdf

Web Sites

National Domestic Violence Hotline: http://www.ndvh.org/

NATIONAL FAMILY VIOLENCE SURVEYS

Social surveys are one source of data on family and intimate partner violence. There have been seven major national surveys that were designed and carried out with the specific purpose of assessing and examining the extent, correlates, causes, and consequences of family violence, intimate partner violence, and/or violence toward children. The majority of these surveys were one-time cross-sectional surveys. In addition, a number of surveys on topics such as youth violence or child and family well-being included one or more questions designed to measure the occurrence of family or intimate partner violence. For example, the National Survey of Families and Households (NSFH) included a single question that can be used to estimate partner violence. The question asked, "During the last year, how many fights with your partner resulted in (you/him/her) hitting, shoving, or throwing things at (you/him/her)?" The NSFH has been examined by some researchers interested in the extent and patterns of partner violence. Sharon Wofford and her colleagues administered the Conflict Tactics Scales during one wave of the National Youth Survey—a longitudinal study of a birth cohort in the United States. Terrie Moffitt and Avshalom Caspi administered a modified version of the Conflict Tactics Scales to a nationally representative birth cohort in Dunedin, New Zealand. The U.S. Department of Justice includes questions on intimate partner violence in the annual National Crime Victimization Survey (NCVS). The U.S. Department of Justice has published a number of reports on intimate violence based on the data collected by the NCVS.

This entry focuses exclusively on those national surveys designed and carried out with the goal of studying family violence, intimate partner violence, or violence toward children.

Family Violence Surveys

Murray Straus and Richard Gelles and their colleagues have carried out three national surveys of family violence: (1) in-person interviews with a nationally representative sample of 2,143 respondents in 1976, (2) telephone interviews with a nationally representative sample of 6,002 respondents in 1985, and (3) telephone interviews with a nationally representative sample of 1,970 respondents in 1992.

Intimate Partner Violence

In terms of intimate partner violence, the rate of minor violence, violence that had a low probability of causing a physical injury, declined from 100 per 1,000 women in 1975 to about 80 per 1,000 in 1985 and then rose to 91 per 1,000 in 1992. More serious or severe acts of violence toward women (acts labeled *severe assaults* or *wife beating* by the investigators) declined from 38 per 1,000 in 1975 to 19 per 1,000 in 1992.

Violence Toward Children

Milder forms of violence, violence that most people think of as physical punishment, were the most common. However, even with the severe forms of violence, the rates were high. Abusive violence was defined as acts that had a high probability of injuring the child. These included kicking, biting, punching, hitting or trying to hit a child with an object, beating up a child, burning or scalding, and threatening to use or using a gun or a knife. Slightly more than two parents in 100 (2.3%) admitted to engaging in one act of abusive violence during the year prior to the 1985 survey. Seven children in 1,000 were hurt as a result of an act of violence directed at them by a parent in the previous year. Projecting the rate of abusive violence to all children under 18 years of age who live with one or both parents means that 1.5 million children experience acts of abusive physical violence each year and 450,000 children are injured each year as a result of parental violence.

National Surveys of Violence Toward Women

The Commonwealth Fund carried out a national survey of violence toward women in the early 1990s. A nationally representative sample of 1,324 was interviewed by telephone. The women's reported rate of victimization was 84 per 1,000 women, with 32 per 1,000 women reporting that they experienced at least one incident of severe violence in the previous year.

The National Violence Against Women Survey (NVAWS) involved telephone interviews with a

nationally representative sample of 8,000 women and 8,000 men. The survey was conducted between November 1995 and May 1996. The NVAWS assessed lifetime prevalence and annual prevalence (violence experienced in the previous 12 months). The NVAWS used a modified version of the Conflict Tactics Scales to measure violence victimization. Nearly 52% of women surveyed (519 per 1,000—52,261,743 women) reported experiencing a physical assault as a child or adult. Nearly 56% of women surveyed (559 per 1,000—56,289,623 women) reported experiencing any form of violence, including stalking, rape, or physical assault. The rate of lifetime assault at the hands of an intimate partner was 221 per 1,000 for physical violence and 254 per 1,000 for any form of violence-victimization. The rates of forms of violence less likely to cause an injury, such as pushing, grabbing, shoving, or slapping, were the highest (between 160 and 181 per 1,000), while the rates of the most severe forms of violence (used a gun, used a knife, beat up) were the lowest (85 per 1,000 for beat up, 7 per 1,000 for used a gun).

The annual prevalence or incidence of violence was 19 per 1,000 for physical assault (1,913,243 women) and 30 per 1,000 for any form of violence victimization (3,020,910 women). The annual prevalence of women victimized by intimate partners was 13 per 1,000 for physical assault (1,309,061) and 18 per 1,000 (1,812,546 women) for all forms of victimization.

National Surveys of Violence Toward Children

Murray Straus and Julie Stewart carried out a national survey of physical punishment of children. A nationally representative sample of 900 adult parents was interviewed in a telephone survey. Straus and Stewart reported that 28.4% of parents of 2- to 4-year-olds and 28.5% of parents of 5- to 8-year-olds used an object to spank their child's bottom. Overall, the survey found that 74% of children less than 5 years old were hit or slapped by their parents.

David Finkelhor and his colleagues conducted a national survey of child victimization in 2002–2003. Interviews were carried with a nationally representative sample of 2,030 parents and children living in the contiguous states in the United States. The survey collected data on children ages 2 to 17 years. Slightly more than 1 in 7 children (138 per 1,000) experienced child maltreatment. Emotional abuse was the most frequent type of maltreatment. The rate of physical abuse (meaning that children experienced physical harm) was 15 per 1,000, while the rate of neglect was 11 per 1,000. The overall projected extent of maltreatment was 8,755,000 child victims. The investigators also found that 35% of children experienced a physical assault at the hands of a sibling in the previous year. Boys and girls were nearly equally likely to be a victim of sibling violence. The rate of assault was highest for children 6 to 12 years of age.

Richard J. Gelles

See also Child Sexual Abuse; Conflict Tactics Scales; Incidence; Intimate Partner Violence; Measurement, Interpersonal Violence; National Crime Victimization Survey; National Institute of Justice; National Violence Against Women Survey; Sexual Abuse

Further Readings

Finkehor, D., Ormrod, R., Turner, H., & Hamby, S. H. (2005). The victimization of children and youth: A comprehensive national survey. *Child Maltreatment, 10,* 5–25.

Gallup Organization. (1995). *Disciplining children in America: A Gallup poll report.* Princeton, NJ: Author.

Gelles, R. J., & Straus, M. A. (1988). *Intimate violence.* New York: Simon & Schuster.

Rennison, C. (2003). *Intimate partner violence: 1993–2001.* Washington, DC: U.S. Department of Justice, Office of Justice Programs.

Tjaden, P., & Thoennes, N. (2000). *Extent, nature, and consequences of intimate partner violence* (NCJ Publication No. 181867). Washington, DC: U.S. Department of Justice.

NATIONAL INCIDENT-BASED REPORTING SYSTEM

The National Incident-Based Reporting System (NIBRS) is the U.S. Department of Justice's incident-based crime reporting system that collects information voluntarily submitted by city, county, and state law enforcement agencies. The NIBRS collects a variety of information or attributes about a crime incident after a participating police agency investigates the incident and finds that it involves at least one of 46 possible crime types. NIBRS grew out of the Federal Bureau of Investigation's (FBI's) Uniform Crime Reporting (UCR) Program, which the International Association of Chiefs of Police designed in 1929 to provide the United States with standardized crime

statistics. The FBI implemented the program in 1930, and since its inception, it has remained virtually unchanged in terms of the summary data collected and format. In the late 1970s, the law enforcement community requested an evaluation of the UCR to understand whether the program could expand so that local police agencies might use it for crime analysis. In 1985, the FBI released the Blueprint for the Future of the Uniform Crime Reporting Program, which it used along with the help of law enforcement executives to formulate additional guidelines for the UCR program. The FBI then developed NIBRS to codify these guidelines and in 1989 began receiving incident-based data from the South Carolina Law Enforcement Division. The NIBRS is currently managed by the FBI's Criminal Justice Information Service Division, which in 1992 was established to serve as its central repository for criminal justice information.

Like its predecessor, the Offenses Known and Clearances by Arrest database, NIBRS contains data from thousands of police departments. But unlike its predecessor, the incident information is not summarized to the agency level. To replace or in concert with the summary information, police departments can submit up to 54 attributes for each incident to their state UCR program or directly to the FBI's UCR program. However, although its name implies a national scope, it is neither a census nor a representative sample of crime incidents known to U.S. law enforcement agencies. By 2004, 4,521 law enforcement agencies contributed records to the NIBRS, or about 27% of the agencies who submitted UCR summary data to the FBI. Nevertheless, this system still provides a substantial amount of standardized incident-level information extracted from police records systems for researchers to analyze at the incident, offense, victim, and offender levels.

For 10 years, the National Archive of Criminal Justice Data (NACJD) has released NIBRS to researchers for analysis. When combined across the first 10 years of usable data (1995–2004), the system has collected information on over 24 million crime incidents, 27 million offenses, and 26 million offenders and victims. For all 24 million incidents, the system contains detailed information about each offense, including type, weapon use, and bias motivation; the quantity and type of property loss, property description, property value, and drug type and quantity; offender information, such as age, sex, and race; arrestee information, such as arrest date and weapon use; and victim information, such as age, sex, ethnicity, and injuries. One of the key victim attributes is the nature of the relationship between the victim and offender. Although not inclusive of all relationship types, this attribute does provide a police officer with a choice of picking one from a list of 25 victim–offender relationships. Among these 25 categories are several key interpersonal relationships, such as spouse, parent, child, boyfriend or girlfriend, and ex-spouse. Thus, NIBRS provides researchers with information to understand the nature and outcomes of interpersonal violence known to the police.

To facilitate analysis of these data, NACJD distributes them by year and organizes them into 13 linked databases. This format allows for a focus on a variety of aspects of a crime incident by the type of law enforcement agency, population size, or the date and time of the incident. Additional data added to the NIBRS by NACJD also facilitate time-series analysis within a selected jurisdiction, aggregated analysis within a geographical area (e.g., metropolitan or micropolitan statistical area), or evaluations of programs implemented in selected jurisdictions from different states.

Christopher D. Maxwell

See also Incidence; National Violence Against Women Survey; Police, Response to Domestic Violence; Prevalence; Prevalence, Measuring; Uniform Crime Reports

Further Readings

Federal Bureau of Investigation. (1999). *The structure of family violence: An analysis of selected incidents* (Report prepared using the National Incident-Based Reporting System to demonstrate utility of NIBRS No. 13). Retrieved from http://www.fbi.gov/ucr/nibrs/famvio21.pdf

Federal Bureau of Investigation. (2000, August). *National Incident-Based Reporting System:* Vol. 1. *Data collection guidelines.* Retrieved from http://www.fbi.gov/ucr/nibrs/manuals/v1all.pdf

National Incident-Based Reporting System resource guide. (n.d.). Retrieved September 1, 2006, from http://www.icpsr.umich.edu/NACJD/NIBRS

Overview of CJIS. (n.d.). Retrieved September 1, 2006, from http://www.fbi.gov/hq/cjisd/about.htm

NATIONAL INSTITUTE OF JUSTICE

The National Institute of Justice (NIJ) is the research, development, and evaluation agency of the U.S. Department of Justice and is dedicated to researching crime control and justice issues. The NIJ was created by the Omnibus Crime Control and Safe Streets Act of 1968. Its principal authorities are derived from this act as amended (42 USC § 3721–3723) and Title II of the Homeland Security Act of 2002.

NIJ's mission is to advance scientific research, development, and evaluation to enhance law enforcement and the administration of justice and to promote public safety. It provides independent, evidence-based knowledge and tools to meet the challenges of crime and justice, particularly at the state and local levels. NIJ's six primary objectives are (1) research, (2) development, (3) evaluation, (4) testing, (5) technical assistance, and (6) dissemination. These objectives are guided by the priorities of the U.S. Department of Justice and the needs of the criminal justice field.

NIJ makes grants and cooperative agreements and enters into contracts with public agencies, institutions of higher education, or private organizations to conduct research, evaluation, or demonstration projects. It also develops new or improved approaches, techniques, systems, equipment, and devices to improve and strengthen the administration of justice. NIJ implements programs of social and behavioral research designed to provide information on the causes of crime and the effectiveness of criminal justice programs designed to prevent or reduce crime. It also provides instructional assistance through its various research fellowship programs. NIJ collects and disseminates data and information obtained by the institute or other federal and public agencies, institutions of higher education, or private organizations engaged in projects supported by the agency. In addition, NIJ makes recommendations for action that can be taken by federal, state, and local governments and by private persons and organizations to improve and strengthen criminal justice.

NIJ accomplishes its objectives through three offices that support and fulfill its mission. The Office of Research and Evaluation (ORE) develops, conducts, directs, and supervises social and behavioral research and evaluation activities. This process occurs through extramural research that involves outside researchers who often collaborate with criminal justice practitioners and intramural research conducted by ORE staff. The ORE consists of the Crime Control and Prevention Research Division, the Evaluation Division, the Justice Systems Research Division, the International Center, and the Violence and Victimization Research Division.

The Crime Control and Prevention Research Division is dedicated to improving law enforcement's response to crime. It supports applied research and evaluation of crime prevention programs. The major program areas for the Crime Control and Prevention Research Division include police, firearms and violence, juvenile delinquency, terrorism (preparedness and response), identity theft, and crime mapping and analysis.

The Evaluation Division was developed in 2003 to oversee NIJ evaluations of other agencies' programs. The goal is to improve the utility of evaluation results for policy, practice, and program development. The Evaluation Division enables NIJ to develop its capacity to conduct cost-effectiveness evaluations of criminal justice programs and enhance the overall quality of its evaluations.

The Justice Systems Research Division is designed to enhance justice systems' responses to crime. The primary program areas of the Division are prosecution, including community prosecution, specialized courts, corrections (institutional and community), the Prison Rape Elimination Act, probation and parole, sex offenders, the Serious/Violent Offender Reentry Initiative, and restorative justice. Through research and evaluation in these program areas, the division helps NIJ achieve its goal of improving the administration of justice in the United States.

NIJ's International Center examines transnational crime and its impact both domestically and globally. A major focus of the International Center is to facilitate the exchange of ideas among criminal justice researchers and practitioners throughout the world. Program areas of the center include terrorism, human trafficking, organized crime and corruption, and emerging issues such as illegal logging and international gang-crime connections.

The Violence and Victimization Research Division seeks to increase the effectiveness and efficiency of justice systems' (criminal and civil) responses to violence, victimization, and victims of crime. The division also promotes the safety of women, children, and families. The major program areas for the division include violence against women (intimate partner violence, sexual violence, and stalking), elder abuse and neglect, victim compensation and assistance, and crime and justice in Indian Country.

The Office of Science and Technology (OST) manages technology research and development, development of technical standards, equipment testing, and forensic sciences capacity building programs. The OST also provides technology assistance to federal, state, and local criminal justice and public safety agencies. It consists of the Research and Technology Development Division, the Investigative and Forensic Sciences Division, and the Technology Assistance Division.

The Research and Technology Development Division develops tools and knowledge to address the technology needs of the criminal justice practitioner community except in the area of forensic science. Its major programs include body armor, cyber crime, explosive detection and remediation, biometrics, sensors and surveillance, pursuit management, and less lethal technology. The Investigative and Forensics Sciences Division develops tools and knowledge to address the technology needs of the forensic science community. The main programs of this division include DNA research and development, cold-case and backlog reduction grants, the Coverdell Forensic Science Improvement Grant Program, and the Forensic Resource Network. The Technology Assistance Division is responsible for NIJ's compliance testing and standards programs. Its two major programs are the Body Armor Initiative and the National Law Enforcement and Corrections Technology Center System.

The Office of the Director sets policy for the institute, identifies priorities, develops strategic plans, allocates budgetary and human resources, oversees management activities, fosters collaboration with other federal agencies, and coordinates the institute's communications with external reviewers and stakeholders. It develops and disseminates all NIJ communication products and activities, including print publications, conference and outreach materials, and electronic products (such as Web materials and CD-ROMs). NIJ conducts these activities through its Planning and Management and Communication Divisions. NIJ is the only federal agency solely dedicated to improving criminal justice policy and practice throughout the country and the world.

Angela Moore Parmley

See also Office on Violence Against Women

Web Sites

National Institute of Justice: http://www.ojp.usdoj.gov/nij

NATIONAL LATINO ALLIANCE FOR THE ELIMINATION OF DOMESTIC VIOLENCE

The National Latino Alliance for the Elimination of Domestic Violence (Alianza) is part of a national effort to address the domestic violence needs and concerns of underserved populations. It represents a growing network of Latina and Latino survivors, advocates, practitioners, researchers, and community activists. As noted on Alianza's Web site, its mission is to "promote understanding, initiate and sustain dialogue, and generate solutions that move toward the elimination of domestic violence affecting Latino communities, with an understanding of the sacredness of all relations and communities."

The Administration for Children and Families of the U.S. Department of Health and Human Services (DHHS) has supported the development of a national network of organizations to support work on domestic violence in specific communities. In addition to Alianza, these include the Institute on Domestic Violence in the African American Community, Asian and Pacific Islander Institute on Domestic Violence, and Sacred Circle National Resource Center to End Domestic Violence Against Native Women.

Alianza evolved from a national steering committee that was established in January 1997 and composed of Latinas and Latinos with a history of national leadership on the issue domestic violence. The steering committee then organized a *National Symposium on La Violencia Doméstica: An Emerging Dialogue Among Latinos* in the fall of 1997. The symposium proceedings, published in 1999, generated a national dialogue on domestic violence in Latino communities. At the symposium, the creation of a national organization was suggested, and in March 1999, the Alianza was formed. The next year, Alianza received funding from DHHS enabling it to hire core staff and to establish an office in New York City. By 2004, Alianza had moved into its own offices and received tax-exempt status as an independent nonprofit organization.

Programs and Projects

Alianza enhances the knowledge and skills of Latino/a service providers, advocates, and survivors and develops culturally and linguistically relevant resource materials. It raises awareness about the devastating effects of domestic violence on Latino families and communities and provides information about existing laws, options, resources, and services.

Alianza supports culturally competent research that informs the development of policies and programs sensitive to the needs of Latino communities. It assists researchers in conducting focus groups and community assessments and supports the mentoring of students and other Latino/a researchers. Alianza

advocates for and helps to formulate policies that help prevent and end domestic violence in Latino communities and advocates for the allocation of adequate resources.

Ricardo Antonio Carrillo and Adelita M. Medina

See also Asian & Pacific Islander Institute on Domestic Violence; Institute on Domestic Violence in the African American Community; Sacred Circle National Resource Center to End Violence Against Native Women

Web Sites

Alianza: http://www.devalianza.org

NATIONAL NETWORK TO END DOMESTIC VIOLENCE

The mission of National Network to End Domestic Violence (NNEDV) is to create a social, political, and economic environment in which domestic violence no longer exists. NNEDV was formed in 1990 by state domestic violence coalitions who initiated early discussions about federal domestic violence policy. NNEDV is a 501(c)(4) membership and advocacy organization that works on behalf of 53 state and U.S. territory domestic violence coalitions, which represent more than 2,500 local domestic violence programs and millions of domestic violence victims.

NNEDV has created a public policy voice for victims of domestic violence, secured increases in federal funding for domestic violence organizations, protected victims from unfair eviction and denial of subsidized housing, argued for recognition of private and privileged communications for victims of domestic violence, and worked to keep firearms out of the hands of abusers. In 1994, NNEDV spearheaded the passage of the Violence Against Women Act (VAWA) and played a leading role in reauthorizing VAWA in 2000 and 2005. NNEDV works with other national organizations and committees working to end domestic violence, such as the Campaign for Funding to End Domestic and Sexual Violence and the committee to reauthorize the Family Violence Prevention and Services Act, and to protect the Victims of Crime Act Fund. NNEDV also acts as a leader in the appropriations process, working with congressional staff to provide funding for programs included in legislation that has been passed by Congress and chairs the National Task Force to End Sexual and Domestic Violence.

In 1995, NNEDV established its sister organization, the NNEDV Fund. The NNEDV Fund is a 501(c)(3) organization that provides training and technical assistance for state and territory domestic violence coalitions and works to increase public awareness of domestic violence issues. The NNEDV Fund's work supports victims by generating support for local domestic violence programs by offering direct financial assistance for victims and by helping victims enhance their safety through technological awareness. The NNEDV Fund also works with coalitions and local programs to change systems by providing training for law enforcement agencies, court officials, judges, prosecutors, state agencies, and housing authorities to ensure that the unique needs of victims are being met and that abusers are being held accountable for their crimes. Additionally, the NNEDV Fund strives to engage communities in the fight to end domestic violence by raising public awareness in communities across the country, training advocates, and changing public attitudes about domestic violence.

NNEDV and the NNEDV Fund bring coalitions together through innovative programming to develop solutions to critical and emerging issues, both locally and nationwide. Key initiatives include economic empowerment and self-sufficiency; emergency financial assistance for domestic violence victims; safe and strategic technology awareness and addressing technology misuse; transitional and long-term housing development; women of color leadership; VAWA implementation and legislative issues; voter education, engagement, and confidentiality; and training and technical assistance planning. Within these initiatives, NNEDV and the NNEDV Fund's work focuses on uniting local, statewide, and national advocates to keep domestic violence at the forefront of national debate.

Sue Else and Allison Randall

See also Family Violence Prevention and Services Act; High-Tech Violence Against Women; Victims of Crime Act; Violence Against Women Act

Web Sites

National Network to End Domestic Violence: http://www.nnedv.org/

NATIONAL ORGANIZATION FOR WOMEN

The National Organization for Women (NOW) was founded on June 30, 1966, by 28 women and men in attendance at the Third National Conference of the Commission on the Status of Women. This conference is the successor to the Presidential Commission on the Status of Women, and although the group made findings of widespread discrimination based on sex, the administration prohibited the delegates from passing resolutions or making any formal recommendations during the 1966 conference. Frustrated by this lack of power, a group of delegates decided to form an independent feminist organization.

The original purpose of the organization, as written by founders Betty Friedan and Pauli Murray, was "to take action to bring women into full participation in the mainstream of American society now, exercising all privileges and responsibilities thereof in truly equal partnership with men." The purpose remains largely unchanged, with the current Statement of Purpose reading: "Our purpose is to take action to bring women into full participation in society—sharing equal rights, responsibilities, and opportunities with men, while living free from discrimination."

Current membership includes 500,000 individuals and 550 chapters around the United States. The entire general membership meets annually in conference and is the supreme governing body of the organization. Four elected officers lead the national level of the organization along with a national board of directors and a national issues committee. Betty Friedan, founder and author of *The Feminine Mystique,* served as the organization's first president. The National Board of Directors governs the organization according to the direction set at the conference. Members are elected to the board by nine regional divisions. Local chapters are located in all 50 states and the District of Columbia and carry out local activism and programming. State organizations work to develop chapters and coordinate activities across the state.

Identification of NOW as a radical feminist organization has its roots in a split in the organization's leadership. The adoption of lesbian, abortion, and contraceptive rights split the leadership of NOW, causing its more conservative leaders to form alternative organizations and shifting the balance of power at NOW. Their platform and legislative and social actions are consistently viewed in light of the political alliances of its leaders.

NOW and Interpersonal Violence

Calling itself "one of the few multi-issue progressive organizations in the United States," NOW works to connect the various forms of oppression, recognizing that racism, homophobia, and classism are intimately connected to sexism. Rather than fighting against other oppressed and marginalized groups, NOW seeks to unite with other people and organizations.

The top six current priorities for NOW are reproductive freedom, diversity and ending racism, ending violence against women, rights for lesbian women, constitutional equality for women, and economic justice.

Interpersonal violence is addressed by NOW as one of several interrelated issues of violence against women. NOW believes that intimate partner violence, like sexual assault, domestic violence, sexual harassment, and gender bias hate crimes, is the result of long-standing patriarchal views on women as subservient to men.

NOW furthers its priorities through education, protest, lobbying, registering voters, and endorsing feminist candidates for office, bringing lawsuits, demanding fair judiciaries, and working in coalition with other progressive organizations. One such priority has been the Violence Against Women Act (VAWA) passed in 1994 and reauthorized in 2000 and 2005. NOW is currently lobbying for adequate federal funding for VAWA programs.

NOW also works to change laws affecting intimate partner violence at the state level. NOW operatives seek to enact more stringent laws recognizing and punishing intimate partner violence. Proposed legislation would include efforts to improve mandatory arrest and report policies and to increase funding for shelters and hotlines. NOW has proposed laws recognizing and punishing crimes like marital rape and stalking. NOW also advocates classification of intimate partner violence as a felony rather than as a misdemeanor offense, a classification that would mandate greater judicial consideration of intimate partner violence in custody and divorce proceedings.

NOW also works to ensure that victims of violent crimes are treated with respect and dignity. NOW pressed legislatures to provide victims of rape with adequate health care, including providing rape victims the morning-after pill to prevent pregnancy. NOW further works with service providers and the media to prevent revictimization of women, endeavoring to ensure that victims are neither treated unfairly nor portrayed as perpetrators.

NOW's legislative initiatives reflect the organization's belief that change must be achieved through both legal and social action. NOW is currently pursuing a public education campaign to better inform society about violence against women and to make it socially unacceptable. Myths surrounding victims of violence are pervasive in society. Victims of rape are often met with preconceived notions about false accusations or moral culpability. Victims of intimate partner violence are similarly faced with assumptions that the violence is just a marital spat in which both parties are responsible. Public education is considered a means of dispelling myths about the perpetrators and victims of violence. NOW is a frequent sponsor of national and local Take Back the Night marches.

NOW is also dedicated to ending violence against women at an international level. NOW has campaigned extensively to protect the women of Ciudad Juarez, Mexico, where hundreds of women disappear under mysterious circumstances, many of whom are discovered to be victims of brutal rape and murder. NOW pressured both American and Mexican officials to investigate and prosecute those responsible, and with the efforts of NOW and its sister organizations, significant progress was made in protecting the women of Juarez.

Juley Fulcher, Jill Fertel, and Sarah K. Brown

See also Feminist Movements to End Violence Against Women; Feminist Theories of Interpersonal Violence; Take Back the Night; Violence Against Women Act

Further Readings

Friedan, B. (1963). *The feminine mystique.* New York: Norton.

Friedan, B. (n.d.). *National Organization for Women's 1966 statement of purpose.* Retrieved from http://www.now.org/history/purpos66.html

National Organization for Women. (n.d.). *About NOW: We want it all.* Retrieved from http://www.now.org/about.html

Web Sites

National Organization of Women: http://www.now.org

NATIONAL RESOURCE CENTER ON DOMESTIC VIOLENCE

The primary focus of the National Resource Center on Domestic Violence (NRCDV) is to inform, coordinate, and strengthen public and private efforts to end domestic violence. Through technical assistance and training and the development of resource materials and special projects, the NRCDV supports and enhances the domestic violence intervention and prevention efforts of communities and institutions. The Pennsylvania Coalition Against Domestic Violence has received core funding to operate the NRCDV since 1993 from the U.S. Department of Health and Human Services (DHHS), with supplemental funds from the Centers for Disease Control and Prevention (CDC) to support VAWnet, its national online resource center.

The NRCDV employs a diverse and multidisciplinary staff supported by a team of nationally recognized consultants and advisors. The technical assistance and training provided by the NRCDV is both reactive and proactive, not only responding to requests from the field, but also anticipating needs for information and guidance around emerging policy and practice issues. The NRCDV's mandate is broad, and training and technical assistance is provided on such diverse topics as teen dating violence, media advocacy, working with the faith community, economic empowerment strategies, culturally competent program design, effective program management strategies, and the building and sustaining of multidisciplinary collaborations, among others. Complementary and closely linked to the provision of technical assistance and training is the NRCDV's development of fact sheets, curricula, policy and practice briefs and manuals, applied research papers, funding alerts, annotated publications lists, information packets, and other materials widely disseminated through VAWnet, the NRCDV's national online resource center, and through other organization Web sites, mailings, and trainings.

The NRCDV has developed a number of special projects designed to focus more deeply on an emerging issue, provide specialized and comprehensive assistance to a particular constituent group, or address a pressing unmet need. In 2006, these projects included the following:

The Domestic Violence Awareness Project—supporting the community awareness and education efforts of domestic violence programs;

Document Our Work—designing tools to capture the scope, value, and impact of local and state domestic violence programs;

The Women of Color Network—promoting and supporting the leadership of women of color activists;

Building Comprehensive Solutions to Domestic Violence—promoting more holistic program and policy responses to domestic violence; and

VAWnet: The National Online Resource Center on Violence Against Women—NRCDV's CDC-funded Web site initiative.

Two toll-free telephone lines (800-537-2238 and TTY 800-553-2508) and a Web site (www.nrcdv.org) enable a caller to access NRCDV's training, technical assistance, and resource materials. The NRCDV is a key member of the Domestic Violence Resource Network to coordinate policy development, training and program planning, and built strong and mutually supportive relationships with the three DHHS-funded culturally specific Institutes and recently funded National Training and TA Center on Domestic Violence, Mental Health and Trauma.

Anne Menard

See also Domestic Violence Resource Network; Women of Color Network

Web Sites

National Resource Center on Domestic Violence: http://www .nrcdv.org
VAWnet: The National Online Resource Center on Violence Against Women: http://www.vawnet.org
Women of Color Network: http://womenofcolornetwork.org/

NATIONAL SEXUAL VIOLENCE RESOURCE CENTER

The National Sexual Violence Resource Center (NSVRC), with funding from the Centers for Disease Control and Prevention, developed as the nation's principal information and resource center regarding all aspects of sexual violence. Founded in 2000 by the Pennsylvania Coalition Against Rape, the NSVRC continues to provide leadership in all aspects of antisexual violence work. It collects and disseminates a wide range of resources on sexual violence, including statistics, research, statutes, training curricula, prevention initiatives, and program information.

The NSVRC assists coalitions, local programs, and others working to end and prevent sexual violence. Allied organizations, government agencies, and the general public also turn to the NSVRC for information and resources. The NSVRC provides national leadership by generating and facilitating the development and flow of information on sexual violence intervention and prevention strategies. It has become a critical resource to the nation, providing technical assistance and professional consultation to sexual violence prevention programs and allied professionals.

The NSVRC develops a variety of resources such as booklets, toolkits, and directories in addition to annual national Sexual Assault Awareness Month campaign materials and its bi-annual news publication, *The Resource*. These and other useful listings, including funding announcements, job opportunities, and scheduled trainings around the country, appear on its Web site. The NSVRC also maintains an extensive online library.

Over the years, the NSVRC has increased its support with additional funding from other organizations, foundations, and governmental agencies as it expanded its involvement in special projects and initiatives. These efforts have led to the production of additional resources, collaborative relationships, and greater national impact.

The NSVRC has become known for its strong emphasis on the prevention of sexual violence. At the same time, it maintains a commitment to supporting the field in its advocacy and intervention work. Throughout its existence, the NSVRC has embraced projects that focus attention on and increase resources for underserved or marginalized communities and culture; these efforts have extended into the U.S. territories and various global issues of sexual violence and trafficking.

Susan Lewis

See also Rape Crisis Centers; Rape/Sexual Assault; Sexual Abuse; Sexual Assault Nurse Examiner; Sexual Assault Response Team

Web Sites

National Sexual Violence Resource Center: http://www .nsvrc.org

NATIONAL VIOLENCE AGAINST WOMEN SURVEY

In an effort to increase knowledge regarding violence against women, the National Institute of Justice and the National Centers for Disease Control and Prevention cosponsored the National Violence Against Women Survey (NVAWS). Using a screener and incident format, principal investigators Patricia Tjaden and Nancy Thoennes estimated lifetime and annual prevalence and annual incidence rates of violence.

Background

The NVAWS, fielded late 1995 through mid-1996, used random digit-dialing and computer-assisted telephone interview to gather victimization data from 8,000 women and 8,005 men, age 18 or older. Participation rates were 72% for females and 69% for males.

Respondents were questioned about their overall fear of violence, about how they managed these fears, and about information on power, control, and emotional abuse sustained from current and former marital and cohabiting partners. Data on forcible rape, stalking, physical assaults perpetrated by adult caretakers when the respondents were children, physical assaults perpetrated by any offender as an adult, and threatened violence were obtained. In addition, respondents' and their current spouse and/or partner's demographic information were collected.

Investigators concluded that the NVAWS sample was similar to the population after a comparison with the U.S. Census Bureau's 1995 Current Population Survey. A lack of representation is noted, as the sample underrepresents older people, those less than 30, less-educated people, African Americans, and Hispanic males.

Estimates

NVAWS findings show that 51.9% of females and 66.4% of males were physically assaulted during their life and that 1.9% of women and 3.4% of men were physically assaulted during the previous year. An estimated 17.6% of females and 3.0% of males sustained a completed or attempted rape during their lifetime, while 0.3% of females and 0.1% of males were victims of the same during the previous year. NVAWS revealed that 8.1% of females and 2.2% of males were stalked during their life, while 1.0% of women and 0.4% of men were stalked in the prior year. Although published estimates are nominally higher than other estimates, many are not statistically different.

Advantages and Disadvantages

The principal investigators state that the NVAWS has advantages over other victim surveys. State-of-the-art techniques were utilized to protect the confidentiality of the data and to minimize risk of additional trauma to respondents. The survey allowed for both prevalence and incidence estimates. And multiple, behaviorally specific screen questions were utilized to increase clarity of the information desired.

One limitation of the NVAWS is the small number of victims from which estimates are calculated. Though 8,000 males and 8,000 females completed interviews, few were victims. Among females, NVAWS annual incidence estimates are based on 24 rape, 80 stalking, 152 physical assault, and 168 rape and/or physical assault victims. In total, estimates come from 240 female victims. Similarly, annual incidence estimates for males come from 312 individuals.

Although lifetime estimates are based on a greater number of victims, sample size problems are evident when comparing subgroups. For example, lifetime estimates of completed or attempted rapes are based on 146 African American, 9 Asian/Pacific Islander, and 30 American Indian/Alaska Native female victims. Lifetime estimates of stalking are based on 51 African American, 6 Asian/Pacific Islander, and 15 American Indian/Alaska Native female victims.

Callie Marie Rennison

See also Assault; Intimate Partner Violence; Rape/Sexual Assault; Stalking; Victimology

Further Readings

Bachman, R. (2000). A comparison of annual incidence rates and contextual characteristics of intimate partner violence against women from the National Crime Victimization Survey (NCVS) and the National Violence Against Women Survey (NVAWS). *Violence Against Women, 6,* 839–867.

Rand, M., & Rennison, C. (2005). Bigger is not necessarily better: An analysis of violence against women estimate from the National Crime Victimization Survey and the National Violence Against Women Survey. *Journal of Quantitative Criminology, 21*(3), 267–291.

Tjaden, P., & Thoennes, N. (2000, November). Full report of the prevalence, incidence and consequences of violence against women: Findings from the National Violence Against Women Survey (Report No. NCJ 183781). Washington, DC: National Institute of Justice and Centers for Disease Control and Prevention. Retrieved from http://www.ncjrs.gov/pdffiles1/nij/183781.pdf

Neuropsychological Factors in Impulsive Aggression and Violent Behavior

Episodically aggressive offenders, both impulsive and predatory, constitute one of the most pressing problems for law enforcement, courts, and corrections, not to mention the general public. This subgroup of offenders is largely responsible for the following: (a) a disproportionate amount of aggressive crimes against persons, (b) high recidivism rates, (c) a significant number of institutional rule violations, (d) high rates of substance abuse, and (e) intractability and poor treatment outcomes. Repetitively aggressive offenders are often diagnosed with antisocial personality disorder (ASPD), and a subset of these as psychopathic. Their personal histories are typified by childhood aggression, insensitivity to punishment, emotional dysregulation, risk taking, and sensation seeking. These inmates are recommitted more often than other inmates, a majority of them recidivate with aggressive offenses, and they are likely to develop an early and more severe course of drug abuse. Yet few community, private, or correctional programs are available to treat these offenders or, more importantly, to prevent the development of these behaviors before they stabilize. There are clear public safety benefits to being able to accurately identify and characterize these offenders in terms of conditions that may underlie or contribute to their dysregulated behavior in order to direct more effectively treatment and prevention resources.

Recent research on underlying mechanisms in aggression may be applicable to this problem and has implications for more effective interventions. Various neuropathological conditions (attenuated frontal P300 amplitude, reduced prefrontal glucose metabolism, subdued physiological responses to alcohol, neuropsychological deficits, differences in neurotransmitter metabolism and activity levels, and heightened stress dampening) have been associated with these dysregulated behaviors, suggesting that neurobiological processes may underlie risky behaviors. In particular, studies have consistently found that deficits in certain neuropsychological functions correlate with and predict aggression, impulsivity, violence, and other forms of persistent misconduct in both children and adults. What is emerging from these studies is that although many offenders may function adequately in terms of basic cognitive skills such as memory, intelligence, and learning ability, those who repeatedly engage in very risky behaviors may have deficits in what is called *executive cognitive functions* (ECFs), higher-order neuropsychological skills. ECFs include a subset of higher-order neuropsychological abilities and their measurement has become more refined, noninvasive, and reliable, making it more amenable to conducting these studies with offenders.

ECF abilities include social skills, impulse control, assessment of and sensitivity to consequences, motivation, attention, and emotional perception and regulation. Deficits in these abilities have been implicated in aggression and are thought to be responsible for a number of traits often seen in aggressive offenders, such as poor social skills and decision-making ability, insensitivity to punishment, impulsivity, inattention, impaired problem solving, cognitive inflexibility, and lack of goal-directed behaviors. And because ECFs regulate and, in most cases, inhibit emotional responses, ECF deficits are also associated with poor emotional regulation and inaccurate perceptions of emotion in others. In essence, impaired ECF may compromise the ability to interpret social cues during interpersonal interactions, which may lead to misperceptions of threat or hostility. As a result, difficulties arise in generating socially adaptive behaviors and in executing responses to avoid aggressive or stressful interactions. Also, compromised cognitive control over behavior may permit hostility, negative affective states, and other maladaptive responses to dominate.

Neural regulatory mechanisms in cognitive impairments that may specifically subserve dysregulated behaviors involve the prefrontal cortex (PFC) and its circuitry to areas of the limbic system. Certain regions of the PFC play a role in neuropsychological functions that support forethought, behavioral inhibition, and capacity to learn from experience. The PFC also plays a role in the regulatory system, controlling emotional perceptions, regulation of emotional responses, and moods. Populations with damage to this circuitry show increased extroversion, impulsivity, irritability, aggressiveness, and various antisocial behaviors, as

well as impairments in ability to make rational decisions and difficulties in processing emotion.

There is evidence that a disconnect between the PFC and structures in the limbic system (an emotional center) may be responsible for these dysregulated behaviors via neuropsychological impairments. Sources of damage to this circuitry that may disrupt ability to assess consequences and regulate impulses include head injury, adversity, prenatal drug exposure, neurotoxins, childhood deprivation, child abuse, and chronic drug use. Many of these factors are environmental, suggesting that the PFC is sensitive to external physical and social influences. Psychosocial stress can alter PFC function and contribute to ECF impairment. The volume and function of particular brain structures, including the PFC and limbic system, are associated with social stress and adversity. Perhaps not coincidentally, the incidence of adverse social (e.g., child abuse) and physical (e.g., head injury) experiences is high in offender populations. Those with brain dysfunction are significantly more likely to have been indicted for violent crimes.

Of particular interest is the connection between neuropsychological impairment and psychopathy. Psychopaths with aggressive behavior have been distinguished from nonpsychopaths on the basis of neuropsychological functioning of the PFC. Prefrontal lobe damage has been reported in a significantly greater percentage of subjects with a history of violent crimes than those with no such damage. Neuroimaging studies report diminished brain activity in the PFC in individuals with persistent violent behavior.

In summary, the prevalence of neuropsychological dysfunction is significantly greater in violent offenders than in nonaggressive offenders and in the general population. This evidence suggests that treatments designed to enhance functionality and connectivity between neural systems may be effective behavioral modifiers.

Diana Fishbein

See also Biochemical Factors in Predicting Violence; Psychophysiological Factors in Predicting Violence

Further Readings

Barratt, E. S., Stanford, M. S., Kent, T. A., & Felthous, A. R. (1997). Neuropsychological and cognitive psychophysiological substrates of impulsive aggression. *Biological Psychiatry, 41*, 1045–1061.

Davidson, R. J., Putnam, K. M., & Larson, C. L. (2000). Dysfunction in the neural circuitry of emotion regulation—A possible prelude to violence. *Science, 289,* 591–594.

Elliott, F. A. (1992). Violence: The neurologic contribution: An overview. *Archives of Neurology, 49,* 595–603.

Fishbein, D. H. (Ed.). (2000). *The science, treatment and prevention of antisocial behaviors: Applications to the criminal justice system.* Kingston, NJ: Civic Research Institute.

Fishbein, D. H. (Ed.). (2004). *The science, treatment and prevention of antisocial behaviors* (Vol. 2). Kingston, NJ: Civic Research Institute.

Kandel, E., & Freed, D. (1989). Frontal-lobe dysfunction and antisocial behavior: A review. *Journal of Clinical Psychology, 45,* 404–413.

Mirsky, A. F., & Siegel, A. (1994). The neurobiology of violence and aggression. In A. J. Reiss, Jr., K. A. Miczek, & J. A. Roth (Eds.), *Violence: Biobehavioral influences* (Vol. 2, pp. 59–172). Washington, DC: National Academy Press.

Raine, A. (1993). *The psychopathology of crime: Criminal behavior as a clinical disorder.* New York: Academic Press.

Raine, A., Buchsbaum, M., & LaCasse, L. (1997). Brain abnormalities in murderers indicated by positron emission tomography. *Biological Psychiatry, 42,* 495–508.

Volavka, J. (1995). *The neurobiology of violence.* Washington, DC: American Psychiatric Press.

NO-DROP PROSECUTION

Prosecutors are said to drop charges when they decline to prosecute, or *nolle prosequi,* a previously filed case, prior to trial. By extension, it is commonly said that victims of intimate partner violence drop charges when they cause criminal charges against abusers to be dismissed, either by a request to the prosecutor or by their unwillingness to participate in criminal proceedings. A no-drop prosecution policy prohibits prosecutors from dismissing charges and thereby denies victims the opportunity to drop charges.

No-drop prosecution has been advocated for cases of domestic violence as a means of ensuring that criminal justice runs its course from arrest through judicial processing. Taken literally, the policy limits the discretion of prosecutors to dispose of cases without holding a defendant accountable. It may be held out as part of a prosecutor's public stance favoring mandatory prosecution or as a commitment to ensuring that

cases of domestic violence get their day in court. In practice, the policy is less a mandate for prosecutors than a tool for ensuring that victims are afforded the protection of criminal justice. It is meant to demonstrate that the crime is a crime against the state, that prosecutors have a duty to pursue charges, and that it will do no good for a defendant to coerce his or her victim into dropping charges, as the victim has no control over the case.

There are jurisdictions in the United States where prosecutors are so committed to this policy that they will coerce victim participation in the prosecution of a case by threatening the victim with possible arrest should he or she fail to appear in court when subpoenaed. Such a *hard* no-drop policy may have the effect of serving to deter prospective batterers from abusing their partners for fear that they will find themselves in a system dedicated to prosecution, irrespective of victim wishes. In reality, however, many prosecutors understand that victims could be endangered if coerced to participate in the prosecution, and so they are allowed to drop charges.

A *soft* no-drop policy is one under which a prosecutor publicly proclaims that, once filed, charges will not be dropped, but the prosecutor then takes into account each victim's special circumstances in determining how best to respond to the victim's request to drop charges. A soft no-drop policy acknowledges that prosecution may jeopardize the victim or the victim's family. Thus, it respects each victim's understanding of her or his own safety, even as it supports the potential for general deterrence, because the no-drop public stance serves to notify abusers of the prosecutor's resolve to pursue domestic violence as a serious crime.

No-drop prosecution is a particularly contentious issue. It seems to pit prosecutors' representation of state interests in justice and accountability against victim expectations for personal justice and protection. Prosecutors act as attorneys for the state with a responsibility to seek justice on behalf of its citizens. It may be that no-drop prosecution is a general deterrent to domestic violence, but extant research challenges the assumption that no-drop prosecution will protect a specific victim from continuing violence. Further research is needed to explore the full range of impacts that no-drop prosecution has in protecting both victims who seek safety through prosecution and those who expect the criminal justice system to reduce the risk of intimate partner violence in the population at large.

David A. Ford

See also Legal System, Criminal Justice System Responses to Intimate Partner Violence; Mandatory Arrest/Pro-Arrest Statutes; Prosecutorial Practices, Intimate Partner Violence

Further Readings

Ford, D. A. (2003). Coercing victim participation in domestic violence prosecutions. *Journal of Interpersonal Violence, 18,* 669–684.

Wills, D. (1997). Domestic violence: The case for aggressive prosecution. *UCLA Women's Law Journal, 7,* 173–182.

NONOFFENDING PARENTS OF MALTREATED CHILDREN

Nonoffending parents of maltreated children are those parents who do not actually commit the abuse against the child, but who are responsible for protecting the child after the abuse. For example, when a child is physically abused by a mother, the father is the nonoffending parent. The majority of literature on nonoffending parents is written about parents of sexually abused children. Sexual abuse is different from other types of child maltreatment in that the vast majority of offenders are male and nonoffending parents are female.

Because of the disproportionate representation of the poor in child welfare, there is also an overrepresentation of poor single mothers. This overrepresentation and the historical bias of considering the mother primarily responsible for the child also contribute to the emphasis by child welfare on nonoffending mothers rather than on nonoffending fathers. Thus, when a child is sexually abused, regardless of whether a mother or father figure is available, the mother is typically assumed to be responsible for the ongoing care, protection, and support of the child.

Nonoffending Mothers and the Early Literature

The historical understanding of the nonoffending mothers' responses to their children's sexual abuse was profoundly influenced by Freudian psychoanalytic theory. To understand how this theory conceptualized mothers, it is helpful to understand how it conceptualized the victim, assumed to be the daughter. Psychoanalytic theory assumed that the daughter seduced her father and then actively participated in the ongoing abuse. Not coincidentally, the mother was assumed to set up the dynamics for the abuse, know about the ongoing abuse, and even allow it to continue. Again, the rationale for this belief system was that the abuse occurred more than one time. Clinicians simply could not understand how the abuse could happen more than one time without the active participation of the child and the active or passive encouragement of the mother.

As theories of human behavior moved away from an intrapsychic (psychoanalytic) perspective in the last half of the 20th century, incest began to be framed within a family systems framework, with the mother being considered the center around which a dysfunctional family system evolved. Again, she was purported not only to set up the dynamics for the abuse but also to contribute to its continuation because of its purported gain for her. Of course, today it is understood that this belief is not the case, but the historic bias against nonoffending mothers of sexually abused children lingers in some areas.

Possible Effects of Early Literature

How much this literature contributed to the belief system of Child Protective Services workers is not known, but what is known is that during this same period of time, child welfare workers appeared to maintain a belief system that the mother was as much to blame for the abuse as the father or perpetrator and that she knew about the ongoing abuse. This belief system may continue, as approximately half of sexually abused children are removed from their homes by Child Protective Services within the first year following the abuse disclosure, and approximately two thirds to three fourths are removed by the end of the second year. For these children to be removed, the nonoffending parents would have to be considered incapable of providing appropriate support and protection to their children. Indeed, in just less than half of all cases of substantiated sexual abuse, mother figures are categorized by Child Protective Services as sexual offenders. In cases of parental incest, over half of mothers are categorized as sex offenders. In comparison, in the more accurate random prevalence studies of child sexual abuse, less than 1% of all sexual abuse is committed by mothers. The inevitable conclusion is that Child Protective Services is categorizing extraordinarily more mothers as being involved in the sexual abuse than actually occurs.

Recent Understanding of Nonoffending Parents

A more holistic understanding of nonoffending parents has emerged in recent years. Many researchers and clinicians recognize the contexts within which the nonoffending parent and victim reside and the complex systems with which they interface. Not only are multiple dynamics occurring within the family, but also families are responding to a Child Protective Services system that is making increased demands upon the family. Nonoffending parents may experience Child Protective Services, as well as other systems designed to support the welfare of the abused child, as hostile to them and to the structure of their family. Further, nonoffending parents may be experiencing their own traumatic responses after finding out that their child was sexually abused.

Even in this enormously difficult environment, most nonoffending parents respond with partial or full support of their children after disclosure. This important finding suggests that most nonoffending parents are capable of and motivated to support their children. Other important studies have found that parental support is amenable even to brief treatment and education. Finally, there is emerging evidence that working with both the child and nonoffending parent in treatment is associated with important reductions in symptoms in children and parents and is also associated with increased parental support.

These emerging findings suggest that Child Protective Services may be able to work more closely and flexibly with nonoffending parents with the hope that eventually more sexually abused children may remain safely in their homes with their nonoffending parents. Doing so is important for helping these children to maintain their very critical attachments with their nonoffending parents while averting the enormous trauma of the rupture of these attachments. Thus, it is hoped that emerging trends in the literature will provide a more holistic understanding of responses of nonoffending parents while also providing enhanced support for the parents and their children.

Rebecca M. Bolen

See also Attachment Disorder; Child Protective Services; Child Sexual Abuse; Failure to Protect; Parental Alienation Syndrome

Further Readings

Bolen, R. M. (2001). *Child sexual abuse: Its scope and our failure.* New York: Kluwer Academic/Plenum Press.

Elliott, A. N., & Carnes, C. N. (2001). Reactions of nonoffending parents to the sexual abuse of their child: A review of the literature. *Child Maltreatment, 6*(4), 314–331.

NOW LEGAL DEFENSE AND EDUCATION FUND

See LEGAL MOMENTUM